W9-BTS-720

Exploring Psychology

Exploring Psychology

Second Edition

David G. Myers

Hope College, Holland, Michigan

WORTH PUBLISHERS

With Thanks to All My Friends at Worth Publishers
for Ten Years of Creative Collaboration

Exploring Psychology, *Second Edition*

Copyright © 1993, 1990 by Worth Publishers, Inc.

All rights reserved.

Manufactured in the United States of Amercia

Library of Congress Catalog Card Number: 92-61385

ISBN: 0-87901-577-2 (Paper edition)

ISBN: 0-87901-578-0 (Cloth edition)

Printing: 2 3 4 5—97 96 95 94 93

Development editor: Christine Brune

Design: Malcolm Grear Designers

Art director: George Touloumes

Production editor: Betsy Mastalski

Production supervisor: Barbara Anne Seixas

Layout: Patricia Lawson

Picture editor: June Lundborg Whitworth

Line art: Bruce P. Maddocks, Warren Budd, and Demetrios Zangos

Composition and separations: York Graphic Services, Inc.

Printing and binding: Von Hoffmann Press, Inc.

Cover and frontispiece: Indonesian batik design; © Michele & Tom Grimm/Int'l. Stock Photo

Illustration credits begin on page IC-1, and constitute an extension of the copyright page.

All royalties from the sale of this book are assigned to the David and Carol Myers Foundation, which exists to receive and distribute funds to other charitable organizations.

Worth Publishers
33 Irving Place
New York, New York 10003

Contents in Brief

Contents

Chapter 7

Chapter 8

Chapter 9

Chapter 13

Chapter 14

Chapter 15

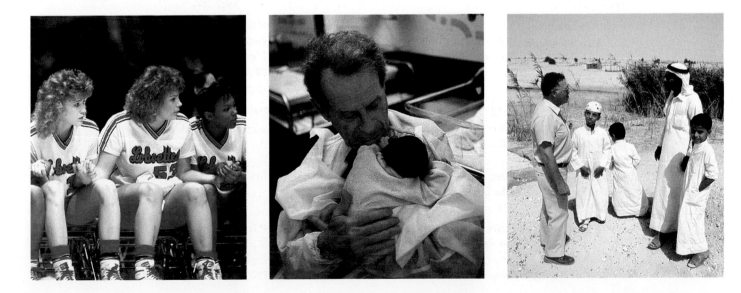

Preface

Of making many books there is no end," observed the philosopher writer of Ecclesiastes. More than two millennia later, these words must still ring true to psychology instructors who take seriously their task of selecting from among the dozens of available textbooks. I have, nevertheless, dared to make another book. Believing with Thoreau that "Anything living is easily and naturally expressed in popular language," I wanted to create a book that communicates psychological science with crisp narrative and vivid story telling. I also wanted to offer students a warmly human book—one that provides insight into phenomena of their everyday lives, that conveys an inquisitive, compassionate, and sometimes playful spirit, and that teaches and exemplifies how to think critically.

Exploring Psychology is my best effort to fulfill those aims in a brief format suited for students with diverse abilities and academic backgrounds. This new edition is

- thoroughly updated: 293 references—17 percent of all citations—are from the 1990s.

- carefully revised: Nearly every paragraph has been edited to make the prose crisper, the voice more active, the reading level more accessible to students with varying abilities.

- modestly reorganized: For example, the material in the first edition Health chapter now appears as a new stress section in the Emotion chapter, an obesity section in the Hunger unit of the Motivation chapter, and a smoking section in the Drugs unit of the States of Consciousness chapter. This reorganization enables instructors who didn't have time for the Health chapter to teach important aspects of health psychology.

- broadened to include a new concluding chapter on Social Diversity. Recognizing the reality of multicultural life in our shrinking global village, this new capstone chapter explores cultural, ethnic, and gender diversity, and shows how people can and do respond when confronting social diversity. In addition to this focused coverage, multicultural and gender material also seep in wherever appropriate throughout the book. (For a page-referenced guide to the integrated coverage of culture and gender, see page 507.)

- expanded to provide even more attention to critical thinking. *Exploring Psychology* presents research as intellectual detective work, exemplifying an inquiring, analytical approach to life. Whether students are studying development, cognition, or statistics, they will see how critical reasoning is used. They will discover how an empirical approach can help them sift competing ideas and publicized claims—ranging from subliminal persuasion and ESP to astrology and hypnotic age regression. In addition, new to this edition are structured Critical Thinking Exercises, prepared by Richard Straub, at the conclusion of each chapter. Each class-tested exercise challenges students to examine a true-to-life problem and use their developing critical-thinking skills to answer pertinent questions. (There is a guide to appropriate answers in Appendix B.)

Exploring Psychology once again offers a running glossary, preview questions, and built-in reviews and self-tests. We integrate these learning aids into an SQ3R structure that augments the narrative without disrupting it. Each chapter opens with a chapter outline that enables students to quickly *Survey* its major topics. Preview *Questions* at the start of each new major topic define the learning objectives that will guide students as they *Read. Rehearse It* quizzes within each chapter offer a novel combination of crisp summary statements regarding key ideas integrated with multiple-choice questions that stimulate students to rehearse what they have learned. The chapter-ending *Review* answers each of the numbered preview questions and is followed by answers for each of the Rehearse It multiple-choice questions. The expanded Studying Psychology section at the end of Chapter 1 explains the format, suggesting how students can survey, question, read, rehearse, and review the material for maximum retention.

The Teaching-Learning Package

Exploring Psychology is accompanied by widely acclaimed materials to enhance teaching and learning. For students who desire additional help mastering the text, there is Richard Straub's (University of Michigan, Dearborn) *Study Guide*. Each chapter uses the SQ3R format to guide students at each step of their study. Progress tests help students check their mastery of the material. The study guide is also computerized in a highly interactive program for use on IBM PC or Macintosh computers.

The *Instructor's Resources* created by Martin Bolt (Calvin College) for *Exploring Psychology* has been hailed as the finest set of psychology teaching resources ever assembled. Now 10 percent bigger, it features dozens of ready-to-use demonstration handouts, along with chapter objectives, lecture/discussion ideas, student projects, classroom exercises, and video and film suggestions. Martin Bolt's new *Lecture Guides*, which come in both printed and easily modifiable IBM PC and Macintosh formats, offer instructors an additional resource for lecture preparation.

The award-winning computer software developed by Thomas Ludwig (Hope College) brings some of psychology's most important concepts and methods to life. *PsychSim: Interactive Graphic Simulations for Psychology* contains 16 programs for use on the IBM PC or Macintosh. Some simulations engage the student as experimenter—conditioning a rat or electrically probing the hypothalamus. Others engage the student as subject—responding to tests of memory or visual illusions. Still others provide a dynamic tutorial/demonstration of, say, hemispheric processing or cognitive development principles. Student worksheets are provided. The *PsychSim* programs for this edition are significantly enhanced over the earlier version that received the 1990 Educom/NCRIPTAL Higher Education Software Award for "Best Psychology Software"—marking the first time that software specifically designed for introductory psychology has been so honored.

The *Test Bank*, by John Brink (Calvin College), provides 2,800 carefully edited factual/definitional, conceptual, and essay questions. Each question is keyed to a learning objective, page-referenced to the textbook, and rated in level of difficulty. (Optional questions are also included for the *PsychSim* exercises and *The Brain* and *The Mind* modules, see below.) The *Test Bank* is available in test-generation systems for IBM PC, Macintosh, and the Apple II family of microcomputers.

Our new Psychology Videodisc package will help you bring to life for your students all of the major topics in *Exploring Psychology*, combining brief, exciting video clips and animated segments with a library of stills. This two-sided CAV videodisc is accompanied by an extensive *Instructor's Guide*, by Martin Bolt and Richard Straub, complete with barcodes; descriptions of each item and suggestions for how to incorporate the material into your lecture; and a subject index, referencing and cross-referencing all items by topic across chapters. A software package by Thomas Ludwig, for use on IBM PC or Macintosh computers, includes an indexing program as well as slide show and lecture template programs. The indexing program makes it easy to assemble a list of relevant video clips and stills for any lecture topic. Instructors may print this list for use with a remote control keypad or barcode reader, or may control the videodisc player directly from the computer to display the clips and stills in "slide show" fashion or as part of a complete, computerized lecture.

In addition, Worth Publishers has produced 38 video modules from *The Mind* series, in association with WNET. These modules were edited by Frank Vattano (Colorado State University) with the consultation of Charles Brewer (Furman University) and myself. Rather than displace the instructor, as do longer films, these brief clips (which can be dubbed onto individual cassettes) dramatically enhance and illustrate lectures. They do so in ways that written and spoken words cannot—by introducing students to a split-brain patient being tested, a sleeping subject being monitored in a lab, a patient suffering the ravages of schizophrenia, and so forth. In addition to the 38 modules on videocassettes available from Worth Publishers, there is now a two-sided CAV videodisc that includes 14 highlights from *The Mind* modules. These are also available from Worth Publishers, accompanied by a barcoded Faculty Guide.

In Appreciation

Hundreds of consultants, reviewers, instructors, and students have helped me to develop far better, more accurate books than I, alone, could have written. I am indebted to each of the teacher-scholars thanked in all three editions of *Psychology*. Their contributions to its improvements have found their way into this book as well.

Exploring Psychology took shape under the tutelage of sensitive and dedicated teachers of psychology who guided us in creating a brief introduction to psychology appropriate for their students. For their generous advice and encouragement in developing the first edition, I remain indebted to the following reviewers:

Martin Bolt, *Calvin College*

Stephen G. Bopp, *Richland Community College*

Peggy R. Brooks, *Kennesaw State College*

Karen Christoff, *University of Mississippi*

John M. Clark, *Macomb Community College*

Daniel G. Crocco, *Mohawk College*

Marc DesLauriers, *Kansas City Kansas Community College*

George Downing, *Gloucester County College*

Ann Ewing, *Mesa Community College*

Robert J. Gregory, *University of Idaho*

Ralph Grippin, *Metropolitan Technical Community College*

William Hampes, *Black Hawk College*

Thomas Lombardo, *University of Mississippi*

Sherry J. Neal, *Oklahoma City Community College*

April W. O'Connell, *Santa Fe Community College*

Dean Schroeder, *Laramie County Community College*

Thomas P. Smith, *Vincennes University*

Elizabeth D. Webb, *Bossier Parish Community College*

This new edition took shape with the fresh perspective of other talented colleagues. A first group of consultants who had classroom experience with the first edition told us what worked best and offered countless criticisms, corrections, and creative suggestions—including wonderful responses from their students. For the resulting improvements I am grateful to:

Robert I. Bermant, *University of Wisconsin Center–Waukesha County*

Stephen G. Bopp, *Richland Community College*

Jane Ewens Holbrook, *University of Wisconsin Center–Waukesha County*

Ray Huebschmann, *Delaware County Community College*

Jane A. Jegerski, *Elmhurst College*

Deborah R. McDonald, *New Mexico State University*

Pennie S. Seibert, *Boise State University*

Timothy P. Tomczak, *Genesee Community College*

Frank J. Vattano, *Colorado State University*

Another group of reviewers critiqued the revised chapters. For their expertise and excellent suggestions I thank:

David R. Beach, *University of Wisconsin, Parkside*

Jean-Jacques D'Aoust, *Ashland Community College*

Robert DaPrato, *Solano Community College*

Nancy A. Dash, *Charles S. Mott Community College*

Vicki Dossett, *Trinity Valley Community College*

Robert A. Frank, *University of Cincinnati*

Barbara B. Grimes, *Pierce Junior College*

Nancey G. Lobb, *Alvin Community College*

Harold L. Mansfield, *Fort Lewis College*

Merrill J. May, *Weber State University*

Gregory J. Mazak, *Bob Jones University*

Cyndi McDaniel, *Northern Kentucky University*

David S. McDougal, *Plymouth State College*

Edward R. Mosley, *Passaic County Community College*

David R. Murphy, *Waubonsee Community College*

Nancy M. Ohuche, *Spokane Falls Community College*

Marilyn J. Reedy, *Alverno College*

Mary Jane Sharp, *Maysville Community College*

At Worth Publishers—a company whose entire staff continues to amaze me with their devotion to the highest standards in everything they do—many people played key supportive roles. John Staley, Phil Reed, and other members of Worth's talented sales staff provided the genesis for this book. Managing editor Anne Vinnicombe helped plan the book and oversee its completion. Editor Christine Brune's combination of enthusiasm and meticulous attention to detail, sustained over two editions, gave this author both pleasure and peace of mind. In this effort she was ably assisted by Barbara Brooks. Debbie Posner, Betsy Mastalski, and Anna Wiese painstakingly checked and polished the final manuscript with skill and good humor. Once again, kudos go to Worth's designers for crafting a beautiful and pedagogically effective book and to the production team, led by George Touloumes and Barbara Seixas, for the layout and production of every page.

At Hope College, the supportive team members included Michelle Nainys, who researched and checked countless items and prepared the name index; Kathy Adamski, who processed hundreds of letters and faxes; Phyllis and Richard Vandervelde, who typed the manuscript drafts with their usual excellence; and poet Jack Ridl, whose influence helped shape the voice you will be hearing in the pages that follow.

To all these colleagues and friends, and to many others who wrote just to say they enjoyed the first edition, I offer my heartfelt thanks.

And to the students who will explore psychology with me, I hope your introduction to psychology will help to enrich your life and enlarge your vision about how we humans perceive, think, feel, and act.

David Myers

Chapter 1

Introducing Psychology

I was relaxing in the barber's black leather chair, enjoying my last haircut before leaving Seattle, when the barber struck up a conversation:

"What do you do?"

"Next week I'll be moving to Iowa to begin graduate school," I replied.

"What are you studying?"

"Psychology."

The haircutting ceased as the friendly barber took a step back, and timidly wondered aloud:

"So what do you think of me?"

For my barber, as for many people whose exposure to psychology comes mostly from popular books, magazines, and TV, psychologists analyze personality, practice psychotherapy, and dispense child-rearing advice.

Do they? Yes, and much more. Consider some of psychology's questions, questions that from time to time you may wonder about:

Have you ever found yourself reacting to something just as one of your parents would—perhaps in a way you vowed you never would—and then wondered how much of your personality you inherited? To what degree are you really like your mother or your father? *To what extent is your parents' influence transmitted through their genes? To what extent through the environment they gave you?*

Have you ever played peekaboo with an infant and wondered why the baby finds the game so delightful? The baby reacts as if, when you momentarily move behind a door, you actually disappear—only to reappear later out of thin air. *What do babies actually perceive and think?*

Have you ever awakened from a nightmare and, with a wave of relief, wondered why we have such crazy dreams? *How often do we dream? Why do we dream?*

Have you ever been to a circus and wondered how someone trained the poodles to dance, the lions to jump through hoops, the chimps to ride bikes? *What are the limits on what we can train animals to do?*

Do you ever get depressed or anxious and wonder whether you'll ever feel "normal"? *What triggers our moods? Can we control our state of mind?*

Have you ever worried about how to act among people of a different culture, race, or sex? In what ways are we alike as members of the human family? How do we differ? And, as citizens of multicultural countries and a shrinking global village, *how can we replace mistrust with understanding and cooperation?*

Such questions provide grist for psychology's mill, for psychology is a science that seeks to answer all sorts of questions about us all: how we think, feel, and act.

Why is this infant so thrilled with a game of peekaboo with his grandmother?

What Is Psychology?

Many academic disciplines study human nature. Among them, psychology is a relative newcomer. What are psychology's roots? Perspectives? Subfields?

Psychology's Roots

Preview Question

1. How did the science of psychology develop?

"I'm a social scientist, Michael. That means I can't explain electricity or anything like that, but if you ever want to know about people, I'm your man."

Drawing by Handelsman; © 1986 The New Yorker Magazine, Inc.

Preview Question

2. What theoretical perspectives do psychologists emphasize?

psychology   The science of behavior and mental processes.

nature-nurture issue   The longstanding controversy over the relative contributions of genes and experience to the development of psychological traits and behaviors.

Psychology is a young science with roots in many countries and disciplines, from physiology to philosophy. Wilhelm Wundt, who founded the first psychology laboratory in 1879 at Germany's University of Leipzig, was both a physiologist and a philosopher. Ivan Pavlov, who pioneered the study of learning, was a Russian physiologist. Sigmund Freud, renowned personality theorist, was an Austrian physician. Jean Piaget, this century's most influential observer of children, was a Swiss biologist. William James, author of an important 1890 psychology textbook, was an American philosopher (Figure 1–1).

Psychology began as the science of mental life. Just over a century ago, Wilhelm Wundt's basic research tool was introspection (self-examination) of one's own emotional states and mental processes. Wundt focused on *inner* sensations, feelings, and thoughts. Thus, until the 1920s, psychology was defined as "the science of mental life."

From the 1920s into the 1960s, American psychologists led by John Watson redefined psychology as "the science of observable behavior." After all, they said, science is rooted in observation. You cannot observe a sensation, a feeling, or a thought, but you *can* observe people's *outer* behavior in reaction to external stimulation.

In the 1960s, psychology began to recapture its initial interest in conscious and unconscious mental processes through studies of how our minds process and retain information. To encompass psychology's concern both with overt behavior and covert thoughts and feelings, we define **psychology** as *the science of behavior and mental processes.*

Perspectives on Behavior and Mental Processes

During its short history, psychology has wrestled with a few big issues that will reappear throughout this book. One of the biggest is this: Are we humans affected more by *internal* or *external* influences? Is your eating or sexual behavior mostly "pushed" by internal drives or "pulled" by external incentives? Is your social behavior better explained by the presence of enduring inner traits or by the temporary demands of external situations? Are your personality and intelligence influenced more by your genes or by your experience? Is your humanness a product of your biology or your culture? The controversy over the relative contributions of genes and experience, called the **nature-nurture issue,** will reappear throughout this book.

Whether psychologists emphasize nature or nurture depends on their theoretical perspective. Each of psychology's major perspectives influences the questions psychologists ask and the kinds of information they consider important. Refer to the six perspectives highlighted in Table 1–1 (page 4), as you consider how each perspective views an emotion such as anger.

Someone working from a **biological perspective** might study the brain circuits that trigger the physical state of being "red in the face" and "hot under the collar."

Someone working from a **psychoanalytic perspective** might view an outburst as an outlet for unconscious hostility.

Figure 1–1 A timeline of psychology's pioneers, 1875–1915.

Hermann Ebbinghaus in Germany reports the first experiments on memory (1885).

Alfred Binet (shown) and **Theodore Simon** devise the first intelligence test for use with Parisian schoolchildren (1905).

Wilhelm Wundt establishes the first psychology laboratory at the University of Leipzig, Germany (1879).

Margaret Floy Washburn, the first woman to receive a Ph.D. in psychology, synthesizes research on animal behavior in *The Animal Mind* (1908).

Edward L. Thorndike in the United States conducts the first experiments on animal learning (1898).

American Psychological Association is founded (1892).

1875 1880 1885 1890 1895 1900 1905 1910 1915

G. Stanley Hall, a student of Wundt's, establishes the first American psychology laboratory at Johns Hopkins University (1883).

Sigmund Freud in Austria introduces his psychoanalytic theory in *The Interpretation of Dreams* (1900).

John B. Watson in the United States champions psychology as the science of behavior (1913).

William James publishes the widely used *Principles of Psychology* in the United States (1890).

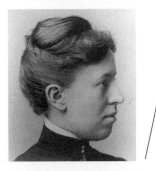

Mary Whiton Calkins creates paired-associates technique for studying memory; becomes president of American Psychological Association (1905).

Ivan Pavlov in Russia begins to publish his classic studies of animal learning (1906)

Table 1-1

Psychology's Perspectives

Perspective	Focus	Emphases
Biological	How the body and brain create emotions, memories, and sensory experiences	How evolution and heredity influence behavior; how messages are transmitted within the body; how blood chemistry is linked with moods and motives
Psychoanalytic	How behavior springs from unconscious drives and conflicts	Analysis of personality traits and disorders in terms of sexual and aggressive drives or as the disguised effects of unfulfilled wishes and childhood traumas
Behavioral	How observable responses are acquired and changed	How we learn to fear particular objects or situations; how we can most effectively alter our behavior, say, to lose weight or stop smoking
Humanistic	Our capacity to choose our life patterns and not just be driven by unconscious forces or shaped by environment	How we seek maturity and fulfillment; how people experience and understand their own lives
Cognitive	How we process, store, and retrieve information	How we use information in remembering, reasoning, and solving problems
Social-cultural	How behavior and thinking vary across situations and cultures	How we are alike as members of one human family, as, say, Africans, Asians, Australians, or North Americans; how we are different, as products of different environments

We can study an emotion such as anger from several perspectives, each of which explores different aspects. Taken together, these studies provide a fuller understanding of the emotion.

Someone working from a **behavioral perspective** might study the facial expressions and body gestures that accompany anger, or determine which external influences trigger angry responses or aggressive acts.

Someone working from a **humanistic perspective** might want to understand what it means to experience and express anger—from the person's own point of view.

Someone working from a **cognitive perspective** might study how our perception of a frustrating situation affects the intensity of our anger, and how an angry mood affects our thinking.

Someone working from a **social-cultural perspective** might explore how anger and its expression vary across cultural groups.

It's obvious that the biological, psychoanalytic, behavioral, humanistic, cognitive, and social-cultural perspectives describe and explain anger very differently. This need not mean that they contradict one another. Rather, they are six useful ways of looking at the same psychological state. By using all six, we gain a fuller understanding of anger than any single perspective can provide.

This important point—that different perspectives can complement one another—is true of all the academic disciplines, each of which provides a different perspective on nature and our place in it. The basic sciences investigate nature's building blocks—atoms, energy forces, living cells—seeking principles based on objective observation. The humanities (literature, philosophy, and the like) address questions of life's meaning and value in human life and use more subjective methods. Psychology lies near the middle of this continuum; it uses scientific methods to explore our thoughts and actions.

clinical psychology A branch of psychology involving the assessment and treatment of those who suffer psychological disorders.

psychiatry A branch of medicine dealing with psychological disorders; practiced by physicians and sometimes involving medical (for example, drug) treatments as well as psychological therapy.

basic research Pure science; aims to increase the scientific knowledge base.

applied research Scientific study that aims to solve practical problems.

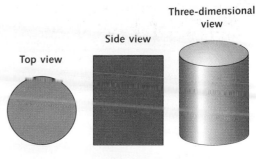

Figure 1–2 What is this object? One person, looking down from the top, says it is a disk. Another, looking at it from the side, says it is a rectangle. Their differing perspectives seem contradictory. In fact, they are complementary, for we can assemble their respective images into a complete three-dimensional view of the object, a cylinder. The views of behavior and mental processes offered by psychology's different perspectives are often like this: A lot depends on your point of view. Each perspective is useful, but none by itself gives the whole picture.

Top view   Side view   Three-dimensional view

Each perspective is useful, but none by itself gives the whole picture (Figure 1–2). If you ignore psychology's limits you will be disappointed. Don't expect psychology to answer the ultimate questions posed by Russian novelist Leo Tolstoy (1904): "Why should I live? Why should I do anything? Is there in life any purpose which the inevitable death that awaits me does not undo and destroy?" Instead, expect that psychology will help you better understand why people feel, think, and act as they do. Then you should find the study of psychology both fascinating and useful.

Psychology's Subfields

Preview Question

3. What are psychology's specialized subfields?

To many people, psychology is a mental health profession devoted to such practical issues as how to have a happy marriage, how to overcome anxiety or depression, and how to raise children. For **clinical psychologists**—psychologists who study, assess, and treat troubled people—such ideas are apt. After their graduate school training, clinical psychologists administer and interpret tests, provide psychotherapy, manage mental health programs, and conduct research. By contrast, **psychiatrists** are medical doctors who are licensed to prescribe drugs and otherwise treat physical causes of psychological disorders along with the psychotherapy they often provide.

Many psychologists work outside the mental health professions. Some conduct **basic research** that builds psychology's knowledge base. In the pages to follow we will meet a wide variety of researchers: *biological psychologists* exploring the links between brain and mind; *developmental psychologists* studying our changing abilities from womb to tomb; *personality psychologists* investigating our inner traits.

Other psychologists conduct **applied research** that tackles practical problems. For example, *industrial/organizational psychologists* study and advise on behavior in the workplace. They use psychology's concepts and methods to help organizations select and train employees, boost morale and productivity, and design products and assess people's responses to them.

With perspectives ranging from the biological to the social, and with settings from the clinic to the laboratory, psychology has become the meeting place for different disciplines. More and more, psychology connects with fields ranging from mathematics and biology to sociology and philosophy. And more and more, psychology's methods and findings aid other disciplines. Psychologists teach in medical schools, law schools, and theological seminaries; they work in hospitals, factories, and corporate offices; they engage in interdisciplinary studies such as psychohistory, the psychological analysis of historical characters, and psycholinguistics, the study of the relation between language and the cognitive or behavioral characteristics of its users.

Aided by a sound-analyzing computer, a developmental psychologist studies the acoustical qualities of a baby's cry. An infant's healthy, normal cries signal a healthy brain.

Rehearse It*

1. Psychology is the science of behavior and mental processes. The perspective in psychology that focuses on how behavior and thought differ from situation to situation and culture to culture is the
a. cognitive perspective.
b. psychoanalytic perspective.
c. social-cultural perspective.
d. biological perspective.

2. In the history of psychology, one of the main debates has been over the nature-nurture issue. Nature is to nurture as
a. personality is to intelligence.
b. genes are to experience.

c. intelligence is to genes.
d. psychological traits are to behaviors.

3. The behavioral perspective in psychology emphasizes observable responses and how they are acquired and modified. A behavioral psychologist would be most likely to study
a. the effect of school uniforms on classroom behaviors.
b. the hidden meaning in children's themes and drawings.
c. the age at which children can learn algebra.
d. whether certain mathematical abilities appear to be inherited.

4. A psychologist who treats emotionally troubled adolescents at the local mental health agency is most likely to be a
a. research psychologist.
b. psychiatrist.
c. industrial/organizational psychologist.
d. clinical psychologist.

*You can find answers to "Rehearse It" questions at the end of each chapter.

The Scientific Approach

With its diverse perspectives and wide-ranging subfields, what unifies psychology? It's the *attitudes* and the *methods* with which psychologists approach the unknown.

The Scientific Attitude

Science is much more than a collection of facts. Science is an attitude, a way of thinking about the world. As a scientist, a psychologist aims to approach the world objectively, with an attitude of *open-minded skepticism*—an openness to new ideas along with skeptical scrutiny of all ideas, new and old.

Consider some familiar claims. Can a theater owner make you hungry by flashing on the screen an imperceptibly brief message—EAT POPCORN? Do lie detectors tell the truth? Can astrologers analyze your character and predict your future based on the position of the planets at the moment of your birth? As you will see in the chapters to follow, we can test all such claims objectively. In the arena of competing ideas, we can discover which ones match the facts.

Putting a scientific attitude into practice requires a good measure of *humility*, because it means that we have to be willing to reject our own ideas. In the last analysis, what matters is not my opinion, or yours, but reality. If animals or people don't behave as our ideas lead us to expect, then so much the worse for our ideas. This is the humble attitude expressed in one of psychology's early mottos: "The rat is always right." Historians of science tell us that these attitudes of open-minded skepticism and humility helped make modern science possible. Many of its founders were people whose religious convictions made them humble before nature yet skeptical of any human authority (Hooykaas, 1972; Merton, 1938).

The rest of this chapter illustrates how this attitude, combined with scientific methods for sifting truth from untruth, prepares us to think critically.

Preview Question

4. What attitudes and basic methods characterize scientific inquiry?

"Truth is arrived at by the painstaking process of eliminating the untrue."

Arthur Conan Doyle's Sherlock Holmes

"My deeply held belief is that if a god anything like the traditional sort exists, our curiosity and intelligence are provided by such a god. We would be unappreciative of those gifts . . . if we suppressed our passion to explore the universe and ourselves."

Carl Sagan (1979a)

critical thinking Thinking that does not blindly accept arguments and conclusions. Rather, it examines assumptions, discerns hidden values, evaluates evidence, and assesses conclusions.

theory An explanation that, through an integrated set of principles, organizes and predicts observations.

hypothesis A testable prediction, often implied by a theory.

replication Repeating the essence of a research study, usually with different subjects in different situations, to see whether the basic finding applies to other subjects and circumstances.

Critical thinking examines assumptions, discerns hidden values, evaluates evidence, and assesses conclusions. Whether reading news reports or listening to conversation, critical thinkers ask questions. They wonder, what ax is this person grinding? Is the conclusion based on mere anecdote and gut feelings? Or on trustworthy evidence? Does the evidence justify a cause-effect conclusion? What alternative explanations are possible? Psychology is less a set of conclusions than a way of thinking our way to conclusions—a way that prefers evidence over anecdote, experimentation over intuition, disciplined investigation over lazy hunch.

Carried to an extreme, critical thinking can degenerate into negative cynicism. But when applied to our own thinking, a critical attitude instead produces humility. It helps us acknowledge our biases, sharpen our analyses, and reach more accurate conclusions.

The Scientific Method

Psychologists apply this scientific ideal as they make observations, form theories, and then refine their theories in the light of new observations.

In everyday conversation, we sometimes use "theory" to mean "mere hunch." In science, a **theory** *explains;* it does so through an integrated set of principles that *organize* and *predict* observable behaviors or events. By organizing isolated facts, a theory simplifies things. There are now so many known facts about behavior—Nobel-laureate psychologist Allen Newell (1988) estimates 3000, including 29 that govern behavior while typing at a keyboard—that we could never hope to remember them all. A theory, however, offers a useful summary.

A good theory of depression, for example, will first organize countless observations concerning depression into a much shorter list of coherent principles. Say we observe over and over that depressed people recall their past, describe their present, and predict their future in gloomy terms. We might therefore theorize that low self-esteem causes depression. So far so good: Our self-esteem principle neatly summarizes a long list of facts about depressed people.

Yet no matter how reasonable a theory may sound—and low self-esteem certainly seems a reasonable explanation of depression—we must put it to the test. A good theory implies *testable predictions*, called **hypotheses.** Such predictions give direction to research by enabling us to test and revise the theory. To test our self-esteem theory of depression we might assess people's self-esteem and see whether, as we hypothesized, people who have poorer self-images are indeed more depressed.

In doing so, we should be aware that our theory can bias our observations. Once we've theorized that depression springs from low self-esteem, we may be tempted to perceive depressed people's comments as self-disparaging. As one check on our biases, we can report our research precisely enough to allow others to **replicate** (repeat) our observations. If other researchers recreate the essence of our study and get similar results, then our confidence in the reliability of our finding grows.

In the end, our theory will be useful if it powerfully organizes and predicts—if it (1) effectively organizes a wide range of observations and (2) implies clear predictions that anyone can use to check the theory or to derive practical applications. (If we boost people's self-esteem, will their depression lift?) Eventually, our theory will probably give way to a revised theory (such as the one on pages 396–398) that better organizes and predicts what we know about depression.

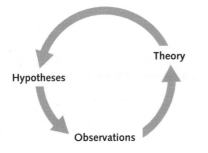

A theory implies hypotheses, which predict observations, which in turn we use to refine the theory.

Good theories explain by:
1. organizing observed facts
2. making testable predictions, sometimes with practical applications

Psychology's Methods

If you want to grasp the essence of psychology and to become a smart consumer of popularized psychology, you must first understand how psychologists ask questions. We test and refine our theories by making *observations* that describe behavior, detecting *correlations* that predict behavior, and doing *experiments* that help explain behavior.

Description

Preview Question

5. How do psychologists observe and describe behavior?

The starting point of any science is description. In everyday life, all of us observe and describe people, often forming hunches about why they behave as they do. Professional psychologists are doing much the same, only more objectively and systematically.

The Case Study

Among the oldest research methods is the **case study,** in which psychologists study one or more individuals in great depth in the hope of revealing things true of us all. Much of our early knowledge about the brain came from case studies of individuals who suffered a particular impairment after damage to a particular brain region. Sigmund Freud constructed his theory of personality from a handful of case studies. Developmental psychologist Jean Piaget taught us about children's thinking after carefully observing and questioning his own three children. Case studies can, however, be time-consuming. Moreover, any given individual may be atypical, making the case misleading.

The Survey

The **survey** method looks at many cases in less depth. A survey asks people to report their behavior or opinions. Questions about everything from sexual practices to opinions about policies and politicians have been put to the public. It's hard to think of a significant question that survey researchers have not asked: Recent surveys reveal that 70 percent of Americans favor prayer in public schools, that 33 percent of women consider themselves feminist, and that 28 percent of men—and 42 percent of women— believe that "most men are basically selfish and inconsiderate" (*American Enterprise,* 1991, 1992a,b). Yet surveys have limitations. They are valid only if the questions are clear and unbiased, the respondents are representative of the total group being studied, and their answers are honest.

Wording Effects   Asking questions is tricky, because even subtle changes in the order or wording of questions can have big effects. For example, 8 in 10 Americans agree that "Women with young children should be able to work outside the home." But 7 in 10 also agree that "Women should stay home if they have young preschool children" (*Public Opinion,* 1984, 1985). Asked, "Which in your opinion is more to blame for crime and lawlessness in this country—individuals or social conditions?" 6 in 10 blame social conditions. But when asked to agree or disagree that "*Individuals* are more to blame than *social conditions* for crime and lawlessness in this country," more than half agree (Krosnick & Schuman, 1988).

   The moral: Wording survey questions is a delicate matter.

Sampling   Like the Harris polls, most surveys sample a target group. If you wished to survey the students at your college you could question them all,

"One final question: Do you own or have you ever owned a fur coat?"

Drawing by M. Stevens; © 1989 The New Yorker Magazine, Inc.

case study Studying one person in depth in the hope of revealing universal principles.

survey A technique for ascertaining the self-reported attitudes or behaviors of people by questioning a representative, random sample of them.

population All the cases or members in a group from which samples may be drawn for study.

random sample A sample that fairly represents a population because each member has an equal chance of inclusion.

naturalistic observation Observing and recording behavior in naturally occurring situations without trying to manipulate and control the situation.

but probably there are too many. Instead, you survey a representative *sample* of the total student **population**—the whole group you want to study and describe. How can you make your sample representative of the population under study? By making it a **random sample,** one in which every person in the entire group has an equal chance of participating.

To sample the students at your institution randomly, you would *not* send them all a questionnaire, because the conscientious people who return it would not represent a random sample. Rather, you would aim for a representative sample by starting at a random point and selecting, say, every tenth or twentieth person from an alphabetical listing and then making sure you get responses from virtually all. Better to have a small, representative sample of 100 than a haphazard, unrepresentative sample of 500.

The random-sampling principle also works in national surveys. Imagine that you had a giant barrel containing 60 million white beans thoroughly mixed with 40 million green beans. A scoop that randomly sampled 1500 of them would contain about 60 percent white and 40 percent green beans, give or take 2 or 3 percent. Sampling voters in a national election survey is like sampling the beans; 1500 randomly sampled people provide a remarkably accurate snapshot of the opinions of a nation.

But getting a random sample can be a huge task. Some people will not be home. Others—often 30 percent or more in urban areas—may refuse to cooperate. Worse, some survey takers make little effort to gather a representative (random) sample. Shere Hite's book *Women and Love* reported survey findings based only on a 4.5 percent response rate from mailings to an unrepresentative sample of 100,000 American women. The response was doubly unrepresentative, because not only did she have a modest, self-selected return, but the women initially contacted were members of women's organizations. Nonetheless, "It's 4500 people. That's enough for me," reported Hite. And it was apparently enough for *Time* magazine, which made a cover story of her findings—that 70 percent of women married 5 years or more were having affairs, and that 95 percent of women feel emotionally harassed by the men they love (Wallis, 1987). Evidently it didn't matter that on less publicized surveys, *randomly* sampled American women express much higher levels of satisfaction: Half or more report feeling "very happy" or "completely satisfied" with their marriage; only 3 percent say they are "not at all happy" (Peplau & Gordon, 1985). And only 1 in 10 reports having had an affair during their current marriage (Greeley, 1991).

The moral: Before believing survey findings, consider the sample.

Psychologists use the survey method to gain information about specific groups of people. Well-done surveys use random sampling to gather information representative of the entire population being studied.

correlation A statistical measure of how much two factors vary together. This statistic indicates how well either factor predicts the other.

"You can see a lot by just looking."

Baseball great Yogi Berra

Naturalistic Observation

Watching and recording the behavior of organisms in their natural environment is known as **naturalistic observation.** Naturalistic observations range from watching chimpanzee societies in the jungle to observing parent-child interactions in different cultures to recording students' self-seating patterns in the lunchrooms of desegregated schools.

Like the case study and survey methods, naturalistic observation does not *explain* behavior. It simply *describes* it. Nevertheless, description can be revealing. We once thought, for example, that only humans use tools. Then naturalistic observation revealed that chimpanzees sometimes insert a stick in a termite mound and withdraw it, eating the stick's load of termites. Chimps and baboons also use deception (a tool of sorts) to achieve their aims. Psychologists Andrew Whiten and Richard Byrne (1988) repeatedly saw one young baboon pretending to have been attacked by another as a tactic to get its mother to drive the other baboon away from its food.

Naturalistic observation can involve activities as different as watching children at play or in the classroom or, as here, studying nesting birds in their natural habitat.

Through naturalistic observations we have also learned that culture shapes child-rearing. In Japan, children learn to "get along" and "go along" with their group. American child-rearing more often emphasizes individual achievement and rewards assertiveness. Naturalistic observation also reveals that at school, students of different races often shun each other outside the classroom (page 501). This suggests that special efforts to engage students in cooperative play and work may be needed to foster social integration.

Correlation

Describing behavior through descriptive methods is a first step toward predicting it. When case studies, surveys, or naturalistic observation reveal that one trait or behavior accompanies another, we say the two *correlate*. A **correlation** is a statistical measure of relationship: It reveals how closely two things vary together and thus how well one *predicts* the other. Knowing how much high school grades correlate with college grades tells us how accurately we can predict college grades from high school grades. A *positive* correlation indicates a *direct* relationship, meaning that two things increase together or decrease together. If amount of violence viewed on television correlates

Preview Question

6. Why do correlations permit prediction but not explanation?

positively with aggressive social behavior (which it does), then people's TV viewing habits will predict their aggressiveness (Figure 1–3). A *negative* correlation—equally predictive—indicates an *inverse* relationship: As one thing increases, the other decreases. Our findings on self-esteem and depression illustrate a negative correlation: People who score *low* on self-esteem tend to score *high* on depression.

The Appendix describes psychology's statistical tools more fully.

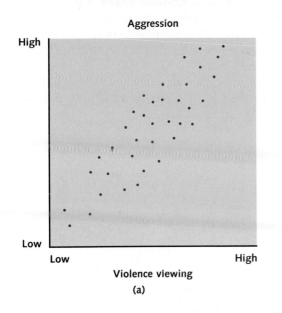

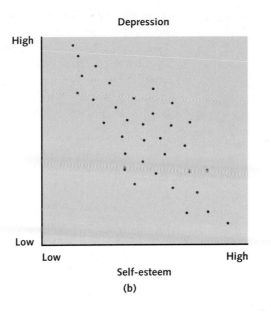

Figure 1–3 Correlation. (a) Positive correlation (direct relationship): Two factors increase (or decrease) together. Thus knowing one (for example, amount of violence viewing) enables us to predict the other (aggression).

(b) Negative correlation (inverse relationship): As one factor rises, the other falls. Again, knowing one (for example, self-esteem) allows us to predict the other (depression).

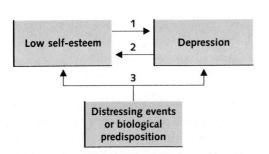

Figure 1–4 People low in self-esteem tend to be more depressed than those high in self-esteem. One possible explanation of this negative correlation is that a bad self-image causes depressed feelings. But, as the diagram indicates, other combinations of cause-effect relationships among these factors are possible.

So, *correlation enables prediction.* But does TV violence *cause* aggression? Does low self-esteem *cause* depression? If, based on the correlational evidence, you assume that they do, you have much company. Perhaps the most irresistible thinking error made both by lay people and by professional psychologists is assuming that correlation proves causation. It does not! If watching TV violence correlates positively with aggressiveness, does this mean that watching TV violence influences aggressive behavior? It may. But might not aggressive people prefer violent programs?

And what about the negative correlation between self-esteem and depression? Perhaps low self-esteem does cause depression. But perhaps instead depression causes people to be down on themselves. Or perhaps self-esteem and depression are causally unrelated. As Figure 1–4 suggests, *both* low self-esteem and depression might be caused by some underlying third factor, such as distressing events or a biological predisposition. Among men, length of marriage correlates positively with hair loss—because both are associated with a third factor, age.

The moral: Although correlation enables prediction, it does not provide explanation. Knowing that two events are correlated need not tell us anything about causation. *Correlation does not imply causation.* Remember this principle and you will be the wiser as you see reports of scientific studies in the news and in this book.

Rehearse It

5. In psychology a good theory implies hypotheses, or predictions that can be tested. When hypotheses are tested the result is typically
a. increased skepticism.
b. rejection of the merely theoretical.
c. refinement or revision of the theory.
d. personal bias on the part of the investigator.

6. Psychology's basic methods are description, correlation, and experimentation. With what type of research would you attempt to predict college grades from high school grades?
a. the case study
b. naturalistic observation
c. correlational research
d. experimental research

7. You wish to take an accurate poll in some country by questioning people who truly represent the country's adult population. Therefore, you need to make sure the people are
a. at least 30 percent urban dwellers.
b. registered voters.
c. predictable.
d. a random sample of the population.

8. Knowing that two events are correlated does not tell us what is the cause and what is the effect. However it does provide
a. a basis for prediction.
b. an explanation of events.
c. proof that one of the two events is the cause.
d. indication that underlying third factors are at work.

9. Suppose a psychologist finds that the *more* natural childbirth training classes a woman attends, the *less* pain medication she requires during childbirth. The relationship between number of training sessions and amount of pain medication required is a
a. positive correlation (direct relationship).
b. negative correlation (inverse relationship).
c. cause-and-effect relationship.
d. controlled experiment.

Preview Question

7. How do experiments clarify or reveal cause-effect relationships?

The color effect is not race-related. Instead, believes cross-cultural researcher John Williams (1992), it stems from our ancestors' associations with the black of night and light of day. Thus, in many African societies, "black" magic is bad magic.

Experimentation

To isolate cause and effect—to *explain* what helps cause, say, depression—psychologists conduct **experiments.** Experiments enable a researcher to focus on the possible effects of a single factor or two *by holding constant other factors and testing the one or two by manipulating them.* If behavior changes predictably when we vary an experimental factor, then that factor is having an effect. Note that unlike correlation studies, which uncover naturally occurring relationships, an experiment manipulates a factor to see its effect. To illustrate, let's consider two experiments.

Do Black Sports Uniforms Affect Perceptions?

Cornell University psychologists Mark Frank and Thomas Gilovich (1988) noticed that in virtually all cultures from central Africa to the Orient to Western Europe, the color black connotes evil. In movies, the bad guys wear black. Iran's Ayatollah Khomeini reportedly referred to the residence of the U.S. president as the "Black House."

Summarizing these varied observations, Frank and Gilovich proposed a simple, small-scale theory: Black garb suggests evil, cuing us to *perceive* people dressed in black as evil and cuing those who wear black to *act out* their evil image. Frank and Gilovich knew that a useful theory must offer testable predictions. So they derived several hypotheses. First, they predicted that people unfamiliar with football and hockey would rate the black uniforms of National Football League and National Hockey League teams as seeming more evil than nonblack uniforms. Indeed, for both sports, people rated black uniforms as bad, mean, and aggressive.

experiment A research method in which the investigator manipulates one or more factors to observe their effect on behavior, while controlling other relevant factors.

control condition The condition of an experiment in which the experimental treatment is absent; serves as a comparison for evaluating the effect of the treatment.

experimental condition The condition of an experiment that exposes subjects to the treatment, that is, to the independent variable.

Second, Frank and Gilovich hypothesized, and found, a positive correlation between black uniforms and total penalties for aggressive play. In all but 1 of the 17 seasons between 1970 and 1986, the football teams with black uniforms were penalized a disproportionate number of yards. Likewise, in all 16 hockey seasons between 1970–1971 and 1985–1986, the teams wearing black uniforms spent more time in the penalty box. Moreover, when the Pittsburgh Penguins switched to black uniforms during the middle of the 1979–1980 season, their penalties increased from an average of 8 minutes per game to 12 minutes. So, in these two sports at least, there definitely has been a correlation between black uniforms and penalized play.

Remember, a correlation is simply a relationship between two factors—in this case, uniform color and penalties. Correlation cannot prove a cause-effect relationship. Maybe there is no cause-effect connection; maybe organizations wanting an aggressive image simply choose black outfits and hire aggressive players. (For the Hell's Angels, white outfits just won't do.) But can you imagine *possible* causes of this correlation? Frank and Gilovich suggested two: The correlation occurs because referees *perceive* acts by players in black as more violent than similar acts by players not wearing black. Or, players who wear black uniforms *enact* the expected tough image.

In experimenting to evaluate these two possibilities, Frank and Gilovich found, first, that uniform color did indeed affect perceptions. They videotaped two staged football plays in which black- or white-clad defenders drove the ball carrier back several yards and then threw him to the ground, or hit the ball carrier violently in midair. For comparison, the experimenters took the color out of the picture to create a **control condition**—a condition lacking the experimental treatment. When all the players' jerseys appeared dull gray, raters judged the tackles of the white- and black-clad defenders as equally aggressive. In the **experimental conditions,** raters saw the same videotape in full color. With the color on, the raters (knowledgeable fans and professional referees) were more likely to judge the tackles as illegal when committed by players wearing black (Figure 1–5). Thus, the control condition of an experiment provides a baseline against which we can compare the effect of the treatment found in the experimental condition.

In a second experiment, Cornell students came to an experiment on "the psychology of competition." Frank and Gilovich randomly assigned them to wear either black or white jerseys and then invited them to choose some games. Those who donned the black jerseys preferred more aggressive games. So, *on average* (such findings tell us only about group trends), wearing black affected not only perceptions but behavior as well.

In traditional westerns you can always tell the good guys from the bad guys by the color of their outfits.

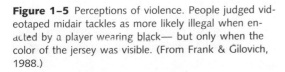

Figure 1–5 Perceptions of violence. People judged videotaped midair tackles as more likely illegal when enacted by a player wearing black— but only when the color of the jersey was visible. (From Frank & Gilovich, 1988.)

independent variable   The experimental factor that is manipulated; the variable whose effect is being studied.

dependent variable   The variable that is being measured; in an experiment, the variable that may change in response to manipulations of the independent variable.

random assignment   Assigning subjects to experimental and control conditions by chance, thus minimizing preexisting differences between those assigned to the different groups.

Note the distinction between random *assignment* in experiments and random *sampling* in surveys. Random assignment helps us infer cause and effect. Random sampling helps us generalize to a population.

"In solving one discovery we never fail to get an imperfect knowledge of others of which we had no idea before, so that we cannot solve one doubt without creating several new ones."

Joseph Priestly
Experiments and Observations on Different Kinds of Air, 1775–1786

The Frank and Gilovich experiments were fairly simple. They manipulated just one factor, jersey color. We call this experimental factor the **independent variable** because we can vary it independently of the other factors, such as the age or size of the players. Experimenters examine the effect of one or more independent variables on some measurable behavior, called the **dependent variable** because it can vary depending on what takes place during the experiment. In Frank and Gilovich's first experiment, the dependent variable was the subjects' perceptions of illegal aggression in response to (a) the control condition (videotape with dull gray jerseys) and to (b) the experimental conditions (videotape showing the black vs. white jerseys). Table 1–2 shows the independent and dependent variables in their second experiment.

Table 1-2

The Design of the Second Frank and Gilovich Experiment

	Condition	Independent variable	Dependent variable
Random assignment of subjects →	Experimental condition	Black jerseys	Aggressiveness
→	Control condition	White jerseys	Aggressiveness

Remember: An experiment has at least two different conditions, a comparison or *control* condition and an *experimental* condition. In this way it tests the effect of at least one *independent* variable (the experimental factor) on at least one *dependent* variable (the response that is measured).

Note that a key feature of experiments is **random assignment.** If enough individuals of different ages and opinions are randomly assigned to two groups, the random assignment will roughly equalize the two groups in age, opinion, and every other characteristic that could possibly affect the results. With random assignment, we can therefore say that if the two groups behave or feel differently at the end of the experiment, it very probably is due to the experiment's independent variable.

Note, too, that in this series of studies a very simple *theory*, inspired by everyday *observations*, generated *hypotheses* that were confirmed by the *correlation* between uniforms and penalties, which in turn stimulated *experiments* that examined causation. Table 1–3 compares the features of psychology's research methods.

How freely can we generalize Frank and Gilovich's findings? Surely we don't perceive Catholic clergy and Hassidic Jews as aggressive, nor does wearing black cause them to act more aggressively. Frank and Gilovich suspect—but can't know without further research—that the effects occur only in situations involving competition and aggressive confrontation.

As so often happens, the answering of one question has led to the asking of another. Scientific inquiry is a voyage of discovery toward a horizon, beyond which yet another horizon beckons.

These concepts—experimental and control condition, independent and dependent variable, random assignment—are important and powerful, yet easily confused. So let's put them to work with another intriguing set of experiments.

Table 1-3
Comparing Research Methods

Research method	Basic purpose	How conducted	What is manipulated
Description	To observe and record behavior	Case studies, surveys, and naturalistic observations	Nothing
Correlation	To detect naturally occurring relationships; to assess how well one variable predicts another	Computing statistical association	Nothing
Experimentation	To explore cause and effect	Manipulating a factor after using random assignment to eliminate preexisting differences among subjects	The independent variable

Can Subliminal Tapes Improve Your Life?

A new generation of entrepreneurs would have you believe so. Mail order catalogs, cable television ads, and bookstores offer tapes with imperceptibly faint messages that will "reprogram your unconscious mind for success and happiness." While underachieving students listen to soothing music, subliminal messages (below the threshold for hearing) persuade the unconscious that "I am a good student. I love learning." Procrastinators can be similarly reprogrammed to think "I set my priorities. I get things done ahead of time!"

Is there *anything* to these wild and sometimes wacky claims? Might positive subliminal messages help us, even a little? In Chapter 4, Sensation and Perception, we will see that subliminal sensation is for real. We do process much information without conscious awareness. And under certain conditions, a stimulus too weak to recognize can subtly affect us.

But does this subtle, fleeting effect extend to the powerful, enduring effects claimed by the subliminal tape merchants? Anthony Greenwald, Eric Spangenberg, Anthony Pratkanis, and Jay Eskenazi (1991) decided to find out. They randomly assigned eager university students to listen daily for 5 weeks to commercial subliminal tapes designed to improve either self-esteem or memory. Then the researchers manipulated an experimental factor. On half the tapes the researchers switched the labels. People given these tapes *thought* they were receiving affirmations of self-esteem, when, actually, they heard the memory enhancement tape. Or they got the memory tape but *thought* their self-esteem was being recharged.

Were the tapes effective? Scores on both self-esteem and memory tests, taken before and after the 5 weeks, revealed no effects. Zilch. Nevertheless, those who *thought* they had a memory tape *believed* their memories had improved. A similar effect occurred with those who thought they had a self-esteem tape. Although the tapes had no effects, people *perceived* themselves receiving the benefits they expected. Reading this research, we can hear echoes of the testimonies that adorn the mail order tape catalogs: "I really know that your tapes were invaluable in reprogramming my mind," wrote one thankful customer.

Our natural tendencies to try new remedies when we are in an emotional slump can further distort a testimonial. When our emotions rebound to nor-

In this experiment, what was the independent variable? The dependent variable? (See page 17.)

placebo [pluh-SEE-bo]   An inert substance that may be administered instead of a presumed active agent, such as a drug; may trigger the effects believed to characterize the active agent.

double-blind procedure   An experimental procedure in which both the subject and the staff are ignorant (blind) about whether the subject has received the treatment or a placebo. Commonly used in drug evaluation studies.

mal, we attribute the rebound to something we have done. If 3 days into a cold we start taking vitamin C tablets and find our cold symptoms lessening, the pills may seem more potent than they are. If, after doing exceptionally poorly on the first exam, we listen to a "peak learning" subliminal tape and find our next exam score improved, we may credit the tape. Whether or not a remedy is effective, enthusiastic users will probably endorse it. To find out whether it actually is effective we must experiment.

And that is precisely how we evaluate new drug treatments and new methods of psychological therapy. In many of these studies, the subjects are "blind" (uninformed) about what treatment, if any, they are receiving. One group might receive the treatment (say, a particular subliminal message or a new drug), while others receive a pseudotreatment—a **placebo** (a tape without the expected message, a pill with no drug in it). Often both the subject and the research assistant who collects the data will not know which group the subject is in. This **double-blind procedure** allows researchers to check the actual effects of a treatment apart from their subjects' and their own enthusiasm for it.

Rehearse It

10. A researcher wants to determine if noise level affects the blood pressure of elderly subjects. In one group she varies the level of noise in the environment and records blood pressures. In this experiment the level of noise is the
a. control condition.
b. dependent variable (or the factor being observed).
c. independent variable (or the factor being manipulated).
d. cause of any blood pressure variations.

11. To test the effect of a new drug on blood cholesterol, we randomly assign subjects to control and experimental conditions. Those in the experimental condition take a pink pill containing the new medication; the control group takes a pink pill that contains no medication. Which statement is true?
a. The medication is the dependent variable.
b. Cholesterol level is the independent variable.
c. The subjects in the control group take a placebo.
d. Neither the experimental nor the control group are told the purpose of the experiment.

12. To eliminate the biasing effect of a researcher's positive expectations on the outcome of a health clinic's research experiment,
a. subjects are randomly assigned to the control and experimental groups (random assignment).
b. the experimental subjects are carefully matched for age, sex, income, and level of education with subjects in the control group (controlled selection).
c. neither the subjects nor the researchers know whether a given subject has been assigned to the experimental or control condition (double-blind procedure).
d. experimental subjects are chosen by selecting every 10th person in an alphabetical listing of all the clinic's patients (random selection).

Questions Commonly Asked About Psychology

We have discussed psychology's historical roots, its current perspectives, and its research methods. We have seen how case studies, surveys, and naturalistic observations allow us to describe behavior. We have noted that correlational studies assess the relationship between two factors, indicating how well we can predict one thing, knowing another. And we have examined the logic that underlies experiments, which use control conditions and random assignment of subjects to isolate the effects of an independent variable on a dependent variable.

This is reasonable preparation for understanding what lies ahead. Yet, knowing this much, students often approach psychology with a mixture of curiosity and apprehension. So before we plunge in, let's address some typical questions and concerns.

Aren't Laboratory Experiments Artificial?

When you see or hear a report of psychological research, do you ever wonder whether people's behavior in the laboratory has anything to do with their behavior in real life? Does detecting the blink of a faint red light in a dark room have anything useful to say about flying a plane at night? Does our tendency to remember best the first and last items in a list of unrelated words tell us anything about how we remember the names of people we meet at a party? After viewing a violent, sexually explicit film, does an angered man's increased willingness to push buttons he thinks electrically shock a woman really say anything about whether violent pornography makes men more likely to abuse women?

Before you answer, consider the intent of laboratory experiments. Far from considering artificiality a problem, the experimenter *intends* the laboratory environment to be a simplified reality—one where important features of everyday life can be simulated and controlled. Like an aeronautical wind tunnel that recreates atmospheric forces under controlled conditions, an experiment enables a psychologist to recreate psychological forces under controlled conditions.

The experiment's purpose is not to recreate the exact behaviors of everyday life but to test theoretical principles (Mook, 1983). *It is the resulting principles—not the specific findings—that help explain everyday behaviors.* When psychologists apply laboratory research on aggression to actual violence, they are applying theoretical *principles* of aggressive behavior, principles refined through many experiments. Similarly, it is the *principles* of the visual system, developed from experiments in artificial settings (such as looking at red lights in the dark), that we apply to more complex behaviors such as night flying.

The point to remember: As research psychologists, our concerns lie less with particular behaviors than with general principles that help explain many behaviors.

Doesn't Everything Depend on One's Culture?

If culture shapes behavior, what can psychological studies done with North Americans—often, white North Americans—really tell us about people in general? As we will see time and again, our cultural diversity greatly affects our specific behaviors and attitudes. Our culture influences our standards of promptness and frankness, our attitudes toward premarital sex and differing body shapes, our tendencies to be casual or formal, and much more. Being aware of such differences can keep us from assuming that others will, or should, think and act as we do. Given the growing mix of cultures and consequent cultural diversity, the need for such awareness becomes urgent.

At the same time, our shared biological heritage unites us as members of a universal human family. The same underlying processes guide people everywhere. A Western woman who wears cologne may not understand a Masai woman who grooms her hair with animal excrement, but both are

Answer to question on page 15: In the subliminal tapes experiment, the primary independent variable was the type of subliminal message, self-esteem vs. memory. (This experiment actually had a second independent variable as well: people's beliefs about which tape they received.) The primary dependent variables were improvement on the self-esteem and memory measures.

One's culture dictates appropriate social behaviors for different situations. This Japanese schoolgirl is simply greeting her teacher, but her behavior would seem unnaturally formal to someone from a Western society.

responding to cultural standards of beauty. Varying languages—verbal and nonverbal— may impede communication across cultures. Yet all languages share deep principles of grammar, and people from opposite sides of the globe can communicate with a smile or a frown. People in different cultures vary in their feelings of loneliness, yet across cultures shyness and low self-esteem magnify loneliness (Jones & others, 1985). Japanese prefer their fish raw while North Americans prefer theirs cooked, but the same principles of hunger and taste influence both. It is truly said that we are each in certain respects like all others, like some others, and like no other. Studying people of all races, sexes, and cultures helps us sort our similarities and differences.

The point to remember: Even when specific attitudes and behaviors vary across cultures, as they often do, the underlying processes are much the same.

Why Do Psychologists Study Animals?

Many psychologists study animals because, like animal lovers everywhere, they find them fascinating. Psychologists also study animals to learn about people. Human physiology resembles that of many other animals. That is why animal experiments have led to treatments for human diseases—insulin for diabetes, vaccines to prevent polio and rabies, transplants to replace defective organs. Likewise, the processes by which humans see, exhibit emotion, and become obese operate in rats and monkeys. To discover more about the basics of human learning, researchers are even studying sea slugs. To understand how a combustion engine works you'd do better to study a lawn mower's engine than a Cadillac's. Humans, like Cadillacs, are more complex. But it is precisely the simplicity of the sea slug's nervous system that makes it so revealing.

Is It Ethical to Experiment on Animals?

During the 1980s, a growing animal protection movement protested the use of animals in psychological, biological, and medical research and teaching—some 20 million animals annually, according to the National Academy of Sciences (1991)—though that's less than 1 percent of the 5 billion animals butchered annually in the United States as a source of food (which means the average American eats roughly 20 animals a year, without allowing for imported meat). Researchers experiment on some 200,000 dogs and cats a year—about 2 percent of the 10 million dogs and cats put to death by animal shelters.

Mobilization for Animals, a network of some 400 animal protection organizations is nevertheless concerned. It has declared that in psychological experiments animals are shocked "until they lose the ability to even scream in pain, . . . deprived of food and water to suffer and die slowly from hunger and thirst, . . . put in total isolation chambers until they are driven insane or even die from despair and terror," and made "the victims of extreme pain and stress, inflicted upon them out of idle curiosity." Psychologists Caroline Coile and Neal Miller (1984) analyzed every animal research article published in the American Psychological Association journals during the preceding 5 years. They found not one study in which any of these allegations was true. Even when researchers used shock, it usually was of a mild intensity that humans can easily endure on their fingers. About 7 percent of psychology's studies have involved animals, 95 percent of which are rats, mice, rabbits, or birds. About 10 percent of these animal studies involved electric shock (Coile

Is it right that researchers use animals to advance our understanding of how humans function? For animal rights activists, no purpose justifies hurting, frightening, or (as here) manipulating an animal. However, most psychologists and medical researchers believe that animal research is both necessary and ethically justified so long as researchers observe strict standards for animal care and inflict no unnecessary pain.

& Miller, 1984; Gallup & Suarez, 1985). In British psychology departments, where animal use has dropped by two-thirds since 1977, electric shock is used in only 4 percent of animal studies—all involving rats (Thomas & Blackman, 1991).

Moreover, say researchers, this is not the morality of good versus evil but of compassion for animals versus compassion for people. How many of us would have attacked Pasteur's experiments with rabies, which in causing some dogs to suffer led to a vaccine that spared millions of people, and dogs, from agonizing death? And would we really wish to have deprived ourselves of the animal research that led to effective methods of training retarded children; of relieving fears and depression; and of controlling stress-related pain and disease?

Out of the heated debate on this subject, two issues emerge. The basic one is whether it is right to place the well-being of humans above that of animals. In experiments on stress and cancer, is it right that mice get tumors so that people might not? Defenders of research on animals argue that anyone who has eaten a hamburger, worn leather shoes, tolerated hunting and fishing, or supported the extermination of crop-destroying or plague-carrying pests has already agreed that, yes, it is sometimes permissible to sacrifice animals for the sake of humans.

If we give human life first priority, the second issue is the priority given the well-being of animals. What safeguards should protect animals? Most researchers today feel ethically obligated to enhance the well-being of captive animals and protect them from needless suffering. They welcomed national animal protection legislation updated by the United States in 1985 and Britain in 1986 and the accompanying regulations and laboratory inspections (Cherfas, 1990; Johnson, 1990).

Ironically, animals have themselves benefitted from animal research. Studies have helped improve their care in laboratories and zoos. By revealing our behavioral kinship with animals, experiments have also increased our empathy with them. At its best, a psychology that is concerned for humans and sensitive to animals can serve the welfare of both.

Is It Ethical to Experiment on People?

If the image of people receiving supposed electric shocks troubles you, you may find it reassuring that most psychological research involves no such stress. Blinking lights, flashing words, and pleasant social interactions are the rule.

Occasionally, though, researchers temporarily stress or deceive people. This is done only when judged essential to a justifiable end, such as understanding and controlling violent behavior or studying mood swings. Such experiments wouldn't work if the participants knew all there was to know about the experiment beforehand. Either the procedures would be ineffective or the participants, wanting to be helpful, might try to confirm the researchers' predictions.

Ethical principles developed by the American Psychological Association and the British Psychological Society urge investigators to (1) obtain the informed consent of potential participants, (2) protect them from harm and discomfort, (3) treat information about individual participants confidentially, and (4) fully explain the research afterward. Moreover, most universities today screen research proposals through an ethics committee that safeguards participants' well-being.

"Please do not forget those of us who suffer from incurable diseases or disabilities who hope for a cure through research that requires the use of animals."

Paraplegic psychologist Dennis Feeney (1987)

"The greatness of a nation can be judged by the way its animals are treated."

Mahatma Gandhi, 1869–1948

hindsight bias The tendency to believe one would have foreseen how something turned out, *after* learning the outcome. (Also known as the *I-knew-it-all-along phenomenon.*)

People interpret ambiguous information to fit their preconceptions. A duck or a rabbit?

"It is doubtless impossible to approach any human problem with a mind free from bias."

Simone de Beauvoir
The Second Sex, 1953

"Life is lived forwards, but understood backwards."

Søren Kierkegaard, 1813–1855

Is Psychology Free of Value Judgments?

Psychology is definitely not value-free. Researchers' values influence their choice of research topics—whether to study worker productivity or worker morale, sex discrimination or sex differences, conformity or independence. Values can also color the "facts." Our preconceptions can bias our observations and interpretations; sometimes we see what we are predisposed to see. Even the words we use to describe a phenomenon can reflect our values. Whether we label sex acts we do not practice as "perversions" or as "sexual variations" conveys a value judgment. The same holds true in everyday speech, as when one person's "terrorists" are another's "freedom fighters." Both in and out of psychology, labels describe and labels evaluate.

Popular applications of psychology also contain hidden values. When people defer to "professional" guidance about how to live—how to raise children, how to achieve self-fulfillment, what to do with sexual feelings, how to get ahead at work—they are accepting value-laden advice. A science of behavior and mental processes can help us reach our goals, but it cannot decide them.

Aren't Psychology's Theories Mere Common Sense?

Perhaps the most common criticism of psychology is that it merely documents the obvious by dressing in jargon what people already know: "So what else is new—you get paid for this?"

In several experiments, psychologist Baruch Fischhoff and others (Slovic & Fischhoff, 1977; Wood, 1979) found that events seem far less obvious and predictable beforehand than in hindsight. Once people learn the outcome of an experiment or an historical episode, it suddenly seems less surprising to them than to people asked to guess the outcome. Finding out that something has happened makes it seem inevitable. So things appear to political columnist George Will (1989), who chides social scientists for "stumbling upon the obvious with a sense of discovery." Psychologists call this 20/20 hindsight vision the **hindsight bias**, also known as the *I-knew-it-all-along phenomenon*.

The phenomenon is easy to demonstrate. Give half the members of a group some purported psychological finding and the other half an opposite result. For example, imagine reading, "Psychologists have found that separation weakens romantic attraction. As the adage says, 'Out of sight, out of mind.'" Could you imagine why this might be? Most people can, and nearly all will then report that the finding is unsurprising.

But what if you had read the opposite: "Psychologists have found that separation strengthens romantic attraction. As the adage says, 'Absence makes the heart grow fonder.'" People given this result can also easily explain it and overwhelmingly see *it* as unsurprising common sense. Obviously, when both a statement and its opposite seem like common sense, there is a problem. It's not that common sense is always wrong, but that it so often is a judgment we make *after* we know the results.

You may have noticed hindsight bias after reading a mystery: The solution, once revealed, appears obvious. We also experience hindsight bias while looking back on history. In contrast to their preelection uncertainty, people *after* a presidential election exude confidence that they could have told you how it would turn out (Powell, 1988). To doctors given case information plus an autopsy report, a cause of death may seem obvious—something they easily could have foreseen, knowing the symptoms. But it is not so obvious to doctors told the same symptoms without the autopsy report (Dawson & oth-

"It is easy to be wise after the event."

Sherlock Holmes, in Arthur Conan
Doyle's "The Problem of Thor Bridge"

ers, 1988). From our 1990s vantage point, it may in hindsight seem obvious that Eastern European countries would exchange communism for democracy. But it wasn't obvious to United Nations ambassador Jeanne Kirkpatrick when in 1980 she warned, "The history of this century provides no grounds for expecting that radical totalitarian regimes will transform themselves."

But sometimes psychological findings *do* jolt our common sense. Throughout this book we will see how research has both inspired and overturned popular ideas—about aging, about sleep and dreams, about personality assessment—and how it has surprised us with discoveries about how the brain's chemical messengers control our moods and memories, about animal abilities, about the effects of stress on our body's capacity to fight disease. If some people see psychology as mere common sense, others have an opposite concern—that it is becoming dangerously powerful.

Isn't Psychology Potentially Dangerous?

Is it an accident, someone once wondered, that astronomy is the oldest science and psychology the youngest? Exploring the external universe is one thing, but exploring our own inner universe is even more dangerous and threatening. Might psychology be used to manipulate people? Might it become the tool of someone seeking to create a totalitarian *Brave New World* or *Nineteen Eighty-Four?*

Knowledge is a power that, like all powers, we can use for good or evil. Nuclear power can light up cities—and destroy them. Persuasive power can educate people—and deceive them. The power of mind-altering drugs can restore sanity—and destroy it.

Although it has the power to deceive, psychology strives to enlighten. Psychologists are exploring ways to enhance moral development, perceptual accuracy, learning, creativity, and compassion. And psychology speaks to many of the world's great problems—war, overpopulation, prejudice, and crime—all of which are problems of attitudes and behavior. Psychology also speaks to humanity's deepest longings—for love, for happiness, even for food and water. Psychology cannot address all the great questions of life, but it speaks to some mighty important ones.

Rehearse It

13. In a laboratory experiment, features of everyday life can be simulated, manipulated, and controlled. The laboratory environment is designed to help us
a. exactly recreate the events of everyday life.
b. examine theoretical principles under controlled conditions.
c. create opportunities for naturalistic observation.
d. minimize the use of animals and humans in psychological research.

14. The animal protection movement has protested the use of animals in all fields of scientific research. In defending their experimental research with animals, psychologists have noted that
a. animals' physiology and behavior can tell us much about our own.
b. psychologists do not torture or needlessly exploit animals.
c. advancing the well-being of humans justifies animal experimentation.
d. all of the above.

15. Psychology is often criticized as telling us what we already know from common sense. Hindsight bias refers to our tendency to
a. perceive events as obvious or inevitable after the fact.
b. assume that because two events are correlated one causes the other.
c. overestimate our abilities to predict the future.
d. make judgments that actually fly in the face of common sense.

SQ3R   An acronym for *Survey, Question, Read, Rehearse, Review*—a method of study

Studying Psychology

The investment you are making in studying psychology has the potential to enrich your life and enlarge your vision. Through painstaking research, psychologists have gained insights into brain and mind, depression and joy, dreams and memories. Even the unanswered questions can enrich us, by renewing our sense of mystery about "things too wonderful" for us yet to understand. What is more, your study of psychology can help teach you *how to ask important questions*—how to think critically as you evaluate competing ideas and pop psychology's claims.

Having your life enriched and your vision enlarged (and getting a decent grade, too) requires effective study. As we will see in Chapter 7, Memory, to master any subject you must *actively process* it. Your mind is not like your stomach, something to be filled passively; it is more like a muscle, which grows stronger with exercise. Countless experiments reveal that people learn and remember material best when they put it in their own words, rehearse it, and then review and rehearse it again.

The famous **SQ3R** study method incorporates these principles (Robinson, 1970). SQ3R is an acronym for its five steps: *Survey, Question, Read, Rehearse, Review*.

To study a chapter, first *survey*, taking a bird's-eye view as you note its headings. Notice how the chapter is organized.

As you prepare to read each section, use its heading or the preview question to form a *question* that you should answer. For this section, you might have asked, "How can I most effectively and efficiently master the information in this book?"

Then *read*, actively searching for the answer. At each sitting, read only as much of the chapter as you can absorb without tiring. Usually, a single main chapter section will do—the "Commonly Asked Questions" section you just finished, for example. Relating what you are reading to your own life will improve understanding and retention. Reading the occasional "Psychology Applied" and "Close-Up" boxed sections will help.

Having read a section, *rehearse* in your own words what you read. Test yourself by trying to answer your question, rehearsing what you can recall, then glancing back over what you can't recall.

Finally, *review:* Read over any notes you have taken, again with an eye on the chapter's organization, and quickly review the whole chapter.

Survey, question, read, rehearse, review. This book's chapters are organized to facilitate your use of the SQ3R study system. Each chapter begins with a chapter outline that aids your *survey*. Headings and preview *questions* suggest issues and concepts you should consider as you *read*. The material is organized into sections of readable length, and the end of a section is the time to *rehearse* what you have learned. The chapter summaries *review* the chapter's essentials and list key terms to help you check your mastery of important concepts. Survey, question, read . . . .

Five additional study tips may further boost your learning:

1. *Distribute your study time.* One of psychology's oldest findings is that "spaced practice" promotes better retention than "massed practice." You'll remember material better if you space your time over several study periods rather than cram it into one long study blitz. Better to give your study of this text one hour a day, with one day off a week, than six hours at a time. Doing this requires a disciplined approach to managing your time. (Richard Straub explains time management in ***Discovering Psychol-***

ogy, the study guide that accompanies this text.) For example, rather than trying to read all of a chapter in a single sitting, read just one of the chapter's sections, and then turn to something else.

2. *Learn to think critically.* Whether reading or in class, note people's *assumptions and values.* What perspective or bias underlies an argument? *Evaluate evidence.* Is it anecdotal? Correlational? Experimental? *Assess conclusions.* Are there alternative explanations? The "Critical Thinking Exercise" at the end of each chapter will help you learn, then practice, these skills.

3. *In class, listen actively.* As psychologist William James urged a century ago, "No reception without reaction, no impression without . . . expression." Listen for the main and sub-ideas of a lecture. Write them down. Ask questions during and after class. In class, as in your private study, process the information actively and you will understand and retain it better.

4. *Overlearn.* Psychology tells us that "overlearning improves retention." Most of us are prone to overestimating how much we know. You may understand a chapter as you read it, but by devoting extra study time to testing yourself and reviewing what you think you know, you will retain your new knowledge long into the future.

5. *Be a smart test-taker.* If a test contains both multiple-choice questions and an essay question, turn first to the essay. Read the question carefully, noting exactly what the instructor is asking. On the back of a page, pencil in a list of points you'd like to make, and then organize them. Before writing, put aside the essay and work through the multiple-choice questions. (As you do so, your mind may continue to mull over the essay question. Sometimes the objective questions will bring pertinent thoughts to mind.) Then reread the essay question, rethink your answer, and start writing. When finished, proofread to eliminate spelling and grammatical errors that make you look less competent than you are. When reading multiple-choice questions, don't confuse yourself by trying to imagine how each of the alternatives might be right. Try instead to recall the answer *before* reading the alternatives given. Answer the question as if it were a fill-in-the-blank; first cover the answers and complete the sentence in your mind, and then find the alternative that best matches your own answer.

While exploring psychology, you will learn much more than effective study techniques. Psychology deepens our appreciation for how we humans perceive, think, feel, and act. By so doing it can indeed enrich our lives and enlarge our vision. Through this book I hope to help guide you toward that end. As educator Charles Eliot said a century ago: "Books are the quietest and most constant of friends, and the most patient of teachers."

Reviewing Your Introduction to Psychology

What Is Psychology?

1. **How did the science of psychology develop?**

   Beginning with the first psychological laboratory, founded in 1879 by German philosopher and physiologist Wilhelm Wundt, psychology's modern roots can be found in many disciplines and countries. Psychology's historic perspectives and current activities lead us to define the field as the science of behavior and mental processes.

2. **What theoretical perspectives do psychologists emphasize?**

There are many disciplines that study human nature. Psychology is one. Within psychology, the biological, behavioral, psychoanalytic, humanistic, cognitive, and social-cultural perspectives are complementary. Each has its own purposes, questions, and limits; together they provide a fuller understanding of mind and behavior.

3. **What are psychology's specialized subfields?**

Psychologists' activities are widely varied, ranging from the diagnoses and therapies of clinical psychologists and psychiatrists to the basic research conducted by biological, developmental, or personality psychologists to the applied research of industrial/organizational psychologists.

The Scientific Approach

4. **What attitudes and basic methods characterize scientific inquiry?**

Scientific inquiry requires an attitude—a mixture of skeptical scrutiny of competing ideas and humility before nature—and basic research methods. Observation stimulates the construction of theories, which in turn organize the observations and imply predictive hypotheses. These hypotheses (predictions) are then tested to validate and refine the theory and to suggest practical applications.

Psychology's Methods

5. **How do psychologists observe and describe behavior?**

Through individual case studies, surveys among random samples of a population, and naturalistic observations, psychologists observe and describe behavior and mental processes.

6. **Why do correlations permit prediction but not explanation?**

Correlations permit prediction because they are a measure of the strength of the relationship of two factors. Knowing how closely two things are correlated tells us how much one predicts the other. But correlation is only a measure of relationship; it does not "explain" the relationship in terms of cause and effect.

7. **How do experiments clarify or reveal cause-effect relationships?**

To examine cause-and-effect relationships more directly, psychologists conduct experiments. By constructing a miniature reality, experimenters can manipulate one or two factors and discover how these independent variables affect a particular behavior, the dependent variable. In many experiments, control is achieved by randomly assigning people either to be experimental subjects who are exposed to the treatment, or control subjects who are not.

Questions Commonly Asked About Psychology

8. **Aren't laboratory experiments artificial?**

By intentionally creating a controlled, artificial environment, experimenters aim to test theoretical principles. These principles help us to understand, describe, explain, and predict everyday behaviors.

9. **Doesn't everything depend on one's culture?**

Although attitudes and behaviors vary across cultures, the principles that underlie them vary much less. Cross-cultural psychology explores both our cultural differences and our human similarities.

10. **Why do psychologists study animals?**

Some psychologists study animals out of an interest in animal behavior. Others do so to gain knowledge of the physiological and psychological processes of animals, which are in certain ways similar to the processes that operate in humans.

11. **Is it ethical to experiment on animals?**

Only about 7 percent of all psychological experiments involve animals, mostly rats, mice, and birds. In only a few of these experiments do the animals experience pain. Nevertheless, opposition to animal experimentation by animal rights groups has raised two important issues: Is the temporary suffering of even a few animals in medical and psychological research justified if it leads to the relief of human suffering? And if indeed human well-being is given first priority, what safeguards should protect animal well-being?

12. **Is it ethical to experiment on people?**

Occasionally researchers temporarily stress or deceive people in order to learn something important. Professional ethical standards provide guidelines concerning the treatment of human subjects.

13. **Is psychology free of value judgments?**

Psychology is not value-free. Psychologists' own values can influence their choice of research topics, their theories and observations, their labels for behavior, and their professional advice.

14. **Aren't psychology's theories mere common sense?**

Experiments reveal a hindsight bias, also called the I-knew-it-all-along phenomenon: Learning the outcome of a study can make it seem like obvious common sense. But things seldom seem so obvious before the results are known.

15. **Isn't psychology potentially dangerous?**

Knowledge is power that can be used for good or evil. Applications of psychology's principles have so far been mostly for the good, and psychology addresses some of humanity's greatest problems and deepest longings.

Terms and Concepts to Remember

psychology, p. 2	applied research, p. 5	experiment, p. 12
nature-nurture issue, p. 2	critical thinking, pp. 6–7	control condition, p. 13
biological perspective, p. 2	theory, p. 7	experimental condition, p. 13
psychoanalytic perspective, p. 2	hypothesis, p. 7	independent variable, p. 14
behavioral perspective, p. 4	replication, p. 7	dependent variable, p. 14
humanistic perspective, p. 4	case study, p. 8	random assignment, p. 14
cognitive perspective, p. 4	survey, p. 8	placebo [pluh-SEE-bo], p. 16
social-cultural perspective, p. 4	population, p. 9	double-blind procedure, p. 16
clinical psychology, p. 5	random sample, p. 9	hindsight bias, p. 20
psychiatry, p. 5	naturalistic observation, p. 10	SQ3R, p. 22
basic research, p. 5	correlation, p. 10	

Rehearse It Answer Key

1. c.　　**2.** b.　　**3.** a.　　**4.** d.　　**5.** c.　　**6.** c.　　**7.** d.　　**8.** a.　　**9.** b.

10. c.　　**11.** c.　　**12.** c.　　**13.** b.　　**14.** d.　　**15.** a.

Critical Thinking Exercise

You have *Surveyed, Questioned, Read, Rehearsed,* and *Reviewed* Chapter 1. Now take your learning a step further by testing your *critical thinking* skills on the following passage. If you need a refresher on the concept of critical thinking, turn to Appendix B before working this exercise.

Your roommate announces that for her senior honors research project: "I'm going to conduct an experiment testing my theory that upperclass men and women do better academically—get better grades—than underclass men and women because they take a more serious approach to their studies. I'm going to survey a random sample of seniors selected from my honors class. I'll ask them whether they agree or disagree with the statement: 'As a senior, I take a more serious and mature approach to college than I did as a freshman.'" More than 90 percent of those surveyed agree with the statement. So your roommate concludes that her study proves that upperclass men and women are, in fact, more serious students.

Understand the Assertion

1. State your roommate's assertion in your own words. Define all important concepts and terms as they are used in this study.

Consider the Evidence

2. Is the evidence for your roommate's assertion empirical (observable)? Is the evidence based on trustworthy research?

Evaluate the Explanation

3. Evaluate the proposed explanation.
   a. Restate it in your own words.
   b. Determine whether the explanation makes sense based on the evidence.
   c. State an alternative explanation.

Check your progress on becoming a critical thinker by comparing your answers to the sample answers found in Appendix B.

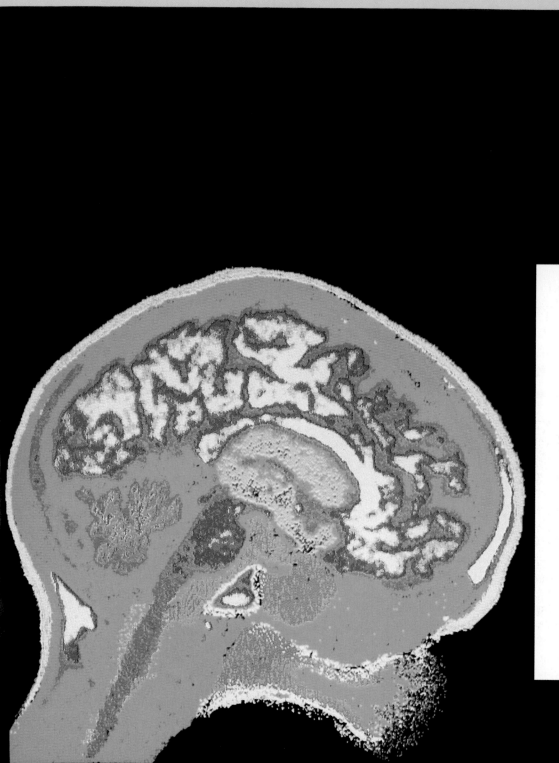

Chapter 2

Biological Roots of Behavior

On the time scale of human existence, the last 150 years are only a few ticks of the clock. But that's how recently a scientific understanding of the biological roots of our behavior began to emerge. We have come far since the early 1800s, when a German physician named Franz Gall invented *phrenology*, an ill-fated theory which held that bumps on the skull could reveal our mental abilities and character traits.

Despite its wrong-headedness, phrenology focused attention on the idea that various brain regions have specific functions. In little more than a century, we have also realized that the body is composed of cells; that among these are nerve cells, which conduct electricity and "talk" to one another by sending chemical messages across a tiny gap that separates them; and that specific areas of the brain serve specific functions (though not the functions that Gall supposed). You and I are privileged to be living at a time when scientific discoveries about the most basic aspects of our biology and behavior are occurring at an exhilarating pace.

Throughout this book you will find examples of how our biology underlies our behavior and mental processes. Every idea, every mood, every memory, every urge that you or I have ever experienced is fundamentally a biological phenomenon. Our thoughts, emotions, and behaviors are all biological events. By studying the links between biology and psychology, **biological psychologists** are gaining new clues about sleep and dreams, depression and schizophrenia, hunger and sex, stress and disease. We therefore begin our study of psychology with a look at its biological roots.

In his theory called phrenology, Gall speculated that the brain's functions were linked with various bumps on the skull.

biological psychologists Psychologists concerned with the links between biology and behavior. (Some biological psychologists call themselves *behavioral neuroscientists, neuropsychologists, physiological psychologists,* or *biopsychologists*.)

nervous system The body's speedy electrochemical communication system, consisting of all the nerve cells of the peripheral and central nervous systems.

neuron A nerve cell; the basic building block of the nervous system.

The Nervous System

Our **nervous system** is an electrochemical communication system that enables us to think, feel, and act. For scientists, it is a happy fact of nature that the nervous systems of humans and other animals operate similarly. All animal nervous systems are constructed of building blocks called **neurons,** or nerve cells. The neurons of various animals are organized in remarkably similar ways. So similar, in fact, that small samples of brain tissue from a person and a monkey are indistinguishable. This similarity allows researchers to study simple animals, such as squids and sea slugs, to discover how neurons operate and communicate, and to study the organization of mammals' brains to understand the organization of our own. Human brains are more complex, but our nervous systems operate according to the same principles that govern the rest of the animal world.

Neurons and Their Messages

Neural Pathways

Preview Question

2. What are the three types of neurons, and how do they work?

Information travels in the nervous system through three types of neurons. The **sensory** or *afferent* (meaning "inward") **neurons** send information from the body's tissues and sensory organs inward to the brain and spinal cord, which process the information. This processing usually involves a second class of neurons, the **interneurons** of the brain and spinal cord. The central nervous system then sends instructions out to the body's tissues via the **motor** or *efferent* (meaning "outward") **neurons.**

Let's slow down, and take a look at a familiar example. The simplest of neural pathways are those that govern our **reflexes,** our automatic responses to stimuli. A simple reflex pathway is composed of a single sensory neuron and a single motor neuron, which often communicate through an interneuron. One such pathway enables the pain reflex (Figure 2–1). When your fingers touch a hot stove, neural activity excited by the heat travels via sensory neurons to interneurons in your spinal cord. These interneurons respond by activating motor neurons to the muscles in your arm, causing you to jerk your hand away.

Figure 2–1 In this simple reflex, information from the skin receptors travels inward via a sensory neuron to an interneuron in the spinal cord, which sends a signal outward to the muscles in the arm via a motor neuron. Because this reflex involves only the spinal cord, you jerk your hand away from the candle flame *before* your brain responds to the information that caused you to experience pain.

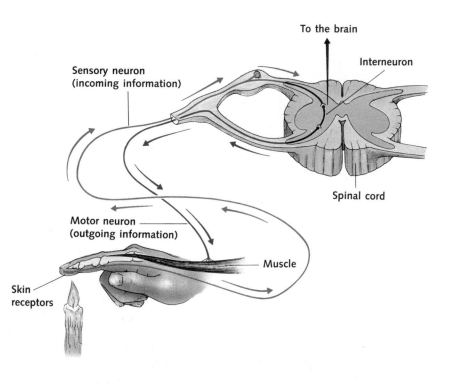

sensory neurons   Neurons that carry incoming information from the sense receptors to the central nervous system.

interneurons   Central nervous system neurons that intervene directly between the sensory inputs and motor outputs.

motor neurons   The neurons that carry outgoing information from the central nervous system to the muscles and glands.

reflex   A simple, automatic, inborn response to a sensory stimulus, such as the knee-jerk response.

Because the simple pain reflex pathway runs through the spinal cord and back out to your muscles, you jerk your hand from the hot stove *before* your brain receives and responds to the information that causes you to feel pain. Information travels to and from the brain mostly by way of the spinal cord's interneurons. Were the top of your spinal cord severed, you would not feel such pain. Or pleasure. If your spinal cord were severed, your brain would literally be out of touch with your body. Thus, you would lose all sensation and voluntary movement in body regions whose sensory and motor neurons connect with the spinal cord below its point of injury. Male paraplegics

dendrite The bushy, branching extensions of a neuron that receive messages and conduct impulses toward the cell body.

axon The extension of a neuron ending in branching terminal fibers through which messages are sent to other neurons or to muscles or glands.

myelin [MY-uh-lin] **sheath** A layer of fatty cells segmentally encasing the fibers of many neurons; makes possible vastly greater transmission speed of neural impulses.

threshold The level of stimulation required to trigger a neural impulse.

(whose legs are paralyzed) are usually capable of an erection (a simple reflex) if their genitals are stimulated. But, depending on where and how completely the spinal cord is severed, they may have no genital feeling and be genitally unresponsive to erotic images (Kennedy & Over, 1990). To feel bodily pain or pleasure, the sensory information must reach the brain.

Generating a Neural Impulse

Each neuron consists of a cell body and one or more branching fibers (Figure 2–2). The fibers are of two types: The **dendrites** receive information from sensory receptors or other neurons, and the **axons** pass it along to other neurons. Unlike the short dendrites, axons may be short or may project through the body up to several feet. For example, the cell body and axon of a motor neuron are roughly on the scale of a basketball attached to a rope 4 miles long. A layer of fatty cells, called the **myelin sheath,** insulates the fibers of some neurons. The sheath helps speed their impulses.

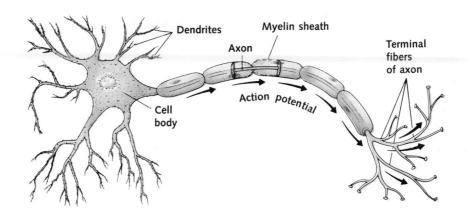

Figure 2–2 A simplified diagram of a motor neuron. Each neuron consists of a cell body and one or more branching extensions or fibers. The dendrites and cell body receive information from sensory receptors or other neurons. If this input exceeds a threshold, the neuron fires an electrical impulse (the action potential) down its axon, whose terminal fibers send this outgoing information to other neurons or to the body's muscles or glands.

You can remember the dendrite-axon sequence as DA—District Attorney.

A neural impulse fires when the neuron is stimulated by pressure, heat, light, or chemical messages from adjacent neurons. The impulse, called the *action potential,* is a brief electrical change that travels down the neuron, rather like a falling line of dominoes, each one tripping the next. The neuron, a miniature decision-making device, receives signals on its dendrites and cell body from hundreds or even thousands of other neurons. The combined signals trigger an impulse if their sum exceeds a minimum intensity, called the **threshold.** If the threshold is reached, the neuron transmits its electrical impulse down the axon, which branches into junctions with hundreds or thousands of other neurons and with the body's muscles and glands.

Increasing the stimulus above the threshold, however, will not increase the impulse's intensity. (The neuron's reaction is an *all-or-none response;* neurons, like guns, either fire or they don't.) Nor does the strength of the stimulus affect the impulse's speed. Depending on the type of nerve fiber, the impulse travels at speeds ranging from a sluggish 2 miles per hour to a breakneck 200 miles or more per hour. But even this top speed is 3 million times slower than the speed of electricity through a wire. That helps to explain why, unlike the nearly instantaneous reactions of a high-speed computer, it may take a quarter-second or more for you to react to a sudden event, such as a child darting in front of your car.

How then do we detect the intensity of a stimulus? How do we distinguish between a gentle touch and a firm hug? Although a strong stimulus cannot trigger a stronger or faster impulse in a neuron, it can trigger more neurons to fire, and to fire more often.

Rehearse It

1. Information travels to and from the brain mostly by way of the spinal cord. The neurons of the spinal cord are called
   a. motor neurons.
   b. sensory neurons.
   c. sending neurons.
   d. interneurons.

2. The neuron fiber that carries messages to other neurons is the
   a. dendrite.
   b. axon.

   c. interneuron.
   d. synapse.

3. The neuron's response to stimulation is an *all-or-none* response. This means that the intensity of the stimulus determines
   a. whether or not an impulse is generated.
   b. how fast an impulse is transmitted.
   c. how intense an impulse will be.
   d. whether the stimulus is excitatory or inhibitory.

Preview Question

3. How do nerve cells communicate?

"All information processing in the brain involves neurons 'talking to' each other at synapses."

Solomon H. Snyder (1984)

synapse [SIN-aps]   The junction between the axon tip of the sending neuron and the dendrite or cell body of the receiving neuron. The tiny gap at this junction is called the *synaptic gap* or *synaptic cleft*.

neurotransmitters   Chemical messengers that traverse the synaptic gaps between neurons. When released by the sending neuron, neurotransmitters travel across the synapse and bind to receptor sites on the receiving neuron, thereby influencing whether it will generate a neural impulse.

How Nerve Cells Communicate

Neurons interweave so intricately that even with a microscope it is hard to see where one neuron ends and another begins. A hundred years ago many scientists believed that the branching axons of one cell fused with the dendrites of another in an uninterrupted fabric. We now know that the axon terminal of one neuron is separated from the receiving neuron by a tiny gap less than a millionth of an inch wide. This junction is the **synapse,** and the gap is called the *synaptic gap* or *synaptic cleft*. To the Nobel laureate, Spanish neuroanatomist Santiago Ramón y Cajal (1832–1934), these near-unions of neurons—"protoplasmic kisses," he called them—were one of nature's marvels. How does the nerve impulse execute the protoplasmic kiss? How does it cross the tiny synaptic gap? The answer is one of the important scientific discoveries of our age.

By an elegant mechanism, the axon's knoblike terminals release chemical messengers, called **neurotransmitters,** into the synaptic gap (Figure 2–3). Within 1/10,000th of a second, the neurotransmitter molecules cross the gap and bind to *receptor sites* on the receiving neuron—as precisely as a key fits a lock. For an instant, the neurotransmitter unlocks tiny "gates" at the receiving site. This allows electrically charged atoms to enter the receiving neuron, thereby either exciting or inhibiting its readiness to fire.

Most neurons have a resting rate of random firing that changes with input from other neurons and from chemicals that affect their sensitivity. Roughly speaking, the neuron is democratic: If it receives more excitatory than inhibitory messages, the cell fires more easily and often. More electrical impulses flash down the axon, releasing more packets of neurotransmitters, which zip across their synaptic gaps to other neurons.

Figure 2-3 Electrical impulses (action potentials) travel from one neuron to another across a junction known as the synaptic gap. When a signal reaches the axon terminal, it stimulates the release of neurotransmitter molecules from the sacs, or vesicles, containing them. These molecules cross the synaptic gap and bind to receptor sites on the receiving neuron. This allows electrically charged atoms (not pictured here) to enter the receiving neuron, thereby influencing its rate of firing.

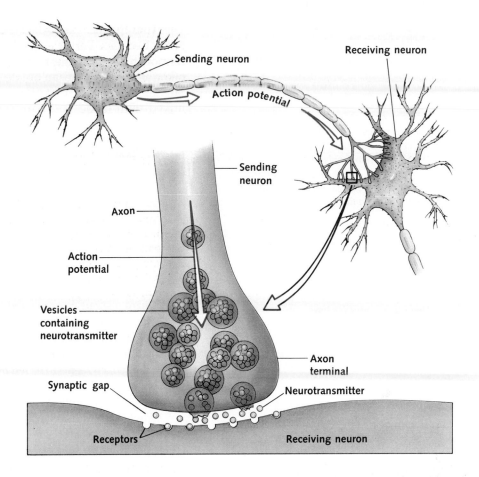

Preview Question

4. How do neurotransmitters influence human behavior?

acetylcholine [ah-seat-el-KO-leen] **(ACh)**
A neurotransmitter that, among its functions, triggers muscle contraction.

How Neurotransmitters Influence Us

The discovery of dozens of different neurotransmitters has created a neuroscience revolution. Why are there so many neural messengers? Are certain neurotransmitters found only in specific places? What are their effects? Can we boost or diminish these effects through drugs or diet? Could such changes affect our moods, memories, or mental abilities? These are questions that intrigue neuroscience researchers and fascinate those of us who are their spectators.

We now know that a particular neural pathway in the brain may use only one or two neurotransmitters, and that particular neurotransmitters may have particular effects on behavior and emotions. One of the best understood neurotransmitters, **acetylcholine (ACh),** is the messenger at every junction between a motor neuron and muscle. With powerful electron microscopes, neurobiologists can magnify thinly sliced specimens of tissue enough to see the sacs that store and release ACh molecules. When ACh is released to the muscle cells, the muscle contracts.

If the transmission of ACh is blocked, muscles cannot contract. Curare, a poison that certain South American Indians put on the tips of their hunting darts, occupies and blocks ACh receptor sites, leaving the neurotransmitter unable to affect the muscles. The result is total paralysis. Botulin, a poison that can form in improperly canned food, causes paralysis by blocking ACh release. The venom of the black widow spider causes a flood of ACh. The result? Violent muscle contractions, convulsions, and possible death.

endorphins [en-DOR-fins] "Morphine within"—natural, opiatelike neurotransmitters linked to pain control and to pleasure.

Physician Lewis Thomas on the endorphins: "There it is, a biologically universal act of mercy. I cannot explain it, except to say that I would have put it in had I been around at the very beginning, sitting as a member of a planning committee."

The Youngest Science, 1983

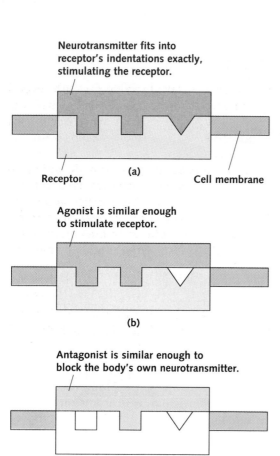

Neurotransmitter fits into receptor's indentations exactly, stimulating the receptor.

Receptor   (a)   Cell membrane

Agonist is similar enough to stimulate receptor.

(b)

Antagonist is similar enough to block the body's own neurotransmitter.

(c)

Figure 2–4 Drugs that mimic or block natural neurotransmitters. Part (a) shows a neurotransmitter molecule stimulating a receptor. Part (b) shows a drug molecule (an *agonist*) that is similar enough to the neurotransmitter to mimic its effects. This may, for example, produce a temporary "high" by amplifying normal sensations of arousal or pleasure (as with opiate drugs). Part (c) shows a drug molecule (an *antagonist*) enough like the natural neurotransmitter to occupy its receptor site and block its effect, but not similar enough to stimulate the receptor. Some poison and snake venoms paralyze by blocking acetylcholine receptors that produce muscle movement.

The Endorphins   An exciting discovery about neurotransmitters occurred when Candace Pert and Solomon Snyder (1973) attached a radioactive tracer to morphine, allowing them to see exactly where in an animal's brain it was taken up. (Morphine, an opiate drug, elevates mood and eases pain.) Pert and Snyder discovered that the morphine was taken up by receptors in areas linked with mood and pain sensations.

It was hard to imagine why the brain would contain these "opiate receptors" unless it had its own naturally occurring opiates. Why would the brain have a chemical lock, unless it also had a key that would fit it? Researchers soon confirmed that the brain indeed contains several types of neurotransmitter molecules similar to morphine. Named **endorphins** (short for *endogenous* [produced within] m*orphine*), these natural opiates are released in response to pain and vigorous exercise (Farrell & others, 1982; Lagerweij & others, 1984). They may therefore help explain all sorts of good feelings, such as the "runner's high," the pain-killing effects of acupuncture, and the indifference to pain in some injured people, such as David Livingstone reported in his 1857 *Missionary Travels*:

I heard a shout. Starting, and looking half round, I saw the lion just in the act of springing upon me. I was upon a little height, he caught my shoulder as he sprang, and we both came to the ground below together. Growling horribly close to my ear, he shook me as a terrier does a rat. The shock produced a stupor similar to that which seems to be felt by a mouse after the first shake of the cat. It caused a sort of dreaminess in which there was no sense of pain nor feeling of terror, though [I was] quite conscious of all that was happening . . . . This peculiar state is probably produced in all animals killed by the carnivora; and if so, is a merciful provision by our benevolent creator for lessening the pain of death.

Drugs and Neurotransmitters   If indeed the endorphins lessen pain and boost mood, why not flood the brain with artificial opiates, thereby intensifying the brain's own "feel good" chemistry? One problem is that when flooded with opiate drugs such as heroin and morphine, the brain may stop producing its own natural opiates. When the drug is withdrawn, the brain may therefore be deprived of any form of opiate. For a drug addict, the result is pain and agony that persists until the brain resumes production of its natural opiates or receives more of the drug.

Cocaine, for instance, floods the brain with substitute excitatory neurotransmitters, producing a "rush." This suppresses the brain's production of its own excitatory neurotransmitters, resulting in a crash of depression when the drug wears off. As we will see in later chapters, many mood-altering drugs share a common effect: They trigger lingering aftereffects. For suppressing the body's own neurotransmitter production, nature charges a price.

Such are the risks inherent in trying to improve our mental state by altering our brain's chemistry. Alert to these dangers, researchers explore the effects of specific neurotransmitters by experimenting first with animals and then verifying the results on people. In this way they are discovering how neurotransmitter abnormalities influence psychological disorders such as depression and schizophrenia.

The good news is that this knowledge is enabling the creation of new therapeutic drugs. Some work by mimicking or blocking a particular neurotransmitter (Figure 2–4). Others work by hampering the neurotransmitter's natural breakdown or its reabsorption by the sending neuron. But designing a drug can be harder than it sounds, because some chemicals don't have the right shape to slither through the blood-brain barrier by which the brain fences off unwanted chemicals circulating in the blood.

Rehearse It

4. There is a minuscule space between the axon of the sending neuron and the dendrite or cell body of the receiving neuron. This small space is called the
a. axon terminal.
b. sac or vesicle.
c. synaptic gap.
d. threshold.

5. When an electrical impulse reaches the axon terminal of a neuron, it stimulates the release of chemical messengers called

a. ions.
b. synapses.
c. neural impulses.
d. neurotransmitters.

6. When the transmission of acetylcholine (ACh) in the brain is blocked,
a. death from convulsions may result.
b. the brain is flooded with substitute excitatory neurotransmitters for a brief "rush."

c. death from paralysis may result.
d. the brain starts producing antagonists, resulting in depression.

7. Endorphins are released in the brain in response to
a. morphine or heroin.
b. pain or vigorous exercise.
c. cocaine.
d. all of the above.

Divisions of the Nervous System

Preview Question

5. What are the major divisions of the nervous system, and what are their basic functions?

The nervous system's building blocks, the neurons, function through several subsystems (Figure 2–5). The **central nervous system (CNS)** includes all the neurons in the brain and spinal cord. But first we will look at the **peripheral nervous system (PNS),** which links the central nervous system with the body's sense receptors, muscles, and glands.

Our peripheral nervous system has two components—somatic and autonomic. The **somatic nervous system** transmits *sensory input* (touch and taste, for example) to the CNS from the outside world and directs *motor output*, the voluntary movements of our skeletal muscles. As you reach the bottom of this page, the somatic nervous system will report to your brain the current position of your hands and will carry instructions back, triggering your hand to turn the page.

Our **autonomic nervous system** influences the glands and the muscles of our internal organs. Like an automatic pilot, it can be consciously overridden. But usually it operates on its own (autonomously) to influence our internal functioning, including our heartbeat, digestion, and glandular activity.

central nervous system (CNS) The brain and spinal cord.

peripheral nervous system (PNS) The neurons that connect the central nervous system to the rest of the body. It consists of the sensory neurons, which carry messages to the central nervous system from the body's sense receptors, and the motor neurons, which carry messages from the central nervous system to the muscles and glands.

somatic [so-MAT-ik] nervous system The division of the peripheral nervous system that receives information from various sense receptors and controls the skeletal muscles of the body.

autonomic [aw-tuh-NAHM-ik] nervous system The part of the peripheral nervous system that controls the glands and the muscles of the internal organs (such as the heart). Its sympathetic division arouses; its parasympathetic division calms.

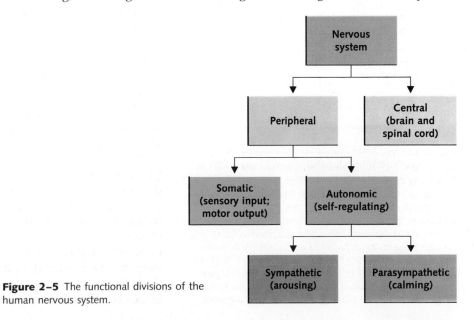

Figure 2–5 The functional divisions of the human nervous system.

sympathetic nervous system The division of the autonomic nervous system that arouses the body, mobilizing its energy in stressful situations.

parasympathetic nervous system The division of the autonomic nervous system that calms the body, conserving its energy.

The autonomic nervous system is a dual system (Figure 2–6). The **sympathetic nervous system** arouses us for defensive action. If something alarms or enrages you, the sympathetic system will accelerate your heartbeat, slow your digestion, raise your blood sugar, dilate your arteries, and cool you with perspiration, making you alert and ready for action. When the stress is over, the **parasympathetic nervous system** produces the opposite effects. It calms you down by decreasing your heartbeat, lowering your blood sugar, and so forth. In everyday situations, the sympathetic and parasympathetic nervous systems work together to keep us in a steady internal state.

Figure 2–6 The autonomic nervous system controls the more autonomous (or self-regulating) internal functions, including those shown here. Its sympathetic division arouses and its parasympathetic division calms, allowing routine maintenance activity. Most organs are affected by both divisions. For example, sympathetic stimulation accelerates heartbeat while parasympathetic stimulation slows it.

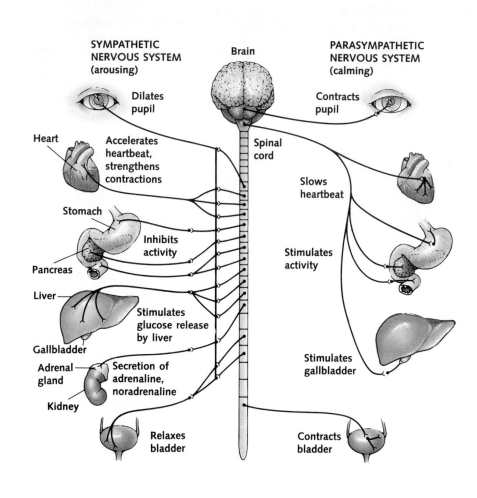

Rehearse It

8. The autonomic nervous system controls internal functions, such as heart rate and glandular activity. The word ''autonomic'' means
a. peripheral.
b. voluntary.
c. self-regulating.
d. arousing.

9. The neurons of the spinal cord are part of the
a. somatic nervous system.
b. CNS (central nervous system).
c. autonomic nervous system.
d. PNS (peripheral nervous system).

10. Usually the sympathetic nervous system arouses us for action, and the parasympathetic nervous system calms us down. Together the two systems make up the
a. autonomic nervous system.
b. somatic nervous system.
c. central nervous system.
d. peripheral nervous system.

The Brain

In a jar on a display shelf in Cornell University's psychology department resides the well preserved brain of Edward Bradford Titchener, a great turn-of-the-century psychologist and proponent of the study of consciousness. Imagine yourself gazing at that wrinkled mass of grayish tissue. Is there any sense in which Titchener is still in there?[1]

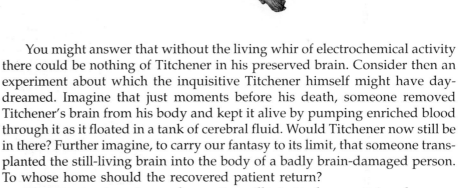

The human brain. Unlike other neural fibers, made white by the fatty covering of myelin sheath, unmyelinated brain tissue is gray.

You might answer that without the living whir of electrochemical activity there could be nothing of Titchener in his preserved brain. Consider then an experiment about which the inquisitive Titchener himself might have daydreamed. Imagine that just moments before his death, someone removed Titchener's brain from his body and kept it alive by pumping enriched blood through it as it floated in a tank of cerebral fluid. Would Titchener now still be in there? Further imagine, to carry our fantasy to its limit, that someone transplanted the still-living brain into the body of a badly brain-damaged person. To whose home should the recovered patient return?

That we can imagine such questions illustrates how convinced we are that we live in our heads. And for good reason: As Woody Allen has said, the brain is a very important organ. The brain makes possible the functions we attribute to the mind: seeing, hearing, remembering, thinking, feeling, speaking, dreaming. But precisely where and how are such mind functions tied to the brain? Let us first see how scientists explore such questions.

"I am a brain, Watson. The rest of me is a mere appendix."

Sherlock Holmes, in Arthur Conan Doyle's "The Adventure of the Mazarin Stone"

How the Brain Governs Behavior

Opening the skull, the first thing we might notice is the brain's size. In dinosaurs the brain represents 1/100,000th of the body's weight, in whales 1/10,000th, in elephants 1/600th, in humans 1/45th. It looks like a principle is emerging. But keep on. In mice the brain is 1/40th the body's weight and in marmosets 1/25th. So there are exceptions to the rule of thumb that the ratio of brain to body weight provides a clue to a species' intelligence.

More useful clues to an animal's capacities come from the brain's structures. In primitive vertebrate (backboned) animals, such as sharks, the brain primarily regulates basic survival functions: breathing, resting, and feeding.

Preview Question

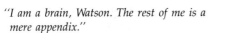

6. How is the brain organized?

[1] Carl Sagan's *Broca's Brain* (1979a) inspired this question.

In lower mammals, such as rodents, a more complex brain enables emotion and greater memory. In advanced mammals, such as humans, the brain processes more information, enabling us to act with foresight. Roughly corresponding to these three stages of brain evolution are three of the vertebrate brain's principal layers—the brainstem, the limbic system, and the cerebral cortex (Figure 2–7).

Figure 2–7 The structures of the human brain with a simplified view of its three principal regions—the brainstem (spinal cord, medulla, reticular formation), the limbic system (hypothalamus, amygdala, hippocampus), and the cerebral cortex. The brainstem region controls automatic survival functions. The limbic system enables memory, emotion, and behaviors that meet basic needs. The cerebral cortex receives, processes, and retrieves information; makes decisions; and directs voluntary actions.

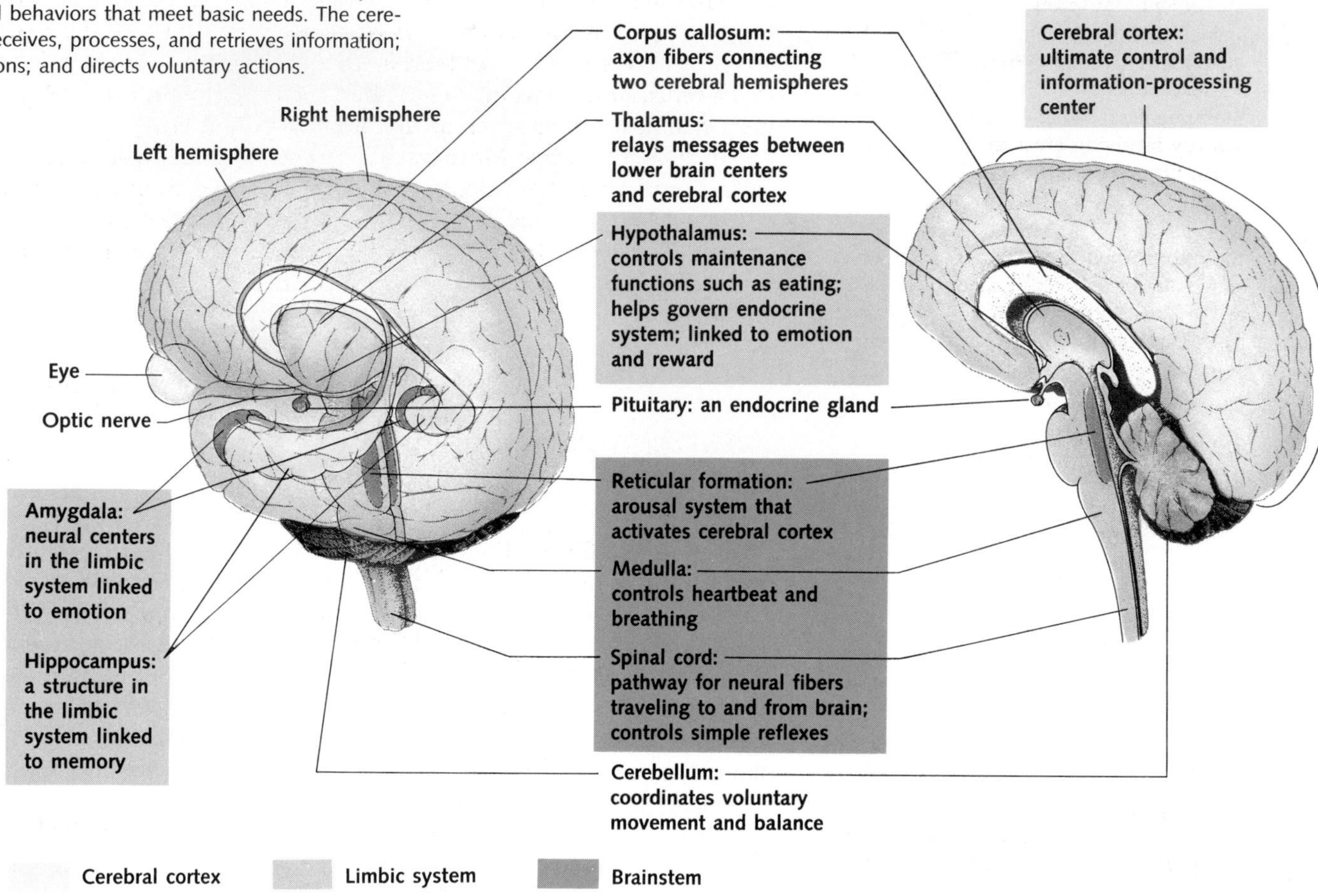

Right hemisphere
Left hemisphere
Eye
Optic nerve

Corpus callosum: axon fibers connecting two cerebral hemispheres

Thalamus: relays messages between lower brain centers and cerebral cortex

Hypothalamus: controls maintenance functions such as eating; helps govern endocrine system; linked to emotion and reward

Pituitary: an endocrine gland

Cerebral cortex: ultimate control and information-processing center

Amygdala: neural centers in the limbic system linked to emotion

Hippocampus: a structure in the limbic system linked to memory

Reticular formation: arousal system that activates cerebral cortex

Medulla: controls heartbeat and breathing

Spinal cord: pathway for neural fibers traveling to and from brain; controls simple reflexes

Cerebellum: coordinates voluntary movement and balance

Cerebral cortex   Limbic system   Brainstem

The Brainstem and Basic Survival

The **brainstem** is the brain's oldest and innermost region. It is therefore also called the *old brain* or *central core*. The brainstem begins where the spinal cord enters the skull and swells slightly, forming the **medulla.** Here lie the controls for your heartbeat and breathing. Here also is the crossover point, where most nerves to and from each side of the brain connect with the body's opposite side. This peculiar cross-wiring is but one of many surprises the brain has to offer.

Extending from the rear of the brainstem is the **cerebellum,** with its two wrinkled hemispheres. The cerebellum influences learning and memory, but its most obvious function is muscular control. On orders from the cortex, the cerebellum coordinates voluntary movement. If you injured your cerebellum, you would probably have difficulty walking, keeping your balance, or shaking hands. Your movements would be jerky and exaggerated.

Preview Question

7. What functions do the structures within the brainstem serve?

brainstem The central core of the brain, beginning where the spinal cord swells as it enters the skull; it is the oldest part of the brain and is responsible for automatic survival functions.

medulla [muh-DUL-uh] The base of the brainstem; controls heartbeat and breathing.

cerebellum [sehr-uh-BELL-um] The ''little brain'' attached to the rear of the brainstem; it helps coordinate voluntary movement and balance.

thalamus [THAL-uh-muss] The brain's sensory switchboard, located on top of the brainstem; directs messages to the sensory receiving areas in the cortex and transmits replies to the cerebellum and medulla.

reticular formation A nerve network (also called the *reticular activating system*) in the brainstem that plays an important role in controlling arousal and attention.

Atop the brainstem sits a joined pair of egg-shaped structures called the **thalamus.** This is the brain's sensory switchboard: It receives information from the sensory neurons and routes it to the higher brain regions that deal with seeing, hearing, tasting, and touching. We can think of the thalamus as being to neural traffic what London is to England's train traffic. Sensory input passes through it en route to various destinations. The thalamus also receives some of the higher brain's replies, which it directs to the cerebellum and medulla.

Inside the brainstem, the **reticular formation** (also known as the *reticular activating system*) extends from the spinal cord right up to the thalamus. This finger-shaped network of neurons helps control arousal and attention. As the spinal cord's sensory input travels up to the thalamus, some of it branches off to the reticular formation, which filters incoming stimuli and relays important information to other areas of the brain (Figure 2–8).

In 1949, Giuseppe Moruzzi and Horace Magoun discovered that electrically stimulating the reticular formation of a sleeping cat almost instantly produced an awake, alert animal. Magoun also severed a cat's reticular formation from higher brain regions without damaging the nearby sensory pathways. The effect? The cat lapsed into a coma from which it never awakened.

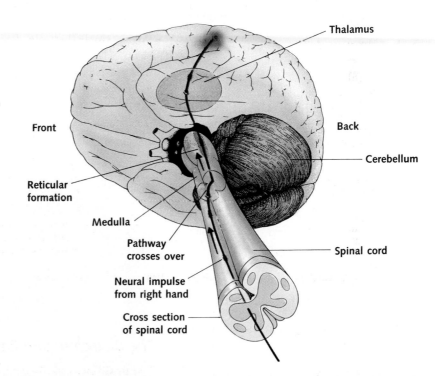

Figure 2–8 We can imagine looking up at the brain from the bottom. First, we see the spinal cord, which then swells to form a tube (the medulla), on which rests a pair of egg-shaped structures (the thalamus), surrounding which, as we will see, are additional layers. Hanging at the back is the baseball-sized cerebellum. Sensory information, say, from your right hand, travels up the spinal cord, crosses over to the left side at the medulla, and is routed to higher brain regions through the thalamus.

The people who first dissected and labeled the brain used the language of scholars, Latin and Greek. Their words are actually attempts at graphic description: For example, ''cortex'' means bark, ''cerebellum'' is little brain, and ''thalamus'' is inner chamber.

Under the influence of the cerebral cortex, the reticular formation controls not only arousal but also attention. While you are concentrating on this paragraph (or for that matter when you are asleep), you are, thanks to your reticular formation, less sensitive to the sound of someone talking nearby. In the same way, a sleeping cat's brain sorts through countless noises, blocking out the irrelevant ones and arousing the animal if it detects a significant sound. This illustrates one of the recurring themes of this book: our brain's capacity to process information without conscious awareness. Remarkably, our brainstem manages these life-sustaining functions with little or no conscious effort. Whether you are asleep or awake, life functions go on, freeing the higher brain regions to dream, to think, to talk, to savor a memory.

Close-Up: The Tools of Discovery

It is exciting to consider how fast and far the neurosciences have progressed within a lifetime. For centuries, the human brain lay largely beyond the reach of science. The neuron is too small to study with the naked eye, its impulses too faint to record with ordinary electrodes. We were able to feel bumps on the skull, dissect and analyze lifeless brains, and observe the effects of specific brain diseases and injuries. But there were no tools high-powered yet gentle enough to explore the living brain. Now, that has all changed. Whether in the interests of science or medicine, we can selectively destroy tiny clusters of normal or defective brain cells, leaving their surroundings unharmed. We can probe the brain with tiny electrical pulses. We can snoop on the messages of individual neurons and on the mass action of billions. We can see color representations of the brain's energy-consuming activity. These new tools and techniques have made possible a neuroscientific revolution.

Clinical Observations   The oldest method of studying brain-mind connections is to observe the effects of brain diseases and injuries. Such observations were first recorded some 5000 years ago. But it was not until the last two centuries that physicians began systematically to record the results of damage to specific brain areas. Some noted that damage to one side of the brain often caused numbness or paralysis on the body's opposite side. Others noticed that damage to the back of the brain disrupted vision, and that damage to the left front part of the brain produced speech difficulties. Gradually, crudely, the brain was being mapped.

Manipulating the Brain   Now, however, scientists need not wait for brain injuries to occur randomly. They can electrically stimulate the brain. Or they can surgically produce a brain **lesion** (destruction of tissue) in specific brain areas in animals. For example, a lesion that destroys one well-defined region of a rat's brain reduces eating, causing the rat to starve unless force-fed. Conversely, a lesion in a nearby area produces overeating.

Recording the Brain's Electrical Activity   Modern researchers have also learned to eavesdrop on the brain. Modern microelectrodes have tips so small they can detect the electrical activity in a single neuron, making possible some astonishingly precise findings. For example, we can now detect exactly where in a cat's brain the information goes when someone strokes its whisker.

This electrical activity in the brain's billions of neurons sweeps in regular waves across its surface. The **electroencephalogram (EEG)** is an amplified tracing of such waves by an instrument called an electroencephalograph. Studying an EEG of the gross activity of the whole brain is like studying the activity of a car engine by listening to the hum of its motor. However, by presenting a stimulus repeatedly and having a computer filter out electrical activity unrelated to the stimulus, one can identify the electrical wave evoked by the stimulus (Figure 2–9). Observing abnormalities in such brain-wave responses is an easy, painless way to diagnose certain forms of brain damage.

Figure 2–9 An electroencephalograph provides amplified tracings of waves of electrical activity in the brain. Here it is detecting brain response to sound, making possible an early evaluation of what may be a hearing impairment.

lesion [LEE-zhuhn] Tissue destruction. A brain lesion is a naturally or experimentally caused destruction of brain tissue.

electroencephalogram (EEG) An amplified recording of the waves of electrical activity that sweep across the brain's surface. These waves are measured by placing electrodes on the scalp.

CAT (computerized axial tomograph) scan A series of x-ray photographs taken from different angles and combined by computer into a composite three-dimensional representation of a slice through the body.

PET (positron emission tomograph) scan A visual display of brain activity that detects where a radioactive form of glucose goes while the brain performs a given task.

MRI (magnetic resonance imaging) A technique that uses magnetic fields and radio waves to produce computer-generated images that distinguish among different types of soft tissue; allows us to see structures within the brain.

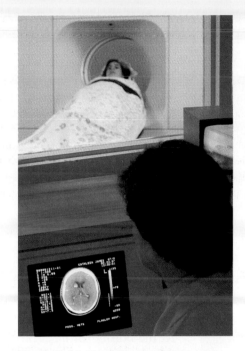

Figure 2–10 The CAT scan examines the brain by taking a series of x-rays from different positions. A computer analyzes the data and arranges them into an image representing a slice through the brain at whatever angle the operator requests.

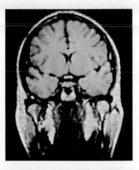
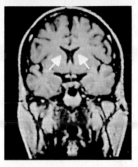

Figure 2–11 MRI scan of a normal person (top) and a schizophrenia patient (bottom). Arrows point to the enlarged fluid-filled brain ventricles in the brain on the bottom.

Brain Scans Other new windows into the brain give us the ability to see inside the brain without lesioning it. For example, the **CAT (computerized axial tomograph) scan** examines the brain by taking x-ray photographs that can reveal brain damage (Figure 2–10). Even more dramatic is the **PET (positron emission tomograph) scan.** A PET scan depicts the activity of different brain areas by showing each area's consumption of its chemical fuel, the sugar glucose (see illustrations, pages 48 and 53). Active neurons burn more glucose. When a person is given a temporarily radioactive form of glucose, the PET scan measures and locates the radioactivity, thereby detecting where this "food for thought" goes.

A new way of looking into the living brain exploits the fact that the centers of atoms, including those in our brains, spin like tops. In **MRI (magnetic resonance imaging)** the head is put in a strong magnetic field, which aligns the spinning atoms. Then a brief pulse of radio waves disorients the atoms momentarily. When the atoms return to their normal spin they release detectable signals, which become computer-generated images of their concentration. The result is a detailed picture of the brain's soft tissues. For example, MRI scans reveal enlarged fluid-filled brain areas in some patients suffering from schizophrenia, a disabling psychological disorder (Figure 2–11).

These new tools have indeed triggered a scientific revolution, most of whose pioneers are still active. To be learning about the neurosciences now is like studying world geography while Magellan was exploring the seas. Every year the explorers announce new discoveries, which also generate new interpretations of old discoveries. Such times can be unsettling, but they are never dull.

Rehearse It

11. The brainstem is the oldest and innermost region of the brain. The brainstem part that controls heartbeat and breathing is the
a. cerebellum.
b. medulla.
c. cortex.
d. limbic system.

12. The part of the brain that coordinates voluntary movement is the
a. cerebellum.
b. medulla.
c. thalamus.
d. reticular formation.

13. The thalamus receives information from the sensory neurons and routes it to the sensory areas of the cortex. The thalamus functions like a(n)
a. memory bank.
b. pleasure center.
c. endocrine gland.
d. switchboard.

14. The structure within the brainstem that governs arousal and attention is the
a. spinal cord.
b. cerebellum.
c. reticular formation.
d. medulla.

The Limbic System: Emotion, Motivation, and Memory

Preview Question

8. What functions do the structures within the limbic system serve?

At the border (or *limbus*) of the brainstem and the cerebral hemispheres is a doughnut-shaped neural system called the **limbic system** (Figure 2–7, page 36). As we will see in Chapter 7, two limbic system components, the amygdala and the hippocampus, enable memory. For now, let's look at the limbic system's links to emotions, such as fear and anger, and to basic motives, such as those for food and sex. As we will see, the limbic system's influence on emotions and motives occurs partly through its control of the body's hormones.

The Amygdala   Two almond-shaped neural clusters in the limbic system, called the **amygdala,** influence aggression and fear. In 1939, psychologist Heinrich Klüver and neurosurgeon Paul Bucy surgically lesioned part of a rhesus monkey's brain that included the amygdala. The operation transformed the normally ill-tempered monkey into the most mellow of creatures. Poke it, pinch it, do virtually anything that normally would trigger a ferocious response, and still the animal remained placid. In later studies with other wild animals, including the lynx, wolverine, and wild rat, researchers noted the same effect. What then might happen if we electrically stimulated the amygdala in a normally placid domestic animal, like a cat? Do so in one spot and the cat prepares to attack, hissing with its back arched, its pupils dilated, its hair on end. Move the electrode only slightly within the amygdala and the cat cowers in terror when caged with a small mouse.

These experiments testify to the amygdala's role in such emotions as rage and fear. Still, we must be careful not to think of the amygdala as *the* control center for aggression and fear. The brain is *not* neatly organized into structures that correspond to our categories of behavior. Aggressive and fearful behavior involve neural activity in all levels of the brain—brainstem, limbic system, and cerebral cortex. Even within the limbic system, stimulating neural structures other than the amygdala can evoke such behavior. Similarly, if

Electrical stimulation of the amygdala provokes physical reactions such as the ones shown in the wild by this threatened penguin. Such stimulation activates which division of the autonomic nervous system— sympathetic or parasympathetic? (See page 44.)

you manipulate your car's carburetor, you can affect how the car runs; but that doesn't mean that the carburetor by itself runs the car. It is merely one link in an integrated system.

The Hypothalamus Another of the limbic system's fascinating structures lies just below (*hypo*) the thalamus, and so is called the **hypothalamus.** By lesioning or stimulating different areas in the hypothalamus, neuroscientists have isolated groups of neurons within it that perform amazingly specific bodily maintenance duties. Some of these neural clusters influence hunger; still others regulate thirst, body temperature, and sexual behavior.

The story of a remarkable discovery about the hypothalamus illustrates how progress in scientific research often occurs—when curious, open-minded investigators make an unexpected observation. Two young neuropsychologists at Canada's McGill University, James Olds and Peter Milner (1954), were trying to implant electrodes in the reticular systems of white rats. One day they made a magnificent mistake. In one rat, they incorrectly placed an electrode in what was later discovered to be a region of the hypothalamus (Olds, 1975). Curiously, the rat kept returning to the place on its tabletop enclosure where it had been stimulated by this misplaced electrode, as if it were seeking more stimulation. Upon discovering their mistake, the alert investigators recognized that they had stumbled upon a brain center that provides a pleasurable reward.

In a meticulous series of experiments, Olds (1958) then went on to locate other "pleasure centers," as he called them. (What the rats actually experience only they know, and they aren't telling.) When Olds allowed rats to trigger their own stimulation in these areas by pressing a pedal, they would sometimes do so at a feverish pace—up to 7000 times per hour—until they dropped from exhaustion. Moreover, they would do anything to get this stimulation, even cross an electrified floor that a starving rat would not cross to reach food (Figure 2–12, page 42).

limbic system A doughnut-shaped system of neural structures at the border of the brainstem and cerebral hemispheres; associated with emotions such as fear and aggression and drives such as those for food and sex.

amygdala [ah-MIG-dah-la] Two almond-shaped neural centers in the limbic system that are linked to emotion.

hypothalamus [hi-po-THAL-uh-muss] A neural structure lying below (*hypo*) the thalamus; it directs several maintenance activities (eating, drinking, body temperature), helps govern the endocrine system via the pituitary gland, and is linked to emotion and reward.

Figure 2–12 A rat readily crosses an electrified grid, accepting the painful shocks, to press a lever that sends electrical impulses to its "pleasure centers." (Adapted from Gazzaniga, Steen, & Volte, 1979.)

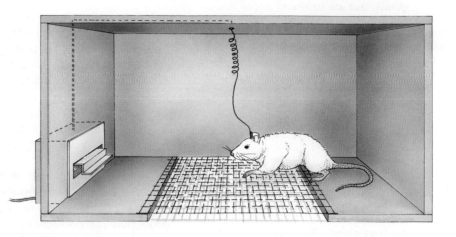

"If you were designing a robot vehicle to walk into the future and survive, . . . you'd wire it up so that behavior that ensured the survival of the self or the species—like sex and eating—would be naturally reinforcing."

Candace Pert (1986)

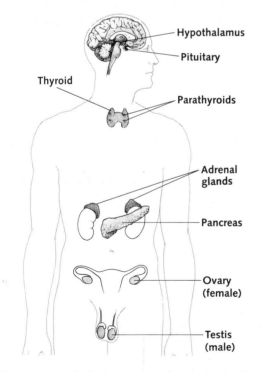

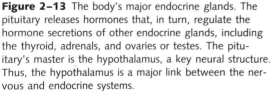

Figure 2–13 The body's major endocrine glands. The pituitary releases hormones that, in turn, regulate the hormone secretions of other endocrine glands, including the thyroid, adrenals, and ovaries or testes. The pituitary's master is the hypothalamus, a key neural structure. Thus, the hypothalamus is a major link between the nervous and endocrine systems.

Similar pleasure centers in or near the hypothalamus were later discovered in many other species, including goldfish, dolphins, and monkeys. In fact, animal research reveals both a general reward system that triggers the release of the neurotransmitter dopamine, and specific centers associated with the pleasures of eating, drinking, and sex. Animals, it seems, come equipped with built-in reward systems for activities essential to survival.

These dramatic findings made people wonder whether humans, too, might have limbic centers for pleasure. Indeed they do. One neurosurgeon has used electrodes to calm violent patients. Stimulated patients report mild pleasure; unlike rats, they are not driven to a frenzy by it (Deutsch, 1972; Hooper & Teresi, 1986).

The Hypothalamus and the Endocrine System   The hypothalamus exerts its control in two ways: electrochemically, by triggering activity in the autonomic nervous system, and chemically, by secreting **hormones.** Hormones are chemical messengers produced in one tissue that travel through the bloodstream and affect other body tissues. Sometimes the affected tissue is the brain: Hormones acting on the brain influence our interest in sex, food, aggression, and nurturance.

Hormones are secreted by the glands of the **endocrine system** (Figure 2–13), the second of the body's communication systems. Unlike the speedy nervous system, which zips messages from eyes to brain to hand in a fraction of a second, endocrine messages use the slow lane. Several seconds or more may elapse before the bloodstream carries a hormone from an endocrine gland to its target tissue. But these endocrine messages are often worth waiting for, because their effects are usually longer-lasting than the effects of a neural message.

The endocrine system's hormones influence many aspects of our lives, from growth to reproduction, from metabolism to mood, keeping everything in balance while responding to stress, exertion, and internal thoughts. In a moment of danger, for example, the autonomic nervous system will order the **adrenal glands** on top of the kidneys to release *epinephrine* and *norepinephrine* (also called *adrenaline* and *noradrenaline*). These hormones increase heart rate, blood pressure, and blood sugar, providing us with a surge of energy. When the emergency passes, the hormones—and the feelings of excitement—linger awhile.

hormones Chemical messengers, such as those manufactured by the endocrine glands, that are produced in one tissue and travel via the bloodstream to affect another.

endocrine [EN-duh-krin] **system** The body's "slow," chemical communication system; a set of glands that secretes hormones into the bloodstream.

adrenal [ah-DREEN-el] **glands** A pair of endocrine glands just above the kidneys. The adrenals secrete the hormones epinephrine (adrenaline) and norepinephrine (noradrenaline), which help to arouse the body in times of stress.

pituitary gland The endocrine system's most influential gland. Under the influence of the hypothalamus, the pituitary regulates growth and controls other endocrine glands.

Imagine a synthetic pituitary growth hormone that had no harmful side effects. Knowing that taller people tend to be more successful in business, politics, and sports, would you give this drug to your children?

The most influential gland in our endocrine system is the **pituitary gland,** a pea-sized structure at the base of the brain. One of its hormones has the important task of regulating body growth. Too little of this hormone will produce a midget; too much, a giant. Since 1985, genetic engineering has made possible the commercial production of pituitary growth hormone, making it available to children who suffer pituitary dwarfism. One recent experiment with older adults who had stopped producing growth hormone suggests that injections of this synthetic hormone may have a rejuvenating effect, reversing the normal pattern of muscle loss and fat gain (Rudman & others, 1990).

Besides releasing its own hormones, the secretions of the pituitary influence the release of hormones by other endocrine glands. This makes the pituitary a sort of master gland. Actually, though, its master is the hypothalamus, a key neural structure that lies just above it. The hypothalamus, in turn, monitors blood chemistry and takes orders from the whole brain. Thinking about sex (in your brain cortex) can stimulate your hypothalamus to influence your pituitary gland. The pituitary triggers your sex glands to release more sex hormones, which may in turn influence your brain and behavior.

This feedback system (brain → pituitary → other glands → hormones → brain) illustrates the intimate connection of the nervous and endocrine systems. The nervous system directs endocrine secretions, which affect the nervous system. Conducting and coordinating this electrochemical orchestra is that maestro we call the brain.

Or should we say the mind? Note how fruitless it is to argue whether our brains or our minds are in charge. In the sex example, the mind influences the brain, which influences the body, which influences the mind. Asking whether brain or mind is in control is like asking whether a computer's output is produced by its hardware or its software. The answer is both, acting together as one whole mind-brain system.

Rehearse It

15. The limbic system, a doughnut-shaped structure at the border of the brainstem and the cerebral hemispheres, is associated with basic drives, emotions, and memory functions. Two parts of the limbic system are the amygdala and the
a. reticular formation.
b. hypothalamus.
c. thalamus.
d. medulla.

16. A ferocious response to electrical brain stimulation would lead you to suppose that the electrode had been touching the
a. medulla.
b. pituitary.
c. hippocampus.
d. amygdala.

17. The "pleasure centers" discovered by Olds and Milner were located in and near the
a. cerebral cortex.
b. brainstem.
c. hypothalamus.
d. spinal cord.

18. The endocrine system, the second and slower bodily communication system, produces chemical messengers that travel through the bloodstream and affect other tissue. These chemical substances are
a. hormones.
b. neurotransmitters.
c. micronutrients.
d. glands.

19. The pituitary gland regulates growth and controls the activity of other glands. The pituitary is part of the
a. endocrine system.
b. limbic system.
c. brainstem.
d. nervous system.

20. The neural structure that most directly controls eating, drinking, and regulating body temperature is the
a. endocrine system.
b. hypothalamus.
c. thalamus.
d. amygdala.

Preview Question

9. How is the cerebral cortex organized?

The penguin on page 41 is aroused via its sympathetic nervous system.

cerebral [seh-REE-bruhl] **cortex** The intricate fabric of interconnected neural cells that covers the cerebral hemispheres; the body's ultimate control and information-processing center.

frontal lobes The portion of the cerebral cortex lying just behind the forehead; involved in speaking and muscle movements and in making plans and judgments.

parietal [puh-RYE-uh-tuhl] **lobes** The portion of the cerebral cortex lying at the top of the head and toward the rear; includes the sensory cortex.

occipital [ahk-SIP-uh-tuhl] **lobes** The portion of the cerebral cortex lying at the back of the head; includes the visual areas, each of which receives visual information from the opposite visual field.

temporal lobes The portion of the cerebral cortex lying roughly above the ears; includes the auditory areas, each of which receives auditory information primarily from the opposite ear.

motor cortex An area at the rear of the frontal lobes that controls voluntary movements.

The Cerebral Cortex and Information Processing

Most of what makes us distinctively human arises from the complex functions of our highly developed cerebral cortex. When the cortex ceases to function, a person vegetates without voluntary movement, without the experiences of sight, sound, and touch, without consciousness.

Structure of the Cortex Opening a human skull and exposing the brain, we would see a wrinkled organ, shaped rather like the meat of an oversized walnut. Covering the brain is the **cerebral cortex,** a ⅛-inch sheet of cells composed of billions of nerve cells and their countless interconnections (Figure 2–7, page 36). To get a feel for the complexity of these interconnections, consider that you could join two 8-studded Lego bricks 24 ways and six bricks nearly 103 million ways. With some 10^{10} neurons, each having roughly 10^4 contacts with other neurons, we end up with something like 10^{14} (100 trillion) cortical synaptic connections. Being human takes a lot of nerve.

The cortex is only the thin outer layer of the ballooning left and right cerebral hemispheres. The hemispheres, which account for 80 percent of the brain's weight, are filled with axons that interconnect the neurons of the cortex with those of other brain regions.

We can view each brain hemisphere as divided into four regions, or *lobes.* Starting at the front of your brain and going around over the top, these are: the **frontal lobes** (behind your forehead), the **parietal lobes** (at the top and to the rear), the **occipital lobes** (at the back of your head), and the **temporal lobes** (just above your ears). These lobes are convenient geographic subdivisions separated by *fissures,* or grooves (Figure 2–14). As we will see, the lobes are not distinct operating units. Each lobe carries out many functions, and some functions require the interplay of several lobes.

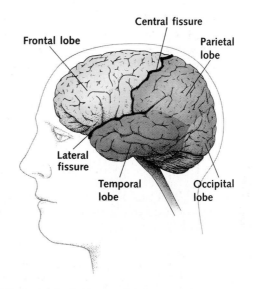

Figure 2–14 The basic subdivisions of the cortex. We can view the cortex as divided into four lobes in each hemisphere, separated by fissures, or grooves.

Preview Question

10. What functions are served by the cerebral cortex?

Functions of the Cortex   More than a century ago, autopsies of partially paralyzed or speechless people revealed damage to specific areas of the cortex. But this rather crude evidence did not convince everyone that specific parts of the cortex perform specific functions. After all, if control of speech and movement were diffused across the entire cortex, damage to almost any area might produce the same effect. Likewise, a television would go dead with its power cord cut, but we would be deluding ourselves if we were to think we had "localized" the source of the picture in the cord. This analogy suggests how easy it is to err when trying to localize brain functions.

Motor Functions   In 1870, German physicians Gustav Fritsch and Eduard Hitzig applied mild electrical stimulation to the cortexes of dogs and made an important discovery: They could make different body parts move. The effects were selective: Stimulation caused movement only when applied to an arch-shaped region at the back of the frontal lobe, running roughly from ear to ear across the top of the brain. This arch we now call the **motor cortex** (Figure 2–15). Moreover, when the researchers stimulated specific parts of this region in the left or right hemisphere, specific body parts moved on the *opposite* side of the body.

A half century ago, neurosurgeons Otfrid Foerster in Germany and Wilder Penfield in Montreal mapped the motor cortex in hundreds of wide-awake patients. The surgeons needed to know the possible side effects of removing different parts of the cortex. So, before putting the knife to the brain, they would painlessly (the brain has no sensory receptors) stimulate different cortical areas and note body responses. Like Fritsch and Hitzig, they found that when they stimulated different areas of the motor cortex at the back of the frontal lobe, different body parts moved. They were therefore able to map the motor cortex according to the body parts it controlled (Figure

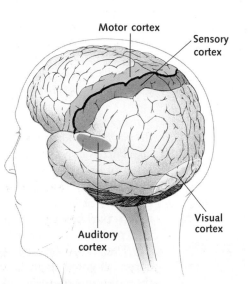

Figure 2–15 The motor cortex, directly in front of the central fissure, controls voluntary muscle movements. The sensory cortex, just behind the central fissure, receives input from the skin and muscles. The occipital lobes at the rear receive input from the eyes. An auditory area of the temporal lobes receives information from the ears.

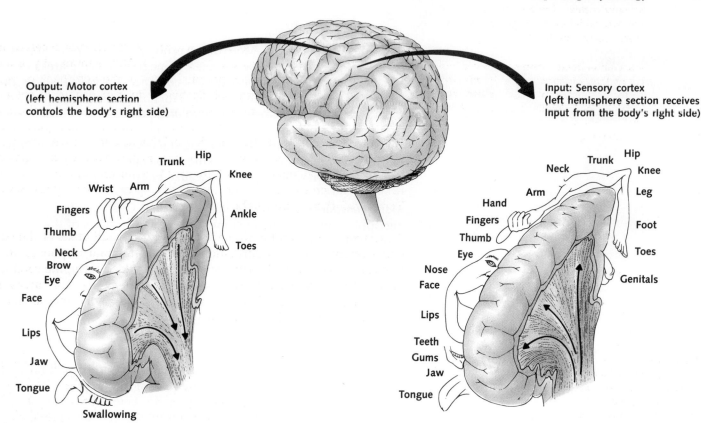

Output: Motor cortex
(left hemisphere section
controls the body's right side)

Input: Sensory cortex
(left hemisphere section receives
input from the body's right side)

Figure 2–16 A depiction of the proportion of left hemisphere tissue devoted to each body part in (a) the motor cortex and (b) the sensory cortex. As you can see, the amount of cortex devoted to a body part is *not* proportional to that part's size. Rather, the brain devotes more tissue to sensitive areas and to areas requiring precise control. For example, the fingers have a greater representation in the cortex than does the upper arm.

The visual and auditory cortex areas also receive sensory input. Thus, the sensory cortex is sometimes called the *somatosensory cortex* to emphasize that its input comes from body (somatic) stimulation.

2–16). Interestingly, those areas of the body requiring precise control, such as the fingers and mouth, occupied the greatest amount of cortical space.

Neuroscientist José Delgado demonstrated the mechanics of motor behavior. In one monkey, he evoked a smiling response over 400,000 times. In a human patient, stimulation of a certain spot on the left motor cortex triggered the right hand to make a fist. Asked to keep the fingers open during the next stimulation, the patient, whose fingers closed despite his best efforts, remarked, ''I guess, Doctor, that your electricity is stronger than my will'' (Delgado, 1969, p. 114).

Sensory Functions   If the motor cortex sends messages out to the body, where do *incoming* messages reach the cortex? Penfield identified a cortical area that specializes in receiving information from the skin senses and from the movement of body parts. This area, parallel to the motor cortex and just behind it at the front of the parietal lobes, we now call the **sensory cortex** (Figure 2–15, page 45). Stimulate a point on the top of this band of tissue, and the person may report being touched on the shoulder; stimulate some point on the side, and perhaps the person will feel something on the face.

The more sensitive a body region, the greater the area of the sensory cortex devoted to it; your supersensitive lips project to a larger brain area than do your toes (Figure 2–16). Similarly, rats have a large area of the brain devoted to whisker sensation, owls to hearing sensations, and so forth. If a monkey or a human loses a finger, the region of the sensory cortex devoted to receiving input from that finger branches to receive sensory input from the adjacent fingers, which now become more sensitive (Fox, 1984). As this illustrates, the brain is sculpted not only by our genes (*nature*) but also by our experience (*nurture*).

sensory cortex The area at the front of the parietal lobes that registers and processes body sensations.

association areas Areas of the cerebral cortex that are not involved in primary motor or sensory functions; rather, they are involved in higher mental functions such as learning, remembering, thinking, and speaking.

Further exploration identified where the cortex first receives messages from the other senses (Figure 2–15, page 45). At this moment you are receiving visual information in the occipital lobes at the very back of your brain. Stimulated there, you might see flashes of light or dashes of color. So, in a sense, we *do* have eyes in the back of our head. From there the visual information you are now processing goes to other brain areas that specialize in tasks such as identifying words, detecting emotions, and recognizing faces.

Any sound you are hearing right now is processed by the auditory areas in your temporal lobes. Most of this auditory information travels a circuitous route from one ear to the auditory receiving area above your opposite ear. Stimulated there, you might hear a sound.

Association Areas So far we have pointed out small areas of the cortex that either receive sensory information or direct muscular responses. In humans, that leaves some three-fourths of the thin wrinkled layer, the cerebral cortex, uncommitted. Neurons in these **association areas** (the gray areas in Figure 2–17) integrate information by communicating with one another and with the cortical neurons of the sensory and motor areas.

Figure 2–17 As animals increase in complexity, there is an increase in the "uncommitted" or association areas of the cortex. These vast areas of the brain are responsible for integrating and acting on information received and processed by sensory areas.

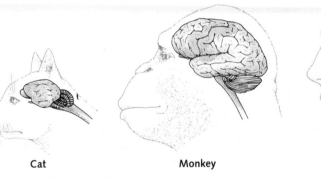

Motor areas

Sensory areas

Association areas

Rat Cat Monkey Human

Electrically probing the association areas doesn't trigger any response. So, unlike the sensory and motor areas, we can't so neatly specify the functions of the association areas. Their silence seems to be what someone had in mind when formulating one of pop psychology's most widespread myths: that we ordinarily use only 10 percent of our brains. The myth implies that if we could activate our whole brain, we would be far smarter than those who drudge along on 10 percent brain power. But from observing surgically lesioned animals and brain-damaged humans, we know that the association areas are not dormant. Rather, they interpret, integrate, and act on information processed by the sensory areas.

Association areas in the frontal lobe enable judging and planning. People with damaged frontal lobes may have intact memories, score high on intelligence tests, and be well able to bake a cake—yet they may be unable to plan ahead to *begin* baking the cake for a birthday party.

Frontal lobe damage can also alter personality, leaving a person uninhibited, coarse, and even promiscuous. The classic case is Phineas Gage, a railroad worker. One afternoon in 1848, 25-year-old Gage was packing gunpowder into a rock with a tamping iron. A spark ignited the gunpowder, shooting the rod up through his left cheek and out the top of his skull, leaving his left frontal lobe massively damaged. To everyone's amazement, Gage was still able to sit up and speak, and after the wound healed he returned to work.

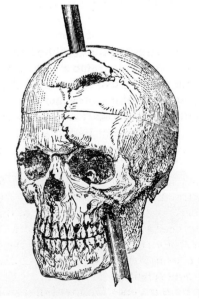

Phineas Gage's skull pierced by a tamping rod.

aphasia Impairment of language, usually caused by left hemisphere damage either to Broca's area (impairing speaking) or to Wernicke's area (impairing understanding).

Broca's area An area of the left frontal lobe that directs the muscle movements involved in speech.

Wernicke's area An area of the left temporal lobe involved in language comprehension.

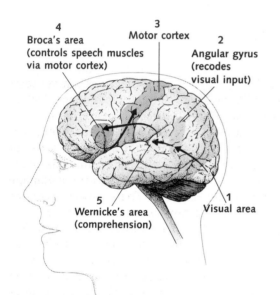

4
Broca's area (controls speech muscles via motor cortex)

3
Motor cortex

2
Angular gyrus (recodes visual input)

5
Wernicke's area (comprehension)

1
Visual area

Figure 2–18 Reading aloud requires the coordination of several brain areas. The arrows show the movement of information in the brain from the time a word is read until it is spoken. (Adapted from "Specialization of the human brain" by N. Geschwind. Copyright © 1979 Scientific American, Inc. All rights reserved.)

Although his mental abilities and memories were intact, his personality was not. The affable, soft-spoken Phineas Gage was now an irritable, profane, capricious person who lost his job and ended up earning his living as a fairground exhibit. This person, said his friends, was "no longer Gage."

The association areas of the other lobes also perform mental functions. For example, an area on the underside of the right temporal lobe enables us to recognize faces. If a stroke or head injury destroyed this area of your brain, you would still be able to describe facial features and to recognize someone's sex and approximate age, yet be strangely unable to identify the person as, say, Boris Yeltsen, your next-door neighbor, or even your spouse. But by and large, complex mental functions such as learning and memory don't reside in any one place. There is no one spot in a rat's (admittedly small) association cortex that, when damaged, will obliterate its ability to learn or remember a maze. Such functions seem spread throughout much of the cortex.

Language Complex human abilities, such as language, result from the intricate coordination of many brain areas. For example, consider the curious finding that damage to any one of several cortical areas can cause **aphasia**, an impaired use of language. It is even more curious that some aphasic people can speak fluently but are unable to read (despite good vision), while others can comprehend what they read but are unable to speak. Still others can write but not read, read but not write, read numbers but not letters, or sing but not speak. These observations are puzzling because we think of speaking and reading, or writing and reading, or singing and speaking, as merely different examples of the same general ability.

Researchers began to sort out how the brain processes language after a discovery by French physician Paul Broca in 1865. Broca discovered that damage to a specific area of the left frontal lobe, later called **Broca's area**, left a person struggling to form words, yet often able to sing familiar songs with ease. A decade later, German investigator Karl Wernicke discovered that damage to a specific area of the left temporal lobe (**Wernicke's area**) would leave people able only to babble meaningless words.

Norman Geschwind assembled these and other clues into an explanation of how we use language. When you read aloud, the words (1) register in the visual area, (2) are relayed to an area called the *angular gyrus,* which then transforms the words into an auditory code that is (3) received and understood in the nearby Wernicke's area, and (4) sent to Broca's area, which (5) controls the motor cortex, creating the pronounced word (Figure 2–18). Depending on which link in this chain is damaged, a different form of aphasia occurs. Damage to the angular gyrus leaves the person able to speak and understand but unable to read. Damage to Wernicke's area disrupts understanding. Damage to Broca's area disrupts speaking. The general principle bears repeating: Complex abilities result from the intricate coordination of many brain areas.

PET scans, such as these, detect the activity of different areas of the brain by measuring their relative consumption of a temporarily radioactive form of the brain's normal fuel, glucose. This series of side-view PET scans of left-facing patients shows levels of increased brain activity in specific areas: (a) when hearing a word—auditory cortex and Wernicke's area; (b) when seeing a word—visual cortex and angular gyrus; and (c) when repeating a word—Broca's area and the motor cortex. The red blotches show where the brain is rapidly consuming glucose.

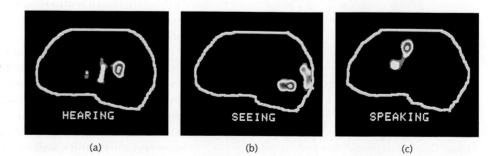

HEARING

SEEING

SPEAKING

(a)

(b)

(c)

Rehearse It

21. Planning is enabled by the
a. occipital lobes.
b. parietal lobes.
c. frontal lobes.
d. temporal lobes.

22. About three-fourths of the cerebral cortex is not committed to any specific sensory or muscular function. The uncommitted areas are called
a. occipital lobes.
b. fissures.
c. association areas.
d. Wernicke's area.

23. The motor cortex is the brain region that controls voluntary movement. If a neurosurgeon stimulated your right motor cortex, you would most likely
a. see light.
b. hear a sound.
c. feel a touch on the right arm.
d. move your left leg.

24. The area in the brain that, if damaged, might impair your speech is
a. Wernicke's area.
b. Broca's area.
c. the left occipital lobe.
d. the angular gyrus.

Preview Question

11. Is the brain capable of reorganizing itself if damaged?

Question: If your Broca's area were damaged, could you write a letter? (See page 52.)

plasticity The brain's capacity for modification, as evident in brain reorganization following damage (especially in children) and in experiments on the effects of experience on brain development.

Brain Reorganization

If injury or illness destroys brain tissue, are its special functions forever lost? If you scrape your knee, new cells will generate to repair the damage. Not so with the neurons of the central nervous system. If the spinal cord is severed or if brain tissue is destroyed, the injured neurons normally will not regenerate.

That's the bad news. The good news is the brain's **plasticity,** or capacity for modification. When one brain area is damaged, other areas may take over some of its functions. Nearby neurons may partly compensate for the damage by making new connections that replace the lost ones. These new connections are one way the brain struggles to recover from, say, a minor stroke.

Our brains are most plastic when we are young children—before cortical regions' functions become fixed (Kolb, 1989). If the speech areas of an infant's left hemisphere are damaged, the right hemisphere will take over much of its customary language function, apparently by making good use of the neuron surplus in a young child's brain. After age 5, however, left hemisphere damage permanently and severely disrupts language.

As an extreme example of plasticity, consider a 5-year-old boy whose severe seizures, caused by a deteriorating left hemisphere, required removing the *entire* hemisphere. Astonishingly, the individual was at last report an executive. Half his skull is filled with nothing but cerebrospinal fluid—functionally it might as well be sawdust—yet he has scored well above average on intelligence tests, completed college, and attended graduate school part-time (Smith & Sugar, 1975; A. Smith, 1987). Although paralyzed on the right side, this man (along with other such cases of "hemispherectomy") testifies to the brain's extraordinary powers of reorganization when damaged before it is fully developed.

Could we enhance the brain's self-repair by transplanting brain tissue? Even in this era of skin grafts and heart transplants, transplanting neural tissue still sounds like science fiction. But in experiments with animals, neuroscientists are now trying, with some success, to mend the brain by replacing destroyed nerve cells with healthy ones (Dunnett, 1989; Gash & others, 1986). In one dramatic experiment, Randy Labbe and her colleagues (1983) found that brain-damaged rats learned a maze twice as fast if given tissue from the corresponding brain areas of rat fetuses.

Might transplants of brain tissue someday enable neurosurgeons to repair the human brain? The tremors of Parkinson's disease and the progressive deterioration of Alzheimer's disease, for example, involve a degeneration of brain tissue that normally produces vital neurotransmitters—dopamine in Parkinson's disease, acetylcholine in Alzheimer's. If we transplanted dopamine-producing tissue into the brains of Parkinson's patients, would the tissue survive and release the needed neurotransmitters? Using such tissue from patients' own adrenal glands or from miscarried fetuses, experimental surgery on dozens of patients in Sweden, Mexico, the United States, and elsewhere has raised hopes that it might (Kimble, 1990; Office of Technology Assessment, 1990).

Our Divided Brains

For more than a century, clinical evidence has shown that the brain's two sides serve differing functions. Accidents, strokes, and tumors in the left hemisphere generally impair reading, writing, speaking, arithmetic reasoning, and understanding. Similar lesions in the right hemisphere do not have such dramatic effects. Small wonder, then, that the left hemisphere became known as the "dominant" or "major" hemisphere, and its silent companion to the right as the "subordinate" or "minor" hemisphere. (With some left-handers, this is reversed—see page 54.) Fascinating experiments on the brain's two hemispheres reveal, however, that each serves important functions.

Splitting the Brain

In 1961, two Los Angeles neurosurgeons, Philip Vogel and Joseph Bogen, were considering surgery for several patients who suffered from epilepsy. The surgeons speculated that major epileptic seizures were caused by an amplification of abnormal brain activity that reverberated back and forth between the two hemispheres. If so, they wondered whether they might control severe epilepsy by cutting communication between the hemispheres. In order to do so, the surgeons would have to sever the **corpus callosum,** the wide band of axon fibers connecting the two hemispheres (Figure 2–19).

They had reason to believe that such an operation would not be seriously incapacitating. Psychologists Roger Sperry, Ronald Myers, and Michael Gazzaniga had divided the brains of cats and monkeys in this manner, without serious ill effects. So Vogel and Bogen operated. The result? Seizures were nearly eliminated and the patients were surprisingly normal, their personalities and intellect hardly affected. Waking from the surgery, one patient even managed to quip that he had a "splitting headache" (Gazzaniga, 1967).

If you chatted with one of these **split-brain** patients you probably would not notice anything unusual. You could understand why only a decade earlier neuropsychologist Karl Lashley jested that maybe the corpus callosum served only "to keep the hemispheres from sagging." But surely a broad band of 200 million nerve fibers capable of transferring more than a billion bits of information per second between the hemispheres must have a more significant purpose. It does, and the ingenious experiments of Sperry and Gazzaniga revealed its purpose and provided a key to understanding the two hemispheres' special functions.

Shortly after one of the split-brain operations, the researchers noted that when they placed an unseen object in a patient's left hand, he denied it was there. This came as no surprise to Sperry and Gazzaniga. They knew that information from the left hand went to the right hemisphere, and their animal

If transplanted brain tissue indeed alleviates Parkinson's disease, would you favor or oppose the use of brain tissue from aborted fetuses?

Preview Question

12. What is a split brain, and what does it reveal about brain functioning?

Corpus callosum

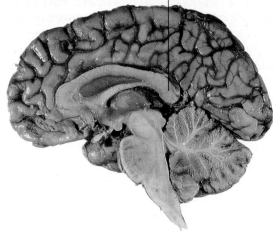

Figure 2–19 The corpus callosum is a large band of neural fibers that connects the two brain hemispheres. To photograph the half brain shown here, the hemispheres were separated by cutting through the corpus callosum and lower brain regions.

corpus callosum [KOR-pus kah-LOW-sum] The largest bundle of neural fibers connecting and carrying messages between the two brain hemispheres.

split-brain A condition in which the two hemispheres of the brain are isolated by cutting the connecting fibers between them (mainly those of the corpus callosum).

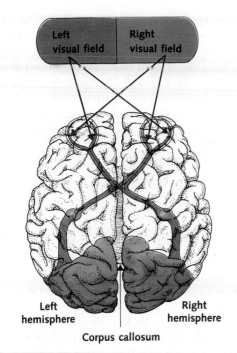

Figure 2–20 Information from the left half of your field of vision is received only by your right hemisphere, and information from the right half of your visual field is received only by your left hemisphere. (Note, however, that each eye receives sensory information from *both* the right and left visual fields.) The data received by either hemisphere is quickly transmitted to the other across the corpus callosum. In a split-brain patient, with a severed corpus callosum, this information sharing does not take place.

experiments suggested that the right hemisphere would be unable to send this information to the speech-controlling areas of the left hemisphere. More extraordinary results came when Sperry and Gazzaniga conducted some perceptual tests.

Our eyes connect to our brains in such a way that, when we look straight ahead, the left half of our field of vision transmits through both eyes to our right hemisphere (Figure 2–20). Likewise, the right side of our field of vision transmits only to our left hemisphere. One woman, having lost a vision-related part of her *right* hemisphere to a massive stroke, sometimes complained that nurses had not put dessert or coffee on her tray. When her head was turned, so that the tray came into view in the right half of her field of vision (where her *left* visual cortex could detect it), she would say, "Oh, there it is—it wasn't there before" (Sacks, 1985, p. 73).

In those of us with healthy, intact brains, information presented only to our right hemisphere quickly gets sent to our left hemisphere, which names it. But what happens in an otherwise healthy person whose corpus callosum has been severed? To find out, experimenters ask a split-brain patient to look at a designated spot. Then they send information to either the left or right hemisphere (by flashing it to the right or left visual field). Finally, they quiz each hemisphere separately.

See if you can guess the results of an experiment using this procedure (Gazzaniga, 1967). While the patients stared at a dot, the word HEART was flashed across the visual field with HE in the left visual field and ART in the right. First, what did the patients *say* they saw? Second, asked to identify with their *left* hands what they had seen, HE or ART, what did they *point* to?

As Figure 2–21 shows, the patients *said* they saw ART, and so were startled when their left hands *pointed* to HE. When given an opportunity to express itself, each hemisphere reported only what *it* had seen.

"Look at the dot."

"What word did you see?"

"Art."

"Point with your left hand to the word you saw."

Figure 2–21 Testing the divided brain. When an experimenter flashes the word HEART across the visual field, the split-brain patient reports seeing the portion of the word transmitted to her left hemisphere. However, if asked to indicate with her left hand what she saw, she points to the portion of the word transmitted to her right hemisphere.

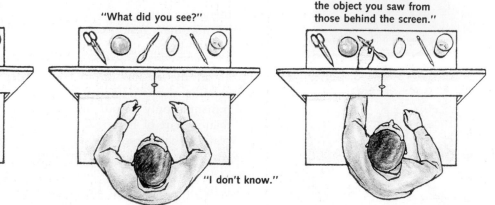

"What did you see?"

"With your left hand, select the object you saw from those behind the screen."

"I don't know."

Figure 2–22 The nonverbal right hemisphere sees the spoon flashed on the screen and directs the left hand to locate it among the objects hidden behind the screen. But the split-brain patient cannot say what he has seen. (From Gazzaniga, 1983.)

Answer to question on page 49: Yes. Broca's area produces a program for controlling the muscles of speech. If damaged, a victim can still understand speech and communicate through gestures or writing.

Figure 2–23 When an experimenter flashes simple commands to the right hemisphere of split-brain patients, they comply. Asked about their response, their left hemisphere, which controls speech and is unaware of what the right hemisphere has seen, invents—and seemingly believes—plausible explanations for what it does not comprehend. Thus, Michael Gazzaniga (1988) concludes that the left hemisphere is an "interpreter" that instantly constructs theories to explain our behavior. (From Gazzaniga, 1983.)

Similarly, when a picture of a spoon was flashed to the right hemisphere, the patients could not say what they saw; but when asked to identify what they had seen by feeling with their left hands an assortment of objects hidden behind a screen, they readily selected the spoon (Figure 2–22). If the experimenter said, "Right!" the patient might reply, "What? Right? How could I possibly pick out the right object when I don't know what I saw?" It is, of course, the left hemisphere doing the talking here, bewildered by what its other half knows. It's as if the patients have "two separate inner visual worlds," noted Sperry (1968). With split brains, each hemisphere truly has a mind of its own.

The left hemisphere, which acts as the brain's press agent, does mental gymnastics to rationalize reactions it does not understand (Figure 2–23). If the patient followed an order sent to the right hemisphere ("Walk"), the interpretive left hemisphere would offer a ready explanation ("I'm going into the house to get a Coke").

These experiments demonstrate that the right hemisphere understands simple requests and easily perceives objects. In fact, the right hemisphere is superior to the left at copying drawings, recognizing faces, and reading emotions. Its perceptual superiority is apparent in one of Sperry's films. A split-brain patient's left hand (directed by the right hemisphere) easily rearranges some blocks to match a drawing. When the right hand (directed by the left hemisphere) tries to perform the same perceptual task, it makes many errors. The bumbling performance frustrates the right hemisphere, which is observing all this. So it triggers the left hand to interrupt the bumbling right hand; but the persistent right hand pushes the left hand away. Outside the labora-

"What was the command?"

"Oh . . itch."

Innocent and carefree, Stuart's left hand didn't know what the right was doing.

THE FAR SIDE © 1990 Universal Press Syndicate. Reprinted with permission. All rights reserved.

"In the normal state, the two hemispheres appear to work closely together as a unit, rather than one being turned on while the other idles."

Roger Sperry (1982)

These PET scans show how active the right hemisphere becomes when the subject is listening to music (right) compared to resting (left). Red signifies the most activity, blue the least.

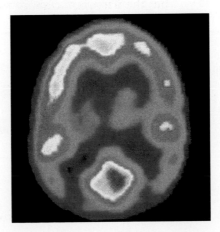
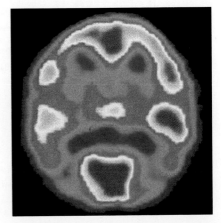

tory, a few split-brain patients have been bothered by the unruly independence of their left hand, which may unbutton a shirt while the right hand buttons it. Split-brain surgery, said Sperry (1964), leaves people "with two separate minds."

To summarize, split-brain patients reveal the special functions of each hemisphere. The left hemisphere is more logical and able to deal with things in sequence. Being verbal, it was the easiest side to get to know—like the side of the moon we see. The right is more emotionally intuitive, skilled at spatial relations, and able to deal with things all at once.

Imaginative writers have had a field day with the left-right dichotomy. Traditional schooling fails to educate the right side of the brain, some have told us. "The left-right dichotomy in cognitive mode is an idea with which it is very easy to run wild," observed Sperry (1982). Complex activities such as practicing science, studying psychology, or creating art emerge from the *integrated* activity of both hemispheres. Creativity involves the frontal lobes of both hemispheres. Although language requires the left hemisphere, the right hemisphere helps us modulate our speech to make meaning clear—asking "What's that in the road ahead?" instead of "What's that in the road, a head?" (Heller, 1990). Even when simply reading a story, both hemispheres are at work—the left understanding the words and finding meaning, the right appreciating humor, imagery, puns, and emotional content (Levy, 1985). Thus, neuropsychologists advise us to beware the fad of locating complex human capacities, such as abilities in science or art, in either hemisphere.

Studying the Normal Brain

What about the 99.99 + percent of us with undivided brains? Have scientists found our hemispheres similarly specialized? They have indeed, by evidence from several different types of studies. For example, when a person performs a *perceptual* task, brain waves, blood flow, and glucose consumption reveal increased activity in the *right* hemisphere; when a person speaks or calculates, activity increases in the left hemisphere.

On occasion, hemispheric specialization has been even more dramatically shown by briefly sedating an entire hemisphere. To check for the locus of language before surgery, a physician may inject a sedative into the neck artery that feeds blood to the hemisphere on its side of the body. Before the drug is injected, the patient is lying down, arms in the air, conversing easily. Can you predict what happens when the drug flows into the artery going to the left hemisphere? Within seconds, the right arm falls limp, and, assuming

Tests reveal that about 95 percent of right-handers process speech primarily in the left hemisphere (Springer & Deutsch, 1985). Left-handers are more diverse. More than half process speech in the left hemisphere, as right-handers do. About one-quarter process language in the right hemisphere; the other quarter use both hemispheres more or less equally. Such left-handers may therefore require better communication between the hemispheres. This might explain the discovery that the corpus callosum averages 11 percent larger in left-handers (Witelson, 1985).

"If the human brain were so simple that we could understand it, we would be so simple that we couldn't."

Emerson M. Pugh, quoted by George E. Pugh *The Biological Origin of Human Values*, 1977

the person's left hemisphere controls language, the subject becomes speechless until the drug wears off. When the drug goes into the artery to the right hemisphere, the *left* arm falls limp, but speech is still possible.

Other tests confirm hemispheric specialization. Most people recognize pictures faster and more accurately when flashed to the right hemisphere, but recognize words faster and more accurately when flashed to the left hemisphere. If a word is flashed to your right hemisphere, perception takes a fraction of a second longer—the length of time it takes to send the information through the corpus callosum to the more verbal left hemisphere.

Finally, which hemisphere would you suppose enables sign language among the deaf? Is it the right hemisphere, because of its visual-spatial superiority? Or the left, because of its preparedness to process language? Studies reveal that just as hearing people use the left hemisphere to process speech, hearing-impaired people use the left hemisphere to read signs (Bellugi & others, 1989). A stroke in the left hemisphere therefore disrupts a deaf person's ability to sign much as it would disrupt a hearing person's use of spoken language.

So, a variety of observations—of people with "split" brains and people with "normal" brains—converge beautifully. There is now little doubt that we have unified brains with specialized parts, and that infants are born with their brains "prewired" accordingly (Hahn, 1987). From looking at the two hemispheres, which look alike to the naked eye, who would suppose that they contribute so uniquely to the harmony of the whole?

From nineteenth-century phrenology to today's neuroscience we have come a long way. Yet what is unknown still dwarfs what is known. We can describe the brain. We can learn the functions of its parts. We can study how the parts communicate. But how does this electrochemical whir give rise to a feeling of elation, a creative idea, or a memory of Grandma's freshly baked cookies?

To judge from one series of interviews with leading brain scientists, feelings of wonder are commonplace, and sometimes lead to mystical and spiritual inspirations. In the words of Candace Pert (1986, p. 390), "I see in the brain all the beauty of the universe and its order—constant signs of God's presence." Others ponder philosophical mysteries: How does the material brain give rise to consciousness? And to what extent can a thing understand itself? The mind seeking to understand the brain—that is the ultimate scientific challenge.

Rehearse It

25. Plasticity refers to the brain's ability to reorganize itself after damage or injury. Especially plastic are the brains of
a. split-brain patients.
b. young adults.
c. young children.
d. right-handed people.

26. The brain structure that enables the right and left hemispheres to communicate is

a. the medulla.
b. Broca's area.
c. Wernicke's area.
d. the corpus callosum.

27. Split-brain patients have enabled us to observe the special functions of each brain hemisphere. The left hemisphere excels in
a. processing language.
b. visual perceptions.

c. recognition of emotion.
d. recognition of faces.

28. Damage to the right hemisphere is most likely to reduce a person's ability to
a. recite the alphabet rapidly.
b. recognize the emotional content of facial expressions.
c. understand verbal instructions.
d. solve arithmetic problems.

Reviewing The Biological Roots of Behavior

1 Why do psychologists study biology?

As a first step in understanding our behavior and mental processes, students of psychology examine the biological roots of how we think, feel, and act.

The Nervous System

2. What are the three types of neurons, and how do they work?

The body's circuitry, the nervous system, consists of billions of nerve cells, called neurons. The sensory neurons transmit information inward to the central nervous system, where it is processed by the interneurons of the brain and spinal cord. Instructions are then sent back out via the motor neurons. Neurons receive signals from external stimuli and from other neurons through their branching dendrites and cell bodies. They then combine these signals in the cell body and transmit electrical impulses down their axons.

3. How do nerve cells communicate?

When electrical signals reach the end of the axon, they stimulate the release of chemical messengers, called neurotransmitters. These molecules traverse the tiny synaptic gap between neurons and combine with receptor sites on neighboring neurons, thus passing on their excitatory or inhibitory messages.

4. How do neurotransmitters influence human behavior?

Dozens of different neurotransmitters have been discovered, and the functions of some have become well-understood. Learning about endorphins, the feel-good neurotransmitters, has helped us understand how drugs affect our brain chemistry.

5. What are the major divisions of the nervous system, and what are their basic functions?

The central nervous system (CNS) neurons of the brain and spinal cord communicate with the sensory and motor neurons of the peripheral nervous system (PNS). The PNS consists of the somatic nervous system, which directs sensory input and motor output, and the autonomic nervous system, whose sympathetic and parasympathetic divisions control our involuntary muscles and our glands.

The Brain

6. How is the brain organized?

The brain can be viewed as having three regions—the brainstem, the limbic system, and the cerebral cortex, each of which represents a stage of brain evolution. The brainstem begins where the spinal cord swells to form the medulla. The limbic system lies at the border of the brainstem and cerebral cortex. The cerebral cortex is the outer layer of the ballooning left and right hemispheres.

7. What functions do the structures within the brainstem serve?

Within the brainstem the medulla controls heartbeat and breathing. The cerebellum, which is attached to the rear of the brainstem, coordinates muscle movement. On top of the brainstem is the thalamus, the brain's sensory switchboard. Within the brainstem, the reticular formation controls arousal and attention.

8. What functions do the structures within the limbic system serve?

The limbic system has been linked primarily to memory, emotions, and drives. For example, one of its neural centers, the amygdala, is involved in aggressive and fearful responses. Another, the hypothalamus, has been linked to various bodily maintenance functions and to pleasurable rewards. The hypothalamus also controls the endocrine system, which is the body's second communication system.

9. How is the cerebral cortex organized?

The cerebral cortex is a thin, wrinkled sheet of neurons with trillions of interconnections. Each of the hemispheres it covers can be viewed as having four geographical areas: the frontal, parietal, occipital, and temporal lobes, which are separated by fissures, or grooves.

10. What functions are served by the cerebral cortex?

Small, well-defined regions within the cerebral lobes control muscle movement and receive information from the body senses. However, most of the cortex—its association areas—is uncommitted to such functions and is therefore free to process other information.

Some brain regions are known to serve specific functions. In general, however, human emotions, thoughts, and behaviors result from the intricate coordination of many brain areas. Language, for example, depends on a chain of events in several brain regions.

11. Is the brain capable of reorganizing itself if damaged?

If one hemisphere is damaged early in life, the other will pick up many of its functions, thus demonstrating the brain's plasticity. Unfortunately, the brain is less plastic later in life. However, nearby neurons can often at least partially compensate for damaged ones, as when a patient recovers from a minor stroke.

12. What is a split brain, and what does it reveal about brain functioning?

A split brain is one whose corpus callosum, the bundle of nerve fibers that connects the two brain hemispheres, has been severed. Clinical observations long ago revealed that the left cerebral hemisphere is crucial for language. More recent experiments on split-brain patients have refined our knowledge of each hemisphere's special functions. By testing the two hemispheres separately, researchers have confirmed that for most people the left hemisphere is indeed the more verbal, and that the right hemisphere excels in visual perception and the recognition of emotion. Controversy still exists regarding the capacities of the right hemisphere, but studies of normal people with intact brains confirm that each hemisphere makes unique contributions to the integrated functioning of the brain.

Terms and Concepts to Remember

biological psychologists, p. 27

nervous system, p. 27

neuron, p. 27

sensory neurons, p. 28

interneurons, p. 28

motor neurons, p. 28

reflex, p. 28

dendrite, p. 29

axon, p. 29

myelin [MY-uh-lin] sheath, p. 29

threshold, p. 29

synapse [SIN-aps], p. 30

neurotransmitters, p. 30

acetylcholine [ah-seat-el-KO-leen] (ACh), p. 31

endorphins [en-DOR-fins], p. 32

central nervous system (CNS), p. 33

peripheral nervous system (PNS), p. 33

somatic [so-MAT-ik] nervous system, p. 33

autonomic [aw-tuh-NAHM-ik] nervous system, p. 33

sympathetic nervous system, p. 34

parasympathetic nervous system, p. 34

brainstem, p. 36

medulla [muh-DUL-uh], p. 36

cerebellum [sehr-uh-BELL-um], p. 36

thalamus [THAL-uh-muss], p. 37

reticular formation, p. 37

lesion [LEE-zhuhn], p. 38

electroencephalogram (EEG), p. 38

CAT (computerized axial tomograph) scan, p. 39

PET (positron emission tomograph) scan, p. 39

MRI (magnetic resonance imaging), p. 39

limbic system, p. 40

amygdala [ah-MIG-dah-la], p. 40

hypothalamus [hi-po-THAL-uh-muss], p. 41

hormones, p. 42

endocrine [EN-duh-krin] system, p. 42

adrenal [ah-DREEN-el] glands, p. 42

pituitary gland, p. 43

cerebral [seh-REE-bruhl] cortex, p. 44

frontal lobes, p. 44

parietal [puh-RYE-uh-tuhl] lobes, p. 44

occipital [ahk-SIP-uh-tuhl] lobes, p. 44

temporal lobes, p. 44

motor cortex, p. 45

sensory cortex, p. 46

association areas, p. 47

aphasia, p. 48

Broca's area, p. 48

Wernicke's area, p. 48

plasticity, p. 49

corpus callosum [kah-LOW-sum], p. 50

split-brain, p. 50

Rehearse It Answer Key

1. d.	2. b.	3. a.	4. c.	5. d.	6. c.	7. b.	8. c.	9. b.
10. a.	11. b.	12. a.	13. d.	14. c.	15. b.	16. d.	17. c.	18. a.
19. a.	20. b.	21. c.	22. c.	23. d.	24. b.	25. c.	26. d.	27. a.
28. b.								

Critical Thinking Exercise

You have *Surveyed, Questioned, Read, Rehearsed,* and *Reviewed* Chapter 2. Now take your learning a step further by testing your *critical thinking* skills on the following passage. If you need a refresher course on the concept of critical thinking, turn to Appendix B before working this exercise.

Your younger brother, who recently read and was fascinated by the book *One Brain, Two Minds,* has decided that some people are "left-brained," and others are "right-brained." The authors studied patients whose epileptic seizures were treated by surgically cutting their corpus callosums. The patients were then quizzed on visual information that was sent to either the left or right hemisphere of their brains. When only the left hemisphere was presented with information, the patients had no trouble verbally identifying words and solving logical problems. When information was presented only to the right hemisphere, the patients were unable to talk or reason about it but were able to copy drawings, recognize faces, and react intuitively. These authors concluded that people who are right-handed, and therefore left-brain dominant, generally are more logical and scientific than left-handers, who are right-brain dominant and therefore less logical, but more creative. Because your brother is left-handed, he has decided to abandon his goal of becoming a science major in college in favor of quitting school and becoming a rap musician.

Understand the Assertion

1. State the researchers' assertion in your own words. Define all important concepts and terms as they are used in this study.

Consider the Evidence

2. Is the evidence for the researchers' assertion empirical (observable)? Is the evidence based on trustworthy research?

Evaluate the Explanation

3. Evaluate the theoretical explanation for the researcher's conclusion.
   a. Restate it in your own words.
   b. Determine whether the explanation makes sense based on the evidence.
   c. State an alternative explanation for the assertion.

Check your progress on becoming a critical thinker by comparing your answers to the sample answers found in Appendix B.

For Further Information

You can find more information regarding the biology of behavior on the following text pages:

Genes and
    aggression, p. 458
    altruism, p. 466
    depression, p. 395
    development, pp. 59–60, 96–99
    fearfulness, p. 311
    gender, p. 488
    intelligence, pp. 260–262
    learning, pp. 184–185, 195–196
    obesity, p. 279
    schizophrenia, p. 403
    evolutionary psychology, pp. 466, 489–490
Neurotransmitters and
    depression, pp. 395–396
    drugs, pp. 169–170
    exercise, p. 335

hunger, p. 274
memory, p. 218
schizophrenia, p. 402
smoking, p. 170
therapy, pp. 435–437
Hormones and
    aggression, pp. 459, 489
    development, pp. 78–79
    emotion, p. 302
    gender, pp. 488–489
    hunger, p. 274
    memory, p. 218
    sex, pp. 284–285
    stress, pp. 324–325, 329

Brain activity and
    aggression, pp. 458–459
    development, pp. 63–65
    dreams, pp. 157–158
    emotion, p. 303
    hunger, pp. 274–275
    hypnosis, p. 165
    memory, pp. 217–220
    sensation, Chapter 4
    psychosurgery, pp. 437–438
    sex, p. 285
    sleep, pp. 151–153
    stress and health, Chapter 11

The Developing Person

In mid-1978, the newest astonishment in medicine, covering all the front pages, was the birth of an English baby nine months after conception in a dish. The older surprise, which should still be fazing us all, is that a solitary sperm and a single egg can fuse and become a human being under any circumstance, and that, however implanted, [this multiplied] cell affixed to the uterine wall will grow and differentiate into eight pounds of baby; this has been going on under our eyes for so long a time that we've gotten used to it; hence the outcries of amazement at this really minor technical modification of the general procedure—nothing much, really, beyond relocating the beginning of the process from the fallopian tube to a plastic container.

Lewis Thomas
The Medusa and Snail, 1979

Preview Question

1. What are the major issues in developmental psychology?

developmental psychology A branch of psychology that studies physical, cognitive, and social change throughout the life span.

The developing person is no less a wonder after birth than in the womb. As we journey through life from womb to tomb, when and how do we change? Usually we notice how we differ. To **developmental psychologists,** who study physical, mental, and social changes throughout the human life cycle, our commonalities are just as important. Virtually all of us—Confucius, Queen Elizabeth, Martin Luther King, Jr., you, and I—began walking around age 1 and talking by age 2. As children we all engaged in social play in preparation for life's serious work. We all smile and cry, love and hate. As adults, we occasionally ponder the fact that someday we will die.

Human development is a lifelong process. Psychology's developmental perspective examines how people are continually developing, from infancy through old age. Much of its research centers on three major issues:

1. *Nature or nurture:* How much is human development influenced by our genetic inheritance (our *nature*) and how much by our experience (the *nurture* we receive)?

2. *Continuity or stages:* Is development a gradual, continuous process, or does it proceed through a sequence of separate stages, like climbing separate steps?

3. *Stability or change:* Do our early personality traits persist through life, or do we become different persons as we age?

At the chapter's end we will reflect on these three developmental issues. But first, our main agenda: to examine human development across the life span, beginning where life begins and ending where life ends.

Prenatal Development and the Newborn

From Life Comes Life

Nothing is more natural than a species reproducing itself. Yet nothing is more wondrous. Consider human reproduction. The process starts when a woman's ovary releases a mature **ovum** (egg), a cell roughly the size of the period at the end of this sentence, and the nearly 300 million sperm deposited during intercourse begin their race upstream toward it.

Like space voyagers approaching a huge planet, the sperm approach a cell 85,000 times their own size. The relatively few sperm that make it to the egg release digestive enzymes that eat away the egg's protective coating, allowing a sperm to penetrate (Figure 3–1). As it does so, an electric charge shoots across the ovum's surface, blocking out all other sperm during the minute or so that it takes the egg to form a barrier. Meanwhile, fingerlike projections sprout around the successful sperm and pull it inward. The egg nucleus and the sperm move toward each other and, before half a day elapses, fuse. The two have become one.

When egg and sperm unite, the 23 **chromosomes** carried in the egg pair up with the 23 chromosomes brought to it by the sperm. These 46 chromosomes contain the master plan for your body. Each chromosome is composed of long threads of a molecule called **DNA (deoxyribonucleic acid).** DNA in turn is made of thousands of **genes,** functional segments capable of synthesizing specific *proteins* (the biochemical building blocks of life).

Your sex is determined by your twenty-third pair of chromosomes, the sex chromosomes. The member of the pair that came from your mother was an *X* **chromosome.** From your father, you received either an *X* chromosome, making you a girl, or a *Y* **chromosome,** making you a boy. The *Y* chromosome contains a single gene that throws a master switch triggering the testes to develop and produce the principal male hormone, **testosterone,** which in turn triggers the development of external male sex organs.

Even at your fortunate moment when one lucky sperm among 300 million won the race, your destiny was not assured. Fewer than half of fertilized eggs, called **zygotes,** survive beyond the first week (Grobstein, 1979). If human life begins at conception, then most people die without being born.

But for you and me good fortune prevailed. Beginning as one cell, each of us became two cells, then four—each cell just like the first. Then, within the first week, when this cell division had produced a zygote of some 100 cells, the cells began to *differentiate*—to specialize in structure and function. Within

ovum   The female reproductive cell, or egg.

chromosomes   Threadlike structures made of DNA molecules that contain the genes.

DNA (deoxyribonucleic acid)   A complex molecule containing genetic information that makes up the chromosomes.

genes   The biochemical units of heredity that make up the chromosomes; a segment of DNA capable of synthesizing a protein.

***X* chromosome**   The sex chromosome found in both men and women. Females have two *X* chromosomes; males have one. An *X* chromosome from each parent produces a female.

***Y* chromosome**   The sex chromosome found only in males. When paired with an *X* chromosome from the mother, the result is a male child.

testosterone   The most important of the male sex hormones. Both males and females have it, but the additional testosterone in males stimulates the growth of the male sex organs in the fetus and the development of the male sex characteristics during puberty.

zygote   The fertilized egg; it enters a 2-week period of rapid cell division and develops into an embryo.

Figure 3–1 Development begins when sperm and egg unite. The result is a single cell that, if all goes well, will become a 100-trillion-cell human being.

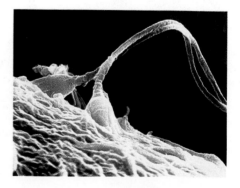

embryo The developing human organism from about 2 weeks after fertilization through the second month.

fetus The developing human organism from 9 weeks after conception to birth.

teratogens Agents, such as chemicals and viruses, that can reach the embryo or fetus during prenatal development and cause harm.

fetal alcohol syndrome Physical and cognitive abnormalities in children caused by a pregnant woman's heavy drinking. In severe cases, symptoms include noticeable facial misproportions.

Prenatal development:
zygote: conception to 2 weeks
embryo: 2 weeks through 8 weeks
fetus: 9 weeks to birth

2 weeks, the increasingly diverse cells became attached to the mother's uterus, beginning approximately 37 weeks of the closest human relationship.

After attaching to the uterine wall, the zygote's outer part becomes the placenta, from which nourishment passes via the umbilical cord. The inner cells become the **embryo** (Figure 3–2). During the next 6 weeks, the embryo's body organs begin to form and function. The heart begins to beat and the liver begins to make red blood cells.

By 9 weeks after conception, the embryo has become unmistakably human and is now a **fetus.** By the end of the sixth month, internal organs such as the stomach have become sufficiently formed and functional to allow a prematurely born fetus a chance of survival.

At each prenatal stage, genetic *and* environmental factors—nature and nurture—affect development. The placenta screens out many potentially harmful substances, while allowing nutrients and oxygen to pass through. But along with nourishment, some damaging agents called **teratogens** pass through with potentially tragic effects. Pregnant women never drink or smoke alone. When the mother takes a drink, alcohol enters her bloodstream—and her fetus's—and depresses activity in both their central nervous systems. When she puffs on a cigarette, she and her fetus both experience reduced blood oxygen and a shot of nicotine. If she is a heavy smoker, her newborn will probably be underweight, sometimes dangerously so. If she is a heroin addict, her baby is born a heroin addict. If she carries the AIDS virus, her baby often does, too.

If the mother drinks heavily, her baby will be at risk for birth defects and mental retardation. For some infants, the effects are visible as **fetal alcohol syndrome,** which involves small, misproportioned heads and lifelong brain abnormalities, often resulting in mental retardation. If the mother uses crack cocaine, her baby, after birth, suffers the pain of withdrawal from an addiction. Having been deprived of nutrients and oxygen while in the womb, the baby may also suffer deformities and growth impairment. In the early 1990s, as the first wave of a new "crack baby" generation began school, urban special education programs struggled to accommodate increasing numbers of withdrawn, impulsive, hyperactive children.

Figure 3–2 Prenatal development.

 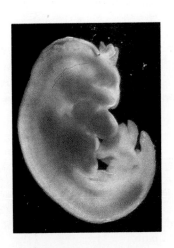 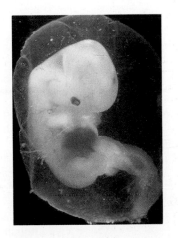 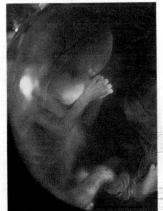

The embryo grows and develops rapidly. At 40 days, the spine is visible and the arms and legs are beginning to grow.

Five days later the inch-long embryo's proportions have begun to change. The rest of the body is now bigger than the head, and the arms and legs have grown noticeably.

By the end of the second month, when the fetal period begins, facial features, hands, and feet have formed.

As the fetus enters the fourth month, it weighs about 3 ounces.

The Competent Newborn

Preview Question

3. What are some of the newborn's capabilities?

Newborns come equipped with reflexes ideally suited for survival. Infants will withdraw a limb to escape pain. Put a cloth over their faces, interfering with their breathing, and they will turn their heads from side to side and swipe at it. New parents are often awed by the coordinated sequence of reflexes by which babies get food. The **rooting reflex** illustrates this: When something touches their cheeks, babies will open their mouths and vigorously "root" for a nipple. Finding one, they will automatically close on it and begin sucking—which itself requires a coordinated sequence of tonguing, swallowing, and breathing. Failing to find satisfaction, the hungry baby may cry—a behavior that parents are predisposed to find highly unpleasant to hear and very rewarding to relieve.

Moreover, a baby's sensory equipment is "wired" to facilitate social responsiveness. Newborns turn their heads in the direction of human voices, but not in response to artificial sounds. They gaze more at a drawing of a human face than at a bull's-eye pattern; yet they gaze more at a bull's-eye pattern—which has contrasts much like that of the human eye—than at a solid disk (Fantz, 1961). They prefer to look at objects 8 to 12 inches away, which, wonder of wonders, just happens to be the approximate distance between a nursing infant's eyes and the mother's (Maurer & Maurer, 1988). Newborns, it seems, arrive perfectly designed to see their mothers' eyes.

Babies' perceptual abilities are continuously developing during the first months of life. Within days of birth, babies can distinguish their mothers' facial expression, odor, and voice. A week-old nursing baby, placed between a gauze pad from its mother's bra and one from another nursing mother, will usually turn toward the smell of its own mother's pad (MacFarlane, 1978). At 3 weeks of age, an infant who sucks on a pacifier that sometimes turns on recordings of its mother's voice and sometimes that of a female stranger will suck more vigorously when it hears its mother's voice (Mills & Melhuish, 1974). So not only can infants see what they need to see, and smell and hear well, but they are already using their sensory equipment to learn. More and more, reports researcher Tiffany Field (1987), psychologists see the baby as "a very sophisticated perceiver of the world, with very sensitive social and emotional qualities and impressive intellectual abilities."

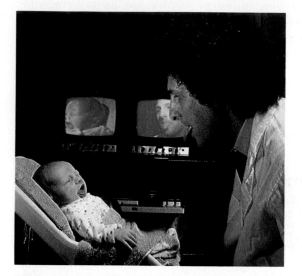

Infant imitation? Researchers have reported the astonishing and controversial finding that infants can mimic facial expression almost from birth. When researcher Andrew Meltzoff (1987) shows his tongue, an 18-day-old boy responds similarly.

Rehearse It

1. The life cycle begins when the egg nucleus and sperm nucleus fuse to create a new individual. The egg and sperm each contribute
a. one chromosome pair.
b. 23 chromosomes.
c. 23 chromosome pairs.
d. an XY chromosome.

2. The fertilized egg will develop into a boy if it receives
a. an X chromosome from its mother.
b. an X chromosome from its father.

c. a Y chromosome from its mother.
d. a Y chromosome from its father.

3. The fertilized egg during the first 2 weeks is called a zygote. Statistically speaking, most zygotes
a. are male.
b. are not fertilized.
c. do not survive to birth.
d. develop into normal fetuses.

4. Teratogens are chemicals that pass through the placenta's screen and may

harm an embryo or fetus. Which of the following is *not* a teratogen?
a. oxygen
b. cocaine
c. alcohol
d. nicotine

5. Stroke a newborn's cheek and he or she will root for a nipple. This illustrates
a. a reflex.
b. sensorimotor learning.
c. perceptual ability.
d. a gender difference.

rooting reflex A baby's tendency, when touched on the cheek, to open the mouth and search for the nipple.

maturation Biological growth processes that enable orderly changes in behavior, relatively uninfluenced by experience.

Infancy and Childhood

During infancy, a baby grows from newborn to toddler, and during childhood from toddler to teenager. Beginning with infancy and childhood and continuing with adolescence through old age, we will see how people of all ages develop—physically, cognitively, and socially.

Physical Development

Brain Development

While you resided in your mother's womb, your body was forming nerve cells at the rate of about one-quarter million per *minute*. On the day you were born you had essentially all the brain cells you will ever have. However, at birth the human nervous system is immature: The neural networks that enable us to walk, talk, and remember are still forming (Figure 3–3). This helps explain why our earliest memories do not predate our third or fourth birthdays (Kihlstrom & Harachkiewicz, 1982).

The nervous system's development enables **maturation,** an orderly sequence of biological growth. Maturation decrees many of our commonalities: standing before walking, using nouns before adjectives. Experience, too, helps develop the brain's neural connections. Although it is "forgotten," early learning is not erased. For example, the first 2 years are critical for learning language. Children who become deaf at age 2, after having been exposed to speech, are later more easily trained in sign language than those deaf from birth (Lenneberg, 1967).

How do early experiences leave their "marks" in the brain? Working at the University of California, Berkeley, Mark Rosenzweig and David Krech caged some rats in solitary confinement and others in a communal playground (Figure 3–4). Rats living in the deprived environment usually developed a lighter, thinner brain cortex with smaller nerve cell bodies and fewer glial cells (the "glue cells" that support and nourish the brain's neurons). Rosenzweig (1984a; Renner & Rosenzweig, 1987) reported being so surprised by these effects of experience on brain tissue that he repeated the experiment several times before publishing his findings—findings that have led to improvements in the environments provided for laboratory, farm, and zoo animals, and institutionalized children. Several research teams have also found that infant rats and premature babies benefit from the stimulation of being touched or massaged (Field & others, 1986; Meaney & others, 1988). "Handled" infants of both species gain weight more rapidly and develop faster neurologically.

Preview Question

4. How do the brain and motor skills develop during infancy and childhood?

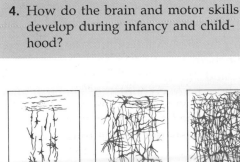
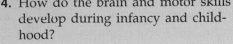
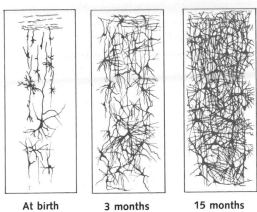

| At birth | 3 months | 15 months |

Figure 3–3 In humans, the brain is immature at birth. These drawings of sections of brain tissue from the cerebral cortex illustrate the increasing complexity of the neural networks in the maturing human brain. The number of nerve cells don't increase, but their interconnections do.

Figure 3–4 Experience affects the brain's development. In pioneering experiments, Mark Rosenzweig and David Krech reared rats either alone in an environment without playthings or with others in an environment enriched with playthings that were changed daily. In 14 out of 16 repetitions of this basic experiment, the rats placed in the enriched environment developed significantly more cerebral cortex (relative to the rest of the brain's tissue) than those in the impoverished environment. (From "Brain changes in response to experience" by M. R. Rosenzweig, E. L. Bennett, and M. C. Diamond. Copyright © 1972 Scientific American, Inc. All rights reserved.)

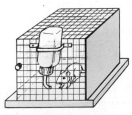

Impoverished environment

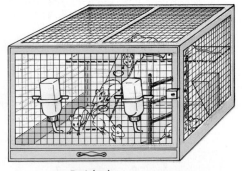

Enriched environment

Throughout life our neural tissue is changing. Sights and smells, touches and tugs activate and strengthen certain neural pathways, while others weaken from disuse. It's like paths through a forest: Less traveled paths are abandoned, popular paths are broadened. Our genes dictate our overall brain architecture, but experience directs the details. If a monkey is trained to push a lever with a finger several thousand times a day, the brain tissue controlling that finger changes to reflect the experience. The wiring of basketball star Michael Jordan's brain reflects the thousands of hours he has spent shooting baskets. Experience nurtures nature.

Motor Development

As the infant's muscles and neural networks mature, ever more complicated skills emerge. Although the age at which infants sit, stand, and walk varies from child to child, the *sequence* in which babies pass these developmental milestones is universal (Figure 3–5).

Can experience retard or speed up the maturation of physical skills? For example, do babies bound to a cradleboard for much of their first year—a traditional practice among the Hopi and Navajo—walk later than do unbound infants? Or, if allowed to spend an hour a day in a walker chair after age 4 months, will babies walk earlier? Amazingly, in view of what we now know about the effects experience has on the brain, the answer seems to be no (Dennis, 1940; Ridenour, 1982).

Figure 3–5 Stages of motor development in infants. Although some infants reach each milestone ahead of others, the order of the stages is the same for all infants. The colored bars show developmental norms. The far left and right sides of the bar indicate the ages by which 25 percent and 90 percent have mastered this movement. Where the colors meet shows the point at which half the infants have mastered the movement.

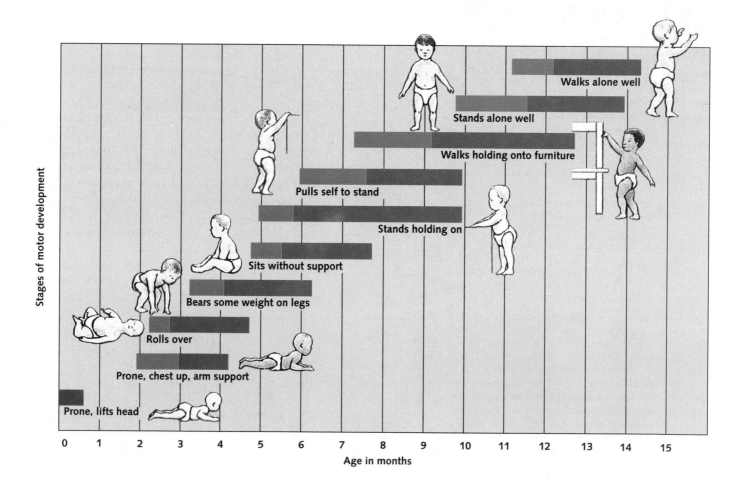

Biological maturation—including the rapid development of the cerebellum at the rear of the brain—creates a readiness to learn walking at about 1 year of age. Experience before that time has no more than a small effect. This is true for other physical skills, including bowel and bladder control. Until the necessary muscular and neural maturation has occurred, no amount of pleading, harassment, or punishment can lead to successful toilet training.

schema A concept or framework that organizes and interprets information.

Preview Question

5. How did Piaget view the mind's development?

Jean Piaget (1930): "If we examine the intellectual development of the individual or of the whole of humanity, we shall find that the human spirit goes through a certain number of stages, each different from the other."

"For everything there is a season, and a time for every matter under heaven."

Ecclesiastes 3:1

Cognitive Development

"Who knows the thoughts of a child?" wondered poet Nora Perry. As much as anyone of his generation, developmental psychologist Jean Piaget (pronounced Pea-ah-ZHAY) knew. His interest began in 1920, when he was working in Paris to develop questions for children's intelligence tests. While administering tests to find out at what age children could answer certain questions correctly, Piaget became intrigued by children's *wrong* answers. Where others saw childish mistakes, Piaget saw intelligence at work. The errors made by children of a given age, he noted, were often strikingly similar.

The more than 50 years Piaget spent with children convinced him that *the child's mind is not a miniature model of the adult's.* Young children actively construct their understandings of the world in radically different ways than adults do, a fact that we sometimes overlook when teaching children. Piaget further believed that the child's mind develops through a series of stages, in an upward march from the newborn's simple reflexes to the adult's abstract reasoning power. An 8-year-old child therefore comprehends things that a 3-year-old cannot. An 8-year-old might grasp the analogy "getting an idea is like having a light turn on in your head," but trying to teach the same analogy to a 3-year-old would be fruitless.

How the Mind of a Child Grows

The driving force behind this intellectual progression is our unceasing struggle to make sense of the world. To this end, the maturing brain builds concepts, which Piaget called **schemas.** Schemas are ways of looking at the world that organize our past experiences and provide a framework for understanding our future experiences. We start life with simple schemas—those involving sense-driven reflexes such as sucking and grasping. With experience we modify our schemas. A toddler may call all four-legged animals *doggies*, but soon learn to refine the category. By adulthood we have built countless schemas that range from knowing how to tie a knot to knowing what it means to be in love.

Look carefully at the "devil's tuning fork" to the right. Now look away—no, better first study it some more—and then look away and draw it. Not so easy, is it? Because this tuning fork is an impossible object, you have no schema to help you assimilate what you see.

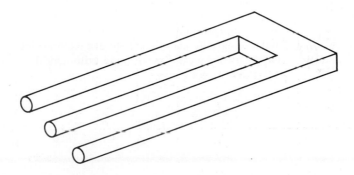

Piaget proposed two concepts to explain how we use and adjust our schemas. First, we interpret our experience in terms of our current understandings; in Piaget's terms, we incorporate, or **assimilate,** new experiences into our existing schemas. Given a simple schema for "dog," a toddler may call all four-legged animals "doggies." But we also adjust, or **accommodate,** our schemas to fit new experiences. The child learns that the original "doggie" schema is too broad, and accommodates by refining the category. When new experiences just will not fit our old schemas, schemas may change or evolve to accommodate the experiences.

Piaget's Theory and Current Thinking on Cognitive Stages

Cognition refers to all the mental activities associated with thinking, knowing, and remembering. Piaget described cognitive development as occurring in four major stages (Table 3–1). The developing child, he believed, moves from one age-related plateau to the next. Each plateau has distinctive characteristics that permit specific kinds of thinking. To appreciate how the mind of a child grows, let's look at each of Piaget's stages in light of current thinking about cognitive development.

Sensorimotor Stage   During the **sensorimotor stage,** from birth to nearly age 2, babies understand the world through their sensory and motor interactions with objects—through looking, touching, mouthing, and grasping. At first they seem unaware that things continue to exist apart from their perceptions.

In one of his tests, Piaget would show an infant an appealing toy and then flop his beret over it to see whether the infant searched for the toy. Much before the age of 8 months, they did not. They lacked **object permanence**—the awareness that objects continue to exist when not perceived. The infant

In the sensorimotor stage of development, from infancy until nearly age 2, children explore the world through their senses. They enjoy the smell, feel, and taste of almost anything they can get their hands on.

Table 3-1

Piaget's Stages of Cognitive Development

Age range	Description of stage	Developmental milestones
Birth to nearly 2 years	**Sensorimotor** Experiencing the world through senses and actions (looking, touching, mouthing)	• Object permanence • Stranger anxiety
About 2 to 6 years	**Preoperational** Representing things with words and images but lacking logical reasoning	• Ability to pretend • Egocentrism
About 7 to 11 years	**Concrete operational** Thinking logically about concrete events; grasping concrete analogies and performing arithmetical operations	• Conservation • Mathematical transformations
About 12 through adulthood	**Formal operational** Abstract reasoning	• Scientific reasoning • Potential for mature moral reasoning

Object permanence. Younger children are still developing the sense that things continue to exist when not in sight; but for this 8½-month-old child, out of sight is not out of mind.

"Children think not of what is past, nor what is to come, but enjoy the present time, which few of us do."

La Bruyère, 1645–1696
Les caractères: De l'homme

assimilation Interpreting one's new experience in terms of one's existing schemas.

accommodation Adapting one's current understandings (schemas) to incorporate new information.

cognition All the mental activities associated with thinking, knowing, and remembering.

sensorimotor stage In Piaget's theory, the stage (from birth to about 2 years of age) during which infants know the world mostly in terms of their sensory impressions and motor activities.

object permanence The awareness that things continue to exist even when not perceived.

stranger anxiety The fear of strangers that infants commonly display beginning by about 8 months of age.

egocentrism In Piaget's theory, the inability of the preoperational child to take another's point of view.

lives in the present. What is out of sight is out of mind. By 8 months, infants begin to develop what psychologists now believe is a memory for things no longer seen. Hide the toy and the infant will momentarily look for it. Within another month or two, the infant will look for it even after being restrained for several seconds.

Object permanence emerges simultaneously with a fear of strangers, called **stranger anxiety.** Watch how infants of different ages react when handed over to a stranger and you will notice that, beginning at 8 or 9 months, they often will cry and reach for their familiar caregivers. Is it a mere coincidence that object permanence and stranger anxiety develop together? Probably not. After about 8 months of age, children have schemas for familiar faces; when they can't associate a new face with these remembered schemas, they become distressed (Kagan, 1984). This illustrates an important principle: The brain, the mind, and social-emotional behavior develop together.

But today's researchers wonder: Do children's cognitive abilities really grow through distinct *stages?* Does object permanence in fact appear rather abruptly, much as a tulip blossoms in spring? Researchers now see development more as a continuous process than the series of *distinct* stages that Piaget recognized. For example, they now view object permanence as unfolding gradually, beginning with young infants looking for a toy where they saw it hidden a second before.

Preoperational Stage Seen through the eyes of Piaget, preschool children are still far from being short grownups. Although aware of themselves, of time, and of the permanence of objects, they are, he said, **egocentric:** They cannot perceive things from another's point of view. Children's conversations may reveal their egocentrism (Phillips, 1969, p. 61):

"Do you have a brother?"

"Yes."

"What's his name?"

"Jim."

"Does Jim have a brother?"

"No."

As the child moves into the preoperational stage, after about 18 months, pretending becomes possible.

The preoperational child cannot perform the mental operations essential to understanding conservation. Closed beakers with identical volumes seem suddenly to hold different amounts after one is merely inverted.

The preschooler who blocks your view of the television while trying to see it herself and the one who asks a question while you are on the phone both assume that you see and hear what they see and hear. When relating to a young child, it may help to remember that such behaviors reflect a cognitive limitation: The egocentric preschooler is not intentionally "selfish" or "inconsiderate," but rather has difficulty taking another's viewpoint. Parents who abuse their children often fail to understand these limits.

Piaget believed that during this preschool period and up to about age 7, children are in what he called the **preoperational stage**—unable to perform mental operations. For a 5-year-old, the quantity of milk that is "too much" in a tall, narrow glass may become an acceptable amount if poured into a short,

preoperational stage   In Piaget's theory, the stage (from about 2 to 6 or 7 years of age) during which a child learns to use language but does not yet comprehend the mental operations of concrete logic.

conservation   The principle (which Piaget believed to be a part of concrete operational reasoning) that properties such as mass, volume, and number remain the same despite changes in the forms of objects.

concrete operational stage   In Piaget's theory, the stage of cognitive development (from about 6 or 7 to 11 years of age) during which children gain the mental operations that enable them to think logically about concrete events.

formal operational stage   In Piaget's theory, the stage of cognitive development (normally beginning about age 12) during which people begin to think logically about abstract concepts.

*"Cut it up into a **LOT** of slices, Mom. I'm really hungry!"*

DENNIS THE MENACE® used by permission of Hank Ketchum and © 1992 by North America Syndicate.

wide glass. This is because the child focuses only on the height dimension and is incapable of performing the *operation* of mentally pouring it back. The child lacks the concept of **conservation**—the principle that the quantity of a substance is *conserved* (remains the same) despite changes in its shape.

Once again, however, researchers have spotted the rudiments of Piaget's cognitive stages at an earlier age than he supposed. Preschoolers are *not* purely egocentric. Given very simple tasks, 4-year-olds will adjust their explanations to make them clearer to a blindfolded listener and will show a toy or picture with the front side facing the viewer (Gelman, 1979; Siegel & Hodkin, 1982). If questioned in a way that makes sense to them, 5- and 6-year-olds will exhibit some understanding of conservation (Donaldson, 1979).

Thus, the abilities to take another's perspective and to perform mental operations are not utterly absent in the preoperational stage—and then suddenly present. Rather, these abilities begin earlier and develop more gradually than Piaget believed.

Concrete Operational Stage   By about 7 years of age, children enter the **concrete operational stage.** They begin to grasp that a given quantity remains the same no matter how its shape changes. By age 11, children can mentally pour the milk back and forth between different-shaped glasses, so they realize that change in shape does not mean change in quantity. They also enjoy jokes that allow them to use their new concepts, such as conservation:

> Mr. Jones went into a restaurant and ordered a whole pizza for his dinner. When the waiter asked if he wanted it cut into 6 or 8 pieces, Mr. Jones said, "Oh, you'd better make it 6, I could never eat 8 pieces!" (McGhee, 1976).

During the concrete operational stage, said Piaget, children fully gain the mental abilities needed to comprehend mathematical transformations and conservation. When my daughter Laura was 6, I was astonished at her inability to reverse arithmetic operations—until considering Piaget. Asked, "What is eight plus four?" she required 5 seconds to compute "twelve," and another 5 seconds to then compute twelve minus four. By age 8, she could reverse the process and answer the second question instantly.

If Piaget was correct—if children construct their understandings and think differently than adults—what are the implications for preschool and elementary school teachers? Piaget contended that teachers should build on what children already know, give them concrete demonstrations, and stimulate them to think for themselves. Future teachers, remember: Young children are incapable of adult logic. Understand how children think, and realize that what is simple and obvious to you—that, say, subtraction is the reverse of addition—may be incomprehensible to a 6-year-old.

Formal Operational Stage   By age 12, reasoning expands from the purely concrete to encompass abstract thinking. As they approach adolescence, said Piaget, children become capable of solving hypothetical propositions and deducing consequences: *If* this, *then* that. Systematic reasoning, which Piaget called **formal operational** thinking, is now within their grasp.

But are younger children incapable of abstract logic? Consider this simple problem:

> If John is in school, then Mary is in school. John is in school. What can you say about Mary?

Many 7-year-olds have no trouble answering correctly (Suppes, 1982). This illustrates why, once again, critics say the rudiments of Piaget's cognitive stages begin earlier than he realized.

Reflections on Piaget's Theory   Piaget's stage theory is controversial. In some ways it gets high marks. Despite cultural variations in the *rate* at which children progress down the developmental highway, Piaget's ideas find support. Studies around the globe, from aboriginal Australia to Algeria to North America, reveal that human cognition everywhere unfolds basically as he proposed (Segall & others, 1990). Today's researchers do, however, see development as more continuous than did Piaget. By detecting the beginnings of each stage at earlier ages, they have revealed conceptual abilities that Piaget missed.

What remains of Piaget's ideas about the child's mind? Plenty. Piaget identified important cognitive milestones and stimulated interest in how the mind develops. That we today are adapting his ideas to accommodate new findings surely would not surprise him.

Rehearse It

6. The orderly sequence of biological growth is called maturation. Maturation explains why
a. children differ greatly in temperament.
b. most children have begun walking by about 12 months.
c. enriching experiences may affect brain tissue.
d. differences between the sexes are minimal.

7. Most of us remember nothing before our third or fourth birthday because
a. we are not born with enough brain cells to form memories.
b. we were not given the extra "handling" and environmental stimulation we needed.
c. the connections between our brain cells had not yet become complex enough to form memories.
d. we do not enter the memory stage until our third year.

8. Object permanence—the awareness that objects continue to exist even when not being perceived—emerges about the same time as stranger anxiety. These two developments occur
a. in the first few months.
b. by about 8 or 9 months.
c. in the second year.
d. after the child has learned to think concretely.

9. According to Piaget, the preoperational stage extends from about age 2 to 6. During this period the young child's thinking is
a. abstract.
b. negative.
c. conservative.
d. egocentric.

10. According to Piaget, the maturing brain builds concepts, or schemas, that help us interpret our experiences. When we adjust or revise an existing schema to make it "fit" new information, we are engaging in
a. accommodation.
b. scientific reasoning.
c. egocentric thinking.
d. assimilation.

11. The principle of conservation explains why a pint of milk remains a pint, whether poured into a tall thin glass or a round goblet. Children acquire the mental operations necessary to understand conservation during
a. infancy.
b. the sensorimotor stage.
c. the preoperational stage.
d. the concrete operational stage.

12. Piaget believed that during adolescence a person becomes capable of thinking logically about abstract concepts. Piaget's final stage of cognitive development is
a. formal operations.
b. concrete operations.
c. scientific reasoning.
d. conventional morality.

13. Piaget's stage theory continues to inform our understanding of cognitive development in childhood. However, many researchers believe that
a. Piaget's "stages" begin earlier and develop more gradually than Piaget realized.
b. children do not progress as rapidly as Piaget predicted.
c. few children really progress to the concrete operational stage.
d. there is no way of testing much of Piaget's theoretical work.

Social Development

Babies are social creatures from birth. Almost from the start, parent and baby communicate through eye contact, touch, smiles, and voice. The resulting social behavior promotes infants' survival and their emerging sense of self, so they, too, eventually may bear and nurture a new generation.

In all cultures, infants develop an intense bond with those who care for them. Beginning with newborns' attraction to humans in general, infants soon come to prefer familiar faces and voices and then to coo and gurgle when given their mothers' or fathers' attention. By 8 months, when object permanence and stranger anxiety fully emerge, infants will crawl wherever the mother or father goes and may become distressed when separated from them. At 12 months many infants cling tightly to a parent when frightened or expecting separation and, when reunited, shower the parent with smiles and hugs. No social behavior is more striking than this intense infant love, called **attachment,** a powerful survival impulse that keeps infants close to their caregivers. Among the early social responses—love, fear, aggression—the first and greatest is this bond of love.

Origins of Attachment

A number of elements work to create the parent-infant bond. Consider three: body contact, familiarity, and temperament.

Body Contact   For many years developmental psychologists reasoned that infants became attached to those who satisfied their need for nourishment. It makes perfect sense. But an accidental finding revealed that this explanation of attachment is incomplete. During the 1950s, University of Wisconsin psychologist Harry Harlow bred monkeys for his learning studies. To equalize the infant monkeys' experiences and to prevent the spread of disease, he separated the monkeys from their mothers shortly after birth and raised them in sanitary, individual cages, which included a cheesecloth baby blanket (Harlow & others, 1971). Surprisingly, the infants became intensely attached to their blankets: When the blankets were taken to be laundered, the monkeys became distressed.

Harlow soon recognized that this attachment to the blanket contradicted the idea that attachment derives from the association with nourishment. But could he show this more convincingly? To pit the drawing power of a food source against the contact comfort of the blanket, Harlow created two artificial mothers. One was a bare wire cylinder with a wooden head, the other a cylinder wrapped with foam rubber and terry cloth. He could associate either with nourishment by attaching a bottle.

When reared with a nourishing wire mother *and* a non-nourishing cloth mother, the monkeys overwhelmingly preferred the cloth mother (Figure 3–6). Like human infants clinging to their mothers, the monkeys would cling to their cloth mother when anxious. They also used her as a secure base from which to venture into the environment, as if attached to the mother by an invisible elastic band that stretches so far and then pulls the infant back. Further studies with Margaret Harlow and others revealed that other qualities—rocking, warmth, and feeding—could make the cloth mother even more appealing.

In human infants, too, attachment usually grows from body contact with parents who are soft and warm and who rock, feed, and pat. All this should reassure the fathers of breast-fed infants: Attachment does not depend on feeding alone.

Preview Question

6. What is attachment, how does it develop, and what effects do early attachment patterns have later in life?

Figure 3–6 Harry Harlow reared monkeys with two artificial mothers—one a bare wire cylinder with a wooden head and an attached feeding bottle, the other a cylinder covered with foam rubber and wrapped with terry cloth but without a feeding bottle. Harlow surprised many psychologists when he reported that the monkeys much preferred contact with the comfortable cloth mother even while feeding from the nourishing wire mother.

attachment   An emotional tie with another person; shown in young children by their seeking closeness to the caregiver and showing distress on separation.

critical period An optimal period during which an organism's exposure to certain influences or experiences will produce proper development.

imprinting The process by which certain animals form attachments during a critical period very early in life.

temperament A person's characteristic emotional reactivity and intensity.

basic trust According to Erik Erikson, a sense that the world is predictable and trustworthy; said to be formed during infancy by appropriate experiences with responsive caregivers.

When imprinting studies go awry . . .

"The Far Side" cartoon is reprinted by permission of Chronical Features, San Francisco.

Figure 3–7 Monkeys raised by artificial mothers were terror-stricken when placed in strange situations without their surrogate mothers.

Familiarity Another key to attachment is familiarity (Rheingold, 1985). In many animals, attachments based on familiarity form during a sensitive, **critical period**—an optimal period shortly after birth when certain events must take place if proper development is to occur (Bornstein, 1989). The first moving object that a gosling, duckling, or chick sees during the hours shortly after hatching is normally its mother. Thereafter the young fowl trails after her, and her alone.

Konrad Lorenz (1937) explored this rigid attachment process, called **imprinting.** He wondered what ducklings would do if *he* was the first moving creature they observed. What they did was follow him around: Everywhere that Konrad went, the ducks were sure to go. Further tests revealed that some species of baby birds would imprint to a variety of moving objects—an animal of another species, a box on wheels, a bouncing ball—and that, once formed, this attachment was often difficult to reverse (Colombo, 1982). Although human infants do not have such precisely timed critical periods, they too become attached to familiar faces and objects.

Temperament and Parent-Infant Relations The quality of parent-child attachment depends not only on comfortable contact and a growing familiarity but also on inborn traits that the child brings into the relationship. The infant's **temperament** includes the inborn rudiments of personality and especially refers to the child's emotional excitability—whether reactive, intense, and fidgety or easygoing, quiet, and placid. From the first weeks of life, "easy" babies are cheerful, relaxed, and predictable in feeding and sleeping. "Difficult" babies are more irritable, intense, and unpredictable (Chess & Thomas, 1987).

Physiological tests reveal that high-strung infants (who often become shy children) have high and variable heart rates and a reactive nervous system (Kagan, 1989). Infant monkeys also vary in temperament. Some are timid and fearful, others more relaxed (Suomi, 1983). And in monkeys as in humans, the timid, anxious ones become more physiologically aroused when facing new or strange situations. With age, many shy, inhibited infants relax, but few fearless, spontaneous infants become shy.

Placed in a strange situation (usually a laboratory playroom), some infants show *secure attachment*. In their mother's presence they play comfortably, happily exploring their new environment. When she leaves, they are distressed; when she returns, they seek contact with her. Other infants show *insecure attachment*. They are less likely to explore the new surroundings and may even cling to their mother. When she leaves, they cry loudly; when she returns, they may be indifferent or even hostile toward her (Ainsworth, 1973, 1989; van IJzendoorn & Kroonenberg, 1988). What accounts for these differences?

Temperament differences are partly responsible. Another possible factor is the mother's behavior. Mary Ainsworth (1979) observed mother-infant pairs at home during the first 6 months and then later observed the 1-year-old infants in a strange situation without their mothers. Sensitive, responsive mothers—mothers who continually noticed what their babies were doing and responded appropriately—had infants who usually became securely attached. Insensitive, unresponsive mothers—mothers who attended to their babies when they felt like doing so but ignored them at other times—had infants who often became insecurely attached. The Harlows' monkey studies, in which the artificial mothers were the ultimate in unresponsiveness, produced even more striking effects. When put in strange situations without their artificial mothers, the deprived infants were more than distressed—they were terrified (Figure 3–7).

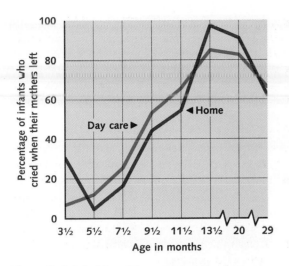

Figure 3-8 Infants' anxiety over separation from parents. In an experiment, groups of infants who had and had not experienced day care were left alone by their mothers in an unfamiliar room. In both groups, the percentage who cried when the mother left peaked at about 13 months. (From Kagan, 1976.)

Monkeys raised in total isolation from the sight or sound of other monkeys for more than 6 months were terrified of other monkeys and either lashed out aggressively or cowered in fright.

In both the monkey experiments (which would not be conducted in today's climate of concern for animals) and in many cases of child abuse, the infants of abusive mothers cling to the only mother they know, as if all were forgiven.

The attachments of early childhood eventually relax. Whether raised entirely at home or also in a day care center, whether living in North America, Guatemala, or the Kalahari Desert, anxiety over being separated from parents peaks at around 13 months and then gradually declines (Kagan, 1976) (Figure 3–8). With time, children become familiar with a wider range of situations and communicate with strangers more freely.

Does this mean that, as we develop, our need for and love of others fades away? Hardly. Yet much of the life cycle story boils down to a rhythm of attachment and separation—from the attachment of fetal life to the separation of birth, from infant attachment to adolescent separation, from the attachment of marriage and parenthood to the separation of death.

Effects of Attachment

Does a trusting, secure attachment have lasting benefits? Does the quality of an infant's attachment predict the child's social competence in the years that follow?

Secure Attachment Promotes Social Competence   At the University of Minnesota, Alan Sroufe and his colleagues (1983) identified infants who were securely attached at 12 to 18 months of age—those who used their mother as a base for comfortably exploring the world and as a haven when distressed. When Sroufe restudied these infants as 2- to 3-year-olds, he saw them functioning more confidently than other toddlers. Given challenging tasks, they were more enthusiastic and persistent. With other children they were more outgoing and responsive.

Developmental theorist Erik Erikson says that securely attached children approach life with a sense of **basic trust**—a sense that the world is predictable and reliable. A child who will let parents leave is a child who trusts they will return. Erikson attributed basic trust not to one's continuing positive environment or to one's inborn temperament, but to early parenting. He theorized that infants blessed with sensitive, loving caregivers form a lifelong attitude of trust rather than fear.

Deprivation of Attachment   If secure attachment nurtures social competence, what are the results of parental deprivation? In all of psychology, no research literature is more saddening. Children reared in institutions without the stimulation and attention of a regular caregiver, or locked away at home under conditions of extreme neglect, are often withdrawn, frightened, even speechless. Adopted into a loving home, they usually progress rapidly, especially in their cognitive development. Nevertheless, they frequently bear scars from their early neglect (Rutter, 1979).

So, too, did the Harlows' monkeys if reared in total isolation, without even an artificial mother. As adults they either cowered in fright or lashed out in aggression when placed with other monkeys their age. Upon reaching sexual maturity, most were incapable of mating. Artificially impregnated females often were neglectful, sadistically cruel, or even murderous toward their firstborn offspring. The unloved had become the unloving.

Most abusive human parents, too, report they were battered or neglected as children (Kempe & Kempe, 1978). Many condemned murderers report the same. One study of 14 young men awaiting execution for juvenile crimes found that "twelve had been brutally physically abused" (Lewis & others, 1988).

Psychology Applied: Father Care

Perhaps you are wondering why mothers are the focus of so much developmental research. Why not fathers, too? The common assumption, long seen in child-custody decisions, has been that fathers are less interested and less competent in child care than mothers. In both subtle and not-so-subtle ways, psychologists have accepted this assumption. Infants who lack mother care are said to suffer "maternal deprivation"; those lacking father care are said merely to experience "father absence."

Across the world mothers do assume more responsibility for infant care, and young children more quickly turn to their mothers for comfort and support (Hartup, 1989). Moreover, a breast-feeding mother and nursing infant have wonderfully coordinated biological systems that predispose their responsiveness to one another. Nevertheless, many modern fathers are becoming more involved in infant care, and researchers are becoming more interested in fathers.

One of the leading father-watchers, Ross Parke (1981), reports that fathers can be as interested in, sensitive to, and affectionate toward their infants as mothers typically are. Although mothers usually do most of the infant care, fathers are as capable (at least when researchers are watching). Although most infants prefer their mothers when anxious, when left alone they are as distressed by their father's departure as by their mother's. Moreover, infants whose fathers have shared in their diapering, bathing, and feeding are more secure when left with a stranger. Preschoolers with involved fathers tend to become adults who are espe-

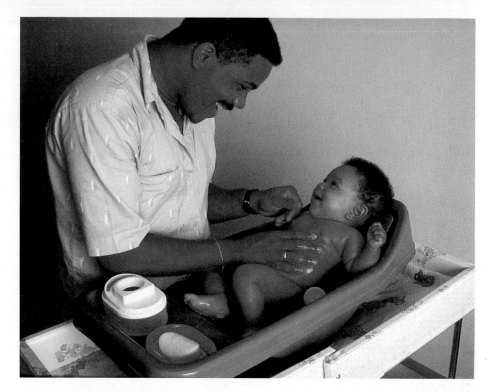

Michael Lamb (1979): "Mothers and fathers can be equally effective as parents. They just have different styles."

cially concerned with being kind, sensitive, and warmhearted (Koestner & others, 1990).

Looking for differences, research psychologists have also uncovered several distinctive ways in which fathers and mothers interact with their infants. Fathers smile less at their babies (males smile less at everyone). They spend more of their interaction in play rather than caregiving (especially with sons). And they play with more physical excitement (Parke, 1981).

However, fathers who are the primary caregivers interact with their babies more, as mothers typically do. This suggests that father-mother dif-

ferences are not biologically fixed, but have social roots as well.

Within two-parent families, both parents have yet another gift to offer: their support of one another. Mothers and fathers who support one another and who sense this mutual support and agreement in child-rearing are more responsive to their infants and feel more competent as parents (Dickie, 1987).

Thanks partly to such research, "fathering" is shifting meaning. "Fathering a child" once meant impregnating, "mothering" meant nurturing. More and more these days, fathering and mothering both mean parenting.

So, do most victims of child abuse become abusive? Is today's victim predictably tomorrow's predator? No. Most abused children do *not* later become violent criminals or abusive parents. But 30 percent do abuse their children—a rate four times higher than the national rate of child abuse (Kaufman & Zigler, 1987; Widom, 1989a,b). Moreover, young children terrorized through sexual abuse or wartime atrocities (being beaten, witnessing torture, and living in constant fear) also suffer scars—often nightmares, depression, and a troubled adolescence (Browne & Finkelhor, 1986; Goleman, 1987).

In a 1989 Gallup poll of Americans, 8 percent of adults said, yes, they had been "a victim" of child abuse.

Self-Concept

Infancy's number one social achievement is attachment. Childhood's major social achievement is a positive sense of self. By the end of childhood, at about age 12, most children have developed a self-concept—a sense of their own personal worth and social identity. When and how does this sense of self develop? And how can parents foster a child's self-esteem?

"Is my baby aware of herself—does she know that she is a person distinct from others?" The baby cannot talk, so we cannot ask her. Perhaps, however, the infant's *behavior* can provide clues to the beginnings of her self-awareness. In 1877, biologist Charles Darwin offered one idea: Self-awareness begins when a child recognizes herself in a mirror. In a simple experiment, researchers sneakily dabbed rouge on children's noses before placing them in front of the mirror. Beginning by 15 to 18 months, children, upon seeing the red spot, will touch their own noses (Gallup & Suarez, 1986). Apparently, 18-month-olds have a schema of how their faces should look. It's as if they wonder, "What is that spot doing on *my* face?"

Beginning with this simple self-awareness, the child's self-concept gradually becomes stronger. By school age, children begin to describe themselves in terms of their gender, their group memberships, and their psychological traits. They come to see themselves as good and skillful in some ways but not others. They form a concept of which traits, ideally, they would like to have. By age 8 or 10, their self-images have become quite stable.

Children's views of themselves affect their actions. Children who form a positive self-concept are more confident, independent, optimistic, assertive, and sociable (Maccoby, 1980). This raises an important question: How can parents encourage a positive self-concept? How does their parenting style affect their children?

Preview Question

7. How does a child's behavior provide evidence of an emerging self-concept?

Mirror images fascinate infants from the age of about 6 months, but the recognition that the child in the mirror is "me" does not occur until about 18 months.

Preview Question

8. What are the links between parenting styles and children's behavior?

Child-Rearing Practices

Parenting styles vary. Some parents spank, some reason. Some parents are strict, some are lax. Some parents seem indifferent to their children, some liberally hug and kiss them. Do such differences affect children?

The most heavily researched aspect of parenting has been how, and to what extent, parents seek to control their children. Several investigators have identified four parenting styles: (1) authoritarian, (2) authoritative, (3) permissive, and (4) rejecting-neglecting.

Authoritarian parents impose rules and expect obedience: "Don't interrupt." "Don't leave your room a mess." "Don't stay out late or you'll be grounded." "Why? Because I said so."

Authoritative parents are both demanding and responsive. They exert control by setting rules and consistently enforcing them, but also by explaining the reasons and, especially with older children, encouraging open discussion when making the rules.

Psychology Applied: Children of Divorce

Nearly half of North American marriages end in divorce. That sad fact makes people wonder and worry: Are children casualties of divorce? Does the stress of divorce and its aftermath erode children's well-being?

Mavis Hetherington and her colleagues (1989, 1992) summarize the available research: Divorce places "children at increased risk for developing social, psychological, behavioral and academic problems." Yet, they report, children's responses are diverse. Whether children cope well after divorce or develop behavior problems depends on such factors as the intensity of parental conflict, the child's temperament, and whether the child is uprooted from familiar friends and classmates in the process.

Following divorce, 9 in 10 children live primarily with their mothers. Although few studies compare children living with single fathers and single mothers, adolescent boys living with a single mother show a higher rate of aggression and other problem behaviors than do boys living with nondivorced parents or with their father (Hetherington & others, 1989; Stevenson & Black, 1988).

One recent study had British parents and teachers rate the behavior of 12,000 children as 7-year-olds and again 4 years later (Cherlin & others, 1991). At the second rating, boys whose parents had divorced during the 4 years had about one-fourth more behavior problems than those whose families remained intact. But the apparent effect of divorce on boys was nearly halved when allowance was made for predivorce behavior differences between the two groups. (For girls, adjusting for preexisting behavior problems did not reduce the apparent divorce effect.) For boys, it seems, family troubles begin taking a toll in advance of divorce.

Typically, divorce provides children with a double dose of stress. Immediately following their parents' divorce, many children feel angry, resentful, and depressed. Young children may blame themselves. Older children may exhibit heightened aggression and noncompliance. Within 2 or 3 years, life typically settles back to a more comfortable equilibrium. Then, often 3 to 5 years after the divorce, there may come a second dose of stress: the custodial parent's remarriage. Because 75 percent of divorced mothers and 80 per-

cent of divorced fathers remarry, most children of divorce will gain a stepparent. Especially for girls, the new stepfather's intrusion into the home may at first be an unwelcome event, disrupting the single mother-daughter relationship and necessitating another period of readjustment.

Data amassed from 92 studies suggest that this double stress does leave its mark on some children (Amato & Keith, 1991; Booth & Edwards, 1989). Compared to those who grew up in intact families, children of divorce grow up with a diminished feeling of well-being. As adults they are more likely to divorce and less likely to say they are "very happy." There is wisdom, it seems, to society's ages-old idea that a loving, stable home life offers the best hope for nurturing children.

But sometimes a stable partnership is not to be. If divorce is stressful for children, so is a conflict-laden marriage, report Hetherington and her associates (1989). Moreover, they say, easygoing children usually cope well with the challenge of divorce and remarriage, and may even emerge better prepared to cope with later challenges.

Permissive parents submit to their children's desires, make few demands, and use little punishment.

Rejecting-neglecting parents are disengaged. They expect little and invest little.

Studies by Stanley Coopersmith (1967), Diana Baumrind (1983, 1991), and John Buri and others (1988) reveal that children with the highest self-esteem, self-reliance, and social competence usually have warm, concerned, authoritative parents. Although in most studies the subjects have been middle-class white families, studies with families of other races confirm the social and academic benefits of authoritative parenting (Baumrind, 1991).

Children who feel enough control to attribute their behaviors to their choices ("I obey because I am good") internalize their behaviors. Coerced children ("I obey or I get in bad trouble") tend not to internalize their actions.

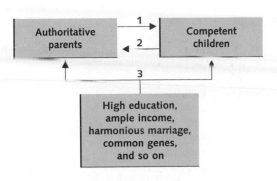

Figure 3–9 Three possible explanations of the correlation between authoritative parenting and social competence in children.

Studies suggest that consistency in enforcing rules, combined with calm discussion and explanation, helps children achieve self-control.

Of the four parenting styles, authoritative parenting provides children with the greatest sense of control, for two reasons. First, authoritative parents openly discuss family rules, by explaining them to younger children and reasoning about them with older children. When rules seem more negotiated than imposed, older children feel more self-control (Baumrind, 1983; Lewis, 1981). Second, when parents enforce rules with consistent, predictable consequences, the child controls the outcome.

Before jumping to conclusions about the results of different parenting styles, we must heed a caution. The evidence is correlational. It tells us that certain parenting styles (say, being firm but open) are associated with certain childhood outcomes (say, social competence). But remember: Correlation need not reveal cause and effect. There may be other possible explanations (Figure 3–9). Perhaps socially mature, agreeable children *elicit* greater trust and more reasonable treatment from their parents than do less competent and less cooperative children.

Or consider this: Authoritative parents are more often well educated and less often enduring the stresses of poverty or recent divorce—factors that can affect children's competence (Hetherington, 1979). Or maybe competent parents and their competent children share genes that predispose social competence. Knowing that parents' behavior relates to their children's behavior does not prove cause and effect.

When considering "expert" child-rearing advice we should also remember that the advice given reflects the advice-giver's values. Should the chief end of childhood be unquestioning obedience? Then an authoritarian style is recommended. Are sociability and self-reliance a higher end? Then firm but open authoritative parenting is advisable. Different experts have different values, which helps explain their disagreements.

Parents everywhere struggle with conflicting advice and with the stresses of child-rearing. Indeed, the personal investment necessary to raise a child yields 20 years not only of joy and love but also of worry and irritation. Yet for most parents, a child is one's biological and social legacy—one's personal investment in the human future. To paraphrase psychiatrist Carl Jung, we reach backward into our parents and forward into our children, and through their children into a future we will never see, but about which we must therefore care.

Rehearse It

14. Body contact facilitates attachment between infant and parent. In a famous series of experiments, Harry Harlow found that monkeys raised with artificial mothers tended, when afraid, to cling to
a. the wire mother.
b. the cloth mother.
c. whichever mother held the feeding bottle.
d. none of the artificial mothers.

15. From the very first weeks of life, infants differ in their characteristic emotional reactions, with some infants being intense and anxious, while others are easygoing and relaxed. These differences are usually explained as differences in

a. attachment.
b. imprinting.
c. temperament.
d. parenting style.

16. Children who in infancy formed secure attachment to their parents
a. are likely to become good parents.
b. prefer the company of adults to that of their peers.
c. become socially competent youngsters.
d. have less stranger anxiety.

17. Most abusive parents report that they were battered or neglected as children. However, statistics show that most abused children

a. are adopted into loving homes.
b. will not have children.
c. will later be arrested for child abuse.
d. do not become abusive parents.

18. Authoritative parenting often is accompanied by high self-esteem and social competence in children. However, parenting style is not the only possible explanation for this finding. Authoritative parents also tend to be
a. economically disadvantaged.
b. divorced or single parents.
c. child care professionals.
d. well educated and financially secure.

adolescence The transition period from childhood to adulthood, extending from puberty to independence.

puberty The early adolescent period of rapid growth and sexual maturation.

primary sex characteristics The body structures (ovaries and testes) that make sexual reproduction possible.

secondary sex characteristics Nonreproductive sexual characteristics such as female breasts and hips, male voice quality, and body hair.

Have you any idea how you will look back on your life 10 years from now? Are you doing the things and making the choices that you will someday recollect with satisfaction?

Preview Question

9. What major physical changes occur during adolescence?

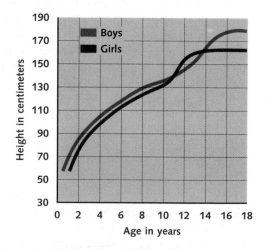

Figure 3–10 Throughout childhood, boys and girls are similar in height. At puberty, girls surge ahead briefly, but then boys overtake them at about age 14. (From Tanner, 1978.)

Adolescence

Among developmental psychologists, the once-popular belief that no important changes in personality occur after childhood has given way to a sense that development is *lifelong.* As today's life-span perspective emerged, psychologists began to look at how nature and nurture shape us in infancy and childhood, *and* in adolescence and beyond. At a 5-year high school reunion, friends may be surprised at the divergence of their paths. A decade after college, two former soul mates may have trouble keeping a conversation going. The old belief that development reaches a plateau after childhood has given way to a realization that as long as we live, we develop.

Adolescence is life between childhood and adulthood. It extends from the physical beginnings of sexual maturity to the social achievement of independent adult status.

Adolescence is a time of transition. At earlier times in Western societies (and in some developing countries today), adolescence was but a brief interlude between the dependence of childhood and the responsibilities of adulthood (Baumeister & Tice, 1986). Adult status and responsibilities were bestowed shortly after sexual maturity, often marked by an elaborate initiation. The new adult worked, married, and had children.

Then, because of improved nutrition, sexual maturity began occurring earlier. And with compulsory schooling, adult independence began occurring later. The resulting gulf between biological maturity and social independence is adolescence.

To G. Stanley Hall (1904), the first American psychologist to describe adolescence, the tension between biological maturity and social dependence created a period of "storm and stress." Indeed, after age 30, many people look back on their teenage years as a time they would not like to relive, a time when the social approval of peers was imperative, one's sense of direction in life was in flux, and alienation from parents was deepest (Macfarlane, 1964).

Other psychologists note that, for many, adolescence is often as Tolstoy described it—a time of vitality without the cares of adulthood, a time of rewarding friendships, a time of heightened idealism and a growing sense of life's exciting possibilities (Coleman, 1980). These psychologists would not be surprised that 9 of 10 high school seniors agree with the statement, "On the whole, I'm satisfied with myself" (*Public Opinion,* 1987a).

Physical Development

Adolescence begins at **puberty,** the time of rapid growth and sexual maturation. Puberty starts with a surge of hormones, which trigger a 2-year growth spurt that usually begins in girls at about age 11 and in boys at about age 13. Boys grow as much as 5 inches a year, compared with about 3 inches for girls—propelling the average male, for the first time in his life, to become distinctly taller than the average female (Figure 3–10). During this growth spurt, the reproductive organs, or **primary sex characteristics,** develop dramatically. So do the **secondary sex characteristics,** the nonreproductive traits of females and males, such as enlarged breasts and hips in girls, facial hair and a deepened voice in boys, pubic and underarm hair in both sexes (Figure 3–11).

The landmarks of puberty are the first ejaculation in boys, which usually occurs by about age 14, and the first menstrual period in girls, by about age 13. The first menstrual period is a memorable event, one that is recalled by nearly all adult women. Most experience and later recall a mixture of feelings—pride, excitement, embarrassment, and apprehension (Greif & Ulman,

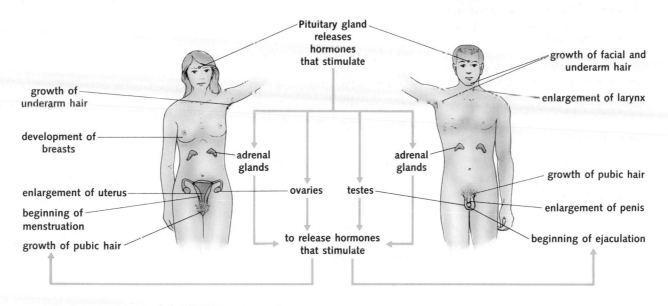

Figure 3–11 At puberty, a surge of hormones triggers a variety of physical changes.

Early maturing girls and late maturing boys may experience social embarrassment.

1982; Woods & others, 1983). For the first few months many keep it a secret from friends, and very few discuss it with their fathers (Brooks-Gunn, 1989). Girls well prepared for menstruation usually experience its onset as a positive life transition. And a transition it is. Regardless of their age, girls afterward increasingly see and present themselves as different from boys and function more independently of their parents (Golub, 1983). Most men similarly recall their first ejaculation, which usually occurs as a nocturnal emission (Fuller & Downs, 1990).

As in the earlier life stages, the *sequence* of physical changes (for example, breast buds before visible pubic hair before first menstrual period) is far more predictable than their *timing*. Some girls start their growth spurt at 9, some boys as late as age 16. Such variations have little effect on height at maturity, but they may have psychological consequences. Studies performed in the 1950s by Mary Cover Jones and her colleagues revealed that early maturation pays dividends for boys. Early-maturing boys, being stronger and more athletic during their early teen years and seemingly less childlike, tend to be more popular, self-assured, and independent.

For girls, early maturation can be stressful. In Sweden, North America, and New Zealand, studies of girls who begin menstruation early (before age 12) or late (at age 14 or after) reveal that early maturation can amplify preexisting problems (Caspi & Moffitt, 1991; Simmons & Blyth, 1987; Stattin & Magnusson, 1990). If a young girl's body is out of sync with her emotional maturity and with what her friends are experiencing, she may, for a time, make older friends and do things considered out-of-bounds for girls her age. Moreover, the 11-year-old who towers over her classmates and becomes the object of sexual attention may temporarily suffer embarrassment and be the object of teasing (Petersen, 1987).

Cognitive Development

Adolescents' developing ability to reason gives them a new level of social awareness and moral judgment. As young teenagers become capable of thinking about their own thinking, and thinking about what other people are thinking, they begin imagining what other people are thinking about *them*. As their cognitive abilities continue to grow, many adolescents begin to think about what is ideally possible and become quite critical of their society, their parents, and their own shortcomings.

Preview Question

10. How did Piaget and Kohlberg describe cognitive and moral development during adolescence?

Developing Reasoning Power

Like physical maturity, cognitive maturity develops over time. Mature reasoning evolves slowly, which helps explain why many adolescents feel immune to the consequences of drug and alcohol use or sexual promiscuity. During the early teen years, reasoning is also egocentric. Adolescents often think their private experiences are unique. They assume their parents or friends (who have suffered the same experiences) just can't understand what it feels like to be dating or to hate school. The adolescent in love for the first time may sigh, "But, Mother, *you* don't really know how it feels to be in love" (Elkind, 1978).

Eventually, though, most achieve the intellectual summit that Piaget called *formal operations.* As we noted earlier, preadolescents reason concretely, but adolescents become capable of abstract, logical thinking. They can reason hypothetically and deduce consequences: *If* this, *then* that. Unlike children, adolescents can deduce that when someone hides a poker chip and says, "Either this chip is green or it is not green," the statement logically must be true (Osherson & Markman, 1974–1975).

Older children may already have enough command of formal operations to learn algebra. But their capacity to reason systematically, as a scientist might in testing hypotheses and deducing conclusions, usually awaits the full development of their adolescent ability for formal reasoning (Inhelder & Piaget, 1958). We can see this new reasoning power in adolescents' pondering and debating such abstract topics as human nature, good and evil, truth and justice. Having perhaps envisioned God as a person in the clouds when first capable of symbolic thinking in early childhood, they may now seek a deeper conception of God and existence (Elkind, 1970; Worthington, 1989). Adolescents' logical thinking also enables them to detect inconsistencies in others' reasoning and between their ideals and actions. Indeed, their newfound ability to spot hypocrisy can lead to heated debates with parents, and silent vows never to lose sight of their own ideals (Peterson & others, 1986).

These adolescents demonstrating for and against abortion rights are illustrating their ability to think logically about abstract topics—in this case, about whose rights are paramount, the mother's or the fetus's. According to Piaget, they are in the final stage of cognitive growth, formal operations.

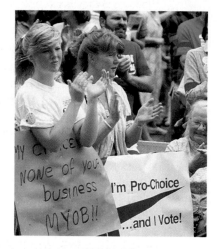 

Developing Morality

A crucial task of childhood is learning right from wrong. To be a moral person is to *think* morally and *act* accordingly. Although as the French essayist Montaigne said, "It is a delightful harmony when doing and saying go together," such harmony often eludes us. "To put one's thoughts into action," noted the German poet Goethe, is "the most difficult thing in the world."

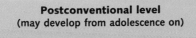

Postconventional level
(may develop from adolescence on)

Morality of abstract principles: to affirm agreed-upon rights and personal ethical principles (Example: "People have a right to live.")

↑

Conventional level
(develops during late childhood and early adolescence)

Morality of law and social rules: to gain approval or avoid disapproval (Example: "If you steal the drug, everyone will think you are a criminal.")

↑

Preconventional level
(develops during early childhood)

Morality of self-interest: to avoid punishment or gain concrete rewards (Example: "If you let your wife die, you will get in trouble.")

Figure 3–12 Kohlberg's moral ladder.

Should we agree that Kohlberg's postconventional, Western morality is indeed the "highest" and most "mature" level? Would society benefit if we all disregarded conventions and followed our own perceptions of universal ethical principles?

"This might not be ethical. Is that a problem for anybody?"

Drawing by Vietor; © 1987 The New Yorker Magazine, Inc.

Moral Thinking   Piaget (1932) believed that children's moral judgments build on their cognitive development. Accordingly, Lawrence Kohlberg (1981, 1984) sought to identify cognitive stages through which moral thinking matures. To study moral thinking, Kohlberg posed moral dilemmas to children, adolescents, and adults. For example, should a poor man steal an overpriced drug to save his dying wife? Kohlberg was not interested in whether people judged such behavior as right or wrong, but rather in the *reasoning process* by which they arrived at their judgment.

Kohlberg's controversial claim was that the levels of moral development form a moral ladder (Figure 3–12). The rungs extend from a young child's immature, preconventional morality at the bottom to, at the top, an adult's self-defined ethical principles. As with all stage theories, the sequence is predictable. We begin on the bottom rung and ascend to varying heights.

Research confirms that children in various cultures do progress sequentially from the level Kohlberg called preconventional (self-centered) into the conventional (rule-bound) level (Edwards, 1981, 1982; Snarey, 1985, 1987). However, the postconventional (principled) level appears mostly in the educated middle class of countries that value individualism, as in Europe and North America. And that is why critics contend the theory is biased against the moral reasoning of those in communal societies such as China and Papua New Guinea—or even against women, whose morality may be less a matter of abstract, impersonal principles, and more an ethic of caring relationships (see Chapter 15, Social Diversity).

Moral Action   Our moral reasoning surely influences our moral talk, but talk is cheap. Morality is also *doing* the right thing, and what we do depends not only on our thinking but on social influences. People's willingness to cheat, to discriminate racially, and to smoke marijuana are not neatly determined by their attitudes toward cheating, race, and drugs. The best predictor of whether a high school student smokes marijuana, for instance, is simply how many of the student's friends smoke it (Oetting & Beauvais, 1987).

Given the loose link between thinking and acting, effective moral education must focus on both. We can stimulate children's moral development through discussions of moral issues and their implications. We can also teach children to restrain their impulses, to delay small gratifications now for the sake of bigger gratifications later. Those who learn to do so become more socially responsible, academically successful, and productive (Funder & Block, 1989; Mischel & others, 1988, 1989.)

And we can focus directly on just and caring moral commitments by both teaching and modeling such behaviors. When parents set high moral standards and practice what they preach, moral principles of justice and caring become forceful. Such was true of the parents of those morally courageous people who protected Jews in Nazi Europe (Oliner & Oliner, 1988).

Social Development

Theorist Erik Erikson (1963) contends that each stage of life has its own "psychosocial" task. Young children wrestle with issues of *trust* (page 73), then *autonomy* (independence), then *initiative* (Table 3–2, page 82). School-age children develop *competence*, the sense that they are able and productive human beings. In adolescence, the task is to synthesize past, present, and future possibilities into a clearer sense of self. Adolescents wonder: "Who am I as an individual? What do I want to do with my life? What values should I live by? What do I believe in?" Erikson calls this quest to more deeply define one's sense of self the adolescent's "search for identity."

Table 3-2
Erikson's Stages of Psychosocial Development

Approximate age	Description of task
Infancy (1st year)	**Trust vs. mistrust** If needs are met, infant develops a sense of basic trust.
Toddler (2nd year)	**Autonomy vs. shame and doubt** Toddler strives to learn independence and self-confidence.
Preschooler (3–5 years)	**Initiative vs. guilt** Preschooler learns to initiate tasks and grapples with self-control.
Elementary school (6 years to puberty)	**Competence vs. inferiority** Child learns either to feel effective or inadequate.
Adolescence (teen years into 20s)	**Identity vs. role confusion** Teenager works at refining a sense of self by testing roles, then integrating them to form a single identity.
Young adulthood (20s to early 40s)	**Intimacy vs. isolation** Young adult struggles to form close relationships and to gain the capacity for intimate love.
Middle adulthood (40s to 60s)	**Generativity vs. stagnation** Middle-aged person seeks a sense of contributing to the world, such as through family and work.
Late adulthood (late 60s and up)	**Integrity vs. despair** When reflecting on his or her life, the elderly person may feel a sense of satisfaction or failure.

Forming an Identity

To refine their sense of identity, adolescents usually try out different "selves" in different situations—perhaps acting out one self at home, another with friends, and still another at school and work. If two of these situations overlap—as when a teenager brings home friends with whom he is Joe Cool—the discomfort can be considerable. The teen asks, "Which self should I be? Which is the real me?" Often, this role confusion gets resolved by the gradual reshaping of a self-definition that unifies the various selves into a consistent and comfortable sense of who one is—an **identity.**

But not always. Erikson believes that some adolescents forge their identity early, simply by taking on their parents' values and expectations. Others may adopt a negative identity that defines itself in opposition to parents and society but in conformity with a particular peer group—complete, perhaps, with shaved head or multicolored hair. Still others never quite seem to find themselves or to develop strong commitments. For most, the struggle for identity continues past the teen years and reappears at turning points during adult life.

The late teen years, when many people begin attending college or working full-time, provide new opportunities for trying out possible roles. As college seniors, many students have achieved a clearer identity than they had as first-year students (Waterman, 1988). Their identity typically incorporates an increasingly positive self-concept. In several nationwide studies, researchers have given young Americans tests of self-esteem (sample item: "I am able

11. What is involved in the adolescent's search for identity, and how does intimacy develop?

"I am becoming still more independent of my parents; young as I am, I face life with more courage than Mummy; my feeling for justice is immovable, and truer than hers. I know what I want, I have a goal, an opinion, I have a religion, and love. Let me be myself and then I am satisfied. I know that I'm a woman, a woman with inward strength and plenty of courage."

Anne Frank
Diary of a Young Girl, 1947

By trying out different roles, adolescents try out different "selves." Although some of their roles are uncomfortable for both the adolescents and their parents, most teenagers eventually forge a consistent and comfortable identity.

to do things as well as most other people"). Between ages 13 and 23, the self-concept usually becomes more positive (O'Malley & Bachman, 1983). A clearer, more self-affirming identity is forming. With it comes a greater sense of control over one's future (Baumgardner, 1990).

Developing Intimacy

Erikson contended that the adolescent identity stage is followed in young adulthood by a developing capacity for **intimacy,** the ability to form emotionally close relationships. Once you have a clear and comfortable sense of who you are, said Erikson, you are ready for close relationships. But to Carol Gilligan and her colleagues (1982, 1990), the "normal" struggle to create one's separate identity describes individualist males more than relationship-oriented females. Gilligan believes females are less concerned than males with viewing themselves as separate individuals and more concerned with "making connections." Thus, females are less likely to exhibit Erikson's identity-before-intimacy sequence (Kahn & others, 1985).

As adolescents seek to form their own identities, they begin to separate themselves from their parents. What their friends are—what "everybody's doing"—they often become. In Western cultures, adolescence is typically a time of growing peer influence and diminishing parental influence, especially on matters of personal taste and life-style. When teen experiences are sampled by beeping them with electronic pagers at random times, most report feeling more free and open with friends than family (Larson & Bradney, 1988).

For a small minority, this means that parents and their adolescents are estranged. But for most, disagreement at the level of bickering is not destructive. One study of 6000 adolescents in 10 countries, from Australia to Bangladesh to Turkey, found that most liked their parents (Offer & others, 1988). "We usually get along but . . . ," adolescents often report (Steinberg, 1987). Positive relations with parents actually support positive peer relations. Although parent-adolescent conflict is most common between mothers and daughters (Tesser & others, 1989), high school girls who have the most affectionate relationships with their mothers tend also to enjoy the most intimate friendships with girlfriends (Gold & Yanof, 1985).

As identity and intimacy mature during the twenties, emotional ties between parents and children continue to loosen. During their early twenties, many still lean heavily on their parents. By their late twenties, most feel more

identity One's sense of self; according to Erikson, the adolescent's task is to solidify a sense of self by testing and integrating various roles.

intimacy In Erikson's theory, the ability to form close, loving relationships; a primary developmental task in late adolescence and early adulthood.

"When I was a boy of 14 my father was so ignorant I could hardly stand to have the old man around. But when I got to be 21, I was astonished at how much he had learnt in seven years."

Mark Twain, 1835–1910

comfortably independent of their parents and better able to empathize with them as fellow adults (Frank, 1988; White, 1983). As the twentieth century winds down, this graduation from adolescence to adulthood is taking longer. Adolescents in Europe and North America are taking longer to finish college, to leave the nest, to establish their careers. From 1960 to 1990, Americans' average age at first marriage increased nearly 4 years (to 26 for men, 24 for women).

By some measures, the late twentieth century is a great time to be an adolescent. Between 1960 and the late 1980s, America's teens enjoyed the benefits of declining family poverty, smaller families, increased parental education, doubled per-pupil school expenditures (in constant dollars), double the number of teachers with advanced degrees, and an 11 percent drop in class size. By other measures, it's not so great. Simultaneously their delinquency rate rose 110 percent, their suicide rate rose 136 percent, their homicide rate rose 194 percent, and their single-parent birthrate rose 245 percent (Myers, 1992; Uhlenberg & Eggebeen, 1986). These are, it seems, the best of times and the worst of times.

Adolescent Sexuality and Pregnancy

Preview Question

12. What factors influence teen pregnancy?

Adolescents' development obviously affects their interests and behavior. In U.S. government-sponsored surveys, the percentage of 15- to 19-year-old women reporting premarital sex rose from 29 percent in 1970 to 52 percent in 1988 (Centers for Disease Control, 1991). Premarital sex rates tend to be even higher in Western Europe and lower in Asian and Arab countries (Buss, 1989). Those who begin having sex at a relatively young age tend to have more sex partners over time and to be more vulnerable to sexually transmitted diseases. Although teen sexual activity occurs with all classes and cultures, it is higher among teens who earn low grades, whose parents are not college graduates, who seldom attend religious services, and who use alcohol or marijuana (Harris & Associates, 1986; Orr & others, 1991).

Partly because most sexually active American teenagers use contraception inconsistently, if at all, the U.S. teen pregnancy rate has surged (Figure 3–13). "Regardless of one's political philosophy or moral perspective, the basic facts are disturbing," reported the National Research Council (1987, p. 1): "More than 1 million teenage girls in the United States become pregnant each year, just over 400,000 teenagers obtain abortions, and nearly 470,000 give birth." (The rest miscarry.)

The increased adolescent pregnancy rate and the often impoverished futures of teenage mothers and their children have prompted research on adolescents' use of contraceptives. Short of "just saying no," contraceptives are the surest strategy of preventing pregnancy. Yet 27 percent of sexually active 12- to 17-year-old Americans never use birth control and another 34 percent do so only occasionally (Harris, 1986). Why? Among the contributing factors are these:

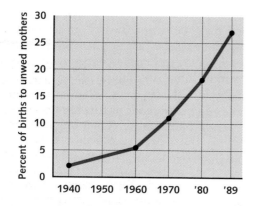

Figure 3–13 In the United States, births to unwed mothers—one-third of whom are teens—have risen sharply since 1960. (Data from National Center for Health Statistics.)

1. *Ignorance:* In eight surveys, fewer than half the adolescents could correctly identify the safe and risky times of the menstrual cycle (Morrison, 1985). Most unwed teen mothers report surprise at finding themselves pregnant (Brooks-Gunn & Furstenberg, 1989). They didn't choose to become pregnant; rather, they and their partners failed to prevent pregnancy.

"Will your child learn to multiply before she learns to subtract?"

Headline on anti-teen-pregnancy poster for the Children's Defense Fund

2. *High sex guilt:* Although sexual inhibitions reduce sexual activity, they also inhibit the planning of birth control for those who do engage in sex (Gerrard, 1987a,b; Mosher & Vonderheide, 1985; Whitley & Schofield, 1986). In their minds, to carry a condom is to decide to have intercourse,

Births to U.S. single mothers have quintupled since 1960, due partly to television's modeling of sexuality, suggests Planned Parenthood.

which sexually conservative teenagers are unlikely to do. When, as sometimes happens, passion overwhelms intentions, the result may be conception.

3. *Minimal communication about birth control:* Many teenagers are uncomfortable discussing contraception with parents, partners, and peers (Kotva & Schneider, 1990; Milan & Kilmann, 1987). Teens are more likely to use contraceptives if they talk freely with friends or parents and are in an exclusive relationship with a partner with whom they communicate openly.

4. *Alcohol use:* Sexually active teens are typically alcohol-using teens (National Research Council, 1987). By depressing brain centers that control judgment, inhibition, and self-awareness, alcohol tends to break down normal restraints, a phenomenon well-known to sexually coercive males.

5. *Mass media norms of unprotected promiscuity:* The Planned Parenthood Federation (1986) has complained that television helps define sexual norms, which today seem to be "Go for it *now*. . . . Don't worry about anything." As noted elsewhere in this book (pages 200 and 461), social behaviors modeled on television have an influence. To find out what sexual behaviors television actually models, Louis Harris and Associates (1988) monitored American prime time network programs. Per hour, they counted 10 sexual innuendos, 5 embraces, and 1.8 implied acts of intercourse, exposing the average viewer to 14,000 sexual events during the 1987–1988 study year. Soap operas, especially, model behavior that would produce unwanted pregnancies. Promiscuity is commonplace. In 1987, unmarried partners outnumbered married partners 24 to 1—with rarely any concern for birth control or sexually transmitted disease (Lowry & Towles, 1989). Planned Parenthood contends that repeated portrayals of unsafe sex, without consequence, amounts to a campaign of sex *dis*information.

Rehearse It

19. Adolescence is marked by the onset of
a. an identity crisis.
b. puberty.
c. separation anxiety.
d. parent-child conflict.

20. According to Piaget, the ability to think logically about abstractions indicates
a. concrete operational thought.
b. assimilation.
c. formal operational thought.
d. accommodation.

21. Moral reasoning based on fear of punishment illustrates
a. preconventional morality.
b. conventional morality.
c. traditional morality.
d. postconventional morality.

22. Erik Erikson contends that each stage of life has its own special psychosocial task or challenge. At adolescence the task is to
a. attain formal operations.
b. forge an identity.
c. develop a sense of industry.
d. live independent of parents.

23. Carol Gilligan contends that adolescent boys are concerned with establishing a separate identity, but girls are more concerned with forming close relationships. In other words, girls at an earlier age are caught up in the search for
a. identity.
b. intimacy.
c. autonomy.
d. self-concept.

24. Aside from abstinence, contraception is the surest way of preventing pregnancy. More than half of all sexually active American teens, however, either do not use contraceptives or do not use them regularly. Among the contributing factors to the epidemic of teen pregnancies in the United States are ignorance about reproduction and contraception, insufficient communication about contraception, and
a. the "just say no" attitude.
b. unavailability of abortion.
c. absence of guilt feelings about sexual activity.
d. alcohol use.

menopause The time of natural cessation of menstruation; also refers to the biological and psychological changes experienced during a woman's years of declining ability to reproduce.

"I am still learning."

Michelangelo's motto, 1560,
at age 85

Preview Question

13. What major physical changes occur during middle and late adulthood?

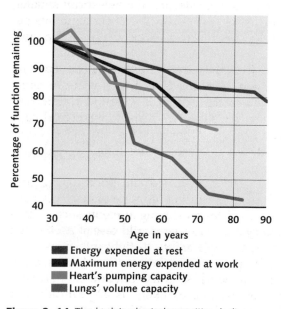

Figure 3–14 The body's physical capacities decline slowly during adulthood. (Adapted from Insel & Roth, 1976.)

- Energy expended at rest
- Maximum energy expended at work
- Heart's pumping capacity
- Lungs' volume capacity

Adulthood

At one time, psychologists viewed adulthood, especially the center-of-life years between adolescence and old age, as one long plateau. No longer. Those who follow the unfolding of people's adult lives now believe development continues. Physically, cognitively, and especially socially, people at age 50 are different from their 25-year-old selves.

Recognizing that adults do change, developmental theorists have proposed various stages of adult development, complete with transition periods. When people become independent of their parents and assume work roles, a transition from adolescence to *early adulthood* occurs. This extends from the twenties (or earlier, depending on the culture and the individual) into the forties, when *middle adulthood* begins. Some developmentalists now distinguish the "young-old" years (age 65 to 75) of *later adulthood* from the "old-old" years (after age 75) of more rapid physical decline.

It's harder to generalize about adulthood than about life's early years. During adulthood, age only modestly correlates with people's traits. If you know that James is a 1-year-old and Jamal is a 10-year-old, you could say a great deal about each child. Not so with adults who differ by a similar number of years. The boss may be 30 or 60; the marathon runner may be 20 or 50; your classmates may be teenagers or grandparents. Likewise, a 19-year-old can be a parent who supports a child or a student who still gets an allowance.

Yet our life courses are in some ways similar. As adults, our bodies, our minds, and our relationships undergo some changes in common with childhood friends, who in other ways now seem so very different.

Physical Changes

Although few of us are aware of it at the time, our physical abilities peak in early adulthood. Muscular strength, reaction time, sensory acuity, and cardiac output all crest by the mid-twenties. Like the declining daylight after the summer solstice, the decline in physical prowess begins imperceptibly. Athletes are often the first to notice. World-class sprinters and swimmers peak in their teens or early twenties. Women, who mature earlier, peak earlier than men. But most people—especially those whose daily lives do not require peak physical performance—hardly perceive the early signs of decline.

Physical Changes in Middle Adulthood

As middle-aged athletes know well, physical decline gradually accelerates (Figure 3–14). "I feel like a 15-year-old trapped in an aging 47-year-old body," said one middle-aged basketball player. But even diminished vigor is sufficient for normal activities. Moreover, during early and middle adulthood physical vigor has less to do with age than with a person's health and exercise habits. Many of today's physically fit 50-year-olds can run for miles with ease, while sedentary 25-year-olds find themselves huffing and puffing on a jog around the block.

For women, the foremost biological change related to aging is **menopause,** the ending of the menstrual cycle, usually beginning within a few years of age 50. Menopause and its occasional physical symptoms, such as hot flashes in some women, accompany a reduction in the hormone estrogen. Like the stereotype of adolescent storm and stress, the image of menopausal emotionality and depression clashes with reality: Menopause usually does *not* create psychological problems for women. One survey of 2500 middle-aged Massachusetts women found them no more or less depressed if experi-

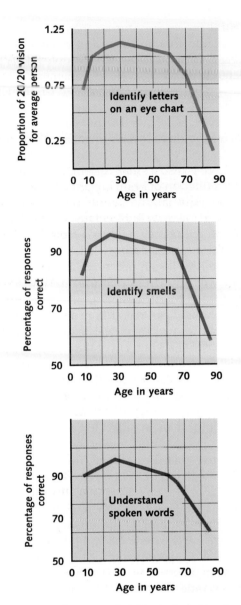

Figure 3–15 The senses of sight, smell, and hearing all decline in later life. (From Doty & others, 1984.)

encing menopause (McKinlay & others, 1987a,b). Apart from occasic shoulders and headaches, Japanese women, too, report few symptoms of menopause (Lock & others, 1988).

What determines the emotional impact of menopause is the woman's attitude toward it. Does she see menopause as a sign that she is losing her femininity and sexual attractiveness and beginning to grow old? Or does she look on it as liberation from contraceptives, menstrual periods, fears of pregnancy, and the demands of children? Social psychologist Jacqueline Goodchilds (1987) appreciates the liberation: "If the truth were known, we'd have to diagnose [older women] as having P.M.F.—Post-Menstrual Freedom."

Men experience no equivalent to the menopause—no cessation of fertility, no sharp drop in sex hormones. But they do experience a more gradual decline in sperm count, testosterone level, and speed of erection and ejaculation. Some may also experience psychological distress related to their perception of decreased virility and declining physical capacities. Nevertheless, after middle age most men and women remain capable of satisfying sexual activity.

Physical Changes in Later Life

Is old age "more to be feared than death" (Juvenal, *Satires*, 100 A.D.)? Or is life "most delightful when it is on the downward slope" (Seneca, *Epistles*, 64 A.D.)? What have we to look forward to? What is it like to grow old?

Sensory Abilities   As we have seen, physical decline begins in early adulthood, but not until later life do people become acutely aware of it. As visual acuity diminishes and adaptation to changes in light level slows, older people have more accidents. Most stairway falls taken by older persons occur on the top step, precisely where the person typically descends from a window-lit hallway into the darker stairwell (Fozard & Popkin, 1978). By using what we know about aging when designing environments, we could reduce such accidents (National Research Council, 1990). Muscle strength, hearing, distance perception, reaction time, sense of smell, and stamina also diminish noticeably (Figure 3–15). In later life, the stairs get steeper, the newsprint smaller, and people seem to mumble more. After age 70, the rate of car accidents per mile increases, reaching the relatively high teenage level by age 75 (National Research Council, 1990).

With age, the eye's pupil shrinks and its lens becomes less transparent, reducing the amount of light reaching the retina. In fact, a 65-year-old retina receives only about one-third as much light as its 20-year-old counterpart (Kline & Schieber, 1985). Thus, to see as well as a 20-year-old when reading, a 65-year-old needs three times as much light. That explains why older people sometimes ask younger people, "Don't you need better light for reading?"

Health   For those growing older, there is both bad and good news about health. The bad news: The body's disease-fighting immune system weakens, making the elderly more susceptible to life-threatening ailments such as cancer and pneumonia. It's as if the very old have a very mild case of AIDS—the immune deficiency that hampers the body's ability to fight infections.

The good news: Thanks to a lifetime's accumulation of antibodies, older people *less* often suffer short-term ailments, such as common flu and cold viruses. For example, those over 65 are half as likely as 20-year-olds and one-fifth as likely as preschoolers to suffer upper respiratory flu each year (U.S. National Center for Health Statistics, 1990). This is one reason why older workers have lower absenteeism rates (Rhodes, 1983).

Alzheimer's disease A progressive and irreversible brain disorder characterized by gradual deterioration of memory, reasoning, language, and, finally, physical functioning.

cross-sectional study A study in which people of different ages are tested or observed at one point in time.

longitudinal study Research in which the same people are restudied over a long time period.

The more active older people remain, the more vigor they retain. Moreover, age per se affects blood pressure and cholesterol less than do the accumulated effects of nutrition, exercise, smoking, and drinking habits (Rowe & Kahn, 1987). Likewise, the loss of hearing, taste, and lung capacity is determined not just by age, but by what we've subjected our ears, tongue, and lungs to.

Aging does, however, slow neural processes. During the early years of life, up to the teen years, we process information more and more speedily (Kail, 1991). But compared to teens and young adults, older people take a bit more time to react, to solve perceptual puzzles, even to remember names (Bashore & others, 1989; Schaie, 1989). Speed slows especially when the task becomes complex (Cerella, 1985; Poon, 1987). At video games, most 70-year-olds are no match for a 20-year-old. (Nor, as I have discovered in play with my daughter, is a 49-year-old a match for a 15-year-old at Nintendo's perceptual speed game, Tetris.)

Beginning in young adulthood, there is also a small, gradual loss of brain cells, contributing to a 5 percent or so reduction of brain weight by age 80. But the proliferation of neural connections, especially in people who remain active, helps compensate for the cell loss (Coleman & Flood, 1986). This helps explain the common finding that adults who remain active—physically, sexually, and mentally—retain more of their capacity for such activities in later years (Jarvik, 1975; Pfeiffer, 1977). "Use it or lose it" is sound advice. We are more likely to rust from disuse than wear out from overuse.

Some adults do, unfortunately, suffer a tragic loss of brain cells. A series of small strokes, a brain tumor, or alcoholism can result in progressive brain damage causing that mental erosion that we call senility. The most feared of all brain ailments, **Alzheimer's disease,** strikes 3 percent of the world's population by age 75. By age 90, nearly 40 percent of the population is afflicted (Jorm and others, 1987). Alzheimer's symptoms are *not* the same as normal aging. (Occasionally forgetting where you laid the car keys or struggling over someone's name is no cause for alarm.)

Alzheimer's destroys even the brightest of minds. First memory, then reasoning and language deteriorate. As the disease runs its course, after 5 to 20 years, the patient becomes disoriented, then incontinent, finally mentally vacant—a sort of living death, preceding actual death, a mere body stripped of its humanity.

In its early stages, Alzheimer's disease is easily mistaken for mental laziness. Robert Sayre (1979) recalls his father shouting at his afflicted mother to "think harder" when she could not remember where she had put something, while his mother, confused, embarrassed, on the verge of tears, randomly searched the house. Caregiving family members of increasingly confused and helpless sufferers themselves often become the disease's exasperated and exhausted hidden victims.

Underlying the symptoms is a deterioration of neurons that produce the neurotransmitter acetylcholine (ACh). Deprived of this vital chemical messenger, memory and thinking suffer. An autopsy reveals two telltale abnormalities in these acetylcholine-producing neurons: shriveled protein filaments in the cell body and placques (globs of degenerating tissue) at the tips of neuron branches. With continuing advances in our understanding of the chemical, neural, and genetic roots of Alzheimer's, hopes for eventual control of this dread disease grow.

Cognitive Changes

One of the most controversial questions in the study of the human life span is whether adult cognitive abilities, such as memory, creativity, and intelligence, parallel the gradually accelerating decline of physical abilities. Employers may wonder about their older workers. Should they encourage senior workers to retire—or capitalize on their experience? In general, people perceive the elderly as mentally less sharp (Kite & Johnson, 1988). Is this stereotype accurate?

Preview Question

14. How are memory and intelligence influenced by aging?

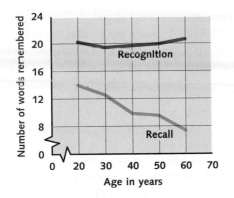

Figure 3–16 In this experiment of recall and recognition in adulthood, the ability to *recall* new information declined during early and middle adulthood, but the ability to *recognize* new information showed no decline. (From Schonfield & Robertson, 1966.)

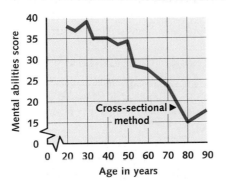

Figure 3–17 On intelligence tests, older adults get fewer questions correct than younger adults. But see Figure 3–18. (From Geiwitz, 1980.)

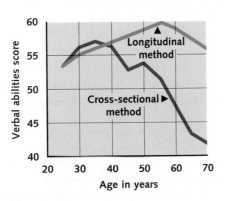

Figure 3–18 In this test of verbal intelligence, the cross-sectional method produced declining scores with age. The longitudinal method (in which the same people were retested over a period of years) produced *rising* scores well into adulthood. (From Schaie & Strother, 1968.)

Aging and Memory

Early adulthood is the peak time for some types of learning and remembering. In one experiment, David Schonfield and Betty-Anne Robertson (1966) asked adults of various ages to learn a list of 24 words. Without giving any clues, the researchers asked some to *recall* as many words as they could from the list. As Figure 3–16 shows, younger adults had better recall—a finding that parallels the greater ease with which younger adults recall new names and process complicated information (Zacks & Hasher, 1988). Others, given multiple-choice questions that asked them simply to *recognize* which words they had seen, exhibited no memory decline with age. So, how well older people remember depends: Are they being asked simply to *recognize* what they have tried to memorize (no decline) or to *recall* it without clues (decline)?

Part of the memory difficulty the elderly complain of may be normal forgetfulness. When a 20-year-old mislays her car keys, she gets frustrated; when her grandfather mislays his, he gets frustrated and blames his age. But the truth is more complicated. If asked to recall meaningless information—remembering nonsense syllables or unimportant events—then the older you are, the more errors you are likely to make. But the elderly's rich web of existing knowledge helps them catch meaningful information. Thus, their capacity to learn and remember skills and *meaningful* material shows less decline (Graf, 1990; Labouvie-Vief & Schell, 1982; Perlmutter, 1983).

Aging and Intelligence

What happens to our broader intellectual powers as we age? Do they gradually decline, like our ability to recall new material? Or do they remain constant, like our ability to recognize meaningful material? The evolving answer to this question makes an interesting research story that illustrates psychology's self-correcting process (Woodruff-Pak, 1989).

Phase I: Cross-Sectional Evidence for Intellectual Decline In **cross-sectional studies,** researchers test people of various ages at the same time. When giving intelligence tests to representative samples of people, researchers consistently find that older adults give fewer correct answers than younger adults (Figure 3–17). David Wechsler (1972), creator of the most widely used adult intelligence test, therefore concluded that "the decline of mental ability with age is part of the general [aging] process of the organism as a whole."

Phase II: Longitudinal Evidence for Intellectual Stability Colleges began giving intelligence tests to entering students about 1920, making it possible to retest older people who had taken an intelligence test years earlier. Several psychologists saw their chance to study intelligence **longitudinally,** by retesting the same people over a period of years. What they expected to find was the usual decrease in intelligence after about age 30 (Schaie & Geiwitz, 1982). What they actually found was a surprise: Until very late in life, intelligence remained stable, and on some tests it even increased (Figure 3–18).

How are we to account for the findings from the cross-sectional studies? In retrospect, researchers saw the problem. When a cross-sectional study compares 70- and 30-year-olds, it compares not only people of two different ages, but of two different eras. It compares generally less educated people (born, say, in the early 1900s) with more educated people (born after 1950), people raised in large families with people raised in smaller families, people growing up in less affluent families with people growing up in more affluent families.

At age 70, John Rock developed the birth control pill. At age 78, Grandma Moses took up painting and was still painting after age 100. At age 81—17 years before the end of his college football coaching career—Amos Alozo Stagg was named coach of the year. At age 89, architect Frank Lloyd Wright designed New York City's Guggenheim Museum.

"In youth we learn, in age we understand."

Marie von Ebner-Eschenbach
Aphorisms, 1883

Phase III: It All Depends   But the controversy is still not over. For one thing, longitudinal studies have their own pitfalls. Those who survive to the end of longitudinal studies may be bright, healthy people whose intelligence is least likely to decline. If so, such studies underestimate the *average* decline in intelligence.

Research is further complicated by the finding that intelligence is not a single trait (see Chapter 8, Thinking, Language, and Intelligence). Intelligence tests that assess speed of thinking may place older adults at a disadvantage because of their slower neural mechanisms for processing information. But slower need not mean less intelligent. Given other tests that assess general vocabulary, knowledge, and ability to integrate information, older adults generally hold their own. German researchers Paul Baltes and Jacqui Smith (1990) are developing "wisdom" tests that assess traits such as expertise and sound judgment in life planning. Their results suggest that older adults more than hold their own on such tests.

So, whether intelligence increases or decreases with age depends on what type of intellectual performance we measure. **Crystallized intelligence**—one's accumulated knowledge as reflected in vocabulary tests—*increases* up to old age. **Fluid intelligence**—one's ability to reason abstractly as when solving logic problems—*decreases* with age (Cattell, 1963; Horn, 1982). We can see this pattern on the intelligence scores of a national sample of adults. After adjusting for education, verbal intelligence held relatively steady from ages 20 to 74, while nonverbal, puzzle-solving intelligence declined (Figure 3–19).

Figure 3-19 After adjustments for education, verbal intelligence holds steady with age, while nonverbal intelligence scores decline. (IQ scores from standardization sample of the Wechsler Adult Intelligence Scale, based on norms for 25- to 34-year-olds.) (Adapted from Kaufman & others, 1989.)

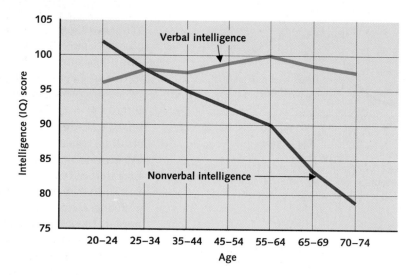

This helps explain why mathematicians and scientists produce much of their notable work during their late twenties or early thirties, while those in literature, history, and philosophy tend to produce their best work later—in their forties, fifties, and beyond, after accumulating more knowledge (Simonton, 1988). History bears out this finding. For example, poets reach their peak output earlier than prose authors—a finding observed in every major literary tradition, for both living and dead languages. So, whether intellectual performance increases or decreases with age depends on how we assess it.

Social Changes

Many differences between younger and older adults are created not by the physical and cognitive changes that accompany aging but by life events associated with family relationships and work. A new job means new relationships, new expectations, and new demands. Marriage brings the joy of inti-

Erik and Joan Erikson have focused their attention on the end of the life cycle as they themselves have aged. Shown here in their eighties, the Eriksons maintain that wisdom has little to do with formal learning: "What is real wisdom? It comes from life experience, well digested. It's not what comes from reading great books. When it comes to understanding life, experiential learning is the only worthwhile kind; everything else is hearsay."

macy and the stress of merging your life with another's. The birth of a child introduces responsibilities and significantly alters your life focus. The death of a loved one creates a sense of irreplaceable loss and a need to reaffirm your own life. Do these normal events of adult life shape a predictable sequence of life changes?

Adulthood's Ages and Stages

Some psychologists describe the human journey through adulthood by intensively studying small samples of people. Daniel Levinson and others (1978, 1986) conducted lengthy interviews with 85 successful, middle-aged men and women. Based partly on their recollections, Levinson concluded that adults progress through periods of stability punctuated by times of upheaval and change. For example, he believes that as people enter their forties, they undergo a "midlife transition" to middle adulthood, which for many is a crisis, a time of great struggle or even of feeling struck down by life. They give up their dreams of fame and fortune (or the illusion that such bring happiness) and question their work and family commitments. The result, says Levinson, is often turmoil and despair. Fortyish people realize that they are no longer starting out, but rather drawing closer to the end. When this painful growth period concludes at about age 45, they again settle into new or deepened attachments, set about completing their careers, and become more compassionate and reflective.

Many researchers are skeptical about such efforts to define adult life as a series of neatly packaged stages, especially stages based merely on interviews with a select few people. To generalize from their career-oriented lives or to use their "midlife crises" to explain or justify the renouncing of old relationships is both misleading and dangerous (Gilligan, 1982). The fact—from large samples of people—is that job dissatisfaction, marital dissatisfaction, divorce, anxiety, and suicide do *not* surge during the early forties (Hunter & Sundel, 1989). Divorce, for example, is most common among those in their twenties, suicide among those in their seventies and eighties.

Are these markers of crisis too crude to detect a more subtle midlife turmoil? National Institute of Aging researchers Robert McCrae and Paul Costa (1990) gave a "Midlife Crisis Scale" assessing sense of meaninglessness and mortality, job and family dissatisfaction, and inner turmoil and confusion to 350 30- to 60-year-old men. They could find "no evidence at all" that such concerns peak at midlife. Surprised, they gave their scale to a new group of 300 men, and a measure of emotional instability to nearly 10,000 men and women. "The results were an exact reconfirmation: There was not the slightest evidence" that distress peaks anywhere in the midlife age range (Figure 3–20).

Moreover, the **social clock**—the cultural prescription of "the right age" to leave home, get a job, marry, have children, and retire—varies from culture to culture and era to era. In Jordan, 44 percent of brides are in their teens; in Hong Kong, only 3 percent are (United Nations, 1990). In contemporary Western nations, women increasingly enter the workplace and college classroom as adults. In earlier times, such ventures outside the home were unusual. Given variations in the social clock and individual experience, the stage theory critics suspect that any proposed timetable of adult ages and stages will have limited applicability.

More important than one's chronological age are life events. Marriage, parenthood, vocational changes, divorce, nest-emptying, relocation, and retirement mark transitions to new life stages whenever they occur—and increasingly they are occurring at unpredictable ages. The social clock is still ticking, but people feel freer to be out of sync with it.

Preview Question

15. Why are age-based stage theories of adult development considered controversial?

"Midway in the journey of our life I found myself in a dark wood, for the straight way was lost."

Dante
The Divine Comedy, 1300–1321

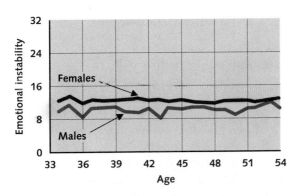

Figure 3–20 Early forties midlife crises? Among 10,000 people responding to a national health survey, there was not even a blip on the trend line of emotional instability ("neuroticism") scores. (From McCrae & Costa, 1990.)

crystallized intelligence One's accumulated knowledge and verbal skills; tends to increase with age.

fluid intelligence One's ability to reason abstractly; tends to decrease during late adulthood.

social clock The culturally preferred timing of social events such as marriage, parenthood, and retirement.

Preview Question

16. What do psychologists view as adulthood's two primary commitments?

"One can live magnificently in this world if one knows how to work and how to love."

Leo Tolstoy, 1856

Since 1960, cohabitation in the United States has increased sixfold, nearly equalling the likelihood of marriage by age 25. Ironically, couples who marry after an apparently successful trial marriage have *higher* divorce rates—36 percent higher in a study of 13,000 U.S. adults, 54 percent higher in a study of 5300 Canadian women, 80 percent higher in a study of 4300 Swedish women (Balakrishan & others 1987; Bennett & others, 1988; Bumpass & Sweet, 1989).

"Marry, and with luck it may go well. But when a marriage fails, then those who marry live at home in hell."

Euripides
Orestes, 408 B.C.

"Appearances notwithstanding, for women, at least, midlife is not a stage tied to chronological age. Rather, it belongs to that point in the life cycle of the family when the children are grown and gone, or nearly so—when, perhaps for the first time in her adult life, a woman can attend to her own needs, her own desires, her own development as a separate and autonomous being."

Sociologist Lillian B. Rubin (1979)

Adulthood's Commitments

Two basic aspects of our lives do, however, dominate adulthood. Erik Erikson called them *intimacy* (forming close relationships) and *generativity* (being productive and supporting future generations). Researchers have chosen various terms—affiliation and achievement, attachment and productivity, commitment and competence. But Sigmund Freud (1935) put it most simply: The healthy adult, he said, is one who can love and work. For most adults, *love* centers on family commitments toward spouse, parents, and children. *Work* encompasses our productive activities, whether for pay or not.

Love   "Traditional" families—father, mother, and children under 18—comprise only 27 percent of U.S. households. Who are the other 73 percent? They include older couples with an empty nest, grandparents caring for grandchildren, single parents and their children, the widowed, singles, cohabiting men and women, and childless or voluntarily child-free married people. To judge from the North American divorce rate—roughly 40 percent of Canadian marriages and half of U.S. marriages end in divorce—marriage has become a union that often defies management. In Europe, too, divorce is nearly as common, after increasing 400 percent between 1960 and 1985 (Inglehart, 1990).

In fact, among Americans married in the early 1970s, only a third in 1986 were still married *and* proclaiming their marriages very happy (Glenn, 1989). Newlyweds beware: Don't take a successful marriage for granted, because the odds are you will *not* live happily ever after. Still, there is brighter news about marriage. More than 9 in 10 adults marry. Of those who divorce, 75 percent remarry—and their second marriages are virtually as happy as the average first marriage (Vemer & others, 1989). And fewer than 25 percent of unmarried adults, but nearly 40 percent of married adults, report being "very happy" with life (Glenn & Weaver, 1988).

Often, love bears children. The most enduring of life changes, having a child, is for most people a happy event. As children begin to absorb time, money, and emotional energy, however, satisfaction with the marriage itself often declines. This is especially so among those employed women who bear the traditional burden of increased chores at home (Belsky & others, 1986). Although U.S. husbands, on average, do one-third of household tasks—up from 15 percent in 1965 (Robinson, 1988)—for most women, work is never done.

Another significant event in family life happens when children leave home. If you have left home, consider your parents' experience: Did they suffer an "empty nest syndrome"—was either of them distressed by a loss of purpose and relationship? Or did your parents discover renewed freedom, relaxation, and satisfaction with their own relationship?

Seven national surveys reveal that the empty nest is for most people a happy place (Adelmann & others, 1989; Glenn, 1975). Compared to middle-aged women who still have children at home, those whose nest has emptied report greater happiness and greater enjoyment of their marriage. Many parents therefore experience what sociologists Lynn White and John Edwards (1990) call a "post-launch honeymoon," especially if they maintain close relationships with their children. Bernice Neugarten (1974) explains, "Most women are glad to see their children grow up, leave home, marry, and have their careers. The notion that they mourn the loss of their reproductive ability and their mother role does not seem to fit modern reality."

For many, a satisfying and interesting occupation enhances happiness.

Work For adults, a large part of the answer to "Who are you?" is the answer to "What do you do?" For most, to feel productive and competent is to raise children and to undertake a career. Career choices are hard to predict. During the first 2 years of college, most students cannot accurately predict their later career path. Most shift from their initially intended majors while in college, many find their postcollege employment in fields not directly related to their majors, and most will change careers (Rothstein, 1980). To many career counselors, this unpredictability means that the best education is not a narrow vocational training, but rather a broad liberal education, an education that fosters "the critical qualities of mind and the durable qualities of character that will serve [people] in circumstances we cannot now even predict" (Gardner, 1984).

Does work, including a career, indeed contribute to fulfillment, as Freud supposed? During the 1970s and 1980s, one approach to answering this question compared self-reported happiness among the roughly equal numbers of North American women who have or have not been employed. Their happiness difference—which slightly favors women who are employed—has always been far smaller than the person-to-person differences within each group (Adelmann, 1988; Campbell, 1981).

For some women and some men, the combined stresses of employment and work at home can overload the circuits (McClanahan & Adams, 1989). For many others, reports Patricia Linville (1987), there are emotional benefits to having multiple roles and identities—as parent, spouse, worker, amateur athlete, community leader, and so forth. When problems arise in any one area, one's whole sense of self feels less threatened. A difficult marriage, say, will be less devastating to the one who can think, "Despite my marital problems, I am a good parent" (or "an effective worker" or "a valuable hospital volunteer").

From their studies at the Wellesley College Center for Research on Women, Grace Baruch and Rosaline Barnett (1986) conclude that what matters is not which roles a woman occupies—as paid worker, wife, and/or mother—but the quality of her experience in that role. Happiness is having work that fits your interests and provides a sense of competence and accomplishment; having a partner who is a close, supportive companion and who sees you as special; having loving children whom you like and feel proud of.

Well-Being Across the Life Span

To live is to grow older, which means that all of us can look backward with satisfaction or sorrow and forward with hope or dread. Adolescents are buffeted by mood swings and insecurity, parental power and peer pressures, identity confusion and career worries. In later life, we presume, income shrinks, work is taken away, the body deteriorates, recall fades, energy wanes, family members and friends die or move away, and the great enemy, death, looms ever closer. Small wonder that we presume the teen and over-65 years to be the worst of times (Freedman, 1978).

Surprisingly, they are not. People of all ages report similar feelings of happiness and satisfaction with life. Ronald Inglehart (1990) confirmed this when he amassed interviews conducted during the 1980s with representative samples of nearly 170,000 people in 16 nations. As Figure 3–21 (page 94) illustrates, age differences in life satisfaction are trivial. Older people report as much happiness and satisfaction with life as younger people do. Given that growing older is one sure consequence of living, an outcome that most of us prefer to its alternative, we can all take comfort in this finding.

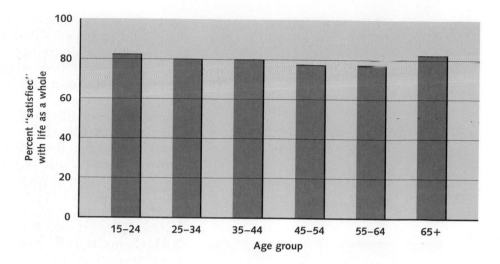

Figure 3–21 Does well-being align itself with any particular age? Multi-national surveys reveal that age differences in life satisfaction (and happiness) are trivial. (Data from Inglehart, 1990.)

Preview Question

17. How are the stages attributed to death and dying comparable to other age-based stage theories of adulthood?

"How many of us older persons have really been . . . prepared for the second half of life, for old age, death and eternity?"

Carl Jung
Modern Man in Search of a Soul, 1933

hospice An organization whose largely volunteer staff provides support for dying people and their families either in special facilities or in people's own homes.

Death and Dying

Most of us will suffer and cope with the deaths of relatives and friends. Usually, the most difficult separation is from one's spouse—a loss suffered by five times more women than men. Grief is especially severe when the death of a loved one comes before its expected time on the social clock. The accidental death of a child or the sudden illness that claims a 45-year-old spouse may trigger a year or more of mourning flooded with memories, eventually subsiding to a mild depression that sometimes continues for several years (Lehman & others, 1987). Contrary to a popular myth, those who express the strongest grief immediately do not resolve their grief more quickly (Wortman & Silver, 1989). The normal range of reactions to a loved one's death is wider than most people suppose. Severe distress is common, but not inevitable.

Those who suffer a terminal illness live with the awareness of their impending death. In analyzing how people cope with the prospect of death, the stage theorists have once again arrived ahead of us. From her interviews with dying patients, Elisabeth Kübler-Ross (1969) proposed that the terminally ill pass through a sequence of five stages: *denial* of the terminal condition; *anger* and resentment ("Why me?"); *bargaining* with God (or physicians) for more time; *depression* stemming from the impending loss of everything and everyone; and, finally, peaceful *acceptance* of one's fate. Others propose similar stages—disbelief, protest, depression, recovery—for coping with a sudden physical impairment (Fitzgerald, 1970).

Critics question the generality of all such stages, stressing that each person's experience is unique. Real people, they say, don't fit into these neat boxes. Moreover, they argue, the simplified stages ignore many important factors—for example, that people who are old usually view death with less expressed fear and resentment than younger people (Wass & others, 1978–1979). Critics also express concern about the eagerness with which the death-and-dying formula has been popularized in courses and books. The danger, they fear, is that rather than having their feelings respected, dying people may be analyzed or manipulated in terms of the stereotyped stages: "She's just going through the anger stage."

Nevertheless, the death-education movement has enabled us to deal more openly and humanely with death and grief. A growing number of individuals are aided by **hospice** organizations, whose staff and volunteers work in special facilities and in people's homes to support and comfort the terminally ill and their families, to help make this a meaningful time "when good-byes can be said, when broken relationships can be healed, when forgiveness can be given or received" (Magno, 1989).

Grief is intense when a loved one's death comes before its expected time on the social clock, whether it be due to war, illness, or accident. The family of Marine Reserve Captain Jonathan Edwards, an investment counselor who became the first Persian Gulf War casualty buried at Arlington National Cemetery, grieves during his burial.

We can be grateful for the waning of death-denying attitudes. Facing death with dignity and openness helps people complete the life cycle with a sense of life's meaningfulness and unity—the sense that their existence has been good and that life and death are parts of an ongoing cycle. Although death may be unwelcome, life itself can be affirmed even at death. This is especially so for people who review their lives not with despair but with what Erik Erikson calls a sense of *integrity*—a feeling that one's life has been meaningful and worthwhile.

Rehearse It

25. By age 75, a person has experienced losses in sight and hearing, and declining heart and muscular strength. However, this "young-old" adult is *less* likely than the young adult to suffer from
a. Alzheimer's disease.
b. accidents and falls.
c. short-term illnesses, such as the flu. ✓
d. chronic illnesses, such as diabetes.

26. Some types of learning and remembering peak in early adulthood. By age 65 a person would be most likely to experience a decline in the ability to
a. recall and list all the items in the chapter glossary.
b. select the correct definition in a multiple choice question.
c. evaluate whether a statement is true or false.
d. exercise sound judgment in answering an essay question.

27. In longitudinal studies the same person is retested at different ages. Longitudinal research suggests that intelligence
a. steadily declines with age.
b. peaks at age 25.
c. generally increases in later life.
d. remains stable until very late in life.

28. Daniel Levinson proposed a "midlife transition," a painful growth period supposedly experienced by most people at about age 45. Levinson's theory is an example of a
a. stage theory of adult development.
b. cross-sectional study.
c. theory of cognitive development.
d. universal pattern in our culture.

29. Freud defined the healthy adult as one who is able to love and work. Erikson agrees; according to him the adult struggles to attain intimacy and
a. affiliation.
b. identity.
c. competence.
d. generativity.

30. Contrary to what many people assume,
a. older people are much happier than adolescents.
b. men in their forties express much greater dissatisfaction than women the same age.
c. people of all ages report similar levels of happiness.
d. those whose children have recently left home—the empty nesters—have the lowest level of happiness of all groups.

identical twins Twins who develop from a single zygote that splits in two, creating two genetic replicas.

fraternal twins Twins who develop from separate zygotes (fertilized eggs); genetically no closer than brothers and sisters, but who have shared the fetal environment.

Preview Question

18. What conclusions can we draw from research on the nature-nurture issue?

Most Navajo babies calmly accept the cradleboard; Caucasian babies protest vigorously. Findings like this suggest that the rudiments of personality are genetically influenced.

Reflections on the Major Developmental Issues

We began our survey of developmental psychology by identifying three pervasive issues: (1) whether development is steered more by nature or nurture, (2) whether development is a gradual, continuous process or a discrete series of stages, and (3) whether development is characterized more by stability over time or by change. Let's conclude by taking stock of current thinking on each issue.

Nature and Nurture

Everyone agrees: We are all influenced by genes *and* experience. The question is, how important is each? For physical attributes such as hair color, the genetic factor predominates. For psychological attributes, the answer is less obvious. In Chapter 8 we will examine the thorny debate over genetic and environmental determinants of intelligence. Here we will consider some provocative findings on how nature and nurture influence the developing personality.

Infants and young children cannot take personality tests, so investigators observe their actual behavior and infer their temperament. As we have seen, children come with differing temperaments. Are such temperamental differences hereditary? They seem to be. Animal breeders selectively mate dogs, horses, and other animals to be either high-strung or easygoing. When researcher Stephen Suomi (1987) placed genetically predisposed "uptight" versus "easygoing" infant monkeys with foster mothers who were themselves uptight or easygoing, heredity overrode rearing. Compared to the naturally easygoing monkeys, the uptight monkeys reacted more anxiously to the stress of separation from their mother, even when raised by easygoing, nurturant foster mothers.

To judge from twin studies (see below), genes influence human temperament, too (Matheny, 1989). Moreover, newborns of different races exhibit differing average temperaments. Babies of Caucasian and African descent tend to be more reactive and irritable than Chinese and Native American babies (who share a common Asian descent). For example, if restrained, undressed, or covered with a cloth, Caucasian babies typically respond more intensely than Navajo infants (Freedman, 1979).

Studies of Twins

Selective breeding varies heredity but not environment, thereby revealing an effect of heredity. Could we do the reverse—vary environment but not heredity—to also see an effect of environment? Happily for our purposes, nature has given us ready-made subjects for this experiment: twins. **Identical twins,** who develop from a single fertilized egg that splits into two, are genetically identical (Figure 3–22). **Fraternal twins,** who develop from separate eggs, are genetically no more similar than ordinary brothers and sisters.

Do identical twins, being genetic replicas of one another, develop more similar personalities than fraternal twins? Studies of 13,000 pairs of Swedish identical and fraternal twins, of 7000 pairs of Finnish twins, and of 850 American twin pairs reveal that identical twins are substantially more similar—in personality, abilities, and even interests (Floderus-Myrhed and others, 1980; Loehlin & Nichols, 1976; Rose & others, 1988). These findings suggest that there is indeed a significant genetic influence.

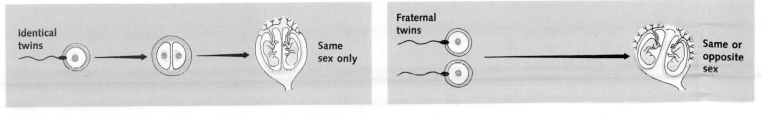

Figure 3–22 Identical twins develop from a single, fertilized egg, fraternal twins from two.

Identical twins Gerald Levey and Mark Newman were separated at birth, 9 months after sharing the same fertilized egg. When reunited at age 31, they discovered that they had chosen the same vocation.

"In some domains it looks as though our identical twins reared apart are . . . just as similar as identical twins reared together. Now that's an amazing finding and I can assure you none of us would have expected that degree of similarity."

Thomas Bouchard (1981)

Coincidences are not unique to twins. Patricia Kern of Colorado was born March 13, 1941, and named Patricia Ann Campbell. Patricia DiBiasi of Oregon also was born March 13, 1941, and named Patricia Ann Campbell. Both had fathers named Robert, worked as bookkeepers, and have children ages 21 and 19. Both studied cosmetology, enjoy oil painting as a hobby, and married military men, within 11 days of each other. They are not genetically related. (From an AP report, May 2, 1983.)

Separated Twins   Imagine a science fiction experiment in which someone, driven by curiosity, decides to separate identical twins at birth and rear them in differing environments. Would such twins differ more from one another than do twins reared together? If so, our mad scientist reasons, one could only credit their differing environments. In reality, circumstances occasionally set up just these conditions.

Thus, in 1979 when University of Minnesota psychologist Thomas Bouchard read a newspaper account of the reuniting of 39-year-old twins who had been separated from infancy, he seized the opportunity and flew them to Minneapolis for extensive tests. Bouchard was looking for differences. What "the Jim twins," Jim Lewis and Jim Springer, presented were amazing similarities (Holden, 1980a,b). Both had married women named Linda, divorced, and married women named Betty. One had a son James Alan, the other a son James Allan. Both had dogs named Toy, chain-smoked Salems, served as sheriff's deputies, drove Chevrolets, chewed their fingernails to the nub, enjoyed stock car racing, had basement workshops, and had built circular white benches around trees in their yards. They also had similar medical histories: Both gained 10 pounds at about the same time and then lost it; both suffered what they mistakenly believed were heart attacks, and both began having late-afternoon headaches at age 18.

Aided by publicity in magazine and newspaper stories, Bouchard and his colleagues (1990) have now located and studied some five dozen pairs of identical twins reared apart. They continue to be impressed by the similarities not only of tastes and physical attributes but also of personality, abilities, and even fears. In Sweden, which has a national registry of 25,000 pairs of adult twins, Nancy Pedersen and her co-workers (1988) identified 99 separated identical twin pairs and more than 200 separated fraternal twin pairs. Compared with equivalent samples of identical twins reared together, the separated identical twins had more dissimilar personalities. Still, separated twins were more alike when genetically identical rather than fraternal. And separation shortly after birth (rather than, say, at age 8) didn't amplify their personality differences.

The cute stories do not impress Bouchard's critics. They contend that if any two strangers of the same sex and age were to spend hours comparing their behaviors and life histories, they would probably discover many coincidental similarities. Even the more impressive data from the personality assessments are clouded by the reunion of many of the separated twins for some years before being tested. Moreover, adoption agencies tend to place separated twins in similar homes. When environments are similar, the impact of environment looks smaller relative to heredity. And as twins age, differing experiences often make their personality differences more noticeable (McCartney & others, 1990). Nevertheless, the twin studies illustrate why scientific opinion has shifted toward a greater appreciation of genetic influences on development.

Ignorant of these findings, popular psychology sometimes encourages parent-blaming: Believing that parents shape their children as a potter molds clay, people praise parents for their children's virtues and blame them for their children's vices. Given our readiness to praise or blame, and to feel pride or shame, we do well to remember a simple principle: Within the normal range of environments, children's genetically predisposed tendencies will assert themselves. Moreover, lives also are formed by environmental influences beyond parents' control—by peer influences, by chance events, by all sorts of life experiences.

It may be scary to realize how risky is the business of having and raising children. In procreation a woman and a man shuffle their gene decks and deal a life-forming hand to their child-to-be, who is then subject to countless influences beyond their control. Keeping in mind that lives are formed by influences both within *and* beyond parents' control, we should, perhaps, be slower to credit parents for their children's achievements and slower still to blame them for their children's problems.

Adoption Studies

Adoption studies offer additional clues to the relative contributions of nature and nurture. For any given trait we can ask whether adopted children are more like their adoptive parents, who contribute a home environment, or their biological parents, who contributed their genes. The stunning finding from studying hundreds of adoptive families in Minnesota, Texas, and Colorado is that people who grow up together do *not* much resemble one another in personality, whether biologically related or not (Rowe, 1990).

What we have here is developmental psychology's newest and one of its biggest puzzles: Why are children in the same family so different? Is it because even though siblings share half their genes, each sibling has a very different combination of genes? Is it because each sibling experiences a different environment (differing peer influences, birth orders, life events)?

Adoption studies show that, although the personalities of adopted children do not much resemble those of their adoptive parents, adoption has many effects. First, the home environment influences adopted children's values, beliefs, and social attitudes. Second, in adoptive homes, child neglect and abuse are rare. (Adoptive parents are carefully screened; natural parents are not.) So it is not surprising that nearly all adopted children thrive. They score higher than their biological parents on intelligence tests, and many become happier and more stable people than they would have in a stressed or neglectful environment. Children need not resemble their adoptive parents to have benefitted from adoption.

Nature and Nurture Interact

To say that genes and experience are *both* important is true, but oversimplified. More precisely, they **interact.** Imagine two babies, one genetically predisposed to be attractive, sociable, and easygoing, the other less so. Assume further that the first baby attracts more affectionate and stimulating care than the second, and so develops into a warmer and more outgoing person. As the two children grow older, the more naturally outgoing one seeks activities and friends that encourage further social confidence.

What has caused their resulting personality difference? We cannot say that their personalities are x percent due to genes and y percent to experience, for the gene-experience effect is combined. Asking which factor is more important is like asking whether the area of a soccer field is due more to its length or to its width. In fact, genes *direct* experience (Scarr & McCartney,

---

"*It's a mistake to look at a child and say, 'I'm going to make this child X or Y.' I say . . . let's see what that child does well at and enjoys. Then let's reinforce those kinds of things . . . what people in the past have called gifts.*"

Thomas Bouchard (1990)

Studies of adoptive families have provided new clues to hereditary and environmental influences on development. How similar would you expect adopted children to be to their adoptive parents? To their biological parents?

interaction effect The effect of one influencing factor (such as experience) depends on another (such as genes). Thus, neither factor operates free of the other.

1983). As we grow older we *select* environments well suited to our natures. Moreover, as in our imaginary example, our genetically influenced traits *evoke* significant responses in others. This helps explain why identical twins reared in different families recall their parents' warmth as remarkably similar—almost as similar as if they had the same parents (Plomin & others, 1988). Fraternal twins recall their early family life more differently—even if reared in the same family! Thus, "children experience us as different parents, depending on their own qualities," notes Scarr (1990).

The moral: Our genes influence the experiences that shape us. The correct view, say behavior genetics researchers, is not nature *versus* nurture, but nature *via* nurture.

Continuity and Stages

Adults are vastly different from infants. But do they differ as a giant redwood differs from its seedling—a difference created by gradual, cumulative growth? Or do they differ as a butterfly differs from a caterpillar—a difference of distinct stages?

Generally speaking, researchers who emphasize experience and learning (nurture) see development as a slow, continuous shaping process. Those who emphasize biological maturation (nature) tend to see development as a sequence of genetically predetermined stages or steps. Although progress through the various stages may be quick or slow, everyone passes through the stages in the same order.

Are there clear-cut stages of psychological development as there are physical stages such as crawling before walking? We have considered the stage theories of Jean Piaget on cognitive development, Lawrence Kohlberg on moral development, and Erik Erikson and Daniel Levinson on psychosocial development. And we have seen their stage theories vigorously criticized. Piaget failed to recognize the early rudiments of later abilities. Kohlberg appeared biased by a worldview characteristic of educated males in individualistic cultures. The ideas of Erikson and Levinson are contradicted by research showing that adult life does not progress through a fixed, predictable series of steps.

Although research casts doubt on the idea that life proceeds through neatly defined, age-linked stages, the concept of stage remains useful. There are spurts of brain growth during childhood and puberty that correspond roughly to Piaget's stages (Thatcher & others, 1987). And stage theories contribute a developmental perspective on the whole life span, by suggesting how people of one age think and act differently when they arrive at a later age.

Stability and Change

This leads us to the final question: Over time, are people's personalities consistent, or do they change? If reunited with a long-lost grade school friend, would you instantly recognize that "it's the same old Andy"? Or is a person during one period of life likely to seem like a different person at a later period?

Researchers who have followed lives through time have found evidence for both stability and change. There is continuity to personality and yet, happily for troubled children and adolescents, human development is life-long: The struggles of the present may be laying a foundation for a happier tomorrow. More specifically, researchers generally agree on the following points:

1. The first 2 years of life provide a poor basis for predicting a person's eventual traits. Even children and adolescents often change: Many con-

Preview Question

19. What conclusions can we draw from research on the issues of continuity versus stages and stability versus change in lifelong development?

fused and troubled children have blossomed into mature, successful adults (Macfarlane, 1964; Thomas & Chess, 1986). As people grow older, however, continuity of personality does gradually increase (Costa & McCrae, 1989; Stein & others, 1986).

2. Some characteristics, such as temperament, are more stable than others, such as social attitudes (Moss & Susman, 1980). But attitudes, too, become more stable with age (Krosnick & Alwin, 1989).

3. In some ways, we all change with age. Most shy, fearful toddlers begin opening up by age 4, and during adulthood most of us mellow. In the years after college, most people become calmer and quieter (Costa & McCrae, 1989). Such changes can occur without changing a person's position *relative* to others of the same age. The hard-driving young adult may mellow by later life yet still be a relatively hard-driving senior citizen.

Finally, we should remember that life contains *both* stability and change. Stability enables us to depend on others, motivates our concern for the healthy development of children, and provides our identity. Change motivates our concerns about present influences, sustains our hope for a brighter future, and enables us to adapt and grow with experience.

"At 70, I would say the advantage is that you take life more calmly. You know that 'this, too, shall pass!'"

Eleanor Roosevelt, 1954

Rehearse It

31. Fraternal twins result when
a. a single egg is fertilized by a single sperm and then splits.
b. a single egg is fertilized by two sperm and then splits.
c. two eggs are fertilized by two sperm.
d. two eggs are fertilized by a single sperm.

32. Studies of identical and fraternal twins have found that identical twins are more alike in personality and ability than fraternal twins. This finding points out the importance of
a. genetics or nature.
b. experience or nurture.

c. similar environments.
d. biological maturation.

33. In studying the relative effects of nature and nurture, developmentalists rely on twin studies and adoption studies. Adoption studies seek to reveal genetic influences on personality by
a. comparing adopted with non-adopted children.
b. evaluating whether adopted children more closely resemble their adoptive or biological parents.
c. studying the effect of prior neglect on adopted children.
d. studying the effect of one's age at adoption.

34. Although development is lifelong, there is stability of personality over time. For example,
a. most personality traits emerge in infancy and persist throughout life.
b. temperamental traits tend to remain stable throughout life.
c. few people change significantly after adolescence.
d. people tend to undergo greater personality changes as they age.

Reviewing The Developing Person

1. What are the major issues in developmental psychology?

Developmental psychologists examine our physical, mental, and social development throughout the life span. Three pervading issues create a backdrop for this study. The first is the nature-nurture issue: To what extent is development influenced by our genes and to what extent by our experiences? Second, is development a continuous process or a sequence of distinct stages? Third, are our traits stable throughout life, or do we change?

Prenatal Development and the Newborn

2. How does life develop before birth?

The life cycle begins as one sperm, out of the some 300 million ejaculated, unites with an egg to form a zygote. The zygote inherits from each parent 23 chromosomes containing DNA, the genetic codes. Two weeks later, the developing embryo attaches to the uterine wall, and after 2 months is a recognizably human fetus. Along with nutrients, teratogens ingested by the mother can reach the developing child and possibly place it at risk.

3. What are some of the newborn's capabilities?

Researchers have discovered that newborns are surprisingly competent. They are born with sensory equipment and reflexes that facilitate their interacting with adults and securing nourishment, and they quickly learn to discriminate the smell and sound of their mothers.

Infancy and Childhood

4. How do the brain and motor skills develop during infancy and childhood?

Within the brain, nerve cells form before birth and, sculpted by experience, their interconnections continue to multiply after birth. Infants' more complex physical skills—sitting, standing, walking—develop in a predictable sequence whose actual timing is a function of individual maturation rate.

5. How did Piaget view the mind's development?

Jean Piaget's observations of children convinced him—and almost everyone else—that the mind of the child is not that of a miniature adult. Piaget theorized that the mind develops by forming schemas that help us assimilate our experiences and that change to accommodate new information. In this way, children progress from the sensorimotor simplicity of the infant to more complex stages of thinking. For example, at about 8 months, an infant becomes aware that things still exist even when out of sight. This sense of object permanence coincides with the development of stranger anxiety, which requires the ability to remember who is familiar and who is not.

Piaget believed that preschool children are egocentric and unable to perform simple logical operations. However, he thought that at about age 7 children become capable of performing concrete operations, such as those required to comprehend the principle of conservation. Recent research indicates that young children are not so cognitively incapable as Piaget believed. It seems that the cognitive abilities that emerge at each stage are developing in a rudimentary form in the previous stage.

6. What is attachment, how does it develop, and what effects do early attachment patterns have later in life?

Infants become attached to their mothers and fathers not simply because mothers and fathers gratify biological needs, but, more important, because they are comfortable, familiar, and responsive. If denied such care, both monkey and human infants may become pathetically withdrawn, anxious, and eventually abusive. Once an attachment forms, infants who are separated from their caregiver will, for a time, be distressed. Human infants who display secure attachment to their mothers generally become socially competent preschoolers. Inborn temperament (emotional excitability) also influences parent-child relations.

7. How does a child's behavior provide evidence of an emerging self-concept?

As with cognitive abilities, the concept of self develops gradually. At about age 18 months, infants will recognize themselves in a mirror. By age 10, children's self-images are quite stable, and are linked with their independence, optimism, assertiveness, and sociability.

8. What are the links between parenting styles and children's behavior?

Children who develop a positive self-image and a happy, self-reliant manner tend to have been reared by parents who are neither permissive nor authoritarian, but authoritative without depriving their children of a sense of control over their own lives.

Adolescence

9. What major physical changes occur during adolescence?

Adolescence typically begins at puberty with the onset of rapid growth and developing sexual maturity. Boys seem to benefit from "early" maturation, and girls from "late" maturation.

10. How did Piaget and Kohlberg describe cognitive and moral development during adolescence?

Piaget theorized that adolescents develop the capacity for formal operations, which enables them to reason abstractly. Following Piaget, Lawrence Kohlberg contended that moral thinking likewise proceeds through a sequence of stages, from a preconventional morality of self-interest, to a conventional morality concerned with gaining others' approval or doing one's duty, to (in some people) a postconventional morality of agreed-upon rights or universal ethical principles. However, say Kohlberg's critics, the postconventional stages represent morality from a Western, middle-class, male, individualistic perspective. Other theorists point out that morality also lies in one's actions, which are influenced by one's social situation and inner attitudes as well as by one's moral reasoning.

11. What is involved in the adolescent's search for identity, and how does intimacy develop?

Erik Erikson theorized that a chief task of adolescence is to form one's identity, or sense of self. This often means "trying on" a number of different roles. Men more than women appear to follow Erikson's identity-before-intimacy pattern. For many people the struggle for identity continues in the adult years as new relationships emerge and new roles are assumed.

12. What factors influence teen pregnancy?

Teens are vulnerable to pregnancy when ignorant or blindly optimistic about the risks of pregnancy, when inhibited from using birth control by guilt and minimal communication with parents and partners, and when under the influence of alcohol and mass media modeling of unprotected promiscuity.

Adulthood

13. What major physical changes occur during middle and late adulthood?

The barely perceptible physical declines of early adulthood begin to accelerate during middle adulthood. For women, a significant physical change of adult life is menopause, which generally seems to be a smooth rather than rough transition. After 65, declining perceptual acuity, strength, and stamina are evident, but short-term ailments are fewer. Although neural processes slow, the brain nevertheless remains healthy, except for those who suffer brain disease, such as the progressive deterioration of Alzheimer's disease.

14. How are memory and intelligence influenced by aging?

As the years pass, recognition memory remains strong, although recall memory begins to decline, especially for novel types of information. Research on how intelligence changes with age has progressed through several phases: cross-sectional studies suggesting a steady intellectual decline after early adulthood; longitudinal studies suggesting intellectual stability until very late in life; and an alternative view that, while fluid intelligence declines in later life, crystallized intelligence does not.

15. Why are age-based stage theories of adult development considered controversial?

Several theorists maintain that adults progress through an orderly sequence of age-related stages. Erikson proposes that after the formation of an identity, the young adult must deal with intimacy, achieve generativity in middle adulthood, and in later adulthood gain a sense of integrity. Daniel Levinson contends that moving from one stage to the next entails recurring times of crisis, such as the early-forties time of transition to midlife. Critics contend that

people are not so predictable; life events involving love and work influence adult development in unanticipated ways. Moreover, feelings of well-being are remarkably stable across the life span.

16. What do psychologists view as adulthood's two primary commitments?

Adulthood's two major commitments are love (intimate relationships, especially with family) and work (productive activity, or what Erikson called "generativity").

17. How are the stages attributed to death and dying comparable to other age-based stage theories of adulthood?

People often experience grief lasting a year or more when a loved one dies, especially if death comes before the expected time on the social clock. Although theories of the stages of dying have been criticized, the resulting death-education movement has enabled us to deal more humanely with death and grief.

Reflections on the Major Developmental Issues

18. What conclusions can we draw from research on the nature-nurture issue?

Adoption studies and studies of twins provide scientific support for the idea that genes influence one's developing personality. Developmentalists generally agree that genes *and* environment, biological *and* social factors, direct our life courses, and that their effects often interact, partly because our genetic predispositions influence our formative experiences.

19. What conclusions can we draw from research on the issues of continuity versus stages and stability versus change in lifelong development?

Although the stage theories of Piaget, Kohlberg, and Erikson have been modified in light of later research, the theories usefully alert us to differences among people of different ages. The discovery that people's traits continue to change in later life has helped create the new emphasis that development is lifelong. Nevertheless, research demonstrates that there is also an underlying consistency in most people's temperaments and personality traits, especially after infancy and early childhood.

Terms and Concepts to Remember

developmental psychologists, p. 59

ovum, p. 60

chromosomes, p. 60

DNA (deoxyribonucleic acid), p. 60

genes, p. 60

X chromosome, p. 60

Y chromosome, p. 60

testosterone, p. 60

zygote, p. 60

embryo, p. 61

fetus, p. 61

teratogens, p. 61

fetal alcohol syndrome, p. 61

rooting reflex, p. 62

maturation, p. 63

schema, p. 65

assimilation, p. 66

accommodation, p. 66

cognition, p. 66

sensorimotor stage, p. 66

object permanence, p. 66

Rehearse It Answer Key

1. b.	2. d.	3. c.	4. a.	5. a.	6. b.	7. c.	8. b.	9. d.
10. a.	11. d.	12. a.	13. a.	14. b.	15. c.	16. c.	17. d.	18. d.
19. b.	20. c.	21. a.	22. b.	23. b.	24. d.	25. c.	26. a.	27. d.
28. a.	29. d.	30. c.	31. c.	32. a.	33. b.	34. b.		

Critical Thinking Exercise

You have *Surveyed, Questioned, Read, Rehearsed,* and *Reviewed* Chapter 3. Now take your learning a step further by testing your *critical thinking* skills on the following passage. If you need a refresher course on the concept of critical thinking, turn back to Appendix B before working this exercise.

A recent study (Lucas and others, 1992) revealed that children who were fed breast milk as infants scored higher on intelligence tests than those who received formula only. The study involved 300 premature babies whose mothers chose whether or not to provide breast milk for their infants. Infants in both the breast-milk and formula groups were fed by tube.

As 8-year-olds, children fed breast milk as infants scored 8 points higher in overall IQ than did those fed formula. This difference was observed after statistically adjusting for the social class and maternal education differences between the two groups.

The authors acknowledged that differences between the groups in parenting skills, genetic potential, or motivation to nurture could explain the results. Yet they believe that human milk contains various hormones and other factors that enhance brain growth and maturation. This nutritional advantage should especially benefit premature babies, who are born at a stage of especially rapid brain growth.

Understand the Assertion

1. State the researchers' assertion in your own words. Define all important concepts and terms as they are used in this study.

Consider the Evidence

2. State the evidence for the researchers' assertion. Is this evidence empirical (observable)? Is it based on trustworthy research?

Evaluate the Explanation

3. Evaluate the researchers' proposed explanation.
   a. Restate it in your own words.
   b. Determine whether the explanation makes sense based on the evidence.
   c. State an alternative explanation.

Check your progress on becoming a critical thinker by comparing your answers to the sample answers found in Appendix B.

Sensation and Perception

sensation The process by which our sense receptors and nervous system receive and represent stimulus energies from our environment.

perception The process of organizing and interpreting sensory information, enabling us to recognize meaningful objects and events.

In a silent, cushioned, inner world of utter darkness floats your brain. From the outer world, myriad stimuli bombard your body. These facts raise a fundamental question that predates psychology by thousands of years and helped inspire its beginnings some 100 years ago: *How does the world out there get in?*

To grasp how the world out there gets represented inside our heads, three computer concepts are useful: input, processing, and output. As Figure 4–1 illustrates, physical objects emit or reflect energy. Our sensory organs detect this energy (input) and encode it into neural signals that our brains organize and interpret (processing) as conscious experiences (output). The resulting perceptions affect our reactions, which may in turn modify our perceptions. The inexperienced softball outfielder who runs in too far to catch fly balls soon learns to judge them better.

Sensation refers to how our sense receptors and nervous system physically represent our external environment. **Perception** refers to how we mentally organize and interpret this information. Although sensation and perception are actually one continuous process, we will look at perception as a mental process that takes up where sensation, its physiological base, leaves off. To recognize, say, an ⌓ and an ⌃ as *A*s and not *H*s or *R*s, we must be capable of sensing (detecting, encoding) and perceiving (organizing, interpreting) information. Sensation provides the raw information that perception constructs into our experiences.

Figure 4–1 How we process sensory input into a meaningful conscious experience.

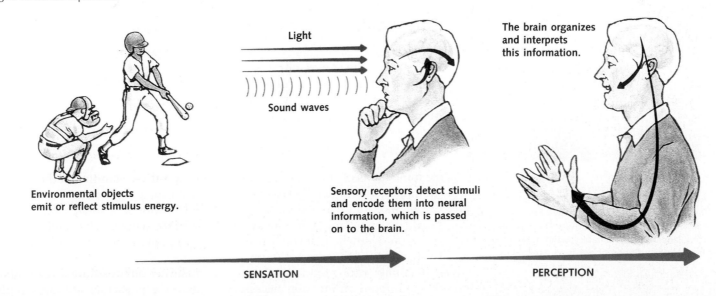

Environmental objects emit or reflect stimulus energy.

Light

Sound waves

Sensory receptors detect stimuli and encode them into neural information, which is passed on to the brain.

The brain organizes and interprets this information.

SENSATION

PERCEPTION

absolute threshold The minimum stimulation needed to detect a particular stimulus.

subliminal Below one's absolute threshold for conscious awareness.

You probably sensed the colors here in an instant. But it takes longer to construct mentally (to perceive) all of the meaningful images in this Bev Doolittle painting, "The Forest Has Eyes."

(a)

(b)

These two photographs show a flower as it appears (a) to the human eye and (b) to the eye of a bee. The bee's ability to perceive ultraviolet wavelengths enables it to see the "landing field" invisible to the human eye, and makes possible more efficient food gathering.

Sensing the World: Some Basic Principles

Sensory systems enable organisms to obtain the information they need to function and survive. A frog, which feeds on flying insects, has eyes with receptor cells that fire only in response to small, dark, moving objects. A frog could starve to death, knee-deep in motionless flies, but let one zoom by and the frog's "bug detector" cells snap awake. A male silkworm moth has receptors so sensitive to the odor of the female sex-attractant that a single female silkworm moth need release only a billionth of an ounce per second to attract every male silkworm moth within a mile. Which is why there continue to be silkworms. We humans are similarly designed to detect what are, for us, the important features of our environments. Nature's sensory gifts suit the needs of each particular recipient. The human ear, thankfully, is most sensitive to the sound frequencies of the human voice.

Thresholds

We exist in a sea of energy. At this moment, you and I are being struck by x-rays and radio waves, ultraviolet and infrared light, very high and very low frequency sound waves. But to all of them we are blind and deaf. The shades on our senses, our windows on the world, are open just a crack, allowing us only a restricted awareness of this vast sea.

Absolute Thresholds

To some kinds of stimuli we are exquisitely sensitive. Standing at the top of a mountain on an utterly dark, clear night, we can, given normal senses, see a candle flame atop another mountain 30 miles away. In a silent room, we can hear a watch ticking 20 feet away. We can feel the wing of a bee falling on our cheek and smell a single drop of perfume in a three-room apartment (Galanter, 1962).

Our awareness of these faint stimuli illustrates our **absolute thresholds**—the minimum stimulation necessary to detect a particular stimulus (light,

Preview Question

1. What is an absolute threshold, and are we influenced by stimuli below it?

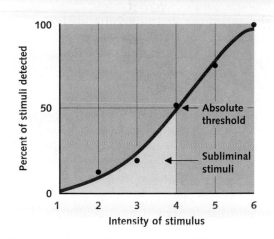

Figure 4–2 The absolute threshold is arbitrarily measured as the intensity at which we perceive a stimulus 50 percent of the time. As you can see from the graph, to be a subliminal stimulus merely means that we perceive it *less* than 50 percent of the time.

Sprinkled throughout the next several chapters you will find evidence that we process enormous amounts of information automatically, unintentionally, without awareness.

"The heart has its reasons which reason does not know."

Pascal
Pensees, 1670

"Finding the occasional straw of truth awash in a great ocean of confusion and bamboozle requires intelligence, vigilance, dedication and courage [without which] we risk becoming a nation of suckers, up for grabs by the next charlatan who comes along."

Carl Sagan (1987)

sound, pressure, taste, odor). To measure absolute threshold, we record the stimulation needed for detection 50 percent of the time. For example, to test your absolute threshold for sounds, a hearing specialist exposes each ear to varying sound levels. For each pitch, the hearing test defines where half the time you correctly detect the sound and half the time you do not. For each of the senses, that 50–50 point defines your absolute threshold.

Subliminal Stimulation

In 1956, controversy erupted over a report that New Jersey movie audiences were unwittingly being influenced by the imperceptible flashed messages DRINK COCA-COLA and EAT POPCORN. Nearly 40 years later, the controversy has erupted anew. Advertisers are said to manipulate consumers by imperceptibly printing the word *sex* on crackers and embedding erotic images in liquor ads. Rock recordings are said to contain "satanic messages" that can be heard if the recordings are played backward and that can unconsciously persuade the unwitting listener, even when played normally. Entrepreneurs offer to help us lose weight, stop smoking, or improve our memories with audiotapes of soothing ocean sounds that contain unheard messages such as, "I am thin," "Smoke tastes bad," and "I do well on tests. I have total recall of information." These claims make two assumptions: that unconsciously we can sense **subliminal** (literally, "below threshold") stimuli (Figure 4–2); and that, without our awareness, these stimuli have extraordinary suggestive powers. Can we? Do they?

Can we be affected by stimuli too weak for us *ever* to notice? Recent experiments hint that, under certain conditions, the answer may be yes. In one experiment, students were repeatedly flashed a series of geometric figures, each for less than 0.01 second—long enough to perceive only a spark of light (Kunst-Wilson & Zajonc, 1980). The students later saw a series of figures which included the ones earlier flashed subliminally. They reported liking the presented figures more than figures that had not been flashed, even though they had no idea which were which. Sometimes we *feel* what we do not know and cannot describe. A weak stimulus evidently triggers a weak response that evokes a feeling, though not conscious awareness of the stimulus.

But does the fact of subliminal *sensation* verify entrepreneurial claims of subliminal *persuasion?* The near-consensus among research psychologists is no. Their verdict is like that of astronomers who say that, yes, astrologers are right that stars and planets are out there, but no, they don't directly affect us. Consider: The laboratory research reveals a subtle, fleeting effect on cognition. Subliminal tape hucksters claim something different: a powerful, enduring effect on behavior.

Moreover, new experiments, such as one described in Chapter 1, show that commercial subliminal tapes have no effect beyond one's belief in them (the placebo effect).

Earlier studies produced similar results, discounting the threat of "hidden persuasion" through subliminal ads (Moore, 1988). Shortly after news of the supposed EAT POPCORN effect swept North America in the mid-50's, the Canadian Broadcasting Corporation used a popular Sunday night TV show to flash a subliminal message 352 times (*Advertising Age,* 1958). Asked to guess the message, none of the almost 500 letter-writers did so. Nearly half, however, did report feeling strangely hungry or thirsty during the show. But this was merely an effect of expectations. The actual message was TELEPHONE NOW. The effect of these 352 subliminal messages on Canadian telephone usage? Zilch. All the evidence considered, say researchers Anthony Pratkanis and Anthony Greenwald (1988), "Subliminal procedures offer little or nothing of value to the marketing practitioner."

Difference Thresholds

To function effectively, we need absolute thresholds low enough to allow us to detect important sights, sounds, textures, tastes, and smells. We also need to detect small differences among stimuli. A musician must detect minute discrepancies in an instrument's tuning. A wine taster must detect the slight flavor difference between two vintage wines.

The **difference threshold** (also called the **just noticeable difference**, or **jnd**) is the minimum difference a person can detect between any two stimuli 50 percent of the time. The difference threshold varies with the magnitude of the stimulus. Add 1 ounce to a 10-ounce weight and you will detect the difference; add 1 ounce to a 10-*pound* weight and you will not, because the difference threshold has increased. More than a century ago, Ernst Weber noted that regardless of their magnitude, two stimuli must differ by a constant proportion for their difference to be perceptible. This principle—that the difference threshold is not a constant amount but some constant *proportion* of the stimulus—is so simple and so widely applicable that we still refer to it as **Weber's law.** The exact proportion varies, depending on the stimulus. For the average person to perceive their differences, two lights must differ in intensity by 8 percent, two objects must differ in weight by 2 percent, and two tones must differ in frequency by only 0.3 percent (Teghtsoonian, 1971).

Weber's law is a rough approximation that works well for nonextreme sensory stimuli. It also parallels some of our life experiences. If the price of a 50-cent candy bar goes up by a nickel, shoppers might notice the change; similarly, a $5,000 price hike in a $50,000 Mercedes-Benz might raise the eyebrows of its potential buyers. In both cases, the price went up by 10 percent. Weber's principle: Our thresholds for detecting differences are a roughly constant proportion of the size of the original stimulus.

Sensory Adaptation

Entering your neighbor's living room, you smell an unpleasant odor. You wonder how she tolerates it, but within minutes you no longer notice it. Jumping into a swimming pool, you shiver and complain how cold it is; a short while later a friend arrives and you exclaim, "C'mon in. Water's fine!" These examples illustrate **sensory adaptation**—our diminishing sensitivity to an unchanging stimulus. (To experience this phenomenon, move your watch up your wrist an inch: You will feel it—but only for a few moments.) After constant exposure to a stimulus, our nerve cells fire less frequently.

Why, then, if we stare at an object without flinching, does it not vanish from sight? Because, unnoticed by us, our eyes are always moving, quivering just enough to guarantee that the retinal image continually changes. (For 9 in 10 people—but only 1 in 3 schizophrenia patients—this eye flutter turns off when the eye is following a moving target [Holzman & Matthysse, 1990].)

What if we could stop our eyes from moving? Would sights seem to vanish, as odors do? To find out, psychologists have devised ingenious instruments for maintaining a constant image on the retina. Imagine that we fitted a subject, Mary, with one of these instruments—a miniature projector mounted on a contact lens (Figure 4–3a). When Mary's eye moves, the projected image moves as well. Thus, everywhere that Mary looks the scene is sure to go.

If we project the profile of a face through such an instrument, what will Mary see? At first she will see the complete profile. But within a few seconds, as her sense receptors begin to fatigue, a strange phenomenon occurs. Bit by bit, the image will vanish, only later to reappear and then disappear—in recognizable fragments or as a whole (Figure 4–3b).

Preview Question

2. How is our threshold for detecting differences affected by the magnitude of the stimuli?

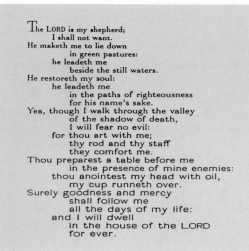

The LORD is my shepherd;
  I shall not want.
He maketh me to lie down
    in green pastures:
    he leadeth me
      beside the still waters.
He restoreth my soul:
    he leadeth me
    in the paths of righteousness
      for his name's sake.
Yea, though I walk through the valley
    of the shadow of death,
    I will fear no evil:
    for thou art with me;
      thy rod and thy staff
      they comfort me.
Thou preparest a table before me
    in the presence of mine enemies:
    thou anointest my head with oil,
      my cup runneth over.
Surely goodness and mercy
      shall follow me
      all the days of my life:
    and I will dwell
      in the house of the LORD
        for ever.

The difference threshold. In this computer-generated copy of Psalm 23, each line of the typeface changes imperceptibly. How many lines are required for you to experience a just noticeable difference?

Preview Question

3. What function does sensory adaptation serve?

"We need above all to know about changes; no one wants or needs to be reminded 16 hours a day that his shoes are on."

Neuroscientist David Hubel (1979)

difference threshold The minimum difference in stimulation that a subject can detect 50 percent of the time. We experience the difference threshold as a just noticeable difference (jnd).

just noticeable difference (jnd) See *difference threshold*.

Weber's law The principle that, to perceive their difference, two stimuli must differ by a constant minimum percentage (rather than a constant amount).

sensory adaptation Diminished sensitivity that is a consequence of constant stimulation.

Although sensory adaptation reduces our sensitivity, it offers an important benefit: It enables us to focus our attention on *informative* changes in our environment without being distracted by the uninformative, constant stimulation of garments, odors, and street noise. Our sense receptors are alert to novelty; bore them with repetition and they free our attention for things more interesting and important. This reinforces a fundamental lesson: We perceive the world not exactly as it is, but as it is useful for us to perceive it.

Sensory thresholds and adaptation are not the only commonalities among the senses. All the senses receive sensory stimulation, transform it into neural information, and deliver that information to the brain. How do the senses work? Let us find out by beginning with vision, the most thoroughly studied of our windows on the world.

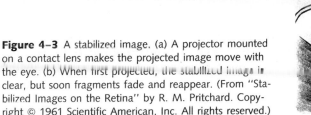
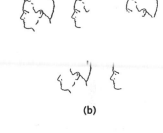

(a) (b)

Figure 4–3 A stabilized image. (a) A projector mounted on a contact lens makes the projected image move with the eye. (b) When first projected, the stabilized image is clear, but soon fragments fade and reappear. (From "Stabilized Images on the Retina" by R. M. Pritchard. Copyright © 1961 Scientific American, Inc. All rights reserved.)

Rehearse It

1. To construct meaning out of our external environment, we organize and interpret sensory information. This process is
a. sensation.
b. persuasion.
c. encoding.
d. perception.

2. The absolute threshold is the minimum stimulation that a person can detect 50 percent of the time. Knowing your absolute threshold for sound tells you
a. the smallest difference you can detect between two sounds.
b. how likely you are to hear a particular faint sound.
c. why you become used to background noise.
d. whether you are being affected by subliminal stimulation.

3. People wonder whether subliminal stimuli, such as undetectably faint sights or sounds, influence us. Subliminal stimuli are
a. too weak to be processed by the brain in any way.
b. below the absolute threshold of awareness.
c. consciously perceived only 50 percent of the time.
d. strong enough to affect our behavior.

4. Confronted with an unchanging stimulus, we experience sensory adaptation. Sensory adaptation explains why
a. we perceive subliminal stimuli.
b. we notice only large differences between two stimuli.
c. we soon get used to an unpleasant smell.
d. we have difficulty keeping our eyes completely still when staring at an object.

5. To be perceived as different, two lights must differ in intensity by at least 8 percent. This illustrates a general principle called Weber's law, which states that for a difference to be perceived, two stimuli must differ by
a. a fixed or constant amount.
b. a constant minimum percentage.
c. a constantly changing amount.
d. more than 7 percent.

6. Sensory adaptation reduces our sensitivity to some stimuli in the environment. However, sensory adaptation has survival benefits. It helps us focus on
a. the world as it really is.
b. underlying phenomena and stimuli.
c. important changes in the environment.
d. constant features of the environment.

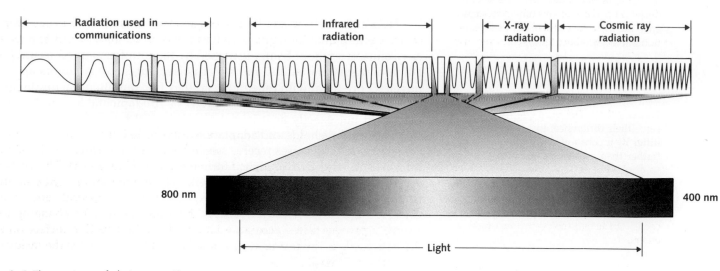

| Radiation used in communications | Infrared radiation | X-ray radiation | Cosmic ray radiation |

800 nm | Light | 400 nm

Figure 4–4 The spectrum of electromagnetic energy ranges from radio waves over a mile long to gamma rays as short as the diameter of an atom. The narrow band of wavelengths visible to the human eye (shown enlarged) extends from the longer waves of red light to the shorter waves of blue-violet light. Other organisms are sensitive to differing portions of the spectrum. As we noted earlier, bees cannot see red, but can see ultraviolet light, the part of the spectrum that causes sunburn in humans.

Preview Question

4. How does the eye transform light energy into neural messages?

Vision

Part of your taken-for-granted genius is your body's ability to convert one sort of energy to another. Our sensory systems convert stimulus energy into neural messages. Your eye, for example, receives light energy and manages an amazing feat: It transforms it into neural messages. Let's see how.

The Stimulus Input: Light Energy

Scientifically speaking, what strikes our eyes is not color but pulses of electromagnetic energy that our visual system experiences as color. What we see as visible light is but a thin slice of the whole spectrum of electromagnetic radiation. As Figure 4–4 illustrates, the electromagnetic spectrum ranges from the long pulses or waves of radio transmission to the narrow band of the spectrum that we see as visible light to the extremely short waves of cosmic rays.

Two physical characteristics of light help determine our sensory experience of it. Its **wavelength**—the distance from one wave peak to the next (Figure 4–5a)—determines its **hue** (the color that we experience, such as blue or green). **Intensity,** the amount of energy in light waves (determined by their *amplitude*), influences brightness (Figure 4–5b). Although the spectrum of vis-

Figure 4–5 The physical properties of electromagnetic energy. (a) Waves vary in wavelength, the distance between successive peaks. Frequency, the number of complete wavelengths that can pass a point in a given time, depends on the wavelength. The shorter the wavelength, the higher the frequency. (b) Waves also vary in amplitude, the height from peak to trough. Wave amplitude determines the intensity of colors and sounds.

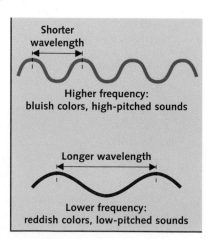

Shorter wavelength

Higher frequency: bluish colors, high-pitched sounds

Longer wavelength

Lower frequency: reddish colors, low-pitched sounds

(a)

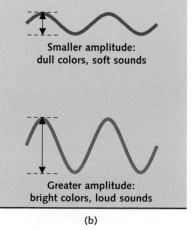

Smaller amplitude: dull colors, soft sounds

Greater amplitude: bright colors, loud sounds

(b)

wavelength The distance from the peak of one light or sound wave to the peak of the next. Electromagnetic wavelengths vary from the long pulses of radio transmission to the short blips of cosmic rays.

hue The dimension of color that is determined by the wavelength of light; what we know as the color names (blue, green, and so forth).

intensity The amount of energy in a light or sound wave, which we perceive as brightness or loudness, as determined by the wave's amplitude.

pupil The adjustable opening in the center of the eye through which light enters.

iris A ring of muscle tissue that forms the colored portion of the eye around the pupil and controls the size of the pupil opening.

lens The transparent structure behind the pupil that changes shape to focus images on the retina.

accommodation 1. The process by which the eye's lens changes shape to focus the image of near objects on the retina. 2. Adapting one's current understandings (schemas) to incorporate new information.

retina The light-sensitive inner surface of the eye, containing the receptor rods and cones plus layers of neurons that begin the processing of visual information.

ible light is a continuum of wavelengths, we humans tend to see four basic colors in it: red, yellow, green, and blue-violet. To understand *how* we transform physical energy into a sensation of color, we first need to understand our visual system's structure.

The Eye

In some ways, the eye functions like a camera. In both eye and camera, light enters through a small opening, behind which a lens focuses the incoming rays into an image on a light-sensitive surface (Figure 4–6). The eye's small opening is the **pupil.** Its size, and therefore the amount of light entering the eye, is regulated by the **iris,** a colored muscle that surrounds and dilates or constricts the pupil. The **lens** focuses the incoming rays by changing its curvature, a process called **accommodation.** The light-sensitive surface on which the rays focus is the **retina,** the multilayered tissue that lines the inside of the back of the eyeball.

For centuries, scientists have known that when the image of a candle passed through a small opening, its mirror image appeared inverted on a dark wall behind. This fact had scholars baffled. If the retina receives an upside-down image as shown in Figure 4–6, how can we see the world right side up? Did the optic nerve twist the image right side up by the time it reached the cortex? Eventually scientists discovered that the retina doesn't read the image as a whole. Rather, its millions of receptor cells convert light energy into neural impulses. These impulses are sent to the brain and assembled *there* to create a perceived, upright-seeming image.

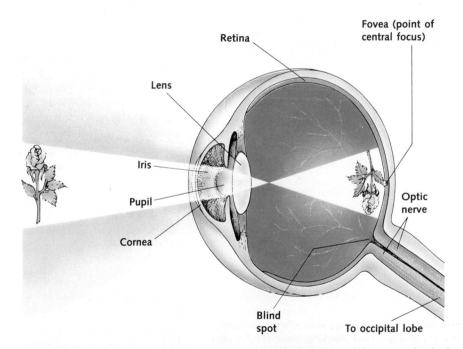

Figure 4–6 The eye. Light rays reflected from the rose pass through the cornea, pupil, and lens. The curvature and thickness of the lens change (accommodate) to bring either nearby or distant objects into focus on the retina. Light rays travel in straight lines. So rays from the top of the rose strike the bottom of the retina and those from the left side of the rose strike the right side of the retina. The rose's retinal image is thus upside-down and reversed.

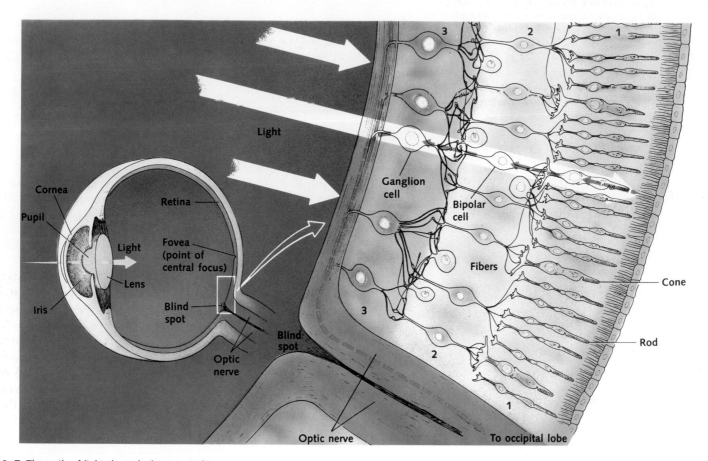

Figure 4–7 The path of light through the eye. Before signals from the retina reach the brain, they pass through a switchboard of neural cells. A ray of light entering the eye triggers a photochemical reaction in the rods and cones (1) at the back of the retina behind the other neural layers. This chemical reaction in turn triggers the bipolar cells (2). The bipolar cells then activate the ganglion cells (3), which converge to form the optic nerve. The optic nerve transmits information to the brain's occipital lobe.

The Retina

If we were to follow a single particle of light energy into the eye, we would see that it first makes its way through the retina's outer layer of cells to its buried receptor cells, the **rods** and **cones** (Figure 4–7). When struck by light energy, chemical changes in the rods and cones generate neural signals that activate the neighboring *bipolar cells,* which in turn activate their neighboring *ganglion cells.* The axons from the network of ganglion cells converge like the strands of a rope to form an **optic nerve** that carries information to the brain. Nearly a million messages can be sent by the optic nerve at once, through nearly a million ganglion fibers. Where the optic nerve leaves the eye there are no receptor cells—creating a **blind spot** (Figure 4–8).

Rods are responsible for black-and-white vision; cones enable you to see color. As illumination diminishes, the cones adjust quickly, the rods more slowly. However, the rods remain more sensitive in dim light, to which the

Figure 4–8 The blind spot. Where the optic nerve leaves the eye (Figure 4–7), there are no receptor cells. This creates a blind spot in our vision. To demonstrate, close your left eye, look at the spot, and move the page to a distance from your face (about 9 inches) at which the oncoming car disappears. In everyday vision the blind spot doesn't impair your vision because your eyes are moving and because one eye covers what the other misses.

rods Retinal receptors that detect black, white, and gray; necessary for peripheral and twilight vision, when cones don't respond.

cones Receptor cells concentrated near the center of the retina that function in daylight or in well-lit conditions, the cones detect fine detail and give rise to color sensations.

optic nerve The nerve that carries neural impulses from the eye to the brain.

blind spot The point at which the optic nerve leaves the eye, creating a "blind" spot because no receptor cells are located there.

Knowing just this much about the eye, can you imagine why a cat sees so much better at night than you do? (See page 114.)

Table 4-1
The Human Eye

	Cones	Rods
Number	6 million	120 million
Location in retina	Center	Periphery
Sensitivity in dim light	Low	High
Color sensitive?	Yes	No

cones do not respond (Table 4–1). That is why you don't see colors in dim light. So when we enter a darkened theater or turn off the light at night, the pupils dilate to allow more light to reach the rods in the retina's periphery. Typically it takes 20 minutes or more before our eyes fully adapt. You can demonstrate dark adaptation by closing one eye for up to 20 minutes, then making the room light not quite bright enough to read this book with your open eye. Now open the dark-adapted eye, and read. This period of dark adaptation is yet another instance of the remarkable adaptiveness of our sensory systems, for it parallels the average twilight transition between the sun's setting and darkness.

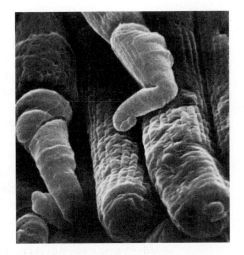

Rod-shaped rods and cone-shaped cones as shown by a scanning electron microscope. Rods are more light-sensitive than the color-sensitive cones, which is why the world looks colorless at night. Some nocturnal animals, such as toads, mice, rats, and bats, have retinas made up almost entirely of rods. Others, such as chickens, have only cones; thus the phrase "to go to bed and get up with the chickens."

Visual Information Processing

We process visual information at progressively more abstract levels. At the entry level, the retina processes information before routing it to the cortex. The retina's neural layers are not just passing along electrical impulses; they also help to encode and analyze the sensory information. The information

Preview Question

5. How is visual information processed in the brain?

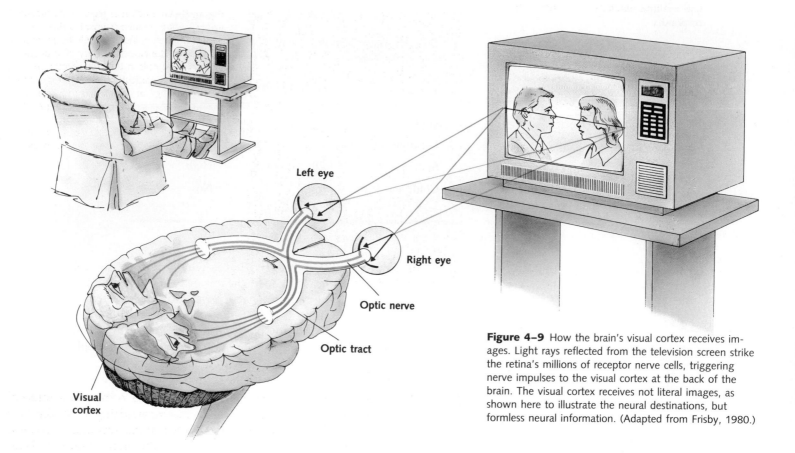

Figure 4–9 How the brain's visual cortex receives images. Light rays reflected from the television screen strike the retina's millions of receptor nerve cells, triggering nerve impulses to the visual cortex at the back of the brain. The visual cortex receives not literal images, as shown here to illustrate the neural destinations, but formless neural information. (Adapted from Frisby, 1980.)

Turn your eyes to the left, close them, and then gently rub the right side of your right eyelid with your fingertip. Note the patch of light to the left, moving as your finger moves. Why do you see light? Why at the left? (See page 117.)

Answer to the question on page 113: There are two reasons: A cat's pupils can open much wider than yours, letting in more light; and a cat has a higher proportion of light-sensitive rods. But there is a trade-off: With its fewer cones, a cat can't see details or color as well as you do.

from the retina's nearly 130 million receptor rods and cones is received and transmitted by the million or so ganglion cells, whose fibers make up the optic nerve. But most information processing occurs in the brain. Any given area of the retina relays its information to a corresponding location in the visual cortex at the back of the brain (Figure 4–9).

Feature Detection

When individual ganglion cells register information in their region of the visual field, they send signals to the visual cortex. Nobelists David Hubel and Torsten Wiesel (1979) believe that when certain cortical neurons, called **feature detectors,** receive this information, they respond only to specific features of a scene—to particular bars, edges, and lines. From these elements the brain assembles the perceived image.

For example, Hubel and Wiesel report that a given brain cell might respond maximally to a line flashed at a particular tilt. If the line is tilted further—say, from a 2 o'clock to a 3 o'clock or 1 o'clock position—the cell quiets down (Figure 4–10). Thus, the feature detector cells record amazingly specific features from the visual information taken in by the eye. Feature detector cells pass this information to other cells that respond only to more complex patterns, such as a particular angle formed by two lines. Still higher level brain cells respond only to specific visual stimuli, such as a face or an arm movement in a particular direction (Perrett & others, 1988). The basic idea, then, is that complex perceptions arise from the interaction of many neural systems, each performing a simple task.

feature detectors Nerve cells in the brain that respond to specific features of the stimulus, such as movement, angle, or shape.

parallel processing Information processing in which several aspects of a problem are processed simultaneously. The brain's natural mode of information processing for many functions, including vision; contrasts with the step-by-step (serial) processing of most computers and of conscious problem solving.

Figure 4–10 Electrodes record how individual cells in this monkey's visual cortex respond to different visual stimuli. Hubel and Wiesel won the Nobel prize for their discovery that most cells in the visual cortex respond only to particular features—for example, to the edge of a surface, or to a line at a 30-degree angle in the upper right part of the field of vision. More complex features trigger higher level detector cells, which integrate information from these simpler ones.

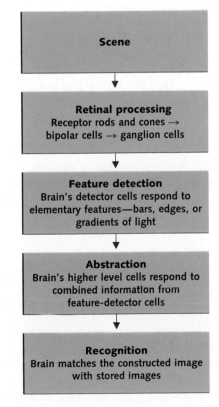

Figure 4–11 A simplified summary of visual information processing.

Parallel Processing

Neural impulses travel a million times slower than a computer's internal messages, yet the brain humbles any computer by recognizing a familiar face instantly. It does this by processing the visual components simultaneously—a procedure called **parallel processing.** For example, the brain divides a visual scene into subdimensions such as color, depth, movement, and form and works on each aspect simultaneously (Livingstone & Hubel, 1988).

The distribution of visual tasks to different neural work teams explains a strange phenomenon. After a stroke, people may lose just one aspect of vision. A person may perceive color but not movement. If something moves, it disappears until it stops. Other brain-damaged victims can tell you all about the subdimensions of an object—the size and color of a rose, for instance, or the features of a family member's face—without recognizing the object or the person. This reminds us of an important truth: Our brains do many things at once, automatically and without our awareness.

The other senses process information with similar speed and intricacy. Opening the back door, you recognize the aroma wafting from the kitchen even before stepping inside. Answering the phone, you recognize the friend calling from the moment she says "hi." Within a fraction of a second after such events stimulate the senses, millions of neurons have simultaneously extracted the essential features, compared them with past experience, and identified the stimulus (Freeman, 1991).

This emerging scientific understanding of the senses illustrates neuropsychologist Roger Sperry's (1985) reflection: The "insights of science give added, not lessened, reasons for awe, respect, and reverence." Think about it: As you look at someone, the visual information is sent to your brain as millions of neural impulses, then reassembled into its component features, and finally, in some as yet mysterious way, composed into a consciously perceived, meaningful image. The whole process (Figure 4–11) is as complex as taking a car apart, piece by piece, transporting it to a different location, then having specialized workers reconstruct it. That all of this happens instantly, effortlessly, and continuously is indeed awesome.

6. What theories contribute to our understanding of color vision, and how are we affected by color constancy?

Color Vision

In the study of vision, one of the most basic and intriguing mysteries is how we see the world in color—and in such a multitude of colors. Our difference threshold for colors is so low that we can discriminate some 7 million different shades (Geldard, 1972).

At least most of us can. For about 1 in 50 people, vision is color-deficient—and that person is probably male, because the defect is genetically sex-linked. To understand why some people have color-deficient vision we must first understand how normal color vision works.

Modern detective work on the mystery of color vision began in the nineteenth century when Hermann von Helmholtz built on the insights of an English physicist, Thomas Young. They recognized a clue in the fact that any color can be created by combining the light waves of three primary colors—red, green, and blue. Young and Helmholtz inferred that the eye must have three types of receptors, one for each primary color (Figure 4–12).

Many years later, researchers measured the response of various cones to different color stimuli and confirmed the **Young-Helmholtz trichromatic (three-color) theory,** which simply states that the retina has three types of color receptors, each especially sensitive to one of three colors. And surprise! Those colors are, indeed, red, green, and blue. When we stimulate combinations of these cones, we see other colors. For example, there are no receptors especially sensitive to yellow. Yet when both red- and green-sensitive cones are stimulated, we see yellow. Most color-deficient people are not actually "color blind." Rather, they simply lack functioning red- or green-sensitive cones. Their vision is dichromatic (two-color) instead of trichromatic, making it difficult to distinguish red and green, as in Figure 4–13 (Boynton, 1979). Dogs, too, lack receptors for the wavelengths of red, giving them only limited, dichromatic color vision (Neitz & others, 1989).

Soon after Young and von Helmholtz proposed the trichromatic theory, physiologist Ewald Hering pointed out that other parts of the color vision mystery remained unsolved. For example, we see yellow when mixing red and green light. But how is it that people blind to red and green can often still see yellow? And why does yellow appear to be a pure color and not a mixture of red and green, as purple does of red and blue?

Hering found one clue in the well-known occurrence of *afterimages*. When you stare at a green square for a while and then look at a white sheet of paper, you will see red, green's *opponent color*. Stare at a yellow square and you will later see its opponent color, blue, on the white paper (as in the flag demonstration in Figure 4–14). Hering surmised that there were two additional color

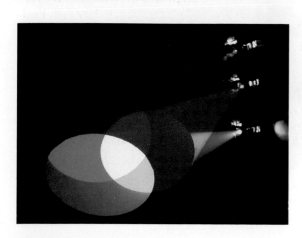

Figure 4–12 The three primary colors of light mix to create other colors. For example, red and green combine to create yellow. All three—red, green, and blue—combine to create white.

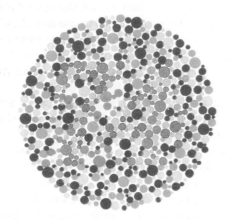

Figure 4–13 Color-deficient vision. People who suffer red-green blindness have trouble perceiving the number within the design above.

Figure 4–14 Afterimage effect. Stare at the center of the flag for a minute and then shift your eyes to the dot in the white space beside it. What do you see?

Young-Helmholtz trichromatic (three-color) theory The theory that the retina contains three different color receptors—one most sensitive to red, one to green, one to blue—which when combined can produce the perception of any color.

opponent-process theory The theory that opposing retinal processes (red-green, yellow-blue, white-black) enable color vision. For example, some cells are stimulated by green and inhibited by red; others are stimulated by red and inhibited by green.

color constancy Perceiving familiar objects as having consistent color, even if changing illumination alters the wavelengths reflected by the object.

Answer to question on page 114: Your retinal cells are so responsive that even pressure triggers them. But your brain interprets their firing as light. Moreover, it interprets the light as coming from the left—which is where light normally comes from when it activates the right side of the retina.

"Only mind has sight and hearing; all things else are deaf and blind."

Epicharmus
Fragments, 550 B.C.

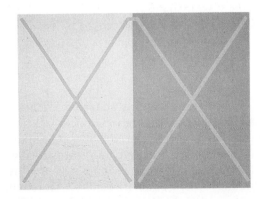

Figure 4–15 Color depends on context. In this painting by Joseph Albers (1975), the unchanging line *seems* to vary from gray to yellow as its surrounding context changes.

processes, one responsible for red versus green perception, and one for blue versus yellow.

A century later, researchers confirmed Hering's **opponent-process theory.** *After* leaving the receptor cells, visual information is analyzed in terms of the opponent colors red and green, blue and yellow, and also black and white. In the retina and in the thalamus (where impulses from the retina are relayed en route to the visual cortex) some neurons are turned "on" by red, but turned "off" by green. Others are turned on by green, but off by red. Both cannot be turned on at the same time. Opponent processes explain afterimages, such as in the flag demonstration, in which we tire our green receptors by staring at green. When we then stare at white (which contains all colors, including red), only the red part of the green/red pairing will fire normally.

The present solution to the mystery of color vision is therefore roughly this: Color processing occurs in two stages. The retina's red, green, and blue cones respond in varying degrees to different color stimuli, as the Young-Helmholtz trichromatic theory suggested. Their signals are then processed by the nervous system's opponent-process cells, en route to the visual cortex.

Color Constancy

Perhaps you have pondered the old question, "If a tree falls in the forest and no one hears it, does it make a sound?" We can ask the same of color: If no one sees a "red" tomato, is it red?

The answer is no. First, the tomato is everything *but* red, because it *rejects* (reflects) the long wavelengths of red. Second, the tomato's color is our mental construction. Color, like all aspects of vision, resides not in the object but in the theater of our brains. Even while dreaming, we may perceive objects in color. Clearly, our experience of color depends on something more than the wavelength information received by our trichromatic cones and transmitted through the opponent-process cells of our thalamus.

That something more is the surrounding *context.* If you view only part of a tomato, without knowing what it is, its color will seem to change as the light changes. But if you see the whole tomato as one item in a bowl of fresh vegetables, its color will remain roughly constant as the lighting shifts—a phenomenon known as **color constancy.** Dorothea Jameson (1985) notes that a green leaf hanging from a brown branch may, when the illumination changes, now reflect the same light energy that formerly came from the brown branch. Yet to us the leaf remains greenish and the branch remains brownish.

We take this color constancy for granted, but the phenomenon is remarkable. It demonstrates that our experience of color comes not just from the object—the color is not in the isolated leaf—but from everything around it as well. You and I see color thanks to our brains' computations of the light reflected by any object *relative to its surrounding objects.*

In an unvarying context, we maintain color constancy. But what if we change the context? Because the brain computes the color of an object relative to its context, the perceived color changes (as is dramatically apparent in Figure 4–15). This principle—that we perceive objects not in isolation but in their environmental context—is especially significant for artists, interior decorators, and clothing designers. The color of a wall or of a swatch of paint on a canvas is determined not just by the paint in the can but by the surrounding colors. The color resides not in the paint, but in our heads.

Rehearse It

7. The blind spot is located in the area of the retina
a. where there are rods but no cones.
b. where there are cones but no rods.
c. where the optic nerve leaves the eye.
d. where the bipolar cells meet the ganglion cells.

8. Rods and cones are the eye's receptor cells. Cones are especially sensitive to _____ light and are responsible for our _____ vision.
a. bright, black and white
b. dim, color
c. bright, color
d. dim, black and white

9. According to Hubel and Wiesel, the brain includes cells that respond maximally to certain bars, edges, and angles. These cells are called

a. rods and cones.
b. feature detector cells.
c. bug detectors.
d. ganglion cells.

10. Unlike most computers, the brain is capable of simultaneously processing separate aspects of an object or problem. This ability we call
a. parallel processing.
b. feature detection.
c. recognition.
d. accommodation.

11. The opponent-process theory of color vision notes that some neurons are turned on by red and turned off by green (or vice versa), and that other opposing color pairs are blue and yellow, and white and black. The theory explains why

a. some people are born with color-deficient vision.
b. different cones respond to different color stimuli.
c. we cannot easily distinguish colors in dim light.
d. staring at a green stimulus, then at white, produces a red afterimage.

12. We perceive well-known objects, for example, tomatoes and stringbeans, as consistently red and green, even though shifting illumination may alter their reflective wavelengths. This demonstrates the phenomenon of
a. afterimages.
b. color constancy.
c. trichromatic vision.
d. color processing.

The Other Senses

For humans, vision is the major sense. More of our brain cortex is devoted to vision than to any other sense. Moreover, when there is a conflict between visual and other sensory information, vision tends to dominate or "capture" the other senses. This phenomenon of **visual capture** is an everyday experience. When viewing a movie for which the projector provides the sound, we nevertheless perceive the sound as coming from the screen, where we *see* the actors talking. While viewing a roller coaster ride on a giant wraparound movie screen, we may brace ourselves, even though our other senses tell us we're not moving. In both cases, vision has captured the other senses. Seeing is believing.

Yet without our senses of hearing, taste, smell, touch, and body motion and position, our capacities for experiencing the world would be vastly diminished.

Preview Question

7. How does the ear transform sound energy into neural messages?

The ear's exquisite sensitivity allows us to detect vibrations of the eardrum as tiny as 0.0000000000003 meter, roughly the diameter of a hydrogen molecule (Kaufman, 1979).

Hearing

Like our other senses, our hearing, or **audition,** is highly adaptive. We hear a wide range of sounds, but we best hear sounds having frequencies within a range that corresponds to the range of the human voice. We also are remarkably sensitive to faint sounds, an obvious boon to our ancestors' survival when hunting or being hunted. (If our ears were much more sensitive, we would hear a constant hiss from the movement of air molecules.) Moreover, we are acutely sensitive to differences in sounds. We can easily detect differences among thousands of human voices, which helps us instantly recognize the voice of almost anyone we know.

For hearing as for seeing, the fundamental question is: How do we do it? How do we transform sound energy into neural messages that the brain interprets as a particular sound coming from a particular place?

visual capture The tendency for vision to dominate the other senses; we perceive filmed voices as coming from the screen we see rather than from the projector behind us.

audition The sense of hearing.

frequency The number of complete wavelengths that pass a point in a given time (for example, per second).

pitch A tone's highness or lowness; depends on frequency.

middle ear The chamber between the eardrum and cochlea containing three tiny bones (hammer, anvil, and stirrup) that concentrate the vibrations of the eardrum on the cochlea's oval window.

The Stimulus Input: Sound Waves

The stimulus energy for hearing is sound waves—jostling molecules of air, each bumping into the next, like a shove being transmitted through the crowded exit tunnel of a football stadium. The resulting waves of compressed and expanded air are like the ripples on a pond circling out from where a tossed stone has broken the surface of the water. The strength, or *amplitude*, of sound waves determines their *loudness*. For sound as for light, we can tolerate stimulus intensities a trillion times more intense than the faintest detectable stimulus. The length and therefore the **frequency** of these waves determines their **pitch:** The longer the waves (thus, the lower their frequency), the lower the pitch; the shorter the waves (thus, the higher their frequency), the higher the pitch (Figure 4–5, page 110). A piccolo produces much shorter sound waves than a kettledrum.

The Ear

To hear, we must somehow convert sound waves into neural activity. The human ear accomplishes this feat through an intricate mechanical chain reaction (Figure 4–16). First, the visible outer ear channels sound waves through the auditory canal to the *eardrum*, a tight membrane that vibrates with the waves. The **middle ear** transmits the eardrum's vibrations through a piston

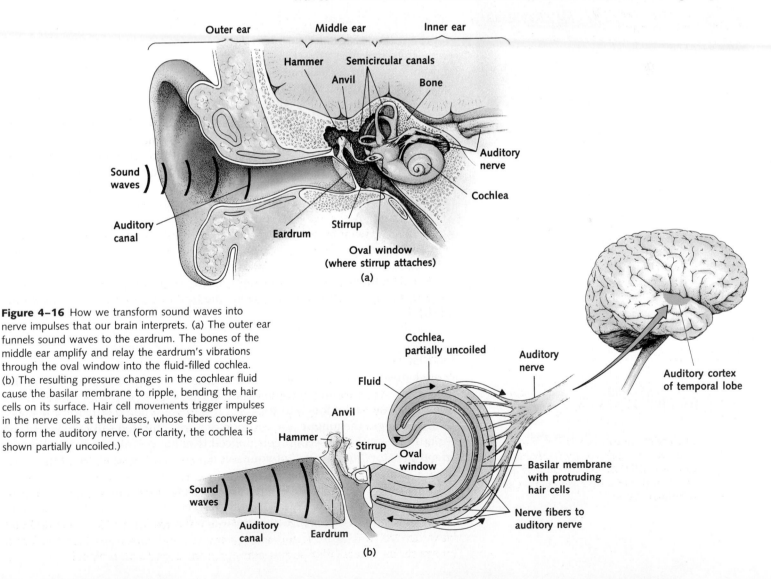

Figure 4–16 How we transform sound waves into nerve impulses that our brain interprets. (a) The outer ear funnels sound waves to the eardrum. The bones of the middle ear amplify and relay the eardrum's vibrations through the oval window into the fluid-filled cochlea. (b) The resulting pressure changes in the cochlear fluid cause the basilar membrane to ripple, bending the hair cells on its surface. Hair cell movements trigger impulses in the nerve cells at their bases, whose fibers converge to form the auditory nerve. (For clarity, the cochlea is shown partially uncoiled.)

inner ear The innermost part of the ear, containing the cochlea, semicircular canals, and vestibular sacs.

cochlea [KOHK-lee-uh] A coiled, bony, fluid-filled tube in the inner ear through which sound waves trigger nerve impulses.

sensory interaction The principle that one sense may influence another, as when the smell of food influences its taste.

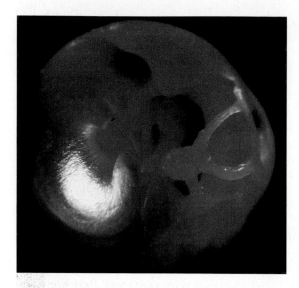

The remarkable details of this photo of the middle ear include the eardrum (at left, curving in a bit), the stirrup (at right), and the oval window (covered by stirrup). The actual distance from eardrum to oval window is less than 1 centimeter.

Preview Question

8. How do we taste and smell?

Are sounds which are equidistant from your two ears—from directly ahead, behind, overhead, or beneath—relatively easy or hard to locate? (See page 123.)

made of three tiny bones (the *hammer, anvil,* and *stirrup*) to a snail-shaped tube in the **inner ear** called the **cochlea** (KOHK-lee-uh). The incoming vibrations cause the cochlea's membrane (the *oval window*) to vibrate the fluid that fills this tube. This motion causes ripples in the *basilar membrane,* which is lined with *hair cells,* so named because of their tiny hairlike projections. At the end of this sequence, the rippling of the basilar membrane bends these hair cells, triggering impulses in the adjacent nerve fibers. Through this mechanical chain of events, sound waves cause the hair cells of the inner ear to send neural messages up to the temporal lobe's auditory cortex. From vibrating air to moving piston to fluid waves to electrical impulses to the brain: We hear.

Brief exposure to extremely intense sounds, such as gunfire near one's ear, and prolonged exposure to intense sounds, such as amplified music, can damage receptor cells (Backus, 1977; West & Evans, 1990). Although rock and roll may be here to stay, the sad truth for some rock musicians is that their hearing may not be. For others, hearing loss, especially for the higher frequencies, accompanies the biology of aging. To many older adults, chirping birds seem quieter and soft conversation becomes frustratingly unintelligible.

How Do We Locate Sounds?

The slightly different messages sensed by the two microphones used in creating a stereophonic recording mimic the slightly different sound messages received by our two ears. As the placement of our eyes allows us to sense depth visually (pages 128 and 129), the placement of our two ears allows us to enjoy stereophonic ("three-dimensional") hearing. For example, if a car to the right honks, your right ear receives a more intense sound slightly sooner than your left ear. Because sound travels 750 miles per hour and our ears are but 6 inches apart, the loudness difference and time lag are extremely small. But our auditory system is so sensitive that our two ears can detect such minute differences (Brown & Deffenbacher, 1979; Middlebrooks & Green, 1991). A just noticeable difference in the direction from which two sounds come corresponds to a time difference of just 0.000027 second!

Taste

Our sense of taste involves four basic sensations—sweet, sour, salty, and bitter (McBurney & Gent, 1979). All other tastes are mixtures of these. Investigators have been frustrated in their search for specialized nerve fibers for each of the four basic taste sensations, but they have found areas of the tongue that have special sensitivities—the tip of the tongue for sweet tastes, the back of the tongue for bitter (Figure 4-17).

Taste is a chemical sense. Inside the little bumps on the top and sides of your tongue are 200 or more taste buds. Each contains a pore that catches food chemicals. These molecules are sensed by 50 taste receptor cells that project antennalike hairs into the pore. Some of these receptors respond mostly to sweet-tasting molecules, others to salty-, sour-, or bitter-tasting ones. It doesn't take much to trigger a response. When a stream of water is pumped across the tongue, the addition of a concentrated salty or sweet taste for but one-tenth of a second gets noticed (Kelling & Halpern, 1983). When a friend asks for "just a taste" of your soft drink, you can squeeze off the straw after a mere fraction of a second.

Taste receptors reproduce themselves every week, so if you burn your tongue with hot food it matters little. However, as you grow older, the number of taste buds decreases, as does taste sensitivity (Cowart, 1981). (No won-

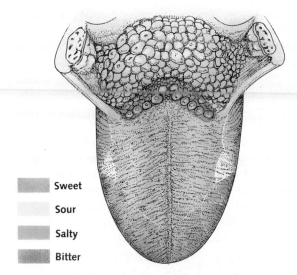

Figure 4–17 Different regions of the tongue have extra sensitivity to one or more of the four basic taste sensations—sweet, sour, salty, and bitter.

Sweet

Sour

Salty

Bitter

der adults enjoy strong-tasting foods that children resist.) Heavy smoking and alcohol use accelerate the decline in taste buds and sensitivities.

Although taste buds are essential for taste, there is more to taste than meets the tongue. Hold your nose, close your eyes, and have someone feed you various foods. A piece of apple may then be indistinguishable from a piece of raw potato; a piece of steak may taste like cardboard. To savor a taste, we normally breathe the aroma through our nose—which is why eating is not much fun when you have a bad cold. Smell not only adds to our perception of taste, it also changes it. A drink's strawberry odor enhances our perception of its sweetness. This is **sensory interaction** at work—the principle that one sense may influence another. Smell influences taste. Similarly, we correctly perceive the location of the voice directly in front of us partly because we also *see* that the person is in front of us, not behind, above, or beneath us.

Smell

Breaths come in pairs—inhale, exhale—except at two moments: birth and death. Each day, as you inhale and exhale nearly 20,000 breaths of life-sustaining air, you bathe your nostrils in a stream of scent-laden molecules. More than you may realize, your resulting experiences of smell (*olfaction*) are intimate ones. To smell someone we must inhale something of the person. Like taste, smell is a chemical sense. We smell something when airborne molecules of a substance reach a tiny cluster of 5 million receptor cells at the top of each of our nasal cavities (Figure 4–18).

These olfactory receptor cells, waving like sea anemones on a reef, respond selectively to the aroma of brownies baking, to a whisp of smoke, to a friend's fragrance, and instantly alert the brain. Even nursing infants and mothers quickly learn to recognize each others' scents (McCarthy, 1986). A mother fur seal returning to a beach crowded with pups will find her own, aided by smell. Yet, unlike the mother fur seal—or a shark or bloodhound—

Figure 4–18 The sense of smell. To smell a rose, molecules of its fragrance must reach receptors at the top of the nose. Sniffing swirls air up to the receptors, enhancing the aroma.

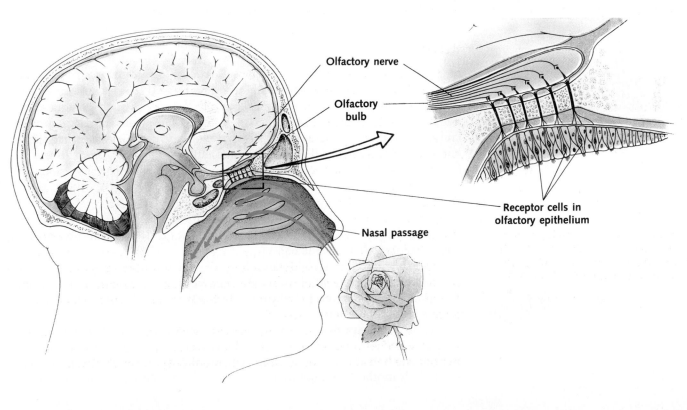

Olfactory nerve

Olfactory bulb

Receptor cells in olfactory epithelium

Nasal passage

the acuteness of our sense of smell is less impressive than that of our vision and our hearing (within the stimulus ranges we detect). Looking out across a garden we see its forms and colors in exquisite detail and hear its singing birds, yet smell little of it without jamming our nose into things.

Precisely how olfactory receptors work is a mystery. Unlike light, which can be separated into its spectral colors, an odor cannot be separated into more elemental odors. Thus, unlike the retina, which detects myriad colors with sensory cells dedicated to red, green, or blue, olfactory receptors recognize odors individually. Odor molecules come in so many shapes and sizes that it takes lots of different receptors to detect them. They do so thanks to a large family of genes that specify the many different smell receptors (Buck & Axel, 1991). The ability to identify scents peaks in early adulthood and gradually declines thereafter (Figure 4–19).

Figure 4–19 Age, sex, and sense of smell. Among the 1.2 million people who responded to a *National Geographic* scratch and sniff survey, women and younger adults most successfully identified six sample odors. (From Wysocki & Gilbert, 1989.)

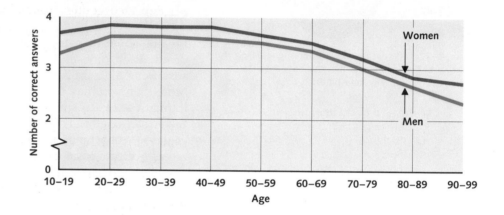

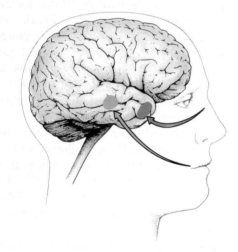

Information from the taste buds (brown arrow) travels to an area of the temporal lobe not far from that where olfactory information is received. The brain's circuitry for smell (magenta arrow) also connects with areas involved in memory storage, which helps explain why a smell can trigger an explosion of memories.

Odors also have the power to evoke memories and feelings. In *Remembrance of Things Past*, the French novelist Marcel Proust described how the aroma and flavor of a bit of cake soaked in tea resurrected long-forgotten memories of his aunt's bedroom in the old family house. "The smell and taste of things," he noted, "bears unfaltering, in the tiny and almost impalpable drop of their essence, the vast structure of recollection."

Laboratory studies confirm that, though it's difficult to recall odors by name, we do indeed have a remarkable capacity to recognize long-forgotten odors and their associated personal episodes (Engen, 1987; Schab, 1991). Students who do a word exercise while smelling the aroma of chocolate remember the words better the next day if the chocolate aroma is again present (Schab, 1990). And pleasant odors evoke pleasant memories (Ehrlichman & Halpern, 1988). The smell of the sea, the scent of a perfume, or an aroma like the floorwax smell in Grandma's kitchen bring to mind happy memories.

Touch

If you had to give up one sense, which would it be? If you could retain only one sense, which would it be?

Touch would be a good candidate for retention. Right from the start, touch is strangely essential to our development. As we noted in Chapter 3, The Developing Person, premature babies gain weight faster and go home sooner if stimulated by hand massage. Infant rats deprived of their mothers' grooming touch produce less growth hormone and have a lower metabolic rate—a good way to keep alive until the mother returns, but resulting in stunted growth if she's delayed. Infant monkeys allowed to see, hear, and smell their mothers, but not touch them, are desperately unhappy; much less

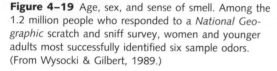

Preview Question

9. How do we sense touch and feel pain?

gate-control theory Melzack and Wall's theory that the spinal cord contains a neurological "gate" that blocks or allows pain signals to pass on to the brain. The "gate" is opened by the activity of pain signals traveling up small nerve fibers and closed by activity in larger fibers or by information coming from the brain.

Answer to question on page 120: Sounds that strike the two ears simultaneously are hard to locate. You can experience this by sitting with eyes closed while a friend snaps fingers at various locations around your head.

so are those separated by a screen with holes, allowing touch. As lovers, we yearn to touch—to kiss, to stroke, to snuggle like spoons.

Our "sense of touch" is actually a mix of at least four distinct skin senses—pressure, warmth, cold, and pain. Touching various spots on the skin with a soft hair, a warm or cool wire, and the point of a pin reveals that some spots are especially sensitive to pressure, others to warmth, others to cold, still others to pain. Within the skin there are different types of specialized nerve endings. Surprisingly, there is no simple relationship between what we feel at a given spot and the type of specialized nerve ending found there. Except for pressure, which does have identifiable receptors, the relationship between warmth, cold, and pain and the receptors that respond to them remains a mystery. Other skin sensations are variations of the basic ones:

Stroking adjacent pressure spots creates a tickle.

Repeated gentle stroking of a pain spot creates an itching sensation.

Touching adjacent cold and pressure spots triggers a sense of wetness, which you can experience by touching dry, cold metal.

Pain

Be thankful for occasional pain. Pain is the body's way of telling us that something has gone wrong. It draws our attention to a burn, a break, or a rupture and tells us to change our behavior immediately. The few people who are born without the ability to feel pain may experience severe injury without ever being alerted by pain's danger signals. More numerous are those who endure chronic pain. The suffering of people with persistent or recurring backaches, arthritis, headaches, and cancer-related pain prompts us to understand pain so that we may better control it.

Pain is not only a property of the senses—of the region where we feel it—but of the brain as well. As the dreamer sees with eyes closed and the listener hears a ringing during utter silence, so amputees may feel pain or movement in their nonexistent limbs. An amputee may try to step off a bed onto a phantom foot or to lift a cup with a phantom hand (Melzack, 1992). These "phantom limb sensations" indicate that with pain, as with sights and sounds, the brain can misinterpret its neural activity.

Unlike vision, however, the pain system is not located in a simple neural cord running from a sensing device to a definable spot in the brain. Moreover, there is no one type of stimulus that triggers pains (as light triggers vision), and there are no special receptors (like the retina's rods and cones) for pain. At low intensities, the stimuli that produce pain cause other sensations, including warmth or coolness, smoothness or roughness.

Although no theory of pain explains all the available findings, psychologist Ronald Melzack and biologist Patrick Wall's (1965, 1983) **gate-control theory** provides a useful model. Melzack and Wall believe that the spinal cord contains a sort of neurological "gate" that either blocks or allows pain signals to pass on to the brain. The spinal cord contains small nerve fibers that conduct most pain signals, and larger fibers that conduct most other sensory signals. When tissue is injured, the small fibers activate and open the neural gate, and you feel pain. Large-fiber activity closes the pain gate, turning pain off.

Thus, one way to treat chronic pain is to stimulate (electrically, by massage, or even by acupuncture) "gate-closing" activity in the large neural fibers. Rub the area around your stubbed toe, and the competing stimulation will block some of the pain messages. Ice on a bruise serves not only to control swelling but also to trigger cold messages that close the gate on the

kinesthesis [kin-ehs-THEE-sehs]   The system for sensing the position and movement of individual body parts.

equilibrium   The sense of body movement and position, including the sense of balance.

"Pain is increased by attending to it."

Charles Darwin
Expression of Emotions in Man and Animals, 1872

Although Lamaze training reduces labor pain, most Lamaze patients request a local anesthetic during labor. Some—having expected a "natural, painless birth"—feel needless guilt and failure (Melzack, 1984). Melzack therefore advocates—as does the Lamaze program itself—childbirth training that prepares a woman "to cope with an event which is often extremely painful and, at the same time, one of the most fulfilling peak experiences in her life."

Preview Question

10. How do we sense our body's position and movement?

pain signals. An arthritic patient, for example, may wear a small portable electrical stimulation unit next to a painful area. When the unit stimulates nerves in the area, the patient feels a vibrating sensation rather than pain (T. Murphy, 1982).

Melzack and Wall believe that the pain gate can also be closed by information from the brain. These brain-to-spinal-cord messages help explain some striking psychological influences on pain. When distracted from pain signals (and soothed by the release of endorphins—see page 32), our experience of pain may be greatly diminished. Football injuries may be unnoticed, until taking the after-game shower. A mere paper cut while doing a dull job may hurt more. Clearly, there is more to pain than meets the sense receptors.

If pain is indeed a physical and a psychological phenomenon, then it should be treatable both physically and psychologically. For example, the widely practiced Lamaze method of prepared childbirth combines several pain control techniques. These include relaxation (through deep breathing and muscle relaxation), counterstimulation (through gentle massage), and distraction (through focusing attention on, say, a pleasant photograph).

Distracting people with pleasant images ("Think of a warm, comfortable environment") or drawing their attention away from the painful stimulation ("Count backward by threes") is an especially effective way to increase pain tolerance (Fernandez & Turk, 1989; McCaul & Malott, 1984). No wonder a well-trained nurse will distract needle-shy patients with chatter and may ask them to look away when inserting the needle.

Body Position and Movement

With only the five familiar senses we have so far considered, we would be helpless. We could not put food in our mouths, stand up, or reach out and touch someone. To know just how to move your arms to grasp someone's hand, you first need to know the current position of your arms and hands and then be aware of their changing positions as you move them. To take just one step requires feedback from and instructions to some 200 muscles.

Humans come equipped with millions of such position and motion sensors. They are all over our bodies—in the muscles, tendons, and joints—and they are continually providing our brains with information. If we twist our wrists 1 degree, the sensors immediately report it. This sense of the position and movement of body parts is **kinesthesis** (kin-ehs-THEE-sehs).

Have you ever considered life without kinesthesis, without, say, being able to sense the positions of your limbs when awakening during the night? Such is the experience of Christina, whose nerve fibers carrying information from muscles, tendons, and joints were destroyed by disease, leaving her floppy as a rag doll (Sacks, 1985). What does it feel like? Like she is disembodied, her body dead, not-real, not-hers. Against all odds, Christina has, however, learned to walk and eat—by visually attending to her limbs and directing them accordingly.

A companion sense called **equilibrium** monitors the position and movement of the whole body. The biological gyroscopes for our sense of equilibrium are in the inner ear. The *semicircular canals*, which look like a three-dimensional pretzel (Figure 4–16, page 119), and the *vestibular sacs*, which connect the canals with the cochlea, contain substances that move when the head rotates or tilts. This movement stimulates hairlike receptors in these organs of the inner ear, which send messages to the brain that enable us continually to sense our body position and thereby maintain our balance.

If you've been twirling around and come to an abrupt halt, the fluid in your semicircular canals and your kinesthetic receptors does not immediately return to its neutral state. The aftereffect fools your dizzy brain with the

Each of these flying trapeze artists must have a highly developed equilibrium and kinesthetic sense.

sensation that you're still spinning. This illustrates a principle that underlies perceptual illusions. Mechanisms that normally give us an accurate experience of the world can, under special conditions, fool us. Understanding how we are fooled provides clues to how our perceptual system works.

Rehearse It

13. The amplitude of a light wave determines our perception of brightness. The amplitude of a sound wave determines our perception of
a. loudness.
b. pitch.
c. audition.
d. frequency.

14. The frequency of soundwaves determines their pitch. The _____ the waves are, the lower their frequency is and the _____ their pitch.
a. shorter, higher
b. longer, lower
c. lower, longer
d. higher, shorter

15. The taste of the food we eat is greatly enhanced by its smell or aroma. One sense influencing another is
a. sensory adaptation.
b. chemical sensation.
c. gate-control theory.
d. sensory interaction.

16. At least four skin senses—pressure, warmth, cold, and pain—make up our sense of touch. Of all the skin senses, the only one that has its own identifiable receptor cells is
a. pressure.
b. warmth.
c. cold.
d. pain.

17. There are no special receptors for pain, no one type of stimuli that triggers pain, and no one definable spot in the brain that interprets pain. Although no theory fully explains our experience of pain, one useful model is the
a. opponent-process theory.
b. Lamaze method.
c. gate-control theory.
d. sensory adaptation theory.

18. Kinesthesis is the body's way of sensing its position movement. The receptors for our companion sense of equilibrium are in the
a. skin.
b. brain.
c. inner ear.
d. skeletal muscles.

Preview Question

11. What did the Gestalt psychologists contribute to our understanding of perception?

gestalt An organized whole. Gestalt psychologists emphasize our tendency to integrate pieces of information into meaningful wholes.

Perceptual Organization

We have examined the processes by which we sense sights and sounds, tastes and smells. Now our central question is, how do we see not just shapes and colors, but a rose in bloom, a familiar face, a sunset? How do we hear not just a mix of pitches and rhythms, but a child's cry of pain, the hum of distant traffic, a symphony? In short, how do we *organize* and *interpret* our sensations so that they become meaningful perceptions?

Early in this century, a group of German psychologists became intrigued with how the mind organizes sensations into perceptions. Given a cluster of sensations, the human perceiver organizes them into a **gestalt**, a German word meaning a "form" or a "whole." The Gestalt psychologists provided

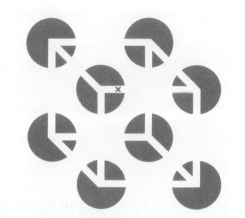

Figure 4–20 What do you see: circles with white lines, or a cube? If you stare at the cube, you may notice that it reverses location, moving the tiny X in the center from the front edge to the back. At times the cube may seem to float in front of the page, with circles behind it; at other times the circles may become holes in the page through which the cube appears, as though it were floating behind the page. (From Bradley, Dumais, & Petry, 1976.)

Preview Question

12. How do the principles of figure-ground and grouping contribute to our perception of form?

many compelling demonstrations of this ability. Look at Figure 4–20. Note that the individual elements of the figure are really nothing but eight blue circles, each containing three white lines. But when we view them all together, we see a *whole* form, a "Necker cube." Note, too, that the figure evokes more than one perception. Because the circles can be organized into several coherent images, each equally plausible, the mind switches back and forth from one to the next. As the Gestalt psychologists were fond of saying, in perception the whole may differ from the sum of its parts. There is far more to perception than meets the senses.

Such demonstrations led the Gestalt psychologists to describe principles by which we organize our sensations into perceptions. As you read about these organizational principles, keep in mind the fundamental truth they illustrate: Our brains do more than merely register information about the world. Perception is not just opening a shutter and letting a picture print itself on the brain. Always, we are filtering sensory information and constructing perceptions in ways that make sense to us.

Form Perception

Imagine that you wanted to design a video/computer system that, like your eye/brain system, could read handwritten addresses or recognize faces. What abilities would it need?

Figure and Ground

To start with, the system would need to recognize the addresses and faces as distinct from their backgrounds. Likewise, our first task in perception is to perceive any object, called the *figure,* as distinct from its surroundings, called the *ground.* Among the voices you hear at a party, the one you attend to becomes the figure, all others part of the ground. As you read, the words are the figure; the white paper, the ground. In Figure 4–21, the **figure-ground**

Figure 4–21 Reversible figure and ground: One face or two? (From Shepard, 1990.)

figure-ground The organization of the visual field into objects (the figures) that stand out from their surroundings (the ground).

grouping The tendency to organize stimuli into coherent groups.

proximity A perceptual tendency to group together visual and auditory events that are near each other.

similarity A perceptual tendency to group together similar elements.

closure The perceptual tendency to fill in gaps, thus enabling one to perceive disconnected parts as a whole object.

continuity A perceptual tendency to group stimuli into smooth, continuous patterns.

connectedness The perceptual tendency to perceive features, such as dots, as a single unit when uniform and linked.

relationship continually reverses—but we always organize the stimulus into a figure seen against a ground. (Is there a candlestick in front of one face, or is that the background between two faces?) Reversible figure and ground demonstrates again that the same stimulus can trigger more than one perception.

Grouping

Having discriminated figure from ground, we (and our video/computer system) must then organize the figure into a meaningful form. Some basic features of a scene, such as color, movement, and light-dark contrast we process instantly and automatically (Treisman, 1987). To bring order and form to these basic sensations, our minds follow certain rules for **grouping** stimuli together. These rules, identified by the Gestalt psychologists, illustrate their idea that the perceived whole differs from the mere sum of its parts (Rock & Palmer, 1990):

Proximity We group nearby figures together. We see below not six separate lines, but three sets of two lines.

Similarity If figures are similar to each other, we group them together. We see the triangles and circles as vertical columns of similar shapes, not as horizontal rows of dissimilar shapes.

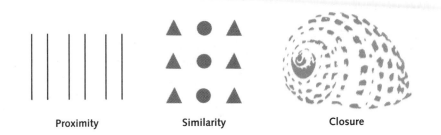

Proximity   Similarity   Closure

Closure If a figure has gaps, we complete it, filling in the gaps to create a complete, whole object. By filling the gaps in the shell's outline here, we see a whole seashell.

Continuity We perceive smooth, continuous patterns rather than discontinuous ones. This pattern could be a series of alternating semicircles, but we perceive it as a wavy line and a straight line.

Connectedness We perceive spots, lines, or areas as a single unit when uniform and linked.

Figure 4–22 You probably perceive this doghouse as a gestalt—a whole (though impossible) structure. As the photo on page 143 shows, Gestalt grouping principles are at work here. [Reprinted from GAMES Magazine (810 Seventh Avenue, New York, NY 10019). Copyright © 1983 PSC Games Limited Partnership.]

Continuity   Connectedness

The grouping principles usually help us perceive reality, but sometimes they lead us astray, as when viewing the doghouse in Figure 4–22.

Depth Perception

Preview Question

13. Why do we see the world in three dimensions?

From the two-dimensional images that fall on our retinas we somehow organize three-dimensional perceptions. The ability to see objects in three dimensions, called **depth perception,** allows us to estimate their distance from us. At a glance, we estimate the distance of an oncoming car or the height of a cliff. This ability is partly innate. Eleanor Gibson and Richard Walk (1960) discovered this using a miniature cliff with a drop-off covered by sturdy glass. The inspiration for these experiments occurred to Gibson as she was eating a picnic lunch on the rim of the Grand Canyon. She wondered: Would a toddler peering over the rim perceive the dangerous drop-off and draw back?

Back in their Cornell University laboratory, Gibson and Walk placed 6- to 14-month-old infants on the edge of a **visual cliff** (Figure 4–23). Their mothers then coaxed them to crawl out on the glass. Most refused to do so, preferring to crawl on the "shallow" side, thereby indicating that they could perceive depth. Newborn animals with virtually no visual experience—including young kittens, a day-old goat, and newly hatched chicks—respond similarly. What is more, during the first month of life, human infants turn to avoid objects coming directly at them but are unbothered by objects approaching at an angle that would not hit them (Ball & Tronick, 1971). Thus, our ability to perceive depth seems innate.

Figure 4–23 Eleanor Gibson and Richard Walk devised this miniature cliff with a glass-covered drop-off to determine whether human infants and newborn animals can perceive depth. Even when coaxed, infants are reluctant to venture onto the glass over the cliff, indicating that even the very young can perceive depth.

How do we do it? How do we transform two-dimensional retinal images into three-dimensional perceptions? Some of the cues we use require both eyes **(binocular cues).** Others are available to each eye separately **(monocular cues).**

Binocular Cues

Because our eyes are about 2½ inches apart, our retinas receive slightly different images of the world. When the brain compares these two images, their **retinal disparity** (the difference in the two images) provides an important cue to distance. When you hold your finger directly in front of your nose, your retinas receive quite different views. (You can see this if you close one eye and then the other.) At greater distance—say, when you hold your finger at arm's length—the disparity is smaller.

depth perception The ability to see objects in three dimensions although the images that strike the retina are two-dimensional; allows us to judge distance.

visual cliff A laboratory device for testing depth perception in infants and young animals.

binocular cues Depth cues, such as retinal disparity and convergence, that depend on the use of two eyes.

monocular cues Distance cues, such as aerial and linear perspective and overlap, available to either eye alone.

retinal disparity A binocular cue for perceiving depth; the greater the disparity (difference) between the two images the retina receives of an object, the closer the object is to us.

convergence A binocular cue for perceiving depth; the extent to which the eyes converge inward when looking at an object.

relative size A monocular cue for perceiving distance; when we assume two objects are the same size, the one that produces the smaller image appears more distant.

overlap A monocular cue for perceiving distance; nearby objects partially block our view of more distant objects.

The creators of 3-D movies and Viewmaster-type 3-D scenes simulate retinal disparity by photographing a scene with two cameras placed a few inches apart (a feature we might want to build into our seeing computer). When viewed through spectacles or a device that allows the left eye to see only the image from the left camera and the right eye the image from the right camera, the 3-D effect mimics normal retinal disparity.

Another binocular cue to distance is **convergence,** a muscular cue that indicates the extent to which the eyes turn inward when we look at an object. By noting the angle of convergence, the brain determines whether you are focusing just past your nose, or on this printed page, or on the person across the room.

Monocular Cues

With both eyes open, we can readily and precisely touch the tip of a pen held in front of us; with one eye closed, the task becomes noticeably more difficult. This demonstrates the importance of binocular cues in judging the distance of nearby objects. How then do we judge whether a person is 100 feet or 100 yards away? In both cases, the retinal disparity while looking straight ahead is slight. At such distances we depend on monocular cues such as the following:

Relative size If we assume that two objects are similar in size, we perceive the one that casts the smaller image on the retina as farther away.

Relative size

Overlap If one object partially covers another, we perceive it as closer. We perceive the young deer as closer than its partially obscured mother.

Overlap

linear perspective A monocular cue for perceiving distance; we perceive the converging of what we know to be parallel lines as indicating increasing distance.

relative height A monocular cue for perceiving distance; we perceive higher objects as farther away.

relative brightness A monocular cue for perceiving distance; dimmer objects seem more distant.

perceptual constancy Perceiving objects as unchanging (having consistent brightness, color, shape, and size) even as illumination and retinal images change.

Linear perspective

Relative height

Linear perspective We interpret the apparent convergence of parallel lines as a clue to distance. The more they converge, the greater the perceived distance. Linear perspective can contribute to rail-crossing accidents, by leading people to overestimate a train's distance (Leibowitz, 1985). (A train's massive size also makes it appear to be moving more slowly than it is.)

Relative height We perceive objects higher in our field of vision as farther away. This may contribute to the illusion that vertical dimensions are longer than identical horizontal dimensions. Is the vertical line here longer, shorter, or equal in length to the horizontal line? Measure and see. To most people, the St. Louis gateway arch appears taller than it is wide. Actually, the height and width of its outer edges are equal.

Relative brightness Nearby objects reflect more light to our eyes. Thus, given two identical objects, the dimmer one seems farther away. Psychologist Helen Ross (1975) demonstrated this by asking passersby to estimate the distances of white disks she had placed on the lawn at Britain's Hull University. Those who judged the distance in the thick morning fog perceived the disks to be farther away than did those who made their estimates in the midday sunshine. This illusion can contribute to accidents, as when a fog-shrouded vehicle, or one with only its parking lights on, seems farther away than it is.

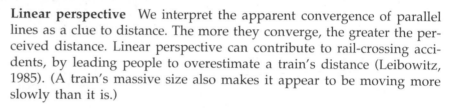

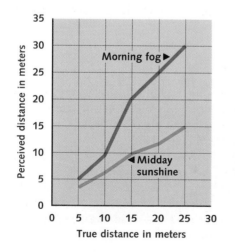

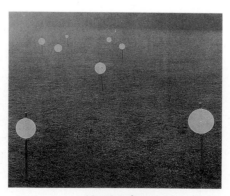

Morning fog

Midday sunshine

Figure 4–24 Ancient Egyptian paintings lacked the monocular cues that later artists used to portray depth. By the time that "Bristol, Broad Quay" was painted (c. 1730, Anonymous), the techniques for showing perspective were well established. Note the effective use of distance cues such as texture gradient, overlap, and relative size and height.

To convey depth on a flat canvas (Figure 4–24), artists use these monocular cues, as do people who must gauge depth with but one eye. In 1960, the University of Washington football team won the Rose Bowl, thanks partly to the superb passing of quarterback Bob Schloredt. Schloredt, who was obviously skilled at judging the distance of his receivers, must have been extremely sensitive to monocular cues for distance, because he is blind in his left eye.

Perceptual Constancy

Preview Question

14. How do perceptual constancies help us to organize our sensations into meaningful perceptions?

So far we have seen that our video/computer system must first perceive objects as we do—as having a distinct form and location. Its next task is even more challenging: to recognize the object, without being deceived by changes in its size, shape, brightness, or color. **Perceptual constancy** allows us to perceive an object as unchanging while the stimuli from it change. You glance at someone ahead of you on the sidewalk and instantly recognize a classmate. In less time than it takes you to draw a breath, the information reaching your eyes has been sent to the brain, where millions of neurons have extracted the essential features, compared them with stored images, and identified the person.

Shape and Size Constancies

Thanks to *shape constancy* we perceive familiar objects as having a constant form, even while our retinal images of them change. When a door opens, it casts a changing shape on our retinas, yet we manage to perceive the door as having a constant doorlike shape (Figure 4–25).

Size constancy—perceiving objects as having a constant size—allows us to perceive a car as big enough to carry people, even when we see it from two blocks away. This illustrates the close connection between an object's perceived *distance* and perceived *size*. Perceiving an object's distance cues us to its size. Likewise, knowing its general size—that the object is, say, a car—provides us with cues to its distance.

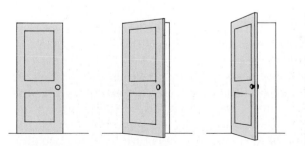

Figure 4–25 Shape constancy. A door casts an increasingly trapezoidal image on our retinas as it opens, yet we still perceive it as rectangular.

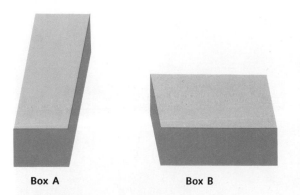

Box A   **Box B**

Perceiving shape. Do the tops of boxes A and B have different dimensions? They appear to. But if you measure, you will see they are identical. With both boxes we adjust our perceptions relative to our viewing angle. (From Shepard, 1981.)

Size-Distance Relationship   The marvel of size perception is how effortlessly it occurs. Given the perceived distance of an object and the size of its image on our retinas, we instantly and unconsciously infer the object's size. Although the monsters in Figure 4–26a cast the same retinal images, their context (linear perspective) cues us that the monster in pursuit is farther away. We therefore perceive it as larger.

This interplay between perceived size and perceived distance helps explain several well-known illusions. For example, can you imagine why the moon looks larger—up to 50 percent larger—near the horizon than when high in the sky? For at least 22 centuries, scholars have wondered, and argued (Hershenson, 1989). A partial reason for the *moon illusion* is that cues to objects' distances at the horizon make the moon behind them seem farther away (Kaufman & Rock, 1962). Thus, the moon on the horizon seems larger (like the distant monster in Figure 4–26a and the distant bar in Figure 4–26b). Take away these distance cues—by looking at the horizon moon (or the monsters) through a paper tube—and it immediately shrinks.

Figure 4–26 The interplay between perceived size and distance. (a) The monocular cues for distance make the pursuing monster look larger than the pursued. It isn't. (From Shepard, 1990.) (b) The Ponzo illusion. The two identical orange bars cast identical images on our retinas. But we believe that a more distant object can only create the same-sized image if it is larger. Thus, we perceive the bar that seems more distant as larger.

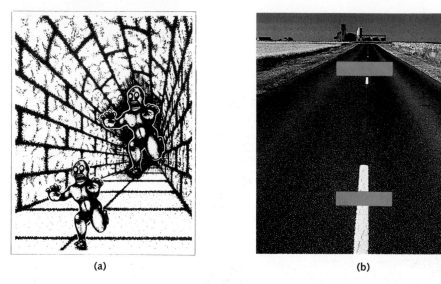

(a)   (b)

The size-distance relationship helps us understand the famous Müller-Lyer illusion: Does either line segment, AB or BC, appear longer?

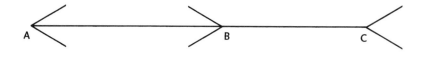

To most people the two segments appear the same length. Surprise! They are not. As your ruler can verify, line AB is a full one-third longer than line BC. In this case, seeing shouldn't be believing.

One explanation is that our experience with the corners of rooms or buildings affects our perceptions of distance and size. Thus, we perceive the vertical line on the ticket booth in Figure 4–27 as closer to us and therefore shorter, and the vertical line by the door as farther away and therefore longer.

Size-distance relationships also explain why, in Figure 4–28, the two girls seem to change size. As the diagram reveals, the room is distorted. But viewed with one eye through a peephole, its trapezoidal walls produce the same images as those of a normal rectangular room viewed with both eyes.

Figure 4–27 The Müller-Lyer illusion. Richard L. Gregory (1968) suggests that the corners in our rectangularly carpentered world teach us to interpret "outward" or "inward" pointing arrowheads at the ends of a line as a cue to the line's distance from us and so to its length. The red line defined by the corner at the ticket windows looks shorter than the red line defined by the corner to the right. But if you measure them, you will see that both are the same length.

Presented with the camera's one-eyed view, the brain makes the reasonable assumption that the room *is* normal, and perceives the girls as changing in size.

Figure 4–28 The illusion of the shrinking and growing girls. When viewed through a peephole with one eye, this distorted room, designed by lawyer-turned-scientist Adelbert Ames, appears to have a normal rectangular shape with both corners the same distance away. Thus, anything in the near corner appears disproportionately large compared to anything in the far corner, because we judge their size based on the false assumption that they are the same distance away.

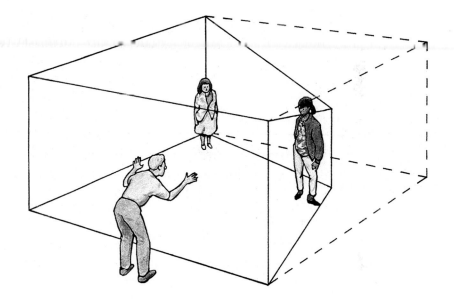

Our occasional misperceptions demonstrate the workings of our normally effective perceptual processes. The perceived relationship between distance and size is generally valid, but under special circumstances can lead us astray—as when helping to create the moon illusion, the Müller-Lyer illusion, and the distorted room illusion. Using distance cues to assess perceived size triggers illusions only if we aren't familiar with the object or if the distance cues are misleading. When we correctly interpret the distance cues—which we normally do—we perceive the size of objects correctly.

Brightness Constancy

White paper reflects 90 percent of the light falling on it; black paper, only 10 percent. In sunlight the black paper may reflect 100 times more light than does the white paper indoors (McBurney & Collings, 1984), but it still looks black. This illustrates *brightness constancy,* our perceiving an object as having a

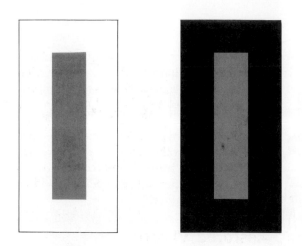

Figure 4–29 Brightness contrast. Although they are in fact identical, the perceived brightness of the interior rectangles differs depending on their surroundings. Like color constancy (page 117), this phenomenon has great significance for artists and interior designers.

constant amount of brightness even while its illumination varies. Perceived brightness depends on *relative luminance*—how much light an object reflects relative to its surroundings. If you view sunlit black paper through a narrow tube so nothing else is visible, it may look gray, because in bright sunshine it reflects a fair amount of light. View it without the tube and it is again black, because it reflects much less light than the objects around it. The phenomenon is similar to that of color constancy (page 117). A red apple in a fruit bowl retains its redness as the light changes, because our brain computes the light reflected by any object relative to its surrounding objects.

If perceived brightness stays roughly constant, given an unchanging context, what happens when the surrounding context changes? The same principle—that the brain computes brightness and color relative to surrounding objects—implies that brightness will change with context. As Figure 4–29 shows, that is precisely what happens.

Form perception, depth perception, and perceptual constancy illustrate how we organize our visual experiences. Perceptual organization applies to other senses, too. It explains why we perceive the clock's steady tick not as tick-tick-tick-tick, but grouped as, say TICK-tick, TICK-tick. Listening to an unfamiliar language, we have trouble hearing where one word stops and the next one begins; listening to our own language, we automatically hear distinct words. This, too, is a form of perceptual organization. But it is more, for we even organize a string of letters—THEDOGATEMEAT—into words that make an intelligible phrase, more likely "The dog ate meat" than "The do gate me at" (McBurney & Collings, 1984). This process involves not only organization but *interpretation*—finding meaning in what we perceive.

Rehearse It

19. In their famous experiments, Gibson and Walk used a visual cliff to test depth perception in infants and young animals. Their results suggest that
a. infants have not yet developed depth perception.
b. crawling infants perceive depth.
c. depth perception depends upon experience.
d. humans differ significantly from animals in being able to perceive depth in infancy.

20. Gestalt psychologists identified the principles by which we organize our perceptions. Our tendency to fill in the gaps, and to perceive a pattern as continuous, are two different examples of the organizing principle called
a. figure-ground.
b. depth perception.
c. shape constancy.
d. grouping.

21. The images that fall on our retinas are two-dimensional, or flat. Yet we perceive the world as having three-dimensional depth. Depth perception underlies our ability to
a. discriminate figure from ground.
b. perceive objects as having a constant shape or form.
c. judge distances.
d. fill in the gaps in a figure.

22. In estimating distances we use both binocular cues, which depend on both eyes, and monocular cues, which are available to either eye alone. Examples of monocular cues are overlap and
a. closure.
b. retinal disparity.
c. linear perspective.
d. convergence.

23. In the Müller-Lyer illusion we misperceive the length of the lines between arrowheads. We do so partly because
a. distance cues do not help us assess size.
b. the visual distance cues (implied by the arrowheads) mislead us.
c. the perceived relationship between distance and size is generally illusory.
d. of our linear perspective.

24. Form perception and perceptual constancy are organizing principles that apply to hearing as well as vision. For example, in listening to a concerto, you follow the solo instrument and perceive the orchestra as accompaniment; this illustrates the organizing principle of
a. figure-ground.
b. shape constancy.
c. grouping.
d. depth or distance perception.

Interpretation

The nature-nurture controversy is not restricted to developmental psychologists. Philosophers interested in perception have long debated the issue. German philosopher Immanuel Kant (1724–1804) believed that we have *innate* (inborn) ways of organizing sensory experiences. British philosopher John Locke (1632–1704) believed that we *learn* how to perceive the world as we experience it. So far we have seen that in some ways Kant was correct (for example, that depth perception is innate) and in other ways John Locke was correct (for example, that through experience we learn to link the distance of an object to its perceived size). But just how important is experience? How radically does it shape our perceptual interpretations?

Sensory Restriction and Restored Vision

Writing to John Locke (1690), William Molyneux wondered whether "a man *born* blind, and now adult, taught by his *touch* to distinguish between a cube and a sphere," could, if made to see, visually distinguish the two. Locke's answer was no, because the man would never have *learned* to see.

Preview Question

15. What does research on sensory restriction and restored vision reveal about the effects of experience on perception?

These blind children are learning to recognize goats by touch. If blind since birth, they probably would be unable to recognize goats by *sight* if their vision were restored.

Molyneux's hypothetical case has since been put to the test with dozens of adults who, though blind from birth, have gained sight (Gregory, 1978; Senden, 1932). Most were patients with cataracts—clouded lenses that enabled them to see only diffused light, rather as you or I might see the world through a Ping-Pong ball sliced in half. When their cataracts were surgically removed, the patients could distinguish figure from ground and could sense colors—suggesting that these aspects of perception are innate. But much as Locke supposed, the formerly blind patients often could not visually recognize objects that were familiar by touch.

perceptual adaptation In vision, the ability to adjust to an artificially displaced or even inverted visual field.

perceptual set A mental predisposition, based on our experiences, assumptions, and expectations, to perceive one thing and not another.

"Let us then suppose the mind to be, as we say, white paper void of all characters, without any ideas: How comes it to be furnished? . . . To this I answer, in one word, from EXPERIENCE."

John Locke
An Essay Concerning Human Understanding, 1690

Preview Question

16. How adaptable is our perception?

Dr. Hubert Dolezal views the world through inverted lenses. Remarkably, people can learn to adapt to an upside-down visual world.

Perhaps in these cases the surgery didn't completely restore the patients' visual equipment. Seeking to gain more control than that provided by clinical cases, researchers have conducted Molyneux's imaginary experiment with animals. To discover whether altering a young animal's normal visual experience would permanently alter its perceptual abilities, they stitched closed the eyelids of infant kittens and monkeys or outfitted them with goggles through which the animals could see only diffuse, unpatterned light (Wiesel, 1982). After infancy, when their visual impairments were removed, these animals exhibited perceptual limitations much like those of human cataract patients. They could distinguish color and brightness, but not the form of a circle from that of a square. Their eyes had not degenerated; their retinas still relayed signals to their visual cortex. But the animals remained functionally blind to shape.

In both humans and animals, a similar period of sensory restriction that occurs later in life is not permanently disruptive. Cover the eye of an animal for several months during adulthood, and vision will be unaffected after removing the eye patch. Remove cataracts that develop after early childhood, and a human, too, will enjoy normal vision. The effects of visual experiences during infancy in cats, monkeys, and humans suggest there is a *critical period* (page 72) for normal perceptual development. Experience guides the organization of the brain's neural connections.

Perceptual Adaptation

Given a new pair of glasses, we may feel slightly disoriented and dizzy. Within a day or two we adjust. Our **perceptual adaptation** to changed visual input makes the world seem normal again. Now imagine a far more dramatic new pair of glasses—one that shifts the apparent location of objects 40 degrees to the left. When you first put them on and toss a ball to a friend, it sails off to the left. Walking forward to shake hands with the person, you veer to the left.

Could you adapt to this distorted world? Chicks cannot. When fitted with such lenses, they continue to peck where food grains *seem* to be (Hess, 1956; Rossi, 1968). But humans adapt to distorting lenses quickly. Within a few minutes your throws would again be accurate, your stride on target. Remove the lenses and you would experience an aftereffect: At first your throws would err in the *opposite* direction, sailing off to the right; but again, within minutes you would readapt.

Indeed, given an even more radical pair of glasses—one that literally turns the world upside down—you could still adapt. Turn-of-the-century psychologist George Stratton (1896) experienced this when he invented and for 8 days wore optical headgear that flipped left to right *and* up to down, making him the first person to experience a right-side-up retinal image while standing upright. At first, Stratton was disoriented. When he wanted to walk, he had to search for his feet, which were now "up." Eating was nearly impossible. He became nauseated and depressed. But Stratton persisted, and by the eighth day he could comfortably reach for something in the right direction and walk without bumping into things. When Stratton finally removed the headgear, he readapted quickly.

In later experiments people wearing the optical gear have even been able to ride a motorcycle, ski the Alps, and fly an airplane. Is this because through experience they perceptually reinvert their upside-down world to an upright position? No, the street, ski slopes, and runway still seem above their heads. But by actively moving about in this topsy-turvy world, they adapt to the context and learn to coordinate their movements.

Figure 4–30 Which do you see in the center picture: the male saxophonist or the woman? Glancing first at one of the two unambiguous versions of the picture would likely influence your interpretation. (From Shepard, 1990.)

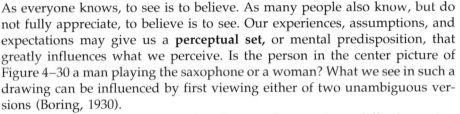

Perceptual Set

As everyone knows, to see is to believe. As many people also know, but do not fully appreciate, to believe is to see. Our experiences, assumptions, and expectations may give us a **perceptual set,** or mental predisposition, that greatly influences what we perceive. Is the person in the center picture of Figure 4–30 a man playing the saxophone or a woman? What we see in such a drawing can be influenced by first viewing either of two unambiguous versions (Boring, 1930).

Once we have formed an idea about reality, we have difficulty seeing things differently. Shown a badly blurred picture of some object, people typically form a hunch about what it is. This expectation then makes it hard to identify the object in a not-so-blurred picture (Bruner & Potter, 1964). (It's much harder to recognize something coming into focus than to ''hang on'' to something going out of focus.)

Even scientists, striving for objectivity, perceive reality through the lenses of their theories. When first viewing the ''canals'' on Mars through telescopes, some astronomers and writers perceived them as the product of intelligent life. They were—but the intelligence was on the viewing end of the telescope.

Everyday examples of perceptual set abound. In 1972, a British newspaper published genuine, unretouched photographs of a ''monster'' in Scotland's Loch Ness—''the most amazing pictures ever taken,'' stated the paper. If this information creates the same perceptual set in you as it did in most of the paper's readers, you, too, will see the monster in the photo reproduced in Figure 4–31. But when Steuart Campbell (1986) approached the photos with a different perceptual set, he saw a curved tree trunk—very likely the same tree

Preview Question

17. How do our assumptions, expectations, and contexts affect our perceptions?

''The temptation to form premature theories upon insufficient data is the bane of our profession.''

Sherlock Holmes, in Arthur Conan Doyle's *The Valley of Fear,* 1914

Figure 4–31 (a) Is this the Loch Ness monster or a log? (b) Are these flying saucers or clouds? We often see what we expect to see.

(a)

(b)

trunk others had seen in the lake the day the photo was shot. Moreover, with this different perceptual set, you may now notice that the object is floating motionless, without any water disturbance or wake around it—hardly what we would expect of a lively monster.

Our perceptual set can influence what we hear as well as what we see. Witness the kindly airline pilot who, on a takeoff run, looked over at his depressed co-pilot and said, "Cheer up." The co-pilot heard the usual "Gear up" and promptly raised the wheels—before they had left the ground (Reason & Mycielska, 1982). When viewing a liquor ad or listening to rock music played backward, people often perceive a sexual image or evil message *if* specifically told what to look for or listen to (Vokey & Read, 1985).

What determines our perceptual set? Our concepts of male saxophonists and women, of monsters and tree trunks, of airplane lights and UFOs, all help us interpret ambiguous sensations. Confronted with an ambiguous moving object in the sky, different people may therefore apply different schemas: "It's a bird." "It's a plane." "It's Superman!"

Context Effects

A given stimulus may trigger radically different perceptions, partly because of our differing expectations, but also because of the immediate context. Some quick examples:

> Did the speaker say "cults and sects" or "cults and sex"? We must discern from the surrounding words.

> Does the pursuing monster in Figure 4–26a on page 132 look aggressive? Does the pursued one seem frightened? If so, you are experiencing a context effect. The two monsters are the same.

> Is the "Magician's Cabinet" in Figure 4–32 sitting on the floor or hanging from the ceiling? How we perceive it depends on the context defined by the bunnies.

Soviet film director Lew Kulechov believed that skilled directors create audience emotion by defining a context in which viewers interpret an actor's expressions. He once produced three short films, each depicting one of three contexts, followed by identical clips of an actor with a neutral expression (Wallbott, 1988). When first shown a dead woman, viewers were struck by the actor's sadness. Shown a dish of soup, viewers judged the actor thoughtful. Shown a playing child, viewers said the actor appeared happy.

In the hospital where I was once an orderly, we occasionally faced the task of transporting a dead body through crowded hallways without alarming the patients or their visitors. Our solution was to exploit the "Kulechov effect" by creating a context that matched people's schemas for sleeping and sedated patients: With the body's face uncovered and the sheet turned down in normal fashion, we could wheel an apparently "sleeping" body past the unsuspecting.

Figure 4–32 Is the box in the far left frame lying on the floor or hanging from the ceiling? The context defined by the inquisitive bunnies guides our perceptions. (From Shepard, 1990.)

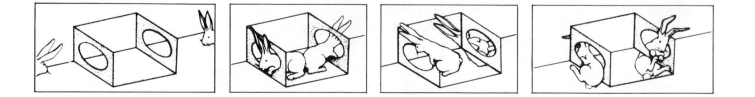

Psychology Applied: The Human Factor in Operating Machines

At the 1991 Cal Tech commencement, President George Bush proposed a national goal: "By the turn of the century, Americans must be able to get their VCRs to stop flashing 12:00."

I love our VCR, though I still haven't figured out how to make it "express record." Our stove is wonderful, except for the moments I spend puzzling over which control works which burner. The push-bar doors on our campus buildings are safe and easy, though occasionally frustrating when I push the wrong end. The extra buttons on my computer-linked phone are handy, though when transferring a call I still must look up which button to press.

Human factors psychologists help to design appliances, machines, and work settings that harness rather than confound our natural perceptions. Psychologist Donald Norman (1988) suggests how simple design changes could reduce some of our frustrations. For example, by exploiting "natural mapping," we could design controls that require no labels.

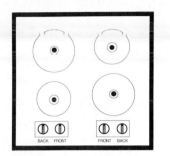

(a) Common stove controls require labeling.

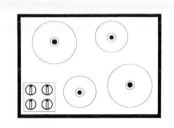

(b) By using a natural map, we needn't read labels.

Understanding human factors can do more than design for reduced frustration; it can help avoid disaster. After beginning commercial flights in the late 1960s, the Boeing 727 was involved in several landing accidents caused by pilot error. Psychologist Conrad Kraft (1978) noted a common feature of these accidents: They took place at night and involved landing short of the runway after crossing a dark stretch of water or unilluminated ground. Beyond the runway, city lights on a rising terrain would have a larger retinal image than would lights on a flat terrain, making the ground seem closer than it was. By recreating these conditions in flight simulations, Kraft discovered that they deceived pilots into thinking they were flying higher than they were (Figure 4–33). Aided by Kraft's finding, the airlines began corrective measures (such as requiring the co-pilot to monitor the altimeter and call out altitudes) and the accidents diminished.

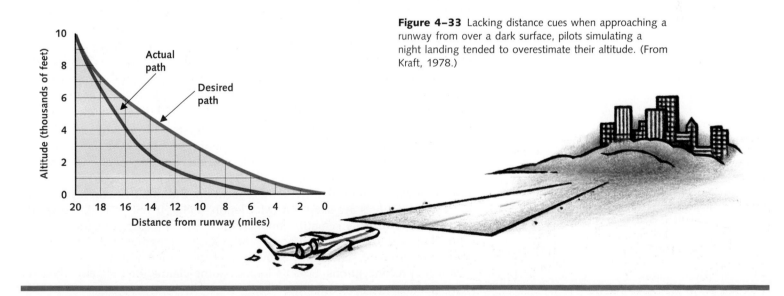

Figure 4–33 Lacking distance cues when approaching a runway from over a dark surface, pilots simulating a night landing tended to overestimate their altitude. (From Kraft, 1978.)

Context effects. What is above the woman's head? In this experiment, nearly all the participants from East Africa thought she was balancing a metal box or can on her head and that the family was sitting under a tree. Westerners, to whom corners and boxlike architecture are more common, were more likely to perceive the family as being indoors, with the woman sitting under a window. (Adapted from Gregory & Gombrich, 1973.)

Amidst conflict, the effect of context can be tragic. During a 1988 military skirmish with Iran's navy, crew members of the U.S. naval destroyer *Vincennes* interpreted radar signals as those from an attacking fighter plane. Actually, they were those of an Iranian airliner flying on course to its scheduled destination. The tragic result of this context effect: the deaths of the 291 people on board.

The effects of perceptual sets and context show how experience helps us construct perception. "We hear and apprehend only what we already half know," said Thoreau. To return to our question—is perception innate or learned?—we can answer simply: It's both.

Is There Perception Without Sensation?

Can we perceive only what we sense? Or, beyond sensory input, are we capable of **extrasensory perception (ESP)?** Half of Americans say they believe in ESP and another quarter aren't sure (Gallup & Newport, 1991). The media overflow with reports of psychic wonders: crimes solved, dreams come true, futures foretold. Are there people who can read minds, see through walls, or foretell the future?

In laboratory experiments, **parapsychologists**—those who study paranormal (literally, beyond the normal) happenings—have sometimes been astonished at psychics who seem capable of discerning the contents of sealed envelopes, influencing the roll of a die, or drawing a picture of what someone else is viewing at an unknown remote location. But other research psychologists and scientists are skeptical (McClenon, 1982). If ESP is real, we would need to overturn the scientific understanding that we are creatures whose minds are tied to our physical brains and whose perceptual experiences of the world are built of sensations. Sometimes new evidence does overturn our scientific preconceptions. So let's look at some claims for ESP, and then see why scientists remain dubious.

extrasensory perception (ESP) The controversial claim that perception can occur apart from sensory input; said to include telepathy, clairvoyance, and precognition.

parapsychology The study of paranormal phenomena including ESP and psychokinesis.

Preview Question

18. What types of ESP have been proposed, and why are most research
psychologists skeptical?

Claims of ESP

Claims of paranormal phenomena include astrological predictions, psychic healing, reincarnation, communication with the dead, and out-of-body travel. Of these, the most respectable, testable, and—for a chapter on sensation and perception—relevant claims are for three varieties of ESP:

Telepathy, or mind-to-mind communication—one person sending thoughts to another or perceiving another's thoughts.

Clairvoyance, or perceiving remote events, such as sensing that a friend's house is on fire.

Precognition, or perceiving future events, such as a political leader's death or a sporting event's outcome.

Closely linked with these are claims of *psychokinesis,* or "mind over matter," such as levitating a table or influencing the roll of a die.

Consider a clairvoyance experiment conducted by Bruce Layton and Bill Turnbull (1975) at the University of North Carolina. Layton and Turnbull had a computer generate a randomized 100-item list of the digits 1, 2, 3, 4, and 5 for each of their 179 student participants. They gave each student such a list in a sealed envelope and asked the student to guess which number was in each of the 100 positions.

By chance, 1 guess in 5, or 20 guesses out of the 100, should be correct. When told beforehand that ESP was beneficial, subjects averaged 20.66 correct out of 100. When told that ESP was harmful, they averaged only 19.49 correct. The difference might seem insignificant. Indeed, you would never notice so small an effect while observing an experiment. But a statistical analysis revealed that a difference that large among so many participants would seldom occur by chance. So Layton and Turnbull concluded that an ESP effect had occurred.

Bolstered by such experiments, believers in ESP accuse research psychologists of the same sort of skepticism that led eighteenth-century scientists to scoff at the idea that meteorites came from outer space. Novelist Arthur Koestler, who in 1983 left more than $700,000 to fund a British professorship in parapsychology, once complained that today's skeptical scientists resemble the Italian philosophers who refused to look at Jupiter's moons through Galileo's telescope—because they "knew" that such moons did not exist. Skepticism sometimes blinds people to the truth.

Skepticism About ESP

The skeptics reply that an uncritical mind is a gullible mind. Time and again, they point out, so-called psychics have exploited unquestioning audiences with amazing performances in which they *appeared* to communicate with the spirits of the dead, read minds, or levitate objects—only to have it revealed that their acts were a hoax, nothing more than the illusions of stage magicians. Indeed, many psychic deceptions have been exposed by magicians, who resent the exploitation of their arts in the name of psychic powers.

Even scientists get hoodwinked. A notable case involved two teenage magicians, Steve Shaw and Michael Edwards (Randi, 1983a,b). In 1979, this young pair approached Washington University's new parapsychology laboratory, offering to demonstrate their "psychic powers." Over the next 3 years, the two pretended to defy the laws of nature. They appeared to project mental images onto film, cause clocks to slide across a table, effortlessly bend metal objects, and move objects in sealed jars. Although forewarned against trickery by the youngsters' magician-adviser, James Randi, the laboratory director

And, as you already know, the Lakers will win tomorrow 98–93. Stay tuned for next week's scores, even though you already know those, too, right HERE on ESP-N, the Psychic Sports Channel!

The Quigmans by Buddy Hickerson; © 1990, Los Angeles Times Syndicate. Reprinted with permission.

"A man does not attain the status of Galileo merely because he is persecuted; he must also be right."

Stephen Jay Gould
Ever Since Darwin, 1973

"A psychic is an actor playing the role of a psychic."

Psychologist-magician Daryl Bem (1984)

"The most eminent scientist, untrained in magic, is putty in the hands of a clever charlatan."

Martin Gardner (1983)

Magicians Steve Shaw and Michael Edwards with their adviser, magician James Randi, after revealing their hoax at a news conference.

More recent experiments in which people attempted to send mental images to dreamers produced some intriguing initial results, but these could not be replicated even with the same subjects. Dream telepathy experiments have therefore been discontinued (Hyman, 1986).

"There comes a point where one has to accept the message of the data, that absence of evidence is evidence of absence."

Frank Close
Too Hot to Handle: The Race for Cold Fusion, 1991

ignored the warnings and for a time proclaimed that "these two kids are the most reliable of the people that we've studied" ("Psychic Abscam," 1983). This parapsychologist's gullibility illustrates how tempting it is to label phenomena *we* don't understand as beyond explanation: "What other explanation could there possibly be but ESP?" the awestruck observer asks.

Premonitions, Pretense, or Coincidence?

Can psychics see into the future? The tallied forecasts of "leading psychics" reveal meager accuracy. Between 1978 and 1985, the New Year's predictions of the *National Enquirer*'s favorite psychics yielded 2 accurate predictions out of 486 (Strentz, 1986). During these years, the psychics foresaw none of the significant unexpected events—that a woman would run for Vice President of the United States, that famine would devastate Ethiopia, that terrorism would plague Europe.

Examinations of psychic visions offered to police departments reveal that these, too, are no more accurate than guesses made by others (Reiser, 1982). Psychics working with the police do, however, generate dozens or even hundreds of predictions; this increases the odds of an occasional correct guess, which psychics can then report to the media. Moreover, vague predictions can later be interpreted to match events, which provide a perceptual set for interpreting them. Nostradamus, a sixteenth-century French psychic, explained in an unguarded moment that his ambiguous prophecies "could not possibly be understood till they were interpreted after the event and by it."

Are the spontaneous "visions" of ordinary people any more accurate? Consider our dreams. Do they foretell the future, as about half of university students believe (Messer & Griggs, 1989)? Or do they only seem to because we are more likely to recall or reconstruct dreams that seem to have come true? More than 50 years ago, two Harvard psychologists (Murray & Wheeler, 1937) tested the prophetic power of dreams. After aviator Charles Lindbergh's baby son was kidnapped and murdered but before the body was discovered, the researchers invited the public to report their dreams about the child. Of the 1300 dream reports submitted, how many accurately envisioned the child dead? A mere 5 percent. And how many also correctly anticipated the body's location—buried among trees? Only 4 of the 1300. Although this number was surely no better than chance, to those four dreamers the accuracy of their *apparent* precognitions must have seemed uncanny.

Every day each of us imagines many events. Occasionally an unlikely imagined event is bound to occur and to astonish us when it does. If you tell everyone in a group of 100 people to think "heads" before each tosses six coins, someone is likely to get all heads (whether thinking heads or not) and to feel eerie afterwards. Given the billions of events that occur in the world each day, and given enough days, some stunning coincidences are sure to occur. As Stephen Jay Gould (1980) noted, "Time converts the improbable to the inevitable."

Finally, consider this, say the skeptics: After tens of thousands of experiments, *there has never been discovered a reproducible ESP phenomenon, nor any individual who can convincingly demonstrate psychic ability* (Marks, 1986). As British psychologist Mark Hansel (1980, p. 314) put it, "After a hundred years of research, not a single individual has been found who can demonstrate ESP to the satisfaction of independent investigators," and, thus, "Today ESP is no nearer to being established than it was a hundred years ago" (1985, p. 124). A recent National Research Council investigation of ESP similarly concludes that "the best available evidence does not support the contention that these phenomena exist" (Druckman & Swets, 1988).

Another view of the impossible doghouse in Figure 4–22 (page 127) reveals the secrets of this illusion. From the photo angle in Figure 4–22, the grouping principle of closure leads us to perceive the boards as continuous.

"At the heart of science is an essential tension between two seemingly contradictory attitudes—an openness to new ideas, no matter how bizarre or counterintuitive they may be, and the most ruthless skeptical scrutiny of all ideas, old and new."

Carl Sagan (1987)

Even parapsychology advocate Charles Tart (1983) acknowledges that "ESP in the laboratory generally shows up weakly or inconsistently, so it has been hard to study its nature."

One skeptic, magician James Randi, has offered $10,000 to anyone who can demonstrate *"any* paranormal ability" before a group of competent experts. Other similar offers total more than a third of a million dollars (Jones, 1985–1986). To anyone whose claims could be authenticated, the scientific seal of approval would be worth far more. Randi's offer has been publicized for well over two decades, and dozens of people have been tested, sometimes under the scrutiny of an independent panel of judges. To refute those who say there is no ESP, one need only produce a single person who can demonstrate a single reproducible ESP phenomenon. As yet, no one has exhibited any such power.

The Mystique of ESP

In times past, there have been all kinds of crazy ideas—that bumps on the head reveal character traits, that bloodletting is a cure-all, that each sperm cell contains a miniature person inside. When faced with such claims—or with claims of mind reading or out-of-body travel or mind-over-matter—how can we separate crazy ideas from those that sound crazy but are true? At the heart of science we find a simple answer: Test them to see if they work. If they do, so much the worse for our skepticism. If they don't, so much the worse for the ideas.

This scientific attitude appears in the agreement of believers and skeptics that what parapsychology needs to give it credibility is a reproducible phenomenon and a theory to explain it. Could the Layton and Turnbull clairvoyance experiment (in which students beat chance in guessing numbers in sealed envelopes) provide such a reproducible phenomenon? The skeptical editor of the *Journal of Experimental Social Psychology*, to which Layton and Turnbull submitted their results for publication, wondered. So he and the authors reached an unusual agreement: The researchers would repeat their experiment, and the journal would then publish the results of both, regardless of the new outcome. (As this illustrates, both ESP researchers and skeptics genuinely seek truth.) The result of the second experiment? Layton and Turnbull summarized honestly and succinctly: "No [statistically] significant effects were present."

Knowing how easily people are deceived, and lacking reproducible results, most research psychologists remain skeptical. Indeed, they are dismayed by all the shows, books, and magazines on paranormal topics. Should we share their skepticism and dismay?

A personal answer: We, too, can be skeptical, but without closing ourselves to all unprovable claims. We can be open to new ideas without being gullible, discerning without being cynical. We can be critical thinkers; yet, knowing that our understanding of nature is incomplete, we can agree with Shakespeare's Hamlet that "there are more things in heaven and earth, Horatio, than are dreamt of in your philosophy."

Why are so many people predisposed to believe that ESP exists? In part, such beliefs may stem from understandable misperceptions, misinterpretations, and selective recall. But for some people there also exists an unsatisfied hunger for wonderment, an itch to experience the magical. In Britain and the United States, the founders of parapsychology were mostly people who, having lost their religious faith, were searching for a scientific basis for believing in the meaningfulness of life and the possibility of life after death (Alcock, 1985; Beloff, 1985).

To be awestruck and to gain a deep reverence for life, we need look no further than our own perceptual system and its capacity for organizing formless nerve impulses into colorful sights, vivid sounds, and evocative smells.

Within our ordinary perceptual experiences lies much that is truly extraordinary! A century of research has revealed many of the secrets of sensation and perception, but for future generations of researchers there remain profound and genuine mysteries.

Rehearse It

25. Experiments in which subjects wear glasses that displace or invert their visual fields show that, after a period of disorientation, they learn to function quite well. This ability is called
a. extrasensory perception.
b. perceptual set.
c. sensory restriction.
d. perceptual adaptation.

26. In some cases, surgeons have restored vision to patients who have been blind from birth. The newly sighted patients were able to sense colors but had difficulty
a. recognizing objects by touch.
b. recognizing the shapes of objects.
c. distinguishing figure from ground.
d. distinguishing between bright and dim light.

27. Our perceptual set influences what we perceive. This mental predisposition reflects our
a. experiences, assumptions, and expectations
b. perceptual adaptation
c. objectivity, realism, and intelligence.
d. extrasensory perception.

28. Locke and other empiricists believed that our perception of the world is learned through experience. Support for their view can be found in
a. the writings of the nativists.
b. research on depth perception.
c. research on perceptual set and context.
d. theories of color vision.

29. More than half of Americans believe in the reality of ESP (extrasensory perception). The response of psychologists to these claims has been to
a. deny the possibility of perception apart from sensation.
b. doubt the existence of mysteries and extraordinary phenomena.
c. test and critique ESP claims.
d. devise a theory that explains why ESP exists.

Reviewing Sensation and Perception

Sensing the World: Some Basic Principles

1. **What is an absolute threshold, and are we influenced by stimuli below it?**

   Each species comes equipped with sensitivities that enable it to survive and thrive. We sense only a portion of the sea of energy that surrounds us, but to this portion we are exquisitely sensitive. Our absolute threshold for any stimulus is the minimum stimulation that is detectable 50 percent of the time. Although recent experiments reveal that we can process some information from subliminal (subthreshold) stimuli, the restricted conditions under which this occurs would not enable unscrupulous opportunists to exploit us with subliminal messages.

2. **How is our threshold for detecting differences affected by the magnitude of the stimuli?**

   To survive and thrive, an organism must have difference thresholds low enough to detect minute changes in important stimuli. In humans, difference thresholds (also called just noticeable differences, or jnd's) remain proportionally constant to the magnitude of the stimulus—a principle known as Weber's law.

3. **What function does sensory adaptation serve?**

   The phenomenon of sensory adaptation helps to focus our attention on changing stimulation by diminishing our sensitivity to constant or routine odors, sounds, and so forth.

Vision

4. **How does the eye transform light energy into neural messages?**

   Each of our senses must receive stimulation, transform it into neural signals, and transmit the neural signals to the brain. In the sense of vision, the energies we experience as light are a small slice from a broad spectrum of electromagnetic waves. After being admitted into the eye through a lens, light waves strike the retina. The retina's rods and cones convert the light energy to neural impulses, which are transmitted by the optic nerve to the brain.

5. How is visual information processed in the brain?

Nerve cells in the retina process information before routing it to the brain. Within the cortex, individual feature detector cells respond to specific aspects of the visual stimulus, and their information is pooled by higher level brain cells for interpretation. Subdimensions of vision (color, movement, depth, and form) are processed separately and simultaneously, illustrating our brain's capacity for parallel processing.

6. What theories contribute to our understanding of color vision, and how are we affected by color constancy?

Research on how we see color supports two theories from the nineteenth century. First, as the Young-Helmholtz three-color theory suggests, the retina contains three types of cones, each of which is most sensitive to one of the three basic colors (red, green, or blue). Second, as opponent-process theory maintains, the nervous system codes the color-related information from the cones into pairs of opponent colors, as demonstrated by the phenomenon of afterimages and as confirmed by measuring opponent processes within visual neurons. Through color constancy, we perceive familiar objects as having consistent color despite changing illumination. Color also depends on its context.

The Other Senses

7. How does the ear transform sound energy into neural messages?

The pressure waves we experience as sound vary in frequency and amplitude, and correspondingly in perceived pitch and loudness. Through a mechanical chain of events, these sound waves traveling down the auditory canal cause minuscule vibrations in the eardrum. Transmitted via the bones of the middle ear to the fluid-filled cochlea, these vibrations create movement in tiny hair cells, triggering neural messages to the brain. We localize sound by detecting minute differences in the loudness and timing of the sounds received by each ear.

8. How do we taste and smell?

Taste, a chemical sense, is a composite of four basic sensations—sweet, sour, salty, and bitter—and of the aromas that interact with information from the taste buds. Like taste, smell is a chemical sense, but there are no basic sensations for smell.

9. How do we sense touch and feel pain?

Our sense of touch is actually four senses—pressure, warmth, cold, and pain—that combine to produce other sensations, such as a tickle. One theory of pain is that a ''gate'' in the spinal cord either opens to permit pain signals traveling up small nerve fibers to reach the brain or closes to prevent their passage. Because pain is both a physiological and psychological phenomenon, it often can be controlled through a combination of medical and psychological treatments.

10. How do we sense our body's position and movement?

Our effective functioning requires a kinesthetic sense, which notifies the brain of the position and movement of body parts, and a sense of equilibrium, which monitors the position and movement of the whole body.

Perceptual Organization

11. What did the Gestalt psychologists contribute to our understanding of perception?

The early Gestalt psychologists were impressed with the seemingly innate way in which we organize fragmentary sensory data into whole perceptions. They studied how our minds structure the information that comes to us.

12. How do the principles of figure-ground and grouping contribute to our perception of form?

To recognize an object, we must first perceive it (see it as a figure) as distinct from surrounding stimuli (the ground). We must also organize the figure into a meaningful form. Several Gestalt principles—proximity, similarity, closure, continuity, and connectedness—describe this process.

13. Why do we see the world in three dimensions?

Research using the visual cliff suggests that in many species the ability to perceive the world in three dimensions is present at, or very shortly after, birth. We transform two-dimensional retinal images into three-dimensional perceptions by use of binocular cues (such as retinal disparity and convergence) and monocular cues (such as overlap; the relative size, height, and brightness of objects; and linear perspective).

14. How do perceptual constancies help us to organize our sensations into meaningful perceptions?

The phenomena of size, shape, and brightness constancy describe how objects appear to have unchanging characteristics regardless of their true distance from us or their actual shape or illumination. These constancies explain several of the well-known visual illusions.

Interpretation

15. What does research on sensory restriction and restored vision reveal about the effects of experience on perception?

If cataract removal restores eyesight to adults who were blind from birth, they are unable to perceive the world normally. Generally, they can distinguish figure from ground and perceive colors, but even with much effort they are unable to distinguish shapes and forms. In better controlled experiments, infant kittens and monkeys have been reared with severely restricted visual input. When their visual exposure is returned to normal they, too, suffer enduring visual handicaps. It appears that for many species infancy is a critical period, during which the brain's innate visual mechanisms must be activated through experience.

16. How adaptable is our perception?

Human vision is remarkably adaptable. Given glasses that shift the world slightly to the left or right, or even turn it upside down, people manage to adapt their movements and, with practice, to move about with ease.

17. How do our assumptions, expectations, and contexts affect our perceptions?

Clear evidence that perception is influenced by our learned assumptions and beliefs as well as by sensory input comes from the many demonstrations of perceptual set. The ideas we have stored in memory help us to interpret otherwise ambiguous stimuli, a fact that helps explain why some of us "see" monsters, faces, and UFOs that others do not.

Is There Perception Without Sensation?

18. What types of ESP have been proposed, and why are most research psychologists skeptical?

Parapsychologists have attempted to document several forms of ESP, including telepathy, clairvoyance, and precognition. For a number of reasons, especially the lack of a reproducible ESP effect, most research psychologists doubt that ESP exists.

Terms and Concepts to Remember

sensation, p. 105

perception, p. 105

absolute threshold, p. 106

subliminal, p. 107

difference threshold, p. 108

just noticeable difference (jnd), p. 108

Weber's law, p. 108

sensory adaptation, p. 108

wavelength, p. 110

hue, p. 110

intensity, p. 110

pupil, p. 111

iris, p. 111

lens, p. 111

accommodation, p. 111

retina, p. 111

rods, p. 112

cones, p. 112

optic nerve, p. 112

blind spot, p. 112

feature detectors, p. 114

parallel processing, p. 115

Young-Helmholtz trichromatic (three-color) theory, p. 116

opponent-process theory, p. 117

color constancy, p. 117

visual capture, p. 118

audition, p. 118

frequency, p. 119

pitch, p. 119

middle ear, p. 119

inner ear, p. 120

cochlea [KOHK-lee-uh], p. 120

sensory interaction, p. 121

gate-control theory, p. 123

kinesthesis [kin-ehs-THEE-sehs], p. 124

equilibrium, p. 124

gestalt, p. 125

figure-ground, p. 126

grouping, p. 127

proximity, p. 127

similarity, p. 127

closure, p. 127

continuity, p. 127

connectedness, p. 127

depth perception, p. 128

visual cliff, p. 128

binocular cues, p. 128

monocular cues, p. 128

retinal disparity, p. 128

convergence, p. 129

relative size, p. 129

overlap, p. 129

linear perspective, p. 130

relative height, p. 130

relative brightness, p. 130

perceptual constancy, p. 131

perceptual adaptation, p. 136

perceptual set, p. 137

extrasensory perception (ESP), p. 140

parapsychology, p. 140

Rehearse It Answer Key

1. d.	2. b.	3. b.	4. c.	5. b.	6. c.	7. c.	8. c.	9. b.
10. a.	11. d.	12. b.	13. a.	14. b.	15. d.	16. a.	17. c.	18. c.
19. b.	20. d.	21. c.	22. c.	23. b.	24. a.	25. d.	26. b.	27. a.
28. c.	29. c.							

Critical Thinking Exercise

You have *Surveyed*, *Questioned*, *Read*, *Rehearsed*, and *Reviewed* Chapter 4. Now take your learning a step further by testing your *critical thinking* skills on the following passage.

Your college roommate, who has been your closest friend since grade school, is convinced she has psychic ability. For years she has claimed to be able to "read your mind," and often does seem to know what you are about to say or do in certain situations. She recently claimed to have experienced a precognitive "vision" a week before you were involved in an automobile accident, although she was too embarrassed to warn you of the impending danger. When pressed for the details of her "vision," she says, "I just felt that something awful was going to happen to you." To prove her psychic ability, she asks you to pick a card at random from a deck of ordinary playing cards and concentrate on its suit (hearts, diamonds, clubs, or spades) while she attempts to read the suit telepathically from your mind. Much to your amazement, and your friend's delight, she correctly identifies the card's suit.

Understand the Assertion

1. State your roommate's assertion in your own words. Define all important concepts and terms as they are used in this example.

Consider the Evidence

2. Is the evidence for your roommate's assertion based on trustworthy research?

Evaluate the Explanation

3. Evaluate the proposed explanation.
   a. Restate it in your own words.
   b. Determine whether the explanation makes sense based on the evidence.
   c. State an alternative explanation.

Check your progress on becoming a critical thinker by comparing your answers to the sample answers found in Appendix B.

Chapter 5

States of Consciousness

consciousness Selective attention to ongoing perceptions, thoughts, and feelings.

selective attention The focusing of conscious awareness on a particular stimulus.

In every science there are concepts so fundamental that they are nearly impossible to define. Biologists agree on what is alive, but not on precisely what life is. In physics, matter and energy elude simple definition. To psychologists, consciousness is similarly a fundamental yet slippery concept. What is consciousness? Is it an awareness of the world? An awareness of one's thoughts? An awareness of being aware?

Studying Consciousness

Preview Question

1. What is consciousness?

"Psychology must discard all reference to consciousness."

Behaviorist John B. Watson (1913)

At its beginning, psychology was sometimes defined as "the description and explanation of states of consciousness" (Ladd, 1887). But the difficulty of studying consciousness scientifically led many psychologists during the first half of this century to turn to direct observations of behavior—an approach favored by an emerging school of psychology called *behaviorism* (page 180). By midcentury, psychology was no longer defined as the study of consciousness or "mental life," but rather as the science of behavior. Psychology had nearly lost consciousness.

By 1960, mental concepts began to reenter psychology. Advances in neuroscience made it possible to relate brain activity to various normal mental states—waking, sleeping, dreaming. Researchers were also beginning to study altered states of consciousness induced by hypnosis and drugs. Psychologists of all persuasions were affirming the importance of mental processes (cognition). Psychology was regaining consciousness.

For most psychologists today, **consciousness** involves awareness and intention. We can define it as *selective attention to ongoing perceptions, thoughts, and feelings.* When learning a complex concept or behavior—say, learning to drive—consciousness focuses our attention on the car and the traffic. With practice, driving becomes automatic and largely unconscious, freeing our consciousness to focus on other tasks.

With experience, many tasks, such as driving, become mostly automatic, freeing our conscious attention for other matters.

Selective Attention

Perceptions come to us moment by moment, one perception vanishing as the next appears. When you were looking at the Necker cube and figure-ground demonstrations in Chapter 4, you could *know* that two interpretations were possible, yet at any moment you consciously experienced only one of them. This illustrates an important principle: Our conscious attention is *selective*. **Selective attention** means that at any moment awareness focuses on only a limited aspect of all that we are capable of experiencing. From among all the stimuli striking your body right now, you select only a few for consciousness.

Until reading this sentence, you have been unaware that your shoes are pressing against your feet or that your nose is in your line of vision. Now, suddenly, your feet feel encased, your nose stubbornly intrudes on the page before you. While attending to these words, you've also been blocking from awareness information coming from your peripheral vision. But you can change that. While staring at the X below, notice what surrounds the book (the edges of the page, your desk top, and so forth).

X

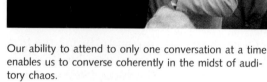

Our ability to attend to only one conversation at a time enables us to converse coherently in the midst of auditory chaos.

Another example of selective attention is the *cocktail party effect*—the ability to attend selectively to only one voice among many. Imagine hearing two conversations over a headset, one in each ear. When you pay attention to what's being said in your left ear, you don't perceive what is said in your right ear. At the level of conscious awareness, whatever has your attention has your undivided attention.

Can unnoticed stimuli affect us? Indeed yes. In one experiment, women students listened through headphones as a prose passage played in one ear. Their task was to repeat its words out loud and to check them against a written transcript (Wilson, 1979). Meanwhile, some simple, novel tunes played in the other ear. The tunes were not subliminal (below threshold)—the women could hear them easily. But with their attention selectively focused on the passage, the women were no more aware of the tunes than you normally are of your shoes. Thus, when they later heard these tunes interspersed among new ones, they could not recognize them (just as people cannot recall a conversation to which they paid no attention). Nevertheless, when asked to rate their fondness for each tune, they *preferred* the ones previously played. Their preferences revealed what their conscious memories could not. So, perception requires attention, but even unattended stimuli sometimes have subtle effects.

States of Consciousness

Many of the topics (perception, learning, memory, thinking, language, emotion) in this course involve the study of normal waking consciousness. Research in each of these areas reveals that we process much information outside of awareness. We register and react to stimuli we do not consciously perceive. We perform well-learned tasks automatically, such as typing without paying attention to where the letters are on the keyboard. We change our attitudes and reconstruct our memories with no awareness of doing so.

As far as our information processing is concerned, consciousness is but the tip of the iceberg. It is the part we are aware of, the part that enables us to exert voluntary control and to communicate our mental states to others (Kihlstrom, 1987). Unlike *unconscious* information processing (which occurs simultaneously on several parallel tracks, without our awareness), *conscious* processing takes place step-by-step, is relatively slow, and has limited capacity. Unconscious processing, like a good team of assistants, takes care of routine business so that consciousness, like a chief executive, can focus on decision making and public relations.

Psychologists may be unsure exactly what consciousness is, but they recognize that it occurs in varied states. Thus, we have not only normal seeing and hearing, reasoning and remembering, but also the altered (distorted or out-of-the-ordinary) consciousness of sleep dreams and daydreams, meditative and hypnotic states, chemically induced hallucinations and near-death visions.

circadian rhythm [ser-KAY-dee-an]   The biological clock; regular bodily rhythms (for example, of temperature and wakefulness) that occur on a 24-hour cycle.

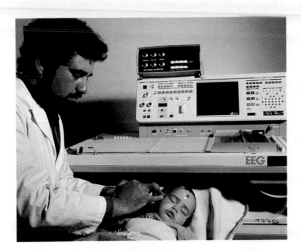

In this sleep laboratory at Technicon Medical School in Israel, a researcher electronically monitors the sleeping subject's physiological state. This information, together with observations made of the sleeper's behavior, provides clues to the mysteries of sleep.

Preview Question

2. What is the biological rhythm we experience, and how does it affect the stages of our sleep?

If our natural circadian rhythm were attuned to a 23-hour cycle, would we instead need to discipline ourselves to stay up later at night and force ourselves to stay in bed longer in the morning?

Sleep and Dreams

Sleep—sweet, renewing, mysterious sleep. Sleep—the irresistible temptation to which we must all succumb. What is it? Why must we have it? Why do we spend a third of our lives—some 25 years, on average—sleeping?

Such questions have intrigued humans for centuries. Now, some of sleep's age-old mysteries are being solved. In laboratories throughout the world, thousands have slept attached to modern gadgetry while others observed. By recording sleepers' brain waves and muscle movements, by observing and awakening them from time to time, the sleep-watchers glimpse things that a thousand years of common sense never told us. Perhaps you can anticipate some of their discoveries. Are the following statements true or false?

1. When people dream of performing some activity, their limbs often move in concert with the dream (pages 152–153).

2. Older adults sleep more than young adults (pages 153–154 and Figure 5–5).

3. After 2 or 3 sleepless days, a person's performance on a brief but demanding intellectual task suffers (page 154).

4. Sleepwalkers are acting out their dreams (pages 152–153).

5. Sleep experts recommend an occasional sleeping pill to break a pattern of insomnia (page 154).

6. The dreams we have before awakening in the morning are similar to those we have soon after falling asleep (page 156).

7. Some people dream every night; others seldom dream at all (page 153).

All these statements (adapted from Palladino & Carducci, 1983) are false. Let's see why.

The Rhythm of Sleep

The rhythm of the day parallels the rhythm of life—from our waking to a new day's birth to our nightly return to what Shakespeare called "death's counterfeit." Our bodies synchronize with the 24-hour cycle of day and night through a biological clock called the **circadian rhythm** (from the Latin *circa*, "about," and *dies*, "day"). Our body temperature, for example, rises as morning approaches, peaks during the day, and then begins to drop before we go to sleep. A transcontinental flight disrupts our circadian rhythm and we experience jet lag, mainly because we are awake when our biological clock cries, "Sleep!" If, on weekends, we stay up late and then sleep in, our biological clock begins to reset itself. When the weekend ends, the result may be "Sunday night insomnia" and "Monday morning blues."

Mysteriously, people isolated without clocks or daylight typically adopt a 25-hour day. This helps explain why most people find it easier to jet west, with an extended day, than east; why rotating shift workers adapt better to progressively later shifts than to earlier shifts; why we often must discipline ourselves to get to bed on time and force ourselves to get up. When placed in a time-free environment under constant illumination, most animals, too, exceed a 24-hour day.

There is also a biological rhythm during our sleep—about every 90 minutes we pass through a cycle of five distinct sleep stages. This fact was unknown until 8-year-old Armond Aserinsky went to bed one night in 1952. His father, Eugene, a University of Chicago graduate student, needed to test an

REM sleep Rapid eye movement sleep, a recurring sleep stage during which vivid dreams commonly occur. Also known as *paradoxical sleep*, because the muscles are relaxed (except for minor twitches) but other body systems are active.

alpha waves The relatively slow brain waves of a relaxed, awake state.

hallucinations False sensory experiences, such as seeing something without any external visual stimulus.

delta waves The large, slow brain waves associated with deep sleep.

electroencephalograph he had been repairing during the day (Aserinsky, 1988; Seligman & Yellen, 1987). He placed electrodes near Armond's eyes to record the electric current produced by the rolling eye movements believed to occur during sleep. Before long, the machine went wild, tracing deep zigzags on the graph paper. Aserinsky thought the machine was still broken. But as the night proceeded, the activity periodically recurred, indicating, Aserinsky finally realized, fast, jerky eye movements accompanied by energetic brain activity. When he awakened Armond during one such episode of *rapid eye movement* sleep (**REM sleep**), the boy reported he was having a dream.

To find out if similar cycles occur during adult sleep, Nathaniel Kleitman (1960) and Aserinsky pioneered procedures that have now been used with thousands of volunteers. To appreciate both their methods and findings, imagine yourself as a subject. When you are ready for bed, the researcher tapes electrodes to your scalp (to measure your brain's electrical waves) and to the corners of your eyes (to detect eye movements) (Figure 5–1). Other devices allow the researcher to record your heart rate, your respiration rate, your muscle tension, and even the degree of your genital arousal.

Figure 5–1 Sleep researchers measure brain-wave activity, eye movements, and muscle tension by taping electrodes to various parts of the head. (From Dement, 1978.)

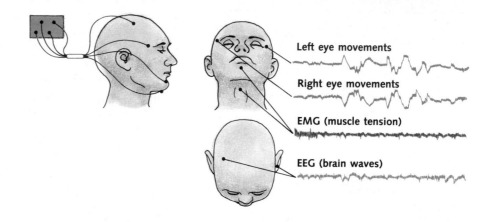

Left eye movements

Right eye movements

EMG (muscle tension)

EEG (brain waves)

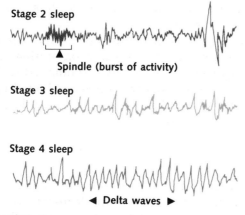

Awake, relaxed

◄ Alpha waves ►

Stage 1 sleep

Stage 2 sleep

Spindle (burst of activity)

Stage 3 sleep

Stage 4 sleep

◄ Delta waves ►

REM sleep

Figure 5–2 Brain waves and sleep stages. The regular alpha waves of an awake, relaxed state are quite different from the slower, larger delta waves of deep Stage 4 sleep. The more rapid REM sleep waves resemble the near-waking Stage 1 sleep. (From Dement, 1978.)

When you are in bed with your eyes closed, the researcher in the next room sees on the EEG the relatively slow **alpha waves** of your awake but relaxed state (Figure 5–2). As you adapt to all this gadgetry and grow tired, your breathing rate slows and your brain waves slow further and show the irregular waves of Stage 1 sleep. During this light sleep, which lasts about 2 minutes, you may experience fantastic images, which are like **hallucinations**— sensory experiences that occur without a sensory stimulus. You may have a sensation of falling (at which moment your body may suddenly jerk) or of floating weightlessly.

Soon, you relax more deeply and begin about 20 minutes of Stage 2 sleep, characterized by the periodic appearance of *sleep spindles*—bursts of brain-wave activity. Although you can still be awakened without too much difficulty during this phase, you are now clearly asleep.

Then for the next few minutes you go through the transitional Stage 3 to the deep sleep of Stage 4. Starting in Stage 3 and increasingly in Stage 4, your brain emits large, slow **delta waves.** These stages together are therefore called *delta sleep.* They last for about 30 minutes, during which you are hard to awaken. Curiously, it is during the deep sleep of Stage 4 that we may talk or walk in our sleep, or (as young children) wet the bed. Moreover, even when we are deeply asleep, our brains somehow process the meaning of certain stimuli. We move around on our beds, but we manage not to fall out of them.

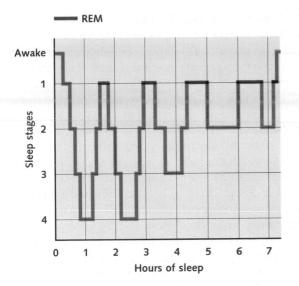

Figure 5–3 The stages in a typical night's sleep. Most people pass through a cycle of the five sleep stages several times, with the periods of Stage 4 sleep and then Stage 3 sleep diminishing and REM sleep periods increasing in duration. (From Cartwright, 1978.)

People rarely snore during dreams. When REM starts, snoring stops.

This piglet, like her companion, needs REM sleep. Deprived of it, she will replenish this deficiency if allowed to sleep undisturbed.

Preview Question

3. What is the function of sleep?

The occasional roar of passing vehicles may leave deep sleep undisturbed, but the cry from a baby's nursery quickly interrupts it.

About an hour after you first fall asleep, a strange thing happens. Rather than continuing in deep slumber, you go back up the sleep ladder. Returning through Stages 3 and 2, you enter the most intriguing sleep phase of all—REM sleep (Figure 5–3). For about 10 minutes, your brain waves become more rapid, like those of the nearly awake Stage 1 sleep. But unlike Stage 1 sleep, your heart rate rises, your breathing becomes more rapid and irregular, and every half minute or so your eyes dart around in a momentary burst of activity behind closed lids. Because anyone watching a sleeper's eyes can notice these REM bursts, it is amazing that science was ignorant of REM sleep until 1952.

During REM sleep, your genitals usually show signs of arousal (either an erection or increased vaginal lubrication). The common "morning erection" stems from the night's last REM period, often just before waking. Except during very scary dreams, genital arousal always occurs, regardless of whether the dream's content is sexual (Karacan & others, 1966). In young men, sleep-related erections outlast REM periods, lasting 30 to 45 minutes on average (Karacan & others, 1983; Schiavi & Schreiner-Engel, 1988). A typical 25-year-old man therefore has an erection during nearly half his night's sleep, a 65-year-old man for one-quarter. Many men troubled by "erectile disorder" (impotence) have morning erections, which suggests that their disorder is not physically based.

Although your brain's motor cortex is active during REM sleep, few of its neural messages reach your muscles, which are therefore very relaxed—so relaxed, in fact, that except for an occasional finger or facial twitch, you are essentially paralyzed. Moreover, you cannot easily be awakened. Thus, REM sleep is sometimes called *paradoxical sleep* because internally the body is aroused but externally it appears calm.

Even more intriguing than the paradoxical nature of REM sleep is what the rapid eye movements announce: the beginning of a dream. Even those who claim they never dream will, more than 80 percent of the time, recall a dream after being awakened during REM sleep. Unlike the fleeting images of Stage 1 sleep, REM sleep dreams are often emotional and usually storylike. (People occasionally recall dreams when awakened from stages other than REM sleep, but these dreams usually involve a single incident, such as, "I was asking George if I could borrow his hammer.")

As the night wears on, this sleep cycle repeats itself about every 90 minutes, with the deep Stage 4 sleep getting briefer and then disappearing and the REM sleep period getting progressively longer. By morning, 20 to 25 percent of our average night's sleep—some 100 minutes—has been REM sleep. This means that those who say, "I never dream" actually spend close to 600 hours a year experiencing some 1500 dreams.

Why Do We Sleep?

Sleep commands roughly one-third of our lives. Deprived of it, we begin to feel terrible; our bodies yearn for it. You can know you are sleep-deprived—as many college students are (Levine & others, 1988)—if most of the following are true: You need an alarm clock to shorten your natural sleep pattern; you feel sleepy while sitting in class or you lack vigor needed for peak performance; you collapse into sleep almost immediately after your head hits the pillow.

Obviously, we need sleep. But why? It seems an easy question to answer: Just keep people awake for several days and note how they deteriorate. The major effect is sleepiness. Given the fatigue and general malaise that accompany sleepiness (Mikulincer & others, 1989), that's no small consequence. Owing to modern light bulbs, TV sets, shift work, and social diversions, people today more than ever suffer from sleep patterns that thwart their having an energized feeling of well-being. As sleep researcher William Dement (1990) laments, "The national sleep debt is larger and more important than the national debt."

Other effects are more subtle: impaired creativity and concentration, diminished immunity to disease, slight hand tremors, irritability, occasional misperceptions on monotonous tasks (Horne, 1989; Webb, 1982a). With some tasks, such as truck driving and controlling air traffic, these effects can be devastating. The *Exxon Valdez* oil spill, the Three Mile Island nuclear accident, and Union Carbide's Bhopal, India, poison gas disaster all occurred after midnight when operators were likely to be drowsiest.

Why, then, must we sleep? We have few definite answers. Sleep probably helps restore body tissues, especially those of the brain. In one study of runners in a 92-kilometer (57-mile) ultramarathon, the competitors averaged 7 hours of sleep during nights before the race and 8½ hours during the two nights after the race. The night after the run, deep Stage 4 sleep doubled (Shapiro & others, 1981).

Sleep may also play a role in the growth process. During deep sleep, the pituitary gland releases a growth hormone. As adults grow older, they release less of this hormone, and they spend less time in deep sleep (Pekkanen, 1982). In addition, the sleeper's lower body temperature conserves energy for the daytime hours. These physiological discoveries are only beginning to solve the ongoing riddle of sleep. As Dement (1978, p. 83) deadpanned, "we have miles to go before we sleep."

Sleep Disorders

The idea that "everyone needs 8 hours of sleep" is untrue. Newborns spend nearly two-thirds of their day asleep, most adults no more than one-third. Age-related differences in average time spent sleeping are rivaled by differences in the normal amount of sleep among individuals at any age. Some people thrive with fewer than 6 hours of sleep per night; others regularly sleep 9 hours or more. (Among various mammals, the need for sleep varies more widely: Horses and cows sleep only 3 to 4 hours per day; rats and cats, 14 to 15 hours [Webb, 1982b].) Human sleep differences are not accompanied by striking personality differences (Webb, 1979). But sleep patterns may be genetically influenced. When Wilse Webb and Scott Campbell (1983) checked the pattern and duration of sleep among fraternal and identical twins, only the identical twins were strikingly similar.

Whatever their normal need for sleep, some 10 to 15 percent of adults complain of **insomnia**—*recurring* problems in falling or staying asleep. True insomnia is not the occasional inability to sleep that we experience when anxious or excited. When stressed, alertness is a natural and adaptive response. We commonly underestimate the amount of sleep we get on restless nights. Even if we've been awake only an hour, we may *think* we've had insomnia much of the night, because that's the part we remember.

The most common quick fixes for true insomnia, sleeping pills and alcohol, aggravate the problem. Both reduce REM sleep; when the drugs are discontinued, the insomnia may worsen. Sleep experts offer other alternatives:

Relax before bedtime.

"Sleep faster, we need the pillows."

Yiddish proverb

Preview Question

4. What are the major sleep disorders?

"The lion and the lamb shall lie down together, but the lamb will not be very sleepy."

Woody Allen in the movie
Love and Death, 1975

"Only about one-third of lost sleep is made up. This recovery sleep contains much of the missing Stage 4 sleep and about half of the missing REM sleep."

James Horne
Why We Sleep, 1988

insomnia A sleep disorder involving recurring problems in falling or staying asleep.

narcolepsy A sleep disorder characterized by uncontrollable sleep attacks in which the sufferer lapses directly into REM sleep, often at inopportune times.

sleep apnea A sleep disorder characterized by temporary cessations of breathing during sleep and consequent momentary reawakenings.

night terrors A sleep disorder characterized by high arousal and an appearance of being terrified; unlike nightmares, night terrors occur during Stage 4 sleep, within 2 or 3 hours of falling asleep, and are seldom remembered.

Avoid caffeine (this means chocolate, too) after late afternoon and avoid rich foods before bedtime. A glass of milk may help. (Milk provides raw materials for the manufacture of serotonin, a neurotransmitter that facilitates sleep.)

Sleep on a regular schedule (rise at the same time even after a restless night) and avoid naps.

Exercise regularly, but not in the late evening.

Reassure yourself that the temporary loss of sleep causes no great harm.

If nothing else works, aim for less sleep; go to bed later or get up earlier.

Rarer but more severe than insomnia are the sleep disorders narcolepsy and sleep apnea. People with **narcolepsy** suffer periodic, overwhelming sleepiness, sometimes at the most inopportune times—perhaps just after taking a terrific swing at a softball or when laughing loudly or shouting angrily (Dement, 1978). The person collapses directly into a brief period of REM sleep, with its accompanying loss of muscular tension. The estimated 100,000 or more Americans who suffer from narcolepsy must live with extra caution. As a traffic menace, "snoozing is second only to boozing," says the American Sleep Disorders Association, and those with narcolepsy are especially at risk (Aldrich, 1989).

A monitor connected to this sleep apnea sufferer sounds an alarm each time he stops breathing. By better understanding this disorder, researchers hope to help those afflicted.

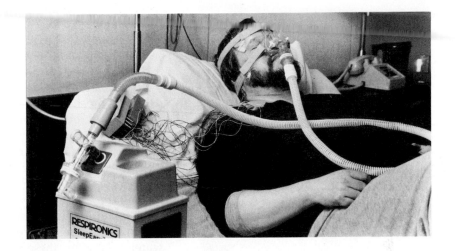

The National Heart, Lung, and Blood Institute reports that some 4 percent of people (mostly overweight men) suffer from **sleep apnea.** They intermittently stop breathing during sleep (*apnea* means "stopping respiration"). After an airless minute or so, decreased blood oxygen arouses the sleeper to snort in air for a few seconds. The process repeats hundreds of times during a night's sleep. Apart from sleepiness during the day—and their mates' complaints about their loud "snoring"—apnea sufferers are often unaware of their disorder.

Still other sleepers, mostly children, experience **night terrors.** The person might sit up or walk around, talk incoherently, experience a doubling of heart and breathing rates, and appear terrified (Hartmann, 1981). The night-terror sufferer very seldom awakens fully and recalls little or nothing the next morning—at most a fleeting, frightening image. Night terrors are not nightmares, which typically occur during early morning REM sleep. Like sleepwalking, night terrors usually occur during the first few hours of sleep and during Stage 4 sleep (Figure 5–4).

Figure 5–4 Night terrors and nightmares in the sleep laboratory. Night terrors occur within 2 or 3 hours of falling asleep, during Stage 4 sleep. Nightmares occur toward morning, during REM sleep. (From Hartmann, 1984.)

manifest content According to Freud, the remembered story line of a dream (as distinct from its latent content).

latent content According to Freud, the underlying but censored meaning of a dream (as distinct from its manifest content). Freud believed that a dream's latent content functions as a safety valve.

Preview Question

5. What do we dream?

Nocturnal mysteries: Francisco de Goya's "The Dream of Reason Produces Monsters."

Preview Question

6. What is the function of dreams?

Dreams

Discovering the link between REM sleep and dreaming opened a new era in dream research. Instead of relying on someone's hazy recall of a dream hours afterward, it became possible to catch dreams as they happen. Researchers could awaken their subjects during a REM sleep period, or within 5 minutes afterward, and get a vivid account of the dream.

What We Dream

REM dreams are vivid, emotional, and bizarre. Several times a night, you are the creator and producer of a surrealistic mental movie, in which events frequently occur in a jumbled sequence, scenes change suddenly, people appear and disappear, and physical laws, such as gravity, may be violated. Yet dreams are so vivid that we may confuse them with reality. Occasionally, we may be sufficiently aware during a dream to wonder whether we are, in fact, dreaming. When experiencing such *lucid dreams,* some people are able to test their state of consciousness. If they can perform some absurd act, such as floating in the air, then they know they are dreaming.

Although we are more likely to be awakened by and to remember our most emotional dreams, many dreams are rather ordinary. When awakened during REM sleep, people report dreams with sexual imagery less often than you might think. In one study, only 1 in 10 dreams among young men and 1 in 30 among young women had sexual overtones (Hall & Van de Castle, 1966). (Recall that genital arousal typically accompanies REM sleep, so it is usually *not* caused by sexual dreams.) More commonly, we dream of daily life events, such as a meeting at work or taking an exam. Six years of our life we spend dreaming, most of which is anything but sweet: People commonly dream of repeatedly failing in an attempt to do something; of being attacked, pursued, or rejected; or of experiencing misfortune (Hall & others, 1982).

The story line of our dreams—what Sigmund Freud called their **manifest content**—often incorporates experiences and preoccupations from the day's events, especially in our first dreams of the night. The sensory stimuli of our sleeping environment may also intrude. A particular odor or the telephone's ringing may be instantly and ingeniously woven into the dream story. In one experiment, William Dement and Edward Wolpert (1958) lightly sprayed cold water on dreamers' faces. Compared to sleepers who did not get the cold water treatment, these subjects were more likely to dream about water— about waterfalls, leaky roofs, or even about being sprayed by someone.

We do not, however, remember taped information played while we are soundly asleep (Eich, 1990). In fact, experiences that occur during the 5 minutes just before falling asleep are typically lost from memory (Roth & others, 1988). This helps explain why dreams that momentarily awaken us are mostly forgotten by morning. To remember a dream, get up and stay awake for a while.

Why We Dream

In his landmark book *The Interpretation of Dreams,* published in 1900, Freud argued that a dream is a psychic safety valve that harmlessly discharges otherwise unacceptable feelings. According to Freud, a dream's manifest content is but a censored, symbolic version of its **latent content,** which consists of unconscious drives and wishes that would be threatening if expressed directly. Although most dreams do not have overt sexual imagery, Freud nevertheless believed that most adult dreams can be "traced back by analysis to

THC The major active ingredient in marijuana; triggers a variety of effects, including mild hallucinations.

Table 5-1

A Guide to Selected Psychoactive Drugs

Drug	Type	Pleasurable effects	Adverse effects
Alcohol	Depressant	Initial high followed by relaxation and disinhibition	Depression, memory loss, organic damage, impaired reactions
Heroin	Depressant	Rush of euphoria, relief from pain	Depressed physiology, agonizing withdrawal
Cocaine	Stimulant	Rush of euphoria, confidence, energy	Cardiovascular stress, suspiciousness, depressive crash
Marijuana	Mild hallucinogen	Enhances sensation, relieves pain, distorts time, relaxed high	Lowered sex hormones, disrupted memory, lung damage
Nicotine	Stimulant	Arouses and relaxes, sense of well-being	Heart disease, cancer (from tars)

Preview Question

14. Why do people use psychoactive drugs?

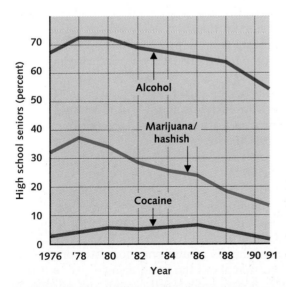

Figure 5–8 The percentage of high school seniors who report having used alcohol, marijuana, or cocaine during the past 30 days has declined since the late 1970s. (From Johnston & others, 1992.)

Influences on Drug Use

Drug use by North American youth increased during the 1970s and declined during the 1980s. In the University of Michigan's annual survey of 16,000 high school seniors, the proportion who believed there is "great risk" in regular marijuana use rose from 35 percent in 1978 to 79 percent in 1991 (Johnston & others, 1992). After peaking in 1979, marijuana use by this age group has since declined (Figure 5–8). In the American Council on Education's annual survey of new college students, support for the legalization of marijuana dropped from 53 percent in 1977 to 18 percent in 1991 (Astin & others, 1987, 1991). Similar attitude and usage changes appear in surveys of Canadian teens (Smart & Adlaf, 1989).

Other studies reveal a changing national attitude toward alcohol. More than at any time since prohibition, health-and safety-conscious Americans see alcohol less as a cheerful beverage than as a drug to be shunned. Gallup surveys show the number of abstainers steadily rising—from 29 percent in 1978 to 43 percent in 1990 (Gallup & Newport, 1990). Likewise, the number of new collegians who reported abstinence from beer during the past year increased from 25 percent in 1981 to 43 percent in 1991. Vigorously inform people about the health hazards of using cocaine, marijuana, alcohol, or tobacco and—without therapy, support groups, or medicines—many will simply stop.

Still, many people continue to use psychoactive drugs. For those adolescents whose focus is on having fun in the here-and-now, occasional drug use may represent thrill-seeking. Others, though, become regular drug users. Why?

Some people may be biologically vulnerable. For example, evidence accumulates that heredity influences alcoholic tendencies. Consider:

Adopted individuals are more susceptible to alcoholism if one or both of their biological parents is alcoholic (Mirin & Weiss, 1989).

Having an alcoholic identical twin also puts one at increased risk (Heath & others, 1989).

Compared to children of nonalcoholics, children of alcoholics appear more sensitive to alcohol's intoxicating effect (Newlin & Thomson, 1990).

Researchers have bred rats that prefer alcoholic drinks to water (Holden, 1991b).

Such findings have fueled the search for a better understanding of genetic and biochemical influences on addiction. The biggest study yet—a $25 million, 5-year analysis of 600 U.S. alcoholics and their relatives—is under way. If biological markers of addiction-proneness can be found, then perhaps young people at risk for specific addictions can be identified and counseled.

Psychological and social factors also have an important influence. In their studies of New Jersey and California youth and young adults, Michael Newcomb and L. L. Harlow (1986) found that one psychological factor is the feeling that one's life is meaningless and directionless, a common feeling among school dropouts who subsist without job skills, without privilege, without hope.

Other studies reveal that heavy users of alcohol, marijuana, and cocaine often have experienced significant stress or failure and are depressed. As we noted earlier, alcohol temporarily dulls the pain of self-awareness, which can make it a way to avoid having to cope with depression, anger, anxiety, or insomnia. The relief may be temporary, but as Chapter 6, Learning, explains, behavior is often more controlled by its immediate than by its later consequences.

Especially for teenagers, drug use also has social roots. Peers influence attitudes about drugs; they also provide the drugs and establish the social context for their use. If an adolescent's friends use drugs, the odds are that he or she will, too. If the friends don't, the temptation may not even arise. Indeed, the peer factor is so powerful that other predictors of adolescent drug use, such as family strength, religiousness, and school adjustment, seem to operate through their effects on peer associations. Those who do use drugs are more likely to stop if indeed their drug use was peer influenced (Kandel & Raveis, 1989). When the friends stop or the social network changes, usage typically ceases. Teenagers who come from happy families and do well in school seldom use drugs, in large part because they rarely associate with those who do (Oetting & Beauvais, 1987, 1990).

Smoking, for example, usually begins during early adolescence and is especially common among those whose friends, parents, and siblings smoke (Chassin & others, 1987). Adolescents learn behaviors through the models they imitate and the social rewards they receive. Teens who start smoking typically have friends who smoke, pressure them to start, and offer cigarettes (Evans & others, 1988). Moreover, many teens perceive teenage smokers as tough, precocious, and sociable (Barton & others, 1982). Self-conscious adolescents, who think the world is watching their every move, may begin smoking to imitate those cool models, to receive the social reward of being accepted by them, and to project a mature image (Covington & Omelich, 1988).

These findings suggest three channels of influence for drug prevention and treatment programs: (1) education about the long-term costs of a drug's temporary pleasures, (2) efforts to boost people's self-esteem and purpose in life, and (3) attempts to modify peer associations or to "inoculate" youth against peer pressures. People are *very* unlikely to abuse drugs if they understand the physical and psychological costs, feel good about themselves and where their lives are heading, and are in a peer group that disapproves of drug use.

Some warning signs of alcoholism:

- drinking binges
- regretting things done or said when drunk
- feeling low or guilty after drinking
- failing to honor a resolve to drink less
- drinking to alleviate depression or anxiety
- avoiding family or friends when drinking

In the real world, alcohol accounts for one-sixth or less of beverage use. In television's world, alcohol drinking occurs more often than the combined drinking of coffee, tea, soft drinks, and water (Gerbner, 1990).

Rehearse It

11. Depressants are drugs that reduce neural activity and slow down body functions. The depressants include alcohol, barbiturates,
a. and opiates.
b. cocaine, and morphine.
c. caffeine, nicotine, and marijuana.
d. and amphetamines.

12. Alcohol is a depressant that, in significant doses, powerfully affects behavior. A few alcoholic drinks may make a person more helpful, more talkative, more "caring"; or it may make a person more aggressive, more stubborn, more daring. These alcohol effects result from
a. alcoholic blackouts or memory losses.

b. deprivation of REM sleep.
c. sensory arousal and hallucination.
d. the lowering of inhibitions.

13. Nicotine, caffeine, the amphetamines, and cocaine stimulate neural activity, arouse bodily functions, and
a. induce sensory hallucinations.
b. interfere with memory.
c. induce a temporary sense of well-being.
d. lead to heroine use.

14. Smoking marijuana can relieve certain kinds of pain and nausea. It also
a. impairs coordination, perception, and memory.

b. inhibits people's reactions.
c. increases male sex hormone levels.
d. stimulates brain cell development.

15. Drug use by young North Americans generally declined during the 1980s. *Social* explanations for drug use today focus on the powerful effect of peer influence. An important *psychological* contributor to drug use is
a. inflated self-esteem.
b. the feeling that life is meaningless or hopeless.
c. academic and job pressures.
d. overprotective parents.

Reviewing States of Consciousness

Studying Consciousness

1. What is consciousness?

Consciousness can be experienced in various normal and altered states, all of which involve a focused awareness of perceptions, thoughts, and feelings as they occur. At any moment we are conscious of a very limited amount of all that we are capable of experiencing. The cocktail party effect—the ability to attend to only one voice among many—is one manifestation of this selective attention.

Sleep and Dreams

2. What is the biological rhythm we experience, and how does it affect the stages of our sleep?

Our daily schedule of waking and sleeping is timed with a body clock known as circadian rhythm. Each night's sleep also has a rhythm of its own, cycling from transitional Stage 1 sleep to deep Stage 4 sleep and back up to the more internally active REM sleep stage about every 90 minutes. Periods of Stage 4 sleep progressively shorten and periods of REM sleep lengthen through the night.

3. What is the function of sleep?

Depriving people of sleep has failed to reveal why, physiologically, we need sleep. Recent research reveals that sleep is linked with the release of pituitary growth hormone and that it may help to restore exhausted tissues.

4. What are the major sleep disorders?

The disorders of sleep include insomnia (recurring wakefulness), narcolepsy (uncontrollable lapsing into REM sleep), sleep apnea (the temporary cessation of breathing while sleeping), and night terrors (high arousal and terrified appearance occurring during Stage 4 sleep).

5. What do we dream?

Although conscious thoughts can occur during any sleep stage, waking people up during REM sleep yields predictable "dreamlike" reports; waking them up during other sleep stages only occasionally yields a fleeting image. Our dreams are mostly of ordinary events; they often relate to everyday experiences and more frequently involve anxiety or misfortune than triumphant achievements.

6. What is the function of dreams?

Freud believed that a dream's manifest content is a censored version of its latent content, which gratifies our unconscious wishes. Newer explanations of why we dream suggest that dreams help process information from the day and fix it in memory, that dreams serve a physiological function, or that dreams are the brain's efforts to string together periodic visual hallucinations due to bursts of activity in the visual cortex. Despite their differences, most theorists agree that REM sleep and its associated dreams serve an important function, as shown by the REM rebound that occurs following REM deprivation.

Daydreams and Meditation

7. What is the function of daydreams and meditation?

Virtually everyone daydreams, especially in times when attention can be freed from the tasks at hand. Daydreaming can be adaptive; it can help us prepare for future events and may substitute for impulsive behavior. Meditation, like deep relaxation, can help relieve stress-related symptoms and illnesses.

Hypnosis

8. What do hypnotized people experience, and how do they behave?

It is now widely agreed that hypnosis is a state of heightened suggestibility; that although hypnosis may help someone to recall something, the hypnotist's beliefs frequently work their way into the subject's recollections; that hypnotized people cannot be made to act against their will any more than nonhypnotized people can; that hypnosis can be at least temporarily therapeutic; that hypnotizable people can enjoy significant pain relief; and that hypnosis can be distinguished from the meditative states.

9. Should hypnosis be considered an extension of normal consciousness or an altered state?

There is still debate on whether hypnosis is a by-product of normal social and cognitive processes or whether it is an altered state of consciousness, perhaps involving a dissociation between levels of consciousness.

Drugs and Consciousness

10. What are psychoactive drugs?

Psychoactive drugs are perception- and mood-altering substances. A surprising number of these drugs, such as caffeine, nicotine, and alcohol, are legal and a part of everyday life. The use of psychoactive drugs often leads to tolerance and physical and/or psychological dependence. Users who are physically dependent will experience withdrawal when trying to stop taking the drug. The three types of psychoactive drugs are depressants, stimulants, and hallucinogens.

11. What are the depressants, and what are their effects?

Alcohol, barbiturates, and the opiates are examples of depressants, which dampen neural activity and slow down body functions. Alcohol seems to enliven by disinhibiting both harmful and helpful tendencies and by impairing judgment. Alcohol also disrupts the processing of recent experiences into long-term memory and reduces self-awareness. User expectation strongly influences alcohol's behavioral effects. Barbiturates can be especially dangerous in combination with alcohol. The harmful aftereffects of opiates oppose and offset the temporary pleasure they induce.

12. What are the stimulants, and what are their effects?

Caffeine, nicotine, the amphetamines, and cocaine are examples of stimulants, which stimulate neural activity and arouse body functions. The reinforcing effects of nicotine make smoking a difficult habit to kick, but increased knowledge of its devastating health effects has led to a decreasing percentage of Americans who smoke. All stimulants, but especially cocaine and crack, produce a crash of agitated depression as the drug wears off. This reinforces taking more drug to get out of the depression, leading regular cocaine and crack users to become addicted. As with nearly all psychoactive drugs, stimulants act at the synapses by influencing the brain's neurotransmitters, and their effects depend on dosage and the user's personality and expectations.

13. What are the hallucinogens, and what are their effects?

LSD and marijuana are examples of hallucinogens, which distort perception and evoke sensory images without sensory input. Both LSD and marijuana can distort the user's judgments of time and, depending on the setting in which they are taken, can alter sensation and perception. Similar hallucinations are reported in near-death experiences, perhaps as a result of oxygen deprivation in the brain. Although marijuana can be therapeutic for those enduring glaucoma or chemotherapy, it has detrimental effects on health, judgment, and memory.

14. Why do people use psychoactive drugs?

Drug use among teenagers and young adults has declined during the 1980s. Nevertheless, psychological factors (such as stress, depression, and hopelessness) and social factors (such as peer pressures) combine to lead many people to experiment with—and become dependent on—drugs. New evidence suggests there may also be genetic and biochemical influences on addiction.

Terms and Concepts to Remember

consciousness, p. 149

selective attention, p. 149

circadian rhythm [ser-KAY-dee-an], p. 151

REM sleep, p. 152

alpha waves, p. 152

hallucinations, p. 152

delta waves, p. 152

insomnia, p. 154

narcolepsy, p. 155

sleep apnea, p. 155

night terrors, p. 155

manifest content, p. 156

latent content, p. 156

REM rebound, p. 158

Rehearse It Answer Key

1. c. **2.** b. **3.** a. **4.** d. **5.** a. **6.** d. **7.** a. **8.** c. **9.** b.

10. c. **11.** a. **12.** d. **13.** c. **14.** a. **15.** b.

Critical Thinking Exercise

You have *Surveyed*, *Questioned*, *Read*, *Rehearsed*, and *Reviewed* Chapter 5. Now take your learning a step further by testing your *critical thinking* skills on the following passage.

Consider the following hypnosis "experiment." "Geraldo the hypnotist" is invited to demonstrate hypnosis to your psychology class. He brings along three volunteers currently enrolled in his hypnosis certification course. Geraldo claims that hypnotists can trigger specific behaviors, perceptions, and memories in subjects because hypnosis involves a unique physiological and psychological state. He then hypnotizes the volunteers and begins a demonstration of age regression. The volunteers are "regressed" back to their first day of kindergarten. Remarkably, their behavior and speech seem childlike. After instructing them to forget everything that happened, Geraldo brings the subjects out of the hypnotic state and invites you and your classmates to question them. To your amazement, the subjects report no memory of the incident. Geraldo concludes that his presentation demonstrates that hypnotic age regression actually causes subjects to relive earlier experiences, while the suggestion of posthypnotic amnesia erases memories from the brain.

Understand the Assertion

1. State the hypnotist's assertion in your own words. Define all important concepts and terms as they are used in this example.

Consider the Evidence

2. Is the evidence for the hypnotist's assertion based on trustworthy research?

Evaluate the Explanation

3. Evaluate the explanation for the hypnotist's conclusion.
   a. Restate the explanation in your own words.
   b. Determine whether the explanation makes sense based on the evidence.
   c. State an alternative explanation.
   d. Suggest a more valid test of hypnosis.

Check your progress on becoming a critical thinker by comparing your answers to the sample answers found in Appendix B.

For Further Information

You can find further information in this text regarding drugs on the following pages:

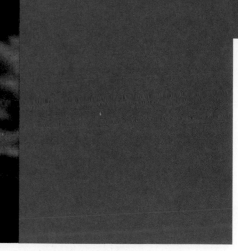

Learning

"Actually, sex just isn't that important to me."
Drawing by Sidney Harris.

learning   A relatively permanent change in an organism's behavior due to experience with the environment.

When a chinook salmon first emerges from its egg in the gravel bed of a stream, its genes provide many of the behavioral instructions it needs for life. It instinctively knows how and where to swim, what to eat, and how to protect itself from predators. Following this built-in plan, the young salmon soon begins a trek to the sea. After some 4 years in the ocean, instinct drives the mature salmon back to its birthplace. It navigates hundreds of miles to the mouth of its home river and then, guided by the scent of its home stream, begins an upstream odyssey to its ancestral spawning ground. Once there, the salmon seeks out the exact conditions of temperature, gravel, and water flow that will maximize the success of its breeding, and then mates and dies.

Unlike the salmon, we are not born with a genetic blueprint for life. Much of what we do we must learn from experience. Although we must struggle to find the life direction a salmon is born with, our learning gives us flexibility. We can learn how to build igloos or grass huts or underwater air chambers and thereby adapt to almost any environment. Indeed, nature's most important gift to us may be our *adaptability*—our capacity to learn new behaviors that enable us to cope with ever-changing circumstances. Were it not for our ability to learn, our migrating ancestors might not have survived their encounters with new animals, new landscapes, new weather patterns.

No topic is closer to the heart of psychology than **learning,** *a relatively permanent change in an organism's behavior due to experience.* Simple animals can learn simple associations. If disturbed by a squirt of water, the sea snail *Aplysia* will protectively withdraw its gill. If the squirts continue, as happens naturally in choppy water, the withdrawal response diminishes as the snail becomes accustomed to it. But if the snail repeatedly receives a shock just after being squirted, its withdrawal response to the squirt alone becomes stronger. Somehow the animal has learned to associate the squirt with the shock that will follow. More complex animals can learn more complex associations, especially those that bring favorable consequences. Sea lions in an aquarium will repeat behaviors, such as slapping and barking, that prompt people to toss them food. Very complex animals, such as chimpanzees, can learn behaviors by merely observing others perform them. We humans can learn in all these ways, and through language we can learn things we have neither experienced nor observed.

In earlier chapters we considered the learning of moral ideas, of self-concept, of visual perceptions. In later chapters we will consider how learning shapes our thought and language, our motivations and emotions, our personalities and attitudes.

Learning in all such realms breeds hope. What is learnable we can potentially teach—a fact that encourages parents, educators, athletic coaches, and animal trainers. What has been learned we can potentially change by new learning—an assumption that underlies counseling, psychotherapy, and re-

behaviorism The view that (1) psychology should be an objective science that (2) studies only overt behavior without reference to mental processes. Most research psychologists today agree with (1) but not (2).

unconditioned response (UCR) In classical conditioning, the unlearned, naturally occurring response to the unconditioned stimulus, such as salivation when food is in the mouth.

unconditioned stimulus (UCS) In classical conditioning, a stimulus that unconditionally—naturally and automatically—triggers a response.

conditioned response (CR) In classical conditioning, the learned response to a conditioned stimulus (CS).

conditioned stimulus (CS) In classical conditioning, an originally neutral stimulus that, after association with an unconditioned stimulus (UCS), comes to trigger a conditioned response.

habilitation. No matter how unhappy, unsuccessful, or unloving we are, that need not be the end of our story. Of all the world's creatures, we humans are the most capable of changing our behavior through learning.

By definition, experience is key to learning. More than 2000 years ago, the classical Greek philosopher Aristotle concluded that we learn by association. Our minds naturally connect events that occur in sequence: We *associate* them. If, after seeing and smelling freshly baked bread, you eat some and find it satisfying, then the next time you see and smell fresh bread, your experience will lead you to expect that eating some will be satisfying again. And if you associate a sound with a frightening consequence, then your fear may be aroused by the sound itself. As one 4-year-old exclaimed after watching a TV character get mugged, "If I had heard that music, I wouldn't have gone around the corner!" (Wells, 1981).

This chapter describes three ways of learning that enable us to adapt to our environments. We learn to expect and prepare for significant events such as food or pain—a basic type of learning called *classical conditioning*. We also learn to repeat acts that bring good results and to avoid acts that bring bad results—a type of learning called *operant conditioning*. And by watching others, we gain new behaviors indirectly—a phenomenon called *observational learning*.

In searching for the laws underlying such learning, psychologist John B. Watson (1913) urged his colleagues to discard reference to inner thoughts, feelings, and motives. Forget the mind, said Watson. Psychology should instead study how organisms respond to stimuli in their environments. "Its theoretical goal is the prediction and control of behavior." Simply said, psychology should be an objective science based on *observable behavior*. This perspective, which dominated American psychology during the first half of this century, Watson called **behaviorism.**

Classical Conditioning

Although the idea of learning by association generated much philosophical discussion, it was not until this century that psychology's most famous research verified it. For many people, the name Ivan Pavlov rings a bell. Pavlov was driven by a lifelong passion for research. After receiving a medical degree at age 33, he spent the next two decades studying the digestive system, work that earned him Russia's first Nobel prize in 1904. But it was the novel experiments on learning, to which he devoted the last three decades of his life, that earned this feisty scientist his place in history.

Pavlov's Experiments

Preview Question

2. How does classical conditioning demonstrate learning by association?

Pavlov's new direction came when his creative mind seized on an incidental finding. After studying salivary secretion in dogs, he knew that when he put food in a dog's mouth the animal would invariably salivate. He also noticed that when he worked with the same dog repeatedly, the dog salivated to food-related stimuli—to the mere sight of the food, to the food dish, to the person who regularly brought the food, or even to the sound of that person's approaching footsteps. Because these "psychic secretions" interfered with his experiments on digestion, Pavlov considered them an annoyance—until he realized they pointed to a simple but important form of learning. From that time on, Pavlov studied learning, which he hoped might enable him to understand better the workings of the brain.

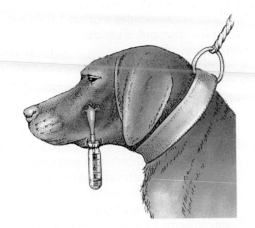

Figure 6–1 Pavlov's device for recording salivation. The isolated dog's saliva was collected drop by drop in a tube. Food was delivered by remote control, and, through a window, the experimenter observed the dog. (Adapted from Goodwin, 1991.)

Remember:

UCS = UnConditioned Stimulus
UCR = UnConditioned Response
CS = Conditioned Stimulus
CR = Conditioned Response

Figure 6–2 Pavlov's classic experiment. By presenting a neutral stimulus—the sound of a tone—just before an unconditioned stimulus (UCS)—food in mouth—the neutral stimulus became a conditioned stimulus (CS). The CS now triggers a conditioned response (CR)—salivation.

At first, Pavlov and his assistants tried to imagine what the dog was thinking and feeling as it drooled in anticipation of the food. This only got them into fruitless debates. So to attack the phenomenon more objectively, they experimented. They paired various neutral stimuli with food in the mouth to see if the dog would begin salivating to the neutral stimuli alone. To eliminate the possible influence of extraneous stimuli, they isolated the dog in a small room, secured it in a harness, and attached a device that diverted its saliva to a measuring instrument (Figure 6–1). From an adjacent room they could present food—at first by sliding in a food bowl, later by blowing meat powder into the dog's mouth at a precise moment. If a neutral stimulus—something the dog could see or hear—now regularly signaled the arrival of food, would the dog eventually begin salivating to the neutral stimulus alone?

The answer proved to be yes. Just before placing food in the dog's mouth to produce salivation, Pavlov would sound a tone. After several pairings of tone and food, the dog began salivating to the tone alone in anticipation of the meat powder. Using this procedure, Pavlov conditioned dogs to salivate to other stimuli—a buzzer, a light, a touch on the leg, even the sight of a circle.

Now for some necessary terminology: Pavlov called the salivation in response to food in the mouth an **unconditioned response (UCR)** because it is innate, or *unlearned*. The UCR is not conditional upon the dog's previous experience (Figure 6–2). Food in the mouth automatically, unconditionally, triggers a dog's salivary reflex. Thus, Pavlov called it an **unconditioned stimulus (UCS)**.

Salivation in response to the tone is conditional upon the dog's learning the association between the tone and the food. This learned response we therefore call the **conditioned response (CR).** The previously neutral tone stimulus that now triggers the conditional salivation is called the **conditioned stimulus (CS).** You can distinguish between these two kinds of stimuli and responses by remembering that conditioned = learned, and *un*conditioned = *un*learned.

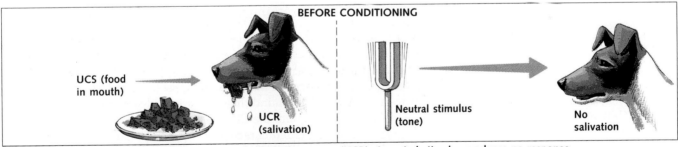

An unconditioned stimulus (UCS) produces an unconditioned response (UCR). A neutral stimulus produces no response.

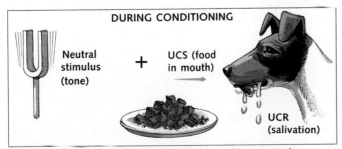

The unconditioned stimulus is presented just after a neutral stimulus. The unconditioned stimulus continues to produce an unconditioned response.

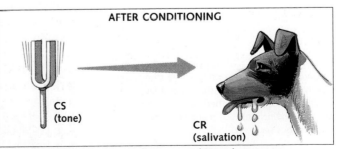

The neutral stimulus now produces a conditioned response (CR), thereby becoming a conditioned stimulus (CS).

classical conditioning Reflexive learning in which an organism comes to associate significant events. A neutral stimulus that signals an unconditioned stimulus (UCS) begins to produce a response that anticipates and prepares for the unconditioned stimulus. (Also known as *Pavlovian conditioning*.)

acquisition The initial stage of learning, during which a response is established and gradually strengthened. In classical conditioning, the phase in which a stimulus comes to evoke a conditioned response. (In operant conditioning, below, the strengthening of a reinforced response.)

Preview Question

3. How do the processes of acquisition, extinction, spontaneous recovery, generalization, and discrimination affect a CR?

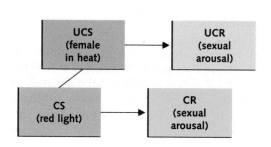

The quail's sexual conditioning. As in Figure 6–2, the top row indicates *before* conditioning, and the bottom row *after* conditioning.

Check yourself: If the aroma of brownies baking sets your mouth to watering, what is the UCS? the CS? the CR? (See page 184.)

For the next three decades Pavlov and his associates explored the causes and effects of this basic type of learning we now call **classical** (or **Pavlovian**) **conditioning.** Their research identified five major conditioning processes: acquisition, extinction, spontaneous recovery, generalization, and discrimination.

Acquisition

Regarding the **acquisition,** or initial learning, of the response, there was first a question of timing: How much time should elapse between presenting the neutral stimulus (the tone, the light, the touch, or whatever) and the unconditioned stimulus? Not much. With many species and procedures, half a second works well. This finding fits the presumption that classical conditioning is biologically adaptive: It helps organisms *prepare* for good or bad events that are about to occur. Because there is no need to prepare for events that have already occurred, acquisition typically does not occur when the neutral stimulus comes after the UCS. When, however, the neutral stimulus comes first, signaling a significant event—say, when the sound of a snapping twig repeatedly precedes danger for a deer—it becomes a CS, and the deer flees more and more rapidly in anticipation of what often follows.

Michael Domjan and his colleagues (1986) showed how this works by conditioning the sexual arousal of male Japanese quail. The researchers turned on a red light before presenting an approachable female. Over time, the quail developed a liking for their cage's red light district. Moreover, when the red light heralded a female's impending arrival, the excited male quail began copulating with her more quickly.

In humans, too, objects, smells, and sights associated with sexual pleasure become conditioned stimuli for sexual arousal. Psychologist Michael Tirrell (1990) recalls: "My first girlfriend loved onions, so I came to associate onion breath with kissing. Before long, onion breath sent tingles up and down my spine. Oh what a feeling!" (Question: What is the unconditioned stimulus here?)

Extinction and Spontaneous Recovery

After conditioning, what happens if the CS occurs repeatedly without the UCS? Will the CS continue to elicit the CR? Pavlov found that when he sounded the tone again and again without presenting food, the dogs salivated less and less. This decline of a CR in the absence of a UCS is called **extinction.** However, Pavlov also found that if he allowed several hours to elapse before sounding the tone again, the CR (salivation) to the tone would reappear (Figure 6–3). This **spontaneous recovery**—the reappearance of a (weakened) CR after a pause—suggested to Pavlov that extinction was suppressing the CR rather than eliminating it.

Figure 6–3 Idealized curve of acquisition, extinction, and spontaneous recovery. The rising curve shows that the CR rapidly grows stronger as the CS and UCS are repeatedly paired (acquisition), then wanes as the CS is presented alone (extinction), but reappears after a rest period (spontaneous recovery).

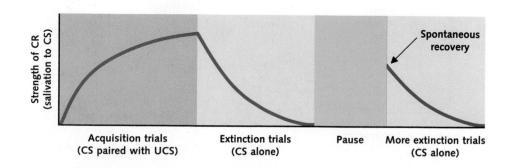

extinction In classical conditioning, the diminishing of a response when an unconditioned stimulus (UCS) does not follow a conditioned stimulus (CS). (In operant conditioning, below, extinction occurs when a response is no longer reinforced.)

spontaneous recovery The reappearance, after a rest period, of an extinguished conditioned response.

generalization The tendency, once a response has been conditioned, for stimuli similar to the conditioned stimulus to evoke similar responses.

discrimination In classical conditioning, the ability to distinguish between a conditioned stimulus and similar stimuli that do not signal an unconditioned stimulus. (In operant conditioning, below, responding differently to stimuli that signal that behavior will be reinforced or nonreinforced.)

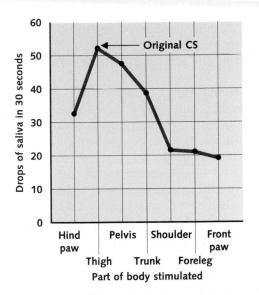

Figure 6–4 Generalization. Pavlov demonstrated generalization after attaching miniature vibrators to various parts of a dog's body. After conditioning salivation to stimulation of the thigh, he stimulated other body areas. The closer they were to the original site of stimulation, the stronger the conditioned response. (From Pavlov, 1927.)

Preview Question

4. What cognitive processes and biological constraints affect classical conditioning?

After breaking up with his fire-breathing heartthrob, Tirrell experienced extinction and spontaneous recovery. He recalls that "the smell of onion breath, no longer paired with the unconditioned stimulus (kissing), lost its ability to shiver my timbers. Occasionally, though, after not sensing the aroma for a long while, smelling onion breath awakens a small version of the emotional response I once felt."

Generalization

Pavlov and his students noticed that a dog conditioned to the sound of one tone also responded somewhat to the sound of a different tone or even to a buzzer never paired with food. Likewise, a dog conditioned to salivate when rubbed would also salivate some when scratched (Windholz, 1989), or when stimulated on a different body part (Figure 6–4). This tendency to respond to stimuli similar to the CS is called **generalization.** Generalization can be adaptive, as when toddlers taught to fear moving cars in the street respond similarly to trucks and motorcycles.

Because of generalization, stimuli that are similar to naturally disgusting or appealing objects will, by association, evoke some disgust or liking. Normally desirable foods, such as fudge, are unappealing when presented in a disgusting form, as when shaped to resemble dog feces (Rozin & others, 1986). We perceive adults with childlike facial features (round face, large forehead, small chin, large eyes) as having childlike warmth, submissiveness, and naiveté (Berry & McArthur, 1986). In both cases, people's emotional reactions to one stimulus generalize to similar stimuli.

Discrimination

Pavlov's dogs also learned to respond to the sound of a particular tone and *not* to other tones. This learned ability to *distinguish* between conditioned stimuli and similar but irrelevant stimuli is **discrimination.** Like generalization, discrimination has survival value. Slightly different stimuli are at times followed by vastly different consequences. Being able to recognize these differences is adaptive. Confronted by a pit bull, your heart may race; confronted by a cocker spaniel, it does not.

Updating Pavlov's Understanding

Pavlov and Watson's disdain for "mentalistic" concepts such as consciousness has given way to a growing realization that they underestimated the importance of cognitive processes (thoughts, perceptions, expectations) and of biological constraints on an organism's capacity for learning.

Cognitive Processes

The early behaviorists believed that the learned behaviors of various organisms could be reduced to universal stimulus-response mechanisms. As recently as 30 years ago, the idea that rats and dogs exhibit cognitive processes struck many psychologists as silly, but no longer. Classical conditioning experiments by Robert Rescorla and Allan Wagner (1972) revealed that animals act as if they mentally associate one event with another, especially if the second event is significant and if the first event *predicts* it. What matters is not how *often* an electric shock, say, follows a tone, but how predictably. The more predictable the association, the stronger the conditioned response. That is, conditioning occurs best when the CS and UCS have just the sort of relationship that would lead a scientist to conclude that the CS *causes* the UCS.

Answer to questions on page 182: Brownies (and their taste) are the UCS. The associated aroma is the CS. Salivation to the aroma is the CR.

It's as if the animal gains an awareness of how likely it is that the UCS will follow the CS. Rescorla (1988) surmises that classical conditioning "is not a stupid process by which the organism willy-nilly forms associations between any two stimuli that happen to occur." Rather, the organism is an information seeker.

Rescorla's analysis helps explain why classical conditioning treatments that ignore cognition often are not completely successful. When, for therapeutic purposes, alcoholics are given alcohol spiked with a nauseating drug, will they always associate alcohol with sickness? If classical conditioning were merely a matter of "stamping in" stimulus-response associations, we might hope so. To some extent, this does occur (as we will see on page 422). However, alcoholics are aware that they can blame their nausea on the drug rather than the alcohol. This cognition often weakens the association between alcohol and sickness. So, even in classical conditioning, it is not only the simple stimulus-response association but also the thought that counts.

Biological Predispositions

Ever since Darwin, most scientists have assumed that animals share a common evolutionary history, as well as the resulting commonalities in their makeup and functioning. Pavlov and Watson, for example, believed the basic laws of learning were essentially similar in all animals. So it should make little difference whether one studied rats, pigeons, or people. Moreover, it seemed that any natural response could be conditioned to any neutral stimulus. As learning researcher Gregory Kimble proclaimed in 1956, "just about any activity of which the organism is capable can be conditioned and . . . these responses can be conditioned to any stimulus that the organism can perceive."

Twenty-five years later, Kimble (1981) humbly acknowledged that "half a thousand" scientific reports had proven him wrong. More than the early behaviorists realized, an animal's capacity for conditioning is constrained by its biology. The biological predispositions of each species dispose it to learn the particular associations that enhance its survival.

John Garcia and Robert Koelling (1966) demonstrated the importance of biological predispositions. They gave rats a particular taste, sight, or sound (CS) and later treated them with radiation or drugs (UCS) causing nausea (UCR). Two startling findings emerged: First, even if sickened as late as several hours after tasting a particular flavor, the rats thereafter avoided that flavor. This violated the notion that for conditioning to occur, the UCS must follow the CS immediately. Second, the sickened rats developed aversions to the tastes but not to the sights or sounds. This contradicted the behaviorists' idea that any perceivable stimulus could serve as a CS. But it made adaptive sense, because for rats taste is a more valuable cue than sight for identifying tainted food. Birds, which hunt by sight, are biologically primed to develop aversions to the *sight* of tainted food (Nicolaus & others, 1983). Humans, too, are biologically prepared to learn some things rather than others. We more readily learn to fear snakes and spiders than to fear flowers (Cook & others, 1986). It makes sense: Such animals harm us more frequently than do flowers. All these cases support the principle that nature prepares each species to learn those associations crucial to its survival.

Garcia's provocative findings stimulated new research, which confirmed his surprising findings and extended them to other species. When coyotes are tempted into eating sheep carcasses laced with a sickening poison, they will develop an aversion to sheep meat (Gustavson & others, 1974). So research on

"Once bitten, twice shy." When coyotes were fed poisoned lamb meat, the poison (UCS) made them sick (UCR). As a result, they developed an aversion (CR) to the lamb (CS) and returned to feeding on their natural prey.

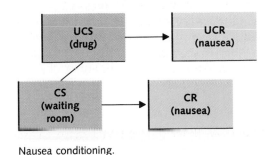

Nausea conditioning.

Ivan Pavlov (1927): "Experimental investigation . . . should lay a solid foundation for a future true science of psychology."

taste aversion suggested ways other than extermination for controlling predators. This is but one instance in which psychological research that began with the discomfort of some laboratory animals enhanced the welfare of many more animals—in this case, saving both the sheep from the coyotes and the coyotes from angry ranchers and farmers, who, with their livestock no longer endangered, were less adamant about destroying the coyotes.

Have such results compelled researchers to abandon the search for universal principles of learning that generalize across species? No, biological predispositions affirm a deeper principle: *Learning enables animals to adapt to their environments.* Adaptation shows us why animals would be responsive to stimuli that announce significant events, such as food or pain. And why animals are predisposed to associate a CS with a UCS that follows predictably and immediately—for causes often immediately precede effects.

Adaptation also helps explain exceptions such as the taste-aversion finding. In this case cause need not precede effect immediately—bad food usually causes sickness quite a while after it has been consumed. Similarly, cancer patients who suffer nausea and vomiting beginning more than an hour following chemotherapy often develop classically conditioned nausea to stimuli associated with taking the drug. Merely returning to the clinic or seeing the nurses can provoke sick feelings (Burish & Carey, 1986).

Pavlov's Legacy

What, then, remains of Pavlov's ideas about conditioning? A great deal. All the researchers we have met so far in this chapter agree that classical conditioning is a basic type of learning. Judged by today's knowledge of cognitive processes and biological predispositions, Pavlov's ideas were incomplete. But if we see further than Pavlov did, it is in large measure because we stand on his shoulders.

Why is Pavlov's work so important? Had he taught us only that old dogs can learn new tricks, his experiments would have long ago been forgotten. Why should anyone care that a dog can be conditioned to drool at the sound of a tone? The importance lies first in this fact: Many other responses to many other stimuli can be classically conditioned in many other organisms—in fact, in every species tested, from worms to fish to dogs to monkeys to people (Schwartz, 1984). Thus, classical conditioning is one way that virtually all organisms learn to adapt to their environment.

Second, Pavlov showed us how an internal process such as learning can be studied objectively. Pavlov was proud that his methods involved virtually no subjective judgments or guesses about what went on in the dogs' minds. The salivary response is an overt behavior measurable as so many drops or cubic centimeters of saliva. Pavlov's success therefore suggested how the young discipline of psychology might proceed—by isolating the elementary building blocks of complex behaviors and studying them with objective laboratory procedures.

Applications of Classical Conditioning

In later chapters on motivation, emotion and health, psychological disorders, and therapy we will see how Pavlov's principles of classical conditioning apply to human health and well-being. For example, former crack cocaine users often feel a craving when they again encounter cues (people, places) associated with previous highs. Thus, drug addicts are advised to steer clear of settings associated with the euphoria of previous drug use. Classical conditioning even works upon the body's disease-fighting immune system. When, say, a particular taste accompanies a drug that influences immune responses, the taste by itself may come to produce an immune response (page 333).

Pavlov's work provided a basis for John Watson's idea that human behavior, though biologically influenced, is also a bundle of conditioned responses. In one famous though ethically troublesome study, Watson and Rosalie Rayner (1920; Harris, 1979) showed how specific fears might be conditioned. Their subject was an 11-month-old infant named Albert. "Little Albert," like most infants, feared loud noises, but not white rats. So Watson and Rayner presented him with a white rat and, as he reached to touch it, struck a hammer against a steel bar just behind his head. After seven repetitions of seeing the rat and then hearing the frightening noise, Albert burst into tears at the mere sight of the rat. What is more, 5 days later Albert showed generalization of his conditioned response by reacting with fear when presented with a rabbit, a dog, and a sealskin coat, but not to dissimilar objects such as toys.

John B. Watson (1924): "Give me a dozen healthy infants, well-formed, and my own specified world to bring them up in and I'll guarantee to take any one at random and train him to become any type of specialist I might select—doctor, lawyer, artist, merchant-chief and, yes, even beggar-man and thief, regardless of his talents, penchants, tendencies, abilities, vocations, and race of his ancestors."

Little Albert's conditioning.

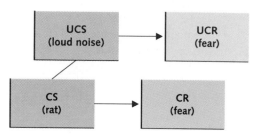

Although some psychologists had difficulty repeating these findings with other children, Watson and Rayner's work with Little Albert has had legendary significance for many psychologists. Some have wondered if each of us might not be a walking repository of conditioned emotions. Might our less adaptive emotions be controlled by the application of extinction procedures or by conditioning new responses to emotion-arousing stimuli? One patient, who for 30 years had feared going into an elevator alone, was told by his therapist to force himself to go in 20 elevators a day. Within 10 days, his fear almost completely vanished (Ellis & Becker, 1982). In Chapter 13, Therapy, we will see more examples of how psychologists use behavioral techniques to treat emotional disorders.

Psychologist Gregory Razran (1940) found that associating political slogans (a CS) with the eating of food (a UCS) made people more approving of them. Similarly, advertisers like to associate their products with naturally pleasing images, such as sexually appealing models.

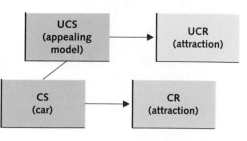

Psychology Applied: Rape as Classical Conditioning

"A burnt child dreads the fire," says a medieval proverb. Experiments with dogs reveal that, indeed, if a painful stimulus is sufficiently powerful, a single event is sometimes enough to traumatize the animal when it again faces the situation. The human counterparts to these experiments can be tragic, as illustrated by one young woman's experience of being attacked and raped, and thereby conditioned to a life of fear. Her fear (CR) is most powerfully associated with particular locations and people (CS), but it generalizes to other places and people. Note, too, how her traumatic experience has robbed her of the normally relaxing associations with such stimuli as home and bed.

Four months ago I was raped. In the middle of the night I awoke to the sound of someone outside my bedroom. Thinking my housemate was coming home, I called out her name. Someone began walking slowly toward me, and then I realized. I screamed and fought, but there were two of them. One held my legs, while the other put a hand over my mouth and a knife to my throat and said, "Shut up, bitch, or we'll kill you." Never have I been so terrified and helpless. They both raped me, one brutally. As they then searched my room for money and valuables, my housemate came home. They brought her into my room, raped her, and left us both tied up on my bed.

We never slept another night in that apartment. We were too terrified. Still, *when I go to bed at night—always with the bedroom light left on—the memory of them entering my room repeats itself endlessly. I was an independent person who had lived alone or with other young women for four years; now I can't even think about spending a night alone. When I drive by our old apartment, or when I have to go into an empty house, my heart pounds and I sweat. I am afraid of strangers, especially men, and the more they resemble my attackers the more I fear them. My housemate shares many of my fears, and is frightened when entering our new apartment. I'm afraid to stay in the same town, I'm afraid it will happen again, I'm afraid to go to bed. I dread falling asleep.*

Rehearse It

1. We adapt to our environment by learning, "a relatively permanent change in behavior due to
a. instinct."
b. mental processes."
c. experience with the environment."
d. education or schooling."

2. Working with dogs, Pavlov paired bells and other neutral stimuli with food-in-the-mouth. The dogs then came to salivate when presented with the neutral stimuli alone. Salivation in response to food-in-the-mouth occurs naturally in dogs, without conditioning: Food is therefore the unconditioned stimulus (UCS). Salivation in response to a bell must be learned; the bell is therefore a
a. conditioned stimulus.
b. unconditioned stimulus.

c. conditioned response.
d. unconditioned response.

3. Dogs can learn to respond to one kind of stimulus and not to another—for example, to salivate at the sight of a circle (the CS) but not a square. Distinguishing between a CS and irrelevant stimuli is
a. generalization.
b. discrimination.
c. acquisition.
d. spontaneous recovery.

4. J. B. Watson classically conditioned fear of a white rat in a small child named Albert. After Watson paired the rat with a frightening noise, Little Albert acted fearful in the presence of the rat (even without the noise). The child later was fearful when presented with a rabbit, a dog, and

a sealskin coat. Little Albert's fear of objects resembling the rat illustrates
a. extinction.
b. generalization of the conditioned response.
c. spontaneous recovery.
d. discrimination between two stimuli.

5. Early behaviorists believed that for conditioning to occur the unconditioned stimulus (UCS) must immediately follow the conditioned stimulus (CS). _____ demonstrated this was not always so.
a. The Little Albert experiment
b. Pavlov's experiments with dogs
c. Watson's behaviorism
d. Garcia's taste-aversion studies

Operant Conditioning

Preview Question

5. What is operant conditioning, and how does it differ from classical conditioning?

Classical conditioning links new stimuli with involuntary responses. But it's one thing to teach an animal to salivate at the sound of a tone or a child to fear cars in the street, and quite another to teach an elephant to walk on its hind legs or a child to say please. How do we learn to perform voluntary behaviors? Through **operant conditioning** an organism becomes more likely to repeat rewarded (reinforced) behaviors and less likely to repeat punished behaviors.

Classical and operant conditioning both involve acquisition, extinction, spontaneous recovery, generalization, and discrimination. Yet their difference is straightforward: Classical conditioning involves **respondent behavior**—reflexive behavior that occurs as an automatic *response* to some stimulus (such as Pavlov's meat powder and tone). Operant conditioning involves voluntary (nonreflexive) action, called **operant behavior** because the act *operates* on the environment to produce rewarding or punishing stimuli.

We can therefore distinguish classical from operant conditioning by asking: Does the controlling stimulus come before or after the response? In classical conditioning, it comes before, no matter what the organism is doing, as when the tone elicits salivation. In operant conditioning, the controlling stimulus, a reinforcer or punisher, comes after the response. This consequence is *contingent* on the animal's behavior, as when a dog performs a trick and obtains food.

Through operant conditioning, these pigs have learned that their running around the racetrack will be rewarded with cookies.

operant conditioning   A type of learning in which behavior is strengthened if followed by reinforcement, or diminished if followed by punishment.

respondent behavior   Behavior that occurs as an automatic response to some stimulus; behavior learned through classical conditioning.

operant behavior   Behavior that operates on the environment, producing consequences.

Skinner box   A chamber containing a bar or key that an animal can manipulate to obtain a food or water reinforcer, and devices to record the animal's rate of bar pressing or key pecking. Used in operant conditioning research.

shaping   An operant conditioning procedure in which reinforcers guide behavior toward closer and closer approximations of a desired goal.

Skinner's Experiments

B. F. Skinner (1904–1990) was a college English major and aspiring writer who, seeking a new direction, entered graduate school in psychology and went on to become modern behaviorism's most influential and controversial figure. Skinner's work elaborated a simple fact of life that turn-of-the-century psychologist Edward L. Thorndike called the *law of effect:* Rewarded behavior

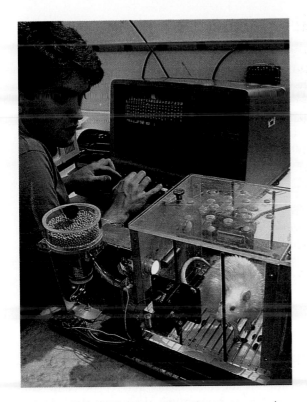

Figure 6–5 Inside the Skinner box, the rat presses a bar for a food reward. Outside, a measuring device records the animal's accumulated responses.

is likely to recur. Using Thorndike's law of effect as a starting point, Skinner developed a "behavioral technology" that enabled him to teach pigeons such unpigeonlike behaviors as walking in a figure 8, playing Ping-Pong, and keeping a missile on course by pecking at a target displayed on a screen.

For his pioneering studies with rats and later with pigeons, Skinner designed the now famous **Skinner box** (Figure 6–5). The "box" is typically a soundproof chamber with a bar or key that an animal presses or pecks to release a food or water reward, and with a device that records these responses. Experiments by Skinner and other operant researchers did far more than teach us how to pull habits out of a rat. They explored the precise conditions that foster efficient and enduring learning.

Shaping

In his experiments, Skinner used **shaping,** a procedure in which successive rewards, such as food, guide an animal's natural behavior toward a desired behavior. Imagine that you wanted to condition a rat to press a bar. After observing how the animal naturally behaves before training, you would build on its existing behaviors. You might, for example, give the rat a food reward each time it approaches the bar. Once the rat is approaching regularly, you would require it to move closer before rewarding it; then closer still, and finally to touch the bar before giving it the food. With this method, you reward responses that are ever-closer to the final desired behavior and ignore all other responses. In this same way, researchers and animal trainers gradually *shape* complex behaviors.

By shaping nonverbal organisms to discriminate between stimuli, a psychologist can also determine what they perceive. Can a dog distinguish colors? Can a baby discriminate sounds? If we can shape them to respond to one stimulus and not to another, then obviously they can perceive the difference. For example, if an experimenter reinforces a pigeon for pecking after seeing a human face, but not after seeing any other image, the pigeon will learn to recognize faces (Herrnstein & Loveland, 1964). With similar training, pigeons have even been taught to discriminate musical selections by Bach from those by Stravinsky (Porter & Neuringer, 1984).

Can a manatee distinguish different shapes and colors? University of Windsor psychologist Dale Woodyard is training this manatee to discriminate between objects of different shapes, colors, and sizes for a food reward. The manatee remembers such lessons for as long as a year.

reinforcer In operant conditioning, any event that *increases* the behavior it follows.

positive reinforcement Strengthening behavior by *presenting* positive stimuli, such as food.

negative reinforcement Strengthening behavior by *removing* negative stimuli, such as a shock.

primary reinforcer An innately reinforcing stimulus, such as food, that satisfies a biological need.

secondary reinforcer A conditioned reinforcer, such as money, that gains its reinforcing power by association with a primary reinforcer.

Parents may use rewards to shape good table manners by praising eating behavior that is more and more adultlike. This sounds simple. But let's compare the essential features of shaping to what often happens at home and at school. In the shaping procedure, the trainer builds on the individual's existing behaviors by immediately rewarding successively closer approximations of a desired behavior. In everyday life, too, we continually reward and shape the behavior of others, said Skinner, but often unintentionally. Sometimes we even reward offensive behavior. Billy's parents, for example, are annoyed and mystified by his loud whining. But look at how they typically deal with Billy—by rewarding the very behavior they find so annoying:

Billy: *"Could you tie my shoes?"*
Father: *(Continues reading paper.)*
Billy: *"Dad, I need my shoes tied."*
Father: *"Uh, yeah, just a minute."*
Billy: *"DAAAAD! TIE MY SHOES!"*
Father: *"How many times have I told you not to whine? Now, which shoe do we do first?"*

Or compare the way learning psychologists shape behavior—by rewarding small improvements—to the way some teachers use rewards. On a wall chart, the teacher pastes gold stars after the names of children scoring 100 percent on spelling tests. All children take the same tests. As everyone can then see, some children, the academic all-stars, easily get 100 percent. The others, no matter how hard they try or how much they improve, get no reward. Better if the teacher would reward poor spellers for gradual improvement (successive approximations toward their potential) or for doing their best.

Principles of Reinforcement

Preview Question

6. What are the basic types of reinforcers?

So far, we have referred rather loosely to the power of "rewards." This idea gains a more precise meaning in Skinner's concept of the **reinforcer,** any event that increases the frequency of a response it follows. A reinforcer may be a tangible reward. It may be praise or attention. It may even be a preferred activity.

Positive and Negative Reinforcers Most people think of reinforcers as rewards. Actually, there are two basic kinds of reinforcers: positive and negative. Positive and negative reinforcers have the same effect; they strengthen behavior.

So, how do they differ? **Positive reinforcement** strengthens a response by *presenting* a positive stimulus after a response. Food is a positive reinforcer for animals; attention, approval, and money are positive reinforcers for most people. **Negative reinforcement** strengthens a response by reducing or *removing* an aversive (unpleasant) stimulus. To an animal in an electrified Skinner box, switching off a foot shock is rewarding: a negative reinforcer. When someone stops nagging or whining, that, too, is a negative reinforcer.

So imagine that whenever a child throws a tantrum, the parent gives in for the sake of peace and quiet. The child's tantrums will be strengthened by positive reinforcement (the parent gives in). The parent's behavior will be strengthened by negative reinforcement (the child stops screaming). Or imagine a worried student who, after goofing off and getting a bad exam grade, studies harder for the next exam. The student may be negatively reinforced by reduced anxiety and positively reinforced by a better grade. *Remember:*

For this young photographer, a first place blue ribbon is positive reinforcement.

Reprinted with special permission of King Features Syndicate.

Negative reinforcement at work. Note that "positive" means *on*set—presenting a stimulus. "Negative" means *off*set—withdrawing a stimulus. *All* reinforcers strengthen behavior. Thus, the removal of an aversive stimulus (such as crying) reinforces the parents' behavior.

Whether it works by giving something positive or reducing something negative, *a reinforcer always strengthens behavior.*

Primary and Secondary Reinforcers **Primary reinforcers**—getting the food or being relieved of the shock—are innately satisfying. We need not learn to like them. **Secondary reinforcers** are learned. They get their power through association with primary reinforcers. If a rat in a Skinner box learns that a light reliably signals that food is coming, the rat will work to turn on the light. The light has become a secondary reinforcer associated with food. Our lives are filled with secondary reinforcers—money, good grades, a pleasant tone of voice, a word of praise—each of which has been linked with more basic rewards. Secondary reinforcers greatly enhance our ability to influence one another.

Immediate and Delayed Reinforcers Consider a typical shaping experiment. Before performing a "wanted" behavior such as pressing the bar, an animal will engage in a sequence of "unwanted" behaviors—scratching, sniffing, and moving around. Whichever of these behaviors immediately precedes the reinforcer becomes more likely to occur again. If we delay the reinforcer for bar pressing for as long as 30 seconds, allowing other behaviors to intervene and be reinforced, virtually no learning of the bar pressing occurs.

Humans learn to respond to reinforcers that are greatly delayed: the paycheck at the end of the week, the grade at the end of the semester, the trophy at the end of the season. Indeed, to function effectively we *must* learn to postpone immediate rewards for greater long-term rewards. Four-year-old children who in laboratory testing show an ability to delay gratification—who'd sooner have a big reward tomorrow than a small one right now—become more socially competent and high achieving as adolescents (Mischel & others, 1989).

The immediacy of reinforcement does influence many of our behaviors, however. Smokers, alcoholics, and other drug users may know that their immediate pleasure—the kick that often comes within seconds—is more than offset by future ill effects. Drugs such as nicotine and cocaine that provide the most immediate reinforcement are also the most strongly addictive (Marlatt, 1991). Likewise, for many teens the immediate gratification of unprotected sex during unplanned passion prevails over the delayed gratifications of "safe" sex or saved sex (Loewenstein & Furstenberg, 1991). And the hour-long enjoyment of staying up to watch another TV show may outweigh the prospect of tomorrow's day-long sluggishness. To our detriment, small but immediate reinforcements are sometimes more effective than powerful but delayed reinforcement.

Preview Question

7. How do partial reinforcement schedules affect behavior?

"The charm of fishing is that it is the pursuit of what is elusive but attainable, a perpetual series of occasions for hope."

Scottish author John Buchan, 1875–1940

continuous reinforcement Reinforcing the desired response every time it occurs.

partial reinforcement Reinforcing a response only part of the time; results in slower acquisition of response but much greater resistance to extinction than does continuous reinforcement. (Also called *intermittent reinforcement*.)

fixed-ratio schedule In operant conditioning, a reinforcement schedule that reinforces behavior only after a specified number of responses.

variable-ratio schedule In operant conditioning, a reinforcement schedule that reinforces behavior after an unpredictable number of responses.

fixed-interval schedule In operant conditioning, a reinforcement schedule that reinforces a response only after a specified time has elapsed.

variable-interval schedule In operant conditioning, a reinforcement schedule that reinforces a response at unpredictable time intervals.

punishment Any event that *decreases* the behavior that it follows.

Reinforcement Schedules So far, most of our examples assume **continuous reinforcement:** The desired response gets reinforced every time it occurs. Under such conditions, learning occurs rapidly. But when the reinforcement stops—when we disconnect the food delivery chute—extinction also occurs rapidly. The rat soon stops pressing the bar. If a normally dependable candy machine fails to deliver a candy bar twice in a row, we stop putting money into it (although a week later we may exhibit spontaneous recovery by trying again).

In real life, continuous reinforcement is rare. A salesperson does not make a sale with every pitch, nor does an angler get a bite with every cast. But they persist because their efforts have occasionally been rewarded. Researchers have explored several **partial reinforcement** schedules in which responses are sometimes reinforced, sometimes not (Nevin, 1988). Initial learning is typically slower with partial reinforcement, which makes continuous reinforcement preferable until a behavior is mastered. But partial reinforcement produces greater persistence—a *resistance to extinction*—than found with continuous reinforcement. Imagine a pigeon that has learned to peck a key to obtain food. When the delivery of food has gradually faded out until it occurs only rarely and unpredictably, pigeons have pecked over 150,000 times without a reward (Skinner, 1953). With partial reinforcement, hope springs eternal.

Corresponding human examples come readily to mind. Slot machines reward gamblers occasionally and unpredictably, and this partial reinforcement affects them much as it affects pigeons: They keep trying, sometimes interminably. There is also a valuable lesson here for parents. *Occasionally* giving in to children's tantrums for the sake of peace and quiet puts the child on a partial reinforcement schedule. That's the very best procedure for making a behavior persist.

Skinner (1961) and his collaborators compared four schedules of partial reinforcement. Some are rigidly fixed, some unpredictably variable. **Fixed-ratio schedules** reinforce behavior after a set number of responses. Like people paid on a piecework basis—say, for every 30 pieces—laboratory animals may be reinforced on a fixed ratio of, say, one reinforcer for every 30 responses. Once conditioned, the animal typically will pause only briefly after a reinforcer and will then return to a high rate of responding. Resting while on a fixed-ratio schedule reduces rewards, and employees typically find such work grueling. Unions have therefore pressured employers to replace piecework pay with hourly wage schedules.

Variable-ratio schedules provide reinforcers after an unpredictable number of responses. This is what gamblers experience—reinforcement after an unpredictable number of bets—and what makes gambling behavior so hard to extinguish. Like the fixed-ratio schedule, it produces high rates of responding, because reinforcers increase as the responding increases.

Fixed-interval schedules feature an equal pause after each reinforcer. During this time no reinforcers are available. When the fixed interval ends, the next response is reinforced. Like people checking more frequently for the mail as the delivery time approaches, pigeons on a fixed-interval schedule peck a key more frequently as the anticipated time for reward draws near, producing a choppy start-stop pattern.

Variable-interval schedules reinforce the first response after *varying* time intervals. Like the unpredictable pop quiz that reinforces studying or the "hello" that finally rewards persistence in calling back a busy phone number, variable-interval schedules tend to produce slow, steady responding. This makes sense, because there is no knowing when the waiting will be over. Should the pop quiz become predictable, students will begin the stop-start work pattern that characterizes fixed-interval schedules.

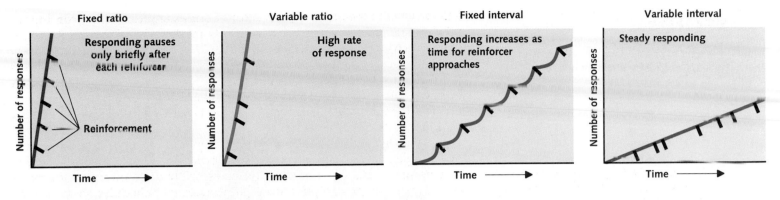

| Fixed ratio | Variable ratio | Fixed interval | Variable interval |

Figure 6–6 Behavior patterns produced by different reinforcement schedules. (Adapted from "Teaching Machines" by B.F. Skinner. Copyright © 1961 by Scientific American, Inc. All rights reserved.)

Question: Airline frequent-flyer programs that offer a free flight after every 20,000 miles of travel use which reinforcement schedule? (See page 194.)

Preview Question

8. How does punishment affect behavior?

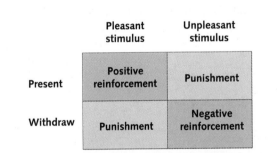

	Pleasant stimulus	Unpleasant stimulus
Present	Positive reinforcement	Punishment
Withdraw	Punishment	Negative reinforcement

Punishment decreases a behavior by delivering an aversive stimulus, or withdrawing a positive stimulus. Negative reinforcement is rewarding, *not* punishing. It strengthens behavior by removing a negative stimulus. Thus, the *delivery* of shock after a response is a punisher; the *termination* of shock after a response is a negative reinforcer. Negative reinforcement is perhaps psychology's most often misunderstood concept.

Check yourself: Which of the following illustrates negative reinforcement? (See page 197.)

1. Matt roughs up his football opponent and draws a penalty.
2. To alleviate the discomfort of nicotine deprivation after a flight, Wilma lights up a cigarette.
3. After Hector makes a big sale, his boss takes him out to lunch.

Figure 6–6 summarizes the response patterns associated with each partial reinforcement schedule. Animal behaviors differ, yet Skinner (1956) contended that the reinforcement principles of operant conditioning are universal. It matters little, he said, what response, what reinforcer, or what species you use. The effect of a given reinforcement schedule is pretty much the same: "Pigeon, rat, monkey, which is which? It doesn't matter . . . . Behavior shows astonishingly similar properties."

Punishment

Punishment has the opposite effect of reinforcement: A punisher is any consequence that *decreases* the frequency of a behavior that it follows. Reinforcement strengthens behavior; punishment weakens behavior. Swift, strong, and consistent punishers can powerfully restrain unwanted behavior. The rat that is shocked after touching the forbidden object and the child who loses a treat after running headlong into the street will learn more quickly not to repeat the behavior.

Nevertheless, punishment, especially physical punishment, has drawbacks. As powerful as punishment can be, punished behavior is not forgotten; it is suppressed. If the punishment is avoidable, the punished behavior may reappear in safe settings. The child who learns through spankings not to swear around the house may swear elsewhere. The driver who is hit with a couple of speeding tickets may buy a radar detector and speed freely when no radar patrol is in the area.

Opponents of physical punishment also say that it increases aggressiveness, by demonstrating aggression as a way to cope with problems. This helps explain why so many aggressive delinquents and abusive parents come from abusive families (Straus & Gelles, 1980). Moreover, harsh punishment can create fear; the person receiving the punishment may associate the fear not only with the undesirable behavior but also with the person who administers it or the situation in which it occurs. Thus, a child may come to fear the punitive teacher and want to avoid school. Worse, when punishments are unpredictable and inescapable, both animals and people may develop the sense that events are beyond their control. As a result, they may come to feel helpless and depressed. (More on "learned helplessness" in later chapters.)

Even when punishment suppresses unwanted behavior, it often does not guide one toward more desirable behavior. Punishment tells you what *not* to do; reinforcement tells you what *to* do. The teacher whose feedback on a paper says, "No, but try this . . . " and "Yes, that's it!" reduces unwanted behavior by reinforcing alternative behaviors.

To sum up, swift and sure punishment can be effective, and may on occasion cause less pain than does the self-destructive behavior it suppresses.

Punishment is most effective when strong, immediate, and consistent, but it can also have undesirable side effects. This teenager's anger at his mother's scolding might, if this were to become their principal mode of communication, translate into a resistance to listening to her.

Reinforcement: The process by which consequences *increase behaviors.*

Positive reinforcement: Increasing behaviors by *presenting positive stimuli* (such as food).

Negative reinforcement: Increasing behaviors by *removing negative stimuli* (such as shock).

Punishment: The process by which aversive consequences *decrease* behaviors.

Answer to question on page 193: Frequent-flyer programs use a fixed-ratio schedule.

However, punished behavior may reappear if the threatened punishment can be avoided. (What punishment often teaches, said Skinner, is how to avoid it.) Physical punishment can also have undesirable side effects, such as creating fear and teaching aggression, and it often fails to teach how to act positively. Thus, most psychologists join Skinner in favoring an emphasis on reinforcement rather than punishment. Catch people doing something right and affirm them for it.

When you stop to think about it, many threats of punishment are just as forceful, and perhaps more effective, if rephrased positively: "Johnny, if you don't clean your room, you may not go outside" could become "Johnny, when you clean your room you may go outside." Likewise, "Maria, if you don't get your homework done, there'll be no TV" could become . . . .

Rehearse It

6. Thorndike's "law of effect" states that "rewarded behavior is likely to recur." This law became the basis for operant conditioning and the behavioral technology developed by
a. Ivan Pavlov.
b. B. F. Skinner.
c. John Garcia.
d. John B. Watson.

7. B. F. Skinner taught hungry rats to press a bar to obtain a food pellet. To guide the rat's natural behavior toward the desired behavior, he used
a. punishment.
b. shaping.
c. taste aversion.
d. bar pressing.

8. A reinforcer is any stimulus presented after a response which makes it more likely that the response will occur again. Imagine that your dog's continual barking disturbs you, and you respond by letting the dog out into the yard. The stopping of the barking is for you the termination of an aversive stimulus, or a
a. positive reinforcer.
b. negative reinforcer.
c. punishment.
d. primary reinforcer.

9. Continuous reinforcement, that is, reinforcement of the desired response every time it occurs, makes for rapid learning and for rapid extinction when reinforce-

ment stops. A partial reinforcement schedule that reinforces a response at unpredictable time intervals is a
a. fixed-interval schedule.
b. variable-interval schedule.
c. fixed-ratio schedule.
d. variable-ratio schedule.

10. A medieval proverb notes that "a burnt child dreads the fire." In behavioral terms, the burning is an example of
a. a primary reinforcer.
b. a negative reinforcer.
c. a punishment.
d. successive approximations.

cognitive map A mental representation of the layout of one's environment. For example, after exploring a maze, rats act as if they learned a cognitive map of it.

latent learning Learning that occurs but is not apparent until there is an incentive to demonstrate it.

Updating Skinner's Understanding

Although Skinner granted both the existence of mental processes and the biological underpinnings of behavior, many psychologists criticized him for discounting their importance.

Preview Question

9. What cognitive processes and biological constraints influence operant conditioning?

Cognition and Operant Conditioning

A mere 8 days before dying of leukemia, Skinner (1990) stood before the American Psychological Association convention for one final blast at "cognitive science," which he viewed as a throwback to turn-of-the-century introspectionism. Skinner died resisting the growing belief that cognitive processes—thoughts, perceptions, expectations—have a necessary place in the science of psychology, and even in our understanding of conditioning. Yet we have seen several hints that cognitive processes are at work in operant learning. For example, animals on a fixed-interval reinforcement schedule respond more and more frequently as the time approaches when a response will produce a reinforcer. The animals behave as if they expect that repeating the response will soon produce the reward.

Other evidence of cognitive processes comes from studies of rats in mazes. Rats exploring a maze, with no obvious reward, are like people driving around a new town. The rats develop a **cognitive map,** a mental representation of the maze. This occurs even if the rats are carried passively through the maze in a wire basket. When an experimenter then places a reward in the maze's goal box, the rats immediately perform as well as rats that have been reinforced with food for running the maze. During their explorations, the rats seemingly experience **latent learning**—learning that becomes apparent only when there is some incentive to demonstrate it. The unavoidable conclusion: Learning can occur without reinforcement. As the cognitive mapping experiments suggest, there is more to learning than associating a response with a tangible consequence. There is also cognition. In Chapter 8, Thinking, Language, and Intelligence, we will encounter striking evidence of animals' cognitive abilities in solving problems and using aspects of language.

Drawing by Nurit; © 1985 The New Yorker Magazine, Inc.

Biological Predispositions

As with classical conditioning, an animal's natural predispositions constrain its capacity for operant conditioning. When reinforced with food, you can easily condition the golden hamster to dig or to rear up, because these actions are among the animal's natural behaviors when searching for food. But it's much harder to use food reinforcers to shape hamster behaviors, such as face washing, that are not normally associated with food or hunger (Shettleworth, 1973). Pigeons easily learn to flap their wings to avoid shock and to peck to obtain food, because they naturally flee with their wings and eat with their beaks. But they have a hard time learning to peck to avoid shock or to flap to obtain food. Biological constraints predispose organisms to learn associations that are naturally adaptive.

Skinner's former associates, Keller Breland and Marian Breland (1961), came to appreciate biological predispositions while using operant procedures to train animals for circuses, TV shows, and movies—procedures that most trained animal shows now apply (Bailey & Bailey, 1980). The Brelands had originally assumed that operant principles would work on almost any response that any animal could make. But after training 6000 animals of 38

"Never try to teach a pig to sing. It wastes your time and annoys the pig."

Mark Twain (1835–1910)

Animals can most easily learn and retain behaviors that draw on their biological predispositions, such as a dolphin's natural leaping behavior.

different species, from chickens to whales, they concluded that biological predispositions were more important than they had supposed. In one act, they trained pigs to pick up large wooden "dollars" and deposit them in a piggy bank. After learning this behavior, however, the animals began to drift back to their natural ways. They would drop the coin, push it with their snouts as pigs are prone to do, pick it up again, and then repeat the sequence—delaying their food reinforcer. As this "instinctive drift" illustrates, "misbehaviors" occurred when the animals reverted to their biologically predisposed patterns.

Skinner's Legacy

B. F. Skinner was one of the most controversial intellectual figures of our time. He stirred a hornet's nest by repeatedly insisting that external influences, not internal thoughts and feelings, shape behavior and by urging the use of operant principles to improve people's behavior at school, work, and home. To help or to manage people effectively, Skinner said, we should worry less about their illusions of freedom and dignity. Recognizing that behavior is shaped by its consequences, we should administer rewards in ways that promote more desirable behavior.

Skinner's critics objected: He dehumanized people, they said, by neglecting their personal freedom and by seeking to control their actions. Skinner's reply: People's behavior is already haphazardly controlled by external consequences, so why not administer those consequences for human betterment? In place of the widespread use of punishment in homes, schools, and prisons,

B.F. Skinner (1983): "I am sometimes asked, 'Do you think of yourself as you think of the organisms you study?' The answer is yes. So far as I know, my behavior at any given moment has been nothing more than the product of my genetic endowment, my personal history, and the current setting."

would not *positive* reinforcers be more humanitarian? And if it is humbling to think that we are shaped by our histories, this very idea also creates the hope that we may actively shape our future.

Applications of Operant Conditioning

We have already seen many everyday applications of operant conditioning principles, and in later chapters we will see how psychologists apply these principles to problems ranging from high blood pressure to social withdrawal. Reinforcement technologies are also at work in schools, businesses, and homes.

At School A generation ago, Skinner and others advocated teaching machines and textbooks that would shape learning in small steps and provide immediate reinforcement for correct responses. These machines and texts, they said, would revolutionize education and free teachers to concentrate on their students' special needs.

To envision Skinner's dream, imagine two mathematics teachers. Faced with a class of academically diverse students, Teacher A gives the whole class the same math lesson. The teacher knows that some students already understand the concepts and that others will be frustrated by their inability to comprehend. But with so many different children, how can one teacher guide them individually? When test time comes, the whiz kids breeze through unchallenged, and the slower learners once again experience failure. Faced with a similar class, Teacher B paces the material according to each student's rate of learning and provides prompt feedback with positive reinforcement to slow and fast learners. Does the individualized instruction of Teacher B sound like an impossible ideal?

Although the predicted revolution has not occurred, to the end of his life Skinner (1986, 1988, 1989) believed the ideal achievable. "Good instruction demands two things," he said. "Students must be told immediately whether what they do is right or wrong and, when right, they must be directed to the step to be taken next." To do this, and to free teachers for uniquely human tasks, computers were his final hope. For reading and math drills, the computer could be Teacher B—engaging the student actively, pacing material according to the student's rate of learning, quizzing the student to find gaps in understanding, providing immediate feedback, and keeping flawless records for the supervising teacher.

Experiments comparing computer-assisted instruction (CAI) to traditional classroom instruction suggest that, for some drill and practice tasks, the computer can indeed be more effective (Kulik & others, 1980, 1985). As microcomputers have become more widely available, so too have new techniques of CAI. A computer can effectively train students to type or play the piano, while tracking progress and providing positive reinforcements. Educational games and computer simulations can also entice students to explore and discover principles on their own. Students can customize their own learning at multimedia work stations by retrieving video and still images from computer-driven laser disks.

At Work Believing that reinforcers influence productivity, business managers have capitalized on psychological research. Many companies now enable their employees to share profits, or even to participate in company ownership. When workers' productivity boosts rewards for all, their motivation and cooperative spirit often increase—leading to improved group morale and friendly feelings (Deutsch, 1991).

Answer to "check yourself" on page 193: Wilma's smoking provides negative reinforcement.

Preview Question

10. How might educators, business managers, and individuals apply operant conditioning?

"You mene I've bin spending this whol term with a defektiv reeding machin?"

Drawing by Sidney Harris © 1992

Drawing by Ziegler; © 1989 The New Yorker Magazine, Inc.

To boost productivity, positively reinforce jobs well done, especially when the desired performance is *well-defined and achievable*. Reward specific behaviors, not vaguely defined "merit." Criticism, too, triggers the least resentment and the greatest performance boost when specific as well as considerate (Baron, 1988).

It's also a good idea to make the reinforcement *immediate*. Thomas Watson, who led IBM during its tremendous growth, would write out a check on the spot for achievements he observed (Peters & Waterman, 1982). But the rewards need not be material, nor so big that they become political and a source of discouragement to those who don't receive them. The effective manager might simply walk the floor and praise people for good work, or write unexpected notes of appreciation for a completed project. As Skinner said, "How much richer would the whole world be if the reinforcers in daily life were more effectively contingent on productive work?"

At Home   Many economists and psychologists view people's spending behavior as controlled by its consequences (what economists call its costs and benefits). Compared with people who rent apartments in buildings where energy costs are paid by the landlord, those who live in comparable buildings but pay their own energy costs (therefore reaping the rewards of their own energy savings) use about 20 percent less energy. Similarly, home electricity users on an "energy diet" are helped by frequent feedback that shows their current usage compared with their past consumption (Darley & others, 1979). In homes, as elsewhere, immediate consequences most effectively influence behavior.

We can also use operant conditioning on ourselves, by reinforcing our most desired behaviors and extinguishing those undesired. To take charge of your own behavior, psychologists suggest these step-by-step procedures:

1. State your goal—say, to stop smoking, lose weight, or study or exercise more—in measurable terms, and make it public. You might, for example, aim to boost your study time by an hour a day. Announce your goal to friends.

2. Record how often you engage in the behavior you wish to promote and note how this behavior is being reinforced. You might log your current study time, noting under what conditions you do and don't study. (When I began writing textbooks, I logged my time and was astonished to discover how much time I was wasting.)

3. Begin systematically to reinforce the desired behavior. To increase your study time, allow yourself a snack (or some other reinforcing activity) only after specified periods of study. Agree with your friends that you will join them for weekend activities only if you have met your weekly studying goal.

4. As your new behaviors become more habitual, gradually reduce the incentives.

Contrasting Conditioning Techniques

The last three decades of research have changed psychology's views of both classical and operant conditioning (summarized in Table 6–1). Learning, like so much else, depends on both nature and nurture. Biological predispositions make certain types of learning easier than others. Animals exhibit more sophisticated cognitive processes than once seemed likely.

observational learning   Learning by observing and imitating the behavior of others.

modeling   The process by which a behavior is observed and imitated.

Table 6-1

Comparison of Classical and Operant Conditioning

	Classical conditioning	Operant conditioning
Behavior	Involuntary (reflexive), including emotions	Voluntary (nonreflexive); produces consequences
Acquisition	Association of events; conditioned stimulus announces unconditioned stimulus; stimuli *precede* response	Association of response with a consequence (reinforcer or punisher); consequence *follows* response
Extinction	CR decreases when CS is repeatedly presented alone	Responding decreases, especially when consistent reinforcement stops
Biological predispositions	Natural predispositions limit what stimuli and responses can easily be associated	Organisms best learn behaviors similar to their natural behaviors; unnatural behaviors instinctively drift back toward natural ones
Cognitive processes	Subjects develop an expectation that the CS signals the arrival of the UCS	Subjects develop an expectation that a response will be reinforced or punished; they also exhibit latent learning without reinforcement

Preview Question

11. What is observational learning?

Albert Bandura (1977): "Learning would be exceedingly laborious, not to mention hazardous, if people had to rely solely on the effects of their own actions to inform them what to do."

Learning by Observation

From drooling dogs, running rats, and pecking pigeons we have learned much about the basic processes of learning. But conditioning principles alone do not tell us the whole story. Among higher animals, especially humans, learning need not occur through direct experience. **Observational learning,** in which we observe and imitate others' behaviors, also plays a big part. The process of observing and imitating a specific behavior is often called **modeling.** By observing and imitating models we learn all kinds of social behaviors. By 9 months of age, infants will imitate novel play behaviors, and by age 14 months will imitate acts modeled on television (Meltzoff, 1988a,b,c). To persuade children to smoke, expose them to parents and older youth who smoke. To encourage children to read, read to them and surround them with books and people who read them. To increase the odds of your children practicing your religion, worship and attend other religious activities with them.

Bandura's Experiments

Picture this scene from a famous experiment devised by Albert Bandura, the pioneering researcher of observational learning (Bandura & others, 1961). A nursery school child is at work on a picture. An adult in another part of the room is working with some Tinker Toys. The adult then gets up and for nearly 10 minutes pounds, kicks, and throws a large inflated Bobo doll around the room, while yelling such remarks as, "Sock him in the nose . . . . Hit him down . . . . Kick him."

Children learn a great deal by observing adult models. This 14-month-old boy in Andrew Meltzoff's laboratory is imitating from TV. (top) On video, the adult pulls apart a novel toy. The infant leans forward and carefully studies the adult's action. (middle) The infant is given the toy. (bottom) The baby pulls the toy apart, imitating what he had seen the adult do.

prosocial behavior Positive, constructive, helpful behavior; the opposite of antisocial behavior.

After observing this outburst, the child is taken to another room where there are many appealing toys. Soon the experimenter interrupts the child's play and explains that she has decided to save these good toys "for the other children." She now takes the frustrated child to an adjacent room containing a few toys, including a Bobo doll. Left alone, what does the child do?

Compared to children not exposed to the adult model, children who observed the aggressive outburst were much more likely to lash out at the doll. Apparently, observing the adult model beating up the doll lowered their inhibitions. But something more than lowered inhibitions is at work, for the children also imitated the very acts and used the identical words that they had observed.

Applications of Observational Learning

The bad news from such studies is that antisocial models—in one's family, neighborhood, or on TV—may have antisocial effects (pages 460–464). This helps us understand how abusive parents might have aggressive children and why men who batter their wives often had wife-battering fathers. The lessons that we learn as children are not easily unlearned as adults, and are often visited on future generations.

The good news is that **prosocial** (positive, helpful) models can have prosocial effects. People who exemplify nonviolent, helpful behavior can prompt similar behavior in others. Mahatma Gandhi and Martin Luther King, Jr., both drew on the power of modeling, making nonviolent action a powerful force for social change. Parents are powerful models. European Christians who risked their lives to rescue Jews from the Nazis and civil rights activists of a generation ago usually had a close relationship with at least one parent who modeled a strong moral or humanitarian concern (London, 1970; Oliner & Oliner, 1988).

Models are most effective when their actions and words are consistent. Sometimes, however, models say one thing and do another. Many parents seem to operate according to the principle "Do as I *say*, not as I do." Experiments suggest that children learn to do both (Rice & Grusec, 1975; Rushton, 1975). When exposed to a hypocrite, they tend to imitate the hypocrisy by doing what the model did and saying what the model said.

What determines whether we will imitate a model? Bandura believes part of the answer is reinforcements and punishments—those received by the model as well as by the imitator. We look and we learn. By looking, we learn to anticipate a behavior's consequences in situations like those we are observing. By watching TV programs, for example, children may "learn" that physical intimidation is an effective way to control others, that free and easy sex brings pleasure without the misery of unwanted pregnancy or disease, or that men are supposed to be tough and women gentle. We are especially likely to imitate those we respect and admire, those we perceive as similar to ourselves, and those we perceive as successful.

Although our knowledge of learning principles comes from the work of thousands of investigators, this chapter has focused on the ideas of a few pioneers—Pavlov, Watson, Skinner, and Bandura. They illustrate the impact that can result from single-minded devotion to a few well-defined problems and ideas. They defined the issues and impressed on us the importance of learning. As their legacy demonstrates, intellectual history is often made by people who, at the risk of overstatement, pursue ideas to their limits.

Rehearse It

11. Although Skinner disputed the idea, most researchers today believe that cognitive processes can play an important role in learning. The effect of cognition (thoughts, perceptions, and expectations) appears most strikingly in rats'
a. spontaneous recovery of previously learned behavior.
b. cognitive maps.
c. respondent behavior.
d. generalization of responses.

12. Animals, like people, can learn from experience, with or without reinforcement. After exploring a maze for 10 days, rats were offered a food reward at the end of the maze. They quickly demonstrated their prior learning of the maze by immediately doing as well as rats that had been reinforced for running the maze. The rats that had learned without reinforcement demonstrate
a. modeling.
b. biological predisposition.
c. shaping.
d. latent learning.

13. Children learn many social behaviors by imitating parents and other models. This type of learning is called
a. observational learning.
b. reinforced learning.
c. operant conditioning.
d. classical conditioning.

Reviewing Learning

1. What is learning?

All animals, but humans especially, adapt to their environments aided by learning. Through classical conditioning, we learn to anticipate events such as being fed or experiencing pain. Through operant conditioning, we learn to repeat acts that bring desired results and avoid acts that bring punishment. Through observational learning, we learn from the experience and example of others.

Classical Conditioning

2. How does classical conditioning demonstrate learning by association?

Although the idea of learning by association was commonly accepted for centuries, it remained for Ivan Pavlov to capture the phenomenon in his classic experiments. In classical conditioning, a neutral stimulus (such as a bell) is repeatedly presented just before an unconditioned stimulus (food) which naturally triggers an unconditioned response (salivation). After several repetitions, the neutral stimulus alone triggers salivation. The tone has become a conditioned stimulus (CS) which produces a conditioned response (CR), salivation. Experiments by Pavlov and others revealed that classical conditioning is usually greatest when the CS is presented just before the UCS, thus preparing the subject for what is coming.

3. How do the processes of acquisition, extinction, spontaneous recovery, generalization, and discrimination affect a CR?

Learned responses may undergo an initial establishment (acquisition); subsequent weakening if not reinforced (extinction); a reappearance after a rest pause (spontaneous recovery); and be triggered by stimuli similar to the conditioned stimulus (generalization) but not by dissimilar stimuli (discrimination).

4. What cognitive processes and biological constraints affect classical conditioning?

Pavlov's experiments bolstered Watson's and other behaviorists' belief that the principles of learning are universal. We now know that classical conditioning is both cognitively and biologically constrained. Rats, for example, are biologically prepared to learn associations between a peculiar taste and a sickening drink, which they will learn to avoid. But they don't learn to avoid a sickening drink announced by a noise. Moreover, animals as well as people appear mentally to associate predictable CS → UCS patterns.

Operant Conditioning

5. What is operant conditioning, and how does it differ from classical conditioning?

Classical (Pavlovian) conditioning works with involuntary (reflexive) behaviors. Operant conditioning works with voluntary behaviors: the learner actively operates on the environment. When rats or pigeons are placed in a Skinner box, researchers can shape their behavior by rewarding successive approximations of the desired behavior. When followed by positive or negative reinforcement, the behavior is strengthened; when followed by punishment, the occurrence of the behavior diminishes.

6. What are the basic types of reinforcers?

Reinforcers can be positive (when presented after a response) or negative (when an aversive stimulus is withdrawn); primary (unlearned) or secondary (learned through association with primary reinforcers); and immediate or delayed. Regardless, all reinforcers strengthen the behaviors that they follow.

7. How do partial reinforcement schedules affect behavior?

Partial reinforcement schedules (fixed-interval, fixed-ratio, variable-interval, and variable-ratio) produce slower acquisition of the target behavior than does continuous reinforcement, but greater resistance to extinction.

8. How does punishment affect behavior?

Like reinforcement, punishment is most effective when strong, immediate, and consistent. Although punishment decreases the frequency of the behavior it follows, it is not simply the logical opposite of reinforcement, for punishment can result in several undesirable side effects, such as lying to avoid punishment, increased aggression, and fear of the punisher.

9. What cognitive processes and biological constraints influence operant conditioning?

Many psychologists have criticized behaviorists, such as Skinner, for underestimating the importance of cognitive and biological processes in operant conditioning. Research on cognitive mapping and latent learning points to the importance of cognitive processes in learning. Research has also made it clear that biological predispositions constrain what an animal can be taught.

10. How might educators, business managers, and individuals apply operant conditioning?

Operant principles are applied successfully in schools, in businesses, and at home. Computer-assisted instruction both shapes and reinforces learning; immediate reinforcement boosts worker productivity; individuals can strengthen desired behavior and extinguish unwanted behavior.

Learning by Observation

11. What is observational learning?

Observational learning results from watching others' behavior. In experiments, children tend to imitate both what a model does and says, whether the behavior is prosocial or antisocial.

Terms and Concepts to Remember

learning, p. 179

behaviorism, p. 180

unconditioned response (UCR), p. 181

unconditioned stimulus (UCS), p. 181

conditioned response (CR), p. 181

conditioned stimulus (CS), p. 181

classical (Pavlovian) conditioning, p. 182

acquisition, p. 182

extinction, p. 182

spontaneous recovery, p. 182

generalization, p. 183

discrimination, p. 183

operant conditioning, p. 188

respondent behavior, p. 188

operant behavior, p. 188

Skinner box, p. 189

shaping, p. 189

reinforcer, p. 190

positive reinforcement, p. 190

negative reinforcement, p. 190

primary reinforcer, p. 191

secondary reinforcer, p. 191

continuous reinforcement, p. 192

partial reinforcement, p. 192

fixed-ratio schedule, p. 192

variable-ratio schedule, p. 192

fixed-interval schedule, p. 192

variable-interval schedule, p. 192

punishment, p. 193

cognitive map, p. 195

latent learning, p. 195

observational learning, p. 199

modeling, p. 199

prosocial behavior, p. 200

Rehearse It Answer Key

1. c.   **2.** a.   **3.** b.   **4.** b.   **5.** d.   **6.** b.   **7.** b.   **8.** b.   **9.** b.

10. c.   **11.** b.   **12.** d.   **13.** a.

Critical Thinking Exercise

You have *Surveyed, Questioned, Read, Rehearsed,* and *Reviewed* Chapter 6. Now take your learning a step further by testing your *critical thinking* skills on the following passage. You may find it helpful to review the text material in the section "Pavlov's Experiments" before completing this exercise.

Psychologists believe that children learn to control their bladders during sleep through classical conditioning, a type of learning in which an organism comes to associate different events. Normally, a wet bed or diaper causes a child to awaken. Through repeated pairings, bladder tension becomes associated with the sensation of wetness and children wake up when they sense full bladders. But some children do not learn the connection between bladder tension and wetness, probably because wetting the bed or diaper does not awaken them. Psychologists have attempted to control bed wetting through classical conditioning by developing a special sheet containing fine electric wires. When the sleeping child wets the bed, the urine (which conducts electricity) immediately completes an electrical circuit and causes a loud bell to ring, awakening the child. Over time, bladder tension becomes associated with the bell and the child wakes up before actually wetting the bed.

Understand the Assertion

1. State the assertion in your own words. Define all important concepts and terms as they are used in this example.

Consider the Evidence

2. Identify the CS, CR, UCS, and UCR for children who learn to wake up without special training, and for children who are conditioned with the special sheet and bell.

Evaluate the Explanation

3. Evaluate the theoretical explanation for the psychologists' conclusion.

   a. Restate the explanation in your own words.

   b. Determine whether the explanation makes sense based on the evidence.

   c. State an alternative explanation.

Check your progress on becoming a critical thinker by comparing your answers to the sample answers found in Appendix B.

Memory

memory The storage and retrieval of information.

amnesia Loss of memory.

Which is more important—your experiences, or your memories of them?

Imagine your life without memories. There would be no savoring remembered joys, no guilt or misery over old pain. Each moment would be a fresh experience. But each person would be a stranger, each task—dressing, cooking, biking—a novel challenge, every language foreign.

Your memory is your mind's storehouse, the reservoir of your accumulated learning. To Cicero, memory was "the treasury and guardian of all things." To a psychologist, **memory** is our ability *to store and retrieve information.*

The Phenomenon of Memory

The range of human memory is evident in some fascinating cases:

Conversing with John, you are impressed by his wit, his intelligence (he might tell you the title of his master's thesis in physics), and his skill at tasks such as typing. It might be some time before you notice that John suffers from a form of **amnesia,** or memory loss, caused by a brain injury suffered in a motorcycle accident. John cannot form new memories. Although he remembers his life before the accident, John otherwise lives in an eternal present. Each morning when his rehabilitation therapist greets him she must reintroduce herself. She must listen patiently as over and over he retells anecdotes from his preaccident life. Each time the need arises, he inquires, "Where is the bathroom?" and is told anew.

At the other extreme are some special people who would be medal winners in a memory Olympics, with the Russian, Shereshevskii, or S as the distinguished Soviet psychologist Alexander Luria (1968) called him, taking home the gold. S's memory earned him a place in virtually every modern book on the subject. You and I can repeat back a string of about seven digits—almost surely no more than nine. S could repeat up to 70 digits or words, provided they were read about 3 seconds apart in an otherwise silent room. Moreover, he could recall them as easily backward as forward. His accuracy was unerring, even when asked to recall a list as much as 15 years later, after having memorized hundreds of other lists. "Yes, yes," he might recall. "This was a series you gave me once when we were in your apartment. . . . You were sitting at the table and I in the rocking chair. . . . You were wearing a gray suit and you looked at me like this. . . ." A journalist, S understandably took no notes at briefing sessions.

Do these memory feats make your own memory seem feeble? If so, consider your capacity for remembering countless voices, sounds, and songs; tastes, smells, and textures; faces, places, and happenings. Imagine viewing more than 2500 slides of faces and places, for only 10 seconds each, and later

WELL, FOR CRYING OUT LOUD! AL TOWBRIDGE! WHAT IS IT, NINE YEARS, SEVEN MONTHS, AND TWELVE DAYS SINCE I LAST RAN INTO YOU? TEN-THIRTY-TWO A.M., A SATURDAY, FELCHER'S HARDWARE STORE. YOU WERE BUYING SEALER FOR YOUR BLACKTOP DRIVEWAY. TELL ME, AL, HOW DID THAT SEALER WORK? DID IT HOLD UP?

MR. TOTAL RECALL

Drawing by Miller; © 1987 The New Yorker Magazine, Inc.

flashbulb memory A clear memory of an emotionally significant moment or event.

"The memory is sometimes so retentive, so serviceable, so obedient; at others, so bewildered and so weak; and at others again, so tyrannic, so beyond control! We are, to be sure, a miracle every way; but our powers of recollecting and forgetting do seem peculiarly past finding out."

Jane Austen
Mansfield Park, 1814

John Dean testifying before the Senate Watergate Committee. When compared to the White House tapes, John Dean's memory was found to be accurate for the substance of most conversations but not for the details.

seeing 280 of these slides one at a time, paired with a previously unseen slide. If you are like the subjects in an experiment by Ralph Haber (1970), you would recognize 90 percent of those you saw before.

Or consider the vividness of your memories of unique and highly emotional moments in your past—perhaps a car accident, your first romantic kiss, or where you were when you heard some tragic news. One such memory of mine is of my only hit in an entire season of Little League baseball. Most Americans over 45 feel sure of exactly what they were doing when they heard the news of President Kennedy's assassination (Brown & Kulik, 1982). You probably remember where you were when you learned that the space shuttle *Challenger* had exploded. This clarity for our memories of surprising, significant events leads some psychologists to call them **flashbulb memories,** because it's as if the brain commands, "Print this!"

How do we accomplish such memory feats? How can we remember things we have not thought about for years, yet forget the name of someone we met a minute ago? How are memories stored in our brains? Why can our memories—even our flashbulb memories—sometimes prove dead wrong? Does what we know about memory give us clues to how we can improve our memories? These will be among our questions as we review insights gleaned from a century of research.

Forming Memories: An Example

History is sometimes determined by what people remember about events. On June 17, 1972, Washington, DC police caught five men trying to tap the telephones of the Democratic National Committee in the Watergate Office Building. In 1973 when President Nixon's legal counselor, John Dean, testified before a U.S. Senate committee investigating White House involvement in "the Watergate scandal," Dean's recall of conversations with the President was so impressive that some writers called him "the human tape recorder." Ironically, it was later revealed that President Nixon's secret taping system had actually recorded the conversations that Dean recounted, providing a rare opportunity to compare an eyewitness's memories with the actual event. Dean's recollection of the essentials proved correct. The highest ranking members of the White House staff went to prison for doing what John Dean said they did, and President Nixon was forced to resign.

However, when Ulric Neisser (1981) compared the details in the tapes to the testimony, he discovered that John Dean was far from a human tape recorder. For example, Dean recalled that entering a September 15 meeting,

> [I] found Haldeman and the President. The President asked me to sit down. Both men appeared to be in very good spirits and my reception was very warm and cordial. The President then told me that Bob—referring to Haldeman—had kept him posted on my handling of the Watergate case. The President told me I had done a good job and he appreciated how difficult a task it had been and the President was pleased that the case had stopped with [his reelection committee's attorney] Liddy.

But almost every detail Dean recalled was wrong. The tape of the meeting revealed that the President did not ask Dean to sit down. He did not say Dean had done a good job. He did not say anything about Liddy or the indictments.

Dean's memory was better for a March 15 conversation during which he delivered a well-prepared report to the President on the unraveling of the White House cover-up. The tape caught Dean actually saying, "We have a cancer within, close to the presidency, that is growing. It is growing daily . . .

encoding The processing of information into the memory system.

storage The maintenance of encoded information over time.

retrieval The process of getting information out of memory storage.

long-term memory The relatively permanent and limitless storehouse of the memory system.

working memory "Short-term" memory that holds a few items briefly, such as the seven digits of a phone number while dialing, before the information is stored long-term or forgotten.

rehearsal The conscious repetition of information, either to maintain it in consciousness or to encode it for storage.

Preview Question

1. How do psychologists describe the human memory system?

because (1) we are being blackmailed, (2) people ar[e] themselves. . . ." In his later congressional testimo[ny] the President that there was a cancer growing on the [...] it was important that this cancer be removed im[mediately?] growing more deadly every day."

How could John Dean have been so right in [recalling] the Watergate discussions, yet, except for the M[...] wrong in recalling the details of most conversations? Why are you likely [to] misrecall a sentence such as, "The angry rioter threw the rock at the window?" To understand Dean's memory (and our own), we need a model for organizing the many aspects of memory.

Memory as Information Processing

To remember any event requires that we *get information into our brains, retain it,* and later *get it back out.* These three steps—**encoding, storage,** and **retrieval**—apply not only to human memory but also to other information-processing systems. Consider how a computer encodes, stores, and retrieves information. First, the computer translates input (via keystrokes, for example) into an electronic language, much like the brain encodes sensory information into a neural language. The computer then permanently stores vast amounts of information on a disk. From this information storehouse it can retrieve a file or document into a working memory, which also receives new information from the keyboard. Part of this working memory is visible on the screen.

Likewise, we store vast amounts of information in **long-term memory.** From our memory storehouse we can retrieve information into a limited-capacity, short-term **working memory,** which also receives information from our current experience. Part of this short-term working memory is displayed on the mental screen we call consciousness. Our working memory typically stores only seven or so bits of information (give or take two), a recall capacity that has been enshrined in psychology as "the Magical Number Seven, plus or minus two" (Miller, 1956). Thus at any given moment we attend to only a very limited amount of information. Without conscious **rehearsal,** information quickly fades from short-term memory.

Figure 7–1 offers a simplified model of the human memory system. Our sensory systems record a precise but fleeting memory of incoming information. We can't focus on everything at once. So we shine the flashlight beam of attention on certain of the incoming stimuli, often informative, novel stimuli.

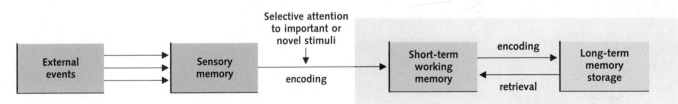

Figure 7–1 A simplified model of human memory.

This information thus gets encoded into a short-term, working memory, much of which is displayed "on screen" in our conscious awareness. Some of this information we then process for long-term storage. From the long-term storehouse, we will be able to retrieve this new information back into working memory.

Sensory Memory: Registering Information

Preview Question

2. How does sensory memory work?

Consider what one intriguing memory experiment revealed about our **sensory memory.** As part of his doctoral research, George Sperling (1960) showed people three rows of three letters each for only 1/20th of a second (Figure 7–2). It was like trying to read by the flashes of a lightning storm. After the nine letters disappeared from the screen, the subjects could recall only about half of them.

```
K   Z   R

Q   B   T

S   G   N
```

Figure 7–2 Momentary photographic memory. When George Sperling flashed a group of letters similar to this for 1/20th of a second, people could recall only about half of the letters. But when signaled to recall a particular row *immediately* after the letters had disappeared, they could do so with near-perfect accuracy.

Why? Was it because they had insufficient time to glimpse them? No, Sperling cleverly demonstrated that even at such lightning-flash speed, people actually *can* see and recall all the letters, but only momentarily. Rather than ask them to recall all nine letters at once, Sperling would sound a high, medium, or low tone immediately *after* flashing the nine letters. This cue directed the subject to report only the letters of the top, middle, or bottom row, respectively. Now the subjects rarely missed a letter, showing that all nine letters were momentarily available for recall.

Sperling's experiment revealed that we have a fleeting photographic memory called **iconic memory.** For an instant, the eyes register an exact representation of a scene, and we can recall any part of it in amazing detail. But only for a few tenths of a second. If Sperling delayed the tone signal by as much as a second, the iconic memory was gone and the subjects once again recalled only about half of the letters. The visual screen clears quickly, as it must, lest new images be superimposed over old ones. The auditory sensory image, called **echoic memory,** also lasts less than a second (Cowan, 1988). But a partially interpreted auditory echo disappears more slowly. The last few words spoken seem to linger for 3 or 4 seconds. Sometimes, just as you ask, "What did you say?" you can hear in your mind the echo of what was said.

Working Memory

Preview Question

3. How does sensory information get encoded and transferred into the memory system?

From our sweeping but fleeting sensory record, we transfer a small portion into working memory. Processing information from sensory memory into working memory is like sorting through the day's mail: We instantly discard some items and open, read, and retain others. To begin with, much of what we sense we never attend to. If you live in the United States, you have probably looked at thousands of pennies in your lifetime. Can you recall what the side with Lincoln's head looks like? If not, let's make the memory test easier: Can you *recognize* the real thing in Figure 7–3?

sensory memory The immediate, initial recording of sensory information in the memory system.

iconic memory A momentary sensory memory of visual stimuli; a photographic or picture-image memory lasting no more than a second or so.

echoic memory A momentary sensory memory of auditory stimuli; even if attention is elsewhere, sounds and words can still be recalled within 3 or 4 seconds.

automatic processing Unconscious encoding of incidental information, such as space, time, and frequency, and of well-learned information, such as word meanings.

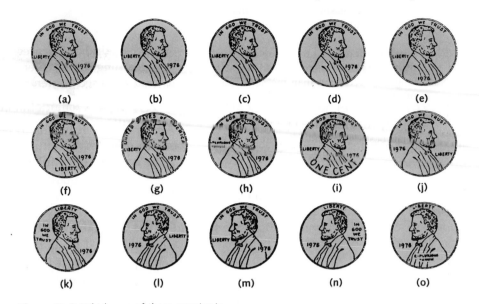

Figure 7-3 Which one of these pennies is the real thing? (From Nickerson & Adams, 1979.) (See page 212.)

Raymond Nickerson and Marilyn Adams (1979) found that most people cannot. The details of a penny are not very meaningful—nor are they essential for distinguishing pennies from other coins—and few of us have made the effort to encode them.

Automatic Processing

Although some information takes attention and effort to remember, other information (a penny's color) gets encoded effortlessly. With little or no effort, you absorb an enormous amount of information about *space, time,* and *frequency:* During an exam, you may recall the place on the textbook page where the forgotten material appears. You can recreate a sequence of the day's events in order to guess where you left your coat. You may realize that "this is the third time I've run into you this afternoon." Memories like these form almost automatically. In fact, not only can **automatic processing** occur effortlessly, but it is also difficult to shut off. When you hear or read a word in your native language, it is virtually impossible not to register its meaning automatically.

Some things we encode automatically, but other things require effort. With practice, however, what takes effort can become automatic.

hippocampus A neural center in the limbic system that helps process explicit memories for storage.

Figure 7–13 The hippocampus processes explicit memories for facts and experiences. This boy's hippocampus is not yet fully mature. Despite his obvious pleasure at his second birthday celebration, he won't remember this event later in life, except through pictures and stories.

Hippocampus

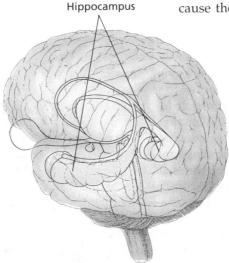

and events into long-term memory (Figure 7–13). When monkeys lose their hippocampus to surgery, they lose most of their recall for things learned during the preceding 8 weeks (Squire, 1990). Chickadees and other birds can store food in hundreds of places and return to these unmarked caches months later, but not if their hippocampus has been removed (Sherry & Vaccarino, 1990). Older memories remain intact, suggesting that the hippocampus is not the permanent storehouse, but a way station that feeds new information to other brain areas for permanent storage. Implicit memories for skills and conditioned associations still form after damage to the hippocampus and seem to be processed in the brain's even more ancient regions.

This dual explicit-implicit memory system helps explain infantile amnesia. Behaviorally, the reactions and skills we learned during infancy reach far into our future. Yet as adults we recall nothing of our first 2 years. Our conscious minds are blank, not only because we index so much of our explicit memory by words that nonspeaking children have not learned but also because the hippocampus is one of the last brain structures to mature.

Rehearse It

8. Ebbinghaus found that retention of novel information such as nonsense syllables drops off quickly; 3 days after such a learning session, we have forgotten much of what we learned. Ebbinghaus's "forgetting curve" shows that as time goes on, our retention of the nonsense syllables tends to
a. increase slightly.
b. decrease noticeably.
c. decrease greatly.
d. level out.

9. The average adult probably has about 1 billion bits of information in long-term memory, which has a capacity perhaps a thousand times greater than that. Evi-

dence suggests that the best way to learn and remember new information is to
a. undergo hypnosis.
b. undergo electrical stimulation of the motor cortex.
c. systematically forget or discard old memories.
d. relate new information to old.

10. An amnesic patient who has suffered damage to the hippocampus typically has difficulties in learning new facts and recalling recent events. (The person may be well able to recall the more distant past and certain well-learned skills, such as how to ride a bicycle or hem a dress.) Memories of skills are
a. explicit memories.

b. implicit memories.
c. semantic memories.
d. episodic memories.

11. The physical basis of memory—how and where memories are physically stored in the brain—is not yet well understood. However, research suggests that the hippocampus, a neural center in the limbic system of the brain, plays an important role. Probably, the hippocampus functions like
a. a way station between short- and long-term explicit memories.
b. a computer's hard disk.
c. the cortex.
d. a processing center for implicit memories.

Retrieval

To most people, memory is **recall,** the ability to retrieve information not in conscious awareness. To a psychologist, memory is any sign that something learned has been retained. So simply *recognizing* or more quickly *relearning* information also indicates memory.

Long after you cannot recall most of the people in your high school graduating class, you may still recognize their yearbook pictures from a photographic lineup and pick their names out from a list of names. Harry Bahrick and his colleagues (1975) reported that people who graduated 25 years earlier could not *recall* many of their old classmates, but they could *recognize* 90 percent of their pictures and names. And if you once learned something and then forgot it, you will probably relearn it more quickly than when you learned it originally. When studying for a final exam or when resurrecting a language used in early childhood, the relearning is easier. Tests of **recognition** and of time spent **relearning** reveal that we remember more than we can recall.

Preview Question

8. How do we get information out of memory storage?

Multiple-choice questions test:
(a) recall.
(b) recognition.
(c) relearning.

Fill-in-the-blank questions
test _____.

(See page 223.)

Even if Madonna and Paul Newman had not become famous, their high school classmates would likely still recognize their yearbook photos.

Madonna Ciccone
Adams High School 1976
Rochester, Mich.
Thespian Society.

Paul Newman
Shaker High School 1943
Shaker Heights, Ohio
Travel Club 2, 3; Booster 3, 4.

recall   A measure of memory in which the person must retrieve information learned earlier, as on a fill-in-the-blank test.

recognition   A measure of memory in which the person need only identify items previously learned, as on a multiple-choice test.

relearning   A memory measure that assesses the amount of time saved when relearning previously learned information.

priming   The activation of particular associations in memory.

Retrieval Cues

To retrieve a fact from a library of stored information, you need a way to gain access to it. In recognition tests, retrieval cues (such as photographs) provide reminders of information (classmates' names) we could not otherwise recall. If you want to know what the pyramid on the back of a dollar bill signifies, you might look in *Collier's Encyclopedia* under "dollar," "currency," or "money." But your efforts would be futile. To get the information you want, you would have to look under the retrieval cue—"Great Seal of the United States" (Hayes, 1981). Like information stored in encyclopedias, memories are inaccessible unless we have cues for retrieving them. The more and better learned the retrieval cues, the more accessible the memory.

You can think of a memory as held in storage by a web of associations (J. R. Anderson, 1983). To retrieve a specific memory, you first need to identify one of the strands that leads to it, a process called **priming** (Bower, 1986).

Figure 7–14 Priming demonstrates implicit memory. The spreading of associations can unconsciously activate related associations. After seeing or hearing *rabbit*, we are later more likely to spell the spoken word *hair* as h-a-r-e. (Adapted from Bower, 1986.)

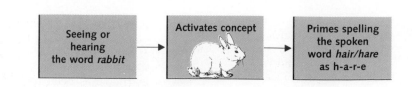

| Seeing or hearing the word *rabbit* | → | Activates concept | → | Primes spelling the spoken word *hair/hare* as h-a-r-e |

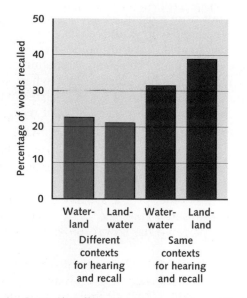

Figure 7–15 The effects of context on memory. Words heard underwater are best recalled underwater; words heard on land are best recalled on land. (Adapted from Godden & Baddeley, 1975.)

"I wonder if you'd mind giving me directions. I've never been sober in this part of town before."

© 1992 John Callahan/distributed by Levin Represents

Often our brains prime (activate) associations without our awareness. Hearing or seeing the word *rabbit* can unconsciously prime people to spell the spoken word *hair* as h-a-r-e. As Figure 7–14 indicates, *rabbit* primes associations with *hare* even though we may not recall having heard *rabbit*.

We can also prime our memories. Before the Watergate hearings, John Dean refreshed his memory "by going through every single newspaper article outlining what had happened and then placing myself in what I had done in a given sequence in time" (Neisser, 1981). Mnemonic chunking devices, such as ROY G. BIV, also provide us with handy retrieval cues.

Context Effects   It does help to put yourself back in the context where you experienced something. Duncan Godden and Alan Baddeley (1975) discovered this by having scuba divers listen to a list of words in two different settings, either 10 feet underwater or sitting on the beach. As Figure 7–15 illustrates, the divers recalled more words when they were retested in the same place. Likewise, taking an exam in the same room where you are taught may help boost recall. You have probably experienced other, similar context effects. Returning to where you once lived or the school you once attended, you may have been flooded with retrieval cues, and then with memories.

Sometimes being in a context similar to one we've been in before may trigger the experience of **déjà vu**—that eerie sense that "I've been in this exact situation before." People who pose the question as, "How could I recognize a situation that I'm experiencing for the first time?" may suppose that something paranormal is occurring. Could it be reincarnation ("I must have experienced this in a previous life") or precognition ("I viewed this scene in my mind before experiencing it")? If we pose the question differently—"Why do I feel as if I recognize this situation?"—we can see how our memory system might produce the déjà vu feeling (Alcock, 1981). If we have previously been in a similar situation, although we can't recall what it was, the current situation may be loaded with cues that unconsciously help us to retrieve the earlier experience. Thus, if you see a stranger who looks and walks like one of your friends, the similarity may give rise to a feeling of recognition. Because the feeling conflicts with your knowledge that the person is a stranger, you may think, "I've seen that person before."

Moods and Memories   It not only helps to get back in the context where you learned something, but back in the mood state. The things we learn in one state—be it joyful or sad, drunk or sober—are sometimes more easily recalled when we are again in the same state, a subtle phenomenon called *state-dependent memory*. What is learned when drunk, high, or depressed is not recalled well in *any* state (drugs and depression interfere with encoding); but it's recalled slightly better when again drunk, high, or depressed. Someone who hides money when drunk may forget where, until drunk again. Cognitive psychologist Gordon Bower (1983) explains: "A specific emotional state is like a specific room in a library into which the subject places memory records, and he can most easily retrieve those records by returning to that same room or emotional state."

déjà vu (From French, literally meaning "already seen.") That eerie sense that "I've experienced this before." Cues from the current situation may subconsciously trigger retrieval of an earlier, similar experience.

mood-congruent memory The tendency to recall experiences that are consistent with one's current good or bad mood.

"When a feeling was there, they felt as if it would never go; when it was gone, they felt as if it had never been; when it returned, they felt as if it had never gone."

George MacDonald
What's Mine's Mine, 1886

Answers to questions on page 221: Multiple-choice questions test recognition. Fill-in-the-blank questions test recall.

More reliable than state-dependent retrieval of specific information is a mood's triggering of emotionally tinged memories (Ellis & Ashbrook, 1989; Ucros, 1989). When sad, we easily recall past events associated with sad emotions. When happy, happy times come to mind. Thus, if people are put in a buoyant mood—whether under hypnosis or just by the day's events (a World Cup soccer victory for the German subjects of one study)—they commonly recall the world through rose-colored glasses (Forgas & others, 1984; Schwarz & others, 1987). They recall and view themselves as competent and effective, other people as benevolent, life in general as wonderful. Put in a bad mood by negative events, the very same people suddenly recall everything more negatively.

So it shouldn't surprise us that *currently* depressed people recall their parents as having been rejecting, punitive, and guilt-promoting, whereas *formerly* depressed people describe their parents as do those who have never suffered severe depression (Lewinsohn & Rosenbaum, 1987). Their memories are **mood-congruent.** Being depressed sours memories by priming negative associations. You and I may nod our heads knowingly. Yet, curiously, when in a good or bad mood, we persist in attributing our changing judgments and memories to reality rather than to our temporary moods.

Moods also influence how we *interpret* other people's behavior. In a bad mood, we read someone's look as a glare; in a good mood we encode the same look as interest. Thus, how we perceive the world depends on our mood. Passions exaggerate.

The effect of mood on encoding and retrieval helps explain why moods persist. When happy, we recall happy events, which help prolong the good mood. When depressed, we recall depressing events, which in turn feeds depressing interpretations of current events. As we will see in Chapter 12, this process maintains depression's vicious cycle.

Finally, our moods affect how attentive we are to new information. Sad people are often preoccupied—less attentive to new information (thus less able to recall it) and more focused on their woes (Salovey & Birnbaum, 1989; Wood & others, 1990). In some respects, that's healthy. A negative mood signals that all's not well, motivating people to ruminate and reassess. Very happy moods can also trigger distracting thoughts, impairing memory for the task at hand (Seibert & Ellis, 1991).

Memory Construction

Picture yourself having the following pleasant experience:

> You decide to go to your favorite restaurant for dinner. You enter the restaurant and are seated at a table with a white tablecloth. You study the menu. You tell the waiter that you want prime rib, medium rare, a baked potato with sour cream, and a salad with blue cheese dressing. You also order some red wine from the wine list. A few minutes later the waiter returns with your salad. Later he brings the rest of the meal, which you enjoy, except that the prime rib is a bit overdone.

Were I immediately to quiz you on this paragraph (from Hyde, 1983), you could surely retrieve considerable detail. For example, without looking back, answer the following questions:

1. What kind of salad dressing did you order?
2. Was the tablecloth red checked?
3. What did you order to drink?
4. Did the waiter give you a menu?

Preview Question

9. How accurate are our memories?

You were probably able to recall exactly what you ordered, and maybe even the color of the tablecloth. Does retrieval therefore consist merely of "reading" the information stored in our brain's library? We do have an enormous capacity for storing and reproducing the incidental details of our daily experience. But as we have seen, we often construct our memories as we encode them, and we may also reconstruct them as we retrieve them. Did the waiter give you a menu? Not in the paragraph given. Nevertheless, many people answer yes. Why? Their concepts of restaurants direct their memory construction, by filtering information and filling in missing pieces.

Elizabeth Loftus has repeatedly shown how eyewitnesses similarly construct their memories at encoding and reconstruct them when asked to recall incidents. In one experiment with John Palmer, Loftus showed a film of a traffic accident and then quizzed the viewers about what they saw (Loftus & Palmer, 1973). Those asked, "How fast were the cars going when they *smashed* into each other?" gave higher speed estimates than those asked, "How fast were the cars going when they *hit* each other?" A week later, the researchers asked the viewers if they recalled seeing any broken glass. Compared to those who had been asked the question with "hit," those asked the question with "smashed" were more than twice as likely to recall broken glass (Figure 7–16). In fact, there was no broken glass.

In many follow-up experiments around the world, people have witnessed an event, received or not received misleading information about it, and then taken a memory test. The repeated result? After exposure to subtle misinformation, many people misremember. They have misrecalled a yield sign as a stop sign, hammers as screwdrivers, Coke cans as peanut cans, *Vogue* magazine as *Mademoiselle,* "Dr. Henderson" as "Dr. Davidson," breakfast cereal as eggs, and a clean-shaven man as having a mustache (Loftus & others, 1989).

So unwitting is the effect that people later find it nearly impossible to discriminate between their memories of real and suggested events (Schooler & others, 1986). This difficulty was strikingly true among those who 3 years later misrecalled their whereabouts upon hearing of the space shuttle *Challenger's* explosion (Neisser & Harsch, 1992). When shown their own handwritten accounts from the day after, many were surprised. Some were so sure of their constructed memories that they insisted their original version must have been flawed. Similarly, the psychologist Jean Piaget was startled as an adult to learn that his vivid, detailed memory of his nursemaid thwarting his kidnapping was utterly false. Piaget apparently constructed the memory from the many retellings of the story he had heard (later confessed by the nursemaid to have been false). Without discounting the horrors of child abuse, critics wonder whether leading questions, therapists' suggestions, and the publicity given child abuse might sometimes similarly contribute to false or distorted memories of early experiences (Doris, 1991).

The moral: Memory is more reconstruction than reproduction. You therefore can't be sure whether a memory is real by how real it feels. Unreal memories feel just like real memories. In experiments on eyewitness testimony, researchers have repeatedly found that the most confident eyewitnesses are the most persuasive, but often not the most accurate. Eyewitnesses, whether right or wrong, express roughly similar self-assurance (Bothwell & others, 1987; Cutler & Penrod, 1989; Wells & Murray, 1984).

Recognizing that memory construction can occur as police and attorneys ask questions framed by their own understandings of an event, Ronald Fisher, Edward Geiselman, and their colleagues (1987, 1989) train police interviewers to ask less suggestive, more effective questions. To activate retrieval cues, the detective first asks witnesses to visualize the scene—the weather,

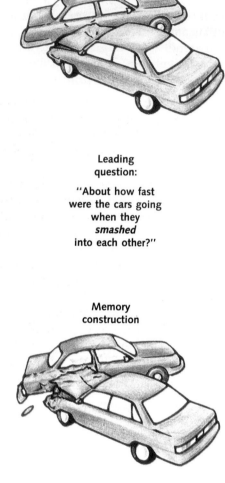

Accident

Leading question:

"About how fast were the cars going when they *smashed* into each other?"

Memory construction

Figure 7–16 Memory construction. When people who saw the film of a car accident were asked a leading question, they recalled a more serious accident than they had witnessed. (From Loftus, 1979.)

time of day, lighting, sounds, smells, positions of objects, and their mood. Then the witness tells in detail, and without interruption, every point recalled, no matter how trivial. Only then does the detective ask evocative follow-up questions: "Was there anything unusual about the person's appearance or clothing?" Using this "cognitive interview" technique, Fisher and Geiselman report that accuracy of recall increases by some 50 percent.

Memory construction helps explain why John Dean's recollections of the Watergate conversations were a mixture of real and imagined events. It explains why "hypnotically refreshed" memories of crimes so easily incorporate errors, some of which originate with the hypnotist's leading questions ("Did you hear loud noises?"). And it explains why dating partners who fall in love *over*estimate their first impressions of one another, while those who break up *under*estimate their earlier liking (McFarland & Ross, 1987).

Knowing What We Know

Sometimes we know more than we are aware of knowing. Other times—perhaps when taking an exam—we discover that we do not know as much as we thought. The difficulties of knowing what you know are exaggerated in the amnesic patients who implicitly know *how* to do things without explicitly knowing *that* they know.

How accurate are we at assessing what we know? John Shaughnessy and Eugene Zechmeister (1992) explored this question in an experiment with two groups of students. Group 1 repeatedly reread dozens of factual statements, then judged the likelihood that they would later remember each fact, and then were tested on their recall. Students in this group felt fairly confident of their knowledge, even on the questions they later missed. Students in group 2 read the statements, but then spent the rest of the time responding to practice tests requiring them to retrieve the facts. Both groups performed equally well on the final recall test, but group 2 students were more accurate in their judgment of what they did and didn't know. Thus, self-testing enhances recall and can help you to know what you know—and thus to focus your study time on what you don't yet know. As the British Prime Minister Benjamin Disraeli once said, "To be conscious that you are ignorant is a great step to knowledge."

Drawing by Cheney, © 1983 *Omni* Magazine, Penthouse Enterprises, Inc.

"Memory is a great betrayer."

Anaïs Nin
The Diary of Anaïs Nin, 1974

Forgetting

Amidst all the applause for memory—all the efforts to understand it, all the books on how to improve it—have any voices been heard in praise of forgetting? William James (1890, p. 680), author of psychology's first textbook, was such a voice: "If we remembered everything, we should on most occasions be as ill off as if we remembered nothing." To discard the clutter of useless or out-of-date information—where we parked the car yesterday, a friend's old phone number, restaurant orders already cooked and served—is surely a blessing (Bjork, 1978). The Russian memory whiz S, whom we met at the beginning of the chapter, was haunted by his junk heap of memories, which continually dominated his consciousness. He found it more difficult than others to think abstractly—to generalize, to organize, to evaluate. A good memory is helpful, but so is the ability to forget.

What causes forgetting? Forgotten events are like old books you can't

proactive interference The disruptive effect of prior learning on the recall of new information. *Proactive* means forward-acting.

retroactive interference The disruptive effect of new learning on the recall of old information. *Retro*active means backward-acting.

Table 7–1
Proactive and Retroactive Interference

Time 1	Time 2	Test	Interference
Study French	Study Spanish	Recall Spanish	French proactively interferes
Study French	Study Spanish	Recall French	Spanish retroactively interferes

find. One possibility is that they decayed and you discarded them from storage. With time, stored memories, too, may decay.

A second possibility is that we failed to encode the information. Thus, it never entered the memory system. At every moment our senses are bombarded with countless stimuli, most of which we retain but for a fleeting moment. Close your eyes and listen for a minute to all the sounds you have been ignoring.

Forgetting as Retrieval Failure

Forgetting occurs when our stored memories decay, when we fail to encode information, *and* when we are unable to retrieve it. Even if the book is stored and available, it may be inaccessible. Perhaps you don't have the needed retrieval clues. Information sometimes gets into our brain and, though we know it is there, we cannot get it out. A person's name may lie poised on the tip of the tongue, waiting to be retrieved. When people who cannot recall information get retrieval cues ("It begins with an *m*"), they will often remember what they could not recall. Retrieval problems help explain the occasional memory failures of older adults. (Chapter 3 notes how older people tend to recall less than do younger adults, but they usually remember as well if given reminders or a recognition test.)

Interference

Learning some items may interfere with retrieving others, especially when the items are similar. If someone gives you a phone number to remember, you may be able to recall it later. But if two more people give you their numbers, each successive number will be more difficult to recall. This **proactive interference** occurs when something you have already learned disrupts your learning something new. As you collect more and more information, your mental attic never fills, but it certainly gets cluttered.

For example, after buying a new combination lock or changing your phone number, the old one may interfere. Benton Underwood (1957) explored this phenomenon. He found that people who learn different lists of words on successive days have more and more difficulty remembering each new list the next day. Proactive interference explains why Ebbinghaus, after memorizing countless lists of nonsense syllables during his career, could remember only about one-fourth of a new list of syllables on the day after he learned it—far fewer than you as a novice could remember after learning a single list.

Retroactive interference occurs when new information makes it harder to recall something you learned earlier. For example, the learning of new students' names typically interferes with a professor's recall of names learned in previous classes. Table 7–1 illustrates both types of interference.

You can minimize retroactive interference by reducing the number of interfering events—say, by learning new information before going to sleep. This is what John Jenkins and Karl Dallenbach (1924) found in a classic experiment. Day after day, two people each learned some nonsense syllables, then tried to recall them after up to 8 hours of being awake or asleep. As Figure 7–17 shows, forgetting occurred more rapidly after being awake and involved with other activities. The investigators surmised that "forgetting is not so much a matter of the decay of old impressions and associations as it is a matter of interference, inhibition, or obliteration of the old by the new" (p. 612). Later experiments confirm that the hour before sleep is a good time to commit information to memory (Fowler & others, 1973).

Figure 7–17 Retroactive interference. More forgetting occurs when a person stays awake and learns other new material. (From Jenkins & Dallenbach, 1924.)

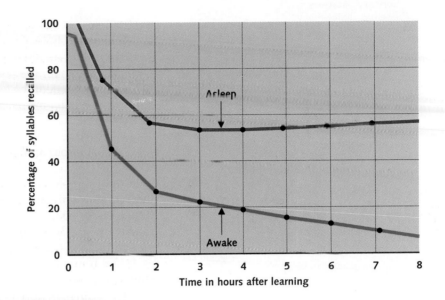

Although interference is an important cause of forgetting, we should not overstate the point. Often, old information facilitates our learning of new information. Knowledge of Latin may aid one's learning of French—a phenomenon called "positive transfer." It's when the old and new information compete with each other that interference occurs.

Motivated Forgetting

The huge cookie jar in our kitchen was jammed with freshly baked chocolate chip cookies. Still more spread across the cooling racks on the counter. Twenty-four hours later, not a crumb was left. Who had taken them? My wife, three children, and I were the only people in the house during that time. So while memories were still fresh, I immediately undertook a little memory test. Andy acknowledged wolfing down as many as 20. Peter admitted eating 15. Laura guessed that she had stuffed her then-6-year-old body with 15 cookies. My wife, Carol, recalled eating 6, and I remembered consuming 15 and taking 18 more to the office. Collectively, our memories sheepishly accepted responsibility for 89 cookies. Still, we had not come close; 160 cookies had been baked.

Why did our memories fail us? Why did we not encode, store, and retrieve almost half the instances of our cookie-eating? As noted earlier, we encode information about frequency fairly automatically. So was it a storage problem? Might our memories of cookies, like Ebbinghaus's memory of nonsense syllables, have vanished almost as fast as the cookies themselves? Or might the information still be intact, but irretrievable because it would be embarrassing to remember?

With his concept of **repression,** Sigmund Freud proposed that our memory systems are indeed self-censoring. To protect our self-concepts and to minimize anxiety, we may repress painful memories. But the submerged memory still lingers, said Freud, and with patience and effort may be retrieved during therapy or by some later cue. One such case involved a woman with an intense, unexplained fear of running water. An aunt solved the mystery one day by whispering, "I have never told." The words cued the woman's memory of an incident when, as a disobedient young child, she wandered away from a family picnic and became trapped under a waterfall —until being rescued by her aunt, who promised not to tell her parents (Kihlstrom, 1990).

After 20 years of apparently repressing the memory, a number of small cues triggered Eileen Franklin-Lipsker's coming forward to claim herself the only witness to her father's molesting and murdering her childhood girlfriend.

repression In psychoanalytic theory, the basic defense mechanism that blocks from consciousness painful memories and anxiety-arousing thoughts.

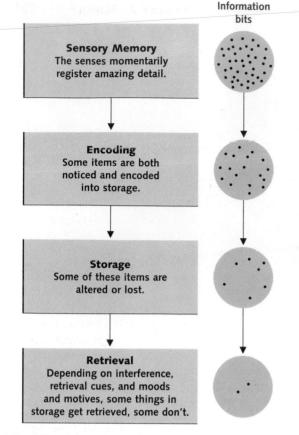

Sensory Memory
The senses momentarily register amazing detail.

Information bits

Encoding
Some items are both noticed and encoded into storage.

Storage
Some of these items are altered or lost.

Retrieval
Depending on interference, retrieval cues, and moods and motives, some things in storage get retrieved, some don't.

Forgetting can occur at any memory stage. As we process information, we filter, alter, or lose much of it.

Evidence of repression comes from torture or war victims who cannot remember their horror-filled moments. The closest laboratory counterpart to repression (and an alternative explanation of it) is the phenomenon of state-dependent memory (page 222): What we learn in one emotional or physiological state we sometimes forget in a radically different state. Thus, what we experience when embarrassed or horror-stricken may be forgotten when we are relaxed.

In experiments that more closely parallel the cookie-memory phenomenon, Michael Ross and his colleagues (1981) found that people unknowingly revise their own histories. After Ross persuaded a group of people that frequent toothbrushing is desirable, they (more than other people) recalled having frequently brushed their teeth in the last 2 weeks. Having taken a highly touted study skills course, students later inflated their estimates of self-improvement. By *de*flating their evaluations of their previous study habits they convinced themselves that they had really benefitted (Conway & Ross, 1984). To remember our past is often to revise it. By recalling events in a desired manner we protect and enhance our self-images.

Our ability to store and retrieve information is a remarkable phenomenon. We have seen that some memories form automatically, others only with effort. Although our working memory capacity is limited, our long-term storage capacity is essentially limitless. Yet it also is imperfect. Between sensation and retrieval, most of the information that confronts us becomes lost, inaccessible, or distorted. Unlike video recordings, memory is a human activity, influenced by heartfelt emotions and mental expectations.

Rehearse It

12. To measure long-term memory, psychologists test a person's ability to *recall* information. They also test ability to *recognize* what has been learned and they measure *relearning* time. A psychologist who asks you to write down as many objects as you can remember having seen a few minutes earlier is testing your
a. recall.
b. recognition.
c. recall and recognition.
d. relearning.

13. To gain access to a memory, a person activates an association that leads to that memory. The association may be activated by a specific odor, visual image, or mnemonic; all of these function as
a. relearning.
b. déjà vu.
c. declarative memories.
d. retrieval cues.

14. When happy, we tend to recall happy times. When depressed, we more often recall depressing events. This tendency to recall experiences that are consistent with our current emotions is called
a. mnemonics.
b. chunking.
c. repression
d. mood-congruent memory.

15. Experiments show that the hour before sleep is a good time to memorize information. For example, studying a vocabulary list before going to sleep minimizes the disrupting effects of all the other new words and terms that might, in the course of a school day, claim our attention. Going to sleep right after learning new material minimizes
a. positive transfer.
b. motivational forgetting.
c. retroactive interference.
d. proactive interference.

16. People unknowingly revise or rearrange their memories of events. According to Sigmund Freud, painful or unacceptable memories are self-censored, or blocked from consciousness, through a mechanism called
a. repression.
b. proactive interference.
c. anxiety.
d. physical decay of the memory trace.

Psychology Applied: Tips for Improving Memory

Repeated study—a little and often—yields more lasting memory than massed study.

"Knit each new thing on to some acquisition already there."

William James
Principles of Psychology, 1890

Much as biology benefits medicine and botany benefits agriculture, so can the psychology of memory benefit education. Sprinkled throughout this chapter and summarized here for easy reference are concrete suggestions for improving your memory. The SQ3R—Study, Question, Read, Recite, Review—study technique introduced in Chapter 1 incorporates several of these strategies.

Study repeatedly to boost long-term recall. Overlearn. To learn a name or a fact, repeat it to yourself after being introduced; wait a few seconds and say it again; wait longer and say it again. To provide many separate study sessions, make use of life's little intervals—riding on the bus, walking across campus, waiting for class to start.

Spend more time rehearsing or actively practicing the material. Speed-reading (skimming) complex material—with minimal rehearsal—yields little retention. Rehearsal helps more. "The act of retrieving an item from memory facilitates subsequent retrieval," advises memory researcher Robert Bjork (1988). It pays to study actively!

Make the material personally meaningful. To build a network of retrieval cues, take thorough text and class notes in your own words. Mindlessly repeating information is relatively ineffective. Better to form images to understand and organize information, to relate the material to what you already know or have experienced, and to put it in your own words. Without such cues, you may

be stuck when a question uses different phrasing than you memorized. To increase retrieval cues, form as many associations as possible.

Use mnemonic devices to remember a list of unfamiliar items. Associate items with peg-words. Make up a story that incorporates vivid images of the items. Chunk information into acronyms. Develop hierarchies.

Refresh your memory by activating retrieval cues. Mentally recreate the situation and the mood in which the original learning occurred. Return to the same location. Jog your memory by allowing one thought to cue the next.

Recall events while they are fresh, before you encounter possible misinformation. If you are an eyewitness to an important event, record your memory before allowing others to suggest what may have occurred.

Test your own knowledge, both to rehearse it and to help you determine what you do not yet know. If you must later *recall* information, do not be lulled into overconfidence by your ability to *recognize* it. Test your recall. Outline sections on a blank page. Define concepts before reading their end-of-chapter definitions. Take practice tests; the study guides that accompany many texts, including this one, can help.

Minimize interference. Study right before sleeping. Don't study topics in close proximity that are likely to interfere with each other, such as Spanish and French.

Reviewing Memory

The Phenomenon of Memory

1. How do psychologists describe the human memory system?

After our sensory systems register information, we encode a small portion for processing in our working memory, much of which appears "on screen" in our conscious awareness. Our attention is especially drawn to novel or meaningful stimuli. Some of this information is then encoded for long-term storage, from which we may retrieve it back into working memory.

Sensory Memory: Registering Information

2. How does sensory memory work?

We have a complete but fleeting iconic (photographic) memory for visual stimuli and a slightly longer-lasting echoic memory for auditory stimuli. Without attention, much of what we sense we don't encode.

Working Memory

3. How does sensory information get encoded and transferred into the memory system?

Information about space, time, and frequency, in addition to well-learned information such as word meanings, is encoded automatically. We retain other types of information only with effort, such as by rehearsing it.

4. How much does rehearsal aid in forming memories?

Without rehearsal, much information that requires effort to remember (such as a new phone number) is lost within 3 seconds. The more we rehearse information, the better we retain it—especially if our rehearsal is spaced out rather than massed.

5. What other methods of effortful processing aid in forming memories?

Effortful encoding of meaning, imagery, and organization enhance long-term retention. Mnemonic devices exploit the memorability of visual images and of information that is organized into chunks. Organizing information into hierarchies also aids memory.

Long-Term Memory

6. How large and durable is our memory storage?

In the short run, our memory span for information just presented is very limited—up to about seven or eight items, depending on the information and how it is presented. Our capacity for storing information permanently is essentially unlimited. The brain does not store information with the durability and exactness of a tape recorder; most of what we learn is soon forgotten.

7. How are memories recorded in the brain?

The search for the physical basis of memory has recently focused on a smaller scale on synapses and neurotransmitters. The reuse of a neural pathway leads to alterations at the synapses that affect neural sensitivity to certain neurotransmitters. On a larger scale, different brain circuits have been found to process different types of memories. One circuit involving the hippocampus processes explicit memories; processing of implicit memories involve other brain structures.

8. How do we get information out of memory storage?

To be remembered, information that is "in there" must be retrieved, with the aid of associations (cues) that serve as reminders. Even mood can be a retrieval cue, leading us to recall happy times when happy, sad times when sad. Moods can also interfere with our recall, as when preoccupation with our feelings—sad or happy—makes us less attentive to new information.

9. How accurate are our memories?

Apparently, memories are not stored as exact copies, and they certainly are not retrieved as such. Rather, we construct our memories, using both stored and new information. Thus, for example, when eyewitnesses are subtly exposed to misleading details after an event, they often believe they *saw* the misleading details as part of the event.

Forgetting

10. Why do we forget?

Memory failure can occur at any stage of the process. Much of what we sense we never encode. Some of what we encode is altered or lost in memory storage. Retrieval failure may be caused by interference, by insufficient cues, or even by motivated forgetting (repression).

Terms and Concepts to Remember

memory, p. 205
amnesia, p. 205
flashbulb memory, p. 206
encoding, p. 207
storage, p. 207
retrieval, p. 207
long-term memory, p. 207
working memory, p. 207
rehearsal, p. 207
sensory memory, p. 208
iconic memory, p. 208

echoic memory, p. 208
automatic processing, p. 209
effortful processing, p. 210
spacing effect, p. 211
serial position effect, p. 211
imagery, p. 213
mnemonics [nih-MON-iks], p. 213
chunking, p. 214
implicit memory, p. 219
explicit memory, p. 219

hippocampus, p. 219
recall, p. 221
recognition, p. 221
relearning, p. 221
priming, p. 221
déjà vu, p. 222
mood-congruent memory, p. 223
proactive interference, p. 226
retroactive interference, p. 226
repression, p. 227

Rehearse It Answer Key

1. b. **2.** c. **3.** a. **4.** b. **5.** a. **6.** d. **7.** c. **8.** d. **9.** d.

10. b. **11.** a. **12.** a. **13.** d. **14.** d. **15.** c. **16.** a.

Critical Thinking Exercise

You have *Surveyed, Questioned, Read, Rehearsed,* and *Reviewed* Chapter 7. Now take your learning a step further by testing your *critical thinking* skills on the following passage.

Danny just happened to be driving into the parking lot of a convenience store the night it was held up and the attendant was killed. He caught a quick glimpse of a man carrying what appeared to be a handgun as he ran from the store. When the police arrived at the scene, Danny was unable to provide much detail regarding the gunman's appearance. Nevertheless, they took him to headquarters and showed him hundreds of mug book photographs. Believing that a man named Raymond had committed the crime, the investigator showed Danny his photograph several times. After many frustrating hours, during which Danny was unable to identify the killer conclusively, the investigator handed Danny a photograph of Raymond, saying "We know this man visited the convenience store the night of the crime. Is this the man you saw running from the store?" When Danny said he wasn't sure, he was allowed to leave and asked to think more carefully about what he had seen that night.

Three weeks later, Danny was asked to pick the killer from a line-up of five men, one of whom was Raymond. Although he remembered feeling uncertain of the identity of the man when he was first questioned, Danny was surprised at how easily and confidently he picked Raymond from the line-up now.

1. Why couldn't Danny identify the gunman right after he witnessed him fleeing from the store?

2. Why was Danny able to identify Raymond from the line-up several weeks later?

Check your progress on becoming a critical thinker by comparing your answers to the sample answers found in Appendix B.

Chapter 8

Thinking, Language, and Intelligence

Throughout history, we humans have deplored the depths of our foolishness and celebrated the heights of our wisdom. In a moment of humility the psalmist wondered, "What is man that thou art mindful of him?" but in the next breath rhapsodized that human beings were "little less than God." The poet T. S. Eliot was struck by "the hollow men . . . Headpiece filled with straw." But Shakespeare's Hamlet extolled the human species as "noble in reason! . . . infinite in faculties! . . . in apprehension how like a god!" In the preceding chapters, we, too, have sometimes marveled at our capabilities, sometimes at our propensity to err.

We have studied the human brain—a mere 3 pounds of tissue containing circuitry more complex than all the planet's telephone networks. We have marveled at the competence of newborn infants. We have appreciated the human sensory system, which disassembles visual stimuli into millions of nerve impulses, distributes them for parallel processing, and then reassembles them into clear and colorful perceived images. We have acknowledged the seemingly limitless capacity of human memory and the ease with which we process information, consciously and unconsciously. Little wonder, then, that our species has the genius to invent the camera, the car, and the computer; to unlock the atom and crack the genetic code; to travel into space and probe the ocean depths.

At the same time, we have seen that our species is kin to the other animals, subject to the same biological impulses and influenced by the same principles of learning as "lesser" creatures. We have noted that we assimilate reality into our preconceptions and succumb to perceptual illusions and distortions. We have seen how easily we deceive ourselves about hypnotic regressions, pseudopsychic claims, and constructed memories. Little wonder, then, that we sometimes imagine we can read minds and travel outside our bodies or that we form distorted images of other ethnic, age, and gender groups.

In this chapter, we encounter further instances of these two images of the human condition—the rational and the irrational. We will see how we form concepts, solve problems, and make judgments. We will look at our flair for language, and ask whether our species alone is capable of language. We will examine controversies regarding the nature and nurture of intelligence. In the end, we reflect on how deserving we are of our name, *Homo sapiens*—wise human.

Thinking

Previous chapters explain how we receive, perceive, store, and retrieve information. Now we consider how our cognitive system uses this information.

Thinking, or *cognition,* is the mental activity associated with understanding, processing, and communicating knowledge. **Cognitive psychologists** study these mental activities. We begin this chapter by considering the logical and sometimes illogical ways in which we create concepts, solve problems, make decisions, and form judgments. First, let's consider the building blocks of thinking: concepts.

Concepts

Preview Question

1. What functions do concepts serve?

To think about the countless events, objects, and people in our world, we simplify things. We organize them into mental groupings called **concepts.** The concept *chair* sums up a variety of items—a baby's high chair, a wing chair, the chairs around a dining room table, and folding chairs.

Imagine life without concepts. We would need a different name for every object and idea. We could not ask a child to "throw the ball" because there would be no concept of ball. Instead of saying, "He was angry," we would have to describe facial expression, vocal intensity, gestures, and words. Concepts such as *ball* and *angry* provide much information with a minimum of cognitive effort. That is why concepts are the basic building blocks of thought.

To simplify things further, we organize concepts into hierarchies. The earliest naturalists simplified and ordered the overwhelming complexity of some 5 million living species by clustering them into two basic categories—the plant kingdom and the animal kingdom. Then they divided these basic categories into smaller and smaller subcategories—vertebrates, fish, and sharks, for instance, in order of increasing specificity.

The urge to classify the world reflects our human tendency to order our environment into hierarchies of concepts. Doing so makes for cognitive efficiency. Using basic physical concepts, physicists speedily classify and solve physics problems. Cab drivers organize their cities into geographical sectors, which subdivide into neighborhoods and again into blocks. Chess masters conceptually organize chess games in ways that help them see the significance of various game positions (Bransford & others, 1986; Chi & others, 1988).

We form some concepts by definition. Told the rule that a triangle has three sides, we thereafter classify all three-sided geometric forms as triangles. By definition, a bird is an animal that has wings, feathers, and hatches from an egg. More often, we form our concepts by developing **prototypes**—a best example of a particular category (Rosch, 1978). The more closely objects

"Attention everyone! I'd like to introduce the newest member of our family."

Drawing by Kaufman; © 1977 The New Yorker Magazine, Inc.

Some birds match our bird prototype better than others.

thinking (or **cognition**) Mental activity associated with understanding, processing, and communicating knowledge.

cognitive psychology The field of psychology that studies mental representations and the processing of information; topics include the mental activities that underlie problem solving, judgments, decision making, and language.

concept A mental grouping of similar objects, events, or people

prototype The best example of a category; matching new items to the prototype provides a quick and easy method for including items in a category (as when comparing feathered creatures to a prototypical bird, such as a robin).

algorithm A methodical, logical rule or procedure for solving a particular problem. May be contrasted with the usually speedier, but also more error-prone use of *heuristics*.

heuristic A rule-of-thumb strategy that often allows us to make judgments and solve problems efficiently; usually speedier, but more error-prone than *algorithms*.

insight A sudden and often novel realization of the solution to a problem; it contrasts with strategy-based solutions.

To search for horseradish in a supermarket you could search every aisle (an algorithm) or check the mustard, spice, and gourmet sections (a heuristic).

Preview Question

2. By what strategies do we solve problems, and what obstacles hinder our problem solving?

match our prototype of a concept, the more readily we recognize them as examples of the concept. A robin and a goose both satisfy our rule for *bird*. Yet people agree more quickly with the statement, "A robin is a bird" than with the statement, "A goose is a bird." For most of us, the robin is the birdier bird; it more closely resembles our prototype of a bird. Likewise, "maternal love" and "self-love" both qualify as love. But people more instantly agree that "maternal love is a type of love," because it better matches their prototype (Fehr & Russell, 1991).

If something fails to match our prototype, we may have trouble classifying it. Thus, we might be slow to recognize nonflying penguins and kiwis as birds. We are much quicker to perceive an illness when our symptoms fit one of our disease prototypes. People whose heart attack symptoms don't precisely match their prototype of a heart attack are therefore slow to seek help (Bishop, 1991).

Solving Problems

One tribute to our rationality is our ability to form and use concepts. Another is our skill at solving problems—at coping with novel situations for which we have no well-established response. We solve some problems through trial and error. Thomas Edison tried thousands of light bulb filaments before stumbling upon one that worked. For other problems, we may follow a step-by-step procedure, called an **algorithm.** Told to find another word using all the letters in CINERAMA, we could systematically try each letter in each position—but generating and examining the 20,160 resulting combinations would take too long. Because algorithms can be laborious, we often solve problems with simple rule-of-thumb strategies, called **heuristics.** Thus, in rearranging the letters of CINERAMA, we might exclude letter combinations such as two *a*'s together or words starting with two consonants, such as *mc* or *nm*. By using rule-of-thumb heuristics and then applying trial and error, many people can come up with the answer (page 242).

Sometimes we are unaware of using any problem-solving strategy; the answer just comes to us. We can all recall occasions when we puzzled over a problem for some time and then, suddenly, the pieces fell together and we perceived the solution. This facility for sudden flashes of inspiration we call **insight.**

We humans aren't the only creatures who display insight. German psychologist Wolfgang Köhler (1925) observed insight while studying chimpanzees placed on an island off the coast of Africa. In one experiment with a chimp named Sultan, Köhler placed a piece of fruit and a long stick outside the chimp's cage, well beyond reach, and placed a short stick inside the cage. Spying the short stick, Sultan grabbed it and tried to reach the fruit with it. But the stick, by design, was too short. After several unsuccessful attempts, the chimp dropped the stick and paused to survey the whole situation. Then suddenly, as if thinking, "Aha!" Sultan jumped up, seized the short stick again, and this time used it to pull in the longer stick—which he then used to reach the fruit. Sultan's actions displayed animal cognition, claimed Köhler, and showed that there is more to learning than conditioning.

In human experience, insight is common. Köhler described it as the sense of satisfaction that accompanies a flash of inspiration. After solving a difficult problem or discovering how to resolve a conflict, we feel happy. The joy of a joke may similarly lie in our capacity for insight—in our sudden comprehension of an unexpected ending or a double meaning, as in the story of Professor Smith, who complained to his colleagues that student interruptions had become a problem. "The minute I get up to speak," he explained, "some fool begins to talk."

confirmation bias A tendency to search for information that confirms one's preconceptions.

fixation The inability to see a problem from a new perspective; an impediment to problem solving.

functional fixedness The tendency to think of things only in terms of their usual functions; an impediment to problem solving.

"The human understanding, when any proposition has been once laid down . . . forces everything else to add fresh support and confirmation."

Francis Bacon
Novum Organum, 1620

Figure 8–1 How would you arrange six matches to form four equilateral triangles? (From ''Problem Solving'' by M. Scheerer. Copyright © 1963 by Scientific American, Inc. All rights reserved.)

Obstacles to Problem Solving

A major obstacle to problem solving is our eagerness to search for information that confirms our ideas, a phenomenon known as **confirmation bias.** In an experiment with British university students, P. C. Wason (1960) demonstrated our reluctance to seek information that might disprove our beliefs. Wason gave students the three-number sequence, 2-4-6, and asked them to guess the rule he had used to devise the series. (The rule was simple: any three ascending numbers.) Before submitting their answers, the students generated their own sets of three numbers, and each time Wason told them whether or not their sets conformed to his rule. Once they had done enough testing to feel *certain* they had the rule, they were to announce it.

The result? Seldom right but never in doubt: Most people convinced themselves of a wrong rule. Typically, they formed an erroneous idea (''Maybe it's counting by twos'') and then searched only for confirming evidence (by testing 6-8-10, 100-102-104, and so forth). Such experiments reveal that we more eagerly seek evidence that will verify our ideas than evidence that might refute them (Klayman & Ha, 1987; Skov & Sherman, 1986). Business managers, for example, are more likely to follow the successful careers of those they've hired than of those they've rejected, which helps them confirm their perceived hiring ability.

Another obstacle to problem solving is **fixation**—the inability to see a problem from a fresh perspective. Once we incorrectly represent the problem, it's hard to restructure how we approach it. Can you overcome fixation in arranging the six matches shown in Figure 8–1 so that they form four equilateral triangles? Next, explain how you would use the materials in Figure 8–2 to mount the candle on a bulletin board. Try both these problems before you read on.

Figure 8–2 Using these materials, how would you mount the candle on a bulletin board? (From Duncker, 1945.)

If your attempts to solve the match problem were fixated on two-dimensional solutions, then the three-dimensional solution shown in Figure 8–3, page 238, will have eluded you.

One type of fixation goes by the awkward but appropriate label, **functional fixedness.** This is our tendency to perceive the functions of objects as fixed and unchanging. A person may ransack the house for a screwdriver when a dime would have done the job. Perhaps you experienced functional fixedness when you tried to solve the candle-mounting problem. If you thought of the matchbox as having only the function of holding matches, you may have overlooked its potential for serving as a platform for the candle, as shown in Figure 8–4, page 238.

Making Decisions and Forming Judgments

Preview Question

3. How do heuristics, overconfidence, and framing influence our decisions and judgments?

When making each day's hundreds of tiny judgments and decisions—Is it worth the bother to take an umbrella? Can I trust this person? Should I shoot the basketball or pass to the player who's hot?—we seldom take the time and effort to reason systematically. Usually, we follow our intuition. After interviewing policymakers in government, business, and education, social psychologist Irving Janis (1986) concluded that they "often do not use a reflective problem-solving approach. How do they usually arrive at their decisions? If you ask, they are likely to tell you . . . they do it mostly by the *seat of their pants*."

Using and Misusing Heuristics

Those mental shortcuts we call heuristics often help us make reasonable seat-of-the-pants judgments. But the price we pay for their efficiency can sometimes be costly bad judgments. To gain an idea of how heuristics determine our intuitive judgments—and how they can lead us astray—consider two heuristics identified by cognitive psychologists Amos Tversky and Daniel Kahneman (1974): *representativeness* and *availability*.

"In creating these problems, we didn't set out to fool people. All our problems fooled us, too."

Amos Tversky (1985)

The Representativeness Heuristic To judge the likelihood of things in terms of how well they represent particular prototypes is to use the **representativeness heuristic.** To illustrate, consider:

> A stranger tells you about a person who is short, slim, and likes to read poetry, and then asks you to guess whether this person is more likely to be a professor of classics at an Ivy League university or a truck driver. Which would be the better guess? (Adapted from Nisbett & Ross, 1980.)

If you are like most people, you answered a professor because the description seems more *representative* of Ivy League scholars than of truck drivers. The representativeness heuristic enabled you to make a snap judgment. But it also led you to ignore other relevant information, such as the total number of classics professors versus truck drivers. When I help people think through this question, their own reasoning usually leads them to an answer that contradicts their immediate intuition. The typical conversation goes something like this:

> *Question:* First, let's figure out how many professors fit the description. How many Ivy League universities do you suppose there are?
>
> *Answer:* Oh, about 10, I suppose.
>
> *Question:* How many classics professors would you guess there are at each?
>
> *Answer:* Maybe four.
>
> *Question:* Okay, that's 40 Ivy League classics professors. What fraction of these are short and slim?
>
> *Answer:* Let's say half.
>
> *Question:* And, of these 20, how many like to read poetry?
>
> *Answer:* I'd say half—10 professors.
>
> *Question:* Okay, now let's figure how many truck drivers fit the description. How many truck drivers do you suppose there are?
>
> *Answer:* Maybe 400,000.
>
> *Question:* What fraction are short and slim?
>
> *Answer:* Not many—perhaps 1 in 8.
>
> *Question:* Of these 50,000, what percentage like to read poetry?

representativeness heuristic A rule of thumb for judging the likelihood of things in terms of how well they seem to represent, or match, particular prototypes; may lead one to ignore other relevant information.

availability heuristic A rule of thumb for estimating the likelihood of events based on their availability in memory; if instances come readily to mind (perhaps because of their vividness), we presume such events are likely.

overconfidence phenomenon The tendency to be more confident than correct—to overestimate the accuracy of one's beliefs and judgments.

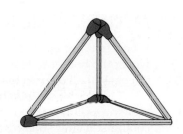

Figure 8–3 Solving the matchstick problem requires breaking a fixation, that of limiting your considerations to two-dimensional solutions. (From "Problem Solving" by M. Scheerer. Copyright © 1963 by Scientific American, Inc. All rights reserved.)

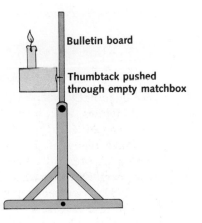

Bulletin board

Thumbtack pushed through empty matchbox

Figure 8–4 Solving the candle-mounting problem requires recognizing that a box need not always serve as a container. (From Duncker, 1945.)

"The information-processing shortcuts—called heuristics—which are normally both highly efficient and immensely time-saving in day-to-day situations, work systematically against us in the marketplace. . . . The tendency to underestimate or altogether ignore past probabilities in making a decision is undoubtedly the most significant problem of intuitive predictions."

David Dreman
Contrarian Investment Strategy: The Psychology of Stock Market Success, 1979

"The human understanding is most excited by that which strikes and enters the mind at once and suddenly, and by which the imagination is immediately filled and inflated. It then begins almost imperceptibly to conceive and suppose that everything is similar to the few objects which have taken possession of the mind."

Francis Bacon
Novum Organum, 1620

Answer: Truck drivers who like poetry? Maybe 1 in 100—oh, oh, I can see where this is going—that leaves me with 500 short, slim, poetry-reading truck drivers.

Question: Yup. So, although the person I described may be much more representative of classics professors than of truck drivers, this person is still (even accepting your stereotypes) 50 times more likely to be a truck driver.

This example illustrates the power of the representativeness heuristic. To judge the likelihood of something, we intuitively compare it to our mental representation of that category—of, say, what a truck driver is like. If the two match, then that fact usually overrides other considerations of statistics or logic.

The Availability Heuristic The **availability heuristic** operates when we base our judgments on the availability of information in our memories. If instances of an event are easily available—if they come to mind readily—we presume such events are common. Usually they are—but not always. To see this, make a guess: Does the letter *k* appear more often as the first or third letter in English words?

Because words beginning with *k* come to mind more easily than words having *k* as their third letter, most people guess that *k* occurs more frequently as the first letter. Actually, *k* is three times more likely to appear as the third letter. So far in this chapter, words such as *know, kingdom,* and *kin* are outnumbered 41 to 14 by words such as *make, likely, asked,* and *acknowledged*.

Those who sell life, health, and theft insurance sometimes exploit our tendency to believe that events are more likely if we can picture them readily (Cialdini & Carpenter, 1981). By having people imagine their families in mourning or their possessions stolen, sellers of insurance may cause the images of these disasters to linger, making them seem more likely to occur and, therefore, to be worth insuring against. In one experiment, Larry Gregory and his colleagues (1982) gave Arizona residents promotional information about cable TV, and asked others to picture themselves enjoying movies on cable instead of spending money on babysitters and gas. The latter group, having readily available images of themselves as subscribers, were more than twice as likely to subscribe.

The availability heuristic also affects our social judgments. Ruth Hamill and her co-workers (1980) presented people with a single, vivid case of wel-

Psychology Applied: Perceiving Risk

"Most people reason dramatically, not quantitatively," said Oliver Wendell Holmes. With horrific television and magazine images of air crashes in mind, many people, petrified of air travel, prefer the safety of their own cars. Of those who did fly during 1989, 44 percent reported feeling fearful (*Gallup Report*, 1989).

Ironically, the statistical reality is that, mile for mile, U.S. travelers during the 1980s were 26 times more likely to die in a car crash than on a commercial flight (National Safety Council, 1991). During 1986 and 1987, for example, 5 scheduled flights out of 13 million—that's 1 flight in every 2.6 million—involved an accident that caused anyone's death (Hebert, 1988).

Still, when overall statistics vie with vivid images of helpless crash victims, many people find the memorable instances more persuasive. It's like judging the likelihood of shark attacks after watching *Jaws*: Regardless of statistics, memorable images have a way of heightening swimmers'

Because vivid events are more available to memory, they seem more common than they are.

feelings of risk. Or like judging, from seeing the faces of missing children on milk cartons, your child's risk of being abducted by a stranger—which the U.S. Justice Department reports actually happens no more than 300 times a year nationwide

(Bonner, 1990). (Virtually all child snatchings are family related.)

In 1988, a terrorist bomb exploded on Pan Am Flight 103 over Scotland, causing many would-be international vacationers to stay home and brave the more dangerous highways. The same fearful public continues to drive without seatbelts, smoke billions of cigarettes a year, guzzle alcohol, and devour foods that put people at risk for the greatest of killers—heart disease. All because people's *perceptions* of risk are virtually unrelated to actual risk (Slovic, 1987)—a phenomenon due partly to our greater fear of things we cannot control and partly to our overestimating the likelihood of dreaded, publicized, and cognitively available events.

And that is why, whether making travel plans or diet decisions, defining safety standards or evaluating environmental hazards, rational people will define risks based not on mentally available media images but on statistical reality.

"What do you mean 'Your guess is as good as mine'? My guess is a hell of a lot better than your guess!"

Drawing by Ross; © 1983 The New Yorker Magazine, Inc.

fare abuse. The case involved a long-term welfare recipient who had several unruly children fathered by different men. The statistical fact is that this case is exceptional: Most Americans who receive welfare do so for 4 years or less (Duncan & others, 1988). Yet when the statistical reality was pitted against the single vivid case, the memorable case proved more persuasive when people later gave their opinions about welfare recipients. A graphic anecdote, it seems, is worth a thousand factual statistics.

Overconfidence

Our use of intuitive heuristics when forming judgments, our eagerness to confirm the beliefs we already hold, and our facility for explaining away failures combine to create **overconfidence,** a tendency to overestimate the accuracy of our knowledge and judgments. Asked factual questions—"Is absinthe a liqueur or a precious stone?"—people's answers are more confident than correct. When 60 percent of people answer such a question correctly, they typically feel 75 percent confident (Fischhoff & others, 1977). (In case you are wondering, absinthe is a licorice-flavored liqueur.)

"We don't like their sound. Groups of guitars are on their way out."

Decca Records, in turning down a recording contract with the Beatles

"When you know a thing, to hold that you know it; and when you do not know a thing, to allow that you do not know it; this is knowledge."

Confucius, 551–479 B.C.
Analects

"This CD player costs less than players selling for twice as much."

Drawing by Weber; © 1989 The New Yorker Magazine, Inc.

Preview Question

4. How do our preexisting beliefs influence our decision making?

Overconfidence plagues decision making outside the laboratory, too. Whether trying to predict the stock market, people's behavior on the basis of an interview, or one's own future actions (will you drop a course this year? call your home more than twice next month?), people are more confident than correct (Dunning & others, 1990; Malkiel, 1985; Vallone & others, 1990).

As do other cognitive limitations, overconfidence has adaptive value. Failing to appreciate one's potential for error when making military, economic, or political judgments can have devastating consequences, but so can *lack* of self-confidence. People who err on the side of overconfidence live more happily and find it easier to make tough decisions (Baumeister, 1989; Taylor, 1989). Moreover, when given prompt and clear feedback on the accuracy of their judgments—as weather forecasters are after each day's predictions—people soon learn to assess their accuracy more realistically (Fischhoff, 1982). The wisdom to know when we know a thing and when we do not is born of experience.

Framing Decisions

A further test of rationality is whether the same issue, presented in two different but logically equivalent ways, will elicit the same answer. For example, whether a surgeon tells someone that 10 percent die during a particular surgery or that 90 percent survive, the information is the same. But the effect is not. The risk seems greater to people who hear that 10 percent will die (Marteau, 1989). This effect of the way we present an issue is called the **framing** effect.

Similarly, consumers respond more positively to ground beef described as "75 percent lean" rather than "25 percent fat" (Levin & Gaeth, 1988). A new medical treatment strikes people as more successful and recommendable if framed as having a "50 percent success rate" rather than a "50 percent failure rate" (Levin & others, 1988). Many people find a 7 percent pay cut when there is no inflation much more objectionable than a 5 percent pay raise when inflation is 12 percent—though the effect is basically the same (Kahneman & others, 1986).

That people's judgments flip-flop so dramatically is startling. It suggests that our judgments and decisions may not be well reasoned, and that those who understand the power of framing can use it to influence important decisions—for example, by framing survey questions to support or reject a particular viewpoint.

Belief Perseverance

An additional source of irrationality is our tendency, called **belief perseverance,** to cling to our beliefs in the face of contrary evidence. Belief perseverance often fuels social conflict. Charles Lord and his colleagues (1979) revealed how this happens in their study of two groups of students. One favored capital punishment, the other opposed it. People on both sides studied two supposedly new research findings, one supporting and the other refuting the claim that the death penalty deters crime. Each side was impressed by the study that supported its beliefs, and readily disputed the other study. Thus, showing the pro- and anti-capital punishment groups the *same* mixed evidence actually *increased* their disagreement.

framing The way an issue is posed. How an issue is framed can significantly affect decisions and judgments.

belief perseverance Clinging to one's initial conceptions after the basis on which they were formed has been discredited.

"Once you have a belief, it influences how you perceive all other relevant information. Once you see a country as hostile, you are likely to interpret ambiguous actions on their part as signifying their hostility."

Political scientist Robert Jervis (1985)

"To begin with, it was only tentatively that I put forward the views I have developed . . . but in the course of time they have gained such a hold upon me that I can no longer think in any other way."

Sigmund Freud
Civilization and Its Discontents, 1930

"I'm happy to say that my final judgment of a case is almost always consistent with my prejudgment of the case."

Drawing by Fradon; © 1973 The New Yorker Magazine, Inc.

For those who wish to rein in the belief perseverance phenomenon, a simple remedy exists: *Consider the opposite.* When Lord and his colleagues (1984) repeated the capital punishment study, they asked some of their subjects to be "as *objective* and *unbiased* as possible." The plea did nothing to reduce the biased evaluation of evidence. They asked another group, however, to consider the opposite—to ask themselves "whether you would have made the same high or low evaluations had exactly the same study produced results on the *other* side of the issue." Having imagined and pondered opposite findings, these people were much less biased in their evaluations of the evidence.

If ambiguous evidence gets interpreted as supporting a person's preexisting belief, would the belief be demolished by information that clearly discredits its basis? Not necessarily. Craig Anderson and Lee Ross discovered that it can be surprisingly difficult to change a false belief once a person has in mind ideas that support it. In one such study with Mark Lepper (1980), they asked subjects to consider whether risk-prone people or cautious people are better fire fighters. Then they told half of the subjects about a risk-taker who was an excellent fire fighter and a cautious person who was a poor fire fighter. From these cases, the subjects surmised that risk-prone people tend to be better fire fighters. "Risk-takers are braver," was a typical explanation. The researchers gave the other subjects two cases suggesting the opposite conclusion, that cautious people are better fire fighters. Subjects typically reasoned, "Cautious people think before they act. They're less likely to make foolish mistakes."

The researchers then discredited the basis for the beliefs by truthfully informing both groups that the cases were simply made up for the experiment. Did discrediting the evidence undermine the subjects' newly formed beliefs? Not by much, because the subjects held on to their explanations for *why* these new beliefs made sense. Although the evidence was gone, their theory survived.

Paradoxically, the more we come to appreciate why our beliefs *might* be true, the more tightly we cling to them. Once people have explained to themselves why they believe that a child is "gifted" or "learning disabled," that presidential candidate *X* or *Y* will be more likely to preserve peace or start a war, or that women are naturally superior or inferior, they tend to ignore evidence that undermines that belief.

The belief perseverance phenomenon does not rule out people's changing their beliefs. It's just that once beliefs form and get justified, it takes more compelling evidence to change them than it did to create them.

We have seen how our irrational thinking can plague our efforts to solve problems, make wise decisions, form valid judgments, and reason logically. For this we might be tempted to conclude that our heads are indeed filled with straw. All in all, the findings we have reviewed—and many more that we have not—suggest "bleak implications for human rationality" (Nisbett & Borgida, 1975). Still, let us not forget that our cognition is effective and efficient: It enables our survival and our inventive genius. Moreover, even the most sophisticated computers are dwarfed by the most ordinary of human mental abilities—recognizing a face, distinguishing a cat from a dog, or knowing whether the word *line* refers to a rope or a fragment of poetry or a social come-on. A computer's capabilities exceed our own at tasks that use its unique strengths—vast memory and precise logic and retrieval. But computers have not duplicated the wide-ranging intelligence of a human mind, a mind that can *all at once* converse naturally, perceive the environment, use common sense, experience emotion, and consciously reflect on the fact of its own existence.

Rehearse It

1. We use the concept "bird" to think and talk about a variety of creatures, all of which have wings and feathers. A concept is
a. a mental grouping of similar things.
b. an example of insight.
c. a fixation on certain characteristics.
d. another word for "prototype."

2. Sometimes we solve problems through trial and error, trying hundreds or even thousands of solutions before finding one that works. At other times we are more methodical or systematic. The most systematic procedure for solving a problem is
a. heuristics.
b. an algorithm.
c. insight.
d. intuition.

3. A major obstacle to problem solving is confirmation bias, the tendency to search for information that confirms our preconceptions, while ignoring information that might prove us wrong. Another obstacle to problem solving is fixation, which is
a. an error we make when we base our judgments on certain vivid memories.
b. the art of framing the same question in two different ways.
c. the inability to view a problem from a new perspective.
d. a rule of thumb for judging the likelihood of a thing in terms of our mental image of it.

4. The way an issue is posed can affect our decisions and judgments. For example, one study found that people perceived worse student cheating if told that 65 percent of students had cheated than if told that 35 percent of students had not cheated (Levin & others, 1988). In this case people's reactions were influenced by
a. belief perseverance.
b. fixation.
c. confirmation bias.
d. framing.

5. Vivid, well-publicized crimes—such as the abduction of a child by a stranger—are perceived as being more common than they are; few people realize that most abductions are carried out by estranged parents. The error illustrates
a. belief perseverance.
b. the availability heuristic.
c. functional fixedness.
d. confirmation bias.

Answer to CINERAMA anagram on page 235: AMERICAN.

Language

The most tangible indication of our thinking power is **language**—our spoken, written, or gestured words and how we combine them as we think and communicate. Humans have long and proudly proclaimed that language sets us above all other animals. "When we study human language," asserted linguist Noam Chomsky (1972), "we are approaching what some might call the 'human essence,' the distinctive qualities of mind that are, so far as we know, unique" to humans.

Language enables us to transmit knowledge and lore from generation to generation.

language Our spoken, written, or gestured words and how we combine them to communicate meaning.

babbling stage Beginning at 3 to 4 months, the stage of speech development in which the infant spontaneously utters various sounds at first unrelated to the household language.

To cognitive scientist Steven Pinker (1990), language is "the jewel in the crown of cognition." When the human vocal tract evolved the capacity to utter the commonest vowels (which chimps cannot), our capacity for language exploded. Complex vocalization boosted our ancestors' ability to communicate information, catapulting our species in a great leap forward (Diamond, 1989). Whether spoken, written, or signed, language enables us to communicate complex ideas from person to person and to transmit civilization's accumulated knowledge from generation to generation.

Language Development

Preview Question

5. When do children acquire language, and how does it develop?

Make a quick guess: How many words did you learn in one average day during the years between your first birthday and your graduation from high school?

The average North American high school graduate knows some 80,000 words (Miller & Gildea, 1987). That averages (after age 1) to nearly 5000 words learned a year, or 13 a day! How you did it—how the 5000 words a year you learned could so far outnumber the roughly 200 words a year that your schoolteachers consciously taught you—is one of the great wonders of human development. Before children can add 2 + 2, they are creating their own original and grammatically appropriate sentences. Most parents would have trouble stating the rules of syntax. Yet their preschoolers comprehend and speak with a facility that puts to shame a college student struggling to learn a foreign language or a scientist struggling to simulate natural language on a computer. How does our astonishing facility for language unfold, and how can we explain it?

Although you probably know more than 100,000 words, you use only 150 words for about half of what you say.

Acquiring Language

Preschoolers have an astonishing capacity to soak up new words and combine them in grammatically sensible sentences.

Children's language development mirrors language structure—by moving from simplicity to complexity. By 4 months of age, babies can read lips and discriminate speech sounds. They prefer to look at a face that matches a sound, so we know they can recognize that *ah* comes from wide open lips and *ee* from a mouth with corners pulled back (Kuhl & Meltzoff, 1982). At about this age, babies enter a **babbling stage** in which they spontaneously utter a variety of sounds such as *ah-goo*. Babbling is not the strict imitation of adult speech, for it includes sounds from various languages, even sounds that do not occur in the household's language. From this early babbling, a listener could not identify an infant as being, say, French, Korean, or Ethiopian. It seems, then, that before nurture molds our speech, nature enables a wide range of possible sounds.

Babbling eventually comes to resemble the characteristic sounds and intonations of the household language. By about age 10 months, a trained ear can identify the language of the household by listening to an infant's babbling (Boysson-Bardies & others, 1989). Sounds outside the infant's native tongue begin to disappear. And infants gradually lose their ability to discriminate sounds that they never hear. An untrained Japanese adult cannot distinguish between the English *ra* and *la* because Japanese uses a single sound intermediate between these two. Clever experiments by Janet Werker (1989) reveal that 6-month old infants can perceive sound differences from any language, but by 12 months they cannot (Figure 8–5, page 244).

Around the first birthday (the exact age varies from child to child), most children enter the **one-word stage.** Having already learned that sounds carry

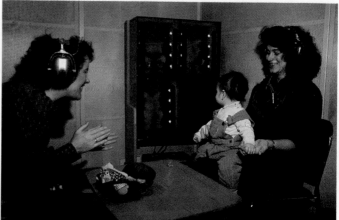

Figure 8–5 We are all born with the ability to recognize speech sounds from all the world's languages. In Janet Werker's lab, an infant is reinforced with applause and by activating toy animals when he looks to the right after hearing a changed sound (as in ba, ba, ba, ba, da, da). Hindi adults and young infants from English-speaking homes can easily discriminate two Hindi *t* sounds not spoken in English. By age 1 and beyond, however, English-speaking listeners rarely perceive the sound difference. (Adapted from Werker, 1989.)

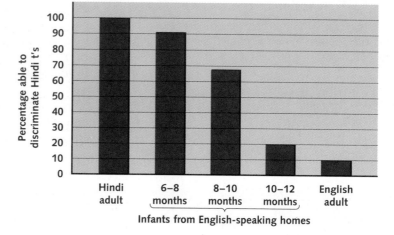

one-word stage The stage in speech development from about age 1 to 2 years during which a child speaks mostly in single words.

two-word stage Beginning about age 2, the stage in speech development during which a child speaks mostly two-word statements.

telegraphic speech Early speech stage in which the child speaks like a telegram—using mostly nouns and verbs and omitting "auxiliary" words.

meanings, they begin to use sounds to communicate meaning. Their first words usually contain but one syllable—*ma* or *da*, for instance—and may be barely recognizable. But family members quickly learn to understand the infant's language, and gradually it conforms more and more to the family's language.

Most of the child's first words refer to things that move or can be played with—things such as a dog or a ball, rather than the table or crib that just sits there (Nelson, 1973). At this one-word stage, an inflected word may equal a sentence. "Doggy!" may mean "Look at the dog out there!"

Children typically use more and more single words during the second year and, by about their second birthday, start uttering two-word sentences (Table 8–1). This **two-word stage** exemplifies **telegraphic speech:** Like telegrams (TERMS ACCEPTED. SEND MONEY.), it contains mostly nouns and verbs (*Want juice*). Also like telegrams, the word order reflects the language of the child's environment. The English-speaking child typically says adjectives before nouns—*big doggy* rather than *doggy big*.

There seems to be no "three-word stage." Once children move out of the two-word stage, they quickly begin uttering longer phrases (Fromkin & Rod-

Table 8–1
Summary of Language Development

Approximate month	Stage
4	Babbles many speech sounds.
10	Babbling reveals household language.
12	One-word stage.
24	Two-word, telegraphic speech.
24+	Language develops rapidly into complete sentences

man, 1983). Although the sentences may still sound like a Western Union message, they continue to make grammatical sense (*Mommy get ball*). By early elementary school, the child understands complex sentences and begins to enjoy the humor conveyed by double meanings: "You never starve in the desert because of all the sand-which-is there."

Explaining Language Development

Those who study language acquisition inevitably wonder how we do it. Attempts to answer this question have sparked a spirited intellectual controversy. The controversy parallels the debate we noted in Chapter 6, Learning, over the behaviorist view of the malleable organism versus the view that each organism comes biologically prepared to learn certain associations. The nature-nurture debate surfaces again, and here, as elsewhere, appreciation for innate predisposition has grown.

Behaviorist B. F. Skinner (1957) believed we can explain language development with familiar learning principles, such as association (of the sights of things with the sounds of words); imitation (of the words and sentence order modeled by others); and reinforcement (with success, smiles, and hugs when the child says something right). Thus, Skinner argued, babies learn to talk in many of the same ways that animals learn to peck keys and press bars. "Verbal behavior evidently came into existence when, through a critical step in the evolution of the human species, the vocal musculature became susceptible to operant conditioning," Skinner (1985) surmised.

Linguist Noam Chomsky (1959, 1987) sees Skinner's view of learning language as naive. Surely, says Chomsky, a Martian scientist observing children in a single-language community would conclude that language is almost entirely inborn. It isn't, because children do learn the language used in their environment. But the rate at which they acquire words and grammar without being taught is too extraordinary to be explained solely by learning principles. Children create all sorts of sentences they have never heard and, therefore, could not be imitating. Moreover, many of their errors result from the application of logical grammatical rules. For example, children overgeneralize the rule about adding *-ed* to a verb to form the past tense (from de Cuevas, 1990):

Child: My teacher holded the baby rabbits and we petted them.

Mother: Did you say your teacher held the baby rabbits?

Child: Yes.

Mother: What did you say she did?

Child: She holded the baby rabbits and we petted them.

Mother: Did you say she held them tightly?

Child: No, she holded them loosely.

Chomsky (1987) likens the behaviorist view of how language develops to filling a bottle with water, and his own view to "helping a flower to grow in its own way." Language development, he believes, is akin to sexual maturation—given adequate nurture, it just "happens to the child." Thanks to their inborn "universal grammar," children readily learn the grammar of whatever language they hear. Other worlds may have languages that, for us humans, are unlearnable, but not our world. Chomsky maintains that our language acquisition capacity is like a box—a "language acquisition device"—in which

"No, Timmy, not 'I sawed the chair.' It's 'I saw the chair' or 'I have seen the chair.'"

Drawing by Glenn Bernhardt.

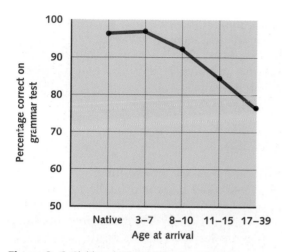

Figure 8-6 Children have a readiness to learn language. Ten years after coming to the United States, Asian immigrants took a grammar test. Those who arrived by age 7 understood grammar as well as native speakers. Those who arrived later did not. (From Johnson & Newport, 1989.)

Deaf children of deaf-signing parents develop language skills at about the same rate as hearing children of hearing-speaking parents. This girl is expressing "not" in her native language—ASL (American Sign Language).

Preview Question

6. Is language unique to humans, or do animals also have language?

grammar switches are thrown as children experience their language. Thus, English-speaking children learn to put the object of a sentence last ("She ate an apple"). Japanese-speaking children put the object before the verb ("She an apple ate").

Those who learn a second language as adults usually speak it with the accent of their first language. Do they more easily master the foreign grammar? To find out, Jacqueline Johnson and Elissa Newport (1989) gave Korean and Chinese immigrants to the United States a grammar test, requiring them to identify each of 276 sentences ("Yesterday the hunter shoots a deer") as grammatically correct or incorrect. Some subjects had immigrated in early childhood, others as adults. Regardless of their age at immigration, the participants had each been in the United States for approximately 10 years. If anything, this gave the adult immigrants—most of whom were professors, researchers, or graduate students—an edge in years of learning English, because they had all studied it in their native country as well. Nevertheless, as Figure 8-6 reveals, those who learned their second language early learned it best. Chomsky would say that once the grammar switches are thrown during a child's developing years, mastering yet another grammar becomes more difficult.

The impact of early experience is also evident among the deaf. Hearing children of hearing-speaking parents, and deaf children of deaf-signing parents, share much in common. Both groups experience language in infancy and develop their early vocabularies at roughly comparable rates (Meier, 1991). But consider the 90+ percent of deaf children born to hearing-nonsigning parents. These children typically do not experience language during their early years. Compared to deaf children exposed to sign language from birth, those who learn signing as teens or adults are like immigrants who learn English after childhood. They can master the basic words and how to order them, but they never become as fluent as native signers in producing and comprehending subtle grammatical differences (Newport, 1990).

To summarize, children are biologically prepared to learn language as they interact with their caregivers. Skinner's emphasis on learning helps explain why infants acquire the language they hear and how they add new words to their vocabularies. Chomsky's emphasis on our built-in readiness to learn grammar rules helps explain why preschoolers acquire language so readily and use grammar so well. Once again, we see biology and experience working together.

Returning to our debate about humanity's thinking powers, let's pause to issue a report card. On decision making and judgment, our error-prone species might rate a C+. On problem solving, where humans are inventive yet vulnerable to fixation, we would probably receive a better mark, perhaps a B+. On cognitive efficiency, our fallible but quick heuristics earn us an A. And when it comes to learning and using language, the awestruck experts would surely award the human species an A+.

Animal Language

If in our use of language we humans are, as the psalmist rhapsodized, "little less than God," where do other animals fit in the scheme of things? Are they "little less than human"? In part, the answer lies in the extent to which animals share our capacity for language. Without doubt, animals communicate. But can they use language?

Washoe, the first sign-language-trained chimpanzee, aroused new interest in the possibility of animal language. Here, she is signing the word "baby."

The Ape Story

A greater challenge to humanity's claim to be the only language-using species has come from reports of apes that "talk" with people. Knowing that chimpanzees could not vocalize more than a few words, University of Nevada researchers Allen and Beatrice Gardner (1969) tried to teach sign language to a chimp named Washoe, as though she were a deaf human child. After 4 years, Washoe could use 132 signs. The Gardners' announcement of the success of their efforts aroused enormous scientific and public interest. One *New York Times* reporter, who had learned sign language from his deaf parents, visited Washoe and exclaimed, "Suddenly I realized I was conversing with a member of another species in my native tongue."

During the 1970s, further evidence of "ape language" surfaced. Not only could apes sign, they could string signs together to form intelligible sentences. Washoe signed, "You me go out, please." Apes even appeared to combine words creatively. Washoe designated a swan as a "water bird." Koko, a gorilla trained by Francine Patterson (1978) in California, reportedly described a long-nosed Pinocchio doll as an "elephant baby." Lana, a chimpanzee that "talks" by punching buttons wired to a computer that translates her punchings into English, wanted her trainer's orange one day. She had no word for *orange*, but she did know her colors and the word for *apple*, so she improvised: "? Tim give apple which-is orange" (Rumbaugh, 1977).

As ape language reports accumulated, it seemed that apes might indeed be "little less than human." Although their vocabularies and sentences were simple compared to ours—corresponding roughly to the capacities of a typical 2-year-old child—apes did seem to share what we humans have considered our unique ability.

Lana, another chimpanzee, has learned to "speak" by punching word symbols on a computer console in a coherent order.

But Can Apes Really Talk?   By the late 1970s, the claims of "talking apes" raised a question: Were the chimps language champs or were the researchers chumps? The ape language researchers were making monkeys out of themselves, said the skeptics. Consider some of their arguments:

Apes gain their limited vocabularies only with great difficulty. They are hardly like speaking or signing children, who effortlessly soak up dozens of new words each week. Saying that apes can learn language because they can sign words is like saying humans can fly because they can jump.

Chimps can make signs or push buttons in sequence to get a reward, but so can pigeons—by pecking a sequence of keys to get grain (Straub & others, 1979)—and no one says that the pigeon is "talking."

Apes can certainly use symbols meaningfully, but the evidence is far from convincing that they can equal even a 3-year-old's ability to order words properly. To the child, "you tickle" and "tickle you" communicate different ideas, but a chimp might sign the phrases interchangeably.

After training a chimp whom he named Nim Chimpsky, Herbert Terrace (1979) concluded that much of chimpanzees' signing is nothing more than their imitating their trainers' signs.

Presented with ambiguous information, people tend to look for and see what they want or expect to see. (Recall the confirmation bias, and the demonstrations of perceptual set in Chapter 4.) Interpreting chimpanzee signs as language may be little more than wishful thinking on the part of their trainers, claims Terrace. (When Washoe signed "water bird," she perhaps was separately naming "water" and "bird.")

Although chimpanzees do not have our facility for language, their thinking and communicating abilities continue to impress their trainers. Loulis, a foster son of Washoe, picked up 68 signs simply by observing Washoe and three other language-trained chimps. Moreover, Washoe, Loulis, and the others now sign spontaneously, as when asking one another to *chase, tickle, hug, come,* or *groom.* People who sign can eavesdrop on these chimp-to-chimp conversations with near-perfect agreement about what the chimps are saying, 90 percent of which pertains to social interaction, reassurance, or play (Fouts & Bodamer, 1987). Moreover, the chimps are modestly bilingual; they can translate spoken English words into signs (Shaw, 1989–1990).

So, trained apes' language capabilities are modest by human standards. Yet their impressive cognitive powers seem indeed to make them "little less than human."

Seeing a doll floating in her water, Washoe signed, "Baby in my drink."

"[Our] egocentric view that [we are] unique from all other forms of animal life is being jarred to the core."

Duane Rumbaugh and Sue Savage-Rumbaugh (1978)

"Although humans make sounds with their mouths and occasionally look at each other, there is no solid evidence that they actually communicate with each other."

© 1979 by Sidney Harris; American Scientist magazine.

Thinking and Language

Preview Question

7. What is the relationship between thinking and language?

Thinking and language intricately intertwine. Asking which comes first is one of psychology's chicken-and-egg questions. Do our ideas come first and wait for words to name them? Or are our thoughts conceived in words and unthinkable without them?

Language Influences Thought

Linguist Benjamin Lee Whorf contended that language determines the way we think. According to Whorf's (1956) **linguistic relativity** hypothesis, different languages impose different conceptions of reality: "Language itself shapes a man's basic ideas."

Whorf's idea seldom occurs to people who speak but one language. To them, language seems only a vehicle for thought. But to those who speak two dissimilar languages, such as English and Japanese, it seems obvious that one thinks differently in different languages (Brown, 1986). For example, the several Japanese words for *give* support important cultural distinctions. Which *give* one uses depends on whether the giver is of higher or lower status and whether or not the giver is a friend or family member.

"All words are pegs to hang ideas on."

Henry Ward Beecher
Proverbs from Plymouth Pulpit,
1887

Another example: In English, there is one word for *snow.* The Eskimo language has many. This, said Whorf, allows Eskimos to *perceive* differences in snow that would go unnoticed by people who speak another language. The language-thought link also occurs at the level of grammar. The Hopi Indians have no past tense for their verbs. Therefore, Whorf contended, the Hopi cannot so readily *think* about the past.

Critics of the language-determines-thought idea claim that words *reflect* rather than create the way we think. The Eskimos' very lives depend on their ability to recognize different conditions of snow and ice, so they need different words for these conditions. (Skiers likewise describe the slopes with such terms as "sticky snow" or "powder.") You lack the Eskimos' rich vocabulary for describing snow, but that does not mean you are incapable of perceiving these differences. Likewise, a New Guinean without our words for shapes and colors nevertheless perceives them much as we do (Rosch, 1974).

"To call forth a concept, a word is needed."

Antoine Lavoisier
Elements of Chemistry, 1789

So, although it is too strong to say that language *determines* the *way* we think, our words certainly can *influence what* we think (Hoffman & others, 1986). We therefore do well to choose our words carefully. When people refer to women as *girls*—as in "the girls at the office"—it perpetuates a view of women's lower status, does it not? Or consider the generic use of the pronoun *he.* Does it make any difference whether I write "A child learns language as *he* interacts with *his* caregivers" or "Children learn language as *they* interact with *their* caregivers"? Some argue that it makes no difference because every reader knows that "the masculine gender shall be deemed and taken to include females" (as the British Parliament declared in 1850).

But is the generic *he* always taken to include females? Twenty studies have consistently found that it is not (Henley, 1989). For example, Janet Hyde (1984) asked children to finish stories for which she gave them a first line such as, "When a kid goes to school, ____ often feels excited on the first day." When Hyde used *he* in the blank, the children's stories were nearly always about males. *He or she* in the blank resulted in female characters about one-third of the time. Studies with adolescents and adults in North America and New Zealand have found similar effects of the generic *he* (Hamilton, 1988; Martyna, 1978; Ng, 1990). Sentences about "the artist and his work" tend to conjure up images of a man.

linguistic relativity Whorf's hypothesis that language determines the way we think.

This girl's efforts to increase her word power will expand her capacity to think.

Consider, too, that people use generic pronouns selectively, as in "the doctor . . . he" and "the secretary . . . she" (MacKay, 1983). If *he* and *his* were truly gender-free, we shouldn't skip a beat when hearing that "a nurse must answer his calls" or that "man, like other mammals, nurses his young." That we are startled indicates that the *his* carries a gender connotation that clashes with our idea of *nurse*.

The power of language to influence thought makes vocabulary building a crucial part of education. To expand language is to expand the ability to think. David Premack (1983) reported that even among chimpanzees, language training enhances the ability to think abstractly and to reason by analogy. Shown a cylinder half filled with water, a chimp not trained in language had difficulty recognizing that half an apple was more like the half-filled cylinder than was three-fourths of an apple. But language-trained chimps could more readily grasp the analogy. In young children, too, thinking develops hand in hand with language (Gopnik & Meltzoff, 1986). What is true for chimpanzees and preschoolers is true for everyone: *It pays to increase your word power*. That is why most textbooks, including this one, introduce new words—to teach new ideas and new ways of thinking.

Thinking Without Language

When you are alone, do you talk to yourself? Is "thinking" simply conversing with yourself? Without a doubt, words convey ideas. But are there not times when ideas precede words? To turn on the cold water in your bathroom, in which direction do you turn the handle?

To answer this question, you probably thought not in words but with a mental picture. Indeed, we often think in images. Artists think in images. So do composers, poets, mathematicians, athletes, and scientists. Albert Einstein reported that he achieved some of his greatest insights through visual images and only later put them into words.

Many successful athletes prepare for contests by imagining themselves performing their events (Mahoney, 1989; Suinn, 1986). Georgia Nigro demonstrated the wisdom of this technique in a laboratory test of mental practice (Neisser, 1984). She had subjects make 24 actual dart throws at a target. She then had half the subjects throw 24 darts mentally. Finally, she had all the subjects again make 24 throws. Only those who had mentally practiced showed any improvement. A National Research Council committee of psychologists investigated claims of performance-enhancement techniques for the U.S. Army and concluded that most (including ESP and "neurolinguistic programming") were of no value (Druckman & Swets, 1988). Based on experiments such as Nigro's, however, they deemed the mental practice of motor skills useful.

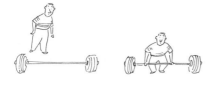

Drawing by Maslin; © 1984 The New Yorker Magazine, Inc.

What, then, should we say about the relationship between thinking and language? We have seen that language influences thinking. But if thinking did not also affect language, there would never be any new words. New words express new ideas. The basketball term *slam dunk* was coined after the act itself had become fairly common. So, let us simply say that *thinking affects our language, which then affects our thought.*

Psychological research on thinking and language mirrors the mixed reviews given our species in literature and religion. The human mind is simultaneously capable of striking intellectual failures and of vast intellectual power. In an age when misjudgments can have disastrous consequences, we do well to appreciate our capacity for error. Yet our heuristics often serve us well, and they certainly are efficient. Moreover, our ingenuity at problem solving and our extraordinary power of language surely, among the animals, rank humankind as almost "infinite in faculties."

Rehearse It

6. Children progress from babbling to sentences of two and then four, five, six or more words. The one-word stage of speech development is usually reached at about
a. 4 months.
b. 6 months.
c. 1 year.
d. 2 years.

7. B. F. Skinner believed that we learn language the same way we learn other behaviors—through association, imitation, and reinforcement. Skinner's behaviorist view is most helpful in explaining.
a. the onset of babbling.
b. the speech behavior of deaf infants.
c. the seemingly effortless mastery of grammatical rules by very young children.
d. the fact that children learn their parents' language.

8. According to Noam Chomsky, we are biologically prepared to acquire language and are born with a readiness to learn the grammatical rules of the language we hear. He believes all that is necessary for us to acquire language is
a. instruction in grammar.
b. exposure to language in early childhood.
c. reinforcement for babbling and other early verbal behaviors.
d. imitation and drill.

9. There is much controversy over whether or not apes can be taught to use language in the way that humans do. However, most researchers of ape sign language agree that apes can
a. communicate through symbols.

b. reproduce most human speech sounds.
c. create new sentences and meanings.
d. surpass a human 3-year-old in language skills.

10. According to Benjamin Lee Whorf, the language we speak determines the way we perceive and think about the world. His linguistic relativity hypothesis suggests an explanation for why
a. a person who learns a second language thinks differently in that language.
b. children have a built-in readiness to learn grammatical rules.
c. apes are able to communicate through sign language.
d. artists, athletes, and others are able to think in visual images.

Intelligence

So far, we have considered how humans, in general, think and communicate. But do we humans not differ from one another in our intellectual capacities? No controversy in psychology has been more heated than the question of whether there exists in each person a general intellectual capacity that can be measured and quantified as a number. School boards, courts, and scientists debate the usefulness and fairness of intelligence and aptitude tests. Should such tests be used to rank individuals and to determine whether to admit them to a particular college or to hire them in a particular job?

"Almost all the joyful things of life are outside the measure of IQ tests."

Madeleine L'Engle
A Circle of Quiet, 1972

aptitude tests Tests designed to predict a person's future performance; aptitude is the capacity to learn.

achievement tests Tests designed to assess what a person has learned.

mental age A measure of intelligence test performance devised by Binet; the chronological age that most typically corresponds to a given level of performance. Thus, a child who does as well as the average 8-year-old is said to have a mental age of 8.

Preview Question

8. How are modern intelligence tests classified, and when and why were they created?

Alfred Binet (Binet & Simon, 1905): "The scale, properly speaking, does not permit the measure of intelligence, because intellectual qualities . . . cannot be measured as linear surfaces are measured."

Let's therefore consider: What is intelligence? How is it assessed? And to what extent does it result from nature (heredity) rather than nurture (environment)? Is intelligence testing society's best means of identifying those who would benefit from special opportunities? Or is intelligence testing a potent discriminatory weapon camouflaged as science?

Assessing Intelligence

By this point in your life, you've faced dozens of different tests of your mental abilities: elementary school tests of basic reading and math skills, course examinations, intelligence tests, driver's license examinations, and college entrance examinations, to mention just a few. Psychologists classify such tests as either **aptitude tests,** intended to *predict* your ability to learn a new skill, or **achievement tests,** intended to *reflect* what you have learned. Thus, a college entrance exam, which seeks to predict your ability to do college work, is an aptitude test. A final exam covering what you have learned in this course would be an achievement test.

The actual differences between aptitude tests and achievement tests are not so clear-cut. Your achieved vocabulary influences your score on most aptitude tests. Similarly, your aptitudes for learning and test-taking influence your grades on tests of your course achievement. Most tests, whether labeled aptitude or achievement, assess both ability and its development. Distinguishing aptitude and achievement is mainly a matter of practicality: We use aptitude tests to predict future performance and achievement tests to assess current performance.

The Origins of Intelligence Tests

To understand intelligence as a psychological concept, it helps first to know the origins and purposes of intelligence testing.

Alfred Binet: Predicting School Achievement The modern intelligence testing movement began at the turn of the century when the French government passed a law requiring that all children attend school. Teachers soon faced a wider range of individual differences than they could handle. Some of the children seemed incapable of benefitting from the regular school curriculum and appeared to need special classes. But how could the schools objectively identify children with special needs?

The government was justifiably reluctant to trust teachers' subjective judgments of children's learning potential. Academic slowness might merely reflect inadequate prior education. Also, teachers might tend to prejudge children on the basis of their social backgrounds. To minimize bias, the Minister of Public Education in 1904 commissioned French psychologist Alfred Binet (1857–1911) to develop an objective test that would identify those children who were likely to have difficulty in the regular classes.

Binet and his collaborator, Théodore Simon, began by assuming that all children follow the same course of intellectual development but that some develop more rapidly than others. "Dull" children, they presumed, were merely "retarded" in their development. On tests, therefore, a dull child should perform like a normal child of a younger age. A "bright" child should perform like a typical older child.

Binet and Simon's task was to measure what came to be called a child's **mental age,** the chronological age that typically corresponds to a given level of performance. The average 9-year-old, then, has a mental age of 9. But some 9-year-olds have mental ages below or above 9. Children below average, such

Stanford-Binet The widely used American revision (by Terman at Stanford University) of Binet's original intelligence test.

intelligence quotient (IQ) Defined originally as the ratio of mental age to chronological age multiplied by 100 (thus, IQ = ma/ca × 100). On contemporary intelligence tests, the average performance for a given age is assigned a score of 100.

"The IQ test was invented to predict academic performance, nothing else. If we wanted something that would predict life success, we'd have to invent another test completely."

Social psychologist Robert Zajonc (1984b)

It was not until World War II that the IQ test became fashionable in France—under the name of Terman, not Binet!

Lewis Terman (1916, p. 115): "The children of successful and cultured parents test higher than children from wretched and ignorant homes for the simple reason that their heredity is better."

"Science must be understood as a social phenomenon, a gutsy, human enterprise, not the work of robots programmed to collect pure information."

Stephen Jay Gould (1981)

as 9-year-olds who perform like the typical 7-year-old, would struggle with normal schoolwork for their age.

In devising a method for measuring mental age, Binet and Simon theorized that mental aptitude, like athletic aptitude, is a general capacity that shows up in various ways. They therefore set about developing various reasoning and problem-solving questions that might predict school achievement. By testing "bright" and "backward" Parisian schoolchildren on these questions, Binet and Simon succeeded in identifying items that did indeed predict how successfully the children handled age-appropriate schoolwork. Binet hoped that his test would be used to improve children's education, but he feared that it would be used to label children and limit their opportunities (Gould, 1981).

Lewis Terman: The Innate IQ What Binet viewed as merely a practical guide for identifying slow learners who needed special help was soon seen by others to be a numerical measure of inherited intelligence. After Binet's death in 1911, Stanford University professor Lewis Terman (1877–1956) decided to use Binet's test. He soon found, however, that the Paris-developed age norms worked poorly with California schoolchildren. So Terman revised the test. He adapted some of Binet's original items, added others, established new age norms, and extended the upper end of the test's range from teenagers to "superior adults." Terman gave his revision the name that it retains today—the **Stanford-Binet.**

For such tests, German psychologist William Stern derived the famous **intelligence quotient,** or **IQ.** The IQ was simply a person's mental age divided by chronological age and multiplied by 100 to get rid of the decimal point:

$$IQ = \frac{\text{mental age}}{\text{chronologic age}} \times 100$$

Thus, an average child, with the same mental and chronological age, has an IQ of 100. But an 8-year-old who answers questions like a typical 10-year-old has an IQ of 125.

Most current intelligence tests, including the Stanford-Binet itself, no longer compute an IQ. The original IQ formula works fairly well for children, but not for adults. Consider: Should a 40-year-old who does as well on the test as the average 20-year-old be assigned an IQ of only 50? Obviously, something is out of whack. Today's intelligence tests therefore produce a mental ability score based on the test-taker's performance relative to the average performance of others the same age. As on the original Stanford-Binet, they define this score to make 100 average, with about two-thirds of all people scoring between 85 and 115. Although there is no longer any intelligence *quotient*, the term "IQ" still lingers in everyday vocabulary as a shorthand expression for "intelligence test score."

Believing that intelligence was measurable, Terman promoted the widespread use of intelligence testing. His motive was to "take account of the inequalities of children in original endowment" by assessing their "vocational fitness" (Terman, 1916).

The U.S. government adapted Binet's and Terman's tests to evaluate World War I army recruits and newly arriving immigrants. Some psychologists misinterpreted the results as documenting the inferiority of people who did not share their Anglo-Saxan heritage. For instance, following his 1913 study of European immigrants arriving at Ellis Island, psychologist Henry Goddard claimed that 83 percent of the Jewish immigrants, 80 percent of the Hungarians, 79 percent of the Italians, and 87 percent of the Russians were "feeble-minded" (Eysenck & Kamin, 1981).

Wechsler Adult Intelligence Scale—Revised (WAIS-R) This revision of the WAIS is the most widely used intelligence test; contains verbal and performance (nonverbal) subtests.

The individually administered Wechsler intelligence test comes in forms suited for adults (WAIS-R) and for children (WISC).

That adaptations of his tests were being used to draw such conclusions would surely have horrified Binet. Indeed, such sweeping judgments eventually became an embarrassment to most of those who championed testing. Terman, for instance, came to appreciate that test scores reflect not only people's innate mental abilities but also their education and their familiarity with the culture assumed by the test. Nevertheless, abuses of the early intelligence tests serve to remind us that science can be value-laden. Behind the screen of scientific objectivity, ideology sometimes hides.

The Most Widely Used Intelligence Test: The WAIS-R Among the supposedly feeble-minded Eastern European immigrants of the early 1900s was a 6-year-old Romanian boy, David Wechsler. Ironically, three decades later psychologist David Wechsler created today's most widely used intelligence test, now known as the **Wechsler Adult Intelligence Scale—Revised (WAIS-R).** Later he developed a similar test for school-age children called the Wechsler Intelligence Scale for Children (WISC), and still later a test for preschool children. The WAIS-R consists of 11 subtests, as illustrated in Figure 8–7. It yields not only an overall intelligence score, as does the Stanford-Binet, but also separate "verbal" and "performance" (nonverbal) scores. Striking differences between the two scores alert the examiner to possible learning problems. For example, a much lower verbal than performance score might indicate a reading or language disability. The tests also give a trained examiner clues to cognitive strengths that a teacher or employer might build upon.

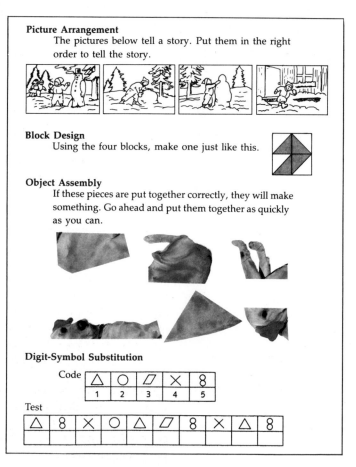

Figure 8–7 Sample subtest items from the Wechsler Adult Intelligence Scale—Revised (WAIS-R) subtests. (From Thorndike & Hagen, 1977.)

Principles of Test Construction

To be widely accepted, psychological tests must meet three criteria: They must be *standardized, reliable,* and *valid.* The Stanford-Binet and the Wechsler tests meet these requirements.

Preview Question

9. What three principles of test construction apply in evaluating a psychological test?

Standardization   Knowing how many questions you got right on an intelligence test would tell us almost nothing. To evaluate your performance, we need a basis for comparing it with others' performance. To enable meaningful comparisons, test makers first give the test to a representative sample of people. When other individuals take the test, we can then compare their scores with the standards defined by this group. This process of defining meaningful scores relative to a pretested group is called **standardization.**

Recall that when Terman realized that the test Binet created in France did not work so well with California schoolchildren, he revised the test and standardized the new version by testing 2300 native-born, white Americans of differing socioeconomic levels. These people defined the performance yardstick for evaluating later test-takers.

A random group of test results typically form a **normal distribution,** a bell-shaped pattern of scores that forms the **normal curve** (Figure 8–8). Whether we are measuring people's heights, weights, or mental aptitudes,

Terman and his colleagues recognized that a scale standardized on Parisians did not provide a satisfactory standard for evaluating Americans. Ironically, they proceeded to evaluate non-white and immigrant groups based on the native-born white American standard (Van Leeuwen, 1982).

Figure 8–8 The normal curve. Scores on aptitude tests tend to form a normal, or bell-shaped, curve. For example, the Wechsler scale calls the average score 100. It defines other scores to make about 68 percent of them fall within 15 points above or below 100. More than 95 percent fall within 30 points above and below 100.

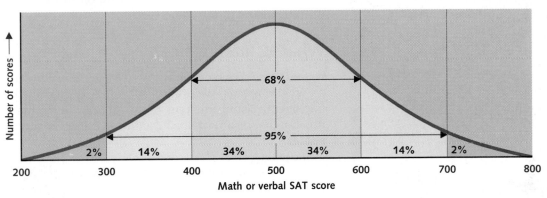

most values tend to cluster around the average. On an intelligence test, we call this average "100." As we move out from the average (toward either extreme) we find fewer and fewer values. Within each age group, the Stanford-Binet and the Wechsler tests assign any person a score according to how much that person's performance "deviates" above or below the average. (See Appendix A for a description of the statistical measure of this deviation called *standard deviation.*) As Figure 8–8 shows, a raw score higher than 98 percent of all scores earns an intelligence score of 130. A raw score that is comparably *below* 98 percent of all the scores earns an intelligence score of 70.

standardization   Defining meaningful scores by comparison with the results of a pretested "standardization group."

normal curve (or **normal distribution**) The symmetrical bell-shaped curve that describes the distribution of many physical and psychological attributes. Most scores fall near the average, and fewer and fewer scores lie near the extremes.

reliability   The extent to which a test yields consistent results, as assessed by the consistency of scores on two halves of the test, on alternate forms of the test, or on retesting.

Reliability   A good test must yield dependably consistent scores; in a word, it must have **reliability.** To check a test's reliability, researchers will retest people using the same test or another form of it. If the two scores generally agree, or *correlate,* the test is reliable. Alternatively, the researcher may split a test in half and see whether scores derived from odd and even questions agree.

validity The extent to which a test measures or predicts what it is supposed to. Thus, Binet's intelligence test was valid because it predicted school achievement.

intelligence The capacity for goal-directed and adaptive behavior. Involves the abilities to profit from experience, solve problems, reason, and successfully meet challenges and achieve goals.

mental retardation A condition of limited mental ability, as indicated by an intelligence score below 70 and difficulty in adapting to the demands of life; varies from mild to profound.

Down syndrome A condition of retardation and associated physical disorders caused by an extra chromosome in one's genetic makeup.

For further information on correlation, see Appendix A.

Preview Question

10. Is intelligence a single general ability, or is it formed from several distinct abilities?

"Intelligence is the particular facility a person has to cope with any given situation."

M. S. Michel
Sweet Murder, 1943

The higher the correlation between the *test-retest* or the *split-half* scores, the higher the test's reliability. The lowest correlation, −1.0, represents perfect disagreement between two sets of scores—as the first score goes up, the second goes down. A correlation of 0 represents no consistency. The highest correlation, +1.0, represents perfect consistency—as the first score goes up, so does the second. The tests we have considered so far—the Stanford-Binet, the WAIS-R, and the WISC—all have reliabilities of about +0.9, which is very high. When retested, people's scores tend to match their first score closely.

Validity High reliability does not ensure a test's **validity**—that it actually measures what it is supposed to measure or predicts what it is supposed to predict. If you use a shrunken tape measure to measure people's heights, your data would have high reliability (consistency) but low validity. How, then, can we determine whether a test is valid? For some tests, it is enough that they tap the behavior they were designed to assess. The road test for a driver's license has content validity because it samples those tasks a driver routinely faces. Your course exams have content validity if they accurately assess your mastery of a representative sample of course material. Other tests are evaluated in terms of how well they *predict* future achievement.

Are general aptitude tests as predictive as they are reliable? As critics are fond of noting, the answer is plainly no. The predictive power of aptitude tests is fairly strong in the early grades, but later it weakens. A better predictor of future grades is past grades, which reflect both aptitude and motivation. More generally, the best predictor of future behavior is a large sample of past behaviors of the same sort.

What Is Intelligence?

So far in this chapter we have used the term *intelligence* as though we all agree on what it means. We don't. Psychologists debate whether we should define intelligence as an inherent brain capacity, an achieved level of intellectual functioning, or an ascribed quality that, like beauty, is in the eye of the beholder.

Intelligence is a concept intended to explain why some people perform better than others on cognitive tasks. In the *Handbook of Human Intelligence,* Robert Sternberg and William Salter (1982, p. 3) reported that most experts view **intelligence** as a person's capacity for "goal-directed adaptive behavior." Intelligent behavior reflects a capacity to adapt, by learning from experience, solving problems, and reasoning clearly. Those behaving intelligently meet challenges and achieve their goals.

Despite this general agreement about the concept, controversy remains over whether intelligence is one dimension, or several.

Is Intelligence One General Ability? Or Several Specific Abilities?

We all know some people talented in mathematics, others in creative writing, and still others in art, music, or dance. Perhaps you have known a talented artist who is dumbfounded by the simplest mathematical problems or a brilliant math student who has little aptitude for literary discussion. We may therefore wonder whether people's mental abilities are too diverse to justify the single label "intelligence" or to quantify them with a single number.

But might there not be a general ability factor that runs throughout our specific mental abilities? To find out, psychologists study how various abilities relate.

Psychology Applied: Extremes of Intelligence

One way to glimpse the validity and significance of any test is to compare people who score at the two extremes of the normal curve. The two groups should differ noticeably, and they do. In one famous project begun in 1921, Lewis Terman studied more than 1500 California schoolchildren with IQ scores over 135. Contrary to the popular myth that intellectually "gifted" children are frequently maladjusted because they are "in a different world" from their nongifted peers, Terman's high-scoring children were unusually healthy, well adjusted, and academically successful. When restudied over the next six decades (Goleman, 1980), most of these people had attained high levels of education. Their vocational success varied, yet the group included many doctors, lawyers, professors, scientists, and writers.

At the other extreme are people whose intelligence scores fall below 70. To be labeled **mentally retarded** a child must have both a low test score *and* difficulty adapting to the normal demands of living independently. Only about 1 percent of the population meets both criteria, with males outnumbering females by 50 percent (American Psychiatric Association, 1987). As Table 8–2 indicates, most such mentally challenged individuals can, with support, live in the mainstream society.

Severe mental retardation, characteristic of only 4 percent of the retarded, usually results from known physical causes, such as **Down syndrome,** a disorder attributable to an extra chromosome in the person's genetic makeup.

During the last two centuries the pendulum of opinion about how best to care for the retarded has made a complete swing. Until the mid-nineteenth century, the mentally challenged were cared for at home. The most severely disabled often died, but the mildly retarded found a place in a farm-based society.

Then, in the United States, residential schools for slow learners were established. By the twentieth century, many of these institutions had become warehouses providing residents no privacy, little attention, and no hope. Parents were often told to separate themselves permanently from a retarded child before they became attached.

Now, in the last half of this century, the pendulum has swung back to normalization—allowing mentally impaired people to live in their own communities as normally as their functioning permits. We educate mildly retarded children in less restrictive environments and we integrate, or *mainstream*, many into regular classrooms. Most grow up with their own families until moving into a protected living arrangement, such as a group home. The hope, and often the reality, is a happier and more dignified life.

Table 8–2
Degrees of Mental Retardation

Level	Typical intelligence scores	Percent of the retarded	Adaptation to demands of life
Mild	50–70	85%	May learn academic skills up to sixth-grade level. Adults may, with assistance, achieve self-supporting social and vocational skills.
Moderate	35–49	10%	May progress to second-grade level academically. Adults may contribute to their own support by labor in sheltered workshops.
Severe	20–34	4%	May learn to talk and to perform simple work tasks under close supervision, but are generally unable to profit from vocational training.
Profound	Below 20	Less than 1%	Require constant aid and supervision.

Source: Adapted from the American Psychiatric Association (1987, pp. 32–33).

general intelligence (g) factor A general underlying intelligence factor believed by Spearman and others to be measured by every task on an intelligence test.

savant syndrome A condition in which a person otherwise limited in mental ability has an amazing specified skill, such as in computation or drawing.

creativity The ability to produce novel and valuable ideas.

Dustin Hoffman's portrayal of a savant in the movie "Rain Man" promoted awareness of these singularly skilled people.

A statistical method called *factor analysis* allows researchers to identify clusters of test items that measure a common ability. For example, people who do well on vocabulary items often do well on paragraph comprehension. This cluster helps define a verbal intelligence "factor." Psychologists have identified several such clusters, including a spatial ability factor and a reasoning ability factor.

Charles Spearman (1863–1945), who helped develop factor analysis, believed there is also a **general intelligence (g) factor** that underlies the specific factors. People often have special abilities that stand out, Spearman allowed. But those who score high on one factor, such as verbal intelligence, typically score higher than average on other factors, such as spatial or reasoning ability. So there is at least a small tendency for different abilities to come in the same package. Spearman believed that this commonality, the g factor, underlies all of our intelligent behavior, from excelling in school to navigating the sea.

Psychologist Howard Gardner (1983) supports the idea that intelligence comes in different packages. He notes that brain damage may diminish one type of ability but not others. He has analyzed the importance of different abilities in different cultures, from hunting societies to Japanese work groups to North American schoolrooms. He has studied people with exceptional abilities, including those who excel in only one. People with **savant syndrome,** for example, score at the low end on intelligence tests but possess incredible specific abilities, such as in computation, drawing, or musical memory (Figure 8–9). These people may have virtually no language ability, yet may be able to compute numbers as quickly and accurately as an electronic calculator or be capable of identifying almost instantly the day of the week that corresponds to any given date in history.

Figure 8–9 The savant syndrome. Although hardly able to talk coherently, 15-year-old Stephen Wiltshire— "possibly the best child artist in Britain"—can draw intricate scenes after just one good look at them. This drawing is of St. Marks in Venice, Italy.

Using such evidence, Gardner argues that we do not have *an* intelligence, but *multiple* intelligences, each independent of the others. In addition to the verbal and mathematical aptitudes assessed by the standard tests, Gardner identifies distinct aptitudes for musical accomplishment, for spatially analyzing the visual world, for mastering movement skills, such as those characteristic of dance, and for insightfully understanding ourselves and others. According to Gardner, the computer programmer, the poet, the street-smart adolescent who becomes a crafty executive, and the point guard on the basketball team exhibit different kinds of intelligence.

Wouldn't it be wonderful if the world were so just, responds intelligence researcher Sandra Scarr (1989), that being weak in any area was likely to be compensated by genius in some other area? Alas, the world is not just, for there remains some tendency for different skills to correlate. Because mentally disadvantaged people often have lesser physical abilities as well, we hold Special Olympics to give them a chance to experience winning.

Robert Sternberg and Richard Wagner (1986; Wagner and Sternberg, 1987) distinguish more simply among three intelligences: the *academic* problem-solving skills assessed by intelligence tests, the *practical* intelligence often required for everyday tasks, and the *creative* intelligence demonstrated in reacting to novel situations. Intelligence tests predict school grades reasonably well but predict vocational success less well. Success in managerial work, for example, depends less on the abilities assessed by an intelligence score (assuming the score is average or above) than on having managerial know-how. Business executives who score high on Sternberg and Wagner's test of practical managerial intelligence (by knowing how to write effective memos, how to motivate people, when to delegate tasks and responsibilities, how to read people, and how to promote their own careers) earn higher salaries and receive better performance ratings than do those who score low. Likewise, Stephen Ceci and Jeffrey Liker (1986) report that racetrack fans' expertise in handicapping the horses—a practical but complex cognitive task—is unrelated to their intelligence scores. So, personal competence in everyday living requires much that traditional intelligence tests do not measure.

We might, then, liken mental abilities to physical abilities. Athleticism is not one thing but many. The ability to run fast is distinct from brute strength, which is distinct from the eye-hand coordination required to throw a ball on target. A champion weightlifter therefore rarely has the potential to be a skilled ice skater. Yet there remains some tendency for good things to come packaged together—for running speed and throwing accuracy to correlate, thanks to general athletic ability. Likewise, intelligence involves several distinct abilities, which cluster together in the same individual often enough to define a small general intelligence factor.

Creativity and Intelligence

Creativity is the ability to produce ideas that are both novel and valuable. The outlets for creativity vary by culture. Samoan culture encourages creativity in dance, Balinese culture in music, the African Ashanti culture in wood carvings (Lubart, 1990). In each, creativity means expressing familiar themes in novel ways.

Results from tests of intelligence and creativity suggest that a certain level of aptitude is necessary but not sufficient for creativity. In general, people with high intelligence scores do well on creativity tests ("How many uses can you think of for a brick?"). But beyond a certain level—a score of about 120—the correlation between intelligence scores and creativity disappears.

"You're wise, but you lack tree smarts."

Drawing by Reilly; © 1988 The New Yorker Magazine, Inc.

On his way home from picking up a Nobel prize in Stockholm, physicist Richard Feynman stopped in Queens, New York, to look at his high school record. "My grades were not as good as I remembered," he reported, "and my IQ was [a good, though unexceptional] 124" (Faber, 1987).

Exceptionally creative architects, mathematicians, scientists, and engineers usually score no higher on intelligence tests than their less creative peers (MacKinnon & Hall, 1972). So there is clearly more to creativity than intelligence scores.

Studies of creative people suggest four other components (Sternberg, 1988; Sternberg & Lubart, 1991). The first is *expertise*—a well-developed base of knowledge. "Chance favors only the prepared mind," observed Louis Pasteur. The second is *imaginative thinking skills*—an ability to see things in new ways, to recognize patterns, to make connections. To be creative you must first master the basic elements of a problem, then redefine the problem in a new way. Copernicus first developed expertise regarding the solar system's sun and planets, then redefined the system as revolving around the sun, not the earth.

Creativity's third ingredient is a *venturesome personality*—one that tolerates ambiguity and risk, perseveres in overcoming obstacles, and seeks new experiences rather than following the pack. Inventors, for example, have a knack for persisting after failures, as Thomas Edison did in trying countless substances for his light bulb filament.

The fourth component is what psychologist Teresa Amabile calls the *intrinsic motivation* principle of creativity: "People will be most creative when they feel motivated primarily by the interest, enjoyment, satisfaction, and challenge of the work itself—and not by external pressures" (Amabile & Hennessey, 1988). Creative people focus not so much on extrinsic motivators—meeting deadlines, impressing people, or making money—as on the intrinsic pleasure and challenge of their work.

Genetic and Environmental Determinants of Intelligence

Intelligence seems to run in families. But why? Are intellectual abilities inherited? Or are they molded by one's environment? To understand why these questions stir up stormy debate, consider how people with differing views sometimes use nature and nurture to further their social agendas.

If, on the one hand, we mainly inherit our differing mental abilities, and if success reflects those abilities, then people's socioeconomic standings will correspond to their inborn differences. Thus, those on top may believe their innate mental superiority justifies their social positions. They may even remind us that it was Thomas Jefferson, not God, who insisted that all people are created equal.

If, on the other hand, mental abilities are primarily nurtured by the environments that raise and school us, then children from disadvantaged environments will often lead disadvantaged lives. In this case, people's socioeconomic standings will result from unequal opportunities, a situation that many regard as basically unjust. Setting aside such political implications as best we can, let's examine the evidence.

Genetic Determinants   Do people who share the same genes also share comparable mental abilities? As you can see from Figure 8–10, which summarizes the accumulated data, the answer is clearly yes. In support of the genetic contribution to intelligence, researchers note that:

> The IQ scores of identical twins are virtually as similar as those of the same person taking the same test twice. Fraternal twins, who share only half their genes, are much less similar in IQ scores.

Preview Question

11. Is intellect influenced more by heredity or environment?

"I am, somehow, less interested in the weight and convolutions of Einstein's brain than in the near certainty that people of equal talent have lived and died in cotton fields and sweatshops."

Stephen J. Gould
The Panda's Thumb, 1980

Figure 8–10 Intelligence: Nature or nurture? How similar are the intelligence scores of identical twins? Of fraternal twins? Of non-twin brothers and sisters? The most genetically similar people have the most similar intelligence scores. But the correlations also reveal an effect of environment: Identical twins reared apart test somewhat less alike than those reared together. Remember: 1.0 indicates a perfect correlation; 0.0 indicates no correlation at all. (From Bouchard, 1982.)

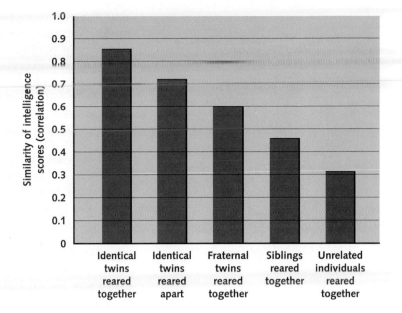

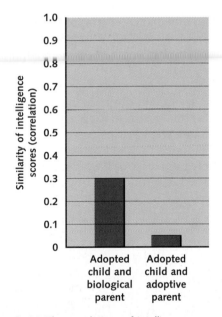

Figure 8–11 The correlations of intelligence scores between 245 adopted Colorado children and their adoptive and biological parents. By age 7, the adopted children had intelligence test scores more like those of their biological parents. (From Fulker & others, 1988.)

heritability The extent to which we can attribute individuals' differences in a trait to genes. The heritability of a trait may vary, depending on the range of populations and environments studied.

Even identical twins whose parents do not dress or treat them identically are virtual carbon copies of one another in IQ score (Loehlin & Nichols, 1976). Likewise, identical twins who have been reared separately have similar IQ scores.

On the other hand, some evidence points to an effect of environment. Fraternal twins, who are genetically no more alike than any other siblings, nevertheless tend to score more alike. As new data accumulate, assessments of the extent to which variation in IQ scores can be attributed to heredity have dropped from earlier estimates of around 80 percent to newer estimates of between 50 percent (Plomin & DeFries, 1980) and 60 percent (Bouchard & Segal, 1988).

As the twin studies illustrate, psychologists struggle to disentangle the effects of genes and environment. In addition to twin studies, several researchers have therefore asked whether adopted children have intelligence scores more like those of their biological parents, from whom they receive their genes, or those of their adoptive parents, who provide their home environment. As Figure 8–11 illustrates, adopted children's intelligence scores are more like their biological parents' scores than like their adoptive parents' (although the relationship is not a strong one). Being reared "together in the same adoptive home does not make you intellectually similar to your brothers and sisters," notes Sandra Scarr (1989); "being genetically related by half of your genes does."

To say that the **heritability** of intelligence—the variation in intelligence scores attributable to genetic factors—is roughly 50 to 60 percent does *not* mean that your genes are responsible for 50 to 60 percent of your intelligence and your environment for the rest. (Likewise, saying that the heritability of height is 90 percent does not mean that a 60-inch-tall woman can credit her genes for 54 inches and her environment for the other 6 inches.) Rather, it means that we can attribute to heredity 50 to 60 percent *of the variation in intelligence within a group of people.* This point is so often misunderstood that I repeat: We can never say what percent of an *individual's* intelligence is inherited. Heritability refers instead to the extent to which *differences among people* are attributable to genes.

Even this conclusion must be qualified. Put on your thinking cap and consider: First, heritability can vary from study to study. Compare people

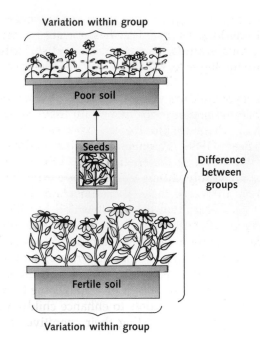

Variation within group

Poor soil

Seeds

Difference between groups

Fertile soil

Variation within group

Figure 8–12 Even if the variation within a group reflects genetic differences (differences between seeds), the average difference between groups may be wholly due to the environment. (From Lewontin, 1976.)

with very different heredities from basically similar environments, and heritability—differences due to genes—will be high. Compare people with not-so-different heredities in drastically different environments and heritability will be low. If everyone had the same heredity, heritability—differences due to genes—would be zero.

Geneticist Richard Lewontin (1976) shows why. If a mixture of seeds is sown in poor soil, the differing heights of the resulting plants will be the result of genetic differences among them. If seeds from the same mixture are sown in fertile soil, the differing heights of these plants will again be the result of genetic differences. But, as Figure 8–12 illustrates, the average height difference *between* the two groups of plants will be due to environmental soil differences. Thus, even if the heritability of a trait is extremely high *within* a particular group, differences in that trait *between* groups may nevertheless have environmental causes.

Remember that genes and environment intertwine. Given the dissimilarities among children who grow up in the same families, researchers infer that our most important experiences are personal. Yet our genetically unique traits affect our experience: They make others react in ways that encourage us to develop our natural gifts, and they lead us to select congenial environments. Students with a natural aptitude for mathematics are more likely to select challenging math courses in high school, and later to score well on math tests—thanks *both* to their natural math aptitude *and* their math experience. Thus, our genes shape the experiences that shape us.

Environmental Determinants   We have seen that our genes make a difference. Were we all raised in the same intellectually stimulating environment, we would not have the same aptitudes. But we have also seen that heredity doesn't tell the whole story. Within the limits dictated by our genes, our life experiences shape us. As Chapter 3 notes, experience literally leaves its mark on the brain: Rats reared in impoverished environments develop lighter and thinner brain cortexes than normal. And as Chapter 7 notes, particular learning experiences have detectable effects on their brains' neural connections.

Human environments are rarely so impoverished as the dark and barren cages inhabited by deprived rats. Yet life experiences also leave marks on a person's mental abilities, as psychologist J. McVicker Hunt (1982) observed in an Iranian orphanage in Tehran. The typical child there could not sit up unassisted at age 2 or walk at age 4. What care the infants received was not in response to their crying, cooing, or other behaviors. The infants were therefore not developing any sense of personal control over their environment, and so were becoming passive "glum lumps." Extreme deprivation was bludgeoning native intelligence.

Aware of the benefits of responsive caregiving, Hunt began a program of "tutored human enrichment." For instance, he trained caregivers to play vocal games with the infants. First, they imitated the babies' babbling. Then they led the babies in vocal follow-the-leader by shifting from one familiar sound to another. Then they began to teach them sounds from the Persian language.

The results were dramatic. All 11 infants who received these language-fostering experiences could name more than 50 objects and parts of the body by 22 months. So charming had the infants become that most were adopted—an unprecedented success for the orphanage.

Hunt's findings testify to the importance of environment. But do they indicate how to "give your child a superior intellect"? Some popular books claim this is possible, but many experts are doubtful. Sandra Scarr (1984)

Intelligence experts dispute claims that special lessons *(top)* can give preschoolers superior minds. But Project Head Start *(bottom)* does help educationally disadvantaged children adjust to school.

Preview Question

12. Are intelligence tests biased and discriminatory?

agrees that neglectful upbringing can have grave long-term consequences. However, she also believes that "as long as an infant has normal human contact and normal exposure to sights, sounds, human speech and so forth, the baby will thrive." As for future intelligence, she maintains: "Parents who are very concerned about providing special educational lessons for their babies are wasting their time." Parents of children with high intelligence scores may be more likely to hang mobiles over their cribs, play with them rather than park them in front of the TV, or whatever. But do such experiences have any effect? We don't know, says Scarr (1986). Parents supply their children with both genes and environment. So even if the environments of children with high intelligence scores are noticeably different from those with low scores, we can't be sure how much difference their environments make.

Hunt would probably agree with Scarr that extra instruction has little effect on the intellectual development of children from stimulating environments. But he was optimistic when it came to children from disadvantaged environments. Indeed, his 1961 book, *Intelligence and Experience*, helped launch Project Head Start in 1965. Head Start is a U.S. government-funded preschool program serving 450,000 children, 90 percent of whom come from families below the poverty level (Horn, 1990). It aims to enhance children's chances for success in school and beyond by boosting their cognitive and social skills.

Does it? Researchers have studied Head Start and other preschool programs by comparing equivalent groups of children who do versus don't experience the intervention. Their findings indicate that high-quality programs for disadvantaged children produce at least short-term cognitive gains, even on intelligence tests (Haskins, 1989). Quality programs also increase school readiness, decreasing the likelihood of a child repeating a grade or being placed in special education. On a less encouraging note, the benefits dissipate over time, reminding us that life experiences *after* Head Start matter, too.

The Question of Bias

Are intelligence tests biased? How we answer depends on what we mean by *bias*. One meaning is that the tests detect not only innate differences in intelligence but also differences caused by cultural experiences. In this sense, everyone agrees that intelligence tests are biased. No one claims that heritability is 100 percent responsible for any test score. An intelligence test measures a person's developed abilities at a particular time. These abilities necessarily reflect that person's experiences and environment. If people's experiences and backgrounds are unequal, the test's results will reflect those inequalities.

It is possible for aptitude tests to be biased in one sense and not in another. Imagine a college—perhaps your own—where courses and teachers share a particular vocabulary and set of assumptions that make it difficult for people from a foreign culture to excel there. Test scores that predict success in such a school will be influenced by a person's cultural background. The test would therefore be culturally biased, because it mirrors the school's cultural bias. Yet the test might be an equally valid predictor of performance for all who take it, and in this sense be unbiased.

Are tests discriminatory? Again, the answer can be yes or no. In one sense, yes, their purpose is to discriminate—to distinguish among individuals. In another sense, their purpose is to reduce discrimination by reducing reliance on the subjective criteria that were once more crucial for school and job placement—criteria such as who you know, what you look like, or how

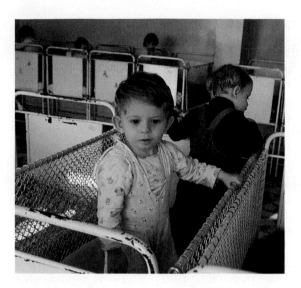

Tests assess developed ability, which is influenced by life experience. Stark neglect, such as these Romanian orphans experienced, takes a toll. Removal from neglect and adoption into stimulating, caring homes pays mental dividends.

much the interviewer happens to like "your kind of person." Banning aptitude tests would force the people who decide on admissions and jobs to rely more on other considerations, such as their personal opinions. Civil service tests, for example, discriminate among individuals, but were devised to do so more fairly and objectively, by reducing the political, racial, and ethnic discrimination that preceded their use. So perhaps our aim should be to realize the benefits that Alfred Binet foresaw for intelligence tests—to enable schools to recognize who might best benefit from early intervention—while sharing Binet's fear that test scores might be misinterpreted as literal measures of a person's worth and fixed potential.

Finally, we must remember that *intelligence scores reflect only one aspect of personal competence.* Other attributes—motivation, character, social skills, artistic talent, athletic ability, sensitivity, emotional maturity—matter. In other words, the competence that intelligence tests sample is important, but far from all-inclusive. The spatial ability of the carpenter differs from the logical ability of the computer programmer, which differs from the verbal ability of the poet. Differences are not deficits. Because there are many ways of being successful, our personal and cultural differences—regardless of their origins— are valuable variations on the human theme of adaptability. Like ice cream, human traits and gifts come in many flavors.

Rehearse It

11. Intelligence quotient, or IQ, was originally defined as the ratio of mental age to chronological age multiplied by 100. Thus, a child of 6 years, whose measured mental age was also 6, had an IQ of 100. A child of 6 whose measured mental age is 9 has an IQ of
a. 67.
b. 133.
c. 86.
d. 150.

12. The Wechsler Adult Intelligence Scale—Revised (WAIS-R) yields a general IQ scale as well as separate scores for verbal and performance (non-verbal) IQs. The WAIS-R is best able to tell us
a. what part of an individual's intelligence is determined by genetic inheritance.
b. whether or not the test-taker will succeed on a job.
c. how the test-taker compares to other adults in vocabulary and arithmetic reasoning.
d. whether or not the test-taker has specific skills for music and the performing arts.

13. The Stanford-Binet, WAIS-R, and WISC are known to have very high reliability (about +.90). This means that
a. a pretest has been given to a representative sample.
b. the test yields consistent results, for example on retesting.
c. the test measures what it is supposed to measure.
d. the results of the test will be distributed on a bell-shaped curve.

14. *Savant syndrome* is retardation combined with incredible ability in one specific area. The existence of savant syndrome seems to support
a. Terman's ideas on "gifted children."
b. Spearman's notion of general intelligence, or g factor.
c. Gardner's theory of multiple intelligences.
d. Binet's conception of mental age.

15. A current view is that roughly 50 percent of intelligence score variation among individuals can be attributed to heredity.

The strongest support for the hereditary influence on intelligence is the finding that
a. identical twins, but not other siblings, have nearly identical IQ scores.
b. the correlation between IQ scores of fraternal twins is higher than that for other siblings.
c. unrelated people living in the same environment do not tend to have similar IQ scores.
d. the IQ scores of adopted children do not closely correlate with those of biological or adoptive parents.

16. Within the limits set by heredity, experiences help shape intelligence. The experience that has the clearest, most profound effect on intellectual development is
a. being enrolled in a Head Start program.
b. growing up in an economically disadvantaged home or neighborhood.
c. being raised in a very neglectful home or institution.
d. being exposed to very stimulating toys and lessons in infancy.

Reviewing Thinking, Language, and Intelligence

Our cognitive system receives, perceives, and retrieves information, which we then use to think and communicate, sometimes wisely, sometimes foolishly. In this chapter we have explored how we form concepts, solve problems, make decisions and judgments, use language, and exhibit intelligence.

Thinking

1. What function do concepts serve?

Concepts are one of the building blocks of thinking. They serve to simplify and order the world by organizing it into a hierarchy of categories. Concepts often form around prototypes, or best examples of a category.

2. By what strategies do we solve problems, and what obstacles hinder our problem solving?

When faced with new situations for which no well-learned response suffices, we may use any of several strategies, such as trial and error, algorithms, and rule-of-thumb heuristics. Insight, a sudden and often novel realization, can also offer solutions to problems. We do, however, face certain obstacles to successful problem solving. The confirmation bias predisposes us to verify rather than challenge our hypotheses. And fixations such as functional fixedness may prevent our taking a needed fresh perspective on a problem.

3. How do heuristics, overconfidence, and framing influence our decisions and judgments?

Our use of heuristics, such as the representativeness and availability heuristics, provides highly efficient but occasionally misleading guides for making quick decisions and forming intuitive judgments. Our tendencies to seek confirmation of our hypotheses and to use quick and easy heuristics can blind us to our vulnerability to error, a phenomenon known as overconfidence. Framing—the way in which a question is presented—can significantly affect our thinking.

4. How do our preexisting beliefs influence our decision making?

As the belief perseverance phenomenon indicates, we sometimes cling to our ideas after their basis has been discredited, because the explanation for their apparent validity lingers in our minds. In general, people tend to accept as more logical those conclusions that agree with their own beliefs.

Language

5. When do children acquire language, and how does it develop?

Among the marvels of nature is our ability to acquire language—our words and how we combine them to communicate meaning. The ease with which children progress from the babbling stage through the one-word stage to the telegraphic speech of the two-word stage and beyond has sparked a lively debate concerning how they do it. The behaviorist explains that language is learned by the familiar principles of association, imitation, and reinforcement. This claim has been challenged by indications that children are biologically prepared to learn words and to organize them according to an inborn readiness to use grammar.

6. Is language unique to humans, or do animals also have language?

Another vigorously debated issue is whether language is a uniquely human ability. Several teams of psychologists provoked enormous interest by teaching various apes, including a number of chimpanzees, to communicate with humans by using sign language or by pushing buttons wired to a computer. The animals have developed considerable vocabularies and are able to string words together to express meaning and requests. Skeptics point out significant differences between apes and humans in their facility with language, especially in their respective abilities to order words grammatically. Nevertheless, these studies have revealed that apes possess considerable cognitive ability.

7. What is the relationship between thinking and language?

Language facilitates and expresses our thoughts. There is no disputing that ideas are associated with words, and that different languages can embody different ways of thinking. Although the linguistic relativity hypothesis suggests that language *determines* thought, it is more correct to say that language *influences* thought. Evidence of the influence of words comes from studies of the effects of using masculine generic pronouns and of how vocabulary enrichment can enhance thinking.

There is also evidence that thinking in images rather than in words is common, especially among artists, poets, athletes, and scientists. Moreover, we sometimes invent new words to describe new ideas. So we might say that our thinking affects our language, which then affects our thoughts.

Intelligence

8. How are modern intelligence tests classified, and when and why were they created?

Today, tests are commonly classified as either aptitude tests (designed to predict ability to learn a particular skill) or achievement tests (designed to assess current competence). In the early 1900s, French psychologist Alfred Binet and his colleague Théodore Simon developed questions in an attempt to help predict children's future progress in the Paris school system. Lewis Terman of Stanford University adapted Binet's test and offered his Stanford-Binet as a way to direct people toward occupations for which they were deemed well suited. Later, David Wechsler developed the most widely used intelligence test, the Wechsler Adult Intelligence Scale—Revised (WAIS-R).

9. What three principles of test construction apply in evaluating a psychological test?

A good test must be standardized, so that a person's performance can be meaningfully compared to others'; reliable, so that it yields dependably consistent scores (over the short run); and valid, so that it measures what it is supposed to measure. Test scores tend to fall into a normal distribution, with the average score given some arbitrary number (such as 100 on an IQ test). Aptitude tests tend to be highly reliable, and to have moderate validity (as judged by their predictive accuracy).

10. Is intelligence a single general ability, or is it formed from several distinct abilities?

Psychologists agree that people possess specific abilities, such as verbal and mathematical aptitudes, but they debate whether a general intelligence (g) factor runs through them all. Statistical analysis and studies of special people, such as those with savant syndrome, have been used to identify various clusters of mental abilities.

11. Is intellect influenced more by heredity or environment?

Because of its political overtones, the nature-nurture debate with regard to intelligence has at times been vehement. Studies of twins, family members, and adopted children together point to a significant hereditary contribution to IQ scores. These same studies, plus others that compare children reared in neglectful or enriched environments, indicate that life experiences also significantly influence test performance.

12. Are intelligence tests biased and discriminatory?

If by "biased" one means sensitive to differences caused by cultural experience, then aptitude tests are necessarily biased. If by biased one means what psychologists commonly mean—that a test predicts less validly for one group than for another—then the current tests we have considered seem not to be biased. Indeed, tests are designed specifically to avoid more subjective forms of discrimination.

Terms and Concepts to Remember

thinking, p. 234

cognition, p. 234

cognitive psychology, p. 234

concept, p. 234

prototype, p. 234

algorithm, p. 235

heuristic, p. 235

insight, p. 235

confirmation bias, p. 236

fixation, p. 236

functional fixedness, p. 236

representativeness heuristic, p. 237

availability heuristic, p. 238

overconfidence phenomenon, p. 239

framing, p. 240

belief perseverance, p. 240

language, p. 242

babbling stage, p. 243

one-word stage, p. 243

two-word stage, p. 244

telegraphic speech, p. 244

linguistic relativity, p. 249

aptitude tests, p. 252

achievement tests, p. 252

mental age, p. 252

Stanford-Binet, p. 253

intelligence quotient (IQ), p. 253

Wechsler Adult Intelligence Scale— Revised (WAIS-R), p. 254

standardization, p. 255

normal curve, p. 255

normal distribution, p. 255

reliability, p. 255

validity, p. 256

intelligence, p. 256

mental retardation, p. 257

Down syndrome, p. 257

general intelligence (g) factor, p. 258

savant syndrome, p. 258

creativity, p. 259

heritability, p. 261

Rehearse It Answer Key

1. a.	2. b.	3. a.	4. d.	5. b.	6. c.	7. d.	8. b.	9. a.

10. a.	11. d.	12. c.	13. b.	14. c.	15. a.	16. c.

Critical Thinking Exercise

You have *S*urveyed, *Q*uestioned, *R*ead, *R*ehearsed, and *R*eviewed Chapter 8. Now take your learning a step further by completing the following exercise. Circle the correct answer to each of the following questions and rate your confidence from 50% ("it's a toss up") to 100% ("I'm certain").

1. What is the tallest office building in the world?

   a. The Sears Tower   **b.** The World Trade Center

   Confidence: _____

2. Which country has the largest population?

   a. South Africa   **b.** Vietnam

   Confidence: _____

3. What color is taupe?

   a. yellowish pink   **b.** brownish gray

   Confidence: _____

4. Who was the last president of the U.S.S.R.?

   a. Boris Yeltsin   **b.** Mikhail Gorbachev

   Confidence: _____

5. Of what country is Canberra the capital?

   a. Australia   **b.** Bolivia

   Confidence: _____

6. Which is the largest planet in our solar system?

   a. Saturn   **b.** Jupiter

   Confidence: _____

7. Which language is used by more people?

   a. Mandarin   **b.** English

   Confidence: _____

8. Which country is the world's largest oil producer?

   a. Saudia Arabia   **b.** The former Soviet Union

   Confidence: _____

9. In which country is the Krone used as the monetary unit?

   a. Finland   **b.** Greenland

   Confidence: _____

10. What is the most frequent cause of death in the United States?

    a. Heart disease   **b.** Cancer

    Confidence: _____

Determine your average confidence level by adding the percentages and dividing by 10, then check your answers with those found in Appendix B.

Average Confidence Level _____

Motivation

motivation A need or desire that energizes and directs behavior toward a goal.

In everyday conversation, the question "What motivated you to do that?" is a way of asking "What *caused* your behavior? *Why* did you act that way?" To psychologists, a **motivation** is a need or desire that serves to *energize* behavior and to *direct* it toward a goal. Like intelligence, motivation is a hypothetical concept. We infer motivation from behaviors we observe:

> David Mandel (1983), a former Nazi concentration camp inmate, recalls how a starving "father and son would fight over a piece of bread. Like dogs." One father, whose 20-year-old son stole his bread from under his pillow while he slept, went into a deep depression, asking over and again how his son could do such a thing. The next day the father died. "Hunger does something to you that's hard to describe. I can't believe it myself today, so how can I expect anyone else to understand it?"

> In the Old Testament's *Song of Solomon* love poems, a man and a woman express their intense sexual passion for one another. "I am sick with love," she declares. "O that his left hand were under my head, and that his right hand embraced me!" He, in turn, pronounces her "delectable." "You are stately as a palm tree, and your breasts are like its clusters. I say I will climb the palm tree and lay hold of its branches."

> In Texas, a school truant officer discovers Alfredo Gonzales, age 14, picking fruit and sends him off to the first day of school in his life. Although placed at the lowest skill level and paddled for asking questions in Spanish—he knows no English—Alfredo decides "I could do better." Indeed, today he is a highly educated college administrator who works to motivate youth to wake up, as he did, to "their own potential and to gain a desire to achieve it."

In this chapter, we will explore motivation by focusing on these three motives—hunger, sex, and achievement. Although other identifiable motives exist (thirst, curiosity, need for approval, and so forth), a close look at just these three reveals the underlying interplay between nature (the biological "push") and nurture (the cognitive and cultural "pulls").

Concepts of Motivation

Early in this century, as the influence of Charles Darwin's evolutionary theory grew, it became fashionable to classify all sorts of behaviors as instincts. If people criticized themselves, it was because of their "self-abasement instinct." If they boasted, it reflected their "self-assertion instinct." After scanning 500 books, one sociologist compiled a list of 5759 supposed human instincts! Before long, the instinct-naming fad collapsed under its own weight. For rather than *explaining* human behaviors, the early instinct theorists were simply *naming* them. It was like "explaining" a bright child's low grades by saying he or she is an "underachiever."

Preview Question

1. What role do biological needs and external incentives play in motivation?

The more complex the nervous system, the more adaptable the organism. The weaver bird's construction skills are instinctual; the human's are learned.

To qualify as an **instinct,** a behavior must have a fixed pattern and not be a product of learning (Tinbergen, 1951). Such behaviors are common in other species (recall imprinting in birds and the return of salmon to their birthplace to spawn). Human behavior, too, exhibits certain innate tendencies, including simple fixed patterns such as an infant's rooting and sucking. Most psychologists, though, view human behavior as directed by biological needs and psychological wants.

Biological Needs: The Internal Pushes

When the instinct theory of motivation collapsed, it was replaced by *drive theory*—the idea that a biological *need* (a deprivation, such as a lack of food) creates an aroused state, or **drive,** which motivates an organism to satisfy the need. The drive prompts the organism to reduce the need by, say, eating or drinking. When a biological need increases, its psychological consequence, a drive, usually increases, too.

The physiological aim of drive reduction is **homeostasis**—the maintenance of a balanced or constant internal state. An example of homeostasis (which literally means "staying the same") is the body's temperature-regulation system, which works much as a thermostat works to keep room temperature constant. Sensors detect the temperature of the room or body and feed this information to a control device. If the room temperature cools, the control device notes this deviation from the desired state and switches on the furnace. If body temperature cools, blood vessels constrict to conserve warmth, and we feel driven to put on more clothes or seek a warmer environment. Likewise, if the water level in our cells drops, sensors detect our need for water and we feel thirsty.

Learning and Culture: The External Pulls

There are, however, motives that do not satisfy any obvious biological need. Monkeys will monkey around trying to figure out how to unlock a latch that opens nothing or how to open a window that allows them to see outside their room (Butler, 1954). The 9-month-old infant who investigates every accessible corner of the house, the scientists whose work this text discusses, and the voyagers who first ventured across and beneath the oceans were all motivated to explore. Asked why he wanted to climb Mt. Everest, George Mallory answered, "Because it is there." Despite having all our biological needs satisfied, we feel driven to experience stimulation.

Curiosity. The activities of young monkeys and children demonstrate the early presence of an insatiable urge to explore—one of several motives that does not fulfill any obvious physiological need.

instinct A behavior that is rigidly patterned and unlearned.

drive An aroused state that typically arises from an underlying need.

homeostasis A tendency to maintain a balanced or constant internal state; refers especially to the body's tendency to maintain an optimum internal state for functioning.

incentives Positive or negative environmental stimuli that motivate behavior.

hierarchy of needs Maslow's pyramid of human needs, beginning at the base with physiological needs that must first be satisfied before higher-level safety needs and then psychological needs become active.

For people who crave the stimulation of ever-increasing tests of their courage or mastery, mental and physical challenges are powerful incentives.

Preview Question

2. What is the basic idea behind Maslow's hierarchy of needs?

Self-actualization needs
To live up to one's fullest and unique potential

Esteem needs
For self-esteem, achievement, competence, and independence; for recognition and respect from others

Belongingness and love needs
To love and be loved, to belong and be accepted; to avoid loneliness and alienation

Safety needs
To feel that the world is organized and predictable; to feel safe, secure, and stable

Physiological needs
To satisfy hunger and thirst

Not only are we pushed by our "need" for optimum stimulation, we are also pulled by **incentives**—any stimulus that has positive or negative value in motivating our behavior. This is where our individual learning histories influence our motives. Depending on our learning, the aroma of fresh roasted peanuts (or toasted ants), the sight of someone we find attractive, and the threat of disapproval can all motivate our behavior. Our internal needs energize and direct our behavior, but so do these external incentives. When there is both a need and an incentive, we feel driven. The food-deprived person who smells bread baking hungers for it. For each motive, we can therefore ask two questions: How is it pushed by our inborn biological needs? How is it pulled by incentives in the environment?

A Hierarchy of Motives

Some needs take priority over others. At this moment, your needs for air and water are probably satisfied, so other motives—such as your desire to achieve a good grade—energize and direct your behavior. If your need for water goes unsatisfied, your thirst will preoccupy you. Deprived of air, your thirst will disappear.

These examples illustrate how the particular needs that motivate our behavior depend on which needs are unmet and, among those, which are the more fundamental. Abraham Maslow (1970) proposed one such **hierarchy of needs** (Figure 9–1). At the base are our physiological needs, such as for food, water, and shelter. Only if these needs are met are we prompted to meet our need for safety, and then to meet the uniquely human needs to give and

Figure 9–1 Maslow's hierarchy of needs. Once our lower-level needs are met, we are prompted to satisfy our higher-level needs. (From Maslow, 1970.)

receive love, and to enjoy self-esteem. Beyond this, said Maslow (1971), lies the highest of human needs: to actualize one's full potential. (More on self-esteem and self-actualization in Chapter 11, Personality.)

Maslow's hierarchy is somewhat arbitrary. Moreover, the order of such needs is not universally fixed. People have starved themselves to make a political statement. Nevertheless, the simple idea that some motives are more compelling than others—until they are satisfied—provides a framework for thinking about motivation. Let's consider three representative motives, beginning at the basic, physiological level with hunger and working up through sexual motivation (which contains both physiological and social elements), to a higher-level motive, achievement. At each level, we will see how psychological factors such as learning interact with what is biologically driven.

Rehearse It

1. Drive reduction motivates many behaviors necessary for survival. A need, or deprivation (for example, a lack of water), leads to an aroused state or drive; and this in turn motivates the organism to act to reduce this drive and restore internal stability. Drive reduction also motivates behaviors such as
a. eating and breathing.
b. curiosity.
c. nest building and other instincts.
d. stimulation seeking.

2. The aim of drive reduction is internal stability. For example, if we are too hot, we perspire; if we are dehydrated, we feel thirsty—and drink. The maintenance of a balanced internal state is called
a. instinct.
b. sensory restriction.
c. a hierarchy of needs.
d. homeostasis.

3. Behavior is also influenced by incentives in the environment. For example, a pile of leaves in the driveway may motivate you to get out the rake; your neighbor's disapproval may motivate you to turn down your radio. To explain the effects of external incentives, we must refer to
a. biological needs.
b. instinct.

c. individual learning histories.
d. homeostasis.

4. According to Abraham Maslow, we are not prompted to satisfy psychological needs, such as the need to be accepted or loved, until we have satisfied more basic needs. Basic needs fall into two categories: physiological needs, including the need for food, water, and oxygen; and
a. safety needs.
b. self-esteem needs.
c. love needs.
d. psychological needs.

During Keys' semistarvation experiment, his conscientious objector subjects became obsessed with food.

Hunger

A vivid demonstration of the priority we give our physiological needs followed reports of starvation in World War II prison camps and occupied areas. To learn more about the results of semistarvation, scientist Ancel Keys and his colleagues (1950) solicited volunteers for an experiment. From among the more than 100 conscientious objectors to the war who applied, they selected 36 men. First, they fed the men just enough to maintain their initial weight. Then, for 6 months, they cut this food level in half.

The effects soon became visible. Without thinking about it, the men began conserving energy; they appeared listless and apathetic. Their body weights dropped rapidly, eventually stabilizing at about 25 percent below their starting weights. The psychological effects were even more dramatic. Consistent with Maslow's idea of a need hierarchy, the men became obsessed with food.

They talked food. They daydreamed food. They collected recipes, read cookbooks, and feasted their eyes on delectable forbidden foods. Meanwhile, they lost their former interests in sex and social activities. They became preoccupied with their unfulfilled basic need. As one subject reported, "If we see a show, the most interesting part of it is contained in scenes where people are eating. I couldn't laugh at the funniest picture in the world, and love scenes are completely dull."

The Physiology of Hunger

Preview Question

3. What makes us hungry?

The hunger Keys' semistarved subjects felt was the response of a homeostatic system designed to maintain normal body weight and an adequate supply of nutrients. But precisely what is it that triggers hunger? Is it the pangs of an empty stomach? So it feels, and so it seemed after A. L. Washburn, working with Walter Cannon (Cannon & Washburn, 1912), intentionally swallowed a balloon. When inflated in his stomach, the balloon transmitted his stomach contractions to a recording device (Figure 9–2). While his stomach was being monitored, Washburn pressed a key each time he felt hungry. This, too, was transmitted to the recording device, which revealed that Washburn was having stomach contractions whenever he felt hungry. (Some diet aids reduce this empty stomach feeling by filling the stomach with indigestible fibers that swell as they absorb water.)

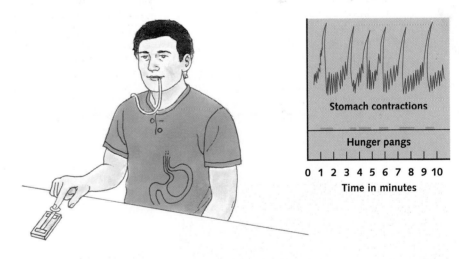

Figure 9–2 The procedure by which Washburn showed that stomach contractions (transmitted by the stomach balloon) accompany our feelings of hunger (indicated by a key press). (From Cannon, 1929.)

Stomach contractions

Hunger pangs

0 1 2 3 4 5 6 7 8 9 10
Time in minutes

Alas, there is more to hunger than the pangs of an empty stomach. Researchers discovered this a quarter-century later when they removed some rats' stomachs and attached their esophagi to their small intestines (Tsang, 1938). Without stomach pangs, did hunger persist? Did the rats continue to eat regularly? Indeed they did. Hunger persists similarly in humans whose ulcerated or cancerous stomachs have been removed. In fact, one can feel hungry even on a full stomach. Animals that fill their stomachs by eating low-calorie food will eat more than animals that consume a less filling, high-calorie diet (McHugh & Moran, 1978). If the pangs of an empty stomach are not the only source of our hunger, what else is involved?

Culture and taste preferences. For Alaskan Eskimos, but not for most other North Americans, whale blubber is a rare and tasty treat.

Body Chemistry

Changes in body chemistry also affect hunger. That people and other animals automatically regulate their caloric intake to maintain a stable body weight suggests that the body is somehow, somewhere keeping tabs on its available resources. One such resource is blood sugar, or **glucose.** Injecting large doses of the hormone **insulin** diminishes the glucose level in the blood, partly by converting it to stored fat, thus causing hunger to increase.

Our preferences for sweet and salty tastes are genetic and universal. Other tastes are conditioned, as when people given highly salted foods develop a liking for excess salt or when people develop an aversion to a food eaten before becoming violently ill. (Recall from Chapter 6 the coyotes that were conditioned to avoid the taste of sheep.) Cultural influences affect taste, too. Bedouins enjoy eating the eye of a camel, which most North Americans would find repulsive. Similarly, North Americans shun dog, rat, and horse meat, all of which are prized elsewhere, but welcome beef, which Hindus wouldn't think of eating.

Body chemistry also influences taste preferences. When feeling tense or depressed, do you crave sweet or starchy carbohydrate-laden foods? Carbohydrates help boost levels of the neurotransmitter serotonin, which has calming effects. Given a drug that similarly increases serotonin, carbohydrate cravers lose their cravings. This suggests that stress-related cravings might be treatable by providing food substitutes that mimic biochemical effects (Hall, 1987).

The Brain and Set Point

Low blood glucose is a source of hunger. But you do not consciously feel your blood chemistry. Rather, the brain monitors information on your body's internal state. Signals from the stomach, the intestines, and the liver (indicating whether glucose is being deposited or withdrawn) all signal the brain to motivate eating or not. But where in the brain are these messages integrated?

glucose The form of sugar that circulates in the blood and provides the major source of energy for body tissues. When its level is low, we feel hunger.

insulin A hormone that, among its effects, helps body tissues convert blood glucose into stored fat. When its level in the body is high, we feel hunger.

set point The point at which an individual's "weight thermostat" is set. When the body falls below this weight, an increase in hunger and a lowered metabolic rate act to restore the lost weight.

metabolic rate The body's rate of energy expenditure at rest.

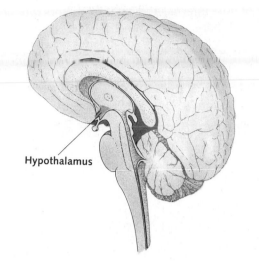

Figure 9–3 As we saw in Chapter 2, the hypothalamus performs various body maintenance functions, including control of hunger. Blood vessels supply the hypothalamus, enabling it to respond to our current blood chemistry as well as to incoming neural information about the body's state.

Destroying the lower middle area of the hypothalamus raised this rodent's set point, causing its weight to triple.

During the 1940s and 1950s, researchers located hunger controls within the hypothalamus, a small but complex neural traffic intersection buried deep in the brain (Figure 9–3).

Actually, there are two distinct hypothalamic centers that help control eating. Activity along the sides of the hypothalamus brings on hunger. When electrically stimulated there, a well-fed animal will begin to eat; when the area is destroyed, even a starving animal has no interest in food. Activity in the lower middle area of the hypothalamus depresses hunger. Stimulate this area and an animal will stop eating; destroy it and the animal's stomach and intestines will process food more rapidly, causing it to eat more often and to become grossly fat (Duggan & Booth, 1986; Hoebel & Teitelbaum, 1966).

How do these complementary areas of the hypothalamus work? One theory is that they influence how much glucose is being converted to fat. Another theory is that manipulating them alters the body's "weight thermostat," which predisposes us to keep our body at a particular weight level, called its **set point** (Keesey & Corbett, 1983). When semistarved rats fall below their normal weight, biological pressures act to restore the lost weight: Hunger increases and energy expenditure decreases. If body weight rises—as happens when rats are force-fed—hunger decreases and energy expenditure increases. This stable weight toward which semistarved and overstuffed rats return is their set point. Some researchers believe that slow, sustained changes in body weight can, however, alter one's set point.

Despite the day-to-day variations in our eating, our bodies are astonishingly good at regulating our weight, much better than we could be through conscious efforts to control food intake precisely. Over the next 40 years you will eat about 20 tons of food. If during those years you daily eat just .01 ounce more than required for your energy needs, you will gain 24 pounds (Martin & others, 1991). The body automatically maintains a remarkable balance of energy intake and expenditure.

Our bodies regulate weight much as rats' bodies do—through the control of food intake and energy output. If our body weight rises above our set point, we tend not to feel so hungry; if our weight drops below, we tend to eat more. To maintain its set-point weight, the body also adjusts its **metabolic rate**—its resting rate of energy expenditure. By the end of their 24 weeks of semistarvation, the subjects in the World War II experiment had stabilized at three-quarters of their normal weight—while eating half what they previously did. The stabilization resulted from reduced energy expenditure, achieved partly by physical lethargy and partly by a 29 percent drop in their resting metabolic rate.

External Incentives and Hunger

Our eagerness to eat is both pushed by our physical state—our body chemistry and hypothalamic activity—and pulled by external stimuli. Like Pavlov's dogs, people learn to salivate in anticipation of appealing foods. When food is abundant, those who are especially responsive to external food stimuli tend to gain the most weight.

Consider the 9- to 15-year-old girls studied by Judith Rodin and Joyce Slochower (1976) at an 8-week summer camp. During the first week of camp, some girls could not resist munching readily visible M&Ms even after a full meal. Such people, whose eating is triggered more by the presence of food than by internal factors, are called *externals*. In the 7 weeks that followed, the "external" girls gained the most weight.

THE EARS HEAR THE CAN OPENER..

RIGHT AWAY THE STOMACH KNOWS THAT SUPPER IS COMING..

HOW DO THE EARS TELL THE STOMACH?

I'VE NEVER BEEN ABLE TO FIGURE THAT OUT..

Drawing by Charles Schultz; © 1989 United Features Syndicate, Inc. Reprinted by permission of UFS, Inc.

Preview Question

4. What factors predispose some people to become and remain obese?

One can weigh more than normal—due to an athletic muscle and bone mass—and not be even slightly obese.

obesity   A surplus of body fat that causes one to be 20 percent or more overweight.

anorexia nervosa   An eating disorder in which a normal-weight person (usually an adolescent female) diets to become significantly underweight (15 percent or more), yet, still feeling fat, continues to starve.

bulimia nervosa   An eating disorder characterized by private, "binge-purge" episodes of overeating, usually of highly caloric foods, followed by vomiting or laxative use.

In a delicious demonstration of how internal and external factors interact, Rodin (1984) invited people to her laboratory for lunch after they went 18 hours without food. While blood samples were being taken, a large, juicy steak was wheeled in, crackling as it finished grilling. As the hungry subjects sat watching, hearing, and smelling the soon-to-be-eaten steak, Rodin monitored their rising blood insulin levels and their accompanying feelings of hunger. When stimulated by the sight, sound, and aroma of the steak, "externals" had the greatest insulin/hunger response. This illustrates how our psychological experience of an external incentive (the steak) can affect our internal physiological state.

Obesity and Weight Control

As Keys' semistarvation experiment demonstrated, caloric intake influences weight. Yet there is more to weight than calories eaten—otherwise, why do some people gain while others who eat the same amount do not? Why do so few overweight people win the battle of the bulge? And what hope is there for the one-quarter of Americans who, according to the National Center for Health Statistics (1985), are **obese**—with surplus body fat causing them to be 20 percent or more over their optimum body weight?

First, the good news about fat. Fat is an ideal form of stored energy that provides the body with a high caloric fuel reserve to carry it through periods when food is scarce—a common occurrence in the feast-or-famine existence of our prehistoric ancestors. Eating three meals every day is a relatively recent phenomenon and a luxury hundreds of millions of people still do not enjoy. In circumstances of alternating feast and famine, overeating and storing the excess as fat is adaptive; it prepares the body to withstand periods of starvation. This may explain why in most developing societies today, as in Europe in earlier centuries, obesity is a sign of affluence and status (Sobal & Stunkard, 1989).

The bad news is that in those parts of the world where food and sweets are now abundantly available, the adaptive tendency to store fat has become maladaptive. Being slightly overweight poses no health risks. But the National Institutes of Health reports that genuine obesity increases the risk of diabetes, high blood pressure and heart disease, gallstones, arthritis, and certain types of cancer (Kolata, 1985). This is more true for apple-shaped people who carry their weight in pot bellies than for pear-shaped people with ample hips and thighs (Greenwood, 1989).

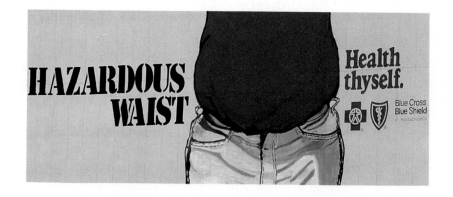

HAZARDOUS WAIST

Health thyself.

Blue Cross Blue Shield

Close-Up: Eating Disorders

Psychological influences on eating behavior are strikingly evident in those who suffer eating disorders. Consider two cases:

Mary is a 5' 3" 15-year-old who, having reached 100 pounds, decided she needed to lose weight to enhance her attractiveness. After gradually reducing her food intake to a few vegetables a day and then adding a vigorous exercise program, she now weighs a mere 80 pounds. Yet she still feels "fat" and plans to continue dieting. Mary has been having difficulty sleeping, has at times been depressed, and no longer has regular menstrual periods. She is socially inactive and seldom dates, but she is very successful academically. Mary does not regard herself as ill or needing treatment.

Alice is a 5' 9", 160-pound 17-year-old who says she has always been a little chubby. For the last 5 years, she has often eaten in binges followed by vomiting. She will eat a quart of ice cream or an entire pie and then, to control her weight, make herself vomit in secret. Alice wants to date, but doesn't because she is ashamed of her looks. She has at times taken diet pills to try to lose weight.

Mary is diagnosed as having **anorexia nervosa**—a disorder in which a person becomes significantly underweight (typically, 15 percent or more) yet feels fat and fears becoming obese. Even when emaciated, the person continues to limit food intake. The disorder usually develops in adolescence, 9 times out of 10 in females.

Alice's condition, which is more common, is **bulimia nervosa**—a disorder characterized by repeated "binge-purge" episodes of overeating followed by vomiting or laxative use. Bulimia patients eat as some alcoholics drink—not steadily nor in moderation, but in spurts, sometimes under the influence of friends who also are binging (Crandall, 1988). Most binge-purge eaters are women in their late teens or twenties. Like those with anorexia, they are preoccupied with food, fearful of becoming overweight, and depressed or anxious (Hinz & Williamson, 1987). The depression and shame are felt most keenly during and following binges. About half of those with anorexia also display the binge-purge-depression symptoms of bulimia. But most bulimics fluctuate within or above normal weight ranges, which makes the condition easy to hide.

Researchers report that the families of bulimia patients have a higher than usual incidence of alcoholism, obesity, and depression. Anorexia patients often come from families that are high-achieving and protective (Yates, 1989, 1990). Mothers of girls with eating disorders are *themselves* often focused on their own, and their daughter's, weight and appearance (Pike & Rodin, 1991).

Biology also may influence susceptibility to eating disorders. When one twin has bulimia, the chances are much greater that the other twin will share the disorder if they are identical rather than fraternal twins (Fichter & Noegel, 1990). People with eating disorders may also have abnormal neurotransmitter supplies that put them at risk for anxiety or depression (Fava & others, 1989).

There is, however, a cultural explanation for the fact that anorexia and bulimia occur mostly in women and mostly in weight-conscious cultures. Anorexia nervosa always begins as a weight-loss diet, and the self-induced vomiting of bulimics nearly always begins after a dieter has broken diet restrictions and gorged. Although ideals of beauty have varied over the centuries, women in every era have struggled to make their bodies conform to the ideal of their day. Thus, the "sickness" of today's eating disorders lies not just within the victims but also within their weight-obsessed culture—a culture that says, in countless ways, "Fat is bad," that motivates millions of women to be "always dieting," and that encourages eating binges by pressuring women to live in a constant state of semistarvation. As obesity researchers Susan Wooley and Orland Wooley (1983) noted, "an increasingly stringent cultural standard of thinness for women has been accompanied by a steadily increasing incidence of serious eating disorders in women."

Singer Karen Carpenter's death of cardiac arrest at age 32 was believed related to her long struggle with anorexia nervosa.

Obesity is not just a threat to physical health. Being perceived as obese can affect how you are treated and how you feel about yourself. Many people think fat people are gluttons. They see obesity as a matter of choice or as a reflection of a personality problem (a maladjusted way of reducing anxiety, dealing with guilt, or gratifying an "oral fixation"). If being obese signifies either a lack of self-discipline or a personality problem, then who would want to hire, date, or associate with such people? And if obese people believe such things about themselves, how could they feel anything but unworthy and undesirable?

The Physiology of Obesity

The arithmetic of weight gain is simple: People get fat by consuming more calories than they expend, and the energy equivalent of a pound of fat is 3500 calories. Therefore, dieters have been told for years that they will lose a pound for every 3500-calorie reduction in their diet. Surprise: This conclusion turns out to be false. To see why, we must examine the physiology of fat.

Fat Cells   The immediate determinants of body fat are the size and number of fat cells. A typical adult has about 30 billion of these miniature fuel tanks, about half of which lie near the skin's surface. A fat cell can vary from relatively empty, like a deflated balloon, to overly full. In the obese, fat cells may swell to two or three times their normal size and then divide. Once the number of fat cells increases—due to genetic predisposition, early childhood eating patterns, or adult overeating—it never decreases. On a diet, fat cells may shrink, but they do not disappear (Sjöstrum, 1980).

The unyielding nature of our fat cells is but one way in which, once we become fat, our bodies maintain fat. Another way is that fat tissue has a low metabolic (energy expenditure) rate. Compared with other tissue, fat takes less food energy to maintain. Thus, once we become fat, we require less food to maintain our weight than we did to attain it.

Set Points and Metabolism   Many scientists believe there is another reason why most obese people find it so difficult to lose weight permanently. Their bodies' weight "thermostats" are set to maintain a higher than average set-point weight. When weight drops below the set point, hunger increases and metabolism decreases.

As many a dieter can testify, the drop in resting metabolic rate can be particularly frustrating. After the rapid weight losses that occur during the initial 3 weeks or so of a rigorous diet, further weight loss comes slowly. In one experiment (Bray, 1969), obese patients whose daily food intake was reduced from 3500 to 450 calories lost only 6 percent of their weight—partly because their metabolic rates dropped 15 percent (Figure 9–4). Thus, the body adapts to starvation by burning off fewer calories, and to extra calories by burning off more. That is why reducing your food intake by 3500 calories may not reduce your weight by 1 pound. And that is why when a diet ends and the body is still conserving energy, amounts of food that only maintained weight before the diet may now increase it.

Individual differences in resting metabolism explain why—contrary to the stereotype of the overweight glutton—it is possible for two people of the same height, age, and activity level to maintain the same weight, even if one of them eats *twice* what the other does. Or why it is possible for a person to eat less than another similarly active person, yet weigh more (Rose & Williams, 1961).

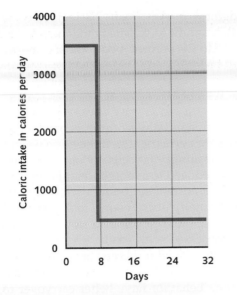

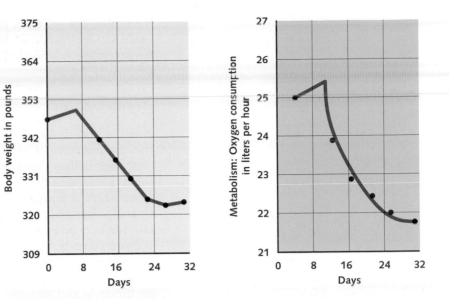

Figure 9–4 The effects of a severe diet on obese patients' body weight and metabolism. After 7 days on a 3500-calorie diet, six obese patients were given only 450 calories a day for the next 24 days. Body weight declined only 6 percent and then leveled off, because metabolism dropped 15 percent. (From Bray, 1969.)

The Barbie fashion doll's unrealistic proportions: 36-18-33 (*Life*, 1991).

The female ideal of 1637 was a rounded contrast to today's thin fashion models. There was biological wisdom in this: A plump woman stored more of the energy and nutrients needed to nourish a fetus and nurse an infant through a famine. However, to many people today, thinness connotes fitness, vitality, and self-control. Naomi Wolf (1991) reports that American models of a generation ago weighed 8 percent less than the average woman; today they weigh 23 percent less—which makes them thinner than 95 percent of women.

The Genetic Factor   Studies of adoptees and twins reveal a genetic influence on body weight. The body fat of adopted people correlates with that of their biological parents, not with that of their adoptive parents (Price, 1987). Brought together in a laboratory and fed an extra 1000 calories a day for 14 weeks, some identical twin pairs gained considerable weight and others didn't (C. Bouchard & others, 1990). If one of an identical twin pair gained extra fat, the other twin responded similarly. Moreover, identical twins have closely similar weights, even if reared apart (Eckert & others, 1987). Being overweight is therefore *not* simply a matter of scarfing too many hot fudge sundaes. And losing weight is not simply a matter of mind over platter.

Genes aren't the whole story, however. Gender and culture play a role in obesity, as they do in eating disorders. Weight resemblance is somewhat less among identical twin women than men. And diet or exercise rather than genes must explain why obesity is six times more common among lower-class than upper-class women, more common among Americans than Japanese and Europeans, and more common among Americans today than in 1900.

Ironically, the growing pudginess of Americans has coincided with an increasing idealization of the thin and fit look. Most models and actresses have hardly more than half the 22 to 26 percent body fat of a normal woman (Brownell, 1991).

Losing Weight

Perhaps you shake your head in sympathy with obese people: Slim chance they (or we) have of losing weight permanently. If they lose weight on a diet, their metabolism slows and their hungry fat cells cry out "Feed me!" Indeed, the condition of a dieter's body reduced to average weight is much like that of a semistarved body. Held under normal set point, each body "thinks" it is starving. Having lost weight, formerly obese people look "normal," but their fat cells may be abnormally small, their metabolism slow, and, like the semi-starved subjects, their minds obsessed with food.

All this explains why most people who succeed on a weight loss program eventually gain it nearly all back (Wing & Jeffery, 1979). Programs that modify life-style and ongoing eating behavior have better carryover to post-diet weight management. However, when cultural ideals of slimness collide with hunger, hunger usually wins. Most commercial weight loss programs can justifiably proclaim that they help people lose weight, *temporarily*. For most people, however, the only long-term result is a thinner wallet.

Nonetheless, the battle of the bulge rages as intensely as ever, especially in North America, where weight concern and dieting are a greater preoccupation than in, say, Australia or Third World countries (Rothblum, 1990; Tiggemann & Rothblum, 1988). Americans spend $33 billion a year trying to lose weight (Scanlan, 1990). In a 1991 poll of adult Americans, 32 percent of men and 44 percent of women said they were trying to lose weight (Castro, 1991). The gender difference is wider for teenagers: 23 percent of boys and 56 percent of girls have dieted (Gallup Organization, 1988). With fat cells, set points, metabolism, and genetic factors all tirelessly conspiring to make losing weight a big problem, what advice can we offer to those who wish to shed excess pounds?

We should first advise assessing the costs. Maintaining weight loss will be difficult. Some researchers believe that the more weight fluctuates from going on and off a diet, the more quickly the body switches on its energy-saving metabolic slowdown with each new diet. Kelly Brownell and his associates (1986) confirmed this effect of yo-yo dieting by making rats obese, putting them on a diet, and then repeating the cycle of weight gain and loss. On the first diet, the rats lost their excess weight in 21 days and took 46 days to regain it. The second time, eating precisely the same amount of food, they took 46 days to lose the weight and 24 days to regain it.

It's as if the body learns from previous diets how to defend its set-point weight, thereby protecting itself from what it interprets as the threat of starvation. (Weight management is unlike love: 'Tis *not* better to have gained and lost than never to have gained at all.) So rather than following the principle of "If at first you don't succeed, try, try again," a dieter's motto should be, "Get it right the first time." Begin a diet only if you feel motivated and self-disciplined enough to restrict your eating permanently. For most people, permanent weight loss requires a lifelong change in eating habits combined with increased exercise. In fact, sustained exercise can be a weapon against the body's normal metabolic slowdown when dieting. Exercise during and after dieting is one of the few predictors of successful long-term weight loss (Brownell, 1989). If you want to lose weight, here are some other things to keep in mind.

Janet Polivy and Peter Herman (1987) believe that widespread, chronic dieting among basically normal-weight girls and women represents the seeds of eating disorder on a massive scale.

Helpful Hints for Dieters

1. *Minimize exposure to tempting food cues.* Keep tempting foods out of the house or out of sight, and go to the supermarket only on a full stomach.

2. *Take steps to boost your metabolism.* Sustained exercise, such as brisk walking, running, and swimming, not only empties fat cells, builds muscle, and makes you feel better, it can also temporarily speed up metabolism (Kolata, 1987; Thompson & others, 1982).

3. *Modify both your metabolic rate and your hunger by changing the food you eat.* Findings suggest that complex carbohydrates (pasta, grains, potatoes) increase metabolism and are less readily converted to body fat than the same calories eaten as fats (Rodin, 1979, 1985). Complex carbohydrates and fructose (in fruits) stimulate less of the hunger-producing insulin jump than refined sugar (sucrose).

4. *Don't starve all day and eat one big meal at night.* This eating pattern, common among overweight people, slows metabolism.

5. *Beware of the binge.* Among people who consciously restrain their eating, drinking alcohol or feeling anxious or depressed can unleash the urge to eat (Herman & Polivy, 1980). Once the diet is broken, binging often follows (Polivy & Herman, 1985, 1987): A lapse becomes a collapse.

6. *Set realistic goals.* Targeting an ambitiously low weight usually dooms a dieter to eventual defeat, but a realistic objective—such as losing a pound a week—can promote effort and persistence.

Finally, we all do well to note what researchers have *not* identified as causes of obesity: guilt, hostility, oral fixation, or any similar personality maladjustment. Nor is obesity simply a matter of a lack of willpower. If obese people are more likely to binge when under stress or after breaking their diets, this may be more a consequence of their constant dieting than a cause of their obesity. "Fat is not a four-letter word," proclaims the National Association to Aid Fat Americans. Although this motto disregards the health risks linked with significant obesity, it does convey a valid point: It may be better to make peace with one's body—accept oneself as a little chubby—than to diet and binge and feel continually out of control and guilty.

In one study of 6671 12- to 17-year-olds, obesity was more common among those who watched the most television. Of course, overweight people may avoid activity, preferring to sit and watch TV. But the association between TV watching and obesity remained when many other factors were controlled, suggesting that the inactivity of TV watching contributes to obesity. (From Dietz & Gortmaker, 1985.)

During a meal of sandwich snacks, the average person swallows every 14 seconds, and chews 19 times per swallow (Stellar, 1985). Ironically, the hungrier people are and the better a food tastes, the *less* time they spend chewing and tasting it.

Rehearse It

5. The hypothalamus, a structure deep within the brain, controls feelings of hunger and satiety, in part by evaluating changes in blood chemistry. Hunger occurs in response to high blood insulin and
a. high blood glucose.
b. low blood glucose.
c. decreased energy expenditure.
d. stimulation of any part of the hypothalamus.

6. Our bodies tend to stay at a particular weight, or set point. Changes in the metabolic rate help keep us at this weight. For example, when we are falling below the set point, we feel hungry (and eat) and lethargic (and reduce our energy expenditure). The operation of this "weight thermostat" is an example of
a. homeostasis.
b. an eating disorder.
c. individual learning.
d. binge-purge episodes.

7. The *worst* life-style change dieters could make would be to:
a. boost their metabolism by regular, vigorous exercise.
b. eat almost no breakfast or lunch in order to be able to enjoy a normal dinner.
c. reduce their consumption of fats.
d. increase the ratio of complex carbohydrates (starches) to simple carbohydrates (sugars) in their diets.

Preview Question

5. How does human sexual behavior vary?

"I lose my respect for the man who can make the mystery of sex the subject of a coarse jest, yet, when you speak earnestly and seriously on the subject, is silent."

Henry David Thoreau
Journal, 1852

Kinsey, shown here giving one of many interviews, did not begin his interviews with sexually explicit questions. Rather, he first helped people feel at ease by asking non-threatening questions about family background, health, and education.

"The psychologist-asker averages up all the lies . . . and everybody in America feels inferior."

Psychologist Sol Gordon (1923–   )

Sexual Motivation

Sex is part of life. Had this not been so for all your ancestors, you would not be reading this book. Sexual motivation is nature's clever way of making people procreate, thus enabling our species to survive. When two people feel attracted, they hardly stop to think of themselves as guided by their genes. Indeed, sexual motivation also satisfies social needs for belongingness and love. To understand this complex motive, we must consider a wide array of human behaviors.

Describing Sexual Behavior

Unable to answer his students' questions about people's sexual practices, Indiana University biologist Alfred Kinsey and his colleagues (1948, 1953) set out to find some answers. Kinsey's confidential interviews with more than 5000 men and nearly 6000 women made history. Social scientists were quick to point out what Kinsey readily acknowledged—that his nonrandom sample contained an overrepresentation of well-educated, white, urban residents of Indiana, Illinois, and several Eastern states. Nevertheless, his statistics-laden volumes became bestsellers. Here readers learned the then surprising news that, among Kinsey's sample at least, most men and nearly half of the women reported having had premarital sexual intercourse, a majority of women and virtually all men reported that they masturbated, and women who reported masturbating to orgasm before marriage seldom had difficulties experiencing orgasm after marriage. One could also find evidence that sexual behavior is enormously varied. For example, Kinsey found some men and women who said they had never had an orgasm, and others who said they had four or more a day. For those who evaluate themselves by comparisons with others, Kinsey's findings—and others showing wide variations in "normal" sexual behavior around the world—are reassuring. Given the range of sex drives and the variety of sexual behaviors, your own sexual interests probably fall well within the range of "normal."

Because we do not know whether Kinsey's sample accurately represented the nation's sexual practices in the 1940s, let alone those of today, it can be misleading to report his precise findings. But Kinsey's surveys were surely less misleading than some of the haphazard sexual surveys that have been reported more recently in the popular press. Recall from Chapter 1 that when popular "sex reports" begin with a biased sample of people (such as subscribers to selected magazines) and receive replies from only 3 percent of this nonrandom sample, there is good reason to doubt the generality of their findings.

Despite variations in sexual frequency, positions, and fantasies, monogamy prevails in American culture. Two new surveys of randomly sampled adults counter the media image of rampant marital infidelity—an image reinforced by media psychologist Joyce Brothers' (1990) pronouncement that two-thirds of married men and half of married women have affairs. Actually, in a recent Gallup survey 9 in 10 married adults claimed to have had sex only with their spouse during their present marriage (Greeley, 1991). When the National Opinion Research Center added an anonymous, self-administered, return envelope sex questionnaire to their annual survey, they found that during the past year only "1.5 percent of married people [had] a sex partner other than their spouse" (Smith, 1990). Faithful attractions greatly outnumbered fatal attractions. And disapproval of extramarital sex, at 91 percent, runs as high as ever among adult Americans (Greeley, 1991).

sexual response cycle The four stages of sexual responding described by Masters and Johnson—excitement, plateau, orgasm, and resolution.

Eager to understand why the AIDS (Acquired Immune Deficiency Syndrome) virus has spread more among some groups than others, researchers undertook new sex surveys at the beginning of this decade. One survey is interviewing a random sample of 20,000 people in Britain (Holden, 1989). The World Health Organization is conducting the first-ever global survey of human sexuality, based on interviews with some 2000 people in each of 20 countries (Carballo & others, 1989). Researchers hope that results from such surveys, including perhaps a much-debated, government-sponsored U.S. sex survey, will help us better understand the behaviors that spread AIDS and other sexually transmitted diseases (STDs).

The Physiology of Sex

As the pleasure we take in eating ensures that our bodies are nourished, the pleasure of sex ensures our species' survival. Research on the biology of sexual motivation concentrates both on internal and external stimuli.

Preview Question

6. What are the biological characteristics of sexual motivation in humans?

The Sexual Response Cycle

The headlines created by Kinsey's 1940s surveys reappeared after some 1960s studies in which scientists recorded the physiological responses of volunteers who masturbated or had intercourse. With the help of 382 female and 312 male volunteers—a somewhat atypical sample, consisting only of people able and willing to display arousal and orgasm while being observed in a laboratory—gynecologist-obstetrician William Masters and his collaborator Virginia Johnson (1966) monitored or filmed more than 10,000 sexual "cycles."

Their description of the **sexual response cycle** identified four stages, similar in men and women (Figure 9–5). During the initial *excitement* phase, the genital areas become engorged with blood, causing the man's penis to become partially erect and the woman's clitoris to swell and the inner lips covering her vagina to open up. Her vagina also expands and secretes lubricant, and her breasts and nipples may enlarge.

Figure 9–5 The sexual response cycle in men and in women. (Adapted from Masters & Johnson, 1966.)

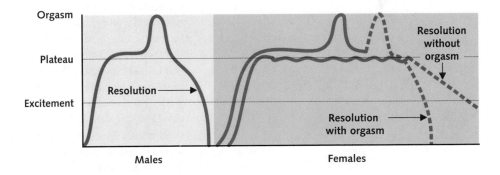

In the *plateau* phase, excitement peaks as breathing, pulse, and blood pressure rates continue to increase. The penis becomes fully engorged and some fluid (frequently containing enough live sperm to enable conception) may appear at the tip of the penis. Vaginal secretion continues to increase, the clitoris retracts, and orgasm feels imminent.

During *orgasm*, Masters and Johnson observed muscle contractions all over the body and further increases in breathing, pulse, and blood pressure

refractory period A resting period after orgasm during which a man cannot achieve another orgasm.

estrogen A sex hormone, secreted in greater amounts by females than males. In nonhuman female mammals, the estrogen peak during ovulation promotes sexual receptivity.

Preview Question

7. What role do hormones play in human sexuality?

Although both males and females produce testosterone, the additional testosterone in males stimulates the growth of male sex characteristics (see Chapter 3) and, especially in nonhuman animals, influences sexual arousal.

rates. The woman's physical reactions facilitate conception, by helping to force all the semen from the penis, positioning the uterus to receive sperm, and helping draw the sperm further inward (Sarnoff & Sarnoff, 1989). In the excitement of the moment, men and women are hardly aware of all this, but are more aware of their rhythmic genital contractions that create a pleasurable feeling of sexual release. The feeling apparently is much the same for both sexes. In one study, a panel of experts could not reliably distinguish between descriptions of orgasm written by men and those written by women (Vance & Wagner, 1976).

After orgasm, the body gradually returns to its unaroused state as the engorged genital blood vessels release their accumulated blood—relatively quickly if orgasm has occurred, relatively slowly otherwise. (It is like the nasal tickle that goes away rapidly if you have sneezed, slowly otherwise.) During this *resolution* phase, the male enters a **refractory period,** lasting from a few minutes to a day or more, during which he is incapable of another orgasm. A female does not have so lengthy a refractory period, which may make it possible for her to have another orgasm if restimulated during or soon after resolution.

Hormones and Sexual Behavior

Sex hormones have two effects: They direct the development of male and female sex characteristics, and (especially in nonhuman animals) they activate sexual behavior. In most mammals, nature neatly synchronizes sex with fertility. The female becomes sexually receptive ("in heat") when production of the female sex hormone **estrogen** peaks at ovulation. (In experiments, researchers simulate this by injecting female animals with estrogen.) Male hormone levels are more constant, and researchers cannot so easily manipulate the sexual behavior of male animals by hormone treatments (Feder, 1984). Nevertheless, castrated male rats—having lost their testes, which manufacture the male sex hormone *testosterone*—gradually lose much of their interest in receptive females, and gradually regain it if injected with testosterone.

Hormones don't so neatly control human sexual behavior. Women's sexual desire is only slightly higher at ovulation (Harvey, 1987) and is actually more responsive to testosterone than to estrogen (Kaplan, 1979; Meyer-Bahlburg, 1980). Normal fluctuations in men's testosterone levels, from man to man and hour to hour, have little effect on sexual drive (Byrne, 1982). Indeed, such fluctuations are partly a response to sexual stimulation. When James Dabbs and his colleagues (1987) had male collegians converse separately with a male and a female student, the men's testosterone levels rose with the social arousal, but especially after talking with the female. Like the effect of the crackling steak on insulin level, sexual arousal can be a cause as well as a consequence of increased testosterone levels.

Although normal short-term hormonal changes have little effect on desire, large hormone shifts have a bigger effect over the life span. A person's interest in dating and sexual stimulation usually increases with the pubertal surge in sex hormones. If the hormonal surge is precluded—as happened with prepubertal boys who were castrated during the 1700s and 1800s to preserve their soprano voices for Italian opera—the normal development of sex characteristics and sexual desire does not occur (Peschel & Peschel, 1987). Among adult men who suffer castration, sex drive typically falls along with declining testosterone levels (Hucker & Bain, 1990). Likewise, male sex offenders lose much of their sexual urge when voluntarily taking Depo-Provera, a drug that reduces testosterone levels to that of a prepubertal boy

(Money & others, 1983). And in later life, the typ... declines as sex hormone levels decline.

Hormones influence sexual arousal via th... monitors variations in blood hormone levels ... neural circuits. In rats, destroying a key area ... sexual activity; stimulating this area, either elec... minute quantities of hormones, may activate ...

To summarize, we might compare human... tosterone, to the fuel in a car. Lacking fuel, the car will... level is minimally adequate, adding more fuel to the gas tank won't change how the car runs. The analogy is imperfect, because the interaction between hormones and sexual motivation is two-way. However, the analogy correctly suggests that biology is a necessary but not sufficient explanation of human sexual behavior. The biological fuel is essential, but so are the psychological stimuli that turn on the engine and shift it into high gear.

The Psychology of Sex

We have seen similarities between hunger and sexual motivation. Both depend on internal biological factors and are also influenced by external stimuli, including gender and culture.

External Stimuli

Many studies confirm that men become aroused when they see, hear, or read erotic material. More surprising to many people (because sexually explicit materials are sold mostly to men) is that most women—at least the less inhibited women who volunteer to participate in such studies (Morokoff, 1986)—report similar arousal to the same stimuli (Harrell & Stolp, 1985).

In one such study, psychologist Julia Heiman (1975) attached instruments that detected arousal (changes in the penis circumference or in vaginal color) to sexually experienced university volunteers. Then the students listened to either a sexually explicit erotic tape, a romantic tape (of a couple expressing love without physical contact), a combined erotic-romantic tape, or a neutral control tape. Which do you suppose the men were most aroused by? And the women? Both the men and the women found the tape of explicit sex most arousing, especially when a woman initiated the sex and when the depiction centered on her responses.

People may find such arousal either pleasing or disturbing. (Those who find it disturbing often limit their exposure to such materials, just as those wishing to control hunger limit their exposure to tempting cues.) Some sexually explicit materials can have additional effects that are not so harmless. First, those depicting women being sexually coerced—and enjoying it—tend to increase viewers' acceptance of the false idea that women enjoy rape and to increase male viewers' willingness to hurt women (see page 463). Second, images of sexually attractive people may lead viewers to devalue their partners and relationships. Several studies (Gutierres & others, 1985; Kenrick & Gutierres, 1980; Weaver & others, 1984) found that after male collegians view TV or magazine depictions of sexually attractive women, they suddenly find an average woman, or their own girlfriends or wives, less attractive. Viewing X-rated sex films similarly tends to diminish people's satisfaction with their sexual partner (Zillmann, 1989). Some sex researchers fear that reading or viewing erotica may create expectations that few men and women can hope to live up to.

Preview Question

8. How do internal and external factors interact to stimulate sexual arousal?

"Ours is a society which stimulates interest in sex by constant titillation. . . . Cinema, television, and all the formidable array of our marketing technology project our very effective forms of titillation and our prejudices about man as a sexy animal into every corner of every hovel in the world."

Germaine Greer (1984)

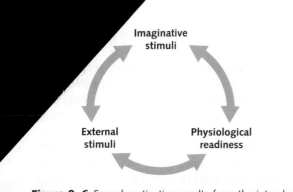

Imaginative
stimuli

External
stimuli

Physiological
readiness

Figure 9–6 Sexual motivation results from the interplay of biology, environment, and imagination. (From Byrne, 1982.)

"There is no difference between being raped and being run over by a truck except that afterward men ask if you enjoyed it."

Marge Piercy
Rape Poem, 1976

sexual dysfunction   A problem that consistently impairs sexual arousal or functioning.

sexual orientation   An enduring sexual attraction toward members of either one's own sex (homosexual orientation) or the other sex (heterosexual orientation).

Imaginative Stimuli

Sexual motivation arises from the interplay of biology and environment. But the stimuli inside our heads—our imaginations—also influence sexual arousal and desire (Figure 9–6). The brain, it has been said, is our most significant sex organ. People who, because of a spinal cord injury, have no genital sensation, can still feel sexual desire (Willmuth, 1987). Consider, too, the erotic potential of dreams. As noted on page 153, genital arousal accompanies all types of dreams, including those that have no sexual content—the vast majority. But in nearly all men and some 40 percent of women (Wells, 1986), dreams sometimes do contain sexual imagery that leads to orgasm. In men, these nocturnal emissions ("wet dreams") are more likely when orgasm has not occurred recently.

Wide-awake people become sexually aroused not only by memories of prior sexual activities but also by fantasies. Fantasies need not correspond to actual behavior. In one survey of masturbation-related fantasies (Hunt, 1974), 19 percent of women and 10 percent of men reported imagining someone forcing them to have sex. Fantasy is not reality, however. To paraphrase Susan Brownmiller (1975), for women there's a big difference between fantasizing that Eddie Murphy or Tom Cruise just won't take no for an answer and having a stranger actually force himself on you. (See also page 463 for a discussion of the "rape myth.")

Sexual Dysfunctions and Therapy

Masters and Johnson sought not only to describe the human sexual response cycle but also to understand and treat the inability to complete it. **Sexual dysfunctions** are problems that consistently impair sexual functioning. Some involve sexual motivation, especially problems of sexual energy and arousability. Men, for example, may experience *premature ejaculation* (reaching orgasm before they or their partners wish) or *impotence* (the inability to have or maintain an erection). Women more often than men experience low sexual desire or *orgasmic dysfunction* (infrequently or never experiencing orgasm).

What causes such problems? The idea that personality disorders are to blame has been largely discounted. Men who experience premature ejaculation are similar, even in their sexual arousal patterns, to men who do not; they simply ejaculate at lower levels of sexual arousal—something that often occurs with young men who have had long periods of sexual abstinence (Spiess & others, 1984).

When Barbara Andersen (1983) reviewed research on the diagnosis and treatment of orgasmic dysfunction in women, she, too, could find no associated personality traits. Furthermore, she reported that treating orgasmic dysfunction through traditional psychotherapy (as though it were a disorder of personality) has been unsuccessful. On the other hand, she reported a nearly 100 percent success rate with a behavioral treatment that trains women to enjoy their bodies and to give themselves orgasms, with a vibrator if necessary. Some of these women can then generalize their new sexual responsiveness to interactions with their mates (LoPiccolo & Stock, 1986; Wakefield, 1987). Success has also been reported in training men to control their premature ejaculations by repeatedly stimulating the penis and then stopping stimulation (or even firmly squeezing the head of the penis) when the urge to ejaculate arises.

Sexual Orientation

Preview Question

9. What factors are involved in sexual orientation?

To motivate is to energize and direct behavior. So far, we have considered the energizing of sexual motivation but not its direction. We express the direction of our sexual interest in our **sexual orientation**—our enduring sexual attraction toward members of a particular sex. As far as we know, virtually all cultures in all times have been predominantly heterosexual (Bullough, 1990), although they vary in their attitudes toward homosexuality. Whether a culture condemns and punishes homosexuality or views it as an acceptable alternative, homosexuality survives and heterosexuality prevails.

Most homosexual people report that they first became aware of their sexual orientation during or shortly after puberty, but they typically do not think of themselves as gay or lesbian until nearer to or after age 20 (Garnets & Kimmel, 1990). How many people are exclusively homosexual? In both Europe and the United States, studies suggest about 4 percent of men and 1 percent of women (Ellis & Ames, 1987). Although the popular press often reports the proportion of homosexuals at 10 percent, a national survey sponsored by the Kinsey Institute in 1970 found that 1.4 percent of men reported having had homosexual relations "fairly often" and another 1.9 percent "occasionally" (Fay & others, 1989). Among sexually active Americans responding to the National Opinion Research Center's confidential survey, 1.6 percent of sexually active people reported having had homosexual contact during the past year (Smith, 1990). If we adjust this figure upward to include homosexuals who are sexually inactive, it roughly concurs with other findings of at least a 2 to 3 percent homosexuality rate (combining men and women).

Some consider themselves bisexual, but a study of 173 male bisexuals in San Francisco found their behavior to be mostly homosexual: 68 percent reported having had no female sex partners over a 6-month period, while only 14 percent had no male partners during that time (Winkelstein & others, 1987). In recent National Opinion Research Center surveys, active bisexual people were scarce—only one-third of one percent of respondents reported (in confidence) having both male and female sexual partners during the past year (Rogers & Turner, 1991). Many more adults report having had an isolated homosexual experience. And most people have occasional homosexual fantasies.

Although health experts find it helpful to know sexual behavior statistics, numbers don't decide issues of human rights. Similarly, it's helpful in manufacturing school desks to know what percent of people are left-handed. But whether left-handers are 3 percent or 10 percent of the population doesn't answer the moral question of whether lefties should enjoy equal rights.

What does it feel like to be homosexual in a heterosexual culture? One way for heterosexual people to understand is to imagine how they would feel if they were to be ostracized or fired for openly admitting or displaying their feelings toward someone of the other sex; if they were to overhear people making crude jokes about heterosexual people; if almost every movie, TV show, and advertisement portrayed (or implied) homosexuality; and if their family members were pleading with them to change their heterosexual lifestyle and to enter into a homosexual marriage.

Facing such reactions, homosexual people often struggle with their sexual orientation. At first, they may try to ignore or deny their desires, hoping they will go away; but they don't. Then they may try to change, through psychotherapy, willpower, or prayer. But the feelings typically persist, as do those of heterosexual people—who, similarly, are incapable of becoming homosexual.

Like heterosexuals, homosexual couples face joys and challenges as their relationship deepens.

The AIDS threat has prompted safer sex among homosexuals. Gay men, especially, report fewer sexual partners (Joseph & others, 1987; Winkelstein & others, 1987). Yet there remains a streak of unrealistic optimism, which explains why so many homosexual men still seldom use condoms (Baumann & Siegel, 1987; Fineberg, 1988). Grand Rapids, Michigan, artist Mark Heckman created a billboard—pasted with 2000 condoms—that people could not ignore—to focus attention on AIDS and one way to reduce exposure to the virus.

Eventually, homosexuals may accept their orientation—by electing celibacy (as do some heterosexuals); by engaging in promiscuous sex (a choice more commonly made by men than women); or by entering into a committed, long-term love relationship (a choice more often made by women than men) (Peplau, 1982; Weinberg & Williams, 1974). Compared with the years preceding the AIDS threat, gay men are now reporting fewer partners. One study of 5000 gay men found that between 1984 and 1986 the number saying they were celibate or monogamous rose from 14 to 39 percent (Fineberg, 1988).

Understanding Sexual Orientation

Sexual orientation in some ways is like handedness: Most people are one way, some the other. A few are ambidextrous. Regardless, the way one is endures. If our sexual orientation is indeed something we do not choose and cannot change, then how does a person move toward either a heterosexual or homosexual orientation? The consensus has emerged from hundreds of research studies on homosexual orientation (Storms 1983):

1. Homosexuality is not linked with problems in a child's relationships with parents, such as with a domineering mother and an ineffectual father, or a possessive mother and a hostile father.

2. Homosexuality does not involve a fear or hatred of the other sex.

3. Sexual orientation is not linked with levels of sex hormones currently in the blood.

4. Sexual victimization of children, by an adult homosexual or others, is not a factor in homosexual orientation.

Consider the findings of lengthy Kinsey Institute interviews with nearly 1000 homosexuals and 500 heterosexuals (Bell & others, 1981; Hammersmith, 1982). The investigators assessed nearly every imaginable psychological cause of homosexuality—parental relationships, childhood sexual experiences, peer relationships, dating experiences, even number of brothers and sisters. Their findings: Apart from homosexuals' somewhat greater nonconformity, the reported backgrounds of homosexuals and heterosexuals were similar.

So, what determines sexual orientation? One theory proposes that people develop erotic associations to their own sex if segregated with their sex at the time their sex drive matures (Storms, 1981). But even in a tribal culture where homosexual behavior is expected of all boys before marriage, heterosexuality prevails (Money, 1987). Another theory proposes the opposite: that people develop romantic attachments to those who are *different* from, and thus more fascinating than, the sex they associated with while growing up (Bell, 1982). But new research indicates that sexual orientation may be at least partly biological. The evidence suggests, first, a genetic influence. In one recent analysis of male homosexual twins, 52 percent of their identical twins and 22 percent of their fraternal twins were also homosexual (Bailey & Pillard, 1991a). That's the sort of pattern we expect to see when genes are having an influence.

The elevated rate of homosexual orientation in the fraternal twins might also result from their sharing the same prenatal environment. In animals and some exceptional human cases, sexual orientation has been altered by abnormal prenatal hormone conditions. Female sheep, for example, will show homosexual behavior if their pregnant mothers are injected with testosterone during a critical gestation period (Money, 1987). With humans, a critical period for the brain's neural-hormonal control system may exist between the middle of the second and fifth months after conception (Ellis & Ames, 1987). It seems that exposure to the hormone levels typically experienced by female fetuses during this time may predispose the person (whether female or male) to become attracted to males.

If genes and prenatal hormones affect sexual orientation, might we identify just how they influence brain development? While studying sections of the hypothalamus taken from deceased heterosexual and homosexual people, researcher Simon LeVay (1991) discovered one cell cluster that was much larger in heterosexual men than in women and homosexual men. During the ensuing media coverage, LeVay acknowledged that it's possible that sexual behavior patterns influence the brain's anatomy. But he believes it more likely that the brain anatomy influences sexual orientation. Future research should soon clarify cause and effect.

Should any combination of these biological influences—genes, prenatal hormones, brain anatomy—prove critical, it would explain why sexual orientation is so difficult to change. It might also lead to changed attitudes toward homosexuals. Most people hesitate to judge another for behaviors they attribute to causes beyond the person's control. As we might expect, those who believe that sexual orientation is uncontrollable express fewer negative attitudes toward homosexuals (Whitley, 1990). This belief is common among homosexual people, many of whom assume their sexual orientation to be biologically influenced (Furnham & Taylor, 1990).

Sex and Human Values

Questions of how we should act, what choices we should make, and what ends are desirable are questions of human values. Recognizing that values are both personal and cultural, most sex researchers and educators strive to keep their writings on sexuality value-free. As scientists and teachers, they aim for objectivity as they help us understand sexual behavior and what motivates it.

Can the study of sex be free of values? Should it be? Those who think not note that the very words we use to describe behavior often reflect our personal values. When sex researchers label sexually restrained individuals as "erotophobic" and as having "high sex guilt," they express their own values.

"Science is rapidly converging on the conclusion that sexual orientation is innate."

J. Michael Bailey and Richard C. Pillard (1991b)

"Were it not for delicately balanced combinations of genetic, neurological, hormonal, and environmental factors, largely occurring prior to birth, each and every one of us would be homosexual."

Lee Ellis and M. Ashley Ames (1987)

Preview Question

10. What roles do personal values play in sex research and sex education?

Whether we label sexual acts we do not practice as "perversions," "deviations," or part of an "alternative sexual life-style" depends on our attitudes toward the behaviors. Labels both describe and evaluate.

When information about sex is separated from the context of human values, some students may get the idea that sexual intercourse is merely recreational activity, or a biological act that is nothing more than "the depositing of seminal fluid, like squirting jam in a doughnut" (Greer, 1984). Diana Baumrind (1982), a University of California child-rearing expert, suspects that adolescents interpret sex education that pretends to be "value-free" as meaning that adults are neutral about adolescent sexual activity. She feels that such an implication is unfortunate, because "promiscuous recreational sex poses certain psychological, social, health, and moral problems that must be faced realistically."

On the other hand, researchers have found that teenagers who have had formal sex education are no more likely to engage in premarital sex than those who have not (Furstenberg & others, 1985; Zelnik & Kim, 1982). Moreover, consider the benefits of sex research and education. We enrich our lives by knowing ourselves, by realizing that others share our feelings, by understanding what is likely to please or displease our loved one. Witness the gradual crumbling of falsehoods about homosexuality. Witness the growing realization that some types of sexually explicit material can lead people to devalue or hurt others.

Perhaps we can agree that the knowledge provided by sex research is preferable to ignorance, yet also agree that researchers' values should be stated openly, enabling us to debate them and to reflect on our own values. We might also remember that although scientific research on sexual motivation has answered important questions, it does not aim to define the personal meaning of sex in our lives. One can know every available fact about sex— that the initial spasms of male and female orgasm come at 0.8-second intervals, that the female nipples expand 10 millimeters at the peak of sexual arousal, that systolic blood pressure rises some 60 points and the respiration rate to 40 breaths per minute—but fail to understand the human significance of sexual intimacy.

Surely one significance of sexual intimacy is its expression of our deeply social nature. Sex is a social as well as a biological act. Men and women can achieve orgasm alone. Yet most people find greater satisfaction in embracing their loved one. As philosopher Bertrand Russell noted in *Marriage and Morals* (1929), "People cannot fully satisfy their sexual instinct without love." Although the yearning for closeness was not part of our description of sexual motivation, sex is a life-uniting and love-renewing experience.

"Let us say with all possible emphasis that human sexuality is a very good thing. . . . It is tied in with and expressive of the urgent desire to love."

Norman Pittenger
Making Sexuality Human, 1970

For most adults, sexual intimacy is not only a biological motive but also a social one—a sharing of love.

Rehearse It

8. In the 1940s, Alfred Kinsey and his colleagues used questionnaires to investigate the sexual behavior of a large sample of men and women in the Midwest and eastern United States. An important discovery made by Kinsey was that
a. premarital sex has tapered off in the 1980s.
b. American teens become pregnant more frequently than teens in other industrialized countries.
c. the sexual response cycle is the same in men and women.
d. there were wide variations in sexual drive and behavior in their "normal" sample.

9. The sexual response cycle in men and women consists of four stages: excitement, plateau, orgasm, and resolution. The sexual response cycle was first clinically observed and described by

a. Alfred Kinsey and his colleagues.
b. William Masters and Virginia Johnson.
c. Walter Cannon.
d. Abraham Maslow.

10. Daily and monthly fluctuations of hormones do not greatly affect sexual desire in humans. Over the life span, however, hormonal changes are significant. The most striking effect of hormonal change on human sexual behavior is
a. the arousing effects of erotic materials.
b. the sharp rise in sexual interests at puberty.
c. the increase in a woman's sexual desire at the time of ovulation.
d. the gradual decrease in frequency of sexual intercourse in later life.

11. Sexual behavior is motivated by internal biological factors, by external stimuli, and by imaginative stimuli. An example of an external stimulus that might influence sexual behavior is

a. blood level of testosterone.
b. the experience of puberty.
c. a sexually explicit film.
d. an erotic fantasy or dream.

12. Sexual orientation refers to the direction of one's sexual interests. There is some evidence to support a "prenatal critical period" theory, which suggests that sexual orientation is significantly influenced by
a. sex hormone levels at puberty and adulthood.
b. sex hormone levels approximately 2 to 5 months after conception.
c. the presence of estrogen at any time in the life span.
d. interaction between mother, father, and newborn.

Preview Question

11. What are the nature and the origins of achievement motivation?

"If my mind can conceive it and my heart can believe it, I know I can achieve it."

Reverend Jesse Jackson
Speech at 1983 civil rights march
on Washington, D.C.

What is your greatest achievement to date? What is your greatest future ambition—to attain fame? Fortune? Creative accomplishment? Security? Love? Power? Wisdom? Spiritual wholeness?

achievement motivation   A desire for accomplishment: for mastery of things, people, or ideas; for attaining a high standard.

Achievement Motivation

The biological perspective on motivation—the idea that biological needs drive us to satisfy those needs—provides only a partial explanation of what energizes and directs our behavior. Sexual motivation has a social as well as a biological component. Moreover, there are motives that, unlike hunger and sex, seem not to satisfy any biological need. Millionaires may be motivated to make ever more money, movie stars to become ever more famous, politicians to achieve ever more power, daredevils to seek ever greater thrills. Such motives seem not to diminish when they are fed. The more we achieve, the more we may need to achieve.

Identifying Achievement Motivation

Think of two of your friends, one who strives to succeed by excelling at any task where evaluation is possible, and one who is less disciplined or driven. Psychologist Henry Murray (1938) defined the first person's high need for achievement, or **achievement motivation,** as a desire for significant accomplishment, for mastering skills or ideas, for control, and for rapidly attaining a high standard.

To study this motive, we first need a way to measure it. But how? Recall from the semistarvation studies that people driven by hunger begin to fantasize about food. Our sexual orientation is similarly reflected in our sexual fantasies. Do these examples suggest a way to assess a person's need to achieve?

Murray and investigators David McClelland and John Atkinson presumed that people's fantasies would reflect their achievement concerns. So they asked subjects to invent stories about ambiguous pictures. If, when shown the daydreaming boy in Figure 9–7, a subject commented that the boy was preoccupied with his pursuit of a goal, that he imagined himself performing a heroic act, or that he was feeling pride in some success, the story was scored as indicating achievement concerns. McClelland and Atkinson regarded people whose stories consistently included such themes as having a high need for achievement.

Would you expect people whose stories express a high need for achievement to prefer tasks that are easy, moderately challenging, or very difficult? People whose stories suggest low achievement motivation tend to choose either very easy or very difficult tasks, where failure is either unlikely or unembarrassing (Geen, 1984). Those whose stories express high achievement motivation tend to prefer moderately difficult tasks, where success is attainable yet attributable to their own skill and effort. In a ring toss game, for instance, they often stand at an intermediate distance from the stake; this allows them some successes, yet provides a suitable challenge. People with a strong need to achieve also are more likely to persist on a task when things get difficult (Cooper, 1983).

As you might expect from their persistence and eagerness for realistic challenge, people with high achievement motivation do achieve more. Compared with children of equal ability, they are more successful. One study of outstanding athletes, scholars, and artists found that all were highly motivated and self-disciplined, willing to dedicate hours every day to the pursuit of their goals (Bloom, 1985). These superstar achievers were distinguished not so much by their extraordinary natural talent as by their extraordinary daily discipline.

When achievement motivation increases, so does achievement. By training the businessmen of a village in India to think, talk, and act like achievement-motivated people, McClelland (1978) and his colleagues were able to boost the villagers' business successes. Compared with other businessmen from a comparable nearby town, those trained in achievement motivation started more new businesses and employed over twice as many new people during the ensuing 2 years.

Sources of Achievement Motivation

Why, despite similar potentials, does one person become more motivated to achieve than another? Highly motivated children often have parents who encourage their independence from an early age and praise and reward them for their successes (Teevan & McGhee, 1972). Such parents encourage their children to dress and feed themselves and to do well in school, and they express their delight when their children achieve. Theorists speculate that the high achievement motivation displayed by such children has *emotional* roots, as children learn to associate achievement with positive emotions. There may also be *cognitive* roots, as children learn to attribute their achievements to their own competence and effort and so to develop higher expectations (Dweck & Elliott, 1983).

These parental influences also help explain a fascinating finding—that birth order correlates with achievement. First-born and only children do slightly better in school and on intelligence tests and are more likely to achieve admission to prestigious colleges than are their later-born brothers and sisters (Falbo & Polit, 1986). This may partly reflect the generally higher socioeconomic status of small families, which have fewer later-born children

Figure 9–7 What is this boy daydreaming about? By analyzing responses to ambiguous photos like this, motivation researchers seek clues to people's levels of achievement motivation.

"They can because they think they can."

Virgil
Aeneid, 19 B.C.

Remember the two people you chose, one who consistently strives to succeed, the other who is less concerned with achievement? Is either a first-born (or only) child?

intrinsic motivation A desire to perform a behavior for its own sake and to be effective.

extrinsic motivation A desire to perform a behavior due to promised rewards or threats of punishment.

(Blake, 1989). However, in separate studies of eminent people from two-child families, 64 percent of "distinguished Americans" were first-born, as were 61 percent of the Rhodes Scholars, and 66 percent of National Merit Scholars. Among the National Merit Scholars who came from three child families, 52 percent were first-born (Altus, 1966).

It is fun to speculate about differences between the experiences of first-born and later-born children. One difference might be the greater parental attention given the first-born during their years as solo children. Perhaps parents are more invested in a first-born child. They may take more pictures of their first child and provide that child with more encouragement and higher expectations. On the other hand, the later-born often have noteworthy social strengths. They tend to be more socially relaxed and popular. Having less power than one's older siblings—less size, strength, verbal facility, and experience—apparently fosters more effective social skills (Miller & Maruyama, 1976).

Moreover, throughout history later-born scientists have been more supportive of new ideas. Charles Darwin, the fifth of six children, found his new ideas supported by most later-born scientists but rejected by his first-born peers. Science historian Frank Sulloway (1990) reports that 23 of 28 such scientific revolutions were led by later-borns. The same was true of the Protestant Reformation, which later-born religious leaders were more likely to support. First-borns, it seems, identify more closely with the views of their parents and of tradition; later-borns tend to be more freewheeling.

Intrinsic Motivation and Achievement

In the classroom, at the workplace, and on the athletic field, two types of achievement motivation operate. **Intrinsic motivation** is the inner desire to be effective and to perform a behavior for its own sake. **Extrinsic motivation** is seeking external rewards and avoiding punishments.

To sense the difference between extrinsic and intrinsic motivation, you might reflect on your own current experience. Are you feeling pressured to get this reading finished before a deadline? Worried about your course grade? Eager for rewards that depend on your doing well? If your answers are yes, then you are extrinsically motivated (as, to some extent, almost all students are). Are you also finding the course material interesting? Does learning it enable you to feel more competent? If there were no grade at stake, might you be curious enough to want to learn the material for its own sake? If your answers are yes, intrinsic motivation also fuels your efforts.

After studying the motivations and achievements of thousands of college students, scientists, pilots, businesspeople, and athletes, Janet Spence and Robert Helmreich (1983) concluded that intrinsic motivation (such as love of the game) produces high achievement, and that extrinsic motivation (such as the desire for a high-paying career) often does not. Spence and Helmreich identified and assessed three facets of intrinsic motivation: people's quests for *mastery* (as shown for example, by their strongly agreeing that "If I am not good at something, I would rather keep struggling to master it than move on to something I may be good at"); their drive to *work* ("I like to work hard"); and their *competitiveness* ("I really enjoy working in situations involving skill and competition").

Despite similar abilities, people oriented toward mastery and hard work typically achieve more. If students, they get better grades; if MBA graduates, they earn more money; if scientists, their work is more often cited by other scientists. No surprise there. But in Spence and Helmreich's studies a high work/mastery orientation proved most productive in people who were *not*

Preview Question

12. What is intrinsic motivation and how can it be nurtured?

Not content with her Emmy Award-winning talk show and estimated $38 million in 1990 earnings, Oprah Winfrey continues to seek new ways to excel through her film-TV company. "I've been blessed—but I create the blessings," she has said.

highly competitive. That is, the effect of competitiveness depends on the degree of work/mastery orientation. Among those who do not intrinsically enjoy mastery and hard work, it pays to be highly competitive; among those driven toward mastery and hard work, it pays to be less competitive.

Motivating People

The growing field of industrial/organizational psychology includes studies of how managers might best:

screen and select motivated, well-suited personnel;

match people with suitable work assignments;

create work environments that boost morale and output and minimize absenteeism and turnover;

evaluate performance and create incentives for excellence;

promote teamwork and group achievement.

What every leader (whether a manager, coach, or teacher) wants to know is: How can I manage in ways that ensure motivated, productive, satisfied people? Among the factors known to affect a leader's effectiveness are the following four.

Cultivating Intrinsic Motivation

If intrinsic motivation stimulates achievement, especially in situations where people work independently (as students, executives, and scientists often do), then how might we encourage it? The consistent answers, from hundreds of studies: First, provide tasks that challenge and trigger curiosity (Malone & Lepper, 1986). Second, avoid snuffing out people's sense of self-determination with an overuse of controlling extrinsic rewards (Deci & Ryan, 1987).

Note that we can use extrinsic rewards in two ways: to *control* ("If you clean up your room, you can have some ice cream") or to *inform* someone of successes ("That was outstanding—we congratulate you"). Attempts to *control* people's behaviors through rewards and surveillance may be successful as long as these controls are present. If taken away, interest in the activity often drops. Ironically, teachers who try hardest to boost their students' achievement on competency tests tend to be most controlling, thus undermining their students' intrinsic interest.

On the other hand, rewards that *inform* people they are doing well can boost their feelings of competence and intrinsic motivation. In one experiment, Thane Pittman and his colleagues (1980) asked college students to work on puzzles. Those given informative compliments ("Compared with most of my subjects, you're doing really well") usually continued playing with the puzzles when left alone. Those given either no praise or a controlling form of praise ("If you keep it up, I'll be able to use your data") were less likely to continue on their own. So, depending on whether we use rewards to control or inform, they can either lower or raise intrinsic motivation.

There is an important practical principle here. Because the controlling use of rewards undermines intrinsic motivation (and creativity—see page 260), parents, teachers, and managers should take care not to be overcontrolling. It is important to expect, support, challenge, and inform; but if you want to encourage internally motivated, self-directed achievements, do not overly control.

Preview Question

13. What motivational strategies are most effective at home, school and work?

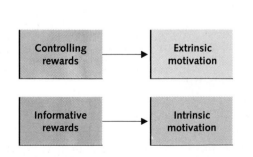

The type of reward affects motivation.

task leadership Goal-oriented leadership that sets standards, organizes work, and focuses attention on goals.

social leadership Group-oriented leadership that builds teamwork, mediates conflict, and offers support.

"Good leaders don't ask more than their constituents can give, but they often ask—and get—more than their constituents intended to give or thought it was possible to give."

John W. Gardner
Excellence, 1984

Keeping an Eye on People's Motives

What managerial style is effective varies with the people managed. To motivate people, Martin Maehr and Larry Braskamp (1986; Braskamp, 1987) advise managers to assess their people's motives and adjust their managerial style accordingly. Challenge employees who value *accomplishment* to try new things and to exhibit excellence. Give those who value *recognition* the attention they desire. Place those who value *affiliation* in a unit that has a trustful family feeling and that shares decision making. Motivate those who value *power* with competition and opportunities for triumphant success. Different strokes for different folks, but for each a way to energize and direct—in a word, to motivate—behavior.

Setting Specific, Challenging Goals

In study after study, specific, challenging goals have motivated higher achievement, especially when combined with progress reports (Locke & Latham, 1990; Mento & others, 1987; Tubbs, 1986). Clear objectives, such as those you might set in planning your coursework, serve to direct attention, promote effort and persistence, and stimulate creative strategies. So, to motivate high productivity, effective leaders work with people to define explicit goals, elicit commitments, and provide feedback on progress.

Choosing an Appropriate Leadership Style

Whether a directive or a democratic leadership style works best depends on the situation and the leader. The best leadership style for leading a discussion is not the best style for leading the troops on a charge (Fiedler, 1981). Some people excel at **task leadership**—setting standards, organizing work, and focusing attention on goals. Being goal-oriented, task leaders are good at keeping a group centered on its mission. Typically, they have a directive style, which can work well if the leader is bright enough to give good orders (Fiedler, 1987).

Other managers excel at **social leadership**—building teamwork, mediating conflicts, and supporting their workforce. Most social leaders have a democratic style: They delegate authority and welcome the participation of team members. Many experiments show that social leadership is good for morale. Subordinates usually feel more satisfied when they can participate in decision making (Spector, 1986). Given some control over their tasks, they also are more motivated to achieve (Burger, 1987). Women more often excel at social leadership, men at task leadership (Eagly & Karau, 1991).

In recent years, many businesses have increased employee participation in making decisions, a management style common in Sweden and Japan (Naylor, 1990; Sundstrom & others, 1990). Ironically, a major influence on the "Japanese-style participative management" now increasingly popular in the United States was M.I.T. social psychologist Kurt Lewin. Lewin and his students demonstrated the effects of worker participation on productivity in laboratory and factory experiments. Shortly before World War II, Lewin visited Japan and explained his findings to industrial and academic leaders (Nisbett & Ross, 1991).

Because effective leadership styles vary with the situation and the person, the once-popular "great person theory of leadership"—that all great leaders share certain traits—fell out of favor. However, Peter Smith and Monir Tayeb (1989) report from recent studies in India, Taiwan, and Iran that effective managers in coal mines, banks, and government offices often exhibit a high

Participative management. General Motors' new Saturn plant in Tennessee has 10-member "teams" of employees. Each work team helps decide such things as new hires for their team and how to run their own area. Part of their salary depends on resulting car quality and company profits.

degree of *both* task and social leadership. As achievement-minded people, they care about how work is progressing, yet they are sensitive to their subordinates' needs. Effective leaders of laboratory groups, work teams, and large corporations also tend to exude a self-confident "charisma" (Bennis, 1984; House & Singh, 1987). Their charisma involves a *vision* of some goal, an ability to *communicate* it clearly and simply, and enough optimism and faith in their group to *inspire* others to follow.

Drawing by Anthony; © 1988 The New Yorker Magazine, Inc.

In this chapter we have seen that identifiable physiological mechanisms drive some motives, such as hunger (though external incentives and learned tastes matter too). Sexual motivation involves both biological and social influences. Other motives, such as achievement, are more obviously driven by psychological factors such as an intrinsic quest for mastery and the external rewards of recognition. What unifies all motives is their common effect: the energizing and directing of behavior toward a goal. Without motivation—without hunger, thirst, sex, curiosity, a drive to achieve, and so forth—life would be dull and aimless. Motivation adds purpose—and zing—to life.

Rehearse It

13. First-borns are more likely than later-borns to
a. have high achievement motivation.
b. become group leaders.
c. have high intrinsic motivation.
d. become revolutionary scientists.

14. Psychologists identify two types of achievement motivation: extrinsic and intrinsic motivation. Intrinsic motivation is a desire to perform a behavior because it is enjoyable and leads to feelings of mastery. For a violinist, an example of an intrinsic motive is the desire to
a. receive a music scholarship.
b. be promoted to concertmaster.
c. perfect a difficult passage.
d. obtain a positive grade or evaluation.

15. Social leaders are group-oriented and welcome participation of team members in decision making. Managers adopting this democratic style make certain assumptions about human motivation in the workplace. For example, they assume that workers are motivated mainly by
a. charisma.
b. the need to demonstrate their skill and creativity.
c. extrinsic rewards, such as money and prizes.
d. productivity goals and other management directives.

Reviewing Motivation

Motivation is the energizing and directing of our behavior, as exemplified in our yearning for food, our longing for sexual intimacy, and our desire to achieve.

Concepts of Motivation

1. What roles do biological needs and external incentives play in motivation?

Early theorists, under Darwin's influence, came to view behavior as being controlled by biological instincts. But when it became clear that people were randomly naming rather than explaining various behaviors by calling them instincts, psychologists turned to a drive theory of motivation: Physiological needs create psychological drives that motivate need satisfaction. The aim of drive reduction is internal stability, or homeostasis. Thus, drive reduction motivates survival behaviors such as eating and drinking but seems not so applicable to motives such as curiosity and achievement, that seek increasing levels of stimulation and are spurred by the external incentives we have learned to value.

2. What is the basic idea behind Maslow's hierarchy of needs?

Maslow's hierarchy of needs expresses the idea that, until satisfied, some motives are more compelling (that is, more basic) than others.

Hunger

3. What makes us hungry?

The inner push of hunger originates not primarily from the stomach's pangs, but from variations in body chemistry. For example, we are likely to feel hungry when our glucose levels are low and our insulin levels are high. This information is monitored by areas within the hypothalamus that regulate the body's weight by influencing our feelings of hunger and satiety. To maintain a set-point weight, the body also adjusts its metabolic rate of energy expenditure. Especially in "external" people, the presence of food can trigger hunger and eating, partly by stimulating a rise in insulin level.

4. What factors predispose some people to become and remain obese?

Fat is a concentrated fuel reserve that is stored in fat cells. The number and size of these cells determine one's body fat. Obese people find it difficult to lose weight permanently because the number of fat cells is not reduced by a diet. Further, the rate of energy expenditure necessary for tissue maintenance is lower in fat than in other tissues, and the overall metabolic rate decreases when body weight drops below the set point. Those who wish to diet anyhow face a life-long commitment to avoiding tempting food, boosting energy expenditure through exercise, and modifying eating patterns.

Sexual Motivation

5. How does human sexual behavior vary?

Sexual motivation is a complex combination, both of physiological and social needs, and of internal and external stimuli. While sex is basic to the survival of the species, individuals can and do live without it. But sexual motivation also satisfies social needs for belongingness and love. Sexual behaviors vary across and within cultures, and the range of "normal" sexual activity is broad.

6. What are the biological characteristics of sexual motivation in humans?

Biologically, the human sexual response cycle normally follows a pattern of excitement, plateau, orgasm, and resolution. During the resolution phase, males enter a refractory period, during which another orgasm is not possible.

7. What role do hormones play in human sexuality?

Sex hormones help our bodies develop and function as either male or female. In nonhuman animals, hormones also help to stimulate sexual activity, but in humans, they influence sexual behavior more loosely, especially once minimally sufficient hormone levels are present.

8. How do internal and external factors interact to stimulate sexual arousal?

External stimuli can trigger sexual arousal in both men and women, although women may be less likely to notice their physiological responses. Sexually explicit materials may also lead people to perceive their partners as comparatively less appealing and to devalue their relationships. In combination with the internal hormonal push and the external pull of sexual stimuli, imagined stimuli (fantasies) help trigger sexual arousal. Some sexual dysfunctions respond well to behavioral treatment, which assumes that people can learn to modify their sexual responses.

9. What factors are involved in sexual orientation?

Social pressures notwithstanding, one's heterosexual or homosexual orientation seems neither willfully chosen nor easily changed. Although it is beginning to look as though biological factors are involved, psychologists are still unsure why one person becomes heterosexual and another homosexual.

10. What roles do personal values play in sex research and sex education?

Sex research and education are not value-free. Sex-related values should therefore be discussed openly, recognizing the social significance of sexual expression.

Achievement Motivation

11. What are the nature and the origins of achievement motivation?

Some human behaviors are energized and directed without satisfying any apparent biological need. Achieving personal goals, for example, may be motivated by a person's social needs for competence and independence. People with a high need to achieve tend to prefer moderately challenging tasks and to persist in accomplishing them. Many achievement-oriented children have parents and teachers who encourage and affirm independent achievement rather than overly controlling them with external rewards and threats. First-born and only children tend to be higher achievers, but later-borns tend to have greater social skills and to be more accepting of new ideas.

12. What is intrinsic motivation and how can it be nurtured?

Intrinsic motivation is the desire to be effective and to perform a behavior for its own sake. Rewards that boost people's sense of competence or inform them of improvement may increase intrinsic motivation. Rewards used to control behavior do not.

13. What motivational strategies are most effective at home, school and work?

People's performance can be increased by increasing their intrinsic motivation, by adjusting leadership style to complement individual motives, by setting specific, challenging goals, and by practicing effective, goal-oriented task leadership and group-oriented social leadership.

Terms and Concepts to Remember

motivation, p. 269

instinct, p. 270

drive, p. 270

homeostasis, p. 270

incentives, p. 271

hierarchy of needs, p. 271

glucose, p. 271

insulin, p. 271

set point, p. 275

metabolic rate, p. 275

obesity, p. 276

anorexia nervosa, p. 277

bulimia nervosa, p. 277

sexual response cycle, p. 283

refractory period, p. 284

estrogen, p. 284

sexual dysfunction, p. 286

sexual orientation, p. 287

achievement motivation, p. 291

intrinsic motivation, p. 293

extrinsic motivation, p. 293

task leadership, p. 295

social leadership, p. 295

Rehearse It Answer Key

1. a.   **2.** d.   **3.** c.   **4.** a.   **5.** b.   **6.** a.   **7.** b.   **8.** d.   **9.** b.

10. b.   **11.** c.   **12.** b.   **13.** a.   **14.** c.   **15.** b.

Critical Thinking Exercise

You have *Surveyed*, *Questioned*, *Read*, *Rehearsed*, and *Reviewed* Chapter 9. Now take your learning a step further by testing your *critical thinking* skills on the following passage.

Janet and Sheila have been good friends since meeting in their introductory psychology class freshman year. They are about the same height and age but vary in weight. Janet, whose parents are both obese, has always struggled with her weight, which fluctuates between 15 and 20 percent above normal. Acquaintances assume she is lazy and gluttonous, but Janet's friends know that she is neither. Sheila is of normal weight, as is her family.

Janet and Sheila have decided to make themselves the subjects of an experiment they need to do as a final project in their Health Psychology class. For a month, they eat the same total number of calories per day, spread across several small, healthy meals that are low in fat and include whole grains, fruits, and vegetables. They also add a brisk 30-minute walk to their daily routine. At the end of the month, Janet and Sheila weigh themselves for the first time since the experiment began. Although Janet is pleased to find that she has lost some weight, Sheila has lost more. After presenting their findings to the class, several students speculate that perhaps Janet simply hadn't employed the willpower that Sheila had, and that was why Sheila lost more weight.

1. What factors in Janet's background might have contributed to her obesity?

2. What factors in Sheila's background might have contributed to her being of normal weight?

3. Why did Sheila lose more weight than Janet while they consumed the same number of calories, the same types of food, and did the same amount of exercise?

Check your progress on becoming a critical thinker by comparing your answers to the sample answers found in Appendix B.

For Further Information

You can find further information regarding industrial/organizational psychology on the following pages:

Chapter 10

Emotions, Stress, and Health

Preview Question

1. What are the components of an emotion?

Feelings—powerful, spontaneous, sometimes unforgettable. Where do feelings come from? Of all the species, we humans seem the most emotional (Hebb, 1980). More often than any other creature, we express fear, anger, sadness, joy, and love. No one needs to tell you that emotions add color to your life, that in times of stress they can disrupt your life or save it. But what are the ingredients of emotion?

Imagine that, while walking home along a deserted street late at night, a motorcycle begins following you. Hearing the rumble of the engine, your heart begins to race, your pace quickens, you wonder about the cyclist's intent, and you feel scared. As your experience illustrates, **emotions** are a mix of (1) physiological arousal (heart pounding), (2) expressive behavior (quickened pace), and (3) conscious experience (interpreting the person's intent and feeling fearful). The puzzle is how these three pieces fit together: Did you first notice your heart racing, your speeded-up walking, and *then* feel afraid? Or did your sense of fear come first, stirring your heart and legs to respond? If prolonged, might such emotions affect your health? Before trying to answer these questions, let's study the individual pieces of the emotion puzzle—its physiology, expression, and conscious experience.

Not only emotion, but most psychological phenomena (vision, sleep, memory, sex, and so forth) can be approached these three ways—physiologically, behaviorally, and cognitively.

The Physiology of Emotion

Arousal

Preview Question

2. What physiological changes accompany emotional arousal?

When emotionally aroused, you are physically aroused. Some physical responses are so obvious that you easily notice them. Hearing the rumble behind you, your muscles tense, your stomach develops butterflies, your mouth becomes dry.

Your body also mobilizes for action in less noticeable ways. To provide energy, your liver pours extra sugar into your bloodstream. To help burn the sugar, your respiration rate increases to supply the needed extra oxygen. Your digestion slows, diverting blood from your internal organs to your muscles. Your pupils dilate, letting in more light. To cool your stirred-up body, you perspire more. If wounded, your blood clots more quickly. Think of this after your next emergency: Without any conscious effort, your body's response to danger was wonderfully coordinated and adaptive—preparing you to fight or flee.

emotion A response of the whole organism, involving (1) physical arousal, (2) expressive behaviors, and (3) conscious experience.

SYMPATHETIC (arousing)		PARASYMPATHETIC (calming)
Pupils dilate	EYES	Pupils contract
Decreases	SALIVATION	Increases
Perspires	SKIN	Dries
Increases	RESPIRATION	Decreases
Accelerates	HEART	Slows
Inhibits	DIGESTION	Activates
Secrete stress hormones	ADRENAL GLANDS	Decrease stress hormones

Figure 10–1 Arousal is involved in both emotional and stress reactions and is controlled by our autonomic nervous system. The sympathetic division activates. The parasympathetic calms.

One explanation of sudden death caused by a voodoo "curse" is that the terrified person's parasympathetic nervous system, which calms the body, overreacts to the extreme arousal by slowing the heart to a stop (Seligman, 1974).

As we learned in Chapter 2 (page 34), our autonomic nervous system controls our arousal. Its sympathetic division (Figure 10–1) activates arousal by directing the adrenal glands atop the kidneys to release the stress hormones epinephrine (adrenaline) and norepinephrine (noradrenaline). The surge in epinephrine and norepinephrine triggers increased heart rate, blood pressure, and blood sugar levels. When the emergency passes, the parasympathetic neural centers become active, calming the body. Even after the parasympathetic division inhibits further release of stress hormones, those already in the bloodstream linger awhile, so arousal diminishes gradually.

As we will see, prolonged arousal, produced by sustained stress, taxes the body. Yet in many situations arousal is adaptive. Too little arousal (say, sleepiness) can be as disruptive as extremely high levels of arousal. When taking an exam, it pays to be moderately aroused—alert but not trembling with nervousness.

Although performance is usually best when arousal is moderate, the level of arousal for optimal performance varies for different tasks. With easy or well-learned tasks, peak performance comes with relatively high arousal. With more difficult or unrehearsed tasks, the optimal arousal is somewhat less. Thus, runners, who perform a well-learned task, usually achieve their peak performances when highly aroused by competition. With less routine skills—say, basketball players shooting free throws—performance declines slightly when a packed fieldhouse makes players hyper-aroused (Sokoll & Mynatt, 1984). Likewise, students who feel great anxiety during exams perform more poorly than equally able but more confident students. Training anxious students how to relax before an exam often enables them to perform better (Hembree, 1988).

Physiological States Accompanying Specific Emotions

Imagine conducting an experiment exploring the physiological signs of arousal. In each of four rooms, you have someone watching a movie: In the first, there's a horror show; in the second, an anger-provoking film; in the third, a sexually arousing film; in the fourth, an utterly boring film. From the control center you monitor each person's physiological responses. By examining the perspiration, breathing, and heart rates of the viewers, could you tell who was frightened, who was angry, who was sexually aroused, and who was bored?

"No one ever told me that grief felt so much like fear. I am not afraid, but the sensation is like being afraid. The same fluttering in the stomach, the same restlessness, the yawning. I keep on swallowing."

C. S. Lewis
A Grief Observed, 1961

In 1966, a young man named Charles Whitman killed his wife and mother and then climbed to the top of a tower at the University of Texas and shot 38 people. An autopsy later revealed he had developed a tumor in his limbic system.

With training, you could probably pick out the bored viewer from the other three. Discerning physiological differences among fear, anger, and sexual arousal is much harder (Zillmann, 1986). Apart from the breathing disruption caused by laughter, experts even have difficulty distinguishing viewers' physiological responses to sad versus funny movies (Averill, 1969).

Fear, anger, sexual arousal, and sadness certainly *feel* different (and, as we will see, cognitively they *are* different). A terrified person may feel a clutching, sinking sensation in the chest and a knot in the stomach. An angry person may feel "hot under the collar" and will probably experience a pressing, inner tension. The sexually stimulated person will experience a genital response. The sad person may be choked up and have an empty, drained feeling (Epstein, 1984). Moreover, frightened, angered, and saddened people often *look* different—"paralyzed with fear," "ready to explode," or "down in the dumps." Knowing this, can we pinpoint some distinct physiological indicators of each emotion?

Fear and rage are accompanied by differing finger temperatures and hormone secretions (Ax, 1953). Scientists increasingly agree that different brain regions and distinct patterns of brain activity also underlie different emotions (Panksepp, 1982). As we saw on page 40, stimulate one area of a cat's limbic system and it will pull back in terror at the sight of a mouse. Stimulate another limbic area and the cat will become enraged—pupils dilated, fur and tail erect, claws out, hissing furiously. As people experience negative emotions, such as disgust, the right hemisphere becomes more electrically active. The left hemisphere activates when processing positive emotions (Davidson & others, 1990, 1991). For some infants and adults, the left frontal lobe shows more activity than the right. These individuals are typically more cheerful and less readily threatened or depressed than those with more active right frontal lobes. "It may be that those people with more left front activity are better able to turn off upsetting feelings," speculates researcher Richard Davidson (1991).

So, although emotions as varied as fear and anger involve a similar general autonomic arousal (thanks to the sympathetic nervous system), there are real, if subtle, physiological differences that help explain why we experience them so differently. Moreover, the physical accompaniments of emotion appear innate and universal—the same in a Sumatran village as in North America (Levenson & others, 1991).

Although one is terrified and the other thrilled by this roller coaster, both riders are experiencing the physiological symptoms of an activated sympathetic nervous system: increased perspiration, racing heart, tense muscles. When the ride is over, the arousal lingers.

Psychology Applied: Lie Detection

Given the physical indicators of emotion, might we, like Pinocchio, give some telltale sign whenever we lie? The *lie detector,* or **polygraph,** was once used mainly in law enforcement and national security work. By the mid-1980s, 2 million Americans annually were reportedly being tested, usually by corporations trying to screen applicants for honesty or to uncover employee theft (Holden, 1986a).

Just what does the polygraph do? It does not literally detect lies. Rather, it measures several of the physiological responses that accompany emotion, such as changes in breathing, pulse rate, blood pressure, and perspiration. While you try to relax, the examiner measures your physiological responses as you answer questions. Some of these, called control questions, are designed to

The polygraph test.

make anyone a little nervous. If asked, "In the last 20 years, have you ever taken something that didn't belong to you?" many people will tell a little white lie and say no, but the polygraph may detect slight physiological changes. If your physiological reactions to the critical questions ("Did you ever steal anything from your previous employer?") are weaker than to the control questions, the examiner infers you are telling the truth. The assumption is that only a thief becomes agitated when denying a theft.

How well does the polygraph work? That depends on whether liars exhibit anxiety while lying. An innocent person might respond with heightened tension to the accusations implied by the relevant questions. When a Yakima, Washington, woman was accused by her ex-husband's new wife of sexually abusing her 4-year-old son, the mother gladly accepted a police offer of a polygraph test "to prove her innocence." Asked, "Did you take Tommy's penis in your mouth?" the accused mother understandably reacted with greater perspiration and blood pressure than when asked "Have you ever told a lie to get out of trouble? This revealed her guilt, explained the police-sergeant-turned-polygrapher to the jury. (Fortunately for the mother, her attorney managed to locate a scientific expert who persuaded the jury that, by itself, this was not credible evidence of guilt.) Many rape victims similarly "fail" lie detector tests when reacting emotionally while telling the truth about their assailant (Lykken, 1992).

The major adversary of lie detector tests is University of Minnesota psychologist David Lykken (1983,

1992). He notes that because physiological response is much the same from one emotion to another, the polygraph cannot distinguish among anxiety, irritation, and guilt. They all appear as arousal. Thus, these tests err about one-third of the time. They more often label the innocent guilty—when the relevant question upsets the honest person—than the guilty innocent (Figure 10–2). Good advice, then, would be never to take a lie detector test if you are innocent. Those who are believed guilty, and are guilty, can welcome the test, because it may exonerate them.

Though more accurate than a 50–50 coin toss, polygraph tests have been deemed too inaccurate for about half of U.S. state courts. The

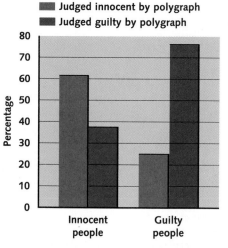

Figure 10–2 How often do lie detectors lie? Benjamin Kleinmuntz and Julian Szucko (1984) had polygraph experts study the polygraph data of 50 theft suspects who later confessed to being guilty and 50 suspects whose innocence was later established by someone's confession. Had the polygraph experts been the judges, more than one-third of the innocent would have been declared guilty, and almost one-fourth of the guilty would have been declared innocent.

polygraph A machine, commonly used in attempts to detect lies, that measures several of the physiological responses accompanying emotion (such as perspiration, heart rate, and breathing changes).

"If you hang them all, you will get the guilty."

Folksinger Tom T. Hall

Congressional Office of Technology Assessment (U.S. Congress, 1983, p. 4) warned that "the available research evidence does not establish the scientific validity of the polygraph test for personnel security screening." The American Psychological Association (1986) similarly "has great reservations about the use of polygraph tests to detect deception," as does the British Psychological Society (1986).

The polygraph functions more appropriately as a tool in criminal investigation. Police sometimes use the polygraph to induce confessions by criminals whom they scare into thinking that any lies will be transparent. A more honest approach uses the *guilty knowledge test*, which assesses a suspect's physiological responses to details of a crime known only to the police and the guilty person. If a camera and money were stolen, the polygraph examiner could see whether the suspect reacts strongly to such details as the specific brand name of the camera and the dollar amounts. Presumably, only a guilty person would. Given enough such specific probes, an innocent person will seldom be wrongly accused. Nevertheless, critics and advocates alike disapprove of widespread commercial use of the polygraph. The truth is that lie detectors sometimes lie. The U.S. Congress recognized this when it passed the Employee Polygraph Protection Act of 1988, prohibiting most nongovernmental polygraph testing.

Expressing Emotion

There is another, simpler method of deciphering people's emotions: We "read" their bodies, listen to their voices, and look at their faces.

Nonverbal Communication

Preview Question

3. Are nonverbal expressions of emotion universally understood?

All of us communicate nonverbally as well as verbally. If irritated, we may tense our bodies, press our lips together, and gesture with our eyebrows. With a gaze, an averted glance, or a stare we can communicate intimacy, submission, or dominance (Kleinke, 1986). Among couples passionately in love, eye-gazing is typically prolonged and mutual (Rubin, 1970). Would intimate gazes stir such feelings between strangers? To find out, Joan Kellerman, James Lewis, and James Laird (1989) asked unacquainted male-female pairs to gaze intently for 2 minutes either at one another's hands or into one another's eyes. After separating, the eye-gazers reported feeling a greater tingle of attraction and affection.

Most of us are good enough at reading nonverbal cues to decipher the emotions in an old silent film. We are especially good at detecting nonverbal threats. In a crowd of faces, a single angry face will "pop out" faster than a single happy one (Hansen & Hansen, 1988). Some of us are more sensitive to these cues than others. Robert Rosenthal, Judith Hall, and their colleagues

Through the silent language of nonverbal expression, the body communicates emotion. Without a word from either one, we know these two spelling bee finalists are anguished.

(1979) discovered this by showing hundreds of people brief film clips of portions of a person's emotionally expressive face or body, sometimes with a garbled voice added. For example, after a 2-second scene revealing only the face of an upset woman, the researchers would ask whether the woman was expressing anger or discussing a divorce. Rosenthal and Hall reported that some people are much better emotion detectors than others, and that women are better at it than men.

Armed with high-tech equipment, psychologists are now linking various emotions with specific facial muscles (Figure 10–3). Hard-to-control facial muscles reveal signs of emotions you may be trying to conceal. Lifting just the inner part of your eyebrows, which few people do consciously, reveals distress or worry. Eyebrows raised and pulled together signal fear. A feigned smile, such as one we make for a photographer, gets switched on more abruptly than a genuine smile (Bugental, 1986), often continues for more than 4 or 5 seconds, by which time most authentic expressions fade, and then abruptly gets switched off.

People learn to recognize these emotional signals. Elisha Babad and his colleagues (1991) videotaped teachers talking to unseen students. A mere 10-second clip of either the teacher's voice or face was enough to clue both young and old viewers as to whether or not this was a child the teacher liked and admired. Although teachers may think they can conceal their feelings and stay objective, their students can sense what their expressions and gestures reveal.

Figure 10–3 Paul Ekman's system for classifying a particular smile consists of a specific code for each of the 80 facial muscles used to create it. Notice how different these smiles are: (a) a smile that masks anger (the woman has just been told she is being dismissed); (b) an overly polite smile (the man is telling a patient to enjoy her hospital stay); (c) a smile softening verbal criticism ("I'd appreciate it if you wouldn't come to rehearsal drunk"); and (d) a reluctant, compliant smile ("I guess I don't have any choice, so OK").

(a)

(b)

(c)

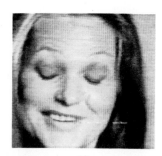

(d)

The growing awareness that we communicate through the body's silent language has led to studies of how job applicants and interviewers communicate (or miscommunicate) nonverbally, and to popular guidebooks on how to interpret nonverbal signals. Whether negotiating a business deal, selling a product, or flirting with someone, it pays to be able to read feelings that "leak through" via subtle facial expressions, body movements, and postures. Fidgeting, for example, may reveal anxiety or boredom. More specific interpretations of postures and gestures are risky. Different expressions may convey the same emotion: Either a cold stare or the avoidance of eye contact may signify hostility. And a given expression can convey very different emotions: Folded arms, for example, can signify irritation or relaxation.

Culture and Emotional Expression

The meaning of gestures varies with the culture. Some years ago, psychologist Otto Klineberg (1938) observed that in Chinese literature people clapped their hands to express worry or disappointment, laughed a great "ho-ho" to express anger, and stuck out their tongues to show surprise. Similarly, the "thumbs up" and "A-OK" signs of North America would be interpreted as insults in certain other cultures. On the other hand, when North Korea in 1968 photographed supposedly happy officers from a captured U.S. Navy spyship, three of the men made the obscene middle finger gesture to communicate their actual emotions. The crew also used the gesture to ridicule their captors, explaining that it was a "Hawaiian good luck sign" (Fleming & Scott, 1991).

Do facial expressions also mean different things in different cultures? To find out, two investigative teams—one led by Paul Ekman and Wallace Friesen (1975, 1987), the other by Carroll Izard (1977)—showed photographs of different facial expressions to people in different parts of the world and asked them to guess the emotion. You can try this yourself. Match the six emotions with the six faces of Figure 10–4.

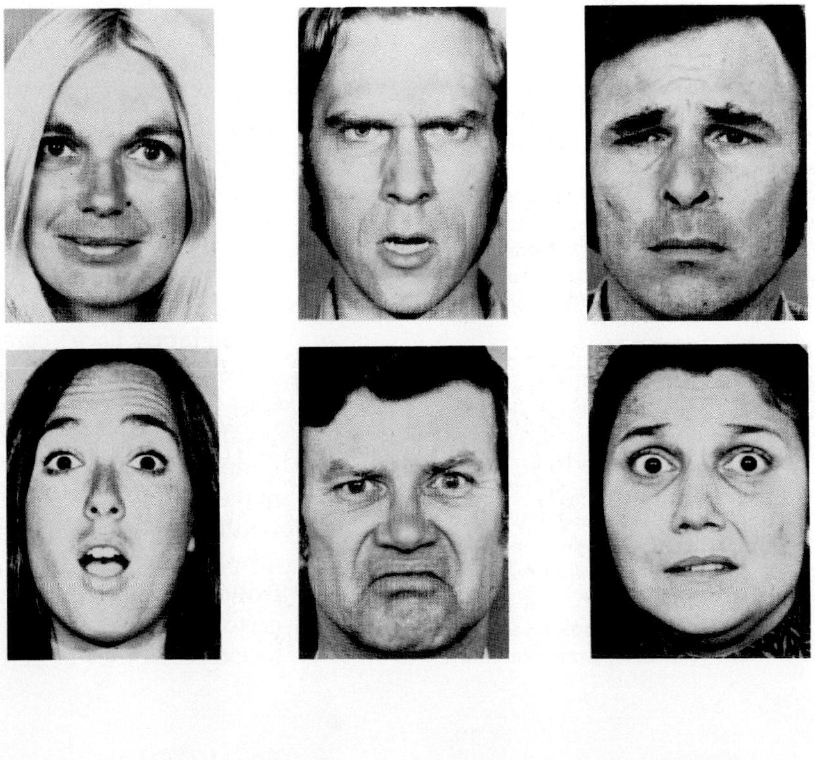

Figure 10–4 Which face expresses disgust? anger? fear? happiness? sadness? surprise? The answers are on page 309.

While astronauts are weightless, their fluids move toward their upper body and their faces become puffy. This makes nonverbal communication more difficult, increasing the risks of misunderstanding, especially among multinational crews (Gelman, 1989).

Paul Ekman (Ekman & Friesen, 1975): "Emotions are shown primarily in the face, not in the body. There is no specific body movement pattern that always signals anger or fear, but there are facial patterns specific to each emotion."

Preview Question

4. Do our facial expressions influence our feelings?

The effect occurs with posture, too (Snodgrass & others, 1986). To demonstrate, walk for a few minutes while taking short, shuffling steps, keeping your eyes downcast. Now walk around taking long strides, with your arms swinging and your eyes looking straight ahead. Can you feel your mood shift?

You probably did pretty well. How do you suppose people from Brazil or Japan did when judging these pictures? About the same as Americans, it turns out. People of different cultures and languages may differ somewhat in how they categorize emotions (Russell, 1991). Yet a smile's a smile the world around. Ditto for the other basic expressions.

Do people from different cultures make and interpret facial expressions similarly because they experience similar influences, such as American movies and CNN? Apparently not. Ekman and his team went to an isolated New Guinea people and asked them to display various emotions by saying, for example, "Pretend your child has died." When they showed videotapes of the New Guineans' facial reactions to American collegians, the Americans could easily read them. Children's facial expressions—even those of blind children who have never seen a face—are also universal (Eibl-Eibesfeldt, 1971). The world over, children cry when distressed, shake their heads when defiant, and smile when happy.

The discovery that the facial muscles speak a universal language would come as no surprise to Charles Darwin. He speculated that in prehistoric times, before our ancestors communicated in words, their ability to convey threats, greetings, and submission with facial expressions helped them to survive. That shared heritage, he believed, is why all humans express the basic emotions by similar facial expressions. A sneer, for example, retains elements of an animal's teeth-baring snarl. Smiles, too, are social communications, not just emotional reflexes. Bowlers don't smile when they score a strike—they smile when they turn to face their companions (Jones & others, 1991; Kraut & Johnston, 1979).

Although cultures share a universal nonverbal language, they differ in how, and how much, they express emotion. In cultures that encourage individuality, as in Western Europe, Australia, New Zealand, and North America, emotional displays often are intense and prolonged. People focus on their own goals and attitudes and express themselves accordingly. In Asian and Third World cultures where social connections and interdependence are emphasized, emotions such as sympathy, respect, and shame are more common than in the West. Moreover, people in such cultures more rarely and more briefly display self-aggrandizing or negative emotions that might disrupt communal feeling within close-knit groups (Markus & Kitayama, 1991; Matsumoto & others, 1988).

The Effects of Facial Expressions

Expressions not only communicate emotion, they also amplify and regulate it. In his 1872 book, *The Expression of the Emotions in Man and Animals*, Darwin contended that "the free expression by outward signs of an emotion intensifies it. . . . He who gives way to violent gestures will increase his rage."

Was Darwin right? I was driving in my car one day when the song "Put On a Happy Face" came on the radio. "How phony," I thought. But I tested Darwin's hypothesis anyway, as you can, too: Fake a big grin. Now scowl. Can you feel the difference?

The subjects in dozens of experiments could feel a difference. When James Laird and his colleagues (1974, 1984, 1989) subtly induced students to make a frowning expression—by asking them to "contract these muscles," "pull your brows together," and the like while he attached electrodes to their faces—the students reported feeling a little angry. Compared with the frowners, students whom he similarly induced to smile felt happier, found cartoons more humorous, and recalled happier memories. People instructed to express other basic emotions react similarly. People report feeling more fear than anger, disgust, or sadness when made to construct an expression of fear: "Raise your eyebrows. And open your eyes wide. Move your whole head back, so that your chin is tucked in a little bit, and let your mouth relax and hang open a little" (Duclos & others, 1989). Going through the motions awakens the emotions.

The effect is subtle, yet detectable in the absence of competing emotions. Just activating one of the smiling muscles by holding a pen in the teeth (rather than with the lips, which activates a frowning muscle) is enough to make cartoons seem more amusing (Strack & others, 1988). A heartier smile, made not just with the mouth but with raised cheeks as well, works even better (Ekman & others, 1990). Smile warmly on the outside and you feel better on the inside. Scowl and the whole world seems to scowl back.

Why might this be so? Paul Ekman and his colleagues (1983) designed an experiment to find out. Their subjects were professional actors trained in the Stanislavsky method, in which they physically (and psychologically) "become" the characters they are playing. The actors would assume an expression and then hold it for 10 seconds while the researchers measured changes in their heart rates and finger temperatures. When they made a fearful expression, their heart rate increased some eight beats per minute and finger temperature was steady. When making an angry expression, both heart rate and finger temperature increased as though the actor were indeed "hot-headed." Our facial expressions, it seems, send signals to our autonomic nervous system, which then responds accordingly.

If assuming an emotional expression triggers a feeling, then imitating others' expressions should help us feel what they are feeling. Again, the laboratory evidence is supportive. Kathleen Burns Vaughn and John Lanzetta (1981) asked some students but not others to make a pained expression whenever an electric shock was apparently delivered to someone they were watching. With each apparent shock, the observers perspired more and had a faster heart rate if grimacing than if not. So one small way to become more empathic—to feel what others feel—is to let your own face mimic the other person's expression. Acting as another acts helps us feel what another feels.

"Refuse to express a passion and it dies. . . . If we wish to conquer undesirable emotional tendencies in ourselves, we must . . . go through the outward movements of those contrary dispositions which we prefer to cultivate."

William James
Principles of Psychology, 1890

Answers to the question in Figure 10–4: From left to right: top row—happiness, anger, sadness; bottom row—surprise, disgust, fear.

Rehearse It

1. Emotions such as fear and anger involve a general autonomic arousal that is orchestrated by the sympathetic nervous system. In many situations, arousal is adaptive. For example, with a challenging task, such as taking an exam or shooting a basket, performance is likely to be best given
a. very high arousal.
b. moderate arousal.
c. low arousal.
d. diminishing arousal.

2. Stimulate one area of a cat's limbic system and the cat draws back in terror; stimulate another area and the cat hisses with rage. This suggests that fear and anger involve
a. different cognitive appraisals.
b. the same hormones.
c. different brain areas.

3. We can successfully interpret nonverbal threats and certain other silent messages regardless of the national origin of the sender. However, some nonverbal behaviors are *not* universal. People in different cultures are most likely to differ in their interpretations of
a. facial expressions.
b. children's facial expressions.

c. smiles.
d. postures and gestures.

4. People who, upon request, assume fearful expressions will feel their heart rates increase. This suggests that the autonomic nervous system responds to
a. signals from the facial muscles.
b. conscious feelings of emotion.
c. physiological responses involved in deception.
d. electrical stimulation.

Experiencing Emotion

The ingredients of emotion include not only physiological arousal and expressive behavior, but also our conscious experience. Psychologists have asked people from different cultures to report their experience of different emotions. Estonians, Poles, Greeks, Chinese, and Canadians, for example, all seem to place emotions along two dimensions—pleasant versus unpleasant and intensely aroused versus sleepy (Russell & others, 1989). On the intensity scale, for example, terrified is more frightened than afraid, enraged is angrier than angry, delighted is happier than happy. To these two dimensions, we might add a third: duration. Among Americans and Japanese, at least, the emotions of joy and sadness typically endure longer than anger and guilt, which outlast fear and disgust (Matsumoto & others, 1988).

Other psychologists have sought to identify emotions that are biologically, facially, and experientially distinct. Carroll Izard (1977) believes there are 10 such basic emotions (joy, anger, interest-excitement, disgust, surprise, contempt, sadness, fear, shame, and guilt), most of which are present in infancy (Figure 10–5). Other emotions, he says, are combinations of these. Love, for instance, is a mixture of joy and interest-excitement.

Let's now examine three important emotions: fear, anger, and happiness. What functions do these emotions serve? And what influences our experience of them?

Figure 10–5 Infants' naturally occurring emotions. To identify the emotions present from birth, Carroll Izard analyzed the facial expressions of very young infants. Shown here are (a) joy (mouth forming smile, cheeks lifted, twinkle in eye); (b) anger (brows drawn together and downward, eyes fixed, mouth squarish); (c) interest (brows raised or knitted, mouth softly rounded, lips may be pursed); (d) disgust (nose wrinkled, upper lip raised, tongue pushed outward); (e) surprise (brows raised, eyes widened, mouth rounded in oval shape); (f) distress (eyes tightly closed; mouth, as in anger, squared); (g) sadness (brows' inner corners raised, mouth corners drawn down); and (h) fear (brows level, drawn in and up, eyelids lifted, mouth corners retracted).

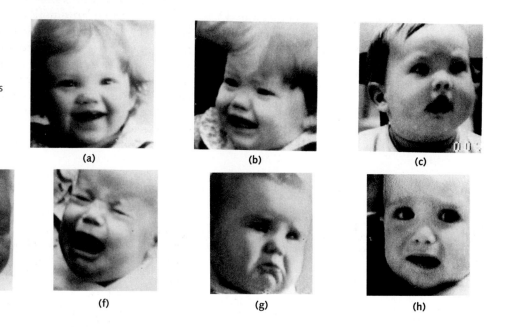

(a)   (b)   (c)

(d)   (e)   (f)   (g)   (h)

Fear

Fear can be a poisonous emotion. It can torment us, rob us of sleep, and preoccupy our thinking. People can be literally scared to death. Fear can also be contagious. In 1903, someone yelled "Fire!" as a fire broke out in Chicago's Iroquois Theater. Eddie Foy, the comedian on stage at the time, tried to reassure the crowd by calling out, "Don't get excited. There's no danger. Take it easy!" Alas, the crowd panicked. During the 10 minutes it took the fire department to arrive and quickly extinguish the flames, more than 500 people perished, most of them trampled or smothered in a stampede. Bodies were piled 7 or 8 feet deep in the stairways, and many of the faces bore heel marks (Brown, 1965).

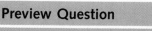

Preview Question

5. What are the causes and consequences of fear?

"He who fears all snares falls into none."

Publilius Syrus
Sententiae, 43 B.C.

More often, fear is an adaptive response. Fear prepares our bodies to flee danger. Fear of real or imagined enemies binds people together as families, tribes, and nations. Fear of injury protects us from harm. Fear of punishment or retaliation constrains us from harming one another.

People can be afraid of almost anything—"afraid of truth, afraid of fortune, afraid of death, and afraid of each other," observed Ralph Waldo Emerson. Why so many fears? Psychologists note that we can learn to fear almost anything. Recall from Chapter 6, Learning, that dogs learn to fear neutral stimuli associated with shock, that an infant can come to fear furry objects associated with frightening noises, and that adults can become terrified of incidental stimuli linked with traumatic experiences such as rape. Through such conditioning, the short list of naturally painful and frightening events can multiply into a long list of human fears—fear of driving or flying, fear of mice or cockroaches, fear of closed or open spaces, fear of failure, fear of another race or nation.

Learning by observation can extend the list even further. Susan Mineka (1985) wondered why nearly all monkeys reared in the wild fear snakes, yet lab-reared monkeys do not. Surely, most wild monkeys do not actually suffer snake bites. Might they learn their fear through observation? To find out, Mineka experimented with six wild-reared monkeys (all strongly fearful of snakes) and their lab-reared offspring (virtually none of which feared snakes). After repeatedly observing their parents or peers refusing to reach for food in the presence of a snake, the younger monkeys developed a similar strong fear of snakes. When retested 3 months later, their learned fear persisted. This suggests that our fears reflect not only our own past traumas but also the fears of our parents and friends.

Moreover, we may be biologically prepared to learn some fears more quickly than others. We humans quickly learn to fear snakes, spiders, and cliffs—fears that probably helped our ancestors survive. We are less predisposed to fear cars, electricity, bombs, and environmental warming, which in modern society are far more dangerous (Lumsden & Wilson, 1983; McNally, 1987). Stone Age fears leave us unprepared for high-tech dangers.

Although a horse encounter may be traumatic for this boy, his fear of large animals is certainly an adaptive response.

Chapters 12 and 13 discuss how such phobias develop and are treated.

Of course, some people's fears of specific things, such as spiders, are greater than others'. For a few people, intense fears of specific objects or situations disrupt their ability to cope. Furthermore, some people are very fearful of threatening or embarrassing situations. Others—courageous heroes and remorseless criminals—are less fearful. Astronauts and adventurers who have "the right stuff"—who can keep their wits and function coolly and effectively in moments of severe stress—seem to thrive on risk. So, too, do con artists and killers who charm their intended victims without a hint of nervousness, and who in laboratory tests exhibit little fear of a tone that predictably precedes a painful electric shock. Experience helps shape such fearfulness or fearlessness, but so do our genes. Even among identical twins reared separately, one twin's level of fearfulness is similar to the other's (Lykken, 1982).

Anger

One problem with chronic hostility is its link with heart disease (pages 330–331).

Anger is said by the sages to be "a short madness" (Horace, 65–8 B.C.) that "carries the mind away" (Virgil, 70–19 B.C.) and can be "many times more hurtful than the injury that caused it" (Thomas Fuller, 1654–1734). But other sages say "noble anger" (William Shakespeare, 1564–1616) "makes any coward brave" (Cato, 234–149 B.C.) and "brings back his strength" (Virgil).

What makes us angry? To find out, James Averill (1983) asked many people to recall or keep careful records of their experiences with anger. Most reported becoming at least mildly angry several times a week; some became angry several times a day. Often the anger was a response to a friend or loved one's perceived misdeed. Anger was especially common when another person's act seemed willful, unjustified, and avoidable. But blameless annoyances—foul odors, high temperatures, aches and pains—also have the power to make us angry (Berkowitz, 1990).

What do people do with their anger? What *should* they do with it? When anger fuels physically or verbally aggressive acts that are later regretted, it is maladaptive. But Averill's subjects recalled that when they were angry they often reacted assertively rather than hurtfully. Their anger frequently led them to talk things over with the offending person and so to lessen the aggravation. Such controlled expressions of anger are more adaptive than either hostile outbursts or just keeping the angry feelings inside.

"Anger will never disappear so long as thoughts of resentment are cherished in the mind."

Buddha, 500 B.C.

Popular books and articles on aggression sometimes advise that even hostile outbursts can be better than keeping anger pent up. If the Roman statesman Seneca was right—"It is hidden anger that harms"—then, when irritated, should we go ahead and curse, tell a person off, or retaliate? Was Ann Landers (1969) right to assert that "youngsters should be taught to vent their anger"?

Such advice is typical of individualized cultures, but would seldom be heard in cultures where people's identity is more group-centered. People who keenly sense their interdependence see anger as a threat to group harmony (Markus & Kitayama, 1991). In Tahiti, for instance, people learn to be considerate and gentle. From infancy on in Japan, expressions of anger are less common than in America.

catharsis   Emotional release. In psychology, the catharsis hypothesis maintains that "releasing" aggressive energy (through action or fantasy) relieves aggressive urges.

The "vent your anger" advice presumes that emotional expression provides emotional release, or **catharsis.** The catharsis hypothesis maintains that we reduce anger after releasing it through aggressive action or fantasy. Experimenters report that this sometimes occurs. When people retaliate against someone who has provoked them, they may indeed calm down—*if* their

Preview Question

6. What are the causes and consequences of anger?

Indiana University basketball coach Bobby Knight's angry outbursts may be temporarily cathartic. If so, they may also be reinforcing.

7. What are the causes and consequences of happiness?

counterattack is directly against the provoker, *if* their retaliation seems justifiable, and *if* their target is not intimidating (Geen & Quanty, 1977; Hokanson & Edelman, 1966). In short, expressing anger can be *temporarily* calming *if* it does not leave us feeling guilty or anxious.

But expressing anger can also breed more anger. For one thing, it may provoke retaliation, thus escalating a minor conflict into a major confrontation. For another, expressing anger can magnify anger. (Recall Darwin's suggestion [page 308] that making violent gestures can increase anger.) Ebbe Ebbesen and his colleagues (1975) saw this when they interviewed 100 frustrated engineers and technicians just laid off by an aerospace company. Some were asked questions that released hostility, such as, "What instances can you think of where the company has not been fair with you?" When these people later filled out a questionnaire that assessed their attitudes toward the company, did this opportunity to "drain off" their hostility reduce it? Quite the contrary. Compared with those who had not vented their anger, those who had done so exhibited more hostility.

Thus, although "blowing off steam" may temporarily calm an angry person, it may also amplify underlying hostility. When angry outbursts do calm us, they may be reinforcing and therefore habit forming. If by berating referees, basketball coaches can drain off some of their tension, then the next time they feel tense with irritation they may be more likely to explode again. Similarly, the next time you are angry you are likely to do whatever has relieved your anger in the past.

What's the best way to handle anger? Experts offer several suggestions. First, bring down the physiological arousal of anger by waiting. "It is true of the body as of arrows," notes Carol Tavris (1982), "what goes up must come down. Any emotional arousal will simmer down if you just wait long enough." Second, deal with anger in a way that involves neither being chronically angry over every little annoyance nor passively sulking, which is merely rehearsing your reasons for anger. Don't be like those who, stifling their feelings over a series of provocations, finally overreact to a single incident (Baumeister & others, 1991). Vent the anger by playing an instrument, exercising, or confiding your feelings to a friend or in a diary.

As we noted earlier, anger can benefit relationships when it expresses a grievance in ways that promote reconciliation rather than retaliation. Civility means not only keeping silent about trivial irritations but also communicating important ones clearly and assertively. A nonaccusing statement of feeling—perhaps letting one's partner know that "I get irritated when you leave your dirty dishes for me to clean up"—can help resolve the conflicts that cause anger.

Happiness

"How to gain, how to keep, how to recover happiness is in fact for most men at all times the secret motive for all they do," observed William James (1902, p. 76). Understandably so, for one's state of happiness or unhappiness colors everything else. People who are happy perceive the world as safer (Johnson & Tversky, 1983), make decisions more easily (Isen & Means, 1983), rate job applicants more favorably (Baron, 1987), and report greater satisfaction with their whole lives (Schwarz & Clore, 1983). When your mood is gloomy, life as a whole seems depressing; but let your mood brighten, and suddenly your relationships, your self-image, and your hopes for the future all seem more promising.

Moreover—and this is one of psychology's most consistent findings—when we feel happy we are more willing to help others. In study after study, people given a mood-boosting experience, such as finding money, succeeding on a challenging task, or recalling a happy event, are more likely to give money, pick up someone's dropped papers, volunteer time, and so forth. It's called the feel-good, do-good phenomenon (Salovey, 1990).

In their pursuit of happiness, psychologists have studied influences upon both our temporary moods and our long-term life satisfaction. Studying people's reports of daily moods confirms that stressful events—an argument with someone, a sick child, a car problem—trigger bad moods. No surprise there. But by the next day, the gloom nearly always lifts. If anything, people tend to rebound from bad days to a *better*-than-usual good mood the following day (Bolger & others, 1989; Stone & Neale, 1984). Have you noticed this effect in your own life? When in a bad mood, can you usually depend on rebounding within a day or two? Are your times of elation similarly hard to sustain?

Apart from prolonged grief over the loss of a loved one or lingering anxiety after traumatic stress, such as child abuse, rape, or the terrors of war, even tragedy is not permanently depressing. The finding is surprising but reliable. People who become blind or paralyzed usually recover near-normal levels of day-to-day happiness. For example, able-bodied University of Illinois students described themselves as happy 50 percent of the time, unhappy 22 percent of the time, and neutral 29 percent of the time. To within 1 percentage point, disabled students rated their emotions identically (Chwalisz & others, 1988). Moreover, students perceive their disabled friends as just as happy as their nondisabled friends (Allman, 1989).

The effect of dramatically positive events is similarly temporary. Once their rush of euphoria wears off, state lottery winners typically find their overall happiness unchanged (Brickman & others, 1978). Other research confirms that there is much more to well-being than being well-off. Many people (including most new collegians, as Figure 10–6 hints) believe they would be happier if they had more money. They probably would be—temporarily. But in the long run, increased affluence hardly affects happiness. Those with lots of money are not much happier than those with only enough money to afford life's necessities. Within a given country there is a slight tendency for the wealthy to be happier than the poor. But people in wealthier countries report feeling only slightly more satisfied with their lives than do those in poorer countries (Inglehart, 1990).

"Weeping may tarry for the night, but joy comes with the morning."

Psalms 30:5

Note that the capacity of people in poor nations to be happy no more justifies poverty than does slaves' capacity to experience moments of happiness justify slavery.

Figure 10–6 Are today's collegians increasingly materialistic? From 1970 through most of the 1980s, annual surveys of more than 200,000 entering American college students revealed an increasing desire for wealth. Although the number is starting to come down, 74 percent in 1991 still rated "Being very well-off financially" as a very important goal. (From Dey & others, 1991.)

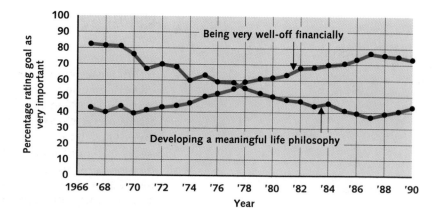

We can also ask whether, over time, our happiness grows with our paychecks. The American experience illustrates the answer: It does not. During the last three decades, the average American's buying power doubled. Their 1957 per person income, expressed in 1991 dollars, was $8,000; by 1991 it was over $16,000. With so much more of what money buys—twice as many cars per capita, and color TVs, VCRs, home computers, microwave ovens, and answering machines galore—did their increased wealth buy more happiness? As Figure 10–7 shows, the average American is now twice as rich, but

Figure 10–7 Does money buy happiness? It surely helps us to avoid certain types of pain. Yet, though buying power has doubled since the 1950s, self-reported happiness has remained almost unchanged. (Happiness data from Niemi, 1989, and T. Smith, 1991; income data from *Historical Statistics of the U.S.* and *Economic Indicators.*)

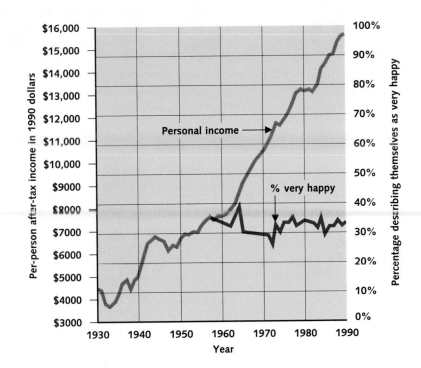

no happier. In 1957, 35 percent said they were "very happy," as did only 31 percent in 1991. Indeed, judging by increased rates of depression (page 393), Americans are more often miserable. It's shocking, and contradicts popular materialism, but how can we deny it: An affluent society's economic growth need not improve its morale.

Two psychological principles explain why more money apparently buys no more than a temporary surge of happiness, and why our emotions seem attached to elastic bands that pull us back from highs or lows. Each principle, in its own way, suggests that happiness is relative.

"No happiness lasts for long."

Seneca
Agamemnon, A.D. 60

adaptation-level principle The tendency for our judgments (of sounds, of lights, of income) to be relative to a "neutral" level defined by our experience.

The Adaptation-Level Principle: Happiness Is Relative to Our Prior Experience

The **adaptation-level principle** describes our tendency to judge various stimuli relative to what we have previously experienced. We adjust our "neutral" levels—the points at which sounds seem neither loud nor soft, lights neither bright nor dim, events neither pleasant nor unpleasant—based on our experience. We then notice and react to variations up or down from these levels.

Thus, if our income, grade-point average, or social prestige increases, we feel an initial surge of pleasure. We then adapt to this new level of achievement, come to see it as normal, and require something better yet to give us another surge of happiness. From my childhood, I can recall the thrill of

Calvin and Hobbes © 1991 Universal Press Syndicate. Reprinted with permission. All rights reserved.

watching my family's first 12-inch, black-and-white television set. Now, if the color goes out on our 25-inch TV, I feel deprived. Having adapted upward, I perceive as negative what I once experienced as positive. Yesterday's luxury has become today's necessity.

It follows that we will never create a social paradise on earth (Campbell, 1975). If you woke up tomorrow to your utopia—perhaps a world with no bills, no ills, all *As*, someone who loves you unreservedly—you would soon recalibrate your adaptation level. Before long you would again sometimes feel gratified (when achievements surpass expectations), sometimes deprived (when they fall below), and sometimes neutral. That helps explain why, despite the realities of triumph and tragedy, million-dollar lottery winners and paraplegics report similar levels of happiness. **The moral:** Satisfaction and dissatisfaction, success and failure—all are relative to our recent experience.

The Relative Deprivation Principle: Happiness Is Relative to Others' Attainments

To explain the frustration expressed by U.S. Air Corps soldiers during World War II, researchers formulated the concept of **relative deprivation** (the sense that we are worse off than others with whom we compare ourselves). Despite a relatively rapid promotion rate, many soldiers were frustrated about their promotion rates (Merton & Kitt, 1950). Apparently, seeing so many others being promoted inflated the soldiers' expectations. And when expectations soar above attainments, the result is frustration. When the Oakland Athletics signed outfielder Jose Canseco to a $4.7 million annual salary, his fellow outfielder Rickey Henderson became openly dissatisfied with his $3 million salary. Refusing to show up on time to spring training, he complained, "I don't think my contract is fair" (King, 1991).

Such comparisons help us understand why the middle- and upper-income people in a given country tend to be slightly more satisfied with life than the relatively poor, with whom the better-off can compare themselves (Diener, 1984). Nevertheless, once a person reaches a moderate income level, further increases do little to increase happiness. Why? Because as people climb the ladder of success they mostly compare themselves with those who are at or above their current level (Gruder, 1977; Suls & Tesch, 1978). For

relative deprivation The perception that one is worse off relative to those with whom one compares oneself.

Rickey Henderson, Jose Canseco was the standard of comparison. As Bertrand Russell (1930, pp. 68–69) observed, "Napoleon envied Caesar, Caesar envied Alexander, and Alexander, I daresay, envied Hercules, who never existed. You cannot, therefore, get away from envy by means of success alone, for there will always be in history or legend some person even more successful than you are."

By "counting our blessings" when we compare ourselves with those less fortunate, we can, however, increase our satisfaction. As comparing ourselves with those better-off creates envy, so comparing ourselves with those less well-off boosts contentment. Marshall Dermer and his colleagues (1979) demonstrated this by asking University of Wisconsin-Milwaukee women to study others' deprivation and suffering. After viewing vivid depictions of how grim life was in Milwaukee in 1900, or after imagining and then writing about various personal tragedies, such as being burned and disfigured, the women expressed greater satisfaction with their own lives. Similarly, when mildly depressed people read about someone who is even more depressed, they feel somewhat better (Gibbons, 1986).

The effect of comparison with others helps us understand why students of a given level of academic ability tend to have a higher academic self-concept if they attend a school where most other students are not exceptionally able (Marsh & Parker, 1984). Having brilliant classmates can make even a bright student feel inferior.

Predictors of Happiness

If, as the adaptation-level principle implies, our emotions tend to balance around normal, then why do some people seem so filled with joy and others so gloomy day after day? What makes one person normally happy and another depressed? In reviewing research, Ed Diener (1984) spotted several variables that correlate with happiness (Table 10–1). Remember, though, that knowing that two variables correlate does not tell us whether one causes the other. For example, many studies indicate that religiously active people tend to report greater happiness and life satisfaction (Myers, 1992). Is happiness conducive to religious commitment? Or, by providing meaning, inner peace, and a sense of ultimate acceptance, does religious faith enhance happiness?

Comparing with those worse off can prompt us to count our blessings, as some people surely did when passing Mike and Jean Richardson and their son, who were lured from Houston to Dallas by a promised job that didn't materialize.

Table 10-1

Happiness Is . . .

Researchers have found that happy people tend to:	However, other factors that seem unrelated to happiness include:
Have high self-esteem	Age
Be optimistic and outgoing	Race
Have a satisfying marriage or other love relationship	Gender (women are more often depressed but also more often joyful)
Have a meaningful religious faith	Educational level
Sleep well	Parenthood (having or not having children)
Exercise	

Source: Summarized from Diener (1984) and Myers (1992).

Whether at work or leisure, most of us derive greatest enjoyment from engaging, challenging activities. Mihaly Csikszentmihalyi (1990; pronounced chick-SENT-me-hi) and his colleagues discovered this after interrupting volunteers several times a day with an electronic paging device. When beeped, the people would note what they were doing and how they were feeling. Usually, they felt happier if mentally engaged by work or active leisure than if passively vegetating. Ironically, the less expensive (and usually more involving) a leisure activity, the more absorbed and happier people are while doing it. People are happier gardening than sitting on a power boat. They're happier talking to friends than watching TV. Indeed, happy are those whose work and leisure absorb them, enabling them unself-consciously to "flow" in focused activity.

Rehearse It

5. Human beings can learn to fear almost anything. However, it appears that some fears are learned more readily—and unlearned with more difficulty—than others. These fears, which appear to have had survival value for humans in the past, include fears of
a. nuclear weapons.
b. snakes, spiders, and cliffs.
c. electricity and explosives.
d. failure.

6. In some situations, venting anger—"blowing up"—seems to calm a person temporarily. In other cases, acting angry increases hostility. Experts suggest that to bring down anger, a good first step is to
a. retaliate verbally or physically.
b. wait or "simmer down."

c. express anger in action or fantasy.
d. review the grievance silently.

7. A philosopher notes that one cannot escape envy by means of success alone: There will always be someone more successful, more accomplished, or richer with whom to compare oneself. In psychology this observation is embodied in
a. the relative deprivation principle.
b. the adaptation-level phenomenon.
c. the list of predictors of life satisfaction.
d. the feel-good, do-good phenomenon.

8. When happy and unhappy people are compared, researchers find that happy people are optimistic, outgoing, and likely to have satisfying close relationships. One

of the most consistent findings of psychological research is that happy people are also
a. more likely to express anger.
b. generally luckier than others.
c. concentrated in the wealthier nations.
d. more likely to help others.

9. Age, race, and gender seem not to be predictably related to subjective feelings of happiness or well-being. However, researchers have found that happy people tend to
a. have children.
b. score high on intelligence tests.
c. have a meaningful religious faith.
d. complete high school and some college.

Theories of Emotion

Preview Question

8. What issue distinguishes the James-Lange and Cannon-Bard theories of emotion?

We have seen that emotions are built from the interplay of physiological arousal, expressive behavior, and conscious experiences. But there is controversy over this interplay. One debate concerns the connection between what we *think* and how we *feel:* Do emotions always grow from thoughts? From our mind's appraisal of a situation? Before considering this question, let's consider an older debate: Does your heart pound because you are afraid, or are you afraid because you feel your heart pounding?

The James-Lange and Cannon-Bard Theories

Common sense tells most of us that we cry because we are sad, lash out because we are angry, tremble because we are afraid. However, to pioneering

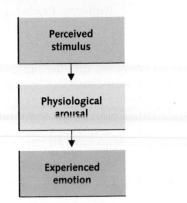

Figure 10–8 The James-Lange theory of emotion.

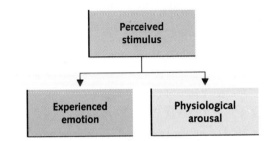

Figure 10–9 The Cannon-Bard theory of emotion.

*"Whenever I feel afraid
I hold my head up high
And whistle a happy tune."*

Richard Rodgers and Oscar
Hammerstein
The King and I

James-Lange theory   The theory that our experience of emotion is our awareness of our physiological responses to emotion-arousing stimuli.

Cannon-Bard theory   The theory that an emotion-arousing stimulus simultaneously triggers (1) physiological responses and (2) the subjective experience of emotion.

psychologist William James the common-sense view of emotion was 180 degrees out of line. According to James, "we feel sorry because we cry, angry because we strike, afraid because we tremble" (1890, p. 1066). If an oncoming car is in your lane, you will swerve sharply to avoid it; *then* you will notice your racing heart and feel shaken with fright. Your feeling of fear follows your body's response (Figure 10–8).

James's idea, which was independently proposed by Danish physiologist Carl Lange and is therefore called the **James-Lange theory,** struck American physiologist Walter Cannon as implausible. For one thing, Cannon thought the body's responses were not distinct enough to evoke the different emotions. Does a racing heart signal fear, anger, or love? For another, changes in heart rate, perspiration, and body temperature seemed to occur too slowly to trigger sudden emotion. Cannon, and later another American physiologist, Philip Bard, concluded that body arousal and the emotional experience occur simultaneously: The emotion-arousing stimulus is routed simultaneously to the brain cortex, causing the subjective awareness of emotion, and to the sympathetic nervous system, causing the body's arousal. Thus, this **Cannon-Bard theory** implies that your heart begins pounding as you experience fear, but one does not cause the other (Figure 10–9).

As long as the evidence suggested that the arousal of one emotion is much the same as another, the James-Lange assumption that we experience our emotions through differing body states seemed improbable. With new evidence showing subtle physiological distinctions among the emotions, the James-Lange theory has become more plausible. As James struggled with his own feelings of depression and grief, he came to believe that we can control emotions by going "through the outward motions" of whatever emotion one wants to experience. "To feel cheerful," he advised, "sit up cheerfully, look around cheerfully, and act as if cheerfulness were already there." The new findings concerning emotional effects of facial expressions (page 308) are precisely what James might have predicted.

To check your understanding of the James-Lange and Cannon-Bard theories, imagine that your brain could not sense your heart pounding or your stomach churning. According to each theory, how would this affect your experienced emotions?

Cannon and Bard would have expected you to experience emotions normally, because they believed emotions occur separately from (though simultaneously with) the body's arousal. James and Lange would have expected greatly diminished emotions because they believed that to experience emotion you must first perceive your body responses.

The condition you imagined actually exists in people with severed spinal cords. Psychologist George Hohmann (1966) interviewed 25 soldiers who received such injuries in World War II. He asked them to recall emotion-arousing incidents that occurred before and after their spinal injuries. Those with injuries in the lower part of the spine, who had lost sensation only in their legs, reported little change in their emotions. Those who could feel nothing below the neck reported a considerable decrease in emotional intensity (as James and Lange would have expected). These soldiers said they might act much the same as before in emotion-arousing situations, but as one confessed about his anger, "It just doesn't have the heat to it that it used to. It's a mental kind of anger." On the other hand, emotions expressed mostly in body areas above the neck are felt more intensely by those with spinal cord injury. Virtually all the men Hohmann interviewed reported increases in weeping, lumps in the throat, and getting choked up when saying good-bye, worshipping, or watching a touching movie.

Although such evidence has breathed new life into the James-Lange theory, many researchers agree with Cannon and Bard that our experienced emotions also involve cognitive activity in the cortex. Whether or not we fear the character in the dark alley depends entirely on whether we interpret his actions as hostile or friendly. So with James and Lange we can say that arousal is an important ingredient of emotion. And with Cannon and Bard we can say that there is more to the experience of emotion than reading our physiology.

Cognition and Emotion

Now, the new controversy: Put simply, what is the connection between what we *think* and how we *feel?*

Can we experience emotion apart from thinking? This issue has practical implications for self-improvement. To change our emotions, must we change our thinking?

Schachter's Two-Factor Theory of Emotion

Most psychologists today believe that our cognitions—our perceptions, memories, and interpretations—are an essential ingredient of emotion. One such theorist is Stanley Schachter, whose **two-factor theory** proposes that emotions have two ingredients: physical arousal and a cognitive label (Figure 10–10). Like James and Lange, Schachter presumed that our experience of emotion grows from our awareness of our body's arousal. But he also believes, like Cannon and Bard, that emotions are physiologically similar, so he argues that an emotional experience requires a conscious interpretation of the arousal.

It is often hard to disentangle our arousal response to an event from our interpretation of the event. Imagine that you attribute some of your arousal to the wrong source. Perhaps after an invigorating run you arrive home to find a message that you got the longed-for job. You are elated. Would you feel the same degree of elation (because your lingering arousal from running spills into your emotion) if you received this news after awakening from a nap?

To find out, Schachter and Jerome Singer (1962) aroused college men with injections of the arousal hormone, epinephrine. Picture yourself as one of their subjects: After receiving the injection, you go to a waiting room, where you find yourself with another person (actually an accomplice of the experimenters) who is acting either euphoric or irritated. As you observe this person, you begin to feel your heart race, your body flush, and your breathing becoming more rapid. If told to expect these effects from the injection, what would you feel? Schachter and Singer's subjects felt little emotion—because they attributed their arousal to the drug. But if told the injection would produce no effects, what would you feel? Perhaps you would react, as another group of subjects did, by "catching" the apparent emotion of the person you are with—becoming happy if the accomplice is acting euphoric and testy if the accomplice is acting irritated.

This discovery—that a stirred-up state can be experienced as one emotion or another very different one, depending on how we interpret and label it—has been replicated in dozens of experiments. Although emotional arousal is not as undifferentiated as Schachter believed, arousal can intensify just about any emotion (Reisenzein, 1983). When people who have just been aroused by pedaling an exercise bike or watching a rock concert film are insulted, they find it easy to misattribute their arousal to the provocation and they feel

Preview Question

9. What is the relationship between thinking and feeling?

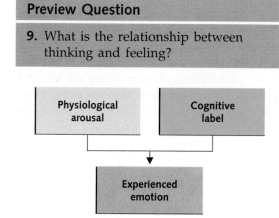

Figure 10–10 A summary of Schachter's two-factor theory of emotion. To experience emotion, we must be aroused and must cognitively label the arousal.

two-factor theory Schachter's theory that to experience emotion one must (1) be physically aroused and (2) cognitively label the arousal.

angrier than do similarly provoked people not previously aroused. Thus, arousal from emotions as diverse as anger, fear, and sexual excitement can indeed spill from one emotion to another (Zillmann, 1986). In anger-provoking situations, sexually aroused people react with more hostility. Similarly, the arousal that lingers after an intense argument or a frightening experience may intensify sexual passion (Palace & Gorzalka, 1990).

Must Cognition Precede Emotion?

So, to experience an emotion, must we first label our arousal? Robert Zajonc (pronounced ZI-yence) (1980, 1984a) contends the answer is no. He argues that our emotional reactions are sometimes quicker than our interpretations of a situation; we therefore feel some emotions *before* we think. (Can you recall immediately liking something or someone without at first knowing why?)

In earlier chapters, we noted that when people repeatedly view stimuli flashed too briefly for them to perceive and recall, they nevertheless come to prefer these stimuli. Without being consciously aware of having seen the stimuli, they rather like them. Moreover, some neural pathways involved in emotion bypass the cortical areas involved in thinking. One such pathway runs from the eye via the thalamus to one of the brain's emotional control centers, the amygdala (LeDoux, 1986). This enables a quick, automatic emotional response, which may then be modified after the cortex has further interpreted a threat (Figure 10–11). In the forest, we warily jump at a cracking sound, leaving the cortex to decide whether it was a falling tree branch or a predator. Such evidence convinces Zajonc that *some* of our emotional reactions involve no deliberate thinking. Cognition, he believes, is not necessary for emotion.

Figure 10–11 The brain's short-cut for emotions. Sensory input may be routed by the thalamus both to the cortex and directly to the amygdala for a more instant emotional reaction.

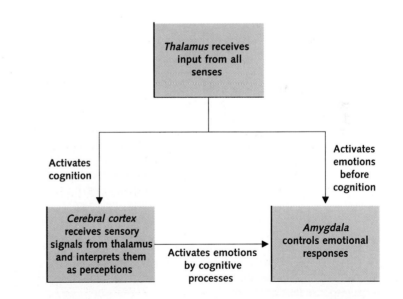

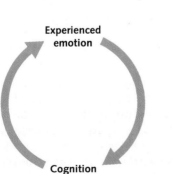

Figure 10–12 Emotion and cognition feed each other. But which is the chicken and which the egg? Lazarus believes that, although emotions influence thinking, our cognitive appraisal of a situation always precedes emotion. Zajonc contends that some of our emotional reactions precede cognitive processing.

Emotion researcher Richard Lazarus (1984, 1991) disagrees. He concedes that our brains process and react to vast amounts of information without our conscious awareness, and he willingly grants that some emotional responses do not require *conscious* thinking (Figure 10–12). Nevertheless, he says, even instantaneously felt emotions require some sort of quick cognitive appraisal of the situation; otherwise, how do we *know* what we are reacting to? The appraisal may be effortless and we may not be conscious of it, but it is still a function of the mind.

Complex emotions, such as anger, guilt, happiness, and love, clearly arise from our conscious interpretations, memories, and inferences. Highly emotional people are intense partly because of their interpretations. They *personalize* events as being somehow directed at them and *generalize* their experiences by blowing single incidents out of proportion (Larsen & others, 1987). How we explain good and bad events affects both our emotions and our motivation. Whether we attribute a low grade to an unfair exam, bad luck, or our own inability or laziness determines whether we feel irritated or depressed (Weiner, 1985). Attributing failure to our own inability erodes motivation. If I just don't have it, why try?

For us, the important conclusion concerns what Lazarus and Zajonc agree on: Some emotional responses—especially simple likes, dislikes, and fears—involve no conscious thinking. We may fear the spider, even if we "know" it is harmless. After conditioning, Little Albert was afraid of furry objects. Such responses are hard to alter by changing our thinking.

Other emotions—including moods such as depression and complex feelings such as hatred and love—are greatly affected by our interpretations, memories, and expectations. For these emotions, as we will see in Chapter 13, learning to *think* more positively about ourselves and the world around us makes us *feel* better.

Regardless of the origins of our emotional responses, how we feel matters to our body. Nervous about a speech or performance, we frequent the bathroom. Smoldering over a family conflict, we get a splitting headache. When such stress endures, it may trigger a skin rash, an asthma attack, or an ulcer. Might it also, as many researchers now believe, put us at risk for one of today's three leading causes of death—heart disease, cancer, and strokes?

Rehearse It

10. Two important theories of emotion are the James-Lange theory and the Cannon-Bard theory. The James-Lange theory states that our experience of an emotion is a consequence of our physiological response to a stimulus; we are afraid because our heart pounds (in response, for example, to an approaching stranger). The Cannon-Bard theory, on the other hand, proposes that the physiological response (like heart pounding) and the subjective experience of, say, fear
a. are unrelated.
b. occur simultaneously.
c. occur in the opposite order (with feelings of fear first).
d. are regulated by the thalamus.

11. According to the two-factor theory, emotions have two components: physical arousal (such as rapid heartbeat) and a cognitive label (such as "nervousness before the exam"). The two-factor theory predicts that becoming physically aroused will
a. weaken an emotion.
b. intensify an emotion.
c. transform an emotion into a different emotion.
d. have no particular effect on the emotion.

12. Research suggests that we can experience an aroused state as one of several different emotions, depending on how we interpret and label the arousal. If physically aroused by swimming, then heckled by an onlooker, we may interpret our arousal as anger and
a. become less physically aroused.
b. feel angrier than usual.
c. feel less angry than usual.
d. feel sexually aroused.

13. Robert Zajonc maintains that some of our emotional reactions occur before we have had the chance to label or interpret them. Richard Lazarus disagrees. The two psychologists differ about whether or not emotional responses occur in the absence of
a. physical arousal.
b. conscious thought.
c. cognitive processing.
d. learning.

Stress and Health

health psychology A subfield of psychology that provides a behavioral approach to medicine. Assumes that biological, psychological, and social factors all contribute to illness and can be a part of preventive strategies.

stress The whole process by which we perceive and respond to certain events, called *stressors*, that we appraise as threatening or challenging.

Walking along the path toward her Rocky Mountain campsite, Karen hears a rustle in the bushes ahead. As she glimpses a rattlesnake, her body mobilizes for fight or flight: Her muscles tense, her adrenaline flows, her heart pounds. Flee she does, racing to the security of camp. Once there, Karen's muscles gradually relax and her heart rate and breathing ease.

Karl leaves his suburban apartment one morning and, delayed by road construction, arrives at the parking lot of the commuter train station just in time to see the 8:05 pull away. Catching the next train, he arrives in the city late and elbows his way through crowds of rush-hour pedestrians. Once at his bank office, he apologizes to his first client, who wonders where Karl has been and why his quarterly investment report is not ready. Karl does his best to mollify the client. Afterward, Karl notices his pent-up emotion—his tense muscles, clenched teeth, and churning stomach.

According to the American Academy of Family Physicians, symptoms related to stress prompt two-thirds of office visits to family doctors (Wallis, 1983).

Karen's response to stress removed her from danger; Karl's, if chronic, could increase his risk of heart disease, high blood pressure, and other stress-linked health problems. Moreover, feeling under pressure, he might sleep and exercise less and smoke and drink more, further endangering his long-term health.

The new subfield of **health psychology** assumes that illness results from the interaction of our biological, psychological, and social systems. Health psychologists ask: How do our emotions and responses to stress influence our risk of disease? What attitudes and behaviors help prevent illness and promote health and well-being? How can we reduce or control stress?

Stress and Stressors

Preview Question

10. What is stress?

Stress is a slippery concept. It sometimes describes threats or challenges ("Karl faced considerable stress") and sometimes describes our responses to them ("When Karen saw the rattler, she experienced acute stress"). To encompass both these meanings, we can define **stress** as the whole process by which we appraise and respond to events, called *stressors*, that threaten or challenge us. Stressors can have positive effects by arousing and motivating us to conquer problems. Championship athletes, successful entertainers, and great teachers and leaders all thrive and excel when aroused by a challenge. But more often stressors threaten our resources—our status and security on the job, our loved ones' health or well-being, our deeply held beliefs, our self-image (Hobfoll, 1989). And when such stress is severe or prolonged, it may also cause mental or physiological harm.

Challenging positive events, such as graduating into the working world, can be stressful. But most stresses arise from negative events that threaten our well-being, such as a child's sudden death from a stray bullet.

general adaptation syndrome (GAS)
Selye's concept of the body's adaptive response to stress as composed of three stages—alarm, resistance, exhaustion.

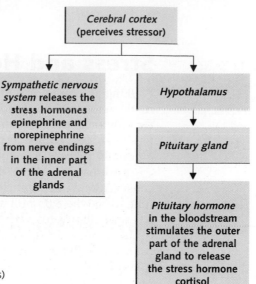

Cerebral cortex (perceives stressor)

Sympathetic nervous system releases the stress hormones epinephrine and norepinephrine from nerve endings in the inner part of the adrenal glands

Hypothalamus

Pituitary gland

Pituitary hormone in the bloodstream stimulates the outer part of the adrenal gland to release the stress hormone cortisol

Figure 10–13 The adrenal glands (atop the kidneys) release stress hormones on orders received through a dual-track system.

The Stress Response System

Although medical interest in stress dates back to Hippocrates (460–377 B.C.), it was not until the 1920s that physiologist Walter Cannon (1929) confirmed that the stress response is part of a unified mind-body system. He observed that a variety of stressors—extreme cold, lack of oxygen, emotion-arousing incidents—trigger an outpouring of epinephrine and norepinephrine. These stress hormones enter the bloodstream from sympathetic nerve endings in the inner part of the adrenal glands. This is but one part of the sympathetic nervous system's response. As we saw in Figure 10–1 (page 302), when alerted by any of a number of brain pathways, the sympathetic nervous system increases heart rate and respiration, diverts blood to skeletal muscles, and releases energy from the body's stores—all to prepare the body for what Cannon called *fight or flight.* All in all, this stress response struck Cannon as wonderfully adaptive. Physiologists have also identified a second stress response system (Figure 10–13). On orders from the cerebral cortex (via the hypothalamus and pituitary gland), the outer (cortex) part of the adrenal gland secretes the stress hormone cortisol.

Canadian scientist Hans Selye's (1936, 1976) 40 years of research on stress extended Cannon's findings and helped make stress a major concept in both psychology and medicine. Selye studied animals' reactions to various stressors, such as electric shock, surgical trauma, and immobilizing restraint. He discovered that the body's adaptive response to stress seemed so general— like a single burglar alarm that would sound no matter what intruded—that he called it the **general adaptation syndrome (GAS).**

Selye saw the GAS as having three phases (Figure 10–14). Let's say you suffer a physical or emotional trauma. In Phase 1, you experience an *alarm reaction* due to the sudden activation of your sympathetic nervous system. Your heart rate zooms, blood is diverted to your skeletal muscles, and you feel the faintness of shock. With your resources mobilized you are now ready to fight the challenge during Phase 2, *resistance.* Your temperature, blood pressure, and respiration remain high, and there is a sudden outpouring of

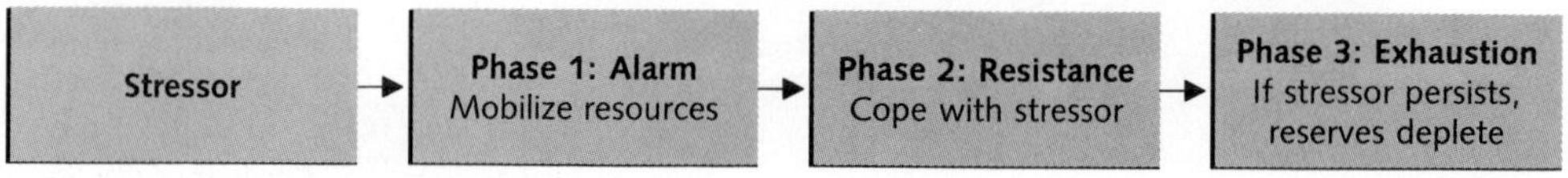

Stressor	Phase 1: Alarm Mobilize resources	Phase 2: Resistance Cope with stressor	Phase 3: Exhaustion If stressor persists, reserves deplete

Figure 10–14 Selye's general adaptation syndrome.

Psychology Applied: The Wounds of War—Post-Traumatic Stress Disorder

During the fighting in Vietnam, Jack's platoon was repeatedly under fire. In one ambush, his closest friend was killed while standing a few feet away. Jack himself killed a young Vietcong soldier by bludgeoning him with a rifle butt. Years later, images of these events intrude as flashbacks and nightmares. He still jumps at the sound of a cap gun or the backfire of a car. When annoyed by family or friends, he lashes out in ways he seldom did before Vietnam. To calm his continuing anxiety, he drinks more than he should.

Such has been the experience of Vietnam combat veterans, Holocaust survivors, and sexual assault victims who suffer from *post-traumatic stress disorder*, symptoms of which include haunting memories and nightmares, social withdrawal, and anxiety or depression (Kaylor & others, 1987; Nadler & Ben-Shushan, 1989; Wilson & others, 1988). To pin down the frequency of such problems, the Centers for Disease Control (1988) compared 7000 Vietnam combat veterans with 7000 noncombat veterans who served during the same years. Combat stress more than doubled a veteran's risk of suffering alcohol abuse, depression, or anxiety.

Studies of Israeli and American soldiers reveal that the more terrifying and prolonged the battle experience, the greater the psychological casualties (King & King, 1991; Solo-

The emotional costs of the Persian War were great, especially for this soldier. He has just been told that the body bag alongside him contains his friend.

mon, 1990). Among Vietnam veterans, the roughly 15 percent rate of post-traumatic stress symptoms was halved among those who never saw combat and tripled among those who experienced heavy combat. For example, more than a decade after the war, one study located 2095 identical twins among Vietnam-era veterans (Goldberg & others, 1990). Compared to co-twins who served noncombat roles in Vietnam, those who experienced heavy combat were 5.4 times more likely to be suffering post-traumatic stress disorder. Although most of these combat-stressed veterans are living produc-

tive lives, many still experience nightmares, have trouble sleeping and concentrating, and find themselves easily startled. This is especially so for those exposed to savage mutilation, torture, or the sight of a friend's death.

Most calculations of the costs of war count fatalities, injuries, and expenditures. There are also emotional costs of fighting. On February 28, 1991, the shooting in the Persian Gulf war stopped. But for many, especially among battle-stressed Iraqi soldiers and citizens and victimized Kuwaitis, the psychological wounds of war had only begun.

hormones. If persistent, the stress may eventually deplete your body's reserves during Phase 3, *exhaustion*. With exhaustion, you are more vulnerable to illness or even, in extreme cases, collapse and death.

Newer research reveals subtle differences in the body's reactions to different stressors. Nevertheless, few medical experts today quarrel with Selye's basic point: Prolonged stress can produce physical deterioration. This leads to the practical concerns of today's health psychologists: What causes stress? What are the effects of stress? And how can we alleviate those effects?

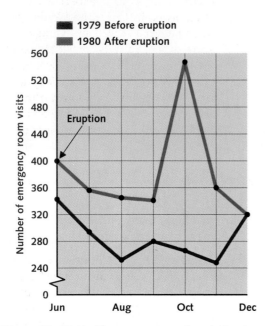

Figure 10–15 Health consequences of a cataclysmic event. During the 7 months following the May 18, 1980, eruption of Mount Saint Helens, emergency room visits in nearby Othello, Washington, rose 34 percent compared to the same 7-month period during the previous year. (From Adams & Adams, 1984.)

Stressful Life Events

The level of stress we experience depends on how we appraise the events of our lives. One person alone in a house dismisses its creaking sounds and experiences no stress; someone else suspects an intruder and becomes alarmed. Research has focused on the health consequences of three types of stressors: catastrophes, significant life changes, and daily hassles.

Catastrophes   Catastrophes are unpredictable, large-scale events such as war and natural disasters. Although people often provide one another with aid and comfort after such events, the health consequences can be significant. Paul and Gerald Adams (1984) documented this by studying the aftermath of the 1980 Mount Saint Helens eruption and ash fall. Compared with the same period during the previous year, emergency room visits in the nearby town of Othello, Washington, rose 34 percent during the 7 months following the eruption (Figure 10–15). Stress-related physical complaints at the local mental health clinic doubled and deaths rose 19 percent.

Do community disasters usually produce effects this great? After digesting data from 52 such studies of catastrophic floods, hurricanes, and fires, Anthony Rubonis and Leonard Bickman (1991) found the typical effect more modest but nonetheless genuine. In disaster's wake, rates of psychological disorders, such as depression and anxiety, rose an average 17 percent. Refugees fleeing their homeland also suffer increased rates of psychological disorder. Their stress stems from the trauma of uprooting and family separation and from the challenges of adjusting to a foreign culture, with its differing language, ethnicity, climate, and social norms (Williams & Berry, 1991).

Significant Life Changes   The second type of life event stressor is personal life changes—the death of a loved one, the loss of a job, a marriage or divorce. Some psychologists study the health effects of life changes by following people over time to see if such events precede illnesses. Others compare the life changes recalled by those who have or have not suffered a specific health problem such as a heart attack. A review of these studies commissioned by the National Academy of Sciences revealed that people recently widowed, fired, or divorced are more vulnerable to disease (Dohrenwend & others, 1982). A Finnish study of 96,000 widowed people confirmed the phenomenon: Their risk of death doubled in the week following their partner's death (Kaprio & others, 1987). Experiencing a cluster of crises puts one even more at risk.

Fortunately, life's major crises are fairly infrequent. When they occur, it's how we appraise them that matters. Retirement may increase stress for one person and reduce it for another. Having an abortion creates stress for women who morally oppose abortion and who lack their partner's or parents' support. Yet most women do not experience severe distress after an abortion (Adler & others, 1990; Major & others, 1990). Thus, notes biologist Robert Sapolsky (1990), "the psychological filters through which external events are perceived can alter physiology at least as profoundly as the external events themselves."

Daily Hassles   As a famous Peanuts book says, "*Happiness is* . . . an *A* on your spelling test . . . finding someone you like at the front door . . . an invitation to a party . . . your first kiss in the rain." As we noted earlier, today's happiness stems less from enduring good fortune than from daily events—a longed-for date, a gratifying letter, your team's winning the big game.

Psychology Applied: The Perceived-Stress Scale

How much stress do you feel in your life? With the help of pollster Louis Harris, researchers Sheldon Cohen and Gail Williamson (1988) asked the following questions of a cross-section of adult Americans.

In the last month, how often have you felt:

a. unable to control the important things in your life?

    0. Never
    1. Almost never
    2. Sometimes
    3. Fairly often
    4. Very often

b. confident about your ability to handle your personal problems?

    0. Very often
    1. Fairly often
    2. Sometimes
    3. Almost never
    4. Never

c. that things were going your way?

    0. Very often
    1. Fairly often
    2. Sometimes
    3. Almost never
    4. Never

d. that difficulties were piling up so high that you could not overcome them?

    0. Never
    1. Almost never
    2. Sometimes
    3. Fairly often
    4. Very often

Your score (from adding the points indicated) provides a crude but quick index to your experienced stress level. In Cohen and Williamson's national study, an average score was 4.7 points for women and 4.2 for men. People with low stress scores were slightly more likely to report themselves in good health and to be practicing good health habits (exercising, not smoking, etc.).

The principle works for negative events, too. Everyday annoyances may be the most significant sources of stress (Lazarus, 1990; Weinberger & others, 1987). These daily hassles include rush-hour traffic, aggravating housemates, long lines at the bank or store, and getting caught in the rain without an umbrella. Although some people can simply shrug them off, others are "driven up the wall" by such inconveniences. Thus, 6 in 10 Americans say they feel "great stress" at least once a week (Harris, 1987; see also Psychology Applied: The Perceived-Stress Scale).

Charles Bukowski (cited by Lazarus in Wallis, 1983): "It's not the large things that send a man to the madhouse . . . no, it's the continuing series of small tragedies . . . not the death of his love but the shoelace that snaps with no time left."

approach-approach conflict Feeling torn between two attractive but incompatible goals.

avoidance-avoidance conflict Feeling torn between which of two unappealing alternatives to avoid.

approach-avoidance conflict Feeling drawn to a goal but also repelled by it, especially when close to it.

Over time, these little stressors can add up and take a toll on health and well-being. Hypertension (high blood pressure) is common among the residents of America's urban ghettos, who endure the daily stresses that accompany poverty, unemployment, single parenting, crime, and overcrowding. There is a correspondingly low rate of heart attacks among those who live the relatively peaceful, monastic life (Henry & Stephens, 1977).

One source of stress comes from everyday conflicts we face between our different motives. Least stressful are the **approach-approach conflicts,** in which two attractive but incompatible goals pull us—to go to a sporting event or out for pizza, to take sociology or anthropology, to wear the green or the raspberry sweater.

Other times we face an **avoidance-avoidance conflict** between two undesirable alternatives. Do you avoid studying a disliked subject or do you avoid failure by opening the book? Do you suffer someone's wrath for admitting the truth or feelings of guilt for having told a fib?

In times of **approach-avoidance conflict** we feel simultaneously attracted and repelled. Some things you may adore about a person you are dating, other things you dislike. Compared to the approach tendency, the avoidance tendency grows more rapidly as you approach the goal (Figure 10–16). Thus, you vacillate. From a distance, the goal—a happy relationship—looks pretty good. Up close, you feel an urge to escape. Stepping back, the negative aspects fade and you again feel attracted. Stress multiplies when we face several approach-avoidance conflicts simultaneously—regarding whom to date, which school to attend, which job to accept.

Figure 10–16 Approach-avoidance conflict. As people approach the goal, their avoidance tendency often rises faster than their approach tendency, causing them to vacillate. This youth's fear is keeping him from diving into the pool.

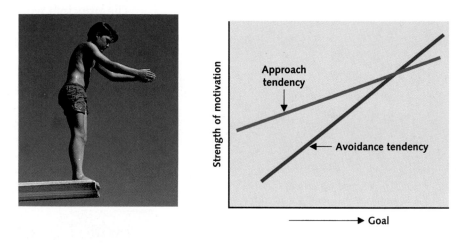

Perceived Control

Catastrophes, important life changes, and daily hassles and conflicts are especially stressful when we appraise them as both negative *and* uncontrollable. If two rats receive simultaneous shocks, but one of them can turn a wheel to stop the shocks, the helpless rat becomes most susceptible to ulcers and lowered immunity to disease (Laudenslager & Reite, 1984) (Figure 10–17).

So it goes in humans: Perceiving a loss of control, we are vulnerable to ill health. Elderly nursing home patients who have little control over their activities tend to decline faster and die sooner than do those given more control over their activities (Rodin, 1986).

Another factor that influences our stress vulnerability is optimism. Psychologists Michael Scheier and Charles Carver (1992) report that optimists—

people who agree with statements such as, "In uncertain times, I usually expect the best"—cope more successfully with stressful events and enjoy better health. During the last month of a semester, students previously identified as optimistic report less fatigue and fewer coughs, aches, and pains. Optimists also respond to stress with smaller increases in blood pressure and recover faster from heart bypass surgery.

Figure 10–17 The health consequences of loss of control. The "executive" rat at the left can switch off the tail shock by turning the wheel. Because it has control over the shock, it is no more likely to develop ulcers than the unshocked control rat on the right. The "subordinate" rat in the center receives the same shocks as the executive rat. But because it has no control over the shocks, the subordinate rat is more likely to develop ulcers. (From Weiss, 1977.)

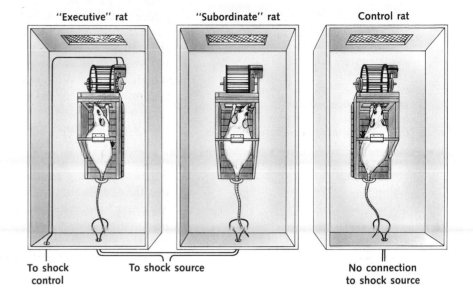

Why do perceived lack of control and a pessimistic outlook contribute to health problems? Animal studies show—and human studies confirm—that losing control provokes an outpouring of stress hormones. When rats cannot control shock or when humans feel unable to control their environment, cortisol levels rise and immune responses drop (Rodin, 1986). Captive animals therefore experience more stress and are more vulnerable to disease than wild animals (Roberts, 1988). The crowding that occurs in high-density neighborhoods, prisons, and college dorms is another source of diminished control—and of increased levels of stress hormones and blood pressure (Fleming & others, 1987; Ostfeld & others, 1987).

Stress and Heart Disease

Although infrequent before this century, **coronary heart disease**—the narrowing of the vessels that nourish the heart muscle—became by the 1950s North America's leading cause of death. In the United States alone, more than half a million people die annually from heart attacks. Why this dramatic increase in coronary deaths? Clearly, people live longer now, and older people are more vulnerable to heart attacks. But changing longevity does not explain why more younger adults are dying of heart disease (Chesney, 1984).

Many factors increase the risk of heart disease—smoking, obesity, family history of the disease, high-fat diet, physical inactivity, elevated blood pressure, and elevated cholesterol level. But even considering all these factors still leaves many instances of heart disease unexplained. Many inactive, overweight smokers do not suffer the disease and many who do suffer heart attacks are active, slender nonsmokers.

Preview Question

12. Who is most vulnerable to heart disease?

coronary heart disease   The clogging of the vessels that nourish the heart muscle; the leading cause of death in the United States.

Type A Friedman and Rosenman's term for competitive, hard-driving, impatient, verbally aggressive, and anger-prone people.

Type B Friedman and Rosenman's term for easygoing, relaxed people.

psychophysiological illness Literally, "mind-body" illness; any physical illness not caused by a known physical disorder. For example, stress can produce hypertension, ulcers, and headaches. Note: This is distinct from *hypochondriasis*—misinterpreting normal physical sensations as symptoms of a disease.

lymphocytes The two types of white blood cells that are part of the body's immune system: B lymphocytes form in the *b*one marrow and release antibodies that fight bacterial infections; T lymphocytes form in the *t*hymus and, among other duties, attack cancer cells, viruses, and foreign substances.

"At ten-thirty, you have an appointment to get even with Ward Ingram. At twelve, you're going to get even with Holus Wentworth at lunch. At three, you're getting even with the Pro-Tech Company at their annual meeting. And at five you're going to get even with Fred Benton over drinks."

Drawing by Fradon; © 1985 The New Yorker Magazine, Inc.

So what else might be involved? In 1956, cardiologists Meyer Friedman, Ray Rosenman, and their colleagues stumbled upon an idea (Friedman & Ulmer, 1984). While studying the eating behavior of white, San Francisco Junior League women and their husbands, Friedman and Rosenman discovered that the women consumed as much cholesterol and fat as their husbands, yet were far less susceptible to heart disease. Was it because of their female sex hormones? No, the researchers surmised, because black women with the same sex hormones but facing more stress are as prone to heart disease as their husbands.

The Junior League president thought she knew the answer. "If you really want to know what is going to give our husbands heart attacks, I'll tell you. It's stress," she said sadly, "the stress they have to face in their businesses, day in, day out. Why, when my husband comes home at night, it takes at least one martini just to unclench his jaws."

To test the idea that stress increases vulnerability to heart disease, Friedman and Rosenman measured the blood cholesterol level and clotting speed of 40 U.S. tax accountants. From January through March, both of these coronary warning indicators were completely normal. Then, as the accountants began scrambling to finish their clients' tax returns before the April 15th filing deadline, their cholesterol and clotting measures rose to dangerous levels. In May and June, with the deadline past, the measures returned to normal. The researchers' hunch had paid off: Stress predicted heart attack risk.

The stage was set for what was to become Friedman and Rosenman's classic 9-year study of more than 3000 healthy men aged 35 to 59. At the start of the study, they interviewed each man for 15 minutes about his work and eating habits. During the interview, they noted the man's manner of talking and other behavioral patterns. Those who seemed the most reactive, competitive, hard-driving, impatient, time-conscious, supermotivated, verbally aggressive, and easily angered they called **Type A.** A roughly equal number who were more easygoing they called **Type B.** Which group do you suppose turned out to be the most coronary-prone? By the time the study was complete, 257 of the men had suffered heart attacks, 69 percent of whom were Type A. Thus, compared to the Type B men, the Type As were more than twice as vulnerable. Moreover, not one of the "pure" Type Bs—the most mellow and laidback of their group—had suffered a heart attack.

As often happens in science, this exciting discovery provoked enormous public interest. But after the honeymoon period, in which the finding seemed definitive and revolutionary, other researchers began the necessary labor of replicating and refining the conclusions.

Why may Type A people be more prone to heart disease? Further research found that reactive Type A individuals are more often "combat ready." When harassed or challenged, their active sympathetic nervous system redistributes blood flow to the muscles and away from the internal organs—including the liver, which removes cholesterol and fat from the blood. Thus, their blood may contain excess cholesterol and fat that later get deposited around the heart. Further stress may then trigger the altered heart rhythms that, in those with weakened hearts, cause sudden death (Kamarck & Jennings, 1991). In such ways, the hearts and minds of people interact.

Newer research reveals that Type A's toxic core is not a fast-paced life but negative emotions, especially the anger associated with an aggressively reactive temperament (Friedman & Booth-Kewley, 1988; Matthews, 1988). The effect of an anger-prone personality appears mostly in studies in which interviewers assess verbal assertiveness and emotional intensity. (If you pause in the middle of a sentence, an intense, anger-prone person may jump in and finish it for you.) Among young and middle-aged adults, those who react with anger over little things are the most coronary-prone. One study followed

"The fire you kindle for your enemy often burns you more than him."

Chinese proverb

Duke University law students over 25 years. Those inclined to be hostile and cynical were five times more likely than their gentler, trusting classmates to die by middle age (Williams, 1989). As Charles Spielberger and Perry London (1982) put it, rage "seems to lash back and strike us in the heart muscle."

Stress and Resistance to Disease

Preview Question

13. How does stress make us vulnerable to disease?

Psychophysiological ("mind-body") **illnesses,** which include certain forms of hypertension, ulcers, and headaches, are not caused by known physical disorders. Instead, the culprit is stress. In people with reactive temperaments, chronic stress produces various changes. In one person, prolonged resentment, anger, or anxiety may stimulate an excess of digestive acids that eats away parts of the lining of the stomach or small intestine, creating ulcers. Another person under stress may retain excess sodium and fluids, which, together with constriction of the arteries' muscle walls, contributes to increased blood pressure (Light & others, 1983).

Stress and the Immune System

"Each patient carries his own doctor inside him."

Albert Schweitzer, 1875–1965

Evidence that psychophysiological ailments are real comes from hundreds of new experiments that reveal the nervous and endocrine systems' influence on the immune system. The immune system is a complex surveillance system that defends the body by isolating and destroying bacteria, viruses, and other foreign substances. It includes two types of white blood cells, called **lymphocytes.** One type releases antibodies that fight bacterial infections. The other attacks cancer cells, viruses, and foreign substances—even "good" ones, such as transplanted organs. Another agent of the immune system is the *macrophage* ("big eater"), which identifies, pursues, and ingests harmful invaders. Age, nutrition, genetics, body temperature, and—we now know—stress all influence the immune system's activity.

The immune system can err in two directions. Responding too strongly, it may attack the body's own tissues, causing arthritis or an allergic attack. Other times, it underreacts, allowing, say, a dormant herpes virus to erupt or cancer cells to multiply.

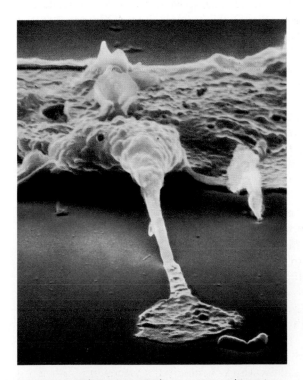

The immune system is not a headless horseman. Rather, it exchanges information with the brain and the hormone-secreting endocrine system. The brain regulates the secretion of stress hormones, which in turn suppress the disease-fighting lymphocytes (Institute of Medicine, 1989). Thus, when animals are physically restrained, given unavoidable electric shocks, or subjected to noise or crowding, they become more susceptible to disease (Jemmott & Locke, 1984).

Does stress similarly depress the immune system of humans? Consider:

Accumulating evidence shows that stress lowers the body's resistance to upper respiratory infections and herpes (Cohen & Williamson, 1991).

The U.S. National Academy of Sciences (1984) reports that the grief and depression that follow the death of a spouse decrease immune defenses and increase the risk of having a heart attack or stroke.

A large macrophage (at top) about to trap and ingest a tiny bacterium (lower right). Macrophages constantly patrol the body in their search for invaders, such as this *Escherichia coli* bacterium, and for debris, such as worn-out red blood cells.

In three separate Skylab missions, the immune systems of the astronauts showed reduced effectiveness immediately after the stress of reentry and splashdown (Kimzey, 1975; Kimzey & others, 1976).

Other studies show that students' disease-fighting mechanisms are weaker during high-stress times, such as exam weeks, and on days when they are upset (Jemmott & Magloire, 1988; Stone & others, 1987). In one experiment, a stressful experience increased the severity of symptoms experienced by volunteers who were knowingly infected with a cold virus (Dixon, 1986). In another, 47 percent of subjects living stress-filled lives caught colds after a virus was dropped in their noses, as did only 27 percent of those who considered themselves relatively stress-free (Cohen & others, 1991).

Can stress depress the immune system? Indeed yes.

Stress and Cancer

To explore the link between stress and cancer, experimenters have given rodents tumor cells or cancer-producing substances. Those rodents also exposed to uncontrollable stress, such as inescapable shocks, are more prone to cancer (Sklar & Anisman, 1981). With their immune systems weakened by stress, their tumors develop sooner and grow larger.

Stress and negative emotions such as depression also have been linked to cancer in humans. Several investigators report that people are at increased risk for cancer a year or so after experiencing depression, helplessness, or bereavement. For example, cancer occurs more often than usual among those widowed, divorced, or separated. One study of the husbands of women with terminal breast cancer pinpointed a possible reason: During the first 2 months after their wives' deaths, the bereaved men's lymphocyte responses dropped (Schleifer & others, 1979). Another study gave a personality test to 2018 middle-aged men employed by the Western Electric Company in 1958. During the next 20 years, 7 percent of those not depressed and 12 percent of those somewhat depressed died of cancer. This difference was not attributable to differences in age, smoking, drinking, or physical characteristics (Persky & others, 1987).

What is more, cancer patients who bottle up their negative emotions may have less chance of survival than those who express them (O'Leary, 1990). A UCLA survey of 649 cancer specialists, who had treated more than 100,000 cancer patients, supported the idea that patients' attitudes matter. Four in five of the physicians rated "a positive approach to the challenge of the illness" and a "strong will to live" as important contributors to longevity (Cousins, 1989).

In the first weeks after receiving their diagnosis, cancer patients are understandably anxious and depressed (Andersen, 1989). Might promoting their fighting spirit and sense of hope aid their survival? Can beliefs boost biology, by alleviating negative emotions that suppress the cancer-fighting

"A cheerful heart is a good medicine, but a downcast spirit dries up the bones."

Proverbs 17:22

This "Sharing Group" is part of California's Wellness Community program, which promotes stress reduction and optimism as possible boosts for its cancer-patient participants.

immune system? Several studies offer hope. Compared to UCLA cancer patients in a control condition, those who participated in support groups and received morale-boosting reeducation became more upbeat, with an accompanying increase in certain immune cells (Cousins, 1989). A study of 86 women undergoing breast cancer therapy at Stanford University Medical School found that those who participated in weekly group therapy survived an average of 37 months, double the 19-month average survival rate among the nonparticipants (Spiegel & others, 1989).

In noting the link between emotions and cancer, we must be careful not to overstep the thin fringe between cutting-edge science and wishful thinking. Researcher Alan Justice (1985) notes that stress does not *create* cancer cells. Rather, it affects their growth by weakening the body's natural defenses against a few proliferating, malignant cells. A relaxed, hopeful state may enhance these defenses. Mastectomy patients who display a determination to conquer their breast cancer more often survive than do those who are stoic or feel hopeless (Hall & Goldstein, 1986; Pettingale & others, 1985).

One danger in publicizing such reports is that they may lead some patients to blame themselves for their cancer—"If only I had been more expressive, relaxed, and hopeful." A corollary danger is a "wellness macho" among the healthy, who credit their health to their healthy character and lay a guilt trip on the ill: "She has cancer? That's what you get for holding your feelings in and being so nice." Dying thus becomes "the ultimate failure."

Actually, the biological processes at work in advanced cancer are *not* likely to be derailed by a relaxed but determined spirit. We can do some things to control our experience of stress, but our emotional reactivity is partly inherited (recall page 72). As theologian Reinhold Niebuhr recognized in his "serenity prayer," we do well to accept those things about ourselves that we cannot change, to change those things that we can, and to seek wisdom to discern the difference. By studying the interplay among emotions, the brain, and the immune system, health psychologists seek the wisdom needed to distinguish between pseudoscientific hocus-pocus and the genuine effects of emotions on health.

Conditioning the Immune System

A hay fever sufferer sees the flower on the restaurant table and, not realizing it is plastic, begins to sneeze. Such experiences hint that stress is not the only psychological influence on the body's ailments. Simple classical conditioning may be an added influence. This raises an intriguing question: If conditioning affects the body's overt physiological responses, might it affect the immune system as well?

Psychologist Robert Ader and immunologist Nicholas Cohen (1985) discovered that the answer is yes. Ader came upon this discovery while researching taste aversion in rats. He paired the rats' drinking of saccharin-sweetened water with injections of a drug which happened to suppress immune functioning. After repeated pairings, sweetened water alone triggered immune suppression as if the drug had been given (Figure 10–18).

Many questions about the role of the immune system and how to harness its healing potential remain unanswered. If it is possible to condition the immune system's suppression, should it not also be possible to condition its enhancement? Might this be one way in which placebos—treatments that have no actual effect—promote healing? Can a placebo sometimes elicit the same healthful state produced by an actual drug? Research now under way may soon answer such questions.

When organic causes of illness are unknown, it is tempting to invent psychological explanations. Before the germ that causes tuberculosis was discovered, personality explanations of TB were popular (Sontag, 1978).

"I didn't give myself cancer."

Mayor Barbara Boggs Sigmund, 1939–1990
Princeton, New Jersey

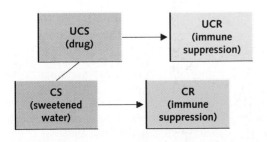

Figure 10–18 The conditioning of immune suppression. Ader and Cohen associated sweetened water with a drug (unconditioned stimulus) that causes immune suppression (unconditioned response). The inert substance alone (conditioned stimulus) then triggered a conditioned immune response.

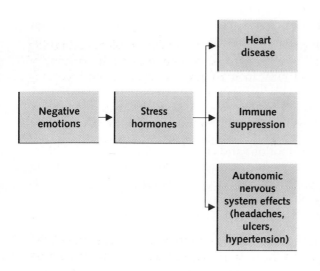

Figure 10–19 Negative emotions can have a variety of health-related consequences. This is especially so when experienced by "disease-prone" angry, depressed, or anxious people. (From Friedman & Booth-Kewley, 1987.)

For now, we can view the toll that stress sometimes takes on our resistance to disease as a price we pay for the adaptive benefits of stress (Figure 10–19). Stress invigorates our lives by arousing and motivating us. An unstressed life would hardly be challenging or productive. Moreover, spending our resources in fighting or fleeing an external challenge aids our immediate survival. But it does so at the cost of diminished resources for fighting internal challenges to our body's health. When the stress is momentary, the cost is negligible. When uncontrollable aggravations persist, however, the cost may become considerable.

Rehearse It

14. The physiologist Walter Cannon described the role of the sympathetic nervous system in preparing the body for fight or flight. Hans Selye extended Cannon's findings by describing the body's adaptive response to stress in general. Selye's general adaptation syndrome (GAS) consists of an alarm reaction followed by
a. fight or flight.
b. resistance and exhaustion.
c. challenge and recovery.
d. stressful life events.

15. In the months following a catastrophe, such as an earthquake or nuclear accident, there is a higher than usual number of emergency hospital admissions, stress-related mental illnesses, and deaths in the local population. Following widowhood, there is an increased risk of illness and death. These findings suggest that
a. daily hassles have adverse health consequences.
b. experiencing a very stressful event increases one's vulnerability to illness and death.
c. being confronted with two undesirable alternatives increases one's vulnerability to illness.

d. having a negative outlook has an adverse effect on recovery from illness.

16. An approach-approach conflict arises when we are confronted with two attractive but incompatible goals—for example, wanting to go away to college and wanting to live near friends and family at home. A child's wanting to pet a dog, while fearing that the dog might bite, is an example of
a. an approach-approach conflict.
b. an approach-avoidance conflict.
c. an avoidance-avoidance conflict.

17. The stress we experience depends on how we perceive the events of our lives. A person (or animal) is most likely to find an event stressful and to suffer reduced immunity and other adverse health effects if the event seems
a. painful or harmful.
b. predictable and bad.
c. uncontrollable and bad.
d. both repellent and attractive.

18. Two cardiologists, Meyer Friedman and Ray Rosenman, observed that heart attacks were more frequent in "Type A" men—in those who appeared to be hard-driving, verbally aggressive, and anger

prone. The terms Type A and Type B, as used by Friedman and Rosenman, refer to
a. kinds of stress.
b. types of coronary heart disease.
c. behavioral patterns.
d. physical types.

19. Recent studies have not always found a significant relationship between Type A behavior and later heart disease. However, a component of Type A behavior linked to coronary heart disease is
a. living a fast-paced life-style.
b. working in a competitive area.
c. meeting deadlines and challenges.
d. feeling angry and negative much of the time.

20. Evidence suggests that disease-fighting mechanisms are weakened during times of high stress, for example, following the death of a loved one. The stress hormones—epinephrine, norepinephrine, and cortisol—suppress the lymphocytes, which ordinarily attack bacteria, viruses, cancer cells, and foreign substances. The stress hormones are released mainly in response to a signal from the
a. lymphocytes and macrophages.
b. cortex.
c. upper respiratory tract.
d. adrenals.

Coping with Stress

Coping with stress can mean confronting or escaping the problem and taking steps to prevent its recurrence. Yet stress is an unavoidable ingredient of modern life. This fact, coupled with the growing awareness that recurring stress correlates with heart disease, lowered immunity, and other bodily ailments, gives us a clear message. If the stress cannot be eliminated by changing or ignoring the situation, we had best learn to manage it. Stress management includes aerobic exercise, biofeedback, relaxation, and social support networks.

Preview Question

14. How do people cope with stress, and what stress management techniques are effective?

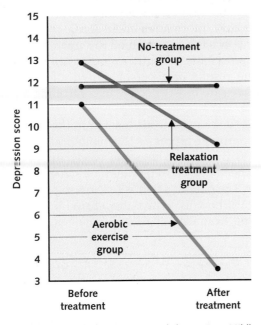

Figure 10–20 Aerobic exercise and depression. Mildly depressed college women who participated in an aerobic exercise program showed markedly reduced depression compared to those who participated in a treatment of relaxation exercises or received no treatment. (From McCann & Holmes, 1984.)

Aerobic Exercise

Many studies suggest that **aerobic exercise**—sustained exercise, such as brisk walking or jogging, that increases heart and lung fitness—can reduce stress, depression, and anxiety. People who exercise regularly cope with stressful events better, exhibit more self-confidence, and are less depressed than those who don't (Brown, 1991; Hogan, 1989). But when stated the other way around—stressed and depressed people exercise less—cause and effect become unclear.

Experiments resolve the ambiguity by randomly assigning stressed, depressed, or anxious people either to aerobic exercise treatments or to other treatments. In one such experiment, Lisa McCann and David Holmes (1984) assigned one third of a group of mildly depressed female college students to a program of aerobic exercise and another third to a treatment of relaxation exercises; the remaining third received no treatment and served as controls. As Figure 10–20 shows, 10 weeks later the women in the aerobic exercise program reported the greatest decrease in depression.

Other research confirms that exercise benefits our sense of well-being. Shipboard sailors report less stress if assigned to an exercise routine (Pavett & others, 1987). Repeated surveys, some by government health agencies, reveal that Canadians and Americans are more self-confident, self-disciplined, and psychologically resilient if physically fit (Stephens, 1988). Even a 10-minute walk stimulates two hours of increased well-being, by raising energy levels and lowering tension (Thayer, 1987).

Still other studies show that exercise also benefits health. One 16-year study of 17,000 middle-aged Harvard alumni found that those who exercised regularly were likely to live longer (Paffenbarger & others, 1986). Another study of 15,000 Control Data Corporation employees found that those who exercised had 25 percent fewer hospital days than those who didn't (Anderson & Jose, 1987). And a digest of data from 43 studies revealed that, compared to inactive adults, people who exercise suffer half as many heart attacks (Powell & others, 1987). The "movement movement" is reaping dividends. Off your duffs, couch potatoes!

Researchers are now wondering *why* aerobic exercise alleviates the effects of stress and negative emotions. They know that exercise strengthens the heart and lowers both blood pressure and the blood pressure reaction to stress (Perkins & others, 1986; Roviario & others, 1984). Perhaps exercise also increases production of mood-boosting neurotransmitters, such as the endorphins. Or the emotional benefits of exercise may be a side effect of increased body warmth or of the muscle relaxation and sounder sleep that occur afterward. Or a sense of accomplishment and an improved physique may enhance one's emotional state. Such possibilities help explain why exercise relieves stress and boosts well-being (Martinsen, 1987).

aerobic exercise Sustained exercise that increases heart and lung fitness; may also alleviate depression and anxiety.

Biofeedback

When a few psychologists started experimenting with ways to train people to bring their heart rate and blood pressure under conscious control, many of their colleagues thought them foolish. These functions are, after all, controlled by the autonomic ("involuntary") nervous system. Then, in the late 1960s, ingenious experiments by respected psychologists began to make the doubters wonder. Neal Miller, for one, found that rats could modify their heartbeat if given pleasurable brain stimulation when their heartbeat increased or decreased. Later research revealed that some paralyzed humans (who cannot use their skeletal muscles) could also learn to control their blood pressure (Miller & Brucker, 1979).

Miller was experimenting with **biofeedback,** a system of electronically recording, amplifying, and feeding back information about subtle physiological responses. Biofeedback instruments have been likened to a mirror (Norris, 1986). The instruments no more control the body than does a mirror comb one's hair. Rather, they reflect the results of a person's own efforts. This allows one to assess which techniques are most effective in controlling a particular physiological response.

In the example in Figure 10–21, a sensor records tension in the forehead muscle of a headache sufferer. A computer processes this biological information and instantly feeds it back to the person in some easily understood image. As a person relaxes the forehead muscle, a pointer on a screen may go lower or a light may grow brighter. The patient's task is to learn to control the pointer or the light and thereby learn how to control the tension in the forehead muscle and the accompanying headaches.

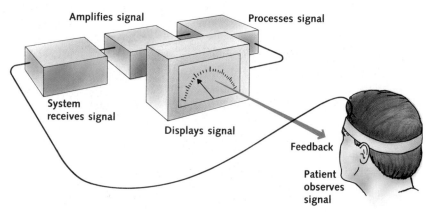

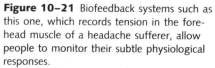

Figure 10–21 Biofeedback systems such as this one, which records tension in the forehead muscle of a headache sufferer, allow people to monitor their subtle physiological responses.

biofeedback A system for electronically recording, amplifying, and feeding back information regarding a subtle physiological state, such as blood pressure or muscle tension.

Initially, biofeedback researchers and practitioners reported that people could learn to increase their production of alpha brain waves, warm their hands, and lower their blood pressure—all signs of a more relaxed state. A decade later, when researchers stepped back to assess the results of hundreds of experiments, the initial claims for biofeedback were found to have been overblown and oversold (Miller, 1985). During biofeedback training, people do enjoy a relaxing tranquility. But this comes about mostly from accompanying factors, such as restricted sensory input (Plotkin, 1979). Biofeedback does enable some people to influence their finger temperature and forehead-muscle tension, and it can help somewhat in reducing the intensity of migraine headaches and chronic pain (King & Montgomery, 1980; Qualls & Sheehan, 1981; Turk & others, 1979). But other, simpler methods of relaxation, which require no expensive equipment, produce many of the same benefits.

Relaxation

If relaxation is an important part of biofeedback, then might not relaxation exercises alone be a natural antidote to stress? Cardiologist Herbert Benson (1976 to 1987) became intrigued with this possibility when he found that experienced meditators could decrease their blood pressure, heart rate, and oxygen consumption and raise their fingertip temperature. You can experience the essence of this *relaxation response*, as Benson called it, right now:

Relaxation training is a component of many stress-reduction programs. At New England Deaconess Hospital, hypertension patients practice deep relaxation.

Assume a comfortable position, close your eyes, breathe deeply, and relax your muscles from foot to face. Now, concentrate on a single phrase—a word, such as "one," or perhaps a prayer, such as "Lord, have mercy." Let other thoughts drift away when they intrude as you repeat this phrase continually for 10 to 20 minutes. Simply by setting aside a quiet time or two each day, many people report enjoying a greater sense of tranquility. In experiments, people who practice relaxation also commonly exhibit lowered blood pressure and strengthened immune defenses (Hyman & others, 1989; Jasnoski & others, 1986).

Type Z behavior

Drawing by Reilly; © 1987 The New Yorker Magazine, Inc.

If Type A heart attack victims could be taught to relax, might their risk of another attack be reduced? To find out, Meyer Friedman and his colleagues randomly assigned hundreds of middle-aged heart attack survivors in San Francisco to one of two groups. The first group received standard advice from cardiologists concerning medications, diet, and exercise habits. The second group received similar advice plus continuing support and counseling on how to slow down and relax—by walking, talking, and eating more slowly; smiling at others and laughing at themselves; admitting mistakes; taking time to enjoy life; and renewing their religious faith. As Figure 10–22 indicates, during the ensuing 3 years the second group experienced only half as many repeat heart attacks as the first group. This, wrote the exuberant Friedman, is "a spectacular reduction in their cardiac recurrence rate" (Friedman & Ulmer, 1984, p. 141). A smaller-scale British study similarly divided heart attack-prone people into control and life-style modification groups (Eysenck & Grossarth-Maticek, 1991). During the next 13 years, it too found a 50 percent reduction in death rate among those trained to alter their thinking and life-style.

Figure 10–22 The San Francisco Recurrent Coronary Prevention Project offered all of their heart attack survivor subjects counseling from a cardiologist. Those who were also guided in modifying their Type A life-style later suffered fewer repeat heart attacks. (From Friedman & Ulmer, 1984.)

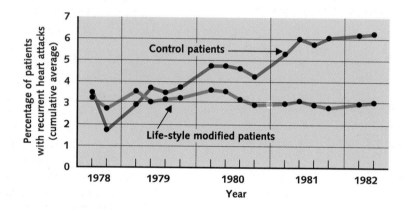

It remains for other researchers to do the painstaking work of identifying which of Friedman's dozens of stress reduction drills are beneficial. Even while Friedman was collecting his data, other investigators were studying specific stress buffers. For example, laughter seems to work in ways similar to exercise—it arouses us, massages muscles, and then leaves us feeling relaxed (Robinson, 1983). This may help explain findings that stressful life events are less disturbing to good-humored people (Lefcourt & Davidson-Katz, 1991; Nezu & others, 1988). Although it would probably be an overstatement to suggest that "laughter is the best medicine," there is reason to suspect that those who laugh, last.

"There ain't much fun in medicine, but there's a heck of a lot of medicine in fun."

Josh Billings, 1818–1885

Social Support

Linda and Emily had much in common. When interviewed for a study conducted by UCLA social psychologist Shelley Taylor (1989), both Los Angeles women had married, raised three children, suffered comparable breast tumors, and recovered from surgery and 6 months of chemotherapy. But there was a difference. Linda, a widow in her early fifties, was living alone, her children scattered in Atlanta, Boston, and Europe. "She had become odd in ways that people sometimes do when they are isolated," reported Taylor. "Having no one with whom to share her thoughts on a daily basis, she unloaded them somewhat inappropriately with strangers, including our interviewer."

Humans aren't the only source of stress-buffering comfort. After stressful events, Medicare patients who have a dog or other companionable pet are less likely to visit their doctor (Siegel, 1990).

Interviewing Emily was difficult in a different way. Phone calls interrupted. Her children, all living nearby, were in and out of the house, dropping things off with a quick kiss. Her husband called from his office for a brief chat. Two dogs roamed the house, greeting visitors enthusiastically. All in all, Emily "seemed a serene and contented person, basking in the warmth of her family."

Three years later the researchers tried to reinterview the women. Linda, they learned, had died 2 years before. Emily was still lovingly supported by her family and friends, and as happy and healthy as ever.

Because no two cancers are identical, we can't be certain that different situations led to Linda and Emily's fates. But they do illustrate a conclusion drawn from several large studies: Social support—feeling liked, affirmed, and encouraged by intimate friends and family—promotes happiness and health.

At the same time we can, however, easily imagine why close relationships could contribute to illness. Relationships are often fraught with stress, especially in crowded living conditions lacking privacy (Evans & others, 1989). "Hell is others," wrote Jean-Paul Sartre. Peter Warr and Roy Payne (1982) at the University of Sheffield asked a representative sample of British adults what, if anything, had emotionally strained them the day before. "Family" was their most frequent answer. Even when well-meaning, family intrusions can be stressful. And stress, as we have seen, contributes to heart disease, hypertension, and a suppressed immune system.

On balance, however, close relationships more often contribute to health and happiness than to illness. Asked what prompted yesterday's times of pleasure, the same British sample, by an even larger margin, again answered "family." For most of us, family relationships provide not only our greatest heartaches, but also our greatest comfort and joy.

Moreover, six massive investigations, each following thousands of people for several years, reveal that close relationships affect health. Compared to those with few social ties, people are less likely to die prematurely if supported by close relationships with friends, family, or fellow members of church, work, or other support groups (Cohen, 1988; House & others, 1988; Nelson, 1988). In a study of leukemia patients preparing to undergo bone marrow transplants, only 20 percent of those who said they had little social support from their family or friends were still alive after two years. Among those who felt strong emotional support the two-year survival rate was 54 percent (Colon, 1991). Social support somehow buffers life's major stresses.

There are several possible reasons for the link between health and social support. Perhaps people with strong social ties eat better, exercise more, and smoke and drink less. Perhaps such relationships help us evaluate and overcome stressful events, such as social rejection. Perhaps they help bolster our self-esteem. When wounded by someone's dislike or the loss of a job, a friend's advice, assistance, and reassurance may be good medicine (Cutrona, 1986; Rook, 1987). Given lots of social support, spouses of cancer patients exhibit stronger immune functioning (Baron & others, 1990).

Close relationships also provide the opportunity to confide painful feelings. In one study, health psychologists James Pennebaker and Robin O'Heeron (1984) contacted the surviving spouses of people who had committed suicide or died in car accidents. Those who bore their grief alone had more health problems than those who openly expressed it. Talking about our troubles can be therapeutic. In a simulated confessional, Pennebaker asked volunteers to share with a hidden experimenter some upsetting events that had been preying on their minds. He asked some of the volunteers to describe

"I get by with a little help from my friends."

John Lennon and Paul McCartney
*Sgt. Pepper's Lonely Hearts
Club Band*, 1967

a trivial event before they divulged the troubling one. Physiological measures revealed that their bodies remained tense the whole time they talked about the trivial event; they relaxed only when they later confided the cause of their turmoil. Even writing about personal traumas in a diary can help. When volunteers in other experiments did this, they had fewer health problems during the ensuing 4 to 6 months (Pennebaker, 1990). As one subject explained, "Although I have not talked with anyone about what I wrote, I was finally able to deal with it, work through the pain instead of trying to block it out. Now it doesn't hurt to think about it."

Friendships are good medicine. Several long-term studies of thousands of people have found that people with close supportive relationships are less likely to die prematurely.

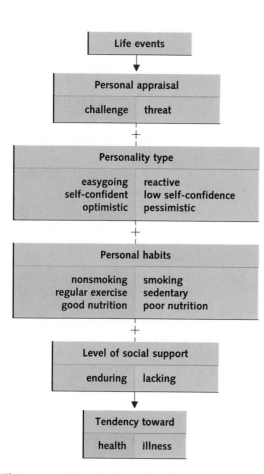

Figure 10–23 Coping with stress. Life events can be debilitating or not, depending on how we appraise them and whether the stresses are buffered by a stress-resistant disposition, healthy habits, and enduring social support.

Suppressed traumas sometimes eat away at us for months or years and affect our physical health. When Pennebaker surveyed more than 700 undergraduate women, he found that about 1 in 12 reported a traumatic sexual experience in childhood. Compared with women who had experienced nonsexual traumas, such as parental death or divorce, the sexually abused women—especially those who had kept their secret to themselves—reported more headaches and stomach ailments. Pennebaker and his colleagues (1989) also invited 33 Holocaust survivors to spend 2 hours recalling their experiences. Many did so in intimate detail never before disclosed, and most watched and showed family and friends a videotape of their recollections in the weeks following. Again, those who were most self-disclosing had the most improved health 14 months later. Confession is good for the soul.

Summing up, sustained emotional reactions to stressful events can be debilitating. However, the level of stress experienced depends on the person and the environment. Because few things are stressful until we appraise them as such, our personalities and interpretations influence how we react emotionally when stressful things happen. Moreover, the negative impact of stressful events can be buffered by a relaxed, healthy life-style and by the comfort and aid provided by supportive friends and family (Figure 10–23).

Rehearse It

21. A number of studies reveal that aerobic exercise raises energy levels and helps alleviate depression and anxiety. The reasons for these emotional effects of exercise are unclear. One explanation is that exercise triggers the release of mood-boosting neurotransmitters called
a. placebos.
b. endorphins.
c. stress hormones.
d. stress buffers.

22. Neal Miller found that rats could learn to control their heart rate when they were rewarded with pleasurable stimulation for doing so. Later research has shown that humans can also learn to control heart rate and blood pressure through biofeedback. Biofeedback teaches people to exercise control over functions that are usually controlled by
a. the autonomic nervous system.
b. conscious thought.
c. the immune system.
d. the nervous system.

23. Biofeedback is a system for electronically recording, amplifying, and feeding back information about physiological states that we are usually not conscious of—including finger temperature and forehead muscle tension. Using a biofeedback system to control finger temperature is most similar to
a. programming a computer to control appliances.
b. using an automatic pilot to fly a plane.
c. using a mirror to practice a dance.
d. using training wheels to learn to ride a bicycle.

24. Long-term studies of thousands of people have shown that people who have close relationships—a strong social support system—are less likely to die prematurely than those who do not. These studies provide evidence that
a. social ties can be a source of stress.
b. people who lose a close relationship are at risk for illness.
c. Type A behavioral patterns are responsible for many premature deaths.
d. social support has a beneficial effect on health.

Reviewing Emotions, Stress, and Health

1. **What are the components of an emotion?**

Emotions are psychological responses of the whole organism that involve an interplay among (1) physiological arousal, (2) expressive behaviors, and (3) conscious experience.

The Physiology of Emotion

2. **What physiological changes accompany emotional arousal?**

In an emergency, the sympathetic nervous system automatically mobilizes the body for fight or flight, directing the adrenals to release hormones that in turn increase heart rate, blood pressure, and blood sugar level. Other changes include tensed muscles, dry mouth, dilated pupils, slowed digestion, and increased sweating. In day-to-day life, our performance on a task is usually best when arousal is moderate, though this varies with the difficulty of the task. The physical arousal that occurs with one emotion is in most ways indistinguishable from that which occurs with another. However, scientists have discovered subtle differences in the brain pathways and hormones associated with different emotions.

Expressing Emotion

3. **Are nonverbal expressions of emotion universally understood?**

Much of our communication is through the silent language of the body. Gestures appear to be culturally determined, but facial expressions, such as those of happiness and fear, are common the world over.

4. **Do our facial expressions influence our feelings?**

Expressions not only communicate emotion to others, they also amplify our own emotions and signal our bodies to respond accordingly.

Experiencing Emotion

5. **What are the causes and consequences of fear?**

Fear is an adaptive emotion, even though it can be traumatic. Although we seem biologically predisposed to acquire some fears, the enormous variety of human fears is best explained by learning.

6. What are the causes and consequences of anger?

Anger is most often aroused by events that are not only frustrating or insulting but also interpreted as willful and unjustified. Although blowing off steam may be temporarily calming, it does not, in the long run, reduce anger. Expressing anger can actually arouse more anger.

7. What are the causes and consequences of happiness?

A good mood boosts people's perceptions of the world and their willingness to help others. The moods triggered by the day's good or bad events seldom last more than that day. Even seemingly significant good events, such as a substantial raise in income, seem not to increase happiness for long. The apparent relativity of happiness can be explained by the adaptation-level principle and the principle of relative deprivation. Nevertheless, some people are usually happier than others, and researchers have identified factors, such as high self-esteem and close personal relationships, that predict such happiness.

Theories of Emotion

8. What issue distinguishes the James-Lange and Cannon-Bard theories of emotion?

One of the oldest theoretical controversies regarding emotion is whether we feel emotion after we notice our body responses (as James and Lange proposed) or at the same time that our bodies respond (as Cannon and Bard believed).

9. What is the relationship between thinking and feeling?

Today's number one controversy among emotion researchers concerns whether human emotions can be experienced apart from cognition. Can we feel before we think? Stanley Schachter's two-factor theory of emotion contends that the cognitive labels we put on our states of arousal are an essential ingredient of emotion. Richard Lazarus agrees that cognition is essential: Many important emotions are rooted in our interpretations or inferences, and other emotions require only a simple cognitive appraisal of the emotion-arousing situation. But Robert Zajonc believes that some simple emotional responses occur instantly, not only outside of conscious awareness but also before any cognitive processing could occur. The issue has practical implications. To the extent that emotions are rooted in thinking, we can hope to change our emotions by changing our thinking.

Stress and Health

10. What is stress?

Stress, the process by which we appraise and respond to events that challenge or threaten us, was conceptualized by Walter Cannon as a fight or flight system and by Hans Selye as a three-stage (alarm/resistance/exhaustion), general adaptation syndrome (GAS).

11. What provokes stress?

Modern research on stress has assessed the health consequences of cataclysmic events, significant life changes, and daily hassles. Events are especially stressful when perceived as both negative and uncontrollable. Optimists cope more successfully with stress and enjoy better health.

12. Who is most vulnerable to heart disease?

Coronary heart disease, the number one cause of death in the United States, has been linked with the competitive, hard-driving, impatient, and (especially) anger-prone Type A personality. Unlike the more relaxed Type B person, under stress the body of the Type A person secretes more of the stress hormones that are believed to accelerate the buildup of plaques on the heart's artery walls.

13. How does stress make us vulnerable to disease?

In addition to contributing to heart disease and a variety of psychophysiological illnesses, stress can suppress the immune system, making a person more vulnerable to infections and cancer. New experiments indicate that the immune system's responses can be influenced by conditioning.

14. How do people cope with stress, and what stress management techniques are effective?

Among the components of stress management programs are exercise, biofeedback, and relaxation. Although the degree of mind control over the body that can be gained through biofeedback has fallen short of early expectations, biofeedback has become one accepted method for helping people control ailments such as tension headaches and high blood pressure. Simple relaxation exercises offer some of the same benefits. Counseling Type A heart attack survivors to slow down and relax has helped them lower their rate of recurring attacks. Social support also helps people cope, partly by buffering the impact of stress.

Terms and Concepts to Remember

emotion, p. 301

polygraph, p. 304

catharsis, p. 312

adaptation-level principle, p. 315

relative deprivation, p. 316

James-Lange theory, p. 319

Cannon-Bard theory, p. 319

two-factor theory, p. 320

health psychology, p. 323

stress, p. 323

general adaptation syndrome (GAS), p. 324

approach-approach conflict, p. 328

avoidance-avoidance conflict, p. 328

approach-avoidance conflict, p. 328

coronary heart disease, p. 329

Type A, p. 330

Type B, p. 330

psychophysiological illness, p. 331

lymphocytes, p. 331

aerobic exercise, p. 335

biofeedback, p. 336

Rehearse It Answer Key

1. b.   **2.** c.   **3.** d.   **4.** a.   **5.** b.   **6.** b.   **7.** a.   **8.** d.   **9.** c.

10. b.   **11.** b.   **12.** b.   **13.** c.   **14.** b.   **15.** b.   **16.** b.   **17.** c.   **18.** c.

19. d.   **20.** b.   **21.** b.   **22.** a.   **23.** c.   **24.** d.

Critical Thinking Exercise

You have *Surveyed*, *Questioned*, *Read*, *Rehearsed*, and *Reviewed* Chapter 10. Now take your learning a step further by testing your *critical thinking* skills on the following passage. You may find it helpful to review the text material in the section "Theories of Emotion" before completing this exercise.

Subjects in a recent study were shown an erotic movie while they were in each of three phases of recovery from aerobic exercise. Subjects first pedaled an exercise bicycle intensely enough to produce significant physical arousal. During each of the three recovery phases, the subjects were asked (1) whether they still felt physically aroused from the exercise, and (2) how sexually excited they felt by the film. The subjects' actual physical arousal (heart rate) was measured throughout the experiment. During the first two phases of recovery, all of the subjects still showed signs of actual physical arousal; although by the second phase, they said they no longer *felt* physically aroused from the exercise. By the third phase, the subjects no longer showed signs of physical arousal from the exercise. The subjects reported feeling significantly more sexually excited by the film during the second phase of exercise recovery than they did during the first and third phases.

1. How well would the James-Lange theory explain the results of this experiment? What variations in reported feelings of sexual excitement would this theory have predicted in the three phases of exercise recovery?

2. How well would the Cannon-Bard theory explain the results of this experiment? What variations in reported feelings of sexual excitement would this theory have predicted in the three phases of exercise recovery?

3. How well would Schachter's two-factor theory explain the results of this experiment? What variations in reported feelings of sexual excitement would this theory have predicted in the three phases of exercise recovery?

Check your progress on becoming a critical thinker by comparing your answers to the sample answers found in Appendix B.

Chapter 11

Personality

Novelist William Faulkner was a master at creating characters with vivid personalities.[1] One of his creations, Ike McCaslin, appears at various ages in more than a dozen novels and short stories. Ike is highly principled, and consistently so. At age 10 he feels a deep reverence for the wilderness and its creatures. At 21 he forfeits a "tainted" inheritance. In his late seventies he counsels his nephew to use his land responsibly. Ike the adult is an extension of Ike the child.

Another Faulkner character, Jason Compson, is a selfish, whining 4-year-old in the opening section of *The Sound and the Fury*, and a selfish, screaming 34-year-old as the novel closes. As head of the Compson household, he verbally abuses family members and household servants. Lying, threatening, conniving, he is a self-centered child who has become a self-centered adult.

Faulkner's characters, as they appear and reappear throughout his fiction, exhibit the distinctiveness and consistency that define personality. Having emphasized in the preceding chapters how we are similar—how we develop, perceive, learn, remember, think, and feel—we now acknowledge that each of us has an individual personality. Your **personality** is your characteristic pattern of thinking, feeling, and acting. If your behavior pattern is unusually distinctive and consistent—if, say, you are strikingly outgoing, whether at a party or in a classroom—people are likely to say that you have a "strong" personality.

Actually, much of this book deals with personality. We have considered biological influences on personality, personality development across the life span, and personality-related aspects of learning, motivation, and emotion. In later chapters we will study disorders of personality, personal and physical well-being, and social influences on personality.

In this chapter we explore and evaluate four major perspectives that seek to explain personality:

Sigmund Freud's *psychoanalytic* theory emphasizes childhood sexuality and unconscious motivations as possible causes of personality.

Trait researchers identify specific dimensions of our personality.

The *humanistic* approach focuses on our inner capacities for growth and self-fulfillment.

Social-cognitive psychologists emphasize how we shape and are shaped by interaction with our environment.

Each perspective offers a distinct view of personality that provides valuable insights and increases our understanding.

personality An individual's characteristic pattern of thinking, feeling, and acting.

---

[1] Faulkner scholar Nancy Nicodemus assisted with these examples.

free association A psychoanalytic method of exploring the unconscious in which the person relaxes and says whatever comes to mind, no matter how trivial or embarrassing.

psychoanalysis The technique of treating psychological disorders by seeking to expose and interpret unconscious tensions. Freud's psychoanalytic theory of personality sought to explain what he observed during psychoanalysis.

unconscious According to Freud, a reservoir of mostly unacceptable thoughts, wishes, feelings, and memories. According to contemporary research psychologists, a level of information processing of which we are unaware.

preconscious Information that is not conscious, but is retrievable into conscious awareness.

Preview Question

2. What role do unconscious dynamics play in Freud's theory of personality?

"Good morning, beheaded—uh, I mean beloved."

Drawing by Fradon; © 1983 The New Yorker Magazine, Inc.

The Psychoanalytic Perspective

Well before entering the University of Vienna in 1873, the youthful Sigmund Freud showed signs of the independence and brilliance that often mark people of eminence. He had a prodigious memory. He so loved serious reading that he once ran up a bookstore debt beyond his means, feeding his insatiable interest in playwrights, poets, and philosophers. As a teen he often took his evening meal in his tiny bedroom, to lose no time from his studies.

After medical school, Freud began a private practice, specializing in nervous disorders. Before long, however, he faced patients whose disorders made no neurological sense. A patient might have lost all feeling in her hand—yet there is no sensory nerve that when damaged would numb the entire hand and nothing else. Noting that hypnosis could also produce such symptoms, Freud wondered whether they might be psychologically rather than physiologically caused. His wonderings set his mind running in a direction that was destined to change human self-understanding.

Exploring the Unconscious

While experimenting with hypnosis, Freud decided that the loss of feeling in one's hand might be caused by the fear of touching one's genitals; that blindness or deafness might be caused by not wanting to see or hear something that aroused intense anxiety. In time, Freud began to see patients with a variety of symptoms. Given patients' uneven capacity for hypnosis, he turned to **free association**—in which he merely told the patient to relax and say whatever came to mind, no matter how embarrassing or trivial. Freud believed that free association produced a chain of thought leading into the patient's unconscious, thereby retrieving and releasing painful unconscious memories, often from childhood. Freud called the process **psychoanalysis.**

Underlying Freud's psychoanalytic conception of personality was his belief that the mind is like an iceberg—mostly hidden. Our conscious awareness is the part of the iceberg that floats above the surface. Below the surface is a much larger, **unconscious** region containing thoughts, wishes, feelings, and memories, of which we are largely unaware. Some of these thoughts we store temporarily in a **preconscious** area, from which we can retrieve them at will into conscious awareness. Of greater interest to Freud was the mass of unacceptable passions and thoughts that we *repress*—forcibly block from our consciousness because they would be so painful to acknowledge. Although we are not consciously aware of these troublesome feelings and ideas, Freud believed they powerfully influence us. In his view, our unacknowledged impulses express themselves in disguised forms—the work we choose, the beliefs we hold, our daily habits, our troubling symptoms. In such ways, the unconscious seeps into our thoughts and actions.

Freud believed he glimpsed the unconscious not only in people's free associations, beliefs, habits, and symptoms but also in their dreams and slips of the tongue and pen. He called dreams the "royal road to the unconscious." By analyzing people's dreams, Freud believed he could reveal the nature of their inner conflicts and release their inner tensions. Slips while reading, writing, and speaking suggested to Freud that what we say and do may reflect the workings of our unconscious minds. Consider his example of a financially stressed patient who, not wanting any large pills, said, "Please do not give me any bills, because I cannot swallow them." Jokes, too, he viewed as a way to express repressed sexual and aggressive tendencies. For Freud the determinist, nothing was ever accidental.

id   A reservoir of unconscious psychic energy that, according to Freud, strives to satisfy basic sexual and aggressive drives.

pleasure principle   The id's demand for immediate gratification.

ego   The largely conscious, "executive" part of personality that, according to Freud, mediates among the demands of the id, superego, and reality.

reality principle   The ego's tendency to satisfy the id's desires in ways that will realistically bring pleasure rather than pain.

superego   The part of personality that, according to Freud, represents internalized ideals and provides standards for judgment (the conscience) and for future aspirations.

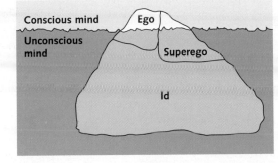

Figure 11–1 Freud's idea of the mind's structure. Consciousness is like an iceberg's visible tip. Note that the id is totally unconscious, but ego and superego operate both consciously and unconsciously.

Preview Question

3. How did Freud view personality structure and development, and what were the defense mechanisms he proposed?

"Fifty is plenty."

"Hundred and fifty."

Drawing by Woodman; © 1987 The New Yorker Magazine, Inc.

Personality Structure

For Freud, human personality—its emotions, strivings, and ideas—arises from a conflict between our aggressive, pleasure-seeking biological impulses and the social restraints against them. In his view, personality results from our efforts to resolve this basic conflict—to express these impulses in ways that bring satisfaction without also bringing guilt or punishment.

Freud theorized that the conflict centers on three interacting systems: id, ego, and superego. Like intelligence and memory, these are abstract psychological concepts (Figure 11–1). They are, said Freud, "useful aids to understanding" that he proposed to help explain the mind's dynamics.

The **id** is a reservoir of unconscious psychic energy that constantly strives to satisfy basic drives to survive, reproduce, and aggress. The id operates on the **pleasure principle:** If unconstrained by reality, it seeks immediate gratification. Think of newborn infants, who, governed by the id, cry out for satisfaction the moment they feel a need, caring nothing for the outside world's conditions and demands.

As the **ego** develops, the young child learns to cope with the real world. The ego operates on the **reality principle,** which seeks to gratify the id's impulses in realistic ways that will bring long-term pleasure rather than pain or destruction. Imagine what would happen if, lacking an ego, we expressed our unrestrained sexual or aggressive impulses whenever we felt them. The ego, which contains our partly conscious perceptions, thoughts, judgments, and memories, is the personality "executive." It decides on our actions as it intervenes among the impulsive demands of the id, the restraining demands of the superego, and the real-life demands of the external world.

Beginning around age 4 or 5, a child's ego recognizes the demands of the newly emerging **superego.** The superego is a voice of conscience that forces the ego to consider not only the real but the ideal. Its sole focus is on how one *ought* to behave. The superego develops as we internalize the morals and values of parents and culture, thereby providing both our sense of right and wrong and our ideals. It strives for perfection and judges our actions, producing positive feelings of pride or negative feelings of guilt. Someone with an exceptionally strong superego may be continually upright yet ironically guilt-ridden; another with a weak superego may be wantonly self-indulgent and remorseless. Because the superego's demands often oppose the id's, the ego

psychosexual stages The childhood stages of development (oral, anal, phallic, latency, genital) during which, according to Freud, the id's pleasure-seeking energies focus on distinct erogenous zones. See Table 11-1 for definitions of these stages.

Oedipus [ED-uh-puss] **complex** According to Freud, a boy's sexual desires toward his mother and feelings of jealousy and hatred for his father.

identification The process by which, according to Freud, children incorporate their parents' values into their developing superegos.

gender identity One's sense of being male or female. Note: One's gender identity is distinct from one's sexual orientation (as heterosexual or homosexual).

fixation According to Freud, a lingering focus of pleasure-seeking energies at an earlier psychosexual stage, where conflicts were unresolved.

defense mechanisms In psychoanalytic theory, the ego's protective methods of reducing anxiety by unconsciously distorting reality.

repression In psychoanalytic theory, the basic defense mechanism that blocks from consciousness painful memories and anxiety-arousing thoughts.

regression In psychoanalytic theory, an individual's retreat, when faced with anxiety, to a more infantile psychosexual stage where some psychic energy remains fixated.

reaction formation In psychoanalytic theory, a defense mechanism by which the ego unconsciously switches unacceptable impulses into their opposites. Thus, people may express feelings that are the opposite of their anxiety-arousing unconscious feelings.

Table 11-1
Freud's Psychosexual Stages

Stage	Focus
Oral (0–18 months)	Pleasure centers on the mouth—sucking, biting, chewing
Anal (18–36 months)	Pleasure focuses on bowel/bladder elimination; coping with demands for control
Phallic (3–6 years)	Pleasure zone is the genitals; coping with incestuous sexual feelings
Latency (6 to puberty)	Repressed sexual feelings
Genital (puberty on)	Maturation of sexual interests

struggles to reconcile the two. The chaste student who is sexually attracted to someone and joins a volunteer organization to work alongside the desired person, satisfies both id and superego.

Personality Development

Analysis of his patients' histories convinced Freud that personality forms during life's first few years. Again and again his patients' symptoms seemed rooted in unresolved conflicts from early childhood. He concluded that children pass through a series of **psychosexual stages** during which the id's pleasure-seeking energies focus on distinct pleasure-sensitive areas of the body called *erogenous zones* (Table 11–1).

During the **oral stage,** which lasts throughout the first 18 months, the infant's sensual pleasures focus on sucking, biting, and chewing.

During the **anal stage,** from about 18 months to 3 years, the sphincter muscles become sensitive and controllable, and bowel and bladder retention and elimination become a source of gratification.

During the **phallic stage,** from roughly ages 3 to 6 years, the pleasure zone shifts to the genitals. Freud believed that during this stage boys seek genital stimulation and develop both unconscious sexual desires for their mother and jealousy and hatred for their father, whom they consider a rival. Boys also were said to feel guilt and a lurking fear that their father would punish them—in particular, by castration. Freud called this collection of feelings the **Oedipus complex** after the Greek legend of Oedipus, who unknowingly killed his father and married his mother. Although some psychoanalysts believed that girls experience a parallel *Electra complex,* Freud (1931, page 229) said no: "It is only in the male child that we find the fateful combination of love for the one parent and simultaneous hatred for the other as a rival."

Children eventually cope with these threatening feelings by repressing them and by identifying with (trying to become like) the rival parent. It's as if

Faced with a mild stress, children and monkeys will regress, by retreating to the comfort of earlier behaviors.

"The lady doth protest too much, methinks."

William Shakespeare
Hamlet, 1600

something inside the child decides, "If you can't beat 'em (the parent of the same sex), join 'em." Through this **identification** process children's superegos gain strength as they incorporate many of their parents' values. Freud believed that identification with the same-sex parent provides our **gender identity**—our sense of being male or female.

With their sexual feelings repressed and redirected, children enter a **latency stage.** Freud maintained that during latency, extending from around age 6 to puberty, sexuality is dormant and children play mostly with peers of the same sex.

At puberty, latency gives way to the final stage, the **genital stage,** as youths begin to experience sexual feelings toward others.

In Freud's view, maladaptive behavior in the adult results from conflicts unresolved during earlier psychosexual stages. At any point in the oral, anal, or phallic stage, strong conflict can lock, or **fixate,** the person's pleasure-seeking energies in that stage. Thus, people who were either orally overindulged or deprived (perhaps by abrupt, early weaning) might fixate at the oral stage. Orally fixated adults are said to exhibit either passive dependence (like that of a nursing infant) or an exaggerated denial of this dependence—perhaps by acting tough and uttering biting sarcasm. They might also continue to seek oral gratification through excessive smoking and eating. Those who never quite resolve the anal conflict, between the desire to eliminate at will and the demands of toilet training, may be either messy and disorganized ("anal expulsive") or highly controlled and compulsively neat ("anal retentive"). In such ways, believed Freud, the twig of personality is bent at an early age.

Defense Mechanisms

To live in social groups, we cannot act out our sexual and aggressive impulses willy-nilly. We must control them. When the ego fears losing control of the inner war between the demands of the id and the superego, the result is anxiety. Anxiety, said Freud, is the price we pay for civilization.

Unlike specific fears, the dark cloud of anxiety is unfocused. Anxiety is therefore hard to cope with, as when we feel unsettled but are not sure why. Freud proposed that the ego protects itself against anxiety with ego **defense mechanisms.** Defense mechanisms reduce or redirect anxiety in various ways, but always by distorting reality. Some examples:

Repression banishes anxiety-arousing thoughts and feelings from consciousness. According to Freud, repression underlies the other defense mechanisms, all of which disguise threatening impulses and keep them from reaching consciousness. Freud believed that repression explains why we do not remember our childhood lust for our parent of the other sex. However, he also believed that repression is often incomplete, with the repressed urges seeping out in dream symbols and slips of the tongue.

We also cope with anxiety through **regression**—retreating to an earlier, more infantile stage of development where some of our psychic energies still fixate. Thus, when facing the anxious first days of school, a child may regress to the oral comfort of thumb sucking or nail biting. Juvenile monkeys, when anxious, retreat to infantile clinging to their mothers or to one another (Suomi, 1987). Even homesick new college students may long for the security and comfort of home.

In **reaction formation,** the ego unconsciously makes unacceptable impulses look like their opposites. En route to consciousness, the unacceptable proposition "I hate him" becomes "I love him." Timidity becomes daring. Feelings of inadequacy become bravado. According to the principle behind this defense mechanism, vehement social crusaders, such as those who ur-

projection In psychoanalytic theory, the defense mechanism by which people disguise their own threatening impulses by attributing them to others.

rationalization In psychoanalytic theory, a defense mechanism that offers self-justifying explanations in place of the real, more threatening, unconscious reasons for one's actions.

displacement In psychoanalytic theory, the defense mechanism that shifts sexual or aggressive impulses toward a more acceptable or less threatening object or person, as when redirecting anger toward a safer outlet.

sublimation In psychoanalytic theory, the defense mechanism by which people rechannel their unacceptable impulses into socially approved activities.

collective unconscious Carl Jung's concept of a shared, inherited reservoir of memory traces from our species' history.

projective tests Personality tests, such as the Rorschach and TAT, for which subjects interpret ambiguous stimuli designed to trigger projection of one's inner dynamics.

gently campaign against gay rights, may be motivated by the very sexual desires against which they are crusading.

Projection disguises threatening impulses by attributing them to others. Thus, "He hates me" may be a projection of the actual feeling "I hate him" or "I hate myself." An El Salvadoran saying captures the idea: "The thief thinks everyone else is a thief." According to Freudian theory, racial prejudice, too, may be the result of projecting one's own unacceptable impulses or characteristics onto members of another group. (As you can imagine, reaction formation and projection have sometimes provided a handy way to ridicule other people's motives.)

The familiar mechanism of **rationalization** lets us unconsciously generate self-justifying explanations so we can hide from ourselves the real reasons for our actions. Thus, habitual drinkers may say they drink with their friends "just to be sociable." Students who fail to study may rationalize, "All work and no play makes Jack [or Jill] a dull person."

Displacement diverts one's sexual or aggressive impulses toward a more psychologically acceptable object than the one that aroused them. Children who can't express anger against their parents may displace their anger onto the family pet. Students upset over an exam may snap at their roommate.

Sublimation is the transformation of unacceptable impulses into socially valued motivations. Sublimation is therefore socially adaptive and may even be a wellspring for great cultural and artistic achievements. Freud suggested that Leonardo da Vinci's paintings of Madonnas were a sublimation of his longing for intimacy with his mother, who was separated from him at an early age.

Note again that all these defense mechanisms function indirectly and unconsciously. They reduce anxiety by disguising our threatening impulses. We never say, "I'm feeling anxious; I'd better project my sexual or hostile feelings onto someone else." Defense mechanisms would not work if we recognized them. As the body unconsciously defends itself against disease, so, believed Freud, the ego unconsciously defends itself against anxiety.

Freud's Descendants and Dissenters

Freud's writings soon attracted followers, mostly young, ambitious physicians who formed an inner circle around their strong-minded leader. These pioneering psychoanalysts and others, whom we now call "neo-Freudians," accepted Freud's basic ideas: the personality structures of id, ego, and superego; the importance of the unconscious; the shaping of personality in childhood; and the dynamics of anxiety and the defense mechanisms. But they veered away from Freud in two important ways. First, they placed more emphasis on the role of the conscious mind in interpreting experience and coping with the environment. What's more, they doubted that sex and aggression were all-consuming motivations. Instead, they placed more emphasis on loftier motives and on social interaction, as the following examples illustrate.

Alfred Adler and Karen Horney agreed with Freud that childhood is important. But they believed that childhood *social*, not sexual, tensions are crucial for personality formation. Adler, who himself struggled to overcome childhood illnesses and accidents, said that much of our behavior is driven by an effort to conquer childhood feelings of inferiority, feelings that trigger strivings for superiority and power. (It was Adler who proposed the still-popular idea of the "inferiority complex.") Horney said that childhood anxiety, caused by the dependent child's sense of helplessness, triggers the desire

Preview Question

4. How did Freud's followers differ from him?

"The female . . . acknowledges the fact of her castration, and with it, too, the superiority of the male and her own inferiority; but she rebels against this unwelcome state of affairs."

Sigmund Freud
Female Sexuality, 1931

Alfred Adler (*Problems of Neurosis*, 1964): "The individual feels at home in life and feels his existence to be worthwhile just so far as he is useful to others and is overcoming feelings of inferiority."

Karen Horney (*Feminine Psychology*, 1923–1937): "The view that women are infantile and emotional creatures, and as such, incapable of responsibility and independence is the work of the masculine tendency to lower women's self-respect."

Carl Jung (*Symbols of Transformation*, 1912): "We can keep from a child all knowledge of earlier myths, but we cannot take from him the need for mythology."

"The forward thrust of the antlers shows a determined personality, yet the small sun indicates a lack of self-confidence. . . ."

© 1983 by Sidney Harris; American Scientist magazine

Preview Question

5. How do projective tests assess personality, and are they considered valid?

for love and security. In countering Freud's assumptions that women have weak superegos and suffer "penis envy," Horney sought to balance the bias she detected in this masculine view of psychology.

Unlike other neo-Freudians, Carl Jung—Freud's disciple-turned-dissenter—placed less emphasis on social factors and agreed with Freud that the unconscious exerts a powerful influence. But to Jung, the unconscious contains more than a person's repressed thoughts and feelings. There is also a **collective unconscious,** he believed, a common reservoir of images derived from our early ancestors' universal experiences. Jung said that the collective unconscious explains why, for many people, spiritual concerns are deep-rooted and why people in different cultures share certain myths and images, such as that of mother as a symbol of nurturance.

Assessing the Unconscious

Those who study personality or provide therapy need ways to evaluate personality characteristics. Different personality theories imply different methods of assessment.

Freud's theory maintains that the significant influences on our personalities arise from the unconscious, which contains residues from early childhood experiences. Psychoanalysts therefore dismiss objective assessment tools, such as agree-disagree or true-false questionnaires, as merely tapping the conscious surface. Needed is a sort of psychological x-ray—a test that can see through our surface pretenses and reveal our hidden conflicts and impulses.

Projective tests aim to provide such a view, by providing people with an ambiguous stimulus and then asking them to describe it or tell a story about it. The stimulus has no inherent meaning, so whatever meaning people read into it presumably reflects their interests and conflicts. Henry Murray (1933) demonstrated a possible basis for such a test at a house party hosted by his 11-year-old daughter. Murray got the children to play a frightening game called "Murder." When shown some photographs after the game, the children perceived the photos as more malicious than they had before the game.

This psychologist presumes that the hopes, fears, and interests expressed in this boy's descriptions of a series of ambiguous pictures in the Thematic Apperception Test (TAT) are projections of his inner feelings.

This woman is taking the most familiar projective test, the Rorschach. Although its reliability and validity are questionable, the Rorschach test is still widely used. Some researchers are working to make its scoring and interpretation more objective.

Thematic Apperception Test (TAT) A projective test in which people express their inner hopes, fears, and interests through the stories they make up about ambiguous scenes.

Rorschach inkblot test The most widely used projective test, designed by Hermann Rorschach; seeks to identify people's projected feelings by analyzing their interpretation of a set of 10 inkblots.

These children, it seemed to Murray, had *projected* their inner feelings onto the pictures. A few years later, Murray introduced the **Thematic Apperception Test (TAT)**—ambiguous pictures about which people make up stories that might explain what the pictured person is thinking and feeling. As you may recall from page 292, one use of the TAT has been to assess achievement motivation. Shown a daydreaming boy, those who imagine him fantasizing an achievement are presumed to be projecting their own personality dynamics.

There are now a variety of projective tests. These tests ask subjects to draw a person, to complete sentences ("My mother . . ."), or to provide the first word that comes to mind after the examiner says a test word. Most widely used is the famous **Rorschach inkblot test,** introduced in 1921 by Swiss psychiatrist Hermann Rorschach. The test assumes that what we see in its 10 inkblots reflects our inner feelings and conflicts. If we see fierce animals or weapons, the examiner may infer that we have aggressive tendencies.

Is this a reasonable assumption? If so, can a psychologist use the Rorschach to understand one's personality and diagnose an emotional disorder? Recall from our discussion of the intelligence tests the two primary criteria of a good test. One is reliability (consistent results). The other is validity (predicting what it's supposed to). On those criteria, how good is the Rorschach?

Most researchers have considered it not very good (Peterson, 1978). There is no one accepted system for scoring and interpreting the test, so unless two raters have been trained in the same scoring system, their agreement on the results of any given test may be minimal. Nor is the test very successful at predicting behavior or at discriminating between groups (for example, identifying who is suicidal and who is not).

Although not as popular as it once was, the Rorschach remains one of the most widely used psychological instruments (Lubin & others, 1984; Piotrowski & Keller, 1989). Some clinicians continue to be confident of the test's validity—not as a device that by itself can provide a diagnosis, but as a source of suggestive leads that supplement other information. Other clinicians believe that even if the Rorschach scoring systems have little validity, the test is still an icebreaker and a revealing interview technique. Promising new research-based, computer-aided scoring and interpretation tools are improving agreement among raters and enhancing the test's validity (Exner,

Sigmund Freud (1856–1939): "I was the only worker in a new field."

Preview Question

6. How do Freud's ideas hold up today?

1986; Parker & others, 1988). But Freud himself would probably have been uncomfortable with trying to assign each patient a test score and more interested in the therapist-patient interactions that take place during the test.

Evaluating the Psychoanalytic Perspective

Knowing what you do about Freud's ideas, listen now to his critics. Bear in mind that we critique Freud from the perspective of the late twentieth century, a perspective that is itself subject to revision. Freud died in 1939 without the benefit of all that we have since learned about human development, thinking, and emotion and without today's research tools. To criticize Freud's theories by comparing them with current concepts is like comparing Henry Ford's Model T with today's Escort.

Freud's Ideas in Light of Modern Research

Recent theories and research contradict many of Freud's specific ideas. Research indicates that human development is lifelong, not fixed in childhood. Developmental psychologists also question Freud's idea that conscience and gender identity form as the child resolves the Oedipus complex at age 5 or 6. Children gain their gender identity earlier. They become strongly masculine or feminine even without a same-sex parent present (Frieze & others, 1978). Freud's ideas about childhood sexuality arose from his rejection of stories of childhood sexual abuse told by his female patients—stories he thought were an expression of their own childhood sexual wishes and conflicts. Today we take reports of sexual abuse seriously. Freud's ideas about the natural superiority of men are widely discounted and considered sexist.

As we saw in Chapter 5, new ideas about why we dream dispute Freud's belief that dreams disguise and fulfill wishes. His belief that repression causes forgetting gains support from reports of memory loss among victims of war trauma and sexual abuse, but other mechanisms of forgetting account for most memory loss (pages 226–227). Even slips of the tongue can be explained as competition between similar verbal choices in our memory network (page 222). Researchers find little support for Freud's idea that people protect themselves against painful self-knowledge by projecting their own unrecognized negative impulses onto others (Holmes, 1978, 1981). And Jerome Kagan (1989b) notes that history has been equally unkind to another idea of Freud's—that sexual repression causes psychological disorder. From Freud's time to ours, sexual repression has diminished, but psychological disorders have not.

History has been kinder to Freud's "iceberg" view of the mind, at least in part. We now know that we indeed have limited access to all that goes on in our minds (Erdelyi, 1985, 1988; Kihlstrom, 1990). However, the "iceberg" notion held by today's research psychologists differs from Freud's. As we saw in earlier chapters, many researchers think of the unconscious not as seething passions and repressive censoring but as information processing that occurs without our awareness. To them, the unconscious involves the schemas that automatically control our perceptions and interpretations; the processing of stimuli to which we have not consciously attended; the right hemisphere activity that enables the split-brain patient's left hand to carry out an instruction the patient cannot verbalize; the simultaneous parallel processing of different aspects of vision and thinking; the implicit memories that operate without need for conscious recall; the conditioned emotions that activate instantly. This understanding of unconscious information processing is more like the pre-Freudian view of an underground stream of unconscious thought from which spontaneous creative ideas surfaced.

Freud's Ideas as Scientific Theory

Psychologists also criticize Freud's theory for its scientific shortcomings. As we noted in Chapter 1, good scientific theories explain observations and offer testable hypotheses. Freud's theory, say the critics, rests on few objective observations and offers few hypotheses to verify or reject. (For Freud, his own recollections and interpretations of patients' free associations, dreams, and slips were evidence enough.)

The most serious problem with Freud's theory, according to critics, is that it offers after-the-fact explanations of any characteristic (of one person's smoking, another's fear of horses, another's sexual orientation), yet fails to *predict* such behavior and traits. If you feel angry at your mother's death, you support the theory because "your unresolved childhood dependency needs are threatened." If you do not feel angry, you again support the theory because "you are repressing your anger." That, said Calvin Hall and Gardner Lindzey (1978, p. 68), "is like betting on a horse after the race has been run."

Such criticisms of Freud's specific concepts and after-the-fact interpretations have led some modern critics to scorn his theory. Peter Medawar (1982, pp. 71–72) compared it to "a dinosaur . . . one of the saddest and strangest of all landmarks in the history of twentieth-century thought." Perhaps we can evaluate Freud less harshly, for three reasons:

1. To criticize Freudian theory for not making testable predictions is like criticizing baseball for not being aerobic exercise. Is it fair to fault something for not being what it was never intended to be? Freud never claimed that psychoanalysis was predictive science. He merely claimed that, looking back, psychoanalysts could find meaning in our state of mind (Rieff, 1979).

2. Some of Freud's ideas are enduring. It was Freud who drew our attention to the unconscious and the irrational, to anxiety and our struggle to cope with it, to the importance of human sexuality, and to the tension between our biological impulses and our social well-being. It was Freud who challenged our self-righteousness, punctured our pretensions, and reminded us of our potential for evil. Few dispute that Freud's ideas were creative, courageous, and comprehensive.

3. Correctly, or incorrectly, Freud influenced our view of human nature. Rightly or wrongly, some ideas that many of us assume to be true—that childhood experiences mold personality, that many behaviors have disguised motives, that dreams have symbolic meaning—are Freud's leg-

"We are arguing like a man who should say, 'If there were an invisible cat in that chair, the chair would look empty; but the chair does look empty; therefore there is an invisible cat in it.'"

C. S. Lewis
Four Loves, 1958

Freud's consulting room was rich with antiquities from around the world, including artwork related to his ideas about our unconscious motives. His famous couch, piled high with pillows, placed patients in a comfortable, reclining position.

acy, which lives on in our own ideas. As Peter Drucker (1982) remarked, "[Many] psychologists have no use for Freud, and I have some grave doubts about him, but he is the only one who created vision and insight and changed our view of ourselves and of the world." For that, Sigmund Freud continues to rank as one of modern history's towering intellectual figures.

Rehearse It

1. According to Freud, we block from consciousness thoughts, wishes, and feelings that are unacceptable or unbearably painful. The blocked material surfaces in disguised forms, for example, in physical symptoms, dreams, or slips of the tongue. This unconscious blocking of unacceptable thoughts is
a. free association.
b. repression.
c. anxiety.
d. reaction formation.

2. Freud described the personality as consisting of three interacting systems, the id, ego, and superego. A term such as "ego" or "id" is best understood as
a. a useful aid in explaining the mind's workings.
b. a name for a region of the brain.
c. a description of a stage in psychosexual development.
d. a testable hypothesis.

3. According to the psychoanalytic view of development, the oral, anal, and phallic stages are followed by a latency stage during which sexuality is largely dormant or submerged. The latency stage extends roughly through
a. the preschool years.
b. the elementary school years.
c. adolescence.

4. Freud proposed an Oedipus complex, which gets resolved in a process called identification, during which the child incorporates parental values. The process is closely associated with the development of the "voice of conscience," that part of the personality which internalizes ideals and which Freud called the
a. ego.
b. superego.

c. reality principle.
d. sublimation.

5. Defense mechanisms identified by Freud include regression (in which a person copes with anxiety by retreating to an earlier stage of development) and projection (in which a person disguises threatening impulses by attributing them to others). There are many other defense mechanisms. All of them have in common some distortion or disguising of reality, and all of them are
a. conscious.
b. unconscious.
c. preconscious.
d. rationalizations.

6. Projective tests are personality tests that present test-takers with an ambiguous stimulus and ask them to respond to it, for example, by describing it or telling a story about it. One well-known projective test, which uses inkblots as stimuli, was created by
a. the neo-Freudians.
b. Freud and his circle.
c. Carl Jung.
d. Hermann Rorschach.

7. Many of Freud's specific ideas—for example, his ideas on the formation of gender identity or the function of dreams—have been modified by the neo-Freudians or challenged by recent research. However, most psychologists would agree with Freud about
a. the existence of unconscious mental processes.
b. the Oedipus and Electra complexes.
c. the predictive value of Freudian theory.
d. adult psychological problems being the result of inadequate psychosexual development.

The Trait Perspective

Preview Question

7. How do trait theorists view personality?

Personality traits can be fundamental to job performance. The outgoing temperament so vital to being a standup comedian is unimportant for a stone carver.

Psychoanalytic theory explains personality in terms of the dynamics that underlie behavior. It peers beneath the surface in search of hidden motives. In 1919, Gordon Allport, a curious 22-year-old psychology student, interviewed Freud in Vienna and discovered just how preoccupied the founder of psychoanalysis was with finding hidden motives, even in Allport's own behavior during the interview. That experience ultimately led Allport to do what Freud did not do—to describe personality in terms of fundamental **traits**—people's characteristic behaviors and conscious motives. Meeting Freud, said Allport, "taught me that [psychoanalysis], for all its merits, may plunge too deep, and that psychologists would do well to give full recognition to manifest motives before probing the unconscious." Allport therefore defined personality in terms of identifiable behavior patterns. He was less concerned with *explaining* and more concerned with *describing* individual traits.

How do psychologists describe and classify personalities? An analogy may help. Imagine that you want to describe and classify apples. Someone might correctly say that every apple is unique. Still, you might find it useful to begin by classifying apples as distinct *types*—Delicious, Granny Smith, McIntosh, and so forth. For example, based on children's physiological and psychological reactivity, Jerome Kagan (1989b) classifies children's temperaments—as either shy-inhibited or fearless-uninhibited types. Some health psychologists find it useful to classify people as intense, "Type A," or as laid back, "Type B" personalities (page 330).

Psychologist William Sheldon (1954) classified people by body type. Santa Claus typifies the plump "endomorph": relaxed and jolly. Superman typifies the muscular "mesomorph": bold and physically active. Sherlock Holmes typifies the thin "ectomorph": high strung and solitary. Are different body types actually associated with different personalities? When researchers assess people's body types and personalities separately, there is a linkage, but it is modest. The stereotypes of the chubby, happy-go-lucky person and of the muscular, confident person turn out to be just that—stereotypes that exaggerate a kernel of truth (Tucker, 1983).

More popular today, especially in business and career counseling, is an effort to classify people based on their responses to 126 questions written by Isabel Briggs Myers (1987) and her mother, Kathleen Briggs. The "Myers-Briggs Type Indicator" is quite simple. It gives choices to its 2 million annual takers, such as "Do you usually value sentiment more than logic, or value logic more than sentiment?" Then it counts their preferences, labels them as indicating, say, a "feeling" or "thinking" type, and describes each type in complimentary terms. Feeling types, for example, are told they are sensitive to values and "sympathetic, appreciative, and tactful"; thinking types are told they "prefer an objective standard of truth" and are "good at analyzing." Most people therefore readily embrace their announced type profile, which mirrors their declared preferences. They may also accept it as a basis for being matched with work partners and tasks that supposedly suit their temperaments. A recent National Research Council report, however, notes that the use of the test has run ahead of research on its value as a predictor of job performance. Thus, the report concludes, "the popularity of this instrument in the absence of proven scientific worth is troublesome" (Druckman & Bjork, 1991, p. 101).

Exploring Traits

If classifying people as one distinct personality type or another fails to fully

trait A characteristic pattern of behavior or conscious motive; assessed by self-report inventories and peer reports.

capture their individuality, how else can we describe their personalities? To return to our apple analogy, we might describe an apple along several trait dimensions—as relatively large or small, red or yellow, sweet or sour. By placing people on several trait dimensions simultaneously, psychologists can describe countless individual personality variations.

What trait dimensions describe personality? Allport and his associate H. S. Odbert (1936) literally counted all the words in an unabridged dictionary with which one could describe people. The list numbered almost 18,000 words! How, then, could psychologists condense the list to a manageable number of basic traits?

One way has been to propose traits, such as anxiety, that some theory regards as basic. A newer technique is *factor analysis,* the statistical procedure described in Chapter 8 to identify clusters of test items that tap basic components of intelligence (such as spatial ability, reasoning ability, or verbal skill). Imagine that people who describe themselves as outgoing also tend to say they like excitement and practical jokes, and that they do not like quiet reading. Such a statistically correlated cluster of behaviors reflects a basic trait, or factor. In this particular case, the identified items are part of a cluster that make up a trait called *extraversion.*

British psychologists Hans and Sybil Eysenck believe that we can reduce many of our normal individual variations to two genetically influenced dimensions: *extraversion-introversion* and *emotional stability-instability* (Figure 11–2). Their Eysenck Personality Questionnaire has been given to people in 35 countries around the world, from China to Uganda to Russia. When people's answers are analyzed, the extraversion and emotionality factors inevitably emerge as basic personality dimensions (Eysenck, 1990). Extraverts, they contend, seek stimulation because their normal levels of brain arousal are relatively low. Emotionally stable people react calmly because their autonomic nervous systems are not so reactive as those of unstable people.

Figure 11–2 In this chart, various combinations of the Eysencks' two primary personality factors—extraversion-introversion and stability-instability—are used to define other, more specific traits. (From Eysenck & Eysenck, 1963.)

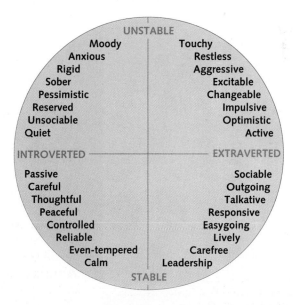

Many other trait theorists, too, view personality traits as biologically rooted. Like Eysenck, Jerome Kagan attributes differences in children's shyness and inhibition to their autonomic nervous system reactivity. Twin and adoption studies of genetic influences on personality traits (pages 96–98) further testify to biology's influence, reminding us that behavior patterns form as a person's genetic endowment interacts with a particular environment.

Most researchers believe the Eysencks' dimensions are important, but don't tell the whole story of someone's personality. They offer a slightly expanded set of factors—dubbed the "Big Five" (John, 1990; Noller & others, 1987). If a test specifies where you are on the five dimensions of Table 11–2, it has said much of what there is to say about your personality. Around the world people describe others in terms roughly consistent with the Big Five—how agreeable they are, how extraverted they are, and so forth. The Big Five may not be the last word, but it's currently our best approximation of the basic trait dimensions.

Table 11-2
The "Big Five" Personality Factors

Trait dimension	Description
Emotional stability	Calm versus anxious Secure versus insecure Self-satisfied versus self-pitying
Extraversion	Sociable versus retiring Fun-loving versus sober Affectionate versus reserved
Openness	Imaginative versus practical Preference for variety versus preference for routine Independent versus conforming
Agreeableness	Soft-hearted versus ruthless Trusting versus suspicious Helpful versus uncooperative
Conscientiousness	Organized versus disorganized Careful versus careless Disciplined versus impulsive

Source: Adapted from "Clinical assessment can benefit from recent advances in personality psychology" by R. McCrae & P. T. Costa, Jr., 1986, *American Psychologist, 41,* p. 1002.

Assessing Traits

Preview Question

8. How do we assess traits?

Assessment techniques derived from trait concepts aim simply to profile a person's behavior patterns, not to reveal the hidden personality dynamics (which is the intent of projective tests). Many trait scales provide quick assessments of a single trait, such as extraversion, anxiety, or self-esteem. Such measures are commonly used in studies of personality and behavior. Alterna-

personality inventory A questionnaire (often with true-false or agree-disagree items) on which people respond to items designed to gauge a wide range of feelings and behaviors; used to assess selected personality traits.

Minnesota Multiphasic Personality Inventory (MMPI) The most widely researched and clinically used of all personality tests. Originally developed to identify the traits of emotionally troubled people (still considered its most appropriate use), this test (recently updated to become the MMPI-2) is now also used for other screening purposes.

empirically derived test A test (such as the MMPI-2) developed by testing a pool of items and then selecting those that discriminate groups of interest.

tively, psychologists can assess several traits at once by administering **personality inventories**—longer questionnaires on which people respond to items designed to gauge a wide range of feelings and behaviors.

The personality inventory that psychologists have most extensively researched and widely used is the **Minnesota Multiphasic Personality Inventory (MMPI).** Although it assesses psychological disorders rather than "normal" personality traits, the MMPI illustrates a good way to develop a personality inventory. One of its creators, Starke Hathaway (1960), compared his effort to that of Alfred Binet. As we learned in Chapter 8, Binet developed the first intelligence test by selecting items that successfully identified children who would have trouble progressing normally in the Parisian school system. The MMPI items, too, were **empirically derived.** That is, from a large pool of items Hathaway and his colleagues selected those that discriminated particular groups.

They initially gave hundreds of true-false statements ("No one seems to understand me," "I get all the sympathy I should," "I like poetry") to groups of psychologically disordered patients and to "normal" people. They retained any item that a patient group answered differently from the normal group, no matter how silly it sounded. "Nothing in the newspaper interests me except the comics" may seem senseless, but it just so happened that depressed people were more likely to answer "true."

Today's new "MMPI-2," renormed on a full cross section of Americans and containing revised items, still contains 10 "clinical scales" (Figure 11–3). It also retains several "validity scales," including a "lie scale" that assesses the extent to which a person is faking a good impression (by responding "false" to statements such as "I get angry sometimes"). And it has 15 "content scales" assessing, for instance, work attitudes, family problems, and anger.

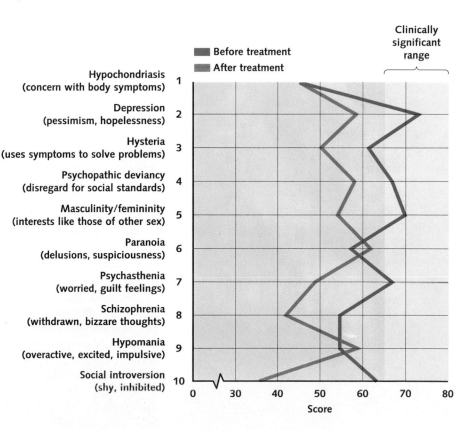

Figure 11–3 Minnesota Multiphasic Personality Inventory (MMPI-2) test profile of Ed, a depressed and anxious young man, before and after psychotherapy. About two-thirds of people taking the MMPI-2 have a score between 40 and 60 on any scale. (Adapted from Butcher, 1990.)

In contrast to the subjectivity of projective tests, personality inventories are scored objectively—so objectively a computer can administer and score them. (The computer can also provide descriptions of people who previously responded similarly.) Objectivity does not, however, guarantee validity. Sophisticated test-takers can fake a good impression if taking the MMPI for employment purposes (by answering in socially desirable ways, except on those items for which nearly anyone would admit to being imperfect). Moreover, the ease of computerized testing tempts untrained administrators—including many personnel officers, educational admissions officers, and physicians—to use the test in ways for which it has not been validated (Matarazzo, 1983). Nevertheless, for better or worse, the objectivity of the MMPI contributes to its rising popularity (Piotrowski & Keller, 1989), and to its translation into more than 100 languages.

Evaluating the Trait Perspective

Are our personality traits stable and enduring? Or does our behavior depend on where we are and whom we're with? Most of us agree that this is not strictly an either/or question: Our behavior is influenced by the interaction of our inner disposition with our environment. Still, the question lingers: which is *more* important? Forced to choose, most people would probably say our traits are stable and enduring. Until recently, most psychologists would have too. Isn't it obvious that some people are dependably conscientious and others unreliable, some cheerful and others dour, some outgoing and others shy?

Remember, to be a genuine personality trait a characteristic must persist over time *and* across situations. If friendliness is a trait, friendly people must act friendly at different times and places. Do they? In Chapter 3, we considered research that has followed lives through time. We noted that some scholars are impressed with personality change (especially those who study infants); others are struck by personality stability from adolescence through adulthood. If people's personalities are assessed in young adulthood and then assessed again several decades later, their characteristics persist.

The consistency of specific behaviors from one situation to the next is another matter. As Walter Mischel (1968, 1984) points out, people do not act with predictable consistency. In one of the first studies to reveal this, Hugh Hartshorne and Mark May (1928b) gave thousands of children opportunities to lie, cheat, and steal while at home, at play, and in the classroom. Were some children consistently honest, others dishonest? Generally not. "Most children will deceive in certain situations and not in others," the researchers reported. A child's "lying, cheating, and stealing as measured by the test situations used in these studies are only very loosely related" (p. 411). More than a half-century later, Mischel's studies of college students' conscientiousness revealed a similar finding. There was virtually no relation between a student's being conscientious on one occasion (say, showing up for class on time) and being similarly conscientious on another occasion (say, turning in assignments on time).

Mischel also points out that people's scores on personality tests only mildly predict their behaviors. For example, people's scores on an extraversion test do not neatly predict how sociable they actually will be on any given occasion. If we remember such results, says Mischel, we will be more cautious about labeling and pigeonholing individuals. We will be more restrained when asked to predict if someone is likely to violate parole, commit suicide, or be an effective employee. Years in advance, science can tell us the phase of the moon for any given date, but we're a long way from being able to predict how you will feel and act tomorrow.

Preview Question

9. Does research support the consistency of personality traits?

Roughly speaking, the temporary, external influences on behavior are the focus of social psychology, and the enduring, inner influences are the focus of personality psychology. In actuality, behavior always depends on the *interaction* of persons with situations (pages 368–369).

"There is as much difference between us and ourselves, as between us and others."

Michel de Montaigne,
Essays, 1588

"Mr. Coughlin over there was the founder of one of the first motorcycle gangs."

Drawing by Miller; © 1984 The New Yorker Magazine, Inc.

In defense of traits, personality psychologist Seymour Epstein (1983a, 1983b) maintains that trying to predict a specific act on the basis of a personality test is like trying to predict your answer to a single test question on the basis of an intelligence test. Your answer to any given question is unpredictable because it depends on so many variables (your reading of the question, your understanding of the topic, your concentration level at the moment, luck). Your *average* accuracy over many questions on several tests is more predictable. Similarly, says Epstein, people's *average* outgoingness, happiness, or carelessness over *many* situations is predictable. When rating someone's shyness or agreeableness, this consistency enables people who know someone well to agree (Kenrick & Funder, 1988). As our best friends can verify, we *do* have personality traits.

In unfamiliar, formal situations—perhaps when eating dinner in a strange home—our traits may remain hidden as we attend carefully to social cues. In familiar, informal situations—just hanging out with friends—we feel less constrained, allowing our traits to emerge (Buss, 1989). In such situations, our expressive styles are impressively consistent. Thus, we often form lasting impressions of people after just a few moments of meeting them or seeing them on TV and noting their animation, manner of speaking, and gestures. Nalini Ambady and Robert Rosenthal (1991, 1992) videotaped 13 Harvard University graduate students teaching undergraduate courses. Observers then viewed three thin slices of each teacher's behavior—more 10-second clips from the beginning, middle, and end of a class—and rated each teachers' confidence, enthusiasm, warmth, and so forth. These behavior ratings, based on *30 seconds* of teaching from an entire semester, predicted amazingly well the teachers' average student ratings at the semester's end.

To sum up, we can say that at any moment the immediate situation powerfully influences a person's behavior, especially when the situation makes clear demands. We can better predict drivers' behavior at traffic lights from knowing the color of the lights than from knowing their personalities. However, averaging people's behavior across many occasions reveals that they do have distinct personalities.

Rehearse It

8. Trait theory describes personality in terms of characteristic behaviors, or traits, such as agreeableness or extraversion. A pioneering trait theorist was
a. Sigmund Freud.
b. Alfred Adler.
c. Gordon Allport.
d. Henry Murray.

9. Trait theorists assess the personality by developing a profile of a person's traits. For example, they administer long questionnaires called personality inventories, which ask people to report their characteristic feelings and behaviors. The most widely used of all personality inventories is the
a. extraversion-introversion scale.
b. TAT.
c. MMPI.
d. Rorschach.

10. The items of the MMPI were empirically derived. This means, for example, that the designers of the test figured out which responses indicated schizophrenia by
a. taking case histories before and after the test.
b. analyzing the content of the items in light of their understanding of the disorder.
c. comparing the responses of known schizophrenia patients with those of normal people.
d. assessing the degree of deception, using validity scales.

11. People's scores on a personality test are only mildly predictive of their behavior. Such tests best predict
a. a person's behavior on a specific occasion.
b. a person's average behavior across many situations.
c. behavior involving a single trait, such as conscientiousness.
d. behavior that depends on situation or context.

The Humanistic Perspective

Preview Question

10. What is the central focus of the humanistic perspective?

By 1960, some prominent personality psychologists became discontented with what they felt was Freud's negativity and with trait psychology's objectivity. In contrast to Freud's study of the "base" motives of "sick" people, these *humanistic psychologists* focused on the strivings of "healthy" people for self-determination and self-realization. In contrast to trait psychologists' profiles, they viewed whole persons as beyond encapsulation as so many test scores. In contrast to behaviorism's mechanistic analysis, which downplayed subjective experience and tied human behavior to conditioned responses, they urged study of personal experiences of sorrow and joy, alienation and intimacy, frustration and fulfillment. Two pioneering theorists illustrate these emphases on human potential and seeing the world through the person's (not the experimenter's) eyes: Abraham Maslow (1908–1970) and Carl Rogers (1902–1987).

Exploring the Self

Abraham Maslow's Self-Actualizing Person

Maslow proposed that we are motivated by a hierarchy of needs (pages 271–272). If our physiological needs are met, we become concerned with personal safety; if we achieve a sense of security, we then seek to love, to be loved, and to love ourselves. Given self-esteem, we ultimately seek **self-actualization,** the process of fulfilling our potential.

Unlike many theorists before him, Maslow (1970) developed his ideas by studying healthy, creative people rather than troubled clinical cases. He based his description of self-actualization on a study of acquaintances and Western cultural figures who seemed notable for their rich and productive lives—Abraham Lincoln, Thomas Jefferson, and Eleanor Roosevelt among them. These people shared certain characteristics. Maslow reported they were self-aware and self-accepting, open and spontaneous, loving and caring, and not paralyzed by others' opinions. Secure in their sense of who they were, their interests were problem-centered rather than self-centered. Often they focused their energies on a particular task, which they regarded as their mission in life. Most enjoyed a few deep relationships rather than many superficial ones. Many had been moved by spiritual or ecstatic *peak experiences* that surpassed ordinary consciousness.

These are mature adult qualities, said Maslow, ones found in those who have learned enough about life to be compassionate, to have outgrown their mixed feelings toward their parents, to have found their calling, to have "acquired enough courage to be unpopular, to be unashamed about being openly virtuous, etc." Maslow's work with college students led him to speculate that those likely to become self-actualizing adults were likable, caring, "privately affectionate to those of their elders who deserve it," and "secretly uneasy about the cruelty, meanness, and mob spirit so often found in young people."

Carl Rogers' Person-Centered Perspective

Fellow humanistic psychologist Carl Rogers agreed with much of Maslow's thinking. Rogers believed that people are basically good and endowed with self-actualizing tendencies. Each of us is like an acorn, containing the poten-

Abraham Maslow (*Motivation and Personality*, 1970): "Any theory of motivation that is worthy of attention must deal with the highest capacities of the healthy and strong person as well as with the defensive maneuvers of crippled spirits."

self-actualization According to Maslow, the ultimate psychological need that arises after basic physical and psychological needs are met and self-esteem is achieved; the motivation to fulfill one's potential.

unconditional positive regard According to Rogers, an attitude of total acceptance toward another person.

self-concept All our thoughts and feelings about ourselves in response to the question, "Who am I?"

When you have empathic listeners, being open and talking freely is easier.

tial for growth and fulfillment, unless thwarted by an environment that inhibits growth. Rogers (1980) surmised that a "growth-promoting" climate required three conditions—genuineness, acceptance, and empathy.

According to Rogers, people nurture others' growth by being *genuine*—by being open with their own feelings, by dropping their facades, by being transparent and self-disclosing.

People also nurture growth by being *accepting*—by offering us what Rogers called **unconditional positive regard.** This is an attitude of grace, an attitude that values us, even knowing our failings. Have you ever experienced the relief of having dropped your pretenses, confessed your worst feelings, and discovered that you were still accepted? We sometimes enjoy this gratifying experience in a good marriage, a close family, or an intimate friendship, when we no longer feel the need to explain ourselves, when we are free to be spontaneous without fear of losing the other's esteem.

Finally, people nurture growth by being *empathic*—by nonjudgmentally reflecting our feelings and meanings. "Rarely do we listen with real understanding, true empathy," said Rogers. "Yet listening, of this very special kind, is one of the most potent forces for change that I know."

Genuineness, acceptance, and empathy are the water, sun, and nutrients that enable people to grow like vigorous oak trees. For "as persons are accepted and prized," Rogers (1980, p. 116) continued, "they tend to develop a more caring attitude toward themselves." As persons are empathically heard, "it becomes possible for them to listen more accurately to the flow of inner experiencings." Rogers would have been pleased by a finding published shortly after his death: Preschool children whose parents exhibit such attitudes usually become creative adolescents (Harrington & others, 1987).

For Maslow, and even more for Rogers, a central feature of personality is one's **self-concept**—all the thoughts and feelings we have in response to the question, "Who am I?" If our self-concept is positive, we tend to act and perceive the world positively. If it is negative—if in our own eyes we fall far short of our "ideal self"—said Rogers, we feel dissatisfied and unhappy. A worthwhile goal for parents, teachers, and friends is, therefore, to help others know, accept, and be true to themselves.

Assessing the Self

Humanistic psychologists sometimes assess personality with questionnaires that evaluate people's self-concepts. One questionnaire, inspired by Carl Rogers, asks people to describe themselves both as they ideally would like to be and as they actually are. When the ideal and the actual self are nearly alike, said Rogers, the self-concept is positive. Thus, he looked for successively closer ratings of actual and ideal self as a way to assess his clients' personal growth during therapy.

Other humanistic psychologists believe that any standardized assessment of personality is depersonalizing. Even a questionnaire detaches the psychologist from the living human. Rather than forcing the person to respond to narrow categories, these humanistic psychologists believe that interviews and intimate conversation enable a better understanding of each person's unique experiences.

Research on the Self

Psychology's concern with people's sense of self dates back at least to William James, who spent more than 100 pages on it in his 1890 *Principles of Psychology*. By 1943, Gordon Allport lamented that the self had become "lost to

Preview Question

11. What have we learned from research on the self?

self-esteem One's feelings of high or low self-worth.

self-serving bias A readiness to perceive oneself favorably.

What possible future selves do you envision? To what extent do these imagined selves motivate you now?

Seneca (*Ad Lucilium*, A.D. 64): "What you think of yourself is much more important than what others think of you."

view." Although humanistic psychology's emphasis on the self did not instigate much scientific research, it did help renew the concept of self and keep it alive. Now, a century after James, the self is one of psychology's most vigorously researched topics. Every year new studies galore appear on "self-esteem," "self-disclosure," "self-awareness," "self-schemas," "self-monitoring," and so forth.

One example of the new thinking about self is the concept of *possible selves* put forth by Hazel Markus and her University of Michigan colleagues (Inglehart & others, 1989; Markus & Nurius, 1986). Your possible selves include your visions of the self you dream of becoming—the fit self, the accomplished self, the loved and admired self. They also include the self you fear becoming—the unemployed self, the alcoholic self, the academically failed self. Such possible selves motivate us by laying out specific goals to pursue and the energy to work toward them. Olympian Carl Lewis concentrated on the achievements of Olympic hero Jesse Owens to give form to his aspirations. Similarly, University of Michigan students in a combined undergraduate/medical school program earn higher grades if they undergo the program with a clear vision of themselves as successful doctors. Those who dream most, achieve most.

Underlying this research is an assumption (shared by humanistic psychologists) that the self, as organizer of our thoughts, feelings, and actions, is a pivotal center of personality. Research studies reveal the benefits of positive self-esteem and the hazards of self-righteous pride.

The Benefits of Self-Esteem   High **self-esteem**—a feeling of self-worth—pays dividends. People who feel good about themselves have fewer ulcers, fewer sleepless nights, succumb less to pressures to conform, are less likely to use drugs, are more persistent at difficult tasks, and are just plain happier (Brockner & Hulton, 1978; Brown, 1991).

Low self-esteem exacts costs. People who feel they are falling short of their hopes are vulnerable to depression. Those whose self-image falls short of what they think they *ought* to be are vulnerable to anxiety (Higgins, 1987). More often than not, unhappiness and despair coexist with a negative self-image.

These correlational links between low self-esteem and life problems have other possible interpretations (maybe life problems cause low self-esteem). However, an *effect* of low self-esteem appears in experiments. Temporarily deflate people's self-image (say, by telling them they did poorly on an aptitude test or by disparaging their personality) and they will be more likely to disparage other people or to express heightened racial prejudice. People who are negative about themselves also tend to be thin-skinned and judgmental (Baumgardner & others, 1989; Crocker & Schwartz, 1985). In experiments, those made to feel insecure often become excessively critical, as if to impress others with their own brilliance (Amabile, 1983). Although some "love their neighbors as themselves," others loathe their neighbors as themselves. Such findings are consistent with Maslow's and Rogers' presumptions that a "healthy" self-image pays dividends. Accept yourself and you'll find it easier to accept others.

The Pervasiveness of Self-Serving Bias   Carl Rogers (1958) once objected to the religious doctrine that humanity's problems arise from excessive self-love, or pride. He noted that most people he had known "despise themselves, regard themselves as worthless and unlovable." Mark Twain had the idea: "No man, deep down in the privacy of his heart, has any considerable respect for himself."

"To love oneself is the beginning of a life-long romance."

Oscar Wilde,
An Ideal Husband, 1895

"It is only our bad temper that we put down to being tired or worried or hungry. We put our good temper down to ourselves."

C. S. Lewis (1898–1963)

"The [self-]portraits that we actually believe, when we are given freedom to voice them, are dramatically more positive than reality can sustain."

Shelley Taylor,
Positive Illusions, 1989

Actually, most of us have a good reputation with ourselves. In studies of self-esteem, even low-scoring people respond in the mid-range of possible scores (Baumeister & others, 1989). (A "low" self-esteem person responds to statements such as "I have good ideas" with qualifying adjectives such as "somewhat" or "sometimes.") Moreover, one of psychology's most provocative yet firmly established recent conclusions concerns our potent **self-serving bias**—our readiness to perceive ourselves favorably (Brown, 1991; Headey & Wearing, 1988; Myers, 1993). Consider:

People accept more responsibility for good deeds than bad, and for successes than failures. Athletes often privately credit their victories to their own prowess, their losses to bad breaks, lousy officiating, or the other team's exceptional performance. After receiving poor exam grades, students in a half dozen studies criticized the exam, not themselves. On insurance forms, drivers have explained accidents in such words as: "An invisible car came out of nowhere, struck my car and vanished." "As I reached an intersection, a hedge sprang up, obscuring my vision, and I did not see the other car." "A pedestrian hit me and went under my car." The question "What have I done to deserve this?" is one we ask of our troubles, not our successes. Success we assume we deserve.

Most people see themselves as better than average. This is true for nearly any subjective and socially desirable dimension. In national surveys, most business executives say they are more ethical than their average counterpart. In several studies, 90 percent of business managers and 90 + percent of college professors rated their performance as superior to their average peer. In Australia, 86 percent of people rate their job performance as above average, 1 percent as below average. And in the United States, most high school seniors rate themselves in the top 10 percent of their agemates in their "ability to get along with others." Although the phenomenon is less striking in Asia, self-serving biases have been observed worldwide: with Dutch, Australian, and Chinese students; Japanese drivers; Indian Hindus; and French people of all ages. The world, it seems, is Garrison Keillor's Lake Wobegon writ large—a place where "all the women are strong, all the men are good-looking, and all the children are above average."

Self-serving bias flies in the face of today's pop psychology. "All of us have inferiority complexes," insists John Powell (1989, p. 15). "Those who seem not to have such a complex are only pretending." But additional streams of evidence remove any doubts: We remember and justify our past actions in self-enhancing ways. We exhibit an inflated confidence in the accuracy of our beliefs and judgments. We overestimate how desirably *we* would act in situations where most people behave less than admirably. We are quicker to believe flattering descriptions of ourselves than unflattering ones, and we are impressed with psychological tests that flatter us. We shore up our self-image by overestimating how much others support our opinions and share our foibles and by *under*estimating the commonality of our strengths. We exhibit group pride—a tendency to see our group (our school, our country, our race) as superior.

Moreover, pride does often go before a fall. The self-serving perceptions that underlie conflicts range from other-blaming marital discord to self-promoting ethnic snobbery. It was "Aryan pride" that fueled Nazi atrocities. It was national self-righteousness that led both the Americans and Soviets during the arms race to say, "Your weapons threaten us, ours are only for defense." No wonder religion and literature so often warn against the perils of excessive pride.

Still, people object. They think of those who do seem to despise themselves, who feel worthless and unlovable. If self-serving bias prevails, why do so many people disparage themselves? For at least two reasons. Sometimes people's self-put-downs are subtly strategic: They elicit reassuring strokes. Usually, a remark such as "No one likes me" will at least elicit a "But not everyone has met you!" Other times, self-disparaging comments, such as before a game or an exam, prepare for possible failure. The coach who extols the superior strength of the upcoming opponent makes a loss understandable, a victory noteworthy.

Even so, it's true: All of us some of the time, and some of us much of the time, *do* feel inferior—especially when comparing ourselves with those who are a step or two higher on the ladder of status, grades, looks, income, or agility. The deeper and more frequently we have such feelings, the more unhappy, even depressed, we are.

We can therefore affirm what humanistic psychologists rightly emphasize: For the individual, self-affirming thinking is generally adaptive. To a point, even our positive illusions are beneficial. They maintain our self-confidence, protect against anxiety and depression, and sustain our sense of well-being. "Life is the art of being well-deceived," observed the English essayist William Hazlitt.

Recognizing both the perils of self-righteousness and the dividends of positive self-esteem, psychologists Roy Baumeister and colleagues (1989), Jonathan Brown (1991), and Shelley Taylor (1989) all suggest that humans function best with modest self-enhancing illusions. We are like the new Japanese and European magnetic levitation trains, says Brown: We function optimally when riding high, just off the rails—not so high that we gyrate and crash, yet not so in touch that we grind to a halt.

Evaluating the Humanistic Perspective

One thing said of Freud can also be said of the humanistic psychologists: Their impact has been pervasive. Their ideas have influenced counseling, education, child-rearing, and management. They have also influenced—sometimes in ways they did not intend—much of today's popular psychology.

It is through popular psychology that many of us absorb some of what Maslow and Rogers so effectively taught—that a positive self-concept is key to happiness and success, that acceptance and empathy help nurture positive feelings about oneself, and that people are basically good and capable of self-improvement. The National Opinion Research Center (1985) reports that by a 4 to 1 margin, Americans believe "human nature is basically good" rather than "fundamentally perverse and corrupt." Humanistic psychologists can also take satisfaction in the dramatically different responses today from those of 50 years ago to one of the MMPI statements (Holden, 1986b): Among those in the 1930s normal standardization sample, only 9 percent agreed that "I am an important person." In the mid-1980s, more than half of the new sample agreed with the statement. And responding to a 1989 Gallup Poll, 85 percent of Americans rated "having a good self-image or self-respect" as *very* important; 0 percent rated it unimportant. Humanistic psychology's message has been heard.

The prominence of the humanistic perspective set off a backlash of criticism. First, said the critics, its concepts are vague and subjective. Consider the description of self-actualizing people as open, spontaneous, loving, self-accepting, and productive. Is this really a scientific description? Or is it

"If you compare yourself with others, you may become vain and bitter; for always there will be greater and lesser persons than yourself."

Desiderata, found in Old St. Paul's Church,
London, 1692

Preview Question

12. What impact has the humanistic perspective had on psychology?

"We do pretty well when you stop to think that people are basically good."

Drawing by Fradon; © 1979 The New Yorker Magazine, Inc.

merely a description of Maslow's personal values and ideals? What Maslow did, noted M. Brewster Smith (1978), was offer impressions of his own personal heroes. Imagine another theorist who began with a different set of heroes—perhaps Napoleon, Alexander the Great, and John D. Rockefeller, Sr. This theorist would likely describe self-actualizing people as "undeterred by the needs of others, motivated to achieve, and obsessed with power."

Second, some critics object to the idea that, as Carl Rogers put it, "The only question which matters is, 'Am I living in a way which is deeply satisfying to me, and which truly expresses me?'" (quoted by Wallach & Wallach, 1985). They fear that the individualism encouraged by humanistic psychology—trusting and acting on one's feelings, being true to oneself, fulfilling oneself—promotes self-indulgence, selfishness, and an erosion of moral restraints (Campbell & Specht, 1985; Wallach & Wallach, 1983). Indeed it is those who focus not on themselves but beyond themselves who are most likely to experience social support, to enjoy life, and to cope effectively with stress (Crandall, 1984).

Humanistic psychologists rebut such objections. They counter that belligerence, hostility, and insensitivity are often traceable to a poor self-concept. Moreover, they argue, self-love is actually the first step toward loving others.

Finally, the humanistic psychologists have been accused of failing to appreciate the reality of our human capacity for evil. Faced with assaults on the environment, overpopulation, and threats of nuclear war, apathy can develop from two rationalizations. One is a naive optimism that denies the threat ("People are basically good; everything will work out"). The other is a dark despair ("It's hopeless; why try?"). Action requires enough realism to fuel concern and enough optimism to provide hope. Humanistic psychology, say the critics, encourages the needed hope, but not the equally necessary realism.

Rehearse It

12. Abraham Maslow theorized that human beings are motivated by a hierarchy of needs. When basic physiological and psychological needs are satisfied, Maslow wrote, people become motivated to fulfill their potential through self-actualization. Maslow based his ideas on
a. Freudian theory.
b. his experiences with patients.
c. a series of laboratory experiments.
d. his study of healthy and creative people.

13. According to Carl Rogers, a growth-promoting environment is one that offers genuineness, acceptance, and empathy.

The total acceptance Rogers advocated is called
a. self-concept.
b. unconditional positive regard.
c. self-actualization.
d. the "ideal self."

14. Researchers have found that people tend to accept responsibility for their successes or good qualities, and blame circumstances or luck for their failures. This is an example of
a. low self-esteem.
b. self-actualization.
c. self-serving bias.
d. empathy.

15. The humanistic perspective is most concerned with the potential for human growth and self-fulfillment; ideas of the humanistic psychologists have found their way into counseling, education, management, and popular psychology. Among the psychologists best known for having made important contributions to humanistic psychology are
a. Abraham Maslow and Carl Rogers.
b. Gordon Allport and Michael Eysenck.
c. Sigmund Freud and Carl Jung.
d. Hermann Rorschach and Hans Eysenck.

The Social-Cognitive Perspective

Preview Question

13. What factors does the social-cognitive perspective emphasize?

Our fourth major perspective on personality derives from psychological principles of learning, cognition, and social behavior. Called the **social-cognitive perspective** by psychologist Albert Bandura (1986), its proponents emphasize the importance of external events. Like learning theorists, they believe that we learn many of our behaviors either by conditioning or by observing others and modeling our behavior after them. Like cognitive and social psychological theorists, they emphasize the importance of mental processes: How we think and feel about the situations we find ourselves in affects our behavior. So instead of focusing solely on how our environment controls us (behaviorism), social-cognitive theorists focus on how we and our environment interact: How do we interpret and respond to external events? How do our schemas, our memories, and our expectations influence our behavior patterns?

Exploring Behavior in Situations

Reciprocal Influences

Bandura (1986) calls the process of interacting with our environment **reciprocal determinism.** "Behavior, internal personal factors, and environmental influences," he says, "all operate as interlocking determinants of each other" (Figure 11–4). For example, children's TV viewing habits (past behavior) influence their viewing preferences (internal personal factor), which influence how television (environmental factor) affects their current behavior. The influences are mutual.

Consider three specific ways in which persons and environments interact:

1. *Different people choose different environments.* The college you attend, the reading you do, the television you watch, the music you listen to, the friends you associate with—all are an environment you have chosen, based partly on your dispositions. You choose it and it shapes you.

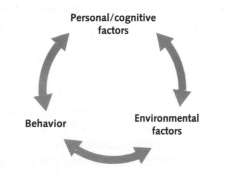

Figure 11–4 Reciprocal determinism. The social-cognitive perspective proposes that our personalities are shaped by the interaction of our situations, our thoughts and feelings, and our behaviors. (From Bandura, 1978).

While this woman is thrilled by her bungee jump, others would be terrified. Our individual personalities are expressed in the distinctive ways we perceive and react to situations.

social-cognitive perspective Applies interactive principles of social learning and cognition to study how the environment shapes people's behavior and beliefs, and how these in turn influence people's situations.

reciprocal determinism The interacting influences between personality and environmental factors.

personal control Our sense of being in control of our environment rather than feeling helpless.

external locus of control The perception that chance or outside forces beyond one's personal control determine one's fate.

internal locus of control The perception that one controls one's own fate.

Preview Question

14. What are the causes and consequences of personal control?

2. *Our personalities shape how we interpret and react to events.* Anxious people are more likely to be attuned to potentially threatening events than are nonanxious people (Eysenck & others, 1987). Thus, anxious people perceive the world as more threatening, and react accordingly.

3. *Our personalities help create situations to which we react.* Many experiments reveal that how we view and treat our families, roommates, and friends influences how they in turn treat us. If we expect someone to be angry with us, we may give the person a cold shoulder, touching off the very behavior we expect.

We are both the products and the architects of our environments. If all this has a familiar ring, it may be because it parallels and reinforces a pervasive theme in psychology and in this book: Behavior emerges from the interplay of external and internal influences. Boiling water turns an egg hard and a potato soft. A threatening environment turns one person into a hero, another into a scoundrel. *At every moment,* our behavior is determined by our experiences *and* our genes, our environments *and* our personalities.

Personal Control

One important aspect of personality is our sense of **personal control**—whether we see ourselves as controlling, or as controlled by, our environments. Studies of people's sense of personal control demonstrate that behavior is affected by whether people perceive the control of their lives as internal (in themselves) or external (at the mercy of the outside world).

Psychologists have two basic ways to study the effect of personal control (or any personality factor). One: *Correlate* people's feelings of control with their behaviors and achievements. Two: *Experiment,* by raising or lowering people's sense of control and noting the effects.

Locus of Control Consider your own feelings of control. Do you feel that your life is beyond your control? That the world is run by a few powerful people? That getting a good job depends mainly on being in the right place at the right time? Or do you more strongly believe that what happens to you is your own doing? That the average person can influence government decisions? That being a success is a matter of hard work, not luck?

Hundreds of studies have compared people who perceive what psychologist Julian Rotter calls an **external locus of control**—that chance or outside forces determine their fate—with those who perceive an **internal locus of control**—that to a great extent they control their own destinies. In study after study, "internals" have achieved more in school (Findley & Cooper, 1983), are more independent, and less depressed (Benassi & others, 1988; Lefcourt, 1982). Moreover, they are better able to delay gratification and cope with various stresses, including marital problems (Miller & others, 1986).

Learned Helplessness Versus Personal Control Helpless, oppressed people often perceive that control is external, and this perception may deepen their feelings of resignation. This is precisely what researcher Martin Seligman (1975, 1991) and others found in experiments with both animals and people. When dogs are strapped in a harness and given repeated shocks, with no opportunity to avoid them, they learn a sense of helplessness. When later placed in another situation where they *could* escape the punishment by merely leaping a hurdle, they cower without hope. Faced with repeated traumatic events over which they have no control, people, too, come to feel helpless, hopeless, and depressed. This passive resignation is called **learned helplessness** (Figure 11–5). In contrast, animals that escape the shocks in the first situation learn personal control and easily escape shocks in the new situation.

Figure 11–5 Learned helplessness.

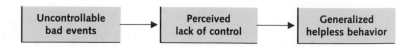

In concentration camps, in prisons, even in factories, colleges, and well-meaning nursing homes, people given little control experience a similar lowering of morale and increased stress. Increasing control—allowing prisoners to move chairs and control room lights and the TV, workers to participate in decision making, nursing home patients to make choices about their environment—noticeably improves health and morale (Miller & Monge, 1986; Ruback & others, 1986; Wener & others, 1987). In one famous study of nursing home patients, 93 percent of those encouraged to exert more control became more alert, active, and happy (Rodin, 1986). As researcher Ellen Langer (1983, p. 291) concluded, "Perceived control is basic to human functioning." Thus "for the young and old alike," we should create environments that enhance a sense of control and personal efficacy.

Nursing home patients who take an active part in their own care and pursue their own interests are more alert and happy than those who do not.

learned helplessness The hopelessness and passive resignation learned when an animal or human is unable to avoid repeated aversive events.

To those who worry that the behavioral sciences might undermine traditional values, the verdict of these studies is reassuring: People thrive under conditions of democracy, personal freedom, and empowerment. Small wonder that the citizens of stable democracies report higher levels of happiness (Inglehart, 1990). Shortly before the democratic revolution in East Germany, psychologists Gabriele Oettingen and Martin Seligman (1990) compared the telltale body language of working-class men in East and West Berlin bars. Compared to their counterparts on the other side of the Wall, the empowered West Berliners much more often sat upright rather than slumped, had upward rather than downward turned mouths, and smiled and laughed. To paraphrase the Roman philosopher Seneca, happy are those who choose their own business.

"O God, give us grace to accept with serenity the things that cannot be changed, courage to change the things which should be changed, and the wisdom to distinguish the one from the other."

Reinhold Niebuhr,
The Serenity Prayer, 1943

Preview Question

15. How do social-cognitive researchers evaluate personality?

Optimism One measure of how helpless or effective you feel is where you stand on the trait dimension of optimism/pessimism. How do you characteristically explain negative and positive events? Perhaps you have known students who blame poor grades on situations beyond their control—their lack of ability ("I can't do this") or "bad" teachers, textbooks, or exam questions. Such students are more likely to persist in getting low grades than are students who adopt the more hopeful attitude that effort, good study habits, and self-discipline can make a difference (Noel & others, 1987; Peterson & Barrett, 1987). Similarly, Seligman and Peter Schulman (1986) compared new life insurance representatives who were more or less optimistic in their outlooks. Those who put an optimistic spin on setbacks—by seeing them as flukes or as suggesting a new approach rather than as signs of incompetence—sold more policies during their first year and were half as likely to quit. Seligman's finding came to life for him when Bob Dell, one of the optimistic recruits who began selling for Metropolitan Life after taking Seligman's optimism test, later dialed him up and sold him a policy.

If positive thinking in the face of adversity pays dividends, so, too, can a realistic dash of pessimism. Anxiety over contemplated failure can actually fuel energetic efforts to avoid the dreaded fate (Cantor & Norem, 1989; Goodhart, 1986; Showers & Ruben, 1987). Overconfident students often perform less well than their equally able peers who, fearing they are going to bomb the upcoming exam, proceed to study furiously and get fabulous grades. Success requires enough optimism to provide hope, but also enough pessimism to prevent complacency.

Assessing Behavior in Situations

Social-cognitive researchers explore the effect of differing situations on people's behavior patterns and attitudes. They study, for example, how viewing aggressive or nonaggressive models affects behavior. They assess the impact of dehumanizing situations on people's attitudes. And they examine the consistency of people's personalities in varying circumstances.

An ambitious example that predates social-cognitive theory is the U.S. Army's World War II strategy for assessing candidates for spy missions. Rather than use paper-and-pencil tests, army psychologists subjected the candidates to simulated undercover conditions. They tested their ability to handle stress, solve problems, maintain leadership, and withstand intense interrogation without blowing their covers. Although time-consuming and expensive, the assessment of behavior in a realistic situation helped predict later success on real spy missions (OSS Assessment Staff, 1948).

Business, military, and educational organizations are continuing this strategy in their evaluations of several hundred thousand people each year. The American Telephone and Telegraph Company observes prospective managers doing simulated managerial work (Bray, 1982). Many colleges assess potential faculty members' teaching abilities by observing them teach. The army assesses its soldiers by observing them during military exercises.

These procedures exploit the principle that the best way to predict people's future behavior is to observe their past behavior patterns in similar situations (Mischel, 1981). So long as the situation as well as the person remain much the same, the best predictor of future job performance is past job performance; the best predictor of future grades is past grades; the best predictor of future aggressiveness is past aggressiveness; the best predictor of drug use in young adulthood is high school drug use. If you can't check the person's past behavior, the next best thing is to create an assessment situation that simulates the task demands so you can see how the person handles them.

Psychology Applied: Pseudo-Assessment—How to Be a "Successful" Astrologer or Palm Reader

Some personality assessment techniques have no validity, though you wouldn't know it by talking to their devotees. Ray Hyman (1981), palm reader turned research psychologist, helps us to see why people get suckered, by revealing the methods of astrologers, palm readers, and crystal-ball gazers.

Their first technique, the "stock spiel," builds on the truth of the observation that each of us is in some ways like no one else and in other ways like everyone. That some things are true of us all enables the "seer" to offer statements that seem impressively accurate: "I sense that you're nursing a grudge against someone; you really ought to let that go." "You worry about things more than you let on, even to your best friends." "You are adaptable to social situations and your interests are wide-ranging."

Such generally true statements can be combined into a personality description. Imagine that you take a personality test and then receive the following character sketch:

You have a strong need for other people to like and to admire you. You have a tendency to be critical of yourself. . . . You pride yourself on being an independent thinker and do not accept other opinions without satisfactory proof. You have found it unwise to be too frank in revealing yourself to others. At times you are extraverted, affable, sociable; at other times you are introverted, wary, and reserved. Some of your aspirations tend to be pretty unrealistic (Forer, 1949).

In experiments, college students have received stock assessments like the one above. When they thought the bogus feedback was prepared just for them and when it was gen-erally favorable, they nearly always rated the description as either "good" or "excellent." Peter Glick and his co-workers (1989) found that even skeptics of astrology, when given a flattering description attributed to an astrologer, begin to think that "maybe there's something to this astrology business after all."

French psychologist Michael Gauguelin placed an ad in a Paris newspaper offering a free personal horoscope. Ninety-four percent of those receiving the horoscope later praised the description as accurate. Actually, all had received the horoscope of France's Dr. Petiot, a notorious mass murderer (Kurtz, 1983).

This acceptance is called the *Barnum effect,* named in honor of master showman P. T. Barnum's dictum, "There's a sucker born every minute." So powerful is the Barnum effect that, given a choice between this stock spiel and an individualized personality description actually based on a real test, most people choose the phony description as being more accurate. Astrologers and palm readers sprinkle their assessments with stock statements, as in the description just quoted, which was drawn from statements in a newsstand astrology book.

Another technique is to "read" the person's clothing, physical features, nonverbal gestures, and reactions to what you are saying. Imagine yourself as the character reader who was visited by a young woman in her late twenties or early thirties. Hyman describes the woman as "wearing expensive jewelry, a wedding band, and a black dress of cheap material. The observant reader noted that she was wearing shoes which were advertised for people with foot trouble." Do these clues suggest anything?

Drawing on these observations, the character reader proceeded to amaze his client with his insights. He assumed that the woman had come to see him, as did most of his female customers, because of a love or financial problem. The black dress and the wedding band led him to reason that her husband had died recently. The expensive jewelry suggested that she had been financially comfortable during marriage, but the cheap dress suggested that her husband's death had left her impoverished. The therapeutic shoes signified that she was now standing on her feet more than she was used to, implying that she had been working to support herself since her husband's death.

If you are not as shrewd as this character reader (who correctly guessed that the woman was wondering if she should remarry in hope of ending her economic hardship), no matter, says Hyman. Just tell people what they want to hear. Memorize some Barnum statements from astrology and fortune-telling manuals and use them liberally. Tell people it is their responsibility to cooperate by relating your message to their specific experiences, and later they will recall that you predicted the specifics. Phrase statements as questions, and when you detect a positive response assert the statement strongly. Be a good listener, and later, in different words, reveal to people what they earlier revealed to you.

Better yet, beware of fortune-tellers, who, by exploiting people with these techniques, become fortune-takers.

While astronomers scoff at the naiveté of astrology, psychologists ask a different question: Does it work? Are birth dates correlated with character traits? Given someone's birth date, can astrologers surpass chance when asked to identify the person from a short lineup of different personality descriptions? Can people pick out their own horoscopes from a lineup of horoscopes? The consistent answers have been: no, no, no, and no (e.g., Carlson, 1985). Graphologists, who make predictions from handwriting samples, have similarly been found to do no better than chance when trying to guess people's occupations, based on several pages of their handwriting (Ben-Shakhar et al., 1986).

"Ah-ha! You are not happy."

Drawing by Fruscino, © 1982 The New Yorker Magazine, Inc.

Preview Question

16. How does the social-cognitive perspective hold up under criticism?

"Nature is always more subtle, more intricate, more elegant than what we are able to imagine."

Carl Sagan
"Science—Who Cares?" 1991

Evaluating the Social-Cognitive Perspective

The social-cognitive perspective on personality sensitizes researchers to how situations affect, and are affected by, individuals. More than the other perspectives, we can also credit it with building on psychological research on learning and cognition.

One criticism is that the theory works *too* well, after the fact. In hindsight, we can "explain" anything as a product of cognition and the social environment. Another criticism is that the theory focuses so much on the situation that it fails to appreciate the person's inner traits. Where is the *person* in this view of personality, ask the dissenters (Carlson, 1984). And where are human emotions? Granted, the situation guides our behavior. But in many instances our unconscious motives, our emotions, and our pervasive traits shine through, say the critics. And so do genetic influences. Twin and adoption studies show that heredity influences personality traits such as extraversion, aggressiveness, and even helpfulness (see Chapter 3).

And that brings us back to the thought with which we began our review of the major personality theories: Each of the perspectives summarized in Table 11–3, page 374, can teach us something. The psychoanalytic perspective draws our attention to the unconscious and irrational aspects of human existence. The trait perspective systematically describes and classifies important personality components. The humanistic perspective reminds us of the pivotal importance of our sense of self and of our healthy potential. The social-cognitive perspective applies psychology's basic concepts of learning and thinking and teaches us that we always act in the context of situations that we help to create.

Seldom in life does a single perspective on any issue give us the complete picture. The kaleidoscope of human personality is mysterious and complex, yet it reveals its different aspects when we view it from different perspectives. Each perspective enlarges our vision of the whole.

Table 11-3
The Four Perspectives on Personality

Perspective	Behavior springs from	Assessment techniques	Evaluation
Psychoanalytic	Processing unconscious conflicts between pleasure-seeking impulses and social restraints	Projective tests aim to reveal unconscious motivations	A speculative, hard-to-confirm theory with enormous cultural impact
Trait	Expressing biologically influenced dispositions, such as extraversion or introversion	Personality inventories assess the strength of different traits; peers rate behavior patterns	A descriptive approach criticized as sometimes underestimating the variability of behavior from situation to situation
Humanistic	Processing conscious feelings about onself in light of one's experiences	(a) Questionnaire assessments of self-concept (b) Empathic understandings of people's unique experiences	A humane theory that reinvigorated contemporary interest in the self; criticized as subjective and sometimes naively self-centered and optimistic
Social-Cognitive	Reciprocal influences between people and their situations; colored by perceptions of control	(a) Questionnaire assessments of people's feelings of control (b) Observations of people's behavior in particular situations	An interactive theory that integrates research on learning, cognition, and social behavior; criticized as underestimating the importance of the unconscious, of emotions, and of enduring traits

Rehearse It

16. Albert Bandura, a social-cognitive theorist, believes that interacting with our environment involves reciprocal determinism, or mutual influences among personal factors, environmental factors, and behavior. An example of an environmental factor is
a. the presence of books in a home.
b. a preference for outdoor play.
c. the ability to read at a fourth-grade level.
d. the fear of violent action on the television.

17. Researchers have found that when elderly patients are given an active part in the management of their care and surroundings, their morale and health tend to improve. The assumption is that the patients do better when they perceive

a. learned helplessness.
b. an external locus of control.
c. an internal locus of control.
d. reciprocal determinism.

18. Martin Seligman described an attitude of passive resignation which he called learned helplessness. Working with animals and people, Seligman identified the circumstances under which learned helplessness develops. For example, a dog will respond with learned helplessness if it has received repeated shocks and has had
a. the opportunity to escape.
b. no control over the shocks.
c. pain or discomfort.

19. We have reviewed four perspectives on personality: the psychoanalytic, trait, humanistic, and social-cognitive perspec-

tives. The perspective that describes personality as a collection of predispositions and behaviors that can be scored on a personality test, is the
a. psychoanalytic perspective.
b. trait perspective.
c. humanistic perspective.
d. social-cognitive perspective.

20. A goal of many personality theories is to be able to predict a person's behavior in a particular situation. A theory that is very sensitive to the way people affect and are affected by particular situations, but says little about enduring traits, is the
a. psychoanalytic theory.
b. trait theory.
c. humanistic theory.
d. social-cognitive theory.

Reviewing Personality

1. **What is personality?**

   Like intelligence, personality is an abstract concept that cannot be seen, touched, or directly measured. To psychologists, personality is one's relatively distinctive and consistent pattern of thinking, feeling, and acting. We have examined four major perspectives on personality, each valuable for the light it sheds on our complex behavior patterns.

The Psychoanalytic Perspective

2. **What role do unconscious dynamics play in Freud's theory of personality?**

   Sigmund Freud's treatment of emotional disorders led him to believe they resulted from unconscious dynamics of personality, dynamics which he sought to analyze through the techniques of free associations and dreams.

3. **How did Freud view personality structure and development, and what were the defense mechanisms he proposed?**

   Freud saw personality as composed of a reservoir of pleasure-seeking psychic impulses (the id), a reality-oriented executive (the ego), and an internalized set of ideals (the superego).

   Freud believed that children develop through several formative psychosexual stages, which he labeled the oral, anal, phallic, latency, and genital stages. He suggested that people's later personalities were influenced by how they resolved conflicts associated with these stages and whether they remained fixated at any stage.

   To cope with anxiety caused by the tensions between the demands of id and superego, the ego has protective, reality-distorting defense mechanisms: repression, regression, reaction formation, projection, rationalization, displacement, and sublimation. Of these, repression is the most basic.

4. **How did Freud's followers differ from him?**

   Neo-Freudians, among them Alfred Adler and Karen Horney, accepted many of Freud's ideas but placed more emphasis on conscious experience and on social motivations other than sex and aggression, such as feelings of inferiority and anxiety. Carl Jung expanded Freud's concept of the unconscious to include a collective unconscious inherited by all humans.

5. **How do projective tests assess personality, and are they considered valid?**

   Psychoanalytic assessment techniques attempt to reveal aspects of personality that are thought to be hidden in the unconscious. Although projective tests such as the Rorschach inkblots have been criticized for their minimal reliability and validity, the Rorschach remains widely used, especially as a technique to promote therapist-patient interaction.

6. **How do Freud's ideas hold up today?**

   Many of Freud's specific ideas have been criticized as implausible or have not been validated. His theory has also been faulted for offering after-the-fact explanations. Nevertheless, Freud succeeded in drawing psychology's attention to the unconscious, to the struggle to cope with anxiety and sexuality, and to the conflict between biological impulses and social restraints. Moreover, his cultural impact has been enormous.

The Trait Perspective

7. **How do trait theorists view personality?**

   Rather than explain the hidden aspects of personality, trait theorists have described the predispositions that underlie our actions. Through factor analysis, these theorists have isolated distinct dimensions of personality: for example, the "big five" trait dimensions—emotional stability, extraversion, openness, agreeableness, and conscientiousness.

8. **How do we assess traits?**

   To assess traits, psychologists have devised objective personality inventories such as the empirically derived MMPI. Computerized testing has made these inventories widely available; however, they are still most helpful when used to assess those who are emotionally troubled.

9. **Does research support the consistency of personality traits?**

   Critics of trait theory question the consistency with which traits are expressed. Although people's traits do seem to persist through time, human behavior varies widely from situation to situation. Despite these variations, people's average behavior across different situations remains fairly consistent.

The Humanistic Perspective

10. **What is the central focus of the humanistic perspective?**

    Humanistic psychologists have sought to turn psychology's attention to the growth potential of healthy people, as seen through the individual's own experiences and self-concept. Abraham Maslow believed that if basic human needs are fulfilled, people will strive to actualize their highest potential. To describe self-actualization, he studied some exemplary personalities and summarized his impressions of their qualities. To nurture growth in others, Carl Rogers advised being genuine, accepting, and empathic. In such a climate, people can develop a deeper self-awareness and a more realistic and positive self-concept. Humanistic psychologists assess personality through questionnaires that rate self-concept and by seeking to understand others' subjective personal experiences in therapy.

11. **What have we learned from research on the self?**

    Through studies of self-esteem and self-serving bias, we know that self-esteem is an adaptive quality, and that most people do perceive and explain themselves favorably.

12. **What impact has the humanistic perspective had on psychology?**

    Humanistic psychology's critics complain that its concepts are vague and subjective, its values self-centered, and its assumptions naively optimistic. Nevertheless, humanistic psychology has helped to renew psychology's interest in the concept of self.

The Social-Cognitive Perspective

13. **What factors does the social-cognitive perspective emphasize?**

    The social-cognitive perspective applies principles of social learning and cognition to personality, with particular emphasis on the ways in which our personalities are influenced by our interaction with the environment. Bandura's reciprocal determinism emphasizes how personal-cognitive factors interact with the environment.

14. **What are the causes and consequences of personal control?**

    By studying variations among people in their perceived locus of control and in their experiences of learned helplessness or mastery and competence, researchers have found that an inner locus of control helps people to cope with life.

15. **How do social-cognitive researchers evaluate personality?**

    Social-cognitive researchers study how people's behaviors and beliefs both affect and are affected by their situations. They have found that the best way to predict someone's behavior in a given situation is to observe that person's behavior in similar situations.

16. **How does the social-cognitive perspective hold up under criticism?**

    Though faulted for underemphasizing the importance of unconscious dynamics and inner traits, the social-cognitive perspective builds on psychology's well-established concepts of learning and cognition and reminds us of the power of social situations.

Terms and Concepts to Remember

personality, p. 345

free association, p. 346

psychoanalysis, p. 346

unconscious, p. 346

preconscious, p. 346

id, p. 347

pleasure principle, p. 347

ego, p. 347

reality principle, p. 347

superego, p. 347

psychosexual stages, p. 348

oral stage, p. 348

anal stage, p. 348

phallic stage, p. 348

Oedipus [ED-uh-puss] **complex**, p. 348

identification, p. 349

gender identity, p. 349

latency stage, p. 349

genital stage, p. 349

fixation, p. 349

defense mechanisms, p. 349

repression, p. 349

regression, p. 349

reaction formation, p. 349

projection, p. 350

rationalization, p. 350

displacement, p. 350

sublimation, p. 350

collective unconscious, p. 351

projective tests, p. 351

Thematic Apperception Test (TAT), p. 352

Rorschach inkblot test, p. 352

trait, p. 356

personality inventory, p. 359

Minnesota Multiphasic Personality Inventory (MMPI), p. 359

empirically derived test, p. 359

self-actualization, p. 362

unconditional positive regard, p. 363

self-concept, p. 363

self-esteem, p. 364

self-serving bias, p. 365

social-cognitive perspective, p. 368

reciprocal determinism, p. 368

personal control, p. 369

external locus of control, p. 369

internal locus of control, p. 369

learned helplessness, p. 370

Rehearse It Answer Key

1. b.	2. a.	3. b.	4. h	5. b.	6. d.	7. a.	8. c.	9. c.
10. c.	11. b.	12. d.	13. b.	14. c.	15. a.	16. a.	17. c.	18. b.
19. b.	20. d.							

Critical Thinking Exercise

You have *Surveyed, Questioned, Read, Rehearsed,* and *Reviewed* Chapter 11. Now take your learning a step further by testing your *critical thinking* skills on the following passage.

Darren is a first-year college student who has a biting, sarcastic manner. He is quite pessimistic and feels that the world is run by a few powerful people. When he received a poor grade on a recent exam, Darren blamed the instructor and claimed the test was unfair. He no longer attends lectures or studies for the course and will probably drop it. He is experiencing similar difficulties in his other courses.

Darren always dreamed of doing well in college. Now he is despondent over his failure and believes his professors hate him. Most of all, he is concerned that if he fails in school his parents will no longer love him. Deciding that he needs guidance, Darren begins weekly counseling sessions with Dr. Roitman, a psychoanalyst. After several weeks, Dr. Roitman decides that Darren's maladaptive behavior and attitude stems from unresolved childhood conflicts. He believes that Darren was orally overindulged and is fixated at this stage of psychosexual development. He also feels that Darren's ego is using the defense mechanisms of projection and rationalization to reduce anxiety. Thus, Darren is unconsciously distorting reality by projecting his own self-hatred onto his professors, and is rationalizing his academic failure with a self-justifying explanation in place of its real, more threatening reason.

Understand the Assertion

1. State the psychoanalyst's assertion in your own words. Define all important concepts and terms as they are used in this example.

Consider the Evidence

2. Is the evidence for the psychoanalyst's assertion empirical (observable)? Is the evidence based on trustworthy research?

Evaluate the Explanation

3. Evaluate the theoretical explanation for the psychoanalyst's conclusion.
   a. Restate it in your own words.
   b. Determine whether the explanation makes sense based on the evidence.
   c. State alternative explanations for Darren's problems.

Check your progress on becoming a critical thinker by comparing your answers to the sample answers found in Appendix B.

Chapter 12

Psychological Disorders

Most people are fascinated by the exceptional, the unusual, and the abnormal. "The sun shines and warms and lights us and we have no curiosity to know why this is so," observed Ralph Waldo Emerson, "but we ask the reason of all evil, of pain, and hunger, and mosquitoes and silly people."

Why this fascination with disturbed people? Perhaps in them we often see something of ourselves. At various moments, all of us feel, think, or act as disturbed people do much of the time. We, too, may be anxious, depressed, withdrawn, suspicious, deluded, or antisocial, although less intensely and enduringly. Studying psychological disorders may therefore at times evoke an eerie sense of self-recognition that illuminates our own personality dynamics. "To study the abnormal is the best way of understanding the normal," proposed William James.

Another reason for our curiosity is that so many of us have felt, either personally or through friends or family members, the bewilderment and pain of a psychological disorder. In all likelihood, you or someone you care about has been disabled by unexplained physical symptoms, overwhelmed by irrational fears, or paralyzed by the feeling that life is not worth living. Each year there are nearly 1.7 million inpatient admissions to U.S. mental hospitals and psychiatric units (Rosenstein & others, 1989). Some 2.4 million others, often troubled but not disabled, seek help as outpatients from mental health organizations and clinics. Many more—15 percent of Americans, according to one government study—are judged to need such help (Robins & Regier, 1991). Such problems are not peculiar to the United States. As far as we know, no human culture is free of the two terrible maladies this chapter examines in depth—depression and schizophrenia (Draguns, 1990a,b). As members of the human family, few of us go through life unacquainted with the reality of psychological disturbance.

"We are all mad at some time or another."

Battista Mantuanus
Eclogues, 1500

Perspectives on Psychological Disorders

Preview Question

1. What criteria are used to judge a person's behavior as disordered?

Most people would agree that someone who is too depressed to get out of bed for weeks at a time suffers a psychological disorder. But what about those who, having experienced a loss, are unable to resume their usual social activities? Where should we draw the line between normality and abnormality? How should we *define* psychological disorders? Equally important, how should we *understand* disorders—as sicknesses that need to be diagnosed and cured, or as natural responses to a troubling environment? Finally, how might we *classify* disordered personalities? Can we do so in a way that allows us to help disturbed people and not merely stigmatize them with labels?

psychological disorder A condition in which behavior is judged atypical, disturbing, maladaptive, and unjustifiable.

Although British street cleaner Snowy Farr's eccentric behavior may indeed be *atypical*, clinicians would not label it disordered because it is not particularly *disturbing* nor is it *maladaptive* or *unjustifiable*.

"If a man is in a minority of one, we lock him up."

Oliver Wendell Holmes, 1841–1935

Defining Psychological Disorders

James Oliver Huberty had been hearing voices. He "talked with God," his wife reported. Although he had never been to Vietnam, he strode into a San Ysidro, California, McDonald's restaurant one summer day in 1984 screaming, "I've killed a thousand in Vietnam and I'll kill a thousand more." In the next few minutes, before police gunned him down, Huberty murdered 21 people.

At the end of World War II, James Forrestal, the first U.S. Secretary of Defense, became convinced that Israeli secret agents were following him. His suspiciousness struck his physicians as bizarre. They diagnosed him as mentally ill and confined him to an upper floor of Walter Reed Army Hospital. From there he plunged to his death. Although Forrestal had problems, it was later discovered that he was, in fact, being followed by Israeli agents, who feared he might secretly negotiate with representatives of Arab nations (Sagan, 1979b). As Woody Allen once said, even paranoids can have enemies.

Both the voices that Huberty heard and the degree of anxiety and depression that Forrestal experienced were deviations from the normal. These were "*ab*normal" (atypical) perceptions. Being different from most other people is *part* of what it takes to define a psychological disorder. But there is more to a disorder than being atypical. Olympic gold medalists are abnormal in their physical capabilities, and they are heroes. To be considered disordered, other people must find the atypical behavior *disturbing.* Certainly the atypical behavior of a James Oliver Huberty is disturbing.

Standards of acceptability for behaviors vary. In some cultures, people routinely behave in ways (such as going about naked) that in other cultures would get them arrested. In at least one cultural context—wartime—even mass killing may be viewed as heroic. One person's homicidal terrorist is another person's freedom fighter. Standards of acceptability vary not only from culture to culture but also from time to time. Two decades ago, the American Psychiatric Association dropped homosexuality as a disorder (because it is now believed unconnected with psychological problems). Later it added tobacco dependence (because it deemed smoking both addictive and self-destructive).

Atypical and disturbing behaviors are more likely to be considered disordered when judged as harmful. Indeed, many clinicians define disorders as behaviors that are *maladaptive*—as when a smoker's nicotine dependence produces physical damage. Accordingly, even typical behaviors, such as the occasional despondency that many college students feel, may signal a psychological disorder if they become disabling.

Finally, abnormal behavior is most likely to be considered disordered when others find it rationally *unjustifiable.* Doctors attributed Forrestal's suspicions to his imagination—and declared him disordered. Had he managed to convince others of his suspicions, he might have been helped, not merely labeled. James Oliver Huberty claimed to hear voices and to talk with God, and we presume he was deranged. But Shirley MacLaine can wear a crystal on her neck and say, "See the outer bubble of white light watching you. It is part of you," and she is not considered disordered because enough people take her seriously (Friedrich, 1987). It is acceptable to be different from others if both you and they can justify or are undisturbed by the difference.

So, mental health workers label behavior **psychologically disordered** when they judge it *atypical, disturbing, maladaptive,* and *unjustifiable.* Huberty's behavior met these criteria, so we have few doubts in judging him a disordered man.

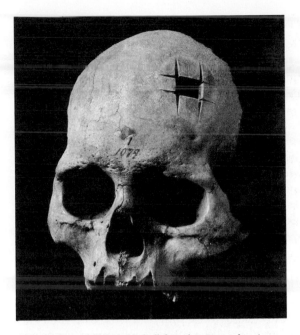

Figure 12–1 An ancient skull found in Peru, showing a hole chipped through the cranium to allow evil spirits to escape. One wonders whether the patient survived the cure.

Preview Question

2. What is the medical model of psychological disorders, and why do critics question it?

medical model The concept that diseases have physical causes that can be diagnosed, treated, and, in many cases, cured. When applied to psychological disorders, the medical model assumes that these "mental" illnesses can be diagnosed on the basis of their symptoms and cured through therapy, which may include treatment in a psychiatric hospital.

Understanding Psychological Disorders

Imagine yourself living hundreds or thousands of years ago. How might you have accounted for the behavior of a James Oliver Huberty? To explain puzzling behavior, our ancestors often presumed that strange forces—the movements of the stars, godlike powers, or evil spirits—were at work. "The devil made him do it," you might have said. The cure might have been to get rid of the evil force—by exorcising the demon or even by chipping a hole in the skull to allow the evil spirit to escape (Figure 12–1). Until the last two centuries, "mad" people were sometimes caged in zoolike conditions or given "therapies" appropriate to a demon. Disordered people have been beaten, burned, and castrated. They have had teeth pulled, lengths of intestines removed, and the clitoris cauterized. They have had their own blood removed and replaced with transfusions of animal blood (Farina, 1982).

The Medical Perspective

In response to such brutal treatment, reformers such as Philippe Pinel (1745–1826) in France insisted that madness was not demon possession but a disease that, like other diseases, we could treat and cure. For Pinel, treatment meant boosting patients' morale by talking with them and by providing humane living conditions. When it was later discovered that an infectious brain disease, syphilis, produced a particular psychological disorder, people came to believe in physical causes for disorders and to search for medical treatments.

Today, Pinel's medical perspective is familiar to us in the medical terminology of the mental *health* movement: A mental *illness* (also called a psychopathology) needs to be *diagnosed* on the basis of its *symptoms* and *cured* through *therapy*, which may include *treatment* in a psychiatric *hospital*. In the 1800s, the assumption of this **medical model**—that psychological disorders are sicknesses—provided the impetus for much-needed reform. The "sick" were unchained and hospitals replaced asylums.

Equating psychological disorders with sickness does, however, have its critics, among them psychiatrist Thomas Szasz. Szasz believes that mental "illnesses" are socially, not medically, defined. When, for many years, Soviet psychiatrists diagnosed dissident citizens as "psychotic," they were using medical metaphors to disguise their contempt for these people's political ideas. Szasz (1984, 1987) concludes that in North America, too, mental health practitioners have too much authority in today's society. When they demean people with the label "mentally ill," their patients may begin to view themselves as "sick" and therefore give up taking responsibility for coping with their problems. Many critics respond similarly to the idea that alcohol abuse, overeating, gambling, and sexual promiscuity are addictive diseases—purely uncontrollable compulsions that require sympathy and treatment. As we will see, labels can be self-fulfilling fables.

Despite such criticisms, the medical perspective survives and even gains renewed credibility from recent discoveries. Genetically influenced abnormalities in brain biochemistry have been linked with two of the most troubling psychological disorders, depression and schizophrenia, both of which are often treated medically.

Those who accept Freud's psychoanalytic perspective agree that psychological disorders are sicknesses that have diagnosable and treatable causes. However, they insist that these causes may include psychological factors. We see such factors in the lingering emotional aftereffects of traumatic stress, such as that caused by rape (page 187) and combat (page 325).

Alternative Perspectives

Psychologists who reject the "sickness" idea typically contend that *all* behavior, whether called normal or disordered, arises from the interaction of nature (genetic and physiological factors) and nurture (past and present experiences). To presume that a person is "mentally ill" attributes the condition solely to an internal problem—to a "sickness" that must be found and cured. Maybe there *is* no deep, internal problem. Maybe there is instead a growth-blocking difficulty in the person's environment, in the person's current interpretations of events, or in the person's bad habits and poor social skills.

When Native Americans were banished from their ancestral lands, forced onto reservations to live in poverty and unemployment, and deprived of personal control, the result was a rate of alcoholism more than five times that of other Americans (May, 1986). Because only some Native Americans become alcoholic, the medical model would attribute such alcoholism to individual "sickness." A psychological perspective would emphasize the interaction between an individual's vulnerability and a particular environment.

Evidence of environmental effects comes from links between disorder and culture. Some major disorders such as depression and schizophrenia are universal. Others are culture-bound (Carson & others, 1988). Different cultures have different stresses and produce different ways of coping. Anorexia nervosa, for example, is mostly a disorder of Western cultures (page 277).

Most mental health workers today assume that disorders are indeed influenced by genetic predispositions and physiological states. And by inner psychological dynamics. And by social circumstances. To get the whole picture, we need an interdisciplinary "bio-psycho-social" perspective.

Classifying Psychological Disorders

In biology and the other sciences, classification creates order. To classify an animal as a mammal says a great deal—that it is warm-blooded, has hair or fur, and nourishes its young with milk. In psychiatry and psychology, too, classification orders and describes clusters of symptoms. To classify a person's disorder as "schizophrenia" suggests that the person talks incoherently, hallucinates or has delusions (bizarre beliefs), shows either little emotion or inappropriate emotion, or is socially withdrawn. Thus, the diagnostic term provides a handy shorthand for describing a complex disorder.

In psychiatry and psychology, diagnostic classification ideally aims to describe a disorder, to predict its future course, to suggest appropriate treatment, and to stimulate research into its causes. Indeed, to study a disorder we must first name and describe it. The current authoritative scheme for classifying psychological disorders is the American Psychiatric Association's *Diagnostic and Statistical Manual of Mental Disorders (Third Edition—Revised)*, nicknamed **DSM-III-R.** This 1987 volume and the book of case illustrations that accompanies it provide the basis for much of the material in this chapter.

DSM-III-R groups some 230 psychological disorders and conditions into 17 major categories of "mental disorder." There are diagnoses for almost every conceivable complaint. In fact, some critics fault DSM-III-R for bringing "almost any kind of behavior within the compass of psychiatry" (Eysenck & others, 1983)—from irrational fear of humiliation and embarrassment (social phobia) to persistently breaking rules at home or school (conduct disorder).

Before establishing the validity of the DSM-III-R categories, we must first confirm their reliability. If one psychiatrist or psychologist diagnoses someone as having, say, a "catatonic schizophrenia disorder," what are the chances that another mental health worker will independently give the same diagnosis? With the DSM-III-R's diagnostic guidelines, the chances are good.

"It's no measure of health to be well adjusted to a profoundly sick society."

Krishnamurti, 1895–1986

Due out by the mid-1990s are new editions of both DSM (DSM-IV) and the World Health Organization's international classification of mental disorders.

DSM-III-R The American Psychiatric Association's *Diagnostic and Statistical Manual of Mental Disorders (Third Edition—Revised)*, a widely used system for classifying psychological disorders. It will be replaced by the forthcoming DSM-IV.

Preview Question

3. Why are psychological disorders classified, and what system is used?

Psychology Applied: The Insanity Defense on Trial

In defining psychological disorders, I have not mentioned insanity. That is because sane and insane are *legal*, not psychological, terms, ones judged either/or. You can be a little depressed or greatly depressed; you cannot be a little insane.

The British created the insanity defense in 1843 after a deluded Scotsman, Daniel M'Naghten, tried to shoot the Prime Minister (who he thought was persecuting him) and killed the Prime Minister's secretary by mistake. A furor erupted after M'Naghten was acquitted as insane and sent to a mental hospital rather than to prison. When the M'Naghten verdict was upheld, an insanity rule emerged. It limited the insanity defense to cases where persons were judged not to have known what they were doing or not to have known that it was wrong. Shakespeare's Hamlet anticipated the defense. If I wrong someone when not myself, he explains, "then Hamlet does it not, Hamlet denies it. Who does it then? His madness."

By the time John Hinckley, Jr., came to trial in 1982 for shooting President Reagan and his press secretary, the insanity defense had been broadened. The prosecution had to prove that Hinckley was sane. Under the Model Penal Code this meant his having "a substantial capacity" not merely to "know" his act was wrong but to "appreciate" its wrongfulness and to act accordingly.

The prosecution was unable to prove sanity to the jurors' satisfaction. So Hinckley, like M'Naghten, was sent to a mental hospital. As in the first insanity case, the public was outraged. One newspaper headlined "Hinckley Insane, Public Mad."

Some news commentators complained that the heinousness of a crime had become the very basis for evading responsibility for it, "like the person who kills his parents and demands mercy because he is an orphan." Are "sick crimes" necessarily the products of sick minds that need treatment, not punishment? Was Jeffrey Dahmer, who in 1991 admitted murdering and eating parts of 15 men, necessarily insane? Are the genuinely bad truly mad? If so, said one commentator, then modern society has become like Aldous Huxley's nightmarish *Brave New World*, in which when someone commits a crime the correct response is, "I did not know he was ill."

In defense of the insanity plea, psychologist David Rosenhan (1983a,b) noted that, actually, such a plea is entered only about 2 times in every 1000 felony cases. In 85 percent of those cases, all parties— mental health experts, prosecutor, and defense attorney—agree that the deranged person was not responsible. In fact, the most important issues that involve psychology and law are not the rare disputes over insanity. They are instead the far more frequent cases concerning child custody (judging who will be the better parent), involuntary commitment to mental hospitals, and predictions about a criminal's future behavior made at the time of sentencing or parole. (When psychiatrists and psychologists use their clinical judgment to predict violence, they are more often wrong than right [Faust & Ziskin, 1988; Monahan, 1988].)

In Canada, and now in the United States under a 1984 law, the insanity defense survives in a restricted format that shifts the burden of proving insanity to the defense. Now defendants must show that they did not understand the wrongfulness of their acts.

By 1987, 13 states instituted a verdict of "guilty but mentally ill." This verdict recognizes a need for treatment but holds people responsible and sends them to prison if they are judged recovered before their sentence is over (Rosenfeld, 1987). Jurors find the verdict a viable option. In mock trials, defendants who otherwise would have been judged either innocent or not guilty by reason of insanity are often judged guilty but mentally ill (Savitsky & Lindblom, 1986).

A posed self-portrait of John W. Hinckley, Jr., former President Reagan's would-be assassin.

The guidelines work by asking clinicians a series of objective questions about observable behaviors, such as, "Is the person afraid to leave home?" In one study, 16 psychologists used this structured interview procedure to diagnose 75 psychiatric patients as suffering either (1) depression, (2) generalized anxiety, or (3) some other disorder (Riskind & others, 1987). Without knowing the first psychologist's diagnosis, another psychologist viewed a videotape of each interview and offered a second opinion. For 83 percent of the patients, the two opinions agreed, indicating good reliability.

Let us now consider a few of the most prevalent and perplexing disorders, remembering that the people we will meet are not sideshow curiosities but real people—troubled people whose loved ones are troubled for them.

Rehearse It

1. Each year more than 600,000 people are admitted to U.S. psychiatric hospitals—and many more seek treatment for psychological disorders at mental health centers or in private counseling. According to one government study, the percentage of people who probably need such help is about
a. 1 percent.
b. 5 percent.
c. 15 percent.
d. 60 percent.

2. To be labeled "disordered," a behavior must usually be atypical, disturbing, unjustified, and maladaptive. For example, we all wash our hands; physicians may well wash their hands 100 times a day. But if a person washes his or her hands 100 times a day for no apparent reason, and is unable to do much else, the behavior will be labeled disordered because it is
a. unjustified and maladaptive.
b. an atypical behavior.
c. not explained by the medical model.
d. harmful and disturbing to others.

3. In the past, people considered to be mad or insane were beaten, punished, or jailed. The more modern approach is to equate psychological disorders with sickness, and to refer the "mentally ill" to hospitals, where they can be treated as patients. This more modern approach is called
a. the insanity defense.
b. the psychological model.
c. the medical model.
d. the diagnostic model.

4. The American Psychiatric Association's system of classifying psychological disorders is found in the *Diagnostic and Statistical Manual of Mental Disorders (Third Edition—Revised)* (DSM-III-R). The DSM-III-R system is more reliable than its predecessors; one study found that psychologists using the manual agreed on a diagnosis for more than 80 percent of patients. The DSM-III-R has improved reliability because it helps mental health workers base their diagnoses on
a. a few well-defined categories.
b. in-depth history of the patients.
c. the patients' observable behaviors.
d. the theories of Pinel, Freud, and others.

Preview Question

4. What behaviors characterize anxiety disorders?

Anxiety Disorders

When speaking in front of a class, when peering down from a ledge, when waiting for a game to begin, any one of us might feel anxious. At one time or another, most of us feel enough anxiety in some social situation that we fail to make eye contact or we avoid talking to someone—"shyness" we call it. But for some people, two-thirds of whom are women, anxiety becomes so distressing and persistent that they suffer an **anxiety disorder.**

Anxiety is part of our everyday experience. Fortunately for most of us, our occasional uneasiness does not entail the intense suffering endured by those with anxiety disorders. There are three important types: **generalized anxiety disorder,** in which a person feels unexplainably tense and uneasy;

anxiety disorders Psychological disorders characterized by distressing, persistent anxiety or maladaptive behaviors that reduce anxiety.

generalized anxiety disorder An anxiety disorder in which a person is continually tense, apprehensive, and in a state of autonomic nervous system arousal.

phobic disorder An anxiety disorder marked by a persistent, irrational fear of a specific object or situation.

obsessive-compulsive disorder An anxiety disorder characterized by unwanted repetitive thoughts (obsessions) and/or actions (compulsions).

panic attack A minutes-long episode of intense dread in which a person experiences terror and accompanying chest pain, choking, or other frightening sensations.

phobic disorder, in which a person feels irrationally afraid of a specific object or situation; and **obsessive-compulsive disorder,** in which a person is troubled by repetitive thoughts or actions.

Generalized Anxiety Disorder

Tom, a 27-year-old electrician, seeks help, complaining of dizziness, sweating palms, heart palpitations, and ringing in the ears. He feels edgy and sometimes finds himself shaking. With reasonable success he hides his symptoms from his family and co-workers. Nevertheless, he has had few social contacts since the symptoms began 2 years ago. Worse, he occasionally has to leave work. His family doctor and neurologist can find no physical problem, and a special diet for those with low blood sugar has not helped.

Tom's unfocused, out-of-control, threatened feelings suggest a generalized anxiety disorder. The symptoms of this disorder are commonplace; their persistence is not. The sufferers are continually tense and jittery, apprehensive about bad things that might happen, and experiencing all the symptoms of autonomic nervous system arousal (racing heart, clammy hands, stomach butterflies). The tension and apprehension may leak out through furrowed brows, twitching eyelids, or fidgeting.

One of the worst characteristics of a generalized anxiety disorder is that the person cannot identify, and therefore cannot avoid, its cause. To use Freud's term, the anxiety is "free-floating." As some 1 in 75 people know, for no apparent reason the anxiety may at times suddenly escalate into a terrifying **panic attack**—an episode of intense dread, usually lasting several minutes. Chest pain, choking or smothering sensations, trembling, dizziness, or fainting typically accompany the panic. The experience is unpredictable and so frightening that the sufferer may then avoid situations where attacks have occurred.

Phobic Disorders

Phobic anxiety focuses on some specific object, activity, or situation. (See Figure 12–2 for a ranking of some common fears.) Phobias—irrational fears—are a common psychological disorder that people often accept and live with.

Figure 12–2 This national survey ranks the relative fear levels of Americans to some common sources of anxiety. A fear becomes a phobia if it provokes a compelling but irrational desire to avoid the dreaded object or situation. (From *Public Opinion*, 1984.)

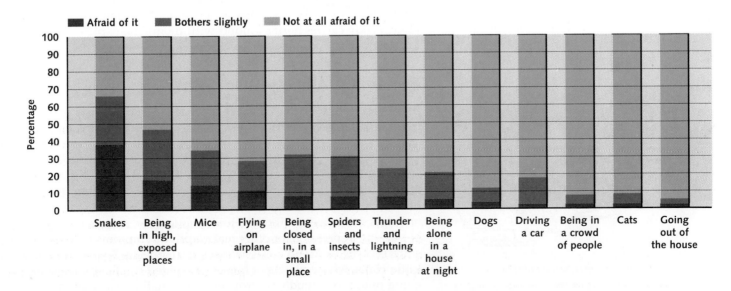

Table 12–1

Common Obsessions and Compulsions

Seventy children and adolescents suffering obsessive-compulsive disorder reported their symptoms.

Obsessions (repetitive thoughts)	Reporting symptom
Concern with dirt, germs, or toxins	40%
Something terrible happening (fire, death, illness)	24%
Symmetry, order, or exactness	17%

Compulsions (repetitive behaviors)	
Excessive hand washing, bathing, tooth brushing, or grooming	85%
Repeating rituals (in/out of a door, up/down from a chair)	51%
Checking doors, locks, appliances, car brake, homework	46%

Source: Adapted from Rapoport, 1989.

Some phobic disorders are incapacitating, however. Marilyn, a 28-year-old homemaker, so fears thunderstorms that she feels anxious as soon as a weather forecaster mentions possible storms later in the week. If her husband is away and a storm is forecast, she sometimes stays with a close relative. During a storm, she hides from windows and buries her head to avoid seeing the lightning. She is otherwise healthy and happy.

Other people with phobic disorders suffer from irrational fears of specific animals or of airplanes or elevators or even public places such as department stores. Sometimes it is possible to avoid the fear-arousing stimulus: One can hide during thunderstorms or avoid air travel. With other phobias, such as an intense fear of being scrutinized by others ("social phobia") or being in open or public places ("agoraphobia"), avoiding fear-arousing situations may dictate never leaving home. Compared to the other disorders discussed in this chapter, phobias have an earlier onset—often by the early teens (Burke & others, 1990).

Obsessive-Compulsive Disorder

As with the generalized anxiety and phobic disorders, we can see aspects of ourselves in the obsessive-compulsive disorder. We may at times be obsessed with senseless or offensive thoughts that will not go away. Or we may engage in compulsive, rigid behavior—rechecking the locked door, stepping over cracks in the sidewalk, or lining up our books and pencils "just so" before studying.

Obsessive thoughts and compulsive behaviors cross the fine line between normality and disorder when they become so persistent that they interfere with the way we live or when they cause distress. Checking to see that the door is locked is normal; checking the door 10 times is not. Hand washing is normal; hand washing so often that one's skin becomes raw is not. (See Table 12–1 for more examples.) At some time during their lives, often during their late teens or in their twenties, 2 to 3 percent cross that line from normal preoccupations and fussiness to debilitating disorder (Karno & others, 1988).

One such person was billionaire Howard Hughes. Hughes would compulsively dictate the same phrases over and over again. Under stress, he developed an obsessive fear of germs. He became reclusive and insisted that his assistants carry out elaborate hand-washing rituals and wear white gloves when handling documents he would later touch. He ordered tape around doors and windows and forbade his staff to touch or even look at him. "Everybody carries germs around with them," he explained. "I want to live longer than my parents, so I avoid germs" (Fowler, 1986).

Explaining Anxiety Disorders

In seeking to understand anxiety disorders, psychologists have emphasized three familiar perspectives—psychoanalytic, learning, and biological.

The Psychoanalytic Perspective

Psychoanalytic theory assumes that, beginning in childhood, intolerable impulses, ideas, and feelings get repressed. This submerged mental energy nevertheless influences our actions and emotions, sometimes producing feelings of anxiety, depression, or other maladaptive symptoms that mystify even the sufferer. One of Freud's classic cases concerned a 5-year-old boy known as Little Hans, whose phobia of horses prevented (in those days before cars) his going outdoors. Freud's controversial speculation was that Little Hans's fear

"He always times '60 Minutes.'"

Drawing by Richter; © 1983 The New Yorker Magazine, Inc.

of horses expressed his underlying fear of his father, whom Hans viewed as a rival for his mother's affections.

Alternatively, the forbidden impulses may break through as thinly disguised thoughts, which may provoke acts aimed at suppressing the associated anxiety. The result: obsessions and compulsions. Repetitive hand washing, for instance, may help suppress anxiety over one's "dirty" urges.

The Learning Perspective

Learning researchers link general anxiety with learned helplessness (page 370). In the laboratory, researchers can create chronically anxious, ulcer-prone rats by giving them unpredictable electric shocks (Schwartz, 1984). Like the rape victim who reported feeling anxious when entering her old neighborhood (page 187), the animals are apprehensive in their lab environment. For many victims of post-traumatic stress disorder (page 325), anxiety swells with any reminder of their trauma.

When the shocks become predictable—when preceded by a particular conditioned stimulus—the animals' fear focuses on *that* stimulus and they relax in its absence. So it can happen with human fears. Recently, my car was struck by another whose driver did not see a stop sign. For months afterward, I felt a twinge of unease with the approach of any car from a side street. Perhaps Marilyn's phobia was similarly conditioned during a terrifying or painful experience associated with a thunderstorm.

Conditioned fears may remain long after we have forgotten the experiences that produced them (Jacobs & Nadel, 1985). Moreover, some fears arise from stimulus generalization. A person who fears heights after a fall may be afraid of airplanes without ever having flown. Someone might also learn such a fear through observational learning—by observing others' fears. As we saw in Chapter 10, Emotions, Stress, and Health, wild monkeys transmit their fear of snakes to their offspring, and human parents transmit their fears to their children. Avoiding or escaping the feared situation reduces anxiety, thus reinforcing the phobic behavior. Compulsive behaviors similarly reduce anxiety. If washing your hands relieves your feelings of unease, you will likely wash your hands again when the feelings return.

The Biological Perspective

Biologically oriented researchers explain our anxiety-proneness in evolutionary, genetic, and physiological terms.

As we noted on page 311, we humans seem biologically prepared to develop fears of heights, storms, snakes, and insects—dangers that our ancestors faced. Compulsive acts typically exaggerate behaviors that contributed to our species' survival. Grooming gone wild becomes hair pulling. Washing up becomes ritual hand washing. Checking territorial boundaries becomes checking and rechecking a door known to be locked (Rapoport, 1989).

Some people more than others seem genetically predisposed to particular fears and high anxiety. Identical twins often develop similar phobias, in some cases even when raised separately (Carey, 1990; Eckert & others, 1981). One pair of 35-year-old identical female twins independently developed claustrophobia. They also became so fearful of water that each would gingerly wade backward into the ocean, only up to the knees. Among monkeys, fearfulness runs in families. Individual monkeys react more strongly to stress if their close relatives are anxiously reactive (Suomi, 1986).

The biology of general anxiety disorder, panic, and even obsessions and compulsions is measurable as overarousal (Baxter & others, 1987; Buchsbaum

Although we seem biologically predisposed to fear heights—certainly an adaptive response—this construction worker seems fearless. Weeks of uneventful existence in his aerial office, and perhaps even an exhilarating moment or two, may have reinforced his comfortable feeling.

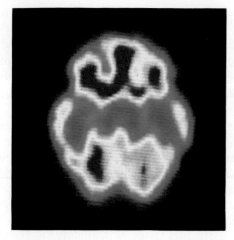

Figure 12–3 A PET scan of a person with obsessive-compulsive disorder reveals abnormally high metabolic activity in the frontal lobes. (Person is facing top of page.) This is visible in a region of the left hemisphere's frontal lobe involved in directing attention.

Preview Question

5. What characterizes the somatoform disorders?

"He was a dreadful hypochondriac."

Punch/Rothco

& others, 1987; Reiman & others, 1989). PET scans of persons with obsessive-compulsive disorder reveal unusually high activity in an area of the frontal lobes just above the eyes (Figure 12–3) and in a more primitive area deep in the brain. Some antidepressant drugs control obsessive-compulsive behavior by muting this activity, through affecting the availability of the neurotransmitter serotonin, one of those messenger molecules that shuttles signals between nerve cells (Rapoport, 1989).

Somatoform Disorders

Ellen becomes dizzy and nauseated in the late afternoon—shortly before she expects her husband home. Her doctor and a neurologist cannot identify a physical cause. They suspect the symptoms have an unconscious psychological origin, possibly triggered by her mixed feelings about her husband. In **somatoform disorders,** such as Ellen's, the distressing symptoms take a somatic (bodily) form, without apparent physical causes. One person may have a variety of complaints—vomiting, dizziness, blurred vision, difficulty in swallowing. Another may experience severe and prolonged pain.

In China, where people less often express the emotional aspects of distress, bodily complaints are common (Draguns, 1990a). Because psychological explanations of anxiety and depression are less socially approved, the Chinese appear more sensitive to and willing to report the bodily symptoms of their distress. Mr. Wu, a 36-year-old technician in Hunan, illustrates one of China's most common psychological disorders (Spitzer & others, 1989). He finds work difficult because of his insomnia, fatigue, weakness, and headaches. Chinese herbs and Western medicines provide no relief. To his Chinese clinician, he seems not so much depressed as exhausted. Similar, generalized bodily complaints have often been observed in African cultures (Binitie, 1975).

Even to people in the West, somatic symptoms are familiar. To a lesser extent, we have all experienced inexplicable physical symptoms under stress. It is little comfort to be told that the problem is "all in your head." Although the symptoms may be psychological in origin, they are nevertheless genuinely felt.

One type of somatoform disorder, more common in Freud's day than ours, is **conversion disorder,** so called because anxiety presumably is converted into a physical symptom. (As we noted in Chapter 11, Freud's effort to treat and understand psychological disorders stemmed from his puzzlement over ailments that had no physiological basis.) A patient with a conversion disorder might, for example, lose sensation in a way that makes no neurological sense. Yet the physical symptoms are real; one could stick pins in the affected area and get no response. Others experience unexplained paralysis, blindness, or an inability to swallow, and are strangely indifferent to their problems.

As you can imagine, somatoform disorders send people not to a psychologist or psychiatrist but to a physician. This is especially true of those who experience **hypochondriasis.** In this relatively common somatoform disorder, people interpret normal sensations (a stomach cramp today, a headache tomorrow) as symptoms of a dreaded disease. Sympathy or temporary relief from everyday demands may reinforce such complaints. No amount of reassurance by any physician convinces the patient not to worry. So the patient moves on to another physician, seeking and receiving more medical attention—but failing to confront the disorder's psychological root.

Dissociative Disorders

Preview Question

6. What is the common characteristic of the dissociative disorders?

Among the most intriguing disorders are the rare **dissociative disorders,** in which a person experiences a sudden loss of memory or change in identity. When a situation becomes too stressful, people may dissociate (detach) themselves from it. Their conscious awareness becomes separated from painful memories, thoughts, and feelings.

Certain symptoms of dissociation are not so rare. Now and then, we may have a sense of being unreal, of being separated from our body, of watching ourselves as in a movie. Facing trauma, such detachment may actually protect a person from being overwhelmed by emotion. Only when such experiences are severe and prolonged do they suggest a dissociative disorder.

Amnesia

Amnesia, the failure to recall events, can be caused by head injuries or alcoholic intoxication. But psychogenic amnesia—a dissociative disorder— usually begins as a response to intolerable psychological stress. One 18-year-old victim was rescued from his sailboat by the Coast Guard and brought to a hospital. He knew he had gone sailing with friends and that he was a college student, but could not recall what happened to his friends. Moreover, he kept forgetting that he was in the hospital; each reminder surprised him. Later, aided by a drug that relaxed him, he remembered: A ferocious storm had washed his companions overboard.

As this case illustrates, the forgetfulness of amnesia is selective: The young man forgot what was intolerably painful. Those with amnesia may be somewhat disoriented and may forget who they are, but they will remember how to drive, count, and talk. Typically, the amnesia vanishes as abruptly as it began and rarely recurs.

Fugue

Like amnesia, **fugue** (pronounced *fewg*, meaning "flight") involves forgetting, but it also involves fleeing one's home and identity for days, months, or years. Gene Saunders, a mid-level manager, had been passed over for promotion, faulted by his supervisor, and rejected by his 18-year-old son, who during a violent argument called him a "failure." Two days later, Saunders disappeared. A month later and 200 miles away, police brought a man who said he was "Burt Tate" to the emergency room. Tate had been hurt in a fight at a diner, where he had been working as a short-order cook since drifting into town a month earlier. He claimed not to recall where he had lived or worked before that. He admitted that was strange but did not seem upset by it. After a missing person's check, Mrs. Saunders confirmed that Burt Tate was Gene Saunders. Though noticeably anxious when faced with his wife, he denied recognizing her. When "awakening" from a fugue state, people such as Gene Saunders remember their old identities but typically deny remembering what occurred during the fugue.

Multiple Personality

Even more mysterious and controversial is the massive dissociation of self from ordinary consciousness in those with **multiple personality disorder.** These people have two or more distinct personalities. The first is usually restrained and dull, the second more impulsive and uninhibited. The person may be prim and proper one moment and loud and flirtatious the next. Each

somatoform disorders Psychological disorders in which the symptoms take a somatic (bodily) form without apparent physical cause.

conversion disorder A rare somatoform disorder in which a person experiences very specific genuine physical symptoms for which no physiological basis can be found.

hypochondriasis A somatoform disorder in which a person misinterprets normal physical sensations as symptoms of a disease.

dissociative disorders Disorders in which conscious awareness becomes separated (dissociated) from painful memories, thoughts, and feelings.

amnesia Loss of memory. Psychogenic amnesia, a dissociative disorder, is selective memory loss often brought on by extreme stress.

fugue [fewg] A dissociative disorder in which flight from one's home and identity accompanies amnesia.

multiple personality disorder A rare dissociative disorder in which a person exhibits two or more distinct and alternating personalities. (Note: Multiple personality disorder is unrelated to schizophrenia.)

"Hillside Strangler" Kenneth Bianchi at his trial.

"Pretense may become reality."

Chinese proverb

The chief of the National Institute of Mental Health unit on dissociative disorders estimates there are 7000 diagnosed cases of multiple personality disorder in the United States (Shulruff, 1990).

personality has its own voice and mannerisms, and the original one typically denies awareness of the other(s).

Although people diagnosed as having multiple personality disorder are usually not violent, there have been cases in which the person reportedly became dissociated into a "good" and a "bad" or aggressive personality—a modern version of the Dr. Jekyll/Mr. Hyde split immortalized in Robert Louis Stevenson's story. Freud would say that, rid of the original "good" personality's awareness, the wanton second personality is free to discharge forbidden impulses. One unusual case that for a time seemed to support this interpretation involved Kenneth Bianchi, who was convicted of the "Hillside Strangler" rapes and murders of 10 California women. During a hypnosis session with Bianchi, psychologist John Watkins (1984) "called forth" a hidden personality:

> *Watkins:* I've talked a bit to Ken, but I think that perhaps there might be another part of Ken that I haven't talked to, another part that maybe feels somewhat differently from the part that I've talked to. . . . Would you talk with me, Part, by saying, "I'm here"?
>
> *Bianchi answered "yes" and engaged in the following interchange:*
>
> *Watkins:* Part, are you the same thing as Ken, or are you different in any way?
>
> *Bianchi:* I'm not him.
>
> *Watkins:* You're not him? Who are you? Do you have a name?
>
> *Bianchi:* Steve. You can call me Steve.

When speaking as Steve, Bianchi stated that he hated Ken because Ken was nice and that he (Steve), aided by a cousin, had murdered women. He also claimed that Ken knew nothing about his existence and that Ken was innocent of the murders.

Was Bianchi's second personality a ruse, simply a way of disavowing responsibility for his actions? Even normal people sometimes act as if they had a multiple personality, as when displaying a goofy, loud-mouthed self when hanging out with friends, and a subdued, respectful self around grandparents. Exploring our normal capacity for personality shifts, Nicolas Spanos (1986b), asked college students to pretend they were accused murderers being examined by a psychiatrist. When given the same hypnotic treatment that Bianchi received, most spontaneously expressed a second personality. This discovery prompted Spanos to wonder (as he does about similar claims of dissociation during hypnosis): Are clinicians who discover multiple personalities merely triggering people to enact a role? If so, can such people then convince themselves of the authenticity of their own role enactments?

Skeptics also find it suspicious that the disorder has just recently become rather popular. There have been at least three times more cases of the disorder reported since 1970 than in the previous 150 years (Orne & others, 1984)—just what one might expect now that the role of multiple personality has been well publicized in books and films, such as *The Three Faces of Eve* and *Sybil.* Moreover, most clinicians have never encountered a multiple personality, and outside North America the disorder is almost nonexistent (Aldridge-Morris, 1989). Yet, strangely, a few North American clinicians claim to encounter them regularly (Levitt, 1988).

With the dissociative disorders as with the anxiety and somatoform disorders, the psychoanalytic and learning perspectives view the symptoms as ways of dealing with anxiety. Psychoanalysts see them as defenses against the anxiety caused by the eruption of unacceptable impulses. Learning theorists see them as behaviors reinforced by anxiety reduction.

Others view dissociative disorders as hypnotic-like states into which people lapse as a protective response to traumatic childhood experiences. Most

"Though this be madness, yet there is method in 't."

William Shakespeare
Hamlet, 1600

people diagnosed as multiple personality are women, many of whom suffered physical, sexual, or emotional abuse as children (Coon & others, 1988; Kluft, 1987). Perhaps, then, multiple personalities are the desperate efforts of the traumatized to flee inward. Maladaptive as they may be, such psychological disorders are expressions of our human struggle to cope with and survive the stresses of life.

Rehearse It

5. About one in 12 people suffers from anxiety so distressing, uncontrollable, or persistent that he or she is said to have an anxiety disorder. If a person's anxiety takes the form of an irrational fear of a specific object or situation—for example, an irrational fear of dogs, thunderstorms, or closed spaces—the disorder is called
a. a phobic disorder.
b. a panic attack.
c. generalized anxiety.
d. an obsessive-compulsive disorder.

6. Rats subjected to unpredictable shocks in the laboratory become chronically anxious. To the learning researcher this suggests that anxiety is a response to
a. a phobia.
b. biological factors.
c. the pressures of the superego.
d. helplessness.

7. Psychologists have different ideas about the causes of phobic disorders. For example, some psychologists stress the importance of biological predispositions, noting that we seem predisposed to fear certain stimuli. Psychologists of the behavioral or learning perspective, on the other hand, maintain that phobias are
a. the result of individual genetic makeup.
b. a way of repressing unacceptable impulses.
c. conditioned fears.
d. a symptom of having been abused as a child.

8. The experience of anxiety often involves physical symptoms, such as trembling, dizziness, chest pains, or sensations of choking or smothering. An episode of intense dread, which is typically accompanied by such symptoms, and by feelings of terror, is called

a. generalized or chronic anxiety.
b. a social phobia.
c. a panic attack.
d. an obsessive fear.

9. A person suffering from a somatoform disorder experiences bodily symptoms which seem to have a psychological, rather than physical, origin. A relatively common somatoform disorder today is
a. conversion disorder.
b. hypochondriasis.
c. unexplained blindness.
d. amnesia.

10. Amnesia, fugue, and multiple personality involve gaps in awareness, for example, sudden loss of memory or change of identity. These psychological disorders are called
a. anxiety disorders.
b. dissociative disorders.
c. mood disorders.
d. memory disorders.

mood disorders Psychological disorders characterized by emotional extremes.

major depression A mood disorder in which a person, for no apparent reason, experiences 2 or more weeks of depressed moods, feelings of worthlessness, and diminished interest or pleasure in most activities.

bipolar disorder A mood disorder in which a person alternates between the hopelessness and lethargy of depression and the overexcited state of mania.

Mood Disorders

The emotional extremes of **mood disorders** come in two principal forms: (1) **major depression,** in which the person experiences the hopelessness and lethargy of prolonged depression until eventually rebounding to normalcy; and (2) **bipolar disorder,** in which the person alternates between depression and *mania,* an overexcited, hyperactive state.

Major Depression

Perhaps you know what depression feels like. If you are like most of the college students studied by Aaron Beck and Jeffrey Young (1978), at some time during this year—more likely the dark months of winter than during summer—you will probably experience a few of the symptoms of depression.

Psychology Applied: Suicide

*"But life, being weary of these worldly bars,
Never lacks power to dismiss itself."*

William Shakespeare
Julius Caesar, 1599

Each year in the United States, more than 25,000 wearied, despairing people will say no to life by electing a permanent solution to what may be a temporary problem. In retrospect, their families and friends may recall signs they now believe should have forewarned them—the suicidal talk, the giving away of possessions, or the withdrawal and preoccupation with death. One-third of those who kill themselves have tried suicide before.

Few of those who talk suicide or think suicidal thoughts (a number that includes one-third of all adolescents and college students) actually attempt suicide, and few of these succeed in killing themselves (Centers for Disease Control, 1989; Westefeld & Furr, 1987). Still, most individuals who do commit suicide have talked of it. And any who do talk suicide are at least sending a signal of their desperate or despondent feelings.

To find out who commits suicide, researchers have compared the suicide rates of different groups.

National differences are puzzling:

Contrary to popular opinion, there are *fewer* suicides on holidays such as Christmas than at other times of the year (Phillips & Wills, 1987).

The suicide rates of Britain, Italy, and Spain are half that in the United States; those of Austria, Denmark, and Switzerland are nearly double (Bureau of the Census, 1990).

Racial differences are intriguing: In the United States, whites are twice as likely as blacks to kill themselves (Figure 12–4).

Group differences are suggestive: Suicide rates are higher among the rich, the nonreligious, and the unmarried—including the widowed and divorced (Gartner & others, 1991; Stengel, 1981).

Gender differences are dramatic: Women are much more likely than men to attempt suicide. Depending on the country, however, men are two to three times more likely to succeed. (Men are more likely to use foolproof methods, such as putting a bullet into the brain.)

Age differences have vanished: Due partly to improved reporting (Gist & Welch, 1989), the known suicide rate among 15- to 19-year-olds has more than doubled since 1950 and now nearly equals the traditionally higher suicide rate among adults (Figure 12–5).

Suicide often occurs not when the person is in the depths of depression, when energy and initiative are lacking, but when the person begins

Preview Question

7. What behaviors characterize mood disorders?

You may feel deeply discouraged about the future, dissatisfied with your life, or isolated from others. You may lack the energy to get things done or even to force yourself out of bed; be unable to concentrate, eat, or sleep normally; or even wonder if you would be better off dead. Perhaps academic success came easily to you in high school, and now you find that disappointing grades jeopardize your goals. Maybe conflicting parental and peer pressures seem intolerable. Perhaps social difficulties, such as loneliness or the breakup of a romance, have plunged you into despair. And maybe your brooding has at times only worsened your self-torment.

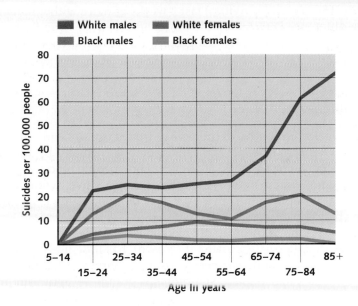

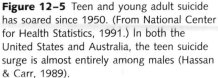

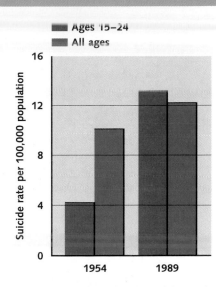

Figure 12-4 In the United States, suicide rates are higher among whites than blacks, and higher among males than females. (From Bureau of the Census, 1990.)

Figure 12-5 Teen and young adult suicide has soared since 1950. (From National Center for Health Statistics, 1991.) In both the United States and Australia, the teen suicide surge is almost entirely among males (Hassan & Carr, 1989).

to rebound and becomes capable of following through. Teenage suicides may follow a traumatic event, such as a romantic breakup or a guilt-provoking antisocial act, and are often linked with drug and alcohol abuse (Fowler & others, 1986; Kolata, 1986). Compared to people who suffer no disorder, alcoholics are roughly 100 times more likely to commit suicide, as some 3 percent of them do (Murphy & Wetzel, 1990). Even among those who have attempted suicide, alcoholics are five times more likely than nonalcoholics eventually to kill themselves (Beck & Steer, 1989). Among the elderly, suicide is sometimes chosen as an alternative to future suffering. In people of all ages, suicide is not necessarily an act of hostility or revenge, as many people think, but may be a way of switching off unendurable pain (Shneidman, 1987).

Social suggestion may trigger the final act. Following highly publicized suicides and TV programs featuring suicide, known suicides increase. So do fatal auto "accidents" and private airplane crashes (page 449).

"My life had come to a sudden stop. I was able to breathe, to eat, to drink, to sleep. I could not, indeed, help doing so; but there was no real life in me."

Leo Tolstoy
My Confession, 1887

If so, you are not alone. Along with the phobias, depression is considered the "common cold" of psychological disorders—an expression that well states its pervasiveness but not its seriousness. Among Americans born since World War II, depression has increased dramatically—tenfold, reports Martin Seligman (1988). Similar trends are evident in Canada, Sweden, Germany, and New Zealand (Klerman & Weissman, 1989). Young adults and women are especially vulnerable.

The line between life's normal "downs" and major depression is difficult to define. Joy, contentment, sadness, and despair are different points on a continuum, points at which any of us may be found at any given moment.

mania A hyperactive, wildly optimistic state.

"I'm always like this, and my family was wondering if you could prescribe a mild depressant."

Drawing by Sidney Harris.

Preview Question

8. What causes mood disorders?

About 50 percent of those who recover from depression will suffer another episode within 2 years. Recovery is more likely to be enduring the longer patients stay well, the fewer their previous episodes, the less stress they experience, and the more social support they have (Belsher & Costello, 1988).

Depression can be an appropriate response to profoundly sad events, such as a significant loss or bereavement. To feel bad in reaction to painful events is to be in touch with reality. Major depression occurs when signs of depression (poor appetite, insomnia, lethargy, feelings of worthlessness, or loss of interest in family, friends, and activities) last 2 weeks or more without any notable cause. The difference between a blue mood after bad news and a mood disorder is like the difference between gasping for breath after exercising and being chronically short of breath.

Bipolar Disorder

After a few weeks or months, depressive episodes usually end with or without therapy. Depressed people typically rebound—usually by returning to their previous behavior patterns. However, some people rebound to or from the opposite emotional extreme—a euphoric, hyperactive, wildly optimistic state of **mania.** If depression is living in slow motion, mania is fast forward. Alternating between depression and mania signals *bipolar disorder.* During the manic phase of a bipolar disorder, the person is typically overtalkative, overactive, elated (though easily irritated if crossed), has little need for sleep, and shows fewer sexual inhibitions. Speech is loud, flighty, and hard to interrupt.

One of mania's maladaptive symptoms is grandiose optimism and self-esteem, which may lead to reckless spending and investment sprees. Although people in a manic state find advice irritating, they need protection from their own poor judgment. In milder forms, however, the energy and free-flowing thinking of mania can fuel creativity. Bipolar disorder is especially common among poets, artists, and playwrights (DeAngelis, 1989; Jamison, 1989). Handel composed his nearly 4-hour-long *Messiah* during 3 weeks of intense, creative energy.

It is as true of emotions as all else: What goes up comes down. Before long, the mood either returns to normal or plunges into a brief depression. Though equally maladaptive as major depression, bipolar disorder is much less common, occurring in about 1 percent of the U.S. population. Unlike major depression, it afflicts as many men as women.

Explaining Mood Disorders

Because depression profoundly affects many people, it has been the subject of thousands of studies. Psychologists are working to develop a theory of mood disorders that will suggest ways to treat or prevent them. Researcher Peter Lewinsohn and his colleagues (1985) summarized the facts that any theory of depression must explain. Among them are:

1. *Many behavioral and cognitive changes accompany depression.* Depressed people are inactive and unmotivated. They also are sensitive to negative happenings. They expect negative outcomes, and they are more likely to recall negative information. When the depression lifts, these behavioral and cognitive accompaniments disappear.

2. *Depression is widespread.* Its commonality suggests that its causes, too, must be common.

3. *Compared to men, women are doubly vulnerable to major depression, even more so if they have been depressed before.* Curiously, the gender difference in depression rates does *not* exist in college students or among bereaved persons (Nolen-Hoeksema, 1990).

Actress Patty Duke spent years suffering with bipolar disorder before she was finally diagnosed and treated. Now she spends her free time educating others about mental illness in thanks ''for having been saved from that pit.'' CBS correspondent Mike Wallace became debilitated by severe depression during a tough libel trial. ''Depression is palpable,'' he says. ''You begin to feel like a fake and a fraud. You second-guess everything about everything.''

4. *Most depressive episodes last less than 3 months.* Although therapy can speed recovery, most people suffering major depression return to normal without out professional help.

5. *Stressful events related to work, marriage, and close relationships often precede depression.* A family member's death, a wage cut, or a physical assault increase one's risk of depression (Shrout & others, 1989). National samples of Israelis, whose tiny nation is a living stress laboratory, revealed greater feelings of depression after the outbreak of the 1982 Israel-Lebanon war (Hobfull & others, 1989).

As you might expect, researchers understand and interpret these facts in ways that reflect their different perspectives.

The Psychoanalytic Perspective

Psychoanalytic theory applies Freud's ideas about the importance of early childhood experiences and unconscious impulses to depression. It suggests that depression occurs when significant losses evoke feelings associated with losses experienced in childhood. Loss of a romantic relationship or job might evoke feelings associated with the loss of the intimate relationship with one's mother. Unresolved anger toward one's parents is also a factor, Freud believed. Some losses, such as a loved one's death, may evoke the anger once felt toward parents who were similarly ''abandoning'' or ''rejecting.'' This anger is unacceptable to the superego, so the emotion turns inward against the self. Combined with the sense of loss, this internalized anger is said to produce depression.

The Biological Perspective

Most of the U.S. government's mental health research dollars of late have funded biological explorations of mood disorders. Depression is clearly a whole-body disorder, involving genetic predispositions, biochemical imbalances, melancholy mood, and negative thoughts.

Genetic Influences We have long known that mood disorders run in families. The risk of major depression increases if you have a parent or sibling who became depressed before age 30 (Weissman & others, 1986). If an identical twin has bipolar disorder, the chances are 7 in 10 that the other twin will at some point be diagnosed similarly. If the identical twin is diagnosed as suffering major depression, the chances are about 1 in 2 that at some time the other twin will be, too. Among fraternal twins, the corresponding odds are just under 1 in 5 (Tsuang & Faraone, 1990). Moreover, adopted people who suffer a mood disorder often have close biological relatives who suffer mood disorders, become alcoholic, or commit suicide (Wender & others, 1986).

Biochemical Influences Genes act by directing biochemical events that, down the line, influence behavior. Through what biochemical processes might genes predispose mood disorders? It more and more looks like a biochemical key is the neurotransmitters, those chemical messenger molecules. Norepinephrine, a neurotransmitter that increases arousal and boosts mood, is overabundant during mania and scarce during depression. A second neurotransmitter, serotonin, sometimes appears scarce during depression. Drugs that alleviate mania reduce norepinephrine; drugs that relieve depression tend to increase norepinephrine or serotonin supplies by blocking either their uptake or chemical breakdown.

Researchers continue to explore the role of these and other neurotransmitters. They hope eventually to identify people who are vulnerable to mood disorders and to prevent their symptoms by counteracting the disorder's biological and psychological underpinnings.

The Social-Cognitive Perspective

Biological factors do not operate in a vacuum: As Figure 12–6 suggests, they accompany psychological reactions to experience. Negative interpretations, created by the mind, somehow influence biochemical events that in a vicious cycle amplify the depressing thoughts.

Recent research reveals the precise sorts of *self-defeating beliefs* that feed the vicious cycle. Depressed people view life through dark glasses. Their intensely negative assumptions about themselves, their situations, and their futures lead them to magnify bad experiences and minimize good ones. As one occasionally depressed young woman put it (Burns, 1980, pp. 28–29):

> My thoughts become negative and pessimistic. As I look into the past, I become convinced that everything that I've ever done is worthless. Any happy period seems like an illusion. My accomplishments appear as genuine as the false facade of a Western movie. I become convinced that the real me is worthless and inadequate. I can't move forward with my work because I become frozen with doubt.

Self-defeating beliefs may arise from *learned helplessness*. As we saw in Chapter 11, both dogs and humans act depressed, passive, and withdrawn after experiencing uncontrollable painful events. Women more often than men have been abused or made to feel helpless, which helps explain why women have been twice as vulnerable to depression as men (Nolen-Hoeksema, 1990, and see Table 12–2 on page 406). (Another explanation is that men more often repress their depressed feelings or drown them in alcohol.)

Maladaptive Explanations Feed Depression   Why do life's unavoidable failures lead some people, but not others, to become depressed? The difference lies partly with people's *attributions* of blame. We have some choice of whom or what to blame for our failures. If you fail a test and blame yourself, you may feel stupid and depressed. If you externalize the blame—if you attribute your failure to an unfair test—you are more likely to feel angry.

In more than 100 studies involving some 15,000 subjects (Sweeney & others, 1986), depressed people have tended to explain bad events in terms that are *stable* ("It's going to last forever"), *global* ("It's going to affect everything I do"), and *internal* ("It's all my fault"). Lyn Abramson, Gerald

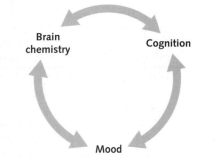

Figure 12–6 Depression—an ailing mind in an ailing body. Altering any component of the chemistry-cognition-mood circuit can alter the others.

"I have learned to accept my mistakes by referring them to a personal history which was not of my making."

B. F. Skinner (1983)

Drawings by Charles Shultz; © 1956 United Feature Syndicate, Inc. Reprinted with permission of UFS, Inc.

Metalsky, and Lauren Alloy (1989) theorize that the result of these pessimistic, overgeneralized, self-blaming attributions is a depressing sense of hopelessness.

Martin Seligman (1988) argues that depression is now common among young Americans because of epidemic hopelessness, which stems from the rise of individualism and the decline of commitment to religion and family. When facing failure or rejection, contends Seligman, the self-focused individual takes on personal responsibility for problems and has nothing to fall back on for hope. In non-Western cultures, where close-knit relationships and co-operation are more common, major depression is less common and less tied to guilt and self-blame over perceived failure. In Japan, for example, depressed people instead tend to report feeling shame over letting down their family or co-workers (Draguns, 1990a).

Depression's Vicious Cycle   Depression is often brought on by stressful experiences—losing a job, being criticized or rejected, physical trauma—anything that disrupts your sense of who you are and why you are a worthy human being (Dohrenwend & others, 1987; Oatley & Bolton, 1985). Depressed people respond to bad events in a more self-focused, self-blaming way (Pyszczynski & others, 1991; Wood & others, 1990a,b). This brooding amplifies negative feelings, which in turn trigger depression's other cognitive and behavioral symptoms.

New evidence suggests that there is two-way traffic between depressed mood and negative thinking. Depression causes self-focused negative thinking, and a self-focused, self-blaming style of explaining events puts one at risk for depression when bad events strike. If you tend to see bad grades, social rejection, and work problems as inevitable and your own fault, and if you ruminate about such things, then when bad events happen you will experience a bad case of the blues. For example, Susan Nolen-Hoeksema and Jannay Morrow (1991) assessed Stanford University students' moods and ruminations 2 weeks before the 1989 earthquake devastated much of their area. Those identified as prone to brood over negative events showed more symptoms of depression both 10 days and 7 weeks after the earthquake. If you have an optimistic way of interpreting events, a failure or stress is unlikely to provoke depression (Seligman, 1991). Even if you do get depressed, you are more likely to recover soon when events brighten (Needles & Abramson, 1990).

Another source of depression's vicious cycle is its social consequences. Being withdrawn, self-focused, and complaining elicits rejection (Coyne & others, 1991). In one study, researchers Stephen Strack and James Coyne (1983) noted that "depressed persons induced hostility, depression, and anxiety in others and got rejected. Their guesses that they were not accepted were not a matter of cognitive distortion." Weary of the depressed person's fatigue, hopeless attitude, and lethargy, a spouse may threaten to leave or a boss may begin to question the person's competence. Indeed, depressed people are at high risk for divorce and job loss, thus compounding their depression. Misery may love another's company, but company does not love another's misery.

We can now assemble the pieces of the depression puzzle (Figure 12–7): (1) Stressful events interpreted through (2) a pessimistic explanatory style create (3) a hopeless, depressed state that (4) hampers the way the person thinks and acts. This, in turn, fuels (1) more negative experiences. On the brighter side, one can break the cycle of depression at any of these points—by moving to a different environment, by reversing one's self-blame and negative attributions, by turning one's attention outward, or by engaging in more pleasant activities and more competent behavior.

"Man never reasons so much and becomes so introspective as when he suffers, since he is anxious to get at the cause of his sufferings."

Luigi Pirandello
Six Characters in Search of an Author, 1922

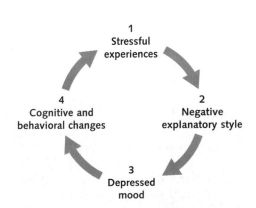

Figure 12–7 The vicious cycle of depression can be broken at any point. The next chapter describes some therapeutic techniques. (Adapted from Lewinsohn & others, 1985.)

Psychology Applied: Loneliness

Loneliness—the painful awareness that one's social relationships are deficient—is both a contributor to depression and a problem in itself. The deficiency stems from a mismatch between one's actual and desired social contacts. One person may feel lonely when isolated and another may feel lonely in a crowd (Peplau & Perlman, 1982). Yet people who are alone—unmarried, unattached, and often young—are more likely to feel lonely. Dutch psychologist Jenny de Jong-Gierveld (1987) therefore speculates that the modern emphasis on individual fulfillment and the downgrading of stable relationships and commitment to others are "loneliness-provoking factors."

People commonly experience one or more of four types of loneliness (Beck & Young, 1978). To be lonely is to feel *excluded* from a group you would like to belong to; to feel *unloved* and uncared about by those around you; to feel *constricted* and unable to share your private concerns with anyone; or to feel *alienated*, or different from, those in your community. Like depressed people, lonely people tend to blame themselves, attributing their deficient so-

Drawing by Cheney; © 1989 The New Yorker Magazine, Inc.

cial relationships to their own inadequacies (Snodgrass, 1987). There may be a basis for this self-blame: Chronically lonely people tend to be shy, self-conscious, and lacking in self-esteem (Check & Melchior, 1990; Vaux, 1988). They often find it hard to introduce themselves, make phone calls, and participate in groups (Rook, 1984; Spitzberg & Hurt, 1987).

In addition, their belief in their social unworthiness restricts their noticing and remembering positive feedback and keeps them from taking steps that would reduce their loneliness (Frankel & Prentice-Dunn, 1990). Thus, factors that work to create and maintain the cycle of depression can also produce a cycle of loneliness.

The several points at which the cycle can be broken are the focus of several different therapeutic methods (Chapter 13, Therapy). Even without therapy, depression will usually end on its own. Winston Churchill called depression a "black dog" that periodically hounded him. Poet Emily Dickinson was so afraid of bursting into tears in public that she spent much of her adult life in seclusion (Patterson, 1951). Abraham Lincoln was so withdrawn and brooding as a young man that his friends feared he might take his own life (Kline, 1974). As each of these lives reminds us, people can and do struggle through depression. Most regain their capacity to love, to work, and even to succeed at the highest levels.

Rehearse It

11. Conversion disorder and multiple personality are relatively rare psychological disorders. An example of a disorder which is so common that it has been called "the common cold" of psychological disorders is
a. amnesia.
b. depression.
c. bipolar disorder.
d. schizophrenia.

12. About 25 percent of us will experience at least one depressive episode, often following a stressful event, such as divorce or job change. In a depressive episode, a person tends to be inactive and unmotivated and overly sensitive to negative thoughts, memories, and events. In most cases the depressive episode lasts
a. less than 3 months.
b. 6 months.
c. 6 months to a year.
d. 2 years.

13. Depression tends to run in families. It can often be alleviated by drugs that block the uptake of the neurotransmitters norepinephrine and serotonin. These findings suggest that an explanation for depression may well be found in
a. psychoanalytic theory.
b. learned helplessness.
c. stressful events.
d. biological factors.

14. Depressed people are more likely than others to blame themselves, rather than external factors, for their failures. Such self-defeating beliefs often arise from feelings of helplessness or futility. Psychologists who emphasize the importance of negative perceptions, beliefs, and thoughts in depression, are working within the
a. psychoanalytic perspective.
b. biological perspective.
c. behavioral perspective.
d. social-cognitive perspective.

Schizophrenia Disorders

Preview Question

9. What behaviors characterize schizophrenia disorders?

If the phobias and depression are the common colds of psychological disorders, chronic schizophrenia is the cancer. About 1 in 100 people will develop schizophrenia, joining the millions who have suffered one of humanity's most dreaded disorders. Schizophrenia is a **psychotic disorder,** in which a person loses contact with reality by experiencing grossly irrational ideas and distorted perceptions. Schizophrenia typically first strikes during adolescence or young adulthood; it knows no national boundaries and it affects the two sexes about equally.

Symptoms of Schizophrenia

Schizophrenia literally translated means "split mind." Split mind refers not to a multiple-personality split, but rather a *split from reality* that shows itself in disorganized thinking, disturbed perceptions, and inappropriate emotions and actions.

Disorganized Thinking

psychotic disorder   Psychological disorder in which a person loses contact with reality, experiencing irrational ideas and distorted perceptions.

schizophrenia   A group of severe psychotic disorders characterized by disorganized and deluded thinking, disturbed perceptions, and inappropriate emotions and actions.

Imagine trying to communicate with Sylvia Frumkin, a young woman whose thoughts spill out in no logical order. Her biographer, Susan Sheehan (1982, p. 25), observed her saying aloud to no one in particular,

> "This morning, when I was at Hillside [Hospital], I was making a movie. I was surrounded by movie stars. The X-ray technician was Peter Lawford. The security guard was Don Knotts. That Indian doctor in Building 40 was Lou Costello. I'm Mary Poppins. Is this room painted blue to get me upset? My grandmother died four weeks after my eighteenth birthday." Miss Frumkin laughed.

delusions False beliefs, often of persecution or grandeur, that may accompany psychotic disorders.

As this strange monologue illustrates, the schizophrenia patient's thinking is fragmented, bizarre, and distorted by false beliefs, called **delusions** ("I'm Mary Poppins"). Jumping from one idea to another may even occur within sentences, creating a sort of "word salad." One young man begged for "a little more allegro in the treatment," and suggested that "liberationary movement with a view to the widening of the horizon" will "ergo extort some wit in lectures."

Many psychologists believe disorganized thoughts result from a breakdown in selective attention. As we noted on page 149, we normally have a remarkable capacity for selective attention—for, say, giving our undivided attention to one voice at a party while filtering out competing sensory stimuli. Schizophrenia sufferers have impaired attention (Gjerde, 1983). Thus, an irrelevant stimulus or an extraneous part of the preceding thought easily distracts them. As one former schizophrenia patient recalled, "What had happened to me . . . was a breakdown in the filter, and a hodge-podge of unrelated stimuli were distracting me from things which should have had my undivided attention" (MacDonald, 1960, p. 218).

Disturbed Perceptions

The schizophrenia victim experiences an altered world. Minute stimuli, such as the grooves on a brick or the inflections of a voice, may distract attention from the whole scene or from the speaker's meaning. Worse, the person may perceive things that are not there.

Such *hallucinations* (sensory experiences without sensory stimulation) are usually auditory. The person may hear voices that seem to come from outside the head and that make insulting statements or give orders. The voices may tell the patient that she is bad or that he must burn himself with a cigarette lighter or even commit murder. Less commonly, people see, feel, taste, or smell things that are nonexistent. Such hallucinations have been compared to dreams breaking into waking consciousness. When the unreal seems real, the resulting perceptions are at best bizarre and at worst terrifying.

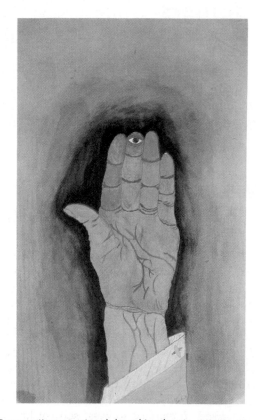

Commenting on artwork by schizophrenia patients, as shown here, poet John Ashbery wrote: "The lure of the work is strong, but so is the terror of the unanswerable riddles it proposes."

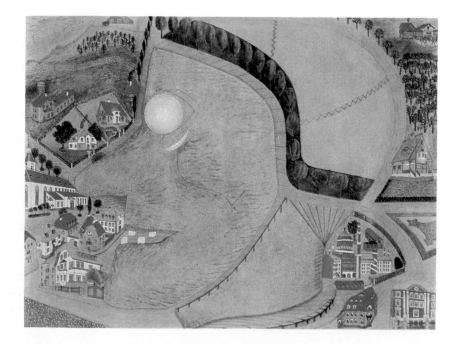

Inappropriate Emotions and Actions

The emotions of schizophrenia are often utterly inappropriate. Sylvia Frumkin's emotions seemed split off from reality. She laughed after recalling her grandmother's death. On occasion, she became angry for no apparent reason or cried when others laughed. Other victims of schizophrenia sometimes lapse into *flat affect*, a zombielike state of apparent apathy.

Motor behavior also may be inappropriate. The person may perform senseless, compulsive acts, such as continually rocking or rubbing an arm. Those who exhibit *catatonia* may remain motionless for hours on end, and then become agitated.

As you can imagine, disorganized thinking, disturbed perceptions, and inappropriate emotions and actions disrupt social relationships. During their most severe periods, schizophrenia sufferers live in a private inner world, preoccupied with illogical ideas and unreal images. Although most people suffer from schizophrenia only intermittently, others remain socially withdrawn and isolated throughout much of their lives. Rarely is there a one-time episode that is "cured," never to return.

People who suffer from schizophrenia often withdraw into an inner world of bizarre thoughts and disturbed perceptions.

Types of Schizophrenia

We have described schizophrenia as if it were a single disorder. Actually, it is a cluster of disorders that have common features but also some distinguishing symptoms. Schizophrenia patients with *positive symptoms* are conspicuously disorganized and deluded in their talk or prone to inappropriate laughter, tears, or rage. Schizophrenia patients with *negative symptoms* have toneless voices, expressionless faces, or mute and rigid bodies. Thus, schizophrenia is not a single disorder for which there could be but one set of causes.

Sometimes, as in the case of Sylvia Frumkin, schizophrenia develops gradually, emerging from a long history of social inadequacy (which partially explains why those predisposed to schizophrenia often end up in the lower socioeconomic levels, or even as homeless people). Other times it appears suddenly, seemingly as a reaction to stress. There is a rule that holds true around the world (World Health Organization, 1979): When the schizophrenia is a slow-developing process (called *chronic*, or *process*, schizophrenia), recovery is doubtful. When, in reaction to particular life stresses, a previously well-adjusted person develops schizophrenia rapidly (*acute*, or *reactive*, schizophrenia), recovery is much more likely.

Close-Up: Experiencing Schizophrenia

These recollections by a recovered schizophrenia patient illustrate the delusions of persecution and grandeur and the hallucinations often experienced by those suffering the positive symptoms of schizophrenia.

One night I was invited to listen to a talk by a worker in the foreign service. I was suspicious of him and thought he thought I was a Communist spy. I didn't say anything. I just leaned over and stared at him.

I thought the Government was spying on my room with a telescope in a building across the street. I thought people were loading down my food in the cafeteria with salt. In criminology class I thought the professor and the other students were laughing about me. I thought they were directing the poisoning of my food in the cafeteria. When I went to the cafeteria my hand shook as

the waitress poured what I thought was poisonous coffee into my cup. I thought everyone in the cafeteria knew I was going to die. They all thought it was too bad but I was so evil it was necessary.

On a Saturday I drank lemonade to try to neutralize the poison. Then I would take showers to try to sweat the poison out. I was so nervous I could hardly think. I thought I might only have hours left to live. I thought of taking a bus home to my parents. But no, I thought, it was too late for that.

One day when my strange behavior landed me in a jail cell, the walls began to buzz like bees. I felt there were thousands of bees in the walls buzzing. The buzzing went on and on. There was no relief. It was maddening. Finally, I felt my father's hand rest on my head and I felt peace. Then voices, like the roar of a crowd came. I felt like Jesus; I was

being crucified. Night settled in. It was dark. I just continued to huddle under the blanket, feeling weak, laid bare and defenseless in a cruel world I could no longer understand.

When someone asks me to explain schizophrenia I tell them, you know how sometimes in your dreams you are in them yourself and some of them feel like real nightmares? My schizophrenia was like I was walking through a dream. But everything around me was real. At times, today's world seems so boring and I wonder if I would like to step back into the schizophrenic dream, but then I remember all the scary and horrifying experiences. (Excerpted with permission from S. Emmons and C. Geiser, *Adventures in Schizophrenia,* unpublished.)

Preview Question

10. What causes schizophrenia?

Understanding Schizophrenia

Schizophrenia is not only the most dreaded psychological disorder but also one of the most heavily researched. Some important new discoveries link schizophrenia with biological factors, such as brain abnormalities and genetic predispositions.

Brain Abnormalities

The idea that imbalances in brain chemistry might underlie schizophrenia has long intrigued scientists. Strange behaviors, they knew, can have strange chemical causes. The saying "Mad as a hatter" refers to the psychological deterioration of British hatmakers whose brains, it was later discovered, were slowly poisoned as they moistened the brims of mercury-laden felt hats with their lips (Smith, 1983). As we saw on page 171, scientists are beginning to understand the mechanism by which chemicals such as LSD produce hallucinations. These discoveries fuel hope that a biochemical key to schizophrenia might be found.

One chemical key to schizophrenia involves the neurotransmitter dopamine. When researchers examined patients' brains after death, they found an excess of receptors for dopamine (Wong & others, 1986). What is more, drugs that block dopamine receptors often lessen schizophrenia symptoms. Drugs that increase dopamine levels, such as amphetamine and cocaine, sometimes intensify schizophrenia symptoms (Swerdlow & Koob, 1987). Such dopamine overactivity may be what makes schizophrenia victims overreactive to irrelevant external and internal stimuli.

Modern brain scanning techniques reveal that many chronic schizophrenia patients have a detectable brain abnormality. Some have abnormally low brain activity in the frontal lobes (Cohen & others, 1988). Others, most often men, have enlarged, fluid-filled areas and a corresponding shrinkage of cerebral tissue (Andreasen & others, 1990a,b; Gur & others, 1991; Raz & Raz, 1990).

Genetic Factors

Naturally, scientists wonder whether people inherit a predisposition to these brain abnormalities. The evidence strongly suggests that some do. The 100-to-1 odds against any person's being diagnosed with schizophrenia become 10-to-1 among those who have an afflicted sibling or parent, and close to 50-50 among those who have an afflicted identical twin (Figure 12–8). Although there are only a dozen such known cases, it appears that an identical twin of a schizophrenia victim retains that 50-50 chance whether they are reared together or apart.

Adoption studies confirm a genetic link (Gottesman, 1991). Children adopted by someone who develops schizophrenia are unlikely to "catch" the disorder. But adopted children do have an elevated risk if a biological parent is diagnosed with schizophrenia.

The genetic contribution to schizophrenia is beyond question. But the genetic role is not so straightforward as the inheritance of eye color. After all, about half the twins who share identical genes with a schizophrenia victim do *not* develop the disorder. Thus, behavior geneticists Susan Nicol and Irving Gottesman (1983) conclude that some people "have a genetic predisposition to the disorder but that this predisposition by itself is not sufficient for the development of schizophrenia."

When twins differ, only the one afflicted with schizophrenia typically has enlarged, fluid-filled cranial cavities (Suddath & others, 1990). The difference between the twins implies some nongenetic factor is also at work.

Figure 12–8 The lifetime risks of suffering from schizophrenia vary with one's genetic relatedness to someone having this disorder. (From Irving Gottesman, 1991, from family and twin studies conducted between 1920 and 1987 in Europe.)

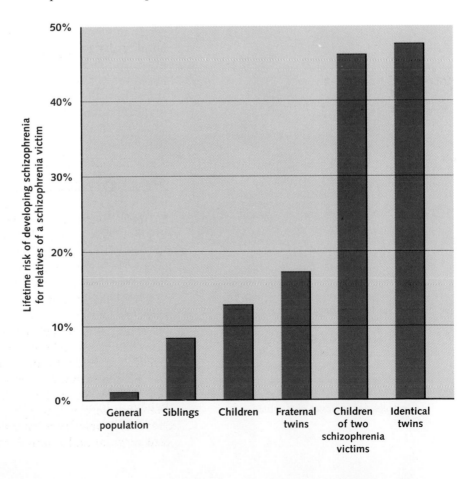

Psychological Factors

If, by themselves, genetically predisposed physiological abnormalities do not cause schizophrenia, neither do psychological factors alone. As Nicol and Gottesman report, "no environmental causes have been discovered that will invariably, or even with moderate probability, produce schizophrenia in persons who are not related to a schizophrenic."

Nevertheless, if genes predispose some people to *react* to particular experiences by developing schizophrenia, then there must be identifiable triggering experiences. Researchers have asked: Can stress trigger schizophrenia? Can difficulties in family communications be a contributing factor?

The answer to each question is a strong, clear maybe. The psychological triggers of schizophrenia have proved elusive, partly because they may vary with the type of schizophrenia and whether it is a slow-developing, chronic schizophrenia, or a sudden, acute reaction to stress. It is true that young people with schizophrenia tend to have unusually disturbed communications with their parents. But is this a cause or a result of their disorder? It is true that stressful experiences, biochemical abnormalities, and schizophrenia's symptoms often occur together. But the traffic between brain biochemistry and psychological experiences runs both ways, so cause and effect are difficult to sort out. It is true that schizophrenic withdrawal often occurs in adolescence or early adulthood, coinciding with the stresses of having to become independent, to assert oneself, and to achieve social success and intimacy. So is schizophrenia the maladaptive coping reaction of biologically vulnerable people?

Most of us can relate more easily to the ups and downs of mood disorders than to the strange thoughts, perceptions, and behaviors of schizophrenia. Sometimes our thoughts do jump around, but we do not talk nonsensically. Occasionally we feel unjustly suspicious of someone, but we do not fear that the world is plotting against us. Often our perceptions are distorted, but rarely do we see or hear things that are not there. We have felt regret after laughing at someone's misfortune, but we rarely giggle in response to bad news. At times we just want to be alone, but we do not live in social isolation. However, millions of people around the world do talk strangely, suffer delusions, hear nonexistent voices, see things that are not there, laugh or cry at inappropriate times, or withdraw into their private imaginary worlds. Because this is true, the scientific quest to solve the cruel puzzle of schizophrenia continues.

The odds of any four people picked at random all suffering from schizophrenia are 1 in 100 million. But the identical Genain quadruplets, (shown here) do. Problems for the sisters began in high school. Since then they have been in and out of hospitals. Of course, these women shared not only identical genes but also a similar environment.

Preview Question

11. What characteristics are typical of personality disorders?

personality disorders Psychological disorders characterized by inflexible and enduring behavior patterns that impair social functioning.

antisocial personality A personality disorder in which the person (usually a man) exhibits a lack of conscience for wrongdoing, even toward friends and family members. May be aggressive and ruthless or a clever con artist.

Personality Disorders

Personality disorders—inflexible and enduring patterns of behavior that impair one's social functioning—sometimes coexist with one of the other psychological disorders, but need not involve anxiety, depression, or loss of contact with reality. For example, a person with a *histrionic personality disorder* displays a shallow, attention-getting emotionality. Histrionic individuals go to great lengths to gain others' praise and reassurance. Those with *narcissistic personality disorder* exaggerate their own importance, aided by success fantasies. They find criticism hard to accept, often reacting with rage or shame.

The most frequent of these disorders, and the most troubling to society, is the **antisocial personality** disorder. The person (formerly called a *sociopath* or a *psychopath*) is typically a male whose lack of conscience becomes plain before age 15, as he begins to lie, steal, fight, or display unrestrained sexual behavior. In adulthood, he may be unable to keep a job, be irresponsible as a spouse and parent, and be assaultive or otherwise criminal. When the antiso-

Cult leader Charles Manson, who with his followers brutally killed nine people over a 2-day period in 1969, is a well known antisocial personality.

cial personality combines a keen intelligence with amorality, the result may be a charming and clever con artist.

Despite their antisocial behavior, most criminals do not fit the description of antisocial personality disorder. Most criminals show responsible concern for their friends and family members; antisocial personalities feel little and fear little. In extreme cases, the results can be tragic. Henry Lee Lucas reported that at age 13 he strangled a woman who refused to have sex with him. He at one time confessed to having bludgeoned, suffocated, stabbed, shot, or mutilated some 360 women, men, and children during his 32 years of crime. During the last 6 years of his reign of terror, Lucas teamed with Elwood Toole, who slaughtered about 50 people whom he "didn't think was worth living anyhow." It ended when Lucas confessed to stabbing and dismembering his 15-year-old common-law wife, who was Toole's niece.

The antisocial personality expresses little regret over violating others' rights. "Once I've done a crime, I just forget it," said Lucas. Toole was equally matter-of-fact: "I think of killing like smoking a cigarette, like another habit" (Darrach & Norris, 1984).

As with mood disorders and schizophrenia, the antisocial personality disorder is woven of biological as well as psychological strands. The usual twin and adoption studies reveal that biological relatives of certain individuals are at increased risk for criminality (DiLalla & Gottesman, 1991; Mednick & others, 1987). Their genetic vulnerability surfaces as minimal arousal under stress, which makes for a rather fearless approach to life. When they await aversive events, such as electric shocks or loud noises, they show little autonomic nervous system arousal (Hare, 1975). Even as youngsters, before committing any crime, it takes more to get them excited (Figure 12–9).

Figure 12–9 Arousability and criminality. Levels of the stress hormone adrenaline were measured in two groups of 13-year-old Swedish boys. In both stressful and nonstressful situations, those who were later convicted of a crime (as 18- to 26-year-olds) showed relatively low reactivity. (From Magnusson, 1990.)

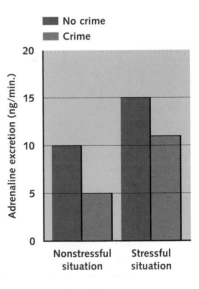

If channeled in more productive directions, such fearlessness may lead to courageous heroism or adventurism. Lacking a sense of social responsibility, the same disposition produces a cool con artist or killer (Lykken, 1982).

Perhaps a biologically based fearlessness, as well as early environment, helps explain the reunion of long-separated sisters Joyce Lott, 27, and Mary Jones, 29—in a South Carolina prison where both were sent on drug charges.

After a newspaper story about their reunion, their long-lost half-brother Frank Strickland called. He explained it would be a while before he could come see them—because he, too, was in jail, on drug, burglary, and larceny charges (Shepherd & others, 1990).

The Commonality of Psychological Disorders

Preview Question

12. How common are the psychological disorders we've discussed?

How prevalent are the various disorders discussed in this chapter? Who is most vulnerable to them? At what times of life? To answer such questions, the National Institute of Mental Health undertook during the 1980s a short census of psychological disorders in America. In five different regions of the country researchers conducted lengthy, structured interviews with a representative sample of people—all told, nearly 20,000 people—and then projected their findings to the entire U.S. population. After asking hundreds of questions that probed for symptoms—"Has there ever been a period of 2 weeks or more when you felt like you wanted to die?"—the researchers estimated both the current and the lifetime prevalence of various disorders.

How many people suffer, or have suffered, a psychological disorder? More than most of us suppose. Sociologist Lee Robins and psychiatrist Darrel Regier (1991, p. 329) report that "one or more of the psychiatric disorders described in this volume had been experienced at some time in their lives by 32% of American adults, and 20% had an active disorder." These surprisingly high rates reflect the inclusion of institutionalized as well as community samples, and surely also reflect how well many people manage to hide disorders such as a phobia, alcohol abuse, or depression. Table 12–2 shows the relative prevalence of most of the disorders we have considered among three ethnic

Table 12–2

Percent of Americans Who Have Ever Experienced Psychological Disorders

	Ethnicity			Sex		
	White	Black	Hispanic	Men	Women	Total
Alcohol abuse or dependence	13.6%	13.8%	16.7%	23.8%	4.6%	13.8%
Generalized anxiety	3.4	6.1	3.7	2.4	5.0	3.8
Phobic disorder	9.7	23.4	12.2	10.4	17.7	14.3
Obsessive-compulsive disorder	2.6	2.3	1.8	2.0	3.0	2.6
Mood disorder	8.0	6.3	7.8	5.2	10.2	7.8
Schizophrenia disorders	1.4	2.1	0.8	1.2	1.7	1.5
Antisocial personality	2.6	2.3	3.4	4.5	0.8	2.6

Source: Data from Robins & Regier, 1991.

groups and among men and women. As you can see, despite differences in their rates of various psychological disorders, all these groups are vulnerable.

Those who experience a psychological disorder usually do so by early adulthood. "Over 75% of our sample with any disorder had experienced its first symptoms by age 24," report Robins and Regier (p. 331). The symptoms of antisocial personality and of phobic disorder appear earliest, by a median age of 8 and 10, respectively. Symptoms of alcohol abuse, obsessive-compulsive disorder, bipolar disorder, and schizophrenia appear at a median age near 20. Major depression often hits somewhat later, at a median age of 25. Such findings make clear the need for research and treatment to help the growing number of people, especially youth and young adults, who suffer the bewilderment and pain of a psychological disorder.

Labeling People: The Power of Preconceptions

Preview Question

13. What potential harm is there in the use of diagnostic labels?

"One of the unpardonable sins, in the eyes of most people, is for a man to go about unlabelled. The world regards such a person as the police do an unmuzzled dog, not under proper control."

T. H. Huxley
Evolution and Ethics, 1893

As noted earlier, the practice of attaching diagnostic labels to people is controversial. Most clinicians believe that classification helps in describing, treating, and researching the causes of psychological disorders. Critics, however, say that these labels are at best arbitrary and at worst value judgments that, thanks to the medical model, masquerade as science. It is better, they say, to study the roots of specific symptoms, such as delusions or hallucinations, than to study catchall categories, such as schizophrenia (Persons, 1986).

Moreover, once we label a person, we view that person differently (Farina, 1982). Labels create preconceptions that can bias our perceptions and interpretations. For example, Ellen Langer and her colleagues (1974, 1980) had people rate an interviewee they thought was either normal (a job applicant) or out of the ordinary (a psychiatric or cancer patient). All subjects saw the identical videotape. Yet those who watched unlabeled interviewees perceived them as normal, while those who watched supposed patients perceived them as "different from most people." Therapists (who thought they were evaluating a psychiatric patient) perceived the interviewee as "frightened of his own aggressive impulses," a "passive, dependent type," and so forth.

Labels can also affect people's self-images and stigmatize them in others' eyes. U.S. Senator Thomas Eagleton experienced this in 1972, when he was dumped as the Democratic party's vice-presidential candidate after it was discovered he had been treated for depression with electroshock therapy. The same stigma surfaced when a female associate of psychologist Stewart Page (1977) called 180 people in Toronto who were advertising furnished rooms for rent. When she merely asked if the room was still available, the answer was nearly always yes. When she said that she was about to be released from a mental hospital, the answer three times out of four was no (as it was when she said she was calling for her brother who was about to be released from jail). When some of those who answered no were called by a second person who simply asked if the room was still available, the advertiser nearly always revealed that it was. Surveys in Western Europe have uncovered similar attitudes toward those labeled mentally ill.

If people form their impressions of psychological disorder from the media, such findings are hardly surprising. Television researcher George Gerbner (1985) reports that 1 in 5 prime-time and daytime programs depicts a psychologically disordered person, and 7 in 10 such programs portray this character as violent or criminal. Movies, too, stereotype mental patients, sometimes as rebellious (Jack Nicholson in *One Flew Over the Cuckoo's Nest*), homicidal (Anthony Perkins in *Psycho*), or as "zoo specimens" (Woody Allen in *Zelig*) (Hyler & others, 1991). More than a few schizophrenia prone people do commit crimes, and some disordered people are amoral and antisocial (Silverton, 1988; Monahan, 1991). However, *most* disordered people are *not* dangerous; instead, they are anxious, depressed, or withdrawn.

Labels not only bias perceptions, they can also change reality. When teachers are told certain students are "gifted," when students expect someone to be "hostile," or when interviewers check to see whether someone is "extraverted," they may act in ways that elicit the very behavior expected (Snyder, 1984). Someone led to think you are nasty may treat you coldly, provoking you to respond as a nasty person would. Labels can serve as self-fulfilling prophecies.

But let us also remember the benefits of diagnostic labels. As Robert Spitzer (1975), the chief author of DSM-III-R, explains:

> There is a purpose to psychiatric diagnosis. It is to enable mental health professionals to (a) communicate with each other about the subject matter of their concern, (b) comprehend the pathological processes involved in psychiatric illness, and (c) control psychiatric outcomes.

We need not dismiss psychological labels in order to be encouraged by the many successful people—including Leonardo da Vinci, Isaac Newton, and Leo Tolstoy—who pursued brilliant careers while enduring psychological difficulties. The bewilderment, fear, and sorrow caused by psychological disorders are real. But, as the next chapter shows, hope is also real.

Rehearse It

15. People who suffer from schizophrenia often show disorganized thinking and disturbed perceptions. They may speak illogically and may hear voices urging self-destruction. Hearing voices in the absence of any auditory stimulation is an example of
a. a delusion or false belief.
b. an inappropriate emotion.
c. a word salad.
d. a hallucination.

16. Stressful events, faulty family communications, and, especially, inherited abnormalities in brain chemistry and structure are all possible factors in the development of schizophrenia. Chances for recovery are best when

a. onset is sudden, in response to stress.
b. deterioration occurs gradually, during childhood.
c. no environmental causes can be identified.
d. there is a detectable brain abnormality.

17. Unlike other psychological disorders, personality disorders need not involve any apparent anxiety, depression, or loss of contact with reality. A personality disorder, such as antisocial personality, is characterized by
a. the presence of multiple personalities.
b. bodily symptoms that have psychological causes.
c. enduring and maladaptive personality traits.
d. mood disturbances.

18. Labels such as "schizophrenic" and "hypochondriac" may be useful in clinical situations. In other contexts, however, labels create preconceptions and biases. From watching television dramas you would never guess that most people who suffer schizophrenia, when encountered in the real world, seem
a. antisocial and amoral.
b. violent or homicidal.
c. accomplished in arts and literature.
d. withdrawn.

Reviewing Psychological Disorders

Perspectives on Psychological Disorders

1. What criteria are used to judge a person's behavior as disordered?

Between normality and abnormality there is not a gulf, but a fine and somewhat arbitrary line. Where the line is drawn is usually based on a variety of criteria, such as how atypical, disturbing, maladaptive, and unjustifiable a person's behavior is.

2. What is the medical model of psychological disorders, and why do critics question it?

The medical model's assumption that psychological disorders are mental illnesses has displaced earlier views that demons and evil spirits were to blame. However, critics question the medical model's labeling of psychological disorders as sicknesses; they argue that the disorders are socially defined and that the labels may be self-fulfilling.

3. Why are psychological disorders classified, and what system is used?

Many psychiatrists and psychologists believe that a system for naming and describing psychological disorders facilitates treatment and research. In the United States, the revised third edition of the *Diagnostic and Statistical Manual of Mental Disorders* (DSM-III-R) is the authoritative classification scheme.

Anxiety Disorders

4. What behaviors characterize anxiety disorders?

Those who suffer an anxiety disorder may for no apparent reason feel uncontrollably tense and uneasy (generalized anxiety disorder). They may be irrationally afraid of a specific object or situation (phobic disorder), or troubled by repetitive thoughts and actions (obsessive-compulsive disorder).

Somatoform Disorders

5. What characterizes the somatoform disorders?

The somatoform disorders involve a somatic (bodily) symptom—a physiologically unexplained but genuinely felt ailment. Freud was particularly fascinated by conversion disorder, in which anxiety appeared to be converted into a symptom that had no physiological basis. Today, hypochondriasis (interpreting one's normal sensations as symptoms of a dreaded disease) is a much more common disorder.

Dissociative Disorders

6. What is the common characteristic of the dissociative disorders?

Under stress, a person's conscious awareness will sometimes become dissociated, or separated, from previous memories, thoughts, and feelings. Dissociative amnesia usually involves selective forgetting in response to stress. Fugue involves not only forgetting one's identity but fleeing one's home. Most mysterious of all dissociative disorders are cases of multiple personality, in which a person is said to have two or more distinct personalities, with the original typically unaware of the other(s).

Mood Disorders

7. What behaviors characterize mood disorders?

In major depression, the person—without apparent reason—descends for weeks or months into deep unhappiness, lethargy, and feelings of worthlessness before rebounding to normality. In the less common bipolar disorder, the person alternates between the hopelessness and lethargy of depression and the hyperactive, wildly optimistic, impulsive phase of mania.

8. What causes mood disorders?

Current research on depression is vigorously exploring (1) genetic predispositions and neurotransmitter abnormalities and (2) cyclic self-defeating beliefs, learned helplessness, negative attributions, and social rejection.

Schizophrenia Disorders

9. What behaviors characterize schizophrenia disorders?

Schizophrenia shows itself in disordered thinking (nonsensical talk and delusions, which may stem from a breakdown of selective attention); disturbed perceptions (including hallucinations); and inappropriate emotions and actions. Schizophrenia is actually a set of disorders that emerge either gradually (*chronic* or *process*) from a long history of social inadequacy (in which case the outlook is dim) or suddenly (*acute* or *reactive*) in reaction to stress (in which case the prospects for recovery are brighter).

10. What causes schizophrenia?

As they have for depression, researchers have identified brain abnormalities (such as in receptors for the neurotransmitter dopamine) that seem linked with certain forms of schizophrenia. Twin and adoption studies also point to a genetic predisposition that, in conjunction with environmental factors, may bring about a schizophrenia disorder.

Personality Disorders

11. What characteristics are typical of personality disorders?

Personality disorders are enduring, maladaptive personality traits. For society, the most troubling of these is the remorseless and fearless antisocial personality.

The Commonality of Psychological Disorders

12. How common are the psychological disorders we've discussed?

A 1980's census of psychological disorders in the United States reports that 32% of adults have experienced a disorder. Although antisocial personality and phobic disorder tend to appear before age 10, most other disorders manifest themselves in the late teens or early twenties.

Labeling People: The Power of Preconceptions

13. What potential harm is there in the use of diagnostic labels?

Critics of diagnostic classification point out that for the benefits we derive from labeling people, we pay a price. Labels facilitate mental health professionals' communications and research. But they also create preconceptions that bias our perceptions of people's past and present behavior and unfairly stigmatize people.

Terms and Concepts to Remember

psychological disorder, p. 380

medical model, p. 381

DSM-III-R, p. 382

anxiety disorders, p. 384

generalized anxiety disorder, p. 384

phobic disorder, p. 385

obsessive-compulsive disorder, p. 385

panic attack, p. 385

somatoform disorders, p. 388

conversion disorder, p. 388

hypochondriasis, p. 388

dissociative disorders, p. 389

amnesia, p. 389

fugue [fewg], p. 389

multiple personality disorder, p. 389

mood disorders, p. 391

major depression, p. 391

bipolar disorder, p. 391

mania, p. 394

psychotic disorder, p. 399

schizophrenia, p. 399

delusions, p. 400

personality disorders, p. 404

antisocial personality, p. 404

Rehearse It Answer Key

1. c.   **2.** a.   **3.** c.   **4.** c.   **5.** a.   **6.** d.   **7.** c.   **8.** c.   **9.** b.

10. b.   **11.** b.   **12.** a.   **13.** d.   **14.** d.   **15.** d.   **16.** a.   **17.** c.   **18.** d.

Critical Thinking Exercise

You have Surveyed, Questioned, Read, Rehearsed, and Reviewed Chapter 12. Now take your learning a step further by testing your *critical thinking* skills on the following passage.

Since her divorce three months ago, sixty-five-year-old Phyllis has felt tired all of the time, has had difficulty sleeping and eating, and has lost all interest in family, friends, and her usual activities. Once proud of her accomplishments and optimistic about her future, Phyllis is now convinced that everything she has ever done, or will do, is worthless. Although her husband was far from a perfect partner, Phyllis has convinced herself that the divorce really was her fault. Her once close friends, who have grown weary of Phyllis's self-absorbed and hopeless attitude, have stopped calling on her. The family physician referred Phyllis to a psychiatrist, who prescribed an antidepressant drug. The drug seemed to help somewhat, but Phyllis was worried that she would become addicted so stopped taking it regularly. Phyllis's son-in-law has grown concerned about her dejected attitude. However, his wife assures him there is no cause for alarm. She says her mother is simply growing old, noting that her mother's listlessness is reminiscent of her deceased maternal grandmother at that age.

1. Should Phyllis's daughter be more concerned about her mother's behavior, or is she correct in attributing it to aging? Explain your reasoning.

2. How might Phyllis's behavior be classified by a clinical psychologist?

3. How might Phyllis's behavior be explained according to the psychoanalytic, biological, and social-cognitive perspectives?

Check your progress on becoming a critical thinker by comparing your answers to the sample answers found in Appendix B.

For Further Information

You can find further information in this text regarding psychological disorders on the following pages:

Therapy

The history of treating psychological disorders reveals how mystifying and intractable these problems are. We have treated psychological disorders with a bewildering variety of methods, harsh and gentle: by cutting holes in the head and by giving warm baths and massages; by restraining, bleeding, or "beating the devil" out of people and by placing them in sunny, serene environments; by administering drugs and electric shocks and by talking—talking about childhood experiences, about current feelings, about maladaptive thoughts and behaviors.

Today's favored treatment depends on the therapist's viewpoint. Those who believe that psychological disorders are learned tend to favor psychological therapies. Those who view disorders as biologically rooted are likely to advocate medication as well. Those who believe that disorders are responses to social conditions will, in addition, want to reform the "sick" environment.

We can classify therapies into two main categories: The *psychological therapies* involve structured interaction (usually verbal) between a trained professional and a client with a problem. The *biomedical therapies* directly affect the nervous system.

William Hogarth's (1697–1764) painting (right) of St. Mary of Bethlehem hospital in London (commonly called Bedlam) depicts the treatment of mental disorders in the eighteenth century. Patients were treated like animals. This chair was designed by Benjamin Rush (1746–1813) "for the benefit of maniacal patients." Rush, considered by many the founder of America's movement for more humane treatment of the mentally ill, believed that they required restraint to regain their sensibilities.

The Psychological Therapies

Psychological therapy, or **psychotherapy,** is "a planned, emotionally charged, confiding interaction between a trained, socially sanctioned healer and a sufferer" (Frank, 1982). From among the 250 or more types of psychotherapy (Parloff, 1987), we will consider the most influential techniques. These derive from psychology's major personality theories: psychoanalytic, humanistic, behavioral, and cognitive.

Each technique is distinctive, yet common threads run through them. Therapists who view disorders as an interplay of bio-psycho-social influences may welcome a combination of treatments. Indeed, half of all psychotherapists describe themselves as taking an **eclectic approach**—as using a blend of therapies (Beitman & others, 1989; Smith, 1982). Depending on the client and the problem, an eclectic therapist will use a variety of techniques.

Psychoanalysis

Although most of today's therapists do not practice as Sigmund Freud did, his psychoanalytic techniques survive. **Psychoanalysis** is part of our modern vocabulary, and its assumptions influence many other therapies.

Aims

As we noted when considering Freud's theory in Chapters 11 and 12, psychoanalysis assumes that many psychological problems are fueled by childhood's residue of repressed impulses and conflicts. Psychoanalysts try to bring these repressed feelings into conscious awareness where the patient can deal with them. By gradually gaining conscious insight into the origins of the disorder—by fulfilling the ancient imperative to "know thyself" in a deep way—the person in analysis "works through" the buried feelings. The theory presumes that healthier, less anxious living becomes possible when patients release the energy previously devoted to id-ego-superego conflicts.

Methods

Psychoanalysis is historical reconstruction. It unearths the past in hopes of unmasking the present. But how?

Drawing by Miller; © 1983 The New Yorker Magazine, Inc.

In this classical Freudian setting, the psychoanalyst minimizes distraction from the inward journey by sitting out of view of the patient on the couch.

psychotherapy An emotionally charged, confiding interaction between a trained therapist and someone who suffers a psychological difficulty.

eclectic approach An approach to psychotherapy that takes advantage of techniques from the various forms of therapy, depending on the client's problems.

psychoanalysis Sigmund Freud's therapeutic technique, in which the patient's free associations, resistances, dreams, and transferences—and the therapist's interpretations of them—release previously repressed feelings, allowing the patient to gain self-insight.

free association A psychoanalytic method of exploring the unconscious in which the person relaxes and says whatever comes to mind, no matter how trivial or embarrassing.

resistance In psychoanalysis, the blocking from consciousness of anxiety-laden material.

interpretation In psychoanalysis, the analyst's assisting the patient to note and understand resistances and other significant behaviors in order to promote insight.

transference In psychoanalysis, the patient's transfer to the analyst of emotions linked with other relationships (such as love or hatred for a parent).

Woody Allen, after awakening from suspended animation in *Sleeper:* "I haven't seen my analyst in 200 years. He was a strict Freudian. If I'd been going all this time, I'd probably almost be cured by now."

When Freud discarded hypnosis as unreliable, he turned to **free association.** Imagine yourself as a patient using the free association technique. The analyst invites you to relax, perhaps by lying on a couch. He or she will probably sit out of your line of vision, helping you focus attention on your internal thoughts and feelings. Beginning with a childhood memory, a dream, or a recent experience, you say aloud whatever comes to your mind from moment to moment. It sounds easy, but soon you notice how often you edit your thoughts as you speak, by omitting material that seems trivial, irrelevant, or shameful. Even in the safe presence of the analyst, you may pause momentarily before uttering an embarrassing thought. You may make a joking remark or change the subject to something less threatening. Sometimes your mind may go blank or you may find yourself unable to remember important details.

To the psychoanalyst, these blocks in the flow of your free associations are **resistances.** They hint that anxiety lurks and that you are repressing sensitive material. The analyst will want to explore these sensitive areas by making you aware of your resistances and by helping you interpret their underlying meaning. The analyst's **interpretations**—suggestions of underlying wishes, feelings, and conflicts—aim to provide rational, nonpsychotic (still in touch with reality) people with *insight.* If offered at the right moment, the analyst's interpretation—of, say, your not wanting to talk about your mother—may illuminate what you are avoiding. You may then discover what your resistances mean and how they fit with other pieces of your psychological puzzle.

Freud believed that another clue to repressed impulses is our dreams' *latent content* (page 156). Thus, after inviting you to report a dream, the analyst may suggest its hidden meaning, thereby adding yet another piece to your developing self-portrait.

During many such sessions you will probably disclose more of yourself to your analyst than you have ever revealed to anyone. Because psychoanalytic theory emphasizes the formative power of childhood experiences, much of what you reveal will pertain to your earliest memories. You will also probably find yourself experiencing strong positive or negative feelings for your analyst. Such feelings may express the dependency or mingled love and anger that you earlier experienced toward family members or other important people in your life. When this happens, Freud would say you are actually "transferring" your strongest feelings from those other relationships to the analyst. Analysts and other therapists believe that this **transference** exposes long-repressed feelings, giving you a belated chance to work through them with your analyst's help. By examining your feelings toward the analyst you may also gain insight into your current relationships.

Critics say that psychoanalysts' interpretations are hard to refute. If, in response to the analyst's suggested interpretation, you say, "Yes! I see now," your acceptance confirms the analyst's interpretation. If you emphatically say, "No! That doesn't ring true," your denial may be taken to reveal more resistance, which would also confirm the interpretation. Psychoanalysts acknowledge that it's hard to prove or disprove their interpretations. But they insist that interpretations often are a great help to patients.

Traditional psychoanalysis is slow and expensive. It requires several years of several sessions a week with a highly trained and well-paid analyst. (Three times a week for just two years at $100 per hour equals about $30,000.) Only those with a high income can afford such treatment.

Although there are relatively few traditional psychoanalysts, psychoanalytic assumptions influence many therapists. We can see this influence in any therapist who tries to understand patients' current symptoms by exploring their childhood experiences; who probes for repressed, emotion-laden infor-

Although in this therapy session the couch has disappeared, the influence of psychoanalytic theory probably has not, especially if the therapist probes for the origin of the patient's symptoms by analyzing repressed information from her past.

mation; who seeks to help people gain insight into the unconscious roots of problems and work through newly resurrected feelings. Although influenced by psychoanalysis, these therapists may talk to people face-to-face (rather than out of the line of vision), once a week (rather than several times weekly), and for only a few weeks or months (rather than several years).

No brief therapy excerpt can exemplify the lengthy process of probing the past. But we can illustrate psychoanalysts' goal of enabling insight by offering interpretations. In the following interaction, therapist David Malan responds to all that he has heard from a depressed patient by suggesting insights into her problems. Note how Malan interprets the woman's earlier remarks and suggests that her relationship with him reveals a characteristic pattern of behavior (1978, pp. 133–134):

> *Malan: I get the feeling that you're the sort of person who needs to keep active. If you don't keep active, then something goes wrong. Is that true?*
>
> *Patient: Yes.*
>
> *Malan: I get a second feeling about you and that is that you must, underneath all this, have an awful lot of very strong and upsetting feelings. Somehow they're there but you aren't really quite in touch with them. Isn't this right? I feel you've been like that as long as you can remember.*
>
> *Patient: For quite a few years, whenever I really sat down and thought about it I got depressed, so I tried not to think about it.*
>
> *Malan: You see, you've established a pattern, haven't you? You're even like that here with me, because in spite of the fact that you're in some trouble and you feel that the bottom is falling out of your world, the way you're telling me this is just as if there wasn't anything wrong.*

Humanistic Therapies

As we noted in Chapter 11, the humanistic perspective emphasizes people's inherent potential for self-fulfillment. Not surprisingly, then, humanistic therapists aim to boost self-fulfillment by helping people grow in self-awareness and self-acceptance. Unlike psychoanalytic therapists, humanistic therapists tend to focus on:

the present instead of the past;

awareness of feelings as they occur rather than achieving insights into the childhood origins of the feelings;

conscious rather than unconscious thoughts;

taking immediate responsibility for one's feelings and actions rather than uncovering hidden determinants; and

promoting growth and fulfillment instead of curing illness.

Person-Centered Therapy

The most widely used humanistic technique is Carl Rogers' (1961, 1980) **person-centered therapy.** Person-centered therapists focus on the client's conscious self-perceptions rather than on their own interpretations as therapists. The therapist listens, without judgment or interpretation, and refrains from directing the client toward certain insights. This strategy has earned person-centered therapy the label *nondirective* therapy.

Believing that most people already have within themselves the resources for growth, Rogers encouraged therapists to exhibit *genuineness, acceptance,* and *empathy.* When therapists drop their facades and genuinely express their

Preview Question

2. What are the basic themes of humanistic therapy, such as Rogers' person-centered approach?

person-centered therapy   A humanistic therapy, developed by Carl Rogers, in which the therapist uses techniques such as active listening within a genuine, accepting, empathic environment to facilitate clients' growth.

The late Carl Rogers, at right, actively listening to a client during a group therapy session.

true feelings, when they enable their clients to feel unconditionally accepted, and when they empathically sense and reflect their clients' feelings, the clients may increase in self-understanding and self-acceptance. Rogers (1980, p. 10) explained:

> Hearing has consequences. When I truly hear a person and the meanings that are important to him at that moment, hearing not simply his words, but him, and when I let him know that I have heard his own private personal meanings, many things happen. There is first of all a grateful look. He feels released. He wants to tell me more about his world. He surges forth in a new sense of freedom. He becomes more open to the process of change.
>
> I have often noticed that the more deeply I hear the meanings of the person, the more there is that happens. Almost always, when a person realizes he has been deeply heard, his eyes moisten. I think in some real sense he is weeping for joy. It is as though he were saying, "Thank God, somebody heard me. Someone knows what it's like to be me."

"Hearing" refers to Rogers' technique of **active listening**—echoing, restating, and seeking clarification of what the person expresses—verbally or nonverbally—and acknowledging the expressed feelings. Active listening is now an accepted part of therapeutic counseling practices in many schools, colleges, and clinics. The counselor listens attentively and interrupts only to restate and confirm the client's feelings, to accept what the client is expressing, or to seek clarification. In his counseling of a 28-year-old male client, Rogers illustrates active listening:

Client: I just ain't no good to nobody, never was, and never will be.

Rogers: Feeling that now, hm? That you're just no good to yourself, no good to anybody. Never will be any good to anybody. Just that you're completely worthless, huh?—Those really are lousy feelings. Just feel that you're no good at all, hm?

Client: Yeah. (Muttering in low, discouraged voice) That's what this guy I went to town with just the other day told me.

Rogers: This guy that you went to town with really told you that you were no good? Is that what you're saying? Did I get that right?

Client: M-hm.

active listening Empathic listening in which the listener echoes, restates, and clarifies. A feature of Rogers' person-centered therapy.

family therapy Therapy that treats the family as a system. Views an individual's unwanted behaviors as influenced by or directed at other family members; encourages family members toward positive relationships and improved communication.

Rogers: I guess the meaning of that if I get it right is that here's somebody that—meant something to you and what does he think of you? Why, he's told you that he thinks you're no good at all. And that just really knocks the props out from under you. (Client weeps quietly.) It just brings the tears. (Silence of 20 seconds)

Client: (Rather defiantly) I don't care though.

Rogers: You tell yourself you don't care at all, but somehow I guess some part of you cares because some part of you weeps over it. (Meador & Rogers, 1984, p. 167)

As this brief excerpt illustrates, the person-centered counselor seeks to provide a psychological mirror that helps clients see themselves more clearly. But can a therapist be a perfect mirror, without selecting and interpreting what is reflected? Rogers conceded that one cannot be *totally* nondirective. Nevertheless, he believed that the therapist's most important contribution is to accept and understand the client. Given a nonjudgmental, grace-filled environment that provides *unconditional positive regard,* people may accept even their worst traits and feel valued and whole.

Group Therapies

Most of the therapies we are considering may also occur in therapist-led small groups. Although it does not provide the same degree of therapist involvement with each client, group therapy saves the therapist's time and the clients' money. More important, the social context allows people to discover that others have problems similar to their own and to try out new ways of behaving. As you have perhaps experienced, it can help to get honest feedback—to be reassured that you look poised even while feeling anxious and self-conscious. And it can be a relief to find that you are not alone—to learn that others, despite their seeming composure, share your problems and your feelings of loneliness, inadequacy, or anger. Such has been the experience of a wide range of people, from cancer patients to dieters to recovering alcoholics (Yalom, 1985).

One popular form of group experience for those not seriously disturbed began as *sensitivity training groups* (*T-groups,* for short) in which teachers, executives, and others practiced relating to one another more sensitively and openly. Leaders encouraged groups of 12 to 20 people to be less inhibited and defensive, to "talk straight," and to listen empathically. Before long, Carl Rogers (1970) and others were offering *encounter groups*—groups that confronted emotion-laden experiences openly and honestly. Although encounter groups are not as popular today as they were during the 1970s, they set the stage for the emergence of countless *self-help* and *support groups*—for substance abusers, divorced people, gamblers, the bereaved, and for those simply seeking personal growth. Each year in the United States, some 7 million people participate in such groups (Jacobs & Goodman, 1989).

One special type of group interaction, **family therapy,** assumes that no person is an island. We live and grow in relation to others, especially our families. We struggle to differentiate ourselves from our families but we also need to connect with them emotionally. Some of our problem behaviors arise from the tension between these two tendencies, which often creates family stress.

Family therapists therefore work with family groups to heal relationships. Their aim is to help family members discover the role they play within their family's social system. A child's rebellion, for example, affects and is affected by other family tensions. Family therapists also aim—usually with some success, research suggests (Hazelrigg & others, 1987; Shadish, 1992)—to open up communication within the family or to help family members discover new ways of preventing or resolving conflicts.

Family therapy often acts as a preventive mental health strategy. The therapist helps family members understand how the ways they relate to each other create problems. The treatment emphasis is not on changing the individuals but rather on changing their relationships and interactions.

Rehearse It

1. All of the psychological therapies involve verbal interactions between a trained professional and a client with a problem. A therapist who encourages clients to relate their dreams and searches for the unconscious roots of their problems is drawing from
a. psychoanalysis.
b. humanistic therapies.
c. person-centered therapy.
d. cognitive therapy.

2. According to psychoanalytic theory, a patient's emotional relationship with the therapist mirrors other important relationships in the patient's life—for example, an early relationship with a parent. In psychoanalysis, the development of strong feelings for the therapist is an important part of the therapeutic process and is called

a. transference
b. resistance.
c. interpretation.
d. empathy.

3. Humanistic therapists focus on present experience—on becoming aware of feelings as they arise and taking responsibility for one's feelings. Compared to psychoanalytic therapists, humanistic therapists are more likely to emphasize
a. hidden or repressed feelings.
b. childhood experiences.
c. psychological disorders.
d. self-fulfillment and growth.

4. Especially important to Carl Rogers' person-centered therapy is the technique of active listening. The therapist who practices active listening

a. engages in free association.
b. exposes the patient's resistances.
c. restates and clarifies the client's statements.
d. directly challenges the client's self-perceptions.

5. A sensitivity training group or encounter group offers participants an opportunity to gain self-awareness and social sensitivity in a group setting. Sensitivity training and encounter groups are most closely associated with
a. psychoanalysis.
b. humanistic therapies.
c. behavior therapies.
d. systematic desensitization.

Preview Question

3. What are the assumptions and techniques of the behavior therapies?

Behavior Therapies

All the therapies we have considered so far assume that, for people who are not seriously disturbed at least, psychological problems diminish as self-awareness grows. The psychoanalyst expects problems to subside as people gain insight into their unresolved and unconscious tensions. So does the humanistic therapist, as people "get in touch with their feelings." Behavior therapists, however, doubt that self-awareness is the key. They assume that the problem behaviors *are* the problems. You can, for example, become aware of why you are highly anxious during exams and still be anxious. Instead of trying to alleviate distressing behaviors by resolving a presumed underlying

behavior therapy   Therapy that applies learning principles to the elimination of unwanted behaviors.

counterconditioning   A behavior therapy procedure that conditions new responses to stimuli that trigger unwanted behaviors; based on classical conditioning. Two such techniques are *systematic desensitization* and *aversive conditioning.*

systematic desensitization   A type of counterconditioning that associates a pleasant, relaxed state with gradually increasing anxiety-triggering stimuli. Commonly used to treat phobias.

problem, **behavior therapy** applies well-established learning principles to eliminate the unwanted behavior. To treat phobias or sexual dysfunctions, for example, behavior therapists do not delve deep below the surface looking for inner causes. Rather, they try to replace problem thoughts and maladaptive behaviors with more constructive ways of thinking and acting.

Classical Conditioning Techniques

One cluster of behavior therapies derives from principles developed in Pavlov's conditioning experiments (pages 180–183). As Pavlov and others showed, we learn various behaviors and emotions through classical conditioning. So, are maladaptive symptoms conditioned responses? If, say, a claustrophobic fear of elevators is a learned response to the stimulus of being in an enclosed space, then might one unlearn the fear by applying extinction principles? Might we countercondition the response? **Counterconditioning** pairs the trigger stimulus with a new response that is incompatible with fear. For example, if we repeatedly pair the enclosed space of the elevator with a relaxed response, the fear response may be displaced. Two such counterconditioning techniques are *systematic desensitization* and *aversive conditioning.*

Systematic Desensitization   Picture this scene reported in 1924 by Mary Cover Jones, an associate of the behaviorist John B. Watson: Three-year-old Peter is woefully afraid of rabbits and other furry objects. (Unlike Little Albert's laboratory-conditioned fear of white rats, described in Chapter 6, Peter's fears arose during the course of his life at home and is more intense.) Jones' aim is to replace Peter's fear of rabbits with a conditioned response that is incompatible with fear. Her strategy is to associate the fear-evoking rabbit with the pleasurable, relaxed response associated with eating.

As the hungry child begins eating his mid-afternoon snack, Jones introduces a caged rabbit on the other side of the huge room. Peter hardly notices as he eagerly munches his crackers and milk. On succeeding days, she gradually moves the rabbit closer and closer. Within 2 months, Peter tolerates the rabbit in his lap and strokes it while he eats. Moreover, his fear of other furry objects subsides as well, having been ''countered'' or replaced by a relaxed state that cannot coexist with fear (Fisher, 1984; Jones, 1924).

Unfortunately for those who might have been helped by her counterconditioning procedures, Jones' story of Peter and the rabbit did not immediately become part of psychology's lore. More than 30 years later, psychiatrist Joseph Wolpe (1958, 1982) refined her technique into what has become the most widely used method of behavior therapy: **systematic desensitization.** Wolpe assumed, as did Jones, that you cannot simultaneously be anxious and relaxed. Therefore, if you can repeatedly relax when faced with anxiety-provoking stimuli, you can gradually eliminate your anxiety. The trick is to proceed gradually.

Let's see how this might work with a common phobia. Imagine yourself afraid of public speaking. A behavior therapist might first ask your help in constructing a hierarchy of anxiety-triggering speaking situations. Your anxiety hierarchy could range from mildly anxiety-provoking situations, such as speaking up in a small group of friends, to panic-provoking situations, such as having to address a large audience.

The therapist would then train you to relax. You learn to relax one muscle group after another, until you achieve a drowsy state of complete relaxation and comfort. Then, with your eyes closed, the therapist asks you to imagine a mildly anxiety-arousing situation: You are having coffee with a group of

Professor Gallagher and his controversial technique of simultaneously confronting the fear of heights, snakes and the dark.

THE FAR SIDE © 1986 Universal Press Syndicate. Reprinted with permission. All rights reserved.

Figure 13–1 Systematic desensitization of a phobia. Beverly, who is terribly afraid of spiders, is gradually able to relax—as shown by her decreasing pulse rate as she spends time in the presence of the aversive object—first at the sight of a spider, then in the presence of a toy spider, a dead spider, and a live one. (From Gilling & Brightwell, 1982.)

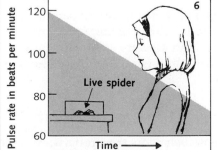

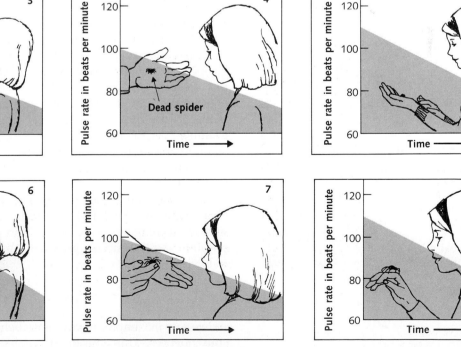

friends and are deciding whether or not to speak up. If imagining the scene causes you to feel any anxiety, you signal your tension by raising your finger, and the therapist instructs you to switch off the mental image and go back to deep relaxation.

This imagined scene is repeatedly paired with relaxation until you can feel no trace of anxiety while imagining it. The therapist progresses up your anxiety hierarchy with this *progressive relaxation* technique, by using the relaxed state to desensitize you to each imagined situation. After several therapy sessions, you practice the imagined behaviors in actual situations, beginning with relatively easy tasks and gradually moving to more anxiety-filled ones (Figure 13–1). Conquering your anxiety in an actual situation, not just in your imagination, raises your self-confidence (Foa & Kozak, 1986; Williams, 1987). Eventually, you may even become a confident public speaker.

Therapists sometimes combine systematic desensitization with other techniques. With phobias, they may have someone model appropriate behavior in a fear-arousing situation. If you were afraid of snakes, you would first observe someone handling a snake. Then you would be coaxed in gradual steps to approach, touch, and handle it yourself (Bandura & others, 1969). By applying this principle of observational learning, therapists have helped people overcome disruptive fears of snakes, spiders, and dogs.

Notice that the systematic desensitization and modeling procedures make no attempt to help you achieve insight into your fear's underlying cause. If you are afraid of heights, the therapist will not spend much time probing when you first experienced this fear or what may have caused it. Nor do behavior therapists worry that eliminating your fear of heights will leave an underlying problem that may now be expressed as, say, a fear of elevators. On the contrary, they find that overcoming maladaptive behaviors helps people feel better about themselves.

aversive conditioning A type of counterconditioning that associates an unpleasant state (such as nausea) with an unwanted behavior (such as drinking alcohol).

Aversive Conditioning   In systematically desensitizing a patient, the therapist seeks to substitute a positive (relaxed) response for a negative (fearful) response to a harmless stimulus. In **aversive conditioning,** the therapist tries to replace a positive response to a harmful stimulus with a negative (aversive) response. Thus, aversive conditioning is the reverse of systematic desensitization.

The procedure is simple: It associates unwanted behavior with unpleasant feelings. In treating an alcoholic, aversion therapists offer appealing drinks laced with a drug that produces severe nausea. By linking the drinking of alcohol with violent nausea, the therapist seeks to transform the alcoholic's reaction to alcohol from positive to negative (see Figure 13–2, and recall the taste aversion experiments with rats and coyotes in Chapter 6). Similarly, by giving child molesters electric shocks as they view photos of nude children, aversion therapists aim to eliminate the molesters' sexual response to children. And by giving withdrawn and self-abusing autistic children harmless "aversives," such as a spray of cold water in the face, therapists hope to suppress self-injury while reinforcing more appropriate behavior. Because this therapy involves an unpleasant experience, it is practiced sparingly and only with the appropriate consent.

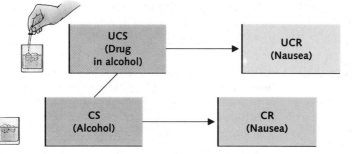

Figure 13–2 Aversion therapy for alcoholics. After repeatedly imbibing an alcoholic drink mixed with a drug that produces severe nausea, some patients develop at least a temporary conditioned aversion to alcohol.

Does aversive conditioning work? In the short run it may. But, as we saw in Chapter 6, the problem is that cognition influences conditioning. People know that outside the therapist's office they can drink without fear of nausea or engage in sexually deviant behavior without fear of shock. The person's ability to discriminate between the aversive conditioning situation and all other situations can limit the treatment's effectiveness.

Aversive conditioning of alcoholics has, nevertheless, enjoyed renewed popularity. For example, Arthur Wiens and Carol Menustik (1983) studied 685 alcoholic patients who completed an aversion therapy program at a Portland, Oregon, hospital. One year later, after returning for several booster treatments of alcohol-sickness pairings, 63 percent were still successfully abstaining. Three years later, 33 percent remained abstinent.

A milder form of classical conditioning, developed by learning theorist O. H. Mowrer, exists for chronic bedwetters. The child sleeps on a liquid-sensitive pad connected to an alarm. Moisture on the pad triggers the alarm, awakening the child. With repetition, this association of urinary relaxation with awakening stops the bedwetting. Usually, the treatment is permanently effective and the success provides a boost to the child's self-image (Sherman & Levin, 1979).

The best candidates for alcoholism treatment programs are people with good jobs, stable relationships, and no history of treatment failures (Holden, 1987).

What might a psychoanalyst say about this therapy for bedwetting? How might a behavior therapist reply?

Operant Conditioning Through Behavior Modification

As we saw in Chapter 6, voluntary behaviors are strongly influenced by their consequences. This simple fact enables behavior therapists to reinforce desired behaviors, while withholding reinforcement for undesired behaviors.

behavior modification The application of operant conditioning principles to the modification of maladaptive human behavior.

token economy An operant conditioning procedure that rewards desired behavior. A patient exchanges a token of some sort, earned for exhibiting the desired behavior, for various privileges or treats.

If this boy completes his work before the timer goes off, the therapist will reward him with a token. He can later exchange the accumulated tokens for special privileges. This form of behavior modification can effectively overcome specific behavior problems.

Using operant conditioning to solve specific behavior problems is called **behavior modification,** a therapy that has raised hopes for some cases thought hopeless. Retarded children have been taught to care for themselves. Autistic children have learned to interact. People with schizophrenia have been helped to behave more rationally on the hospital ward.

In extreme cases, the treatment must be intensive. For 19 withdrawn, uncommunicative, 3-year-old autistic children in one study, it involved a 2-year, 40-hour-a-week shaping program by their parents (Lovaas, 1987). But the combination of positive reinforcement of desired behaviors and the ignoring or punishing of aggressive and self-abusive behaviors worked wonders. By first grade, 9 of the 19 children were functioning successfully in school and exhibiting normal intelligence. Only 1 of 40 comparable children who did not undergo this treatment showed similar improvement.

The rewards used to modify behavior vary. With some people the reinforcing power of attention or praise is sufficient. Others require more concrete rewards, such as food. In institutional settings, therapists may create a **token economy.** When people display appropriate behavior, such as getting out of bed, washing, dressing, eating, talking coherently, cleaning up their rooms, or playing cooperatively, they receive a token or plastic coin (Kazdin, 1982). Later, they can exchange their accumulated tokens for various rewards, such as candy, television watching, trips to town, or better living quarters. Therapists use tokens to shape behavior in the step-by-step manner described on page 189. Token economies have been successfully applied in various settings (classrooms, hospitals, homes for the delinquent) and with various populations (disturbed children, the mentally retarded, schizophrenia patients).

Critics of behavior modification express two concerns. One concern is practical: What happens when the reinforcers stop, as when the person leaves the institution? Might the person have become so dependent on the extrinsic rewards that the appropriate behaviors quickly disappear? If so, how can behavior therapists make the appropriate behaviors durable? First, they may wean patients from the tokens by shifting them toward rewards, such as social approval, more typical of life outside the institution. They may also train patients to behave in ways that are intrinsically rewarding. As a withdrawn person becomes more socially competent, for example, the intrinsic satisfactions of social interaction may help maintain the behavior.

The second concern is ethical: Is it right for one human to control another's behavior? Those who set up token economies typically deprive people of something they desire and then decide which behaviors they will reinforce. To critics, the whole behavior modification process has a totalitarian taint. Advocates reply that control already exists; rewards and punishers are already maintaining destructive behavior patterns. So why not reinforce adaptive behavior instead? What is more, behavior modification increases *self-control.* They argue that treatment with positive rewards is more humane than being institutionalized or punished, and that the right to effective treatment and to an improved life justifies temporary deprivation.

Cognitive Therapies

We have seen how behavior therapists treat specific fears and problem behaviors. But how do they deal with major depression or general anxiety? One can reinforce healthier behaviors and train people to avoid "high risk" situations. Still, when anxiety has no focus, making a hierarchy of anxiety-triggering situations is difficult. The "cognitive revolution" that has so changed psychology during the last three decades has influenced how therapists treat these less clearly defined psychological problems.

Preview Question

4. What are the goals and techniques of the cognitive therapies?

cognitive therapy Therapy that teaches people new, more adaptive ways of thinking and acting; based on the assumption that thoughts intervene between events and our emotional reactions.

rational-emotive therapy A confrontational cognitive therapy, developed by Albert Ellis, that vigorously challenges people's illogical, self-defeating attitudes and assumptions.

The **cognitive therapies** assume that our thinking colors our feelings (Figure 13–3). As we noted in the last chapter's discussion of depression, self-blaming and overgeneralized explanations of bad events are an integral part of the vicious cycle of depression. The depressed person interprets a suggestion as criticism, disagreement as dislike, praise as flattery, friendliness as pity. If such thinking patterns are learned, then surely they can be replaced (Brewin, 1989). Thus, cognitive therapists try in various ways to teach people new, more constructive ways of thinking.

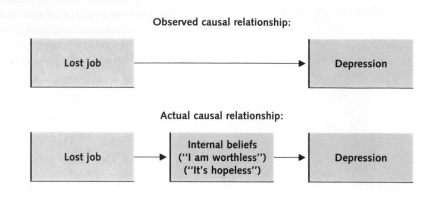

Figure 13–3 A cognitive perspective on psychological disorders. The person's emotional reactions are produced not directly by the event, but by the person's thoughts in response to the event.

Rational-Emotive Therapy

According to Albert Ellis (1962, 1987), the creator of **rational-emotive therapy,** many problems arise from irrational thinking. For example, he describes a disturbed woman (1984, p. 198):

> [She] does not merely believe it is *undesirable* if her love partner is rejecting. She tends to believe, also, that (1) it is *awful;* (2) she *cannot stand* it; (3) she *should not,* must not be rejected; (4) she will *never* be accepted by any desirable partner; (5) she is a *worthless person* because one lover has rejected her; and (6) she *deserves to be damned* for being so worthless. Such common covert hypotheses are nonsensical. . . . They can be easily elicited and demolished by any scientist worth his or her salt; and the rational-emotive therapist is exactly that: an exposing and nonsense-annihilating scientist.

Does this sound like the opposite of the warm, caring, reflective acceptance of feelings expressed by Carl Rogers? It very nearly is. Ellis intends to "make mincemeat" of people's illogical ideas—that we must be loved by everyone, that we must be thoroughly competent and successful at everything, that it is a disaster when things do not go as we wish. Change people's thinking by revealing the "absurdity" of their self-defeating ideas, he believes, and you will change their self-defeating feelings and actions. Let's eavesdrop as tart-tongued Ellis exhibits his confrontational style with a 25-year-old female client who suffers feelings of guilt, unworthiness, and depression (1989, p. 219):

> *Ellis:* The same crap! It's always the same crap. Now if you would look at the crap—instead of "Oh, how stupid I am! He hates me! I think I'll kill myself!"—then you'd get better right away.
>
> *Client:* You've been listening! (laughs)
>
> *Ellis:* Listening to what?
>
> *Client:* (laughs) Those wild statements in my mind, like that, that I make.

Ellis: That's right! Because I know that you have to make those statements—because I have a good theory. And according to my theory, people couldn't get upset unless they made those nutty statements to themselves. . . . Even if I loved you madly, the next person you talk to is likely to hate you. So I like brown eyes and he likes blue eyes, or something. So you're then dead! Because you really think: "I've got to be accepted! I've got to act intelligently!" Well, why?

Client: (very soberly and reflectively) True.

Ellis: You see?

Client: Yes.

Ellis: Now, if you will learn that lesson, then you've had a very valuable session. Because you don't have to upset yourself. As I said before: If I thought you were the worst [expletive] who ever existed, well that's my opinion. And I'm entitled to it. But does it make you a turd?

Client: (reflective silence)

Ellis: Does it?

Client: No.

Ellis: What makes you a turd?

Client: Thinking *that* you are.

Ellis: That's right! Your belief *that you are*. That's the only thing that could ever do it. And you never have to believe that. See? You control your thinking. I control my thinking—my *belief about you*. But you don't have to be affected by that. You always control what you think.

Values in Psychotherapy   As the preceding dialogue illustrates, therapists' personal beliefs and values are an inevitable part of psychotherapy. Ellis (1980), for example, assumes that "no one and nothing is supreme," that "self-gratification" should be encouraged, and that "unequivocal love, commitment, service, and . . . fidelity to any interpersonal commitment, especially marriage, leads to harmful consequences." Allen Bergin (1980), co-editor of the *Handbook of Psychotherapy and Behavior Change*, makes opposite assumptions. He believes that "because God is supreme, humility and the acceptance of divine authority are virtues," that "self-control and committed love and self-sacrifice are to be encouraged," and that "infidelity to any interpersonal commitment, especially marriage, leads to harmful consequences." Despite their differences, Ellis, Bergin, and others agree that psychotherapists' personal attitudes, beliefs, and values influence their therapy. Values are an inevitable, if sometimes hidden, part of therapy and should be more openly acknowledged.

Cognitive Therapy for Depression

Like Ellis, cognitive therapist Aaron Beck was originally trained in Freudian techniques. As Beck analyzed his depressed patients' dreams, negative themes of loss, rejection, and abandonment recurred and extended into their waking thoughts. So in his form of cognitive therapy, Beck and his colleagues (1979) seek to reverse clients' catastrophizing beliefs about themselves, their situations, and their futures. Beck shares with Ellis the goal of getting depressed people to take off the dark glasses through which they view life. But his technique is a kinder, gentler questioning that aims to help people discover their irrationalities (Beck & others, 1979, pp. 145–146):

Patient: I agree with the descriptions of me but I guess I don't agree that the way I think makes me depressed.

Beck: How do you understand it?

Patient: I get depressed when things go wrong. Like when I fail a test.

Beck: How can failing a test make you depressed?

Patient: Well, if I fail I'll never get into law school.

Beck: So failing the test means a lot to you. But if failing a test could drive people into clinical depression, wouldn't you expect everyone who failed the test to have a depression? . . . Did everyone who failed get depressed enough to require treatment?

Patient: No, but it depends on how important the test was to the person.

Beck: Right, and who decides the importance?

Patient: I do.

Beck: And so, what we have to examine is your way of viewing the test (or the way that you think about the test) and how it affects your chances of getting into law school. Do you agree?

Patient: Right.

Beck: Do you agree that the way you interpret the results of the test will affect you? You might feel depressed, you might have trouble sleeping, not feel like eating, and you might even wonder if you should drop out of the course.

Patient: I have been thinking that I wasn't going to make it. Yes, I agree.

Beck: Now what did failing mean?

Patient: (tearful) That I couldn't get into law school.

Beck: And what does that mean to you?

Patient: That I'm just not smart enough.

Beck: Anything else?

Patient: That I can never be happy.

Beck: And how do these thoughts make you feel?

Patient: Very unhappy.

Beck: So it is the meaning of failing a test that makes you very unhappy. In fact, believing that you can never be happy is a powerful factor in producing unhappiness. So, you get yourself into a trap—by definition, failure to get into law school equals "I can never be happy."

Drawing by Ziegler; © 1984 The New Yorker Magazine, Inc.

A new variety of cognitive therapy builds on the finding that depressed people do not exhibit the self-serving bias common in nondepressed people (page 365). Instead, they often attribute their failures to themselves and their successes to external circumstances. Thus, Adele Rabin and her colleagues (1986) first explained to 235 depressed adults the advantages of interpreting events as nondepressed people do. She then trained them to reform their habitually negative patterns of thinking and labeling. For example, she gave

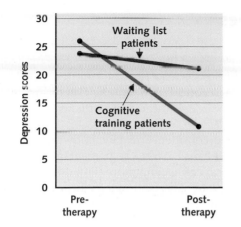

Figure 13–4 Cognitive therapy for depression. After undergoing a program that trained them to think more like nondepressed people—by noticing and taking personal credit for good events and by not taking blame for or overgeneralizing from bad events—patients' depression dropped dramatically. (From Rabin & others, 1986.)

the patients homework assignments that required them to record each day's positive events and to write down how they contributed to each. Compared with depressed people who remained on a waiting list, those who went through the positive thinking exercises became much less depressed (Figure 13–4).

The more people change their negative thinking styles, the more their depression lifts (Seligman, 1989). Cognitive therapists often combine the reversal of self-defeating thinking with efforts to modify behavior. *Cognitive behavior therapy* aims to make people aware of their irrational negative thinking, to replace it with new ways of thinking and talking, *and* to practice the more positive approach in everyday settings.

Because we often think in words, notes Donald Meichenbaum (1977, 1985), getting people to change what they say to themselves is an effective way to change their thinking. Perhaps you can identify with the anxious students who before an exam make matters worse with self-defeating thoughts: "This exam is probably going to be impossible. All these other students seem so relaxed and self-confident. I wish I were better prepared. Anyhow, I'm so nervous I'll forget everything." To change such negative patterns, Meichenbaum trains people to restructure the way they think in stressful situations. Sometimes it may be enough simply to say more positive things to oneself: "Relax. The exam may be hard, but it will be hard for everyone else, too. I studied harder than most people. Besides, I don't need a perfect score to get a good grade."

Rehearse It

6. Behavior therapies apply learning principles to the treatment of problems such as sexual dysfunction, phobias, and addiction. In treating people with these problems, the goal of the behavior therapist is to
a. identify and treat the underlying causes of dysfunction.
b. improve learning and insight.
c. eliminate the unwanted behavior.
d. improve communication and social sensitivity.

7. Behavior therapists assume that fears and other maladaptive behaviors are conditioned responses. Behaviorists attempt either to extinguish these responses or to countercondition a client by conditioning a new response to stimuli that trigger maladaptive or unwanted responses. Two counterconditioning techniques are systematic desensitization and
a. behavior modification.
b. aversive conditioning.
c. sensitivity or T-groups.
d. token economy.

8. The technique of systematic desensitization, developed by Joseph Wolpe, teaches people to relax in the presence of progressively more anxiety-provoking stimuli. Systematic desensitization has been found to be especially effective in the treatment of
a. phobias.
b. depression.
c. alcoholism.
d. bedwetting.

9. In institutions such as homes for the mentally retarded or for juvenile delinquents, a token economy may be used to shape behavior. Tokens, which may later be exchanged for other rewards, are given when a person displays a desired behavior, or takes a step in the right direction. The token economy is an application of
a. classical conditioning.
b. counterconditioning.
c. cognitive therapy.
d. operant conditioning.

10. Cognitive therapists assume that our internal beliefs and characteristic ways of thinking strongly influence our responses to events. They treat emotional problems by teaching people new and more adaptive ways of thinking. An example of a cognitive therapy is rational-emotive therapy, which was developed by
a. Carl Rogers.
b. Joseph Wolpe.
c. Albert Ellis.
d. Allen Bergin.

11. Aaron Beck and other cognitive therapists teach people to stop attributing failures to personal inadequacy and success to external circumstances. Beck's form of cognitive therapy has been shown to be especially effective in treating
a. mental retardation.
b. phobia.
c. alcoholism.
d. depression.

Evaluating Psychotherapies

Preview Question

5. What does research on psycho-therapy reveal about its effectiveness?

Advice columnist Ann Landers frequently advises her troubled letter writers to get professional help. One response urged the writer "not to give up. Hang in there until you find [a psychotherapist] who fills the bill. It's worth the effort." She advised the same day's second letter writer, "There are many excellent mental health facilities in your city. I urge you to make an appointment at once" (Farina & Fisher, 1982).

Many people share Ann Landers' confidence in psychotherapy's effectiveness. Between the mid-1950s and the mid-1980s, the percentage of Americans who had ever sought psychological counseling more than doubled, from 13 to almost 30 percent (Meredith, 1986). The National Institute of Mental Health estimates that 15.5 million Americans undergo psychotherapy each year (Trafford, 1988).

Before 1950, the main mental health providers were psychiatrists. Since then the demand has outgrown the psychiatric profession, so most psychotherapy is now done by clinical and counseling psychologists; clinical social workers; pastoral, marital, abuse, and school counselors; and psychiatric nurses (Table 13–1). Is the faith that Ann Landers and millions of other Americans have placed in these therapists justified?

Table 13-1

A Consumer's Guide to Psychotherapists

If you are looking for a therapist, you may wish to shop around by having a preliminary consultation with two or three therapists, during which you can describe your problem, gather information about their treatment approaches, credentials, and fees, and assess your feelings about each.

Type	Description	Number practicing in U.S.	Approximate average hourly fee in U.S. $
Psychiatrists	Physicians who specialize in the treatment of psychological disorders. Not all psychiatrists have had extensive training in psychotherapy, but as M.D.s they can prescribe medications. Thus, they tend to see those with the most serious problems. Many have a private practice.	38,000	$100+
Clinical psychologists	Most are Ph.D. psychologists with expertise in research, assessment, and therapy, usually supplemented by a supervised internship. About half work in agencies and institutions, half in private practice.	90,000	$80+
Clinical or psychiatric social workers	A 2-year Master of Social Work graduate program plus postgraduate supervision prepares some social workers to offer psychotherapy, mostly to people with everyday personal and family problems. About half have earned the National Association of Social Workers designation of clinical social worker.	80,000	$65
Counselors	Marriage and family counselors specialize in problems arising from family relations. Pastoral counselors, some certified by the American Association of Pastoral Counselors, provide counseling to countless people. Abuse counselors work with substance abusers, spouse and child abusers, and their victims.	55,000+	0–$70

Note: Numbers and fees from Hunt (1987), Gates (1989), and *Psychiatric News* (1989). Fees adjusted for inflation.

Is Psychotherapy Effective?

The question, though simply put, is not simply answered. For one thing, measuring therapy's effectiveness is not like taking your body's temperature. If you and I were to undergo psychotherapy, how would we gauge its effectiveness? By how we feel about our progress? How our therapist feels about it? How our friends and family feel about it? How our behavior has changed?

Clients' Perceptions   If clients' testimonials were the only yardstick, we could strongly affirm the effectiveness of psychotherapy. Three out of four clients report themselves satisfied, and one in two say they are "very satisfied" (Lebow, 1982). We have their word for it—and who should know better?

We should not dismiss these testimonials lightly. People enter therapy because they are suffering, and most leave feeling better about themselves. But there are several reasons why client testimonials do not persuade psychotherapy's skeptics:

> People often enter therapy in crisis. When, with the normal ebb and flow of events, the crisis passes, they may attribute their improvement to the therapy.

> Clients may need to believe the therapy was worth the effort. To admit investing time and money in something ineffective is like admitting to having one's car serviced repeatedly by a mechanic who never fixed it. Self-justification is a powerful human motive.

> Clients generally like their therapists and speak kindly of them. Even if the clients' problems remain, say the therapy critics, "they work hard to find something positive to say. The therapist had been very understanding, the client had gained a new perspective, he learned to communicate better, his mind was eased, anything at all so as not to have to say treatment was a failure" (Zilbergeld, 1983, p. 117).

Clinicians' Perceptions   If clinicians' perceptions accurately reflected their own therapeutic effectiveness, we would have even more reason to celebrate. Case studies of successful treatment abound. Furthermore, every therapist treasures compliments from clients as they say goodbye or later express their gratitude. The problem is that clients justify entering psychotherapy by emphasizing their woes, justify leaving therapy by emphasizing their well-being, and stay in touch only if satisfied. Therapists are aware of failures—mostly the failures of *other* therapists, those whose clients, having experienced only temporary relief, are now seeking a new therapist for their recurring problems. Thus, the same person with the same recurring difficulty—the same old weight problem, depression, or marital difficulty—may represent "success" stories in several therapists' files.

Outcome Research   How, then, can we objectively measure the effectiveness of psychotherapy? What types of people and problems are best helped, and by what type of psychotherapy? The questions have both academic and personal relevance. If you or someone you care about feels anxious or depressed, or suffers some psychological disorder, how likely is it that psychotherapy will help?

In hopes of better assessing psychotherapy's effectiveness, psychologists have turned to controlled research studies. Similar research in the 1800s transformed medicine from concocted treatments (bleeding, purging, infusions of plant and metal substances) into a science. The transformation occurred when skeptical physicians began to realize that many patients got better on their own, that most of the fashionable treatments were doing no good, and that sorting sense from nonsense required closely following illnesses—with and without a particular treatment.

In psychology, the opening volley in what became a spirited debate over such research was fired by British psychologist Hans Eysenck (1952). His conclusion: Studies show that after undergoing eclectic psychotherapy, two-thirds of those suffering nonpsychotic disorders improve markedly. To this day, no one disputes that optimistic estimate.

So why are we still debating psychotherapy's effectiveness? Because Eysenck also reported similar improvement among *untreated* persons, such as those who were on waiting lists. With or without psychotherapy, he said, roughly two-thirds improved noticeably. Time was a great healer.

The avalanche of criticism prompted by Eysenck's conclusions revealed shortcomings in his analyses. Also, in 1952 Eysenck could find only 24 studies of psychotherapy outcomes to analyze. Today, there are hundreds. The best of these studies randomly assign people on a waiting list to alternative treatments or to no treatment. Afterward, researchers evaluate.

In the first statistical digest of these studies, Mary Lee Smith and her colleagues (1980) combined the results of 475 investigations. For psychotherapists, the welcome result was that "the evidence overwhelmingly supports the efficacy of psychotherapy" (p. 183). Figure 13–5 depicts their finding—that the average therapy client ends up better off than 80 percent of the untreated individuals on waiting lists. The claim is more modest than it first appears—by definition, about 50 percent of untreated people also are better off than the average untreated person. Nevertheless, Smith and her collaborators concluded that "psychotherapy benefits people of all ages as reliably as schooling educates them, medicine cures them, or business turns a profit" (p. 183).

"Fortunately, [psycho]analysis is not the only way to resolve inner conflicts. Life itself still remains a very effective therapist."

Karen Horney
Our Inner Conflicts, 1945

Figure 13–5 The two normal distribution curves based on data from 475 studies show the improvement of untreated people and psychotherapy clients. The outcome for the average therapy client surpasses that for 80 percent of the untreated people. (Adapted from Smith & others, 1980.)

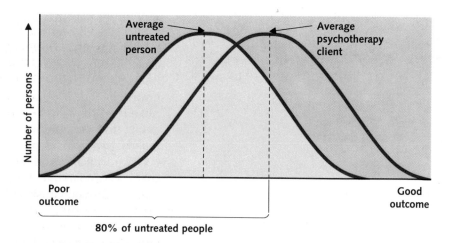

Newer research summaries confirm this optimism (McLean & Carr, 1989; Robinson & others, 1990). The most ambitious of the new psychotherapy studies is a National Institute of Mental Health evaluation of three depression treatments: cognitive therapy, interpersonal therapy (which focuses on social relations), and a standard drug therapy. Twenty-eight experienced therapists at research sites in Norman, Oklahoma, Washington, DC, and Pittsburgh were trained in one of the three methods and randomly assigned their share of the 239 depressed patients who participated. Patients in all three groups improved more than did those in a control condition who received merely an inert medication and supportive attention, encouragement, and advice. Among patients who completed a full 16-week treatment program, the depression had lifted for slightly more than half of those in each treatment group—but only for 29 percent of those in the control group (Elkin & others, 1989). This verdict echoes the results of the earlier outcome studies: *Those not undergoing therapy improved, but those undergoing therapy improved more*.

So, while extravagant expectations that psychotherapy will transform your life and personality seem unwarranted, Eysenck's pessimism also seems unwarranted. On the average, psychotherapy is somewhat effective—and is also cost-effective compared with the greater costs of medical care for psychologically related ailments (Turkington, 1987). The annual cost of psychological disorders and substance abuse is staggering—in the United States, $273 billion annually in crime, accidents, and lost productivity, says the Alcohol, Drug Abuse, and Mental Health Administration (1990). Thus, as an investment in prenatal and well-baby care *reduces* long-term costs, so will an investment in almost any effective treatment for psychological problems. Anything that boosts employees' psychological well-being will reduce medical costs, improve work efficiency, and diminish absenteeism.

But note that "on the average" refers to no one therapy in particular. It is like saying "surgery is somewhat effective," or like reassuring lung cancer patients that "on the average" medical treatment of health problems is effective. What people want to know is not the effectiveness of therapy in general but the effectiveness of particular treatments for their particular problems.

In general, therapy is most effective when the problem is clear-cut and specific (Singer, 1981). Those who suffer phobias, who are unassertive, or who are frustrated by sexual performance problems can hope for improvement. Those who suffer chronic schizophrenia or who wish to change their whole personality are unlikely to benefit from psychotherapy alone (Zilbergeld, 1983).

The Relative Effectiveness of Different Therapies

People considering therapy also want to know *which* psychotherapy will be most effective for their problem. The meta-analysis conducted by Mary Lee Smith and her colleagues (1977, 1980) allowed a comparison of the effectiveness of different therapies. What do you suppose they found? Did one therapeutic technique get the best results? Did people benefit more from group or individual therapy? From sustained or short-term therapy? From therapy with experienced or novice therapists?

Despite claims of superiority by advocates of different types of therapy, Smith's comparison of the therapies revealed no clear winner. No one type of therapy proved consistently superior. Moreover—and more astonishing—it made no discernible difference whether the therapy was group or individual, whether many or few sessions were offered, or how well trained and experienced the therapist was.

Some therapies are, however, well suited to particular disorders. With specific behavior problems such as phobias, compulsions, or sexual dysfunctions, behavioral conditioning therapies achieve especially favorable results (Bowers & Clum, 1988; Giles, 1983). With depression, the cognitive therapies prove most successful (Dobson, 1989; Shapiro & Shapiro, 1982). Just as physicians offer particular treatments for specific problems rather than treating every complaint with the same drug or surgical procedure, so psychotherapists increasingly offer particular treatments for specific problems (Stiles & others, 1986).

Commonalities Among Psychotherapies

Some clinicians suggest a reason why no one therapeutic method proves generally superior or inferior to another. Despite their differences, each therapy's effectiveness may derive from underlying commonalities. Jerome Frank (1982), Marvin Goldfried (Goldfried & Padawer, 1982), and Hans Strupp (1986) studied common ingredients of various therapies and suggested that they all offer at least three benefits: hope for demoralized people; a new perspective on oneself and the world; and an empathic, trusting, caring relationship. These "nonspecific" factors aren't all that therapy offers (Barker & others, 1988; Jones & others, 1988), but they are important aspects. They also are part of what the growing numbers of mutual help and support groups offer their members.

Hope for Demoralized People   People who seek therapy typically are anxious, depressed, lacking in self-esteem, and feeling incapable of turning things around. What any therapy offers is the expectation that, with commitment from the patient, things can and will get better. Apart from the particular therapeutic technique, this belief may itself promote improved morale, new feelings of self-efficacy, and diminished symptoms (Prioleau & others, 1983). This benefit of a person's belief in a treatment is the *placebo effect*. As we saw in Chapter 1, a placebo is an inert treatment often used as a control treatment in drug experiments. The placebo has no effect apart from a person's belief in it. In psychotherapy experiments, the placebo treatment may be listening to inspirational tapes, attending group discussions, or taking a fake pill.

The finding that placebo-treated people improve more than do untreated people, although not as much as those receiving actual psychotherapy, suggests that one reason therapies help is the hope they offer. In their individual ways, each therapy may harness the person's own healing powers. And that, says psychiatrist Jerome Frank, helps us understand why all sorts of treatments—including some folk healing rites known to be powerless apart from the patient's belief—may in their own time and place produce cures.

A New Perspective on Oneself and the World   Every therapy offers people a plausible explanation of their symptoms and an alternative way of looking at themselves or responding to their worlds. Therapy also offers new experiences that help people change their views of themselves and their behaviors. Armed with a believable fresh perspective, they may approach life with a new attitude.

An Empathic, Trusting, Caring Relationship   To say that all therapies are about equally effective is not to say all *therapists* are equally effective. Regardless of their therapeutic technique, effective therapists are empathic people who seek to understand another's experience; whose care and concern the client feels; and whose respectful listening, reassurance, and advice earn the client's trust and respect. Indeed, some believe that warmth and empathy are hallmarks of healers everywhere, whether psychiatrists, witch doctors, or shamans (Torrey, 1986).

The notion that all therapies offer *hope* through the *fresh perspective* offered by a *caring person* gains support from a digest of 39 studies. Each study compared treatment offered by professional therapists with treatment offered by lay people. These lay people included friendly professors, people who have had a few hours' training in empathic listening skills, and college students supervised by a professional clinician. The result? The "paraprofessionals," as we call these briefly trained people, typically proved as effective as the professionals (Berman & Norton, 1985; Hattie & others, 1984). Most of the problems they treated were mild. In these studies, however, trained paraprofessionals were—believe it or not—as effective as professionals, even when dealing with more disturbed adults, such as those diagnosed as seriously depressed.

Effective therapists form a bond of trust with their clients.

To sum up, people who seek help usually improve. So do many of those who do not undergo psychotherapy, and that is a tribute to our human resourcefulness and to our capacity to care for one another. Nevertheless, though it appears not to matter much which type of therapy is practiced, how much is received, or how experienced the therapist, those who receive some psychotherapy usually improve more than those who do not. Mature, articulate people with specific emotional or behavior problems often improve the most.

Part of what all therapies offer is hope, a fresh way of looking at life, and an empathic, caring relationship. That may explain why the empathy and friendly counsel of paraprofessionals are so often as helpful as professional psychotherapy. And that may also explain why those who feel supported by close relationships—who enjoy the fellowship and friendship of caring people—are less likely to need or seek therapy (Frank, 1982; O'Connor & Brown, 1984).

Rehearse It

12. The question "Is psychotherapy effective?" has been the subject of hundreds of scientific studies and innumerable personal accounts. The most enthusiastic or optimistic view of psychotherapy comes from
a. outcome research.
b. psychologist Hans Eysenck.
c. reports of clinicians and clients.
d. an NIMH study of treatment for depression.

13. On average, troubled people who undergo therapy are more likely to improve than those who do not, and therapy tends to be most effective when the problem is clear-cut and specific. Studies show that _____ therapy is most effective.
a. behavior
b. humanistic
c. individual as opposed to group
d. no one type of

14. Psychologists have observed that people's belief that a treatment will help them is often sufficient to cause some improvement. When a neutral treatment, such as an inert pill, results in improved morale and diminished symptoms, psychologists call this
a. a placebo effect.
b. preventive mental health.
c. behavior modification.

The Biomedical Therapies

Psychotherapy is one way to treat psychological disorders. The other is to physically alter the brain's functioning—by altering its electrochemical transmissions with drugs, by overloading its circuits with electroconvulsive shock, or by disconnecting its circuits through psychosurgery.

Drug Therapies

Preview Question

6. What are the most common forms of drug therapy?

By far the most widely used biomedical treatments today are the drug therapies. When introduced in the 1950s, drug therapy greatly reduced the need for psychosurgery or hospitalization. Discoveries in **psychopharmacology** (the study of drug effects on mind and behavior) revolutionized the treatment of severely disordered people, liberating hundreds of thousands from confinement in mental hospitals. Thanks to drug therapy—and to political and legal efforts to minimize involuntary hospitalization and to return hospitalized people to their communities, aided by community mental health programs—the resident population of state and county mental hospitals in the United States today is but 20 percent of what it was 30 years ago (Figure 13–6).

Figure 13–6 The emptying of America's mental hospitals. After the widespread introduction of antipsychotic drugs, starting in about 1955, the number of residents in state and county mental hospitals declined sharply. But the rush to "deinstitutionalize" the mentally ill left many people who are ill-equipped to care for themselves homeless on city streets. (Data from NIMH.)

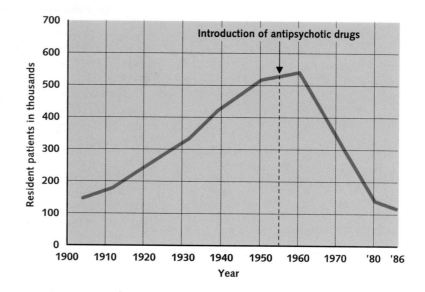

For those still unable to care for themselves, however, release from hospitals has meant not liberation but homelessness. Studies suggest that about one-third of the homeless suffer disabling psychological disorders (not including alcohol and drug abuse, which also plague about 1 in 3 homeless people—Fischer & Breakey, 1991; Levine & Rog, 1990; McCarty & others, 1991). Unlike the homeless on yesterday's skid rows in major cities, 3 percent of whom were female, 25 percent of today's homeless are female.

With almost any new treatment, including drug therapy, there is a first wave of enthusiasm as many people apparently improve. But that enthusiasm often diminishes after researchers subtract the rate of (1) normal recovery among untreated persons, and (2) recovery due to the placebo effect, which arises from the positive expectations of patients and staff alike. So, to evaluate the effectiveness of any new drug, researchers use the double-blind technique. Half the patients receive the drug, the other half a similar-appearing placebo. Neither the staff nor the patients know who gets which. In double-blind studies, several types of drugs have proved useful in treating psychological disorders.

psychopharmacology The study of the effects of drugs on mind and behavior.

"The mentally ill were out of the hospital, but in many cases they were simply out on the streets, less agitated but lost, still disabled but now uncared for."

Lewis Thomas
Late Night Thoughts on Listening to Mahler's Ninth Symphony, 1983

Antipsychotic Drugs

The revolution in drug therapy for psychological disorders began when it was accidentally discovered that certain drugs, used for other medical purposes, also calmed psychotic patients. These antipsychotic drugs, such as chlorpromazine (sold as Thorazine), provide most help to people experiencing the positive symptoms of auditory hallucinations and paranoia, by dampening their responsiveness to irrelevant stimuli (Lenzenweger & others, 1989). Schizophrenia patients with the negative symptoms of apathy and withdrawal often do not respond well to these antipsychotic drugs. A new drug, clozapine (marketed as Clozaril), does help reanimate such people and has been effectively used in Europe.

The molecules of the Thorazine-like antipsychotic drugs are similar enough to molecules of the neurotransmitter dopamine to occupy its receptor sites and block its activity (Pickar & others, 1984). This finding—that most antipsychotic drugs block dopamine receptors—reinforces the idea that, as psychopharmacologist Soloman Snyder (1984) put it, "dopamine systems in the brain are closely related to whatever is fundamentally abnormal in schizophrenic brains—either an excess of dopamine formation or perhaps a supersensitivity of dopamine receptors."

Antipsychotics such as Thorazine are powerful drugs that can produce sluggishness, tremors, and muscular coordination problems similar to those of Parkinson's disease (Kaplan & Saddock, 1989). What is an effective dose for some people may be an overdose for others. Asians, for example, seem to require lower doses than Caucasians (Holden, 1991b). By carefully monitoring the dosage and its effects, therapist and patient tread the fine line between relieving the symptoms and causing some extremely unpleasant side effects. In this way, and with the help of supportive people, hundreds of thousands of schizophrenia patients who had been consigned to the back wards of mental hospitals have returned to jobs and to near-normal lives.

Antianxiety Drugs

Among the most heavily prescribed and abused drugs are the antianxiety agents, such as Valium and Librium. Like alcohol, these drugs depress central nervous system activity. Because they reduce tension and anxiety without causing excessive sleepiness, they have been prescribed even for minor emo-

lithium A chemical that provides an effective drug therapy for the mood swings of bipolar (manic-depressive) disorders.

electroconvulsive therapy (ECT) Shock treatment. A biomedical therapy for severely depressed patients in which a brief electric current is sent through the brain of an anesthetized patient.

tional stresses. Used in combination with other therapy, an antianxiety drug sometimes helps a person learn to cope successfully with frightening situations. Calmed with the help of a drug, the person may learn to deal with fear-triggering stimuli.

The criticism sometimes made of the behavior therapies—that they reduce symptoms without resolving underlying problems—is also made of antianxiety drugs. Unlike the behavior therapies, they may even be used as a continuing treatment. Routinely "popping a Valium" at the first sign of tension can produce psychological dependence on the drug. When heavy users stop taking the drug, they may experience increased anxiety and insomnia, driving them back to the drug for relief.

Antidepressant Drugs

If the antianxiety drugs calm anxious people down, the antidepressants lift depressed people up. Most of the antidepressants increase the availability of the neurotransmitters norepinephrine and serotonin, which appear scarce during depression. For example, the popular new antidepressant fluoxetine (marketed as Prozac) blocks the reabsorption and removal of serotonin from the synapse. Patients who begin taking antidepressants do not wake up the next day singing "Oh, what a beautiful morning!" The full effect often requires 3 or 4 weeks, sometimes aided by cognitive therapy to help the patient reverse a now-habitual negative thinking style.

For those suffering the manic-depressive mood swings of a bipolar disorder, the simple salt **lithium** is often an effective mood stabilizer. An Australian physician, John Cade, discovered this in the 1940s when he administered lithium to a severely manic patient. Although his reason for doing so was misguided—he thought lithium had calmed excitable guinea pigs when actually it made them sick—Cade found that in less than a week the patient became perfectly well (Snyder, 1986). With continued lithium use, the emotional highs and lows typically level. After suffering mood swings for years, many people find relief with a daily dose of this cheap salt.

Electroconvulsive Therapy

Preview Question

7. How effective are electroconvulsive therapy and psychosurgery?

The medical use of electricity is an ancient practice. Physicians treated the Roman Emperor Claudius (10 B.C.–A.D. 54) for headaches by pressing electric eels to his temples.

A more controversial brain manipulation occurs through shock treatment, or **electroconvulsive therapy (ECT).** When ECT was first introduced in 1938, the wide-awake patient was strapped to a table and jolted with roughly 100 volts of electricity to the brain, producing racking convulsions and momentary unconsciousness. ECT therefore gained a barbaric image that lingers to the present. Today, however, the patient first receives a general anesthetic and a muscle relaxant to prevent injury from convulsions. Then a psychiatrist electrically shocks the unconscious patient's brain for a fraction of a second. Within 30 minutes the patient awakens and remembers nothing of the treatment or of the hours preceding.

Psychiatrists give ECT to severely depressed patients. (It is usually ineffective in treating other psychological disorders.) After three such treatments a week for 2 to 4 weeks, 80 percent or more of depressed people improve markedly and without discernible brain damage (Bergsholm & others, 1989; Coffey & Weiner, 1990). "A miracle had happened in two weeks," reported noted research psychologist Norman Endler (1982) after ECT alleviated his deep depression. A 1985 panel of the National Institutes of Health reported that for many others, too, ECT is an effective treatment for severe depression that has not responded to drug therapy (Consensus Conference, 1985). Thus, ECT has regained respectability as a "major treatment" for depression, according to the American Psychiatric Association (1990).

psychosurgery Surgery that removes or destroys brain tissue in an effort to change behavior.

lobotomy A now-rare psychosurgical procedure once used to calm uncontrollably emotional or violent patients. In this procedure, the nerves that connect the frontal lobes to the emotion-controlling centers of the inner brain are cut.

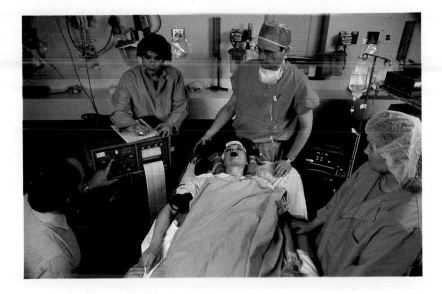

Electroconvulsive therapy remains a controversial treatment that can provide relief from serious depression.

How does ECT work? After more than 50 years, no one knows for sure. Perhaps electrical shock increases the release of norepinephrine, the neurotransmitter that elevates arousal and mood and seems in short supply during depression. Or perhaps the shock-induced seizures cause the brain to react by calming neural centers where overactivity produces depression (Sackeim, 1988).

Although ECT is credited with saving many from suicide and is now used on some 100,000 Americans a year (S. Squire, 1987), its Frankenstein-like image continues. No matter how impressive the results, the idea of electrically shocking people into convulsions still strikes many as barbaric, especially given our ignorance about why ECT works. Moreover, ECT-treated patients, like other formerly depressed patients, are vulnerable to relapse. Nevertheless, electroconvulsive therapy is, in the minds of many psychiatrists and patients, a godsend—or at least a lesser evil than depression's misery, anguish, and risk of suicide.

Psychosurgery

Because its effects are irreversible, **psychosurgery**—surgery that removes or destroys brain tissue to change behavior—is the most drastic and the least-used biomedical intervention. In the 1930s, Portuguese physician Egas Moniz developed what became the best known psychosurgical operation: the **lobotomy.** Moniz found that cutting the nerves connecting the frontal lobes with the emotion-controlling centers of the inner brain calmed uncontrollably emotional and violent patients. During the 1940s and 1950s, tens of thousands of severely disturbed people were "lobotomized," and Moniz was honored with a Nobel prize (Valenstein, 1986).

Although the intention was simply to disconnect emotion from thought, the effect was often more drastic: The lobotomy produced a permanently lethargic, immature, impulsive personality. During the 1950s, when calming drugs became available, psychosurgery was largely abandoned. Today, lobotomies are very rarely performed. Other psychosurgery is used only in extreme cases. For example, if a patient suffers uncontrollable seizures, surgeons can deactivate the specific nerve clusters that cause or transmit the convulsions. Because such beneficial operations are irreversible, however, neurosurgeons perform them only as a last resort.

The effectiveness of the biomedical therapies reminds us of a fundamental lesson: We find it convenient to talk of separate psychological and biological influences, but everything psychological *is* biological. Every thought and feeling depends on the functioning brain. Every creative idea, every moment of joy or anger, every period of depression emerges from the electrochemical activity of the brain.

The biomedical therapies assume that mind and body are a unit: Affect one and you will affect the other.

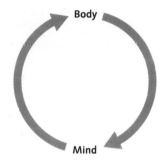

Preventing Psychological Disorders

Preview Question

8. What is the rationale for preventive mental health programs?

Psychotherapies and biomedical therapies tend to locate the cause of psychological disorders within the disordered person. We infer that people who act cruelly must be cruel and that people who act "crazy" must be "sick." We attach labels to such people, thereby distinguishing them from "normal" folks. It follows, then, that we try to treat "abnormal" people by giving them insight into their problems, by changing their thinking, or by controlling them with drugs.

There is another way to view many psychological disorders: as an understandable response to a disturbing and stressful society. According to this view, it is not just the person who needs treatment, but also the person's social context. Better to prevent a problem by reforming a sick situation than to wait for a problem to arise and then treat it.

A story about the rescue of a drowning person from a rushing river illustrates the need for prevention. Having successfully administered first aid, the rescuer spots another struggling person and pulls her out, too. After a half dozen repetitions, the rescuer suddenly turns and starts running away while the river sweeps yet another floundering person into view. "Aren't you going to rescue that fellow?" asks a bystander. "Heck no," the rescuer replies. "I'm going upstream to find out what's pushing all these people in."

Preventive mental health is upstream work. It seeks to prevent psychological casualties by identifying and alleviating the conditions that cause them. George Albee (1986), a past president of the American Psychological Association, believes there is abundant evidence that poverty, meaningless work, constant criticism, unemployment, racism, and sexism undermine people's sense of competence, personal control, and self-esteem. Such stresses increase their risk of depression, alcoholism, and suicide.

Albee contends that those who care about preventing psychological casualties should therefore support programs that alleviate poverty, discrimination, and other demoralizing situations. We eliminated smallpox not by treating the afflicted but by inoculating the unafflicted. We conquered yellow fever by controlling mosquitoes. Prevention of psychological problems means empowering those who have learned an attitude of helplessness, changing environments that breed loneliness, and bolstering parents' and teachers' skills at nurturing children's self-esteem. Indeed, "everything aimed at improving the human condition, at making life more fulfilling and meaningful, may be considered part of primary prevention of mental or emotional disturbance" (Kessler & Albee, 1975, p. 557).

Albee reminds us again of one of this book's themes: A human being is an integrated bio-psycho-social system. For years we have trusted our bodies to physicians and our minds to psychiatrists and psychologists. That neat separation no longer seems valid. Chemical imbalances can produce schizophrenia and depression. And anger, depression, and stress, as we learned in Chapter 10, can threaten our physical health. "*Mens sana in corpore sano*," says an ancient Latin adage: a healthy mind in a healthy body.

"Mental disorders arise from physical ones, and likewise physical disorders arise from mental ones."

The Mahabharata, c. 200 A.D.

Rehearse It

15. Antipsychotic drugs are used to calm schizophrenia patients so that they can live outside the hospital. The drugs often bring relief from auditory hallucinations and other troubling symptoms. However they can have unpleasant side effects, most notably
a. hyperactivity.
b. convulsions and momentary memory loss.
c. tremors and muscular coordination problems.
d. paranoia.

16. The antidepressant drugs seem to increase the availability of the neurotransmitters norepinephrine and serotonin, which appear to be scarce during depression. An example of an antidepressant

drug that often brings relief to patients suffering the manic-depressive mood swings of a bipolar disorder is
a. dopamine.
b. Librium.
c. lithium.
d. Valium.

17. Two controversial biomedical therapies are electroconvulsive therapy (shock treatment) and lobotomy (an example of psychosurgery). Lobotomy, once used to treat uncontrollably violent patients, is no longer an accepted treatment. Electroconvulsive therapy, however, remains in use as a treatment for

a. depression.
b. severe depression.
c. schizophrenia.
d. anxiety disorders.

18. Being poor or unemployed undermines a person's self-esteem and fosters feelings of helplessness. An approach that seeks to alleviate poverty and other stresses that put people at high risk for developing psychological disorders is
a. biomedical therapy.
b. the humanistic approach.
c. empathy and active listening.
d. preventive mental health.

Reviewing Therapy

Treatment for psychological disorders encompasses both the psychological therapies, involving verbal interactions, and the biomedical therapies, which alter the structure or functioning of the central nervous system.

The Psychological Therapies

1. **What are the aims and methods of psychoanalysis?**

The goal of psychoanalysts is to help people gain insight into the unconscious origins of their disorders and to work through the accompanying feelings. To do so, analysts

draw on techniques such as free association, the interpretation of dreams and resistances, and the transference to the therapist of long-repressed feelings. Like the psychoanalytic perspective on personality, psychoanalysis is criticized for its after-the-fact interpretations as well as for being time-consuming and costly. Although traditional psychoanalysis is not widely practiced, its influence can be seen in therapists who explore childhood experiences, who assume that certain emotion-laden information is repressed, and who seek to help their clients achieve insight into the root of their problems.

2. **What are the basic themes of humanistic therapy, such as Rogers' person-centered approach?**

Unlike psychoanalysts, humanistic therapists tend to focus on clients' current conscious feelings and on their taking responsibility for their own growth. Carl Rogers, in his person-centered therapy, used active listening to express genuineness, acceptance, and empathy. These and other therapeutic techniques can also be applied in group therapy, such as sensitivity training, self-help, and support groups. Family therapy focuses not on changing individuals, but on changing their relationships and interactions.

3. **What are the assumptions and techniques of the behavior therapies?**

Behavior therapists worry less about promoting self-awareness and more about directly modifying problem behaviors. Thus, they may countercondition behaviors through systematic desensitization or aversive conditioning. Or they may apply operant conditioning principles along with behavior modification techniques such as in token economies.

4. **What are the goals and techniques of the cognitive therapies?**

The newer cognitive therapies, such as Ellis's rational-emotive therapy and Beck's cognitive therapy for depression, aim to change self-defeating thinking by training people to look at themselves in new, more positive ways.

5. **What does research on psychotherapy reveal about its effectiveness?**

Because the positive testimonials of clients and therapists cannot prove that therapy is actually effective, psychologists have conducted hundreds of studies of the outcomes of psychotherapy. These studies indicate that (1) people who remain untreated often improve; (2) those who receive psychotherapy are somewhat more likely to improve, regardless of what kind of therapy they receive and for how long; (3) mature, articulate people with specific behavior problems often receive the greatest benefits from therapy; but (4) placebo treatments or the sympathy and friendly counsel of "paraprofessionals" also tend to produce more improvement than occurs in untreated people.

The Biomedical Therapies

6. **What are the most common forms of drug therapy?**

Drugs are the most widely used biomedical therapy. Antipsychotic drugs block dopamine activity; antianxiety drugs depress central nervous system activity; antidepressant drugs increase availability of seratonin and norepinephrine, and lithium is a mood stabilizer.

7. **How effective are electroconvulsive therapy and psychosurgery?**

Although controversial, a growing body of evidence indicates that ECT is an effective treatment for many severely depressed people who do not respond to drug therapy. Brain surgery is occasionally used to alleviate specific problems, but the effects of radical psychosurgical procedures such as lobotomy are irreversible and potentially drastic. Thus, psychosurgery is seldom performed.

Preventing Psychological Disorders

8. **What is the rationale for preventive mental health programs?**

Psychologists concerned with preventive mental health argue that many psychological disorders could be prevented by changing oppressive, esteem-destroying environments into more benevolent, nurturing environments that would foster individual growth and self-esteem.

Terms and Concepts to Remember

Rehearse It Answer Key

1. a.	2. a.	3. d.	4. c.	5. b.	6. c.	7. b.	8. a.	9. d.
10. c.	11. d.	12. c.	13. d.	14. a.	15. c.	16. c.	17. b.	18. d.

Critical Thinking Exercise

You have *Surveyed*, *Questioned*, *Read*, *Rehearsed*, and *Reviewed* Chapter 13. Now take your learning a step further by testing your *critical thinking* skills on the following passage.

> Deborah is very satisfied with the large amount of time and money she has invested in psychotherapy. When she began therapy, her life was in crisis and she was desperate for help in overcoming her depressed, pessimistic attitude. After shopping around, she finally found an understanding cognitive therapist who made her feel hopeful she could get her life back on track. After three months of psychotherapy, Deborah is once again enjoying her life and attributes her recovery to the psychotherapy.
>
> Vincent is a middle-aged manager of an auto parts store. He is under a lot of pressure at work, has a very pessimistic attitude toward life, and "blows up" frequently at minor family annoyances. Although he admits that he is depressed and complains to his family a lot, he doesn't feel there is anything wrong with him. His family disagrees and is concerned that he is increasingly showing signs of psychologically disordered behavior. At their insistence, Vincent reluctantly agrees to see a psychotherapist. He picks a name at random from the phone book and grudgingly endures several weeks of "overpriced gibberish" to appease his family. Despite the good efforts of the psychotherapist, who attempts to countercondition Vincent's maladaptive behaviors, Vincent shows no improvement following psychotherapy.

1. Assuming their initial problems were equally serious, what could account for Deborah and Vincent's very different experiences with psychotherapy?

2. Deborah now swears by cognitive therapy, while Vincent is very critical of behavior therapy. Are their recommendations acceptable as scientific evidence regarding the effectiveness of psychotherapy? Why or why not?

Check your progress on becoming a critical thinker by comparing your answers to the sample answers found in Appendix B.

Chapter 14

Social Psychology

"We cannot live for ourselves alone," remarked the novelist Herman Melville, for "our lives are connected by a thousand invisible threads." **Social psychologists** explore these connections by scientifically studying how we *think about, influence,* and *relate* to one another.

Social Thinking

Especially when the unexpected occurs, we analyze and discuss why people act as they do. In everyday life we do the same. Does her warmth reflect romantic interest in me, or is that how she relates to everyone? Does his absenteeism signify laziness or an oppressive work atmosphere?

Attributing Behavior to Persons or to Situations

After studying how people explain others' behavior, Fritz Heider (1958) proposed **attribution theory.** Heider noted that people often attribute others' behavior either to their internal *dispositions* or to their external *situations.* A teacher, for example, may wonder whether a child's hostility reflects an aggressive personality (a *dispositional attribution*) or whether the child is reacting to stress or abuse (a *situational attribution*).

In class, we notice that Julie doesn't say much; over coffee, Jack talks nonstop. Attributing their behaviors to their personal dispositions, we decide that Julie is shy and Jack is outgoing. Because people do have enduring personality traits, such attributions are sometimes valid. However, we often overestimate the influence of personality and underestimate the impact of the situation. In class, Jack may be as quiet as Julie. Catch Julie at a party and you may hardly recognize your quiet classmate. Underestimating situational influences is known as the **fundamental attribution error.**

An experiment by David Napolitan and George Goethals (1979) illustrates this principle. The researchers had Williams College students talk, one at a time, with a young woman who acted either aloof and critical or warm and friendly. Beforehand, they told half the students that the woman's behavior would be spontaneous. They told the other half the truth—that she had been instructed to *act* friendly (or unfriendly). What effect do you suppose this information had?

None. The students disregarded the information. If the woman acted friendly, they inferred she really was a warm person. If she acted unfriendly, they inferred she really was a cold person. In other words, they attributed her behavior to her personal disposition, *even when told that her behavior was situational*—that she was merely acting that way for purposes of the experiment.

Preview Question

1. How do we err when explaining the behavior of others?

social psychology The scientific study of how we think about, influence, and relate to one another.

attribution theory The theory that we tend to give a causal explanation for someone's behavior, often by crediting either the situation or the person's disposition.

fundamental attribution error The tendency for observers, when analyzing another's behavior, to underestimate the impact of the situation and to overestimate the impact of personal disposition.

Knowing about the fundamental attribution error is helpful, yet committing it is almost irresistible. In a high school play I attended recently, a talented 16-year-old girl convincingly played the part of a bitter old woman—so convincingly that, although I reminded myself of the fundamental attribution error, I still assumed that the young actress was typecast because she was well-suited for the part. Meeting her later at a cast party, I discovered she actually has a very pleasant disposition. I then remembered that several months earlier I had seen her play the part of a charming 10-year-old in *The Sound of Music*. Leonard Nimoy of *Star Trek* fame would not have been surprised by my error. He titled one of his books *I Am Not Spock*.

You, too, have surely committed the fundamental attribution error. In judging, say, whether your psychology instructor is shy or outgoing, you perhaps inferred from your class experience that he or she has an outgoing personality. But you know your instructor only from the classroom, a situation that demands outgoing behavior. Catch the instructor in a different situation and you might be surprised (as some of my students are when confronting me in a pick-up basketball game). Outside of their assigned roles, professors seem less professorial, presidents less presidential, servants less servile.

The instructor, on the other hand, observes his or her own behavior in many different situations—in the classroom, in meetings, at home, and the like—and so might say, "Me, outgoing? It all depends on the situation. In class or with good friends, yes, I'm outgoing. But at conventions I'm really rather shy."

So, when explaining *our own* behavior, we are sensitive to how our behavior changes with the situations we encounter. When explaining *others'* behavior, particularly after observing them in only one type of situation, we often commit the fundamental attribution error. We disregard the situation and leap to unwarranted conclusions about their personality traits. We do so partly because our attention focuses on the person more than on the situational context. Meanwhile, the person's own attention focuses more on the situation to which he or she is reacting.

So, what do you suppose happens when we reverse the perspectives of actor and observer—by having each view a videotape replay of the situation from the other's perspective? As the focus-of-attention explanation predicts, this reverses the attributions (Lassiter & Irvine, 1986; Storms, 1973). By seeing the world from the actor's perspective, the observers better appreciate the situation. Given an observer's point of view, the actors better appreciate their own initiative and personal style.

The Effects of Attribution

In everyday life we often struggle to explain why others act as they do. A jury must decide whether a shooting was malicious or in self-defense. An unhappy wife and husband each ponder why the other behaves so selfishly. An interviewer must judge whether the applicant's geniality is genuine. When making such judgments, our attributions—either to the person or to the situation—have important consequences (Bradbury & Fincham, 1990; Fletcher & others, 1990). Happily married couples attribute their spouse's tart-tongued remark to a temporary situation ("She must have had a bad day at work"). Unhappily married persons attribute the same remark to a mean disposition ("Why ever did I marry such a cold and hostile person?").

Or consider the political effects of attribution: How do you explain poverty or unemployment? Researchers in Britain, India, Australia, and the United States (Furnham, 1982; Pandey & others, 1982; Wagstaff, 1982) report that political conservatives tend to attribute these and other social problems

Recall from Chapter 11 that personality psychologists study the enduring, inner determinants of behavior that help to explain why different people act differently in a given situation. Social psychologists study the social influences that help explain why a given person will act differently in different situations.

attitude A belief and feeling that predisposes one to respond in a particular way to objects, people, and events.

to the personal dispositions of the poor and unemployed themselves: "People generally get what they deserve. Those who don't work are often lazy freeloaders. People who take initiative can still get ahead." Political liberals are more likely to blame past and present situations: "If you or I had to live with the same poor education, lack of meaningful opportunity, and outright discrimination, would we be any better off?"

And how do you explain homelessness? Some people—45 percent in one survey (Lee & others, 1990)—attribute homelessness to society's failure to provide adequate jobs and housing. Others—33 percent—blame the homeless themselves. President Reagan (1988), for example, believed that many homeless people "make it their own choice" not to seek shelter. Clearly, there are political implications to whether we attribute people's behavior to social conditions or to their own choices and shortcomings.

In evaluating employees, managers must also make attributions. They are likely to attribute the poor performance of workers to personal factors such as low ability or lack of motivation. Workers who are doing poorly on a job recognize situational influences: inadequate supplies, poor working conditions, difficult co-workers, impossible or ambiguous demands (Rice, 1985).

The point to remember: Our attributions—to individuals' dispositions or to their situations—have practical consequences.

Attitudes and Behavior

Social psychology's single most important concept has been that of *attitudes*. **Attitudes** are beliefs and feelings that predispose our reactions to objects, people, and events. If we *believe* that someone is mean, we may *feel* dislike for the person and *act* unfriendly. "Change the way people think," said South African civil rights martyr Steve Biko, "and things will never be the same."

Do Our Attitudes Guide Our Behavior?

Although most persuasive appeals assume that changed attitudes can indeed change behavior, dozens of studies during the 1960s challenged this idea (Wicker, 1971). Moreover, studies of people's attitudes and behaviors regarding cheating, the church, and racial minorities revealed that folks often talk and act a different game. "Thinking is easy," said the German poet Goethe (1749–1832), "acting difficult, and to put one's thoughts into action, the most difficult thing in the world."

But the seeming hypocrisy did startle social psychologists, most of whom shared Steve Biko's belief that there is a close connection between thought and action, character and conduct, private words and public deeds. So they conducted many follow-up studies during the 1970s and 1980s (Kraus, 1991). These studies reveal that our attitudes *will* guide our actions if:

> *Outside influences on what we say and do are minimal.* Social pressures may blur the underlying connection between our attitudes and actions by affecting either what we say or what we do (Figure 14–1). In 1990, 4 weeks before a congressional election, President Bush and political leaders from both parties asked members of the U.S. House of Representatives to pass a compromise deficit-reducing budget. Privately, most members of Congress agreed that the painful cuts and tax increases were essential to the nation's health: Among those retiring or unopposed for reelection and thus facing little external pressure, 86 percent voted for the bill. For others, voting their privately held attitudes was more difficult. Among the 36 representatives who were about to face angry voters in close races back home, there were no profiles in courage: All 36 voted against it.

Preview Question

2. Under what conditions do our attitudes guide our behavior?

"I do not understand my own actions. For I do not do what I want, but I do the very thing I hate."

St. Paul
Romans 7:15

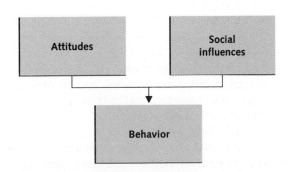

Figure 14–1 Our behavior is affected by both our inner attitudes and by external social influences.

The attitude is specifically relevant to the behavior. People readily profess *general* attitudes that are inconsistent with their behavior. They proclaim love while practicing hate, cherish honesty while cheating on their income tax returns, and value good health while smoking and not exercising. Attitudes about the specific act do, however, guide action. Attitudes toward exercise predict exercising behavior.

We are keenly aware of our attitudes. When we mindlessly follow habit or social expectations, our attitudes lie dormant. If something makes us self-conscious or reminds us of how we feel, we are truer to our convictions. For example, Martha Powell and Russell Fazio (1984) had people rate their attitudes about gun control and about the Equal Rights Amendment. They found that repeating an attitude makes it come to mind more quickly. And attitudes that come quickly to mind are more likely to guide our behavior (Fazio, 1990). When we know what we believe and are conscious of its implications for our actions, we probably will be true to ourselves.

Do Our Actions Affect Our Behavior?

Preview Question

3. Under what conditions does our behavior affect our attitudes?

So, under certain circumstances—when other influences are minimal, when the attitude is specific to the behavior, and when people are mindful of their attitudes—people will stand up for what they believe. Attitudes can affect behavior. Now consider a surprising related principle: People also come to believe in what they have stood up for. Many streams of evidence confirm that *attitudes follow behavior.* Here are two.

The Foot-in-the-Door Phenomenon   During the Korean War, 7200 captured American soldiers were imprisoned in war camps run by Chinese communists. Without using brutality, the captors secured their prisoners' collaboration in ways ranging from running errands and accepting favors to making radio appeals and false confessions to informing on fellow prisoners and divulging military information. When the war ended, 21 prisoners chose to stay with the communists. Many others returned home "brainwashed"—convinced that communism was a good thing for Asia.

A key ingredient of the Chinese "thought-control" program was their effective use of the **foot-in-the-door phenomenon**—a tendency for people who agree to a small request to comply later with a larger one. The Chinese harnessed this phenomenon by gradually escalating their demands on the prisoners, beginning with harmless requests (Schein, 1956). Having "trained" the prisoners to speak or write trivial statements, the communists then asked them to copy or create something more important, noting, perhaps, the flaws of American capitalism. The prisoners then participated in group discussions, wrote self-criticisms, or uttered public confessions. Once they did so, perhaps to gain privileges, the prisoners then often adjusted their beliefs toward consistency with their public acts.

Research studies show that the foot-in-the-door tactic also helps boost charitable contributions, blood donations, and product sales. In one experiment, researchers posing as safety-drive volunteers asked Californians to permit the installation of a large, poorly lettered "Drive Carefully" sign in their front yards. Only 17 percent consented. Others were first approached with a small request: Would they display a 3-inch "Be a Safe Driver" sign? Nearly all readily agreed. When reapproached 2 weeks later to allow the large, ugly sign in their front yards, 76 percent consented (Freedman & Fraser, 1966).

foot-in-the-door phenomenon The tendency for people who have first agreed to a small request to comply later with a larger request.

role A set of expectations about a social position, defining how those in the position ought to behave.

"If the King destroys a man, that's proof to the King it must have been a bad man."

Thomas Cromwell in Robert Bolt's
A Man for All Seasons, 1960

Both the obedient recruit and the abusive sergeant may have begun by consciously adopting the behavior expected of them in these roles, but they often end up becoming the characters they are playing.

The moral is simple, says Robert Cialdini (1988): To get people to agree to something big, "start small and build." And be wary of those who would exploit you with the tactic. This chicken-and-egg spiral of actions feeding attitudes feeding actions enables behavior to escalate. A trifling act makes the next act easier. Succumb to a temptation and the next temptation will be harder to resist.

Dozens of experiments have simulated part of the war prisoners' experience, by coaxing people into acting against their attitudes or violating their moral standards. The nearly inevitable result: Most subjects begin to rationalize their behavior by persuading themselves that they were justified in saying or doing what they did. If induced to speak or write on behalf of a point of view they have doubts about, they begin to believe their own words. Saying becomes believing. Similarly, subjects induced to harm an innocent victim—by making cutting comments or by delivering electric shocks—typically begin to disparage their victim.

Fortunately, the attitudes-follow-behavior principle works as well for good deeds as for bad. In the years immediately following the introduction of school desegregation and the passage of the U.S. Civil Rights Act of 1964, white Americans expressed diminishing racial prejudice. And as Americans in different regions came to act more alike—thanks to more uniform national standards against discrimination—they began to think more alike. Experiments reveal that moral action has positive effects on the actor, and that doing favors for another person often leads to greater liking of the person. We love people for the good we do them as well as for the good they do us. Evil acts shape the self, but so do moral acts.

Role Playing Affects Attitudes In psychology, as in the theatre, a **role** refers to a cluster of prescribed actions—the behaviors we expect of those who occupy a particular social position. When you adopt a new role—when you become a college student, marry, or begin a new job—you strive to follow the social prescriptions. At first, the behaviors may feel phony, because you are *acting* the role. The first weeks in the military feel artificial—as if one is pretending to be a soldier. The first weeks of a marriage may feel like "playing house." Before long, however, your behavior no longer feels forced. What began as play-acting in the theater of life becomes you.

Researchers have confirmed this effect by assessing people's attitudes before and after they adopt a new role. Sometimes this occurs in laboratory situations, sometimes in everyday situations, such as before and after taking a job. In one laboratory study, college students volunteered to spend time in a simulated prison devised by psychologist Philip Zimbardo (1972). Some he randomly designated as guards; he gave them uniforms, billy clubs, and whistles and instructed them to enforce certain rules. The remainder became prisoners; they were locked in barren cells and forced to wear humiliating outfits. After a day or two of self-consciously "playing" their roles, the simulation became real—too real. The guards devised cruel and degrading routines, and one by one the prisoners either broke down, rebelled, or passively grew resigned to their roles, causing Zimbardo to call the study off after only 6 days.

Meanwhile, in real life, the military junta then in power in Greece was training another group of men to become torturers (Staub, 1989). The men's indoctrination into their roles occurred in small steps. First, the trainee stood guard outside the interrogation cells—the "foot in the door." Next, he stood guard inside. Only then was he ready to become actively involved in the questioning and torture. As the nineteenth-century writer Nathaniel Hawthorne noted, "No man, for any considerable period, can wear one face to

cognitive dissonance theory The theory that we act to reduce the discomfort (dissonance) we feel when two of our thoughts (cognitions) are inconsistent—as when we respond to our having acted contrary to our attitudes by changing our attitude.

"Sit all day in a moping posture, sigh, and reply to everything with a dismal voice, and your melancholy lingers. . . . If we wish to conquer undesirable emotional tendencies in ourselves, we must . . . go through the outward movements of those contrary dispositions which we prefer to cultivate."

William James
Principles of Psychology, 1890

himself and another to the multitude without finally getting bewildered as to which may be true." Behavior affects attitudes. What we do we gradually become.

Why Does Our Behavior Affect Our Attitudes?   Without doubt, then, behavior can affect attitudes, sometimes turning prisoners into collaborators, doubters into believers, or mere acquaintances into friends. But why? One explanation is that we feel motivated to justify our actions. When aware that our thoughts and actions don't coincide, we experience tension, called *cognitive dissonance*. To relieve this tension, according to the **cognitive dissonance theory** proposed by Leon Festinger, people will bring their attitudes into line with their actions. It's as if people rationalize, "If I chose to do it (or say it), I must believe in it." The less coerced and more responsible we feel for a troubling act, the more dissonance we feel. The more dissonance we feel, the more our attitudes change to justify the act.

The attitudes-follow-behavior principle has heartening implications as well. Although we cannot directly control all our feelings, we can influence them by altering our behavior. If we are unloving, we can become more loving by behaving as if we were so—by doing thoughtful things, expressing affection, giving affirmation. If we are down in the dumps, we can do as cognitive therapists advise and talk in more positive, self-accepting ways with fewer self put-downs. **The moral:** We can as easily act ourselves into a way of thinking as think ourselves into a way of acting.

Rehearse It

1. In explaining a person's behavior we tend to make the fundamental attribution error—we overestimate the impact of internal factors (such as disposition, or personality) and underestimate the impact of the situation in which the behavior occurs. Thus, if we encounter a cocaine addict, we might attribute the person's behavior to
a. moral weakness or an addictive personality.
b. peer pressure.
c. the easy availability of the drug on city streets.
d. society's acceptance of drug use.

2. Whether or not our actions are really guided by our attitudes depends on several factors. For example, attitudes that are specifically relevant to a behavior are most likely to predict that behavior. Thus we could best predict whether or not someone will vote in a mayoral election if we knew the person's attitude on
a. the importance of voting in a democracy.
b. the benefits of efficient city government.
c. corruption in municipal affairs.
d. the importance of this particular election.

3. When we are aware that there is a discrepancy between our attitudes and our behavior, cognitive dissonance theory predicts that we will act to reduce the discomfort or dissonance we feel. The theory explains why
a. people who act against their attitudes tend to change their attitudes.
b. attitudes predict actions when social pressures are minimized.
c. changing an attitude, for example, through persuasion often fails to result in behavioral changes.
d. people are hypocritical, talking one way and acting another.

Social Influence

Social psychology's great lesson—the enormous power of social influence on our attitudes, beliefs, decisions, and actions—can be seen in our conformity, compliance, and group behavior. Suicides, bomb threats, airplane hijackings, and UFO sightings all have a curious tendency to come in waves. Armed with principles of social influence, advertisers and salespeople aim to sway our decisions to buy, to donate, to vote. Isolated with others who share their grievances, dissenters may gradually become rebels and rebels may become terrorists. Let's examine these potent social forces.

Conformity and Obedience

Preview Question

4. What do experiments on conformity and compliance reveal about the power of social influence?

Behavior is contagious. One person giggles, coughs, or yawns, and others in the group are soon doing the same. A cluster of people stands gazing upward, and passersby pause to do likewise. Laughter, even canned laughter, can be infectious. Bartenders and street musicians know to "seed" their tip cups with money that suggests that others have given.

Sometimes, the effects of suggestibility are more serious. Sociologist David Phillips and his colleagues (1985, 1989) found that known suicides increase following a highly publicized suicide (Figure 14–2). So do fatal auto accidents and private airplane crashes (some of which disguise suicides).

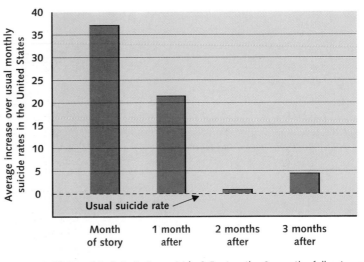

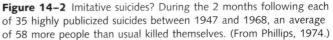

Figure 14–2 Imitative suicides? During the 2 months following each of 35 highly publicized suicides between 1947 and 1968, an average of 58 more people than usual killed themselves. (From Phillips, 1974.)

"The person we have to thank is Arthur here. He's the one with the infectious grin."

Drawing by Handelsman; © 1984 The New Yorker Magazine, Inc.

These increases occur only in the areas where the suicide is publicized, and the victims tend to be near the age of the publicized suicide victim. Following film star Marilyn Monroe's suicide on August 6, 1962, there were 200 more August suicides in the United States than normal. In Germany and the United States, escalated suicide rates have also followed fictional suicides on soap operas, and even on well-intentioned dramas dealing with the issue (Gould & Shaffer, 1986; Hafner & Schmidtke, 1989; Phillips, 1982). Such outbreaks of copycat suicides help explain the clusters of teenage suicides that occasionally occur in some communities.

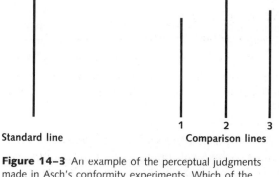

Standard line   Comparison lines

Figure 14–3 An example of the perceptual judgments made in Asch's conformity experiments. Which of the three comparison lines is equal to the standard line? What do you suppose most people would say after hearing four others say "line 3"?

In this photo from the Asch experiment, the subject (center) shows the severe discomfort that comes from disagreeing with the responses of other group members.

"It is too easy to go over to the majority."

Seneca
Ad Lucilium Epistula, A.D. 63–65

Group Pressure and Conformity

Suggestibility is a subtle type of **conformity**, adjusting our thinking or behavior to bring it into line with some group standard. To study conformity Solomon Asch (1955) devised a simple test. As one of his subjects, you arrive at the experiment location in time to take a seat at the end of a row where four people are already seated. The experimenter asks which of three comparison lines is identical to the standard line (Figure 14–3). You see clearly that the answer is line 2 and await your turn to say so after the others. Your boredom with this experiment begins to show when the next set of lines proves equally easy.

Now comes the third trial, and the correct answer seems just as clear-cut, but the first person gives what strikes you as a wrong answer: "Line 3." When the second person and then the third give the same wrong answer, you sit straight up and squint. When the fourth person agrees with the first three, you feel your heart begin to pound. The experimenter then looks to you for your answer. Torn between the unanimity of your four fellow subjects and the evidence of your own eyes, you feel tense and much less sure of yourself than you were moments ago. You hesitate before answering, wondering whether you should suffer the discomfort of being viewed as an oddball. What answer do you give?

In the experiments conducted by Asch and others after him, thousands of college students have experienced this conflict. Answering such questions alone, they erred less than 1 percent of the time. But it was a different story when several others—who were actually confederates working for the experimenter—answered incorrectly. Asch reports that his "intelligent and well-meaning" college subjects were then "willing to call white black" more than one-third of the time by going along with the group.

Conditions That Strengthen Conformity   Asch's procedure became the model for later investigations. Although experiments have not always found such a high degree of blind conformity, they reveal that conformity increases when:

We are made to feel incompetent or insecure.

The group has at least three people. (Further increases in the group size do not yield much increase in conformity.)

The group is unanimous. (The support of a single fellow dissident greatly increases our social courage.)

We admire the group's status and attractiveness.

We have made no prior commitment to any response.

Others in the group observe our behavior.

Our culture strongly encourages respect for social standards.

Thus, we might predict the behavior of Joe, an eager but insecure new member of a prestigious fraternity: Noting that the 40 other members appear unanimous in their plans for an upcoming fund-raiser, Joe is unlikely to voice his dissent.

Reasons for Conforming Why do people comply with social pressure? Why do we clap when others clap, eat as others eat, believe what others believe, even see what others see? Frequently, it is to avoid rejection or to gain social approval. In such cases, we are responding to what social psychologists call **normative social influence.** We are sensitive to social **norms**—understood rules for accepted and expected behavior—because the price we pay for being different may be severe. Marco Lokar knows. During the 1991 Persian Gulf War, Lokar, an Italian, was the only Seton Hall University basketball player who chose not to display an American flag on his uniform. When, as the team traveled about, the fan abuse over his nonconforming behavior became unbearable, he quit the team and returned to Italy.

But there is another reason: We may conform because the group can provide valuable information. When we accept others' opinions about reality, we are responding to **informational social influence.** "Those who never retract their opinions love themselves more than they love truth," observed Joseph Joubert, an eighteenth-century French essayist.

As these reasons for conformity suggest, social influence can be either constructive or destructive. When influence supports what we approve, then we applaud those who are "open-minded" and "sensitive" enough to be "responsive." When influence supports what we disapprove, then we scorn the "submissive conformity" of those who comply with others' wishes. As we will see in Chapter 15, Social Diversity, cultures vary in the value they place on independence versus responsiveness to others. Europeans and those in most English-speaking countries tend to prize independence more than conformity and obedience.

Obedience

Social psychologist Stanley Milgram (1974) knew that people often comply with social pressures. But how would they respond to outright commands? To find out, he undertook what have become social psychology's most famous and controversial experiments. Imagine yourself as one of the nearly 1000 participants in Milgram's 20 experiments.

Responding to an advertisement, you come to Yale University's psychology department to participate in an experiment. Professor Milgram's assistant explains that the study concerns the effect of punishment on learning. You and another subject draw slips out of a hat to see who will be the "teacher" (which your slip says) and who will be the "learner." The learner is then led to an adjoining room and strapped into a chair that is wired through the wall to an electric shock machine. You sit down in front of the machine, which has switches labeled with voltages. Your task: to teach and then test the learner on a list of word pairs. You are to punish the learner for wrong answers by delivering brief electric shocks, beginning with a switch labeled "15 Volts—Slight Shock." After each error by the learner you are to move up to the next higher voltage. With each flick of a switch, lights flash, relay switches click on, and an electric buzzing fills the air.

"'The way to get along,' I was told when I entered Congress, 'is to go along.'"

John F. Kennedy
Profiles in Courage, 1956

---

conformity Adjusting one's behavior or thinking to coincide with a group standard.

normative social influence Influence resulting from a person's desire to gain approval or avoid disapproval.

norms Understood rules for accepted and expected behavior. Norms prescribe "proper" behavior.

informational social influence Influence resulting from one's willingness to accept others' opinions about reality.

Stanley Milgram (1933–1984), whose obedience experiments now "belong to the self-understanding of literate people in our age" (Sabini, 1986).

If you comply with the experimenter's instructions, you hear the learner grunt when you flick the third, fourth, and fifth switches. After you activate the eighth switch (labeled "120 Volts"), the learner shouts that the shocks are painful. After the tenth switch ("150 Volts—Strong Shock"), he cries, "Experimenter, get me out of here! I won't be in the experiment anymore! I refuse to go on!" You draw back when you hear these pleas, but the experimenter prods you: "Please continue—the experiment requires that you continue." If you still resist, he insists, "It is absolutely essential that you continue," or "You have no other choice, you *must* go on."

If you obey, you hear the learner's protests escalate to shrieks of agony as you continue to raise the shock level with each succeeding error. After the 330-volt level, the learner refuses to answer and soon falls silent. Still, the experimenter pushes you toward the final, 450-volt switch, ordering you to ask the questions and, if a correct answer is not given, to administer the next shock level.

How far do you think you would follow the experimenter's commands? When Milgram surveyed people before conducting the experiment, most declared they would stop playing such a sadistic role soon after the learner first indicates pain and certainly before he shrieks in agony. This also was the prediction made by each of 40 psychiatrists whom Milgram asked to guess the outcome. When Milgram actually conducted the experiment with men aged 20 to 50, he was astonished to find that 63 percent complied fully—right up to the last switch.

Did the teachers figure out the hoax—that no shock was being delivered? Did they guess that the learner was a confederate who only pretended to feel the shocks? Did they realize that the experiment was really testing their willingness to comply with commands to inflict punishment? No, the teachers typically displayed genuine agony: They sweated, trembled, laughed nervously, and bit their lips. In defense of his use of deception, Milgram pointed out that, after learning of the deception and actual research purposes, virtually none regretted participating. When 40 of the subjects who had agonized most were later interviewed by a psychiatrist, none appeared to be suffering emotional aftereffects.

Perhaps the subjects obeyed because the learners' protests were not convincing. To preclude this possibility, Milgram repeated the experiment. This time his confederate mentioned a "slight heart condition" while being strapped into the chair and then complained and screamed more intensely as the shocks became more punishing. Still, when 40 new teachers were tested, 65 percent complied fully (Figure 14–4).

In later experiments, Milgram discovered that when he varied the social conditions, the proportion of fully compliant subjects varied from 0 to 93 percent. Obedience was highest when:

The one giving the orders was close at hand and perceived as a legitimate authority figure.

The authority figure was supported by a prestigious institution. (Milgram got somewhat less compliance when he dissociated his experiments from Yale University.)

The victim was depersonalized or at a distance, even in another room. (Similarly, in combat with an enemy they can see, many soldiers will either not fire their rifles or not aim them properly. Such refusals to kill are rare among those who operate the more distant weapons of artillery or aircraft [Padgett, 1989].)

There were no role models for defiance; that is, there were no other subjects seen disobeying the experimenter.

"Drive off the cliff, James, I want to commit suicide."

Drawing by Mel Yauk; © 1981

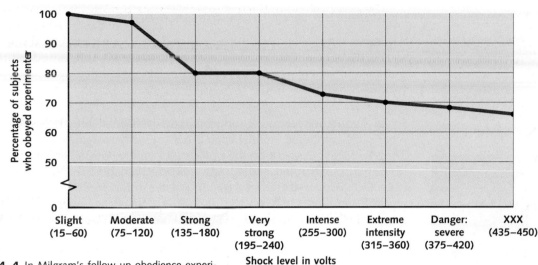

Figure 14-4 In Milgram's follow-up obedience experiment, 65 percent of the adult male subjects fully obeyed the experimenter's commands to continue. This was despite the victim's "heart condition" and despite hearing cries of protest after 150 volts and agonized protests after 330 volts. (Data from Milgram, 1974.)

"I was only following orders."

Adolf Eichmann, director of Nazi deportation of Jews to concentration camps

". . . the Milgram experiment is really a valuable attack on the denial and indifference of all of us. Whatever upset follows facing the truth, we must eventually face up to the fact that so many of us are, in fact, available to be genociders or their assistants."

Israel W. Charny
Executive Director, International Conference on the Holocaust and Genocide, 1982

Lessons from the Conformity and Obedience Studies

What do these experiments teach us about ourselves? How does judging the length of a line or flicking a shock switch relate to everyday social behavior? Recall from Chapter 1 that psychological experiments aim not to recreate the literal behaviors of everyday life but to capture and explore the underlying processes that shape those behaviors. Asch and Milgram devised experiments in which the subjects had to choose between holding to their own standards and being responsive to others, a dilemma we all face frequently.

In Milgram's experiments, subjects were also torn between what they should respond to—the pleas of the victim or the orders of the experimenter. Their moral sense warned them not to harm another, but it also prompted them to obey the experimenter and to be a good subject. With kindness and obedience on a collision course, obedience usually won.

These experiments demonstrate that social influences can be strong enough to make people conform to falsehoods or capitulate to cruelty. "The most fundamental lesson of our study," Milgram noted, is that "ordinary people, simply doing their jobs, and without any particular hostility on their part, can become agents in a terrible destructive process" (1974, p. 6). Milgram entrapped his subjects not by asking them first to zap someone with enough electricity to stand their hair on end. Rather, he exploited the foot-in-the-door effect, beginning with a little tickle of electricity and escalating step by step. In the subjects' minds, the little action became justified, making the next act tolerable.

So it happens when people succumb, gradually, to evil. In any society, great evils sometimes grow out of people's compliance with little evils. The Nazi leaders suspected that most German civil servants would resist shooting or gassing Jews directly, but found them surprisingly willing to handle the paperwork of the Holocaust (Silver & Geller, 1978). Likewise, when Milgram asked 40 men to administer the learning test while someone else did the shocking, 93 percent complied.

Group Influence

How do groups affect our behavior? To find out, social psychologists study the various influences that operate in the simplest of groups—one person in the presence of another—and those that operate in more complex groups, such as families, teams, and committees.

Individual Behavior in the Presence of Others

Appropriately, social psychology's first experiments focused on the simplest of all questions about social behavior: How are we influenced by the mere presence of others—by people watching us or joining us as we engage in various activities?

Social Facilitation   Having noticed that cyclists' racing times were faster when they competed against each other rather than against a clock, Norman Triplett (1898) guessed that the presence of others boosts performance. To test his hypothesis, Triplett had adolescents wind a fishing reel as rapidly as possible. He discovered that they wound faster in the presence of someone who worked simultaneously on the same task. This stronger performance in the presence of others is known as social facilitation. For example, after a light turns green, drivers take about 15 percent less time to travel the first 100 yards when another car is beside them at the intersection than when they are alone (Towler, 1986). But on certain other tasks, such as learning nonsense syllables or solving complex multiplication problems, people perform less well when there are observers or co-workers present.

Further studies revealed why the others' presence sometimes helps and sometimes hinders performance (Guerin, 1986; Zajonc, 1965). When observed by others, people become aroused. This arousal strengthens the most likely response—the correct one on an easy task, an incorrect one on a difficult task. Thus, when observed, people perform well-learned tasks more quickly and accurately and unmastered tasks less quickly and accurately. James Michaels and his associates (1982) found that expert pool players who made 71 percent of their shots when alone made 80 percent when four people came up to watch them. Poor shooters, who made 36 percent of their shots when alone, made only 25 percent when watched. **The moral:** What you do well, you are likely to do even better in front of an audience; what you normally find difficult may seem impossible when others are watching.

Social facilitation also helps explain a funny effect of crowding: Comedy records that are mildly amusing to people in an uncrowded room seem funnier to people in a densely packed room (Aiello & others, 1983; Freedman & Perlick, 1979). As comedians and actors know, a "good house" is a full one. The arousal triggered by crowding amplifies other reactions, too. If sitting close, experimental subjects like a friendly person more, an unfriendly person less (Schiffenbauer & Schiavo, 1976; Storms & Thomas, 1977).

Social Loafing   The social facilitation experiments test the effect of others' presence on *individual* effort in tasks ranging from winding fishing reels to shooting pool. But what happens in situations that require a *team* effort to achieve a common goal? In a team tug-of-war, do you suppose people would individually exert more, less, or the same effort as they would in a one-on-one tug-of-war?

To find out, Alan Ingham and his fellow researchers (1974) asked blind-folded University of Massachusetts students to "pull as hard as you can" on a rope. When Ingham fooled the students into believing three others were also pulling behind them, they exerted only 82 percent as much effort as when they knew they were pulling alone.

To describe the diminished effort by those submerged in a group, Bibb Latané and his colleagues (1981; Jackson & Williams, 1988) coined the term social loafing. In more than four dozen experiments conducted in the United States, India, Thailand, Japan, and Taiwan, social loafing occurred on various tasks (Gabrenya & others, 1983). For example, blindfolded subjects seated in a group have clapped or shouted as loud as they could while listening through

Preview Question

5. In what ways are we affected by the mere presence of others?

Athletes often find they are "on" before a crowd. Spectators inspire them to excel, illustrating the principle that emotional arousal leads to better performance on well-learned tasks.

social facilitation   Improved performance of tasks in the presence of others; occurs with simple or well-learned tasks but not with tasks that are difficult or not yet mastered.

social loafing   The tendency for people in a group to exert less effort when pooling their efforts toward attaining a common goal than when individually accountable.

headphones to the sound of loud clapping or shouting. When told they were doing it with the others, the subjects produced about one-third less noise than when they thought their individual efforts were identifiable.

Why? First, people acting as part of a group feel less accountable and therefore worry less about what others think. Second, they may view their contribution as dispensable (Harkins & Szymanski, 1989; Kerr & Bruun, 1983). As many leaders of organizations know, if group members share equally in the group's benefits regardless of how much they contribute, they may slack off and "free-ride" on the other group members' efforts.

Deindividuation   We have seen that the presence of others can arouse people (as in the social facilitation experiments) or can diminish their feelings of responsibility (as in the social loafing experiments). Sometimes the presence of others both arouses people *and* diminishes their sense of responsibility. The result can be uninhibited behavior ranging from a food fight in the dining hall or screaming at a basketball referee to vandalism or rioting. Abandoning normal restraints to the power of the group is termed **deindividuation.** To be deindividuated is to be less self-conscious and less restrained in a group situation.

Deindividuation often occurs when group participation makes people feel aroused and anonymous. In one experiment, New York University women dressed in depersonalizing Ku Klux Klan style hoods delivered twice as much electric shock to a victim as did identifiable women (Zimbardo, 1970). (As in all such experiments, the "victim" did not actually receive the shocks.) Similarly, tribal warriors who depersonalize themselves with face paints or masks are more likely than those with exposed faces to kill, torture, or mutilate captured enemies (Watson, 1973). Whether in a mob, at a rock concert, at a dance, or at worship, to lose one's self-consciousness (to become deindividuated) is to become more responsive to the group experience and—for better or for worse—to give up some self-control.

Deindividuation. Whether in experiments or in real-life situations like this rock concert, people made anonymous act on their impulses with less restraint.

Preview Question

6. What are group polarization and groupthink?

deindividuation The loss of self-awareness and self-restraint occurring in group situations that foster arousal and anonymity.

group polarization The enhancement of a group's prevailing attitudes through discussion.

Effects of Group Interaction

We have examined the conditions under which the presence of others can fuel mob violence and enhance humor, make easy tasks easier and difficult tasks harder, tempt people to free-ride on the efforts of others and motivate them to cycle faster. Research shows how group interaction, too, can have both bad and good effects.

Group Polarization   Educational researchers have noted that, over time, initial differences between groups of college students often grow. If the first-year students at College *X* tend to be more intellectually oriented than those at College *Y*, chances are this difference will be amplified by the time they are seniors. Similarly, if the political conservatism of students who join fraternities and sororities is greater than that of students who do not, the gap in the political attitudes of the two groups will probably widen as they progress through college (Wilson & others, 1975).

This enhancement of a group's prevailing tendencies—called **group polarization**—occurs when people within a group discuss attitudes that most of them favor or oppose. For example, George Bishop and I discovered that when prejudiced high school students discussed racial issues, their attitudes became more prejudiced. When low-prejudice students discussed the same issues, they became more tolerant (Myers & Bishop, 1970).

Group polarization can have beneficial results, as when it strengthens the resolve of those in a self-help group. But it can also have dire consequences. From their analysis of terrorist organizations around the world, psychologists

groupthink The mode of thinking that occurs when the desire for harmony in a decision-making group overrides a realistic appraisal of alternatives.

"One's impulse to blow the whistle on this nonsense was simply undone by the circumstances of the discussion."

Arthur M. Schlesinger, Jr. (1965, p. 255)

Clark McCauley and Mary Segal (1987) note that the terrorist mentality does not erupt suddenly. Rather, it arises among people who have come together because of a grievance and who become more and more extreme as they interact in isolation from moderating influences.

Groupthink   Does group interaction ever distort important group decisions? Social psychologist Irving Janis thought so when he first read historian Arthur M. Schlesinger, Jr.'s, account of how President John F. Kennedy and his advisers blundered into an ill-fated plan to invade Cuba with 1400 CIA-trained Cuban exiles. When the invaders were easily captured and soon linked to the American government, Kennedy wondered aloud, "How could we have been so stupid?"

To find out, Janis (1982) studied the decision-making procedures that led to the fiasco. He discovered that the high morale of the recently elected President and his advisers fostered a sense that the plan would succeed. To preserve the good group feeling, dissenting views were suppressed or self-censored, especially after the President voiced his enthusiasm for the scheme. Since no one spoke sharply against the idea, everyone assumed there was consensus support for it. To describe this harmonious but unrealistic group thinking, Janis coined the term **groupthink**.

Janis and others then examined other historical fiascos—the failure to anticipate the Pearl Harbor attack, the escalation of the Vietnam war, the Watergate cover-up, the Chernobyl reactor accident (Reason, 1987), and the space shuttle *Challenger* explosion (Esser & Lindoerfer, 1989). They discovered that in these cases, too, groupthink was fed by overconfidence, conformity, self-justification, and group polarization. Buoyed by a string of successful space shuttle launches, the NASA management team approached the 1985 *Challenger* mission brimming with confidence but frustrated by launch delays. When the rocket booster's engineers opposed the launch because of dangers posed by freezing temperatures, group pressures to go ahead effectively silenced their warnings. Unless the engineers could *prove* that the rocket seals would not hold, the management group would not agree to another delay. Moreover, managers shielded the NASA executive who made the final "go" decision from information about the warnings. Wrongly assuming that the support was unanimous, he launched the *Challenger* on its one-way flight to annihilation.

Despite such fiascos and tragedies, Janis also knew that, with some types of problems, two heads are better than one. So he also studied instances in which American presidents and their advisers collectively made good decisions. Examples were the Truman administration's formulation of the Marshall Plan for getting Europe back on its feet after World War II and the Kennedy administration's actions to keep the Soviets from installing missiles in Cuba. In such instances—and in the business world, too, Janis believed—groupthink is prevented by a leader who welcomes various opinions, invites experts' critiques of developing plans, or even assigns people to identify possible problems. As the suppression of dissent bends a group toward bad decisions, so open debate often shapes good decisions.

In affirming the power of social influence, we must not overlook our power as individuals. As we noted in Chapter 11, Personality, *social control* (the power of the situation) and *personal control* (the power of the individual) interact. Many of the situations that influence us are ones we choose to help create. If we expect people to be uncooperative and hostile, we may treat them in ways that elicit such behavior. Thus, our expectations may be self-fulfilling. In one experiment, men talked more charmingly over the phone to women they believed to be beautiful. This led the women to respond more

Standing against a group. Facing strong pressures to conform, obey, or concur with a group, most will do so. Yet some individuals resist coercion, as did this unarmed Beijing man challenging a line of tanks after the 1989 Tiananmen Square uprising was crushed.

warmly—confirming the men's idea that attractive people are likable (Snyder & others, 1977).

Minority Influence

The powers of individuals also appear in their influence over their groups. Social history is often made by a minority that sways the majority. Were this not so, women would still not have the right to vote in the United States, communism would have remained a political theory, and Christianity would be a small Middle Eastern sect. Technological history, too, is often made by innovative minorities who overcome the majority's resistance to change. To many folks, the railroad was a nonsensical idea; some farmers feared that train noise would prevent hens from laying eggs. People derided Robert Fulton's steamboat as "Fulton's Folly." As Fulton later said, "Never did a single encouraging remark, a bright hope, a warm wish, cross my path." Much the same reaction greeted the printing press, the telegraph, the incandescent lamp, and the typewriter (Cantril & Bumstead, 1960).

To understand better how minorities can sway majorities, social psychologists in Europe have investigated groups in which an individual or two consistently expresses a controversial attitude or an unusual perceptual judgment. They have repeatedly found that a minority that unswervingly holds to its position is far more successful in swaying the majority than is a minority that waffles. Holding consistently to a minority opinion will not make you popular, but it may make you influential. This is especially so if your self-confidence stimulates others to consider why you react as you do. Although people often follow the majority view publicly, they may privately develop sympathy for the minority view. Even when a minority's influence is not yet visible, it may be persuading some members of the majority to rethink their views (Maass & Clark, 1984; Nemeth, 1986). Thus, although the combined powers of social thinking and social influence are enormous, so are the powers of the committed individual.

Preview Question

7. Can a minority sway a majority?

As the life of Mahatma Gandhi (1869–1948) powerfully testifies, a consistent and persistent minority voice can sometimes sway the majority. Gandhi was often vilified and imprisoned. But his nonviolent appeals and fasts eventually won independence for India.

Rehearse It

4. In a classic experiment on obedience, Stanley Milgram tested his subjects' willingness to comply with a command to deliver painful high-voltage shocks to another person. Although no shocks were given, the subjects believed that they were—and more than 60 percent complied with the experimenter's instruction to deliver stronger and stronger shocks. In subsequent experiments, Milgram's obedience studies showed that the rate of compliance was highest when
a. the victim was at a distance.
b. the experimenter was in another room.
c. other subjects refused to go along with the experimenter.
d. the subjects believed that the victim had a heart condition or some other vulnerability.

5. Conformity involves adjusting our thinking and behavior toward others in the group. Conformity studies have found that a person is most likely to conform to a group that consists of
a. people with diverse opinions.
b. social equals or inferiors.
c. at least three people.
d. people who will not observe the person's response.

6. In the presence of others we become emotionally aroused: Before an audience, a swimmer swims faster. Social facilitation—improved performance in the presence of others—occurs with
a. any physical task.
b. new learning.
c. a well-learned task.
d. competitive sports or activities only.

7. In a group situation that fosters arousal and anonymity, a person sometimes loses self-consciousness and self-control. This phenomenon, called deindividuation, is best illustrated by
a. improved performance in front of an audience.
b. unrestrained behavior at a mass rally.
c. evasion of responsibility in a group clean-up effort.
d. denial of one's own perceptions in the face of an opposing consensus.

8. If a group is like-minded, discussion strengthens its prevailing opinion. This effect is called
a. groupthink.
b. minority influence.
c. group polarization.
d. social facilitation.

aggression Any physical or verbal behavior intended to hurt or destroy.

Social Relations

Having sampled how we *think* about and *influence* one another, we come finally to social psychology's third focus—how we *relate* to one another. We will consider the bad and the good: aggression, helpfulness, and attraction.

Aggression

In psychology, aggression has a more precise meaning than it does in everyday usage. The assertive, persistent salesperson is not aggressive. Nor is the dentist who makes you wince with pain. But the person who passes along a vicious rumor about you and the attacker who mugs you are. **Aggression** is any physical or verbal behavior intended to hurt or destroy, whether done out of hostility or as a calculated means to an end. Some of the 25,000 murders and more than one million assaults recorded in the United States during 1991 were cool, calculated acts, but more were hostile outbursts.

Time and again, we have seen that behavior emerges from the interaction of our biology and experience. Research on aggression reinforces that theme. For a gun to fire, the trigger must be pulled; with some people, as with hair-trigger guns, it doesn't take much to trip an explosion. Let us look first at biological factors that influence our thresholds for aggressive behavior. Then we will examine the psychological factors that pull the trigger.

The Biology of Aggression

According to one view, argued by Sigmund Freud among others, our species has a volcanic potential to erupt in aggression. Freud thought that, along with positive survival instincts, we harbor a self-destructive "death instinct" that we usually displace toward others as aggression or release in socially approved activities such as painting or sports.

Although aggression varies too widely from culture to culture and person to person to be considered an unlearned instinct, biology does influence aggression. Stimuli that trigger aggressive behavior operate through our biological system. We can look for physiological influences at three levels—genetic, neural, and biochemical. Our genes engineer our individual nervous systems, which operate electrochemically.

Genetic Influences Animals have been bred for aggressiveness, sometimes for sport, sometimes for research. Twin studies suggest that genes influence human aggression as well (Rushton & others, 1986). If one identical twin admits to "having a violent temper," the other twin will often independently admit the same. Fraternal twins are much more likely to respond differently.

Neural Influences Animal and human brains have neural systems that, when stimulated, produce aggressive behavior (Moyer, 1983). Consider:

> A cat lives harmoniously with a rat until one day an implanted electrode stimulates a specific spot in its hypothalamus. Immediately, the cat attacks its cagemate and kills it as would a wild cat, by biting through its spinal cord at the neck.

> A mild-mannered woman has an electrode implanted deep in her brain's limbic system (in the amygdala) by neurosurgeons seeking to diagnose a disorder. Because the brain has no sensory receptors, she cannot feel any stimulation. But at the flick of a switch she snarls, "Take my blood pressure. Take it now," and then stands up and begins to strike the doctor.

Preview Question

8. What biological factors influence aggressive behavior?

Intensive evaluation of 15 death-row inmates reveals that all 15 have suffered severe head injury. Researcher Dorothy Lewis and her colleagues (1986) infer that many condemned criminals suffer unrecognized neurological disorders.

Biochemical Influences Hormones and other substances in the blood influence the neural systems that activate and inhibit aggression. A raging bull will become a gentle Ferdinand when castration reduces its testosterone level. The same is true of castrated mice. When injected with testosterone, the castrated mice again become aggressive.

Although humans are less sensitive to hormonal changes, violent criminals tend to be muscular young males with lower than average intelligence scores and higher than average testosterone levels (Dabbs & others, 1987; Wilson & Herrnstein, 1985). Drugs that sharply reduce their testosterone levels subdue their aggressive tendencies. Among the normal range of teenage boys and adult men, high testosterone levels correlate with delinquency, hard drug use, and aggressive, bullying responses to provocation (Archer, 1991; Dabbs & Morris, 1990; Olweus & others, 1988).

For both biological and psychological reasons, alcohol unleashes aggressive responses to provocation (Bushman & Cooper, 1990; Taylor & Leonard, 1983). Police data and prison surveys reinforce conclusions from experiments on alcohol and aggression. Intoxicated people commit 65 percent of murders, 88 percent of knifings, 65 percent of spouse beatings, and 55 percent of physical child abuse (Steele, 1990).

The traffic between hormones and behavior is two-way. Testosterone heightens dominance and aggressiveness, but dominating or defeating also boosts testosterone levels (Gladue & others, 1989).

"He that is naturally addicted to Anger, let him Abstain from Wine; for it is but adding Fire to Fire."

Seneca
De Ira, A.D. 49

A 1985 riot at a soccer game in Brussels left 38 dead and 437 injured. Aroused by the competition and loaded with alcohol, English fans lost all restraint when provoked by Italian fans. They attacked the Italians, who retreated and were then crushed against a wall.

The Psychology of Aggression

Biological factors influence the ease with which psychological aggravations pull the aggression trigger. But what psychological factors do the pulling?

Aversive Events Although suffering sometimes builds character, it may also bring out the worst in us. Studies in which animals or humans experience unpleasant, uncontrollable events reveal that those made miserable often make others miserable (Berkowitz, 1983, 1989).

Preview Question

9. What psychological factors influence aggressive behavior?

Aversive events can trigger aggression, especially when blamed on another.

Being unable to achieve a goal also increases people's readiness to behave aggressively. This phenomenon has led to the **frustration-aggression principle:** Frustration creates anger, which may generate aggression. When social psychologists realized that events such as physical pain and personal insults also trigger aggression, they saw that frustrations are instances of aversive events. Foul odors, hot temperatures, cigarette smoke, and a host of other aversive stimuli can also evoke hostility (Figure 14–5).

Figure 14–5 Uncomfortably hot weather can elicit and heighten aggressive reactions. More violent crime and spouse abuse occurs in summer than in winter, in hot years than in cooler years, in hot cities than in cooler cities, and on hotter days than on colder days (Anderson 1989). For example, between 1980 and 1982 in Houston, murders and rapes were more common on days over 91° F. This finding is consistent with those from laboratory experiments in which people working in a hot room react to provocations with greater hostility. (From Anderson & Anderson, 1984.)

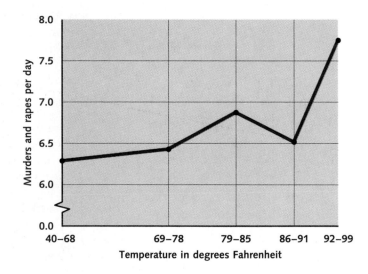

frustration-aggression principle The principle that frustration—the blocking of an attempt to achieve some goal—creates anger, which can generate aggression.

Learning to Express and Inhibit Aggression Aggression may be a natural response to aversive events, but learning can alter natural reactions. Animals naturally eat when they are hungry. But if appropriately rewarded or punished, they can be taught either to overeat or to starve.

Aggressive reactions are more likely in situations where experience has taught us that aggression pays. Children whose aggression successfully intimidates other children may become more aggressive. Violent demonstrations that provide demonstrators with desired attention may recur.

Aggressive behavior can be learned through direct rewards, as when animals that have fought successfully to get food or mates become increasingly ferocious. It can also be learned through observation. Children who grow up observing aggressive models often imitate the behaviors they see. For example, parents of delinquent youngsters typically rely on beatings for discipline, thus modeling aggression as a method of dealing with problems (Patterson & others, 1982). Once established, aggressive behavior patterns are difficult to change. To foster a kinder, gentler world we had best model and reward sensitivity and cooperation from an early age, perhaps by training parents how to discipline without modeling violence.

Television Watching and Aggression Parents aren't the only ones who model aggression. During their first 18 years, most children spend more time watching television than they spend in school. In urban homes across the world, including those of South America and Asia, television is now commonplace. In Beijing, for example, the percentage of homes with television skyrocketed from 32 percent in 1980 to 95 percent by the end of the decade (Lull, 1988). Prime-time U.S. programs offer about 6 violent acts per hour; children's weekend programs about 26 (Gerbner & Signorielli, 1990). During their impressionable elementary and junior high school years, the average child therefore views some 13,000 TV murders among more than 100,000 acts of violence. This is life as rendered by a rather peculiar storyteller, one who reflects the culture's mythology but not its reality. In action-oriented crime shows, TV cops fire their guns in almost every episode; in Chicago, the average police officer fires a gun once every 27 years (Radecki, 1989).

Does viewing aggression on TV influence some people to commit aggression? To find out, researchers have conducted correlational and experimental studies (Hearold, 1986; Wood & others, 1991).

Correlational studies reveal a link between young boys' violence-viewing and their combativeness as teenagers and young adults (Eron, 1987; Turner & others, 1986). In the United States and Canada, a doubling of homicide rates between 1957 and 1974 coincided with the introduction and spread of violent television. Moreover, census regions that acquired television late showed the homicide jump correspondingly later. Among white South Africans, who were first introduced to television in 1975, a similar near-doubling of the homicide rate did not begin until after 1975 (Centerwall, 1989).

Critics respond that these correlational studies do not prove that viewing violence *causes* aggression (Freedman, 1988; McGuire, 1986). Maybe aggressive children prefer violent programs. Maybe children of neglectful or abusive parents are both more aggressive and more often left in front of the TV. And maybe television merely reflects violent trends.

To pin down causation, experimenters have exposed some viewers to violence and others to entertaining nonviolence and then observed their reactions. Does viewing murder and mayhem make people react more cruelly when irritated? "The consensus among most of the research community," reported the National Institute of Mental Health (1982), "is that violence on television does lead to aggressive behavior by children and teenagers who watch the programs." Statements by the American Psychological Association, American Medical Association, and American Pediatric Association concur. The violence effect stems from a combination of factors—from *arousal* by the violent excitement, from the triggering of violence-related *ideas*, from the erosion of one's *inhibitions*, and from *imitation* (Geen & Thomas, 1986).

Television's unreal world, in which acts of aggression greatly outnumber acts of affection, can also affect our thinking about the real world. Those who

"The problem with television is that the people must sit and keep their eyes glued to a screen: the average American family hasn't time for it. Therefore the showmen are convinced that . . . television will never be a serious competitor of [radio] broadcasting."

The New York Times, 1939

In the days before television

Drawing by Gary Larson: "The Far Side" cartoon is reprinted by permission of Chronicle Features, San Francisco.

TV's greatest effect may stem from what it displaces. Children and adults who spend 4 hours a day watching television spend 4 fewer hours in active pursuits—talking, studying, playing, reading, or socializing with friends. What would you have done with your extra time if you had never watched television?

Stayskal/Tampa Tribune

In other surveys, about half of women report some form of unwanted sexual coercion and most report experiencing verbal sexual harassment (Craig & others, 1989; Koss & Burkhart, 1989; Sandberg & others, 1985).

Pornography means different things to different people. Consistent with Webster's dictionary, some define pornography as erotic depictions intended to excite sexual arousal. Others define it as sexual materials that exploit, degrade, or subordinate women.

watch a great deal of prime-time crime regard the world as more dangerous (Gerbner & Signorielli, 1990; Heath & Petraitis, 1987; Singer & Singer, 1986). Prolonged exposure to violence also desensitizes viewers; they become more indifferent to it when later viewing a brawl, whether on TV or in real life (Rule & Ferguson, 1986). Indeed, suggest Edward Donnerstein and his co-researchers (1987), an evil psychologist could hardly imagine a better way to make people indifferent to brutality than to expose them to a graded series of scenes, from fights to killings to the mutilations of slasher movies.

Sexual Aggression and the Media   Over the last 30 years, America's known rape rate has quadrupled. Recent surveys of both women and men reveal that unreported rapes, most committed by dates or acquaintances, greatly outnumber those reported. In surveys among a nationwide sample of 6200 college students and 2200 Ohio working women, Mary Koss and her colleagues (1987, 1988, 1990) found that 27.5 percent of the women reported an experience that met the legal definition of rape or attempted rape (although one-fourth of them labeled it as such). Only 1 of 4 victims of stranger rape and 1 of 30 victims of acquaintance rape reported the incident to the police. In a 1990 national survey of 4000 women, 1 in 8 reported experiencing rape, most while younger than 18 (National Victim Center, 1992).

Does the dramatic surge in reported rapes reflect an actual increase in sexual violence, or merely a greater willingness to report them? The increase appears real. First, in the government's annual National Crime Survey, the percentage of acknowledged rapes reported to police has *not* been increasing (Koss, 1992). Second, if the number of young females subjected to rape has been increasing, then young women today should be more likely than today's older women ever to have been raped. Indeed, adult women under 45 are two to three times more likely than those over 65 to report ever having been raped (Sorenson & others, 1987). Third, the quadrupling of the known rape rate parallels the quintupling of America's overall violent crime rate since 1960.

What factors might explain the modern epidemic of sexual aggression? Alcohol consumption—often linked with aggression—has not increased. Might changes in the media be a contributing factor? Coincident with the increase in sexual aggression has been, thanks partly to the home video business, easier access to R-rated "slasher films" and X-rated pornographic films. Content analyses reveal that X-rated films mostly depict quick, casual sex between strangers, but that scenes of rape and sexual exploitation of women by men are also common (Cowan & others, 1988; NCTV, 1987; Yang & Linz, 1990). Rape scenes often portray the victim at first fleeing and resisting her attacker, then becoming aroused and finally driven to ecstasy. Most men are not sexually aroused (as measured by a *penile plethysmograph*) while viewing rape depictions. But convicted rapists are. So are normal men if they have been drinking or, if after pedaling an exercise bike, they are angered by a woman's insults (Barbaree, 1991). In less graphic form, the same unrealistic, women-enjoy-being-taken myth is commonplace on TV programs and in romance novels. The woman who first pushes the insistent man away ends up passionately kissing him.

Do such films and other similar materials influence sexual aggression? When interviewed, Canadian and American sex offenders (rapists, child molesters, and serial killers) do report a greater-than-usual appetite for sexually explicit and sexually violent materials—materials typically labeled as "pornography" (Marshall, 1989; Ressler & others, 1988). But are the sexual offenders merely, as sex researcher John Money (1988) believes, using pornography "as an alibi to explain to themselves and their captors what otherwise is inexplicable"?

In follow-up studies, Zillmann (1989) found that after massive exposure to X-rated sexual films, men and women became more accepting of extramarital sex, of women's sexual submission to men, and of a man's seducing a 12-year-old girl. As people heavily exposed to televised crime perceive the world as more dangerous, so people heavily exposed to pornography see the world as more sexual—as a place where, say, extramarital and group sex are commonplace.

Experiments on the effects of viewing violent pornography raise concerns about society's acceptance of its degradation of women.

Laboratory experiments, which do pin down cause and effect, reveal that repeated viewing of X-rated films (even if nonviolent) makes one's own partner seem less attractive (page 285) and makes sexual aggression seem less serious. In one such experiment, Dolf Zillmann and Jennings Bryant (1984) showed undergraduates six brief, sexually explicit films a week for 6 weeks. A control group viewed nonerotic films during the same 6-week period. Three weeks later, both groups read a newspaper report about a man convicted but not yet sentenced for raping a hitchhiker. When asked to suggest an appropriate prison term, those who had viewed sexually explicit films recommended sentences half as long as the control group's.

In search of possible effects of films on men's willingness to aggress against women, experimenters examined, first, the effect of film viewing on men's acceptance of the "rape myth" (the idea that some women would enjoy being raped). Neil Malamuth and James Check (1981) compared University of Manitoba men who were shown either two nonsexual movies or two movies depicting a man sexually overpowering a woman. A week later, when surveyed by a different experimenter, those who had seen the films with mild sexual violence were more accepting of violence against women. Further experiments showed that viewing slasher movies, such as *The Texas Chainsaw Massacre*, can also lead viewers to trivialize rape.

Experiments have also explored the effect of violent versus nonviolent films on men's willingness to deliver supposed electric shocks to women who earlier provoked them. (Although such experiments cannot study actual sexual violence, they can assess a man's willingness to hurt a woman.) These experiments suggest that it's not eroticism but depictions of sexual *violence* (whether in R-rated slasher films or X-rated films) that most affect men's acceptance and performance of aggression against women. A 1986 conference of 21 social scientists, including many of the researchers who conducted these experiments, produced a consensus that "pornography that portrays sexual aggression as pleasurable for the victim increases the acceptance of the use of coercion in sexual relations." Moreover, "in laboratory studies measuring short-term effects, exposure to violent pornography increases punitive behavior toward women" (Surgeon General, 1986).

Because significant behaviors such as sexual violence usually have many determinants, any single explanation is probably an oversimplification. Child abuse, hostility, dominance motives, sexual promiscuity, and disinhibition by alcohol are among the known predictors of sexual violence (Malamuth & others, 1991). Still, if media depictions of violence can disinhibit and desensitize, if viewing sexual violence fosters attitudes and behaviors that degrade women, and if viewing pornography can lead viewers to trivialize rape and devalue their partners, then the issue of violence in the media is not a minor one.

Television and pornography researchers have therefore urged teaching people to be critical viewers. The American Psychological Association advises parents not only to limit their children's TV watching but also to watch and discuss programs with their children. Some researchers advocate "media awareness training." "Our utopian and perhaps naive hope," say pornography researchers Edward Donnerstein, Daniel Linz, and Steven Penrod (1987, p. 196), "is that in the end the truth revealed through good science will prevail and the public will be convinced that these images not only demean those portrayed but also those who view them."

Might public consciousness be raised by making people aware of the information you have just been reading? In the 1940s, movies often depicted African Americans as childlike, superstitious buffoons. Today, such images are offensive. In the 1960s and 1970s, entertainment from Beatles' music to

"What we're trying to do is raise the level of awareness of violence against women and pornography to at least the level of awareness of racist and Ku Klux Klan literature."

Gloria Steinem (1988)

movies such as *Easy Rider* glamorized drug use. No longer. Responding to a tidal change in cultural attitudes, the entertainment industry now portrays drugs as dangerous. Is it too much to hope that, without violating artistic freedom, society might soon look back with similar embarrassment on the days when movies "entertained" people with scenes of torture, mutilation, and sexual coercion?

Altruism

Altruism—an unselfish regard for others' welfare—became a major concern of social psychologists after a vile act of sexual violence. A knife-wielding stalker repeatedly stabbed Kitty Genovese, then raped her as she lay dying outside her Queens, New York, apartment at 3:30 A.M. on March 13, 1964. "Oh, my God, he stabbed me!" she screamed into the early-morning stillness. "Please help me!" Windows opened and lights went on as 38 of her neighbors heard her screams. One couple pulled chairs up to the window and turned out the light to see better. Her attacker fled and then returned to stab her eight more times and rape her again. Not until he departed for good did anyone so much as call the police, at 3:50 A.M.

"Probably no single incident has caused social psychologists to pay as much attention to an aspect of social behavior as Kitty Genovese's murder."

R. Lance Shotland (1984)

Bystander Intervention

Reflecting on the Genovese murder and other such tragedies, most commentators lamented the bystanders' "apathy" and "indifference." Rather than blaming them, social psychologists John Darley and Bibb Latané (1968b) attributed onlooker inaction to an important situational factor—the presence of others. Given the right circumstances, they suspected, most of us might behave similarly.

Preview Question

10. What is the bystander effect?

After staging emergencies under various conditions, Darley and Latané assembled their findings into a decision scheme: We will help if and only if the situation enables us first to *notice* the incident, then to *interpret* it as an emergency, and finally to *assume responsibility* for helping (Figure 14–6).

At each step, the presence of other bystanders turns people away from the path that leads to helping. In laboratory experiments and on the street, people in groups of strangers are more likely than solitary individuals to keep their eyes on what they are doing or where they are going. If they notice an unusual situation, they may infer from the blasé reactions of the other passersby that the situation is not an emergency. "The person lying on the sidewalk must be drunk," they think, and move on.

Figure 14–6 The decision-making process for bystander intervention. (From Darley & Latané, 1968b.)

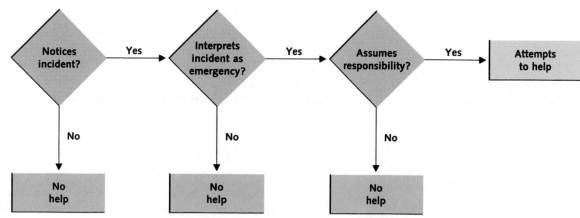

altruism Unselfish regard for the welfare of others.

bystander effect The tendency for any given bystander to be less likely to give aid if other bystanders are present.

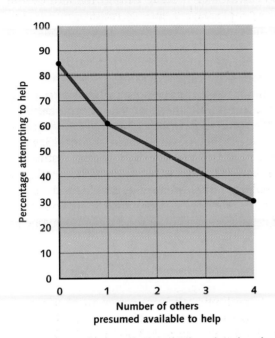

Figure 14–7 When people thought they alone heard an epileptic seizure victim calling for help, they usually helped. But when they thought four others were hearing it, too, fewer than a third responded. (From Darley & Latané, 1968a.)

"Oh, make us happy and you make us good!"

Robert Browning
The Ring and the Book, 1868

Preview Question

11. What other factors influence helping?

But sometimes, as with the Genovese murder, the emergency is unambiguous and people still fail to help. The witnesses looking out through their windows noticed the incident, correctly interpreted the emergency, yet failed to assume responsibility. To find out why, Darley and Latané (1968a) simulated a physical emergency in their laboratory. University students participated in a discussion over an intercom. Each student was in a separate cubicle, and only the person whose microphone was switched on could be heard. One of the students was an accomplice of the experimenters. When his turn came, he called for help and made sounds as though he were having an epileptic seizure.

How did the other students react? As Figure 14–7 shows, those who believed they were the only one who could hear the victim—and therefore thought they bore total responsibility for helping—usually went to his aid. Those who thought others could also hear were more likely to react as did Kitty Genovese's neighbors. The more people shared the responsibility for helping, the less likely any single listener was to help.

In hundreds of additional experiments, psychologists have studied the factors that influence bystanders' willingness to relay an emergency phone call, aid a stranded motorist, donate blood, pick up dropped books, contribute money, and give time to someone. For example, Latané, James Dabbs (1975), and 145 collaborators took 1497 elevator rides in three American cities and "accidentally" dropped coins or pencils in front of 4813 fellow passengers. The women coin-droppers were more likely to receive help than the men—a gender difference often reported by other researchers (Eagly & Crowley, 1986). But the major finding was the **bystander effect**—any particular bystander was less likely to give aid with other bystanders present. When one other person was on the elevator, those who dropped the coins were helped 40 percent of the time. When there were six passengers, help came less than 20 percent of the time.

From their observations of behavior in tens of thousands of such "emergencies," altruism researchers have discerned some additional patterns. The odds of our helping someone are best when:

We have just observed someone else being helpful.

We are not in a hurry.

The victim appears to need and deserve help.

The victim is in some way similar to ourselves.

We are in a small town or rural area.

We are feeling guilty.

We are focused on others and not preoccupied.

We are in a good mood.

This last result, that happy people are helpful people, is one of the most consistent findings in all psychology. No matter how people are cheered—whether by having been made to feel successful and intelligent, by thinking happy thoughts, by finding money, or even by receiving a posthypnotic suggestion—they become more generous and more eager to help (Carlson & others, 1988).

The Psychology of Helping

Why do we help? One widely held view is that self-interest underlies all human interactions, that our constant goal is to maximize rewards and minimize costs. Accountants call it cost-benefit analysis. Philosophers call it utilitarianism. Social psychologists call it *social exchange theory*. If you are pondering whether to donate blood, you may weigh the costs of doing so (time, discomfort, and anxiety) against the benefits (reduced guilt, social approval, good feelings). If the anticipated rewards of helping exceed the anticipated costs, you help.

Social norms also influence helping. They prescribe how we ought to behave, often to our mutual benefit. Through socialization, we learn the *reciprocity norm*, the expectation that we should return help, not harm, to those who have helped us. In our relations with others of similar status, the reciprocity norm compels us to give (in favors, gifts, or social invitations) about as much as we receive. With young children, the disabled, and others who cannot give as much as they receive, we also learn a *social responsibility norm*—that we should help those who need our help, even if the costs outweigh the benefits.

The Evolutionary Psychology of Helping   Evolutionary psychologists suggest that our genes predispose us to act in ways that enhance their chance of surviving and spreading. As novelist Samuel Butler said a century ago, "a hen is only an egg's way of making another egg."

Although heroes who sacrifice their lives for another leave fewer descendants, evolutionary psychologists contend that some forms of altruism help perpetuate our genes. One example is being good to those who can later reciprocate our helpfulness—benefitting us both. An even more obvious example is devotion to our children—the carriers of our genes. Natural selection favors parents who care deeply about their children's survival and welfare. People usually feel empathy toward other relatives, too, in proportion to their genetic closeness. In experiments, people also give more empathy and help to a stranger who looks, acts, and thinks like themselves—someone whose genetic similarities they detect, an evolutionary psychologist would say (Rushton, 1989).

Nevertheless, for some heroic people, a sense of *human* kinship entails the risk of self-sacrifice. The Holocaust memorial in Jerusalem honors 8000 "Righteous Gentiles"—those whose identities are known among the many more Europeans who gave refuge to Jews during World War II. These people knew that if the Nazis learned of their subterfuge, they might suffer a common fate with their guests, as many did. For decades afterward, social scientists interviewed rescuers, searching for the patterns of personality and belief that predict why these heroes acted as so few did.

Where did these people gain the compassion to care and the courage to defy power and authority? Among the predictors were having caring parental models, close-knit families, allegiance to religious or humanitarian convictions, and friendships with Jews who confronted them with the need for help (London, 1970; Oliner & Oliner, 1988). Long after the war, rescuers more than bystanders were caring in new ways—feeding the sick and aged, supporting groups and causes, leading recreational activities, offering counsel. Their lives remind us that some attributes of character shine through differing situations.

Attraction

Pause a moment and think about your relationships with two people—a close friend, and someone who has stirred in you feelings of romantic love. What factors lead to friendship and romance? What factors help us sustain these relationships?

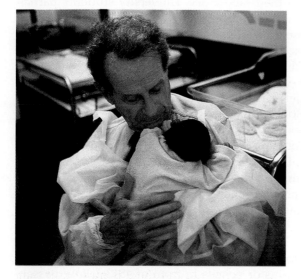

Volunteers are motivated to help if the rewards, whether psychological or social, are greater than the costs. This volunteer finds satisfaction in time spent comforting "boarder babies"—infants born to crack-addicted mothers who cannot care for them.

"I prefer my daughters to my nieces, my nieces to my cousins, my cousins to my neighbors, my neighbors to my fellow citizens, my fellow citizens to foreigners. What's wrong with that?"

Jean-Marie Le Pen, leader of France's far-right National Front, 1992

mere exposure effect The phenomenon that repeated exposure to novel stimuli increases liking of them.

We endlessly wonder how we can win others' affection and what makes our own affections flourish or fade. Do birds of a feather flock together, or do opposites attract? Does familiarity breed contempt or liking? Does absence make the heart grow fonder, or is out of sight out of mind? Social psychology suggests some answers.

The mere exposure effect applies even to ourselves. Have you ever noticed that you never look quite right in photographs? Most of us prefer our familiar mirror-image look to our photo. Most of our friends prefer an actual photo over its mirror-image (Mita & others, 1977). Arsenio Hall is at the left. But, if asked, Arsenio Hall would probably prefer the self at the right, the one he sees in the mirror each morning.

"Personal beauty is a greater recommendation than any letter of introduction."

Aristotle
Apothegems, 330 B.C.

The Psychology of Attraction

What is the psychological chemistry that binds two people together in that special sort of friendship that helps one cope with all other relationships? Consider three ingredients of our liking for one another.

Proximity Before friendships become close, they must begin. Proximity—geographic nearness—is perhaps the most powerful predictor of friendship. Of course, proximity also provides opportunities for aggression. But much more often it instigates liking. Study after study reveals that people are most likely to like, and even to marry, those who live in the same neighborhood, who sit nearby in class, who work in the same office, who share the same parking lot. Look around.

Why is proximity so conducive to liking? Obviously, part of the answer is the greater availability of those we often meet. But there is more to it than that. For one thing, repeated exposure to novel stimuli—be they nonsense syllables, musical selections, geometric figures, Chinese characters, human faces, or the letters of our own name—increases our liking for them (Moreland & Zajonc, 1982; Nuttin, 1987). This phenomenon is known as the **mere exposure effect.** Within certain limits (Bornstein, 1989), familiarity breeds fondness.

Physical Attractiveness Once proximity affords you contact, what most affects your first impressions: the person's sincerity? Intelligence? Personality? Hundreds of experiments reveal that it is probably something more superficial: appearance.

For people taught that "beauty is only skin deep" and that "appearances can be deceiving," the power of physical attractiveness is unnerving. In one early study, Elaine Hatfield and her co-workers (Walster & others, 1966) randomly matched new University of Minnesota students for a "Welcome Week" dance. Before the dance, all took a battery of personality and aptitude tests. On the night of the blind date, the couples danced and talked for more than 2 hours and then took a brief intermission to rate their dates. What determined whether they liked each other? So far as the researchers could determine, only one thing mattered: physical attractiveness (which had been rated by the researchers beforehand). Both the men and the women liked good-looking dates best. Later research confirms that, although women are more likely than men to *say* that another's looks don't affect them, a man's looks do affect women's behavior (Feingold, 1990; Sprecher, 1989; Woll, 1986).

Later studies also reveal that people's physical attractiveness predicts their dating frequency, their feelings of popularity, and others' initial impressions of their personalities. We perceive attractive people, even children and those of our own sex, to be happier, more sensitive, more successful, and more socially skilled, though not more honest or compassionate (Dion, 1986; Eagly & others, 1991; Hatfield & Sprecher, 1986). Attractive and well-dressed people are also more likely to make a favorable impression on potential employers (Cash & Janda, 1984; Solomon, 1987). To judge from their gazing

Couples tend to be matched in attractiveness. If un-matched, the less attractive member often has compensating assets.

"The thin, narrow-shouldered ectomorph who was yesterday's spinster librarian is today's high fashion model; the plump and buxom endomorph who was a Victorian romantic ideal today is eating cottage cheese and grapefruit, and weighing in every Tuesday at Weight Watchers."

Phyllis Bronstein-Burrows (1981)

"Love is a dirty trick played on us to achieve the continuation of the species."

Novelist W. Somerset Maugham (1874–1965)

"Love has ever in view the absolute loveliness of that which it beholds."

George MacDonald
Unspoken Sermons, 1867

times, even babies prefer attractive over unattractive faces (Langlois & others, 1987).

If looks matter so much, who dates and marries those less attractive? Although people might prefer someone superattractive, they tend not to approach those who are "out of their league." Thus, we often match up with people who are about as attractive as we are (Murstein, 1986). When partners are noticeably unequal in attractiveness, the less physically attractive person often has compensating assets, such as greater wealth, status, or social competence. This helps explain why beautiful young women sometimes marry older men whose social or financial status is higher than their own (Elder, 1969).

That looks are important may seem unfair and unenlightened. Two thousand years ago the Roman statesman Cicero felt the same way: "The final good and the supreme duty of the wise person is to resist appearance." Cicero might be reassured by two other findings about attractiveness.

First, people's attractiveness is surprisingly unrelated to their self-esteem (Major & others, 1984). One reason may be that few people view themselves as unattractive. (Thanks, perhaps, to the mere exposure effect, most of us become accustomed to our own faces.) Another reason is that strikingly attractive people are sometimes suspicious that praise may be simply a reaction to their looks. When less attractive people are praised for their work, they are more likely to accept it as sincere.

Cicero might also find comfort in knowing that judgments about attractiveness are relative. They depend first on the accepted standards of beauty in one's place and time. Hoping to look attractive, people in different places have pierced their noses, lengthened their necks, bound their feet, dyed their skin and hair, eaten to achieve a full figure, and liposuctioned fat to achieve a slim one. (The standards by which judges crown "Miss Universe" hardly even apply to the whole planet.) In North America, the ultra-thin ideal of the Roaring Twenties gave way to the soft, voluptuous Marilyn Monroe ideal of the '50s, to be replaced by the lean, athletic ideal of the '80s.

Some aspects of attractiveness, however, cross place and time. It comes as no surprise to evolutionary psychologists that men in 37 cultures, from Australia to Zambia, judge women as more attractive if they have a youthful appearance (Buss, 1989; Cunningham, 1986). Evolutionary psychologists say that men drawn to healthy, fertile-appearing women have stood a better chance of sending their genes into the future. To women, men seem more attractive if they appear mature and dominant. This connotes, say the evolutionary psychologists, a capacity to support and protect (Sadalla & others, 1987).

Cultural differences and similarities aside, attractiveness also depends on our feelings about the person. In a Rodgers and Hammerstein musical, Prince Charming asks Cinderella, "Do I love you because you're beautiful, or are you beautiful because I love you?" Chances are it is both. As we discover someone's similarities to us, see them again and again, and come to like them, their physical imperfections grow less noticeable and their attractiveness grows more apparent (Beaman & Klentz, 1983; Gross & Crofton, 1977). As Shakespeare put it in *A Midsummer Night's Dream,* "Love looks not with the eyes, but with the mind." E.T. is as ugly as Darth Vader, until you get to know him.

Similarity   Let's say that proximity has brought you into contact with someone and that your appearance has made a favorable first impression. What now influences whether acquaintances develop into friends? For example, as

Conceptions of attractiveness vary by culture as well as by time. What may be attractive in one culture may seem strange or unattractive in another, and each of these cultures' concepts of beauty—in Kenya, Morocco, and the United States—may well change in the future.

you get to know someone better, is liking more probable if you are opposites, or if you are alike?

It makes a good story—extremely different types living in harmonious union: Rat, Mole, and Badger in *The Wind in the Willows*, Frog and Toad in Arnold Lobel's books. The stories delight us by expressing what we seldom experience, for we tend to dislike dissimilar people (Rosenbaum, 1986). In real life, birds that flock together are usually of a feather. Friends and couples are far more likely than randomly paired people to share common attitudes, beliefs, and interests (and, for that matter, age, religion, race, education, intelligence, smoking behavior, and economic status). Moreover, the greater their likeness, the more their liking will endure (Byrne, 1971). Similarity breeds content.

Proximity, attractiveness, and similarity are not the only determinants of attraction. We also like those who like us, especially when our self-image is low. When we believe someone likes us, we respond to them more warmly, which leads them to like us even more (Curtis & Miller, 1986). To be liked is powerfully rewarding. Indeed, a simple reward theory of attraction—that we will like those whose behavior is rewarding to us and that we will continue relationships that offer more rewards than costs—can explain all the findings we have considered so far. When a person lives or works in close proximity with someone else, it costs less time and effort to develop the friendship and enjoy its benefits. Attractive people are aesthetically pleasing, and associating with them can be socially rewarding. Those with similar views reward us by validating our own.

Romantic Love

Occasionally, people progress quickly from initial impressions to friendship to the more intense, complex, and mysterious state of romantic love. Elaine Hatfield (1988) distinguishes two types of love: temporary passionate love, and the more enduring *companionate* love.

Passionate Love Noting that arousal is a key ingredient of **passionate love,** Hatfield suggests that the two-factor theory of emotion (page 320) can help us understand this intense positive absorption in another. The theory assumes that emotions have two ingredients—physical arousal plus cognitive ap-

Preview Question

13. What is the distinction between passionate and companionate love?

passionate love An aroused state of intense positive absorption in another, usually present at the beginning of a love relationship.

companionate love The deep affectionate attachment we feel for those with whom our lives are intertwined.

equity A condition in which people receive from a relationship in proportion to what they give to it.

self-disclosure Revealing intimate aspects of oneself to others.

"When two people are under the influence of the most violent, most insane, most delusive, and most transient of passions, they are required to swear that they will remain in that excited, abnormal, and exhausting condition continuously until death do them part."

George Bernard Shaw
Man and Superman, 1903

"When a match has equal partners then I fear not."

Aeschylus
Prometheus Bound, 478 B.C.

praisal—and that arousal from any source can enhance one emotion or another, depending on how we interpret and label the arousal.

In tests of this theory, college men have been aroused by fright, by running in place, by viewing erotic materials, or by listening to humorous or repulsive monologues. They are then introduced to an attractive woman and asked to rate her, or are simply asked to rate their girlfriends. Unlike unaroused men, those who are stirred up attribute some of their arousal to the woman or girlfriend and feel more attracted toward her (Carducci & others, 1978; Dermer & Pyszczynski, 1978; White & others, 1981; White & Kight, 1984).

Outside the laboratory, Donald Dutton and Arthur Aron (1974, 1989) went to two bridges across British Columbia's rocky Capilano River. One was a swaying footbridge 230 feet above the rocks; the other was a low, solid bridge. An attractive young female accomplice intercepted men coming off each bridge, sought their help in filling out a short questionnaire, and then offered her phone number in case they wanted to hear more about her project. Far more of those who had just crossed the high bridge—which left their hearts pounding—accepted the number and later called the woman. To be revved up and to associate some of that arousal with a desirable person is to feel the pull of passion. As lovers who take a thrilling roller coaster ride together know, adrenaline makes the heart grow fonder.

Companionate Love Inevitably, the passion of romantic love subsides. The intense absorption in the other, the thrill of the romance, the giddy "floating on a cloud" feeling fades. JUST MARRIED becomes just married, the magic lost. So, are the French correct in saying that "love makes the time pass and time makes love pass"?

Hatfield notes that if love matures it becomes a warmer, steadier **companionate love**—a deep, affectionate attachment. There may be adaptive wisdom to this change from passion to affection. Passionate love often brings children, whose survival is aided by the parents' waning obsession with one another. Social psychologist Ellen Berscheid and her colleagues (1984) note that the failure to appreciate passionate love's limited half-life can doom a relationship: "If the inevitable odds against eternal passionate love in a relationship were better understood, more people might choose to be satisfied with the quieter feelings of satisfaction and contentment."

One key to a gratifying and enduring relationship is **equity:** Both partners receive in proportion to what they give. When equity exists—when both partners freely give and receive, when they share decision making—their chances for sustained and satisfying companionate love are good (Gray-Little & Burks, 1983; Van Yperen & Buunk, 1990). Mutually sharing self and possessions, giving and getting emotional support, promoting and caring about one another's welfare, are at the core of every type of loving relationship, whether between lovers, parent and child, or intimate friends (Sternberg & Grajek, 1984).

Another vital ingredient of loving relationships is intimacy (Sternberg, 1986). A strong friendship or marriage permits **self-disclosure,** a revealing of intimate details about ourselves—our likes and dislikes, our dreams and worries, our proud and shameful moments. "When I am with my friend," noted the Roman statesman Seneca, "me thinks I am alone, and as much at liberty to speak anything as to think it. . . ." Self-disclosure grows as a relationship deepens. As one person reveals a little, the other reciprocates, the first person reveals more, and on and on, as friends or lovers move to deeper intimacy. Given self-disclosing intimacy plus mutually supportive equality, the odds favor enduring companionate love.

Rehearse It

9. Aggression is physical or verbal behavior that is intended to hurt someone. We find physiological influences on aggression at three levels: the genetic, the neural, and the biochemical. Evidence of a biochemical influence on aggressiveness is the finding that
a. aggressiveness varies widely from culture to culture.
b. animals can be bred for aggressiveness.
c. stimulation of an area of the limbic system in the brain produces aggressive behavior.
d. a high level of the hormone testosterone is associated with violent behavior in males.

10. Studies show that delinquent young people tend to have parents who relied on beatings to enforce discipline. This demonstrates that aggression can be
a. learned through direct rewards.
b. learned through observation of aggressive models.
c. triggered by exposure to violent media.
d. caused by hormone changes at puberty.

11. There is considerable controversy about the effects of heavy exposure to violent television programming. However, most experts would agree that repeated viewing of television violence

a. makes all viewers significantly more aggressive.
b. has little effect on viewers.
c. dulls the viewer's sensitivity to violence.
d. makes viewers angry and frustrated.

12. Social scientists have studied the effects of pornography on ordinary adults in the laboratory. After reviewing results of many experiments, they generally agree that violent pornography
a. has little effect on most viewers.
b. is the primary cause of reported and unreported rapes.
c. leads viewers to be more accepting of coercion in sexual relations.
d. has no short-term effects, other than arousal and entertainment.

13. Psychologists have studied the factors that determine whether or not a bystander will come to the aid of a stranger in an "emergency." They have found that people who are in a good mood are most likely to extend their help. Perhaps the most important finding, though, is the bystander effect, which states that a particular bystander is *less* likely to give aid if
a. the victim is similar to him or her in appearance.
b. there is no one else present.

c. other bystanders are present.
d. the incident occurs in a deserted or rural area.

14. Repeated exposure to a stimulus—including a new human face—increases our liking of the stimulus. This *mere exposure effect* helps explain why proximity is a powerful predictor of friendship and marriage, and why, for example, people tend to marry
a. someone about as attractive as themselves.
b. someone who lives or works nearby.
c. someone of similar religious or ethnic background.
d. someone who has similar attitudes and habits.

15. Male subjects who are aroused by various stimuli, and then introduced to an attractive woman, tend to attribute their arousal to the woman, and to report positive feelings toward her. This supports the two-factor theory of emotion, which assumes that emotions such as passionate love consist of physical arousal plus
a. a reward.
b. our interpretation of that arousal.
c. proximity.
d. companionate love.

Reviewing Social Psychology

Social psychologists study how people think about, influence, and relate to one another.

Social Thinking

1. **How do we err when explaining the behavior of others?**

   We generally explain people's behavior by attributing it either to internal dispositions or to external situations. In accounting for others' actions, we tend to underestimate the influence of the situation, thus committing the fundamental attribution error. When we explain our own behavior, however, we more often point to the situation and not to ourselves.

2. **Under what conditions do our attitudes guide our behavior?**

   Initially, social psychologists agreed with the popular wisdom that attitudes determine behavior. Now they note that attitudes predict behavior only under certain conditions, such as when other influences are minimized, when the attitude is specific to the behavior, and when people are aware of their attitudes.

3. **Under what conditions does our behavior affect our attitudes?**

Studies of role playing and of performing uncharacteristic acts reveal that our behavior can modify our attitudes, especially when we feel responsible for that behavior. Cognitive dissonance theorists explain that behavior shapes attitudes because people feel discomfort when their actions go against their feelings and beliefs; they reduce the discomfort by bringing their attitudes more into line with their behavior.

Social Influence

4. **What do experiments on conformity and compliance reveal about the power of social influence?**

Solomon Asch and others learned that under certain conditions people will conform to a group's judgment even when it is clearly incorrect. In Milgram's famous experiments, people who were torn between obeying an experimenter and responding to another's pleas usually chose to obey orders, even though obedience appeared to involve harming another person. These classic experiments demonstrate the potency of social forces, and they highlight the fact that we conform either to gain social approval (normative social influence) or because we depend on the information that others provide (informational social influence).

5. **In what ways are we affected by the mere presence of others?**

Experiments on social facilitation indicate that the presence of others can arouse individuals, slightly boosting their performance on easy tasks but hindering it on difficult ones. When people pool their efforts toward a group goal, social loafing may occur as individuals free-ride on others' efforts. When aroused and made anonymous by a group, people may become less self-aware and self-restrained, a psychological state known as deindividuation.

6. **What are group polarization and groupthink?**

Discussions with like-minded others often produce group polarization, an enhancement of the group's prevailing attitudes. This is one cause of groupthink, the tendency for harmony-seeking groups to make unrealistic decisions after suppressing unwelcome information.

7. **Can a minority sway a majority?**

The power of the group is great, but so can be the power of a minority, especially when its views are expressed consistently.

Social Relations

8. **What biological factors influence aggressive behavior?**

Like all behavior, aggression is a product of both nature and nurture. Although the idea that aggression is an instinct is not looked upon favorably, there is ample evidence that aggressiveness is genetically and biochemically influenced, and that certain areas of the brain, when stimulated, activate or inhibit aggression.

9. **What psychological factors influence aggressive behavior?**

A variety of aversive events are known to heighten people's hostility. Frustration and aversive stimuli are especially likely to trigger aggression in those who have been rewarded for aggression in the past or who have observed role models acting aggressively. Violent television and violent pornography present numerous aggressive models. Viewers of such media are somewhat more likely, when provoked, to behave aggressively, and they tend to become desensitized to the cruelties depicted.

10. **What is the bystander effect?**

In response to incidents of bystander nonintervention in emergencies, social psychologists undertook experiments that revealed a bystander effect: Any given bystander is less likely to help if others are present. The bystander effect is especially apparent in situations where the presence of others inhibits one's noticing the event, interpreting it as an emergency, or assuming responsibility for helping. Many factors, including mood, also influence willingness to help someone in distress.

11. **What other factors influence helping?**

Both psychological and biological explanations have been offered for why we help others. Social exchange theory proposes that our social behaviors—even our helpful acts—maximize our benefits (which may include our own good feelings) and minimize our costs. Our desire to help is also affected by social norms, which prescribe reciprocating the help we receive and being socially responsible toward those who are in need. Evolutionary psychologists believe that a genetic predisposition to preserve our genes, through devotion to those with whom we share them, underlies altruism.

12. **What psychological factors promote attraction?**

Three factors are known to influence our attraction to one another. Geographical proximity is conducive to attraction, partly because mere exposure to a stimulus enhances liking. Physical attractiveness influences both social opportunities and the way one is perceived. As acquaintanceship moves toward friendship, similarity of attitudes and interests greatly increases attraction.

13. **What is the distinction between passionate and companionate love?**

Passionate love can be viewed as a temporary, aroused state that we cognitively label as love. The strong affection of companionate love, which often emerges as a relationship matures, is enhanced by an equitable relationship and by intimate self-disclosure.

Terms and Concepts to Remember

Rehearse It Answer Key

1. a.   **2.** d.   **3.** a.   **4.** a.   **5.** c.   **6.** c.   **7.** b.   **8.** c.   **9.** d.

10. b.   **11.** c.   **12.** c.   **13.** c.   **14.** b.   **15.** b.

Critical Thinking Exercise

You have *Surveyed, Questioned, Read, Rehearsed,* and *Reviewed* Chapter 14. Now take your learning a step further by testing your *critical thinking* skills on the following passage.

When Mary and Kathy met as college roommates, they discovered they had a lot in common and quickly became close friends. They spent many hours discussing their innermost feelings and were pleased to find they shared a dislike of all forms of prejudice. At the beginning of their sophomore year, they pledged with different sororities. Despite Mary's protests, Kathy pledged with a sorority that has a reputation for being elitist and somewhat prejudiced against minority groups, including Mary's. Although initially Kathy was concerned about her sorority's reputation, she felt after the first meeting with her new sorority sisters her concern was undeserved and went on to become a full member of the sorority. As weekly meetings continued, however, the discussions at Kathy's sorority became increasingly tinged with bigotry. Kathy gradually found herself thinking more and more like her sorority sisters and even openly making a few contemptuous remarks about minority groups. Although she sometimes felt troubled by her behavior, Kathy had worked so hard to

become a member of the sorority that she decided she must really have felt this way about minority groups all along.

Being immersed in their separate sororities, Kathy and Mary did not see each other for several months, until their sororieties met at an intramural softball game. Running over to greet her friend, Mary was hurt by Kathy's cool, almost haughty manner toward her and other minority members of Mary's sorority. In the midst of her sorority sisters, Kathy seemed a different person altogether. Later that evening, Mary confided in her journal that she must have initially misjudged Kathy as sharing her beliefs and that Kathy had finally displayed her true personality as a very prejudiced person.

1. What social psychological principles might help explain why Mary and Kathy became friends?

2. What social psychological principles might help explain why Mary and Kathy grew apart?

3. Did Mary initially misjudge Kathy's personality?

Check your progress on becoming a critical thinker by comparing your answers to the sample answers found in Appendix B.

Chapter 15

Social Diversity

"Good news, Mr. Vanderfirth. We've traced your lineage back to a woman who lived in East Africa two hundred thousand years ago."

Drawing by Mankoff; © 1991 The New Yorker Magazine, Inc.

To review cultural and gender similarities and differences mentioned in previous chapters, see page 507.

Some 100,000 to 200,000 years ago, we humans were members of one African race. Anticipating the ancient injunction to "be fruitful and multiply, and fill the earth," many of our ancestors moved out of Africa. In adapting to their new environments, our forebears developed differences that, measured on anthropological scales, are relatively recent and superficial. Those who went far north of the equator, for example, evolved lighter skins capable of synthesizing vitamin D in less direct sunlight. Still, historically, we all are Africans.

As descendants of common ancestors, we in the human family share not only a common biological heritage but also common behavioral tendencies. Our shared brain architecture predisposes us to sense the world, develop language, and feel hunger through identical mechanisms. Coming from opposite sides of the globe, we know how to read one another's smiles and frowns. Whether our last name is Wong, Nkomo, Gonzales, or Smith, we fear strangers beginning at about 8 months of age and as adults prefer the company of individuals whose attitudes and attributes are similar to our own. Regardless of our culture or gender, we regard female features that signify youth and health—and reproductive potential—as attractive. Whether we live in the Arctic or the tropics, we prefer sweet tastes to sour, shiver when cold, and feel drawn to behaviors that produce and protect offspring. As members of one species, we affiliate, conform, and organize hierarchies of status. A visitor from outer space could drop in anywhere and find humans playing sports and games, dancing and feasting, singing and worshipping, living in families and forming groups. To be human is to be more alike than different. Taken together, such universal behavior tendencies define human nature.

Among our similarities, the most important—the behavioral hallmark of our species—is our enormous capacity to learn and adapt. Ironically, this fundamental likeness enables human diversity. Go barefoot for a summer and you will develop toughened, calloused feet—a biologically disposed adaptation to friction. Meanwhile, your shoed neighbor will remain a tenderfoot. Is the difference between the two of you an effect of environment? Yes, of course. Is it also the product of a biological mechanism? Yes again. Our shared biology enables our adaptive diversity (Buss, 1991). Likewise, depending on their experiences in particular environments, one person may become aggressive, another gentle; one may value freedom, another order and control; one may prize individuality, another the social ties that bind people together.

As citizens in a multicultural world, we need to understand our similarities. We also need to understand our differences. At various points throughout this book we have examined our *individual differences* in traits such as temperament, intelligence, personality, and health. Time and again we have also glimpsed a second dimension of diversity—our *group differences* in tend-

encies ranging from expressing anger to concern about weight. Having examined individual diversity in some depth, let us conclude our journey through psychology by further exploring our social diversity and how we respond to it. How do culture and gender shape our social identities and behaviors? What leads us to loathe or to love those who are different?

Preview Question

1. How do cultural norms and roles differ?

A multicultural space station community of 1000 people fairly sampled from today's global village would have 585 Asians, 151 Europeans, 123 Africans, 81 North Americans, 55 South Americans, and 5 Australians and New Zealanders.

culture The enduring behaviors, ideas, attitudes, and traditions shared by a large group of people and transmitted from one generation to the next.

personal space The buffer zone we like to maintain around our bodies.

Cultural Diversity

A **culture** is the composite of the enduring behaviors, ideas, attitudes, and traditions shared by a large group of people and transmitted from one generation to the next (Brislin, 1988). If we all lived as homogeneous ethnic groups in separate regions of the world, as some people still do, cultural diversity would be largely irrelevant. Riding along with a unified culture is like riding a bike with the wind: As it carries you along, you hardly notice it's there. It's when we try riding *against* it that we feel its force. Face-to-face with a different culture, people become aware of the cultural winds. Visiting Europe, most North Americans are struck by the smallness of the cars, the left-handed use of the fork, the uninhibited attire on the beaches. Stationed in Saudi Arabia, European and American soldiers realized the liberality of their home cultures. Visiting North America, visitors from some cultures struggle to understand why people wear their dirty *street* shoes in the house, or why people find it fun to eat a picnic lunch out in the bush amid flies and ants.

Increasingly, cultural diversity surrounds us. More and more we live in a global village, connected to our fellow villagers by telecommunications, jumbo jets, and international trade. Cultural diversity exists within nations, too. As Iraqis, Indians, and Israelis know well, conflicts stemming from cultural differences are longstanding. But migration and refugee evacuations make this more true today than ever. "East is East and West is West, and never the twain shall meet," wrote nineteenth-century author Rudyard Kipling. But today, East and West, and North and South, meet all the time. Italy is

A universal behavior. You know the meaning of this facial expression, and each of these people would understand the same expression on your face.

home to many Albanians, Germany to Turks, England to Pakistanis and West Indians. For Canadians, Americans, and Australians, too, one's country is more and more a mix of cultures. One in six Canadians is an immigrant. In half the 100 largest U.S. cities, ethnic minorities will together have become the majority by the end of this decade (Jones, 1990). As we work, play, and live with people from diverse cultural backgrounds, it becomes helpful to understand how our cultures influence us and to appreciate important ways in which cultures differ.

Cultural Norms

All cultural groups, from homogeneous nations to motorcycle gangs, evolve their own social norms—their rules for accepted and expected behavior. Muslims use only the right hand's fingers for eating. The Japanese have norms for taking shoes off, for giving and opening gifts, and for showing respect to one's social superiors. Sometimes social expectations seem oppressive. Westerners wonder: Wouldn't Middle Eastern women prefer to come out from behind their veils and express their individuality? However, norms also grease the social machinery. Prescribed, well-learned behaviors free us from self-preoccupation. Knowing when to clap or bow, which fork to pick up first at the dinner party, and what sorts of gestures and compliments are appropriate enables us to relax and enjoy one another without fear of embarrassment or insult.

When cultures collide, their differing norms often bemuse or befuddle. If someone invades our **personal space**—the portable buffer zone we like to maintain around our bodies—we feel uncomfortable. Most Americans, Scandinavians, and the British prefer more personal space than do Latin Americans, Arabs, and the French (Sommer, 1969). At a social gathering, a Mexican seeking a comfortable conversation distance may waltz around a room with a back-pedaling American. To the American, the Mexican may seem a space invader; to the Mexican, the American may seem cold and standoffish.

Culture influences personal space. In Arabic countries, such as Morocco, people typically require less personal space than do North Americans.

Cultures also vary in their expressiveness and pace of life. People whose roots are in northern European culture often perceive people from Mediterranean cultures as warm and charming but inefficient. The Mediterraneans, in turn, see the northern Europeans as efficient, but cold and preoccupied with punctuality (Triandis, 1981). When cultures mix, misunderstandings are commonplace. The British businessperson may feel frustrated by a Latin American client who arrives 30 minutes late for lunch. People from time-conscious Japan—where bank clocks keep exact time, pedestrians walk briskly, and post office clerks fill requests speedily—may find themselves growing impatient when visiting Indonesia, where clocks keep less exact time and the pace of life is slower (Levine, 1990). In adjusting to their host countries, American Peace Corps volunteers report that two of their greatest culture shocks, after the language difference, are the slower pace of life and the differing punctuality of the people (Spradley & Phillips, 1972).

Recall from Chapter 14 that when a whole set of norms accompanies a social position, such as parent or professor, we consider that social category a *role.* In some cultures, such as in Japan, meeting the expectations of one's various roles is an overriding life priority. One's behavior and identity shift, depending on whether one is with a supervisor, a colleague, or a spouse. Other societies define roles more loosely. People therefore develop a more stable sense of self and feel freer to express themselves as individuals (de Rivera, 1989). Thus, compared to students in Japan and China, American university students are much more likely to complete the sentence "I am . . ." with personal traits ("I am sincere," "I am confident") and much less likely to declare their social identities ("I am a Keio University student," "I am the third son in my family") (Cousins, 1989; Triandis, 1989a,b). The priority we place on our individual versus our collective identity is an important aspect of cultural diversity.

Preview Question

2. What distinguishes collectivist and individualist cultures?

Individualism Versus Collectivism

Some animals, like wolves, are communal. Others, like tigers, are solitary. Although we humans are basically gregarious, our social styles vary from stressing individual control and achievement to emphasizing social intimacy and solidarity. Most industrialized cultures, especially those based on north-

People in individualist Western cultures sometimes see the Japanese as straitjacketed by their culture's norms. But from the Japanese perspective, the same tradition expresses a "serenity that comes to people who know exactly what to expect from each other" (Weisz & others, 1984).

"We must delight in each other, make others' conditions our own, rejoyce together, mourn together, labor and suffer together, always having before our eyes our community as members of the same body."

Puritan leader John Winthrop at Salem Harbor, just before his people set foot on American soil in 1630

"No mind can take the same interest in his neighbor's me as in his own. The neighbor's me falls together with all the rest of things in one foreign mass, against which his own me stands out in startling relief."

William James
Principles of Psychology, 1890

individualism Giving priority to one's own goals over group goals, and defining one's identity in terms of personal attributes rather than group identifications.

collectivism Giving priority to the goals of one's groups (often one's extended family or work group) and defining one's identity accordingly.

ern European norms and roles, nurture **individualism.** Individualists give priority to personal goals and define their identity mostly in terms of their personal attributes, not their social groups. Western literature, from the *Iliad and Odyssey* to *The Adventures of Huckleberry Finn,* celebrates self-reliant individuals who seek their own fulfillment rather than follow others' expectations.

Other cultures—especially those native to Asia, Africa, and Central and South America—nurture **collectivism.** Collectivists give priority to the goals of their groups—often their family, clan, or work group—and define their identity accordingly. Like athletes who take more pleasure in their team's victory than in their own performance, collectivists find satisfaction in advancing their group's interests, even at the expense of personal needs. Eastern literature expresses these ideals by celebrating those who do their duty to others, despite temptations to self-indulgence. Although there are individualists and collectivists in every culture, this cultural difference affects self-concept, attitudes, and family relations.

Culture and the Self

If someone were to rip away your social connections, say, by making you a solitary refugee in a foreign land, how much of your identity would remain intact? For individualists, a great deal—the very core of their being, their sense of "me," their awareness of their personal convictions and values. In many ways, Western psychology reflects the individualism of its cultures. In Chapter 3, we examined Western adolescents' struggle to separate from parents and define their personal identity. In Chapter 11, we focused on personality—the distinctiveness and consistency that make each of us in some ways unique. At each of these points, we assumed—and if you are a product of Western culture, you probably did not question the assumption—that the individual is supreme. This individualist perspective on the self also appears in humanistic psychology's emphasis on getting in touch with oneself, accepting oneself, and being true to oneself.

For the collectivist, one's social network provides one's bearings. Cut off from their family, their groups, and their loyal friends, collectivists would lose the connections that define who they are. Individualist cultures give priority to personal identity, by putting the personal name first ("John Brink"). Collectivist cultures give priority to one's family identity, sometimes

No wonder, says Triandis (1989b), that modern world colonization was led not by Asians, who were reluctant to cut social and family ties, but by the more individualist Europeans. And no wonder that once-colonized countries, such as Canada, the United States, and Australia, are today among the most individualist.

"Over the years, I learned to choose from the best opinions. Chinese people had Chinese opinions. American people had American opinions. And in almost every case, the American version was much better.

It was only later that I discovered there was a serious flaw with the American version. There were too many choices, so it was easy to get confused and pick the wrong thing."

Amy Tan
The Joy Luck Club, 1989

by putting the family name first ("Hui Harry"). Individualists easily move in and out of social groups. They feel relatively free to switch churches, leave one job for another, or even to leave their extended families and migrate to a new place. Collectivists have fewer but deeper, more stable attachments to their groups and friends. Relationships are long-term. Thus, loyalties run strong between employer and employees. And compared with American students, university students in Hong Kong talk with half as many people during a day, but for longer periods (Wheeler & others, 1989).

Because they value communal solidarity, people in collectivist cultures place a premium on maintaining harmony and allowing others to save face. Direct confrontation and blunt honesty are rare, as are expressions of personal egotism. Elders and superiors command respect. To preserve group spirit, people avoid touchy topics, defer to others' wishes, and display a polite, self-effacing humility (Markus & Kitayama, 1991). People remember those who have done them favors and make reciprocation a social art. The collectivist self is not independent but *inter*dependent. Among collectivists, no person is an island.

In terms of the self, individualism and collectivism each offers benefits—at a cost. People in competitive, individualist cultures have more personal freedom, take more pride in personal achievements, are less geographically bound to their families, and enjoy more privacy. Their less unified cultures offer a smorgasbord of life-styles and invite individuals to construct their own identities. But compared to collectivists, individualists are also lonelier, more alienated, more likely to divorce, more homicidal, and more vulnerable to stress-related diseases, such as heart attacks (Triandis & others, 1988). Thus, Martin Seligman (1988) notes that "rampant individualism carries with it two seeds of its own destruction. First, a society that exalts the individual to the extent ours now does will be ridden with depression. . . . Second, and perhaps most important, is meaninglessness [which occurs when there is no] attachment to something larger than you are."

Culture and Social Judgment

Culture also affects our readiness to prejudge others. Individualists idealize *not* **stereotyping** people based on their group memberships. Because Jane is an individual, you shouldn't prejudge her attitudes and beliefs just from knowing her background and affiliations. Collectivists respond that in their culture it *helps* to know a person's group identifications: "If I know Yasumasa's family, work group, and schooling, I know a good deal about Yasumasa."

Individualists tend to see causes residing in personal traits ("He is lazy; she needs therapy"). Collectivists are somewhat less vulnerable to this fundamental attribution error (Zebrowitz-McArthur, 1988). When told of someone's actions, Hindus in India are less likely than Americans to offer dispositional explanations ("She is sociable") and more likely to propose situational explanations ("Her friends were with her") (Miller, 1984). Because group identifications are important in judging others, personal attributes, such as physical attractiveness, matter less to collectivists (Dion & others, 1990).

Culture and Parent-Child Relations

Right from the start, Japanese and Chinese parents foster interdependence. Even after birth, mother and child continue to be joined—sleeping, bathing, and moving about together. The traditional Japanese mother carries her child on her back for much of the first 2 years, a practice that may account for the

stereotype A generalized (often over-generalized) belief about a group of people.

While collectivists teach their children *inter*dependence, children in individualist cultures learn from an early age to be independent and competitive and to take pride in their personal achievements.

Preview Question

3. How does cultural diversity affect the ethnic groups that make up a society?

ethnicity That part of one's social identity defined by the ancestors, heritage, and traits one shares with others.

greater separation stress experienced by Japanese than American infants (Markus & Kitayama, 1991).

In modern individualist cultures, parents want their children to become independent and "have good judgment." They express less concern for training conformity and submissiveness—or, as a collectivist might say, for communal sensitivity and cooperation (Alwin, 1990). Schools teach children to clarify their own values so they can make good decisions for themselves. Thus, in Western restaurants, parents and children decide their own orders individually. In Western homes, adolescents open their own mail, refuse parental guidance in choosing their own boyfriends and girlfriends, and often seek the privacy of their own rooms. As adults they chart their own goals and separate from their parents, who already live apart from the grandparents. If a child fails, the embarrassed parents will nevertheless be able to discuss the child's problems openly.

All of this seems strange to Asian collectivists, whose parents more actively guide or decide their children's choices and whose schools are less bashful about teaching accepted cultural values (Hui, 1990). So close is the mutual identification of parent and child that the crushed parents of an errant child seldom discuss their feelings of shame.

Ethnicity

The distinct traditions and styles contributed by different ethnic and racial groups add another dimension to cultural diversity. When groups of people migrate, they do not leave their cultural values behind. Over time and generations, they will absorb many cultural norms from their new homeland. Yet, especially if connected to fellow immigrants, they also will retain much of their original ethnic identity and cultural heritage. Thus, they make their new homeland a more culturally diverse place.

A culture, as we've seen, is a people's shared behaviors, ideas, attitudes, and traditions. **Ethnicity,** an aspect of one's social identity, is defined by the common ancestors and cultural heritage one shares with others. Culture and ethnicity are at times hard to disentangle, but they can be distinguished. A family living in Boston, for example, may be ethnically Italian and culturally East Coast urban Americans who define themselves as Italian Americans.

Ethnicity and Race

In practice, race is socially as well as physically defined. For example, North Americans typically regard those whose ancestors are mostly white, but who retain features that reveal African ancestry, as "black." Brazilians regard anyone whose features reveal a partial Caucasian ancestry as "white." Thus, studies that purport to compare races often are comparing groups defined socially, not biologically. Moreover, in nearly every trait studied, from blood proteins to intelligence test scores, individual differences within racial groups greatly exceed the small differences between groups. Different "racial groups are much more alike than they are different," concludes Marvin Zuckerman (1990). For these reasons, it is difficult to draw conclusions about biologically based racial differences.

Although we can't really compare groups that differ only on biological race, we *can* explore cultural differences within and between socially defined racial or ethnic groups. In adapting to the geographical and social circumstances of their past, ethnic groups have developed differing styles of communicating and relating. Between East and West, the norms of individualism or collectivism define one such difference. In North America, the language, literature, music, foods, religion, and style of today's white culture incorporate African influences, just as today's black culture incorporates European influences. *The World They Made Together* is the book title by which Mechal Sobel describes the African and European streams that fed the American South. Nevertheless, notes social psychologist James Jones (1988), partly as a result of its African heritage and partly as an adaptation to the prevailing attitudes of the larger culture, black American culture has evolved its own style. It tends to be present-oriented, expressive, spiritual, and emotion-driven. White culture is more often future-oriented, reserved, rationalistic, and achievement-driven. Because people so often judge others by their own standards, Jones argues that we are wiser to accept diversity than to pretend such differences don't matter or don't exist. Differing cultures have something to offer each other. In some situations expressiveness is an advantage and in others future-orientation is an advantage. The capacity for each enriches a multicultural society.

Ethnic Self-Awareness

Self-concept is a mix of personal identity (self-esteem, outgoingness, appearance) and social identity (identification with certain people and groups). Which aspects we're aware of at any moment depend not only on our culture but also on the immediate context. When invited by researchers to "tell us about yourself," children emphasize their distinctive attributes. Foreign-born children mention their birthplace, redheads their hair color, skinny or obese children their body weight, minority children their ethnicity (McGuire & others, 1978, 1979).

Surely you've noticed. You become conscious of your gender when alone among people of the other sex. You are more racially self-aware when among people of another race but may give no thought to it when everyone around you is the same race. Indeed, notes Jean Phinney (1990), in an ethnically homogeneous society, "ethnic identity is a virtually meaningless concept." The simple principle, say William McGuire and colleagues (1978), is that

> one is conscious of oneself insofar as, and in the ways that, one is different. . . . If I am a Black woman in a group of White women, I tend to think of myself as Black; if I move to a group of Black men, my blackness loses salience and I become more conscious of being a woman.

Self-awareness of our distinctiveness explains why *any* minority group is conscious of itself in contrast with the majority. One way to appreciate the minority experience is to become a minority. One doesn't realize how American one is until, as an American Jew, one lives for a time in Israel, or until as an African American, one sojourns in Africa. Living for a year in Scotland, I was conscious on a daily basis of what I hardly noticed at home—the Americanness of my accent, clothing, and personal style. I also wondered how people were reacting to my obvious difference: Is she being extra polite because I am a foreigner? Is he snubbing me because he doesn't happen to like Americans?

In multicultural settings, those who share a minority status may enjoy one another's company. Canadians who have little in common back home in British Columbia will talk like old friends upon discovering one another at a sidewalk cafe in Prague. To the majority culture, the minority may seem peculiarly sensitive or clannish. But that behavior only reflects that unpeculiar tendency for people to be oblivious to their commonalities and conscious of their distinctiveness.

James Jones (1990): "Color makes a difference. Gender makes a difference. Ethnicity makes a difference. Acting as if they don't will create more problems than it will solve."

At the moment this man may not be conscious of his maleness, but he is probably extremely aware of his Americanness. In a given situation, we tend to be conscious of how we are distinct.

These ethnically conscious French Canadians—supporting Bill 101 "to live in French in Quebec"—may or may not also feel strongly Canadian. As countries become more ethnically diverse, people debate how we can build societies that are both pluralistic and unified.

E pluribus unum: Out of many, one. Motto of the United States

Ethnic Identity and Cultural Identity

In ethnically diverse cultures, how do people balance their ethnic identities and their national identities? "Meet the Press" (1984) interviewer Marvin Kalb asked the question of then presidential candidate Jesse Jackson:

> *Kalb: Are you a black man who happens to be an American running for the presidency, or are you an American who happens to be a black man running for the presidency?*
>
> *Jackson: Well, I'm both an American and a black at one and the same time. I'm both of these . . .*
>
> *Kalb: What I'm trying to get at is . . . are your priorities deep inside yourself, to the degree that anyone can look inside himself, those of a black man who happens to be an American or the reverse?*
>
> *Jackson: Well, I was born black in America, I was not born American in black! You're asking a funny kind of Catch-22 question. My interests are national interests.*

Jackson's response reflects what identity researcher Phinney (1990) calls a "bicultural" identity, one that identifies both with the ethnic culture and the larger culture. Ethnically conscious Asians living in England may or may not also feel strongly British (Hutnik, 1985). French Canadians who identify with their ethnic roots may or may not also feel strongly Canadian (Driedger, 1975). Hispanic Americans who retain a strong sense of their "Cubanness" (or of their Mexican, Puerto Rican, or Spanish heritage) may or may not feel strongly American (Roger & others, 1991).

Researchers have wondered, as did Marvin Kalb, whether pride in one's ethnic group competes with identification with the larger culture. Does a strong ethnic identification displace other social identities? Social psychologist John Turner (1987) notes that we evaluate ourselves partly in terms of our group memberships. Seeing our own group as superior and deserving helps us feel good about ourselves. A positive ethnic identity can therefore contribute to positive self-esteem. So can a positive mainstream social identity among those who have lost touch with their mixed ethnic roots. "Marginal" people, who have neither an ethnic nor a mainstream identity (see table below), often have low self-esteem. Bicultural people, who affirm both identities, typically have a strongly positive self-concept (Phinney, 1990).

By forging national identities and unifying ideals, immigrant countries such as the United States, Canada, and Australia have avoided ethnic wars like those in India, Yugoslavia, and Iraq. In North America, Irish and Italians, Swedes and Scots, Asians and Africans, seldom kill in defense of their ethnic identities. When overemphasized, diversity becomes destructive. Nevertheless, even the immigrant nations struggle between separation and assimilation, between pride in one's distinct heritage and unity as one nation, between acknowledging the reality of diversity and questing for shared values.

		Identification with ethnic group	
		Strong	**Weak**
Identification with majority group	**Strong**	Bicultural	Assimilated
	Weak	Separated	Marginal

Rehearse It

1. Cultures vary in their social norms—their rules for expected behavior. For example, people in some cultures prefer more *personal space*, that is
a. larger bedrooms.
b. more privacy.
c. greater distance from others during conversation.
d. independence from parents.

2. Cultures also vary in the priority they give to personal versus group goals. Collectivists especially value
a. their groups.
b. their freedom.
c. their independence.
d. self-indulgence.

3. Individualists and collectivists have differing identities. Compared to collectivists, individualists more often define themselves in terms of their
a. family connections.
b. nationality.
c. social roles.
d. personal achievements.

4. Individualists and collectivists also differ in their social judging and child-rearing. Compared to individualists, collectivists are more likely to
a. confront and criticize others.
b. actively guide their children's choices and train social sensitivity.
c. avoid judging people based on their group affiliations.
d. encourage their children to think for themselves.

5. Our self-concept blends our personal identity and our social identity. At any given time, we are most likely to be conscious of
a. our personal identity.
b. our social identity.
c. our race.
d. how we differ from those around us.

6. Our social identity includes our ethnic identity and our identification with the larger culture. People who strongly identify with both their ethnic group and their larger culture are referred to as
a. bicultural.
b. assimilated.
c. separated.
d. marginal.

Gender Diversity

As noted in Chapter 8, Thinking, Language, and Intelligence, we humans have an urge to organize our complex worlds into simple categories. We categorize people as well as things. Among all the ways we classify people—as tall or short, fair-haired or dark, slim or muscular or rotund, blue-eyed or brown-eyed—two dimensions are especially potent. For people's self-concepts and identities, for selecting friends and mates, and for how others regard and treat them, height and hair color may matter, but ethnicity and sex matter much more. Among the dimensions of diversity, people first attune to another's ethnicity and, especially, to another's sex. When you were born, the first thing people wanted to know about you was, "Is it a boy or a girl?" When your sex was ambiguous—say, when not cued by a pink or blue outfit—people were unsure how to react.

As common ancestry and cultural heritage define our ethnicity, our biological sex dictates our **gender**—the characteristics by which people identify us as male or female. In considering how culture creates social diversity, let's look at the nature and nurture of gender. How different *are* males and females at different life stages? How does our culture's concept of gender affect how we see ourselves? How others see us?

Gender Similarities and Differences

gender In psychology, the characteristics, whether biologically or socially influenced, by which people define male and female.

In many traits, the sexes are alike. Whether you are male or female had no bearing on when you sat up, teethed, or walked (Maccoby, 1980). Tell me your sex and you've given me no clues to your vocabulary, intelligence, or happiness. But there are some intriguing differences. Compared to the average man, the average woman has 70 percent more fat, 40 percent less muscle,

Even in physical traits, individual differences among men and among women far exceed the average differences between the sexes. Don Schollander's world-record-setting 4 minutes, 12 seconds in the 400-meter freestyle swim at the 1964 Olympics would have placed him 6th against the women racing in the 1992 Olympics and 5 seconds behind the winner, Germany's Dagmar Hafe.

Preview Question

4. What broad cognitive and social differences exist between the sexes?

More often than others their age, whiz kids such as these also are left-handed, nearsighted, and allergic or asthmatic—traits that some brain scientists attribute to excess testosterone during prenatal development (Geschwind & Behan, 1984).

and is 5 inches shorter. Compared to women, men enter puberty 2 years later, are 20 times more likely to have color-deficient vision, and, depending on the country, die up to 10 years sooner. Unlike women, half of men are balding by age 50. If it's any consolation, men are twice as likely to be capable of wiggling their ears.

In earlier chapters we also noted some other gender differences. Women are more likely to dream equally of men and women, to become sexually rearoused immediately after orgasm, and to smell faint odors. Women are twice as vulnerable to anxiety disorders and depression, and perhaps 10 times more susceptible to eating disorders. Men are five times more likely to become alcoholic, three times more likely to commit suicide, and far more likely to be diagnosed as hyperactive as children and to display antisocial personalities as adults.

Gender and Cognitive Abilities

In science, as in everyday life, differences, not similarities, excite interest. To some, it is news that there is no gender gap in average verbal ability as assessed by tests of vocabulary, reading comprehension, and solving analogies (Hyde & Linn, 1988). But most people find it more newsworthy that boys outnumber girls at the low extremes. Boys are more often slow to talk. In remedial reading classes, boys outnumber girls three to one (Finucci & Childs, 1981).

In math grades, the average girl typically equals or surpasses the average boy (Kimball, 1989). And on math tests given to more than 3 million representatively sampled people in 100 independent studies, males and females have obtained nearly identical average scores (Hyde & others, 1990). But again group differences make the news. Although females have an edge in math computation, males in various cultures score higher in math problem solving (Benbow, 1988; Lummis & Stevenson, 1990). For example, male high school seniors average 50 points higher on the SAT math aptitude test (which literally means that they average four more correct answers on the 60-question test). The differences are sharpest at the extremes. Among precocious 12-year-olds scoring above 700 on SAT math, boys outnumber girls 13 to 1 (Holden, 1991a). Even the *average* male-female difference becomes striking at one particular ability—speedily rotating three-dimensional objects in one's mind (Halpern, 1986; Linn & Peterson, 1986; Sanders & Soares, 1986) (Figure 15-1). Such spatial ability helps when fitting suitcases into a car trunk, playing chess, or doing certain types of geometry problems.

Figure 15–1 A test of spatial abilities: the mental rotation test. Which two responses show a different view of the standard? (From Vandenberg & Kuse, 1978.) (See page 487 for answers.)

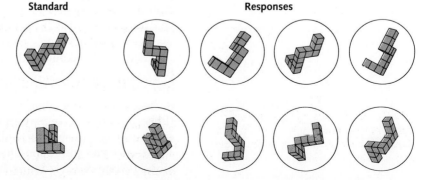

Which two circles contain a configuration of blocks identical to the one in the circle at the left?

Standard   Responses

Do natural sex differences therefore explain why most mathematicians and more than 9 in 10 rated chess players and American architects are men? Before concluding yes, consider how social expectations shape boys' and girls' interests and abilities (Eccles & others, 1990). Many North American parents send their sons to computer camps and give their daughters more encouragement in English. As you might expect, the male edge in math problem solving grows with age, becoming detectable only after elementary school. As more and more girls are encouraged to develop their abilities in math and science, the gender gap is narrowing. Among representative national samples of high school juniors taking the Preliminary Scholastic Aptitude Test (PSAT), the male edge nearly disappeared between 1960 and the mid-1980s (Linn & Hyde, 1991).

Gender and Social Behavior

Research on the psychology of women and men evokes the concern that studies of male-female differences might exaggerate people's gender stereotypes. Others assert that gender differences are not women's deficits. If women, for example, are more socially connected, well, in most cases maybe that is healthy rather than a symptom of an overly supportive ("co-dependent") personality. Whether biologically rooted or socially constructed, such diversity can be accepted, even valued. Let's consider, then, gender comparisons in independence, aggression, social dominance, and sexual initiative.

Independence Versus Interdependence Individual men and women vary from gently nurturant to fiercely competitive. Yet diversity exists between as well as within the sexes. After listening to women's reasoning and concerns, psychologists Nancy Chodorow (1978, 1989), Jean Baker Miller (1986), and Carol Gilligan and her colleagues (1982, 1990) concluded that women more than men give priority to relationships. Unlike boys, who must define themselves in separation from their usually female caregiver, girls more easily identify with their mothers and develop an identity based on their social connections. Later experiences reinforce the sense of independent self among men and of interdependent self among women. Women use conversation to explore relationships, men use it to convey solutions. Women emphasize caring and they provide most of the care to the very young and the very old. Although 69 percent of people say they have a close relationship with their father, 90 percent say they're close to their mother (Hugick, 1989). Men, like empowered people generally, emphasize freedom and self-reliance.

Women's social connectedness appears greater not only in the care and support women more often give to their young children and aging parents but also in women's career choices and attitudes. In most of the caregiving professions—social worker, teacher, nurse—women outnumber men. Among the 211,000 first-year American college students surveyed in 1991 (Astin & others, 1992), 50 percent of males but 69 percent of females said it was very important to "help others who are in difficulty."

The greater connectedness of females surfaces early, in children's play. Boys typically play in large groups with an activity focus and little intimate discussion. Girls play in smaller groups, often with a single friend. Girls' play is less competitive than boys' and more imitative of social relationships (Lever, 1978). Both in play and in later achievement settings, females are more open and responsive to feedback than are males (Maccoby, 1990; Roberts, 1991). As teens, girls spend more time than do boys with friends and less time alone (Wong & Csikszentmihalyi, 1991).

"There should be no qualms about the forthright study of racial and gender differences; science is in desperate need of good studies that . . . inform us of what we need to do to help underrepresented people to succeed in this society. Unlike the ostrich, we cannot afford to hide our heads for fear of socially uncomfortable discoveries."

Developmental psychologist
Sandra Scarr (1988)

"The phrase 'working mother' is redundant."

Jane Sellman,
American writer

Women *report* more empathy. Do they actually *feel* more empathy? Studies do show that women surpass men at reading others' emotions.

Answers to the mental rotation test on page 485: For the top standard, the first and fourth alternatives; for the bottom standard, the second and third alternatives.

When surveyed, women also are far more likely than men to describe themselves as having empathy. If you are empathic, you identify with others. You rejoice with those who rejoice and weep with those who weep. You imagine what it must feel like to live with that handicap, what it must be like to try so hard to impress people, what a thrill it must be to win that award. Physiological measures of empathy, such as one's heart rate while seeing another's distress, reveal a much smaller gender gap than reported in surveys (Eisenberg & Lennon, 1983). Nevertheless, females are more likely to *express* empathy—to cry and to report distress when observing someone in distress.

Moreover, studies consistently find females better at reading people's emotional cues (Hall, 1987). Shown a silent, 2-second film clip of an upset woman's face, women are better than men at sensing whether she is angry or discussing a divorce. Women's nonverbal sensitivity helps explain why both men and women report their friendships with women to be more intimate, enjoyable, and nurturing (Rubin, 1985; Sapadin, 1988). When wanting understanding and someone with whom to share worries and hurts, both men and women usually turn to women.

Given the low value that Western societies place on caregiving (as reflected in the low pay of traditionally female helping occupations, such as preschool teacher or social worker), some psychologists wonder: Doesn't affirming women's connectedness reinforce what should be changed? Should Western women be out of step with their culture's individualism? Better, they say, that women stop being dependent on others and become self-reliant individualists. Other psychologists argue that women's approach to life holds the promise of transforming power-oriented, individualist societies into more caring communities. With the growing problems of homelessness, child neglect and abuse, and depression, one doesn't get the impression that too much caring is a massive social problem.

The renewed valuing of human connectedness is strikingly similar to the traditional values that predominate in collectivist cultures. Together, the feminist and cross-cultural scholars are forging what Hazel Markus and Shinobu Kitayama (1991) call a new understanding of dependence. "Being dependent does not invariably mean being helpless, powerless, or without control. It often means being *inter*dependent." It means affecting others and being responsive to them, giving and receiving support, confiding and being confided in. It means defining oneself in relation to others, seeing oneself not as a lone island but as attached to important others.

Aggression In surveys, men admit to considerably more hostility and aggression than do women. In laboratory experiments that assess *physical* aggression, men indeed behave more aggressively, by administering what they think are higher levels of hurtful electric shock (Eagly, 1987; Hyde, 1986). In every society that keeps crime records, males commit far more physical violence (Kenrick, 1987). In the United States during 1990, the male-to-female arrest ratio was 8.1 to 1 for murder and 11.3 to 1 for robbery. Throughout the world, hunting, fighting, and warring are primarily men's activities.

Social Dominance Around the world, men are also perceived as more dominant. From Finland to France, Peru to Pakistan, Nigeria to New Zealand, people rate men as more dominant, aggressive, and achievement-driven, and women as more deferential, nurturant, and affiliative (Williams & Best, 1990). Indeed, in virtually every society, men *are* socially dominant. When groups are formed, leadership tends to go to males. As leaders, men tend to be directive, even autocratic, and women tend to be more democratic (Eagly & Johnson, 1990). When people interact, men are more likely to utter opinions, women to express support (Aries, 1987; Wood, 1987). In everyday behavior, men are more likely to act as powerful people do—to talk assertively, to interrupt, to initiate touching, to smile less, to stare (J. Hall, 1987; Major & others, 1990).

These behavior differences lessen with maturity, as middle-aged women become more assertive and men more empathic (Pratt & others, 1990). Nevertheless, the behaviors help maintain the inequities of social power. When political leaders are elected, they usually are men. When salaries are paid, those in traditionally male occupations receive more. When asked what pay they deserve, women often expect less than do similarly qualified men (Major, 1987). In one recent month, only 6 percent of people quoted on the front page of *The New York Times* were women. In self-defense, the paper's executive editor said it wasn't the *Times'* fault that the national and global power players involved in page one issues were mostly men (Leo, 1990).

In one recent count, 87 percent of the world's legislators were men (Harper's Index, 1989).

Sexual Initiative   "With few exceptions anywhere in the world," report cross-cultural psychologist Marshall Segall and his colleagues (1990, p. 244), "males are more likely than females to initiate sexual activity." Susan Hendrick and her colleagues (1985) report a corresponding gender gap in sexual attitudes: Women are "moderately conservative" about casual sex, men "moderately permissive." The annual survey of new American college students illustrates: "If two people really like each other, it's all right for them to have sex even if they've known each other for only a very short time," agreed 66 percent of men but only 38 percent of women (Astin & others, 1991).

Men also have a lower threshold for perceiving someone's warmth as a sexual come-on. Here we find another practical consequence of how we attribute behavior (page 443). In study after study, men more often than women attribute a woman's friendliness to sexual interest (Abbey, 1987; Saal & others, 1989). Such misattribution of a woman's cordiality helps explain men's greater sexual assertiveness (Kenrick & Trost, 1987). The unfortunate results can range from sexual harassment to date rape (Kanekar & Nazareth, 1988; Muehlenhard, 1988; Shotland, 1989).

Is Biology Destiny?

To explain our sex-related differences, let's first consider some biological possibilities. Do men's and women's physical differences influence their social behavior? The "biosocial" view of gender says yes—perhaps indirectly, via the social consequences of mere physical differences—but yes.

Preview Question

5. How do biological sex differences influence social behavior?

Sex Hormones and Social Behavior

Males and females are variations on a single form. Eight weeks after conception, they are anatomically indistinguishable. (For example, both sexes have nipples, although only women will ever nurse.) Then, our genes activate our biological sex. *XY* sex chromosomes direct development of a male; *XX* chromosomes produce a female. After a male embryo's testes form internally, they begin to secrete testosterone, the principal male sex hormone. Testosterone triggers the development of external male sex organs. Otherwise, the embryo continues its course toward the development of female sex organs.

Note to computer geeks: The sex variable has a default value of female.

What, then, do you suppose happens when glandular malfunction or hormone injections expose a female embryo to excess testosterone? Genetically female infants are born with masculine-appearing genitals, which can be corrected surgically. Until puberty, such females typically act in more aggressive "tomboyish" ways than most girls, and dress and play in ways more typical of boys than girls (Ehrhardt, 1987; Money, 1987).

Is their behavior due to the prenatal hormones? Perhaps. (Experiments with many species, from rats to monkeys, confirm that female embryos given male hormones later exhibit more masculine appearance and behavior [Hines, 1982].) But these girls frequently look masculine and are known to be "different," so perhaps people also treat them more like boys. Early exposure to sex hormones thus affects us both directly (physically) and indirectly—by influencing the experiences that shape us. Biological appearances have social consequences.

Researchers debate the influence of sex hormones on spatial ability. Melissa Hines (1990) reports that girls whose glands overproduce testosterone have spatial abilities more like those of the average boy. Doreen Kimura (1989) reports that boys whose glands underproduce testosterone (and who therefore fail to undergo normal puberty) have spatial abilities more like those of the average girl. Moreover, there is some tendency—at best a small tendency, say skeptics (Benderly, 1989)—for women's spatial performance to vary with hormonal changes during the menstrual cycle.

Somewhat less controversial is testosterone's influence on aggression. In various animal species, one can increase aggressiveness by administering testosterone. In humans, violent male criminals average higher than normal testosterone levels (Dabbs & others, 1987). National Football League players have higher testosterone levels than ministers (Dabbs & others, 1990). Moreover, the gender difference in aggression appears early in life and across many species of mammals. In humans it wanes as men's testosterone levels decline during adulthood. No one of these findings is conclusive, but the convergence of evidence suggests that male aggressiveness does have biological roots. As we will see, it also has social roots.

Evolution and Sex Differences

Working from the perspective of evolution, some psychologists attribute gender diversity to males' and females' differing reproductive strategies (Kenrick & Trost, 1989). Natural selection favors organisms which send their genes into the future, by producing offspring that survive to reproduce. Men, they suggest, are quicker to perceive friendliness as sexual interest and to initiate sexual relations because sperm are cheap. (Males will produce about 2000 new sperm during the time it takes to read this sentence.) Males who compete successfully with other males to fertilize the most females will be winners in the genetic sweepstakes, by producing more offspring who carry their genes and their traits. Thus, nature's mating game favors male sexual initiative toward females and aggressive dominance in competing with other males.

Female reproductive strategy differs radically, say the evolutionary psychologists. A female has relatively few eggs and invests enormous time and energy in carrying and nursing a single offspring. To avoid squandering their few reproductive chances, females are cautiously selective in their choice of mates. They respond to signs of health and strength, and, in our own species, an ability to commit time and resources to protecting and nurturing their young. This helps explain the differing sexual values, mate preferences, and mating behaviors of women and men, suggests psychologist David Buss (1989). Cultural and individual differences show that genes do not rigidly determine sex differences, he cautions. Yet studies in 37 cultures revealed worldwide similarities in what men find attractive in women (features that

"There is little doubt that we would all be safer if the world's weapon systems were controlled by average women instead of by average men."

Melvin Konner
The Tangled Wing: Biological Constraints of the Human Spirit, 1982

The male bowerbird of New Guinea and Australia attracts its mates by building an elaborate bower decorated with flowers, fruits, and leaves. Before selecting a mate, the female inspects several of these bowers, which indicate their builder's strength, dexterity, and ability to defend his bower from other males, and, thus, the potential of his genes. Evolutionary psychologists believe that studying such bird behavior helps us better understand human mating and sexual behavior.

gender identity One's sense of being male or female. Note: One's gender identity is distinct from one's sexual orientation (as heterosexual or homosexual) and from the strength of one's gender-typing.

gender-typed Exhibiting masculine or feminine gender identity and role.

gender schema theory The theory that children learn from their cultures a concept of what it means to be male and female and adjust their behavior accordingly.

Preview Question

6. What accounts for individual variations in gender-typing and gender roles?

suggest fertility) and what women find attractive in men (wealth, power, ambition). And that, says Buss, indicates that our evolutionary heritage matters, too.

Critics question this evolutionary psychology. Granted, our common biology endows us with universal similarities. But when it comes to complex social behaviors, such as fathers' investment in infant care or relations between the sexes, cultural diversity is enormous. Marriage patterns vary from monogamy (one spouse) to serial monogamy (a succession of spouses) to polygamy (several wives) to polyandry (several husbands) to spouse-swapping.

Furthermore, say critics, evolutionary explanations are after the fact. Knowing the sexual double standard, we can imagine how natural selection might predispose men's promiscuous inclinations. But let's also explain the many men who are faithful to one woman. Of course!—the offspring of two invested parents who support each other have better survival chances. Or, imagine that women were the more aggressive sex. But of course, someone might explain, strong and aggressive women more successfully protect their children.

Both sides agree, however, that men and women are the products of their mammalian and human history, *and* of their cultural history. Nature's special gift to humans is our great capacity to learn and adapt. Therein lies a culture's power to create our concept of gender.

The Social Construction of Gender

What biology initiates, environment accentuates. Society assigns us each—even those few whose biological sex is ambiguous at birth—to the social category of male or female. The inevitable result is our strong gender identity (our sense of being male or female). To varying extents, we also become gender-typed. That is, some boys more than others exhibit traditionally masculine traits and interests, and some girls more than others become distinctly feminine.

Gender-Typing

Freud explained gender-typing with his theory that 5-to 6-year-old children resolve tensions linked with their attraction to the other-sex parent by identifying with the same-sex parent and adopting his or her characteristics. But this can't be the entire explanation, because children become gender-typed well before age 6 and even in the absence of a same-sex parent (Frieze & others, 1978; Stevenson & Black, 1988).

Social learning theory assumes that children learn gender-linked behaviors by observing and imitating, and being rewarded or punished. "Susie, you're such a good mommy to your dolls"; "Big boys don't cry, Dick." But this can't be the whole story either, because differences in the way parents rear boys and girls aren't enough to explain gender-typing (Lytton & Romney, 1991). Even when their families discourage traditional gender-typing, children organize themselves into boy worlds and girl worlds, each guided by rules for what boys and girls do.

Gender schema theory (Figure 15–2) combines cognitive theory with social learning theory: Out of children's struggles to comprehend the world come concepts, or *schemas*, including a schema for their own gender (Bem, 1987). Gender becomes a lens through which children view their experience. By age 3, they begin organizing their worlds on the basis of gender. Language forces them to. English uses the pronouns he and she. Other languages clas-

Around the world, from Indonesia to North America, children learn gender-typed behaviors partly by observing and imitating, and being rewarded or punished.

sify objects as masculine ("*le* train") or feminine ("*la* table"). Through language, dress, toys, and songs, social learning shapes gender schemas. Children then compare themselves to their concept of gender ("I am male—thus, masculine, strong, aggressive" or "I am female—therefore, feminine, sweet, and helpful") and adjust their behavior accordingly.

Gender Roles

In becoming gender-typed we learn the social role that our culture deems appropriate to our sex. Traditionally, men initiate dates, drive the car, and pick up the check; women cook the meals, buy the children's clothes, and do the laundry. Such formulas smooth social relations, saving awkward decisions about who does what. But at a cost. When deviating from social convention, as when a woman initiates a formal date with a man, we may feel anxious or be viewed as weird (Green & Sandos, 1983).

Figure 15–2 Three theories of gender-typing.

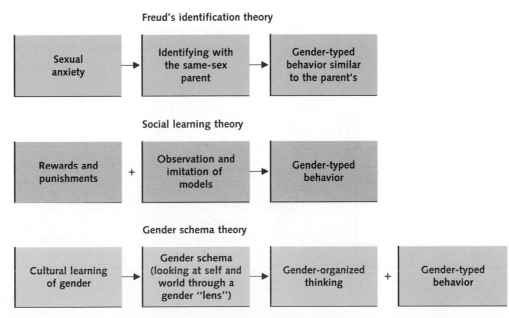

gender role A set of expected behaviors for males and for females.

Experiments show that many people do act to fulfill **gender role** expectations. For example, Mark Zanna and Susan Pack (1975) had college women write descriptions of themselves for a tall, unattached, male senior whom they anticipated meeting. Those expecting to meet a man who liked nontraditional women described themselves as relatively nontraditional. Those led to think he favored traditional gender roles described themselves as more traditionally feminine; they also performed more modestly on an aptitude test, solving 15 percent fewer problems. Gender expectations help create a gender difference.

Unlike biological differences, gender roles vary across cultures and over time. Such variations illustrate the social construction of gender.

Cultural Variations in Gender Roles   Around the world, men predominate in fighting wars and hunting, women in caring for infants. Yet different societies socialize children for varying gender roles. In nomadic societies of food-gathering people, there is little division of labor by sex. Thus, boys and girls receive much the same upbringing. In agricultural societies, women stay close to home, in the fields and with the children; men roam more freely. Such societies typically socialize children into more distinct gender roles (Segall & others, 1990; Van Leeuwen, 1978).

Men and women who assume distinct roles develop skills and attitudes that help explain their differing social behaviors (Eagly & Wood, 1991). In the United States, women are 3 percent of top executives at Fortune 1000 corporations, 4 percent of the Marine Corps, 97 percent of nurses, and 99 percent of secretaries (Castro, 1990; Williams, 1989). Such roles enacted by men and women have psychological consequences. Leadership roles foster assertiveness; caregiving roles foster nurturance.

Roles vary enormously among the industrialized countries. In North America, medicine and dentistry are predominantly male occupations; in Russia, most medical doctors are women, as are most dentists in Denmark. Socialization practices vary just as widely. In countries around the world, girls spend more time than boys helping with housework and child care; boys spend more time in unsupervised play (Edwards, 1991). In rural central India, for example, girls spend two-thirds of their time doing household work, including a daily hour and a half fetching water; boys spend two-thirds of their time in leisure (Sarawathi & Dutta, 1988). In Israel, Arab adolescents favor more distinct gender roles than do Jewish adolescents, thus anticipating the adult Arab world's more distinct norms for male and female behavior (Seginer & others, 1990). Similarly, compared with American 14-year-olds, Mexico City youth have more strongly gender-typed ideals (Figure 15–3).

Figure 15–3 Drawing of an ideal man by (a) an American girl, and (b) a Mexican girl (translation: "What is most valued in a man is that he be a chivalrous man and that he give his place to the woman"). (From Stiles & others, 1990.)

(a)   (b)

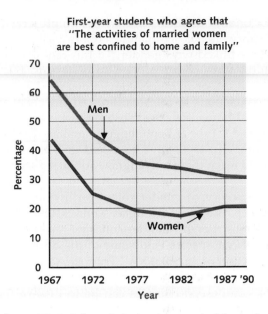

First-year students who agree that "The activities of married women are best confined to home and family"

Figure 15–4 College student endorsement of the traditional view of women's role has declined dramatically. (From Dey & others, 1991.)

Variations in Gender Roles over Time   Gender roles vary over time as well as across cultures. In 1938, only 1 in 5 Americans approved of "a married woman earning money in business or industry if she has a husband capable of supporting her"; by 1988, 4 in 5 approved (Niemi & others, 1989). In the flick of an apron, the number of American college women hoping to be full-time homemakers plunged during the late '60s and early '70s (Figure 15–4).

The change is behavioral as well. The number of women earning education degrees fell sharply after 1970, while the number of women awarded business degrees rose sharply (Figure 15–5). Moreover, between 1960 and 1990, the proportion of American women in the work force increased from 1 in 3 to nearly 3 in 5. Over the same period, these trends contributed to a 7-fold increase in the number of female doctors and a 24-fold increase in the numbers of female lawyers and engineers (Wallis, 1989).

A more subtle revolution has also been occurring in men's roles. Since 1965, American men have been devoting more and more time to family work (Figure 15–6). Increasingly, men are found in front of the stove, behind the vacuum cleaner, and over the diaper-changing table. But cultural differences remain huge: The average Japanese husband devotes 3 to 5 hours a week to domestic chores (one-ninth as much as his spouse); Swedish husbands clock 18 domestic hours per week (Juster & Stafford, 1991). Even in countries that have promoted equality, gender distinctions persist. Whether in Russia, China, or Sweden, answers to "Who works in the child care nurseries?" "Who cooks dinner?" and "Who leads the country?" remain the same as in North America.

"Like an ethnic culture in danger of being swallowed up by the culture of the dominant group, the contribution of the traditional homemaker has been devalued first by men and now by more women," reports sociologist Arlie Hochschild (1989, p. 267). "One way to reverse this devaluation is for men to share in that devalued work, and thereby to revalue it." Men's increasing sharing in homemaking chores may bode well for marriage, too. Women in mutually supportive marriages are less likely to consider divorce, reports Hochschild.

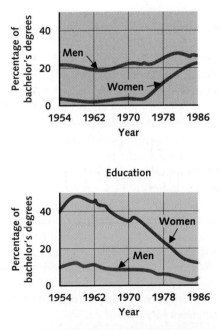

Figure 15–5 The shrinking gender gap in American bachelor's degrees awarded in education and business. (From Turner & Bowen, 1990.)

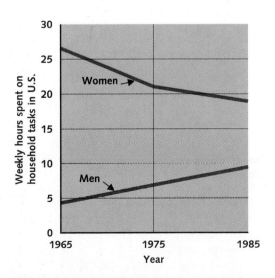

Figure 15–6 Time spent by American men and women on household tasks. (Data from Robinson, 1988.)

The Quigmans by Buddy Hickerson; © 1990, Los Angeles Times Syndicate.
Reprinted with Permission.

"This fundamental truth—that women are not just men who can have babies and men are not just women who spike footballs—gives marriage its vitality, its dynamics, its delights, and its divorce."

Bill Cosby
Love and Marriage, 1989

Should There Be Gender Roles?   Should distinct gender roles be preserved? Psychologist Sandra Bem (1985) answers no: "Human behaviors and personality attributes should no longer be linked with gender." If this requires imposing one's egalitarian values on one's children, then so be it, says Bem. Parents who have deep social, political, or religious convictions need not be timid about transmitting their convictions to their children. If the children don't absorb ideology and values at home, they will absorb them elsewhere. To raise children who are less gender-typed, Bem suggests making gender irrelevant to cooking, dishwashing, and toys. Give boys and girls the same privileges and responsibilities. And teach them to recognize subtle sex stereotyping and discrimination.

Noting the strength and persistence of gender roles worldwide, some psychologists doubt they will ever disappear. Douglas Kenrick (1987) believes that, try as we might to reconstruct our gender concepts, "we cannot change the evolutionary history of our species, and some of the differences between us are undoubtedly a function of that history." True, the sexes share many traits and abilities in common. But each sex also bears special gifts. To distinguish between two wines, composers, or sexes can be to discern the virtues of each. Equality and freedom of individual choice, yes; sameness, no.

Others say that biological differences are socially trivial. Human beings—both women *and* men—should be unshackled from all that constrains their being fully human—assertive *and* nurturant, self-confident *and* tender, independent *and* compassionate. Bem (1987) acknowledges that there may be "biologically based sex differences in behavior." But she believes that the social construction of gender greatly exaggerates them. Thus, she says, if under egalitarian social conditions,

> it turns out that more men than women become engineers or that more women than men decide to stay at home with their children, I'll live happily with those sex differences as well as with any others that emerge. But I am willing to bet that the sex differences that emerge under those conditions will not be nearly as large or as diverse as the ones that currently exist in our society.

So, what can we conclude about gender differences? First, gender similarities are impressive. Compared with the huge differences among individuals, differences between the sexes are small. Second, we can appreciate the detectable differences, without using them to judge individuals. Consider: When guessing someone's life expectancy, we prefer to note particulars of this individual—whether the person drinks heavily or smokes, whether the person's parents died young or old, whether the person eats a high fat diet. Because most of the cognitive and social differences are smaller than the life expectancy difference, it makes even more sense to judge people as individuals on these dimensions. Could you become a competent engineer? A child care worker? Knowing that you are a man or a woman tells us little; knowing you as an individual tells us much more.

The overlapping distributions of male and female qualities caused researcher Lauren Harris (1978) to caution against thinking of females and males as *opposite* sexes: "Neither in any physiological nor in any psychological sense are males and females 'contrary or antithetical in nature or tendency, diametrically opposed, or altogether different.'" Instead we might think of our own sex and the *other* sex as like the two halves of an oyster shell—similar but not identical, equally important, and fitting together because they grow together and change around each other.

Rehearse It

7. Although men and women are more alike than different, gender differences arouse most interest. Nevertheless, men and women do *not* differ significantly in
a. mathematical and spatial performance.
b. vulnerability to eating disorders and alcoholism.
c. caregiving.
d. verbal ability.

8. The differences among individuals of each sex are much greater than the differences between men and women. Nevertheless, women more than men exhibit a concern for
a. independence and self-reliance.
b. tending to social connections.
c. competitive achievement.
d. social stereotyping.

9. And men more than women
a. read people's subtle emotional cues.
b. express empathy.
c. commit physical violence.
d. lead a group democratically rather than autocratically.

10. Biological factors influence gender differences directly (by influencing our body and brain architecture) and indirectly (by influencing the experiences that shape us). An ample or excess supply of the sex hormone, testosterone, for example, is linked with
a. aggressiveness.
b. intelligence.
c. feminine appearance and behavior.
d. heavy beard growth.

11. Some boys are more gender-typed than others—they exhibit traditionally masculine traits and interests. Which theory of gender typing emphasizes children's resolving anxiety by identifying with their same-sex parent?
a. Freud's identification theory
b. social learning theory
c. gender schema theory

12. Gender is socially as well as biologically influenced. The "social construction of gender" is strikingly apparent in
a. the evolutionary psychology of sex differences.
b. "tomboyish" behavior among girls prenatally exposed to an excess of the hormone testosterone.
c. changing gender roles over time and across cultures.
d. the gender difference in social dominance.

Responding to Diversity

As we noted in Chapter 14, similarity promotes attraction. If likeness leads to liking, do differences foster disliking? If so, how can people of differing cultures or sexes accept, embrace, and enjoy their diversity? In today's world, few questions are more important. Thus, notes Carl Sagan (1980),

> Human history can be viewed as a slowly dawning awareness that we are members of a larger group. Initially our loyalties were to ourselves and our immediate family, next, to bands of wandering hunter-gatherers, then to tribes, small settlements, city-states, nations. We have broadened the circle of those we love. . . . If we are to survive, our loyalties must be broadened further, to include the whole human community, the entire planet Earth.

Together we all face the challenges of environmental pollution, global warming, resource depletion, and weapons proliferation. Yet seldom do we identify with our common humanity. Conscious of our diversity, we instead divide the world into "us"—our own nation, culture, creed, ethnic group, and sex—and "them." In a time when ethnic and national loyalties hinder our solving global problems, we need to ask: How can we replace attitudes that lead us to reject diversity with those that promote its acceptance?

"The growing diversity of the American population makes the quest for unifying ideals and a common culture all the more urgent. In a world savagely rent by ethnic and racial antagonisms, the U.S. must continue as an example of how a highly differentiated society holds itself together."

Historian Arthur Schlesinger
The Cult of Ethnicity, Good and Bad, 1991

Rejecting Diversity

How much prejudice persists? What causes it? What steps can we take to replace destructive conflict with constructive peace and good will?

Earth Day celebrations help us to see beyond our own small communities and to identify with the *global* community in all its unity and diversity.

Prejudice

Prejudice means prejudgment. It is an unjustifiable and usually negative attitude toward a group—typically a different cultural, ethnic, or gender group. Like all attitudes, **prejudice** is a mixture of beliefs (often overgeneralized stereotypes), emotions (hostility, envy, or fear), and predispositions to action (to discriminate). To believe that overweight people are gluttonous, to feel unattracted to an overweight person, and to be hesitant to hire or date an overweight person is to be prejudiced.

Like other forms of prejudgment, prejudices are schemas that influence how we notice and interpret events. In one study, most whites perceived a white man shoving a black as "horsing around." The same shove by the black to the white man was more often seen as "violent" (Duncan, 1976). Our preconceived ideas about people, sometimes formed by labels put on them, bias our impressions of their behavior. Prejudgments color perceptions.

How prejudiced are people? To find out, we can assess what they say and what they do. To judge by what Americans say, racial and gender attitudes have changed dramatically in the last half century (Figure 15–7). Nearly everyone agrees that children of all races should attend the same schools and that women and men should receive the same pay for the same job.

Figure 15–7 Americans today express much less racial and gender prejudice than they did a generation ago. (Responses to the racial questions are from non-African Americans only.) (From Gallup & Hugick, 1990; Niemi & others, 1989; Tom Smith, National Opinion Research Center, personal correspondence.)

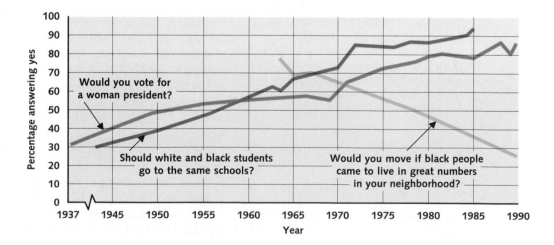

prejudice An unjustifiable (and usually negative) attitude toward a group and its members. Prejudice generally involves stereotyped beliefs, negative feelings, and a predisposition to discriminatory action.

ingroup bias The tendency to favor one's own group.

Preview Question

7. What are the social and emotional roots of prejudice?

"It is understandable that the suppressed people should develop an intense hostility toward a culture whose existence they make possible by their work, but in whose wealth they have too small a share."

Sigmund Freud
The Future of an Illusion,
1927

"Evil is anyone outside the tribe. Evil works by dehumanizing the Other. A perverse, efficient logic: identifying others as evil justifies all further evil against them."

Lance Morrow
Evil, 1991

Despite these more accepting attitudes, prejudice persists. In socially intimate settings (dating, dancing, marrying), many white people admit they would feel uncomfortable with someone of another race. Since the late 1980s, prejudice occasionally has resurfaced in public settings as well. American cities and college campuses have experienced significant increases in "hate crimes" (slurs, vandalism, and physical violence) against African Americans and homosexuals (Goleman, 1990; Herek, 1989, 1990; Levine, 1990). In other countries, hate rages even more openly—between Israel's Palestinians and Jews, Northern Ireland's Protestants and Catholics, Yugoslavia's Serbs and Croatians, South Africa's Zulus and African National Congress members. In Europe, hostility toward ethnic immigrants has been on the rise. The German government counted 246 crimes motivated by hatred of foreigners in 1990, and 2074 in 1991 (Graff, 1992).

Around the world, gender prejudice and discrimination persist too. In the Sudan, a woman may not leave the country without permission of her husband, father, or brother (Beyer, 1990). In Saudi Arabia, women are forbidden to drive. Nowhere are female infants left out on a hillside to die of exposure, as was the practice in Ancient Greece. Yet even today boys are often valued more than their sisters. During the 1976–77 famine in Bangladesh, preschool girls were more malnourished than boys, and in many developing countries death rates are higher for girls than boys (Bairagi, 1987). In South Korea, where testing often reveals the sex of an abortable fetus, male births exceed female births by 14 percent. Under China's one-child policy, unmarried men now greatly exceed the number of unmarried women (*Time,* 1990).

Once established, prejudice is maintained both by the inertia of social influence and by emotional and cognitive mechanisms. But why does prejudice arise in the first place?

Social Inequalities   When some people have money, power, and prestige and others do not, the "haves" usually develop attitudes that justify things as they are. In the extreme case, United States slave owners perceived slaves as lazy, ignorant, and irresponsible—as having the very traits that "justified" enslaving them. More commonly, women may be seen as unassertive but sensitive and therefore fit for the tasks they often perform (Hoffman & Hurst, 1990). In short, prejudice rationalizes inequalities.

Discrimination also increases prejudice through the reactions it provokes in its victims. In his classic 1954 book, *The Nature of Prejudice,* Gordon Allport noted that being a victim of discrimination can produce either self-blame or anger. Both reactions may create new grounds for prejudice through the classic "blame the victim" dynamic. If the circumstances of ghetto life breed a higher crime rate, someone can then use the higher crime rate to justify continuing the discrimination that helped to create the ghetto.

Us and Them: Ingroup and Outgroup   Group identifications typically promote an **ingroup bias**—a tendency to favor one's own group. The social definition of who you are—your ethnicity, gender, religion, academic major—also implies who you are not. Mentally drawing a circle that defines "us" excludes "them." In experiments, creating even an arbitrary us-them distinction—say, by grouping people with the toss of a coin—leads people to show favoritism to their own group when dividing rewards (Tajfel, 1982; Wilder, 1981).

To Greeks of the classical era, all non-Greeks were "barbarians." Most citizens in the coalition of countries fighting in the 1991 Persian Gulf War felt more pain over the few hundred allied soldiers who died than over the reported 100,000 Iraqi dead. In Africa, where some 700 traditional societies

"Actually, Lou, I think it was more than just my being in the right place at the right time. I think it was my being the right race, the right religion, the right sex, the right socioeconomic group, having the right accent, the right clothes, going to the right schools . . ."

Drawing by W. Miller; © 1992 The New Yorker Magazine, Inc.

"If the Tiber reaches the walls, if the Nile does not rise to the fields, if the sky doesn't move or the earth does, if there is famine, if there is plague, the cry is at once: 'The Christians to the lion!'"

Tertullian
Apologeticus, A.D. 197

Preview Question

8. What are the cognitive roots of prejudice?

cluster into fewer than 50 nations, people typically like and admire their own group and direct their hostility toward other groups (Segall & others, 1990). Most children believe their school is better than the other schools in town. Even chimpanzees have been seen to wipe themselves clean where touched by a chimp from another group (Goodall, 1986).

Ingroup bias is especially potent in collectivist cultures (Triandis, 1989a). Because group identity runs strong, outsiders receive cautious treatment. Ingroup members—friends, colleagues, and extended family—receive favors and other forms of support. Compared to individualist cultures, conflict in collectivist cultures less often occurs within groups (such as families) and more often between groups. Collectivists also feel more awkward relating to outgroup members. In one study, North American students experienced smoother and more intimate interactions with ingroup members (classmates) than with strangers. But this ingroup/outgroup difference was considerably greater among students in collectivist South Korea (Gudykunst & others, 1987).

Scapegoating   Prejudice can spring from the passions of the heart as well as the divisions of society. Prejudice may express anger: When things go wrong, finding someone to blame can provide an outlet. Evidence for this **scapegoat theory** of prejudice comes from high prejudice levels among economically frustrated people and from experiments in which a temporary frustration intensifies prejudice. Nazi leader Hermann Rausching once explained the Nazis' need to scapegoat: "If the Jew did not exist, we should have to invent him" (quoted by Koltz, 1983). Passions produce prejudice.

Despised outgroups not only provide a handy emotional outlet for anger, they can also boost self-esteem. In experiments, students who experience failure or are made to feel insecure will often restore their self-esteem by disparaging a rival school or another person (Cialdini & Richardson, 1980; Crocker & others, 1987). To boost our own sense of status, it helps to have others to denigrate. For this reason, a rival's misfortune sometimes provides a twinge of pleasure. To a Chicago Cubs baseball fan, happiness is the Cubs winning—and the Chicago White Sox losing.

Cognitive Roots of Prejudice   New research has focused on another source of prejudice. Stereotyped beliefs are a natural by-product of how we cognitively simplify the world.

Categorization   One way we simplify our world is to categorize things. A chemist classifies molecules as organic and inorganic. A mental health professional classifies people's psychological disorders by types. In categorizing people into groups we often stereotype them. We overestimate the similarity of people within groups other than our own. "They"—the members of some other group—seem to look and act alike, but "we" are diverse (Bothwell & others, 1989). To us on the outside, the members of fraternity *X* are jocks and those in fraternity *Y* are intellectuals. Members of each fraternity see their own diversity. To those in one ethnic group, those of another often seem more alike in appearance, personality, and attitudes than they are.

Vivid Cases   As noted in Chapter 8's discussion of the availability heuristic, we often judge the frequency of events by instances that readily come to mind. If asked whether blacks run faster than whites, many people may think of Carl Lewis, Leroy Burrell, and Florence Griffith Joyner. From such vivid but exceptional cases they overgeneralize that "yes, blacks run faster."

In an experiment with University of Oregon students, Myron Rothbart and his colleagues (1978) showed how we overgeneralize from vivid, memorable cases. They divided the students into two groups and showed them information about 50 men. The first group's list included 10 men arrested for nonviolent crimes, such as forgery. The second group's list included 10 men arrested for violent crimes, such as assault. When both groups later recalled how many men on their list had committed any sort of crime, the second group overestimated how many there were. Vivid (violent) cases, being readily available to memory, influence our judgments of a group.

The Just-World Phenomenon   We noted earlier that people often justify their prejudice by blaming its victims. Impartial observers may also blame victims, by assuming the world is just and that people get what they deserve. In laboratory experiments, merely observing someone receive painful shocks has led many people to think less of the victim (Lerner, 1980). This **just-world phenomenon** reflects an idea we commonly teach our children—that good is rewarded and evil is punished. From this it is a short leap to assume that those who succeed must be good and those who suffer must be bad. Such reasoning enables the rich to see their wealth, and the poor's misfortune, as justly deserved. As one German civilian is said to have remarked when visiting the Bergen-Belsen concentration camp shortly after World War II, "What terrible criminals these prisoners must have been to receive such treatment."

People of another race often seem to look alike. Australian sunbathers on Bali's beaches appreciate the Balinese masseuses wearing numbers, so they can recognize them.

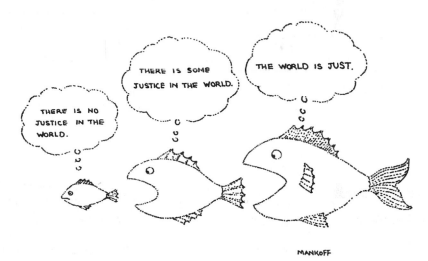

Drawing by Mankoff; © 1981 The New Yorker Magazine, Inc.

scapegoat theory The theory that prejudice provides an outlet for anger by providing someone to blame.

just-world phenomenon The tendency of people to believe the world is just and that people therefore get what they deserve and deserve what they get.

Hindsight bias is also at work here (Carli & Leonard, 1989). Have you ever heard people say that rape victims, abused spouses, or people with AIDS got what they deserved? An experiment by Ronnie Janoff-Bulman and her collaborators (1985) illustrates victim-blaming. When given an account of a date that ended with the woman being raped, people perceived the woman as partly to blame. In hindsight, they thought, "She should have known better." (Victim-blaming also reassures people that it couldn't happen to them.) Others who were given the same account, without the rape, did not perceive the woman as inviting rape. Only when she was victimized was she faulted for her behavior.

Conflict

We live in surprising times. With astonishing speed, democratic movements have swept away totalitarian rule in Eastern European countries. The hope of a "new world order" has replaced the Cold War chill. Yet world spending for arms and armies continues to drain $3 billion per day from spending for housing, nutrition, education, and health. Knowing that, as the UNESCO motto declares, wars begin in human minds, psychologists have wondered what steps might reverse destructive spirals of conflict. How might the perceived threats of social diversity be replaced by a spirit of cooperation?

To a social psychologist, a **conflict** is a seeming incompatibility of actions, goals, or ideas. The elements of conflict are much the same at all levels, from nations in an arms race to cultural disputes within a society to individuals in marital strife. In each situation, people become enmeshed in a destructive social process that produces results no one wants. Among these destructive processes are social traps and distorted perceptions.

Social Traps   In some situations, we can enhance our collective well-being by pursuing our personal interests. As capitalist Adam Smith wrote in *The Wealth of Nations* (1776), "It is not from the benevolence of the butcher, the brewer, or the baker that we expect our dinner, but from their regard to their own interest." In other situations, the parties involved—be they individuals or nations—may become caught up in mutually harmful behavior as they pursue their own ends. Such situations are **social traps.**

Consider the simple game matrix in Figure 15–8, which is similar to those used in experiments with thousands of people. Pretend that you are person 1, and that you and person 2 will each receive the amount of money shown after separately choosing either *A* or *B*. (You might invite someone to look at the matrix with you and take the role of person 2.) Which do you choose—*A* or *B*?

As you ponder the game, you discover that you and person 2 are caught in a dilemma. You both benefit if you both choose *A,* by making 50 cents each, and neither of you benefits if you both choose *B*, for you both make nothing. Nevertheless, on any single trial you serve your own interests if you choose *B*. If you choose *B* you can't lose, and you might make $1. But the same is true for the other person. Hence, the social trap: As long as you both pursue your own immediate best interest and choose *B*, you will both end up with nothing—the typical result—when you could have made 50 cents.

Many real-life situations similarly pit people's individual interests against their communal well-being. Individual whalers reason that the few whales they take don't threaten the species and that if they didn't take them others would anyway. The result: A species of whales becomes endangered. The individual car owner and home owner reasons, "It would cost me comfort or money to buy a more fuel-efficient car and furnace. Besides, the fossil fuels I burn don't noticeably add to the greenhouse gases." When others reason similarly, the collective result threatens disaster—global warming.

Social traps challenge us to find ways of reconciling our right to pursue our personal well-being with our responsibility for the well-being of all. Psychologists are therefore exploring ways to convince people to cooperate for their mutual betterment—through agreed-upon regulations, through better communication, and through promoting awareness of our responsibilities toward community, nation, and the whole of humanity (Dawes, 1980; Linder, 1982; Sato, 1987). Under such conditions, people more often cooperate, whether playing laboratory games or playing the game of real life.

"Every gun that is made, every warship launched, every rocket fired signifies, in the final sense, a theft from those who hunger and are not fed, those who are cold and are not clothed."

President Dwight Eisenhower, in a speech to the American Society of Newspaper Editors, 1953

Preview Question

9. What social processes fuel conflict?

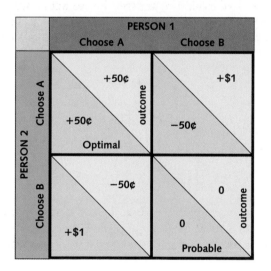

Figure 15–8 By pursuing our self-interest and not trusting others, we can end up losers. To illustrate this, play the game above. The pink triangles show the outcomes for person 1, which depend on the choices made by both persons. If you were person 1, would you choose *A* or *B*? (This game is called a "non-zero-sum game" because the outcomes need not add up to zero; both sides can win or both can lose.)

conflict A perceived incompatibility of actions, goals, or ideas.

social traps Situations in which the conflicting parties, by each rationally pursuing their self-interest, become caught in mutually destructive behavior.

mirror-image perceptions Distinct but similar views of one another often held by parties in conflict; each views itself as moral and peace-loving, the other as evil and aggressive.

HOPES FOR PEACE GROW

WELL... IF IT ISN'T THE TERRORIST DICTATOR AND BUTCHER OF BAGHDAD

AND YOU MUST BE THE SATANIC IMPERIALIST AND DEFILER OF ALL THINGS HOLY

Drawing by Wasserman; © 1990 Boston Globe. Distributed by Los Angeles Times Syndicate. Reprinted with permission.

Preview Question

10. What circumstances facilitate the resolution of conflict?

"You cannot shake hands with a clenched fist."

Indira Gandhi, 1971

Mirror-Image Perceptions Psychologists have noted a curious tendency for those in conflict to form diabolical images of each other. These distorted images are so similar that we call them **mirror-image perceptions:** As we see them—as untrustworthy and evil intentioned—so they see us. Thus, during the early 1980s, the U.S. government viewed the Communist support of guerrillas trying to overthrow the government of El Salvador as evidence of an "evil empire" at work. Meanwhile, the Soviets saw the U.S. support of guerrillas trying to overthrow the government of Nicaragua as the work of "imperialist warmongers." As enemies change, so do perceptions. In American minds and media, the "bloodthirsty, cruel, treacherous," Japanese of World War II later became our "intelligent, hardworking, self-disciplined, resourceful allies" (Gallup, 1972) who, in some minds, are now turning into our unfair, cutthroat business competitors.

In recent chapters we have considered the psychological roots of biased perceptions. The *self-serving bias* leads each party to accept credit for good deeds and to shuck the blame for bad deeds. Although two nations admit to a buildup of military forces, the *fundamental attribution error* leads each to see the other's actions as arising from its aggressive disposition, but its own buildup as necessary self-defense. Information about one another's actions is then filtered, interpreted, and remembered through preconceived *stereotypes*. Group interaction among like-minded policymakers may *polarize* these tendencies, leading to *groupthink* that sees one's own group as more moral, thereby justifying one's retaliation.

The result of such perceptions is a vicious cycle of hostility. If John believes Mary is annoyed at him, he may snub her, causing her to act in ways that justify his perception. As with individuals, so with countries. Perceptions confirm themselves by influencing the other country to react in ways that seem to justify them.

Accepting Diversity

"Come, my friends,
'Tis not too late to seek
a newer world."
Alfred, Lord Tennyson
Ulysses, 1842

How, then, can we transform antagonisms fed by prejudice, social traps, and misperceptions into constructive attitudes that promote peace? Such transformations are most likely in situations characterized by cooperation, communication, and conciliation.

Cooperation

Does it help to put two conflicting parties into close contact so they might get to know and like each other? It depends. When the contact is noncompetitive and between parties of equal status, such as fellow store clerks, it may help. Initially prejudiced co-workers of different races have, in such circumstances, usually learned to accept one another (Pettigrew, 1969). However, mere contact is sometimes not enough. In most desegregated junior high schools, whites and blacks resegregate themselves in the lunchrooms and on the school grounds (Schofield, 1986).

Mere contact was not enough to defuse intense conflicts instigated by researcher Muzafer Sherif (1966). He placed 22 Oklahoma City boys in two separate areas of a Boy Scout camp. He then put the two groups through a

superordinate goals Shared goals that override differences among people and require their cooperation.

GRIT Graduated and Reciprocated Initiatives in Tension-Reduction: a strategy designed to decrease international tensions.

series of competitive activities, with prizes going to the victors. Before long, each group became intensely proud of itself and hostile to the "sneaky," "smart-alecky" "stinkers" in the other group. Food wars broke out during meals. Cabins were ransacked. Fistfights had to be broken up by members of the camp staff. When Sherif brought the two groups together, they avoided one another, except to taunt and threaten.

Nevertheless, within a few days Sherif transformed these young enemies into jovial comrades by giving them **superordinate goals**—shared goals that overrode their differences and that could only be achieved through cooperation. A disruption of the camp water supply necessitated that all 22 boys work together to restore water. Renting a movie in those pre-VCR days required their pooled resources. A truck stalled until all the boys pulled and pushed together to get it moving. Having used isolation and competition to make strangers into enemies, Sherif used shared predicaments and goals to reconcile the enemies and make them friends. What reduced conflict was not contact itself, but *cooperative* contact.

Extending these findings, Samuel Gaertner and his co-workers (1989) report that cooperation has especially positive effects when it leads people to define a new, inclusive group that dissolves their former subgroups. Seat the members of two groups not on opposite sides, but alternately around the table. Give them a new, shared name. Have them work together. Such experiences change "us and them" into "we." People once perceived as in another group now are part of one's own group.

During the 1970s, several teams of educational researchers simultaneously wondered: If cooperative contacts between members of rival groups encourage positive attitudes, could we apply this principle in multicultural schools? Could we promote interracial friendships by replacing competitive classroom situations with cooperative ones? And could cooperative learning maintain or even enhance student achievement? Many experiments confirm that the answers are yes (Johnson & Johnson, 1987; Slavin, 1989). Members of interracial groups who work together on projects and play together on athletic teams typically come to feel friendly toward those of the other race. So do those who engage in cooperative classroom learning. So encouraging are these results that more than 25,000 teachers have introduced interracial cooperative learning into their classrooms (Kohn, 1987). Working with fellow students in all their diversity sets the stage, declared the Carnegie Council on Adolescent Development (1989), for "adult work life and for citizenship in a multicultural society."

Cooperative efforts to achieve superordinate goals break down social barriers.

"I am prepared this day to declare myself a citizen of the world, and to invite everyone everywhere to embrace this broader vision of our interdependent world, our common quest for justice, and ultimately for Peace on Earth."

Father Theodore Hesburgh
The Human Imperative, 1974

The power of cooperative activity to make friends of former enemies has led psychologists to urge increased international exchange and cooperation (Klineberg, 1984). As we engage in mutually beneficial trade, as we work to protect our common destiny on this fragile planet, and as we become more aware that our hopes and fears are shared, we will change misperceptions into a solidarity based on common interests.

Communication

In the social trap game matrix we considered earlier, people usually are distrustful and pursue their individual interests as a defense against exploitation. However, when allowed to discuss the dilemma and to negotiate a commitment to cooperate, cooperation increases (Jorgenson & Papciak, 1981).

When conflicts become intense, a third-party mediator—a marriage counselor, labor mediator, diplomat, community volunteer—may facilitate communication (Pruitt & Rubin, 1986). Mediators help each party to voice its viewpoint and, in the process, to understand the other's. Such understanding is most needed, yet least likely, in times of crisis (Tetlock, 1988). When conflicts grow intense, images become more stereotyped, communication becomes more difficult, and judgments become more rigid. Iraq's President Saddam Hussein, America's friend while attacking Iran in the 1980s, became to George Bush "another Hitler" after attacking oil-producing Kuwait in 1990. To Hussein, Bush became "Satan in the White House."

Conciliation

When tension and suspicion peak, cooperation and communication may become impossible. Each party is likely to threaten, coerce, or retaliate—the very actions that will worsen the conflict. In the weeks before the Persian Gulf War, President Bush threatened, in the full glare of publicity, to "kick Saddam's ass." Saddam Hussein communicated in kind, threatening to make Americans "swim in their own blood."

Under such conditions, is there an alternative to war or surrender? Social psychologist Charles Osgood (1962, 1980) advocates a strategy of "Graduated and Reciprocated Initiatives in Tension-Reduction," nicknamed **GRIT.** In applying GRIT, one side first announces its recognition of mutual interests and its intent to reduce tensions. It then initiates one or more small, conciliatory acts. Without weakening one's retaliatory capability, this modest beginning opens the door for reciprocation by the other party. Should the enemy respond with hostility, one reciprocates in kind. But so, too, with any conciliatory response. Thus, President Kennedy's gesture of stopping atmospheric nuclear tests began a series of reciprocated conciliatory acts that culminated in the atmospheric test-ban treaty.

In laboratory experiments, GRIT is the most effective strategy known for increasing trust and cooperation (Lindskold & others, 1978–1988). Even during intense personal conflict, when communication has been nonexistent, a small conciliatory gesture—a smile, a touch, a word of apology—may work wonders. Conciliations allow both parties to begin edging down the tension ladder to a safer rung where communication and mutual understanding can begin.

And how good that such can happen, for civilization advances not by cultural isolation—maintaining walls around ethnic enclaves—but by tapping the knowledge, the skills, and the arts that are each culture's legacy to the whole human race. Thomas Sowell (1991) notes that, thanks to cultural

"To begin with, I would like to express my sincere thanks and deep appreciation for the opportunity to meet with you. While there are still profound differences between us, I think the very fact of my presence here today is a major breakthrough."

Drawing by W. Miller; © 1983 The New Yorker Magazine, Inc.

sharing, every modern society is enriched by a cultural mix. We have China to thank for paper and printing, and for the magnetic compass that opened the great explorations. We have Egypt to thank for trigonometry. We have the Hindus of India and the Islamic world to thank for our Arabic numerals, which, except for numbering Superbowls and Kings and Queens, really are superior to the Roman numerals they replaced. While celebrating and claiming these cultural legacies, we can also welcome the enrichment of today's social diversity. We can view ourselves as individual instruments in a human orchestra. And we can therefore affirm our own culture's heritage while building bridges of communication, understanding, and cooperation across cultural traditions.

Rehearse It

13. Experiments show that when people are temporarily frustrated, they express more intense prejudice. When things go wrong, prejudice provides an outlet for our anger—and gives us someone to blame. This effect is best described by
a. ingroup bias.
b. scapegoat theory.
c. Freud's theory on the death instinct.
d. the just-world phenomenon.

14. Stereotypes are a natural by-product of our usual ways of thinking. For example, we tend to judge the frequency of events in terms of cases that come readily to memory. Thus, if several well-publicized murders are committed by members of a particular group, we tend to react with fear and suspicion toward all members of the group. In other words, we
a. blame the victim.
b. overgeneralize from vivid, memorable cases.
c. create a scapegoat.
d. categorize people incorrectly.

15. Conflicts often arise from destructive social processes. In many situations, individuals, in rationally pursuing their self-interests, get caught up in a behavior that harms both themselves and others. This destructive social process is called
a. gameplaying.
b. mirror image perception.
c. a social trap.
d. the fundamental attribution error.

16. Social psychologists have attempted to define the circumstances that facilitate conflict resolution. One way of fostering cooperation is by providing contentious groups with superordinate goals, which are
a. the goals of friendly competition.
b. shared goals that override differences.
c. goals for winning at negotiations.
d. goals for reducing conflict through increased contact.

Reviewing Social Diversity

Cultural Diversity

1. How do cultural norms and roles differ?

Our shrinking world, with its increasingly multicultural countries, more and more confronts us with our diversity. Cultural rules for accepted and expected behavior vary in ways that can befuddle outsiders. Cultures differ, for example, in their requirements for personal space, their pace of life, and the strength of their role expectations.

2. What distinguishes collectivist and individualist cultures?

Individuals and cultures also vary in whether they emphasize individual self-reliance and control or collective solidarity. This cultural factor affects how people define their self-concepts, make judgments of others, and relate to their families. Industrialized cultures derived from northern Europe are predominantly individualist; those native to Asia, Africa, and Central and South America are more collectivist.

3. How does cultural diversity affect the ethnic groups that make up a society?

Common ancestors and cultural heritage define one's ethnicity. Ethnic groups have developed differing cultural styles. For example, African Americans tend to be more emotionally expressive than European Americans. Yet one's ethnic awareness varies with the situation. In general, we are conscious of our distinctiveness and oblivious to our commonalities. We become especially conscious of our nationality, our sex, or our ethnicity when we are the different ones. People tend to favor the group with which they identify. Thus, people who see themselves as separate from the main culture as well as those who are either assimilated or bicultural typically enjoy more positive self-esteem than do socially marginal people. As countries become more diverse, we struggle with how to maintain a multicultural yet unified society.

Gender Diversity

4. What broad cognitive and social differences exist between the sexes?

The sexes are in many ways alike, but their differences excite more interest. Although fewer girls than boys have reading and speech disorders, males and females don't noticeably differ in average verbal ability. Males do, however, retain a small edge in the ability to solve math problems and a more significant edge on some spacial tasks. Women and men, like Asians and North Americans, differ in their social connectedness. Boys define themselves apart from their caregivers and playmates; girls through their social ties. As adults, women typically become more caring, supportive, and empathic, and men more independent, self-reliant, and unexpressive. Research studies also reveal male-female diversity in aggressiveness, social dominance, and sexual initiative.

5. How do biological sex differences influence social behavior?

Hormonal differences help explain certain sex differences. But biology is not destiny. What biology initiates, culture accentuates.

6. What accounts for individual variations in gender-typing and gender roles?

Cultural socialization helps explain why some children become more gender-typed than others and why gender roles vary so sharply across cultures and over time.

Responding to Diversity

7. What are the social and emotional roots of prejudice?

Prejudice often arises as those who enjoy social and economic superiority attempt to justify the status quo. Even the temporary assignment of people to groups can cause an ingroup bias. Once established, the inertia of social influence can help maintain prejudice. Prejudice may also serve the emotional functions of draining off the anger caused by frustration and of boosting self-esteem.

8. What are the cognitive roots of prejudice?

Newer research reveals how our ways of processing information—for example, by overestimating similarities when we categorize people or by noticing and remembering vivid cases—work to create stereotypes. In addition, favored social groups often rationalize their higher status by the just-world phenomenon.

9. What social processes fuel conflict?

Conflicts often arise from destructive social processes that include social traps, in which each party, by protecting and pursuing its self-interest, creates a result that no one wants. The vicious spiral of conflict both feeds and is fed by distorted mirror-image perceptions, in which each party views itself as moral and the other as untrustworthy and full of evil intentions.

10. What circumstances facilitate the resolution of conflict?

Enemies sometimes become friends, especially when the circumstances favor cooperation toward superordinate goals, understanding through communication, and reciprocated conciliatory gestures.

Terms and Concepts to Remember

culture, p. 476

personal space, p. 477

individualism, p. 478

collectivism, p. 479

stereotype, p. 480

ethnicity, p. 481

gender, p. 484

gender identity, p. 490

gender-typed, p. 490

gender schema theory, p. 490

gender role, p. 492

prejudice, p. 496

ingroup bias, p. 497

scapegoat theory, p. 498

just-world phenomenon, p. 499

conflict, p. 500

social traps, p. 500

mirror-image perceptions, p. 501

superordinate goals, p. 502

GRIT, p. 503

Rehearse It Answer Key

1. c.   **2.** a.   **3.** d.   **4.** b.   **5.** d.   **6.** a.   **7.** d.   **8.** b.   **9.** c.

10. a.   **11.** a.   **12.** c.   **13.** b.   **14.** b.   **15.** c.   **16.** b.

Critical Thinking Exercise

You have *Surveyed, Questioned, Read, Rehearsed,* and *Reviewed* Chapter 15. Now take your learning a step further by completing the following exercise (Zechmeister & Johnson, 1992).

Write down three characteristics or descriptions that you associate with each of the following groups of people.

Physicians   _____   _____   _____

Athletes   _____   _____   _____

Artists   _____   _____   _____

Vegetarians   _____   _____   _____

College students   _____   _____   _____

Lawyers   _____   _____   _____

From the above list of groups, choose one or more groups with which you identify closely and one or more that you are least able to identify with. The groups with which you most closely identify can be considered your ingroups; those that you feel most unlike are your outgroups. List your ingroup and outgroup descriptions in the space below and then answer the following questions.

Ingroup descriptions   _____   _____   _____

                         _____   _____   _____

Outgroup descriptions   _____   _____   _____

                         _____   _____   _____

1. Was it easier to come up with descriptions for your ingroups or for your outgroups? Why do you think this is so?

2. Are your descriptions of your ingroups and outgroups equally favorable? If not, why do you think this is so?

3. Compare your descriptions with those made by other college students (Appendix B). Which of your descriptions matches those of the other college students better—your ingroup or outgroup descriptions? What explanation can you offer for this phenomenon?

For Further Information

For further information in this text on culture and multicultural experience, see:

Adolescence, p. 78
Aggression, p. 458
Anger, p. 312
Attachment, p. 73
Attribution, pp. 444–445
Depression, pp. 379, 393, 397
Dieting, p. 280
Divorce, p. 92
Eating disorders, pp. 277, 382
Expressing emotion, pp. 307–308
Healer commonalities, p. 432
Intelligence, pp. 258–259, 262–264

Language, pp. 243–244, 246
Menopause, p. 87
Moral development, p. 81
Multiple personality, p. 390
Norms, p. 451
Obesity, pp. 276, 279–280
Perception, p. 140
Personality dimensions, p. 357
Physiology of emotion, p. 303
Premarital sex, p. 84
Psychological disorders, pp. 379, 382, 388, 390, 395

Roles, p. 447
Schizophrenia, p. 401
Self-serving bias, p. 365
Social clock, p. 91
Somatoform disorders, p. 388
Speech perception, pp. 243–244
Suicide, pp. 392–393
Temperament, p. 96
Weight concern, pp. 279–280
Work-related values, p. 295

For further information in this text on the psychology of women and men, see:

Abortion stress, p. 326
Adult development of women and men, p. 86
Alcoholism, pp. 168, 406
Body image, p. 277
Bonding, pp. 71–72
Depression, pp. 393–394
Dieting, p. 280
Dreams of men and women, p. 156
Early versus late maturation of boys and girls, p. 79
Eating disorders, p. 277
Emotion detection, pp. 305–306

Employment of women, p. 93
Empty nest, p. 92
Fatherhood, p. 74
Freud's views, pp. 350, 353
Generic pronoun "he," p. 249
Happiness, p. 317
Heart disease, p. 330
Help-receiving, p. 465
Hormones and aggression, sexual behavior, sexual development, pp. 78, 284–285, 459
Intimacy and identity, pp. 82–83
Leadership, p. 295

Menopause, pp. 86–87
Menstruation, pp. 78–79
Pornography, pp. 462–464
Rape, pp. 187, 462–464
Sensitivity to smells, p. 122
Self-concept, p. 75
Sexual coercion, pp. 167, 462–464
Sexual development, pp. 78–79
Sexual dysfunction, p. 286
Sexual orientation, pp. 287–288
Sexuality, pp. 282–286
Suicide by men and women, pp. 392–393

Statistical Reasoning in Everyday Life

Science fiction writer H. G. Wells predicted that "statistical thinking will one day be as necessary for efficient citizenship as the ability to read and write." If by statistical thinking Wells meant not a technical knowledge of how to compute statistics but rather an understanding of the principles of statistical reasoning, then that day has arrived. Today's statistics are tools that help us see and interpret what the unaided eye might miss.

My aim in this appendix is not to make you a statistical wizard. Rather, it is to help you use the power of statistical reasoning in your own everyday thinking so that you can:

accurately organize and interpret events;

realistically generalize from instances;

improve your critical thinking skills; and

become a more discerning consumer of research reported in the media.

First, I will introduce you to a few basic statistical concepts and formulas. If you are not mathematically inclined, stay with me, rereading where necessary. You will be amazed at how easy it is to grasp the basics.

Describing Data

Researchers or not, we all make observations or gather data that we must organize and interpret. Let's see how we might effectively do this.

Distributions

Laura is a college admissions officer. Attempting to predict which applicants will probably succeed at her school, she sorts through their high school grades, aptitude scores, biographical statements, and recommendation letters. But there is too much information to remember. Moreover, she knows that impressions are swayed by the information available to memory, often the vivid or extreme instances (see the "availability heuristic," page 238).

So instead of trusting her impressions, she begins by organizing the applicants' high school grade point averages (GPAs) into a **frequency distribution** (Figure A–1a). To do this, she breaks the entire range of scores into equal intervals and then counts the number of scores that fall in each interval. (Figure A–1a, in fact, presents a frequency distribution of the actual high school GPAs of 50 randomly selected sophomores at my own college.)

frequency distribution A listing of the number of individual scores that occur within each equal-sized interval within a distribution.

percentile rank The percentage of the sources in a distribution that a given score exceeds.

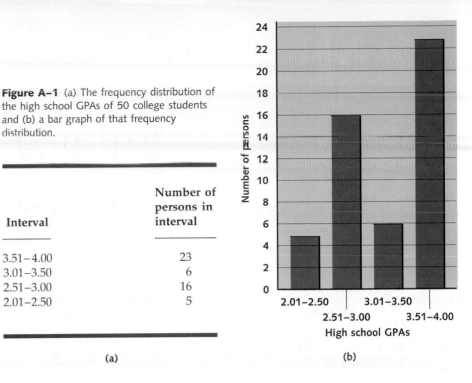

Figure A–1 (a) The frequency distribution of the high school GPAs of 50 college students and (b) a bar graph of that frequency distribution.

Interval	Number of persons in interval
3.51–4.00	23
3.01–3.50	6
2.51–3.00	16
2.01–2.50	5

(a)

(b)

To make the general picture easier to see, Laura displays this frequency distribution in a graph (Figure A–1b). Here she represents the frequency of scores within a particular interval as a bar. This bar graph also helps Laura see about where any particular student's score falls relative to the others. She can express any student's ranking as a **percentile rank,** which is simply the percentage of scores that fall below a particular score. A student whose percentile rank is 99 has a GPA that exceeds those of 99 percent of all the students. (You can never have a percentile rank of 100. Your score can never exceed those of 100 percent of the people because you are one of them.)

A note of caution: Take care when reading statistical graphs. Depending on what people want to emphasize, they can design the graph to make the same difference look small or big. For example, Laura can make the difference in the average high school GPAs of male and female students seem small or large depending on the units she chooses for the vertical axis (Figure A–2).

The moral: When looking at statistical graphs in books and magazines and on television ads and news broadcasts, always read the labels.

Figure A–2 Two bar graphs comparing the average high school GPAs of males and females in a sample of 50 students. Notice how a difference in the vertical dimension of the two graphs can make the gap seem either (a) small or (b) large.

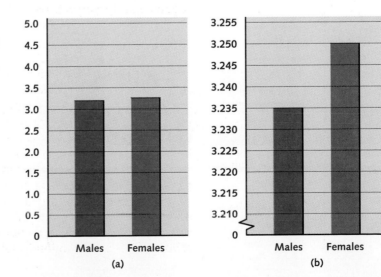

Close-Up: Florence Nightingale: Pioneer in the Use of Statistics

The world remembers Florence Nightingale as a pioneering nurse and hospital reformer. Less well known is her equally pioneering use of statistics. In advocating medical reform, Nightingale also promoted statistical description: She developed a uniform procedure for hospitals to report statistical information. She invented the pie chart, which represents proportions as wedges of a circular diagram. And she struggled to get the study of statistics introduced into higher education.

One of Nightingale's analyses compared the peacetime death rates of British soldiers and civilians. She discovered and showed that the soldiers, who lived in barracks under unhealthy conditions, were twice as likely to die as civilians of the same age and sex (Figure A–3). She then used the soldiers' 2 percent death rate to persuade the Queen and Prime Minister to establish a Royal Commission on the Health of the Army. It is just as criminal, she wrote, for the Army to have a mortality of 20 per 1000 "as it would be to take 1,100 men per annum out upon Salisbury Plain and shoot them."

Bernard Cohen (1984) reports that "Nightingale's commitment to statistics transcended her interest in health care reform, and it was closely tied to her religious convictions. To her, laws governing social phenomena, 'the laws of our moral progress,' were God's laws, to be revealed by statistics."

Florence Nightingale (1820–1910)

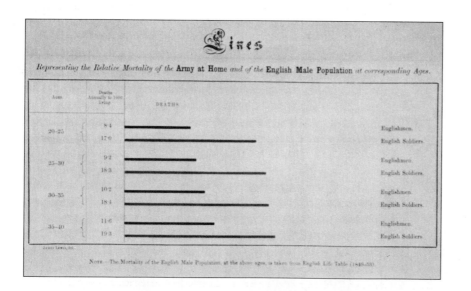

Figure A–3 Florence Nightingale's bar graph comparing peacetime death rates of British soldiers and civilian males illustrates her innovative approach to the presentation of statistics.

mode The most frequently occurring score in a distribution.

mean The arithmetic average of a distribution, obtained by adding the scores and then dividing by the number of scores.

median The middle score in a distribution; half the scores are above it and half are below it.

range The difference between the highest and lowest scores in a distribution.

standard deviation A measure of score variability; computed by (1) calculating the deviation of each score from the mean, (2) squaring those deviations, (3) finding their average, and (4) finding the square root of this average.

In Brazil, the mean income in 1984 was $1720 and the median income was $808. What does this tell you about the distribution of income in Brazil?

Central Tendencies

Andrew is a government official. To determine the level of poverty in the various small towns in his region, he gathers data about the residents' incomes. To simplify things, he might decide first to calculate the typical income level or *central tendency* for each town. For any distribution of *scores* (in this case, incomes), there are three commonly used measures of the central tendency. The simplest is the **mode,** the most frequently occurring score. The most commonly reported is the **mean,** or arithmetic average (the total sum of all the scores divided by the number of scores). The **median** is the midmost score—the 50th percentile; if you arrange all the scores in order from the highest to the lowest, half will be above the median and half will be below it.

When the distribution of scores (or incomes) is not symmetrical, the three measures of central tendency tell different stories. Suppose, for instance, that the mean annual family income in the first town Andrew studies is $19,000, whereas mean income in the second town is only $13,000. At first Andrew might assume there are more families living in poverty in the second town. But as Figure A–4 shows, the first town, in which a few wealthy employers and quite a few poorly paid employees live, actually has many families struggling to live on less than $10,000.

The moral: Always take note of the reported measure of central tendency, and consider: Could a few atypical scores be distorting it?

Variation

In any distribution of scores it is often useful to know how much variation there is. Are scores similar or widely spread out? The **range** of scores—the gap between the lowest and highest score—provides only a crude estimate of variation, because just one extreme score in an otherwise uniform group will create a deceptively large range. If, in a small class, all the scores on an exam were between 70 and 80 except for one score of 20, the range of 60 (80 − 20 = 60) would mislead us about the actual amount of variation.

The more standard measure of how much scores deviate from one another is the **standard deviation.** It better gauges whether scores are packed together or dispersed, because it uses information from each score, by squaring the difference, or deviation, between each score and the mean.

Figure A–4 This graphic representation of the distribution of incomes in Andrew's first town illustrates the three measures of central tendency—mode, mean, and median. Note how just a few high incomes make the mean—the fulcrum point which balances the incomes above and below—deceivingly high.

9 10 12 15 19 30 45 140

Mode Median Mean

One family

Income per family in thousands of dollars

normal curve (or **normal distribution**) The symmetrical bell-shaped curve that describes the distribution of many physical and psychological attributes. Most scores fall near the average, and fewer and fewer scores lie near the extremes.

As an example, consider Peter, the punter on his college football team. To keep track of his progress, he records the distance of each of his punts. He does not trust his gut-level impression of how consistent his punting is. After his first football game of the season, Peter therefore calculates the standard deviation for his four punts.

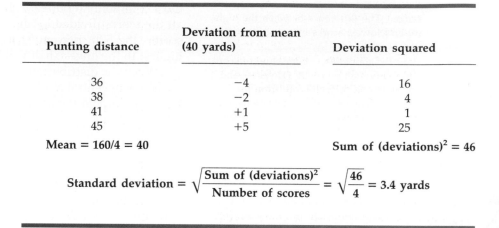

Punting distance	Deviation from mean (40 yards)	Deviation squared
36	−4	16
38	−2	4
41	+1	1
45	+5	25
Mean = 160/4 = 40		**Sum of (deviations)² = 46**

$$\text{Standard deviation} = \sqrt{\frac{\text{Sum of (deviations)}^2}{\text{Number of scores}}} = \sqrt{\frac{46}{4}} = 3.4 \text{ yards}$$

To grasp the meaning of this statistic, Peter would need to understand how scores tend to be distributed. In nature, large amounts of data—heights, weights, IQ scores, grades (though not incomes)—often form a roughly symmetrical, bell-shaped distribution. Most cases fall near the mean and fewer cases fall near either extreme. This bell-shaped distribution is so typical that we call the curve it forms the **normal curve.** As Figure A–5 shows, a useful property of the normal curve is that roughly 68 percent of the cases fall within 1 standard deviation on either side of the mean—in Peter's case, within 3.4 yards of his 40-yard average. About 95 percent of cases fall within 2 standard deviations. Thus, Chapter 8, Thinking, Language, and Intelligence, notes that about 68 percent of people taking an intelligence test will score within ±15 IQ points (1 standard deviation) of 100. About 95 percent will score within ±30 points (2 standard deviations).

Figure A–5 The normal curve. Data often form a normal or bell-shaped curve in which 68 percent of the cases fall within 1 standard deviation of the mean and 95 percent fall within 2 standard deviations. For example, on an IQ test such as the WAIS, we assign the mean a value of 100 and 1 standard deviation we call 15 points; therefore, 68 percent of the scores fall between 85 and 115, and 95 percent fall between 70 and 130.

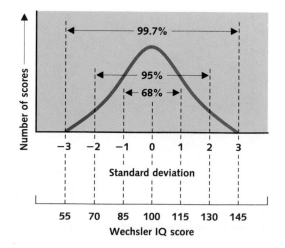

scatterplot A graphed cluster of dots each of which represents the values of two variables (such as a student's high school and college GPAs). The slope of the points suggests the degree and direction of the relationship between the two variables. (Also called a *scattergram* or *scatter diagram*.)

correlation coefficient A measure of the direction and extent of the relationship between two sets of scores. Scores with a *positive correlation coefficient* go up and down together (as with high school and college GPAs). A *negative correlation coefficient* indicates that one score falls as the other rises (as in the relationship between self-esteem and depression).

Correlation

In this book we often ask how much two things relate: How closely do the personality scores of twins relate to one another? How well do IQ scores predict school grades? How often does stress portend disease? To get a feel for whether one set of scores relates to a second set, let's once again begin graphically, with a **scatterplot.** Figure A–6a depicts the actual relationship between SAT scores and college first-year GPAs for the 50 college students we met earlier. Each point on the graph represents these two numbers for one student. Figure A–6b is a scatterplot of the relationship between these students' high school and college GPAs.

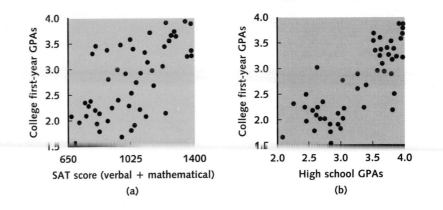

Figure A–6 Scatterplots of (a) the relationship between total SAT scores (verbal and mathematical) and first-year college GPAs and (b) the closer relationship between high school and first-year GPAs of 50 college students. Each point represents the data for one student.

The **correlation coefficient** is a statistical measure of how strongly related any two sets of scores are. It can range from

+1.00, which means that one set of scores increases in direct proportion to the other,

through 0.00, meaning that the scores are unrelated,

to −1.00, which means that one set of scores goes up precisely as the other goes down.

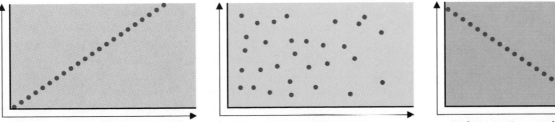

Perfect positive correlation (+1.00)   No relationship (0.00)   Perfect negative correlation (−1.00)

(Note that a correlation being negative has nothing to do with its strength or weakness; a negative correlation means two things relate inversely. A weak correlation, indicating little or no relationship, is one that has a coefficient near zero.) Now look again at the scatterplots in Figure A–6. Do the correlations look as if they were positive or negative?

Some examples of positive correlations:
Child abuse and children's
aggressiveness
Education and income
Achievement motivation and grades

Some examples of negative correlations:
Self-esteem and depression
Age and deep sleep
Stress and health

Subject	Height in inches	Temper-ament
1	80	75
2	63	66
3	61	60
4	79	90
5	74	60
6	69	42
7	62	42
8	75	60
9	77	81
10	60	39
11	64	48
12	76	69
13	71	72
14	66	57
15	73	63
16	70	75
17	63	30
18	71	30
19	68	84
20	70	39

In each scatterplot in Figure A–6, the upward slope of the cluster of points as one moves to the right shows that the two sets of scores tend to rise together. This means the correlations are positive: +.64 for the SAT-college GPA relationship shown in Figure A–6a, and a stronger +.80 for the high school GPA-college GPA relationship shown in A–6b. As SAT scores and, especially, high school grades go up, so do college grades. (The GPA-GPA relationship, incidentally, illustrates the common finding that the best predictor of people's future behavior is usually their behavior in similar situations in the past. Still, people can and do change.)

I said at the beginning that statistics can help us see what the naked eye sometimes misses. To demonstrate this for yourself, try to discern what relationship, if any, exists between two sets of scores not yet organized into a scatterplot:

Alessandra wonders whether men's heights correlate with their temperaments. She measures the heights of 20 men, has someone else independently assess their temperaments (from 0 for extremely calm to 100 for highly reactive), and obtains the data in the table to the left.

With all the relevant data right in front of you, can you tell whether there is (1) a positive correlation between height and reactive temperament, (2) very little or no correlation, or (3) a negative correlation?

Comparing the columns in the table, most people detect very little relationship between height and temperament. In fact, the correlation in this imaginary example is moderately positive, +.57, as you could see if you made a scatterplot of the data. If we fail to see a relationship when data are presented as systematically as in this table, how much less likely are we to notice them in everyday life? To see what is right in front of us, we sometimes need statistical illumination. People can easily see evidence of sex discrimination when given statistically summarized information about job level, seniority, performance, sex, and salary. But they will often see no sex discrimination when the same information dribbles in, case by case (Twiss & others, 1989).

The moral: Although the correlation coefficient tells us nothing about cause and effect, it can help us see the world more clearly by revealing the actual extent to which two things relate.

Illusory Correlations

We sometimes also "see" relationships that do not exist. A perceived correlation that does not really exist is an **illusory correlation.** When we *believe* there is a relationship between two things, we are likely to *notice* and *recall* instances that confirm our belief (Troilier & Hamilton, 1986). In one experiment, people saw the results of a hypothetical, 50-day experiment (Ward & Jenkins, 1965). For each of the 50 days, the subjects learned whether or not the clouds had been "seeded" to produce rain and whether or not it had rained. The "results" given were actually random; they showed no relationship between cloud seeding and rainfall. Nevertheless, the subjects typically perceived—in keeping with what they expected—a positive relationship between cloud seeding and rainfall.

Because we are sensitive to dramatic or unusual events, we are especially likely to notice and remember the occurrence of two such events in sequence—say, a premonition of an unlikely phone call followed by the call. When the call does not follow the premonition, we are less likely to note and remember the nonevent.

Likewise, instances of positive-thinking people being cured of cancer impress those who believe positive attitudes counter disease. But to assess

illusory correlation The perception of a relationship where none exists.

regression toward the mean The tendency for extreme or unusual scores to fall back (regress) toward the average.

whether positive thinking actually affects cancer, we need three more types of information. First, we need an estimate of how many positive thinkers *weren't* cured. And among those *not* trying to heal themselves through positive thinking, we need to know how many were and weren't cured. Without these comparison figures, positive examples of a few hope-filled people tell us nothing about the actual correlation between attitudes and disease.

The moral: When we notice and remember vivid, random coincidences, we may forget that they are random and see them as correlated. Thus, we can easily deceive ourselves by seeing what is not there.

Regression Toward the Mean

Illusory correlations feed another illusion—that chance events are subject to our personal control. Gamblers, remembering their lucky rolls, may come to believe they can influence the roll of the dice by again, say, throwing gently for low numbers and hard for high numbers. The illusion that uncontrollable events correlate with our actions is also fed by a statistical phenomenon called **regression toward the mean.** Average results are more typical than extreme results. Thus, after an unusual event, things tend to return toward their average level; that is, extraordinary happenings tend to be followed by more ordinary ones.

Examples are abundant: Basketball players who make or miss all their shots in the first half of the game are likely to "regress" (fall back) to their more usual performance level during the second half. Students who score much lower or higher on an exam than they usually do are likely, when retested, to regress toward their average. Unusual ESP subjects who defy chance when first tested nearly always lose their "psychic powers" when retested (a phenomenon that parapsychologists have called the "decline effect").

The point may seem obvious, yet we regularly miss it. Thus, we may attribute what may be a normal statistical regression (the expected falling back to normal) to something we have done:

After doing miserably on the first test, we may stop reading the chapter summaries before reading the chapters and then do better on the second test. We may then attribute our improvement to the new study technique.

After a sudden crime wave, the town council initiates a "stop crime" drive and the crime rate then returns to previous levels. The drive may therefore appear more successful than it was.

Coaches who yell at their players after an unusually bad first half may feel rewarded for having done so when the team's performance improves (returns to normal) during the second half.

Scientists who win a Nobel prize often have diminished accomplishments thereafter, leading some to wonder whether winning a Nobel hinders creativity.

Some people believe there is a *"Sports Illustrated* jinx"— that athletes whose peak performances get them on the cover of the magazine will then suffer a decline in their performance.

In each of these cases, it is possible that the effect is genuine. It is more likely, however, that these represent the natural tendency for behavior to regress from the unusual to the more usual.

Failure to recognize regression is the source of many superstitions and some ineffective practices as well. When day-to-day behavior has a large element of chance fluctuation, we may notice that others' behavior improves (regresses toward average) after we criticize them for very bad performance, and worsens (regresses toward average) after we warmly praise them for an exceptionally fine performance. Ironically, then, regression toward the average can mislead us into feeling rewarded for having criticized others and punished for having praised them (Tversky & Kahneman, 1974).

The moral: When a fluctuating behavior returns to normal, there is no need to invent fancy explanations for why it does. Regression toward the mean is probably at work.

Generalizing from Instances

So far we have seen how statistical reasoning helps us digest and describe information more accurately. Statistical reasoning also helps in a second important way: to make correct leaps of understanding from our samples of information to what is generally true.

Populations and Samples

A **population** is the whole group we are interested in. For convenience, we often observe just a small sample drawn from a population and then generalize about the whole population. We meet a few students and attend a few classes during a visit to a college and infer from those instances how friendly the campus is and how good the teaching is. We observe the weather during a week-long visit to Seattle and then tell our friends about the climate there. Obviously, we had better be careful when drawing conclusions from specific people or events. Let's take a look at some principles that can guide us when generalizing from instances.

Principle 1: Representative Samples Are Better Than Biased Samples

It is often tempting to overgeneralize from highly select samples. For example, we can delude ourselves about the actual difference between two groups when we compare members drawn from their extremes. In the 1992 Olympics, the competitors in the finals of the men's 100-meter dash were all black. How much would this tell us about the sprinting abilities of the different races? As you can see from the hypothetical illustration in Figure A–7, even a very small average difference between two races will lead to one race predominating at the high extreme. Thus, knowing that any individual is a member of race X or race Y may tell us virtually nothing about the person's sprinting abilities. The same is true when the superstars in some nonathletic pursuit come mostly from a given race, culture, or gender. Though it seems obvious, this principle is often missed in everyday life.

We are particularly prone to overgeneralize when the extremes are vivid cases. Given (a) a statistical summary of the evaluations of all of Professor Zeno's students, and (b) the vivid comments of two irate students, an administrator's impression of the professor may be as much influenced by the two unhappy students as by many favorable evaluations in the statistical summary. Driving into Chicago from the south, many people see the miles of tenement houses near the highway and think, "What an ugly city this is."

population All the cases or members in a group from which samples may be drawn for study.

"Once you become sensitized to it, you see regression everywhere."

Psychologist Daniel Kahneman (1985)

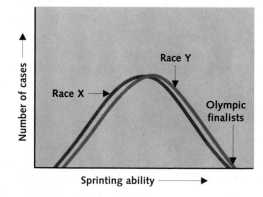

Figure A–7 Hypothetical normal curves for sprinting ability for two races. As you can see, sampling from the extremes is not the best basis for inferring general racial differences.

Standing in the checkout line at the supermarket, George sees the woman in front of him pay with food stamps and then drive away in a Cadillac. "What an easy life these welfare cheats have!" he later tells his friends. In each of these situations, the temptation to generalize from a few unrepresentative but vivid cases is nearly irresistible.

The moral: The best basis for generalizing is not from the exceptional cases one finds at the extremes, but from a representative sample of cases.

Principle 2: Random Sequences May Not Look Random

Your chances of being dealt either of these exact hands is precisely the same: 1 in 2,598,960.

As we noted in Chapter 1, we generate a representative sample of any population by gathering a *random* sample—one in which each person in the population has an equal chance of being selected. As chance would have it, though, random sequences often do not look random. If someone flipped a coin six times, would one of the following sequences of heads (H) and tails (T) be more likely than the other two: HHHTTT or HTTHTH or HHHHHH?

Daniel Kahneman and Amos Tversky (1972) found that most people believe HTTHTH would be the most likely random sequence. Actually, all possible sequences are equally likely to occur (or, you might say, equally unlikely). A bridge or poker hand of 10 through Ace, all of hearts, would seem extraordinary; actually, it would be no more or less likely than any other specific hand of cards.

The failure to recognize random occurrences for what they are can predispose people to seek extraordinary explanations for ordinary events. Imagine that on one warm spring day 4000 college students gather for a coin-tossing contest. Their task is to flip heads. On the first toss, 2000 students do so and advance to the second round. As you might expect, about 1000 of these progress to a third round, 500 to a fourth, 250 to a fifth, 125 to a sixth, 62 to a seventh, 31 to an eighth, 15 to a ninth, and 8 amazing individuals, having flipped heads nine times in a row with ever-increasing displays of concentration and effort, advance to the tenth round.

By now, the crowd of losers is in awestruck silence as these expert coin tossers prepare to display their amazing ability yet again. The proceedings are temporarily halted so that a panel of impartial scientists can observe and document the incredible achievement of these gifted individuals. Alas, on succeeding tosses they each flip one or more tails. "But, of course," their admirers say, "coin tossing is a highly sensitive skill. The tense, pressured atmosphere created by the scientific scrutiny has disturbed their fragile gift."

BIZARRE SEQUENCE OF COMPUTER-GENERATED RANDOM NUMBERS

Bizarre-looking, perhaps. But actually no more unlikely than any other number sequence.

© 1990 by Sidney Harris/American Scientist Magazine

Sometimes, though, events seem so extraordinary that we struggle to conceive an ordinary, chance-related explanation. In such cases, statisticians often are less mystified. When Evelyn Marie Adams won the New Jersey lottery twice, newspapers reported the odds of her feat as 1 in 17 trillion. Bizarre? Actually, 1 in 17 trillion are the odds that a given person who buys a single ticket for two New Jersey lotteries will win both times. But statisticians Stephen Samuels and George McCabe (1989) report that, given the millions of people who buy U.S. state lottery tickets, it was "practically a sure thing" that someday, somewhere, someone would hit a state jackpot twice. Indeed, say fellow statisticians Persi Diaconis and Frederick Mosteller (1989), "With a large enough sample, any outrageous thing is likely to happen." Ron Vachon was astounded during a September, 1990, baseball game in Boston. Oakland A's outfielder Rickey Henderson hit foul balls right to him on successive pitches. That something like that should have happened to Vachon (who dropped them both) was incredibly unlikely. That it sometime would happen to someone was not. In North America, an event that happens to but 1 in 100 million people every day occurs about three times a day, 1000 times a year.

The moral: Whether watching basketball, choosing stocks, or flipping coins (see Close-Up), remember: Random sequences often don't look random. Expect streaks.

Principle 3: More Cases Are Better Than Fewer

I have seen it happen: An eager high school senior visits two college campuses, each for a day. At the first, the student randomly attends three classes and discovers each instructor to be witty and engaging. At the next campus, the three instructors sampled seem dull and uninspiring. Returning home, the student tells friends what "great teachers" there are at the first school, and what "bores" the faculty are at the second school. Again, we know it but we ignore it: Small samples provide less reliable estimates of the average than do large samples. The proportion of heads in samples of 10 coin tosses varies more than in samples of 100 tosses.

Said differently, *averages based on more cases are more reliable* (less variable) than averages based on only a few cases. Knowing this, maybe you will come up with different answers to a question posed by Christopher Jepson, David Krantz, and Richard Nisbett (1983) to University of Michigan introductory psychology students:

> The registrar's office at the University of Michigan has found that usually about 100 students in Arts and Sciences have a 4.00 GPA at the end of their first term at the University. However, only about 10–15 students graduate with a 4.00 GPA. What do you think is the most likely explanation for the fact that there are more 4.00 GPAs after one term than at graduation?

Most of the students come up with plausible causes for the drop in GPA, such as, "Students tend to work harder at the beginning of their college careers than toward the end." Fewer than a third recognized the statistical phenomenon clearly at work: Averages based on fewer courses are more variable, which guarantees a greater number of extremely low and high GPAs at the end of the first term.

The moral: Don't be overly impressed by a few anecdotes. Generalizations based on only a few cases are unreliable.

Principle 4: Less Variable Observations Are Better Than Highly Variable Observations

Averages derived from scores with low variability are more reliable than averages based on scores with high variability. If a basketball player scored between 13 and 17 points in each of her first 10 games in a season, we would be pretty confident that she would score near 15 points in her next game—more confident than if her scores had varied from 5 to 30 points.

Intuitively, you know this to be the case. You might therefore respond much as did the students in another experiment by Nisbett and his colleagues (1983): Imagine that you are an explorer who has landed on a little-known island in the southeastern Pacific. You encounter three natives, each obese and brown-skinned. What percentage of all the natives on the island would you expect to be obese? Brown-skinned? Knowing that body weight is more variable than skin color within a geographical group, the students in the experiment much more often inferred that all the people of the island were brown-skinned than that all were obese.

Close-Up: When You're Hot You're Hot, Right? Random Sequences That Don't Look Random

Every basketball player and fan "knows" that players have hot and cold streaks. Players who have "hot hands" can't seem to miss while those who have "cold" ones can't find the center of the hoop. When Thomas Gilovich, Robert Vallone, and Amos Tversky (1985) interviewed team members of the Philadelphia 76ers, the players estimated they were about 25 percent more likely to make a shot after they had just made one than after a miss. In one survey, 9 in 10 basketball fans agreed that a player "has a better chance of making a shot after having just *made* his last two or three shots than he does after having just *missed* his last two or three shots." Believing in shooting streaks, players will feed the ball to a teammate who has just made two or three shots in a row, and many coaches will bench the player who has just missed three in a row.

The only trouble is, it isn't true.

When Gilovich and his collaborators studied detailed individual shooting records, they found that the 76ers—and the Boston Celtics, the New Jersey Nets, the New York Knicks, and Cornell University's men's and women's basketball players—were equally likely to score after a miss as after a basket. A typical 50 percent shooter averages 50 percent after just missing three shots, and 50 percent after just making three shots.

Why, then, do players and fans alike believe that players are more likely to score after scoring and miss after missing? In any series of 20 shots by a 50 percent shooter (or 20 flips of a coin), there is a 50-50 chance of four baskets (or heads) in a row, and it is quite possible that 1 person out of 5 will have a streak of five or six. Players and fans notice these random streaks and so form the myth that "when you're hot you're hot" (Figure A–8).

The same misinterpretation of random sequences is common in other settings. Hospital workers sometimes notice streaks of male births or female births. Not realizing that random sequences usually contain such streaks, they may attribute them to mysterious forces, such as phases of the moon.

Likewise, many investors believe that a mutual fund which has had a string of good years will likely outperform one that has had a string of bad years. Based on that assumption, investment magazines report mutual funds' performance. But, as economist Burton Malkiel (1989a) documents, past performances of mutual funds do *not* predict their future performance. When funds have streaks of several good or bad years, we may nevertheless be fooled into thinking that past success predicts future success.

Figure A–8 Who is the chance shooter? Here are 21 consecutive shots, each scoring either a basket or a miss, by two players who each make 50 percent. Within this sample of shots, which player's sequence looks more like what we would expect in a random sequence? (See page 520.) (Adapted from Barry Ross, *Discover*, 1987.)

statistical significance A statistical statement of how likely it is that an obtained result occurred by chance.

Well and good. The problem comes when we falsely assume groups to be relatively homogeneous. And that is typically what we do with unfamiliar "outgroups." Many experiments show that we perceive groups we don't know—for example, people of another race—as being more homogeneous than groups we know well.

The moral: Less variable observations do indeed provide a better basis for generalizing than highly variable observations; nevertheless, we often misperceive people in other groups as being more uniform than they are.

Testing Differences

We have seen that we can have more confidence in the generalizations we make from samples that are (1) representative of the population we wish to study, (2) larger rather than smaller, and (3) less rather than more variable. These principles extend to the inferences we make about differences between groups. So, when can we generalize from a difference we have observed—say, from the male versus female GPA difference in Figure A–2 (page 509) to the whole campus population of males and females?

Statistical tests help us decide by indicating the reliability of such differences. You needn't understand how they are computed to understand the logic behind them: When *averages* from two samples are each *reliable* measures of their respective populations (as when each is based on many observations that have a small standard deviation), then the difference between the samples is likely to be reliable as well. When the *difference* between the averages for the two samples is *large,* we have even more confidence that the difference between them reflects a real difference in their populations.

In short, when the sample averages are reliable and the difference between them is large, we say the difference has **statistical significance.** This simply means that the difference very likely reflects a real difference and is not due to chance variation between the samples.

When reading about research, you should remember that, given large enough or homogeneous enough samples, a difference between them may be "significant" yet unimportant. For example, when comparing the IQs among several hundred thousand first-born and later-born individuals, there is a highly significant tendency for first-born individuals within a family to have higher average scores than their later-born siblings, but only by a single IQ point or two (Zajonc & Markus, 1975).

The moral: "Statistical significance" does not equal importance; rather it means the difference is very probably not due to chance.

Using the basic statistical tools discussed in this appendix can help you to think critically—to see more clearly what you might otherwise miss or misinterpret and to generalize more accurately from your observations. People who understand and use the principles of statistics think more rationally (Nisbett & others, 1987). It requires training and practice, but developing the ability to think clearly and critically is part of becoming an educated person. The report of the Project on Redefining the Meaning and Purpose of Baccalaureate Degrees (1985) eloquently asserts why there are few higher priorities in a college education:

> If anything is paid attention to in our colleges and universities, thinking must be it. Unfortunately, thinking can be lazy. It can be sloppy. . . . It can be fooled, misled, bullied. . . . Students possess great untrained and untapped capacities for logical thinking, critical analysis, and inquiry, but these are capacities that are not spontaneous: They grow out of wide instruction, experience, encouragement, correction, and constant use.

Answer to Figure A–8 (page 519): Player *B*, whose outcomes may look more random, actually has fewer streaks than would be expected by chance. For these players, chance shooting, like chance coin tossing, should produce a change in outcome about 50 percent of the time. But 70 percent of the time (14 times out of 20) Player *B*'s outcome changes on successive shots. Player *A*, on the other hand, is scoring randomly; 10 times out of 20 Player *A*'s next outcome is different.

Reviewing Statistical Reasoning in Everyday Life

To be an educated person today is to be able to apply simple statistical principles to everyday reasoning. One needn't remember complicated formulas to think more clearly and critically about data.

From our consideration of how we can organize and describe data—by constructing distributions and computing measures of central tendency, variation, and correlation—we derived five practical morals for statistical reasoning:

1. When looking at statistical graphs in books and magazines and on TV ads and news broadcasts, always read the labels.

2. Note which measure of central tendency is reported, and consider: Could a few atypical scores be distorting it?

3. Although the correlation coefficient tells us nothing about cause and effect, it *can* help us see the world more clearly by revealing the actual extent to which two things relate.

4. When we notice and remember vivid, random events, we may forget that they are random and see them as correlated. Thus, we can easily be deceived into seeing what is not there.

5. When a fluctuating behavior returns to normal, there is no need to invent fancy explanations for why it does. Regression toward the mean is probably at work.

From our consideration of how we can appropriately leap from samples of data to conclusions about what is generally true we derived five more practical morals:

6. The best basis for generalizing is not from the exceptional, memorable cases one finds at the extremes but from a representative sample of cases.

7. Whether watching basketball, choosing stocks, or flipping coins, remember the statistical principle that random sequences often don't look random. Expect streaks.

8. Don't be overly impressed by a few anecdotes. Generalizations based on only a few cases are unreliable.

9. Less variable observations provide a better basis for generalizing than highly variable observations; nevertheless, we often misperceive people in other groups as being more uniform than they actually are.

10. "Statistical significance" does not equal importance; rather, it means the observed difference is probably not due to chance.

Terms and Concepts to Remember

frequency distribution, p. 508

percentile rank, p. 509

mode, p. 511

mean, p. 511

median, p. 511

range, p. 511

standard deviation, p. 511

normal curve (or **normal distribution**), p. 512

scatterplot, p. 513

correlation coefficient, p. 513

illusory correlation, p. 514

regression toward the mean, p. 515

population, p. 516

statistical significance, p. 520

Sample Answers to Critical Thinking Exercises

Introduction to Critical Thinking Exercises

Most psychology courses have two major goals: (1) to help you acquire a basic understanding of psychology's knowledge base and (2) to help you learn to think like a psychologist. The second goal—learning to think like a psychologist—involves critical thinking. Critical thinking refers to an attitude of healthy skepticism that should guide your study of psychology, or of any topic. As a critical thinker, you learn not to accept any explanation or conclusion about behavior as true until you have evaluated the evidence.

To learn to think critically, you must first recognize that psychological information is transmitted through persuasive arguments. An argument consists of three parts: an *assertion, evidence,* and an *explanation* (Mayer and Goodchild, 1990).

Assertion   An assertion states a relationship between some aspect of behavior, such as intelligence, and another factor, such as age. A good test of your understanding of an assertion is to try to restate it in your own words. As you do so, pay close attention to how terms and concepts are defined. When a researcher asserts that "intelligence declines with age," for example, what is meant by "intelligence"? Assertions such as this one may be true when a critical term ("intelligence") is defined one way (for example, "speed of thinking"), but not when defined in another way (for example, "general knowledge"). One of the strengths of psychology is the use of *operational definitions*—definitions of terms and concepts that specify how they are to be measured, thus eliminating any ambiguity about their meaning. "Intelligence," for example, is often operationally defined as a person's score on a test that measures specific abilities. Whenever you encounter an assertion that is ambiguous, be skeptical of its accuracy.

Evidence   When you have a clear understanding of an argument's assertion, evaluate the second component of an argument, its supporting evidence. Is it *empirical;* that is, is it based on actual experience—an observation or an experiment, for example? Does it, in fact, support the assertion? Psychologists accept only *empirical (observable) evidence* that is based on direct assessment of behavior. Hearsay, intuition, and personal anecdotes are not acceptable evidence. Chapter 1 contains a thorough discussion of the various research methods used by psychologists to gather empirical evidence. Some examples include surveys and tests, observations of behavior in natural settings, and experiments.

As you study psychology, you will become aware of another important issue in evaluating evidence—determining whether the research on which it is based is faulty. Research can be faulty for many reasons, including the use of an unrepresentative sample of subjects, experimenter bias, and inadequate control of unanticipated factors that might influence results. Evidence based on faulty research should be discounted. Appendix A, Statistical Reasoning in Everyday Life, discusses these and other examples of faulty research.

Explanation   The third component of an argument is the explanation provided for an assertion, which is based on the evidence that has been presented. While the argument's assertion merely *describes* how two things (such as intelligence and age) are related, the explanation tells *why*, often by proposing some theoretical mechanism that causes the relationship. Empirical evidence that thinking speed slows with age (the assertion), for example, may be explained as being caused by age-related changes in the activity of brain cells (a physiological explanation).

Be cautious in accepting explanations. In order to think critically about an argument's explanation, ask yourself three questions: (1) Can I restate the explanation in my own words?; (2) Does the explanation make sense based on the stated evidence?; and (3) Are there alternative explanations that adequately explain the assertion? Consider this last point in relation to our sample assertion: It is possible that the slower thinking speed of older adults is due to their having less recent experience than younger people with tasks that require quick thinking.

Some Suggestions for Becoming a Critical Thinker

1. Adopt an attitude of healthy skepticism in evaluating psychological arguments.

2. Insist on unambiguous operational definitions of an argument's important concepts and terms.

3. Be cautious in accepting supporting evidence for an argument's assertion.

4. Refuse to accept evidence for an argument if it is based on faulty research.

5. Ask yourself if the theoretical explanation provided for an argument makes sense based on the empirical evidence.

6. Determine whether there are alternative explanations that adequately explain an assertion.

7. Use critical thinking to construct your own effective arguments when writing term papers, answering essay questions, and speaking.

8. Polish your critical thinking skills by applying them to each of your college courses, and to other aspects of life as well. Learn to think critically about advertising, political speeches, and the material presented in popular periodicals.

You should now be ready to test your understanding of critical thinking by completing the exercises presented at the end of each chapter in this text. For some chapters, the exercise presents a hypothetical situation you will need to think through. For others, you will be asked to evaluate arguments that are derived from actual psychological research. And for some chapters, your comprehension of what you have read will be tested by asking you to apply it to a new situation. Carefully read the passage for each exercise and then answer the questions that follow. Finally, compare your answers with those that appear in this Appendix.

Chapter 1   Introducing Psychology

1. Your roommate asserts that upperclass men and women do better academically, defined as higher overall grade point average, because they are more serious. "Seriousness" is not defined.

2. She bases her conclusion on the large percentage of upperclass men and women who agreed with the statement, "As a senior, I take a more serious and mature approach to college than I did as a freshman." Although empirical (based on a measured response to a question), her evidence is not based on trustworthy research. One problem is that this is not an experiment. An experiment has random assignment to at least two different conditions, a comparison or control condition and an experimental condition. In the present situation there is only one condition—the seniors—with no comparison group. Furthermore, no evidence is provided regarding the seniors' actual grade point averages. It would have been better to compare the grade point averages and questionnaire responses of the seniors to the grade point averages and questionnaire responses of a sample of freshman.

    A second problem reflects an error in sampling. Seniors selected from an honors class are neither a random nor a representative sample of all upperclass men and women.

    A third problem relates to wording effects in survey research. The wording of the statement, which the students were asked to agree or disagree with, might have biased the students' responses. "Serious" and "mature" are likely to be perceived by the majority of students as desirable attributes, so it is not surprising that such a large percentage agreed with the statement as worded.

3a. Your roommate stated that seniors have higher grade point averages because they take a more serious approach to their studies.

  b. Although it is quite plausible that seriousness as a student leads to higher grades, the evidence provided does not necessarily verify this explanation nor rule out alternative explanations of the results.

  c. Assuming that the upperclass men and women do, in fact, have high grade point averages, it is quite possible that this group agrees with the statement on seriousness, not because they are seniors, but because their academic talent (presumably based on their high level of motivation and serious approach to academics) earned them admission into the honors program.

Chapter 2   Biological Roots of Behavior

1. The researchers have made several assertions: (1) that the two hemispheres of the brain function independently in people with severed corpus callosums, *and* in those with intact brains; (2) that one or the other of the two hemispheres is "dominant" in each person; and (3) that the left hemisphere is verbal and more logical than the right hemisphere, which is more intuitive and skilled at perceptual relations. "Left-" and "right-brained" are equated with right- and left-handedness, respectively. Scientific and creative ability are equated with the specialized functions of the two hemispheres of the brain, as revealed in tests that present visual information separately to each.

2. The researchers base their assertion on evidence that is empirical (based on measured results from laboratory studies) and, presumably, trustworthy. Given similar evidence from the split-brain studies cited in the

chapter, there is no reason to doubt the specialized functions of the right- and left-hemispheres, or that people whose corpus callosums have been severed are unable to integrate information received independently by each side of the brain.

3a. The researchers maintain that right-handed people are more scientific than left-handers because their left hemispheres, which process speech and logic, are "dominant." Left-handed people, in whom the more intuitive right hemisphere is presumably dominant, are believed to be less logical and more creative.

b. Although the authors build a foundation of careful observations, they leap from it to unwarranted conclusions. Consider: For one thing, it is questionable whether results from tests with split-brain patients can be generalized to people with intact brains. In normal people, the corpus callosum ensures that both sides of the brain are aware of all sensory input. A second problem is the assertion that one hemisphere is "dominant" in each person. As noted in the chapter, complex activities emerge from the integrated activity of both hemispheres in normal people. A third problem is the researchers' assertion that left-handed people naturally process speech and logic only in the right hemisphere. As noted in the chapter, more than half of all left-handers process speech in the left hemisphere, as right-handers do. It does not follow from the evidence cited that left-handers have a "dominant" right hemisphere. Finally, the authors present no evidence that left-handed people who process language in their right hemisphere are less logical and fluent.

c. Obviously, people differ in their scientific and creative abilities. Still, we can't equate these differences to which of the two sides of the brain is "dominant" in a person. The researchers might instead examine each individual's personality and background—their interests, role models, and early experiences—for factors contributing to a scientific or creative nature.

Chapter 3   The Developing Person

1. The researchers assert that breast milk offers a nutritional advantage over formula, resulting in increased intelligence, which they define as performance on an IQ test.

2. The evidence is based on empirical correlational research comparing IQ test scores of children who, as premature infants were fed breast milk, with those who were fed formula. The research appears solid; and it attempts to rule out factors that might have influenced the results, such as the mother's social and educational status.

3a. The authors state that the IQ advantage of infants fed breast milk is the result of nutritional factors that promote brain growth and thereby facilitate cognitive development.

b. Based on the evidence presented, the assertion makes sense. However, because the evidence is correlational, not based on experimental data, we can't be sure that breast milk actually affects intelligence. An experiment would be simple—mothers who intend to bottle feed, rather than nurse, could be given free milk for their babies. Half could be given formula and half breast milk from a donor.

c. It is possible that breast milk alone does not cause increased intelligence test scores. Despite the researchers' efforts to rule out group differences in mothers' social class and educational level, it is still possible that mothers who nurse their babies are more generally nurturing and produce better cared-for infants.

Chapter 4   Sensation and Perception

1. Your roommate asserts that extrasensory perception actually occurs. She defines ESP as perception that occurs outside of normal sensory experiences. She also asserts that she has psychic ability, including the ability to perceive future events (precognition) and to read your mind (telepathy).

2. Your roommate bases her belief on: (1) her ability to predict what you will say and do in certain situations, (2) her having known that you were in danger a week before your automobile accident, and (3) her identifying the suit of a playing card you randomly selected. None of these constitutes trustworthy evidence that would support her assertion. (1) When we have known someone for many years, we often are able to predict what that person will say and do simply because we have observed him or her in similar situations in the past. (2) It is common for close friends to fear that bad things may happen to one another. Occasionally an unlikely event (such as an automobile accident) occurs, and what had been a vague feeling of dread is interpreted after the fact as a precognitive experience. (3) Although empirical, the telepathy "experiment" is not based on solid research. Since there are only four suits in a deck of playing cards, by chance 1 guess in 4 should be correct. Based on only 1 guess, it is impossible to determine whether your friend's accuracy was greater than chance. Had the "experiment" continued, it is likely that your friend's guesses would be correct about 25 percent of the time.

3a. Your roommate believes that her precognitive "visions" and her ability to predict what you will say and do in certain situations can only be the result of paranormal phenomena, including extrasensory perception.

 b. The explanation provided does not verify the existence of extrasensory perception, nor does it rule out alternative explanations for your roommate's experiences.

 c. An alternative explanation is that your roommate's experiences are the result of perfectly normal phenomena. Being predisposed to believe that ESP exists, it is likely your roommate selectively recalls those few predictions that later "come true" and discounts (or just plain forgets) those that do not. Her occasional ability to predict your thoughts and actions is not necessarily anything more than familiarity with you in past situations. And finally, her accuracy in identifying the suit of one card you selected at random is not necessarily greater than chance.

Chapter 5   States of Consciousness

1. Geraldo asserts that hypnotists have the power to trigger specific behaviors, perceptions, and memories in people because hypnosis induces an altered state of consciousness involving unique physiological and psychological changes. He further claims that hypnotic age regression allows people to relive earlier experiences and that posthypnotic suggestions can erase memories from the brain. Hypnosis is defined as a unique physiological and psychological state in which people become more suggestible. Age regression is defined as the reliving of earlier experiences, such as in early childhood. Posthypnotic amnesia is defined as the inability of subjects to recall their experiences while hypnotized.

2. The research is not trustworthy for several reasons. First, Geraldo's belief in the power of hypnosis prevents him from being an objective and unbiased experimenter. His expectations of what people will do when hypnotized could bias the outcome of his "experiment." Second, enrollment in a hypnosis course signifies belief in its effectiveness. So the beliefs of the "volunteers" could also affect the outcome. Finally, because there is no control group of fully conscious subjects who are given the same suggestions as the hypnotized volunteers, this is not a true experiment.

3a. The hypnotist's explanation for the subjects' childlike behavior is that the altered state of hypnosis allows subjects to "relive" earlier experiences. Posthypnotic amnesia is explained as due to the power of hypnosis to erase memories from the brain.

b. The explanation provided does not prove that hypnosis involves a unique state of consciousness, nor does it rule out alternative explanations for the hypnotized subjects' behavior. No actual evidence of physiological change in the hypnotized subjects was presented. Nor was evidence presented that the behaviors attributed to age regression and posthypnotic amnesia could not be induced in fully conscious subjects or in those who do not have a preexisting belief in the power of hypnosis.

c. An alternative explanation is that hypnotic phenomena may be nothing more than the workings of normal consciousness. It is possible that the "hypnotized" people were merely acting the role of "good hypnotic subjects" as they confirmed the hypnotist's, and their own, beliefs about hypnotic behavior.

d. A more valid test of hypnosis must control for the possibility that the subjects' and the hypnotist's beliefs could influence the results. One way of doing so would be to pre-test volunteers by asking them whether they believe that hypnosis "works" and whether it involves a unique state of consciousness. "Believers" and "non-believers" would then undergo hypnosis. Another more valid test of hypnosis would compare the suggestibility of unhypnotized subjects with that of hypnotized subjects given the same "hypnotic suggestions."

Chapter 6   Learning

1. The assertion is that children are classically conditioned to wake up when their bladders are full. Classical conditioning is learning through the association of different events.

2. For children who learn to wake up without special training, the sensation of a wet bed or diaper functions as a UCS that elicits awakening, which is the UCR. Bladder tension (unless painful) is an initially neutral stimulus that becomes associated with the UCS. Over time, bladder tension becomes a CS and will cause the child to awaken before the bed or diaper is wet. This learned awakening is the CR. For children who are trained with the sheet and bell, the UCS is the bell which causes them to wake up, the UCR is waking up in response to the bell, the CS is bladder tension, and the CR is waking up in response to bladder tension.

3a. The explanation of how children learn to control their bladders during sleep is that waking up is a classically conditioned response to bladder tension, which has naturally been associated with the unconditioned stimulus of a wet bed or diaper.

b. The explanation appears to make sense based on the evidence. It is clear that bladder tension, unless painful, is not an unconditioned stimulus that automatically awakens a sleeping child. From the evidence cited, it is also clear that a bell can be made sufficiently loud to function as a UCS and elicit awakening as a UCR. Because the pairing of bladder tension (a neutral stimulus) with an effective UCS (the bell) eventually results in the child waking up before the bed is wet (or the bell rings), the criteria of classical conditioning have been satisfied.

c. Although the classical conditioning explanation for this example makes sense based on the evidence, an explanation based on operant conditioning is also possible. Although in very young children waking up is naturally a reflexive act (and therefore subject to classical conditioning), in older children it can be considered a *nonreflexive* act (and therefore subject to operant conditioning). Children may learn to wake up because this behavior *operates* on the environment to produce rewarding stimuli, such as the pleasurable sensation of relieving one's bladder.

Chapter 7   Memory

1. Danny was probably unable to identify the gunman shortly after seeing him run from the store because his fleeting glimpse of the man did not allow him to encode the details of his appearance. It is also possible that the confusion of the moment prevented Danny from rehearsing his mental image of the perpetrator so that his memory quickly decayed. Moreover, seeing hundreds of mug book photographs so soon after the crime could have retroactively interfered with whatever real memory Danny had of the gunman's appearance. Finally, the mug book may not actually have contained the gunman's photograph.

2. The misleading questioning and repeated exposure to Raymond's photograph may have caused Danny to misremember the actual event and to reconstruct his memory of it to include Raymond's involvement. Seeing the line-up of men several weeks later, Danny may have been unable to discriminate his eyewitness memory from his memory of the mug book photographs. This would also account for Danny's new-found confidence in the accuracy of his memory.

Chapter 8   Thinking, Language, and Intelligence

The correct answers are: 1. a; 2. b; 3. b; 4. b; 5. a; 6. b; 7. a; 8. b; 9. b; 10. a. Determine the percentage of questions you answered correctly by dividing the number correct by 10 and multiplying this figure by 100. Compare this percentage with your average confidence level. Were you more confident than correct? More correct than confident?

If your confidence level exceeded your accuracy, your thinking may be plagued by overconfidence. Overconfidence in the correctness of knowledge that is wrong hinders critical thinking, interferes with your ability to learn new information, and lowers academic performance. High-achieving students are less susceptible to overconfidence.

Several reasons have been suggested for overconfidence. One is our eagerness to confirm beliefs we already hold. Another is that we often fail to think critically about what it is we actually know. Good students are more likely to mentally "cross-examine" their evidence for choosing answers. Students who are not fully realizing their academic potential often consider only evidence that supports their belief that an answer is correct and ignore reasons why it might be wrong. Simply becoming aware of this tendency will help you think more critically about your own knowledge and reasoning. This should improve the accuracy of your confidence judgments and help you make better decisions.

You can train yourself to think more critically by imagining that you will have to explain to other students why you have made a particular decision or chosen an answer to a question such as those in this exercise. Researchers have shown that this helps to reduce overconfidence and eventually becomes a spontaneous approach to decision-making.

Chapter 9   Motivation

1. Since her parents are both obese, it is likely that Janet inherited a genetic predisposition toward obesity and possibly a lower metabolic rate than Sheila. Janet may also have a higher body weight set point than Sheila.

2. Because her parents are of normal weight, it is likely that Sheila herself is genetically predisposed to be of normal body weight. It is also likely that Sheila has a lower body weight set point and a higher metabolic rate than Janet.

3. The diet Janet and Sheila chose was effective, but more effective for Sheila due to her genetic background. Janet and her parents are all obese, so it is likely that her body has a higher percentage of fat than does Sheila's. Because fat tissue has a low metabolic rate (and therefore takes less food energy to maintain), Janet's body probably requires fewer calories to maintain its weight than does Sheila's. There is no reason to believe that Janet cheated on her diet for lack of willpower. Those genetically predisposed to obesity can eat the same foods, do the same amount of exercising, and still not lose weight as easily as those of normal body weight.

Chapter 10   Emotions, Stress, and Health

1. The James-Lange theory proposes that the experience of emotion derives from our awareness of our physiological responses to emotion-arousing stimuli. It also equates different emotions with specific body states. Assuming that sexual excitement can be triggered by the physical changes induced by exercise, this theory would predict greater reported feelings of sexual excitement during the first two phases of exercise recovery, when the subjects were actually physically aroused, than during the third phase, when the subjects were no longer aroused. The fact that sexual excitement was low during the first phase of recovery, when physical arousal was high, seems to conflict with the theory.

2. The Cannon-Bard theory proposes that an emotion-arousing stimulus simultaneously triggers physical arousal and the subjective experience of emotion. Assuming that the film was an emotion-arousing stimulus, this theory would predict greater reported feelings of sexual excitement during all three phases of the experiment because subjects viewed the film in each phase. However, this explanation is inconsistent with the finding that subjects reported being sexually excited only during the second phase of the experiment. The theory offers no explanation of why the emotional experiences of subjects during phases one and two differed.

3. According to Schachter's two-factor theory, to experience emotion one must be physically aroused and cognitively label that arousal as an emotion. Of the three theories, this one seems to explain the results of the experiment most fully. During the first phase, subjects were physically aroused, and a potential "emotional" explanation for their arousal (the film) was available. Because they *perceived* that they were still aroused from the exercise, however, subjects during this phase attributed their arousal to the exercise rather than to sexual excitement. By the third phase, the subjects had fully recovered from the exercise and lacked the physical arousal necessary to trigger the emotion-attribution process. In phase two, the subjects were physically aroused but did not subjectively perceive this arousal. According to the two-factor theory, this unexplained arousal was attributed to sexual excitement.

Chapter 11   Personality

1. The psychoanalyst has made several assertions regarding Darren's behavior and attitude: 1) The roots of Darren's problems are in unresolved childhood conflicts; 2) Darren was orally overindulged as a child; 3) Darren's personality development is fixated in the oral stage of psychosexual development; and 4) Darren is rationalizing his academic failure and projecting his own self-hatred onto his professors. Rationalization is defined as the ego's attempt to protect itself from anxiety by offering a self-justifying explanation ("the test was unfair") in place of the real, more threatening reason for failure ("I was unprepared"). Projection is defined as a defense mechanism in which a threatening impulse ("I hate myself") is disguised and attributed to others ("they hate me"). The psychoanalyst's views also imply that unconscious forces are a part of personality and that children pass through a series of psychosexual stages as their personalities are formed.

2. There really is no evidence for the various assertions made by the psychoanalyst. Dr. Roitman's conclusions are based entirely on a psychoanalytic interpretation of the behaviors and attitudes Darren displays during counseling. Although many of these behaviors are observable, they do not constitute empirical evidence for the *specific* assertions made. For this reason the evidence is not trustworthy.

3a. The theoretical explanation for Dr. Roitman's assertion is derived from Freud's psychoanalytic theory. According to this view, Darren's problems are attributed to unresolved oral conflict during his childhood. Believing that Darren was overindulged during this stage of psychosexual development, Dr. Roitman maintains that Darren's personality became fixated. Darren's self-justifying explanation for his failure and his feeling that his professors dislike him are explained as his ego's protective method of coping with unresolved conflict by unconsciously distorting reality.

b. As is generally true of psychoanalytic theory, Dr. Roitman's explanation can neither be proved nor disproved. This is because after-the-fact explanations of behavior are not based on *objective* observations and do not offer testable hypotheses. To someone who accepts psychoanalytic theory, Dr. Roitman's explanation would make sense based on the evidence; to a critically thinking scientist, however, the evidence does not necessarily support the explanation nor rule out alternative explanations.

c. Several alternative explanations can be found in the other personality theories discussed in this chapter. Humanistic theorists might explain Darren's pessimism and sarcastic manner as a result of low self-esteem and perhaps not having his basic needs met as his personality was formed. Darren's insecure feelings about his parents might mean these caregivers did not provide him with unconditional positive regard. Humanistic theorists might also suggest that Darren has a negative self-concept because his ideal self (a successful college student) differs from his actual self (an academic failure). Darren's unwillingness to accept responsibility for his failure might be described as a self-serving bias.

According to the social-cognitive perspective, Darren's personal/cognitive factors and behavior interacted with environmental influences to shape his personality. Darren's attitude about the world and unwillingness to accept responsibility for failure indicate that he perceives himself as being controlled by, rather than controlling, his environment.

Chapter 12   Psychological Disorders

1. Phyllis's daughter may be wrongfully attributing to old age what is really psychologically disordered behavior. Mental health workers label behavior as psychologically disordered when they judge it atypical, disturbing, maladaptive, and unjustifiable. Phyllis's behavior would certainly satisfy the first three of these criteria. Furthermore, although her hopeless attitude was triggered by the stress of her divorce, it has persisted too long and is too extreme to be considered a normal, justifiable response to a stressful event. Phyllis's daughter also hasn't realized there is evidence of biological factors in her mother's condition—her grandmother had similar symptoms, and the antidepressant drug prescribed by her mother's psychiatrist had been effective.

2. Phyllis is showing many classic symptoms of major depression—including poor appetite, insomnia, lethargy, feelings of worthlessness, and loss of interest in family and friends. Furthermore, these symptoms have persisted much longer than would normally be expected following a stressful event.

3. Psychoanalysts would attribute Phyllis's behavior to early childhood experiences and unconscious impulses. They might suggest, for example, that the loss of her husband evoked feelings associated with troubling losses she experienced in childhood.

Two pieces of evidence suggest the existence of biological factors in Phyllis's depression: 1) Since her mother seems to have suffered depression as well, Phyllis may have a genetic predisposition to this condition; and 2) the fact that an antidepressant drug made her feel less depressed suggests Phyllis's depression may be caused by a biochemical imbalance.

According to the social-cognitive perspective, Phyllis may be caught in a vicious cycle of overgeneralized, self-focused negative thinking that is fueling her depression. Like many depressed people, Phyllis has explained a stressful experience (her divorce) in terms that are *stable* and *global* ("Everything I have ever done, or will do, is worthless") and *internal* ("The divorce is my fault"). The result of these self-blaming attributions is a depressing sense of hopelessness that has elicited social rejection, hampered her behavior and thinking, and is likely to lead to further negative experiences.

Chapter 13   Therapy

1. There are several possible reasons psychotherapy was apparently effective for Deborah, but not for Vincent. One is that cognitive therapies, such as Deborah's, have proven most successful in treating depression. Behavior therapies, such as the counterconditioning Vincent experienced, have proven to be more effective in treating specific behavior problems, such as phobias, compulsions, or sexual dysfunctions. A second reason is that Deborah actively sought and entered therapy at a time of personal crisis, while Vincent felt that there was nothing unusual about his behavior or attitude. Deborah's depression may have lifted partly as a result of the passage of time and the lessening of the crisis. A third reason is that Deborah chose her therapist carefully, and she worked with someone who offered hope that things would improve. Vincent picked his therapist randomly, maintained a skeptical attitude throughout therapy, and never admitted he needed help. Thus, Deborah's belief in her treatment could have created a powerful placebo effect that harnessed her own healing powers and led to improvement. Finally, Deborah invested considerably more time and money in her therapy than Vincent did. This would probably result in a stronger need to justify the therapy and, thus, in a more favorable evaluation of its effectiveness.

2. Clients' perceptions of the effectiveness of psychotherapy are not acceptable as scientific evidence. One reason is that people who are suffering nonpsychotic disorders often improve whether or not they receive treatment. Psychotherapy clients who would have improved anyway might misattribute their improvement to therapy. Furthermore, people who go into therapy with the expectation that it will be effective may fall victim to the confirmation bias and remember only information that confirms their expectation.

Chapter 14   Social Psychology

1. Several principles of social psychology help explain why Mary and Kathy became friends. Through the mere exposure effect, their proximity in the dormitory would have encouraged their friendship. Their similarity in attitudes, beliefs, interests, and education probably helped cement their fondness for one another.

2. The strongest factor in the disintegration of Mary and Kathy's friendship was probably the social influence of Kathy's sorority on her attitudes and behavior. Being a sorority sister created a role with specific norms that Kathy strived to adopt. This role included an expectation that she would harbor prejudiced attitudes toward minority groups. Although Kathy was initially troubled by these attitudes, she experienced normative social influence as her desire to gain the approval of her sorority sisters created pressure to conform to their expectations. Over time the hateful attitudes became more acceptable (through mere exposure), and Kathy found herself going along with the group—feeling more and more comfortable in her new role. Kathy probably also experienced cognitive dissonance when she first joined the sorority, as her beliefs and actions conflicted. She may have been inclined to change her beliefs regarding minority groups in order to reduce this dissonance. The weekly meetings of the like-minded sorority sisters also may have contributed to both groupthink and group polarization. This would help explain the increasingly hateful attitudes of both Kathy and her sorority sisters. Finally,

Kathy's cool attitude toward Mary at the softball game may have been the result of a loss of self-awareness and self-restraint (deindividuation) in the presence of her sorority sisters.

3. It is difficult to say whether Kathy's changed behavior is the result of her true beliefs surfacing or the situational influence of the sorority. Mary may be making the fundamental attribution error by attributing Kathy's behavior at the softball game to an inner disposition of bigotry. That is, she may be underestimating the situational influence of Kathy's sorority sisters at the time of their reunion.

Chapter 15   Social Diversity

1. If you are like many people, you found it more difficult to generate descriptions of groups with which you less closely identify. This may be the result of having more limited contact with individuals in such groups.

2. Your ingroup descriptions are probably more favorable than your outgroup descriptions. This tendency to favor one's own group, called the ingroup bias, may also be reflected in prejudicial descriptions of outgroup members.

3. When 50 college students were asked to describe each of these groups, their top five descriptions were as follows:

Physicians: (1) intelligent/smart; (2) caring/understanding/compassionate; (3) wealthy/rich; (4) busy/ hardworking; (5) well-educated

Athletes: (1) athletic/fit/strong; (2) driven/highly-motivated/dedicated; (3) competitive; (4) agile/quick; (5) glorified/famous/popular and egotistical/proud

Artists: (1) creative; (2) bizarre/strange; (3) free-spirited/nonconforming/individualistic; (4) liberal/tolerant/open-minded; (5) talented/gifted

Vegetarians: (1) healthy/health-conscious; (2) environmentally or ecologically conscious; (3) limited in diet/picky about food; (4) caring/sensitive; (5) liberal

College Students: (1) fun/wild/exciting; (2) stressed/pressured/fatigued; (3) intelligent/bright; (4) diligent/dedicated/studious; (5) poor/broke and open-minded/tolerant/liberal

Lawyers: (1) articulate/convincing/persuasive; (2) deceptive/dishonest; (3) wealthy/rich; (4) intelligent/smart; (5) strong-willed/powerful and ambitious/success-oriented

Your outgroup descriptions probably match better with the above than your ingroup descriptions. People tend to form stereotyped beliefs in order to simplify the world. In categorizing people into groups, they overestimate the similarity of people within groups other than their own. "They"—the members of the outgroup—are all alike, while "we"—the members of the ingroup—are much more diverse. This tendency is one of several cognitive roots of prejudice.

Glossary

absolute threshold The minimum stimulation needed to detect a particular stimulus. (p. 106)

accommodation 1. The process by which the eye's lens changes shape to focus the image of near objects on the retina. (p. 111) 2. Adapting one's current understandings (schemas) to incorporate new information. (p. 66)

acetylcholine [ah-seat-el-KO-leen] **(ACh)** A neurotransmitter that, among its functions, triggers muscle contraction. (p. 31)

achievement motivation A desire for accomplishment; for mastery of things, people, or ideas; for attaining a high standard. (p. 291)

achievement tests Tests designed to assess what a person has learned. (p. 252)

acquisition The initial stage of learning, during which a response is established and gradually strengthened. In classical conditioning, the phase in which a stimulus comes to evoke a conditioned response. In operant conditioning, the strengthening of a reinforced response. (p. 182)

active listening Empathic listening in which the listener echoes, restates, and clarifies. A feature of Rogers' person-centered therapy. (p. 417)

adaptation-level principle The tendency for our judgments (of sounds, of lights, of income) to be relative to a "neutral" level defined by our experience. (p. 315)

adolescence The transition period from childhood to adulthood, extending from puberty to independence. (p. 78)

adrenal [ah-DREEN-el] **glands** A pair of endocrine glands just above the kidneys. The adrenals secrete the hormones epinephrine (adrenaline) and norepinephrine (noradrenaline), which help to arouse the body in times of stress. (p. 42)

aerobic exercise Sustained exercise that increases heart and lung fitness; may also alleviate depression and anxiety. (p. 335)

age regression In hypnosis, the supposed reliving of earlier experiences, such as in early childhood; greatly susceptible to false recollections. (p. 161)

aggression Any physical or verbal behavior intended to hurt or destroy. (p. 458)

algorithm A methodical, logical rule or procedure for solving a particular problem. May be contrasted with the usually speedier, but also more error-prone use of *heuristics*. (p. 235)

alpha waves The relatively slow brain waves of a relaxed, awake state. (p. 152)

altruism Unselfish regard for the welfare of others. (p. 464)

Alzheimer's disease A progressive and irreversible brain disorder characterized by gradual deterioration of memory, reasoning, language, and, finally, physical functioning. (p. 88)

amnesia Loss of memory. Psychogenic amnesia, a dissociative disorder, is selective memory loss often brought on by extreme stress. (pp. 205, 389)

amphetamines Drugs that stimulate neural activity, causing speeded-up body functions and associated energy and mood changes. (p. 169)

amygdala [ah-MIG-dah-la] Two almond-shaped neural centers in the limbic system that are linked to emotion. (p. 40)

anal stage The second of Freud's psychosexual stages, from about 18 months to 3 years, during which pleasure focuses on bowel and bladder elimination, retention, and control. (p. 348)

anorexia nervosa An eating disorder in which a normal-weight person (usually an adolescent female) diets to become significantly underweight (15 percent or more), yet, still feeling fat, continues to starve. (p. 277)

antisocial personality A personality disorder in which the person (usually a man) exhibits a lack of conscience for wrongdoing, even toward friends and family members. May be aggressive and ruthless or a clever con artist. (p. 404)

anxiety disorders Psychological disorders characterized by distressing, persistent anxiety or maladaptive behaviors that reduce anxiety. (p. 384)

aphasia Impairment of language, usually caused by left hemisphere damage either to Broca's area (impairing speaking) or to Wernicke's area (impairing understanding). (p. 48)

applied research Scientific study that aims to solve practical problems. (p. 5)

approach-approach conflict Feeling torn between two attractive but incompatible goals. (p. 328)

approach-avoidance conflict Feeling drawn to a goal but also repelled by it, especially when close to it. (p. 328)

aptitude tests Tests designed to predict a person's future performance; aptitude is the capacity to learn. (p. 252)

assimilation Interpreting one's new experience in terms of one's existing schemas. (p. 66)

association areas Areas of the cerebral cortex that are not involved in primary motor or sensory functions; rather, they are involved in higher mental functions such as learning, remembering, thinking, and speaking. (p. 47)

attachment   An emotional tie with another person; shown in young children by their seeking closeness to the caregiver and showing distress on separation. (p. 71)

attitude   A belief and feeling that predisposes one to respond in a particular way to objects, people, and events. (p. 445)

attribution theory   The theory that we tend to give a causal explanation for someone's behavior, often by crediting either the situation or the person's disposition. (p. 443)

audition   The sense of hearing. (p. 118)

automatic processing   Unconscious encoding of incidental information, such as space, time, and frequency, and of well-learned information, such as word meanings. (p. 209)

autonomic [aw-tuh-NAHM-ik] **nervous system**   The part of the peripheral nervous system that controls the glands and the muscles of the internal organs (such as the heart). Its sympathetic division arouses; its parasympathetic division calms. (p. 33)

availability heuristic   A rule of thumb for estimating the likelihood of events based on their availability in memory; if instances come readily to mind (perhaps because of their vividness), we presume such events are likely. (p. 238)

aversive conditioning   A type of counterconditioning that associates an unpleasant state (such as nausea) with an unwanted behavior (such as drinking alcohol). (p. 422)

avoidance-avoidance conflict   Feeling torn between which of two unappealing alternatives to avoid. (p. 328)

axon   The extension of a neuron ending in branching terminal fibers through which messages are sent to other neurons or to muscles or glands. (p. 29)

babbling stage   Beginning at 3 to 4 months, the stage of speech development in which the infant spontaneously utters various sounds at first unrelated to the household language. (p. 243)

barbiturates   Drugs that depress the activity of the central nervous system, reducing anxiety, but impairing memory and judgment. (p. 169)

basic research   Pure science; aims to increase the scientific knowledge base. (p. 5)

basic trust   According to Erik Erikson, a sense that the world is predictable and trustworthy; said to be formed during infancy by appropriate experiences with responsive caregivers. (p. 73)

behavior modification   The application of operant conditioning principles to the modification of maladaptive human behavior. (p. 423)

behavior therapy   Therapy that applies learning principles to the elimination of unwanted behaviors. (p. 420)

behavioral perspective   Emphasizes environmental influences on observable behaviors. (p. 4)

behaviorism   The view that (1) psychology should be an objective science that (2) studies only overt behavior without reference to mental processes. Most research psychologists today agree with (1) but not (2). (p. 180)

belief perseverance   Clinging to one's initial conceptions after the basis on which they were formed has been discredited. (p. 240)

binocular cues   Depth cues, such as retinal disparity and convergence, that depend on the use of two eyes. (p. 128)

biofeedback   A system for electronically recording, amplifying, and feeding back information regarding a subtle physiological state, such as blood pressure or muscle tension. (p. 336)

biological perspective   Emphasizes the influences of heredity and physiology upon our behaviors, emotions, memories, and sensory experiences. (p. 2)

biological psychologists   Psychologists concerned with the links between biology and behavior. (Some biological psychologists call themselves *behavioral neuro-scientists, neuropsychologists, physiological psychologists,* or *biopsychologists.*) (p. 27)

bipolar disorder   A mood disorder in which a person alternates between the hopelessness and lethargy of depression and the overexcited state of mania. (p. 391)

blind spot   The point at which the optic nerve leaves the eye, creating a "blind" spot because no receptor cells are located there. (p. 112)

brainstem   The central core of the brain, beginning where the spinal cord swells as it enters the skull; it is the oldest part of the brain and is responsible for automatic survival functions. (p. 36)

Broca's area   An area of the left frontal lobe that directs the muscle movements involved in speech. (p. 48)

bulimia nervosa   An eating disorder characterized by private, "binge-purge" episodes of overeating, usually of highly caloric foods, followed by vomiting or laxative use. (p. 277)

bystander effect   The tendency for any given bystander to be less likely to give aid if other bystanders are present. (p. 465)

Cannon-Bard theory   The theory that an emotion-arousing stimulus simultaneously triggers (1) physiological responses and (2) the subjective experience of emotion. (p. 319)

case study   Studying one person in depth in the hope of revealing universal principles. (p. 8)

CAT (computerized axial tomograph) scan   A series of x-ray photographs taken from different angles and combined by computer into a composite three-dimensional representation of a slice through the body. (p. 39)

catharsis   Emotional release. In psychology, the catharsis hypothesis maintains that "releasing" aggressive energy (through action or fantasy) relieves aggressive urges. (p. 312)

central nervous system (CNS)   The brain and spinal cord. (p. 33)

cerebellum [sehr-uh-BELL-um]   The "little brain" attached to the rear of the brainstem; it helps coordinate voluntary movement and balance. (p. 36)

cerebral [seh-REE-bruhl] **cortex**   The intricate fabric of interconnected neural cells that covers the cerebral hemispheres; the body's ultimate control and information-processing center. (p. 44)

chromosomes   Threadlike structures made of DNA molecules that contain the genes. (p. 60)

chunking   Organizing items into familiar, manageable units; often done automatically. (p. 214)

circadian rhythm [ser-KAY-dee-an]   The biological clock; regular bodily rhythms (for example, of temperature and wakefulness) that occur on a 24-hour cycle. (p. 151)

classical conditioning   Reflexive learning in which an organism comes to associate significant events. A neutral stimulus that signals an unconditioned stimulus (UCS) begins to produce a response that anticipates and prepares for the unconditioned stimulus. (Also known as *Pavlovian conditioning*.) (p. 182)

clinical psychology   A branch of psychology involving the assessment and treatment of those who suffer psychological disorders. (p. 5)

closure   The perceptual tendency to fill in gaps, thus enabling one to perceive disconnected parts as a whole object. (p. 127)

cochlea [KOHK-lee-uh]   A coiled, bony, fluid-filled tube in the inner ear through which sound waves trigger nerve impulses. (p. 120)

cognition   All the mental activities associated with thinking, knowing, and remembering. (p. 66)

cognitive dissonance theory   The theory that we act to reduce the discomfort (dissonance) we feel when two of our thoughts (cognitions) are inconsistent—as when we respond to our having acted contrary to our attitudes by changing our attitude. (p. 448)

cognitive map   A mental representation of the layout of one's environment. For example, after exploring a maze, rats act as if they learned a cognitive map of it. (p. 195)

cognitive perspective   Emphasizes how we process, store, and retrieve information and how we use it to reason and solve problems. (p. 4)

cognitive psychology   The field of psychology that studies mental representations and the processing of information; topics include the mental activities that underlie problem solving, judgments, decision making, and language. (p. 234)

cognitive therapy   Therapy that teaches people new, more adaptive ways of thinking and acting; based on the assumption that thoughts intervene between events and our emotional reactions. (p. 424)

collective unconscious   Carl Jung's concept of a shared, inherited reservoir of memory traces from our species' history. (p. 351)

collectivism   Giving priority to the goals of one's groups (often one's extended family or work group) and defining one's identity accordingly. (p. 479)

color constancy   Perceiving familiar objects as having consistent color, even if changing illumination alters the wavelengths reflected by the object. (p. 117)

companionate love   The deep affectionate attachment we feel for those with whom our lives are intertwined. (p. 470)

concept   A mental grouping of similar objects, events, or people. (p. 234)

concrete operational stage   In Piaget's theory, the stage of cognitive development (from about 6 or 7 to 11 years of age) during which children gain the mental operations that enable them to think logically about concrete events. (p. 69)

conditioned response (CR)   In classical conditioning, the learned response to a conditioned stimulus (CS). (p. 181)

conditioned stimulus (CS)   In classical conditioning, an originally neutral stimulus that, after association with an unconditioned stimulus (UCS), comes to trigger a conditioned response. (p. 181)

cones   Receptor cells concentrated near the center of the retina that function in daylight or in well-lit conditions, the cones detect fine detail and give rise to color sensations. (p. 112)

confirmation bias   A tendency to search for information that confirms one's preconceptions. (p. 236)

conflict   A perceived incompatibility of actions, goals, or ideas. (p. 500)

conformity   Adjusting one's behavior or thinking to coincide with a group standard. (p. 450)

connectedness   The perceptual tendency to perceive features, such as dots, as a single unit when uniform and linked. (p. 127)

consciousness   Selective attention to ongoing perceptions, thoughts, and feelings. (p. 149)

conservation   The principle (which Piaget believed to be a part of concrete operational reasoning) that properties such as mass, volume, and number remain the same despite changes in the forms of objects. (p. 69)

continuity   A perceptual tendency to group stimuli into smooth, continuous patterns. (p. 127)

continuous reinforcement   Reinforcing the desired response every time it occurs. (p. 192)

control condition   The condition of an experiment in which the experimental treatment is absent; serves as a comparison for evaluating the effect of the treatment. (p. 13)

convergence   A binocular cue for perceiving depth; the extent to which the eyes converge inward when looking at an object. (p. 129)

conversion disorder   A rare somatoform disorder in which a person experiences very specific genuine physical symptoms for which no physiological basis can be found. (p. 388)

coronary heart disease   The clogging of the vessels that nourish the heart muscle; the leading cause of death in the United States. (p. 329)

corpus callosum [KOR-pus kah-LOW-sum]   The largest bundle of neural fibers connecting and carrying messages between the two brain hemispheres. (p. 50)

correlation   A statistical measure of how much two factors vary together. This statistic indicates how well either factor predicts the other. (p. 10)

correlation coefficient   A measure of the direction and extent of the relationship between two sets of scores. Scores with a *positive correlation coefficient* go up and down together (as with high school and college GPAs). A *negative correlation coefficient* indicates that one score falls as the other rises (as in the relationship between self-esteem and depression). (p. 513)

counterconditioning   A behavior therapy procedure that conditions new responses to stimuli that trigger unwanted behaviors; based on classical conditioning. Two such techniques are *systematic desensitization* and *aversive conditioning*. (p. 420)

creativity The ability to produce novel and valuable ideas. (p. 259)

critical period An optimal period during which an organism's exposure to certain influences or experiences will produce proper development. (p. 72)

critical thinking Thinking that does not blindly accept arguments and conclusions. Rather, it examines assumptions, discerns hidden values, evaluates evidence, and assesses conclusions. (p. 7)

cross-sectional study A study in which people of different ages are tested or observed at one point in time. (p. 89)

crystallized intelligence One's accumulated knowledge and verbal skills; tends to increase with age. (p. 90)

culture The enduring behaviors, ideas, attitudes, and traditions shared by a large group of people and transmitted from one generation to the next. (p. 476)

defense mechanisms In psychoanalytic theory, the ego's protective methods of reducing anxiety by unconsciously distorting reality. (p. 349)

deindividuation The loss of self-awareness and self-restraint occurring in group situations that foster arousal and anonymity. (p. 455)

déjà vu (From French, literally meaning "already seen.") That eerie sense that "I've experienced this before." Cues from the current situation may subconsciously trigger retrieval of an earlier, similar experience. (p. 222)

delta waves The large, slow brain waves associated with deep sleep. (p. 152)

delusions False beliefs, often of persecution or grandeur, that may accompany psychotic disorders. (p. 400)

dendrite The bushy, branching extensions of a neuron that receive messages and conduct impulses toward the cell body. (p. 29)

dependent variable The variable that is being measured; in an experiment, the variable that may change in response to manipulations of the independent variable. (p. 14)

depressants Drugs (such as alcohol, barbiturates, and opiates) that reduce neural activity and slow body functions. (p. 167)

depth perception The ability to see objects in three dimensions although the images that strike the retina are two-dimensional; allows us to judge distance. (p. 128)

developmental psychology A branch of psychology that studies physical, cognitive, and social change throughout the life span. (p. 59)

difference threshold The minimum difference in stimulation that a subject can detect 50 percent of the time. We experience the difference threshold as a just noticeable difference (jnd). (p. 108)

discrimination In classical conditioning, the ability to distinguish between a conditioned stimulus and similar stimuli that do not signal an unconditioned stimulus. (In operant conditioning, below, responding differently to stimuli that signal that behavior will be reinforced or nonreinforced.) (p. 183)

displacement In psychoanalytic theory, the defense mechanism that shifts sexual or aggressive impulses toward a more acceptable or less threatening object or person, as when redirecting anger toward a safer outlet. (p. 350)

dissociation A split in consciousness, which allows some thoughts and behaviors to occur simultaneously with others. (p. 164)

dissociative disorders Disorders in which conscious awareness becomes separated (dissociated) from painful memories, thoughts, and feelings. (p. 389)

DNA (deoxyribonucleic acid) A complex molecule containing genetic information that makes up the chromosomes. (p. 60)

double-blind procedure An experimental procedure in which both the subject and the staff are ignorant (blind) about whether the subject has received the treatment or a placebo. Commonly used in drug evaluation studies. (p. 16)

Down syndrome A condition of retardation and associated physical disorders caused by an extra chromosome in one's genetic makeup. (p. 257)

drive An aroused state that typically arises from an underlying need. (p. 270)

DSM-III-R The American Psychiatric Association's *Diagnostic and Statistical Manual of Mental Disorders (Third Edition—Revised)*, a widely used system for classifying psychological disorders. It will be replaced by the forthcoming DSM-IV. (p. 382)

echoic memory A momentary sensory memory of auditory stimuli; even if attention is elsewhere, sounds and words can still be recalled within 3 or 4 seconds. (p. 208)

eclectic approach An approach to psychotherapy that takes advantage of techniques from the various forms of therapy, depending on the client's problems. (p. 414)

effortful processing Encoding that requires attention and conscious effort. (p. 210)

ego The largely conscious, "executive" part of personality that, according to Freud, mediates among the demands of the id, superego, and reality. (p. 347)

egocentrism In Piaget's theory, the inability of the preoperational child to take another's point of view. (p. 67)

electroconvulsive therapy (ECT) Shock treatment. A biomedical therapy for severely depressed patients in which a brief electric current is sent through the brain of an anesthetized patient. (p. 436)

electroencephalogram (EEG) An amplified recording of the waves of electrical activity that sweep across the brain's surface. These waves are measured by placing electrodes on the scalp. (p. 38)

embryo The developing human organism from about 2 weeks after fertilization through the second month. (p. 61)

emotion A response of the whole organism, involving (1) physical arousal, (2) expressive behaviors, and (3) conscious experience. (p. 301)

empirically derived test A test (such as the MMPI-2) developed by testing a pool of items and then selecting those that discriminate groups of interest. (p. 359)

encoding The processing of information into the memory system. (p. 207)

endocrine [EN-duh-krin] **system** The body's "slow," chemical communication system; a set of glands that secretes hormones into the bloodstream. (p. 42)

endorphins [en DOR fins] "Morphine within"—natural, opiatelike neurotransmitters linked to pain control and to pleasure. (p. 32)

equilibrium The sense of body movement and position, including the sense of balance. (p. 124)

equity A condition in which people receive from a relationship in proportion to what they give to it. (p. 470)

estrogen A sex hormone, secreted in greater amounts by females than males. In nonhuman female mammals, the estrogen peak during ovulation promotes sexual receptivity. (p. 284)

ethnicity That part of one's social identity defined by the ancestors, heritage, and traits one shares with others. (p. 481)

experiment A research method in which the investigator manipulates one or more factors to observe their effect on behavior, while controlling other relevant factors. (p. 12)

experimental condition The condition of an experiment that exposes subjects to the treatment, that is, to the independent variable. (p. 13)

explicit memory Memory of facts and experiences that one can consciously know and "declare" in words. (Also called *declarative memory*.) (p. 219)

external locus of control The perception that chance or outside forces beyond one's personal control determine one's fate. (p. 369)

extinction In classical conditioning, the diminishing of a response when an unconditioned stimulus (UCS) does not follow a conditioned stimulus (CS). (In operant conditioning, below, extinction occurs when a response is no longer reinforced.) (p. 182)

extrasensory perception (ESP) The controversial claim that perception can occur apart from sensory input; said to include telepathy, clairvoyance, and precognition. (p. 140)

extrinsic motivation A desire to perform a behavior due to promised rewards or threats of punishment. (p. 293)

family therapy Therapy that treats the family as a system. Views an individual's unwanted behaviors as influenced by or directed at other family members; encourages family members toward positive relationships and improved communication. (p. 418)

feature detectors Nerve cells in the brain that respond to specific features of the stimulus, such as movement, angle, or shape. (p. 114)

fetal alcohol syndrome Physical and cognitive abnormalities in children caused by a pregnant woman's heavy drinking. In severe cases, symptoms include noticeable facial misproportions. (p. 61)

fetus The developing human organism from 9 weeks after conception to birth. (p. 61)

figure-ground The organization of the visual field into objects (the figures) that stand out from their surroundings (the ground). (p. 126)

fixation 1. According to Freud, a lingering focus of pleasure-seeking energies at an earlier psychosexual stage, where conflicts were unresolved. (p. 349) 2. The inability to see a problem from a new perspective; an impediment to problem solving. (p. 236)

fixed-interval schedule In operant conditioning, a reinforcement schedule that reinforces a response only after a specified time has elapsed. (p. 192)

fixed-ratio schedule In operant conditioning, a reinforcement schedule that reinforces behavior only after a specified number of responses. (p. 192)

flashbulb memory A clear memory of an emotionally significant moment or event. (p. 206)

fluid intelligence One's ability to reason abstractly; tends to decrease during late adulthood. (p. 90)

foot-in-the-door phenomenon The tendency for people who have first agreed to a small request to comply later with a larger request. (p. 446)

formal operational stage In Piaget's theory, the stage of cognitive development (normally beginning about age 12) during which people begin to think logically about abstract concepts. (p. 69)

framing The way an issue is posed. How an issue is framed can significantly affect decisions and judgments. (p. 210)

fraternal twins Twins who develop from separate zygotes (fertilized eggs); genetically no closer than brothers and sisters, but who have shared the fetal environment. (p. 96)

free association A psychoanalytic method of exploring the unconscious in which the person relaxes and says whatever comes to mind, no matter how trivial or embarrassing. (pp. 346, 415)

frequency distribution A listing of the number of individual scores that occur within each equal-sized interval within a distribution. (p. 508)

frequency The number of complete wavelengths that pass a point in a given time (for example, per second). (p. 119)

frontal lobes The portion of the cerebral cortex lying just behind the forehead; involved in speaking and muscle movements and in making plans and judgments. (p. 44)

frustration-aggression principle The principle that frustration—the blocking of an attempt to achieve some goal—creates anger, which can generate aggression. (p. 460)

fugue [fewg] A dissociative disorder in which flight from one's home and identity accompanies amnesia. (p. 389)

functional fixedness The tendency to think of things only in terms of their usual functions; an impediment to problem solving. (p. 236)

fundamental attribution error The tendency for observers, when analyzing another's behavior, to underestimate the impact of the situation and to overestimate the impact of personal disposition. (p. 443)

gate-control theory Melzack and Wall's theory that the spinal cord contains a neurological "gate" that blocks or allows pain signals to pass on to the brain. The "gate" is opened by the activity of pain signals traveling up small nerve fibers and closed by activity in larger fibers or by information coming from the brain. (p. 123)

gender identity One's sense of being male or female. Note: One's gender identity is distinct from one's sexual orientation (as heterosexual or homosexual) and from the strength of one's gender-typing. (pp. 349, 490)

gender In psychology, the characteristics, whether biologically or socially influenced, by which people define male and female. (p. 484)

gender role A set of expected behaviors for males and for females. (p. 492)

gender schema theory The theory that children learn from their cultures a concept of what it means to be male and female and adjust their behavior accordingly. (p. 490)

gender-typed Exhibiting masculine or feminine gender identity and role. (p. 490)

general adaptation syndrome (GAS) Selye's concept of the body's adaptive response to stress as composed of three stages—alarm, resistance, exhaustion. (p. 324)

general intelligence (g) factor A general underlying intelligence factor believed by Spearman and others to be measured by every task on an intelligence test. (p. 258)

generalization The tendency, once a response has been conditioned, for stimuli similar to the conditioned stimulus to evoke similar responses. (p. 183)

generalized anxiety disorder An anxiety disorder in which a person is continually tense, apprehensive, and in a state of autonomic nervous system arousal. (p. 384)

genes The biochemical units of heredity that make up the chromosomes; a segment of DNA capable of synthesizing a protein. (p. 60)

genital stage The last of Freud's psychosexual stages, beginning in puberty, during which sexuality matures and the person seeks pleasure through sexual contact with others. (p. 349)

gestalt An organized whole. Gestalt psychologists emphasize our tendency to integrate pieces of information into meaningful wholes. (p. 125)

glucose The form of sugar that circulates in the blood and provides the major source of energy for body tissues. When its level is low, we feel hunger. (p. 274)

GRIT Graduated and Reciprocated Initiatives in Tension-Reduction: a strategy designed to decrease international tensions. (p. 503)

group polarization The enhancement of a group's prevailing attitudes through discussion. (p. 455)

grouping The tendency to organize stimuli into coherent groups. (p. 127)

groupthink The mode of thinking that occurs when the desire for harmony in a decision-making group overrides a realistic appraisal of alternatives. (p. 456)

hallucinations False sensory experiences, such as seeing something without any external visual stimulus. (p. 152)

hallucinogens Psychedelic ("mind-manifesting") drugs, such as LSD, that distort perceptions and evoke sensory images in the absence of sensory input. (p. 167)

health psychology A subfield of psychology that provides a behavioral approach to medicine. Assumes that biological, psy-chological, and social factors all contribute to illness and can be a part of preventive strategies. (p. 323)

heritability The extent to which we can attribute individuals' differences in a trait to genes. The heritability of a trait may vary, depending on the range of populations and environments studied. (p. 261)

heuristic A rule-of-thumb strategy that often allows us to make judgments and solve problems efficiently; usually speedier, but more error-prone than *algorithms*. (p. 235)

hierarchy of needs Maslow's pyramid of human needs, beginning at the base with physiological needs that must first be satisfied before higher-level safety needs and then psychological needs become active. (p. 271)

hindsight bias The tendency to believe one would have foreseen how something turned out, *after* learning the outcome. (Also known as the *I-knew-it-all-along phenomenon*.) (p. 20)

hippocampus A neural center in the limbic system that helps process explicit memories for storage. (p. 220)

homeostasis A tendency to maintain a balanced or constant internal state; refers especially to the body's tendency to maintain an optimum internal state for functioning. (p. 270)

hormones Chemical messengers, such as those manufactured by the endocrine glands, that are produced in one tissue and travel via the bloodstream to affect another. (p. 42)

hospice An organization whose largely volunteer staff provides support for dying people and their families either in special facilities or in people's own homes. (p. 94)

hue The dimension of color that is determined by the wavelength of light; what we know as the color names (blue, green, and so forth). (p. 110)

humanistic perspective Emphasizes people's capacities for choice and growth—studies people's subjective experiences. (p. 4)

hypnosis A state of apparently heightened suggestibility in which some people narrow their focus of attention and claim to experience imaginary happenings as if they were real. (p. 159)

hypochondriasis A somatoform disorder in which a person misinterprets normal physical sensations as symptoms of a disease. (p. 388)

hypothalamus [hi-po-THAL-uh-muss] A neural structure lying below (*hypo*) the thalamus; it directs several maintenance activities (eating, drinking, body temperature), helps govern the endocrine system via the pituitary gland, and is linked to emotion and reward. (p. 41)

hypothesis A testable prediction, often implied by a theory. (p. 7)

iconic memory A momentary sensory memory of visual stimuli; a photographic or picture-image memory lasting no more than a second or so. (p. 208)

id A reservoir of unconscious psychic energy that, according to Freud, strives to satisfy basic sexual and aggressive drives. (p. 347)

identical twins Twins who develop from a single zygote that splits in two, creating two genetic replicas. (p. 96)

identification The process by which, according to Freud, children incorporate their parents' values into their developing superegos. (p. 349)

identity One's sense of self; according to Erikson, the adolescent's task is to solidify a sense of self by testing and integrating various roles. (p. 82)

Illusory correlation The perception of a relationship where none exists. (p. 514)

imagery Mental pictures. A powerful aid to effortful processing, especially when combined with semantic encoding. (p. 213)

implicit memory Retention (of skills, preferences, and dispositions) without conscious recollection. (Also called *nondeclarative memory*.) (p. 219)

imprinting The process by which certain animals form attachments during a critical period very early in life. (p. 72)

incentives Positive or negative environmental stimuli that motivate behavior. (p. 271)

independent variable The experimental factor that is manipulated; the variable whose effect is being studied. (p. 14)

individualism Giving priority to one's own goals over group goals, and defining one's identity in terms of personal attributes rather than group identifications. (p. 479)

informational social influence Influence resulting from one's willingness to accept others' opinions about reality. (p. 451)

ingroup bias The tendency to favor one's own group. (p. 497)

inner ear The innermost part of the ear, containing the cochlea, semicircular canals, and vestibular sacs. (p. 120)

insight A sudden and often novel realization of the solution to a problem; it contrasts with strategy-based solutions. (p. 235)

insomnia A sleep disorder involving recurring problems in falling or staying asleep. (p. 154)

instinct A behavior that is rigidly patterned and unlearned. (p. 270)

insulin A hormone that, among its effects, helps body tissues convert blood glucose into stored fat. When its level in the body is high, we feel hunger. (p. 274)

intelligence quotient (IQ) Defined originally as the ratio of mental age to chronological age multiplied by 100 (thus, IQ = (ma/ca) × 100). On contemporary intelligence tests, the average performance for a given age is assigned a score of 100. (p. 253)

intelligence The capacity for goal-directed and adaptive behavior. Involves the abilities to profit from experience, solve problems, reason, and successfully meet challenges and achieve goals. (p. 256)

intensity The amount of energy in a light or sound wave, which we perceive as brightness or loudness, as determined by the wave's amplitude. (p. 110)

interaction effect A result in which the effect of one factor depends on the level of another. (p. 98)

internal locus of control The perception that one controls one's own fate. (p. 369)

interneurons Central nervous system neurons that intervene directly between the sensory inputs and motor outputs. (p. 28)

interpretation In psychoanalysis, the analyst's assisting the patient to note and understand resistances and other significant behaviors in order to promote insight. (p. 415)

intimacy In Erikson's theory, the ability to form close, loving relationships; a primary developmental task in late adolescence and early adulthood. (p. 83)

intrinsic motivation A desire to perform a behavior for its own sake and to be effective. (p. 293)

iris A ring of muscle tissue that forms the colored portion of the eye around the pupil and controls the size of the pupil opening. (p. 111)

James-Lange theory The theory that our experience of emotion is our awareness of our physiological responses to emotion-arousing stimuli. (p. 319)

just noticeable difference (jnd) See *difference threshold*. (p. 108)

just-world phenomenon The tendency of people to believe the world is just and that people therefore get what they deserve and deserve what they get. (p. 499)

kinesthesis [kin-ehs-THEE-sehs] The system for sensing the position and movement of individual body parts. (p. 124)

language Our spoken, written, or gestured words and how we combine them to communicate meaning. (p. 242)

latency stage The fourth of Freud's psychosexual stages, from about age 6 to puberty, during which sexual impulses are repressed. (p. 349)

latent content According to Freud, the underlying but censored meaning of a dream (as distinct from its manifest content). Freud believed that a dream's latent content functions as a safety valve. (p. 156)

latent learning Learning that occurs but is not apparent until there is an incentive to demonstrate it. (p. 195)

learned helplessness The hopelessness and passive resignation learned when an animal or human is unable to avoid repeated aversive events. (p. 370)

learning A relatively permanent change in an organism's behavior due to experience with the environment. (p. 179)

lens The transparent structure behind the pupil that changes shape to focus images on the retina. (p. 111)

lesion [LEE-zhuhn] Tissue destruction. A brain lesion is a naturally or experimentally caused destruction of brain tissue. (p. 38)

limbic system A doughnut-shaped system of neural structures at the border of the brainstem and cerebral hemispheres; associated with emotions such as fear and aggression and drives such as those for food and sex. (p. 40)

linear perspective A monocular cue for perceiving distance; we perceive the converging of what we know to be parallel lines as indicating increasing distance. (p. 130)

linguistic relativity Whorf's hypothesis that language determines the way we think. (p. 249)

lithium A chemical that provides an effective drug therapy for the mood swings of bipolar (manic-depressive) disorders. (p. 436)

lobotomy A now-rare psychosurgical procedure once used to calm uncontrollably emotional or violent patients. In this procedure the nerves that connect the frontal lobes to the emotion-controlling centers of the inner brain are cut. (p. 437)

long-term memory The relatively permanent and limitless storehouse of the memory system. (p. 207)

longitudinal study Research in which the same people are restudied over a long time period. (p. 89)

LSD A powerful hallucinogenic drug; also known as *acid*. (p. 171)

lymphocytes The two types of white blood cells that are part of the body's immune system: B lymphocytes form in the *bone* marrow and release antibodies that fight bacterial infections; T lymphocytes form in the *thymus* and, among other duties, attack cancer cells, viruses, and foreign substances. (p. 331)

major depression A mood disorder in which a person, for no apparent reason, experiences 2 or more weeks of depressed moods, feelings of worthlessness, and diminished interest or pleasure in most activities. (p. 391)

mania A hyperactive, wildly optimistic state. (p. 394)

manifest content According to Freud, the remembered story line of a dream (as distinct from its latent content). (p. 156)

maturation Biological growth processes that enable orderly changes in behavior, relatively uninfluenced by experience. (p. 63)

mean The arithmetic average of a distribution, obtained by adding the scores and then dividing by the number of scores. (p. 511)

median The middle score in a distribution; half the scores are above it and half are below it. (p. 511)

medical model The concept that diseases have physical causes that can be diagnosed, treated, and, in many cases, cured. When applied to psychological disorders, the medical model assumes that these "mental" illnesses can be diagnosed on the basis of their symptoms and cured through therapy, which may include treatment in a psychiatric hospital. (p. 381)

medulla [muh-DUL-uh] The base of the brainstem; controls heartbeat and breathing. (p. 36)

memory The storage and retrieval of information. (p. 205)

menopause The time of natural cessation of menstruation; also refers to the biological and psychological changes experienced during a woman's years of declining ability to reproduce. (p. 86)

mental age A measure of intelligence test performance devised by Binet; the chronological age that most typically corresponds to a given level of performance. Thus, a child who does as well as the average 8-year-old is said to have a mental age of 8. (p. 252)

mental retardation A condition of limited mental ability, as indicated by an intelligence score below 70 and difficulty in adapting to the demands of life; varies from mild to profound. (p. 257)

mere exposure effect The phenomenon that repeated exposure to novel stimuli increases liking of them. (p. 467)

metabolic rate The body's rate of energy expenditure at rest. (p. 275)

middle ear The chamber between the eardrum and cochlea containing three tiny bones (hammer, anvil, and stirrup) that concentrate the vibrations of the eardrum on the cochlea's oval window. (p. 119)

Minnesota Multiphasic Personality Inventory (MMPI) The most widely researched and clinically used of all personality tests. Originally developed to identify the traits of emotionally troubled people (still considered its most appropriate use), this test (recently updated to become the MMPI-2) is now also used for other screening purposes. (p. 359)

mirror-image perceptions Distinct but similar views of one another often held by parties in conflict; each views itself as moral and peace-loving, the other as evil and aggressive. (p. 501)

mnemonics [nih-MON-iks] Memory aids, especially those techniques that use vivid imagery and organizational devices. (p. 213)

mode The most frequently occurring score in a distribution. (p. 511)

modeling The process by which a behavior is observed and imitated. (p. 199)

monocular cues Distance cues, such as aerial and linear perspective and overlap, available to either eye alone. (p. 128)

mood disorders Psychological disorders characterized by emotional extremes. (p. 391)

mood-congruent memory The tendency to recall experiences that are consistent with one's current good or bad mood. (p. 223)

motivation A need or desire that energizes and directs behavior toward a goal. (p. 269)

motor cortex An area at the rear of the frontal lobes that controls voluntary movements. (p. 45)

motor neurons The neurons that carry outgoing information from the central nervous system to the muscles and glands. (p. 28)

MRI (magnetic resonance imaging) A technique that uses magnetic fields and radio waves to produce computer-generated images that distinguish among different types of soft tissue; allows us to see structures within the brain. (p. 39)

multiple personality disorder A rare dissociative disorder in which a person exhibits two or more distinct and alternating personalities. (Note: Multiple personality disorder is unrelated to schizophrenia.) (p. 389)

myelin [MY-uh-lin] **sheath** A layer of fatty cells segmentally encasing the fibers of many neurons; makes possible vastly greater transmission speed of neural impulses. (p. 29)

narcolepsy A sleep disorder characterized by uncontrollable sleep attacks in which the sufferer lapses directly into REM sleep, often at inopportune times. (p. 155)

naturalistic observation Observing and recording behavior in naturally occurring situations without trying to manipulate and control the situation. (p. 10)

nature-nurture issue The longstanding controversy over the relative contributions of genes and experience to the development of psychological traits and behaviors. (p. 2)

near-death experience An altered state of consciousness reported after a close brush with death (such as through cardiac arrest); often similar to drug-induced hallucinations. (p. 171)

negative reinforcement Strengthening behavior by *removing* negative stimuli, such as a shock. (p. 190)

nervous system The body's speedy electrochemical communication system, consisting of all the nerve cells of the peripheral and central nervous systems. (p. 27)

neuron A nerve cell; the basic building block of the nervous system. (p. 27)

neurotransmitters Chemical messengers that traverse the synaptic gaps between neurons. When released by the sending neuron, neurotransmitters travel across the synapse and bind to receptor sites on the receiving neuron, thereby influencing whether it will generate a neural impulse. (p. 30)

night terrors A sleep disorder characterized by high arousal and an appearance of being terrified; unlike nightmares, night terrors occur during Stage 4 sleep, within 2 or 3 hours of falling asleep, and are seldom remembered. (p. 155)

normal curve (or **normal distribution**) The symmetrical bell-shaped curve that describes the distribution of many physical and psychological attributes. Most scores fall near the average, and fewer and fewer scores lie near the extremes. (pp. 255, 512)

normative social influence Influence resulting from a person's desire to gain approval or avoid disapproval. (p. 451)

norms Understood rules for accepted and expected behavior. Norms prescribe ''proper'' behavior. (p. 451)

obesity A surplus of body fat that causes one to be 20 percent or more overweight. (p. 276)

object permanence The awareness that things continue to exist even when not perceived. (p. 66)

observational learning Learning by observing and imitating the behavior of others. (p. 199)

obsessive-compulsive disorder An anxiety disorder characterized by unwanted repetitive thoughts (obsessions) and/or actions (compulsions). (p. 385)

occipital [ahk-SIP-uh-tuhl] **lobes** The portion of the cerebral cortex lying at the back of the head; includes the visual areas, each of which receives visual information from the opposite visual field. (p. 44)

Oedipus [ED-uh-puss] **complex** According to Freud, a boy's sexual desires toward his mother and feelings of jealousy and hatred for his father. (p. 348)

one-word stage The stage in speech development from about age 1 to 2 years during which a child speaks mostly in single words. (p. 243)

operant behavior Behavior that operates on the environment, producing consequences. (p. 188)

operant conditioning A type of learning in which behavior is strengthened if followed by reinforcement, or diminished if followed by punishment. (p. 188)

opiates Opium and its derivatives, such as morphine and heroin; they depress neural activity, temporarily lessening pain and anxiety. (p. 169)

opponent-process theory The theory that opposing retinal processes (red-green, yellow-blue, white-black) enable color vision. For example, some cells are stimulated by green and inhibited by red; others are stimulated by red and inhibited by green. (p. 117)

optic nerve The nerve that carries neural impulses from the eye to the brain. (p. 112)

oral stage The first of Freud's psychosexual stages, from birth to about 18 months, during which sensual pleasure centers on the mouth via sucking, biting, and chewing. (p. 348)

overconfidence The tendency to be more confident than correct—to overestimate the accuracy of one's beliefs and judgments. (p. 239)

overlap A monocular cue for perceiving distance; nearby objects partially block our view of more distant objects. (p. 129)

ovum The female reproductive cell, or egg. (p. 60)

panic attack A minutes-long episode of intense dread in which a person experiences terror and accompanying chest pain, choking, or other frightening sensations. (p. 385)

parallel processing Information processing in which several aspects of a problem are processed simultaneously. The brain's natural mode of information processing for many functions, including vision; contrasts with the step-by-step (serial) processing of most computers and of conscious problem solving. (p. 115)

parapsychology The study of paranormal phenomena including ESP and psychokinesis. (p. 140)

parasympathetic nervous system The division of the autonomic nervous system that calms the body, conserving its energy. (p. 34)

parietal [puh-RYE-uh-tuhl] **lobes** The portion of the cerebral cortex lying at the top of the head and toward the rear; includes the sensory cortex. (p. 44)

partial reinforcement Reinforcing a response only part of the time; results in slower acquisition of response but much greater resistance to extinction than does continuous reinforcement. (Also called *intermittent reinforcement*.) (p. 192)

passionate love An aroused state of intense positive absorption in another, usually present at the beginning of a love relationship. (p. 469)

percentile rank The percentage of the sources in a distribution that a given score exceeds. (p. 509)

perception The process of organizing and interpreting sensory information, enabling us to recognize meaningful objects and events. (p. 105)

perceptual adaptation In vision, the ability to adjust to an artificially displaced or even inverted visual field. (p. 136)

perceptual constancy Perceiving objects as unchanging (having consistent brightness, color, shape, and size) even as illumination and retinal images change. (p. 131)

perceptual set A mental predisposition, based on our experiences, assumptions, and expectations, to perceive one thing and not another. (p. 137)

peripheral nervous system (PNS) The neurons that connect the central nervous system to the rest of the body. It consists of the sensory neurons, which carry messages to the central nervous system from the body's sense receptors, and the motor neurons, which carry messages from the central nervous system to the muscles and glands. (p. 33)

person-centered therapy A humanistic therapy, developed by Carl Rogers, in which the therapist uses techniques such as active listening within a genuine, accepting, empathic environment to facilitate clients' growth. (p. 416)

personal control Our sense of being in control of our environment rather than feeling helpless. (p. 369)

personal space The buffer zone we like to maintain around our bodies. (p. 477)

personality An individual's characteristic pattern of thinking, feeling, and acting. (p. 345)

personality disorders Psychological disorders characterized by inflexible and enduring behavior patterns that impair social functioning. (p. 404)

personality inventory A questionnaire (often with true-false or agree-disagree items) on which people respond to items designed to gauge a wide range of feelings and behaviors; used to assess selected personality traits. (p. 359)

PET (positron emission tomograph) scan A visual display of brain activity that detects where a radioactive form of glucose goes while the brain performs a given task. (p. 39)

phallic stage The third of Freud's psychosexual stages, from about ages 3 to 6, during which the pleasure zone is the genitals and sexual feelings arise toward the parent of the other sex. (p. 348)

phobic disorder An anxiety disorder marked by a persistent, irrational fear of a specific object or situation. (p. 385)

physical dependence A developed, physiological need for a drug that results in unpleasant withdrawal symptoms when use of the drug is discontinued. (p. 167)

pitch A tone's highness or lowness; depends on frequency. (p. 119)

pituitary gland The endocrine system's most influential gland. Under the influence of the hypothalamus, the pituitary regulates growth and controls other endocrine glands. (p. 43)

placebo [pluh-SEE-bo] An inert substance that may be administered instead of a presumed active agent, such as a drug; may trigger the effects believed to characterize the active agent. (p. 16)

plasticity The brain's capacity for modification, as evident in brain reorganization following damage (especially in children) and in experiments on the effects of experience on brain development. (p. 49)

pleasure principle The id's demand for immediate gratification. (p. 347)

polygraph A machine, commonly used in attempts to detect lies, that measures several of the physiological responses accompanying emotion (such as perspiration, heart rate, and breathing changes). (p. 304)

population All the cases or members in a group from which samples may be drawn for study. (pp. 9, 516)

positive reinforcement Strengthening behavior by *presenting* positive stimuli, such as food. (p. 190)

posthypnotic amnesia Supposed inability to recall what one experienced during hypnosis, induced by the hypnotist's suggestion. (p. 160)

posthypnotic suggestion A suggestion, made during a hypnosis session, to be carried out after the subject is no longer hypnotized; used by some clinicians to help control undesired symptoms and behaviors. (p. 163)

preconscious Information that is not conscious, but is retrievable into conscious awareness. (p. 346)

prejudice An unjustifiable (and usually negative) attitude toward a group and its members. Prejudice generally involves stereotyped beliefs, negative feelings, and a predisposition to discriminatory action. (p. 496)

preoperational stage In Piaget's theory, the stage (from about 2 to 6 or 7 years of age) during which a child learns to use language but does not yet comprehend the mental operations of concrete logic. (p. 68)

primary reinforcer An innately reinforcing stimulus, such as food, that satisfies a biological need. (p. 191)

primary sex characteristics The body structures (ovaries and testes) that make sexual reproduction possible. (p. 78)

priming The activation of particular associations in memory. (p. 221)

proactive interference The disruptive effect of prior learning on the recall of new information. *Pro*active means forward-acting. (p. 226)

projection In psychoanalytic theory, the defense mechanism by which people disguise their own threatening impulses by attributing them to others. (p. 350)

projective tests Personality tests, such as the Rorschach and TAT, for which subjects interpret ambiguous stimuli designed to trigger projection of one's inner dynamics. (p. 351)

prosocial behavior Positive, constructive, helpful behavior; the opposite of antisocial behavior. (p. 200)

prototype The best example of a category; matching new items to the prototype provides a quick and easy method for including items in a category (as when comparing feathered creatures to a prototypical bird, such as a robin). (p. 234)

proximity A perceptual tendency to group together visual and auditory events that are near each other. (p. 127)

psychiatry A branch of medicine dealing with psychological disorders; practiced by physicians and sometimes involving medical (for example, drug) treatments as well as psychological therapy. (p. 5)

psychoactive drug A chemical substance that alters mood and perceptions. (p. 166)

psychoanalysis Sigmund Freud's therapeutic technique, in which the patient's free associations, resistances, dreams, and transferences—and the therapist's interpretations of them—release previously repressed feelings, allowing the patient to gain self-insight. (pp. 346, 414)

psychoanalytic perspective Emphasizes unconscious drives and conflicts, many of which may stem from childhood experiences. (p. 2)

psychological dependence A developed, psychological need for a drug, such as to relieve negative emotions. (p. 167)

psychological disorder   A condition in which behavior is judged atypical, disturbing, maladaptive, and unjustifiable. (p. 380)

psychology   The science of behavior and mental processes. (p. 2)

psychopharmacology   The study of the effects of drugs on mind and behavior. (p. 434)

psychophysiological illness   Literally, "mind-body" illness; any physical illness not caused by a known physical disorder. For example, stress can produce hypertension, ulcers, and headaches. Note: This is distinct from *hypochondriasis*—misinterpreting normal physical sensations as symptoms of a disease. (p. 331)

psychosexual stages   The childhood stages of development (oral, anal, phallic, latency, genital) during which, according to Freud, the id's pleasure-seeking energies focus on distinct erogenous zones. (p. 348)

psychosurgery   Surgery that removes or destroys brain tissue in an effort to change behavior. (p. 437)

psychotherapy   An emotionally charged, confiding interaction between a trained therapist and someone who suffers a psychological difficulty. (p. 414)

psychotic disorders   Psychological disorder in which a person loses contact with reality, experiencing irrational ideas and distorted perceptions. (p. 399)

puberty   The early adolescent period of rapid growth and sexual maturation. (p. 78)

punishment   Any event that *decreases* the behavior that it follows. (p. 193)

pupil   The adjustable opening in the center of the eye through which light enters. (p. 111)

random assignment   Assigning subjects to experimental and control conditions by chance, thus minimizing preexisting differences between those assigned to the different groups. (p. 14)

random sample   A sample that fairly represents a population because each member has an equal chance of inclusion. (p. 9)

range   The difference between the highest and lowest scores in a distribution. (p. 511)

rational-emotive therapy   A confrontational cognitive therapy, developed by Albert Ellis, that vigorously challenges people's illogical, self-defeating attitudes and assumptions. (p. 424)

rationalization   In psychoanalytic theory, a defense mechanism that offers self-justifying explanations in place of the real, more threatening, unconscious reasons for one's actions. (p. 350)

reaction formation   In psychoanalytic theory, a defense mechanism by which the ego unconsciously switches unacceptable impulses into their opposites. Thus, people may express feelings that are the opposite of their anxiety-arousing unconscious feelings. (p. 349)

reality principle   The ego's tendency to satisfy the id's desires in ways that will realistically bring pleasure rather than pain. (p. 347)

recall   A measure of memory in which the person must retrieve information learned earlier, as on a fill-in-the-blank test. (p. 221)

reciprocal determinism   The interacting influences between personality and environmental factors. (p. 368)

recognition   A measure of memory in which the person need only identify items previously learned, as on a multiple-choice test. (p. 221)

reflex   A simple, automatic, inborn response to a sensory stimulus, such as the knee-jerk response. (p. 28)

refractory period   A resting period after orgasm during which a man cannot achieve another orgasm. (p. 284)

regression   In psychoanalytic theory, an individual's retreat, when faced with anxiety, to a more infantile psychosexual stage where some psychic energy remains fixated. (p. 349)

regression toward the mean   The tendency for extreme or unusual scores to fall back (regress) toward the average. (p. 515)

rehearsal   The conscious repetition of information, either to maintain it in consciousness or to encode it for storage. (p. 207)

reinforcer   In operant conditioning, any event that *increases* the behavior it follows. (p. 190)

relative brightness   A monocular cue for perceiving distance; dimmer objects seem more distant. (p. 130)

relative deprivation   The perception that one is worse off relative to those with whom one compares oneself. (p. 316)

relative height   A monocular cue for perceiving distance; we perceive higher objects as farther away. (p. 130)

relative size   A monocular cue for perceiving distance; when we assume two objects are the same size, the one that produces the smaller image appears more distant. (p. 129)

relearning   A memory measure that assesses the amount of time saved when relearning previously learned information. (p. 221)

reliability   The extent to which a test yields consistent results, as assessed by the consistency of scores on two halves of the test, on alternate forms of the test, or on retesting. (p. 255)

REM rebound   The tendency for REM sleep to increase following REM sleep deprivation (created by repeated awakenings during REM sleep). (p. 158)

REM sleep   Rapid eye movement sleep, a recurring sleep stage during which vivid dreams commonly occur. Also known as *paradoxical sleep*, because the muscles are relaxed (except for minor twitches) but other body systems are active. (p. 152)

replication   Repeating the essence of a research study, usually with different subjects in different situations, to see whether the basic finding applies to other subjects and circumstances. (p. 7)

representativeness heuristic   A rule of thumb for judging the likelihood of things in terms of how well they seem to represent, or match, particular prototypes; may lead one to ignore other relevant information. (p. 237)

repression   In psychoanalytic theory, the basic defense mechanism that blocks from consciousness painful memories and anxiety-arousing thoughts. (pp. 227, 349)

resistance   In psychoanalysis, the blocking from consciousness of anxiety-laden material. (p. 415)

respondent behavior   Behavior that occurs as an automatic response to some stimulus; behavior learned through classical conditioning. (p. 188)

reticular formation A nerve network (also called the *reticular activating system*) in the brainstem that plays an important role in controlling arousal and attention. (p. 37)

retina The light-sensitive inner surface of the eye, containing the receptor rods and cones plus layers of neurons that begin the processing of visual information. (p. 111)

retinal disparity A binocular cue for perceiving depth; the greater the disparity (difference) between the two images the retina receives of an object, the closer the object is to us. (p. 128)

retrieval The process of getting information out of memory storage. (p. 207)

retroactive interference The disruptive effect of new learning on the recall of old information. *Retro*active means backward-acting. (p. 226)

rods Retinal receptors that detect black, white, and gray; necessary for peripheral and twilight vision, when cones don't respond. (p. 112)

role A set of expectations about a social position, defining how those in the position ought to behave. (p. 447)

rooting reflex A baby's tendency, when touched on the cheek, to open the mouth and search for the nipple. (p. 62)

Rorschach inkblot test The most widely used projective test, designed by Hermann Rorschach; seeks to identify people's projected feelings by analyzing their interpretation of a set of 10 inkblots. (p. 352)

savant syndrome A condition in which a person otherwise limited in mental ability has an amazing specified skill, such as in computation or drawing. (p. 258)

scapegoat theory The theory that prejudice provides an outlet for anger by providing someone to blame. (p. 498)

scatterplot A graphed cluster of dots, each of which represents the values of two variables (such as a student's high school and college GPAs). The slope of the points suggests the degree and direction of the relationship between the two variables. (Also called a *scattergram* or *scatter diagram*.) (p. 513)

schema A concept or framework that organizes and interprets information. (p. 65)

schizophrenia A group of severe psychotic disorders characterized by disorganized and deluded thinking, disturbed perceptions, and inappropriate emotions and actions. (p. 399)

secondary reinforcer A conditioned reinforcer, such as money, that gains its reinforcing power by association with a primary reinforcer. (p. 191)

secondary sex characteristics Nonreproductive sexual characteristics such as female breasts and hips, male voice quality, and body hair. (p. 78)

selective attention The focusing of conscious awareness on a particular stimulus. (p. 149)

self-actualization According to Maslow, the ultimate psychological need that arises after basic physical and psychological needs are met and self-esteem is achieved; the motivation to fulfill one's potential. (p. 362)

self-concept All our thoughts and feelings about ourselves in response to the question, "Who am I?" (p. 363)

self-disclosure Revealing intimate aspects of oneself to others. (p. 470)

self-esteem One's feelings of high or low self-worth. (p. 364)

self-serving bias A readiness to perceive oneself favorably. (p. 365)

sensation The process by which our sense receptors and nervous system receive and represent stimulus energies from our environment. (p. 105)

sensorimotor stage In Piaget's theory, the stage (from birth to about 2 years of age) during which infants know the world mostly in terms of their sensory impressions and motor activities. (p. 66)

sensory adaptation Diminished sensitivity that is a consequence of constant stimulation. (p. 108)

sensory cortex The area at the front of the parietal lobes that registers and processes body sensations. (p. 46)

sensory interaction The principle that one sense may influence another, as when the smell of food influences its taste. (p. 121)

sensory memory The immediate, initial recording of sensory information in the memory system. (p. 208)

sensory neurons Neurons that carry incoming information from the sense receptors to the central nervous system. (p. 28)

serial position effect Our tendency to recall best the last and first items in a list. (p. 211)

set point The point at which an individual's "weight thermostat" is set. When the body falls below this weight, an increase in hunger and a lowered metabolic rate act to restore the lost weight. (p. 275)

sexual dysfunction A problem that consistently impairs sexual arousal or functioning. (p. 286)

sexual orientation An enduring sexual attraction toward members of either one's own sex (homosexual orientation) or the other sex (heterosexual orientation). (p. 287)

sexual response cycle The four stages of sexual responding described by Masters and Johnson—excitement, plateau, orgasm, and resolution. (p. 283)

shaping An operant conditioning procedure in which reinforcers guide behavior toward closer and closer approximations of a desired goal. (p. 189)

similarity A perceptual tendency to group together similar elements. (p. 127)

Skinner box A chamber containing a bar or key that an animal can manipulate to obtain a food or water reinforcer, and devices to record the animal's rate of bar pressing or key pecking. Used in operant conditioning research. (p. 189)

sleep apnea A sleep disorder characterized by temporary cessations of breathing during sleep and consequent momentary reawakenings. (p. 155)

social clock The culturally preferred timing of social events such as marriage, parenthood, and retirement. (p. 91)

social facilitation Improved performance of tasks in the presence of others; occurs with simple or well-learned tasks but not with tasks that are difficult or not yet mastered. (p. 454)

social leadership Group-oriented leadership that builds teamwork, mediates conflict, and offers support. (p. 295)

social loafing The tendency for people in a group to exert less effort when pooling their efforts toward attaining a common goal than when individually accountable. (p. 454)

social psychology The scientific study of how we think about, influence, and relate to one another. (p. 443)

social traps Situations in which the conflicting parties, by each rationally pursuing their self-interest, become caught in mutually destructive behavior. (p. 500)

social-cognitive perspective Applies interactive principles of social learning and cognition to study how the environment shapes people's behavior and beliefs, and how these in turn influence people's situations. (p. 368)

social-cultural perspective Emphasizes the differences and similarities of thinking and behavior in diverse social situations and cultures. (p. 4)

somatic [so-MAT-ik] **nervous system** The division of the peripheral nervous system that receives information from various sense receptors and controls the skeletal muscles of the body. (p. 33)

somatoform disorders Psychological disorders in which the symptoms take a somatic (bodily) form without apparent physical cause. (p. 388)

spacing effect The tendency for distributed study or practice to yield better long-term retention than massed study or practice. (p. 211)

split-brain A condition in which the two hemispheres of the brain are isolated by cutting the connecting fibers between them (mainly those of the corpus callosum). (p. 50)

spontaneous recovery The reappearance, after a rest period, of an extinguished conditioned response. (p. 182)

SQ3R An acronym for *Survey, Question, Read, Rehearse, Review*—a method of study. (p. 22)

standard deviation A measure of score variability; computed by (1) calculating the deviation of each score from the mean, (2) squaring those deviations, (3) finding their average, and (4) finding the square root of this average. (p. 511)

standardization Defining meaningful scores by comparison with the performance of a pretested "standardization group." (p. 255)

Stanford-Binet The widely used American revision (by Terman at Stanford University) of Binet's original intelligence test. (p. 253)

statistical significance A statistical statement of how likely it is that an obtained result occurred by chance. (p. 520)

stereotype A generalized (often overgeneralized) belief about a group of people. (p. 480)

stimulants Drugs (such as caffeine, nicotine, and the more powerful amphetamines and cocaine) that excite neural activity and speed up body functions. (p. 167)

storage The maintenance of encoded information over time. (p. 207)

stranger anxiety The fear of strangers that infants commonly display beginning by about 8 months of age. (p. 67)

stress The whole process by which we perceive and respond to certain events, called *stressors*, that we appraise as threatening or challenging. (p. 323)

sublimation In psychoanalytic theory, the defense mechanism by which people rechannel their unacceptable impulses into socially approved activities. (p. 350)

subliminal Below one's absolute threshold for conscious awareness. (p. 107)

superego The part of personality that, according to Freud, represents internalized ideals and provides standards for judgment (the conscience) and for future aspirations. (p. 347)

superordinate goals Shared goals that override differences among people and require their cooperation. (p. 502)

survey A technique for ascertaining the self-reported attitudes or behaviors of people by questioning a representative, random sample of them. (p. 8)

sympathetic nervous system The division of the autonomic nervous system that arouses the body, mobilizing its energy in stressful situations. (p. 34)

synapse [SIN-aps] The junction between the axon tip of the sending neuron and the dendrite or cell body of the receiving neuron. The tiny gap at this junction is called the *synaptic gap* or *synaptic cleft*. (p. 30)

systematic desensitization A type of counterconditioning that associates a pleasant, relaxed state with gradually increasing anxiety-triggering stimuli. Commonly used to treat phobias. (p. 420)

task leadership Goal-oriented leadership that sets standards, organizes work, and focuses attention on goals. (p. 295)

telegraphic speech Early speech stage in which the child speaks like a telegram—using mostly nouns and verbs and omitting "auxiliary" words. (p. 244)

temperament A person's characteristic emotional reactivity and intensity. (p. 72)

temporal lobes The portion of the cerebral cortex lying roughly above the ears; includes the auditory areas, each of which receives auditory information primarily from the opposite ear. (p. 44)

teratogens Agents, such as chemicals and viruses, that can reach the embryo or fetus during prenatal development and cause harm. (p. 61)

testosterone The most important of the male sex hormones. Both males and females have it, but the additional testosterone in males stimulates the growth of the male sex organs in the fetus and the development of the male sex characteristics during puberty. (p. 60)

thalamus [THAL-uh-muss] The brain's sensory switchboard, located on top of the brainstem; directs messages to the sensory receiving areas in the cortex and transmits replies to the cerebellum and medulla. (p. 37)

THC The major active ingredient in marijuana; triggers a variety of effects, including mild hallucinations. (p. 172)

Thematic Apperception Test (TAT) A projective test in which people express their inner hopes, fears, and interests through the stories they make up about ambiguous scenes. (p. 352)

theory   An explanation that, through an integrated set of principles, organizes and predicts observations. (p. 7)

thinking (or **cognition**)   Mental activity associated with understanding, processing, and communicating knowledge. (p. 234)

threshold   The level of stimulation required to trigger a neural impulse. (p. 29)

token economy   An operant conditioning procedure that rewards desired behavior. A patient exchanges a token of some sort, earned for exhibiting the desired behavior, for various privileges or treats. (p. 423)

tolerance   The diminishing of a drug's effect with regular use of the same dose, requiring the user to take larger and larger doses to experience the drug's effect. (p. 167)

trait   A characteristic pattern of behavior or conscious motive; assessed by self-report inventories and peer reports. (p. 356)

transference   In psychoanalysis, the patient's transfer to the analyst of emotions linked with other relationships (such as love or hatred for a parent). (p. 415)

two-factor theory   Schachter's theory that to experience emotion one must (1) be physically aroused and (2) cognitively label the arousal. (p. 320)

two-word stage   Beginning about age 2, the stage in speech development during which a child speaks mostly two-word statements. (p. 244)

Type A   Friedman and Rosenman's term for competitive, hard-driving, impatient, verbally aggressive, and anger-prone people. (p. 330)

Type B   Friedman and Rosenman's term for easygoing, relaxed people. (p. 330)

unconditional positive regard   According to Rogers, an attitude of total acceptance toward another person. (p. 363)

unconditioned response (UCR)   In classical conditioning, the unlearned, naturally occurring response to the unconditioned stimulus, such as salivation when food is in the mouth. (p. 181)

unconditioned stimulus (UCS)   In classical conditioning, a stimulus that unconditionally—naturally and automatically—triggers a response. (p. 181)

unconscious   According to Freud, a reservoir of mostly unacceptable thoughts, wishes, feelings, and memories. According to contemporary research psychologists, a level of information processing of which we are unaware. (p. 346)

validity   The extent to which a test measures or predicts what it is supposed to. (p. 256)

variable-interval schedule   In operant conditioning, a reinforcement schedule that reinforces a response at unpredictable time intervals. (p. 192)

variable-ratio schedule   In operant conditioning, a reinforcement schedule that reinforces behavior after an unpredictable number of responses. (p. 192)

visual capture   The tendency for vision to dominate the other senses; we perceive filmed voices as coming from the screen we see rather than from the projector behind us. (p. 118)

visual cliff   A laboratory device for testing depth perception in infants and young animals. (p. 128)

wavelength   The distance from the peak of one light or sound wave to the peak of the next. Electromagnetic wavelengths vary from the long pulses of radio transmission to the short blips of cosmic rays. (p. 110)

Weber's law   The principle that, to perceive their difference, two stimuli must differ by a constant minimum percentage (rather than a constant amount). (p. 108)

Wechsler Adult Intelligence Scale—Revised (WAIS-R) This revision of the WAIS is the most widely used intelligence test; contains verbal and performance (nonverbal) subtests. (p. 254)

Wernicke's area   An area of the left temporal lobe involved in language comprehension. (p. 48)

withdrawal   The discomfort and distress that follow discontinued use of addictive drugs. (p. 167)

working memory   "Short-term" memory that holds a few items briefly, such as the seven digits of a phone number while dialing, before the information is stored long-term or forgotten. (p. 207)

X chromosome   The sex chromosome found in both men and women. Females have two X chromosomes; males have one. An X chromosome from each parent produces a female. (p. 60)

Y chromosome   The sex chromosome found only in males. When paired with an X chromosome from the mother, the result is a male child. (p. 60)

Young-Helmholtz trichromatic (three-color) theory   The theory that the retina contains three different color receptors—one most sensitive to red, one to green, one to blue—which when combined can produce the perception of any color. (p. 116)

zygote   The fertilized egg; it enters a 2-week period of rapid cell division and develops into an embryo. (p. 60)

References

Abbey, A. (1987). Misperceptions of friendly behavior as sexual interest: A survey of naturally occurring incidents. *Psychology of Women Quarterly, 11*, 173–194. (p. 488)

Abrams, D. B., & Wilson, G. T. (1983). Alcohol, sexual arousal, and self-control. *Journal of Personality and Social Psychology, 45*, 188–198. (p. 168)

Abramson, L. Y., Metalsky, G. I., & Alloy, L. B. (1989). Hopelessness depression: A theory-based subtype. *Psychological Review, 96, 358–372.* (p. 207)

Adams, P. R., & Adams, G. R. (1984). Mount Saint Helens's ashfall: Evidence for a disaster stress reaction. *American Psychologist, 39*, 252–260. (p. 326)

Adelmann, P. K. (1988). Work and psychological well-being: A meta-analysis. Unpublished manuscript, University of Michigan. (p. 93)

Adelmann, P. K., Antonucci, T. C., Crohan, S. F., & Coleman, L. M. (1989). Empty nest, cohort, and employment in the well-being of midlife women. *Sex Roles, 20*, 173–189. (p. 92)

Ader, R., & Cohen, N. (1985). CNS-immune system interactions: Conditioning phenomena. *Behavioral and Brain Sciences, 8*, 379–394. (p. 333)

Adler, N. E., David, H. P., Major, B. N., Roth, S. H., Russo, N. F., & Wyatt, G. E. (1990). Psychological responses after abortion. *Science, 248*, 41–44. (p. 326)

Advertising Age (1958, February 10). "Phone now," said CBC subliminally—but nobody did. p. 8. (p. 107)

Aiello, J. R., Thompson, D. D., & Brodzinsky, D. M. (1983). How funny is crowding anyway? Effects of room size, group size, and the introduction of humor. *Basic and Applied Social Psychology, 4*, 193–207. (p. 454)

Ainsworth, M. D. S. (1973). The development of infant-mother attachment. In B. Caldwell & H. Ricciuti (Eds.), *Review of child development research* (Vol. 3). Chicago: University of Chicago Press. (p. 72)

Ainsworth, M. D. S. (1979). Infant-mother attachment. *American Psychologist, 34*, 932–937. (p. 72)

Ainsworth, M. D. S. (1989). Attachments beyond infancy. *American Psychologist, 44*, 709–716. (p. 72)

Albee, G. W. (1986). Toward a just society: Lessons from observations on the primary prevention of psychopathology. *American Psychologist, 41*, 891–898. (p. 438)

Alcock, J. E. (1981). *Parapsychology: Science or magic?* Oxford: Pergamon. (p. 222)

Alcock, J. E. (1985, Spring). Parapsychology: The "spiritual" science. *Free Inquiry*, pp. 25–35. (p. 143)

Alcohol, Drug Abuse, and Mental Health Administration. (1990). *Economic costs of alcohol and drug abuse and mental illness: 1985.* Rockville, MD: National Clearinghouse for Alcohol and Drug Information. (p. 431)

Aldrich, M. S. (1989). Automobile accidents in patients with sleep disorders. *Sleep, 12*, 487–494. (p. 155)

Aldridge-Morris, R. (1989). *Multiple personality: An exercise in deception.* Hillsdale, NJ: Erlbaum. (p. 390)

Alexander, C. N., Cranson, R. W., Boyer, R. W., & Orme-Johnson, D. W. (1987). Transcendental consciousness: A fourth state of consciousness beyond sleep, dreaming and waking. In J. Gackenbach (Ed.), *Sleep and dreams: A source-book.* New York: Garland Press. (p. 159)

Alexander, C. N., Langer, E. J., Newman, R. I., Chandler, H. M., & Davies, J. L. (1989). Transcendental meditation, mindfulness, and longevity: An experimental study with the elderly. *Journal of Personality and Social Psychology, 57*, 950–964. (p. 159)

Alkon, D. L. (1989, July). Memory storage and neural systems. *Scientific American*, pp. 42–50. (p. 218)

Allard, F., & Burnett, N. (1985). Skill in sport. *Canadian Journal of Psychology, 39*, 294–312. (p. 214)

Allman, A. L. (1989). *Subjective well-being of students with and without disabilities.* Paper presented at the Midwestern Psychological Association convention. (p. 314)

Allport, G. W., & Odbert, H. S. (1936). Trait-names: A psycho-lexical study. *Psychological Monographs, 47*(1). (p. 357)

Altman, L. K. (1990, May 29). The evidence mounts on passive smoking. *New York Times*, pp. C1, C8. (p. 169)

Altus, W. D. (1966). Birth order and its sequelae. *Science, 151*, 44–49. (p. 293)

Alwin, D. F. (1990). Historical changes in parental orientations to children. In N. Mandell (Ed.), *Sociological studies of child development* (Vol. 3). Greenwich, CT: JAI Press. (p. 481)

Amabile, T. M. (1983). *The social psychology of creativity.* New York: Springer-Verlag. (p. 364)

Amabile, T. M., & Hennessey, B. A. (1988). The motivation for creativity in children. In A. K. Boggiano & T. Pittman (Eds.), *Achievement and motivation: A social-developmental perspective.* New York: Cambridge University Press. (p. 260)

Amato, P. R., & Keith, B. (1991).   Parental divorce and the well-being of children: A meta-analysis. *Psychological Bulletin, 110,* 26–46. (p. 76)

Ambady, N., & Rosenthal, R. (1991).   Half a minute: Predicting teacher effectiveness from nonverbal classroom behavior. Unpublished manuscript, Harvard University. (p. 361)

Ambady, N., & Rosenthal, R. (1992).   Thin slices of expressive behavior as predictors of interpersonal consequences: A meta-analysis. *Psychological Bulletin, 111,* 256–274. (p. 361)

American Enterprise. (1991, November/December).   What women think about the feminist label. p. 92. (p. 8)

American Enterprise. (1992, January/February).   Similarities and differences. p. 104. (a) (p. 8)

American Enterprise. (1992, March/April).   30 years after the Supreme Court's school prayer decision. pp. 102–4. (b) (p. 8)

American Psychiatric Association. (1987).   *Diagnostic and statistical manual of mental disorders (Third Edition—Revised).* Washington, DC: American Psychiatric Association. (p. 257)

American Psychiatric Association. (1990).   *The practice of ECT: Recommendations for treatment, training, and privileging.* Washington, DC: American Psychiatric Press. (p. 436)

American Psychological Association. (1986).   Council of Representatives statement cited by N. Abeles, Proceedings of the American Psychological Association, Incorporated, for the Year 1985: Minutes of the annual meeting of the Council of Representatives August 22 and 25, 1985, Los Angeles, California, and January 31–February 2, 1986, Washington, DC. *American Psychologist, 41,* 633–663. (p. 305)

Andersen, B. L. (1989).   Health psychology's contribution to addressing the cancer problem: Update on accomplishments. *Health Psychology, 8,* 683–703. (p. 332)

Anderson, B. L. (1983).   Primary orgasmic dysfunction: Diagnostic considerations and review of treatment. *Psychological Bulletin, 93,* 105–136. (p. 286)

Anderson, C. A. (1989).   Temperature and aggression: Ubiquitous effects of heat on occurrence of human violence. *Psychological Bulletin, 106,* 74–96. (p. 460)

Anderson, C. A., & Anderson, D. C. (1984).   Ambient temperature and violent crime: Tests of the linear and curvilinear hypotheses. *Journal of Personality and Social Psychology, 46,* 91–97. (p. 460)

Anderson, C. A., Lepper, M. R., & Ross, L. (1980).   Perseverance of social theories: The role of explanation in the persistence of discredited information. *Journal of Personality and Social Psychology, 39,* 1037–1049. (p. 241)

Anderson, D. R., & Jose, W. S., II (1987, December).   Employee lifestyle and the bottom line: Results from the StayWell evaluation. *Fitness in Business,* pp. 86–91. (p. 335)

Anderson, J. R. (1983).   Retrieval of information from long-term memory. *Science, 220,* 25–30. (p. 221)

Andreasen, N. C., Ehrhardt, J. C., Swayze, V. W., Alliger, R. J., Yuh, W. T. C., Cohen, G., & Ziebell, S. (1990a).   Magnetic resonance imaging of the brain in schizophrenia. *Archives of General Psychiatry, 47,* 35–44. (p. 403)

Andreasen, N. C., Swayze, V. W., Flaum, M., Yates, W. R., Arndt, S., & McChesney, C. (1990b).   Ventricular enlargement in schizophrenia evaluated with computed tomographic scanning. *Archives of General Psychiatry, 47,* 1008–1015. (p. 403)

Archer, J. (1991).   The influence of testosterone on human aggression. *British Journal of Psychology, 82,* 1–28. (p. 459)

Aries, E. (1987).   Gender and communication. In P. Shaver & C. Henrick (Eds.), *Review of Personality and Social Psychology, 7,* 177–200. (p. 488)

Asch, S. E. (1955).   Opinions and social pressure. *Scientific American, 193,* 31–35. (p. 450)

Aserinsky, E. (1988, January 17).   Personal communication. (p. 152)

Astin, A. W. & Others (1991).   *The American freshman: National norms for Fall 1990.* Los Angeles: American Council on Education and Higher Education Research Institute, UCLA. (pp. 173, 314)

Astin, A. W., Dey, E. L., Korn, W. S., & Riggs, E. (1991).   *The American freshman: National norms for Fall 1991.* Los Angeles: American Council on Education and Higher Education Research Institute, UCLA. (pp. 486, 488, 493)

Astin, A. W., Green, K. C., & Korn, W. S. (1987).   *The American freshman: Twenty year trends.* Los Angeles: American Council on Education and Higher Education Research Institute, UCLA. (pp. 173, 314)

Astin, A. W., Korn, W. S., & Berz, E. R. (1989).   *The American freshman: National norms for Fall 1989.* Los Angeles: American Council on Education and Higher Education Research Institute, UCLA. (p. 314)

Atwell, R. H. (1986, July 28).   Drugs on campus: A perspective. *Higher Education & National Affairs,* p. 5. (p. 168)

Averill, J. R. (1969).   Autonomic response patterns during sadness and mirth. *Psychophysiology, 5,* 399–414. (p. 303)

Averill, J. R. (1983).   Studies on anger and aggression: Implications for theories of emotion. *American Psychologist, 38,* 1145–1160. (p. 312)

Ax, A. F. (1953).   The physiological differentiation of fear and anger in humans. *Psychosomatic Medicine, 15,* 433–442. (p. 303)

Babad, E., Bernieri, F., & Rosenthal, R. (1991).   Students as judges of teachers' verbal and nonverbal behavior. *American Educational Research Journal, 28,* 211–234. (p. 306)

Backus, J. (1977).   *The acoustical foundations of music* (2nd ed.). New York: Norton. (p. 120)

Baddeley, A. D. (1982).   *Your memory: A user's guide.* New York: Macmillan. (p. 211)

Bahrick, H. P. (1984a).   Memory and people. In J. Harris (Ed.), *Everyday memory, actions, and absentmindedness.* Orlando, FL: Academic Press. (p. 211)

Bahrick, H. P. (1984b).   Semantic memory content in permastore: 50 years of memory for Spanish learned in school. *Journal of Experimental Psychology: General, 111,* 1–29. (pp. 216, 217)

Bahrick, H. P., & Hall, L. K. (1991).   Lifetime maintenance of high school mathematics content. *Journal of Experimental Psychology: General, 120,* 20–33. (p. 211)

Bahrick, H. P., Bahrick, P. O., & Wittlinger, R. P. (1975).   Fifty years of memory for names and faces: A cross-sectional approach. *Journal of Experimental Psychology: General, 104,* 54–75. (p. 221)

Bailey, J. M., & Pillard R. C. (1991a).   A genetic study of male sexual orientation. *Archives of General Psychiatry, 48,* 1089–1096. (p. 289)

Bailey, J. M., & Pillard, R. C. (1991b, December 17). Are some people born gay? *New York Times*, p. A21. (p. 289)

Bailey, R. E., & Bailey, M. B. (1980). A view from outside the Skinner box. *American Psychologist, 35*, 942–946. (p. 195)

Bairagi, R. (1987). Food crises and female children in rural Bangladesh. *Social Science, 72*, 48–51. (p. 497)

Baker, E. L. (1987). The state of the art of clinical hypnosis. *International Journal of Clinical and Experimental Hypnosis, 35*, 203–214. (p. 163)

Balakrishnan, T. R., Rao, K. V., Lapierre-Adamcyk, E., & Krotki, K. J. (1987). A hazard model analysis of the covariates of marriage dissolution in Canada. *Demography, 24*, 395–406. (p. 92)

Ball, W., & Tronick, E. (1971). Infant responses to impending collision: Optical and real. *Science, 171*, 818–820. (p. 128)

Baltes, P. B., & Smith, J. (1990). Toward a psychology of wisdom and its ontogenesis. In R. J. Sternberg (Ed.), *Wisdom: Its nature, origins, and development.* New York: Cambridge University Press. (p. 90)

Bandura, A. (1977). *Social learning theory.* Englewood Cliffs, NJ: Prentice-Hall. (p. 199)

Bandura, A. (1978). The self-system in reciprocal determinism. *American Psychologist, 33*, 344–358. (p. 368)

Bandura, A. (1986). *Social foundations of thought and action: A social-cognitive theory.* Englewood Cliffs, NJ: Prentice-Hall. (p. 368)

Bandura, A., Blanchard, E. B., & Ritter, B. (1969). Relative efficacy of desensitization and modeling approaches for inducing behavioral, affective, and attitudinal changes. *Journal of Personality and Social Psychology, 13*, 173–199. (p. 421)

Bandura, A., Ross, D., & Ross, S. A. (1961). Transmission of aggression through imitation of aggressive models. *Journal of Abnormal and Social Psychology, 63*, 575–582. (p. 199)

Barbaree, H. E., & Marshall, W. L. (1991). The role of male sexual arousal in rape: Six models. Special Section: Theories of sexual aggression. *Journal of Consulting and Clinical Psychology, 59*, 621–630. (p. 462)

Barker, S. L., Funk, S. C., & Houston, B. K. (1988). Psychological treatment versus nonspecific factors: A meta-analysis of conditions that engender comparable expectations for improvement. *Clinical Psychology Review, 8*, 579–594. (p. 432)

Baron, R. A. (1987). Interviewer's mood and reaction to job applicants: The influence of affective states on applied social judgments. *Journal of Applied Social Psychology, 17*, 911–926. (p. 313)

Baron, R. A. (1988). Negative effects of destructive criticism: Impact on conflict, self-efficacy, and task performance. *Journal of Applied Psychology, 73*, 199–207. (p. 198)

Baron, R. S., Cutrona, C. E., Hicklin, D., Russell, D. W., & Lubaroff, D. M. (1990). Social support and immune function among spouses of cancer patients. *Journal of Personality and Social Psychology, 59*, 344–352. (p. 339)

Barton, J., Chassin, L., Presson, C. C., & Sherman, S. J. (1982). Social image factors as motivators of smoking initiation in early and middle adolescence. *Child Development, 53*, 1499–1511. (p. 174)

Baruch, G. K., & Barnett, R. (1986). Role quality, multiple role involvement, and psychological well-being in midlife women. *Journal of Personality and Social Psychology, 51*, 578–585. (p. 93)

Bashore, T. R., Osman, A., & Heffley, E. F. (1989). Mental slowing in elderly persons: A cognitive psychophysiological analysis. *Psychology and Aging, 4*, 235–244. (p. 88)

Bauman, L. J., & Siegel, K. (1987). Misperception among gay men of the risk for AIDS associated with their sexual behavior. *Journal of Applied Social Psychology, 17*, 329–350. (p. 288)

Baumeister, R. F. (1989). The optimal margin of illusion. *Journal of Social and Clinical Psychology, 8*, 176–189. (p. 240)

Baumeister, R. F., & Tice, D. M. (1986). How adolescence became the struggle for self: A historical transformation of psychological development. In J. Suls & A. G. Greenwald (Eds.), *Psychological perspectives on the self* (Vol. 3). Hillsdale, NJ: Erlbaum. (p. 78)

Baumeister, R. F., Stillwell, A., & Wotman, S. R. (1991). Victim and perpetrator accounts of interpersonal conflict: Autobiographical narratives about anger. *Journal of Personality and Social Psychology, 59*, 994–1005. (p. 313)

Baumeister, R. F., Tice, D. M., & Hutton, D. G. (1989). Self-presentational motivations and personality differences in self-esteem. *Journal of Personality, 57*, 547–579. (pp. 365, 366)

Baumgardner, A. H. (1990). To know oneself is to like oneself: Self-certainty and self-affect. *Journal of Personality and Social Psychology, 58*, 1062–1072. (p. 83)

Baumgardner, A. H., Kaufman, C. M., & Levy, P. E. (1989). Regulating affect interpersonally: When low esteem leads to greater enhancement. *Journal of Personality and Social Psychology, 56*, 907–921. (p. 364)

Baumrind, D. (1982). Adolescent sexuality: Comment on Williams' and Silka's comments on Baumrind. *American Psychologist, 37*, 1402–1403. (p. 290)

Baumrind, D. (1983). Rejoinder to Lewis's reinterpretation of parental firm control effects: Are authoritative families really harmonious? *Psychological Bulletin, 94*, 132–142. (pp. 76, 77)

Baumrind, D. (1991). Parenting styles and adolescent development. In J. Brooks-Gunn, R. Lerner, & A. C. Petersen (Eds.), *The encyclopedia of adolescence.* New York: Garland. (p. 76)

Baxter, L. R., Jr., Phelps, M. E., Mazziotta, J. C., Guze, B. H., Schwartz, J. M., & Selin, C. E. (1987). Local cerebral glucose metabolic rates in obsessive-compulsive disorder. *Archives of General Psychiatry, 44*, 211–218. (p. 387)

Beaman, A. L., & Klentz, B. (1983). The supposed physical attractiveness bias against supporters of the women's movement: A meta-analysis. *Personality and Social Psychology Bulletin, 9*, 544–550. (p. 468)

Beck, A. T., & Steer, R. A. (1989). Clinical predictors of eventual suicide: A 5- to 10-year prospective study of suicide attempters. *Journal of Affective Disorders, 17*, 203–209. (p. 393)

Beck, A. T., & Young, J. E. (1978, September). College blues. *Psychology Today*, pp. 80–92. (pp. 391, 398)

Beck, A. T., Rush, A. J., Shaw, B. F., & Emery, G. (1979). *Cognitive therapy of depression.* New York: Guilford Press. (p. 425)

Beitman, B. D., Goldfried, M. R., & Norcross, J. C. (1989). The movement toward integrating the psychotherapies: An overview. *American Journal of Psychiatry, 146*, 138–147. (p. 414)

Bell, A. P. (1982, November/December). Sexual preference: A postscript. (SIECUS Report, 11, No. 2) *Church and Society*, pp. 34–37. (p. 289)

Bell, A. P., Weinberg, M. S., & Hammersmith, S. K. (1981). *Sexual preference: Its development in men and women*. Bloomington: Indiana University Press. (p. 288)

Bellugi, U., Poizner, H., & Klima, E. S. (1989). Language, modality and the brain. *Trends in Neurosciences, 12*, 380–388. (p. 54)

Beloff, J. (1985, Spring). Science, religion and the paranormal. *Free Inquiry*, pp. 36–41 (p. 143)

Belsher, G., & Costello, C. G. (1988). Relapse after recovery from unipolar depression: A critical review. *Psychological Bulletin, 104*, 84–96. (p. 394)

Belsky, J., Lang, M., & Huston, T. L. (1986). Sex typing and division of labor as determinants of marital change across the transition to parenthood. *Journal of Personality and Social Psychology, 50*, 517–522. (p. 92)

Bem, D. J. (1984). Quoted in the *Skeptical Inquirer, 8*, 194. (p. 141)

Bem, S. L. (1985). Androgyny and gender schema theory: A conceptual and empirical integration. *Nebraska Symposium on Motivation, 32*, 179–226. (p. 494)

Bem, S. L. (1987). Masculinity and femininity exist only in the mind of the perceiver. In J. M. Reinisch, L. A. Rosenblum, & S. A. Sanders (Eds.), *Masculinity/femininity: Basic perspectives*. New York: Oxford University Press. (pp. 490, 494)

Ben-Shakhar, G., Bar-Hillel, M., Bilu, Y., Ben-Abba, E., & Flug, A. (1986). Can graphology predict occupational success? Two empirical studies and some methodological ruminations. *Journal of Applied Psychology, 71*, 645–653. (p. 373)

Benassi, V. A., Sweeney, P. D., & Dufour, C. L. (1988). Is there a relation between locus of control orientation and depression? *Journal of Abnormal Psychology, 97*, 357–367. (p. 369)

Benbow, C. P. (1988). Sex differences in mathematical reasoning ability in intellectually talented preadolescents: Their nature, effects, and possible causes. *Behavioral and Brain Sciences, 11*, 169–182. (p. 485)

Benderly, B. L. (1989, November). Don't believe everything you read: A case study of how the politics of sex-difference research turned a small finding into a major media flap. *Psychology Today*, pp. 67–69. (p. 489)

Bennett, N. G., Blanc, A. K., & Bloom, D. E. (1988). Commitment and the modern union: Assessing the link between premarital cohabitation and subsequent marital stability. *American Sociological Review, 53*, 127–138. (p. 92).

Bennis, W. (1984). Transformative power and leadership. In T. J. Sergiovani & J. E. Corbally (Eds.), *Leadership and organizational culture*. Urbana: University of Illinois Press. (p. 296)

Benson, H., & Klipper, M. Z. (1976). *The relaxation response*. New York: Morrow. (p. 337)

Benson, H., & Proctor, W. (1987). *Your maximum mind*. New York: Times Books/Random House. (p. 337)

Bergsholm, P., Larsen, J. L., Rosendahl, K., & Holsten, F. (1989). Electroconvulsive therapy and cerebral computed tomography. *Acta Psychiatrica Scandinavia, 80*, 566–572. (p. 436)

Berkowitz, L. (1983). Aversively stimulated aggression: Some parallels and differences in research with animals and humans. *American Psychologist, 38*, 1135–1144. (p. 459)

Berkowitz, L. (1989). Frustration-aggression hypothesis: Examination and reformulation. *Psychological Bulletin, 106*, 59–73. (p. 459)

Berkowitz, L. (1990). On the formation and regulation of anger and aggression: A cognitive-neoassociationistic analysis. *American Psychologist, 45*, 494–503. (p. 312)

Berman, J. S., & Norton, N. C. (1985). Does professional training make a therapist more effective? *Psychological Bulletin, 98*, 401–407. (p. 433)

Berry, D. S., & McArthur, L. Z. (1986). Perceiving character in faces: The impact of age-related craniofacial changes on social perception. *Psychological Bulletin, 100*, 3–18. (p. 183)

Berscheid, E., Gangestad, S. W., & Kulakowski, D. (1984). Emotion in close relationships: Implications for relationship counseling. In S. D. Brown & R. W. Lent (Eds.), *Handbook of counseling psychology*. New York: Wiley. (p. 470)

Beyer, L. (1990, Fall issue on women). Life behind the veil. *Time*, p. 37. (p. 497)

Binet, A., & Simon, T. (1905; reprinted 1916). New methods for the diagnosis of the intellectual level of subnormals. In A. Binet & T. Simon, *The development of intelligence in children*. Baltimore: Williams & Wilkins. (p. 252)

Binitie, A. (1975). A factor-analytical study of depression across cultures (African and European). *British Journal of Psychiatry, 127*, 559–563. (p. 388)

Bishop, G. D. (1991). Understanding the understanding of illness: Lay disease representations. In J. A. Skelton & R. T. Croyle (Eds.), *Mental representation in health and illness*. New York: Springer-Verlag. (p. 235)

Bjork, R. A. (1978). The updating of human memory. In G. H. Bower (Ed.), *The psychology of learning and motivation* (Vol. 12). New York: Academic Press. (p. 225)

Bjork, R. A. (1988). Retrieval practice and the maintenance of knowledge. In M. M. Bruneberg, P. E. Morris, & R. N. Sykes (Eds.), *Practical aspects of memory: Current research and issues*. New York: Wiley. (p. 229)

Blackmore, S. (1991, Fall). Near-death experiences: In or out of the body? *Skeptical Inquirer*, pp. 34–45. (p. 171)

Blake, J. (1989). Number of siblings and educational attainment. *Science, 245*, 32–36. (p. 293)

Bloom, B. S. (Ed.). (1985). *Developing talent in young people*. New York: Ballantine. (p. 292)

Bolger, N., DeLongis, A., Kessler, R. C., & Schilling, E. A. (1989). Effects of daily stress on negative mood. *Journal of Personality and Social Psychology, 57*, 808–818. (p. 314)

Bonner, E. (1990, May 4). Missing-child study: Relative often to blame. *Chicago Tribune*. (p. 239)

Booth, A., & Edwards, J. N. (1989). Transmission of marital and family quality over the generations: The effect of parental divorce on unhappiness. *Journal of Divorce, 12*, 41–58. (p. 76)

Boring, E. G. (1930). A new ambiguous figure. *American Journal of Psychology, 42*, 444–445. (p. 137)

Bornstein, M. H. (1989). Stability in early mental development: From attention and information processing in infancy to language and cognition in childhood. In M. G. Bornstein & N. A. Krasnegor (Eds.), *Stability and continuity in mental development; Behavioral and biological perspectives.* Hillsdale, NJ: Erlbaum. (p. 72)

Bornstein, R. F. (1989). Exposure and affect: Overview and meta-analysis of research, 1968–1987. *Psychological Bulletin, 106,* 265–289. (p. 467)

Bothwell, R. K., Brigham, J. C., & Malpass, R. S. (1989). Cross-racial identification. *Personality and Social Psychology Bulletin, 15,* 19–25. (p. 498)

Bothwell, R. K., Deffenbacher, K. A., & Brigham, J. C. (1987). Correlation of eyewitness accuracy and confidence: Optimality hypothesis revised. *Journal of Applied Psychology, 72,* 691–695. (p. 224)

Bouchard, C., Tremblay, A., Despres, J-P., Nadeau, A., Lupien, P. J., Theriault, G., Dussault, J., Moorjani, S., Pinault, S., & Fournier, G. (1990). The response to long-term overfeeding in identical twins. *The New England Journal of Medicine, 322,* 1477–1482. (p. 279)

Bouchard, T. (1990). Interview with T. M. Skovholt, Counseling implications of genetic research: A dialogue with Thomas Bouchard. *Journal of Counseling and Development, 68,* 633–636. (p. 98)

Bouchard, T. J., Jr. (1991, December 6). Interview on *Nova: Twins* [program broadcast by the Public Broadcasting Service]. (p. 97)

Bouchard, T. J., Jr. (1982). Twins—Nature's twice told tale. In *1983 Yearbook of science and the future.* Chicago: Encyclopaedia Britannica. (p. 261)

Bouchard, T. J., Jr., & Segal, N. L. (1988). Heredity, environment, and IQ. In *Instructor's Resource Manual* to accompany G. Lindzey, R. Thompson, & B. Spring, *Psychology* (3rd ed.). New York: Worth Publishers. (p. 261)

Bouchard, T. J., Lykken, D. T., McGue, M., Segal, N. L., & Tellegen, A. (1990). Sources of human psychological differences: The Minnesota study of twins reared apart. *Science, 250,* 223–228. (p. 97)

Bower, G. H. (1983). Affect and cognition. *Philosophical Transaction: Royal Society of London, Series B, 302,* 387–402. (p. 222)

Bower, G. H. (1986). Prime time in cognitive psychology. In P. Eelen (Ed.), *Cognitive research and behavior therapy: Beyond the conditioning paradigm.* Amsterdam: North Holland Publishers. (pp. 221, 222)

Bower, G. H., & Morrow, D. G. (1990). Mental models in narrative comprehension. *Science, 247,* 44–48. (p. 212)

Bower, G. H., Clark, M. C., Lesgold, A. M., & Winzenz, D. (1969). Hierarchical retrieval schemes in recall of categorized word lists. *Journal of Verbal Learning and Verbal Behavior, 8,* 323–343. (p. 214)

Bowers, K. S. (1984). Hypnosis. In N. Endler & J. M. Hunt (Eds.), *Personality and behavioral disorders* (2nd ed.). New York: Wiley. (pp. 160, 163)

Bowers, K. S. (1987, July). Personal correspondence. (p. 161)

Bowers, K. S. (1990). Unconscious influences and hypnosis. In J. E. Singer (Ed.), *Repression and dissociation: Implications for personality theory, psychopathology, and health.* Chicago: University of Chicago Press. (p. 165)

Bowers, K. S., & LeBaron, S. (1986). Hypnosis and hypnotizability: Implications for clinical intervention. *Hospital and Community Psychiatry, 37,* 457–467. (p. 165)

Bowers, T. G., & Clum, G. A. (1988). Relative contribution of specific and nonspecific treatment effects: Meta-analysis of placebo-controlled behavior therapy research. *Psychological Bulletin, 103,* 315–323. (p. 431)

Boynton, R. M. (1979). *Human color vision.* New York: Holt, Rinehart & Winston. (p. 116)

Bradbury, T. N., & Fincham, F. D. (1990). Attributions in marriage: Review and critique. *Psychological Bulletin, 107,* 3–33. (p. 444)

Bradley, D. R., Dumais, S. T., & Petry, H. M. (1976). Reply to Cavonius. *Nature, 261,* 78. (p. 126)

Bransford, J. D., & Johnson, M. K. (1972). Contextual prerequisites for understanding: Some investigations of comprehension and recall. *Journal of Verbal Learning and Verbal Behavior, 11,* 717–726. (p. 212)

Bransford, J., Sherwood, R., Vye, N., & Rieser, J. (1986). Teaching thinking and problem solving. *American Psychologist, 41,* 1078–1089. (p. 234)

Braskamp, L. A. (1987). *Spectrum: Utility for educational selection and organizational development.* Paper presented at the American Psychological Association convention. (p. 295)

Bray, D. W. (1982). The assessment center and the study of lives. *American Psychologist, 37,* 180–189. (p. 371)

Bray, G. A. (1969). Effect of caloric restriction on energy expenditure in obese patients. *Lancet, 2,* 397–398. (pp. 278, 279)

Breland, K., & Breland, M. (1961). The misbehavior of organisms. *American Psychologist, 16,* 661–664. (p. 195)

Brewer, W. F. (1977). Memory for the pragmatic implications of sentences. *Memory & Cognition, 5,* 673–678. (p. 212)

Brewin, C. F. (1989). Cognitive change processes in psychotherapy. *Psychological Review, 96,* 379–394. (p. 424)

Brickman, P., Coates, D., & Janoff-Bulman, R. J. (1978). Lottery winners and accident victims: Is happiness relative? *Journal of Personality and Social Psychology, 36,* 917–927. (p. 314)

Brislin, R. W. (1988). Increasing awareness of class, ethnicity, culture, and race by expanding on students' own experiences. In I. S. Cohen (Ed.), *The G. Stanley Hall Lecture Series* (Vol. 8). Washington, DC: American Psychological Association. (p. 476)

British Psychological Society. (1986). Report of the working group on the use of the polygraph in criminal investigation and personnel screening. *Bulletin of the British Psychological Society, 39,* 81–94. (p. 305)

Brockner, J., & Hulton, A. J. B. (1978). How to reverse the vicious cycle of low self-esteem: The importance of attentional focus. *Journal of Experimental Social Psychology, 14,* 564–578. (p. 364)

Bronstein-Burrows, P. (1981). *Introductory psychology: A course in the psychology of both sexes.* Paper presented at the American Psychological Association convention. (p. 468)

Brooks-Gunn, J. (1989). Adolescents as daughters and as mothers: A developmental perspective. In I. Sigel & G. Brody (Eds.), *Family research.* Hillsdale, NJ: Erlbaum. (p. 79)

Brooks-Gunn, J., & Furstenberg, F. F., Jr. (1989). Adolescent sexual behavior. *American Psychologist, 44,* 249–257. (p. 84)

Brothers, J. (1990, February 18). Why wives have affairs. *Parade,* pp. 4–7. (p. 282)

Brown, E. L., & Deffenbacher, K. (1979). *Perception and the senses.* New York: Oxford University Press. (p. 120)

Brown, J. D. (1991). Accuracy and bias in self-knowledge. In C. R. Snyder & D. F. Forsyth (Eds.), *Handbook of social and clinical psychology: The health perspective.* New York: Pergamon Press. (pp. 364, 365, 366)

Brown, J. D. (1991). Staying fit and staying well: Physical fitness as a moderator of life stress. *Journal of Personality and Social Psychology, 60,* 555–561. (p. 335)

Brown, R. (1965). *Social psychology.* New York: Free Press. (p. 310)

Brown, R. (1986). Linguistic relativity. In S. H. Hulse & B. F. Green, Jr. (Eds.), *One hundred years of psychological research in America.* Baltimore: Johns Hopkins University Press. (p. 249)

Brown, R., & Kulik, J. (1982). Flashbulb memories. In U. Neisser (Ed.), *Memory observed.* San Francisco: Freeman. (p. 206)

Browne, A., & Finkelhor, D. (1986). Impact of child sexual abuse: A review of the research. *Psychological Bulletin, 99,* 66–77. (p. 75)

Brownell, K. D. (1989). Weight control and your health. *World Book Encyclopedia,* pp. 369–384. (p. 280)

Brownell, K. D. (1991). Dieting and the search for the perfect body: Where physiology and culture collide. *Behavior Therapy, 22,* 1–12. (p. 280)

Brownell, K. D., Greenwood, M. R. C., Stellar, E., & Shrager, E. E. (1986). The effects of repeated cycles of weight loss and regain in rats. *Physiology and Behavior, 38,* 459–464. (p. 280)

Brownmiller, S. (1975). *Against our will: Men, women, and rape.* New York: Simon and Schuster. (p. 286)

Bruner, J. S., & Potter, M. C. (1964). Interference in visual recognition. *Science, 144,* 424–425. (p. 137)

Buchsbaum, M. S., Wu, J., Haier, R., Hazlett, E., Ball, R., Katz, M., Sokolski, K., Lagunas-Solar, M., & Langer, D. H. (1987). Positron emission tomography assessment of effects of benzodiazepines on regional glucose metabolic rate in patients with anxiety disorder. *Life Sciences, 40,* 2393–2400. (p. 387)

Buck, L., & Axel, R. (1991). A novel multigene family may encode odorant receptors: A molecular basis for odor recognition. *Cell, 65,* 175–187. (p. 122)

Bugelski, B. R., Kidd, E., & Segmen, J. (1968). Image as a mediator in one-trial paired-associate learning. *Journal of Experimental Psychology, 76,* 69–73. (p. 213)

Bugental, D. B. (1986). Unmasking the "polite smile": Situational and personal determinants of managed affect in adult-child interaction. *Personality and Social Psychology Bulletin, 12,* 7–16. (p. 306)

Bullough, V. (1990). The Kinsey scale in historical perspective. In D. P. McWhirter, S. A. Sanders, & J. M. Reinisch (Eds.), *Homosexuality/heterosexuality: Concepts of sexual orientation.* New York: Oxford University Press. (p. 287)

Bumpass, L. L., & Sweet, J. A. (1989). National estimates of cohabitation. *Demography, 26,* 615–625. (p. 92)

Bureau of the Census. (1990). *Statistical abstract of the U.S.* Washington, DC: Superintendent of Documents, U.S. Government Printing Office. (pp. 392, 393)

Burger, J. M. (1987). Increased performance with increased personal control: A self-presentation interpretation. *Journal of Experimental Social Psychology, 23,* 350–360. (p. 295)

Buri, J. R., Louiselle, P. A., Misukanis, T. M., & Mueller, R. A. (1988). Effects of parental authoritarianism and authoritativeness on self-esteem. *Personality and Social Psychology Bulletin, 14,* 271–282. (p. 76)

Burish, T. G., & Carey, M. P. (1986). Conditioned aversive responses in cancer chemotherapy patients: Theoretical and developmental analysis. *Journal of Counseling and Clinical Psychology, 54,* 593–600. (p. 185)

Burke, K. C., Burke, J. D., Regier, D. A., & Rae, D. S. (1990). Age at onset of selected mental disorders in five community populations. *Archives of General Psychiatry, 47,* 511–518. (p. 386)

Burns, D. D. (1980). *Feeling good: The new mood therapy.* New York: Signet. (p. 396)

Bushman, B. J., & Cooper, H. M. (1990). Effects of alcohol on human aggression: An integrative research review. *Psychological Bulletin, 107,* 341–354. (p. 459)

Buss, A. H. (1989). Personality as traits. *American Psychologist, 44,* 1378–1388. (p. 361)

Buss, D. M. (1989). Sex differences in human mate preferences: Evolutionary hypotheses tested in 37 cultures. *Behavioral and Brain Sciences, 12,* 1–49. (pp. 84, 468, 489)

Buss, D. M. (1991). Evolutionary personality psychology. *Annual Review of Psychology, 42,* 459–491. (p. 475)

Butcher, J. N. (1990). *The MMPI-2 in psychological treatment.* New York: Oxford University Press. (p. 359)

Butler, R. A. (1954, February). Curiosity in monkeys. *Scientific American,* pp. 70–75. (p. 270)

Byrne, D. (1971). *The attraction paradigm.* New York: Academic Press. (p. 469)

Byrne, D. (1982). Predicting human sexual behavior. In A. G. Kraut (Ed.), *The G. Stanley Hall Lecture Series* (Vol. 2). Washington, DC: American Psychological Association. (pp. 284, 286)

Cameron, P., & Biber, H. (1973). Sexual thought throughout the life-span. *Gerontologist, 13,* 144–147. (p. 159)

Campbell, A. (1981). *The sense of well-being in America.* New York: McGraw-Hill. (p. 93)

Campbell, D. T. (1975). On the conflicts between biological and social evolution and between psychology and moral tradition. *American Psychologist, 30,* 1103–1126. (p. 316)

Campbell, D. T., & Specht, J. C. (1985). Altruism: Biology, culture, and religion. *Journal of Social and Clinical Psychology, 3*(1), 33–42. (p. 367)

Campbell, S. (1986). *The Loch Ness Monster: The evidence.* Willingborough, Northamptonshire, U.K.: Acquarian Press. (p. 137)

Camper, J. (1990, February 7). Drop pompom squad, U. of I. rape study says. *Chicago Tribune,* p. 1. (p. 167)

Cannon, W. B. (1929). *Bodily changes in pain, hunger, fear, and rage.* New York: Branford. (pp. 273, 324)

Cannon, W. B., & Washburn, A. (1912). An explanation of hunger. *American Journal of Physiology, 29,* 441–454. (p. 273)

Cantor, N., & Norem, J. K. (1989). Defensive pessimism and stress and coping. *Social Cognition, 7*, 92–112. (p. 371)

Cantril, H., & Bumstead, C. H. (1960). *Reflections on the human venture.* New York: New York University Press. (p. 457)

Carballo, M., Cleland, J., Carael, M., & Albrecht, G. (1989). A cross national study of patterns of sexual behaviour. Unpublished manuscript, Social and Behavioural Research Unit, Global Programme on AIDS, World Health Organization, 1211 Geneva 27, Switzerland. (p. 283)

Carducci, B. J., Cosby, P. C., & Ward, D. C. (1978). Sexual arousal and interpersonal evaluations. *Journal of Experimental Social Psychology, 14*, 449–457. (p. 470)

Carey, G. (1990). Genes, fears, phobias, and phobic disorders. *Journal of Counseling and Development, 68*, 628–632. (p. 387)

Carli, L. L., & Leonard, J. B. (1989). The effect of hindsight on victim derogation. *Journal of Social and Clinical Psychology, 8*, 331–343. (p. 499)

Carlson, M., Charlin, V., & Miller, N. (1988). Positive mood and helping behavior: A test of six hypotheses. *Journal of Personality and Social Psychology, 55*, 211–229. (p. 465)

Carlson, R. (1984). What's social about social psychology? Where's the person in personality research? *Journal of Personality and Social Psychology, 47*, 1304–1309. (p. 373)

Carlson, S. (1985). A double-blind test of astrology. *Nature, 318*, 419–425. (p. 373)

Carnegie Council on Adolescent Development. (1989, June). *Turning points: Preparing American youth for the 21st century.* (The report of the Task Force on Education of Young Adolescents.) New York: Carnegie Corporation. (p. 502)

Carson, R. C., Butcher, J. N., & Coleman, J. C. (1988). *Abnormal psychology and modern life* (8th ed.). Glenview, IL: Scott, Foresman. (p. 382)

Cartwright, R. D. (1978). *A primer on sleep and dreaming.* Reading, MA: Addison-Wesley. (p. 153)

Cash, T., & Janda, L. H. (1984, December). The eye of the beholder. *Psychology Today*, pp. 46–52. (p. 467)

Caspi, A., & Moffitt, T. E. (1991). Individual differences are accentuated during periods of social change: The sample case of girls at puberty. *Journal of Personality and Social Psychology, 61*, 157–168. (p. 79)

Castro, J. (1990, Fall issue on women). Get set: Here they come. *Time*, pp. 50–52. (p. 492)

Castro, J. (1991, October 28). Vox pop. *Time*, p. 23. (p. 280)

Cattell, R. B. (1963). Theory of fluid and crystallized intelligence: A critical experiment. *Journal of Educational Psychology, 54*, 1–22. (p. 90)

Ceci, S. J., & Liker, J. K. (1986). A day at the races: A study of IQ, expertise, and cognitive complexity. *Journal of Experimental Psychology: General, 115*, 255–266. (p. 259)

Centers for Disease Control Vietnam Experience Study. (1988). Health status of Vietnam veterans. *Journal of the American Medical Association, 259*, 2701–2709. (p. 325)

Centers for Disease Control. (1983). Behavioral risk factor prevalence surveys—United States. Reported in *Behavior Today Newsletter*, October 29, 1984, p. 7. (p. 168)

Centers for Disease Control. (1989). Results from the national adolescent student health survey. *Morbidity and Mortality Weekly Report, 38*(9), 147–150. (p. 392)

Centers for Disease Control. (1989). Weekly report summarized in *Detroit Free Press*, November 25, p. A1. (p. 168)

Centers for Disease Control. (1991, January 5). Data from the National Survey of Family Growth as reported by Associated Press release. (p. 84)

Centerwall, B. S. (1989). Exposure to television as a risk factor for violence. *American Journal of Epidemiology, 129*, 643–652. (p. 461)

Cerella, J. (1985). Information processing rates in the elderly. *Psychological Bulletin, 98*, 67–83. (p. 88)

Chase, W. G., & Simon, H. A. (1973). Perception in chess. *Cognitive Psychology, 4*, 55–81. (p. 214)

Chassin, L., Presson, C. C., Sherman, S. J., & McGrew, J. (1987). The changing smoking environment for middle and high school students: 1980–1983. *Journal of Behavioral Medicine, 10*, 581–593. (p. 174)

Chaves, J. F. (1989). Hypnotic control of clinical pain. In N. P. Spanos & J. F. Chaves (Eds.), *Hypnosis: The cognitive-behavioral perspective.* Buffalo, NY: Prometheus Books. (p. 164)

Cheek, J. M., & Melchior, L. A. (1990). Shyness, self-esteem, and self-consciousness. In H. Leitenberg (Ed.), *Handbook of social and evaluation anxiety.* New York: Plenum. (p. 398)

Cherfas, J. (1990). Two bomb attacks on scientists in the U.K. *Science, 248*, 1485. (p. 19)

Cherlin, A. J., Furstenberg, F. F., Jr., Chase-Landale, P. L., Kiernan, K. E., Robins, P. K., Morrison, D. R., & Teitler, J. O. (1991). Longitudinal studies of effects of divorce on children in Great Britain and the United States. *Science, 252*, 1386–1389. (p. 76)

Chesney, M. A. (1984). *Behavioral factors in coronary heart disease separating benign from malignant.* Paper presented at the American Psychological Association convention. (p. 329)

Chess, S., & Thomas, A. (1987). *Know your child: An authoritative guide for today's parents.* New York: Basic Books. (p. 72)

Chi, M. T. H., Glaser, R., & Farr, M. J. (Eds.). (1988). *The nature of expertise.* Hillsdale, NJ: Erlbaum. (p. 234)

Chodorow, N. J. (1978). *The reproduction of mothering: Psychoanalysis and the sociology of gender.* Berkeley, CA: University of California Press. (p. 486)

Chodorow, N. J. (1989). *Feminism and psychoanalytic theory.* New Haven, CT: Yale University Press. (p. 486)

Chomsky, N. (1959). Review of B. F. Skinner's *Verbal behavior. Language, 35*, 26–58. (p. 245)

Chomsky, N. (1972). *Language and mind.* New York: Harcourt Brace Jovanovich. (p. 242)

Chomsky, N. (1987). Language in a psychological setting. Sophia Linguistic Working Papers, No. 22, Sophia University, Tokyo. (p. 245)

Chwalisz, K., Diener, E., & Gallagher, D. (1988). Autonomic arousal feedback and emotional experience: Evidence from the spinal cord injured. *Journal of Personality and Social Psychology, 54,* 820–828. (p. 314)

Cialdini, R. B. (1988). *Influence: Science and practice* (2nd ed.). Glenview, IL: Scott, Foresman. (p. 447)

Cialdini, R. B., & Carpenter, K. (1981). The availability heuristic: Does imagining make it so? In P. H. Reingen & A. G. Woodside (Eds.), *Buyer-seller interactions: Empirical issues and normative issues.* Chicago: American Marketing Association. (p. 238)

Cialdini, R. B., & Richardson, K. D. (1980). Two indirect tactics of image management: Basking and blasting. *Journal of Personality and Social Psychology, 39,* 406–415. (p. 498)

Coe, W. C. (1989a). Posthypnotic amnesia: Theory and research. In N. P. Spanos & J. F. Chaves (Eds.), *Hypnosis: The cognitive-behavioral perspective.* Buffalo, NY: Prometheus Books. (p. 160)

Coe, W. C. (1989b). Hypnosis: The role of sociopolitical factors in a paradigm clash. In N. P. Spanos & J. F. Chaves (Eds.), *Hypnosis: The cognitive-behavioral perspective.* Buffalo, NY: Prometheus Books. (p. 165)

Coffey, C. E., & Weiner, R. D. (1990). Electroconvulsive therapy: An update. *Hospital and Community Psychiatry, 41,* 515–521. (p. 436)

Cohen, I. B. (1984, March). Florence Nightingale. *Scientific American,* pp. 128–137. (p. 510)

Cohen, R. M., Semple, W. E., Gross, M., & Nordahl, T. E. (1988). From syndrome to illness: Delineating the pathophysiology of schizophrenia with PET. *Schizophrenia Bulletin, 14,* 169–178. (p. 403)

Cohen, S. (1988). Psychosocial models of the role of social support in the etiology of physical disease. *Health Psychology, 7,* 269–297. (p. 339)

Cohen, S., & Williamson, G. M. (1988). Perceived stress in a probability sample of the United States. In S. Spacapan & S. Oskamp (Eds.), *The social psychology of health.* Newbury Park, CA: Sage. (p. 327)

Cohen, S., & Williamson, G. M. (1991). Stress and infectious disease in humans. *Psychological Bulletin, 109,* 5–24. (p. 331)

Cohen, S., Tyrrell, D. A. J., & Smith, A. P. (1991). Psychological stress and susceptibility to the common cold. *New England Journal of Medicine, 325,* 606–612. (p. 332)

Coile, D. C., & Miller, N. E. (1984). How radical animal activists try to mislead humane people. *American Psychologist, 39,* 700–701. (pp. 18, 19)

Coleman, J. C. (1980). *The nature of adolescence.* London: Methuen. (p. 78)

Coleman, P. D., & Flood, D. G. (1986). Dendritic proliferation in the aging brain as a compensatory repair mechanism. In D. F. Swaab, E. Fliers, M. Mirmiram, W. A. Van Gool, & F. Van Haaren (Eds.), *Progress in brain research* (Vol. 20). New York: Elsevier. (p. 88)

Colombo, J. (1982). The critical period concept: Research, methodology, and theoretical issues. *Psychological Bulletin, 91,* 260–275. (p. 72)

Colon, E. A., Callies, A. L., Popkin, M. K., & McGlave, P. B. (1991). Depressed mood and other variables related to bone marrow transplantation survival in acute leukemia. *Psychosomatics, 32,* 420–425. (p. 339)

Consensus Conference. (1985). Electroconvulsive therapy. *Journal of the American Medical Association, 254,* 2103–2108. (p. 436)

Conway, M., & Ross, M. (1984). Getting what you want by revising what you had. *Journal of Personality and Social Psychology, 47,* 738–748. (p. 228)

Cook, E. W., III, Hodes, R. L., & Lang, P. J. (1986). Preparedness and phobia: Effects of stimulus content on human visceral conditioning. *Journal of Abnormal Psychology, 95,* 195–207. (p. 184)

Coon, P. M., Bowman, E. S., & Milstein, V. (1988). Multiple personality disorder: A clinical investigation of 50 cases. *Journal of Nervous and Mental Disease, 176,* 519–527. (p. 391)

Cooper, W. H. (1983). An achievement motivation nomological network. *Journal of Personality and Social Psychology, 44,* 841–861. (p. 292)

Coopersmith, S. (1967). *The antecedents of self-esteem.* San Francisco: Freeman. (p. 76)

Costa, P. T., Jr., & McCrae, R. R. (1989). Personality continuity and the changes of adult life. In M. Storandt & G. R. VandenBos (Eds.), *The adult years: Continuity and change.* Washington, DC: American Psychological Association. (p. 100)

Cousins, N. (1989). *Head first: The biology of hope.* New York: Dutton. (pp. 332, 333)

Cousins, S. D. (1989). Culture and self-perception in Japan and the United States. *Journal of Personality and Social Psychology, 56,* 124–131. (p. 478)

Covington, M. V., & Omelich, C. L. (1988). I can resist anything but temptation: Adolescent expectations for smoking cigarettes. *Journal of Applied Social Psychology, 18,* 203–227. (p. 174)

Cowan, G., Lee, C., Levy, D., & Snyder, D. (1988). Dominance and inequality in X-rated videocassettes. *Psychology of Women Quarterly, 12,* 299–311. (p. 462)

Cowan, N. (1988). Evolving conceptions of memory storage, selective attention, and their mutual constraints within the human information-processing system. *Psychological Bulletin, 104,* 163–191. (p. 208)

Cowart, B. J. (1981). Development of taste perception in humans: Sensitivity and preference throughout the life span. *Psychological Bulletin, 90,* 43–73. (p. 120)

Coyne, J. C., Burchill, S. A. L., & Stiles, W. B. (1991). An interactional perspective on depression. In C. R. Snyder & D. O. Forsyth (Eds.), *Handbook of social and clinical psychology: The health perspective.* New York: Pergamon. (p. 397)

Craig, M. E., Kalichman, S. C., & Follingstad, D. R. (1989). Verbal coercive sexual behavior among college students. *Archives of Sexual Behavior, 18,* 421–434. (p. 462)

Craik, F. I. M., & Watkins, M. J. (1973). The role of rehearsal in short-term memory. *Journal of Verbal Learning and Verbal Behavior, 12,* 599–607. (p. 211)

Crandall, C. S. (1988). Social contagion of binge eating. *Journal of Personality and Social Psychology, 55,* 588–598. (p. 277)

Crandall, J. E. (1984). Social interest as a moderator of life stress. *Journal of Personality and Social Psychology, 47,* 164–174. (p. 367)

Crocker, J., & Schwartz, I. (1985). Effects of self-esteem on prejudice and ingroup favoritism in a minimal intergroup situation. *Personality and Social Psychology Bulletin, 11*(4). (p. 364)

Crocker, J., Thompson, L. L., McGraw, K. M., & Ingerman, C. (1987). Downward comparison, prejudice, and evaluation of others: Effects of self-esteem and threat. *Journal of Personality and Social Psychology, 52,* 907–916. (p. 498)

Crowe, L. C., & George, W. H. (1989). Alcohol and human sexuality: Review and integration. *Psychological Bulletin, 105,* 374–386. (p. 168)

Csikszentmihalyi, M. (1990). *Flow: The psychology of optimal experience.* New York: Harper & Row. (p. 318)

Cunningham, M. R. (1986). Measuring the physical in physical attractiveness: Quasi-experiments on the sociobiology of female facial beauty. *Journal of Personality and Social Psychology, 50,* 925–935. (p. 468)

Curtis, R. C., & Miller, K. (1986). Believing another likes or dislikes you: Behaviors making the beliefs come true. *Journal of Personality and Social Psychology, 51,* 284–290. (p. 469)

Cutler, B. L., & Penrod, S. D. (1989). Forensically relevant moderators of the relation between eyewitness identification accuracy and confidence. *Journal of Applied Psychology, 74,* 650–652. (p. 224)

Cutrona, C. E. (1986). Behavioral manifestations of social support: A microanalytic investigation. *Journal of Personality and Social Psychology, 51,* 201–208. (p. 389)

Dabbs, J. M., Jr., & Morris, R. (1990). Testosterone, social class, and antisocial behavior in a sample of 4,462 men. *Psychological Science, 1,* 209–211. (p. 459)

Dabbs, J. M., Jr., de La Rue, D., & Williams, P. M. (1990). Testosterone and occupational choice: Actors, ministers, and other men. *Journal of Personality and Social Psychology, 59,* 1261–1265. (p. 489)

Dabbs, J. M., Jr., Frady, R. L., Carr, T. S., & Besch, N. F. (1987). Saliva testosterone and criminal violence in young adult prison inmates. *Psychosomatic Medicine, 49,* 174–182. (pp. 459, 489)

Dabbs, J. M., Jr., Ruback, R. B., & Besch, N. F. (1987). *Male saliva testosterone following conversations with male and female partners.* Paper presented at the American Psychological Association convention. (p. 284)

Darley, J. M., & Latané, B. (1968a). Bystander intervention in emergencies: Diffusion of responsibility. *Journal of Personality and Social Psychology, 8,* 377–383. (p. 465)

Darley, J. M., & Latané, B. (1968b, December). When will people help in a crisis? *Psychology Today,* pp. 54–57, 70–71. (p. 464)

Darley, J. M., Seligman, C., & Becker, L. J. (1979, April). The lesson of twin rivers: Feedback works. *Psychology Today,* pp. 16, 23–24. (p. 198)

Darrach, B., & Norris, J. (1984, August). An American tragedy. *Life,* pp. 58–74. (p. 405)

Davidson, R. J. (1991, February 12). Quoted by Daniel Goleman, Feeling cheerful? Thank brain's left lobe. *New York Times,* pp. C1, C10. (p. 303)

Davidson, R. J., Ekman, P., Saron, C. D., Senulis, J. A., & Friesen, W. V. (1990). Approach-withdrawal and cerebral asymmetry: Emotional expression and brain physiology I. *Journal of Personality and Social Psychology, 58,* 330–341. (p. 303)

Dawes, R. M. (1980). Social dilemmas. *Annual Review of Psychology, 31,* 169–193. (p. 500)

Dawson, N. V., Arkes, H. R., Siciliano, C., Blinkhorn, R., Lakshmanan, M., & Petrelli, M. (1988). Hindsight bias: An impediment to accurate probability estimation in clinicopathologic conferences. *Medical Decision Making, 8,* 259–264. (p. 20)

de Boysson-Bardies, B., Halle, P., Sagart, L., & Durand, C. (1989). A cross linguistic investigation of vowel formats in babbling. *Journal of Child Language, 16,* 1–17. (p. 243)

de Cuevas, J. (1990, September-October). "No, she holded them loosely." *Harvard Magazine,* pp. 60–67. (p. 245)

de Jong-Gierveld, J. (1987). Developing and testing a model of loneliness. *Journal of Personality and Social Psychology, 53,* 119–128. (p. 398)

de Rivera, J. (1989). Comparing experiences across cultures: Shame and guilt in America and Japan. Symposium presentation to the American Psychological Society convention. (p. 478)

DeAngelis, T. (1989, January). Mania, depression, and genius. *The APA Monitor,* pp. 1, 24. (p. 394)

Deci, E. L., & Ryan, R. M. (1987). The support of autonomy and the control of behavior. *Journal of Personality and Social Psychology, 53,* 1024–1037. (p. 294)

Delgado, J. M. R. (1969). *Physical control of the mind: Toward a psychocivilized society.* New York: Harper & Row. (p. 46)

Dement, W. (1990). In the PBS film, *Sleep alert.* Quoted by *Behavior Today,* March 12, p. 8. (p. 154)

Dement, W. C. (1978). *Some must watch while some must sleep.* New York: Norton. (pp. 152, 154, 155)

Dement, W. C., & Wolpert, E. A. (1958). The relation of eye movements, body mobility, and external stimuli to dream content. *Journal of Experimental Psychology, 55,* 543–553. (p. 156)

Dempster, F. N. (1988). The spacing effect: A case study in the failure to apply the results of psychological research. *American Psychologist, 43,* 627–634. (p. 211)

Dennis, W. (1940). Does culture appreciably affect patterns of infant behavior? *Journal of Social Psychology, 12,* 305–317. (p. 64)

Denton, K., & Krebs, D. (1990). From the scene to the crime: The effect of alcohol and social context on moral judgment. *Journal of Personality and Social Psychology, 59,* 242–248. (p. 168)

D'Eon, J. L. (1989). Hypnosis in the control of labor pain. In N. P. Spanos & J. F. Chaves (Eds.), *Hypnosis: The cognitive-behavioral perspective.* Buffalo, NY: Prometheus Books. (p. 164)

Dermer, M., & Pyszczynski, T. A. (1978). Effects of erotica upon men's loving and liking responses for women they love. *Journal of Personality and Social Psychology, 36,* 1302–1309. (p. 470)

Dermer, M., Cohen, S. J., Jacobsen, E., & Anderson, E. A. (1979). Evaluative judgments of aspects of life as a function of vicarious exposure to hedonic extremes. *Journal of Personality and Social Psychology, 37,* 247–260. (p. 317)

Deutsch, J. A. (1972, July). Brain reward: ESP and ecstasy. *Psychology Today,* pp. 46–48. (p. 42)

Deutsch, M. (1991). Egalitarianism in the laboratory and at work. In R. Vermunt & H. Steensma (Eds.), *Social justice in human relations.* New York: Plenum. (p. 197)

Dey, E. L., Astin, A. W., & Korn, W. S. (1991). *The American freshman: Twenty-five year trends.* Los Angeles: Higher Education Research Institute, UCLA. (p. 493)

Diaconis, P., & Mosteller, F. (1989). Methods for studying coincidences. *Journal of the American Statistical Association, 84,* 853–861. (p. 519)

Diamond, J. (1989, May). The great leap forward. *Discover,* pp. 50–60. (p. 243)

Dickie, J. R. (1987). Interrelationships within the mother-father-infant triad. In P. W. Berman & F. A. Pedersen (Eds.), *Men's transitions to parenthood: Longitudinal studies of early family experience.* Hillsdale, NJ: Erlbaum. (p. 74)

Diener, E. (1984). Subjective well-being. *Psychological Bulletin, 95,* 542–575. (p. 316, 317)

Dietz, W. H., Jr., & Gortmaker, S. L. (1985). Do we fatten our children at the television set? Obesity and television viewing in children and adolescents. *Pediatrics, 75,* 807–812. (p. 281)

DiLalla, L. F., & Gottesman, I. I. (1991). Biological and genetic contributors to violence—Widom's untold tale. *Psychological Bulletin, 109,* 125–129. (p. 405)

Dion, K. K. (1986). Stereotyping based on physical attractiveness: Issues and conceptual perspectives. In C. P. Herman, M. P. Zanna, & E. T. Higgins (Eds.), *Physical appearance, stigma, and social behavior: The Ontario symposium on personality and social psychology* (Vol. 3). Hillsdale, NJ: Erlbaum. (p. 467)

Dion, K. K., Pak, A. W-P., & Dion, K. L. (1990). Stereotyping physical attractiveness: A sociocultural perspective. *Journal of Cross-Cultural Psychology, 21,* 378–398. (p. 480)

Dixon, B. (1986, April). Dangerous thoughts: How we think and feel can make us sick. *Science, 86,* pp. 63–66. (p. 332)

Dobson, K. S. (1989). A meta-analysis of the efficacy of cognitive therapy for depression. *Journal of Consulting and Clinical Psychology, 57,* 414–419. (p. 431)

Dohrenwend, B. P., Levav, I., Shrout, P. E., Link, B. G., Skodol, A. E., & Martin, J. L. (1987). Life stress and psychopathology: Progress on research begun with Barbara Snell Dohrenwend. *American Journal of Community Psychology, 15,* 677–715. (p. 397)

Dohrenwend, B., Pearlin, L., Clayton, P., Hamburg, B., Dohrenwend, B. P., Riley, M., & Rose, R. (1982). Report on stress and life events. In G. R. Elliott & C. Eisdorfer (Eds.), *Stress and human health: Analysis and implications of research* (A study by the Institute of Medicine/National Academy of Sciences). New York: Springer. (p. 326)

Dolezal, H. (1982). *Living in a world transformed.* New York: Academic Press. (p. 136)

Domjan, M., Lyons, R., North, N. C., & Bruell, J. (1986). Sexual Pavlovian conditioned approach behavior in male Japanese quail (*Coturnix coturnix japonica*). *Journal of Comparative Psychology, 100,* 413–421. (p. 182)

Donaldson, M. (1979, March). The mismatch between school and children's minds. *Human Nature,* pp. 60–67. (p. 69)

Donnerstein, E., Linz, D., & Penrod, S. (1987). *The question of pornography.* New York: Free Press. (pp. 462, 463)

Doris, J. (Ed.) (1991). *The suggestibility of children's recollections: Implications for eyewitness testimony.* Washington, DC: American Psychological Association. (p. 224)

Doty, R. L., Shaman, P., Applebaum, S. L., Giberson, R., Siksorski, L., & Rosenberg, L. (1984). Smell identification ability: Changes with age. *Science, 226,* 1441–1443. (p. 87)

Draguns, J. G. (1990a). Normal and abnormal behavior in cross-cultural perspective: Specifying the nature of their relationship. *Nebraska Symposium on Motivation 1989, 37,* 235–277. (pp. 379, 388, 397)

Draguns, J. G. (1990b). Applications of cross-cultural psychology in the field of mental health. In R. W. Brislin (Ed.), *Applied cross-cultural psychology.* Newbury Park, CA: Sage. (p. 379)

Driedger, L. (1975). In search of cultural identity factors: A comparison of ethnic students. *Canadian Review of Sociology and Anthropology, 12,* 150–161. (p. 483)

Drucker, P. F. (1982, December). A conversation with Peter F. Drucker. *Psychology Today,* pp. 60–67. (p. 355)

Druckman, D., & Bjork, R. A. (1991). *In the mind's eye: Enhancing human performance.* Washington, DC: National Academy Press. (p. 356)

Druckman, D., & Swets, J. A. (Eds.). (1988). *Enhancing human performance: Issues, theories, and techniques.* Washington, DC: National Academy Press. (pp. 142, 250)

Duclos, S. E., Laird, J. D., Sexter, M., Stern, L., & Van Lighten, O. (1989). Emotion-specific effects of facial expressions and postures on emotional experience. *Journal of Personality and Social Psychology, 57,* 100–108. (p. 309)

Duggan, J. P., & Booth, D. A. (1986). Obesity, overeating, and rapid gastric emptying in rats with ventromedial hypothalamic lesions. *Science, 231,* 609–611. (p. 275)

Duncan, B. L. (1976). Differential social perception and attribution of intergroup violence: Testing the lower limits of stereotyping of blacks. *Journal of Personality and Social Psychology, 34,* 590–598. (p. 496)

Duncan, G. J., Hill, M. S., & Hoffman, S. D. (1988). Welfare dependence within and across generations. *Science, 239,* 467–471. (p. 239)

Duncker, K. (1945). On problem solving. *Psychological Monographs, 58* (Whole no. 270). (pp. 236, 238)

Dunnett, S. B. (1989). Neural transplantation: Normal brain function and repair after damage. *The Psychologist, 1,* 4–8. (p. 49)

Dunning, D., Griffin, D. W., Milojkovic, J. D., & Ross, L. (1990). The overconfidence effect in social prediction. *Journal of Personality and Social Psychology, 58,* 568–591. (p. 240)

Dutton, D. G., & Aron, A. (1989). Romantic attraction and generalized liking for others who are sources of conflict-based arousal. *Canadian Journal of Behavioural Sciences, 21,* 246–257. (p. 470)

Dutton, D. G., & Aron, A. P. (1974). Some evidence for heightened sexual attraction under conditions of high anxiety. *Journal of Personality and Social Psychology, 30,* 510–517. (p. 470)

Dweck, C. S., & Elliott, E. S. (1983). Achievement motivation. In P. Mussen & E. M. Hetherington (Eds.), *Handbook of child psychology* (Vol. IV). New York: Wiley. (p. 292)

Dywan, J., & Bowers, K. (1983). The use of hypnosis to enhance recall. *Science, 222,* 184–185. (p. 161)

Eagly, A. H. (1987). *Sex differences in social behavior: A social-role interpretation.* Hillsdale, NJ: Erlbaum. (p. 487)

Eagly, A. H., & Crowley, M. (1986). Gender and helping behavior: A meta-analytic review of the social psychological literature. *Psychological Bulletin, 100,* 283–308. (p. 465)

Eagly, A. H., & Johnson, B. T. (1990). Gender and leadership style: A meta-analysis. *Psychological Bulletin, 108,* 233–256. (p. 487)

Eagly, A. H., & Karau, S. J. (1991). Gender and the emergence of leaders: A meta-analysis. *Journal of Personality and Social Psychology, 60,* 685–710. (p. 295)

Eagly, A. H., & Wood, W. (1991). Explaining sex differences in social behavior: A meta-analytic perspective. *Personality and Social Psychology Bulletin, 17,* 306–315. (p. 492)

Eagly, A. H., Ashmore, R. D., Makhijani, M. G., & Kennedy, L. C. (1991). What is beautiful is good, but . . .: A meta-analytic review of research on the physical attractiveness stereotype. *Psychological Bulletin, 110,* 109–128. (p. 467)

Ebbesen, E. B., Duncan, B., & Konecni, V. J. (1975). Effects of content of verbal aggression on future verbal aggression: A field experiment. *Journal of Experimental Social Psychology, 11,* 192–204. (p. 313)

Ebbinghaus, H. (1885). *Über das Gedachtnis.* Leipzig: Duncker & Humblot. Cited in R. Klatzky (1980), *Human memory: Structures and processes.* San Francisco: Freeman. (pp. 216–267)

Eccles, J. S., Jacobs, J. E., & Harold, R. D. (1990). Gender role stereotypes, expectancy effects, and parents' socialization of gender differences. *Journal of Social Issues, 46,* 183–201. (p. 486)

Eckert, E. D., Bouchard, T. J., Jr., Segal, N. L., Lykken, D. T., & Heston, L. L. (1987). Sex differences in genetic influence on body weight in monozygotic twins reared apart. Unpublished manuscript, University of Minnesota. (p. 279)

Eckert, E. D., Heston, L. L., & Bouchard, T. J., Jr. (1981). MZ twins reared apart: Preliminary findings of psychiatric disturbances and traits. In L. Gedda, P. Paris, & W. D. Nance (Eds.), *Twin research: Vol. 3. Pt. B. Intelligence, personality, and development.* New York: Alan Liss. (p. 387)

Edwards, C. P. (1981). The comparative study of the development of moral judgment and reasoning. In R. H. Munroe, R. L. Munroe, & B. B. Whiting (Eds.), *Handbook of cross-cultural human development.* New York: Garland Press. (p. 81)

Edwards, C. P. (1982). Moral development in comparative cultural perspective. In D. A. Wagner & H. W. Stevenson (Eds.), *Cultural perspectives on child development.* San Francisco: Freeman. (p. 81)

Edwards, C. P. (1991). Behavioral sex differences in children of diverse cultures: The case of nurturance to infants. In M. Pereira & L. Fairbanks (Eds.), *Juveniles: Comparative socioecology.* Oxford: Oxford University Press. (p. 492)

Ehrhardt, A. A. (1987). A transactional perspective on the development of gender differences. In J. M. Reinisch, L. A. Rosenblum, & S. A. Sanders (Eds.), *Masculinity/femininity: Basic perspectives.* New York: Oxford University Press. (p. 489)

Ehrlichman, H., & Halpern, J. N. (1988). Affect and memory: Effects of pleasant and unpleasant odors on retrieval of happy and unhappy memories. *Journal of Personality and Social Psychology, 55,* 769–779. (p. 122)

Eibl-Eibesfeldt, I. (1971). *Love and hate: The natural history of behavior patterns.* New York: Holt, Rinehart & Winston. (p. 308)

Eich, E. (1990). Learning during sleep. In R. R. Bootzin, J. F. Kihlstrom, & D. L. Schacter (Eds.), *Sleep and cognition.* Washington, DC: American Psychological Association. (p. 156)

Eich, J. E. (1980). The cue-dependent nature of state-dependent retrieval. *Memory and Cognition, 8,* 157–173. (p. 168)

Eisenberg, N., & Lennon, R. (1983). Sex differences in empathy and related capacities. *Psychological Bulletin, 94,* 100–131. (p. 487)

Ekman, P., & Friesen, W. V. (1975). *Unmasking the face.* Englewood Cliffs, NJ: Prentice-Hall. (pp. 307, 308)

Ekman, P., Davidson, R. J., & Friesen, W. V. (1990). The Duchenne smile: Emotional expression and brain physiology II. *Journal of Personality and Social Psychology, 58,* 342–353. (p. 309)

Ekman, P., Friesen, W. V., O'Sullivan, M., Chan, A., Diacoyanni-Tarlatzis, I., Heider, K., Krause, R., LeCompte, W. A., Pitcairn, T., Ricci-Bitti, P. E., Scherer, K., Tomita, M., & Tzavaras, A. (1987). Universals and cultural differences in the judgments of facial expressions of emotion. *Journal of Personality and Social Psychology, 53,* 712–717. (p. 307)

Ekman, P., Levenson, R. W., & Friesen, W. V. (1983). Autonomic nervous system activity distinguishes among emotions. *Science, 221,* 1208–1210. (p. 309)

Elder, G. H., Jr. (1969). Appearance and education in marriage mobility. *American Sociological Review, 34,* 519–533. (p. 468)

Elkin, I., Shea, T., Watkins, J. T., Imber, S. D., Sotsky, S. M., Collins, J. F., Glass, D. R., Pilkonis, P. A., Leber, W. R., Docherty, J. P., Fiester, S. J., & Parloff, M. B. (1989). National Institute of Mental Health treatment of depression collaborative research program. *Archives of General Psychiatry, 46,* 971–983. (p. 431)

Elkind, D. (1970). The origins of religion in the child. *Review of Religious Research, 12,* 35–42. (p. 80)

Elkind, D. (1978). *The child's reality: Three developmental themes.* Hillsdale, NJ: Erlbaum. (p. 80)

Ellis, A. (1962). *Reason and emotion in psychotherapy.* Secaucus, NJ: Citadel Press. (p. 424)

Ellis, A. (1980). Comment on A. E. Bergin's Psychotherapy and religious values. *Journal of Consulting and Clinical Psychology, 48,* 635–638. (p. 425)

Ellis, A. (1984). Rational-emotive therapy. In R. J. Corsini (Ed.), *Current psychotherapies* (3rd ed.). Itasca, IL: Peacock. (p. 424)

Ellis, A. (1987). The impossibility of achieving consistently good mental health. *American Psychologist, 42,* 364–375. (p. 424)

Ellis, A. (1989). Rational-emotive therapy. In R. J. Corsini & D. Wedding (Eds.), *Current psychotherapies* (4th ed.). Itasca, IL: Peacock. (p. 424)

Ellis, A., & Becker, I. M. (1982). A guide to personal happiness. North Hollywood, CA: Wilshire Book Co. (p. 186)

Ellis, H. C., & Ashbrook, P. W. (1989). The "state" of mood and memory research: A selective review. *Journal of Social Behavior and Personality, 4,* 1–21. (p. 223)

Ellis, L., & Ames, M. A. (1987). Neurohormonal functioning and sexual orientation: A theory of homosexuality-heterosexuality. *Psychological Bulletin, 101*, 233–258. (pp. 287, 289)

Empson, J. A. C., & Clarke, P. R. F. (1970). Rapid eye movements and remembering. *Nature, 227*, 287–288. (p. 157)

Endler, N. S. (1982). *Holiday of darkness: A psychologist's personal journey out of his depression.* New York: Wiley. (p. 436)

Engen, T. (1987). Remembering odors and their names. *American Scientist, 75*, 497–503. (p. 122)

Eppley, K. R., Abrams, A. I., & Shear, J. (1989). Differential effects of relaxation techniques on trait anxiety: A meta-analysis. *Journal of Clinical Psychology, 45*, 957–974. (p. 159)

Epstein, S. (1983a). Aggregation and beyond: Some basic issues on the prediction of behavior. *Journal of Personality, 51*, 360–392. (p. 361)

Epstein, S. (1983b). The stability of behavior across time and situations. In R. Zucker, J. Aronoff, & A. I. Rabin (Eds.), *Personality and the prediction of behavior.* San Diego: Academic Press. (p. 361)

Epstein, S. (1984). Controversial issues in emotions. In P. Shaver (Ed.), *Review of Personality and Social Psychology.* Beverly Hills, CA: Sage. (p. 303)

Erdelyi, M. H. (1985). *Psychoanalysis: Freud's cognitive psychology.* New York: Freeman. (p. 353)

Erdelyi, M. H. (1988). Repression, reconstruction, and defense: History and integration of the psychoanalytic and experimental frameworks. In J. Singer (Ed.), *Repression: Defense mechanism and cognitive style.* Chicago: University of Chicago Press. (p. 353)

Erikson, E. H. (1963). *Childhood and society.* New York: Norton. (p. 81)

Eron, L. D. (1987). The development of aggressive behavior from the perspective of a developing behaviorism. *American Psychologist, 42*, 435–442. (p. 461)

Esser, J. K., & Lindoerfer, J. S. (1989). Groupthink and the space shuttle *Challenger* accident: Toward a quantitative case analysis. *Journal of Behavioral Decision Making, 2*, 167–177. (p. 456)

Evans, G. W., Palsane, M. N., Lepore, S. J., & Martin, J. (1989). Residential density and psychological health: The mediating effects of social support. *Journal of Personality and Social Psychology, 57*, 994–999. (p. 339)

Evans, R. I., Dratt, L. M., Raines, B. E., & Rosenberg, S. S. (1988). Social influences on smoking initiation: Importance of distinguishing descriptive versus mediating process variables. *Journal of Applied Social Psychology, 18*, 925–943. (p. 174)

Exner, J. E., Jr. (1986). *The Rorschach: A comprehensive system. Volume 1: Basic Foundations* (2nd ed.). New York: Wiley. (p. 352)

Eysenck, H. J. (1952). The effects of psychotherapy: An evaluation. *Journal of Consulting Psychology, 16*, 319–324. (p. 430)

Eysenck, H. J. (1990, April 30). An improvement on personality inventory. *Current Contents: Social and Behavioral Sciences, 22*(18), 20. (p. 357)

Eysenck, H. J., & Grossarth-Maticek, R. (1991). Creative novation behaviour therapy as a prophylactic treatment for cancer and coronary heart disease: Part II—Effects of treatment. *Behaviour Research and Therapy, 29*, 17–31. (p. 338)

Eysenck, H. J., & Kamin, L. (1981). *The intelligence controversy: H. J. Eysenck vs. Leon Kamin.* New York: Wiley. (p. 253)

Eysenck, H. J., Wakefield, J. A., Jr., & Friedman, A. F. (1983). Diagnosis and clinical assessment: The DSM-III. *Annual Review of Psychology, 34*, 167–193. (p. 382)

Eysenck, M. W., MacLeod, C., & Mathews, A. (1987). Cognitive functioning and anxiety. *Psychological Research, 49*, 189–195. (p. 369)

Eysenck, S. B. G., & Eysenck, H. J. (1963). The validity of questionnaire and rating assessments of extraversion and neuroticism, and their factorial stability. *British Journal of Psychology, 54*, 51–62. (p. 357)

Faber, N. (1987, July). Personal glimpse. *Reader's Digest*, p. 34. (p. 259)

Falbo, T., & Polit, D. F. (1986). Quantitative review of the only child literature: Research evidence and theory development. *Psychological Bulletin, 100*, 176–189. (p. 292)

Fantz, R. L. (1961, May). The origin of form perception. *Scientific American*, pp. 66–72. (p. 62)

Farina, A. (1982). The stigma of mental disorders. In A. G. Miller (Ed.), *In the eye of the beholder.* New York: Praeger. (pp. 381, 407)

Farina, A., & Fisher, J. D. (1982). Beliefs about mental disorders: Findings and implications. In G. Weary & H. L. Mirels (Eds.), *Integrations of clinical and social psychology.* New York: Oxford University Press. (p. 428)

Farley, F. (1986, May). The big T in personality. *Psychology Today*, pp. 44–52. (p. 271)

Farrell, P. A., Gates, W. K., Maksud, M. G., & Morgan, W. P. (1982). Increases in plasma beta-endorphin/beta-lipotropin immunoreactivity after treadmill running in humans. *Journal of Applied Physiology, 52*, 1245–1249. (p. 32)

Faust, D., & Ziskin, J. (1988). The expert witness in psychology and psychiatry. *Science, 241*, 31–35. (p. 383)

Fava, M., Copeland, P. M., Schweiger, U., & Herzog, D. B. (1989). Neurochemical abnormalities of anorexia nervosa and bulimia nervosa. *American Journal of Psychiatry, 146*, 963–971. (p. 277)

Fay, R. E., Turner, C. F., Klassen, A. D., & Gagnon, J. H. (1989). Prevalence and patterns of same-gender sexual contact among men. *Science, 243*, 338–348. (p. 287)

Fazio, R. H. (1990). Multiple processes by which attitudes guide behavior: The MODE model as an integrative framework. In M. P. Zanna (Ed.), *Advances in experimental social psychology* (Vol. 23). San Diego: Academic Press. (p. 446)

Feder, H. H. (1984). Hormones and sexual behavior. *Annual Review of Psychology, 35*, 165–200. (p. 284)

Feeney, D. M. (1987). Human rights and animal welfare. *American Psychologist, 42*, 593–599. (p. 19)

Fehr, B., & Russell, J. A. (1991). The concept of love viewed from a prototype perspective. *Journal of Personality and Social Psychology, 60*, 425–438. (p. 235)

Feingold, A. (1990). Gender differences in effects of physical attractiveness on romantic attraction: A comparison across five research paradigms. *Journal of Personality and Social Psychology, 59*, 981–993. (p. 467)

Fernandez, E., & Turk, D. C. (1989). The utility of cognitive coping strategies for altering pain perception: A meta-analysis. *Pain, 38,* 123–135. (p. 124)

Fichter, M. M., & Noegel, R. (1990). Concordance for bulimia nervosa in twins. *International Journal of Eating Disorders, 9,* 255–263. (p. 277)

Fiedler, F. E. (1981). Leadership effectiveness. *American Behavioral Scientist, 24,* 619–632. (p. 295)

Fiedler, F. E. (1987, September). When to lead, when to stand back. *Psychology Today,* pp. 26–27. (p. 295)

Field, T. M. (1987, May). Baby research comes of age. *Psychology Today,* p. 46. (p. 62)

Field, T. M., Schanberg, S. M., Scafidi, F., Bauer, C. R., Vega-Lahr, N., Garcia, R., Nystrom, J., & Kuhn, C. M. (1986). Tactile/kinesthetic stimulation effects on preterm neonates. *Pediatrics, 77,* 654–658. (p. 63)

Findley, M. J., & Cooper, H. M. (1983). Locus of control and academic achievement: A literature review. *Journal of Personality and Social Psychology, 44,* 419–427. (p. 369)

Fineberg, H. V. (1988). Education to prevent AIDS: Prospects and obstacles. *Science, 239,* 592–596. (p. 288)

Finucci, J. M., & Childs, B. (1981). Are there really more dyslexic boys than girls? In A. Ansara, N. Geschwind, A. Galaburda, M. Albert, & N. Gartrell (Eds.), *Sex differences in dyslexia.* Towson, MD: The Orton Dyslexia Society. (p. 485)

Fischer, P. J., & Breakey, W. R. (1991). The epidemiology of alcohol, drug, and mental disorders among homeless persons. *American Psychologist, 46,* 1115–1128. (p. 434)

Fischhoff, B. (1982). Debiasing. In D. Kahneman, P. Slovic, & A. Tversky (Eds.), *Judgment under uncertainty: Heuristics and biases.* New York: Cambridge University Press. (p. 240)

Fischhoff, B., Slovic, P., & Lichtenstein, S. (1977). Knowing with certainty: The appropriateness of extreme confidence. *Journal of Experimental Psychology: Human Perception and Performance, 3,* 552–564. (p. 239)

Fisher, H. T. (1984). Little Albert and Little Peter. *Bulletin of the British Psychological Society, 37,* 269. (p. 420)

Fisher, R. P., Geiselman, R. E., & Amador, M. (1989). Field test of the cognitive interview: Enhancing the recollection of actual victims and witnesses of crime. *Journal of Applied Psychology, 74,* 722–727. (pp. 224, 225)

Fisher, R. P., Geiselman, R. E., & Raymond, D. S. (1987). Critical analysis of police interview techniques. *Journal of Police Science and Administration, 15,* 177–185. (pp. 224, 225)

Fitzgerald, R. C. (1970). Reactions to blindness: An exploratory study of adults with recent loss of sight. *Archives of General Psychiatry, 22,* 370–379. (p. 94)

Fleming, I., Baum, A., & Weiss, L. (1987). Social density and perceived control as mediator of crowding stress in high-density residential neighborhoods. *Journal of Personality and Social Psychology, 52,* 899–906. (p. 329)

Fleming, J. H., & Scott, B. A. (1991). The costs of confession: The Persian Gulf War POW tapes in historical and theoretical perspective. *Contemporary Social Psychology, 15,* 127–138. (p. 307)

Fletcher, G. J. O., Fitness, J., & Blampied, N. M. (1990). The link between attributions and happiness in close relationships: The roles of depression and explanatory style. *Journal of Social and Clinical Psychology, 9,* 243–255. (p. 444)

Floderus-Myrhed, B., Pedersen, N., & Rasmuson, I. (1980). Assessment of heritability for personality, based on a shortform of the Eysenck Personality Inventory: A study of 12,898 twin pairs. *Behavior Genetics, 10,* 153–162. (p. 96)

Foa, E. B., & Kozak, M. J. (1986). Emotional processing of fear: Exposure to corrective information. *Psychological Bulletin, 99,* 20–35. (p. 421)

Forer, B. R. (1949). The fallacy of personal validation: A classroom demonstration of gullibility. *Journal of Abnormal and Social Psychology, 44,* 118–123. (p. 372)

Forgas, J. P., Bower, G. H., & Krantz, S. E. (1984). The influence of mood on perceptions of social interactions. *Journal of Experimental Social Psychology, 20,* 497–513. (p. 223)

Fouts, R. S., & Bodamer, M. (1987). Preliminary report to the National Geographic Society on: "Chimpanzee intrapersonal signing." *Friends of Washoe, 7*(1), 4–12. (p. 248)

Fowler, M. J., Sullivan, M. J., & Ekstrand, B. R. (1973). Sleep and memory. *Science, 179,* 302–304. (p. 226)

Fowler, R. C., Rich, C. L., & Young, D. (1986). San Diego suicide study: II. Substance abuse in young cases. *Archives of General Psychiatry, 43,* 962–965. (p. 393)

Fowler, R. D. (1986, May). Howard Hughes: A psychological autopsy. *Psychology Today,* pp. 22–33. (p. 386)

Fox, J. L. (1984). The brain's dynamic way of keeping in touch. *Science, 225,* 820–821. (p. 46)

Fozard, J. L., & Popkin, S. J. (1978). Optimizing adult development: Ends and means of an applied psychology of aging. *American Psychologist, 33,* 975–989. (p. 87)

Frank, J. D. (1982). Therapeutic components shared by all psychotherapies. In J. H. Harvey & M. M. Parks (Eds.), *The Master Lecture Series: Vol. 1. Psychotherapy research and behavior change.* Washington, DC: American Psychological Association. (pp. 414, 432, 433)

Frank, M. G., & Gilovich, T. (1988). The dark side of self and social perception: Black uniforms and aggression in professional sports. *Journal of Personality and Social Psychology, 54,* 74–85. (pp. 12–14)

Frank, S. J. (1988). Young adults' perceptions of their relationships with their parents: Individual differences in connectedness, competence, and emotional autonomy. *Developmental Psychology, 24,* 729–737. (p. 84)

Frankel, A., & Prentice-Dunn, S. (1990). Loneliness and the processing of self-relevant information. *Journal of Social and Clinical Psychology, 9,* 303–315. (p. 398)

Freedman, D. G. (1979). *Human sociobiology: A holistic approach.* New York: Free Press. (p. 96)

Freedman, J. L. (1978). *Happy people.* San Diego: Harcourt Brace Jovanovich. (p. 93)

Freedman, J. L. (1988). Television violence and aggression: What the evidence shows. In S. Oskamp (Ed.), *Television as a social issue.* Newbury Park, CA: Sage. (p. 461)

Freedman, J. L., & Fraser, S. C. (1966).   Compliance without pressure: The foot-in-the-door technique. *Journal of Personality and Social Psychology, 4,* 195–202. (p. 446)

Freedman, J. L., & Perlick, D. (1979)   Crowding, contagion, and laughter. *Journal of Experimental Social Psychology, 15,* 295–303. (p. 454)

Freeman, W. J. (1991, February).   The physiology of perception. *Scientific American,* pp. 78–85. (p. 115)

Freud, S. (1931; reprinted 1961).   Female sexuality. In J. Strachey (Trans.), *The standard edition of the complete psychological works of Sigmund Freud.* London: Hogarth Press. (pp. 348, 350)

Frezza, M., DiPadova, C., Possato, G., Terpin, M., Buraona, E., & Lieber, C. (1990).   High blood alcohol levels in women. *New England Journal of Medicine, 322,* 95–99. (p. 168)

Friedman, H. S., & Booth-Kewley, S. (1987).   The "disease-prone personality": A meta-analytic view of the construct. *American Psychologist, 42,* 539–555. (p. 334)

Friedman, H. S., & Booth-Kewley, S. (1988).   Validity of the Type A construct: A reprise. *Psychological Bulletin, 104,* 381–384. (pp. 330, 334)

Friedman, M., & Ulmer, D. (1984).   *Treating Type A behavior—and your heart.* New York: Knopf. (pp. 330, 338)

Friedrich, O. (1987, December 7).   New age harmonies. *Time,* pp. 62–72. (p. 380)

Frieze, I. H., Parsons, J. E., Johnson, P. B., Ruble, D. N., & Zellman, G. L. (1978).   *Women and sex roles: A social psychological perspective.* New York: Norton. (pp. 353, 490)

Frisby, J. P. (1980).   *Seeing: Illusion, brain and mind.* New York: Oxford University Press. (p. 114)

Fritsch, G., & Hitzig, E. (1870; reprinted 1960).   On the electrical excitability of the cerebrum. In G. Von Bonin (Trans.), *Some papers on the cerebral cortex.* Springfield, IL: Charles C. Thomas. (p. 45)

Fromkin, V., & Rodman, R. (1983).   *An introduction to language* (3rd ed.). New York: Holt, Rinehart & Winston. (p. 244)

Fulker, D. W., DeFries, J. C., & Plomin, R. (1988).   Genetic influence on general mental ability increases between infancy and middle childhood. *Nature, 336,* 767–769. (p. 261)

Fuller, M. J., & Downs, A. C. (1990).   *Spermarche is a salient biological marker in men's development.* Poster presented at the American Psychological Society convention. (p. 79)

Funder, D. C., & Block, J. (1989).   The role of ego-control, ego-resiliency, and IQ in delay of gratification in adolescence. *Journal of Personality and Social Psychology, 57,* 1041–1050. (p. 81)

Furnham, A. (1982).   Explanations for unemployment in Britain. *European Journal of Social Psychology, 12,* 335–352. (p. 444)

Furnham, A., & Taylor, L. (1990).   Lay theories of homosexuality: Aetiology, behaviours, and 'cures.' *British Journal of Social Psychology, 29,* 135–147. (p. 289)

Furstenberg, F. F., Jr., Moore, K. A., & Peterson, J. L. (1985).   Sex education and sexual experience among adolescents. *American Journal of Public Health, 75,* 1331–1332. (p. 290)

Gabrenya, W. K., Jr., Latané, B., & Wang, Y-E. (1983).   Social loafing in cross-cultural perspective. *Journal of Cross-Cultural Psychology, 14,* 368–384. (p. 454)

Gaertner, S. L., Mann, J., Murrell, A., & Dovidio, J. F. (1989).   Reducing intergroup bias: The benefits of recategorization. *Journal of Personality and Social Psychology, 57,* 239–249. (p. 502)

Galanter, E. (1962).   Contemporary psychophysics. In R. Brown, E. Galanter, E. H. Hess, & G. Mandler (Eds.), *New directions in psychology.* New York: Holt, Rinehart & Winston. (p. 106)

Gallup, G. G., & Suarez, S. D. (1985).   Alternatives to the use of animals in psychological research. *American Psychologist, 40,* 1104–1111. (p. 19)

Gallup, G. G., & Suarez, S. D. (1986).   Self-awareness and the emergence of mind in humans and other primates. In J. Suls & A. G. Greenwald (Eds.), *Psychological perspectives on the self* (Vol. 3.). Hillsdale, NJ: Erlbaum. (p. 75)

Gallup, G. H., Jr. (1972).   *The Gallup poll: Public opinion 1935–1971* (Vol. 3). New York: Random House. (p. 501)

Gallup, G. H., Jr., & Newport, F. (1991, Winter).   Belief in paranormal phenomena among adult Americans. *Skeptical Inquirer,* pp. 137–146. (p. 140)

Gallup, G. H., Jr., & Hugick, L. (1990, June).   Racial tolerance grows, progress on racial equality less evident. *Gallup Poll Monthly,* pp. 23–32. (p. 496)

Gallup, G. H., Jr., & Newport, F. (1990, December).   Americans now drinking less alcohol. *Gallup Poll Monthly,* pp. 2–6. (p. 173)

Gallup Organization. (1988).   *America's youth 1977–1988.* Princeton, NJ. (pp. 170, 280)

Gallup Report. (1989, March/April).   Commercial aviation. pp. 32–33. (p. 239)

Gallup Report. (1989, March/April).   Importance of social values (self-image). p. 42. (p. 366)

Gallup Report. (1989, May).   Fifteen percent cite personal knowledge of child abuse cases. Report No. 284. (p. 75)

Garcia, J., & Koelling, R. A. (1966).   Relation of cue to consequence in avoidance learning. *Psychonomic Science, 4,* 123–124. (p. 184)

Gardner, H. (1983).   *Frames of mind: The theory of multiple intelligences.* New York: Basic Books. (pp. 258, 259)

Gardner, J. W. (1984).   *Excellence: Can we be equal and excellent too?* New York: Norton. (pp. 93, 295)

Gardner, M. (1983, Summer).   Lessons of a landmark PK hoax. *The Skeptical Inquirer,* pp. 16–19. (p. 141)

Gardner, R. A., & Gardner, B. I. (1969).   Teaching sign language to a chimpanzee. *Science, 165,* 664–672. (p. 247)

Garnets, L., & Kimmel, D. (1990).   *Lesbian and gay dimensions in the psychological study of human diversity.* Master lecture, American Psychological Association convention. (p. 287)

Gartner, J., Larson, D. B., Allen, G. D., & Gartner, A. F. (1991).   Religious commitment and psychopathology: A review of the empirical literature. *Journal of Psychology and Theology, 19,* 6–25. (p. 392)

Gash, D. M., Notter, M. F. D., Okawara, S. H., Kraus, A. L., & Joynt, R. J. (1986).   Amniotic neuroblastoma cells used for neural implants in monkeys. *Science, 233,* 1420–1421. (p. 49)

Gates, M. (1989, December 10).   Psychiatrists not where patients are. *Grand Rapids Press* (Newhouse News Service), p. D8. (p. 428)

Gawin, F. H. (1991). Cocaine addiction: Psychology and neurophysiology. *Science, 251,* 1580–1586. (p. 170)

Gazzaniga, M. S. (1967, August). The split brain in man. *Scientific American,* pp. 24–29. (pp. 50, 51)

Gazzaniga, M. S. (1983). Right hemisphere language following brain bisection: A 20-year perspective. *American Psychologist, 38,* 525–537. (pp. 51, 52)

Gazzaniga, M. S. (1988). *Mind matters: How mind and brain interact to create our conscious lives.* Boston: Houghton Mifflin. (p. 52)

Geen, R. G. (1984). Human motivation: New perspectives on old problems. In A. M. Rogers & C. J. Scheirer (Eds.), *The G. Stanley Hall Lecture Series* (Vol. 4). Washington, DC: American Psychological Association. (p. 292)

Geen, R. G., & Quanty, M. B. (1977). The catharsis of aggression: An evaluation of a hypothesis. In L. Berkowitz (Ed.), *Advances in experimental social psychology* (Vol. 10). New York: Academic Press. (p. 313)

Geen, R. G., & Thomas, S. L. (1986). The immediate effects of media violence on behavior. *Journal of Social Issues, 42*(3), 7–28. (p. 461)

Geiwitz, J. (1980). *Psychology: Looking at ourselves* (2nd ed.). Boston: Little, Brown. (p. 89)

Geldard, F. A. (1972). *The human senses* (2nd ed.). New York: Wiley. (p. 116)

Gelman, D. (1989, May 15). Voyages to the unknown. *Newsweek,* pp. 66–69. (p. 308)

Gelman, R. (1979). Preschool thought. *American Psychologist, 34,* 900–905. (p. 69)

Gerard, R. W. (1953, September). What is memory? *Scientific American,* pp. 118–126. (p. 217)

Gerbner, G. (1985). *Dreams that hurt: Mental illness in the mass media.* Keynote address to the First Rosalynn Carter Symposium on Mental Health Policy, Emory University School of Medicine, Atlanta. (p. 407)

Gerbner, G. (1990). Stories that hurt: Tobacco, alcohol, and other drugs in the mass media. In H. Resnik (Ed.), *Youth and drugs: Society's mixed messages.* Rockville, MD: Office for Substance Abuse Prevention, U.S. Department of Health and Human Services. (p. 174)

Gerbner, G., & Signorielli, N. (1990). *Profile 1967 through 1988–89:* Enduring patterns. Unpublished report, Annenberg School of Communications, University of Pennsylvania. (pp. 461, 462)

Gerrard, M. (1987a). Emotional and cognitive barriers to effective contraception: Are males and females really different. In K. Kelley (Ed.), *Females, males, and sexuality: Theories and research.* Albany: State University of New York Press. (p. 84)

Gerrard, M. (1987b). Sex, sex guilt, and contraceptive use revisited: The 1980s. *Journal of Personality and Social Psychology, 52,* 975–980. (p. 84)

Geschwind, N. (1979, September). Specializations of the human brain. *Scientific American,* pp. 180–199. (p. 48)

Geschwind, N., & Behan, P. O. (1984). Laterality, hormones, and immunity. In N. Geschwind & A. M. Galaburda (Eds.), *Cerebral dominance: The biological foundations.* Cambridge, MA: Harvard University Press. (p. 485)

Gfeller, J. D., Lynn, S. J., & Pribble, W. E. (1987). Enhancing hypnotic susceptibility: Interpersonal and rapport factors. *Journal of Personality and Social Psychology, 52,* 586–595. (p. 165)

Giambra, L. M. (1974). Daydreaming across the life span: Late adolescent to senior citizen. *Aging and Human Development, 5,* 115–140. (p. 159)

Gibbons, F. X. (1986). Social comparison and depression: Company's effect on misery. *Journal of Personality and Social Psychology, 51,* 140–148. (p. 317)

Gibson, E. J., & Walk, R. D. (1960, April). The "visual cliff." *Scientific American,* pp. 64–71. (p. 128)

Giles, T. R. (1983). Probable superiority of behavioral interventions—II: Empirical status of the equivalence of therapies hypothesis. *Journal of Behavior Therapy and Experimental Psychiatry, 14,* 189–196. (p. 431)

Gilligan, C. (1982). *In a different voice: Psychological theory and women's development.* Cambridge, MA: Harvard University Press. (pp. 83, 91, 486)

Gilligan, C., Lyons, N. P., & Hanmer, T. J. (Eds.). (1990). *Making connections: The relational worlds of adolescent girls at Emma Willard School.* Cambridge, MA: Harvard University Press. (pp. 83, 486)

Gilling, D., & Brightwell, R. (1982). *The human brain.* New York: Facts on File. (p. 421)

Gilovich, T., Vallone, R., & Tversky, A. (1985). The hot hand in basketball: On the misperception of random sequences. *Cognitive Psychology, 17,* 295–314. (p. 518)

Gist, R., & Welch, Q. B. (1989). Certification change versus actual behavior change in teenage suicide rates, 1955–1979. *Suicide and Life Threatening Behavior, 19,* 277–288. (p. 392)

Gjerde, P. F. (1983). Attentional capacity dysfunction and arousal in schizophrenia. *Psychological Bulletin, 93,* 57–72. (p. 400)

Gladue, B. A., Boechler, M., & McCaul, K. D. (1989). Hormonal response to competition in human males. *Aggressive Behavior, 15,* 409–422. (p. 459)

Glenn, N. D. (1975). Psychological well-being in the postparental stage: Some evidence from national surveys. *Journal of Marriage and the Family, 37,* 105–110. (p. 92)

Glenn, N. D. (1989). The social and cultural meaning of contemporary marriage. In B. Christensen (Ed.), *The retreat from marriage.* Rockford, IL: The Rockford Institute. (p. 92)

Glenn, N. D., & Weaver, C. N. (1988). The changing relationship of marital status to reported happiness. *Journal of Marriage and the Family, 50,* 317–324. (p. 92)

Glick, P., Gottesman, D., & Jolton, J. (1989). The fault is not in the stars: Susceptibility of skeptics and believers in astrology to the Barnum effect. *Personality and Social Psychology Bulletin, 15,* 572–583. (p. 372)

Godden, D. R., & Baddeley, A. D. (1975). Context-dependent memory in two natural environments: On land and underwater. *British Journal of Psychology, 66,* 325–331. (p. 222)

Gold, M., & Yanof, D. S. (1985). Mothers, daughters, and girlfriends. *Journal of Personality and Social Psychology, 49,* 654–659. (p. 83)

Gold, P. E. (1987). Sweet memories. *American Scientist, 75,* 151–155. (p. 218)

Goldberg, J., True, W. R., Eisen, S. A., & Henderson, W. G. (1990). A twin study of the effects of the Vietnam War on posttraumatic stress disorder. *Journal of the American Medical Association, 263,* 1227–1232. (p. 325)

Goldfried, M. R., & Padawer, W. (1982). Current status and future directions in psychotherapy. In M. R. Goldfried (Ed.), *Converging themes in psychotherapy: Trends in psychodynamic, humanistic, and behavioral practice.* New York: Springer. (p. 432)

Goleman, D. (1980, February). 1,528 little geniuses and how they grew. *Psychology Today,* pp. 28–53. (p. 257)

Goleman, D. (1987, February 24). Terror's children: Mending mental wounds. *New York Times,* pp. C1, C12. (p. 75)

Goleman, D. (1990, May 29). As bias crime seems to rise, scientists study roots of racism. *The New York Times,* pp. C1, C5. (p. 497)

Golub, S. (1983). *Menarche: The transition from girl to woman.* Lexington, MA: Lexington Books. (p. 79)

Goodall, J. (1986). *The chimpanzees of Gombe: Patterns of behavior.* Cambridge, MA: Harvard University Press. (p. 498)

Goodchilds, J. (1987). Quoted by Carol Tavris, Old age is not what it used to be. *The New York Times Magazine: Good Health Magazine,* September 27, pp. 24–25, 91–92. (p. 87)

Goodhart, D. E. (1986). The effects of positive and negative thinking on performance in an achievement situation. *Journal of Personality and Social Psychology, 51,* 117–124. (p. 371)

Goodwin, C. J. (1991). Misportraying Pavlov's apparatus. *American Journal of Psychology, 104,* 135–141. (p. 181)

Gopnik, A., & Meltzoff, A. N. (1986). Relations between semantic and cognitive development in the one-word stage: The specificity hypothesis. *Child Development, 57,* 1040–1053. (p. 250)

Gottesman, I. I. (1991). *Schizophrenia genesis: The origins of madness.* New York: Freeman. (p. 403)

Gould, M. S., & Shaffer, D. (1986). The impact of suicide in television movies: Evidence of imitation. *New England Journal of Medicine, 315,* 690–694. (p. 449)

Gould, S. J. (1981). *The mismeasure of man.* New York: Norton. (p. 253)

Graf, P. (1990). Life-span changes in implicit and explicit memory. *Bulletin of the Psychonomic Society, 28,* 353–358. (p. 89)

Graff, J. L. (1992, January 13). Surge to the right. *Time,* pp. 22–24. (p. 497)

Gray-Little, B., & Burks, N. (1983). Power and satisfaction in marriage: A review and critique. *Psychological Bulletin, 93,* 513–538. (p. 470)

Greeley, A. M. (1991). *Faithful attraction.* New York: Tor Books. (pp. 9, 282)

Green, S. K., & Sandos, P. (1983). Perceptions of male and female initiators of relationships. *Sex Roles, 9,* 849–852. (p. 491)

Greene, R. L. (1987). Effects of maintenance rehearsal on human memory. *Psychological Bulletin, 102,* 403–413. (p. 211)

Greenwald, A. G., Spangenberg, E. R., Pratkanis, A. R., & Eskenazi, J. (1991). Double-blind tests of subliminal self-help audiotapes. *Psychological Science, 2,* 119–122. (p. 15)

Greenwood, M. R. C. (1989). Sexual dimorphism and obesity. In A. J. Stunkard & A. Baum (Eds.), *Perspectives in behavioral medicine: Eating, sleeping, and sex.* Hillsdale, NJ: Erlbaum. (p. 276)

Greer, G. (1984, April). The uses of chastity and other paths to sexual pleasures. *MS,* pp. 53–60, 96. (pp. 285, 290)

Gregory, R. L. (1968, November). Visual illusions. *Scientific American,* pp. 66–76. (p. 133)

Gregory, R. L. (1978). *Eye and brain: The psychology of seeing* (3rd ed.). New York: McGraw-Hill. (p. 135)

Gregory, R. L., & Gombrich, E. H. (Eds.). (1973). *Illusion in nature and art.* New York: Charles Scribner's Sons. (p. 140)

Gregory, W. L., Cialdini, R. B., & Carpenter, K. M. (1982). Self-relevant scenarios as mediators of likelihood estimates and compliance: Does imagining make it so? *Journal of Personality and Social Psychology, 43,* 89–99. (p. 238)

Greif, E. B., & Ulman, K. J. (1982). The psychological impact of menarche on early adolescent females: A review of the literature. *Child Development, 53,* 1413–1430. (p. 78)

Grobstein, C. (1979, June). External human fertilization. *Scientific American,* pp. 57–67. (p. 60)

Gross, A. E., & Crofton, C. (1977). What is good is beautiful. *Sociometry, 40,* 85–90. (p. 468)

Gruder, C. L. (1977). Choice of comparison persons in evaluating oneself. In J. M. Suls & R. L. Miller (Eds.), *Social comparison processes.* New York: Hemisphere. (p. 316)

Gudykunst, W., Yoon, Y. C., & Nishida, T. (1987). The influence of individualism-collectivism on perceptions of communication in ingroup and outgroup relationships. *Communication Monographs, 54,* 295–306. (p. 498)

Guerin, B. (1986). Mere presence effects in humans: A review. *Journal of Personality and Social Psychology, 22,* 38–77. (p. 454)

Gur, R. E., Mozley, D., Resnick, S. M., Shtasel, D., Kohn, M., Zimmerman, R., Herman, G., Atlas, S., Grossman, R., Erwin, R., Gur, R. C. (1991). Magnetic resonance imaging in schizophrenia. *Archives of General Psychiatry, 48,* 407–412. (p. 403)

Gustavson, C. R., Garcia, J., Hankins, W. G., & Rusiniak, K. W. (1974). Coyote predation control by aversive conditioning. *Science, 184,* 581–583. (p. 184)

Gutierres, S. E., Kenrick, D. T., & Goldberg, L. (1985). *Adverse influence on exposure to popular erotica: Effects on judgments of others and judgments of one's spouse.* Paper presented at the meeting of the Midwestern Psychological Association. (p. 285)

Haber, R. N. (1970, May). How we remember what we see. *Scientific American,* pp. 104–112. (p. 206)

Hafner, H., & Schmidtke, A. (1989). Do televised fictional suicide models produce suicides? In D. R. Pfeffer (Ed.), *Suicide among youth: Perspectives on risk and prevention.* Washington, DC: American Psychiatric Press. (p. 449)

Hahn, W. K. (1987). Cerebral lateralization of function: From infancy through childhood. *Psychological Bulletin, 101,* 376–392. (p. 54)

Hall, C. S., & Lindzey, G. (1978). *Theories of personality* (2nd ed.). New York: Wiley. (p. 354)

Hall, C. S., & Van de Castle, R. L. (1966). *The content analysis of dreams.* New York: Appleton-Century-Crofts. (p. 156)

Hall, C. S., Dornhoff, W., Blick, K. A., & Weesner, K. E. (1982). The dreams of college men and women in 1950 and 1980: A comparison of dream contents and sex differences. *Sleep, 5,* 188–194. (p. 156)

Hall, G. S. (1904). *Adolescence: Its psychology and its relations to physiology, anthropology, sex, crime, religion and education* (Vol. I). New York: Appleton-Century-Crofts. (p. 78)

Hall, J. A. (1987). On explaining gender differences: The case of nonverbal communication. In P. Shaver & C. Hendrick (Eds.), *Review of Personality and Social Psychology, 7,* 177–200. (pp. 487, 488)

Hall, N. R., & Goldstein, A. L. (1986, March/April). Thinking well: The chemical links between emotions and health. *The Sciences,* pp. 34–40. (p. 333)

Hall, T. (1987, September 27). Cravings: Does your body know what it needs? *The New York Times Magazine: Good Health Magazine,* pp. 23, 62–65. (p. 274)

Halpern, D. F. (1986). *Sex differences in cognitive abilities.* Hillsdale, NJ: Erlbaum. (p. 485)

Hamill, R., Wilson, T. D., & Nisbett, R. E. (1980). Insensitivity to sample bias: Generalizing from atypical cases. *Journal of Personality and Social Psychology, 39,* 578–589. (p. 238)

Hamilton, M. C. (1988). Using masculine generics: Does generic "he" increase male bias in the user's imagery? *Sex Roles, 19,* 785–799. (p. 249)

Hammersmith, S. K. (1982). *Sexual preference: An empirical study from the Alfred C. Kinsey Institute for Sex Research.* Paper presented at the American Psychological Association convention. (p. 288)

Hansel, C. E. M. (1980). *ESP and parapsychology: A critical reevaluation.* Buffalo, NY: Prometheus. (p. 142)

Hansel, C. E. M. (1985). The search for a demonstration of ESP. In P. Kurtz (Ed.), *A skeptic's handbook of parapsychology.* Buffalo, NY: Prometheus. (p. 142)

Hansen, C. H., & Hansen, R. D. (1988). Finding the face-in-the-crowd: An anger superiority effect. *Journal of Personality and Social Psychology, 54,* 917–924. (p. 305)

Hare, R. D. (1975). Psychophysiological studies of psychopathy. In D. C. Fowles (Ed.), *Clinical applications of psychophysiology.* New York: Columbia University Press. (p. 405)

Harkins, S. G., & Szymanski, K. (1989). Social loafing and group evaluation. *Journal of Personality and Social Psychology, 56,* 934–941. (p. 455)

Harlow, H. F., Harlow, M. K., & Suomi, S. J. (1971). From thought to therapy: Lessons from a primate laboratory. *American Scientist, 59,* 538–549. (p. 71)

Harper's Index. (1989, November). *Harper's,* p. 15. (p. 488)

Harrell, T. H., & Stolp, R. D. (1985). Effects of erotic guided imagery on female sexual arousal and emotional response. *Journal of Sex Research, 21,* 292–304. (p. 285)

Harrington, D. M., Block, J. H., & Block, J. (1987). Testing aspects of Carl Rogers's theory of creative environments: Child-rearing antecedents of creative potential in young adolescents. *Journal of Personality and Social Psychology, 52,* 851–856. (p. 363)

Harris, D. (1979). Whatever happened to Little Albert? *American Psychologist, 34,* 151–160. (p. 186)

Harris, L. (1987). *Inside America.* New York: Random House. (p. 327)

Harris, L., & Associates. (1986). American teens speak: Sex, myths, TV, and birth control: The Planned Parenthood Poll. Available from Planned Parenthood, 810 Seventh Avenue, New York, NY 10019. (p. 84)

Harris, L., & Associates. (1988, January 26). Sexual material on American network television during the 1987–88 season. Available from Planned Parenthood, 810 Seventh Avenue, New York. (p. 85)

Harris, L. J. (1978). Sex differences in spatial ability: Possible environmental, genetic, and neurological factors. In M. Kinsbourne (Ed.), *The asymmetrical function of the brain.* New York: Cambridge University Press. (p. 494)

Hartmann, E. (1981, April). The strangest sleep disorder. *Psychology Today,* pp. 14, 16, 18. (p. 155)

Hartmann, E. (1984). *The nightmare: The psychology and biology of terrifying dreams.* New York: Basic Books. (p. 155)

Hartshorne, H., & May, M. A. (1928). *Studies in deceit.* New York: Macmillan. (p. 360)

Hartup, W. W. (1989). Social relationships and their developmental significance. *American Psychologist, 44,* 120–126. (p. 74)

Harvey, S. M. (1987). Female sexual behavior: Fluctuations during the menstrual cycle. *Journal of Psychosomatic Research, 31,* 101–110. (p. 284)

Haskins, R. (1989). Beyond metaphor: The efficacy of early childhood education. *American Psychologist, 44,* 274–282. (p. 263)

Hassan, R., & Carr, J. (1989). Changing patterns of suicide in Australia. *Australian and New Zealand Journal of Psychiatry, 23,* 226–234. (p. 393)

Hatfield, E. (1988). Passionate and companionate love. In R. J. Sternberg & M. L. Barnes (Eds.), *The psychology of love.* New Haven: Yale University Press. (p. 469)

Hatfield, E., & Sprecher, S. (1986). *Mirror, mirror . . . The importance of looks in everyday life.* Albany: State University of New York Press. (p. 467)

Hathaway, S. R. (1960). *An MMPI Handbook* (Vol. 1, Foreword). Minneapolis: University of Minnesota Press. (Revised edition, 1972). (p. 359)

Hattie, J. A., Sharpley, C. F., & Rogers, H. J. (1984). Comparative effectiveness of professional and paraprofessional helpers. *Psychological Bulletin, 95,* 534–541. (p. 433)

Hayes, J. R. (1981). *The complete problem solver.* Philadelphia: Franklin Institute Press. (p. 221)

Hazelrigg, M. D., Cooper, H. M., & Borduin, C. M. (1987). Evaluating the effectiveness of family therapies: An integrative review and analysis. *Psychological Bulletin, 101,* 428–442. (p. 418)

Headey, B., & Wearing, A. (1988). The sense of relative superiority—central to well-being. *Social Indicators Research, 20,* 497–516. (p. 365)

Hearold, S. (1986). A synthesis of 1043 effects of television on social behavior. In G. Comstock (Ed.), *Public communication and behavior.* New York: Academic Press. (p. 461)

Heath, A. C., Jardine, R., & Martin, N. G. (1989). Interactive effects of genotype and social environment on alcohol consumption in female twins. *Journal of Studies on Alcohol, 50,* 38–48. (p. 174)

Heath, L., & Petraitis, J. (1987). Television viewing and fear of crime: Where is the mean world? *Basic and Applied Social Psychology, 8,* 97–123. (p. 462)

Hebb, D. O. (1980). *Essay on mind.* Hillsdale, NJ: Erlbaum. 9–16. (p. 301)

Hebert, H. J. (1988, January 13). Airlines hit 5-year high in fatalities. *Detroit Free Press,* pp. 1A, 16A. (p. 239)

Heider, F. (1958). *The psychology of interpersonal relations.* New York: Wiley. (p. 443)

Heiman, J. R. (1975, April). The physiology of erotica: Women's sexual arousal. *Psychology Today,* 90–94. (p. 285)

Heller, W. (1990, May/June). Of one mind: Second thoughts about the brain's dual nature. *The Sciences,* pp. 38–44. (p. 53)

Helzer, J. E., Canino, G. J., Eng-Kung, Y., Bland, R. C., Lee, C. K., Hwu, H-G., & Newman, S. (1990). Alcoholism—North America and Asia. *Archives of General Psychiatry, 47,* 313–319. (p. 168)

Hembree, R. (1988). Correlates, causes, effects, and treatment of test anxiety. *Review of Educational Research, 58,* 47–77. (p. 302)

Hendrick, S. S., Hendrick, C., Slapion-Foote, J., & Foote, F. H. (1985). Gender differences in sexual attitudes. *Journal of Personality and Social Psychology, 48,* 1630–1642. (p. 488)

Henley, N. M. (1989). Molehill or mountain? What we know and don't know about sex bias in language. In M. Crawford & M. Gentry (Eds.), *Gender and thought: Psychological perspectives.* New York: Springer-Verlag. (p. 249)

Henry, J. P., & Stephens, P. M. (1977). *Stress, health, and the social environment.* New York: Springer-Verlag. (p. 328)

Herek, G. M. (1989). Hate crimes against lesbians and gay men: Issues for research and policy. *American Psychologist, 44,* 948–955. (p. 497)

Herman, C. P., & Polivy, J. (1980). Restrained eating. In A. J. Stunkard (Ed.), *Obesity.* Philadelphia: Saunders. (p. 281)

Herrnstein, R. J., & Loveland, D. H. (1964). Complex visual concept in the pigeon. *Science, 146,* 549–551. (p. 189)

Hershenson, M. (1989). *The moon illusion.* Hillsdale, NJ: Erlbaum. (p. 132)

Hess, E. H. (1956, July). Space perception in the chick. *Scientific American,* pp. 71–80. (p. 136)

Hetherington, E. M. (1979). Divorce: A child's perspective. *American Psychologist, 34,* 851–858. (p. 77)

Hetherington, E. M., & Clingempeel, W. G. (1992). Coping with marital transitions: A family systems perspective. *Society for Research in Child Development Monographs,* in press. (p. 76)

Hetherington, E. M., Stanley-Hagan, M., & Anderson, E. R. (1989). Marital transitions: A child's perspective. *American Psychologist, 44,* 303–312. (p. 76)

Higgins, E. T. (1987). Self-discrepancy: A theory relating self and affect. *Psychological Review, 94,* 319–340. (p. 364)

Hilgard, E. R. (1986). *Divided consciousness: Multiple controls in human thought and action.* New York: Wiley. (p. 165)

Hines, M. (1982). Prenatal gonadal hormones and sex differences in human behavior. *Psychological Bulletin, 92,* 56–80. (p. 489)

Hines, M. (1990). Gonadal hormones and human cognitive development. In J. Balthazart (Ed.), *Hormones, brain and behaviour in vertebrates, I. Sexual differentiation, neuroanatomical aspects, neurotransmitters and neuropeptides.* Basel, Switzerland: Karger. (p. 489)

Hintzman, D. L. (1978). *The psychology of learning and memory.* San Francisco: Freeman. (p. 213)

Hinz, L. D., & Williamson, D. A. (1987). Bulimia and depression: A review of the affective variant hypothesis. *Psychological Bulletin, 102,* 150–158. (p. 277)

Hirst, W., Neisser, U., & Spelke, E. (1978, June). Divided attention. *Human Nature,* pp. 54–61. (p. 165)

Hobfoll, S. E. (1989). Conservation of resources: A new attempt at conceptualizing stress. *American Psychologist, 44,* 513–524. (p. 323)

Hobfoll, S. E., Lomranz, J., Eyal, N., Bridges, A., & Tzemach, M. (1989). Pulse of a nation: Depressive mood reactions of Israelis to the Israel-Lebanon war. *Journal of Personality and Social Psychology, 56,* 1002–1012. (p. 395)

Hobson, J. A. (1988). *The dreaming brain.* New York: Basic Books. (p. 158)

Hochschild, A. (1989). *The second shift: Working parents and the revolution at home.* New York: Viking. (p. 493)

Hoebel, B. G., & Teitelbaum, P. (1966). Effects of forcefeeding and starvation on food intake and body weight in a rat with ventromedial hypothalamic lesions. *Journal of Comparative and Physiological Psychology, 61,* 189–193. (p. 275)

Hoffman, C., & Hurst, N. (1990). Gender stereotypes: Perception or rationalization? *Journal of Personality and Social Psychology, 58,* 197–208. (p. 497)

Hoffman, C., Lau, I., & Johnson, D. R. (1986). The linguistic relativity of person cognition: An English-Chinese comparison. *Journal of Personality and Social Psychology, 51,* 1097–1105. (p. 249)

Hogan, J. (1989). Personality correlates of physical fitness. *Journal of Personality and Social Psychology, 56,* 284–288. (p. 335)

Hohmann, G. W. (1966). Some effects of spinal cord lesions on experienced emotional feelings. *Psychophysiology, 3,* 143–156. (p. 319)

Hokanson, J. E., & Edelman, R. (1966). Effects of three social responses on vascular processes. *Journal of Personality and Social Psychology, 3,* 442–447. (p. 313)

Holden, C. (1980a). Identical twins reared apart. *Science, 207,* 1323–1325. (p. 97)

Holden, C. (1980b, November). Twins reunited. *Science, 80,* 55–59. (p. 97)

Holden, C. (1986a). Days may be numbered for polygraphs in the private sector. *Science, 232,* 705. (p. 304)

Holden, C. (1986b). Researchers grapple with problems of updating classic psychological test. *Science, 233*, 1249–1251. (p. 366)

Holden, C. (1987). Is alcoholism treatment effective? *Science, 236*, 20–22. (p. 422)

Holden, C. (1989) Private sector to do British sex survey. *Science, 246*, 450. (p. 283)

Holden, C. (1991a). Is "gender gap" narrowing? *Science, 253*, 959–960. (p. 485)

Holden, C. (1991b). New center to study therapies and ethnicity. *Science, 251*, 748. (pp. 174, 435)

Holmes, D. S. (1978). Projection as a defense mechanism. *Psychological Bulletin, 85*, 677–688. (p. 353)

Holmes, D. S. (1981). Existence of classical projection and the stress-reducing function of attributive projection: A reply to Sherwood. *Psychological Bulletin, 90*, 460–466. (p. 353)

Holmes, D. S. (1984). Meditation and somatic arousal reduction: A review of the experimental evidence. *American Psychologist, 39*, 1–10. (p. 159)

Holzman, P. S., & Matthysse, S. (1990). The genetics of schizophrenia: A review. *Psychological Science, 1*, 279–286. (p. 108)

Hooper, J., & Teresi, D. (1986). *The three pound universe.* New York: Macmillan. (p. 42)

Hooykaas, R. (1972). *Religion and the rise of modern science.* Grand Rapids, MI: Eerdmans. (p. 6)

Horn, J. L. (1982). The aging of human abilities. In J. Wolman (Ed.), *Handbook of developmental psychology.* Englewood Cliffs, NJ: Prentice-Hall. (p. 90)

Horn, W. F. (1990, October). Psychology can help kids get a Head Start. *APA Monitor*, p. 3. (p. 263)

Horne, J. A. (1989). Sleep loss and "divergent" thinking ability. *Sleep, 11*, 528–536. (p. 154)

House, J. S., Landis, K. R., & Umberson, D. (1988). Social relationships and health. *Science, 241*, 540–545. (p. 339)

House, R. J., & Singh, J. V. (1987). Organizational behavior: Some new directions for I/O psychology. *Annual Review of Psychology, 38*, 669–718. (p. 296)

Hubel, D. H. (1979, September). The brain. *Scientific American*, pp. 45–53. (p. 108)

Hubel, D. H., & Wiesel, T. N. (1979, September). Brain mechanisms of vision. *Scientific American*, pp. 150–162. (p. 114)

Hucker, S. J., & Bain, J. (1990). Androgenic hormones and sexual assault. In W. Marshall, R. Law, & H. Barbaree (Eds.), *The handbook on sexual assault.* New York: Plenum. (p. 284)

Hugick, L. (1989, July). Women play the leading role in keeping modern families close. *Gallup Report*, No. 286, pp. 27–34. (p. 486)

Hui, C. H. (1990). *West meets East: Individualism versus collectivism in North America and Asia.* Invited address, Hope College. (p. 481)

Hull, J. G., & Bond, C. F., Jr. (1986). Social and behavioral consequences of alcohol consumption and expectancy: A meta-analysis. *Psychological Bulletin, 99*, 347–360. (p. 168)

Hull, J. G., Young, R. D., & Jouriles, E. (1986). Applications of the self-awareness model of alcohol consumption: Predicting patterns of use and abuse. *Journal of Personality and Social Psychology, 51*, 790–796. (p. 168)

Hunt, J. M. (1982). Toward equalizing the developmental opportunities of infants and preschool children. *Journal of Social Issues, 38*(4), 163–191. (p. 262)

Hunt, M. (1974). *Sexual behavior in the 1970s.* Chicago: Playboy Press. (p. 286)

Hunt, M. (1987, August 30). Navigating the therapy maze. *The New York Times Magazine*, pp. 28–49. (p. 428)

Hunter, S., & Sundel, M. (Eds.). (1989). *Midlife myths: Issues, findings, and practice implications.* Newbury Park, CA: Sage. (p. 91)

Hutnik, N. (1985). Aspects of identity in a multi-ethnic society. *New Community, 12*, 298–309. (p. 483)

Hyde, J. S. (1983, November). *Bem's gender schema theory.* Paper presented at GLCA Women's Studies Conference, Rochester, IN. (p. 223)

Hyde, J. S. (1984, July). Children's understanding of sexist language. *Developmental Psychology, 20*(4), 697–706. (p. 249)

Hyde, J. S. (1986). Gender differences in aggression. In J. S. Hyde & M. C. Linn (Eds.), *The psychology of gender: Advances through meta-analysis.* Baltimore: Johns Hopkins University Press. (p. 487)

Hyde, J. S., & Linn, M. C. (1988). Gender differences in verbal ability: A meta-analysis. *Psychological Bulletin, 104*, 53–69. (p. 485)

Hyde, J. S., Fennema, E., & Lamon, S. J. (1990). Gender differences in mathematics performance: A meta-analysis. *Psychological Bulletin, 107*, 139–155. (p. 485)

Hyler, S., Gabbard, G. O., & Schneider, I. (1991). Homicidal maniacs and narcissistic parasites: Stigmatization of mentally ill persons in the movies. *Hospital and Community Psychiatry, 42*, 1044–1048. (p. 408)

Hyman, R. (1981). Cold reading: How to convince strangers that you know all about them. In K. Frazier (Ed.), *Paranormal borderlands of science.* Buffalo, NY: Prometheus. (p. 372)

Hyman, R. (1986). Maimonides dream-telepathy experiments. *Skeptical Inquirer, 11*, 91–92. (p. 142)

Hyman, R. B., Feldman, H. R., Harris, R. B., Levin, R. F., & Malloy, G. B. (1989). The effects of relaxation training on clinical symptoms: A meta-analysis. *Nursing Research, 38*, 216–220. (p. 337)

Ingham, A. G., Levinger, G., Graves, J., & Peckham, V. (1974). The Ringelmann effect: Studies of group size and group performance. *Journal of Experimental Social Psychology, 10*, 371–384. (p. 454)

Inglehart, M. R., Markus, H., & Brown, D. R. (1989). The effects of possible selves on academic achievement—a panel study. In J. P. Forgas & J. M. Innes (Eds.), *Recent advances in social psychology: An international perspective.* North-Holland: Elsevier Science Publishers. (p. 364)

Inglehart, R. (1990). *Culture shift in advanced industrial society.* Princeton, NJ: Princeton University Press. (p. 92, 93, 94, 314, 370)

Inhelder, B., & Piaget, J. (1958). *The growth of logical thinking.* New York: Basic Books. (p. 80)

Insel, P. M., & Roth, W. T. (1976). *Health in a changing society.* Palo Alto, CA: Mayfield Press. (p. 86)

Institute of Medicine. (1989). *Behavioral influences on the endocrine and immune systems.* Washington, DC: National Academy Press. (p. 331)

Isen, A. M., & Means, B. (1983). The influence of positive affect on decision making strategy. *Social Cognition, 2,* 28–31. (p. 313)

Izard, C. E. (1977). *Human emotions.* New York: Plenum Press. (pp. 307, 310)

Jackson, J. M., & Williams, K. D. (1988). Social loafing: A review and theoretical analysis. Unpublished manuscript, Fordham University. (p. 454)

Jacobs, B. L. (1987). How hallucinogenic drugs work. *American Scientist, 75,* 386–392. (p. 171)

Jacobs, M. K., & Goodman, G. (1989). Psychology and self-help groups: Predictions on a partnership. *American Psychologist, 44,* 536–545. (p. 418)

Jacobs, W. J., & Nadel, L. (1985). Stress-induced recovery of fears and phobias. *Psychological Bulletin, 92,* 512–531. (p. 387)

James, W. (1890). *The principles of psychology* (Vol. 2). New York: Holt. (pp. 2, 3, 23, 166, 225, 229, 309, 319, 363, 448, 479)

James, W. (1902; reprinted 1958). *Varieties of religious experience.* New York: Mentor Books. (p. 313)

Jameson, D. (1985). Opponent-colors theory in light of physiological findings. In D. Ottoson & S. Zeki (Eds.), *Central and peripheral mechanisms of color vision.* New York: Macmillan. (p. 117)

Jamison, K. R. (1989). Mood disorders and patterns of creativity in British writers and artists. *Psychiatry, 52,* 125–134. (p. 394)

Janis, I. L. (1982). *Groupthink: Psychological studies of policy decisions and fiascoes.* Boston: Houghton Mifflin. (p. 456)

Janis, I. L. (1986). Problems of international crisis management in the nuclear age. *Journal of Social Issues, 42*(2), 201–220. (p. 237)

Janoff-Bulman, R., Timko, C., & Carli, L. L. (1985). Cognitive biases in blaming the victim. *Journal of Experimental Social Psychology, 21,* 161–177. (p. 499)

Jarvik, L. F. (1975). Thoughts on the psychobiology of aging. *American Psychologist, 30,* 576–583. (p. 88)

Jasnoski, M. L., Kugler, J., & McClelland, D. C. (1986). *Power imagery and relaxation affect psychoneuroimmune indices.* Paper presented at the American Psychological Association convention. (p. 337)

Jemmott, J. B., III, & Locke, S. E. (1984). Psychosocial factors, immunologic mediation, and human susceptibility to infectious diseases: How much do we know? *Psychological Bulletin, 95,* 78–108. (p. 331)

Jemmott, J. B., III, & Magloire, K. (1988). Academic stress, social support, and secretory immunoglobulin A. *Journal of Personality and Social Psychology, 55,* 803–810. (p. 331)

Jenkins, J. G., & Dallenbach, K. M. (1924). Obliviscence during sleep and waking. *American Journal of Psychology, 35,* 605–612. (pp. 226, 227)

Jepson, C., Krantz, D. H., & Nisbett, R. E. (1983). Inductive reasoning: Competence or skill. *The Behavioral and Brain Sciences, 3,* 494–501. (p. 519)

Jervis, R. (1985, April 2). Quoted by D. Goleman, Political forces come under new scrutiny of psychology. *The New York Times,* pp. C1, C4. (p. 241)

John, O. P. (1990). The "big five" factor taxonomy: Dimensions of personality in the natural language and in questionnaires. In L. A. Pervin (Ed.), *Handbook of personality: Theory and research.* New York: Guilford Press. (p. 358)

Johnson, D. (1990). Animal rights and human lives: Time for scientists to right the balance. *Psychological Science, 1,* 213–214. (p. 19)

Johnson, D. W., & Johnson, R. T. (1987). *Learning together and alone: Cooperative, competitive, and individualistic learning* (2nd ed.). Englewood Cliffs, NJ: Prentice-Hall. (p. 502)

Johnson, E. J., & Tversky, A. (1983). Affect, generalization, and the perception of risk. *Journal of Personality and Social Psychology, 45,* 20–31. (p. 313)

Johnson, J. S., & Newport, E. L. (1989). Critical period effects in second language learning: The influence of maturational state on the acquisition of English as a second language. *Cognitive Psychology, 21,* 60–99. (p. 246)

Johnston, L. D., O'Malley, P. M., & Bachman, J. G. (1992, January 27). *Annual report of drug use survey.* Ann Arbor: University of Michigan News and Information Services. (pp. 170, 173)

Jones, E. E., Cumming, J. D., & Horowitz, M. J. (1988). Another look at the nonspecific hypothesis of therapeutic effectiveness. *Journal of Consulting and Clinical Psychology, 56,* 48–55. (p. 432)

Jones, J. M. (1988). *Piercing the veil: Bi-cultural strategies for coping with prejudice and racism.* Invited address, national conference, "Opening doors: An appraisal of race relations in America," University of Alabama. (p. 482)

Jones, J. M. (1990). *Promoting diversity in an individualistic society.* Keynote address, Great Lakes College Association conference, "Multiculturalism transforming the 21st century." (pp. 477, 482)

Jones, L. (1985–86). CSICOP's international conference in London: Investigation and belief, past lives and prizes. *Skeptical Inquirer, 10,* 98–104. (p. 143)

Jones, M. C. (1924). A laboratory study of fear: The case of Peter. *Journal of Genetic Psychology, 31,* 308–315. (p. 420)

Jones, M. C. (1957). The later careers of boys who were early or late maturing. *Child Development, 28,* 113–128. (p. 79)

Jones, S. S., Collins, K., & Hong, H-W. (1991). An audience effect on smile production in 10-month-old infants. *Psychological Science, 2,* 45–49. (p. 308)

Jones, W. H., Carpenter, B. N., & Quintana, D. (1985). Personality and interpersonal predictors of loneliness in two cultures. *Journal of Personality and Social Psychology, 48,* 1503–1511. (p. 18)

Jorgenson, D. O., & Papciak, A. S. (1981). The effects of communication, resource feedback, and identifiability on behavior in a simulated commons. *Journal of Experimental Social Psychology, 17,* 373–385. (p. 503)

Jorm, A. F., Korten, A. E., & Henderson, A. S. (1987). The prevalence of dementia: A quantitative integration of the literature. *Acta Psychiatrica Scandinavica, 76,* 465–479. (p. 88)

Joseph, J. G., Montgomery, S. B., Emmons, C-A., Kirscht, J. P., Kessler, R. C., Ostrow, D. G., Wortman, C. B., O'Brien, K., Eller, M., & Eshleman, S. (1987). Perceived risk of AIDS: Assessing the behavioral and psychosocial consequences in a cohort of gay men. *Journal of Applied Social Psychology, 17,* 231–250. (p. 288)

Jung, C. (1933). *Modern man in search of a soul*. New York: Harcourt Brace Jovanovich. (p. 94)

Juster, F. T., & Stafford, F. P. (1991). The allocation of time: Empirical findings, behavioral models, and problems of measurement. *Journal of Economic Literature, 29*, 471–522. (p. 493)

Justice, A. (1985). Review of the effects of stress on cancer in laboratory animals: Importance of time of stress application and type of tumor. *Psychological Bulletin, 98*, 108–138. (p. 333)

Kagan, J. (1976). Emergent themes in human development. *American Scientist, 64*, 186–196. (p. 73)

Kagan, J. (1984). *The nature of the child*. New York: Basic Books. (p. 67)

Kagan, J. (1989a). Temperamental contributions to social behavior. *American Psychologist, 44*, 668–674. (p. 72)

Kagan, J. (1989b). *Unstable ideas: Temperament, cognition, and self.* Cambridge, MA: Harvard University Press. (pp. 353, 356)

Kahn, S., Zimmerman, G., Csikszentmihalyi, M., & Getzels, J. W. (1985). Relations between identity in young adulthood and intimacy in midlife. *Journal of Personality and Social Psychology, 49*, 1316–1322. (p. 83)

Kahneman, D. (1985, June). Quoted by K. McKean, Decisions, decisions. *Discover*, pp. 22–31. (p. 516)

Kahneman, D., & Tversky, A. (1972). Subjective probability: A judgment of representativeness. *Cognitive Psychology, 3*, 430–454. (p. 517)

Kahneman, D., Knetsch, J. L., & Thaler, R. (1986). Fairness as a constraint on profit seeking: Entitlements in the market. *American Economic Review, 76*, 728–741. (p. 240)

Kail, R. (1991). Developmental change in speed of processing during childhood and adolescence. *Psychological Bulletin, 109*, 490–501. (p. 88)

Kamarck, T., & Jennings, J. R. (1991). Biobehavioral factors in sudden cardiac death. *Psychological Bulletin, 109*, 42–75. (p. 330)

Kandel, D. B., & Raveis, V. H. (1989). Cessation of illicit drug use in young adulthood. *Archives of General Psychiatry, 46*, 109–116. (p. 174)

Kandel, E. R., & Schwartz, J. H. (1982). Molecular biology of learning: Modulation of transmitter release. *Science, 218*, 433–443. (p. 218)

Kanekar, S., & Nazareth, A. (1988). Attributed rape victim's fault as a function of her attractiveness, physical hurt, and emotional disturbance. *Social Behaviour, 3*, 37–40. (p. 488)

Kaplan, H. I., & Saddock, B. J. (Eds.). (1989). *Comprehensive textbook of psychiatry, V.* Baltimore, MD: Williams and Wilkins. (p. 435)

Kaplan, H. S. (1979). *Disorders of sexual desire*. New York: Brunner/Mazel. (p. 284)

Kaprio, J., Koskenvu, M., & Rita, H. (1987). Mortality after bereavement: A prospective study of 95,647 widowed persons. *American Journal of Public Health, 77*, 283–287. (p. 326)

Karacan, I., Aslan, C., & Hirshkowitz, M. (1983). Erectile mechanisms in man. *Science, 220*, 1080–1082. (p. 153)

Karacan, I., Goodenough, D. R., Shapiro, A., & Starker, S. (1966). Erection cycle during sleep in relation to dream anxiety. *Archives of General Psychiatry, 15*, 183–189. (p. 153)

Karno, M., Golding, J. M., Sorenson, S. B., & Burnam, A. (1988). The epidemiology of obsessive-compulsive disorder in five US communities. *Archives of General Psychiatry, 45*, 1094–1099. (p. 386)

Kaufman, A. S., Reynolds, C. R., & McLean, J. E. (1989). Age and WAIS-R intelligence in a national sample of adults in the 20- to 74-year age range: A cross-sectional analysis with educational level controlled. *Intelligence, 13*, 235–253. (p. 90)

Kaufman, J., & Zigler, E. (1987). Do abused children become abusive parents? *American Journal of Orthopsychiatry, 57*, 186–192. (p. 75)

Kaufman, L. (1979). *Perception: The world transformed*. New York: Oxford University Press. (p. 118)

Kaufman, L., & Rock, I. (1962). The moon illusion I. *Science, 136*, 953–961. (p. 132)

Kaylor, J. A., King, D. W., & King, L. A. (1987). Psychological effects of military service in Vietnam: A meta-analysis. *Psychological Bulletin, 102*, 257–271. (p. 325)

Kazdin, A. E. (1982). The token economy: A decade later. *Journal of Applied Behavior Analysis, 15*, 431–445. (p. 423)

Keesey, R. E., & Corbett, S. W. (1983). Metabolic defense of the body weight set-point. In A. J. Stunkard & E. Stellar (Eds.), *Eating and its disorders*. New York: Raven Press. (p. 275)

Kellerman, J., Lewis, J., & Laird, J. D. (1989). Looking and loving: The effects of mutual gaze on feelings of romantic love. *Journal of Research in Personality, 23*, 145–161. (p. 305)

Kelling, S. T., & Halpern, B. P. (1983). Taste flashes: Reaction times, intensity, and quality. *Science, 219*, 412–414. (p. 120)

Kempe, R. S., & Kempe, C. C. (1978). *Child abuse*. Cambridge, MA: Harvard University Press. (p. 73)

Kennedy, S., & Over, R. (1990). Psychophysiological assessment of male sexual arousal following spinal cord injury. *Archives of Sexual Behavior, 19*, 15–27. (p. 29)

Kenrick, D. T. (1987). Gender, genes, and the social environment. In P. C. Shaver & C. Hendrick (Eds.), *Review of Personality and Social Psychology, 8*, 14–43. (pp. 487, 494)

Kenrick, D. T., & Funder, D. C. (1988). Profiting from controversy: Lessons from the person-situation debate. *American Psychologist, 43*, 23–34. (p. 361)

Kenrick, D. T., & Gutierres, S. E. (1980). Contrast effects and judgments of physical attractiveness: When beauty becomes a social problem. *Journal of Personality and Social Psychology, 38*, 131–140. (p. 285)

Kenrick, D. T., & Trost, M. R. (1987). A biosocial theory of heterosexual relationships. In K. Kelly (Ed.), *Females, males, and sexuality*. Albany: State University of New York Press. (p. 488)

Kenrick, D. T., & Trost, M. R. (1989). Reproductive exchange model of heterosexual relationships: Putting proximate economics in ultimate perspective. In C. Hendrick (Ed.), *Review of personality and social psychology* (Vol. 10). Newbury Park, CA: Sage. (p. 489)

Kerr, N. L., & Bruun, S. E. (1983). Dispensability of member effort and group motivation losses: Free-rider effects. *Journal of Personality and Social Psychology, 44*, 78–94. (p. 455)

Kessler, M., & Albee, G. (1975). Primary prevention. *Annual Review of Psychology, 26*, 557–591. (p. 439)

Keys, A., Brozek, J., Henschel, A., Mickelsen, O., & Taylor, H. L. (1950). *The biology of human starvation.* Minneapolis: University of Minnesota Press. (p. 272)

Kihlstrom, J. F. (1985). Hypnosis. *Annual Review of Psychology, 36,* 385–418. (pp. 160, 163)

Kihlstrom, J. F. (1987). The cognitive unconscious. *Science, 237,* 1445–1452. (p. 150)

Kihlstrom, J. F. (1990). The psychological unconscious. In L. A. Pervin (Ed.), *Handbook of personality: Theory and research.* New York: Guilford Press. (p. 353)

Kihlstrom, J. F., & Harachkiewicz, J. M. (1982). The earliest recollection: A new survey. *Journal of Personality, 50,* 134–148. (p. 63)

Kihlstrom, J. F., & McConkey, K. M. (1990). William James and hypnosis: A centennial reflection. *Psychological Science, 1,* 174–177. (pp. 166, 227)

Kimball, M. M. (1989). A new perspective on women's math achievement. *Psychological Bulletin, 105,* 198–214. (p. 485)

Kimble, D. P. (1990). Functional effects of neural grafting in the mammalian central nervous system. *Psychological Bulletin, 108,* 462–479. (p. 50)

Kimble, G. A. (1956). *Principles of general psychology.* New York: Ronald Press. (p. 184)

Kimble, G. A. (1981). *Biological and cognitive constraints on learning.* In L. T. Benjamin, Jr. (Ed.), *The G. Stanley Hall Lecture Series* (Vol. 1). Washington, DC: American Psychological Association. (p. 184)

Kimura, D. (1989, November). How sex hormones boost—or cut—intellectual ability. *Psychology Today,* pp. 62–66. (p. 489)

Kimzey, S. L. (1975). The effects of extended spaceflight on hematologic and immunologic systems. *Journal of the American Medical Women's Association, 30*(5), 218–232. (p. 331)

Kimzey, S. L., Johnson, P. C., Ritzman, S. E., & Mengel, C. E. (1976, April). Hematology and immunology studies: The second manned Skylab mission. *Aviation, Space, and Environmental Medicine,* pp. 383–390. (p. 331)

King, D. W., & King, L. A. (1991). Validity issues in research on Vietnam veteran adjustment. *Psychological Bulletin, 109,* 107–124. (p. 325)

King, N. J., & Montgomery, R. B. (1980). Biofeedback-induced control of human peripheral temperature: A critical review of the literature. *Psychological Bulletin, 88,* 738–752. (p. 337)

King, P. (1991, March 18). Bawl players. *Sports Illustrated,* pp. 14–17. (p. 316)

Kinsey, A. C., Pomeroy, W., & Martin, C. (1948). *Sexual behavior in the human male.* Philadelphia: Saunders. (p. 282)

Kinsey, A. C., Pomeroy, W., Martin, C., & Gebhard, P. (1953). *Sexual behavior in the human female.* Philadelphia: Saunders. (p. 282)

Kite, M. E., & Johnson, B. T. (1988). Attitudes toward older and younger adults: A meta-analysis. *Psychology and Aging, 3,* 233–244. (p. 88)

Klayman, J., & Ha, Y-W. (1987). Confirmation, disconfirmation, and information in hypothesis testing. *Psychological Review, 94,* 211–228. (p. 236)

Kleinke, C. L. (1986). Gaze and eye contact: A research review. *Psychological Bulletin, 100,* 78–100. (p. 305)

Kleinmuntz, B., & Szucko, J. J. (1984). A field study of the fallibility of polygraph lie detection. *Nature, 308,* 449–450. (p. 304)

Kleitman, N. (1960, November). Patterns of dreaming. *Scientific American,* pp. 82–88. (p. 152)

Klerman, G. L., & Weissman, M. M. (1989). Increasing rates of depression. *Journal of the American Medical Association, 261,* 2220–2235. (p. 393)

Kline, D., & Schieber, F. (1985). Vision and aging. In J. E. Birren & K. W. Schaie (Eds.), *Handbook of the psychology of aging.* New York: Van Nostrand Reinhold. (p. 87)

Kline, N. S. (1974). *From sad to glad.* New York: Ballantine Books. (p. 398)

Klineberg, O. (1938). Emotional expression in Chinese literature. *Journal of Abnormal and Social Psychology, 33,* 517–520. (p. 307)

Klineberg, O. (1984). Public opinion and nuclear war. *American Psychologist, 39,* 1245–1253. (p. 503)

Kluft, R. P. (1987). An update on multiple personality disorder. *Hospital and Community Psychiatry, 38,* 363–373. (p. 391)

Klüver, H., & Bucy, P. C. (1939). Preliminary analysis of functions of the temporal lobes in monkeys. *Archives of Neurology and Psychiatry, 42,* 979–1000. (p. 40)

Koestner, R., Franz, C., & Weinberger, J. (1990). The family origins of empathic concern: A 26-year longitudinal study. *Journal of Personality and Social Psychology, 58,* 709–717. (p. 74)

Kohlberg, L. (1981). *The philosophy of moral development: Essays on moral development* (Vol. I). San Francisco: Harper & Row. (p. 81)

Kohlberg, L. (1984). *The psychology of moral development: Essays on moral development* (Vol. II). San Francisco: Harper & Row. (p. 81)

Köhler, W. (1925; reprinted 1957). *The mentality of apes.* London: Pelican. (p. 235)

Kohn, A. (1987, October). It's hard to get left out of a pair. *Psychology Today,* pp. 53–57. (p. 502)

Kolata, G. (1985). Obesity declared a disease. *Science, 227,* 1019–1020. (p. 276)

Kolata, G. (1986). Youth suicide: New research focuses on a growing social problem. *Science, 233,* 839–841. (p. 393)

Kolata, G. (1987). Metabolic catch-22 of exercise regimens. *Science, 236,* 146–147. (p. 281)

Kolb, B. (1989). Brain development, plasticity, and behavior. *American Psychologist, 44,* 1203–1212. (p. 49)

Kolers, P. A. (1975). Specificity of operations in sentence recognition. *Cognitive Psychology, 7,* 289–306. (p. 210)

Koltz, C. (1983, December). Scapegoating. *Psychology Today,* pp. 68–69. (p. 498)

Koss, M. P. (1992). The underdetection of rape: Methodological choices influence incidence estimates. *Journal of Social Issues, 48,* 61–75. (p. 462)

Koss, M. P., & Burkhart, B. R. (1989). A conceptual analysis of rape victimization. *Psychology of Women Quarterly, 13,* 27–40. (p. 462)

Koss, M. P., Dinero, T. E., Seibel, C. A., & Cox, S. L. (1988). Stranger and acquaintance rape: Are there differences in the victim's experience? *Psychology of Women Quarterly, 12,* 1–24. (p. 462)

Koss, M. P., Gidycz, C. A., & Wisniewski, N. (1987). The scope of rape: Incidence and prevalence of sexual aggression and victimization in a national sample of higher education students. *Journal of Consulting and Clinical Psychology, 55,* 162–170. (p. 462)

Koss, M. P., Koss, P., & Woodruff, W. J. (1990). Relation of criminal victimization to health perceptions among women medical patients. *Journal of Consulting and Clinical Psychology, 58,* 147–152. (p. 462)

Kotva, H. J., & Schneider, H. G. (1990). Those "talks"—general and sexual communication between mothers and daughters. *Journal of Social Behavior and Personality, 5,* 603–613. (p. 85)

Kraft, C. (1978). A psychophysical approach to air safety: Simulator studies of visual illusions in night approaches. In H. L. Pick, H. W. Leibowitz, J. E. Singer, A. Steinschneider, & H. W. Stevenson (Eds.), *Psychology: From research to practice.* New York: Plenum Press. (p. 139)

Kraus, S. J. (1991). Attitudes and the prediction of behavior. Doctoral dissertation, Harvard University. (p. 445)

Kraut, R. E., & Johnston, R. E. (1979). Social and emotional messages of smiling: An ethological approach. *Journal of Personality and Social Psychology, 37,* 1539–1553. (p. 308)

Krosnick, J. A., & Alwin, D. F. (1989). Aging and susceptibility to attitude change. *Journal of Personality and Social Psychology, 57,* 416–425. (p. 100)

Krosnick, J. A., & Schuman, H. (1988). Attitude intensity, importance, and certainty and susceptibility to response effects. *Journal of Personality and Social Psychology, 54,* 940–952. (p. 8)

Kübler-Ross, E. (1969). *On death and dying.* New York: Macmillan. (p. 94)

Kuhl, P. K., & Meltzoff, A. N. (1982). The bimodal perception of speech in infancy. *Science, 218,* 1138–1141. (p. 243)

Kuiper, N.A., & Rogers, T. B. (1979). Encoding of personal information: Self-other differences. *Journal of Personality and Social Psychology, 37,* 499–514. (p. 212)

Kulik, J. A., Kulik, C. C., & Bangert-Drowns, R. L. (1985). Effectiveness of computer-based education in elementary schools. *Computers in Human Behavior, 1,* 59–74. (p. 197)

Kulik, J. A., Kulik, C. C., & Cohen, P. A. (1980). Effectiveness of computer-based college teaching: A meta-analysis of findings. *Review of Educational Research, 50,* 525–544. (p. 197)

Kunst-Wilson, W. R., & Zajonc, R. B. (1980). Affective discrimination of stimuli that cannot be recognized. *Science, 207,* 557–558. (p. 107)

Kurtz, P. (1983, Spring). Stars, planets, and people. *The Skeptical Inquirer,* pp. 65–68. (p. 372)

Labbe, R., Firl, A., Jr., Mufson, E. J., & Stein, D. G. (1983). Fetal brain transplants: Reduction of cognitive deficits in rats with frontal cortex lesions. *Science, 221,* 470–472. (p. 49)

Labouvie-Vief, G., & Schell, D. A. (1982). Learning and memory in later life. In B. B. Wolman (Ed.), *Handbook of developmental psychology.* Englewood Cliffs, NJ: Prentice-Hall. (p. 89)

Ladd, G. T. (1887). *Elements of physiological psychology.* New York: Scribner's. (p. 149)

Lagerweij, E., Nelis, P. C., van Ree, J. M., & Wiegant, V. M. (1984). The twitch in horses: A variant of acupuncture. *Science, 225,* 1172–1174. (p. 32)

Laird, J. D. (1974). Self-attribution of emotion: The effects of expressive behavior on the quality of emotional experience. *Journal of Personality and Social Psychology, 29,* 475–486. (p. 308)

Laird, J. D. (1984). The real role of facial response in the experience of emotion: A reply to Tourangeau and Ellsworth, and others. *Journal of Personality and Social Psychology, 47,* 909–917. (p. 308)

Laird, J. D., Cuniff, M., Sheehan, K., Shulman, D., & Strum, G. (1989). Emotion specific effects of facial expressions on memory for life events. *Journal of Social Behavior and Personality, 4,* 87–98. (p. 308)

Lamb, M. (1979, June 17). Quoted by G. Collins, A new look at life with father. *The New York Times Magazine,* pp. 30–31, 48–52, 65. (p. 74)

Landauer, T. K. (1986). How much do people remember? Some estimates of the quantity of learned information in long-term memory. *Cognitive Science, 10,* 477–493. (p. 216)

Landers, A. (1969, April 8). Syndicated newspaper column. Cited by L. Berkowitz, The case for bottling up rage. *Psychology Today,* September, 1973, pp. 24–31. (p. 312)

Landfield, P., Cadwallader, L. B., & Vinsant, S. (1988). Quantitative changes in hippocampal structure following long-term exposure to Delta-9-tetrahydrocannabinol: Possible mediation by glucocorticoid systems. *Brain Research,* Vol. 443, 47–62. (p. 172)

Langer, E. J. (1983). *The psychology of control.* Beverly Hills, CA: Sage. (p. 370)

Langer, E. J., & Abelson, R. P. (1974). A patient by any other name . . . : Clinician group differences in labeling bias. *Journal of Consulting and Clinical Psychology, 42,* 4–9. (p. 407)

Langer, E. J., & Imber, L. (1980). The role of mindlessness in the perception of deviance. *Journal of Personality and Social Psychology, 39,* 360–367. (p. 407)

Langlois, J. H., Roggman, L. A., Casey, R. J., Ritter, J. M., Rieser-Danner, L. A., & Jenkins, V. Y. (1987). Infant preferences for attractive faces: Rudiments of a stereotype? *Developmental Psychology, 23,* 363–369. (p. 468)

Larsen, R. J., Diener, E., & Cropanzano, R. S. (1987). Cognitive operations associated with individual differences in affect intensity. *Journal of Personality and Social Psychology, 53,* 767–774. (p. 322)

Larson, R. W., & Bradney, N. (1988). Precious moments with family members and friends. In R. M. Milardo (Ed.), *Families and social networks.* Newbury Park, CA: Sage. (p. 83)

Lassiter, G. D., & Irvine, A. A. (1986). Video-taped confessions: The impact of camera point of view on judgments of coercion. *Journal of Personality and Social Psychology, 16,* 268–276. (p. 444)

Latané, B. (1981). The psychology of social impact. *American Psychologist, 36,* 343–356. (p. 454)

Latané, B., & Dabbs, J. M., Jr. (1975). Sex, group size and helping in three cities. *Sociometry, 38,* 180–194. (p. 465)

Laudenslager, M. L., & Reite, M. L. (1984). Losses and separations: Immunological consequences and health implications. *Review of Personality and Social Psychology, 5,* 285–312. (p. 328)

Laurence, J-R., & Perry, C. (1988). *Hypnosis, will and memory: A psycho-legal history.* New York: Guilford. (p. 161)

Layton, B. D., & Turnbull, B. (1975). Belief, evaluation, and performance on an ESP task. *Journal of Experimental Social Psychology, 11,* 166–179. (pp. 141, 143)

Lazarus, R. S. (1984). On the primacy of cognition. *American Psychologist, 39,* 124–129. (p. 321)

Lazarus, R. S. (1990). Theory-based stress measurement. *Psychological Inquiry, 1,* 3–13. (p. 327)

Lazarus, R. S. (1991). Progress on a cognitive-motivational-relational theory of emotion. *American Psychologist, 46,* 819–834. (p. 321)

Lebow, J. (1982). Consumer satisfaction with mental health treatment. *Psychological Bulletin, 91,* 244–259. (p. 429)

LeDoux, J. E. (1986). Sensory systems and emotions: A model of affective processing. *Integrative Psychiatry, 4,* 237–243. (p. 321)

Lee, B. A., Lewis, D. W., & Jones, S. H. (1990). *Blaming the homeless: A test of two theories.* Paper presented at the American Psychological Association convention. (p. 445)

Lefcourt, H. M. (1982). *Locus of control: Current trends in theory and research.* Hillsdale, NJ: Erlbaum. (p. 369)

Lefcourt, H. M., & Davidson-Katz, K. (1991). The role of humor and the self. In C. R. Snyder & D. R. Forsyth (Eds.), *Handbook of social and clinical psychology: The health perspective.* New York: Pergamon Press. (p. 338)

Lehman, D. R. Wortman, C. B., & Williams, A. F. (1987). Long-term effects of losing a spouse or child in a motor vehicle crash. *Journal of Personality and Social Psychology, 52,* 218–231. (p. 94)

Leibowitz, H. W. (1985). Grade crossing accidents and human factors engineering. *American Scientist, 73,* 558–562. (p. 130)

Leigh, B. C. (1989). In search of the seven dwarves: Issues of measurement and meaning in alcohol expectancy research. *Psychological Bulletin, 105,* 361–373. (p. 168)

Lenneberg, E. H. (1967). *Biological foundations of language.* New York: Wiley. (p. 63)

Lenzenweger, M. F., Dworkin, R. H., & Wethington, E. (1989). Models of positive and negative symptoms in schizophrenia: An empirical evaluation of latent structures. *Journal of Abnormal Psychology, 98,* 62–70. (p. 435)

Leo, J. (1990, May 14). No, don't give me a number. *U.S. News & World Report,* p. 22. (p. 488)

Lerner, M. J. (1980). *The belief in a just world: A fundamental delusion.* New York: Plenum Press. (p. 499)

LeVay, S. (1991). A difference in hypothalamic structure between heterosexual and homosexual men. *Science, 253,* 1034–1037. (p. 289)

Levenson, R. W., Ekman, P., Heider, K., & Friesen, W. V. (1991). Emotion and autonomic nervous system activity in an Indonesian culture. Unpublished manuscript, University of California, Berkeley. (p. 303)

Lever, J. (1978). Sex differences in the complexity of children's play and games. *American Sociological Review, 43,* 471–483. (p. 486)

Levin, I. P., & Gaeth, G. J. (1988). How consumers are affected by the framing of attribute information before and after consuming the product. *Journal of Consumer Research, 15,* 374–378. (p. 240)

Levin, I. P., Schnittjer, S. K., & Thee, S. L. (1988). Information framing effects in social and personal decisions. *Journal of Experimental Social Psychology, 24,* 520–529. (pp. 240, 242)

Levine, A. (1990, May 7). America's youthful bigots *U.S. News and World Report,* pp. 59–60. (p. 497)

Levine, B., Roehrs, T., Zorick, F., & Roth, T. (1988). Daytime sleepiness in young adults. *Sleep, 11,* 39–46. (p. 153)

Levine, I. S., & Rog, D. J. (1990). Mental health services for homeless mentally ill persons: Federal initiatives and current service trends. *American Psychologist, 45,* 963–968. (p. 434)

Levine, R. V. (1990). The pace of life. *American Scientist, 78,* 450–459. (p. 478)

Levinson, D. J. (1986). A conception of adult development. *American Psychologist, 41,* 3–13. (p. 91)

Levinson, D. J., Darow, C. N., Klein, E. B., Levinson, M. H., & McKee, B. (1978). *The seasons of a man's life.* New York: Knopf. (p. 91)

Levitt, E. E. (1986). *Coercion, voluntariness, compliance and resistance: The essence of hypnosis twenty-seven years after Orne.* Invited address to the American Psychological Association convention. (p. 163)

Levitt, E. E. (1988). Questions about multiple personality. *Harvard Medical School Mental Health Letter, 4*(10), 8. (p. 390)

Levy, J. (1985, May). Right brain, left brain: Fact and fiction. *Psychology Today,* pp. 38–44. (p. 53)

Lewinsohn, P. M., & Rosenbaum, M. (1987). Recall of parental behavior by acute depressives, remitted depressives, and nondepressives. *Journal of Personality and Social Psychology, 52,* 611–619. (p. 223)

Lewinsohn, P. M., Hoberman, H., Teri, L., & Hautziner, M. (1985). An integrative theory of depression. In S. Reiss & R. Bootzin (Eds.), *Theoretical issues in behavior therapy.* Orlando, FL: Academic Press. (pp. 394, 397)

Lewis, C. C. (1981). The effects of parental firm control: A reinterpretation of findings. *Psychological Bulletin, 90,* 547–563. (p. 77)

Lewis, D. O., Pincus, J. H., Bard, B., Richardson, E., Prichep, L. S., Feldman, M., & Yeager, C. (1988). Neuropsychiatric, psychoeducational, and family characteristics of 14 juveniles condemned to death in the United States. *American Journal of Psychiatry, 145,* 584–589. (p. 73)

Lewis, D. O., Pincus, J. H., Feldman, M., Jackson, L., & Bard, B. (1986). Psychiatric, neurological, and psychoeducational characteristics of 15 death row inmates in the United States. *American Journal of Psychiatry, 143,* 838–845. (p. 459)

Lewontin, R. (1976). Race and intelligence. In N. J. Block & G. Dworkin (Eds.), *The IQ controversy: Critical readings.* New York: Pantheon. (p. 262)

Life (1991, January). Barbie fashion doll proportions. p. 78. (p. 279)

Lifton, R. J. (1986). *The Nazi doctors.* New York: Basic Books. (p. 168)

Light, K. C., Koepke, J. P., Obrist, P. A., & Willis, P. W., Jr. (1983). Psychological stress induces sodium and fluid retention in men at high risk for hypertension. *Science, 220,* 429–431. (p. 331)

Linder, D. (1982). Social trap analogs: The tragedy of the commons in the laboratory. In V. J. Derlega & J. Grzelak (Eds.), *Cooperative and helping behavior: Theories and research.* New York: Academic Press. (p. 500)

Lindskold, S. (1978). Trust development, the GRIT proposal, and the effects of conciliatory acts on conflict and cooperation. *Psychological Bulletin, 85, 772–793.* (p. 503)

Lindskold, S. (1986). GRIT: Reducing distrust through carefully introduced conciliation. In S. Worchel & W. G. Austin (Eds.), *Psychology of intergroup relations* (2nd ed.). Chicago: Nelson-Hall. (p. 503)

Lindskold, S., & Han, G. (1988). GRIT as a foundation for integrative bargaining. *Personality and Social Psychology Bulletin, 14, 335–345.* (p. 503)

Lindskold, S., Han, G., & Betz, B. (1986). Repeated persuasion in interpersonal conflict. *Journal of Personality and Social Psychology, 51,* 1183–1188. (p. 503)

Lindskold, S., Walters, P. S., & Koutsourais, H. (1983). Cooperators, competitors, and response to GRIT. *Journal of Conflict Resolution, 27,* 521–532. (p. 503)

Linn, M. C., & Hyde, J. S. (1991). Trends in cognitive and psychosocial gender differences. In R. M. Lerner, A. C. Petersen, & J. Brooks-Gunn (Eds.), *The encyclopedia of adolescence.* New York: Garland Publishing. (p. 486)

Linn, M. C., & Petersen, A. C. (1986). A meta-analysis of gender differences in spatial ability: Implications for mathematics and science achievement. In J. S. Hyde & M. C. Linn (Eds.), *The psychology of gender: Advances through meta-analysis.* Baltimore: Johns Hopkins University Press. (p. 485)

Linville, P. W. (1987). Self-complexity as a cognitive buffer against stress-related illness and depression. *Journal of Personality and Social Psychology, 52, 663–676.* (p. 93)

Livingstone, M., & Hubel, D. (1988). Segregation of form, color, movement, and depth: Anatomy, physiology, and perception. *Science, 240, 740–749.* (p. 115)

Lock, M., Kaufert, P., & Gilbert, P. (1988). Cultural construction of the menopausal syndrome: The Japanese case. *Maturitas, 10, 317–332.* (p. 87)

Locke, E. A., & Latham, G. P. (1990). Work motivation and satisfaction: Light at the end of the tunnel. *Psychological Science, 1, 240–246.* (p. 295)

Loehlin, J. C., & Nichols, R. C. (1976). *Heredity, environment, and personality.* Austin: University of Texas Press. (pp. 96, 260)

Loewenstein, G., & Furstenberg, F. (1991). Is teenage sexual behavior rational? *Journal of Applied Social Psychology, 21, 957–986.* (p. 191)

Loftus, E. F. (1979). The malleability of human memory. *American Scientist, 67, 313–320.* (p. 224)

Loftus, E. F. (1980). *Memory: Surprising new insights into how we remember and why we forget.* Reading, MA: Addison-Wesley. (p. 161)

Loftus, E. F., & Loftus, G. R. (1980). On the permanence of stored information in the human brain. *American Psychologist, 35, 409–420.* (p. 217)

Loftus, E. F., & Palmer, J. C. (1973). Reconstruction of automobile destruction: An example of the interaction between language and memory. *Journal of Verbal Learning and Verbal Behavior, 13, 585–589.* (p. 224)

Loftus, E. F., Donders, K., Hoffman, H. G., & Schooler, J. W. (1989). Creating new memories that are quickly accessed and confidently held. *Memory and Cognition, 17, 607–616.* (p. 224)

London, P. (1970). The rescuers: Motivational hypotheses about Christians who saved Jews from the Nazis. In J. Macaulay & L. Berkowitz (Eds.), *Altruism and helping behavior.* New York: Academic Press. (pp. 200, 466)

LoPiccolo, J. L., & Stock, W. E. (1986). Treatment of sexual dysfunction. *Journal of Consulting and Clinical Psychology, 54, 158–167.* (p. 286)

Lord, C. G., Lepper, M. R., & Preston, E. (1984). Considering the opposite: A corrective strategy for social judgment. *Journal of Personality and Social Psychology, 47, 1231–1247.* (p. 241)

Lord, C. G., Ross, L., & Lepper, M. (1979). Biased assimilation and attitude polarization: The effects of prior theories on subsequently considered evidence. *Journal of Personality and Social Psychology, 37,* 2098–2109. (p. 240)

Lord, L. J. (1987, November 30). Coming to grips with alcoholism. *U. S. News and World Report,* pp. 56–63. (p. 167)

Lorenz, K. (1937). The companion in the bird's world. *Auk, 54,* 245–273. (p. 72)

Lovaas, O. I. (1987). Behavioral treatment and normal educational and intellectual functioning in young autistic children. *Journal of Consulting and Clinical Psychology, 55, 3–9.* (p. 423)

Lowry, D. T., & Towles, D. E. (1989). Soap opera portrayals of sex, contraception, and sexually transmitted diseases. *Journal of Communication, 39*(2), 76–83. (p. 85)

Lubart, T. I. (1990). Creativity and cross-cultural variation. *International Journal of Psychology, 25, 39–59.* (p. 259)

Lubin, B., Larsen, R. M., & Matarazzo, J. D. (1984). Patterns of psychological test usage in the United States: 1935–1982. *American Psychologist, 39, 451–454.* (p. 352)

Lucas, A., Morley, R., Cole, T. J., Lister, G., & Leeson-Payne, C. (1992). Breast milk and subsequent intelligence quotient in children born preterm. *The Lancet, 339, 261–264.* (p. 103)

Lull, J. (Ed.). (1988). *World families watch television.* Newbury Park, CA: Sage. (p. 461)

Lummis, M., & Stevenson, H. W. (1990). Gender differences in beliefs and achievement: A cross-cultural study. *Developmental Psychology, 26, 254–263.* (p. 485)

Lumsden, C. J., & Wilson, E. O. (1983). *Promethean fire: Reflections on the origin of mind.* Cambridge, MA: Harvard University Press. (p. 311)

Luria, A. M. (1968). In L. Solotaroff (Trans.), *The mind of a mnemonist.* New York: Basic Books. (p. 205)

Lykken, D. T. (1982, September). Fearlessness: Its carefree charm and deadly risks. *Psychology Today,* pp. 20–28. (pp. 312, 405)

Lykken, D. T. (1983, April). Polygraph prejudice. *APA Monitor,* p. 4. (p. 304)

Lykken, D. T. (1992). *Science, lies, and controversy: An epitaph for the polygraph.* Invited address to the American Psychological Association convention. (p. 304)

Lynch, G. (1990). *The many shapes of memory and the several forms of synaptic plasticity.* Invited address to the American Psychological Society convention. (p. 218)

Lynch, G., & Baudry, M. (1984). The biochemistry of memory: A new and specific hypothesis. *Science, 224,* 1057–1064. (p. 218)

Lynn, M. (1988). The effects of alcohol consumption on restaurant tipping. *Personality and Social Psychology Bulletin, 14,* 87–91. (p. 167)

Lynn, S. J., & Rhue, J. W. (1986). The fantasy-prone person: Hypnosis, imagination, and creativity. *Journal of Personality and Social Psychology, 51,* 404–408. (p. 161)

Lytton, H., & Romney, D. M. (1991). Parents' differential socialization of boys and girls: A meta-analysis. *Psychological Bulletin, 109,* 267–296. (p. 490)

Maass A., & Clark, R. D., III. (1984). Hidden impact of minorities: Fifteen years of minority influence research. *Psychological Bulletin, 95,* 428–450. (p. 457)

Maccoby, E. (1980). *Social development: Psychological growth and the parent-child relationship.* New York: Harcourt Brace Jovanovich. (pp. 75, 484)

Maccoby, E. E. (1990). Gender and relationships: A developmental account. *American Psychologist, 45,* 513–520. (p. 486)

MacDonald, N. (1960). Living with schizophrenia. *Canadian Medical Association Journal, 82,* 218–221. (p. 400)

Macfarlane, J. W. (1964). Perspectives on personality consistency and change from the guidance study. *Vita Humana, 7,* 115–126. (pp. 78, 100)

MacFarlane, A. (1978, February). What a baby knows. *Human Nature,* pp. 74–81. (p. 62)

MacKay, D. G. (1983). Prescriptive grammar and the pronoun problem. In B. Thorne, C. Kramarae, & N. Henley (Eds.), *Language, gender and society.* Rowley, MA: Newbury House. (p. 250)

MacKinnon, D. W., & Hall, W. B. (1972). Intelligence and creativity. *Proceedings, XVIIth International Congress of Applied Psychology* (Vol. 2, pp. 1883–1888). Brussels: Editest. (p. 260)

Maehr, M. L., & Braskamp, L. A. (1986). *The motivation factor: A theory of personal investment.* Lexington, MA: Lexington Books. (p. 295)

Magno, J. B. (1989, April 15). *The Hospice concept of care: Facing the 1990's.* Keynote address to the Association for Death Education and Counseling. (p. 94)

Magnusson, D. (1990). Personality research—challenges for the future. *European Journal of Personality, 4,* 1–17. (p. 405)

Mahoney, M. J. (1989). Sport psychology. In I. S. Cohen (Ed.), *G. Stanley Hall Lecture Series* (Vol. 9). Washington, DC: American Psychological Association. (p. 250)

Major, B. (1987). Gender, justice, and the psychology of entitlement. In P. Shaver & C. Hendrick (Eds.), *Sex and gender.* Beverly Hills, CA: Sage. (p. 488)

Major, B., Carrington, P. I., & Carnevale, P. J. D. (1984). Physical attractiveness and self-esteem: Attribution for praise from an other-sex evaluator. *Personality and Social Psychology Bulletin, 10,* 43–50. (p. 468)

Major, B., Cozzarelli, C., Sciacchitano, A. M., Cooper, M. L., Testa, M., & Mueller, P. M. (1990). Perceived social support, self-efficacy, and adjustment to abortion. *Journal of Personality and Social Psychology, 59,* 452–463. (p. 326)

Major, B., Schmidlin, A. M., & Williams, L. (1990). Gender patterns in social touch: The impact of setting and age. *Journal of Personality and Social Psychology, 58,* 634–643. (p. 488)

Malamuth, N. M., & Check, J. V. P. (1981). The effects of media exposure on acceptance of violence against women: A field experiment. *Journal of Research in Personality, 15,* 436–446. (p. 463)

Malamuth, N. M., Sockloskie, R. J., Koss, M. P., & Tanaka, J. S. (1991). Characteristics of aggressors against women: Testing a model using a national sample of college students. *Journal of Consulting and Clinical Psychology, 59,* 670–681. (p. 463)

Malan, D. H. (1978). "The case of the secretary with the violent father." In H. Davanloo (Ed.), *Basic principles and techniques in short-term dynamic psychotherapy.* New York: Spectrum. (p. 416)

Malkiel, B. (1985). *A random walk down Wall Street* (4th ed.). New York: Norton. (p. 240)

Malkiel, B. G. (1989a). Is the stock market efficient? *Science, 243,* 1313–1318. (p. 518)

Malone, T. W., & Lepper, M. R. (1986). Making learning fun: A taxonomy of intrinsic motivations for learning. In R. E. Snow & M. J. Farr (Eds.), *Aptitude, learning, and instruction: III. Cognitive and affective process analysis.* Hillsdale, NJ: Erlbaum. (p. 294)

Mandel, D. (1983, March 13). One man's holocaust: Part II. The story of David Mandel's journey through hell as told to David Kagan. *Wonderland Magazine* (Grand Rapids Press), pp. 2–7. (p. 269)

Manning, W. G., Keefer, E. B., Newhouse, J. P., Sloss, E. M., & Wasserman, J. (1989). The taxes of sin: Do smokers and drinkers pay their way? *Journal of the American Medical Association, 261,* 1604–1609. (p. 169)

Marks, D. F. (1986). Investigating the paranormal. *Nature, 320,* 119–124. (p. 142)

Markus, H., & Kitayama, S. (1991). Culture and the self: Implications for cognition, emotion, and motivation. *Psychological Review, 98,* 224–253. (pp. 308, 312, 480, 481, 487)

Markus, H., & Nurius, P. (1986). Possible selves. *American Psychologist, 41,* 954–969. (p. 364)

Marlatt, G. A. (1991). *Substance abuse: Etiology, prevention, and treatment issues.* Master lecture, American Psychological Association convention. (pp. 168, 191)

Marschark, M., Richman, C. L., Yuille, J. C., & Hunt, R. R. (1987). The role of imagery in memory: On shared and distinctive information. *Psychological Bulletin, 102,* 28–41. (p. 213)

Marsh, H. W., & Parker, J. W. (1984). Determinants of student self-concept: Is it better to be a relatively large fish in a small pond even if you don't learn to swim as well? *Journal of Personality and Social Psychology, 47,* 213–231. (p. 317)

Marshall, W. L. (1989). Pornography and sex offenders. In D. Zillmann & J. Bryant (Eds.), *Pornography: Research advances and policy considerations.* Hillsdale, NJ: Erlbaum. (p. 462)

Marteau, T. M. (1989). Framing of information: Its influences upon decisions of doctors and patients. *British Journal of Social Psychology, 28,* 89–94. (p. 240)

Martin, R. J., White, B. D., & Hulsey, M. G. (1991). The regulation of body weight. *American Scientist, 79,* 528–541. (p. 275)

Martinsen, E. W. (1987). The role of aerobic exercise in the treatment of depression. *Stress Medicine, 3,* 93–100. (p. 335)

Martyna, W. (1978). What does "he" mean? Use of generic masculine. *Journal of Communication, 28*(1), 131–138. (p. 249)

Maslow, A. H. (1970). *Motivation and personality* (2nd ed.). New York: Harper & Row. (pp. 271, 362)

Maslow, A. H. (1971). *The farther reaches of human nature.* New York: Viking Press. (p. 272)

Masters, W. H., & Johnson, V. E. (1966). *Human sexual response.* Boston: Little, Brown. (p. 283)

Matarazzo, J. D. (1983). Computerized psychological testing. *Science, 221,* 323. (p. 360)

Matheny, A. P., Jr. (1989). Children's behavioral inhibition over age and across situations: Genetic similarity for a trait during change. *Journal of Personality, 57,* 215–235. (p. 96)

Matsuda, L., Lolait, S. J., Brownstein, M. J., Young, A. C., & Bonner, T. I. (1990). Structure of a cannabinoid receptor and functional expression of the cloned CDNA. *Nature, 346,* 561–564. (p. 172)

Matsumoto, D., Kudoh, T., Scherer, K., & Wallbott, H. (1988). Antecedents of and reactions to emotions in the United States and Japan. *Journal of Cross-Cultural Psychology, 19,* 267–286. (pp. 308, 310)

Matthews, K. A. (1988). CHD and Type A behaviors: Update on and alternative to the Booth-Kewley and Friedman quantitative review. *Psychological Bulletin, 104,* 373–380. (p. 330)

Maurer, D., & Maurer, C. (1988). *The world of the newborn.* New York: Basic Books. (p. 62)

May, P. A. (1986). Alcohol and drug misuse prevention programs for American Indians: Needs and opportunities. *Journal of Studies on Alcohol, 47,* 187–195. (p. 382)

Mayer, R., & Goodchild, F. (1990). *The critical thinker: Thinking and learning strategies for psychology students.* Dubuque, IA: Wm. C. Brown Publishers. (p. 522)

McBurney, D. H., & Collings, V. B. (1984). *Introduction to sensation and perception* (2nd ed.). Englewood Cliffs, NJ: Prentice-Hall. (pp. 133, 134)

McBurney, D. H., & Gent, J. F. (1979). On the nature of taste qualities. *Psychological Bulletin, 86,* 151–167. (p. 120)

McCann, I. L., & Holmes, D. S. (1984). Influence of aerobic exercise on depression. *Journal of Personality and Social Psychology, 46,* 1142–1147. (p. 335)

McCarthy, C. (1988, December 31). Koop versus booze. *Washington Post,* p. A19. (p. 168)

McCarthy, P. (1986, July). Scent: The tie that binds? *Psychology Today,* pp. 6, 10. (p. 121)

McCartney, K., Harris, M. J., & Bernieri, F. (1990). Growing up and growing apart: A developmental meta-analysis of twin studies. *Psychological Bulletin, 107,* 226–237. (p. 97)

McCarty, D., Argeriou, M., Huebner, R. B., & Lubran, B. (1991). Alcoholism, drug abuse, and the homeless. *American Psychologist, 46,* 1139–1148. (p. 434)

McCaul, K. D., & Malott, J. M. (1984). Distraction and coping with pain. *Psychological Bulletin, 95,* 516–533. (p. 124)

McCauley, C. R., & Segal, M. E. (1987). Social psychology of terrorist groups. In C. Hendrick (Ed.), *Group processes and intergroup relations.* Beverly Hills, CA: Sage. (p. 450)

McClanahan, S., & Adams, J. (1989). The effects of children on adults' psychological well-being: 1957–1976. *Social Forces, 68,* 124–146. (p. 93)

McClelland, D. C. (1978). Managing motivation to expand human freedom. *American Psychologist, 33,* 201–210. (p. 292)

McClenon, J. (1982). A survey of elite scientists: Their attitudes toward ESP and parapsychology. *Journal of Parapsychology, 46,* 127–152. (p. 140)

McCloskey, M., Wible, C. G., & Cohen, N. J. (1988). Is there a special flashbulb-memory mechanism? *Journal of Experimental Psychology: General, 117,* 171–181. (p. 206)

McCrae, R. R., & Costa, P. T., Jr. (1986). Clinical assessment can benefit from recent advances in personality psychology. *American Psychologist, 41,* 1001–1003. (p. 358)

McCrae, R. R., & Costa, P. T., Jr. (1990). *Personality in adulthood.* New York: Guilford. (p. 91)

McFarland, C., & Ross, M. (1987). The relation between current impressions and memories of self and dating partners. *Psychological Bulletin, 13,* 228–238. (p. 225)

McGaugh, J. L. (1990). Significance and remembrance: The role of neuromodulatory systems. *Psychological Science, 1,* 15–25. (p. 218)

McGhee, P. E. (1976). Children's appreciation of humor: A test of the cognitive congruency principle. *Child Development, 47,* 420–426. (p. 69)

McGrath, M. J., & Cohen, D. G. (1978). REM sleep facilitation of adaptive waking behavior: A review of the literature. *Psychological Bulletin, 85,* 24–57. (p. 157)

McGuire, W. J. (1986). The myth of massive media impact: Savings and salvagings. In G. Comstock (Ed.), *Public communication and behavior.* Orlando, FL: Academic Press. (p. 461)

McGuire, W. J., & Padawer-Singer, A. (1978). Trait salience in the spontaneous self-concept. *Journal of Personality and Social Psychology, 33,* 743–754. (p. 482)

McGuire, W. J., McGuire, C. V., & Winton, W. (1979). Effects of household sex composition on the salience of one's gender in the spontaneous self-concept. *Journal of Experimental Social Psychology, 15,* 77–90. (p. 482)

McHugh, P. R., & Moran, T. H. (1978). Accuracy of the regulation of caloric ingestion in the rhesus monkey. *American Journal of Physiology, 235,* R29–34. (p. 273)

McKinlay, J. B., McKinlay, S. M., & Brambilla, D. J. (1987a). Health status and utilization behavior associated with menopause. *American Journal of Epidemiology, 125,* 110–121. (p. 87)

McKinlay, J. B., McKinlay, S. M., & Brambilla, D. (1987b). The relative contributions of endocrine changes and social circumstances to depression in mid-aged women. *Journal of Health and Social Behavior, 28,* 345–363. (p. 87)

McLean, P. D., & Carr, S. (1989). The psychological treatment of unipolar depression: Progress and limitations. *Canadian Journal of Behavioural Science, 21,* 452–469. (p. 430)

McNally, R. J. (1987). Preparedness and phobias: A review. *Psychological Bulletin, 101,* 283–303. (p. 311)

Meador, B. D., & Rogers, C. R. (1984). Person-centered therapy. In R. J. Corsini (Ed.), *Current psychotherapies* (3rd ed.). Itasca, IL: Peacock. (p. 418)

Meaney, M. J., Aitken, D. H., Van Berkel, C., Bhatnagar, S., & Sapolsky, R. M. (1988). Effect of neonatal handling on age-related impairments associated with the hippocampus. *Science, 239,* 766–768. (p. 63)

Medawar, P. (1982). *Pluto's republic.* New York: Oxford University Press. (p. 354)

Mednick, S. A., Moffitt, T. E., & Stack, S. (1987). *The causes of crime: New biological approaches.* Cambridge: Cambridge University Press. (p. 405)

Meet the Press. (1984, February 13). Quoted by J. M. Jones (1990), *Promoting diversity in an individualistic society.* Keynote address, Great Lakes College Association conference, "Multiculturalism transforming the 21st century." (p. 483)

Meichenbaum, D. (1977). *Cognitive-behavior modification: An integrative approach.* New York: Plenum Press. (p. 427)

Meier, R. P. (1991). Language acquisition by deaf children. *American Scientist, 79,* 60–70. (p. 246)

Meltzoff, A. N. (1987, May). Baby research comes of age. *Psychology Today,* p. 47. (p. 62)

Meltzoff, A. N. (1988a). Infant imitation and memory: Nine-month-olds in immediate and deferred tests. *Child Development, 59,* 217–225. (p. 199)

Meltzoff, A. N. (1988b). Infant imitation after a 1-week delay: Long-term memory for novel acts and multiple stimuli. *Developmental Psychology, 24,* 470–476. (p. 199)

Meltzoff, A. N. (1988c). Imitation of televised models by infants. *Child Development, 59,* 1221–1229. (p. 199)

Melzack, R. (1984). The myth of painless childbirth. *Pain, 19,* 321–337. (p. 124)

Melzack, R. (1992, April). Phantom limbs. *Scientific American,* pp. 120–126. (p. 123)

Melzack, R., & Wall, P. D. (1965). Pain mechanisms: A new theory. *Science, 150,* 971–979. (p. 123)

Melzack, R., & Wall, P. D. (1983). *The challenge of pain.* New York: Basic Books. (p. 123)

Mento, A. J., Steel, R. P., & Karren, R. J. (1987). A meta-analytic study of the effects of goal setting on task performance: 1966–1984. *Organizational Behavior and Human Decision Processes, 39,* 52–83. (p. 295)

Meredith, N. (1986, June). Testing the talking cure. *Science,* pp. 31–37. (p. 428)

Merton, R. K. (1938; reprinted 1970). *Science, technology and society in seventeenth-century England.* New York: Fertig. (p. 6)

Merton, R. K., & Kitt, A. S. (1950). Contributions to the theory of reference group behavior. In R. K. Merton & P. F. Lazarsfeld (Eds.), *Continuities in social research: Studies in the scope and method of the American soldier.* Glencoe, IL: Free Press. (p. 316)

Messer, W. S., & Griggs, R. A. (1989). Student belief and involvement in the paranormal and performance in introductory psychology. *Teaching of Psychology, 16,* 187–191. (p. 142)

Meyer-Bahlburg, H. F. L. (1980). Sexuality in early adolescence. In B. B. Wolman & J. Money (Eds.), *Handbook of human sexuality.* Englewood Cliffs, NJ: Prentice-Hall. (p. 284)

Michaels, J. W., Bloomel, J. M., Brocato, R. M., Linkous, R. A., & Rowe, J. S. (1982). Social facilitation and inhibition in a natural setting. *Replications in Social Psychology, 2,* 21–24. (p. 454)

Middlebrooks, J. C., & Green, D. M. (1991). Sound localization by human listeners. *Annual Review of Psychology, 42,* 135–159. (p. 120)

Mikulincer, M., Babkoff, H., Caspy, T., & Sing, H. (1989). The effects of 72 hours of sleep loss on psychological variables. *British Journal of Psychology, 80,* 145–162. (p. 154)

Milan, R. J., Jr., & Kilmann, P. R. (1987). Interpersonal factors in premarital contraception. *Journal of Sex Research, 23,* 289–321. (p. 85)

Milgram, S. (1974). *Obedience to authority.* New York: Harper & Row. (pp. 451, 453)

Miller, G. A. (1956). The magical number seven, plus or minus two: Some limits on our capacity for processing information. *Psychological Review, 63,* 81–97. (p. 207)

Miller, G. A., & Gildea, P. M. (1987, September). How children learn words. *Scientific American,* pp. 94–99. (p. 243)

Miller, J. B. (1986). *Toward a new psychology of women* (2nd ed.). Boston, MA: Beacon Press. (p. 486)

Miller, J. G. (1984). Culture and the development of everyday social explanation. *Journal of Personality and Social Psychology, 46,* 961–978. (p. 480)

Miller, K. I., & Monge, P. R. (1986). Participation, satisfaction, and productivity: A meta-analytic review. *Academy of Management Journal, 29,* 727–753. (p. 370)

Miller, N., & Maruyama, G. (1976). Ordinal position and peer popularity. *Journal of Personality and Social Psychology, 33,* 123–131. (p. 293)

Miller, N. E. (1985, February). Rx: biofeedback. *Psychology Today,* pp. 54–59. (p. 337)

Miller, N. E., & Brucker, B. S. (1979). A learned visceral response apparently independent of skeletal ones in patients paralyzed by spinal lesions. In N. Birbaumer & H. D. Kimmel (Eds.), *Biofeedback and self-regulation.* Hillsdale, NJ: Erlbaum. (p. 336)

Miller, P. C., Lefcourt, H. M., Holmes, J. G., Ware, E. E., & Saleh, W. E. (1986). Marital locus of control and marital problem solving. *Journal of Personality and Social Psychology, 51,* 161–169. (p. 369)

Mills, M., & Melhuish, E. (1974). Recognition of mother's voice in early infancy. *Nature, 252,* 123–124. (p. 62)

Mineka, S. (1985). The frightful complexity of the origins of fears. In F. R. Brush & J. B. Overmier (Eds.), *Affect, conditioning and cognition: Essays on the determinants of behavior.* Hillsdale, NJ: Erlbaum. (p. 311)

Mirin, S. M., & Weiss, R. D. (1989). Genetic factors in the development of alcoholism. *Psychiatric Annals, 19,* 239–242. (p. 173)

Mischel, W. (1968). *Personality and assessment.* New York: Wiley. (p. 360)

Mischel, W. (1981). Current issues and challenges in personality. In L. T. Benjamin, Jr. (Ed.), *The G. Stanley Hall Lecture Series* (Vol. 1). Washington, DC: American Psychological Association. (p. 371)

Mischel, W. (1984). Convergences and challenges in the search for consistency. *American Psychologist, 39*, 351–364. (p. 360)

Mischel, W., Shoda, Y., & Peake, P. K. (1988). The nature of adolescent competencies predicted by preschool delay of gratification. *Journal of Personality and Social Psychology, 54*, 687–696. (p. 81)

Mischel, W., Shoda, Y., & Rodriguez, M. L. (1989). Delay of gratification in children. *Science, 244*, 933–938. (pp. 81, 191)

Mita, T. H., Dermer, M., & Knight, J. (1977). Reversed facial images and the mere-exposure hypothesis. *Journal of Personality and Social Psychology, 35*, 597–601. (p. 467)

Monahan, J. (1983). *Predicting violent behavior: An assessment of clinical techniques.* Beverly Hills, CA: Sage. (p. 383)

Monahan, J. (1992). Mental disorder and violent behavior: Perceptions and evidence. *American Psychologist, 47*, 511–521. (p. 408)

Money, J. (1987). Sin, sickness, or status? Homosexual gender identity and psychoneuroendocrinology. *American Psychologist, 42*, 384–399. (pp. 289, 489)

Money, J. (1988). *Gay, straight, and in-between.* New York: Oxford University Press. (p. 462)

Money, J., Berlin, F. S., Falck, A., & Stein, M. (1983). *Antiandrogenic and counseling treatment of sex offenders.* Baltimore: Department of Psychiatry and Behavioral Sciences, The Johns Hopkins University School of Medicine. (p. 285)

Moody, R. (1976). *Life after life.* Harrisburg, PA: Stackpole Books. (p. 171)

Mook, D. G. (1983). In defense of external invalidity. *American Psychologist, 38*, 379–387. (p. 17)

Moore, T. E. (1988). The case against subliminal manipulation. *Psychology and Marketing, 5*, 297–316. (p. 107)

Moreland, R. L., & Zajonc, R. B. (1982). Exposure effects in person perception: Familiarity, similarity, and attraction. *Journal of Experimental Social Psychology, 18*, 395–415. (p. 467)

Morokoff, P. J. (1986). Volunteer bias in the psychophysiological study of female sexuality. *Journal of Sex Research, 22*, 35–51. (p. 285)

Morrison, D. M. (1985). Adolescent contraceptive behavior: A review. *Psychological Bulletin, 98*, 538–568. (p. 84)

Moruzzi, G., & Magoun, H. W. (1949). Brain stem reticular formation and activation of the EEG. *Electroencephalography and Clinical Neurophysiology, 1*, 455–473. (p. 37)

Mosher, D. L., & Anderson, R. D. (1986). Macho personality, sexual aggression, and reactions to guided imagery of realistic rape. *Journal of Research in Personality, 20*, 77–94. (p. 167)

Mosher, D. L., & Vonderheide, S. G. (1985). Contributions of sex guilt and masturbation guilt to women's contraceptive attitudes and use. *Journal of Sex Research, 21*, 24–39. (p. 84)

Moss, H. A., & Susman, E. J. (1980). Longitudinal study of personality development. In O. G. Brim, Jr., & J. Kagan (Eds.), *Constancy and change in human development.* Cambridge, MA: Harvard University Press. (p. 100)

Moyer, K. E. (1983). The physiology of motivation: Aggression as a model. In C. J. Scheier & A. M. Rogers (Eds.), *G. Stanley Hall Lecture Series* (Vol. 3). Washington, DC: American Psychological Association. (p. 458)

Muehlenhard, C. L. (1988). Misinterpreted dating behaviors and the risk of date rape. *Journal of Social and Clinical Psychology, 6*, 20–37. (p. 488)

Murphy, G. E., & Wetzel, R. D. (1990). The lifetime risk of suicide in alcoholism. *Archives of General Psychiatry, 47*, 383–392. (p. 393)

Murphy, T. N. (1982). Pain: Its assessment and management. In R. J. Gatchel, A. Baum, & J. E. Singer (Eds.), *Handbook of psychology and health: Vol. I. Clinical psychology and behavioral medicine: Overlapping disciplines.* Hillsdale, NJ: Erlbaum. (p. 124)

Murray, H. (1938). *Explorations in personality.* New York: Oxford University Press. (pp. 291, 292)

Murray, H. A. (1933). The effect of fear upon estimates of the maliciousness of other personalities. *Journal of Social Psychology, 4*, 310–329. (p. 351)

Murray, H. A., & Wheeler, D. R. (1937). A note on the possible clairvoyance of dreams. *Journal of Psychology, 3*, 309–313. (p. 142)

Murstein, B. L. (1986). *Paths to marriage.* Newbury Park, CA: Sage. (p. 468)

Myers, D. G. (1992). *The pursuit of happiness: Who is happy—and why.* New York: William Morrow. (pp. 84, 317)

Myers, D. G. (1993). *Social psychology,* 4th ed. New York: McGraw-Hill. (p. 365)

Myers, D. G., & Bishop, G. D. (1970). Discussion effects on racial attitudes. *Science, 169*, 778–779. (p. 455)

Myers, I. B. (1987). *Introduction to type: A description of the theory and applications of the Myers-Briggs Type Indicator.* Palo Alto, CA: Consulting Psychologists Press. (p. 356)

Nadler, A., & Ben-Shushan, D. (1989). Forty years later: Long-term consequences of massive traumatization as manifested by Holocaust survivors from the city and the Kibbutz. *Journal of Consulting and Clinical Psychology, 57*, 287–293. (p. 325)

Nadon, R., Hoyt, I. P., Register, P. A., & Kihlstrom, J. F. (1991). Absorption and hypnotizability: Context effects reexamined. *Journal of Personality and Social Psychology, 60*, 144–153. (p. 161)

Napolitan, D. A., & Goethals, G. R. (1979). The attribution of friendliness. *Journal of Experimental Social Psychology, 15*, 105–113. (p. 443)

Nash, M. (1987). What, if anything, is regressed about hypnotic age regression? A review of the empirical literature. *Psychological Bulletin, 102*, 42–52. (p. 161)

National Academy of Science. (1984). *Bereavement: Reactions, consequences, and cure.* Washington, DC: National Academy Press. (p. 331)

National Academy of Sciences, Institute of Medicine. (1982). *Marijuana and health.* Washington, DC: National Academy Press. (p. 172)

National Academy of Sciences. (1991). *Science, medicine, and animals.* Washington, DC: National Academy Press. (p. 18)

National Center for Health Statistics. (1985). *Health: United States, 1985.* DHHS Pub. No. (PHS) 86–1232. Washington, DC: U.S. Government Printing Office. (p. 276)

National Center for Health Statistics. (1990, November 28). Advance report of final mortality statistics, 1988. *Monthly Vital Statistics Report, 39,* Table 5. (p. 393)

National Institute of Mental Health. (1982). *Television and behavior: Ten years of scientific progress and implications for the eighties.* Washington, DC: U.S. Government Printing Office. (p. 461)

National Opinion Research Center. (1985, October/November). Images of the world. *Public Opinion,* p. 38. (p. 366)

National Research Council. (1987). *Risking the future: Adolescent sexuality, pregnancy, and childbearing.* Washington, DC: National Academy Press. (pp. 84, 85)

National Research Council. (1990). *Human factors research needs for an aging population.* Washington, DC: National Academy Press. (p. 87)

National Safety Council. (1991). *Accident facts.* Chicago: National Safety Council. (p. 239)

National Victim Center and Crime Victims Research and Treatment Center. (1992). *Rape in America: A Report to the Nation.* Arlington, VA: National Victim Center. (p. 462)

Naylor, T. H. (1990). Redefining corporate motivation, Swedish style. *Christian Century, 107,* 566–570. (p. 295)

NCTV News. (1987, July-August). More research links harmful effects to non-violent porn. National Coalition on Television Violence, p. 12. (p. 462)

Needles, D. J., & Abramson, L. Y. (1990). Positive life events, attributional style, and hopefulness: Testing a model of recovery from depression. *Journal of Abnormal Psychology, 99,* 156–165. (p. 397)

Neisser, U. (1981). John Dean's memory: A case study. *Cognition, 9,* 1–22. (pp. 206, 222)

Neisser, U. (1984). The role of invariant structures in the control of movement. In M. Frese & J. Sabini (Eds.), *Goal directed behavior: The concept of action in psychology.* Hillsdale, NJ: Erlbaum. (p. 250)

Neisser, U., & Harsch, N. (1992). Phantom flashbulbs: False recollections of hearing the news about *Challenger.* In E. Winograd & U. Neisser (Eds.), *Affect and accuracy in recall: Studies of "flashbulb" memories.* New York: Cambridge University Press. (pp. 206, 224)

Neisser, U., Winograd, E., & Weldon, M. S. (1991). *Remembering the earthquake: "What I experienced" vs. "How I heard the news."* Paper presented to the Psychonomic Society convention. (p. 218)

Neitz, J., Geist, T., & Jacobs, G. H. (1989). Color vision in the dog. *Visual Neuroscience, 3,* 119–125. (p. 116)

Nelson, K. (1973). Structure and strategy in learning to talk. *Monographs of the Society for Research in Child Development, 38*(1 & 2, Serial No. 149). (p. 244)

Nelson, N. (1988). *A meta-analysis of the life-event/health paradigm: The influence of social support.* Philadelphia: Temple University Ph.D. dissertation. (p. 339)

Nemeth, C. J. (1986). Differential contributions of majority and minority influence. *Psychological Review, 93,* 23–32. (p. 457)

Neugarten, B. L. (1974). The roles we play. In American Medical Association, *Quality of life: The middle years.* Acton, MA: Publishing Sciences Group. (p. 92)

Nevin, J. A. (1988). Behavioral momentum and the partial reinforcement effect. *Psychological Bulletin, 103,* 44–56. (p. 192)

Newcomb, M. D., & Bentler, P. M. (1988). Impact of adolescent drug use and social support on problems of young adults: A longitudinal study. *Journal of Abnormal Psychology, 97,* 64–75. (p. 172)

Newcomb, M. D., & Harlow, L. L. (1986). Life events and substance use among adolescents: Mediating effects of perceived loss of control and meaninglessness in life. *Journal of Personality and Social Psychology, 51,* 564–577. (p. 174)

Newell, A. (1988, March 9). Quoted by D. L. Wheeler, From years of work in psychology and computer science, scientists build theories of thinking and learning. *Chronicle of Higher Education,* pp. A4, A6. (p. 7)

Newlin, D. B., & Thomson, J. B. (1990). Alcohol challenge with sons of alcoholics: A critical review and analysis. *Psychological Bulletin, 108,* 383–402. (p. 174)

Newport, E. L. (1990). Maturational constraints on language learning. *Cognitive Science, 14,* 11–28. (p. 246)

Nezu, A. M., Nezu, C. M., & Blissett, S. E. (1988). Sense of humor as a moderator of the relation between stressful events and psychological distress: A prospective analysis. *Journal of Personality and Social Psychology, 54,* 520–525. (p. 338)

Ng, S. H. (1990). Androcentric coding of *man* and *his* in memory by language users. *Journal of Experimental Social Psychology, 26,* 455–464. (p. 249)

Nickerson, R. S., & Adams, M. J. (1979). Long-term memory for a common object. *Cognitive Psychology, 11,* 287–307. (p. 209)

Nicol, S. E., & Gottesman, I. I. (1983). Clues to the genetics and neurobiology of schizophrenia. *American Scientist, 71,* 398–404. (pp. 403, 404)

Nicolaus, L. K., Cassel, J. F., Carlson, R. B., & Gustavson, C. R. (1983). Taste-aversion conditioning of crows to control predation on eggs. *Science, 220,* 212–214. (p. 184)

Niemi, R. G., Mueller, J., & Smith, T. W. (1989). *Trends in public opinion: A compendium of survey data.* New York: Greenwood Press. (pp. 169, 315, 493, 496)

Nisbett, R., & Ross, L. (1991). *The person and the situation.* New York: McGraw-Hill. (p. 295)

Nisbett, R. E., & Borgida, E. (1975). Attribution and the psychology of prediction. *Journal of Personality and Social Psychology, 32,* 932–943. (p. 241)

Nisbett, R. E., & Ross, L. (1980). *Human inference: Strategies and shortcomings of social judgment.* Englewood Cliffs, NJ: Prentice-Hall. (p. 237)

Nisbett, R. E., Fong, G. T., Lehman, D. R., & Cheng, P. W. (1987). Teaching reasoning. *Science, 238,* 625–631. (p. 521)

Nisbett, R. E., Krantz, D. H., Jepson, C., & Kunda, Z. (1983). The use of statistical heuristics in everyday inductive reasoning. *Psychological Review, 90,* 339–363. (p. 520)

Noel, J. G., Forsyth, D. R., & Kelley, K. N. (1987). Improving the performance of failing students by overcoming their self-serving attributional biases. *Basic and Applied Social Psychology, 8,* 151–162. (p. 371)

Nolen-Hoeksema, S. (1990). *Sex differences in depression.* Stanford, CA: Stanford University Press. (pp. 394, 396)

Nolen-Hoeksema, S., & Morrow, J. (1991). A prospective study of depression and post-traumatic stress symptoms following a natural disaster: The 1989 Loma Prieta earthquake. *Journal of Personality and Social Psychology, 61,* 115–121. (p. 397)

Noller, P., Law, H., & Comrey, A. L. (1987). Cattell, Comrey, and Eysenck personality factors compared: More evidence for the five robus factors? *Journal of Personality and Social Psychology, 53,* 1208–1217. (p. 358)

Norman, D. A. (1988). *The psychology of everyday things.* New York: Basic Books. (p. 139)

Norris, P. A. (1986). On the status of biofeedback and clinical practice. *American Psychologist, 41,* 1009–1010. (p. 336)

Nuttin, J. M., Jr. (1987). Affective consequences of mere ownership: The name letter effect in twelve European languages. *European Journal of Social Psychology, 17,* 381–402. (p. 467)

Oatley, K., & Bolton, W. (1985). A social-cognitive theory of depression in reaction to life events. *Psychological Review, 92,* 382–388. (p. 397)

O'Connor, P., & Brown, G. W. (1984). Supportive relationships: Fact or fancy? *Journal of Social and Personal Relationships, 1,* 159–175. (p. 433)

Oetting, E. R., & Beauvais, F. (1987). Peer cluster theory, socialization characteristics, and adolescent drug use: A path analysis. *Journal of Counseling Psychology, 34,* 205–213. (pp. 61, 171)

Oetting, E. R., & Beauvais, F. (1990). Adolescent drug use: Findings of national and local surveys. *Journal of Consulting and Clinical Psychology, 58,* 385–394. (p. 174)

Oettingen, G., & Seligman, M. E. P. (1990). Pessimism and behavioural signs of depression in East versus West Berlin. *European Journal of Social Psychology, 20,* 207–220. (p. 370)

Offer, D., Ostrov, E., Howard, K. I., & Atkinson, R. (1988). *The teenage world: Adolescents' self-image in ten countries.* New York: Plenum. (p. 83)

Office of Technology Assessment. (1990). *Neural grafting: Repairing the brain and spinal cord,* OTA-BA-462, U.S. Congress. Washington, DC: U.S. Government Printing Office. (p. 50)

Olds, J. (1958). Self-stimulation of the brain. *Science, 127,* 315–324. (p. 41)

Olds, J. (1975). Mapping the mind onto the brain. In F. G. Worden, J. P. Swazey, & G. Adelman (Eds.), *The neurosciences: Paths of discovery.* Cambridge, MA: MIT Press. (p. 41)

Olds, J., & Milner, P. (1954). Positive reinforcement produced by electrical stimulation of the septal area and other regions of rat brain. *Journal of Comparative and Physiological Psychology, 47,* 419–427. (pp. 41, 43)

O'Leary, A. (1990). Stress, emotion, and human immune function. *Psychological Bulletin, 108,* 363–382. (p. 332)

Oliner, S. P., & Oliner, P. M. (1988). *The altruistic personality: Rescuers of Jews in Nazi Europe.* New York: Free Press. (pp. 81, 200, 466)

Olweus, D., Mattsson, A., Schalling, D., & Low, H. (1988). Circulating testosterone levels and aggression in adolescent males: A causal analysis. *Psychosomatic Medicine, 50,* 261–272. (p. 459)

O'Malley, P. M., & Bachman, J. G. (1983). Self-esteem: Change and stability between ages 13 and 23. *Developmental Psychology, 19,* 257–268. (p. 83)

Orne, M. T. (1982, April 28). Affidavit submitted to State of Pennsylvania. (p. 162)

Orne, M. T., & Evans, F. J. (1965). Social control in the psychological experiment: Antisocial behavior and hypnosis. *Journal of Personality and Social Psychology, 1,* 189–200. (p. 163)

Orne, M. T., Dinges, D. F., & Orne, E. C. (1984). On the differential diagnosis of multiple personality in the forensic context. *International Journal of Clinical and Experimental Hypnosis, 32,* 118–169. (p. 390)

Orne, M. T., Soskis, D. A., Dinges, D. F., & Orne, E. C. (1984). Hypnotically induced testimony. In G. L. Wells & E. F. Loftus (Eds.), *Eyewitness testimony: Psychological perspectives.* New York: Cambridge University Press. (p. 161)

Orr, D. P., Beiter, M., & Ingersoll, G. (1991). Premature sexual activity as an indicator of psychosocial risk. *Pediatrics, 87,* 141–147. (p. 84)

Osgood, C. E. (1962). *An alternative to war or surrender.* Urbana: University of Illinois Press. (p. 503)

Osgood, C. E. (1980). *GRIT: A strategy for survival in mankind's nuclear age?* Paper presented at the Pugwash Conference on New Directions in Disarmament. (p. 503)

Osherson, D. N., & Markman, E. (1974–1975). Language and the ability to evaluate contradictions and tautologies. *Cognition, 3,* 213–226. (p. 80).

OSS Assessment Staff. (1948). *The assessment of men.* New York: Rinehart. (p. 371)

Ostfeld, A. M., Kasl, S. V., D'Atri, D. A., & Fitzgerald, E. F. (1987). *Stress, crowding, and blood pressure in prison.* Hillsdale, NJ: Erlbaum. (p. 329)

Padgett, V. R. (1989). *Predicting organizational violence: An application of 11 powerful principles of obedience.* Paper presented to the American Psychological Association convention. (p. 452)

Paffenbarger, R. S., Jr., Hyde, R. T., Wing, A. L., & Hsieh, C-C. (1986). Physical activity, all-cause mortality, and longevity of college alumni. *New England Journal of Medicine, 314,* 605–612. (p. 335)

Page, S. (1977). Effects of the mental illness label in attempts to obtain accommodation. *Canadian Journal of Behavioral Science, 9,* 84–90. (p. 407)

Paivio, A. (1986). *Mental representations: A dual coding approach.* New York: Oxford University Press. (p. 213)

Palace, E. M., & Gorzalka, B. B. (1990). The enhancing effects of anxiety on arousal in sexually dysfunctional and functional women. *Journal of Abnormal Psychology, 99,* 403–411. (p. 321)

Palladino, J. J., & Carducci, B. J. (1983). *"Things that go bump in the night": Students' knowledge of sleep and dreams.* Paper presented at the Southeastern Psychological Association convention. (p. 151)

Palmer, S., Schreiber, C., & Fox, C. (1991). *Remembering the earthquake: "Flashbulb" memory for experienced vs. reported events.* Paper presented to the Psychonomic Society convention. (p. 218)

Palumbo, S. R. (1978). *Dreaming and memory: A new information-processing model.* New York: Basic Books. (p. 157)

Pandey, J., Sinha, Y., Prakash, A., & Tripathi, R. C. (1982). Right-left political ideologies and attribution of the causes of poverty. *European Journal of Social Psychology, 12,* 327–331. (p. 444)

Panksepp, J. (1982).   Toward a general psychobiological theory of emotions. *Behavioral and Brain Sciences, 5,* 407–467. (p. 303)

Parke, R. D. (1981).   *Fathers.* Cambridge, MA: Harvard University Press. (p. 74)

Parker, K. C., Hanson, R. K., & Hunsley, J. (1988).   MMPI, Rorschach, and WAIS: A meta-analytic comparison of reliability, stability, and validity. *Psychological Bulletin, 103,* 367–373. (p. 353)

Parloff, M. B. (1987, February).   Psychotherapy: An import from Japan. *Psychology Today,* pp. 74–75. (p. 414)

Patterson, F. (1978, October).   Conversations with a gorilla. *National Geographic,* pp. 438–465. (p. 247)

Patterson, G. R., Chamberlain, P., & Reid, J. B. (1982).   A comparative evaluation of parent training procedures. *Behavior Therapy, 13,* 638–650. (p. 461)

Patterson, R. (1951).   *The riddle of Emily Dickinson.* Boston: Houghton Mifflin. (p. 398)

Pavett, C. M., Butler, M., Marcinik, E. J., & Hodgdon, J. A. (1987).   Exercise as a buffer against organizational stress. *Stress Medicine, 3,* 87–92. (p. 335)

Pavlov, I. P. (1927).   In G. V. Anrep (Trans.), *Conditioned reflexes.* London: Oxford University Press. (pp. 183, 185)

Pedersen, N. L., Plomin, R., McClearn, G. E., & Friberg, L. (1988).   Neuroticism, extraversion, and related traits in adult twins reared apart and reared together. *Journal of Personality and Social Psychology, 55,* 950–957. (p. 97)

Pekkanen, J. (1982, June).   Why do we sleep? *Science, 82,* p. 86. (p. 154)

Penfield, W. (1969).   Consciousness, memory, and man's conditioned reflexes. In K. Pigram (Ed.), *On the biology of learning.* New York: Harcourt, Brace & World. (p. 217)

Pennebaker, J. (1990).   *Opening up: The healing power of confiding in others.* New York: William Morrow. (p. 340)

Pennebaker, J. W., & O'Heeron, R. C. (1984).   Confiding in others and illness rate among spouses of suicide and accidental death victims. *Journal of Abnormal Psychology, 93,* 473–476. (p. 339)

Pennebaker, J. W., Barger, S. D., & Tiebout, J. (1989).   Disclosure of traumas and health among Holocaust survivors. *Psychosomatic Medicine, 51,* 577–589. (p. 340)

Peplau, L. A. (1982).   Research on homosexual couples: An overview. *Journal of Homosexuality, 8*(2), 3–8. (p. 288)

Peplau, L. A., & Gordon, S. L. (1985).   Women and men in love: Gender differences in close heterosexual relationships. In V. E. O'Leary, R. K. Unger, & B. S. Wallston (Eds.), *Women, gender, and social psychology.* Hillsdale, NJ: Erlbaum. (p. 9)

Peplau, L. A., & Perlman, D. (1982).   *Loneliness: A sourcebook of current theory, research and therapy.* New York: Wiley. (p. 398)

Perkins, K. A., Dubbert, P. M., Martin, J. E., Faulstich, M. E., & Harris, J. K. (1986).   Cardiovascular reactivity to psychological stress in aerobically trained versus untrained mild hypertensives and normotensives. *Health Psychology, 5,* 407–421. (p. 335)

Perlmutter, M. (1983).   Learning and memory through adulthood. In M. W. Riley, B. B. Hess, & K. Bond (Eds.), *Aging in society: Selected reviews of recent research.* Hillsdale, NJ: Erlbaum. (p. 89)

Perrett, D. I., Harries, M., Misflin, A. J., & Chitty, A. J. (1988).   Three stages in the classification of body movements by visual neurons. In H. B. Barlow, C. Blakemore, & M. Weston Smith (Eds.), *Images and understanding.* Cambridge: Cambridge University Press. (p. 114)

Persky, V. W., Kempthorne-Rawson, J., & Shekelle, R. B. (1987).   Personality and risk of cancer: 20-year follow-up of the Western Electric study. *Psychosomatic Medicine, 49,* 435–449. (p. 332)

Persons, J. B. (1986).   The advantages of studying psychological phenomena rather than psychiatric diagnoses. *American Psychologist, 41,* 1252–1260. (p. 407)

Pert, C. (1986).   Quoted in J. Hooper & D. Teresi, *The three-pound universe.* New York: Macmillan. (pp. 42, 54)

Pert, C. B., & Snyder, S. H. (1973).   Opiate receptor: Demonstration in nervous tissue. *Science, 179,* 1011–1014. (p. 32)

Peschel, E. R., & Peschel, R. E. (1987).   Medical insights into the castrati in opera. *American Scientist, 75,* 578–583. (p. 284)

Peters, T. J., & Waterman, R. H., Jr. (1982).   *In search of excellence: Lessons from America's best-run companies.* New York: Harper & Row. (p. 198)

Petersen, A. C. (1987, September).   Those gangly years. *Psychology Today,* pp. 28–34. (p. 79)

Peterson, C., & Barrett, L. C. (1987).   Explanatory style and academic performance among university freshmen. *Journal of Personality and Social Psychology, 53,* 603–607. (p. 371)

Peterson, C., Peterson, J., & Skevington, S. (1986).   Heated argument and adolescent development. *Journal of Social and Personal Relationships, 3,* 229–240. (p. 80)

Peterson, L. R., & Peterson, M. J. (1959).   Short-term retention of individual verbal items. *Journal of Experimental Psychology, 58,* 193–198. (p. 210)

Peterson, R. (1978).   Review of the Rorschach. In O. K. Buros (Ed.), *The eighth mental measurements yearbook* (Vol. I). Highland Park, NJ: Gryphon Press. (p. 352)

Pettigrew, T. F. (1969).   Racially separate or together? *Journal of Social Issues, 25,* 43–69. (p. 501)

Pettingale, K. W., Morris, T., Greer, S., & Haybittle, J. L. (1985, March 30).   Mental attitudes to cancer: An additional prognostic factor. *Lancet,* p. 750. (p. 333)

Pfeiffer, E. (1977).   Sexual behavior in old age. In E. W. Busse & E. Pfeiffer (Eds.), *Behavior and adaptation in late life* (2nd ed.). Boston: Little, Brown. (p. 88)

Phillips, D. P. (1974).   The influence of suggestion on suicide: Substantive and theoretical implications of the Werther effect. *American Sociological Review, 39,* 340–354. (p. 449)

Phillips, D. P. (1982).   The impact of fictional television stories on U.S. adult fatalities: New evidence on the effect of the mass media on violence. *American Journal of Sociology, 87,* 1340–1359. (p. 449)

Phillips, D. P. (1985).   Natural experiments on the effects of mass media violence on fatal aggression: Strengths and weaknesses of a new approach. In L. Berkowitz (Ed.), *Advances in experimental social psychology* (Vol. 19). Orlando, FL: Academic Press. (p. 449)

Phillips, D. P., & Wills, J. S. (1987).   A drop in suicides around major national holidays. *Suicide and Life-Threatening Behavior, 17,* 1–12. (p. 392)

Phillips, D. P., Carstensen, L. L., & Paight, D. J. (1989). Effects of mass media news stories on suicide, with new evidence on the role of story content. In D. R. Pfeffer (Ed.), *Suicide among youth: Perspectives on risk and prevention*. Washington, DC: American Psychiatric Press. (p. 449)

Phillips, J. L. (1969). *Origins of intellect: Piaget's theory*. San Francisco: Freeman. (p. 67)

Phinney, J. S. (1990). Ethnic identity in adolescents and adults: Review of research. *Psychological Bulletin, 108,* 499–514. (pp. 482, 483)

Piaget, J. (1930). *The child's conception of physical causality*. London: Routledge & Kegan Paul. (p. 65)

Piaget, J. (1932). *The moral judgment of the child*. New York: Harcourt, Brace & World. (p. 81)

Piccione, C., Hilgard, E. R., & Zimbardo, P. G. (1989). On the degree of stability of measured hypnotizability over a 25-year period. *Journal of Personality and Social Psychology, 56,* 289–295. (p. 161)

Pickar, D., Labarca, R., Linnoila, M., Roy, A., Hommer, D., Everett, D., & Payl, S. M. (1984). Neuroleptic-induced decrease in plasma homovanillic acid and antipsychotic activity in schizophrenic patients. *Science, 225,* 954–957. (p. 435)

Pike, K. M., & Rodin, J. (1991). Mothers, daughters, and disordered eating. *Journal of Abnormal Psychology, 100,* 198–204. (p. 277)

Pinker, S. (1990, September-October). Quoted by J. de Cuevas, "No, she held them loosely." *Harvard Magazine*, pp. 60–67. (p. 243)

Piotrowski, C., & Keller, J. W. (1989). Psychological testing in outpatient mental health facilities: A national study. *Professional Psychology: Research and Practice, 20,* 423–425. (pp. 352, 360)

Pittman, T. S., Davey, M. E., Alafat, K. A., Vetherill, K. V., & Kramer, N. A. (1980). Informational versus controlling verbal rewards. *Personality and Social Psychology Bulletin, 6,* 228–233. (p. 294)

Planned Parenthood Federation of America. (1986, December 15). Sex education for parents. *USA Today*, p. 11A. (p. 85)

Plomin, R., & DeFries, J. C. (1980). Genetics and intelligence: Recent data. *Intelligence, 4,* 15–24. (p. 261)

Plomin, R., McClearn, G. E., Pedersen, N. L., Nesselroade, J. R., & Bergeman, C. S. (1988). Genetic influence on childhood family environment perceived retrospectively from the last half of the life span. *Developmental Psychology, 24,* 37–45. (p. 99)

Plotkin, W. B. (1979). The alpha experience revisited: Biofeedback in the transformation of psychological state. *Psychological Bulletin, 86,* 1132–1148. (p. 337)

Polivy, J., & Herman, C. P. (1985). Dieting and binging: A causal analysis. *American Psychologist, 40,* 193–201. (p. 281)

Polivy, J., & Herman, C. P. (1987). Diagnosis and treatment of normal eating. *Journal of Personality and Social Psychology, 55,* 635–644. (pp. 280, 281)

Pomerleau, O. F., & Pomerleau, C. S. (1984). Neuroregulators and the reinforcement of smoking: Towards a biobehavioral explanation. *Neuroscience and Biobehavioral Reviews, 8,* 503–513. (p. 170)

Poon, L. W. (1987). Myths and truisms: Beyond extant analyses of speed of behavior and age. Address to the Eastern Psychological Association convention. (p. 88)

Porter, D., & Neuringer, A. (1984). Music discriminations by pigeons. *Journal of Experimental Psychology: Animal Behavior Processes, 10,* 138–148. (p. 189)

Powell, J. (1989). *Happiness is an inside job*. Valencia, CA: Tabor. (p. 365)

Powell, J. L. (1988). A test of the knew-it-all-along effect in the 1984 Presidential and statewide elections. *Journal of Applied Social Psychology, 18,* 760–773. (p. 20)

Powell, K. E., Thompson, P. D., Caspersen, C. J., & Kendrick, J. S. (1987). Physical activity and the incidence of coronary heart disease. *Annual Review of Public Health, 8,* 253–287. (p. 335)

Powell, M. C., & Fazio, R. H. (1984). Attitude accessibility as a function of repeated attitudinal expression. *Personality and Social Psychology Bulletin, 10,* 139–148. (p. 446)

Pratkanis, A. R., & Greenwald, A. G. (1988). Recent perspectives on unconscious processing: Still no marketing applications. *Psychology and Marketing, 5,* 337–353. (p. 107)

Pratt, M. W., Pancer, M., Hunsberger, B., & Manchester, J. (1990). Reasoning about the self and relationships in maturity: An integrative complexity analysis of individual differences. *Journal of Personality and Social Psychology, 59,* 575–581. (p. 488)

Premack, D. (1983). The codes of man and beasts. *The Behavioral and Brain Sciences, 6,* 125–167. (p. 250)

Price, R. A. (1987). Genetics of human obesity. *Annals of Behavioral Medicine, 9,* 9–14. (p. 279)

Prioleau, L., Murdock, M., & Brody, N. (1983). An analysis of psychotherapy versus placebo studies. *The Behavioral and Brain Sciences, 6,* 275–310. (p. 432)

Pritchard, R. M. (1961, June). Stabilized images on the retina. *Scientific American*, pp. 72–78. (p. 109)

Project on Redefining the Meaning and Purpose of Baccalaureate Degrees. (1985). *Integrity in the college curriculum*. Washington, DC: Association of American Colleges. (p. 521)

Pruitt, D. G., & Rubin, J. Z. (1986). *Social conflict: Escalation, stalemate, and settlement*. New York: Random House. (p. 503)

Psychiatric News. (1989, September 1). Reported by *Behavior Today*, September 25, 1989, pp. 3–4. (p. 428)

Psychic Abscam. (1983, March). *Discover*, p. 10. (p. 142)

Public Opinion. (1984, August/September). Phears and Phobias, p. 32. (p. 385)

Public Opinion. (1984, August/September). Tradeoffs, p. 36. (p. 8)

Public Opinion. (1985, February/March). Defining woman's place, p. 40. (p. 8)

Public Opinion. (1987, May/June). Teen angels (report of University of Michigan survey), p. 32. (p. 78)

Pyszczynski, T., Hamilton, J. C., Greenberg, J., & Becker, S. E. (1991). Self-awareness and psychological dysfunction. In C. R. Snyder & D. O. Forsyth (Eds.), *Handbook of social and clinical psychology: The health perspective*. New York: Pergamon. (p. 397)

Qualls, P. J., & Sheehan, P. W. (1981). Electromyograph biofeedback as a relaxation technique: A critical appraisal and reassessment. *Psychological Bulletin, 90,* 21–42. (p. 337)

Rabin, A. S., Kaslow, N. J., & Rehm, L. P. (1986). *Aggregate outcome and follow-up results following self-control therapy for depression.* Paper presented at the American Psychological Association convention. (pp. 426, 427)

Radecki, T. (1989, February-March). On picking good television and film entertainment. *NCTV News, 10*(1–2), p. 5. (p. 461)

Randi, J. (1983a, Summer). The Project Alpha experiment: Part 1. The first two years. *The Skeptical Inquirer,* pp. 24–33. (p. 141)

Randi, J. (1983b, Fall). The Project Alpha experiment: Part 2. Beyond the laboratory. *The Skeptical Inquirer,* pp. 36–45. (p. 141)

Rapoport, J. L. (1989, March). The biology of obsessions and compulsions. *Scientific American,* pp. 83–89. (pp. 386, 387, 388)

Ray, O., & Ksir, C. (1990). *Drugs, society, and human behavior* (5th ed.). St. Louis: Times Mirror/Mosby. (p. 170)

Raz, S., & Raz, N. (1990). Structural brain abnormalities in the major psychoses: A quantitative review of the evidence from computerized imaging. *Psychological Bulletin, 108,* 93–108. (p. 403)

Razran, G. H. S. (1940). Conditioned response changes in rating and appraising sociopolitical solutions. *Psychological Bulletin, 37,* 481. (p. 186)

Reagan, R. (1988, December 21). Television interview with David Brinkley, broadcast December 22, and reported by wire services on December 23. (p. 445)

Reason, J. (1987). The Chernobyl errors. *Bulletin of the British Psychological Society, 40,* 201–206. (p. 456)

Reason, J., & Mycielska, K. (1982). *Absent-minded? The psychology of mental lapses and everyday errors.* Englewood Cliffs, NJ: Prentice-Hall. (p. 138)

Reiman, E. M., Fusselman, M. J., Fox, P. T., & Raichle, M. E. (1989). Neuroanatomical correlates of anticipatory anxiety. *Science, 243,* 1071–1074. (p. 388)

Reisenzein, R. (1983). The Schachter theory of emotion: Two decades later. *Psychological Bulletin, 94,* 239–264. (p. 320)

Reiser, M. (1982). *Police psychology.* Los Angeles: LEHI. (p. 142)

Renner, M. J., & Rosenzweig, M. R. (1987). *Enriched and impoverished environments: Effects on brain and behavior.* New York: Springer-Verlag. (p. 63)

Rescorla, R. A. (1988). Pavlovian conditioning: It's not what you think it is. *American Psychologist, 43,* 151–160. (p. 184)

Rescorla, R. A., & Wagner, A. R. (1972). A theory of Pavlovian conditioning: Variations in the effectiveness of reinforcement and nonreinforcement. In A. H. Black & W. F. Perokasy (Eds.), *Classical conditioning II: Current theory.* New York: Appleton-Century-Crofts. (p. 183)

Ressler, R. K., Burgess, A. W., & Douglas, J. E. (1988). *Sexual homicide patterns.* Boston: Lexington Books. (p. 462)

Reveen, P. J. (1987–88). Fantasizing under hypnosis: Some experimental evidence. *The Skeptical Inquirer, 12,* 181–183. (p. 162)

Rheingold, H. L. (1985). Development as the acquisition of familiarity. *Annual Review of Psychology, 36,* 1–17. (p. 72)

Rhodes, S. R. (1983). Age-related differences in work attitudes and behavior: A review and conceptual analysis. *Psychological Bulletin, 93,* 328–367. (p. 87)

Rice, B. (1985, September). Performance review: The job nobody likes. *Psychology Today,* pp. 30–36. (p. 445)

Rice, M. E., & Grusec, J. E. (1975). Saying and doing: Effects on observer performance. *Journal of Personality and Social Psychology, 32,* 584–593. (p. 200)

Ridenour, M. (1982). Infant walkers: Developmental tool or inherent danger. *Perceptual and Motor Skills, 55,* 1201–1202. (p. 64)

Rieff, P. (1979). *Freud: The mind of a moralist* (3rd ed.). Chicago: University of Chicago Press. (p. 354)

Ring, K. (1980). *Life at death: A scientific investigation of the near-death experience.* New York: Coward, McCann & Geoghegan. (p. 171)

Riskind, J. H., Beck, A. T., Berchick, R. J., Brown, G., & Steer, R. A. (1987). Reliability of DSM-III diagnoses for major depression and generalized anxiety disorder using the structured clinical interview for DSM-III. *Archives of General Psychiatry, 44,* 817–820. (p. 384)

Roberts, L. (1988). Beyond Noah's ark: What do we need to know? *Science, 242,* 1247. (p. 329)

Roberts, T-A. (1991). Gender and the influence of evaluations on self-assessments in achievement settings. *Psychological Bulletin, 109,* 297–308. (p. 486)

Robins, L., & Regier, D. (Eds.). (1991). *Psychiatric disorders in America.* New York: Free Press. (pp. 379, 406, 407)

Robinson, F. P. (1970). *Effective study.* New York: Harper & Row. (p. 22)

Robinson, J. P. (1988, December). Who's doing the housework? *American Demographics,* pp. 24–28, 63. (pp. 92, 493)

Robinson, L. A., Berman, J. S., & Neimeyer, R. A. (1990). Psychotherapy for the treatment of depression: A comprehensive review of controlled outcome research. *Psychological Bulletin, 108,* 30–49. (p. 430)

Robinson, V. M. (1983). Humor and health. In P. E. McGhee & J. H. Goldstein (Eds.), *Handbook of humor research: Vol. II. Applied studies.* New York: Springer-Verlag. (p. 338)

Rock, I., & Palmer, S. (1990, December). The legacy of Gestalt psychology. *Scientific American,* pp. 84–90. (p. 127)

Rodin, J. (1979). *Obesity theory and behavior therapy: An uneasy couple?* Paper presented at the meeting of the Association for the Advancement of Behavior Therapy. (p. 281)

Rodin, J. (1984, December). A sense of control [interview]. *Psychology Today,* pp. 38–45. (p. 276)

Rodin, J. (1985). Insulin levels, hunger and food intake: An example of feedback loops in body weight regulation. *Health Psychology, 4,* 1–18. (p. 281)

Rodin, J. (1986). Aging and health: Effects of the sense of control. *Science, 233,* 1271–1276. (pp. 328, 329, 370)

Rodin, J., & Slochower, J. (1976). Externality in the non-obese: Effects of environmental responsiveness on weight. *Journal of Personality and Social Psychology, 33,* 338–344. (p. 275)

Roger, L. H., Cortes, D. E., & Malgady, R. B. (1991). Acculturation and mental health status among Hispanics: Convergence and new directions for research. *American Psychologist, 46,* 585–597. (p. 483)

Rogers, C. R. (1958). Reinhold Niebuhr's *The self and the dramas of history:* A criticism. *Pastoral Psychology, 9,* 15–17. (p. 364)

Rogers, C. R. (1961). *On becoming a person: A therapist's view of psychotherapy.* Boston: Houghton Mifflin. (p. 416)

Rogers, C. R. (1970). *Carl Rogers on encounter groups.* New York: Harper & Row. (p. 418)

Rogers, C. R. (1980). *A way of being.* Boston: Houghton Mifflin. (pp. 363, 416, 417)

Rogers, S. M., & Turner, C. F. (1991). Male-male sexual contact in the U.S.A.: Findings from five sample surveys, 1970–1990. *Journal of Sex Research, 28,* 491–519. (p. 287)

Rook, K. S. (1984). Promoting social bonding: Strategies for helping the lonely and socially isolated. *American Psychologist, 39,* 1389–1407. (p. 398)

Rook, K. S. (1987). Social support versus companionship: Effects on life stress, loneliness, and evaluations by others. *Journal of Personality and Social Psychology, 52,* 1132–1147. (p. 339)

Rosch, E. (1974). Linguistic relativity. In A. Silverstein (Ed.), *Human communication: Theoretical perspectives.* New York: Halsted Press. (p. 249)

Rosch, E. (1978). Principles of categorization. In E. Rosch & B. L. Lloyd (Eds.), *Cognition and categorization.* Hillsdale, NJ: Erlbaum. (p. 204)

Rose, G. A., & Williams, R. T. (1961). Metabolic studies on large and small eaters. *British Journal of Nutrition, 1,* 1–9. (p. 278)

Rose, R. J., Koskenvuo, M., Kaprio, J., Sarna, S., & Langinvainio, H. (1988). Shared genes, shared experiences, and similarity of personality: Data from 14,228 adult Finnish co-twins. *Journal of Personality and Social Psychology, 54,* 161–171. (p. 96)

Rosenbaum, M. (1986). The repulsion hypothesis: On the nondevelopment of relationships. *Journal of Personality and Social Psychology, 51,* 1156–1166. (p. 469)

Rosenfeld, S. P. (1987, March 29). Insanity defense is riskier now and can turn winners to losers. Associated Press release (*Grand Rapids Press,* p. A17). (p. 383)

Rosenhan, D. L. (1983a). Psychological abnormality and law. In C. J. Scheirer & B. C. Hammonds (Eds.), *The master lecture series: Vol. 2. Psychology and the law.* Washington, DC: American Psychological Association. (p. 383)

Rosenhan, D. L. (1983b). *Psychological realities and judicial policy.* Paper presented at the American Psychological Association convention. (p. 383)

Rosenstein, M. J., Milazzo-Sayre, L. J., & Manderscheid, R. W. (1989). Care of persons with schizophrenia: A statistical profile. *Schizophrenia Bulletin, 15,* 45–58. (p. 379)

Rosenthal, R., Hall, J. A., Archer, D., DiMatteo, M. R., & Rogers, P. L. (1979). The PONS test: Measuring sensitivity to nonverbal cues. In S. Weitz (Ed.), *Nonverbal communication* (2nd ed.). New York: Oxford University Press. (p. 305)

Rosenzweig, M. R. (1984). Experience, memory, and the brain. *American Psychologist, 39,* 365–376. (p. 63)

Rosenzweig, M. R., Bennett, E. L., & Diamond, M. C. (1972, February). Brain changes in response to experience. *Scientific American,* 22–29. (p. 63)

Ross, H. (1975, June 19). Mist, murk, and visual perception. *New Scientist,* pp. 658–660. (p. 130)

Ross, M., McFarland, C., & Fletcher, G. J. O. (1981). The effect of attitude on the recall of personal histories. *Journal of Personality and Social Psychology, 40,* 627–634. (p. 228)

Rossl, P. J. (1960). Adaptation and negative aftereffect to lateral optical displacement in newly hatched chicks. *Science, 160,* 430–432. (p. 136)

Roth, T., Roehrs, T., Zwyghuizen-Doorenbos, A., Stpeanski, E., & Witting, R. (1988). Sleep and memory. In I. Hindmarch & H. Ott (Eds.), *Benzodiazepine receptor ligans, memory and information processing.* New York: Springer-Verlag. (p. 156)

Rothbart, M., Fulero, S., Jensen, C., Howard, J., & Birrell, P. (1978). From individual to group impressions: Availability heuristics in stereotype formation. *Journal of Experimental Social Psychology, 14,* 237–255. (p. 499)

Rothblum, E. D. (1990). Women and weight: Fad and fiction. *Journal of Psychology, 124,* 5–24. (p. 280)

Rothstein, W. G. (1980). The significance of occupations in work careers: An empirical and theoretical review. *Journal of Vocational Behavior, 17,* 328–343. (p. 93)

Roviaro, S., Holmes, D. S., & Holmsten, R. D. (1984). Influence of a cardiac rehabilitation program on the cardiovascular, psychological, and social functioning of cardiac patients. *Journal of Behavioral Medicine, 7,* 61–81. (p. 335)

Rowe, D. C. (1990). As the twig is bent? The myth of child-rearing influences on personality development. *Journal of Counseling and Development, 68,* 606–611. (p. 98)

Rowe, J. W., & Kahn, R. L. (1987). Human aging: Usual and successful. *Science, 237,* 143–149. (p. 88)

Rozin, P., Millman, L., & Nemeroff, C. (1986). Operation of the laws of sympathetic magic in disgust and other domains. *Journal of Personality and Social Psychology, 50,* 703–712. (p. 183)

Ruback, R. B., Carr, T. S., & Hopper, C. H. (1986). Perceived control in prison: Its relation to reported crowding, stress, and symptoms. *Journal of Applied Social Psychology, 16,* 375–386. (p. 370)

Rubin, L. B. (1979). *Women of a certain age: The midlife search for self.* New York: Harper & Row. (p. 92)

Rubin, L. B. (1985). *Just friends: The role of friendship in our lives.* New York: Harper & Row. (p. 487)

Rubin, Z. (1970). Measurement of romantic love. *Journal of Personality and Social Psychology, 16,* 265–273. (p. 305)

Rubonis, A. V., & Bickman, L. (1991). Psychological impairment in the wake of disaster: The disaster-psychopathology relationship. *Psychological Bulletin, 109,* 384–399. (p. 326)

Rudman, D., Feller, A. G., Nagraj, H. S., Gergans, G. A., Lalitha, P. Y., Goldberg, A. F., Schlenker, R. A., Cohn, L., Rudman, I. W., & Mattson, D. E. (1990). Effects of human growth hormone in men over 60 years old. *New England Journal of Medicine, 323,* 1–6. (p. 43)

Rulc, B. G., & Ferguson, T. J. (1986). The effects of media violence on attitudes, emotions, and cognitions. *Journal of Social Issues, 42*(3), 29–50. (p. 462)

Rumbaugh, D. M. (1977). *Language learning by a chimpanzee: The Lana project.* New York: Academic Press. (p. 247)

Rumbaugh, D. M., & Savage-Rumbaugh, S. (1978). Chimpanzee language research: Status and potential. *Behavior Research Methods & Instrumentation, 10,* 119–131. (p. 248)

Rushton, J. P. (1975).   Generosity in children: Immediate and long-term effects of modeling, preaching, and moral judgment. *Journal of Personality and Social Psychology, 31,* 459–466. (p. 200)

Rushton, J. P. (1989)   Genetic similarity, human altruism, and group selection. *Behavioral and Brain Sciences, 12,* 503–559. (p. 466)

Rushton, J. P., Fulker, D. W., Neale, M. C., Nias, D. K. B., & Eysenck, H. J. (1986).   Altruism and aggression: The heritability of individual differences. *Journal of Personality and Social Psychology, 50,* 1192–1198. (p. 458)

Russell, B. (1930/1985).   *The conquest of happiness.* London: Unwin Paperbacks. (p. 317)

Russell, J. A. (1991).   Culture and the categorization of emotions. *Psychological Bulletin, 110,* 426–450. (p. 308)

Russell, J. A., Lewicka, M., & Niit, T. (1989).   A cross-cultural study of a circumplex model of affect. *Journal of Personality and Social Psychology, 57,* 848–856. (p. 310)

Rutter, M. (1979).   Maternal deprivation, 1972–1978: New findings, new concepts, new approaches. *Child Development, 50,* 283–305. (p. 73)

Saal, F. E., Johnson, C. B., & Weber, N. (1989).   Friendly or sexy? It may depend on whom you ask. *Psychology of Women Quarterly, 13,* 263–276. (p. 488)

Sabini, J. (1986).   Stanley Milgram (1933–1984).   *American Psychologist, 41,* 1378–1379. (p. 452)

Sackeim, H. A. (1988).   Mechanisms of action of electroconvulsive therapy. In A. J. Frances & R. E. Hales (Eds.), *Review of Psychiatry* (Vol. 7). Washington, DC: American Psychiatric Press. (p. 437)

Sacks, O. (1985).   *The man who mistook his wife for a hat.* New York: Summit Books. (pp. 51, 124, 218, 219)

Sadalla, E. K., Kenrick, D. T., & Vershure, B. (1987).   Dominance and heterosexual attraction. *Journal of Personality and Social Psychology, 52,* 730–738. (p. 468)

Sagan, C. (1979a).   *Broca's brain.* New York: Random House. (pp. 6, 35)

Sagan, C. (1979b).   *Dragons of Eden.* New York: Random House. (p. 380)

Sagan, C. (1980).   *Cosmos.* New York: Random House. (p. 495)

Sagan, C. (1987, February 1).   The fine art of baloney detection. *Parade.* (pp. 107, 143)

Salovey, P. (1990, January/February).   Interview. *American Scientist,* pp. 25–29. (p. 314)

Salovey, P., & Birnbaum, D. (1989).   Influence of mood on health-relevant cognitions. *Journal of Personality and Social Psychology, 57,* 539–551. (p. 223)

Samuels, S., & McCabe, G. (1989).   Quoted by P. Diaconis & F. Mosteller, Methods for studying coincidences. *Journal of the American Statistical Association, 84,* 853–861. (p. 519)

Sandberg, G. G., Jackson, T. L., & Petretic-Jackson, P. (1985).   *Sexual aggression and courtship violence in dating relationships.* Paper presented at the Midwestern Psychological Association convention. (p. 462)

Sanders, B., & Soares, M. P. (1986).   Sexual maturation and spatial ability in college students. *Developmental Psychology, 22,* 199–203. (p. 485)

Sapadin, L. A. (1988).   Friendship and gender: Perspectives of professional men and women. *Journal of Social and Personal Relationships, 5,* 387–403. (p. 487)

Sapolsky, R. M. (1990, January).   Stress in the wild. *Scientific American,* pp. 116–123. (p. 326)

Sarawathi, T. S., & Dutta, R. (1988).   *Invisible boundaries: Grooming for adult roles.* New Delhi: Northern Book Centre. Cited by R. Larson & M. H. Richards (1989). Introduction: The changing life space of early adolescence. *Journal of Youth and Adolescence, 18,* 501–509. (p. 492)

Sarnoff, I., & Sarnoff, S. (1989).   *Love-centered marriage in a self-centered world.* New York: Hemisphere. (p. 284)

Sato, K. (1987).   Distribution of the cost of maintaining common resources. *Journal of Experimental Social Psychology, 23,* 19–31. (p. 500)

Savitsky, J. C., & Lindblom, W. D. (1986).   The impact of the guilty but mentally ill verdict on juror decisions: An empirical analysis. *Journal of Applied Social Psychology, 16,* 686–701. (p. 383)

Sayre, R. F. (1979).   The parents' last lessons. In D. D. Van Tassel (Ed.), *Aging, death, and the completion of being.* Philadelphia: University of Pennsylvania Press. (p. 88)

Scanlan, C. (1990, March 27).   Weight-loss industry diagnosed as unhealthy. *Detroit Free Press,* pp. 1A, 6A. (p. 280)

Scarr, S. (1984, May).   What's a parent to do? [Conversation with E. Hall.] *Psychology Today,* pp. 58–63. (p. 262)

Scarr, S. (1986).   *Mother care/other care.* New York: Basic Books. (p. 263)

Scarr, S. (1988).   Race and gender as psychological variables: Social and ethical issues. *American Psychologist, 43,* 56–59. (p. 486)

Scarr, S. (1989).   Protecting general intelligence: Constructs and consequences for interventions. In R. J. Linn (Ed.), *Intelligence: Measurement, theory, and public policy.* Champaign: University of Illinois Press. (pp. 259, 261)

Scarr, S. (1990).   Back cover comments on J. Dunn & R. Plomin (1990).   *Separate lives: Why siblings are so different.* New York: Basic Books. (p. 99)

Scarr, S., & McCartney, K. (1983).   How people make their own environments: A theory of genotype → environment effects. *Child Development, 54,* 424–435. (p. 98)

Schab, F. R. (1990).   Odors and the remembrance of things past. *Journal of Experimental Psychology: Learning, Memory, and Cognition, 16,* 648–655. (p. 122)

Schab, F. R. (1991).   Odor memory: Taking stock. *Psychological Bulletin, 109,* 242–251. (p. 122)

Schachter, S., & Singer, J. E. (1962).   Cognitive, social and physiological determinants of emotional state. *Psychological Review, 69,* 379–399. (p. 320)

Schacter, D. L. (1987).   Implicit memory: History and current status. *Journal of Experimental Psychology: Learning, Memory, and Cognition, 13,* 501–518. (p. 219)

Schaie, K. W. (1989).   Perceptual speed in adulthood: Cross-sectional and longitudinal studies. *Psychology and Aging, 4,* 443–453. (p. 88)

Schaie, K. W., & Geiwitz, J. (1982).   *Adult development and aging.* Boston: Little, Brown. (p. 89)

Schaie, K. W., & Strother, C. R. (1968). A cross-sequential study of age changes in cognitive behavior. *Psychological Bulletin, 70,* 671–680. (p. 89)

Scheerer, M. (1963, April). Problem solving. *Scientific American,* pp. 118–128. (pp. 236, 238)

Scheier, M. F., & Carver, C. S. (1992). Effects of optimism on psychological and physical well-being: Theoretical overview and empirical update. *Cognitive Therapy and Research, 16,* 201–228. (p. 328)

Schein, E. H. (1956). The Chinese indoctrination program for prisoners of war: A study of attempted brainwashing. *Psychiatry, 19,* 149–172. (p. 446)

Schiavi, R. C., & Schreiner-Engel, P. (1988). Nocturnal penile tumescence in healthy aging men. *Journal of Gerontology: Medical Sciences, 43,* M146–150. (p. 153)

Schiffenbauer, A., & Schiavo, R. S. (1976). Physical distance and attraction: An intensification effect. *Journal of Experimental Social Psychology, 12,* 274–282. (p. 454)

Schleifer, S. J., Keller, S. E., McKegney, F. P., & Stein, M. (1979). *The influence of stress and other psychosocial factors on human immunity.* Paper presented at the 36th Annual Meeting of the American Psychosomatic Society. (p. 332)

Schlesinger, A. M., Jr. (1965). *A thousand days.* Boston: Houghton Mifflin. (p. 456)

Schnaper, N. (1980). Comments germane to the paper entitled "The reality of death experiences" by Ernst Rodin. *Journal of Nervous and Mental Disease, 168,* 268–270. (p. 171)

Schofield, J. W. (1986). Black-White contact in desegregated schools. In M. Hewstone & R. Brown (Eds.), *Contact and conflict in intergroup encounters.* Oxford: Basil Blackwell Ltd. (p. 501)

Schonfield, D., & Robertson, B. A. (1966). Memory storage and aging. *Canadian Journal of Psychology, 20,* 228–236. (p. 89)

Schooler, J. W., Gerhard, D., & Loftus, E. F. (1986). Qualities of the unreal. *Journal of Experimental Psychology: Learning, Memory, and Cognition, 12,* 171–181. (p. 224)

Schwartz, B. (1984). *Psychology of learning and behavior* (2nd ed.). New York: Norton. (pp. 185, 387)

Schwarz, N., & Clore, G. L. (1983). Mood, misattribution, and judgments of well-being: Informative and directive functions of affective states. *Journal of Personality and Social Psychology, 45,* 513–523. (p. 313)

Schwarz, N., Strack, F., Kommer, D., & Wagner, D. (1987). Soccer, rooms, and the quality of your life: Mood effects on judgments of satisfaction with life in general and with specific domains. *European Journal of Social Psychology, 17,* 69–79. (p. 223)

Segall, M. H., Dasen, P. R., Berry, J. W., & Poortinga, Y. H. (1990). *Human behavior in global perspective: An introduction to cross-cultural psychology.* New York: Pergamon. (pp. 70, 488, 492, 498)

Seginer, R., Karayanni, M., & Mar'i, M. M. (1990). Adolescents' attitudes toward women's roles. *Psychology of Women Quarterly, 14,* 119–133. (p. 492)

Seibert, P. S., & Ellis, H. C. (1991). Irrelevant thoughts, emotional mood states, and cognitive task performance. *Memory and Cognition, 19,* 507–513. (p. 223)

Seligman, M. E. P. (1974, May). Submissive death: Giving up on life. *Psychology Today,* pp. 80–85. (p. 302)

Seligman, M. E. P. (1975). *Helplessness: On depression, development and death.* San Francisco: Freeman. (p. 369)

Seligman, M. E. P. (1988, October). Boomer blues. *Psychology Today,* pp. 50–55. (p. 480)

Seligman, M. E. P. (1988). Why is there so much depression today? The waxing of the individual and the waning of the commons. In I. S. Cohen (Ed.), *The G. Stanley Hall Lectures* (Vol. 9). Washington, DC: American Psychological Association. (pp. 393, 397)

Seligman, M. E. P. (1989). Explanatory style: Predicting depression, achievement, and health. In M. D. Yapko (Ed.), *Brief therapy approaches to treating anxiety and depression.* New York: Brunner/Mazel. (p. 427)

Seligman, M. E. P. (1991). *Learned optimism.* New York: Knopf. (pp. 369, 397)

Seligman, M. E. P., & Schulman, P. (1986). Explanatory style as a predictor of productivity and quitting among life insurance sales agents. *Journal of Personality and Social Psychology, 50,* 832–838. (p. 371)

Seligman, M. E. P., & Yellen, A. (1987). What is a dream? *Behavior Research and Therapy, 25,* 1–14. (pp. 152, 158)

Selye, H. (1936). A syndrome produced by diverse nocuous agents. *Nature, 138,* 32. (p. 324)

Selye, H. (1976). *The stress of life.* New York: McGraw-Hill. (p. 324)

Senden, M., von (1932; reprinted 1960). In P. Heath (Trans.), *Space and sight: The perception of space and shape in the congenitally blind before and after operation.* Glencoe, IL: Free Press. (p. 135)

Shadish, W. R., Jr. (1992). Do family and marital psychotherapies change what people do? A meta-analysis of behavioral outcomes. In T. D. Cook, H. M. Cooper, D. S. Cordray, H. Hartman, L. V. Hedges, R. J. Light, T. A. Louis, & F. Mosteller (Eds.), *Meta-analysis for explanation: A casebook.* New York: Russell Sage. (p. 418)

Shapiro, C. M., Bortz, R., Mitchell, D., Bartel, P., & Jooste, P. (1981). Slow-wave sleep: A recovery period after exercise. *Science, 214,* 1253–1254. (p. 154)

Shapiro, D. A., & Shapiro, D. (1982). Meta-analysis of comparative therapy outcome studies: A replication and refinement. *Psychological Bulletin, 92,* 581–604. (p. 431)

Shaughnessy, J. J., & Zechmeister, E. (1992). Memory monitoring accuracy as influenced by the distribution of retrieval practice. *Bulletin of the Psychonomic Society, 30,* 125–128. (p. 225)

Shaw, H. L. (1989–90). Comprehension of the spoken word and ASL translation by chimpanzees (Pan troglodytes). *Friends of Washoe, 9*(1/2), 8–19. (p. 248)

Sheehan, S. (1982). *Is there no place on earth for me?* Boston: Houghton Mifflin. (p. 399)

Sheldon, W. H. (1954). *Atlas of man: A guide for somatotyping the adult male of all ages.* New York: Harper & Row. (p. 356)

Shepard, R. N. (1981). Psychophysical complementarity. In M. Kubovy & J. R. Pomerantz (Eds.), *Perceptual organization.* Hillsdale, NJ: Erlbaum. (p. 132)

Shepard, R. N. (1990). *Mind sights.* New York: Freeman. (pp. 126, 132, 137, 138)

Shepherd, C., Kohut, J. J., & Sweet, R. (1990). *More news of the weird*. New York: Penguin/Plume Books. (p. 406)

Sherif, M. (1966). *In common predicament: Social psychology of intergroup conflict and cooperation*. Boston: Houghton Mifflin. (p. 501)

Sherman, A. R., & Levin, M. P. (1979). *In vivo* therapies for compulsive habits, sexual difficulties, and severe adjustment problems. In A. P. Goldstein & F. H. Kanfer (Eds.), *Maximizing treatment gains: Transfer enhancement in psychotherapy*. New York: Academic Press. (p. 422)

Sherry, D., & Vaccarino, A. L. (1989). Hippocampus and memory for food caches in black-capped chickadees. *Behavioral Neuroscience, 103*, 308–318. (p. 220)

Shettleworth, S. J. (1973). Food reinforcement and the organization of behavior in golden hamsters. In R. A. Hinde & J. Stevenson-Hinde (Eds.), *Constraints on learning*. London: Academic Press. (p. 195)

Shneidman, E. (1987, March). At the point of no return. *Psychology Today*, pp. 54–58. (p. 393)

Shotland, L. (1984, March 12). Quoted by Maureen Dowd, 20 years after the murder of Kitty Genovese, the question remains: Why? *The New York Times*, p. B1. (p. 464)

Shotland, R. L. (1989). A model of the causes of date rape in developing and close relationships. In C. Hendrick (Ed.), *Review of Personality and Social Psychology* (Vol. 10). Newbury Park, CA: Sage. (p. 488)

Showers, C., & Ruben, C. (1987). *Distinguishing pessimism from depression: Negative expectations and positive coping mechanisms*. Paper presented at the American Psychological Association convention. (p. 371)

Shrout, P. E., Link, B. G., Dohrenwend, B. P., Skodol, A. E., Stueve, A., & Mirotznik, J. (1989). Characterizing life events as risk factors for depression: The role of fateful loss events. *Journal of Abnormal Psychology, 98*, 460–467. (p. 395)

Shulruff, L. I. (1990, August 10). In sex case, focus is on multiple personalities. *New York Times*. (p. 390)

Siegel, J. M. (1990). Stressful life events and use of physician services among the elderly: The moderating role of pet ownership. *Journal of Personality and Social Psychology, 58*, 1081–1086. (p. 339)

Siegel, L. S., & Hodkin, B. (1982). The garden path to the understanding of cognitive development: Has Piaget led us into the poison ivy? In S. Modgil & C. Modgil (Eds.), *Jean Piaget: Consensus and controversy*. New York: Praeger. (p. 69)

Siegel, R. K. (1977, October). Hallucinations. *Scientific American*, pp. 132–140. (p. 171)

Siegel, R. K. (1980). The psychology of life after death. *American Psychologist, 35*, 911–931. (p. 171)

Siegel, R. K. (1984, March 15). Personal communication. (p. 171)

Siegel, R. K. (1990). *Intoxication*. New York: Pocket Books. (pp. 168, 170, 171, 172)

Siegel, R. K. Quoted by J. Hooper (1982, October), Mind tripping. *Omni*, pp. 72–82, 159–160. (p. 171)

Silver, M., & Geller, D. (1978). On the irrelevance of evil: The organization and individual action. *Journal of Social Issues, 34*, 125–136. (p. 453)

Silverman, P. S., & Retzlaff, P. D. (1986). Cognitive stage regression through hypnosis: Are earlier cognitive stages retrievable? *International Journal of Clinical and Experimental Hypnosis, 34*, 192–204. (p. 161)

Silverton, L. (1988). Crime and the schizophrenia spectrum: A study of three Danish cohorts. In T. E. Moffitt & S. A. Mednick (Eds.), *Biological contributions to crime causation*. New York: Martinus-Nijhoff. (p. 408)

Simmons, R. G., & Blyth, D. A. (1987). *Moving into adolescence: The impact of pubertal change and school context*. New York: Aldine De Gruyter. (p. 79)

Simonton, D. K. (1988). Age and outstanding achievement: What do we know after a century of research? *Psychological Bulletin, 104*, 251–267. (p. 90)

Singer, J. L. (1975). Navigating the stream of consciousness: Research in daydreaming and related inner experience. *American Psychologist, 30*, 727–738. (p. 159)

Singer, J. L. (1976, July). Fantasy: The foundation of serenity. *Psychology Today*, pp. 32–37. (p. 159)

Singer, J. L. (1981). Clinical intervention: New developments in methods and evaluation. In L. T. Benjamin, Jr. (Ed.), *The G. Stanley Hall Lecture Series* (Vol. 1). Washington, DC: American Psychological Association. (p. 431)

Singer, J. L. (1986). Is television bad for children? *Social Science, 71*, 178–182. (p. 159)

Singer, J. L., & Singer, D. G. (1986). Family experiences and television viewing as predictors of children's imagination, restlessness, and aggression. *Journal of Social Issues, 42*(3), 7–28. (p. 462)

Sjöstrom, L. (1980). Fat cells and body weight. In A. J. Stunkard (Ed.), *Obesity*. Philadelphia: Saunders. (p. 278)

Skinner, B. F. (1953). *Science and human behavior*. New York: Macmillan. (p. 192)

Skinner, B. F. (1956). A case history in scientific method. *American Psychologist, 11*, 221–233. (p. 193)

Skinner, B. F. (1957). *Verbal behavior*. Englewood Cliffs, NJ: Prentice-Hall. (p. 245)

Skinner, B. F. (1961, November). Teaching machines. *Scientific American*, pp. 91–102. (pp. 192, 193)

Skinner, B. F. (1983, September). Origins of a behaviorist. *Psychology Today*, pp. 22–33. (pp. 196, 396)

Skinner, B. F. (1985). Cognitive science and behaviorism. Unpublished manuscript, Harvard University. (p. 245)

Skinner, B. F. (1986). What is wrong with daily life in the western world? *American Psychologist, 41*, 568–574. (p. 197)

Skinner, B. F. (1988). *The school of the future*. Address to the American Psychological Association convention. (p. 197)

Skinner, B. F. (1989). Teaching machines. *Science, 243*, 1535. (p. 197)

Skinner, B. F. (1990). Can psychology be a science of the mind? *American Psychologist, 45*, 1206–1210. (p. 195)

Sklar, L. S., & Anisman, H. (1981). Stress and cancer. *Psychological Bulletin, 89*, 369–406. (p. 332)

Skov, R. B., & Sherman, S. J. (1986). Information-gathering processes: Diagnosticity, hypothesis-confirmatory strategies, and perceived hypothesis confirmation. *Journal of Experimental Social Psychology, 22,* 93–121. (p. 236)

Slavin, R. E. (1989). Cooperative learning and student achievement. In R. E. Slavin (Ed.), *School and classroom organization.* Hillsdale, NJ: Erlbaum. (p. 502)

Slovic, P. (1987). Perception of risk. *Science, 236,* 280–285. (p. 239)

Slovic, P., & Fischhoff, B. (1977). On the psychology of experimental surprises. *Journal of Experimental Psychology: Human Perception and Performance, 3,* 544–551. (p. 20)

Small, M. F. (1991, July). Sperm wars. *Discover,* pp. 48–53. (p. 489)

Smart, R. G., & Adlaf, E. M. (1989). The Ontario student drug use survey: Trends between 1977–1989. 33 Russell Street, Toronto, Ontario M5S: Addiction Research Foundation of Ontario. (p. 173)

Smith, A. (1983). Personal correspondence. (p. 402)

Smith, A. (1987). Personal communication. (p. 49)

Smith, A., & Sugar, O. (1975). Development of above normal language and intelligence 21 years after left hemispherectomy. *Neurology, 25,* 813–818. (p. 49)

Smith, D. (1982). Trends in counseling and psychotherapy. *American Psychologist, 37,* 802–809. (p. 414)

Smith, M. B. (1978). Psychology and values. *Journal of Social Issues, 34,* 181–199. (p. 367)

Smith, M. C. (1983). Hypnotic memory enhancement of witnesses: Does it work? *Psychological Bulletin, 94,* 387–407. (p. 161)

Smith, M. L., & Glass, G. V. (1977). Meta-analysis of psychotherapy outcome studies. *American Psychologist, 32,* 752–760. (p. 431)

Smith, M. L., Glass, G. V., & Miller, R. L. (1980). *The benefits of psychotherapy.* Baltimore: Johns Hopkins Press. (pp. 430, 431)

Smith, P. B., & Tayeb, M. (1989). Organizational structure and processes. In M. Bond (Ed.), *The cross-cultural challenge to social psychology.* Newbury Park, CA: Sage. (p. 295)

Smith, T. (1991). Personal communication. Chicago: National Opinion Research Center. (pp. 315, 496)

Smith, T. W. (1990). Adult sexual behavior in 1989: Number of partners, frequency, and risk. General Social Survey Topic Report No. 18, National Opinion Research Center, University of Chicago. (pp. 282, 287)

Snarey, J. (1987, June). A question of morality. *Psychology Today,* pp. 6–7. (p. 81)

Snarey, J. R. (1985). Cross-cultural universality of social-moral development: A critical review of Kohlbergian research. *Psychological Bulletin, 97,* 202–233. (p. 81)

Snodgrass, M. A. (1987). The relationships of differential loneliness, intimacy and characterological attributional style to duration of loneliness. *Journal of Social Behavior and Personality, 2,* 173–186. (p. 398)

Snodgrass, S. E., Higgins, J. G., & Todisco, L. (1986). *The effects of walking behavior on mood.* Paper presented at the American Psychological Association convention. (p. 308)

Snyder, M. (1984). When belief creates reality. In L. Berkowitz (Ed.), *Advances in experimental social psychology* (Vol. 18). New York: Academic Press. (p. 408)

Snyder, M., Tanke, E. D., & Berscheid, E. (1977). Social perception and interpersonal behavior: On the self-fulfilling nature of social stereotypes. *Journal of Personality and Social Psychology, 35,* 656–666. (p. 457)

Snyder, S. H. (1984). Neurosciences: An integrative discipline *Science, 225,* 1255–1257. (pp. 30, 435)

Snyder, S. H. (1986). *Drugs and the brain.* New York: Scientific American Library. (p. 436)

Sobal, J., & Stunkard, A. J. (1989). Socioeconomic status and obesity: A review of the literature. *Psychological Bulletin, 105,* 260–275. (p. 276)

Sokoll, G. R., & Mynatt, C. R. (1984). *Arousal and free throw shooting.* Paper presented at the Midwestern Psychological Association convention. (p. 302)

Solomon, M. (1987, December). Standard issue. *Psychology Today,* pp. 30–31. (p. 467)

Solomon, Z. (1990). Does the war end when the shooting stops? The psychological toll of war. *Journal of Applied Social Psychology, 20,* 1733–1745. (p. 325)

Sommer, R. (1969). *Personal space.* Englewood Cliffs, NJ: Prentice-Hall. (p. 477)

Sontag, S. (1978). *Illness as metaphor.* New York: Farrar, Straus, & Giroux. (p. 333)

Sorenson, S. B., Stein, J. A., Siegel, J. M., Golding, J. M., & Burnam, M. A. (1987). Prevalence of adult sexual assault: The Los Angeles Epidemiologic Catchment Area Study. *American Journal of Epidemiology, 126,* 1154–1164. (p. 462)

Sowell, T. (1991, May/June). Cultural diversity: A world view. *American Enterprise,* pp. 44–55. (p. 503)

Spanos, N. & Chaves, J. F. (Eds.) (1989). Hypnosis: The cognitive-behavioral perspective. Buffalo, NY: Promotheus Books. (p. 165)

Spanos, N. P. (1982). A social psychological approach to hypnotic behavior. In G. Weary & H. L. Mirels (Eds.), *Integrations of clinical and social psychology.* New York: Oxford University Press. (p. 163)

Spanos, N. P. (1986a). Hypnotic behavior: A social-psychological interpretation of amnesia, analgesia, and "trance logic." *Brain and Behavioral Sciences, 9,* 449–502. (p. 164)

Spanos, N. P. (1986b). Hypnosis, nonvolitional responding, and multiple personality: A social psychological perspective. *Progress in Experimental Personality Research, 14,* 1–62. (p. 390)

Spanos, N. P. (1987–88). Past-life hypnotic regression: A critical view. *The Skeptical Inquirer, 12,* 174–180. (p. 162)

Spanos, N. P. (1991). Hypnosis, hypnotizability, and hypnotherapy. In C. R. Snyder & D. R. Forsyth (Eds.), *Handbook of social and clinical psychology: The health perspective.* New York: Pergamon Press. (p. 163)

Spanos, N. P., Radtke, L., & Bertrand, L. D. (1985). Hypnotic amnesia as a strategic enactment: Breaching amnesia in highly susceptible subjects. *Journal of Personality and Social Psychology, 47,* 1155–1169. (p. 160)

Spector, P. E. (1986). Perceived control by employees: A meta-analysis of studies concerning autonomy and participation at work. *Human Relations, 39,* 1005–1016. (p. 295)

Spence, J. T., & Helmreich, R. L. (1983). Achievement-related motives and behavior. In J. T. Spence (Ed.), *Achievement and achievement motives: Psychological and sociological approaches*. New York: Freeman. (p. 293)

Sperling, G. (1960). The information available in brief visual presentations. *Psychological Monographs, 74* (Whole No. 498). (p. 208)

Sperry, R. W. (1964). *Problems outstanding in the evolution of brain function*. James Arthur Lecture, American Museum of Natural History, New York. Cited by R. Ornstein (1977), *The psychology of consciousness* (2nd ed.). New York: Harcourt Brace Jovanovich. (p. 53)

Sperry, R. W. (1968). Hemisphere deconnection and unity in conscious awareness. *American Psychologist, 23,* 723–733. (p. 52)

Sperry, R. W. (1982). Some effects of disconnecting the cerebral hemispheres. *Science, 217,* 1223–1226. (p. 53)

Sperry, R. W. (1985). Changed concepts of brain and consciousness: Some value implications. *Zygon, 20,* 41–57. (p. 115)

Spiegel, D., Bloom, J. R., Kraemer, H. C., & Gottheil, E. (1989, October 14). Effect of psychosocial treatment on survival of patients with metastatic breast cancer. *The Lancet,* pp. 888–891. (p. 333)

Spielberger, C., & London, P. (1982). Rage boomerangs. *American Health, 1,* 52–56. (p. 331)

Spiess, W. F. J., Greer, J. H., & O'Donohue, W. T. (1984). Premature ejaculation: Investigation of factors in ejaculatory latency. *Journal of Abnormal Psychology, 93,* 242–245. (p. 286)

Spitzberg, B. H., & Hurt, H. T. (1987). The relationship of interpersonal competence and skill to reported loneliness across time. *Journal of Social Behavior and Personality, 2,* 157–172. (p. 398)

Spitzer, R. L. (1975). On pseudoscience in science, logic in remission, and psychiatric diagnosis: A critique of Rosenhan's "On being sane in insane places." *Journal of Abnormal Psychology, 84,* 442–452. (p. 408)

Spitzer, R. L., Gibbon, M., Skodol, A. E., Williams, J. B. W., & First, M. B. (1989). *DSM-III-R casebook*. Washington, DC: American Psychiatric Press. (p. 388)

Spradley, J. P., & Phillips, M. (1972). Culture and stress: A quantitative analysis. *American Anthropologist, 74,* 518–529. (p. 478)

Sprecher, S. (1989). The importance to males and females of physical attractiveness, earning potential, and expressiveness in initial attraction. *Sex Roles, 21,* 591–607. (p. 467)

Springer, S. P., & Deutsch, G. (1985). *Left brain, right brain*. San Francisco: Freeman. (p. 54)

Squire, L. (1990). *Memory and brain systems*. Invited address to the American Psychological Society convention. (pp. 219, 220)

Squire, L. R. (1987). *Memory and brain*. New York: Oxford University Press. (pp. 218, 219)

Squire, S. (1987, November 22). Shock therapy's return to respectability. *The New York Times Magazine,* pp. 78–89. (p. 437)

Sroufe, L. A., Fox, N. E., & Pancake, V. R. (1983). Attachment and dependency in developmental perspective. *Child Development, 54,* 1615–1627. (p. 73)

Stattin, H., & Magnusson, D. (1990). *Pubertal maturation in female development*. Hillsdale, NJ: Erlbaum. (p. 79)

Staub, E. (1989). *The roots of evil: The psychological and cultural sources of genocide*. New York: Cambridge University Press. (p. 447)

Steele, C. (1990b). *Protecting the self: Implications for social psychological theory and minority achievement*. Address to the American Psychological Association convention. (p. 459)

Steele, C. M., & Josephs, R. A. (1990). Alcohol myopia: Its prized and dangerous effects. *American Psychologist, 45,* 921–933. (p. 167)

Stein, J. A., Newcomb, M. D., & Bentler, P. M. (1986). Stability and change in personality: A longitudinal study from early adolescence to young adulthood. *Journal of Research In Personality, 20,* 276–291. (p. 100)

Steinberg, L. (1987, September). Bound to bicker. *Psychology Today,* pp. 36–39. (p. 83)

Steinem, G. (1988). Six great ideas that television is missing. In G. Comstock (Ed.), *Public communication and behavior*. New York: Academic Press. (p. 464)

Stellar, E. (1985). *Hunger in animals and humans*. Distinguished lecture to the Eastern Psychological Association convention. (p. 281)

Stengel, E. (1981). Suicide. In *The new encyclopaedia britannica, macropaedia* (Vol. 17, pp. 777–782). Chicago: Encyclopaedia Britannica. (p. 392)

Stephens, T. (1988). Physical activity and mental health in the United States and Canada: Evidence from four population surveys. *Preventive Medicine, 17,* 35–47. (p. 335)

Sternberg, R. J. (1986). A triangular theory of love. *Psychological Review, 93,* 119–135. (p. 470)

Sternberg, R. J. (1988). Applying cognitive theory to the testing and teaching of intelligence. *Applied Cognitive Psychology, 2,* 231–255. (p. 260)

Sternberg, R. J., & Grajek, S. (1984). The nature of love. *Journal of Personality and Social Psychology, 47,* 312–329. (p. 470)

Sternberg, R. J., & Lubart, T. I. (1991). An investment theory of creativity and its development. *Human Development,* 1–31. (p. 260)

Sternberg, R. J., & Salter, W. (1982). Conceptions of intelligence. In R. J. Sternberg (Ed.), *Handbook of human intelligence*. New York: Cambridge University Press. (p. 256)

Sternberg, R. J., & Wagner, R. K. (Eds.). (1986). *Practical intelligence: Origins of competence in the everyday world*. New York: Cambridge University Press. (p. 259)

Stevenson, M. R., & Black, K. N. (1988). Paternal absence and sex-role development: A meta-analysis. *Child Development, 59,* 793–814. (pp. 76, 490)

Stiles, D. A., Gibbons, J. L., & Schnellmann, J. D. G. (1990). Opposite-sex ideal in the U.S.A. and Mexico as perceived by young adolescents. *Journal of Cross-Cultural Psychology, 21,* 180–199. (p. 492)

Stiles, W. B., Shapiro, D. A., & Elliott, R. (1986). "Are all psychotherapies equivalent?" *American Psychologist, 41,* 165–180. (p. 431)

Stone, A. A., & Neale, J. M. (1984). Effects of severe daily events on mood. *Journal of Personality and Social Psychology, 46,* 137–144. (p. 314)

Stone, A. A., Cox, D. S., Valdimarsdottir, H., Jandor, L., & Neale, J. M. (1987). Evidence that secretory IgA antibody is associated with daily mood. *Journal of Personality and Social Psychology, 52,* 988–993. (p. 331)

Storms, M. D. (1973).   Videotape and the attribution process: Reversing actors' and observers' points of view. *Journal of Personality and Social Psychology, 27,* 165–175. (p. 444)

Storms, M. D. (1981).   A theory of erotic orientation development. *Psychological Review, 88,* 340–353. (p. 289)

Storms, M. D. (1983).   *Development of sexual orientation.* Washington, DC: Office of Social and Ethical Responsibility, American Psychological Association. (p. 288)

Storms, M. D., & Thomas, G. C. (1977).   Reactions to physical closeness. *Journal of Personality and Social Psychology, 35,* 412–418. (p. 454)

Strack, F., Martin, L., & Stepper, S. (1988).   Inhibiting and facilitating conditions of the human smile: A nonobtrusive test of the facial feedback hypothesis. *Journal of Personality and Social Psychology, 54,* 768–777. (p. 309)

Strack, S., & Coyne, J. C. (1983).   Social confirmation of dysphoria: Shared and private reactions to depression. *Journal of Personality and Social Behavior, 44,* 798–806. (p. 397)

Stratton, G. M. (1896).   Some preliminary experiments on vision without inversion of the retinal image. *Psychological Review, 3,* 611–617. (p. 136)

Straub, R. O., Seidenberg, M. S., Devei, T. G., & Terrace, H. S. (1979).   Serial learning in the pigeon. *Journal of the Experimental Analysis of Behavior, 32,* 137–148. (p. 248)

Straus, M. A., & Gelles, R. J. (1980).   *Behind closed doors: Violence in the American family.* New York: Anchor/Doubleday. (p. 193)

Strentz, H. (1986, January 1).   Become a psychic and amaze your friends! *Atlanta Journal,* p. 15A. (p. 142)

Strupp, H. H. (1986).   Psychotherapy: Research, practice, and public policy (How to avoid dead ends). *American Psychologist, 41,* 120–130. (p. 432)

Suddath, R. L., Christison, G. W., Torrey, E. F., Casanova, M. F., & Weinberger, D. R. (1990).   Anatomical abnormalities in the brains of monozygotic twins discordant for schizophrenia. *New England Journal of Medicine, 322,* 789–794. (p. 403)

Suedfeld, P., & Mocellin, J. S. P. (1987).   The "sensed presence" in unusual environments. *Environment and Behavior, 19,* 33–52. (p. 172)

Suinn, R. M. (1986).   *Seven steps to peak performance.* Toronto: Hogrefe. (p. 250)

Sulloway, F. J. (1990).   *Orthodoxy and innovation in science: The influence of birth order in a multivariate context.* Paper delivered at the American Association for the Advancement of Science annual meeting. (p. 293)

Suls, J. M., & Tesch, F. (1978).   Students' preferences for information about their test performance: A social comparison study. *Journal of Experimental Social Psychology, 8,* 189–197. (p. 316)

Sundstrom, E., De Meuse, K. P., & Futrell, D. (1990).   Work teams: Applications and effectiveness. *American Psychologist, 45,* 120–133. (p. 295)

Suomi, S. J. (1983).   Social development in rhesus monkeys: Consideration of individual differences. In A. Oliverio & M. Zappella (Eds.), *The behavior of human infants.* New York: Plenum Press. (p. 72)

Suomi, S. J. (1986).   Anxiety-like disorders in young nonhuman primates. In R. Gettleman (Ed.), *Anxiety disorders of childhood.* New York: Guilford Press. (p. 387)

Suomi, S. J. (1987).   Genetic and maternal contributions to individual differences in rhesus monkey biobehavioral development. In N. A. Krasnegor & others (Eds.), *Perinatal development: A psychobiological perspective.* Orlando, FL: Academic Press. (pp. 96, 349)

Suppes, P. Quoted by R. H. Ennis (1982).   Children's ability to handle Piaget's propositional logic: A conceptual critique. In S. Modgil & C. Modgil (Eds.), *Jean Piaget: Consensus and controversy.* New York: Praeger. (p. 69)

Surgeon General. (1986).   *The Surgeon General's workshop on pornography and public health,* June 22–24. Report prepared by E. P. Mulvey & J. L. Haugaard and released by Office of the Surgeon General on August 4, 1986. (p. 463)

Surgeon General. (1989).   *Reducing the health consequences of smoking: 25 years of progress.* Rockville, MD: U.S. Department of Health and Human Services. (p. 169)

Swann, W. B., Jr., & Miller, L. C. (1982).   Why never forgetting a face matters: Visual imagery and social memory. *Journal of Personality and Social Psychology, 43,* 475–480. (p. 213)

Sweeney, P. D., Anderson, K., & Bailey, S. (1986).   Attributional style in depression: A meta-analytic review. *Journal of Personality and Social Psychology, 50,* 974–991. (p. 396)

Swerdlow, N. R., & Koob, G. F. (1987).   Dopamine, schizophrenia, mania, and depression: Toward a unified hypothesis of corticostiato-pallido-thalamic function (with commentary). *Behavioral and Brain Sciences, 10,* 197–246. (p. 402)

Szasz, T. (1984).   *The therapeutic state: Psychiatry in the mirror of current events.* Buffalo, NY: Prometheus. (p. 381)

Szasz, T. (1987).   *Insanity: The idea and its consequences.* New York: Wiley. (p. 381)

Tajfel, H. (Ed.). (1982).   *Social identity and intergroup relations.* New York: Cambridge University Press. (p. 497)

Tanner, J. M. (1978).   *Fetus into man: Physical growth from conception to maturity.* Cambridge, MA: Harvard University Press. (p. 78)

Tart, C. T. (1983).   *OpenMind, 1*(1), 6. (p. 143)

Tavris, C. (1982, November).   Anger defused. *Psychology Today,* pp. 25–35. (p. 313)

Taylor, S. E. (1989).   *Positive illusions.* New York: Basic Books. (pp. 240, 338, 365, 366)

Taylor, S. P., & Leonard, K. E. (1983).   Alcohol and human physical aggression. In R. Geen & E. Donnerstein (Eds.), *Aggression: Theoretical and empirical reviews* (Vol. 1). New York: Academic Press. (p. 459)

Teevan, R. C., & McGhee, P. E. (1972).   Childhood development of fear of failure motivation. *Journal of Personality and Social Psychology, 21,* 345–348. (p. 292)

Teghtsoonian, R. (1971).   On the exponents in Stevens' law and the constant in Ekman's law. *Psychological Review, 78,* 71–80. (p. 108)

Terman, L. M. (1916).   *The measurement of intelligence.* Boston: Houghton Mifflin. (p. 253)

Terrace, H. S. (1979, November).   How Nim Chimpsky changed my mind. *Psychology Today,* pp. 65–76. (p. 248)

Tesser, A., Forehand, R., Brody, G., & Long, N. (1989).   Conflict: The role of calm and angry parent-child discussion in adolescent adjustment. *Journal of Social and Clinical Psychology, 8,* 317–330. (p. 83)

Tetlock, P. E. (1988). Monitoring the integrative complexity of American and Soviet policy rhetoric: What can be learned? *Journal of Social Issues, 44*, 101–131. (p. 503)

Thatcher, R. W., Walker, R. A., & Giudice, S. (1987). Human cerebral hemispheres develop at different rates and ages. *Science, 236*, 1110–1113. (pp. 99)

Thayer, R. E. (1987). Energy, tiredness, and tension effects of a sugar snack versus moderate exercise. *Journal of Personality and Social Psychology, 52*, 119–125. (p. 335)

Thomas, A., & Chess, S. (1986). The New York Longitudinal Study: From infancy to early adult life. In R. Plomin & J. Dunn (Eds.), *The study of temperament: Changes, continuities, and challenges.* Hillsdale, NJ: Erlbaum. (p. 100)

Thomas, G. V., & Blackman, D. (1991). Are animal experiments on the way out? *The Psychologist, 14*, 208–212. (p. 19)

Thompson, J. K., Jarvie, G. J., Lahey, B. B., & Cureton, K. J. (1982). Exercise and obesity: Etiology, physiology, and intervention. *Psychological Bulletin, 91*, 55–79. (p. 281)

Thompson, R. F. (1985). *The brain.* New York: Freeman. (p. 218)

Thorndike, A. L., & Hagen, E. P. (1977). *Measurement and evaluation in psychology and education.* New York: Macmillan. (p. 254)

Tiggemann, M., & Rothblum, E. D. (1988). Gender differences in social consequences of perceived overweight in the United States and Australia. *Sex Roles, 18*, 75–86. (p. 280)

Time (1990, Fall issue on women). Asia: Discarding daughters. P. 40. (p. 497)

Tinbergen, N. (1951). *The study of instinct.* Oxford: Clarendon. (p. 270)

Tirrell, M. E. (1990). Personal communication. (p. 182, 183)

Tolstoy, L. (1904). *My confessions.* Boston: Dana Estes. (p. 5)

Torrey, E. F. (1986). *Witchdoctors and psychiatrists.* New York: Harper & Row. (p. 432)

Towler, G. (1986). From zero to one hundred: Coaction in a natural setting. *Perceptual and Motor Skills, 62*, 377–378. (p. 454)

Trafford, A. (1988, August 11). Why the beef? Psychotherapy gets bad rap in political campaigns. *Grand Rapids Press* (via *Washington Post*), p. A11. (p. 428)

Treisman, A. (1987). Properties, parts, and objects. In K. R. Boff, L. Kaufman, & J. P. Thomas (Eds.), *Handbook of perception and human performance.* New York: Wiley. (p. 127)

Triandis, H. C. (1981). *Some dimensions of intercultural variation and their implications for interpersonal behavior.* Paper presented at the American Psychological Association convention. (p. 478)

Triandis, H. C. (1989a). The self and social behavior in differing cultural contexts. *Psychological Review, 96*, 506–520. (pp. 478, 498)

Triandis, H. C. (1989b). Cross-cultural studies of individualism and collectivism. In J. J. Berman (Ed.), *Nebraska symposium on motivation 1989* (Vol. 37). Lincoln, NE: University of Nebraska Press. (pp. 478, 480)

Triandis, H. C., Brislin, R., & Hui, C. H. (1988). Cross-cultural training across the individualism-collectivism divide. *International Journal of Intercultural Relations, 12*, 269–289. (p. 480)

Triplett, N. (1898). The dynamogenic factors in pacemaking and competition. *American Journal of Psychology, 9*, 507–533. (p. 454)

Trolier, T. K., & Hamilton, D. L. (1986). Variables influencing judgments of correlational relations. *Journal of Personality and Social Psychology, 50*, 879–888. (p. 514)

True, R. M. (1949). Experimental control in hypnotic age regression states. *Science, 110*, 583–584. (p. 162)

Tsang, Y. C. (1938). Hunger motivation in gastrectomized rats. *Journal of Comparative Psychology, 26*, 1–17. (p. 273)

Tsuang, M. T., & Faraone, S. V. (1990). *The genetics of mood disorders.* Baltimore, MD: Johns Hopkins University Press. (p. 395)

Tubbs, M. E. (1986). Goal setting: A meta-analytic examination of the empirical evidence. *Journal of Applied Psychology, 71*, 474–483. (p. 295)

Tucker, L. A. (1983). Muscular strength and mental health. *Journal of Personality and Social Psychology, 45*, 1355–1360. (p. 356)

Turk, D. C., Meichenbaum, D. H., & Berman, W. H. (1979). Application of biofeedback for the regulation of pain: A critical review. *Psychological Bulletin, 86*, 1322–1338. (p. 337)

Turkington, C. (1987, August). Help for the worried well. *Psychology Today*, pp. 44–48. (p. 431)

Turner, C. W., Hesse, B. W., & Peterson-Lewis, S. (1986). Naturalistic studies of the long-term effects of television violence. *Journal of Social Issues, 42*(3), 7–28. (p. 461)

Turner, J. C. (1987). *Rediscovering the social group: A self-categorization theory.* New York: Basil Blackwell. (p. 483)

Turner, S. E., & Bowen, W. G. (1990). The flight from the arts and sciences: Trends in degrees conferred. *Science, 250*, 517–521. (p. 493)

Tversky, A. (1985, June). Quoted by K. McKean, Decisions, decisions. *Discover*, pp. 22–31. (p. 237)

Tversky, A., & Kahneman, D. (1974). Judgment under uncertainty: Heuristics and biases. *Science, 185*, 1124–1131. (pp. 237, 516)

Twiss, C., Tabb, S., & Crosby, F. (1989). Affirmative action and aggregate data: The importance of patterns in the perception of discrimination. In F. Blanchard & F. Crosby (Eds.), *Affirmative action: Social psychological perspectives.* New York: Springer-Verlag. (p. 514)

Ucros, C. G. (1989). Mood state-dependent memory: A meta-analysis. *Cognition and Emotion, 3*, 139–167. (p. 223)

Uhlenberg, P., & Eggebeen, D. (1986). The declining well-being of adolescents. *Public Interest, 82*, 25–38. (p. 84)

Underwood, B. J. (1957). Interference and forgetting. *Psychological Review, 64*, 49–60. (p. 226)

United Nations. (1990). *Demographic yearbook.* New York: Department of Economic and Social Affairs, Statistical Office, United Nations. (p. 91)

U.S. Congress, Office of Technology Assessment. (1983, November). *Scientific validity of polygraph testing: A research review and evaluation—A technical memorandum*, p. 4. Washington, DC: U.S. Government Printing Office. (p. 305)

U.S. National Center for Health Statistics. (1990). *Vital and health statistics.* Series 10. (p. 87)

Valenstein, E. S. (1986). *Great and desperate cures: The rise and decline of psychosurgery.* New York: Basic Books. (p. 437)

Vallone, R. P., Griffin, D. W., Lin, S., & Ross, L. (1990). Overconfident prediction of future actions and outcomes by self and others. *Journal of Personality and Social Psychology, 58,* 582–592. (p. 240)

Vance, E. B., & Wagner, N. N. (1976). Written descriptions of orgasm: A study of sex differences. *Archives of Sexual Behavior, 5,* 87–98. (p. 284)

Vandenberg, S. G., & Kuse, A. R. (1978). Mental rotations, a group test of three-dimension spacial visualization. *Perceptual and Motor Skills, 47,* 599–604. (p. 485)

Van Dyke, C., & Byck, R. (1982, March). Cocaine. *Scientific American,* pp. 128–141. (p. 171)

van IJzendoorn, M. H., & Kroonenberg, P. M. (1988). Cross-cultural patterns of attachment: A meta-analysis of the strange situation. *Child Development, 59,* 147–156. (p. 72)

Van Leeuwen, M. S. (1978). A cross-cultural examination of psychological differentiation in males and females. *International Journal of Psychology, 13,* 87–122. (p. 492)

Van Leeuwen, M. S. (1982). IQism and the just society: Historical background. *Journal of the American Scientific Affiliation, 34,* 193–201. (p. 255)

Van Yperen, N. W., & Buunk, B. P. (1990). A longitudinal study of equity and satisfaction in intimate relationships. *European Journal of Social Psychology, 20,* 287–309. (p. 470)

Vaughn, K. B., & Lanzetta, J. T. (1981). The effect of modification of expressive displays on vicarious emotional arousal. *Journal of Experimental Social Psychology, 17,* 16–30. (p. 309)

Vaux, A. (1988). Social and personal factors in loneliness. *Journal of Social and Clinical Psychology, 6,* 462–471. (p. 398)

Vemer, E., Coleman, M., Ganong, L. H., & Cooper, H. (1989). Marital satisfaction in remarriage: A meta-analysis. *Journal of Marriage and the Family, 51,* 713–725. (p. 92)

Venn, J. (1986). Hypnosis and the Lamaze method: A reply to Wideman and Singer. *American Psychologist, 41,* 475–476. (p. 164)

Vokey, J. R., & Read, J. D. (1985). Subliminal messages: Between the devil and the media. *American Psychologist, 40,* 1231–1239. (p. 138)

Wagner, R. K., & Sternberg, R. J. (1987). Tacit knowledge in managerial success. *Journal of Business and Psychology, 14,* 301–312. (p. 259)

Wagstaff, G. (1982). Attitudes to rape: The "just world" strikes again? *Bulletin of the British Psychological Society, 13,* 275–283. (p. 444)

Wakefield, J. C. (1987). The semantics of success: Do masturbation exercises lead to partner orgasm? *Journal of Sex and Marital Therapy, 13,* 3–14. (p. 286)

Wallace, R. K., & Benson, H. (1972, February). The physiology of meditation. *Scientific American,* pp. 84–90. (p. 159)

Wallach, M. A., & Wallach, L. (1983). *Psychology's sanction for selfishness: The error of egoism in theory and therapy.* New York: Freeman. (p. 367)

Wallach, M. A., & Wallach, L. (1985, February). How psychology sanctions the cult of the self. *Washington Monthly,* pp. 46–56. (p. 367)

Wallbott, H. G. (1988). In and out of context: Influences of facial expression and context information on emotion attributions. *British Journal of Social Psychology, 27,* 357–369. (p. 138)

Wallis, C. (1983, June 6). Stress: Can we cope? *Time,* pp. 48–54. (pp. 323, 327)

Wallis, C. (1987, October 12). Back off, buddy: A new Hite report stirs up a furor over sex and love in the '80s. *Time,* pp. 68–73. (p. 9)

Wallis, C. (1989, December 4). Onward, women! *Time,* pp. 80–89. (p. 493)

Walster (Hatfield), E., Aronson, V., Abrahams, D., & Rottman, L. (1966). Importance of physical attractiveness in dating behavior. *Journal of Personality and Social Psychology, 4,* 508–516. (p. 467)

Ward, W. C., & Jenkins, H. M. (1965). The display of information and the judgment of contingency. *Canadian Journal of Psychology, 19,* 231–241. (p. 514)

Warr, P., & Payne, R. (1982). Experiences of strain and pleasure among British adults. *Social Science and Medicine, 16,* 1691–1697. (p. 339)

Wason, P. C. (1960). On the failure to eliminate hypotheses in a conceptual task. *Quarterly Journal of Experimental Psychology, 12,* 129–140. (p. 236)

Wass, H., Christian, M., Myers, J., & Murphey, M. (1978–1979). Similarities and dissimilarities in attitudes toward death in a population of older persons. *Omega, 9,* 337–354. (p. 94)

Waterman, A. S. (1988). Identity status theory and Erikson's theory: Commonalities and differences. *Developmental Review, 8,* 185–208. (p. 82)

Watkins, J. G. (1984). The Bianchi (L. A. Hillside Strangler) case: Sociopath or multiple personality? *International Journal of Clinical and Experimental Hypnosis, 32,* 67–101. (p. 390)

Watson, J. B. (1913). Psychology as the behaviorist views it. *Psychological Review, 20,* 158–177. (pp. 149, 180)

Watson, J. B. (1924). *Behaviorism.* New York: Norton. (p. 186)

Watson, J. B., & Rayner, R. (1920). Conditioned emotional reactions. *Journal of Experimental Psychology, 3,* 1–14. (p. 186)

Watson, R. I., Jr. (1973). Investigation into deindividuation using a cross-cultural survey technique. *Journal of Personality and Social Psychology, 25,* 342–345. (p. 455)

Weaver, J. B., Masland, J. L., & Zillmann, D. (1984). Effect of erotica on young men's aesthetic perception of their female sexual partners. *Perceptual and Motor Skills, 58,* 929–930. (p. 285)

Webb, W. B. (1982a). Sleep and biological rhythms. In W. B. Webb (Ed.), *Biological rhythms, sleep, and performance* (pp. 87–110). Chichester, England: Wiley. (p. 154)

Webb, W. B. (1982b). Sleep and dreaming. In *Encyclopedia of Science and Technology* (pp. 470–474). New York: McGraw-Hill. (p. 154)

Webb, W. B., & Campbell, S. S. (1983). Relationships in sleep characteristics of identical and fraternal twins. *Archives of General Psychiatry, 40,* 1093–1095. (p. 154)

Webb, W. G. (1979). Are short and long sleepers different? *Psychological Reports, 44,* 259–264. (p. 154)

Wechsler, D. (1972). "Hold" and "Don't Hold" tests. In S. M. Chown (Ed.), *Human aging.* New York: Penguin. (p. 89)

Weinberg, M. S., & Williams, C. (1974). *Male homosexuals: Their problems and adaptations.* New York: Oxford University Press. (p. 288)

Weinberger, M., Hiner, S. L., & Tierney, W. M. (1987). In support of hassles as a measure of stress in predicting health outcomes. *Journal of Behavioral Medicine, 10,* 19–31. (p. 327)

Weiner, B. (1985). An attributional theory of achievement motivation and emotion. *Psychological Review, 92,* 548–573. (p. 322)

Weingartner, H., Rudorfer, M. V., Buchsbaum, M. S., & Linnoila, M. (1983). Effects of serotonin on memory impairments produced by ethanol. *Science, 221,* 472–473. (p. 218)

Weiss, J. M. (1977). Psychological and behavioral influences on gastrointestinal lesions in animal models. In J. D. Maser & M. E. P. Seligman (Eds.), *Psychopathology: Experimental models.* San Francisco: Freeman. (p. 329)

Weissman, M. M., Merikangas, K. R., Wickramaratne, P., Kidd, K. K., Prusoff, B. A., Leckman, J. F., & Pauls, D. L. (1986). Understanding the clinical heterogeneity of major depression using family data. *Archives of General Psychiatry, 43,* 430–434. (p. 395)

Weisz, J. R., Rothbaum, F. M., & Blackburn, T. C. (1984). Standing out and standing in: The psychology of control in America and Japan. *American Psychologist, 39,* 955–969. (p. 479)

Wells, B. L. (1986). Predictors of female nocturnal orgasms: A multivariate analysis. *Journal of Sex Research, 22,* 421–437. (p. 286)

Wells, G., & Murray, D. M. (1984). Eyewitness confidence. In G. L. Wells & E. F. Loftus (Eds.), *Eyewitness testimony: Psychological perspectives.* New York: Cambridge University Press. (p. 224)

Wells, G. L. (1981). Lay analyses of causal forces on behavior. In J. Harvey (Ed.), *Cognition, social behavior and the environment.* Hillsdale, NJ: Erlbaum. (p. 180)

Wender, P. H., Kety, S. S., Rosenthal, D., Schulsinger, F., Ortmann, J., & Lunde, I. (1986). Psychiatric disorders in the biological and adoptive families of adopted individuals with affective disorders. *Archives of General Psychiatry, 43,* 923–929. (p. 395)

Wener, R., Frazier, W., & Farbstein, J. (1987, June). Building better jails. *Psychology Today,* pp. 40–49. (p. 370)

Werker, J. F. (1989). Becoming a native listener. *American Scientist, 77,* 54–59. (pp. 243, 244)

West, P. D. B., & Evans, E. F. (1990). Early detection of hearing damage in young listeners resulting from exposure to amplified music. *British Journal of Audiology, 24,* 89–103. (p. 120)

Westefeld, J. S., & Furr, S. R. (1987). Suicide and depression among college students. *Professional Psychology: Research and Practice, 18,* 119–123. (p. 392)

Wheeler, L., Reis, H. T., & Bond, M. H. (1989). Collectivism-individualism in everyday social life: The middle kingdom and the melting pot. *Journal of Personality and Social Psychology, 57,* 79–86. (p. 480)

White, G. L., & Kight, T. D. (1984). Misattribution of arousal and attraction: Effects of salience of explanations for arousal. *Journal of Experimental Social Psychology, 20,* 55–64. (p. 470)

White, G. L., Fishbein, S., & Rutstein, J. (1981). Passionate love and the misattribution of arousal. *Journal of Personality and Social Psychology, 41,* 56–62. (p. 470)

White, K. M. (1983). Young adults and their parents: Individuation to mutuality. *New Directions for Child Development, 22,* 61–76. (p. 84)

White, L., & Edwards, J. (1990). Emptying the nest and parental well-being: An analysis of national panel data. *American Sociological Review, 55,* 235–242. (p. 92)

Whiten, A., & Byrne, R. W. (1988). Tactical deception in primates. *Behavioral and Brain Sciences, 11,* 233–244, 267–273. (p. 10)

Whitley, B. E., Jr. (1990). The relationships of heterosexuals' attributions for the causes of homosexuality to attitudes toward lesbians and gay men. *Personality and Social Psychology Bulletin, 16,* 369–377. (p. 289)

Whitley, B. E., Jr., & Schofield, J. W. (1986). A meta-analysis of research on adolescent contraceptive use. *Population and Environment, 8,* 173–203. (p. 84)

Whorf, B. L. (1956). Science and linguistics. In J. B. Carroll (Ed.), *Language, thought, and reality: Selected writings of Benjamin Lee Whorf.* Cambridge, MA: MIT Press. (p. 249)

Wickelgren, W. A. (1977). *Learning and memory.* Englewood Cliffs, NJ: Prentice-Hall. (p. 212)

Wicker, A. W. (1971). An examination of the "other variables" explanation of attitude-behavior inconsistency. *Journal of Personality and Social Psychology, 19,* 18–30. (p. 445)

Widom, C. S. (1989a). Does violence beget violence? A critical examination of the literature. *Psychological Bulletin, 106,* 3–28. (p. 75)

Widom, C. S. (1989b). The cycle of violence. *Science, 244,* 160–166. (p. 75)

Wiens, A. N., & Menustik, C. E. (1983). Treatment outcome and patient characteristics in an aversion therapy program for alcoholism. *American Psychologist, 38,* 1089–1096. (p. 422)

Wiesel, T. N. (1982). Postnatal development of the visual cortex and the influence of environment. *Nature, 299,* 583–591. (p. 136)

Wilder, D. A. (1981). Perceiving persons as a group: Categorization and intergroup relations. In D. L. Hamilton (Ed.), *Cognitive processes in stereotyping and intergroup behavior.* Hillsdale, NJ: Erlbaum. (p. 497)

Wilentz, A. (1987, March 23). Teen suicide: Two death pacts shake the country. *Time,* p. 12. (p. 393)

Will, G. (1989, December 12). Scary to consider horror fixation. *Grand Rapids Press* (Washington Post Writers Group), p. A17. (p. 20)

Williams, C. L. (1989). *Gender differences at work: Women and men in nontraditional occupations.* Berkeley: University of California Press. (p. 492)

Williams, C. L., & Berry, J. W. (1991). Primary prevention of acculturative stress among refugees. *American Psychologist, 46,* 632–641. (p. 326)

Williams, J. E. (1992). Culture and behavior: Sense and nonsense. Presidential address to the Southeastern Psychological Association convention. (p. 12)

Williams, J. E., & Best, D. L. (1990). *Measuring sex stereotypes: A multination study.* Newbury Park, CA: Sage. (p. 487)

Williams, R. (1989). *The trusting heart: Great news about Type A behavior.* New York: Random House. (p. 331)

Williams, R. L., Karacan, I., & Hursch, C. J. (1974). *Electroencephalography (EEG) of human sleep: Clinical applications.* New York: Wiley. (p. 157)

Williams, S. L. (1987). *Self-efficacy and mastery-oriented treatment for severe phobias.* Paper presented to the American Psychological Association convention. (p. 421).

Willmuth, M. E. (1987). Sexuality after spinal cord injury: A critical review. *Clinical Psychology Review, 7,* 389–412. (p. 286)

Wilson, J. P., Harel, Z., & Kahana, B. (1988). *Human adaptation to extreme stress: From the Holocaust to Vietnam.* New York: Plenum Press. (p. 325)

Wilson, J. Q., & Herrnstein, R. J. (1985). *Crime and human nature.* New York: Simon and Schuster. (p. 459)

Wilson, R. C., Gaft, J. G., Dienst, E. R., Wood, L., & Bavry, J. L. (1975). *College professors and their impact on students.* New York: Wiley. (p. 455)

Wilson, S. C., & Barber, T. X. (1983). The fantasy-prone personality: Implications for understanding imagery, hypnosis, and parapsychological phenomena. In A. A. Sheikh (Ed.), *Imagery: Current theory, research, and applications.* New York: Wiley. (p. 172)

Wilson, W. R. (1979). Feeling more than we can know: Exposure effects without learning. *Journal of Personality and Social Psychology, 37,* 811–821. (p. 150)

Windholz, G. (1989, April–June). The discovery of the principles of reinforcement, extinction, generalization, and differentiation of conditional reflexes in Pavlov's laboratories. *Pavlovian Journal of Biological Science, 26,* 64–74. (p. 183)

Wing, R. R., & Jeffrey, R. W. (1979). Outpatient treatments of obesity: A comparison of methodology and clinical results. *International Journal of Obesity, 3,* 261–279. (p. 280)

Winkelstein, W., Jr., Samuel, M., Padian, N. S., & Wiley, J. A. (1987). Selected sexual practices of San Francisco heterosexual men and risk of infection by the human immunodeficiency virus. *Journal of the American Medical Association, 257,* 1470. (pp. 287, 288)

Witelson, S. F. (1985). The brain connection: The corpus callosum is larger in left-handers. *Science, 229,* 665–667. (p. 54)

Wolf, N. (1991). *The beauty myth: How images of beauty are used against women.* NY: Morrow. (p. 279)

Woll, S. (1986). So many to choose from: Decision strategies in videodating. *Journal of Social and Personal Relationships, 3,* 43–52. (p. 467)

Wolpe, J. (1958). *Psychotherapy by reciprocal inhibition.* Stanford, CA: Stanford University Press. (p. 420)

Wolpe, J. (1982). *The practice of behavior therapy.* New York: Pergamon. (p. 420)

Wong, D. F., & Associates. (1986). Positron emission tomography reveals elevated D2 dopamine receptors in drug-naive schizophrenics. *Science, 234,* 1588–1563. (p. 402)

Wong, M. M., & Csikszentmihalyi, M. (1991). Affiliation motivation and daily experience: Some issues on gender differences. *Journal of Personality and Social Psychology, 60,* 154–164. (p. 486)

Wood, G. (1979). The knew-it-all-along effect. *Journal of Experimental Psychology: Human Perception and Performance, 4,* 345–353. (p. 20)

Wood, J. V., Saltzberg, J. A., & Goldsamt, L. A. (1990a). Does affect induce self-focused attention? *Journal of Personality and Social Psychology, 58,* 899–908. (pp. 223, 397)

Wood, J. V., Saltzberg, J. A., Neale, J. M., Stone, A. A., & Rachmiel, T. B. (1990b). Self-focused attention, coping responses, and distressed mood in everyday life. *Journal of Personality and Social Psychology, 58,* 1027–1036. (pp. 223, 397)

Wood, W. (1987). Meta-analytic review of sex differences in group performance. *Psychological Bulletin, 102,* 53–71. (p. 488)

Wood, W., Wong, F. Y., & Chachere, J. G. (1991). Effects of media violence on viewers' aggression in unconstrained social interaction. *Psychological Bulletin, 109,* 371–383. (p. 461)

Woodruff-Pak, D. S. (1989). Aging and intelligence: Changing perspectives in the twentieth century. *Journal of Aging Studies, 3,* 91–118. (p. 89)

Woods, N. F., Dery, G. K., & Most, A. (1983). Recollections of menarche, current menstrual attitudes, and premenstrual symptoms. In S. Golub (Ed.), *Menarche: The transition from girl to woman.* Lexington, MA: Lexington Books. (p. 79)

Wooley, S., & Wooley, O. (1983). Should obesity be treated at all? *Psychiatric Annals, 13*(11), 884–885, 888. (p. 277)

World Health Organization. (1979). *Schizophrenia: An international follow-up study.* Chicester, England: Wiley. (p. 401)

Worthington, E. L., Jr. (1989). Religious faith across the life span: Implications for counseling and research. *The Counseling Psychologist, 17,* 555–612. (p. 80)

Wortman, C. B., & Silver, R. C. (1989). The myths of coping with loss. *Journal of Consulting and Clinical Psychology, 57,* 349–357. (p. 94)

Wu, T-C., Tashkin, D. P., Djahed, B., & Rose, J. E. (1988). Pulmonary hazards of smoking marijuana as compared with tobacco. *New England Journal of Medicine, 318,* 347–351. (p. 172)

Wysocki, C. J., & Gilbert, A. N. (1989). *National Geographic* survey: Effects of age are heterogeneous. *Annals of the New York Academy of Sciences, 561,* 12–28. (p. 122)

Yalom, I. D. (1985). *The theory and practice of group psychotherapy* (3rd ed.). New York: Basic Books. (p. 418)

Yang, N., & Linz, D. (1990). Movie ratings and the content of adult videos: The sex-violence ratio. *Journal of Communication, 40*(2), 28–42. (p. 462)

Yarnell, P. R., & Lynch, S. (1970, April 25). Retrograde memory immediately after concussion. *Lancet,* pp. 863–865. (p. 217)

Yates, A. (1989). Current perspectives on the eating disorders: I. History, psychological and biological aspects. *Journal of the American Academy of Child and Adolescent Psychiatry, 28,* 813–828. (p. 277)

Yates, A. (1990). Current perspectives on the eating disorders: II. Treatment, outcome, and research directions. *Journal of the American Academy of Child and Adolescent Psychiatry, 29,* 1–9. (p. 277)

Zacks, R. T., & Hasher, L. (1988). Capacity theory and the processing of inferences. In L. Light & D. Burke (Eds.), *Language, memory, and aging.* New York: Cambridge University Press. (p. 89)

Zajonc, R. B. (1965). Social facilitation. *Science, 149,* 269–274. (p. 454)

Zajonc, R. B. (1980). Feeling and thinking: Preferences need no inferences. *American Psychologist, 35,* 151–175. (p. 321)

Zajonc, R. B. (1984a). On the primacy of affect. *American Psychologist, 39,* 117–123. (p. 321)

Zajonc, R. B. (1984b, July 22).   Quoted by D. Goleman, Rethinking IQ tests and their value. *The New York Times*, p. D22. (p. 253)

Zajonc, R. B., & Markus, G. B. (1975).   Birth order and intellectual development. *Psychological Review, 82*, 74–88. (p. 520)

Zanna, M. P., & Pack, S. J. (1975).   On the self-fulfilling nature of apparent sex differences in behavior. *Journal of Experimental Social Psychology, 11*, 583–591. (p. 492)

Zebrowitz-McArthur, L. (1988).   Person perception in cross-cultural perspective. In M. H. Bond (Ed.), *The cross-cultural challenge to social psychology.* Newbury Park, CA: Sage. (p. 480)

Zelnick, M., & Kim, Y. J. (1982).   Sex education and its association with teenage sexual activity, pregnancy, and contraceptive use. *Family Planning Perspectives, 14*(3), 117–126. (p. 290)

Zilbergeld, B. (1983).   *The shrinking of America: Myths of psychological change.* Boston: Little, Brown. (pp. 429, 431)

Zillmann, D. (1986).   Effects of prolonged consumption of pornography. Background paper for *The Surgeon General's workshop on pornography and public health,* June 22–24. Report prepared by E. P. Mulvey & J. L. Haugaard and released by Office of the Surgeon General on August 4, 1986. (pp. 303, 321)

Zillmann, D. (1989).   Effects of prolonged consumption of pornography. In D. Zillmann & J. Bryant (Eds.), *Pornography: Research advances and policy considerations.* Hillsdale, NJ: Erlbaum. (pp. 285, 463)

Zillmann, D., & Bryant, J. (1984).   Effects of massive exposure to pornography. In N. Malamuth & E. Donnerstein (Eds.), *Pornography and sexual aggression.* Orlando, FL: Academic Press. (p. 463)

Zimbardo, P. G. (1970).   The human choice: Individuation, reason, and order versus deindividuation, impulse, and chaos. In W. J. Arnold & D. Levine (Eds.), *Nebraska Symposium on Motivation, 1969.* Lincoln: University of Nebraska Press. (p. 455)

Zimbardo, P. G. (1972, April).   Pathology of imprisonment. *Transaction/Society,* pp. 4–8. (p. 447)

Zuckerman, M. (1990).   Some dubious premises in research and theory on racial differences: Scientific, social, and ethical issues. *American Psychologist, 45,* 1297–1303. (p. 481)

Illustration Credits

Frontmatter

p. ix Richard Pasley/Stock, Boston **p. x** Carl Purcell/Photo Researchers **p. xi** M. & E. Bernheim/Woodfin Camp & Associates **p. xii** Stephen Wade/Allsport USA **p. xiii** (left) Bob Daemmrich/Stock, Boston; (center) Joel Gordon, 1990; (right) David Austen/Stock, Boston

Chapter 1

Opener: J. Ramey/The Image Bank **p. 1** Laura Dwight **p. 3** (from top left) National Library of Medicine; National Library of Medicine; National Library of Medicine; Brown Brothers; National Library of Medicine; National Library of Medicine; National Library of Medicine; Archives of the History of American Psychology; National Library of Medicine; Wellesley College Archives; National Library of Medicine **p. 4** Topham/The Image Works **p. 5** Richard Howard 1984 **p. 9** Elsa Peterson 1989/Design Conceptions **p. 10** Cary Wolinsky/Stock, Boston **p. 13** Movie Still Archives **Fig. 1–5** From Frank, M. G., & Gilovich, T. (1988). The dark side of self and social perceptions: Black uniforms and aggression in professional sports. *Journal of Personality and Social Psychology*, 54, 74–85. Copyright 1988 by the American Psychological Association. Adapted by permission. **p. 17** Mark S. Wexler/Woodfin Camp & Associates **p. 18** Jim Amos/Photo Researchers **p. 20** From Shepard, Roger N. (1990). *Mind sights*. New York: W. H. Freeman and Company. Reprinted by permission of W. H. Freeman and Company.

Chapter 2

Opener: New York Hospital/Peter Arnold, Inc. **p. 35** A. Glauberman/Photo Researchers **Fig. 2–9** Alexander Tsiaras/Stock, Boston **Fig. 2–10** Jim Pickerell/Tony Stone Worldwide/Chicago, Ltd. **Fig. 2–11** Daniel R. Weinberger, M.D., CBDB, NIMH **p. 41** Martin Rogers/Woodfin Camp & Associates **Fig. 2–12** From Gazzaniga, M. S., Steen, D., & Volpe, B. T. (1979). *Functional neuroscience* (p. 278). New York: Harper & Row. Copyright © 1979 by Harper & Row, Publishers, Inc. Reprinted by permission of HarperCollins Publishers. **p. 47** (bottom) The Warren Anatomical Museum, Harvard Medical School **p. 48** (bottom) Courtesy of Marcus Raichle, M.D., Mallinckrodt Institute of Radiology, St. Louis **Figs. 2–21, 2–22 & 2–23** Gazzaniga, Michael. S. (1983). Right hemisphere language following brain bisection: A 20-year perspective. *American Psychologist*, 38, 525–537. Copyright © 1983 by the American Psychological Association. Adapted by permission. **p. 53** Courtesy of Drs. Michael E. Phelps and John C. Mazziotta, UCLA School of Medicine

Chapter 3

Opener: Sobel/Klonsky/The Image Bank **Fig. 3–1** Per Sundstrom/Gamma Liaison **Fig. 3–2** (far left, left, right) Petit Format, Science Source/Photo Researchers; (far right) Donald Yaeger/Camera MD Studios **p. 62** © Enrico Feorelli **Fig. 3–3** From Conel, J. L. (1939–1963). *The postnatal development of the human cerebral cortex* (Vols. I–VI). Cambridge, MA: Harvard University Press. Reprinted by permission. **Fig. 3–5** Adapted from Frankenburg, W. K., & Dodds, J. B. (1967). The Denver developmental screening test. *Journal of Pediatrics*, 71 (2), 181–191. **p. 65** Bill Anderson/Monkmeyer Press Photo Service **p. 66** David M. Grossman **p. 67** Hazel Hankin **p. 68** (top) Joel Gordon 1990; (bottom) Ontario Science Centre **p. 71, 72, 73** Harlow Primate Laboratory, University of Wisconsin **Fig. 3–8** From Kagan, J. (1976). Emergent themes in human development. *American Scientist*, 64, 186–196. Reprinted by permission of Sigma Xi, The Scientific Research Society. **p. 74** Laura Dwight 1989 **p. 75** Sybil Shackman/Monkmeyer Press Photo Service **p. 77** Laura Dwight **Fig. 3–10** From Tanner, J. M. (1978). *Fetus into man: Physical conception to maturity*. Cambridge, MA: Harvard University Press.

Copyright © 1978 by J. M. Tanner. Reprinted by permission. **p. 79** J. Gerard Smith/Monkmeyer Press Photo Service **p. 80** (left) Charles Harbutt/Actuality; (right) Bob Daemmrich/The Image Works **p. 83** (left) Richard Pasley/Stock, Boston; (right) Bob Daemmrich/The Image Works **Fig. 3–13** Data from National Center for Health Statistics (1991). *Vital statistics of the United States* (Natality issue). Washington, DC: U.S. Government Printing Office. **p. 85** Reprinted with the permission of Planned Parenthood Federation of America, Inc. **Fig. 3–14** Adapted from Insel, P. M., & Roth, W. T. (1976). *Health in a changing society* (p. 98). Mountain View, CA: Mayfield. **Fig. 3–15** Adapted from Doty, R. L., et al. (1984). Smell identification ability: Changes with age. *Science*, 226, 1441–1443. Copyright © 1984 by the American Association for the Advancement of Science. **p. 88** David Wells/The Image Works **Fig. 3–16** From Schonfield, D., & Robertson, B. A. (1966). Memory storage and aging. *Canadian Journal of Psychology*, 20, 228–236. Copyright © 1966 Canadian Psychological Association. **Fig. 3–17** From Geiwitz, J. (1980). *Psychology: Looking at ourselves*. Boston: Little, Brown & Co. **Fig. 3–18** From Schaie, K. W., & Strother, C. R. (1968). A cross-sequential study of age changes in cognitive behavior. *Psychological Bulletin*, 70, 671–680. Copyright © 1968 by the American Psychological Association. Reprinted by permission. **Fig. 3–19** Adapted from Kaufman, A. S., Reynolds, C. R. & McLean, J. E. (1989). Age and WAIS-R intelligence in a national sample of adults in the 10- to 74-year age range: A cross-sectional analysis with educational level controlled. *Intelligence*, 13, 235–253. **p. 90** Sarah Putnam/NYT Pictures **Fig. 3–20** From McCrae, R. R., & Costa, P. T., Jr. (1990). *Personality in adulthood*. New York: Guilford. **p. 93** (top) Joe McNally; (center) Bob Daemmrich/The Image Works; (bottom) Charles Harbutt/Actuality **Fig. 3–21** Data from Inglehart, R. (1990). *Culture shift in advanced industrial society*. Princeton, NJ: Princeton University Press. **p. 95** Martin Simon/SABA **p. 96** Doris Pinney **p. 97** Bob Sacha **p. 98** Kathleen Marie Menke/Crystal Images, Monkmeyer Press Photo Service

Chapter 4

Opener: O'Rourke/The Image Bank **p. 106** (bottom) Thomas Eisner **p. 113** From E. R. Lewis, Y. Y. Zeevi & F. S. Werblin. *Brain Res.*, 15, 559–562. **Fig. 4–9** Adapted from Frisby, J. P. (1980). *Seeing: Illusion, brain and mind* (p. 157). New York: Oxford University Press. Reprinted by permission. **Fig. 4–10** Fritz Goro, LIFE Magazine © 1971 Time Warner, Inc. **Fig. 4–12** (top) Fritz Goro, LIFE Magazine © 1944 Time Warner, Inc. **Fig 4–13** From Richmond Products, Boca Raton, FL. **Fig. 4–15** From Albers, J. (1975). *The interaction of color* (revised pocket edition) (Plate VI–3). New Haven: Yale University Press. Photo courtesy of the Josef Albers Foundation. **p. 120** From Nilsson, Lennart. *Behold man*. New York: Little, Brown and Company. Photo courtesy Bonnier Fakta. **Fig. 4–19** From Wysocki, C. J., & Gilbert, A. W. (1989). National Geographic smell survey: Effects of age are heterogeneous. In C. Murphy & W. S. Cain (Eds.), *Proceedings of the conference on nutrition and the chemical senses in aging (Annals of the New York Academy of Sciences)*, Vol. 561. New York: New York Academy of Sciences. **p. 125** Addison Geary/Stock, Boston **Fig. 4–20** From Bradley, D. R., Dumais, S. T., & Petry, H. M. (1976). Reply to Cavonius. *Nature*, 261, 78. Copyright © 1976 by Macmillan Journals Limited. Reprinted by permission. **Fig. 4–21** From Shepard, Roger N. (1990). *Mind sights*. New York: W. H. Freeman and Company. Reprinted by permission of W. H. Freeman and Company. **p. 129** (top) Otto Greule, Jr./Allsport USA; (bottom) Ron Watts/Black Star **p. 130** (top) Rainer Grosskopf/Tony Stone Worldwide/Chicago, Ltd.; (center) Rick Friedmann/Black Star; (bottom, both) From Ross, H. E. (1975). Mist, murk and visual perception. *New Scientist*, 66, 658–660. Photos courtesy Helen E. Ross. **Fig. 4–24** City Art Gallery, Bristol/The Bridgeman Art Library, Superstock **p. 132** (top) From Shepard, R. N. (1981).

Psychophysical complimentarity. In M. Kubovy & J. R. Pomerantz (Eds.), *Perceptual organization* (pp. 279–341). Hillsdale, NJ: Lawrence Erlbaum. Copyright © 1981 by Lawrence Erlbaum Associates **Fig. 4–26** *(left)* From Shepard, Roger N. (1990). *Mind sights.* New York: W. H. Freeman and Company. Reprinted by permission of W. H. Freeman and Company; *(right)* Alan Choisnet/The Image Bank **Fig. 4–28** Photo by S. Schwartzenberg, © The Exploratorium **p. 135** Michael Hayman/Stock, Boston **p. 136** Courtesy Dr. Hubert Dolezal **Fig. 4–30** From Shepard, Roger N. (1990). *Mind sights.* New York: W. H. Freeman and Company. Reprinted by permission of W. H. Freeman and Company **Fig 4–31** *(left)* © Frank Searle, photo supplied by Steuart Campbell; *(right)* Dick Ruhl **p. 138** From Shepard, Roger N. (1990). *Mind sights.* New York: W. H. Freeman and Company. Reprinted by permission of W. H. Freeman and Company. **p. 139** *(top)* From Norman, D. A. (1988). *The psychology of everyday things.* New York: Basic Books, Inc. Reprinted with permission of Basic Books, Inc., a division of HarperCollins Publishers. **Fig. 4–33** From Kraft, C. (1978). A psychophysical approach to air safety: Simulator studies of visual illusions in night approaches. In H. L. Pick, H. W. Liebovitz, J. E. Singer, A. Steinschneider, & H. W. Stevenson (Eds.), *Psychology: From research to practice.* New York: Plenum Press. **p. 140** Adapted from Gregory, R. L., & Gombrich, E. H. (Eds.). (1974). *Illusion in nature and art.* Copyright © 1973 by C. Blakemore, J. D. Deregowski, E. H. Gombrich, R. L. Gregory, H. P. Hinton, & R. Primrose. Reprinted by permission of Duckworth. **p. 142** Dana Fineman/Sygma

Chapter 5

Opener: David M. Grossman **p. 149** Will and Deni McIntyre/Photo Researchers **p. 150** Ellis Herwig/Stock, Boston **p. 151** R. Nowitz/Phototake **Figs. 5–1 & 5–2** From Dement, W. (1972). *Some must watch while some must sleep.* Stanford, CA: Portable Stanford Book Series, 1972. Reprinted by permission of the Stanford Alumni Association, Stanford University. **Fig. 5–3** From Cartwright, R. D. (1978). *A primer on sleep and dreaming* (Fig. 1–6). Reading, MA: Addison-Wesley. Reprinted by permission. **p. 153** Susan Copen Oken **Fig. 5–4** From Hartmann, E. (1984). *The nightmare: The psychology and biology of terrifying dreams.* Copyright © 1984 by Ernest Hartmann. Reprinted by permission. **p. 155** Peter Menzel/Stock, Boston **p. 156** National Gallery of Art, Washington, DC, Rosenwald Collection **Fig. 5–5** Adapted from Williams, R. L., Karacan, I., & Hursch, C. J. (1974). *Electroencephalography (EEG) of human sleep: Clinical applications.* New York: Wiley. **p. 160** James Wilson/Woodfin Camp & Associates **p. 161** Mimi Forsyth/Monkmeyer Press Photo Service **p. 164** Joel Gordon 1990 **p. 165** Courtesy News Service, Stanford University **p. 168** Courtesy MADD, Minnesota State Office **Fig. 5–7** From Siegel, R. K. (1977, October). Hallucinations. *Scientific American,* p. 134. **Fig. 5–8** From Johnston, L. D., O'Malley, P. M., & Bachman, J. G. (1992, January 27). Annual report of drug use survey. Ann Arbor: University of Michigan News and Information Services.

Chapter 6

Opener: Charles Harbutt/Actuality **Fig. 6–1** Adapted from Goodwin, C. J. (1991). Misportraying Pavlov's apparatus. *American Journal of Psychology, 104,* 135–141. **Fig. 6–4** Data from I. P. Pavlov (1927). In G. P. Anrep (Trans.), *Conditioned reflexes* (p. 185). London: Oxford University Press. Reprinted by permission. **p. 184** James Balog/Black Star **p. 185** Sovfoto **p. 186** Archives of the History of American Psychology **p. 188** AP/Wide World Photos **Fig. 6–5** Richard Wood/The Picture Cube **p. 189** *(bottom)* Fred Bavendam/Peter Arnold, Inc. **p. 190** Richard Hutchings/Photo Researchers **p. 194** Joan Liftin/Actuality **p. 196** *(top)* W. M. Curtsinger/Photo Researchers; *(center)* Carl Purcell/Photo Researchers; *(bottom)* Joe McNally **p. 199** Courtesy Albert Bandura, Stanford University **p. 200** From A. N. Meltzoff, 1988. Imitation of televised models by infants. *Child Development, 59,* 1221–1229. Photos courtesy A. N. Meltzoff and M. Hanak.

Chapter 7

Opener: John Lewis Stage/The Image Bank **p. 206** Fred Ward/Black Star **Fig. 7–3** From Nickerson, R. S., & Adams, M. J. (1979). Long-term memory for a common object. *Cognitive Psychology, 11,* 287–307. **p. 209** *(left)* Erika Stone; *(right)* Bob Daemmrich/Stock, Boston **Fig. 7–4** From Peterson, L. R., & Peterson, M. J. (1959). Short-term retention of individual verbal items. *Journal of Experimental Psychology, 58,* 193–198. **Fig. 7–5** Reprinted with permission from Macmillan Publishing Company from *Your memory: A user's guide* by Alan Baddeley. Copyright © 1982 by Multimedia Publications (UK) Ltd. **Fig. 7–6** From Craik, F. I. M., & Watkins, M. J. (1973). The role of rehearsal in short-term memory. *Journal of Verbal Learning and Verbal Behavior, 12,* 599–607. **Fig. 7–7** From Hintzman, Douglas L. (1978). *The psychology of learning and*

memory. Copyright © 1978 W. H. Freeman and Company. Reprinted by permission. **Fig. 7–10** Data from Ebbinghaus, E. (1885). Über das Gedächtnis. Leipzig: Dunker. Cited in R. Klatzky (1980). *Human memory: Structures and processes.* Copyright © 1980 by W. H. Freeman and Company. All rights reserved. **Fig. 7–11** From Bahrick, H. P. (1984). Semantic memory content in permastore: 50 years of memory for Spanish learned in school. *Journal of Experimental Psychology: General, 113,* 1–29. Copyright © 1984 by the American Psychological Association. Adapted by permission. **p. 218** Lynn Johnson 1986/Black Star **p. 220** George Goodwin/Monkmeyer Press Photo Service **p. 221** Seth Poppel/Yearbook Archives **Fig. 7–14** Adapted from Bower, G. H. (1986). Prime time in cognitive psychology. In P. Eelen (Ed.), *Cognitive research and behavior therapy: Beyond the conditioning paradigm.* Amsterdam: North Holland Publishers. **Fig. 7–15** Adapted from Godden, D. R., & Baddeley, A. D. (1975). Context-dependent memory in two natural environments: On land and under water. *British Journal of Psychology, 66,* 325–331. **Fig. 7–16** From Loftus, E. F. (1979). The malleability of human memory. *American Scientist, 67,* 313–320. Reprinted by permission of *American Scientist,* journal of Sigma XI, The Scientific Research Society. **Fig. 7–17** From Jenkins, J. G., & Dallenbach, K. M. (1924). Oblivescence during sleep and waking. *American Journal of Psychology, 35,* 605–612. **p. 227** Shahn Kermani/Gamma Liaison **p. 229** Hugh Rogers/Monkmeyer Press Photo Service

Chapter 8

Opener: Sybil Shackman/Monkmeyer Photo Service **p. 234** *(left)* J. Messerschmidt/The Picture Cube; *(right)* Ron Sanford/Black Star **Figs. 8–2 & 8–4** From Duncker, K. (1945). On problem solving. *Psychological Monographs, 58,* 289–291. **p. 239** Chip Peterson/Sygma **p. 242** M. & E. Bernheim/Woodfin Camp & Associates **p. 243** Camilla Smith/Rainbow **Fig. 8–5** Peter McLeod **Fig. 8–5** Adapted from Werker, J. F. (1989). Becoming a native listener. *American Scientist, 77,* 54–59. Reprinted by permission of *American Scientist,* journal of Sigma Xi, The Scientific Research Society. **Fig. 8–6** From Johnson, J. S., & Newport, E. L. (1989). Critical period effects in second language learning: The influence of maturational state on the acquisition of English as a second language. *Cognitive Psychology, 21,* 60–99. **p. 246** *(bottom)* © George Ancona **p. 247** *(top)* Paul Fusco/Magnum Photos; *(bottom)* Language Research Center, Yerkes Regional Primate Research Center **p. 250** Elizabeth Crews/The Image Works **p. 252** National Library of Medicine **p. 253** News Service, Stanford University **p. 254** *(top)* Will & Deni McIntyre/Science Source/Photo Researchers; *(center)* Lew Merrim/Monkmeyer Press Photo Service **Fig. 8–7** From Thorndike, A. L. & Hagen, E. P. (1977). *Measurement and evaluation in psychology and education* (fourth edition). New York: Macmillan. Reprinted with permission from Macmillan Publishing Company. Photo of dog © Russ Kinne/Comstock. **Table 8–2** Adapted from the American Psychiatric Association (1987). Diagnostic and statistic manual of mental disorders (Third Edition Revised). Washington, DC: American Psychiatric Association. **Fig. 8–9** From Wiltshire, Stephen (1991). *Floating cities.* London: Michael Joseph Ltd. **Fig. 8–10** From Bouchard, T. J., Jr. (1982). Twins—Nature's twice-told tale. In *1983 Yearbook of science and the future.* Copyright © 1982 by Encyclopaedia Britannica, Inc. Adapted by permission. **Fig. 8–11** Based upon data from Fulker, D. W., DeFries, J. C., & Plomin, R. (1988). Genetic influence on general mental ability increases between infancy and middle childhood. *Nature, 336,* 767–769. Copyright © 1988 by Macmillan Magazines Limited. **Fig. 8–12** From Lewontin, R. (1976). Race and intelligence. In N. J. Block & D. Dworken (Eds.), *The IQ controversy: Critical readings.* New York: Pantheon. Copyright © 1976. Reprinted by permission. **p. 263** Jacques Chenet/Woodfin Camp & Associates **p. 264** Tomas Muscionico/Contact Press Images, Woodfin Camp & Associates

Chapter 9

Opener: Gautreau/A.F.P. **Fig. 9–1** From Maslow, A. H. (1970). *Motivation and personality* (2nd ed.). New York: Harper & Row. Copyright © 1954 by Harper & Row Publishers, Inc. Copyright © 1970 by Abraham H. Maslow. Reprinted by permission of HarperCollins Publishers. **p. 270** *(top)* Tony Brandenburg/Bruce Coleman, Inc.; *(center)* Bob Daemmrich/The Image Works; *(bottom left)* Harlow Primate Laboratory, University of Wisconsin; *(bottom right)* Hazel Hankin **p. 271** *(left)* Jeff Hall/Bowling Green State University, with permission of Marlon Wells. Photo courtesy Scholastic, Inc.; *(right)* David Lokey/Comstock **p. 272** Wallace Kirkland, LIFE Magazine © 1945 Time Warner Inc. **Fig. 9–2** Adapted from Cannon, W. B. (1929). *Bodily changes in pain, hunger, fear, and rage.* New York: Branford. **p. 274** Richard Olsenius/Black Star **p. 275** Richard Howard 1980 **p. 276** Lincoln Russell/Stock, Boston **p. 277** Lynn McAfee/Globe Photos **Fig. 9–4** From Bray, G. A. (1969). Effect of caloric restriction on energy expenditure in obese patients. *Lancet, 2,* 397–398. **p. 279** *(left)* The Garden of Love (detail), Peter Paul Rubens, The Prado, Madrid/The Bridgeman Art Library, Superstock; (right) J. Baes/Photo Researchers **p. 282** Photo by Dellenbeck. Reprinted by permission of the Kinsey Institute for Research in Sex, Gender and Reproduction, Inc. **Fig. 9–5** Adapted from Masters, W. H., & Johnson, V. E. (1966). *Human sexual response.* Boston: Little, Brown & Co. **Fig. 9–6** From Byrne, D. (1982). Predicting human sexual behavior. In A. G. Kraut, *The G. Stanley Hall Lecture Series* (Vol. 2). Copyright © 1982 by the American Psychological Association. Reprinted by permission. **p. 287** (top) Joel Gordon; (bottom) Herb Snitzer/The Stock Shop **p. 288** David Kryszak/Black Star **p. 290** Nathaniel Antman/The Image Works **Fig. 9–7** From McClelland, D. C., et al. (1953). *The achievement motive.* New York: Appleton-Century-Crofts. Reprinted with permission of Irvington Publishers, New York. **p. 293** Rob Nelson/Black Star **p. 296** Ted Thai/TIME Magazine

Chapter 10

Opener: Michael Kevin Daly/The Stock Market **p. 303** M. Grecco/Stock, Boston **Fig. 10–2** From Kleinmuntz, B., & Szucko, J. J. (1984). A field study of the fallability of polygraph lie detection. *Nature*, 308, 449–450. Copyright © 1984 by Macmillan Journals Limited. **p. 304** Rob Kinmoth **p. 306** (top) Craig Ruttle **Fig. 10–3** Courtesy Dr. Paul Ekman, University of California at San Francisco **Fig. 10–4** From Ekman P., and Friesen, W. V. (1984). *Unmasking the face* (reprint edition). Palo Alto, CA: Consulting Psychologists Press Courtesy. Photos courtesy Dr. Paul Ekman. **p. 308** Benjamin E. Bobblett **Fig. 10–5** Courtesy Carroll Izard, University of Delaware **p. 311** Peter Vandermark/Stock, Boston **p. 313** Focus on Sports **Fig. 10–6** From Dey, E., et al. (1991). *The American freshman: Twenty-five year trends.* Los Angeles: Higher Education Research Institute, UCLA. **Table 10–1** From Diener, E. (1984). Subjective well-being. *Psychological Bulletin*, 95, 542–575. Copyright © 1984 by the American Psychological Association. Adapted by permission. **p. 317** Shelly Katz 1990/Black Star **p. 323** (left) Andy Levin 1991/Photo Researchers; (right) Arlene Collins/Monkmeyer Press Photo Service **p. 325** David Turnley/Black Star **Fig. 10–15** From Adams, P. R., & Adams, G. R. (1984). Mount St. Helens ashfall: Evidence for a disaster stress reaction. *American Psychologist*, 29, 252–260. Copyright © 1984 by the American Psychological Association. Reprinted by permission. **p. 327** Peter Glass/Monkmeyer Press Photo Service **Fig. 10–16** Bill Bachman/Photo Researchers **Fig. 10–17** From Weiss, J. M. (1977). Psychological and behavioral influences on gastrointestinal lesions in animal models. In J. D. Maser and M. E. P. Seligman (Eds.), *Psychopathology: Experimental models.* Copyright © 1977 by W. H. Freeman and Company. All rights reserved. **p. 331** Lennart Nilsson © Boehringer Ingelheim International GmbH **p. 332** Paul Fusco/Magnum Photos **Fig. 10–19** Based on information presented in Friedman, H. S., & Booth-Kewley, S. (1987). The "disease-prone personality": A meta-analytic view of the construct. *American Psychologist*, 42, 539–555. **Fig. 10–20** Adapted from McCann, I. L., & Holmes, D. S. (1984). Influence of aerobic exercise on depression. *Journal of Personality and Social Psychology*, 46, 1142–1147. Copyright © 1984 by the American Psychological Association. Reprinted by permission. **Fig. 10–21** (right) Dan McCoy/Rainbow **p. 337** Steve Liss/TIME Magazine **Fig. 10–22** From Friedman, M., & Ulmer, D. (1984). Treating type A behavior—and your heart. New York: Alfred A. Knopf, Inc. Reprinted by permission. **p. 340** Bob Krist/Black Star

Chapter 11

Opener: Eastcott/Momatiuk/Woodfin Camp & Associates **p. 349** (top) Rick Friedman/Black Star; (bottom) Harlow Primate Laboratory, University of Wisconsin **p. 351** (left) National Library of Medicine; (center) The Bettmann Archive; (right) Archives of the History of American Psychology **p. 352** (top) Sing-Si Schwartz/Betty Dornheim Picture Service; (bottom) Will & Deni McIntyre/Photo Researchers **p. 353** Culver Pictures **p. 354** Edmund Engelman **p. 356** (top) Arthur Grace/Sygma; (bottom) Rhoda Sidney/The Image Works **Fig. 11–2** From Eysenck, S. B. G., & Eysenck, H. J. (1963). The validity of questionnaire and rating assessments of extraversion and neuroticism, and their factorial stability. *British Journal of Psychology*, 54, 51–62, Fig. 1. **Table 11–2** From McCrae, R., & Costa, P. T. (1986). Clinical assessment can benefit from recent advances in personality psychology. *American Psychologist*, 41, 1002. Copyright © 1986 by the American Psychological Association. Adapted by permission. **Fig. 11–3** Adapted from Butcher, J. N. (1990). *The MMPI-2 in psychological treatment.* New York: Oxford University Press. **p. 362** Ted Polumbaum/LIFE Magazine © 1968 Time Warner, Inc. **p. 363** Antman/The Image Works **p. 364** Victor Engelbert/Photo Researchers **Fig. 11–4** From Bandura, A. (1978). The self-system in reciprocal determinism. *American Psychologist*, 33, 344–358. Copyright © 1978 by the American Psychological Association. Adapted by permission. **p. 368** Stephen Wade/Allsport USA **p. 370** (left) Joe McNally; (right) Bob Daemmrich

Chapter 12

Opener: Joel Gordon 1991 **p. 380** Tony Ray Jones/Magnum Photos **Fig. 12–1** J. Otis Wheelock; courtesy Department of Library Services, American Museum of Natural History (neg. no.: 31565) **p. 383** AP/Wide World Photos **Fig. 12–2** From Roper report 84-3, February 11–25, 1984. *Public Opinion*, August/September, 25. Reprinted with permission of the American Enterprise Institute for Public Policy Research, Washington, DC. **Table 12–1** Adapted from "The Biology of Obsessions and Compulsions" by J. L. Rapoport. Copyright © 1989 by Scientific American, Inc. All rights reserved. **p. 387** Paul Fusco/Magnum Photos **Fig. 12–3** From Baxter, L. R. (1987). *Archives of General Psychology*, 44 (3), p. 211–218. Copyright 1987 AMA. **p. 390** AP/Wide World Photos **Fig. 12–4** Bureau of the Census (1990). *Statistical abstract of the United States.* Washington, DC: Superintendent of Documents, United States Government Printing Office. **Fig. 12–5** From National Center for Health Statistics. **p. 395** (top) AP/Wide World Photos; (bottom) Stephen P. Allen/Gamma Liaison **Fig. 12–7** Adapted from Lewinsohn, P. M., et al. (1985). An integrative theory of depression. In S. Reiss and R. Bootzin (Eds.), *Theoretical issues in behavior therapy.* Orlando, FL: Academic Press. **p. 400** (left) Berthold, L., Untitled. The Prinzhorn Collection, University of Heidelberg; (right) August Natterer, *Witch's Head.* The Prinzhorn Collection, University of Heidelberg. Photos: Krannert Museum, University of Illinois at Urbana. **p. 401** Grunnitus/Monkmeyer Press Photo Service **Fig. 12–8** Data from *Schizophrenia genesis: The origins of madness* by I. I. Gottesman. Copyright © 1991 by W. H. Freeman and Company. Reprinted by permission. **p. 404** Courtesy of the Genäin Family **p. 405** Phil Huber/Black Star **Fig. 12–9** Adapted from Magnusson, D. (1990). Personality research—Challenges for the future. *European Journal of Personality*, 4, 1–17. Copyright © 1990 by John Wiley & Sons, Ltd. Reprinted by permission. **Table 12–2** Reprinted with permission of The Free Press, a Division of Macmillan, Inc., from *Psychiatric Disorders in America* by Lee N. Robins and Darrel A. Regier. Copyright © 1991 by Lee N. Robins and Darrel A. Regier.

Chapter 13

Opener: Stacy Pickerell/Tony Stone Worldwide/Chicago Ltd. **p. 413** (left) The Bettmann Archive; (right) The Granger Collection **p. 414** Paul Meredith/TSW Click/Chicago, Ltd. **p. 416** Steve Goldberg/Monkmeyer Press Photo Service **p. 417** Michael Rougier, LIFE Magazine © Time Warner, Inc. **p. 419** Stacy Pick/Stock, Boston **Fig. 13–1** Gilling, D. & Brightwell, R. (1982). *The human brain.* London: Little, Brown & Co. **p. 423** Sybil Shelton/Monkmeyer Press Photo Service **Fig. 13–4** Rabin, A. S., et al. (1986). Aggregate outcome and follow-up results following self-control therapy for depression. Paper presented at the American Psychological Association Convention. **Table 13–1** Numbers and fees from Hunt, M. (1987, August 30). Navigating the therapy maze. *The New York Times Magazine*, pp. 28–49, and Gates, M. (1989, December 10). Psychiatrists not where patients are. *Grand Rapids Press* (Newhouse News Service), p. D8, and *Psychiatric News* (1989, September 1). Reported by *Behavior Today*, September 25, 1989, pp. 3–4. **Fig. 13–5** Adapted from Smith, M. L., et al. (1980). *The benefits of psychotherapy* (p. 88). Baltimore, MD: Johns Hopkins University Press. Reprinted by permission. **p. 433** Mark Antman/The Image Works **Fig. 13–6** Data from NIMH—PSC collaborative study I. **p. 435** Leesnider/The Image Works **p. 437** James Wilson/Woodfin Camp & Associates

Chapter 14

Opener: Hugh Rogers/Monkmeyer Press Photo Service **p. 447** Thomas Hopker/Magnum Photos **Fig. 14–2** From Phillips, D. P. (1974). The influence of suggestion on suicide: Substantive and theoretical implications of the Werther effect. *American Sociological Review*, 39, 340–354. Reprinted by permission of the American Sociological Association. **p. 450** William Vandivert and Scientific American. **p. 452** Courtesy Graduate School and University Center of the City University of New York **Fig. 14–4** Data from Milgram, S. (1974). *Obedience to authority.* Copyright © 1974 by Stanley Milgram. Reprinted by permission of HarperCollins Publishers. **p. 454** Focus on Sports **p. 455** Keystone Press Agency, Inc. **p. 456** AP/Wide World Photos **p. 457** Margaret Bourke-White, LIFE Magazine © 1946 Time Warner, Inc. **p. 459** Presse-Sports **p. 460** Serge de Sazo/Rapho, Photo Researchers **Fig. 14–5** From Anderson, C. A., & Anderson, D. C. (1984). Ambient temperature and violent crime: Tests on the linear and curvilinear hypotheses. *Journal of Personality and Social Psychology*, 46, 91–97. Copyright © 1984 by the American Psychological Association. Reprinted by permission. **p. 462** Stayskal/Tampa Tribune **p. 463** Joel Gordon **Fig. 14–6** From Darley, J. M., & Latané, B. (1968b, December). When will people help in a crisis? *Psychology Today*, pp. 54–57, 70–71. Reprinted with permission from Psychology Today Magazine. Copyright © 1968

(Sussex Publishers, Inc.).   **Fig. 14–7** From Darley, J. M., & Latané, B. (1968a). Bystander intervention in emergencies: Diffusion of responsibility. *Journal of Personality and Social Psychology, 8,* 377–383. Copyright © 1968 by the American Psychological Association. Reprinted by permission.   **p. 466** Joel Gordon 1990   **p. 467** Sygma   **p. 468** James Kamp/Black Star   **p. 469** *(left)* Margaret Gowan/Tony Stone Worldwide/Chicago Ltd.; *(center)* Victor Englebert/Photo Researchers; *(right)* Nancy Brown/The Image Bank

Chapter 15

Opener: N. Markus/Photo Researchers   **p. 476** *(left)* Joe Carini/The Image Works; *(center)* Robert Caputo/Stock, Boston; *(right)* Brett Froomer/The Image Bank   **p. 477** *(top left)* Willie L. Hill, Jr./Stock, Boston; *(top center)* Sally Cassidy/The Picture Cube; *(top right)* Lawrence Migdale/Stock, Boston; *(center left)* Sally Cassidy/The Picture Cube; *(bottom left)* Owen Franken/Stock, Boston   **p. 478** Gary Rogers/The Image Bank   **p. 479** Fujifotos/The Image Works   **p. 481** Bob Daemmrich/The Image Works   **p. 482** *(top)* Courtesy James Jones; *(bottom)* David Austen/Stock, Boston   **p. 483** Jonathan Wenk/Black Star   **Fig. 15–1** From Vandenberg, S. G., & Kuse, A. R. (1978). Mental rotations, a group test of three-dimensional spacial visualization. *Perceptual and Motor Skills, 47,* 599–604. Reprinted with permission.   **p. 487** Susan Lapides 1990/Design Con-ceptions   **p. 489** National Museum of Natural History/Photo Researchers   **p. 491** *(left)* Lindsay Hebberd/Woodfin Camp and Associates; *(right)* L. Townshend/The Picture Cube   **Fig. 15–4** From Dey, E., et al. (1991). *The American Freshman: Twenty-Five Year Trends.* Los Angeles: Higher Education Research Institute, UCLA.   **Fig. 15–5** From Turner, S. E., & Bowen, W. G. (1990). The flight from the arts and sciences: Trends in degrees conferred. *Science, 250,* 517–521. Copyright © 1990 by the American Association for the Advancement of Science.   **Fig. 15–6** From Robinson, J. P. (1988, December). Who's doing the housework? *American Demographics,* pp. 24–28, 63.   **p. 496** Elsa Peterson/Design Conceptions   **Fig. 15–7** From Gallup, G., Jr., & Hugick, L. (1990, June). Racial tolerance grows, progress on racial equality less evident. *Gallup Poll Monthly,* pp. 23–32, and Niemi, R. G., Moeller, J., & Smith, T. W. (1989). *Trends in public opinion: A compendium of survey data.* Westport, CT: Greenwood Publishing Group.   **p. 499** Michael S. Yamashita/Woodfin Camp & Associates   **p. 502** Bob Daemmrich/Stock, Boston

Appendix

p. 510 *(top)* The Bettmann Archive   **Fig. A–3** By permission of the Houghton Library, Harvard University.   **Fig. A–8** Adapted from Ross, B. (1987). In K. McKean, The orderly pursuit of pure disorder. *Discover,* January, 72–81. Copyright © 1987 Discover Magazine.

Name Index

Subject Index